University Casebook Series

ACCOUNTING AND THE LAW, Third Edition (1964), with Problem Pamphlet
The late James L. Dohr, Director, Institute of Accounting, Columbia University,
Ellis L. Phillips, Jr., Professor of Law, Columbia University.
George C. Thompson, Professor, Columbia University Graduate School of Business, and
William C. Warren, Professor of Law, Columbia University.

ACCOUNTING, LAW AND (1949)
Donald Schapiro, Instructor in Law, Yale University, and
Ralph Wienshienk, Visiting Lecturer in Law, Yale University.

ACCOUNTING, MATERIALS ON, (1959), with 1968 Supplement
Robert Amory, Jr., Esq.,
W. Covington Hardee, Esq., Third Edition by
David R. Herwitz, Professor of Law, Harvard University, and
Donald T. Trautman, Professor of Law, Harvard University.

ADMINISTRATIVE LAW, Fifth Edition (1970), with Problems Supplement
Walter Gellhorn, Professor of Law, Columbia University, and
Clark Byse, Professor of Law, Harvard University.

ADMIRALTY (1969)
Jo Desha Lucas, Professor of Law, University of Chicago.

ADMIRALTY (1954)
The late Stanley Morrison, Professor of Law, Stanford University, and
The late George W. Stumberg, Professor of Law, University of Texas.

ADVOCACY, INTRODUCTION TO (1970) with Supplementary Cases Pamphlet
Board of Student Advisers, Harvard Law School.

ANTITRUST LAW (1967), with 1969 Supplement
Harlan M. Blake, Professor of Law, Columbia University.
Robert Pitofsky, Professor of Law, New York University.

ARBITRATION (1968)
Shelden D. Elliott, Professor of Law, New York University.

BANKRUPTCY ACT (Annotated) 1967 Edition
The late James Angell MacLachlan, Professor of Law Emeritus, Harvard University.

BIOGRAPHY OF A LEGAL DISPUTE, THE: An Introduction to American Civil Procedure (1968)
Marc A. Franklin, Professor of Law, Stanford University.

UNIVERSITY CASEBOOK SERIES — Continued

BUSINESS ORGANIZATION: EMPLOYMENT—AGENCY—PARTNERSHIP—ATTORNEYS, Third Edition (1965)
Alfred F. Conard, Professor of Law, University of Michigan, and
Robert L. Knauss, Associate Professor of Law, University of Michigan.

BUSINESS ORGANIZATION: CORPORATIONS (1948)
A. A. Berle, Jr., Professor of Law, Columbia University, and
William C. Warren, Professor of Law, Columbia University.

BUSINESS PLANNING (1966) with 1971 Problem Supplement
David R. Herwitz, Professor of Law, Harvard University.

CIVIL PROCEDURE, see Procedure

COMMERCIAL AND INVESTMENT PAPER, Third Edition (1964) with Statutory Materials
Roscoe T. Steffen, Professor of Law, University of California, Hastings College of the Law.

COMMERCIAL LAW, CASES & MATERIALS ON, Second Edition (1968) with Statutory Supplement
E. Allan Farnsworth, Professor of Law, Columbia University.
John Honnold, Professor of Law, University of Pennsylvania.

COMMERCIAL PAPER (1968), with Statutory Supplement
E. Allan Farnsworth, Professor of Law, Columbia University.

COMMERCIAL PAPER AND BANK DEPOSITS AND COLLECTIONS (1967) with Statutory Supplement
William D. Hawkland, Professor of Law, University of Illinois.

COMMERCIAL TRANSACTIONS—Text, Cases and Problems, Fourth Edition (1968)
Robert Braucher, Professor of Law, Harvard University, and
Arthur E. Sutherland, Jr., Professor of Law, Harvard University.

COMPARATIVE LAW, Third Edition (1970)
Rudolf B. Schlesinger, Professor of Law, Cornell University.

CONFLICT OF LAWS, Sixth Edition (1971)
Willis L. M. Reese, Professor of Law, Columbia University, and
Maurice Rosenberg, Professor of Law, Columbia University.

CONSTITUTIONAL LAW, Third Edition (1963) with 1971 Supplement
Edward L. Barrett, Jr., Dean of the Law School, University of California, Davis,
Paul W. Bruton, Professor of Law, University of Pennsylvania, and
John O. Honnold, Professor of Law, University of Pennsylvania.

CONSTITUTIONAL LAW, Eighth Edition (1970) with 1971 Supplement
Gerald Gunther, Professor of Law, Stanford University.
Noel T. Dowling, late Professor of Law, Columbia University.

CONSTITUTIONAL LAW, INDIVIDUAL RIGHTS IN (1970) with 1971 Supplement
Gerald Gunther, Professor of Law, Stanford University.
Noel T. Dowling, late Professor of Law, Columbia University.

UNIVERSITY CASEBOOK SERIES — Continued

CONTRACTS, (1965) (Successor Volume to Patterson, Goble & Jones, Cases on Contracts) with Statutory Supplement

Harry W. Jones, Professor of Law, Columbia University.
E. Allan Farnsworth, Professor of Law, Columbia University.
William F. Young, Professor of Law, Columbia University.

CONTRACTS (1971) with Statutory and Administrative Law Supplement

Ian R. Macneil, Professor of Law, Cornell University.

CONTRACT LAW AND ITS APPLICATION (1971)

Addison Mueller, Professor of Law, University of California, Los Angeles.
Arthur I. Rosett, Professor of Law, University of California, Los Angeles.

CONTRACT LAW, STUDIES IN (1970)

Edward J. Murphy, Professor of Law, University of Notre Dame.
Richard E. Speidel, Professor of Law, University of Virginia.

CONTRACTS AND CONTRACT REMEDIES, Fourth Edition (1957)

Harold Shepherd, Professor of Law Emeritus, Stanford University, and
Harry H. Wellington, Professor of Law, Yale University.

CONTRACTS AND CONTRACT REMEDIES, Second Edition (1969)

John P. Dawson, Professor of Law, Harvard University, and
Wm. Burnett Harvey, Dean of the Law School, Indiana University.

CONVEYANCES, Second Edition (1941)

Marion R. Kirkwood, Professor of Law Emeritus, Stanford University.

COPYRIGHT, Unfair Competition, and Other Topics Bearing on the Protection of Literary, Musical, and Artistic Works (1960)

Benjamin Kaplan, Professor of Law, Harvard University, and
Ralph S. Brown, Jr., Professor of Law, Yale University.

CORPORATE REORGANIZATION, with Statutory Supplement (1950)

The late E. Merrick Dodd, Professor of Law, Harvard University, and
DeForest Billyou, Professor of Law, New York University.

CORPORATIONS, Fourth Edition—Unabridged, 1969

William L. Cary, Professor of Law, Columbia University.

CORPORATIONS, Fourth Edition—Abridged (1970)

William L. Cary, Professor of Law, Columbia University.

CORRECTIONAL PROCESS (1971) (Pamphlet)

Reprinted from Miller, Dawson, Dix and Parnas's Criminal Justice Administration & Related Processes

CREDITORS' RIGHTS, Fifth Edition (1957)

The late John Hanna, Professor of Law Emeritus, Columbia University, and
The late James Angell MacLachlan, Professor of Law Emeritus, Harvard University.

UNIVERSITY CASEBOOK SERIES — Continued

CREDITORS' RIGHTS AND CORPORATE REORGANIZATION, Fifth Edition (1957)

    The late John Hanna, Professor of Law Emeritus, Columbia University, and The late James Angell MacLachlan, Professor of Law Emeritus, Harvard University.

CREDITORS' RIGHTS AND SECURED TRANSACTIONS, 1967

    William E. Hogan, Professor of Law, Cornell University.
    William D. Warren, Professor of Law, University of California Los Angeles.

CRIMINAL JUSTICE, THE ADMINISTRATION OF, CASES AND MATERIALS ON, Second Edition (1969)

    Francis C. Sullivan, Professor of Law, Louisiana State University.
    Paul Hardin III, Professor of Law, Duke University.
    John Huston, Professor of Law, University of Washington.
    Frank R. Lacy, Professor of Law, University of Oregon.
    Daniel E. Murray, Professor of Law, University of Miami.
    George W. Pugh, Professor of Law, Louisiana State University.

CRIMINAL JUSTICE, Third Edition, 1968, two volumes: I. Criminal Law, II. Criminal Law Administration, with 1971 Supplement

    Fred E. Inbau, Professor of Law, Northwestern University.
    James R. Thompson, Professor of Law, Northwestern University, and Claude R. Sowle, President, Ohio University.

CRIMINAL JUSTICE ADMINISTRATION AND RELATED PROCESSES (1971)

    Frank W. Miller, Professor of Law, Washington University.
    Robert O. Dawson, Professor of Law, University of Texas.
    George E. Dix, Professor of Law, Arizona State University.
    Raymond I. Parnas, Professor of Law, University of California, Davis.

CRIMINAL LAW (1969)

    Lloyd L. Weinreb, Professor of Law, Harvard University.

CRIMINAL LAW AND ITS ADMINISTRATION (1940), with 1956 Supplement

    The late Jerome Michael, Professor of Law, Columbia University, and Herbert Wechsler, Professor of Law, Columbia University.

CRIMINAL LAW AND PROCEDURE, Third Edition (1966)

    Rollin M. Perkins, Professor of Law, University of California, Hastings College of the Law.

CRIMINAL PROCESS (1969)

    Lloyd L. Weinreb, Professor of Law, Harvard University.

DAMAGES, Second Edition (1952)

    The late Charles T. McCormick, Professor of Law, University of Texas, and William F. Fritz, Professor of Law, University of Texas.

DECEDENTS' ESTATES AND TRUSTS, Fourth Edition (1971)

    John Ritchie III, Dean and Professor of Law, Northwestern University, Neill H. Alford, Jr., Professor of Law, University of Virginia, and Richard W. Effland, Professor of Law, Arizona State University.

UNIVERSITY CASEBOOK SERIES — Continued

DECEDENTS' ESTATES AND TRUSTS (1968)
  Howard R. Williams, Professor of Law, Stanford University.

DOMESTIC RELATIONS (1970), with Statutory Supplement
  Monrad G. Paulsen, Dean of the Law School, University of Virginia.
  Walter Wadlington, Professor of Law, University of Virginia.
  Julius Goebel, Jr., Professor of Law Emeritus, Columbia University.

DOMESTIC RELATIONS: STATUTORY MATERIALS
  Monrad G. Paulsen, Dean of the Law School, University of Virginia.
  Walter Wadlington, Professor of Law, University of Virginia.

DOMESTIC RELATIONS—Civil and Canon Law (1963)
  Philip A. Ryan, Professor of Law, Georgetown University, and
  Dom David Granfield, Associate Professor, Catholic University of America.

DYNAMICS OF AMERICAN LAW, THE: Courts, the Legal Process and Freedom of Expression (1968)
  Marc A. Franklin, Professor of Law, Stanford University.

EQUITY, Fifth Edition (1967)
  The late Zechariah Chafee, Jr., Professor of Law, Harvard University, and
  Edward D. Re, Professor of Law, St. John's University.

EQUITY, RESTITUTION AND DAMAGES (1969)
  Robert Childres, Professor of Law, Northwestern University.

ETHICS, see Legal Profession

EVIDENCE (1968) with 1969 Supplement
  David W. Louisell, Professor of Law, University of California, Berkeley,
  John Kaplan, Professor of Law, Stanford University,
  Jon R. Waltz, Professor of Law, Northwestern University.

EVIDENCE, Fifth Edition (1965) with 1970 Supplement
  John M. Maguire, Professor of Law Emeritus, Harvard University.
  Jack B. Weinstein, Professor of Law, Columbia University.
  James H. Chadbourn, Professor of Law, Harvard University.
  John H. Mansfield, Professor of Law, Harvard University.

EVIDENCE (1968)
  Francis C. Sullivan, Professor of Law, Louisiana State University,
  Paul Hardin, III, Professor of Law, Duke University.

FEDERAL COURTS, FIFTH EDITION (1970) with 1971 Supplement
  The late Charles T. McCormick, Professor of Law, University of Texas,
  James H. Chadbourn, Professor of Law, Harvard University, and
  Charles Alan Wright, Professor of Law, University of Texas.

FEDERAL COURTS AND THE FEDERAL SYSTEM (1953)
  The late Henry M. Hart, Jr., Professor of Law, Harvard University and
  Herbert Wechsler, Professor of Law, Columbia University.

FEDERAL RULES OF CIVIL PROCEDURE, 1971 Edition

UNIVERSITY CASEBOOK SERIES — Continued

FEDERAL TAXATION, see Taxation

FREE ENTERPRISE AND ECONOMIC ORGANIZATION, Third Edition (1966)
two volumes: I. Concentration & Restrictive Practices, II. Regulation of Entry, Rates and Discrimination
Louis B. Schwartz, Professor of Law, University of Pennsylvania.

FUTURE INTERESTS AND ESTATE PLANNING (1961) with 1962 Supplement
W. Barton Leach, Professor of Law, Harvard University, and
James K. Logan, Dean of the Law School, University of Kansas.

FUTURE INTERESTS (1958)
The late Philip Mechem, Professor of Law Emeritus, University of Pennsylvania.

FUTURE INTERESTS (1970)
Howard R. Williams, Professor of Law, Stanford University.

HOUSING (THE ILL-HOUSED) (1971)
Peter W. Martin, Professor of Law, University of Minnesota.

INSURANCE (1971)
William F. Young, Professor of Law, Columbia University.

INTERNATIONAL LAW: See also Transnational Legal Problems and United Nations Law

INTERNATIONAL TRADE AND INVESTMENT, REGULATION OF (1970)
Carl H. Fulda, Professor of Law, University of Texas,
Warren F. Schwartz, Professor of Law, University of Virginia.

INTERNATIONAL TRANSACTIONS AND RELATIONS (1960)
Milton Katz, Professor of Law, Harvard University, and
Kingman Brewster, Jr., President, Yale University.

INTRODUCTION TO THE STUDY OF LAW (1970)
E. Wayne Thode, Professor of Law, University of Utah.
J. Leon Lebowitz, Professor of Law, University of Texas.
Lester J. Mazor, Professor of Law, University of Utah.

INTRODUCTION TO LAW, see also Legal Method, also On Law in Courts, also Dynamics of American Law

JUDICIAL CODE: Rules of Procedure in the Federal Courts with Excerpts from the Criminal Code, 1971 Edition
The late Henry M. Hart, Jr., Professor of Law, Harvard University, and
Herbert Wechsler, Professor of Law, Columbia University.

JURISPRUDENCE (Temporary Edition Hard Bound) (1949)
Lon L. Fuller, Professor of Law, Harvard University.

JUVENILE COURTS (1967)
Hon. Orman W. Ketcham, Juvenile Court of the District of Columbia.
Monrad G. Paulsen, Dean of the Law School, University of Virginia.

UNIVERSITY CASEBOOK SERIES—Continued

JUVENILE JUSTICE PROCESS (1971) (Pamphlet)
> Reprinted from Miller, Dawson, Dix & Parnas's Criminal Justice Administration & Related Processes

LABOR LAW, Seventh Edition 1969 with Statutory Supplement
> Archibald Cox, Professor of Law, Harvard University, and
> Derek C. Bok, President, Harvard University.

LABOR LAW (1968) with Statutory Supplement
> Clyde W. Summers, Professor of Law, Yale University.
> Harry H. Wellington, Professor of Law, Yale University.

LABOR RELATIONS (1949)
> The late Harry Shulman, Dean of the Law School, Yale University, and
> Neil Chamberlain, Professor of Economics, Columbia University.

LAND FINANCING (1970)
> Norman Penney, Professor of Law, Cornell University.
> Richard F. Broude, Professor of Law, Georgetown University.

LEGAL DRAFTING (1951)
> Robert N. Cook, Professor of Law, University of Cincinnati.

LEGAL METHOD, Second Edition (1952)
> Noel T. Dowling, late Professor of Law, Columbia University,
> The late Edwin W. Patterson, Professor of Law, Columbia University, and
> Richard R. B. Powell, Professor of Law, University of California, Hastings College of the Law.
> Second Edition by Harry W. Jones, Professor of Law, Columbia University.

LEGAL METHODS (1969)
> Robert N. Covington, Professor of Law, Vanderbilt University,
> E. Blythe Stason, Professor of Law, Vanderbilt University,
> John W. Wade, Dean of Law School, Vanderbilt University,
> Elliott E. Cheatham, Professor of Law, Vanderbilt University,
> Theodore A. Smedley, Professor of Law, Vanderbilt University.

LEGAL PROFESSION (1970)
> Samuel D. Thurman, Dean of the College of Law, University of Utah.
> Ellis L. Phillips, Jr., Professor of Law, Columbia University.
> Elliott E. Cheatham, Professor of Law, Vanderbilt University.

LEGISLATION, Second Edition (1959)
> Horace E. Read, Vice President, Dalhousie University.
> John W. MacDonald, Professor of Law, Cornell Law School, and
> Jefferson B. Fordham, Professor of Law, University of Pennsylvania.

LOCAL GOVERNMENT LAW (1949)
> Jefferson B. Fordham, Professor of Law, University of Pennsylvania.

MENTAL HEALTH PROCESS (1971) (Pamphlet)
> Reprinted from Miller, Dawson, Dix & Parnas's Criminal Justice Administration & Related Processes

UNIVERSITY CASEBOOK SERIES — Continued

MODERN REAL ESTATE TRANSACTIONS, Second Edition (1958)
Allison Dunham, Professor of Law, University of Chicago.

MUNICIPAL CORPORATIONS, see Local Government Law

NEGOTIABLE INSTRUMENTS, see Commercial Paper

NEW YORK PRACTICE, Second Edition (1968)
Herbert Peterfreund, Professor of Law, New York University,
Joseph M. McLaughlin, Professor of Law, Fordham University.

OIL AND GAS, Second Edition (1964)
Howard R. Williams, Professor of Law, Stanford University,
Richard C. Maxwell, Professor of Law, University of California, Los Angeles, and
Charles J. Meyers, Professor of Law, Stanford University.

ON LAW IN COURTS (1965)
Paul J. Mishkin, Professor of Law, University of Pennsylvania.
Clarence Morris, Professor of Law, University of Pennsylvania.

OWNERSHIP AND DEVELOPMENT OF LAND (1965)
Jan Krasnowiecki, Professor of Law, University of Pennsylvania.

PARTNERSHIP PLANNING (1970) (Pamphlet)
William L. Cary, Professor of Law, Columbia University.

PATENT, TRADEMARK AND COPYRIGHT LAW (1959)
E. Ernest Goldstein, Professor of Law, University of Texas.

PLEADING & PROCEDURE: STATE AND FEDERAL, Second Edition (1968)
David W. Louisell, Professor of Law, University of California, Berkeley, and
Geoffrey C. Hazard, Jr., Professor of Law, Yale University.

POLICE FUNCTION (1971) (Pamphlet)
Reprinted from Miller, Dawson, Dix & Parnas's Criminal Justice Administration and Related Processes

PROCEDURE—Biography of a Legal Dispute (1968)
Marc A. Franklin, Professor of Law, Stanford University.

PROCEDURE—CIVIL PROCEDURE (1961)
James H. Chadbourn, Professor of Law, Harvard University, and
A. Leo Levin, Professor of Law, University of Pennsylvania.

PROCEDURE—CIVIL PROCEDURE, Temporary Second Edition (1968)
Richard H. Field, Professor of Law, Harvard University, and
Benjamin Kaplan, Professor of Law, Harvard University.

PROCEDURE—CIVIL PROCEDURE, Second Edition (1970)
Maurice Rosenberg, Professor of Law, Columbia University,
Jack B. Weinstein, Professor of Law, Columbia University.
Hans Smit, Professor of Law, Columbia University.

UNIVERSITY CASEBOOK SERIES — Continued

PROCEDURE—FEDERAL RULES OF CIVIL PROCEDURE, 1971 Edition

PROCEDURE PORTFOLIO (1962)
James H. Chadbourn, Professor of Law, Harvard University, and
A. Leo Levin, Professor of Law, University of Pennsylvania.

PRODUCTS AND THE CONSUMER: Defective and Dangerous Products (1970)
W. Page Keeton, Dean of the School of Law, University of Texas,
Marshall S. Shapo, Professor of Law, University of Virginia.

PROPERTY, Second Edition (1966)
John E. Cribbet, Dean of the Law School, University of Illinois,
William F. Fritz, Professor of Law, University of Texas, and
Corwin W. Johnson, Professor of Law, University of Texas.

PROPERTY—PERSONAL (1953)
The late S. Kenneth Skolfield, Professor of Law Emeritus, Boston University.

PROPERTY—PERSONAL, Third Edition (1954)
Everett Fraser, Dean of the Law School Emeritus, University of Minnesota
—Third Edition by
Charles W. Taintor II, late Professor of Law, University of Pittsburgh.

PROPERTY—REAL—INTRODUCTION, Third Edition (1954)
Everett Fraser, Dean of the Law School Emeritus, University of Minnesota.

PROPERTY—REAL PROPERTY AND CONVEYANCING (1954)
Edward E. Bade, late Professor of Law, University of Minnesota.

PROPERTY, REAL, PROBLEMS IN (Pamphlet) (1969)
Edward H. Rabin, Professor of Law, University of California, Davis.

PUBLIC UTILITY LAW, see Free Enterprise, also Regulated Industries

RECEIVERSHIP AND CORPORATE REORGANIZATION, see Creditors' Rights

REGULATED INDUSTRIES (1967) with Statutory Supplement
William K. Jones, Professor of Law, Columbia University.

RESTITUTION, Second Edition (1966)
John W. Wade, Dean of the Law School, Vanderbilt University.

SALES AND SECURITY, Fourth Edition (1962), with Statutory Supplement
George G. Bogert, James Parker Hall Professor of Law Emeritus, University of Chicago.
The late William E. Britton, Professor of Law, University of California, Hastings College of the Law, and
William D. Hawkland, Professor of Law, University of Illinois.

SALES AND SALES FINANCING, Third Edition (1968) with Statutory Supplement
John Honnold, Professor of Law, University of Pennsylvania.

UNIVERSITY CASEBOOK SERIES — Continued

SECURITY, Third Edition (1959)
    The late John Hanna, Professor of Law Emeritus, Columbia University.

SECURITIES REGULATION, Second Edition (1968) with 1971 Supplement
    Richard W. Jennings, Professor of Law, University of California, Berkeley.
    Harold Marsh, Jr., Professor of Law, University of California, Los Angeles.

SOCIAL WELFARE AND THE INDIVIDUAL (1971)
    Robert J. Levy, Professor of Law, University of Minnesota.
    Thomas P. Lewis, Professor of Law, University of Minnesota.
    Peter W. Martin, Professor of Law, University of Minnesota.

TAXATION, FEDERAL, Sixth Edition (1966) with 1970 Supplement
    Erwin N. Griswold, Solicitor General of the United States.

TAXATION, FEDERAL ESTATE AND GIFT, 1961 Edition with 1965 Supplement
    William C. Warren, Professor of Law, Columbia University, and
    Stanley S. Surrey, Professor of Law, Harvard University.

TAXATION, FEDERAL INCOME, 1960 Edition integrated with 1961 Supplement and a 1964 Supplement
    Stanley S. Surrey, Professor of Law, Harvard University, and
    William C. Warren, Professor of Law, Columbia University.

TORT LAW AND ALTERNATIVES: INJURIES AND REMEDIES (1971)
    Marc A. Franklin, Professor of Law, Stanford University.

TORTS, Second Edition (1952)
    The late Harry Shulman, Dean of the Law School, Yale University, and
    Fleming James, Jr., Professor of Law, Yale University.

TORTS, Fifth Edition (1971)
    William L. Prosser, Professor of Law, University of California, Hastings College of the Law.
    John W. Wade, Dean of the School of Law, Vanderbilt University.

TRADE REGULATION, Fourth Edition (1967) with 1970 Supplement
    Milton Handler, Professor of Law, Columbia University.

TRADE REGULATION, see Free Enterprise

TRANSNATIONAL LEGAL PROBLEMS (1968) with Documentary Supplement
    Henry J. Steiner, Professor of Law, Harvard University,
    Detlev F. Vagts, Professor of Law, Harvard University.

TRIAL ADVOCACY (1968)
    A. Leo Levin, Professor of Law, University of Pennsylvania,
    Harold Cramer, Esq., Member of the Philadelphia Bar. (Maurice Rosenberg, Professor of Law, Columbia University, as consultant).

TRUSTS, Fourth Edition (1967)
    George G. Bogert, James Parker Hall Professor of Law Emeritus, University of Chicago.
    Dallin H. Oaks, Professor of Law, University of Chicago.

UNIVERSITY CASEBOOK SERIES — Continued

TRUSTS AND SUCCESSION, Second Edition (1968)
George E. Palmer, Professor of Law, University of Michigan.

UNITED NATIONS IN ACTION (1968)
Louis B. Sohn, Professor of Law, Harvard University.

UNITED NATIONS LAW, Second Edition (1967) with Documentary Supplement (1968)
Louis B. Sohn, Professor of Law, Harvard University.

WATER RESOURCE MANAGEMENT (1971)
Charles J. Meyers, Professor of Law, Stanford University.
A. Dan Tarlock, Professor of Law, Indiana University.

WILLS AND ADMINISTRATION, 5th Edition (1961)
The late Philip Mechem, Professor of Law, University of Pennsylvania, and
The late Thomas E. Atkinson, Professor of Law, New York University.

WORLD LAW, see United Nations Law

University Casebook Series

EDITORIAL BOARD

LON L. FULLER
DIRECTING EDITOR
Professor of Law, Harvard University

EDWARD L. BARRETT, Jr.
Dean of the Law School, University of California, Davis

JEFFERSON B. FORDHAM
Professor of Law, University of Pennsylvania

HARRY W. JONES
Professor of Law, Columbia University

PAGE KEETON
Dean of the Law School, University of Texas

BAYLESS A. MANNING
Professor of Law, Stanford University

LOUIS H. POLLAK
Professor of Law, Yale University

WILLIAM L. PROSSER
Professor of Law, University of California, Hastings College of the Law

JOHN RITCHIE, III
Dean of the Law School, Northwestern University

SAMUEL D. THURMAN
Dean of the Law School, University of Utah

WILLIAM C. WARREN
Professor of Law, Columbia University

CASES AND MATERIALS
ON
CRIMINAL LAW
AND
PROCEDURE

By

ROLLIN M. PERKINS

Professor of Law
University of California, The Hastings College of Law
Connell Professor of Law Emeritus, UCLA

THIRD EDITION

Brooklyn
THE FOUNDATION PRESS, INC.
1966

Copyright © 1952, 1959
by
THE FOUNDATION PRESS, INC.

Copyright © 1966
by
THE FOUNDATION PRESS, INC.
All rights reserved

PREFACE TO THE THIRD EDITION

Either of two recent developments would have required a new edition of this casebook. One has been in the form of recent Supreme Court decisions which have made such a great change in the rights of one accused of crime. An introduction of the law student to the field of Criminal Law and Procedure today would be incomplete without a careful study of some of these cases and the implications to be drawn therefrom.

The other has been the completion of the Model Penal Code prepared by the American Law Institute. "Completion" is perhaps not the appropriate word since even as these pages go to press the Official Draft is not yet available. For that reason all references to the Code herein, unless otherwise indicated, are to the Proposed Official Draft of 1962, as amended at the 1962 meeting. It was stated at that time, it may be added, that the official form "will be the Code as amended at this meeting" except that "the Reporters may make further editorial revision in matters not affecting substance. . . ."[1]

The Model Penal Code must not be confused with the Restatements by the Institute which are of importance in such courses as Contracts, Property and Torts. The Model Penal Code does not purport to be a restatement of existing law. Its very purpose is to make significant changes in the law. It is recommended legislation, and great care must be taken to insure that students do not confuse it with existing law. But the need for changes in the criminal law, long recognized, has been receiving ever increasing attention and in the years ahead the Model Penal Code will be the starting point for all studies of this nature. Hence the law student of today needs to have an introduction to that Code as well as a thorough grounding in the existing criminal law.

So long as the present law remains effective the study of the cases should come first. Only after the student is well acquainted with the present law in some part of the field should his attention be directed to the pertinent provisions of the Code—to see what significant differences are found therein. If the Code should be adopted the effective date will no doubt be a year or two later. Except for a few matters which could not operate to the prejudice of one accused of crime the Code will not apply to offenses committed prior to its effective date. And since many years may elapse before a case is finally disposed of on appeal, and perhaps retrial, the importance of the present law will continue well into the future. It will continue to demand the attention of lawyers, moreover, until changed by both state and federal statutes.

[1] 39 ALI Proceedings 226(1962). The Proposed Final Draft was copyrighted by the American Law Institute in 1962. The quotations herein are with its permission.

PREFACE TO THE THIRD EDITION

Some years ago a university president complained that all of his professors of political science wanted to teach law and all of his law professors wanted to teach political science. He made it quite clear that he did not expect those in either field to ignore the other; his objection was that each seemed inclined to ignore his own. In recent years a comparable situation has come into prominence. Some of those in charge of the criminal-law course have become so interested in criminology that it seems to them not important to give the students any real familiarity with the existing law of crimes. This is not something entirely new in the law-school world but seems to have assumed unusual proportions at the present time. Needless to say, the teacher of criminal law cannot ignore criminology, but the first-year classroom is not the place for extensive inter-disciplinary collaboration between the behavioral sciences and the administration of justice.

The compiler has been teaching criminal law for half a century and must confess that during that time there have been occasions when his class tended to become a seminar in criminology. Such a digression is interesting, without a doubt, but conversations about it with lawyers who had no other introduction to criminal law while in school are enlightening, but very disheartening. The target of the criminal-law class should be the common law of crimes, as modified by statutes which have been rather widely enacted. In the words of Dean Pound, first in the legal profession to emphasize the importance of non-legal disciplines, the law teacher must teach "the actual law by which courts decide".[2] However, a seminar on criminology for upper-class students would seem to have a strong claim for a place in the law-school curriculum.[3]

An invitation to make suggestions was sent to all teachers known to be using the second edition at the time this revision was undertaken (which was several years ago) and much help was received. As was to be expected some opinions were in sharp contrast, and where this happened an effort was made to follow what seemed to be the prevailing desire. Thus while one suggestion called for a major change in the arrangement, there seemed to be very general satisfaction with the plan of taking up the specific offenses before the general principles, and with the plan of placing the major emphasis upon the substantive law, but also giving a brief introduction to the field of criminal procedure up to the point of trial. The appendix, which seemed important for the first edition because my text was not then available, and was continued in the second edition for no apparent reason, has been omitted. A different appendix, much better suited to the needs of today, has been substituted.

[2] Pound, The Need for a Sociological Jurisprudence, 19 Green Bag 607, 612 (1907).
[3] See Glueck, On the Conduct of a Seminar in the Administration of Criminal Justice, 16 J.Legal Ed. 71 (1963).

PREFACE TO THE THIRD EDITION

It is expected that the student will supplement his study of the cases with a careful examination of the treatment of the same field in the text. The two books have been keyed together chapter by chapter and section by section with two exceptions. As the plan of the casebook is to give "case treatment" to selected offenses only, in order to give adequate consideration to the general principles of the criminal law, there are a few deviations in the first four chapters, although not such as to cause the student any difficulty in coordinating the two. And the casebook gives an introduction to criminal procedure which is beyond the scope of the text.

For the most part citations in opinions are of no help to a first-year law student and serve only to distract his attention. Hence citations in the opinions have been omitted unless there was some special reason for inclusion. Furthermore the purpose of a casebook seemed not to make it important to use ellipsis marks where only citations have been omitted, hence they are employed only to indicate an omission of part of the opinion proper. And it seemed unimportant to indicate whether the omissions were of paragraphs or parts of a paragraph. Frequently the parts omitted dealt with matters other than the primary point for which the case was included. At other times space limitations required the omission of part of the opinion dealing with that point. The student, without fail, should go to the original reports now and then, to study the full opinion of a case which has been abbreviated for casebook use.

The very drastic cutting of the long cases at the end of the book, although quite unfortunate, was necessary for reasons obvious to any experienced teacher. And for the benefit of the teacher who has been using the second edition it may be mentioned that 63 of the following cases did not appear therein (most of them having been decided since the earlier publication), while 68 second-edition cases have been omitted.

The Revised Penal Law of New York, to become effective on September 1, 1967, was not available until the following pages had been set in type and hence is not included in any of the footnote references to New York law.

An additional acknowledgment is due to my wife, Florence Payne Perkins, who not only edited the manuscript, with annual changes, while the cases were being used in mimeograph form for three years before the first printed edition, but since then has done the typing, cutting and pasting, as well as the editing and proofreading. Without her painstaking help the work could not have been completed

ROLLIN M. PERKINS

San Francisco
April, 1966

PREFACE TO THE FIRST EDITION

THE LAW school course known as criminal law and procedure, or simply as criminal law, has had a wide range of treatment and experimentation. At one extreme has been the plan by which each case is "squeezed dry" before the following case is presented. This involves not only an exhaustive consideration of the actual holding of the case and any dictum found in the opinion but also of numerous problems developed by analogy from either. In its most extreme form this plan starts with the first case in the book and proceeds case by case, with no deviation of method until the end of the school year. This permits consideration of only a small fraction of the field but the explanation offered is that the important consideration is not the extent of coverage but only the method of study. Outside reading is not emphasized. In fact there have been times when outside reading has been frowned upon as something comparable to the use of a "pony" in a Latin class. The study of a course by this method is an intellectual experience but the sacrifices are too great, at least for criminal law. The student ends the course with no appreciation of the field as a whole and the calls upon his time outside the classroom have been entirely inadequate.

At the other extreme is the plan which undertakes to cover the entire field of criminal law and procedure, prorating the time to each topic according to its relative importance. This may be suited to a class of students who do not intend to become lawyers, and who seek merely an introduction to the field as a background for other purposes, but with the time limitations of the present schedule it has no place in the law school program.

Between these two extremes are many possibilities. What seems to be the best adopts much from each. This plan contemplates digging deeply and exhaustively here and there while other parts of the field are covered much more generally,—to a large extent by assignments for outside reading. This has the advantage of both depth and breadth. Substantially the entire field is covered but the student also acquires that appreciation of the subject which comes only with intensive and thorough study.

No doubt every major course in the curriculum has run this gamut but criminal law has had even wider experimentation. At one extreme is the approach which assumes that the existing law is entirely adequate and satisfactory. The plan is to teach the common law, with

PREFACE TO THE FIRST EDITION

reference to changes made by some of the more widely adopted statutes, but with no effort to question the desirability of existing rules. At the other extreme is the attitude that the existing law of crimes and punishments is so entirely bad that attempting to grasp it is not worth while. Hence the cases in the book are used as mere pegs on which to hang general discussions of criminology. While there have been deviations in the practice of some instructors the general history of the teaching of criminal law appears to be this: The starting point was the first of the two extremes which held sway for many years. Before World War I there was a trend away from that extreme which gradually moved to solid ground between the two. Then the swing of the pendulum carried further until there was a tendency to reach the second extreme. Now, quite fortunately, there is a trend back toward the middle position. Rules which have come down to us as a result of historical accident, and which tend to hinder rather than to promote the general scheme of social discipline, should not be presented as the "perfection of reason." On the other hand the teacher should not forget that the first need of the lawyer is to know what the law is. And with a field as vast and as complicated as criminal law and procedure it will tax the skill of the instructor and the ability of the student to give the latter even a fair grasp of the law as it now exists. The student will not close his mind to the need for changes in the law if the teacher makes any reasonable effort to keep it open. On the other hand, great care must be taken to avoid an emphasis which will result in confusion. A class made up of beginning law students must not be conducted as if it were a lawyer's seminar. The teacher must make a studious effort to avoid placing such stress upon his notions of what the law should be that these ideas will be recalled by the student at a later time in the form of misconceptions of existing law. And so far as criminology is concerned the greatest contribution to be made in the criminal law classroom is for the teacher to raise questions which he persistently refuses to foreclose by any categorical answers. In the classroom, as elsewhere in life, he who is the jack of all trades is master of none. And he who undertakes to teach knowledge in general, rather than some very small fragment thereof, actually succeeds in teaching nothing.

A casebook is a "study tool" as well as a "teaching device". And in a course on criminal law and procedure, offered to first-year students, it is important for the "study tool" to change as the work progresses. A determined effort has been made to fill that need in these pages. At the start the same subject is presented both in cases and in text form (in the appendix). The need at this point is to get something of an introduction to the field rather rapidly. After this introduction the plan is changed. Some subjects are presented only by cases and others only in text form (for outside reading). Still later

PREFACE TO THE FIRST EDITION

another change is made. Both text and cases are used to present the same subject,—but not the same parts of the subject. Some of the simpler problems are disposed of by text statements while certain of the more difficult problems are left entirely to the cases. Thus in the section on Intoxication the older problems are presented in text form while the cases deal with the newer problems arising out of the automobile cases. And in the section on Prevention of Crime the use of deadly force for this purpose, which is the difficult part of the subject, is left to the cases after a simple text statement of the other matters.

A few of the cases used have official footnotes. These are included unless there seemed to be some reason for their omission. If the official footnote indication is other than that regularly used herein (if, for example, it is ª, or *) this has been deemed sufficient to show that it is official. The extreme variation in the use of footnote material in different parts of the book is due to intentional changes in the form of the "study tool" as mentioned above.

It is impossible to give due acknowledgment to all the contributions to these pages. Many of them have come, through the years, from ordinary conversations with teachers, lawyers, judges, peace officers, probation officers, prison officials, criminologists and others. Two specific references, however, are in order. Grateful acknowledgment is due to my wife who painstakingly read the manuscript in three different drafts. Without this generous help the work could not have been completed. And during most of the time when the manuscript was being prepared my office was directly across the hall from that of the greatest legal scholar of our time. As those doors were never closed there was hardly a day during that period when I was not in his office or he in mine. I may have failed to take full advantage thereof but I certainly had the opportunity to get Dean Roscoe Pound's ideas on a multitude of problems of criminal law and procedure, as well as his ideas on classroom presentation and casebook construction. These have made outstanding contributions to this volume.

ROLLIN M. PERKINS

LOS ANGELES
June 20, 1952

INTRODUCTION

By
ROSCOE POUND

IT IS REASSURING to find a book coming from a university law school of today in which criminal law and criminal procedure as a whole are presented as a basis for the training of lawyers with an adequate knowledge of a necessary and highly important department of the law they are to practice, all as counselors, if not also as advocates, some as prosecutors, some as judges, and some are to expound as writers and others impart as teachers. That the newly admitted lawyer is potentially all these demands that he have the foundation on which alone competent performance in any of these capacities can be built.

Because of the crowding of the law-school curriculum through pressure from public law and of administrative law and tax law with the rise of the service state, there is a tendency to diminish the attention formerly given to fundamental subjects of private law and if not to leave them out entirely, to join subjects with no systematic connection, each expounded independently, but put together in order to give enough content for a "course", since there is felt to be no room for full presentation of either. In this practice there is hardly even the beginning of system, which has been the only way out when a body of law becomes too bulky and too complicated for effective teaching. But joining criminal law and criminal procedure in one course and in one casebook, as Professor Beale did originally is another matter. Here there is an intimate connection, and in the pressure for time for new subjects to give criminal law and criminal procedure as two is wasteful as leaving both out or reducing one to a skeleton is too great a sacrifice. Professor Perkins wisely includes both in a unified presentation in which each is adequately developed.

That a reasonably full teaching of the fundamentals of each belongs in the law-school curriculum, now that the university law schools have control over training of lawyers, ought to go without saying. Courts in finding the law must depend much on help from the advocates who practice before them. It is competent presentation of the law as well as of the facts by advocates in argument which enables a relatively small number of judges to dispose well of an enormous number of cases in our large cities. Raising up of a body of lawyers, who are to be advocates, prosecutors, and judges, with no thorough training in criminal law, is nothing short of a threat to the administration of justice. Today there is pressure to find a place in the curriculum for the newer administrative methods of individualization. That these

INTRODUCTION

have great importance for the administration of justice I should be the last to deny. But the training should be built up from the bottom, not over built at the top with weak foundation. The need is to give competent fundamental training in criminal law to those who are to take part as counsel, prosecutors and judges so that they have a legal basis for handling the newer individualized methods we are developing. For in our polity these methods must be exercised under a constitutional system of guaranteed rights and the supremacy of the law. To dilute a superficial sketch of Anglo-American criminal law with superficial expositions of our developing administrative preventive and correctional procedures and institutions will achieve nothing but fumbling. All lawyers need a sound fundamental grasp of criminal law. Those who are to be teachers, or prosecutors, or judges, or officials in the administrative agencies of law enforcement and prevention, can build on this a sound training in the principles and procedures of recent preventive and rehabilitating agencies. Criminology and penal methods should be put in graduate courses for teachers and administrative officials. They can only confuse students who have more than enough to do in learning the lawyer's technique and the starting points of legal reasoning.

Sir William Holdsworth considered that the characteristic method of exposition of Anglo-American law by subjects independently set forth arranged in alphabetical order was better suited to our law than the method which obtains in the domain of the civil law, namely, systematic exposition according to a general plan regarding each subject as a part to be expounded in logical connection with each other and with the whole. The latter method was highly developed in the last century by the Pandectists who divided their treatment into a general part, setting forth general principles from which to start in all subjects and in all details of each, and a special part taking up details. This was taken over in codes since 1900. Professor Beale used it in his Cases in Criminal Law. It had advantages for a school with a national student body, for which the general part, having been developed by the courts, was characteristically consistent and uniform, whereas the special part, the detailed body of precepts as to particular offenses, was largely, if not chiefly, legislative in form, even if developed from a basis of common law, was full of local variations, anomalies from a general standpoint, and so did not lend itself too well to general as contrasted with broad study and exposition.

There is always temptation to begin with a general systematic outline which is supposed to lay out the ground for the student to fill in with details as he takes up the special part. But there is a danger that beginning students will fill in the abstract systematic outline with mistaken or misunderstood concrete contents. Wrong ideas acquired

INTRODUCTION

in this way at the outset are very hard to dislodge, as the teacher who has to teach first-year law students, fresh from pre-legal courses in college, becomes painfully aware. Satisfactory as Beale's Cases (particularly the first edition) used to be, I can testify from some fifteen years teaching from that book in three law schools that there was a like difficulty. Teaching act, intent, imputability, responsibility, justification, excuses, modifying circumstances, and the like from cases involving all manner of specific offenses, required eternal vigilance to prevent premature wrong ideas as to the general features of those particular offences being acquired incidentally. In Anglo-American law the generalized starting point for legal reasoning must be drawn from concrete cases, not derived *a priori*. Professor Perkins, as a result of his long experience of teaching criminal law, has developed a method of meeting this difficulty which can well prove effective. Exposition of the general questions as they come up incidentally in the study of particular offences may be made to afford a sound basis for later detailed exposition of the general part. Thus the several offences will be well understood in their general aspects and the student will know how to distinguish local peculiarities of legislation or decision and will not carry them over into the general part.

Law teachers today are much concerned about reorganizing curricula by working a number of subjects, traditionally taught separately and separately expounded in textbooks, into smaller number of integrated courses in order to make room for many things not taught in the past. In this process there is a risk that the newly devised courses will have no internal unity and so will achieve nothing except in form. Such unity must be brought about by system in each subject developed to system to make a systematic group. Systematizing is an evident need of our law in the complexity it has attained. It must be looked forward to now that training of the profession has definitely become a function of the universities. If the teacher has not learned it, the inquiring student who persists in bringing over to one subject what he has been taught in others will in time make him aware that the different subjects of the law and the different details in each subject are interrelated. We cannot know any one of them completely without knowledge of many others.

Our Anglo-American law has grown up in the courts and so has developed initially from decision of concrete controversies and so has been a body of authoritative precepts in the form of models or patterns of decision of particular cases to be applied directly or by analogy to other cases by an authoritative technique. Thus starting points for legal reasoning are established and there comes to be a body of principles. Teachers work out broad doctrines to unify these principles, and the teacher's ideal of a body of logically interdependent pre-

INTRODUCTION

cepts leads to organization of them in order to make them teachable, which has the practical result of making them easier to find and apply. A resulting tradition of organization of the law through principles and doctrines makes for certainty and uniformity in the judicial process and assures stability. On the other hand professional and judicial application to concrete cases continually unsettles the details of the teacher's logical organization and requires overhauling of his doctrines. This meets the inevitable need of change, since law governs life and the essence of life is adaptation to change. Teaching on the one hand and practical application on the other hand correct each other and achieve a balance between the general security, which calls for stability, and the individual life which demands change.

In the long run there will be a systematizing of a body of law corresponding to the complexity and number of its precepts. This has been evident in the history of the modern Roman or, as we call it, civil law. When study of Roman law was revived in the Italian universities of the twelfth century the medieval jurist developed an elaborate system of glosses or commentaries as a consequence of which there came to be an enormous mass of detail which it became difficult to teach. The detail had grown beyond what could be brought within the term of a reasonable period of instruction. In the sixteenth century jurists, postulating a body of logically interdependent precepts, began to write systematic treatises on the whole law instead of systematic exposition of particular subjects as they were found in the titles of Justinian's Digest. This culminated in the writings of the Pandectists in the nineteenth century. But they over-systematized so that there has been a reaction from their method in the present century. We have repeated something of this in Anglo-American law. The method of Coke's Institutes and of Serjeant Williams' notes to Saunders' Reports was that of the medieval glossators and commentators on the Roman law. The great English and American textbooks of the nineteenth century developed system in each subject as system had been developed by civilians in the titles of Justinian's Digest devoted to particular subjects. We have come to a situation where the resulting mass of detail is such that the teaching of the whole law to students in the time that can be given for a reasonable professional training has become quite impossible. We must be moving to systematizing of the law as a whole, and the work of the American Law Institute has been laying a foundation for this by completing the systematizing of particular subjects for many of the larger and more important subjects.

Unhappily we are still far from the thorough-going modernizing and systematizing of the several subjects of criminal law to be ready for overall systematizing of the whole. Criminal procedure has moved

INTRODUCTION

rapidly to a stage of maturity in the Federal Rules. The substantive criminal law still lags. There are three reasons for this lag. Two of them apply to the substantive criminal law in both of the legal systems of the world. The third applies only in America.

From its very nature criminal law suffers from an inherent internal conflict which has stood in the way of its reaching the full maturity of development which we find in the law governing the relations of man with man in private law. In criminal law we encounter the antinomy of the general security and security of the individual life; of the general security on the one hand and justice as the ideal relation among men on the other hand. Either of these carried to full logical development negates the other, and a balance which does not sacrifice too much of either has always been hard to find and to maintain. If we look only or too much to the general security we regard detection of offenders and bringing them to justice as justifying extreme measures of interfering with individual personality. Extortion of confessions, forcible extractings from the person, what is called the "third degree", invasion of homes, unreasonable searches and seizures, entrapments and *agents provocateurs,* and summary modes of trial are thought to be required in order to protect society from anti-social conduct. If, on the other hand, we consult only our humanitarian feelings and look only at an ideal relation among men which values the individual personality instead of the general security, we bring about a regime of secured individual rights at the expense of efficient investigation and prosecution, and an overtechnical procedure for assuring protection of the accused, which was for a time carried too far in Anglo-American criminal law. Indeed we have but recently emerged from such a condition. Criminal law everywhere is troubled by the difficulty of reconciling efficient maintaining of the general security with assured security of what we feel are fundamental rights of individuals. This stands in the way of system since so much of criminal law takes the form of legislation, now moved by the idea of security and now by the ideal of justice, and hence too often wanting in consistent adherence to the needed balance or sometimes either to one or the other even in a single statute.

Again, criminal law has suffered from not having the assured foundation in the work of the Roman jurists in the classical era which has served so well for the builders of modern law on its civil side. Roman criminal law had no such matured development as had the Roman law of private relations. The texts as to criminal law which came down to us in Justinian's Digest were few and relatively crude. The later Middle Ages, the formative era of modern law, which could build private law on the matured Roman system, could build criminal law only on the crude ideas and methods of the peoples who overthrew the

Roman empire. There was no long tradition of experience developed by reason and reason tested by experience to which medieval jurists and lawmakers could turn for criminal law. As a result criminal law had by no means kept up with the general march of the law from the Middle Ages to the present century.

Furthermore both the criminal law and the administration of justice in criminal cases in the United States suffer from a growing neglect of teaching and study of criminal law in our law schools. Both the further development and the administration of the criminal law need more and better training of the lawyers, who are to be the prosecutors and judges of tomorrow, than the law schools are giving them today. Much less time is given to the required work in criminal law. Much less is covered, and the tendency is to cover less thoroughly what is taught. It cannot be a wise policy that, as is the general practice, sets the superior judges to the criminal docket in rotation and expects them to learn on the bench the criminal law they ought to have known well when they came to the bar. It is true in their neglect of criminal law the law schools reflect the attitude of the legal profession and the demands of the students. Economic causes have been turning the leaders of the profession more and more away from the trial courts and almost wholly away from the criminal courts. Hence no ambitious student in a national law school today seeks to prepare himself to practice in criminal cases. He knows that such practice as a major activity is the business of a type of politician lawyer of little standing at the bar and is regarded as appropriate to the lower stratum of the profession. Accordingly he wishes no more than that minimum knowledge of criminal law required by the examiners for admission to the bar. But university law schools, and our better law schools are now of that type, certainly should not think of themselves as simply training students to pass bar examinations. They have a duty to the public to turn out competent, well trained lawyers equal to the tasks which will come to them as counsel to defend accused persons, as prosecutors, or as judges. It is a serious matter that the department of the law which is to maintain the general security is so little regarded in the training of the profession.

In the Soviet polity punitive justice has been substantially taken away from the courts and made a matter of administrative action. With the rise of the service state and development of a humanitarian ideal of justice, signs are not wanting that the further development of criminal law may run in the same direction. If advocates, prosecutors, and judges are not well trained in the law they take part in administering, a general inefficiency in the work of the courts in criminal cases may well turn us from the traditional judicial path of the common law into the administrative path.

INTRODUCTION

In our American legal constitutional polity we may assume that criminal justice will remain justice according to law. It may be admitted that we must look forward to further development of individualized treatment of offenders and to further development of preventive justice on the criminal side. This may be had only through a better development of the administrative element in our criminal law and procedure and in the organization of our law enforcing agencies. Undoubtedly the substantive criminal law will have to be adjusted to development of the administrative side of the regime of criminal justice. But the administrative element must rest on and have its limits defined by law in order to be tolerable. Otherwise administrative punitive justice without law will take us far on the road to absolute government.

ROSCOE POUND

University of California
Los Angeles, California

SUMMARY OF CONTENTS

PART 1. THE SUBSTANTIVE CRIMINAL LAW

	Page
CHAPTER 1. DEFINITION AND CLASSIFICATION	1
Section	
1. Definition	1
2. Classification	4
CHAPTER 2. OFFENSES AGAINST THE PERSON	13
Section	
1. Homicide	13
2. Assault and Battery	75
3. Other Offenses Against the Person	85
CHAPTER 3. OFFENSES AGAINST THE HABITATION	93
Section	
1. Burglary	93
2. Arson	120
CHAPTER 4. LARCENY AND KINDRED OFFENSES (LARCENY, EMBEZZLEMENT, FALSE PRETENSES, ROBBERY, RECEIVING)	124
Section	
1. The Subject of Larceny	124
2. Property "Of Another"	131
3. The Caption and Asportation	132
4. The Trespass	137
5. The Intent	187
CHAPTER 5. OTHER OFFENSES	204
Section	
1. Offenses Against Morality and Decency	204
2. Offenses Against the Public Peace	207
3. Offenses Affecting Sovereignty or the Administration of Governmental Functions	210
CHAPTER 6. Imputability	217
Section	
1. The Necessity of an Act	217
2. What Contitutes an Act	220
3. Attempt and Kindred Problems	224
4. Negative Acts	250
5. Conspiracy	264
6. Agency	283
7. Incorporation	288
8. Parties to Crime	296
9. Causation	312

SUMMARY OF CONTENTS

	Page
CHAPTER 7. RESPONSIBILITY: IN GENERAL	343
Section	
1. Mens Rea	343
2. Criminal Negligence	352
3. Specific Intent	359
4. Other Particular States of Mind	371
5. Strict Liability	388
6. Unlawful Conduct	409
7. "Transferred Intent"	418
8. Motive	429
9. Concurrence of Mens Rea and Actus Reus	438
CHAPTER 8. RESPONSIBILITY: LIMITATIONS ON CRIMINAL CAPACITY	445
Section	
1. Immaturity (Infancy)	445
2. Mental Disease or Defect (Insanity)	463
3. Drunkenness (Intoxication)	487
4. Coverture	497
CHAPTER 9. RESPONSIBILITY: MODIFYING CIRCUMSTANCES	501
Section	
1. Ignorance or Mistake	501
2. Compulsion or Necessity	535
3. Consent of the Other Party	541
4. Guilt of the Injured Party	555
5. Conduct of the Injured Party	558
6. Condonation by Injured Party	563
CHAPTER 10. SPECIAL DEFENSES	571
Section	
1. Public Authority	571
2. Domestic Authority	581
3. Prevention of Crime	590
4. Self-Defense	598
5. Defense of Others	619
6. Defense of Property	628
7. Entrapment	638

PART 2. PROCEDURE AND ENFORCEMENT

CHAPTER 11. THE LIMITATIONS OF PROSECUTION	653
Section	
1. Jurisdiction	653
2. Extradition	694

SUMMARY OF CONTENTS

CHAPTER 11. THE LIMITATIONS OF PROSECUTION—Continued

Section	Page
3. Statute of Limitations	714
4. Former Jeopardy	725
5. Ex Post Facto Laws	759

CHAPTER 12. PROCEEDINGS PRELIMINARY TO TRIAL 769

Section	
1. Steps by the Prosecution Prior to Indictment	769
2. The Indictment or Information	822
3. Steps by the Prosecution After Indictment	828
4. Steps by the Defendant	832

CHAPTER 13. CERTAIN RIGHTS AND PRIVILEGES OF THE ACCUSED 861

Section	
1. The Right to Counsel	861
2. The Privilege Against Self-Incrimination	872
3. The Right of Privacy (To be Free from Unreasonable Search and Seizure)	891
4. Rights as to the Time of Trial	903
5. Right to be Present During Trial	905
6. Right to a Public Trial	906
7. Right to a Trial by Jury	909
8. Right to a Fair and Impartial Trial	912
9. The Interplay of Rights and Privileges	913

APPENDIX—A.L.I.A. MODEL CODE OF PRE-ARRAIGNMENT PROCEDURE—TENTATIVE DRAFT NO. 1 931

INDEX 957

TABLE OF CONTENTS

PART 1. THE SUBSTANTIVE CRIMINAL LAW

	Page
CHAPTER 1. DEFINITION AND CLASSIFICATION	1

Section
1. Definition _____ 1
2. Classification _____ 4

CHAPTER 2. OFFENSES AGAINST THE PERSON _____ 13

Section
1. Homicide _____ 13
2. Assault and Battery _____ 75
3. Other Offenses Against the Person _____ 85
    (A) Abduction _____ 85
    (B) Abortion and Contraceptivism _____ 86
        (i) Abortion _____ 86
        (ii) Contraceptivism _____ 87
        (iii) Indecent Advertising _____ 87
        (iv) Federal Offenses _____ 87
    (C) Rape _____ 88
    (D) False Imprisonment _____ 88
    (E) Kidnaping _____ 89
        (i) Simple Kidnaping _____ 89
        (ii) Kidnaping for Ransom _____ 90
        (iii) Child Stealing _____ 90
        (iv) Consent _____ 90
        (v) The Federal Kidnaping Act (The Lindbergh Law) _____ 90
    (F) Mayhem _____ 91
    (G) Dueling _____ 92

CHAPTER 3. OFFENSES AGAINST THE HABITATION _____ 93

Section
1. Burglary _____ 93
2. Arson _____ 120

CHAPTER 4. LARCENY AND KINDRED OFFENSES (LARCENY, EMBEZZLEMENT, FALSE PRETENSES, ROBBERY, RECEIVING) _____ 124

Section
1. The Subject of Larceny _____ 124
2. Property "Of Another" _____ 131
3. The Caption and Asportation _____ 132
4. The Trespass _____ 137
    (A) The Necessity of Trespass (And the Meaning of the Word "Trespass" in Larceny) _____ 137

TABLE OF CONTENTS

Chapter 4. Larceny and Kindred Offenses (Larceny, Embezzlement, False Pretenses, Robbery, Receiving)—Continued

Page

    (B) Appropriation of Delivered Goods 141
        (i) In General 141
        (ii) Distinction Between Custody and Possession 143
        (iii) The Breaking Bulk Doctrine 150
        (iv) Goods Delivered by Mistake 150
        (v) Goods Obtained by Fraud 157
    (C) Appropriation of Lost or Mislaid Goods 178
    (D) The Doctrine of Continuing Trespass 184
  5. The Intent 187

Chapter 5. Other Offenses 204

Section
1. Offenses Against Morality and Decency 204
    (A) Adultery, Fornication and Illicit Cohabitation 205
    (B) Bigamy 205
    (C) Incest 205
    (D) Seduction 205
    (E) Sodomy 206
    (F) Prostitution, Obscenity and Indecency 206
2. Offenses Against the Public Peace 207
    (A) Breach of the Peace 207
    (B) Fighting 207
    (C) Unlawful Assembly, Rout and Riot 208
    (D) Disturbance of Public Assembly 208
    (E) Disorderly House 209
    (F) Forcible Entry and Detainer 209
    (G) Libel 209
3. Offenses Affecting Sovereignty or the Administration of Governmental Functions 210
    (A) Treason 210
    (B) Perjury and Subornation 210
    (C) Bribery 210
    (D) Misconduct in Office (Official Misconduct) 211
    (E) Embracery 211
    (F) Counterfeiting 211
    (G) Obstruction of Justice 212
    (H) Escape and Kindred Offenses 212
    (I) Misprision of Felony 212
    (J) Compounding Crime 213
    (K) Maintenance, Champerty and Barratry 213
    (L) Contempt 214
    (M) Other Offenses 216

TABLE OF CONTENTS

	Page
CHAPTER 6. IMPUTABILITY	217
Section	
1. The Necessity of an Act	217
2. What Constitutes an Act	220
3. Attempt and Kindred Problems	224
(A) Attempt	224
(i) In General	224
(ii) Perpetrating Act	225
(iii) Impossibility	231
(iv) Intent	239
(B) Aggravated Assault	241
(C) Solicitation	244
(D) Abandonment	246
4. Negative Acts	250
5. Conspiracy	264
6. Agency	283
7. Incorporation	288
8. Parties to Crime	296
9. Causation	312
CHAPTER 7. RESPONSIBILITY: IN GENERAL	343
Section	
1. Mens Rea	343
2. Criminal Negligence	352
3. Specific Intent	359
4. Other Particular States of Mind	371
(A) Malice	371
(B) Knowledge	380
(C) Wilfulness	385
5. Strict Liability	388
6. Unlawful Conduct	409
7. "Transferred Intent"	418
8. Motive	429
9. Concurrence of Mens Rea and Actus Reus	438
CHAPTER 8. RESPONSIBILITY: LIMITATIONS ON CRIMINAL CAPACITY	445
Section	
1. Immaturity (Infancy)	445
2. Mental Disease or Defect (Insanity)	463
3. Drunkenness (Intoxication)	487
4. Coverture	497

TABLE OF CONTENTS

	Page
CHAPTER 9. RESPONSIBILITY: MODIFYING CIRCUMSTANCES	501

Section
1. Ignorance or Mistake _____ 501
    (A) Ignorance or Mistake of Law _____ 501
    (B) Ignorance or Mistake of Fact _____ 520
2. Compulsion or Necessity _____ 535
3. Consent of the Other Party _____ 541
4. Guilt of the Injured Party _____ 555
5. Conduct of the Injured Party _____ 558
6. Condonation by Injured Party _____ 563

CHAPTER 10. SPECIAL DEFENSES _____ 571

Section
1. Public Authority _____ 571
2. Domestic Authority _____ 581
3. Prevention of Crime _____ 590
4. Self-Defense _____ 598
5. Defense of Others _____ 619
6. Defense of Property _____ 628
7. Entrapment _____ 638

PART 2. PROCEDURE AND ENFORCEMENT

CHAPTER 11. THE LIMITATIONS OF PROSECUTION _____ 653

Section
1. Jurisdiction _____ 653
    (A) The Extent of the Authority of the State _____ 653
        (i). In General _____ 655
        (ii). Basis of Criminal Jurisdiction _____ 657
        (iii). The Situs of Crime _____ 666
        (iv) Jurisdiction Over Boundary Rivers _____ 675
    (B) Venue _____ 677
    (C) Courts _____ 691
2. Extradition _____ 694
3. Statute of Limitations _____ 714
4. Former Jeopardy _____ 725
    (A) Problems Peculiar to the Proceedings _____ 727
    (B) "The Same Offense" _____ 743
5. Ex Post Facto Laws _____ 759

CHAPTER 12. PROCEEDINGS PRELIMINARY TO TRIAL ____ 769

Section
1. Steps by the Prosecution Prior to Indictment _____ 769
    (A) Introduction _____ 769
    (B). The Complaint _____ 771
    (C) The Warrant _____ 776

TABLE OF CONTENTS

CHAPTER 12. PROCEEDINGS PRELIMINARY TO TRIAL—Continued

1. Steps by the Prosecution Prior to Indictment—Continued

		Page
(D)	Arrest	786
(i)	What Constitutes Arrest	786
(ii)	Who May Arrest	788
(1)	Under a Warrant	788
(2)	On Oral Order of a Magistrate	789
(3)	Assisting an Officer	790
(4)	"Without a Warrant"	791
(a)	Committed in His Presence	791
(b)	On Charge Preferred by Another	797
(c)	On Probable Cause	799
(d)	For Felony by Arrestee	801
(e)	On Official Information	802
(iii)	Place of Arrest	802
(iv)	Time of Arrest	805
(v)	Rights, Privileges and Duties	805
(1)	Manifestation of Purpose and Authority	805
(2)	Use of Force	806
(3)	Breaking Doors and Windows	809
(4)	Search of Prisoner	811
(5)	The "Frisk"	812
(6)	"Held for Questioning"	813
(7)	Disposition of Prisoner	815
(8)	Rights and Duties of Arrestee	816
(vi)	The Third Degree	817
(E)	Summons	818
(F)	Summary Trial and Preliminary Examination	820
(G)	Discharge, Commitment and Bail	821

2. The Indictment or Information ... 822
   (A) The Grand Jury ... 822
   (B) The Indictment ... 823
   (C) The Coroner's Inquest ... 826
   (D) The Information ... 826
3. Steps by the Prosecution After Indictment ... 828
   (A) The Bench Warrant ... 828
   (B) The Arraignment ... 829
   (C) Motions ... 830
   (D) Demurrer ... 831
   (E) Nolle Prosequi ... 831
4. Steps by the Defendant ... 832
   (A) Bail ... 832
   (B) Habeas Corpus ... 834
   (C) Demurrer ... 843
   (D) Motions ... 845

TABLE OF CONTENTS

CHAPTER 12. PROCEEDINGS PRELIMINARY TO TRIAL—Continued

    4. Steps by the Defendant—Continued
       (D) Motions—Continued

	Page
(i) Motion to Quash	845
(ii) Motion to Dismiss	846
(iii) For Change of Venue	846
(iv) For Change of Judge	847
(v) For Other Purposes	847
(E) Pleas	848
(i) Plea of Sanctuary	849
(ii) Plea of Benefit of Clergy	849
(iii) Plea to the Jurisdiction	849
(iv) Plea in Abatement	850
(v) Plea of Pardon	850
(vi) Pleas of Former Conviction, Former Acquittal or Former Jeopardy	850
(vii) Plea of Agreement to Turn State's Evidence	851
(viii) Plea of Not Guilty by Reason of Insanity	852
(ix) Plea of Not Guilty	852
(x) Plea of Guilty	853
(xi) Plea of Nolo Contendere	854
(xii) Plea of Guilty to a Lesser Offense	855
(F) Discovery	855

CHAPTER 13. CERTAIN RIGHTS AND PRIVILEGES OF THE ACCUSED ... 861

Section
1. The Right to Counsel ... 861
2. The Privilege Against Self-Incrimination ... 872
3. The Right of Privacy (to be Free from Unreasonable Search and Seizure) ... 891
4. Rights as to the Time of Trial ... 903
5. Right to be Present During Trial ... 905
6. Right to a Public Trial ... 906
7. Right to a Trial by Jury ... 909
   (A) Waiver ... 910
   (B) Alternate Jurors ... 911
8. Right to a Fair and Impartial Trial ... 912
9. The Interplay of Rights and Privileges ... 913

APPENDIX—A.L.I.A. MODEL CODE OF PRE-ARRAIGNMENT PROCEDURE—TENTATIVE DRAFT NO. 1 ... 931

Index ... 957

TABLE OF CASES

The principal cases are in italic type. Roman type indicates cases cited or discussed in the text and footnotes. References are to pages.

Abbate v. United States, 753
Accardi v. United States, 650
Adams, Commonwealth v., 414
Adamson v. California, 884
Ah Gee, People v., 301
Allen v. State, 169
Allison v. State, 48
Almeida, Commonwealth v., *333*
Altiere, United States v., 783
Andersen v. United States, 476
Anderson, State ex rel. v. Fousek, 9
Ann v. State, 34
Argent v. United States, 485
Arp v. State, 536
Ashley, People v., 165
Azzopardi, Regina v., 658

Bailey v. State, 153
Balint, United States v., 397
Ball, United States v., 735
Ballentine, People v., 854
Banks, Rex v., 142
Banks v. State, 36
Banovitch v. Commonwealth, *361*
Barnett, People v., 172
Barnett, State v., 357
Bartkus v. Illinois, 753
Bazeley, King, The v., 143
Beard v. United States, 604
Beard, Director of Public Prosecutions v., 487
Beattie v. State, 670
Beckham, State v., 633
Beggs, People v., 373
Behrman, United States v., 397
Belk v. People, 325
Bell v. State, 139
Benesch, Commonwealth v., 509
Benge and Another, Regina v., 338
Bennett, State v., 673
Betts v. Brady, 862
Birdsell, State v., 405
Bleasdale, Regina v., 284
Blechman, State v., 244
Bloom v. Marciniak, 711
Blyler, Holmes v., 783
Boies, State v., 377
Booth v. State, 235
Borchers, People v., 45

Bostick, People v., 886
Botkin, People v., 671
Brandenburg, United States v., 114
Breithaupt v. Abram, 924
Brewer v. State, 536
Brisbane, United States v., 745
Broadhurst, State v., 616
Brock v. State of North Carolina, 751
Brooks v. State, 178
Brown v. State, 377
Brown v. United States, 603
Brown v. Walker, 888
Brown, People v., 187, 318
Brown, State v., 490
Burrows v. State, 493
Bush v. Commonwealth, 340

Cahan, People v., 891
Calhoun v. State, 182
Cali, Commonwealth v., 433
Camodeca, People v., 236
Campbell v. United States, 858
Canadian Fur Trappers Corporation, People v., 290
Carbo v. State, 559
Caridis, People v., 125
Caritativo v. California, 464
Carmen's Petition, In re, 655
Carmody v. Seventh Judicial District Court in and for Lincoln County, 755
Carroll v. United States, 925
Chandler, State ex rel. v. Main, 662
Chavex, People v., 27
Chiarello, State v., 625
Chicago, Milwaukee & St. Paul R. Co., State v., 345
Chisser, Rex v., 544
Cicenia v. Lagay, 862
Ciucci v. Illinois, 754
Clarke v. Commonwealth, 95
Cleary v. Booth, 585
Clemon v. State, 33
Clyde, State v., 613
Cohen, State v., 131
Collum v. State, 60
Conde, Regina v., 250
Connors, People v., 367
Conrad v. State, 68
Cook, People v., 324, 546
Coombs, State v., 186

TABLE OF CASES

Cooper v. Commonwealth, 150
Cooper v. State, 604
Cores, United States v., 686
Corkran, Hyatt v. People ex rel., 699
Cornell v. State, 254
Cornett, People v., 64
Cowan v. State, 128
Creeks, People v., 274
Crooker v. California, 862
Cross v. State, 540
Crotty & Others, Commonwealth v., 780
Cude, State v., 503
Cummins v. Commonwealth, 134
Cunningham v. United States, 450
Currens, United States v., 477
Curtis, People v., 627
Cutter v. State, 505

Daniels v. State, 106
Davis, Rex v., 107
Davis v. Commonwealth, 98
Davis v. State, 471
Davis, State v., 56, 608
Davis, Tennessee v., 843
Dee, Regina v., 550
Decina, People v., 221
Dege, United States v., 266, 499
Dennison, Kentucky v., 699
Dilger v. Commonwealth, 795
Disbrow, State v., 717
Dixon, United States v., 684
Dobbs' Case, 364
Donahue, Commonwealth v., 631
Donoghue, Commonwealth v., 264
Dorado, People v., 921
Doughty v. Maxwell, 892
Douglas v. California, 867
Downes, Regina v., 252
Downey v. People, 13
Drew v. Thaw, 701
Drew, State v., 383
Drum, Commonwealth v., 61
Dudley and Stephens, Regina v., 538
Duncan v. State, 376
Dupree, People v., 101
Durham v. United States, 473
Duroncelay, People v., 923
Duty, In re, 656
Dye v. Johnson, 713

Easton v. Iowa, 656
Egginton, R. v., 545
Emmons, Commonwealth v., 592
Errington and Others' Case, 30
Escobedo v. Illinois, 916

Estreich, People v., 405, 530
Etter v. State, 727
Evans v. United States, 438
Eversole v. Commonwealth, 583
Ewart, King, The v., 523

Fahy v. Connecticut, 922
Fain v. Commonwealth, 222
Falcone, United States v., 272
Faulkner, Regina v., 426
Faustina v. Superior Court, 233
Favors, State v., 679
Fears v. State, 377
Feguer v. United States, 479
Feldkamp, People v., 767
Ferguson, People v., 517
Fields v. United States, 386
Finkelstein, People v., 235
Fisher v. United States, 466
Flaherty v. Thomas, 761
Fong Foo v. United States, 737
Fontaine, People v., 903
Forbs, People v., 922
Fox, United States v., 276
Frazier, State v., 322
Freddo v. State, 45
Frisbie v. Collins, 707

Gaines, In re, 886
Gallegos, State v., 2
Ganaposki, United States v., 719
Gargare, State v., 383
Gay v. State, 315
Gebardi v. United States, 269
Gendusa, State v., 99
George F. Fish, Inc., United States v., 289
Gideon v. Wainwright, 863
Gill, People v., 768
Gillow, Rex v., 433
Giordenello v. United States, 771
Gisske v. Sanders, 813
Glover v. Commonwealth, 246
Glover, State v., 329
Godfrey, Rex v., 701
Golden v. State, 438
Goldman, State v., 381
Gore v. United States, 744
Gorshen, People v., 483
Gould, People v., 566
Grafton v. United States, 748
Gray v. State, 109
Green v. United States, 735
Gregory, Commonwealth v., *550*
Grierson, State v., 611

TABLE OF CASES

Griffin v. California, 883
Grimes v. State, 16
Grogan v. State, 730
Grugin, State v., 42
Gut, State v., 571
Gwynne, Horton v., 391

Hadley v. State, 28
Hairston v. State, 369
Hall, Regina v., 191
Hall, State v., 666, 696
Hamilton v. Alabama, 863
Hands, Regina v., 175
Hanks v. State, 662
Hardie, State v., 51
Hardy v. Betz, 704
Harmon, People v., 761
Harris v. State, 58
Harris, People v., 40
Harrison, People v., 333
Hartgraves, People v., 921
Hawkins v. United States, 434
Hayner, People v., 24
Hays, Commonwealth v., 154
Hegeman, People ex rel. v. Corrigan, 430
Heigho, Ex parte, 318
Hemphill, State v., 77
Henderson, People v., 469, 738
Henderson v. State, 198
Henry v. United States, 814
Hermann v. State, 135
Hernandez, People v., 530
Hill v. State, 78
Hoag v. New Jersey, 749
Hobbs v. Winchester Corp., 394
Hogan, Regina v., 251
Holbrook, Regina v., **285**
Holdren, State v., 293
Holland, Regina v., 562
Holloway, Regina v., 192
Holmes, Joseph, In re, 449
Holmes, United States v., 538
Holsey v. State, 565
Horton, State v., 411
Howk, People v., 273
Hubbard v. Commonwealth, 561
Hudson, State v., 492
Huggins, Rex v., 283
Hüter, People v., 66
Hyde, People v., 383

Innes v. Tobin, 703

Jackson v. Commonwealth, 439
Jackson v. Denno, 873

Jacobs, State v., 677
Jaffe, People v., 233
James v. Louisiana, 812
Jencks v. United States, 858
Johnson, State v., 375
Johnson v. Zerbst, 862
Jones v. United States, 254, 774

Karp, People v., 164
Katz, United States v., 267
Kealy, State v., 709
Keaton v. State, 331
Keefer, People v., 304
Kelly, Rex v., 428
Kelly, State v., 391
Kennedy, Commonwealth v., 226
Ker v. California, 891, 896
Ker v. Illinois, 708
Kilham, Queen, The v., 160
Killough v. United States, 922
Kindle, State v., 21
Knight, State v., 698
Koczwara, Commonwealth v., 405
Konigsberg, United States v., 922
Koons, People ex rel. v. Elling, 127
Kremer, State v., 408

Lambert v. California, 511
Lambert, State v., 377
Langford v. United States, 433
Lankford, State v., 549
Lanza, United States v., 748
Lascelles v. Georgia, 710
Lauglin, State v., 372
La Voie, People v., 601
Law v. Commonwealth, 307
Laws v. State, 435
Learned, State v., 747
Lee v. United States, 901
Lee Kong, People v., 244
Leland v. Oregon, 485
Leopold, State v., 328
Lesley, Regina v., 573
Letner v. State, 326
Lewis, People v., 315, 447
Lewis, Rex v., 419
Ligouri, People v., 606
Limicy v. State, 350
Linkletter v. Walker, 892
Long v. State, 514
Lopez v. United States, 899

McAfee, Commonwealth v., 584
McCann, United States ex rel. Adams v., 866

TABLE OF CASES

McCord v. People, 557
McGavic, United States v., 898
McGee, People v., 715
McLaughlin, Commonwealth v., 31
McNabb v. United States, 879
Macloon, Commonwealth v., 671
Maish, State v., 483
Malcomson v. Scott, 804
Mallory v. United States, 881
Malloy v. Hogan, 872
Mapp v. Ohio, 891
Markiewicz v. Black, 729
Martin, Rex v., 218
Martin, State v., 420
Martinis, People v., 749
Masciale v. United States, 648
Mason v. Commonwealth, 137
Massey v. Moore, 463
Massiah v. United States, 913
Masters v. State, 137
Matthews, State v., 48
Meath v. State, 383
Merritt v. Commonwealth, 239
Merry v. Green, 152
Michael, Regina v., 339
Mills, State v., 196
Mink, Commonwealth v., 409
Mitchell, Commonwealth v., 787
Mitchell v. Gladden, 455
Mitchell v. State, 620
Mitchell, State v., 231
Mizner, State v., 587
Modesto, People v., 884
Monroe, State v., 337
Mooney v. Holohan, 838
Moore v. Dempsey, 838, 912
Moore, State v., 721
Moore, People v., 75
Moreland v. State, 261
Moreland, United States v., 5
Morgan v. Commonwealth, 145
Morgan, United States v., 848
Morissette v. United States, 396
Morrill & Another, Commonwealth v., 555
Morse, People v., 738
Mortensen v. United States, 433
Moyer, Commonwealth v., 329
Mulcahy, People v., 414
Mulhall, State v., 421
Mullins v. Sanders, 780
Murdock, United States v., 385, 872
Murphy v. State, 623
Murphy v. Waterfront Commission of New York Harbor, 872

Nall v. Commonwealth, 539
Nash, State v., 521
Neagle, In re, 842
Neal v. State of California, 726
Neely, State v., 920
Neff, State v., 93
Nicholls v. State, 103
Nielson v. Oregon, 675
Noble, State v., 481
Noblett, People v., 164
Norris v. United States, 267

Odenwald, People v., 128
Oliver, State v., 584
Olmstead v. United States, 649
Olshefski, Commonwealth v., 394
O'Neal v. United States, 434
O'Neil, State v., 518
On Lee v. United States, 901
Osborn, United States v., 903

Pacheco, State v., 903
Pack, People v., 923
Padilla, State v., 471
Palermo, United States v., 385
Palko v. Connecticut, 740
Park, State v., 479
Patton v. United States, 910
Payne v. Arkansas, 841
Pear, King, The v., 157
Peaslee, Commonwealth v., 245
Peery, State v., 347
Pembliton, Regina v., 424
Penman, People v., 491
Penny, People v., 55
Peoni, United States v., 307
Perryman v. State, 540
Peterson, State v., 247
Phetheon, Regina v., 194
Pickus, State v., 385
Pierce, Commonwealth v., 353
Pierce, People v., 266
Pilkington v. United States, 450
Pinkerton v. United States, 275
Plachy v. State, 761
Podolski, People v., 333
Pointer v. Texas, 927
Porter v. State, 377
Porter, Queen, The v., 39
Powell v. Alabama, 861, 914
Preddy v. Commonwealth, 238
Price v. Tehan, 793
Price, State v., 747
Prince, Queen, The v., 158
Prince, State v., 402
Pulley, People v., 38
Putch, Commonwealth v., 262
Putnam v. United States, 683

xxxviii

TABLE OF CASES

Quick, State v., *217*

Rabinowitz, United States v., 812
Rankin, State v., 748
Raven's Case, 141
Reade, People v., *137*
Reck v. Pate, 892
Redline, Commonwealth v., *333*
Reese, State v., 680
Revard v. State, 477
Richardson, King, The v., 309
Rider, State v., 218
Riley, Regina v., 184
Rizzo, People v., 228
Robinson, Application of, 702
Robinson v. State, 152
Robles, People v., 111
Rochin v. California, 812
Rockwell, People v., 336
Rodriguez, People v., 54
Rojas, People v., 232
Romig, Commonwealth v., 414
Roper, People v., 451
Roth v. United States, 433
Ruhl, State v., 528
Russell, Rex v., 258
Russell, Trial of Earl, 660
Ryan, Commonwealth v., 148

Salmon, Regina v., 355
Samuel v. Payne, 797
Samuels v. McCurdy, 767
Santa Rita Store Co., United States v., 266
Saunders and Archers, Regina v., *310*
Savage, State v., 189
Scales v. United States, 278
Scofield, Rex v., 224
Scott v. Commonwealth, 641
Sealfon v. United States, 752
Sealy, State v., 413
Shepherd v. People, 760
Sherman v. United States, 643
Shook v. United States, 787
Siegel, People v., 721
Silverman v. United States, 893
Simpson v. State, 668
Singer v. United States, 911
Sipes, State v., 610
Smiley, United States v., 660
Smith v. California, 394
Smith v. Crouse, 892
Smith, Regina v., 424
Smith v. State, 80, 545
Sorrells v. United States, 640
Spannell v. State, 745

Spano v. New York, 913
Spreckels, People v., 693
Stanford v. Texas, 783
Statley, People v., 497
Stein v. New York, 875
Stephens, Queen, The v., 388
Stephens, State v., 692
Storey v. State, 592
Stowell v. People, 100
Striggles, State v., 517
Stuart, People v., 414
Sullens, Rex v., 147

Taft, State v., 220
Tateo, United States v., 734
Terrell v. State, *373*
Thabo Meli v. Regina, 441
Thacker v. Commonwealth, 365
Thompson v. Missouri, 763
Thompson v. People, 908
Thompson v. State, 132
Thompson v. Utah, 763
Thurborn, Regina v., 180
Tinkler, Regina v., 529
Tolson, Regina v., 533
Townley, Queen, The v., 138
Townsend v. Sain, 922
Travis v. United States, 690
Trogdon v. State, 437
Turley, United States v., 175
Turvey, Rex v., 544

Ullmann v. United States, 886

Van Schaick, United States v., 256
Ventresca, United States v., 775
Viliborghi v. State, 594
Vogel, People v., 525

Wade v. Hunter, 734
Wadsworth, Commonwealth ex rel. *v.* Shortall, 574
Waina and Swatoa, Regina v., 657
Walker v. State, 107
Walls v. State, 433
Walsh, Rex v., 133
Ward, People v., 760
Warmke v. Commonwealth, *18*
Warren, People v., 785
Washington v. People, 919
Washington, People v., 333
Wayne v. United States, 897
Weeks v. United States, 891
Weisengoff, State v., 39
Weiss, People v., 507
White, Commonwealth v., *82*

xxxix

TABLE OF CASES

White v. Maryland, 928
White, Queen, The v., 256
White, State v., 481
White, United States v., 784
Whitmore v. State, 170
Whittington, In re, 703
Wild's Case, 629
Wiley v. United States, 435
Wilkinson v. State, 161
Williams v. State, 135
Williams, Commonwealth v., 414
Williams, State v., 305, 408
Williamson, State v., 421
Willis, Rex v., 132
Wilson v. State, 225

Wilson, State v., 241
Windisch v. United States, 362
Winn v. State, 743
Wolf v. Colorado, 891
Wolff, People v., 484
Wong Sun v. United States, 892
Wood, People v., 333
Wood, State v., 314
Woodrow, Regina v., 394
Woods v. State, 93
Woo Wai v. United States, 640
Wright, People v., 112
Wright v. State, 376

Young, People v., 624

CASES AND MATERIALS ON CRIMINAL LAW AND PROCEDURE

Part 1

THE SUBSTANTIVE CRIMINAL LAW

Chapter 1

DEFINITION AND CLASSIFICATION

SECTION 1. DEFINITION

A crime is any social harm defined and made punishable by law.

The definition suggested by Blackstone is as follows: "A crime or misdemeanour is an act committed or omitted, in violation of a public law either forbidding or commanding it."[1] Although definitions of crime have tended to follow the Blackstone pattern, with variations as to the exact wording, the emphasis is faulty. Suppose, for example, D stabbed X unlawfully, inflicting a serious injury that resulted in X's death six weeks thereafter. Under the theory of the common law of crimes, unchanged by statute, D should be punished for the unlawful killing of X, but X's death was the result of D's

---

1. 4 Bl.Comm. *5.

act rather than the act itself, which was thrusting the knife.[2] If, quite by accident, a surgeon should have come upon X so soon after the wounding as to be able to save his life this would not in any way change D's act. The knife thrust by D would be unaltered by this fortuitous occurrence although the difference in the consequences would be tremendous. And although D's act would be the same in either case his crime would be entirely different because under the first assumption he is to be punished for an unlawful killing whereas under the second, there would be no killing and the punishment would be for unlawful wounding. In other words it is more accurate to define crime in terms of the social harm caused rather than the act committed.[3]

To repeat: A crime is any social harm defined and made punishable by law.

STATE v. GALLEGOS

Supreme Court of Wyoming, 1963.
384 P.2d 967.

Before PARKER, C. J., and HARNSBERGER, GRAY and McINTYRE, JJ.

MR. JUSTICE McINTYRE delivered the opinion of the court.

Johnny Gallegos, defendant, along with two others, was charged in the District Court of Albany County, by information, with the violation of § 14–23(d), W.S.1957, of the state's child protection act. The provisions of this section are these:

"It shall be unlawful for any person (including but not limited to parent, guardian, or custodian) knowingly to commit any of the following acts with respect to a child under the age of 19 years:

* * * * * * * * * *

"(d) To cause, encourage, aid or contribute to the endangering of the child's health, welfare, or morals."

Gallegos entered a demurrer to the information claiming the portion of the statute under which he was charged was so vague and indefinite that an accused could not know the nature of a crime charged against him, and that the essentials of due process were thereby violated.

---

2. "The word 'act' is used throughout the Restatement of this Subject to denote an external manifestation of the actor's will and does not include any of its results even the most direct, immediate and intended." Restatement, Second, Torts § 2(1965).

3. For this reason Bishop defined crime in terms of the "wrong" done. "A crime is any wrong which the government deems injurious to the public at large, and punishes through a judicial proceeding in its own name." 1 Bishop, New Criminal Law § 32 (8th ed. 1892).

The district court sustained this contention and dismissed the charge. The county and prosecuting attorney took an exception to the ruling and has filed a bill of exceptions in this court, pursuant to the provisions of §§ 7-288 to 7-290, W.S.1957.

The matter of definiteness required in criminal statutes was fully discussed by us in Day v. Armstrong, Wyo., 362 P.2d 137, 147-148. The principles adhered to in that opinion are directly applicable here and sufficient to resolve the question which we are asked to decide.

For example, recognition was given in the Day case to these principles:

1. The requirement of a reasonable degree of certainty in legislation, especially in the criminal law, is a well-established element of the guarantee of due process of law.

2. No one may be required at peril of life, liberty or property to speculate as to the meaning of penal statutes.

3. All are entitled to be informed as to what the state commands or forbids.

4. A statute which either forbids or requires the doing of an act in terms so vague that men of common intelligence must necessarily guess at its meaning and differ as to its application violates the first essential of due process of law.

5. The constitutional guarantee of equal rights under the law (see Art. 1, §§ 2 and 3, Wyoming Constitution) will not tolerate a criminal law so lacking in definition that each defendant is left to the vagaries of individual judges and juries.

The statute here in question forbids any person to "cause, encourage, aid or contribute to the endangering of the child's health, welfare, or morals." The objection to the statute is that it furnishes no standard as to what the endangering of a child's health, welfare or morals is, and hence it leaves decision to arbitrary judgment, whim and caprice. . . .

The American Cancer Society has in recent times made reports showing that cigarette smoking may lead to lung cancer. Hence, the question might be asked, would the offering of a cigarette to a person under the age of 19 be considered as endangering the health of a child and therefore punishable under this statute? Or again, since we have statutes forbidding the serving of intoxicating liquor to minors, would the serving of cocktails to friends in one's home, in the presence of a minor, be thought of as encouraging or contributing to the endangering of the child's health, welfare or morals?

These questions, as representative of many more which could be asked, serve to illustrate how utterly impossible it would be to know just what acts are and what acts are not forbidden by the statute under which defendant was charged. Since men must necessarily guess at its meaning and differ as to its application, the statute violates an essential of due process of law. . . .

Section 14–21, W.S.1957, a part of the child protection act, declares it is the policy of the act to protect children from all types of abuse which jeopardize their health, welfare or morals. Without doubt statutes directed to that end are essential for the safeguarding of youth and for the preservation of health and moral standards. However, criminal statutes cannot be couched in terms so vague and indefinite as to deny due process to an accused. . . .

We realize there is respectable authority from some of our sister states approving legislation somewhat similar, but not exactly the same, as the statute here involved. Without attempting to distinguish such legislation, we prefer to rely upon the fact that general principles with respect to due process, as heretofore announced in this jurisdiction and in the Supreme Court of the United States, prompts us to hold subsection (d) of § 14–23 in violation of the due process clause of Art. 1, § 6, Wyoming Constitution.

Exceptions overruled.[a]

SECTION 2. CLASSIFICATION

The common law divided crime into three major groups: (1) treason, (2) felony and (3) misdemeanor. To remove the uncertainty which had developed in the ancient law, the Statute of Treasons enacted in 1350 [1] specified exactly what should constitute this offense including, among certain other wrongs, a manifested intent to kill the king, queen or prince, levying war against the king, adhering to his enemies, giving them aid and comfort. The original determinant of felony was forfeiture of lands and goods, although three influences tended to obscure this fact: (1) under the English common law all felonies carried also the death penalty except mayhem for which mutilation was substituted,[2] (2) misdemeanors were never punished

---

[a] A statute prohibiting the Sunday sale of goods, wares or merchandise except "drugs or medicines, provisions, *or other articles of immediate necessity*" is void for vagueness because the words emphasized do not have a meaning determinable by any objective standard. "To attempt to enforce the statute would be the equivalent of an effort to carry out a statute which in terms penalized and punished all acts detrimental to the public interest when unjust and unreasonable in the estimation of the court and jury (United States v. L. Cohen Grocery Co., 225 U.S. 81, 41 S.Ct. 298, 65 L.Ed. 516, 14 A.L.R. 1045)". State v. Hill, 189 Kan. 403, 369 P.2d 365, 91 A.L.R.2d 750 (1962).

An ordinance providing that "no person shall loiter . . . in or upon any street, park or public place, or in any public building; . . ." with no definition of the word "loiter", is void for vagueness. State v. Caez, 81 N.J. Super. 315, 195 A.2d 496 (1963).

1. 25 Edw. 111 c. 2.

2. Whipping was substituted for death as the penalty for petit larceny, but this was a change from the common law resulting from an early statute. Statute of Westminster, 1, c. 15 (1275).

capitally and (3) early statutes creating new felonies regularly imposed and emphasized the penalty of death. Because of these facts there has been a tendency to say that under the common-law plan all offenses punished by death were felonies whereas those punished only by some milder penalty were misdemeanors. This is very nearly accurate but it is well to bear in mind that the actual determinant was forfeiture.[3]

What has been said shows the common-law classification to be unsound because one category was determined by the nature of the wrong perpetrated and the other two by the penalty provided. In fact, since treason was punished by forfeiture of lands and goods (and by death) it was strictly speaking a felony, although it was convenient to deal with it as a separate category for procedural reasons. Statutes in this country commonly divide offenses into two classes: (1) felony and (2) misdemeanor. The determinant is usually the penalty imposed although the exact nature of the penalty employed for this purpose is not uniform and nowhere has any resemblance to the common law in this regard except that a capital offense is a felony. Very few felonies are capital today and the other type of penalty used to distinguish felony from misdemeanor usually follows one of two patterns. It is based upon either: (1) the type of institution in which the offender may be incarcerated (such as the state prison), or (2) the length of term which may be imposed (as, for example, a term exceeding one year).

For certain purposes quite a different plan of classification may be employed. For a consideration of the specific offenses, for example, it is common to have the categories dependent upon the particular type of social harm involved, such as (1) offenses against the person, (2) offenses against the habitation, (3) offenses against property, and so forth, as indicated in the following chapters. Another dichotomy in crime classification is based upon the concept of infamy and divides the field into (1) infamous crimes and (2) noninfamous crimes.

UNITED STATES v. MORELAND

Supreme Court of the United States, 1922.
258 U.S. 433, 42 S.Ct. 368.

MR. JUSTICE MCKENNA delivered the opinion of the Court.

The question in the case is what procedure, in the prosecution and conviction for crime, the Fifth Amendment of the Constitution of the United States makes dependent upon the character of punishment assigned to the crime.

3. In the words of Blackstone, "the true criterion of felony is forfeiture".
4 Bl.Comm. *97.

The amendment provides that—

"No person shall be held to answer for a capital, or otherwise infamous crime, unless on a presentment or indictment of a grand jury, except in cases arising in the land or naval forces, or in the militia, when in actual service in time of war or public danger. . . ."

The respondent, Moreland, was proceeded against in the juvenile court of the District of Columbia by information, not by presentment or indictment by a grand jury, for the crime of willfully neglecting or refusing to provide for the support and maintenance of his minor children. The statute prescribes the punishment to be "a fine of not more than $500 or by imprisonment in the workhouse of the District of Columbia at hard labor for not more than twelve months or by both such fine and imprisonment." 34 Stat. 86.

He was tried by a jury and found guilty, and, after certain proceedings with which we have no concern, he was sentenced to the workhouse at hard labor for six months.

The Court of Appeals reversed the judgment and remanded the case to the juvenile court, with directions to dismiss the complaint. The court considered that it was constrained to decide that the judgment was in violation of the Fifth Amendment, and, therefore, to reverse it on the authority of Wong Wing v. United States, 163 U.S. 228, 16 S.Ct. 977, 41 L.Ed. 140.

The United States resists both the authority and extent of that case by the citation of others, which, it asserts, modify or overrule it. A review of it, therefore, is of initial importance.

Certain statutes of the United States made it unlawful under certain circumstances for a Chinese laborer to be in the United States, and provided for his deportation by certain officers, among others, a commissioner of a United States court. And one of them (Act of 1892 [Comp.St. § 4318]) provided that, if a Chinese person or one of that descent was "convicted and adjudged to be not lawfully entitled to be or remain in the United States," he should "be imprisoned at hard labor for a period not exceeding one year, and thereafter removed from the United States."

Wong Wing, a Chinese person (there were others arrested, but for the purpose of convenience of reference we treat the case as being against him only), was arrested and taken before a commissioner of the Circuit Court for the Eastern District of Michigan and adjudged to be unlawfully within the United States and not entitled to remain therein. It was also adjudged that he be imprisoned at hard labor at and in the Detroit House of Correction for the period of 60 days.

The court, considering the statutes, said they operated on two classes—one which came into the country with its consent; the other which came in without consent and in disregard of law—and that

Congress had the constitutional power to deport both classes and to commit the enforcement of the law to executive officers.

This power of arrest by the executive officers and the power of deportation were sustained; but the punishment provided for by the act, and which was pronounced against Wong Wing, that is, imprisonment at hard labor, was decided to be a violation of the Fifth Amendment; he not having been proceeded against by presentment or indictment by a grand jury.

The court noted the argument and the cases cited and sustained the power of exclusion, but said that when Congress went further, and inflicted punishment at hard labor, it "must provide for a judicial trial to establish the guilt of the accused." And this because such punishment was infamous and prohibited by the Fifth Amendment; the conditions prescribed by the amendment not having been observed. The necessity of their observance was decided, because, to repeat, imprisonment at hard labor was an infamous punishment. . . .

The ultimate contention of the United States is that the provision of the Act of March 23, 1906, for punishment by fine or imprisonment are severable, and that, therefore, it was error in the Court of Appeals in holding the act unconstitutional, and in directing the dismissal of the case, instead of sending it back for further proceedings.

The contention is untenable. It is what sentence can be imposed under the law, not what was imposed, that is the material consideration. When an accused is in danger of an infamous punishment, if convicted, he has a right to insist that he be not put upon trial, except on the accusation of a grand jury. Ex parte Wilson and Mackin v. United States, supra.

Judgment affirmed.[1]

MR. JUSTICE CLARKE took no part in the consideration and decision of this case.

MR. JUSTICE BRANDEIS, with whom concurs MR. CHIEF JUSTICE TAFT and MR. JUSTICE HOLMES, dissenting. . . .

It is not the provision for hard labor, but the imprisonment in a penitentiary, which now renders a crime infamous. Commitment to a penitentiary, with or without hard labor, connotes infamy, because it is proof of the conviction of a crime of such a nature that infamy was a prescribed consequence. Confinement in a penitentiary is the modern substitute for the death penalty and for the other forms of corporal punishment which, at the time of the adoption of the Fifth Amendment, were still administered in America for most

---

[1]. The statute making a sentence to an infamous punishment a ground for divorce means the sentence actually imposed and not the potential sentence. Hull v. Donze, 164 La. 199, 113 So. 816 (1927).

of the crimes deemed serious. It was then believed that even capital punishment should be inflicted under conditions involving public disgrace. Largely for this reason hangings were public, as in earlier days men had been drawn and quartered. If the life of an offender was spared, it was then thought that some other punishment involving disgrace must be applied to render his loss of reputation permanent. When in 1786 Pennsylvania, shrinking from the physical cruelties inflicted under sentence of the courts, took the first step in reform by substituting imprisonment for death as the penalty for some of the lesser felonies, the exposure to infamy was still deemed an essential of punishment. The measure then enacted provided specifically that the imprisonment should be attended by "continuous hard labor publicly and disgracefully imposed." Hard labor as thus prescribed and practiced was merely an instrument of disgrace. The statutory direction was carried out by employing the convicts in gang labor along the public roads, chained by fetters with bomb shells attached and iron collars, with shaved heads, and wearing a distinctive infamous dress. The demoralizing influence both upon the community and the convict of these public manifestations of disgrace was soon realized, and led, shortly after the adoption of our Constitution, to their discontinuance in Pennsylvania and to the establishment in Philadelphia of America's first penitentiary.

Hard labor was not considered an essential element of the penitentiary punishment; and experience proved that it was in fact an alleviation. The most severe punishment inflicted was solitary confinement without labor. Hard labor regularly pursued and productively employed had for two centuries been applied as a corrective measure in the effort to deal with social delinquents. Then the belief spread that it might be effectively employed also in the reformation of criminals—a class of persons theretofore generally considered incorrigible. And when reform and rehabilitation of those convicted of serious crimes became a chief aim of the penal system, the dignity of labor was proclaimed and the practices of the workhouse were adopted and developed in the penitentiary. Thus hard labor, which, in inflicting punishment for serious crimes, had first been introduced as a medium of disgrace, became the means of restoring and giving self-respect. . . .

Imprisonment in a penitentiary where the convict is (or used to be) "subject to solitary imprisonment, to have his hair cropped, to be clothed in conspicuous prison dress, subjected to hard labor without pay, to hard fare, coarse and meager food, and to severe discipline" is a punishment deemed infamous; but commitment to a "house of correction, under that and the various names of workhouse or bridewell," although some of the incidents of the confinement are identical, "has not the same character of infamy attached to it." There is thus no basis for the contention that sentence to hard labor as an incident of confinement necessarily renders a punishment infamous, or that commitment to a workhouse at hard labor can be made only upon indictment by a grand jury. . . .

STATE ex rel. ANDERSON v. FOUSEK, MAYOR

Supreme Court of Montana, 1932.
91 Mont. 448, 8 P.2d 791.

ANGSTMAN, J. Defendant is mayor of the city of Great Falls, a city of the first class. Relator, Anderson, was appointed as lieutenant of the police force of the city and acted as such from March 18, 1929, until suspended as hereinafter stated. On December 17, 1930, relator, with other members of the police force, was charged by indictment filed in the District Court of the United States for the District of Montana with the crime of willfully, wrongfully, unlawfully, knowingly, and feloniously conspiring, combining, confederating, and agreeing together and with each other and with divers other persons, to possess, keep for sale, and sell intoxicating liquors containing more than one-half of 1 per cent. of alcohol by volume and fit for beverage purposes, and to maintain in the city of Great Falls a large number of common nuisances, to wit, rooms, houses, buildings, structures, and places where intoxicating liquors were to be possessed, kept for sale, and sold for beverage purposes, and of doing acts to effect the object of the conspiracy, all in violation of the act of Congress commonly known as the Jones Act (27 U.S.C.A. §§ 91, 92). He was found guilty by verdict of a jury, and was adjudged to pay a fine of $100 and to be imprisoned in case of default in payment. The judgment of conviction has not been reversed, modified, or set aside, and no appeal therefrom has been prosecuted. The time for paying the fine was extended beyond the time of the proceedings in the District Court from which this appeal was taken.

After the conviction of relator, defendant here suspended relator from the police force and filed charges against him with the police commission of the city. Thereafter a hearing was had before the police commission, and, while the commission found that relator had been found guilty of the crime charged, it also found that the crime did not involve moral turpitude, and ordered his reinstatement. Within five days thereafter defendant ordered his permanent discharge from the police force. Relator applied to the district court for a writ of mandate to compel defendant to comply with the order of the commission by reinstating him. An alternative writ was issued. Defendant's motion to quash the alternative writ was granted, and the proceedings were dismissed. This appeal followed.

There is no dispute concerning the facts. While other questions are argued in the excellent briefs of counsel, the determinative question is one of law, viz.: Must the judgment of the court be sustained because of section 511, Revised Codes 1921? That section in part provides: "An office becomes vacant on the happening of either of the following events before the expiration of the term of the incumbent: . . . 8. His conviction of a felony, or of any offense involving moral turpitude, or a violation of his official duties."

The first point of difference between the parties is whether a member of the police force of a city is the incumbent of an office within the meaning of section 511. . . . It follows that relator, as a policeman, was the incumbent of an office within the meaning of section 511. The almost universal rule announced by the authorities generally is that a policeman is a public officer.

If, then, relator was convicted of a felony, it operated as an automatic limitation upon the duration of his office. . . .

Was relator convicted of a felony? The statutory offense for which he was convicted is found in section 88, 18 U.S.C.A., which reads: "If two or more persons conspire either to commit any offense against the United States, or to defraud the United States in any manner or for any purpose, and one or more of such parties do any act to effect the object of the conspiracy, each of the parties to such conspiracy shall be fined not more than $10,000, or imprisoned not more than two years, or both." One who commits the crime denounced by section 88 is guilty of a felony, for "all offenses which may be punished by death or imprisonment for a term exceeding one year, shall be deemed felonies." Section 541, 18 U.S.C.A. All felonies are infamous crimes. Falconi v. United States (C.C.A.) 280 F. 766. And the test to be applied in determining whether a crime is infamous under the Fifth Amendment to the Constitution of the United States is the punishment that may be inflicted, and not what was actually imposed. . . . And that is the test to be applied in determining whether a person has been convicted of a felony or a misdemeanor [1] when he has violated a federal statute on conspiracy. State ex rel. Beckman v. Bowman, 38 Ohio App., 237, 175 N.E. 891.

A different rule is prescribed by our statute which classifies crimes after judgment as felonies or misdemeanors by the punishment actually imposed.[2] Section 10723, Rev.Codes 1921; State v.

---

1. A person finally adjudged guilty of a felony in Oklahoma is not entitled to register and vote in a state primary or general election and therefore is not a qualified elector of the state; and it is the potential punishment rather than that actually imposed which determines whether the offense is a felony or a misdemeanor. Braly v. Wingard, Okl., 326 P.2d 775 (1958).

2. Such a provision is not uncommon. E. g., "A felony is a crime which is punishable with death or by imprisonment in the state prison. Every other crime is a misdemeanor. When a crime, punishable by imprisonment in the state prison, is also punishable by fine or imprisonment in a county jail, in the discretion of the court, it shall be deemed a misdemeanor for all purposes after a judgment imposing a punishment other than imprisonment in the state prison." West's Ann.Cal.Pen.Code, § 17.

Under such a provision the offense is regarded as a felony for all purposes until judgment. The judge can make it a misdemeanor by a misdemeanor sentence, but if no judgment is pronounced it remains a felony. People

Atlas, 75 Mont. 547, 244 P. 477. But that statute has to do only with crimes under our state statutes, and has nothing to do with crimes classified by the federal statutes. The character of an offense, i. e., whether a felony or a misdemeanor, must be determined by the laws of the jurisdiction where the crime was committed. State ex rel. Beckman v. Bowman, supra.

The crime for which relator stands convicted is a felony in the jurisdiction where committed, and we cannot regard it otherwise. Under the plain provisions of section 511 the office of relator became vacant upon his conviction, unless, as relator contends, section 511 has to do only with felonies or other crimes under our state laws, and does not cover felonies under the federal laws.

This same contention was advanced in the case of In re Peters, 73 Mont. 284, 235 P. 772, 774, which was a disbarment proceeding under a statute very similar to section 511, and it was there held that the state statute, section 8961, authorizing the suspension of an attorney upon "conviction of a felony or misdemeanor involving moral turpitude," required the suspension of an attorney when the conviction was in the federal court. That case is determinative of the question against the contention of the relator.

The judgment appealed from is affirmed.

CALLAWAY, C. J., and GALEN, FORD, and MATTHEWS, JJ., concur.

MODEL PENAL CODE *

Section 1.04. Classes of Crimes; Violations.

(1) An offense defined by this Code or by any other statute of this State, for which a sentence of [death or of] [1] imprisonment is authorized,

v. Banks, 53 Cal.2d 370, 1 Cal.Rptr. 669, 348 P.2d 102 (1959). D's plea of guilty resulted in three-years probation, with twelve months imprisonment in the county jail as a condition. The probation period had expired and no sentence had been pronounced, nor had advantage been taken of the dismissal proceedings authorized by the Penal Code under such circumstances. It was held that the offense remains a felony. For a classification of such an offense for various purposes see the Court's note 7 in the case cited above.

Unless a misdemeanor sentence is entered against a defendant found guilty of forgery of a narcotics prescription, the offense stands provisionally as a felony, but if probation is granted without pronouncement of sentence, the probationer retains his ordinary civil rights. In re Trummer, 60 Cal. 2d 658, 36 Cal.Rptr. 281, 388 P.2d 177 (1964).

* Prepared by the American Law Institute. The student must not confuse the Model Penal Code with the Restatements prepared by the Institute. This does not purport to be a statement of existing law; it is recommended legislation. As the Official Draft will not be available in time for this edition, all references to the Model Penal Code herein are to the Proposed Official Draft (1962, as amended at the 1962 meeting) unless otherwise indicated. This and the other quotations from the Code have been expressly authorized by the American Law Institute.

1. Since a few jurisdictions do not have capital punishment all references to the death sentence are bracketed in the Code.

constitutes a crime. Crimes are classified as felonies, misdemeanors or petty misdemeanors.

(2) A crime is a felony if it is so designated in this Code or if persons convicted thereof may be sentenced [to death or] to imprisonment for a term which, apart from an extended term, is in excess of one year.[2]

(3) A crime is a misdemeanor if it is so designated in this Code or in a statute other than this Code enacted subsequent thereto.

(4) A crime is a petty misdemeanor if it is so designated in this Code or in a statute other than this Code enacted subsequent thereto or if it is defined by a statute other than this Code which now provides that persons convicted thereof may be sentenced to imprisonment for a term of which the maximum is less than one year.

(5) An offense defined by this Code or by any other statute of this State constitutes a violation if it is so designated in this Code or in the law defining the offense or if no other sentence than a fine, or fine and forfeiture or other civil penalty is authorized upon conviction or if it is defined by a statute other than this Code which now provides that the offense shall not constitute a crime. A violation does not constitute a crime and conviction of a violation shall not give rise to any disability or legal disadvantage based on conviction of a criminal offense.

(6) Any offense declared by law to constitute a crime, without specification of the grade thereof or of the sentence authorized upon conviction, is a misdemeanor.

(7) An offense defined by any statute of this State other than this Code shall be classified as provided in this Section and the sentence that may be imposed upon conviction thereof shall hereafter be governed by this Code.

Section 6.08. Sentence of Imprisonment for Misdemeanors and Petty Misdemeanors; Ordinary Terms.

A person who has been convicted of a misdemeanor or a petty misdemeanor may be sentenced to imprisonment for a definite term which shall be fixed by the Court and shall not exceed one year in the case of a misdemeanor or thirty days in the case of a petty misdemeanor.

2. A felony punished by death is a separate category. Aside from this, felonies are divided into three degrees. For a felony of the first degree the maximum penalty is life imprisonment; for a felony of the second degree the maximum is ten years; and for a felony of the third degree the maximum is five years.

Chapter 2

OFFENSES AGAINST THE PERSON

SECTION 1. HOMICIDE

DOWNEY v. PEOPLE

Supreme Court of Colorado, en Banc, 1950.
121 Colo. 307, 215 P.2d 892.

MOORE, JUSTICE. David Albert Downey, the defendant in the lower court and to whom we hereinafter refer as defendant, or by name, was charged by information filed in the district court of El Paso county on July 28, 1947, with having "feloniously, wilfully and of his malice aforethought" killed and murdered one Lolly Lila Downey. Defendant entered a plea of not guilty and the cause came on for trial October 7, 1947. The jury returned a verdict of guilty of murder in the first degree and fixed the penalty at "life imprisonment at hard labor in the State Penitentiary." Motion for new trial was thereafter filed, argued, and denied, and appropriate judgment was entered by the court. Defendant brings the cause here by writ of error, and relies for reversal upon alleged errors of the lower court in the conduct of the trial as follows: . . .

3rd. The court erred in overruling defendant's motion for a directed verdict upon the ground that the corpus delicti had not been established. . . .

Between one and two o'clock in the afternoon of July 18, 1947, a Dr. Wilson was driving on the Rampart Range road when he observed the defendant being assisted into a car by a Mr. Hubbard from Texas. Dr. Wilson stopped his automobile and noticed blood on the left side of defendant's shirt. He testified that defendant stated, "I am not hurt—that is my wife's blood. . . . She may be dead." Dr. Wilson and Mr. Hubbard were unable to find Mrs. Downey and returned to defendant's automobile and he thereupon assisted them in locating the body. According to Dr. Wilson the body was not disarranged. It was placed out very carefully. Mrs. Downey was dead but the body was warm. Defendant complained of injuries received from a fall, police authorities were notified, and defendant was taken to a hospital in Colorado Springs where he remained until Saturday, July 19, when he was lodged in the county jail. Dr. Wilson testified that while at the hospital defendant asked him, "if her tongue was out" and when the doctor asked the reason for the question defendant stated, "She seemed to be strangling and I tried to remove her tongue." The terrain where the body was found was rugged, being a mass of rocks and boulders. It was not, however, a dangerous area as to being precipitous. The body was lying at the foot of a ledge of rock about three feet in height, on the surface of which there was a considerable amount of blood. About thirty-four feet up the hill from the point where the body was found there was some evidence that a scuffle had occurred. An autopsy was performed which disclosed superficial scratches and bruises. There was a two inch wound in the back of the head which penetrated the scalp but did no further damage and was not the cause of death, which, as testified by the experts performing the autopsy, was asphyxia due to strangulation. . . .

Second: *Was the corpus delicti sufficiently established by the evidence?*

At the close of all the evidence the defendant moved for a directed verdict of not guilty "for the reason that the corpus delicti has not been established without recourse to the alleged confession of the defendant." The motion was overruled and error is assigned on the ruling.

In Bruner v. People, 113 Colo. 194, 156 P.2d 111, 117, we said: "It is well settled in this jurisdiction that the corpus delicti consists of two components: death as a result and the criminal agency of another as the means, and it is equally settled that the corpus delicti may be established by either direct or circumstantial evidence. . . ." [1]

---

[1]. Whether the *uncorroborated confession of the accused* in a criminal case is alone sufficient to support a conviction is a question which for more than a hundred years was left unsettled in English law. . . .

"The proposed rule appeared in two variations: by the one, the corroborative evidence might be of *any sort* whatever; by the other, it must specifically relate to the '*corpus delicti*', *i. e.* the fact of injury. The latter form tended to prevail; but in neither form did the rule obtain a general footing. So far as it can be supposed to obtain at all today in the English and Irish courts, it is apparently restricted to the case of homicide: . . .

"The conflicting state of the English rulings left the Courts and the Legislatures of the United States to choose which rule might commend itself. Except in a few jurisdictions, they seem to have preferred, wherever the question has come up for decision, to adopt the fixed rule that corroboration was necessary,—chiefly moved, in all probability, by Professor Greenleaf's suggestion that 'this opinion certainly best accords with the humanity of the criminal code and with the great degree of caution applied in receiving and weighing the evidence of confessions in other cases.'

"In a few jurisdictions, the rule is properly not limited to evidence concerning the 'corpus delicti'; *i. e.* the corroborating facts may be of *any sort whatever*, provided only that they tend to produce a confidence in the truth of the confession: . . .

"The meaning of the phrase '*corpus delicti*' has been the subject of much loose judicial comment, and an apparent sanction has often been given to an unjustifiably broad meaning. It is clear that an analysis of every crime, with reference to this element of it, reveals three component parts, *first*, the *occurrence* of the specific

Sec. 1　　　　　　　　*HOMICIDE*　　　　　　　　15

The Bruner case is authority for the rule prevailing in this jurisdiction that circumstantial evidence is sufficient to establish the corpus delicti in a homicide case if it is such as to prove the essentials thereof to a reasonable certainty.

In Lowe v. People, 76 Colo. 603, 234 P. 169, 173, we stated:

"Proof that one charged committed a felonious homicide involves three elements; First, the death; Second, the criminal agency of another as the cause; Third, the identity of the accused as that other. The first two constitute what is known in law as the corpus delicti . . . Each of these elements must be established by the prosecution to the satisfaction of the jury beyond a reasonable doubt. The court, however, is not the judge of the weight of the evidence. When sufficient has been produced to justify a submission to the jury and support a verdict of guilty, should such a verdict be returned thereon, the requirements of the law have been met. This rule applies to each of the elements of the corpus delicti as it does to the proof of the identity of the accused as the perpetrator; no more no less."

"That proof may be made by any legal evidence, the same as proof of other facts."

It is true that a conviction of crime cannot be upheld where it is based upon the uncorroborated confession of the person accused. There must be evidence of the corpus delicti apart from the statements contained in the confession. In the case at bar there is ample evidence, apart from the confession, from which the jury might properly find that the wife of defendant was dead, and that her death was brought about by "the criminal agency of another as the means." Defendant was the sole companion of his wife at the time of her death. There was blood on his shirt, which he stated was that of his wife. He directed those first upon the scene to the place where her body was found. The body was still warm. The position of the body, the

---

kind of injury or loss (as, in homicide, a person deceased; in arson, a house burnt; in larceny, property missing); *secondly*, somebody's criminality (in contrast, *e. g.* to accident) as the source of the loss,—these two together involving the commission of a crime by *somebody;* and *thirdly*, the accused's *identity* as the doer of this crime.

"(1) Now, the term 'corpus delicti' seems in its orthodox sense to signify merely the first of these elements, namely, the *fact of the specific loss or injury sustained:* . . .

"(2) But by most judges the term is made to include the second element also, *i. e. somebody's criminality:* . . .

"This broader form makes the rule much more difficult for the jury to apply amid a complex mass of evidence, and tends to reduce the rule to a juggling-formula.

"(3) A third view, indeed, too absurd to be argued with, has occasionally been advanced, at least by counsel, namely, that the 'corpus delicti' includes the third element also, *i. e.*, the *accused's identity* or agency as the criminal. By this view, the term 'corpus delicti' would be synonymous with the whole of the charge, and the rule would require that the whole be evidenced in all three elements independently of the confession, which would be absurd." VII Wigmore on Evidence, §§ 2070–2072 (3d ed. 1940). Reprinted by permission of the publisher, Little, Brown and Company.

fact that her clothing was not disarranged, the fact that pressure had been applied to both of her wrists and her throat, the general topography of the terrain where she was found, were all inconsistent with the theory of accidental death. The ragged scalp wound in the back of the head of deceased corroborated the statement of defendant that he struck her a blow with a "rock about the size of two teacups." The defendant directed an inquiry to Dr. Wilson as to whether deceased's tongue was out when he first observed the body, and this unusual question was wholly the thought of defendant. The doctors who performed the autopsy testified that the cause of death was strangulation produced by pressure applied to the throat. Competent evidence tending to establish these facts was sufficient to establish the corpus delicti of the crime of murder, and the trial court did not commit error in overruling defendant's motion for a directed verdict on the ground that the corpus delicti had not been sufficiently proven. . . .

The defendant was capably represented at the trial, and here, by counsel of ability and experience, and we are persuaded that he was afforded a fair trial in accordance with established rules of law. The assignments upon which he relies for reversal are overruled, and accordingly the judgment is affirmed.

GRIMES v. STATE

Supreme Court of Georgia, 1949.
204 Ga. 854, 51 S.E.2d 797.

Isaiah Grimes was indicted for murder and convicted with a recommendation to mercy. He was charged with throwing kerosene oil upon Fluke Catlin, setting fire to his clothing, burning his body and limbs, thereby producing mortal wounds.

The deceased lived near the town of Loganville on the Atlanta Highway. Some time in the early part of the night of May 31, 1947, Charles A. Kelly, Jr., a neighbor, was attracted by some commotion at the home of the deceased. He testified: "I went to the door. . . . Fluke came out the [his] back door . . . of the kitchen, and I couldn't see him until he was out in the yard, and he was hollering, 'Somebody help me, I'm afire,' . . . and I started running towards Fluke's yard. I was approximately two hundred feet from Fluke when I first saw him. . . . I saw he was on fire . . . from his knees burning down and up. . . . The flames reached five or six inches from him. . . . I got some water and helped put out the fire. . . . As to whether I smelled anything, it smelled to me like kerosene. I could smell it in the yard, and when I got to Fluke it smelled like kerosene. We also smelled it in the house when we went in there an hour or more later. . . . Two or three of us knocked the door open, . . . and found an overstuffed chair burning and found . . . the mattress of the bed was burning right around the outer edges in the center, and we found this lamp that was broken and looked like it was broken into a hundred or two hundred pieces; it looked like it was both broken and melted. I did not see any sign of any wick or burner on the lamp. . . . I did not look for the burner or wisk. . . . He [Fluke] was adepted to drinking. . . . While Fluke was lying there I asked him how did he catch afire, and he said the house was afire and he tried to put it out. . . . I could not tell whether he was drinking on that occasion." . . .

[The testimony was corroborated by other witnesses. One witness added that defendant had been drinking, but did not elaborate.]

The accused was the stepson of the deceased. Two or three days prior to the fire the deceased and his wife had trouble over some whisky, and the wife was arrested. Following her arrest she did not return to the home of the deceased, but went to the home of her son, the accused, and was staying there at the time of the fire. The home of the accused was on the same road as that of the deceased and about half a mile away. There was no evidence that the accused was seen at or near the home of the deceased at the time of the fire. There was evidence that the deceased died about thirty days after the fire as a result of his burns.

The accused was arrested about six months after the fire and placed in jail. After his arrest he made two statements to the officers about the fire, the first being made December 15, and the second some days later, to wit: "The first statement . . . was he said he went to Fluke's house and got into an argument with him about a debt which Fluke claimed he owed him, . . . and Fluke struck at him, and that he picked up a lamp that was lighted and he struck him in the face and bursted the lamp and set Fluke afire. . . . He changed that to some extent the second time; in the second statement he said he went there and got in a discussion about this debt, . . . and that an argument followed, and that Fluke struck at him and then he struck Fluke and knocked him down back in the chair and Fluke passed out, . . . and that then he got this lamp and took the burner out and poured kerosene on him from the bowl of the lamp and struck the lighted burner to him and ignited the kerosene."

The defense interposed by the accused was an alibi.

ATKINSON, PRESIDING JUSTICE. (After stating the foregoing facts.) 1. The record in this case presents the question of whether there is sufficient evidence to corroborate the confession of the accused. The Code, § 38–420, provides: "A confession alone, uncorroborated by any other evidence, shall not justify a conviction." However, proof of the corpus delicti is held to be sufficient corroboration. . . . To prove the corpus delicti in a charge of murder, it is essential to establish that the person alleged to have been killed is actually dead, and that death was caused or accomplished by violence or other direct criminal agency of another human being; that is, it was not accidental, nor due to natural causes, nor to the act of the deceased, and that the accused caused the death in the manner charged.[1] Independently of the confession, there is no evidence in this record to show that the accused [deceased] was killed by violence or other direct criminal agency of another. He was seen coming from his house with his clothing afire, and died from the burns. There was the smell of kerosene upon him and in the house. The lamp containing kerosene was shown to have been broken. There was no evidence that anyone else was in the house at that time. Witnesses for the State testified that immediately after coming out of the house, and when asked how did he catch afire, the deceased stated, "The house was afire and he tried to put it out." Certainly these facts, standing alone, do not establish the corpus delicti. The corpus delicti must be proved beyond a reasonable doubt. One element of the corpus delicti is just as essential as the other, and if dependent on circumstantial evidence, it must be established to the exclusion of every other reasonable hypothesis. A confession may authorize a conviction, if corroborated, and as above stated, proof of the corpus delicti is sufficient corroboration; but the proof to establish all the elements of the corpus delicti must be from a source or sources other than the confession. "A confession alone, however, being insufficient to convict, makes other evidence in corroboration necessary." Smith v. State, 64 Ga. 605, 606. In the absence of extraneous evidence of all elements of the corpus delicti, the proof is insufficient to corroborate the confession. . . .

Judgment reversed. All the Justices concur.

WARMKE v. COMMONWEALTH

Court of Appeals of Kentucky, 1944.
297 Ky. 649, 180 S.W.2d 872.

FULTON, CHIEF JUSTICE. This appeal is from a manslaughter sentence of nine years imposed on the appellant in connection with the death of her infant child. The sole ground urged for reversal was that the corpus delicti was not sufficiently shown.

The appellant resided in Utica, a village in Davies County. Some weeks prior to July 8, 1943 she went to Louisville and there gave birth to an illegitimate child. On July 8, 1943, she traveled to Clover-

---

1. The corpus delicti in a homicide case requires proof of two facts: (1) that the person alleged to have been killed is actually dead, and (2) that the death was due to criminal agency. For a conviction it is necessary to prove also that the defendant caused the death, but this is not an element of the corpus delicti despite loose statements in some of our prior cases. McVeigh v. State, 205 Ga. 326, 53 S.E.2d 462 (1949).

port, in Breckenridge County, by bus arriving about 8 o'clock p. m. It was raining very hard and she went into a drug store for shelter. A. T. Couch, an employee of the store, loaned her a coat in which to wrap her baby. She went out leaving her suitcase in the store. She called Couch by telephone about 10:30, requesting him to come to the store so that she might get her suitcase. When she met Couch at the store she did not have the baby but returned the borrowed coat. Early the next morning she went to the home of a kinswoman, Mrs. Pate. The town marshal, having learned that the baby was missing, went to Mrs. Pate's home and questioned the appellant. She told him that after she left the drug store she started to cross a railroad trestle near the town in an effort to get to the home of a friend and that while she was crossing a train approached and she crawled over on the edge of the ties and accidentally dropped the baby. The town marshal and a highway patrolman then took the appellant to the trestle and she pointed out where the baby had been dropped. There was a creek under the trestle at this point. It was flooded and the current was swift. A baby's cap was found on the bank of the creek and the appellant exclaimed, "There is my little baby's cap". The baby's body was never found.

When the officers returned to town with the appellant she told them, after some questioning, that she purposely threw the baby into the creek because she was unable to face the humiliation of going home with an illegitimate child.

On the trial she repudiated the confession she had made to the officers and testified that she dropped the baby accidentally, in the manner she first told the officers. She testified that she was scared and excited and didn't remember saying she dropped the baby purposely. She said that after she dropped the baby she wandered around all night barefooted and in a dazed condition and that in the morning she put on her shoes and stockings and went to Mrs. Pate's. She gave as a reason for stopping off at Cloverport that it was her father's home town and that she desired to talk to a friend, Mrs. Atwill, and obtain advice. She did not see Mrs. Atwill but says that she was looking for her house when she dropped the baby and that thereafter she remembered nothing until early morning.

It is axiomatic that the corpus delicti must be shown. This term means the body of the offense, the substance of the crime. Proof of the corpus delicti in homicide cases involves two principal facts, namely, that the person is dead and that he died as a result of the injury alleged to have been received. In short, there must be proof of a death and proof that such death was caused by the criminal agency of the accused.

But the law does not subscribe to the rigid formula that the body must be found or seen after death. The death may be established by circumstantial evidence. 26 Amer.Juris. 376. As said in 13 R.C.L.

737, the death may be shown "by proof of criminal violence adequate to produce death and which accounts for the disappearance of the body. In short, the body must be found or there must be proof of death which the law deems to be equivalent to direct evidence that it was found."

We think there was sufficient proof of the death of the baby in the case before us. It was dropped, either purposely or accidentally, by the appellant from the railroad trestle into the flooded creek below and was never found. It seems beyond the bounds of possibility that the baby survived this ordeal and was never thereafter heard of. At least, we think the evidence was ample to justify the jury's finding that death ensued.

It is argued for the appellant, however, that the corpus delicti must be established by evidence other than the confession of the accused out of court and that there was no other evidence here. The soundness of the legal proposition thus advanced may be admitted. There must be proof of the component elements of the corpus delicti, a death and the criminal agency of the accused, by proof in addition to the confession of the accused made out of court. But, as indicated above, the appellant testified that the baby was dropped into the creek. Thus there was proof of the death independent of the appellant's confession made out of court.

The remaining question is whether there was proof, in addition to the appellant's confession made out of court, of her criminal agency in causing the death. Her agency in causing the death was admitted from the witness stand. Was there evidence, independent of her confession out of court, that this agency was criminal? We think there was an abundance of such evidence. Such independent evidence may be circumstantial as well as direct.

Circumstances pointing clearly to the fact that the appellant purposely dropped the baby from the trestle may be thus summarized. She had an impelling motive, concealment of the birth of the illegitimate child. Her reason for going to Cloverport instead of her home is rather vague and unsatisfactory. This reason was that she decided to consult her friend, Mrs. Atwill, yet she never did so. She eventually wound up at Mrs. Pate's and not at Mrs. Atwill's. But most illuminating of all is her failure to notify any one that she had dropped the baby from the trestle, if it was dropped accidentally. She accounts for this by saying she was in a dazed condition, nevertheless she called Mr. Couch by telephone to come to the drug store so that she might get her suitcase. She returned the coat to him. She had borrowed this coat to wrap the baby in. It is singular that she would have accidentally dropped the baby without dropping the coat. It is even more singular that she never notified Mrs. Pate, her kinswoman, the next morning of the loss of the baby. These circumstances and the justifiable inferences to be drawn from them, amply warranted the jury in finding that the dropping of the baby from the trestle was purposely, and not accidentally, done by the appellant.

Affirmed.[1]

STATE v. KINDLE

Supreme Court of Montana, 1924.
71 Mont. 58, 227 P. 65.

MR. CHIEF JUSTICE CALLAWAY delivered the opinion of the court.

By information Simeon E. Kindle and W. Edwin Kindle were charged with the murder of Gilbert Gilbertson. The case is here upon the state's appeal as the result of a verdict of not guilty returned by the court's direction. The main question presented is whether upon the trial the state proved the *corpus delicti*. . . .

News of the shooting having reached Malta, the county seat, the sheriff, county attorney and others left for the scene. On the way they met Fred Kindle, a brother of the defendants, driving a Ford automobile. Where Fred Kindle was going does not appear, but when the sheriff reached the scene of the shooting Fred Kindle was there with the defendants. After leaving Fred Kindle the sheriff went to the Gilbertson house and from there to the east side of the ranch. Upon arriving there the sheriff observed three men on a hill who proved to be the defendants and Fred Kindle. Of them he inquired as to the whereabouts of Gilbertson, whose body was not then in sight. One of the defendants, Edwin, according to the sheriff's recollection, answered, and as a result of the conversation the party went toward the body, northwest about 100 feet. The body was lying in the decedent's own field 85 feet north of his south (the east and west) fence. Gilbertson was lying on his back, arms and legs outstretched, his head to the south. He had been shot through the head. The bullet entered directly between the eyes; there the skin was torn evenly, while at the point of exit directly in the back of the head "the skin was irregular and pushed out." The physician who examined the body did not observe any powder burns. There was not a gun or weapon of any kind near the body. On the contrary, Gilbertson's rifle and also a Springfield rifle belonging to Edwin Kindle were found in the possession of the defendants. The gun belonging to the deceased did not have either a cartridge or a shell in the barrel. There was a shell in the magazine, but the sheriff was unable to ex-

---

1. "The rule requiring a confession to be corroborated by proof of the '*corpus delicti*' has no application to infrajudicial confessions." Manning v. United States, 215 F.2d 945, 950 (10th Cir. 1954). The offense was transporting a motor vehicle in interstate commerce, knowing it to have been stolen.

"It is, of course, elementary and unquestioned that a defendant who chooses to testify is just as competent to establish the corpus delicti as any other witness". People v. Ditson, 57 Cal.2d 415, 445–46, 20 Cal.Rptr. 165, 182, 369 P.2d 714, 731 (1962). The offense was first-degree murder.

tract that as it was lodged. In the barrel of the Kindle gun there was an empty shell.

After viewing the body, at the suggestion of the defendants the sheriff went to the fence and then to the edge of a coulee near by. The fence was found to be cut in several places. A pair of nippers was found there. The "Kindle boys" mentioned the fact that the fence was cut. About 100 yards distant the sheriff found the grub hoe, called by him an "adz," with the handle broken. The sheriff searched for cartridges or shells; he "went down to the edge of this coulee and followed around the point of the hill up around this way and down to where the body was (indicating on the map)," accompanied by the county attorney, a Mr. Mills, and the three Kindle boys. A question as to whether he made the trip at the suggestion of "the Kindles" was objected to and the objection sustained. The sheriff was asked whether he learned the cause of Gilbertson's death, to which he answered: "Yes, sir. Q. From whom? A. Edwin Kindle. Q. And what did he give as the cause of his death?" This was objected to, the objection being that the state had failed to prove the *corpus delicti*. The court thought the objection well taken. Thereupon counsel for the state offered to prove by the testimony of Mr. Wolfe, the sheriff, the substance of a conversation between himself and Edwin Kindle in which the latter said he had shot Gilbertson, and in which the circumstances of the affray were described at some length. Further: "That upon approaching the defendants there at or near the place where the body was found and a little way from it, he asked one of the defendants where Gilbertson was and he replied: 'He is damned easy found now; he is right over the hill there.' That the witness asked him what happened, to which he replied: 'I killed him; it was either get killed or kill him.'[1] . . ."

The offer was denied, the court holding that the *corpus delicti* must be proved before the prosecution may give in evidence any statement of the defendants. Commenting on the situation, the court remarked: "There is only one question: As to whether there can be an inference drawn from the testimony so far, as to whether there was a criminal agency. I am frank to say to you until State v. Riggs

---

[1]. Defendant's extrajudicial admissions of essential facts are of the same character as confessions and require corroboration. This is true even if in the form of an "exculpatory statement." But in such a case it is sufficient if there is evidence *aliunde* which tends to establish the trustworthiness of the admission and to establish every element of the *corpus delicti*. Opper v. United States, 348 U.S. 84, 75 S.Ct. 158 (1954).

"Once prima facie proof of the corpus delicti is made, the extrajudicial statements, admissions and confessions of a defendant may be considered in determining whether all the elements of a crime have been established." People v. Duncan, 51 Cal.2d 523, 528, 334 P. 2d 858, 861 (1959).

D's admissions at the time of the arrest, and at the place where evidence of the crime then being perpetrated was found, were part of the *res gestae* and admissible for that reason. State v. La Rue, 67 N.M. 149, 353 P.2d 367 (1960). The charge was operating a game of chance.

was announced you had abundant testimony here for a *corpus delicti*." The learned judge was of the opinion that this court, in State v. Riggs, 61 Mont. 25, 201 P. 272, had laid down a more stringent rule respecting proof of the *corpus delicti* than had been indicated in some of its earlier decisions.

Generally speaking, the term *"corpus delicti,"* when applied to any particular offense means that the specific crime charged has actually been committed by someone, and it is made up of two elements: First, that a certain result has been produced, as that a man has died; second, that someone is criminally responsible for the result, as for the death.

Section 10962, Revised Codes of 1921, reads as follows: "No person can be convicted of murder or manslaughter unless the death of the person, alleged to have been killed, and the fact of the killing by the defendant as alleged, are established as independent acts; the former by direct proof, and the latter beyond a reasonable doubt."

In a prosecution for murder proof of the *corpus delicti* does not necessarily carry with it the identity of the slain nor of the slayer. Under the statute the only fact required to be proved directly is the death of the person alleged to have been killed. The identity of such person, if in doubt, and of the killing by the defendant, may be proved by direct or by indirect or circumstantial evidence. The Riggs Case is to the same effect. To sustain the charge against the defendants it was, of course, necessary for the state to prove that the crime charged had been committed and the defendants, or one of them, committed it. In such case a mere showing of the fact of death is not sufficient; it must appear also that it came about through criminal agency. As said in the Riggs Case, in order to sustain a conviction proof of the criminal agency is as indispensable as the proof of death. But no universal and invariable rule can be laid down as to what will amount to proof of criminal agency, as each case must depend upon its own peculiar circumstances; and when there is any evidence, direct, indirect or circumstantial, tending to prove the fact, it is for the jury to pass upon its sufficiency. If however, the evidence is fairly susceptible to the construction that death was accidental, or the result of suicide, or due to a natural cause, then it is not sufficient to warrant a conviction, for the reason that in order to convict a defendant he must be proven guilty of the crime charged beyond a reasonable doubt. He cannot be convicted when the evidence is fairly susceptible to a construction which will prove innocence as well as guilt. The Riggs Case did not attempt to, nor did it, go any further than this.

There was not a fact or circumstance indicating that Gilbertson's death was the result of other than criminal agency. Suicide was out of the question. If he met death through accident, surely it was not of his own causing.

The proffered testimony should have been admitted. But counsel for defendants say if the testimony had been admitted it would have proven that Edwin Kindle in shooting the deceased acted in self-defense. Possibly a jury would have come to that conclusion; but by its action in excluding the proffered testimony the court precluded the state from developing its case, and we may not assume that it did not have other testimony tending to show the guilt not only of Edwin Kindle but of Simeon. . . .

Counsel for defendants also suggests that the state should not have been permitted to introduce the proffered testimony for the reason that it consists of a confession of Edwin Kindle, and there was no preliminary proof that it was made voluntarily. Whether it consists of a confession or an admission the record does not indicate that any inducement was held out to cause Kindle to make it; on the contrary, it appears that he talked voluntarily, freely, even eagerly. There does not seem to be any merit in the objection.

The judgment is reversed and the cause is remanded to the district court of Phillips county, with directions to grant a new trial.

Reversed and remanded.

ASSOCIATE JUSTICES HOLLOWAY, GALEN and STARK concur.

MR. JUSTICE COOPER, being absent, did not hear the argument and takes no part in the foregoing decision.

PEOPLE v. HAYNER

Court of Appeals of New York, 1949.
300 N.Y. 171, 90 N.E.2d 23.

LOUGHRAN, CH. J. At a Trial Term of the Supreme Court held in Broome County, the defendant on February 22, 1949, was convicted of the murder of a male child of which his fourteen-year-old daughter had been delivered by him early on the morning of May 17, 1948. Soon after that birth, the defendant summoned a doctor who took him and his daughter to a hospital where injuries done to her by the delivery were repaired. Meantime in the reception room of the hospital the defendant was questioned by the Sheriff of Broome County and by one of his deputies. The Sheriff says the defendant there "stated that his daughter had given birth to a baby and he had pulled the top of the baby's head off." According to the deputy sheriff, the defendant on the same occasion said: "I deliberately killed that baby. I didn't want to bring any disgrace upon the family." A little later, the Sheriff and three deputies accompanied the defendant to his home in the town of Chenango where he pointed out a grave from which one of the deputies removed a male baby with the umbilical cord still attached and wound around the neck loosely.

The defendant next (about 10 o'clock of the same morning) made at the Sheriff's office a further statement which was read and sworn to by him after it had been written down by a deputy sheriff. In part that statement is as follows: "At about 11 P.M. yesterday my daughter Kaye started to have labor pains, same continuing on until about 5:15 A.M. on this date [May 17, 1948] at which time the baby started to be born. As the head came out my wife and I tried to help it along as it came very slowly and Kaye was in terrible pain screaming for help and bleeding badly. As I pulled on the head, the skin came off from a portion of the skull on top of the head and some of the brains came out running on the bed. The baby started to cry just after being born. I then cut the umbilical cord from the mother, using a pair of shears. I then took the umbilical cord which was still attached to the baby, from the mother, and wound it tightly around the baby's neck for purpose of strangulation (drew it tightly) and the baby stopped crying. The baby was being born over a period of 45 minutes to one hour. Some time after I wrapped the baby in a turkish towel, carried it across the driveway a few rods from the house . . . and buried it in a shallow hole covering same with dirt and three large stones. . . . Just after the baby had emerged completely from its mother's womb, I tied the cord about its neck probably within 10 or 12 seconds. Then within 20 or 30 seconds it stopped crying and I believe it was dead. There was not motion at that time. Then about 10 or 12 minutes I carried it away and buried it. . . . I'm admitting to having intercourse with my daughter. I'm admitting to that."

The defendant's wife and daughter were witnesses for the People. The wife said the defendant had been sleeping with the daughter for a time before the daughter became pregnant and the daughter said he had sexual intercourse with her during that period. Thus there was an adequate basis for a finding by the jury of an emotion in the defendant that might well have led him to the commission of the crime charged. Moreover, he had an opportunity to commit that crime and the dead body of the child was found where he said he had buried it. These items of evidence plus the defendant's confessions were not, however, sufficient warrant for the verdict herein. For the People were bound to establish by proof outside the confessions (Code Crim.Pro., § 395) that the child was born alive in the legal sense, that is, had been wholly expelled from its mother's body and possessed or was capable of an existence by means of a circulation independent of her own. "The true test of separate existence in the theory of the law (whatever it may be in medical science) is the answer to the question 'whether the child is carrying on its being without the help of the mother's circulation.'" (1 Russell on Crime [9th ed.], p. 349, note u. See the cases there cited.)

The defendant and his wife were the only persons who were with their daugher at the time her child was born. As witnesses for the

People, the wife and daughter said they never saw the child and did not hear it cry. The defendant did not take the stand. Consequently, the People were constrained to attempt the necessary corroboration of his confessions solely through medical opinions that were based upon nothing more than a post-mortem examination.

Four physicians were witnesses for the People. One of them performed an autopsy upon the body of the child. In substance his findings were as follows: There was one faint bruise on the right side of the neck and two faint bruises on the left side thereof; these were the only marks on the body; there was no ring of discoloration around the neck; there was a scalp wound about an inch and a half in diameter which, however, was no part of the cause of death; there was no skull fracture; no hemorrhage in the skull; no evidence of injury to brain or skull; no hemorrhage in the brain; nothing abnormal in the conjunctiva of the eyes; no discharge of any kind from the nose or mouth; no foreign object in any part of the body; no evidence of any fracture of the neck; there was a slight blue cast under the nails, but no blueness of the face such as often results from suffocation; the color of the skin was normal except for the three faint bruises on the neck.

On the strength of the autopsy report alone, the medical expert witnesses called by the People took it upon themselves to declare their ability to express "with reasonable certainty" an opinion to this effect: (1) The child was born alive and had a living existence separate and independent from its mother; and (2) the cause of death was an external force which shut off the air supply to the lungs. The pathologist who made the autopsy report gave this testimony: "Q. Will you tell us whether in your post-mortem examination findings . . . there is positive evidence that this baby suffered from traumatic asphyxia as the result of the air supply being shut off? . . . A. Yes, there is. Q. What is that evidence? A. The evidence is that the lungs were fully expanded, but even more than that, there was interstitial emphysema of the lungs. Q. By that you mean what? A. Tearing of the wall sacs and escape of air into the connective tissue of the framework of the lung." But the People admitted the absence of hemorrhage in the wall sacs and connecting tissue of either lung—a strong circumstance on the side of the defendant since bleeding naturally follows rupture of a blood vessel of a living person. The expansion of the lungs was of no great moment because the legal test of live birth—possession by the child of a separate circulation—made irrelevant the question whether the child had breathed or not (see Winfield, "The Unborn Child", 8 Cambridge L.J., 76, 79; Stephen's Digest of the Criminal Law, supra; 21 Am. & Eng.Encyc. Law [2d ed.], p. 102).

The foregoing, we believe, is a sufficient analysis of the case for the People. The testimony of their medical experts was necessarily of slight or merely conjectural significance. For here no one claiming to be an eye or ear witness came forth and, where that is the case evidence of live birth precedent to speedy death is of a nature practically impossible to medical science (see Atkinson, "Life, Birth and Live-Birth", 20 Law Quarterly Rev. 134, 146, 149). Hence we are ourselves wholly unconvinced that the jury were justified in finding the fact of live birth to have been established beyond a reasonable doubt, and, this being so, the conviction of the defendant cannot be allowed to stand (People v. Crum, 272 N.Y. 348, 350, 6 N.E.2d 51).

The judgment of conviction should be reversed and a new trial ordered.[1]

LEWIS, CONWAY, DESMOND, DYE, FULD and BROMLEY, JJ., concur.

Judgment of conviction reversed, etc.

---

1. "The desired and rational view as to the burden placed on the State in proving that the deceased child was born alive is reflected in an enlightened opinion by the District Court of Appeal of California, Fourth District, in People v. Chavez, 77 Cal.App.2d 621, 176 P.2d 92, 94, wherein Barnard, P. J., after reviewing the common law doctrines developed by the decisions in England and this country as to the question now being considered wrote:

"'Beyond question, it is a difficult thing to draw a line and lay down a fixed general rule as to the precise time at which an unborn infant, or one in the process of being born, becomes a human being in the technical sense. There is not much change in the child itself between a moment before and a moment after its expulsion from the body of its mother, and normally, while still dependent upon its mother, the child, for some time before it is born, has not only the possibility but a strong probability of an ability to live an independent life. It is well known that a baby may live and grow when removed from the body of its dead mother by a Caesarian operation. The mere removal of the baby in such a case of its birth in a normal case does not, of itself and alone, create a human being. While before birth or removal it is in a sense dependent upon its mother for life, there is another sense in which it has started an independent existence after it has reached a state of development where it is capable of living and where it will, in the normal course of nature and with ordinary care, continue to live and grow as a separate being. While it may not be possible to draw an exact line applicable to all cases, the rules of law should recognize and make some attempt to follow the natural and scientific facts to which they relate. As Judge Cardozo once said: "Let the facts be known as they are, and the law will sprout from the seed and turn its branches toward the light." There is no sound reason why an infant should not be considered a human being when born or removed from the body of its mother, when it has reached that stage of development where it is capable of living an independent life as a separate being, and where in the natural course of events it will so live if given normal and reasonable care. It should equally be held that a viable child in the process of being born is a human being within the meaning of the homicide statutes, whether or not the process has been fully completed. It should at least be considered a human being where it is a living baby and where in the natural course of events a birth which is already started would naturally be successfully completed. While the question of whether death by criminal means has resulted while the process of birth was being carried out, or shortly thereafter, may present difficult questions of fact, those questions should be met and decided on the basis of whether or not a living baby with the natural possibility and probability of growth and development was being born, rather than on any hard and fast technical rule establishing a legal fiction that the infant being born was not a human being because some part of the process of birth had not been fully completed.

HADLEY v. STATE

Supreme Court of Alabama, 1876.
55 Ala. 31.

The defendants in this case, James Hadley and James M. Hadley, were jointly indicted and tried, together with Jesse Hadley, Thomas Stewart, and Howell Pitcher, for the murder of Green B. Bryars; pleaded not guilty to the indictment; were convicted of murder in the second degree, and sentenced to imprisonment in the penitentiary for the term of ten years, while a verdict of not guilty was returned as to the other defendants. . . .

"The court charged the jury, among other things, as follows: 'If one man shoot another with a gun, or other deadly weapon, and death ensues, the law implies, or considers, or presumes, that the act was done maliciously, and imposes upon the slayer the burthen of rebutting this presumption, unless the evidence which proves the killing itself shows it to have been done without malice. Hence, if you believe, from the evidence, that the prisoners at the bar shot Green B. Bryars with a shot gun, or other deadly weapon, and thereby caused his death, the law presumes that the act was done maliciously, and

---

" 'The question presented has not been decided in this state. Section 192 of the Penal Code provides: "Manslaughter is the unlawful killing of a human being without malice . . ." In Scott v. McPheeters, 33 Cal.App.2d 629, 92 P.2d 678, 93 P.2d 562, it was pointed out that the theory under another statute that an unborn child is a human being separate and distinct from its mother is something more than a fiction and is based upon scientific fact, common experience and knowledge. In fact, it would be a mere fiction to hold that a child is not a human being because the process of birth has not been fully completed, when it has reached that state of viability when the destruction of the life of its mother would not end its existence and when, if separated from the mother naturally or by artificial means, it will live and grow in the normal manner. In practical effect, the rules that have developed at common law furnish a presumption that the baby in question is, or will be, born dead. This presumption is not only contrary to common experience and the ordinary course of nature, but it is contrary to the usual rule with respect to presumptions followed in this state. Section 1963(28) of the Code of Civil Procedure provides that, while it may be disputed, it is to be presumed "That things have happened according to the ordinary course of nature and the ordinary habits of life." While this presumption may not be sufficient for every purpose it is not only some evidence, but it suggests the proper manner of approach in considering all of the evidence.'

"The views expressed above by the California Court of Appeal in our opinion present a logical approach and invite a rational conclusion to determining the viability of a new born child. Adopting such view it is our conclusion that the State met the burden of proof cast upon it to establish that the infant in the present case was born alive." Singleton v. State, 33 Ala.App. 536, 35 So.2d 375 (1948).

"It has always been difficult to procure conviction in cases like these. The necessary evidence is hard to obtain. In England there is a statute making it a crime to conceal the birth of an infant, and reference to the English cases will show that most of the convictions obtained are of concealment and not of murder." Morgan v. State, 148 Tenn. 417, 421, 256 S.W. 433, 434 (1923).

Now, in England, such convictions are usually of a new statutory offense—infanticide. Royal Commission on Capital Punishment (1949–1953) 57–59.

imposes upon the prisoners the burthen of rebutting this presumption, unless the evidence which proves the killing itself shows it to have been done without malice. Now, then, if you believe from the evidence that the prisoners took the life of Green B. Bryars with a shot gun, or other deadly weapon, willfully, deliberately, maliciously, and premeditatedly, as tested by what I have said to you, and you find that it was done in this county, and before the finding of this indictment, they would be guilty of murder in the first degree, and it would be your duty so to find them. Should you find them guilty of murder in the first degree,' etc. To this charge the defendants excepted."

STONE, J. Mr. Wharton, the able author of the works on Criminal Law, and on Homicide, has contributed an article to the "Forum," April number, 1875, in which he attempts to show that there has been a revolution in criminal law, in the matter of presumed malice. In his work on Homicide, 2d ed., § 671, he asserts the same doctrine, and says, "If it be said that the use of a weapon, likely to inflict a mortal blow, implies, as a presumption of law, in its technical sense, a deadly design, this is an error; and *a fortiori* is it so, when it is said the use of such a weapon implies a malicious design."

Malice, design, and motive, are, as a rule, but inferential facts. They are inferred from facts and circumstances, positively proven. If direct, positive proof of them were required, it could rarely be given. Still, we know they exist; and when sufficient facts are in evidence to justify us in drawing such inference, we rest as securely in the conviction, as if it were forced upon us by positive proof. The measure of evidence, however, to justify such abiding conviction, must be very full,—so full as to exclude every other reasonable hypothesis.

That every one must be held to intend the known consequences of his intentional act is a recognized canon of moral accountability, and of municipal law. Malice, as an ingredient of murder, is but a formed design, by a sane mind, to take life unlawfully, without such impending danger, to be averted thereby, as will render it excusable, and without such provocation as will repel the imputation of formed design. Hence, when life is taken by the direct use of a deadly weapon, the canon, stated above, comes to its aid; and if there be nothing else in the transaction—no qualifying or explanatory circumstance—the conclusion is irresistible, that the killing was done pursuant to a formed design; in other words, with malice aforethought; for malice, in such connection, is but the absence of impending peril to life or member, which would excuse the homicide, and of sufficient provocation to repeal the imputation of its existence.

In Foster's Crown Law, it is said, "In every charge of murder, *the fact of killing being first proved*, all the circumstances of accident, necessity, or infirmity, are to be satisfactorily proved by the prisoner, unless they arise out of the evidence produced against him; for the law presumeth the fact to have been founded in malice, until the contrary appeareth; and very right it is that the law should so presume." The same doctrine is affirmed in all the older writers and adjudications on criminal law.

Sir Wm. Blackstone (4 Com. 201) says: "We may take it for a general rule, that all homicide is malicious, and, of course, amounts to murder, unless when justified, excused, or alleviated into manslaughter; and all these circumstances of justification, excuse, or alleviation, it is incumbent on the prisoner to make out to the satisfaction of the court and jury." . . . [1]

There is no error in the record. The judgment of the Circuit Court is affirmed, and the sentence of the law must be executed.

ERRINGTON and OTHERS' CASE

Newcastle Assizes, 1838.
2 Lewin C.C. 217, 168 Eng.Rep. 1133.

. . .

The case against the prisoners was a very serious one. It appeared, that the deceased, being in liquor, had gone at night into a glass-house, and laid himself down upon a chest: and that while he was there asleep the prisoners covered and surrounded him with straw, and threw a shovel of hot cinders upon his belly; the consequence of which was, that the straw ignited, and he was burnt to death.

There was no evidence in the case of express malice; but the conduct of the prisoners indicated an entire recklessness of consequences, hardly consistent with anything short of design.

PATTESON, J., cited from the text books the law applicable to the case, and pointed the attention of the jury to the distinctions which characterise murder and manslaughter. He then adverted to the fact of there being no evidence of express malice; but told them, that if they believed the prisoners really intended to do any serious injury to the deceased, although not to kill him, it was murder; but if they believed their intention to have been only to frighten him in sport, it was manslaughter.

The jury took a merciful view of the case, and returned a verdict of manslaughter only.

---

[1]. In a murder trial, proof of defendant's commission of the homicide by evidence not tending to show any justification, excuse or mitigation, places upon him the burden of establishing the existence of any such factor if he can. State v. Burris, 80 Idaho 395, 331 P.2d 265 (1958).

COMMONWEALTH v. McLAUGHLIN

Supreme Court of Pennsylvania, 1928.
293 Pa. 218, 142 A. 213.

Opinion by MR. JUSTICE SCHAFFER, May 7, 1928.

Defendant, a young man, twenty years of age at the time of the occurrence we are to deal with, appeals from his conviction and sentence for murder of the second degree, contending that the evidence produced against him did not establish this crime.

With two companions he was driving his father's automobile about half past ten o'clock at night along Northampton Street in Wilkes-Barre Township in the County of Luzerne. His progress was down grade and was at the rate of twenty or twenty-five miles an hour. The highway was well lighted. Frank Ravitt and his wife were walking in the cartway of the street ahead of and in the same direction as the automobile, their presence within the street limits and not on the sidewalk being due to the pavement's bad condition. They were at the right-hand side of the center of the cartway, the wife in or near the street car track, the husband on her right. He was pushing a baby coach in which was their infant child. Defendant so drove his automobile that it struck the group in the cartway, killing the husband and the baby and seriously injuring the wife. The impact was with such force as to knock the bodies of the man and woman a distance of from twenty-five to fifty feet and the child out of the coach and over onto the pavement. There was a dispute in the testimony as to whether the lights on the automobile were lit and as to whether defendant sounded his horn as he approached the stricken people; whether he was intoxicated was likewise a controverted fact.

One of the Commonwealth's most material witnesses, Lawrence Brosinski, the only person except defendant and the two others who were in the car with him who actually saw the tragedy, testified that if defendant "had swung his machine toward the side instead of the middle of the road he would never have struck these people." Defendant's story in amplification of this was that he blew his horn and noticed the two persons walking in the center of the road, that he had ample room to pass them to the right, that when he blew his horn "they seemed to be going to the left, and all of a sudden they veered to the right, and as they did I applied my brakes, but it was too late. I had already struck them—he [the husband] seemed to dart to the right quicker than I could get the machine stopped." In this recital he was corroborated by the two young men who were in the car with him. The automobile ran some distance, perhaps 200 feet beyond the point of the collision. Defendant and his companions ascribed this to the circumstance that in his excitement he took his foot off the brake. It appeared in the prosecution's case by the testimony of more than one witness that the brakes were applied, as they heard their screeching before the crash. Immediately after the automobile stopped, defendant ran back, picked up the woman and aided in placing her and the husband in automobiles, one of them in his own, to convey them to the hospital. Upon this evidence the jury found defendant guilty of murder of the second degree and the question to be decided is whether that finding can be sustained.

Murder, as defined by the common law, consists of the unlawful killing of a human being with malice aforethought, express or implied: Com. v. Harman, 4 Pa. 269, 271. Malice is a legal term which comprehends not only a particular ill will, but every case where there is wickedness of disposition, hardness of heart, cruelty, recklessness of consequences, or a mind regardless of social duty: Com. v. Drum, 58 Pa. 9, 15. In this State the legislature has divided the common law crime of murder into two degrees. The statute defines murder of the first degree, and then provides that "all other kinds of murder shall be deemed murder of the second degree": Act of March 31, 1860, P.L. 332, section 74. Thus murder of the second degree is common law murder, but the killing is not accompanied by the distinguishing features of murder of the first degree. The crime includes every element which enters into murder of the first degree except the intention to kill. "Premeditation is essential as in other cases of murder". It is apparent, therefore, that malice is a necessary element of the crime of murder of the second degree, and it was with this in view that we recently said "it is rarely that the facts in a motor vehicle accident will sustain a charge of murder. The element of malice is usually missing. There must be a consciousness of peril or probable peril to human life imputed to the operator of a car before he can be held for murder". In the present case one of the things which seems to have been given much weight by the court below in its opinion sustaining the conviction was defendant's failure to see the people on the road in time to avoid striking them. This negatives any specific intent to injure them. Unless he intended to strike them, which we think it manifest from the evidence he did not, or was recklessly disregardful of their safety, which the testimony does not establish, he could not legally be convicted of murder. Malice may be inferred from the wanton and reckless conduct of one who kills another from wicked disregard of the consequences of his acts, but here defendant's actions after the collision negative the idea of wickedness of disposition or hardness of heart. He endeavored as best he knew how to care for those he had injured. Moreover, it cannot be implied from the circumstances of the accident that defendant was driving his car with wanton disregard of the rights and safety of others upon the highway. The mere fact that he was intoxicated (conceding this to have been proved), without more being shown, would not sustain the conviction. Consequently, we are of the opinion that it could not properly be found, upon the evidence presented, that defendant either purposely, intentionally, recklessly, or wantonly drove his car upon the deceased, and therefore that he should not have been convicted of murder.

If defendant was guilty of any crime, it was that of involuntary manslaughter, which consists in "the killing of another without malice and unintentionally, but in doing some unlawful act not amounting to a felony nor naturally tending to cause death or great bodily harm, or in negligently doing some act lawful in itself, or by the negligent omission to perform a legal duty".

Defendant may still be tried on the indictment charging involuntary manslaughter, notwithstanding that the district attorney entered a nolle prosequi on the indictment. A nolle prosequi is a voluntary withdrawal by the prosecuting attorney of present proceedings on a particular bill. At common law it might at any time be retracted, and was not a bar to a subsequent prosecution on another indictment, but it might be so far cancelled as to permit a revival of the proceedings on the original bill. Whatever the rule may be elsewhere, such action in this jurisdiction is not a bar to a subsequent indictment for the same offense, or may be so far cancelled as to permit a revival of proceedings on the original bill.

The first assignment of error is sustained and the judgment of sentence is reversed without prejudice to the Commonwealth's right to proceed against defendant for the crime of involuntary manslaughter.[1]

Dissenting Opinion by MR. JUSTICE SIMPSON:

The majority opinion states that defendant, while driving his father's automobile struck three persons who were travelling in front of him and going in the same direction he was, killing two of them and greatly injuring the third; that the car then ran some 200 feet further, after which he returned and helped convey two of the three to the hospital, and from this concludes that "defendant's actions after the collision negative the idea of wickedness of disposition or hardness of heart." With all due respect, the jury and trial judge who saw the witnesses when they testified, and the colleagues of the latter who obtained from him a clear picture of their conduct on the witness stand, were far better able to draw the true inferences, than the judges of this court who must rely upon what appears in cold type only. At least as possible an inference from the facts above stated is that the defendant, while running the 200 feet beyond the place of the accident, concluded he would be better off if he came back than if he fled further, and hence the fact of his return did not negative the

---

[1]. D and another were engaged in an automobile race on a state highway at a speed of from 100 to 120 miles an hour. While traveling almost abreast they overtook the deceased who was riding a motorcycle and both cars struck him while he was crossing a bridge, killing him instantly and knocking the motorcycle 300 feet or more from the point of collision. A conviction of murder was affirmed. Clemon v. State, 218 Ga. 755, 130 S.E. 2d 745 (1963).

conclusion, which the jury drew from all the evidence, that defendant's "wanton and reckless conduct . . . [*at the time of the accident* shows his] wicked disregard of the consequences of his acts," and this, if found to be true, as it was, the majority agree would be sufficient to sustain the verdict and sentence. For this reason I dissent.

The chief justice concurred in this dissent.

ANN v. STATE

Supreme Court of Tennessee, 1850.
30 Tenn. 159.

McKINNEY, J., delivered the opinion of the court.

The plaintiff in error was indicted jointly with another slave named Tom, in the circuit court of Williamson, for the murder of Mary E. B. Marr, the infant child of their master and mistress. The jury acquitted Tom, and found the plaintiff in error guilty as charged in the indictment. The court refused to grant a new trial, and pronounced judgment of death upon the prisoner, from which an appeal in error has been prosecuted to this court. It is not necessary, in the view we have taken of the case, to state the evidence in detail; a mere outline will be sufficient to raise the questions of law presented for our determination, except the question in relation to the admissibility of the prisoner's confession.

The infant, of whose murder the prisoner stands convicted, was of extremely tender age, only five weeks old; and the death was caused by an over-dose of laudanum administered by the prisoner, without the knowledge of any one, and contrary to a general command, not to give the child anything whatever.

The prisoner is of immature age, being at the time of the alleged murder, not over fifteen years. A day or two preceding the death of the infant, the prisoner was taken from the negro-quarter on the plantation and put in the house to serve in the capacity of nurse. On the day of the infant's death, Mrs. Marr went into another room to attend to some of her domestic affairs, leaving the child, asleep in the cradle in care of the prisoner. She remained absent about fifteen minutes as she supposes, during which time the laudanum was administered. The child survived about four hours. A physician was immediately sent for, but did not arrive until about two hours after the laudanum was given, and his efforts to counteract its effect were unavailing. He states, that the death was caused by an over-dose of laudanum, and that half a drop was as large a dose as the infant could have borne. . . .

2nd. The next question is, was the law correctly stated to the jury? We think not. The errors of the charge will be obvious from the mere statement of a few plain elementary principles.

To constitute the crime of murder by the common law, and by that law this case is to be governed, the killing must be with malice aforethought: no matter by which of the thousand means adequate to the destruction of life, the death may have been effected. Malice, in its legal sense, is the sole criterion by which murder is distinguished from every other species of homicide. The malice essential to constitute the crime of murder, however, is not confined to an intention to take away the life of the deceased; but includes an intent to do any unlawful act which may probably result in depriving the party of life. It is not, in the language of Blackstone, so properly spite or malevolence to the individual in particular, as an evil design in general, the dictate of a wicked, depraved, and malignant heart; and it may be either express or implied in law. 4 Bl.Com. 199–200.

If an action, unlawful in itself, be done deliberately and with intention of mischief, or great bodily harm, to particulars, or of mischief indiscriminately, fall where it may, and death ensue; against or beside the original intention of the party, it will be murder. But, if such mischievous intention do not appear, (which is matter of fact to be collected from the circumstances,) and the act was done heedlessly and incautiously, it will be manslaughter only. But, if the death ensue in the performance of a lawful act, it may amount either to murder, manslaughter, or misadventure, according to the circumstances by which it is accompanied.

These general principles apply as much to a case where death ensues by means of a medicine of poisonous qualities, as to any other species of homicide. It is true, that where one wilfully poisons another, from such deliberate act the law presumes malice, though no particular enmity can be proved. But this presumption may be displaced in a case of death from poison, as in other cases, by direct proof, or by the circumstances of the particular case.

If, as Blackstone says, the poison were wilfully administered, that is, with intent that it should have the effect of destroying the life of the party: or if, in the language of Foster, the act were "done deliberately and with intention of mischief, or great bodily harm," and death ensue, it will be murder. But if it were not wilful, and such deliberate mischievous intention do not appear; and the act was done heedlessly and incautiously, it will be only manslaughter at most.

Testing the charge by these familiar principles, it is manifestly incorrect in several respects. It assumes, that if the prisoner administered the laudanum in violation of her master's order, for the purpose of "producing unnecessary sleep," and death ensued, contrary to her intention, she is guilty of murder. This is not law. In the first place, the charge puts the disobedience to the master's order, on the same footing with a violation of a command or prohibition of the law. This is a great mistake. Such violation of the master's order, is not an "unlawful act" in the sense of the rule above stated. It is no offence against the law of the land: nor is it cognizable by any tribunal created by law. It is an offence simply against the private authority of the master, and is cognizable and punishable alone in the domestic forum. Again: the criminality of the act is made to depend upon an intent, with reference to the deceased infant, which may be in law, if not positively innocent, at least comparatively so.

The laudanum may have been given by the prisoner in utter ignorance of the fact that it possessed any poisonous quality; and there may have been a total absence of any intention to do serious injury, or indeed injury of any sort, much less to destroy the life of the child. If the prisoner's purpose really was, to superinduce a state of temporary quietude or sleep, without more, in order to afford better opportunity, or greater facility, for carrying on her own illicit intercourse with Tom, this, however culpable in morals, would not involve her in the guilt of murder. . . .

In the case of the prisoner, her relation as a slave, taken in connection with her disregard of her master's positive direction, and the gross heedlessness and incautiousness of the act, might constitute her offence manslaughter, but certainly nothing more. . . .

The judgment of the Circuit Court will be reversed.

BANKS v. STATE
Court of Criminal Appeals of Texas, 1919.
85 Tex.Cr.R. 165, 211 S.W. 217.

LATTIMORE, JUDGE. In this case appellant was convicted in the District Court of Polk County of the offense of murder and his punishment fixed at death.

On his appeal but one question is presented and but one question was contained in the motion for new trial, namely, that the evidence does not show appellant guilty of that character of homicide which should be punished by the extreme penalty of death.

It appears from the record that on the night of the homicide, and while at his post of duty on a moving railroad train one Hawkins, a negro brakeman was shot and killed by some member of a party of negroes who were walking along a dirt road near to the railroad track. No reason is assigned for such shooting and it does not appear that appellant or any member of the party was acquainted with any of the parties on the train and that any specific malice could be directed toward the deceased, but under our law the same is not necessary.

One who deliberately uses a deadly weapon in such reckless manner as to evince a heart regarless [sic] of social duty and fatally bent on mischief, as is shown by firing into a moving railroad train upon which human beings necessarily are, cannot shield himself from the consequences of his acts by disclaiming malice. Malice may be toward a group of persons as well as toward an individual. It may exist without former grudges or antecedent menaces. The intentional doing of any wrongful act in such manner and under such circumstances as that the death of a human being may result therefrom is malice. In the instant case the appellant admits his presence and participation in the shooting which resulted in the death of the deceased. . . .

An examination of this statement shows a deliberate unprovoked shooting into a moving train—an act which could reasonably result in the destruction of human life. No excuse or justification is pleaded or shown in the evidence for the act. It is true that appellant says that he shot each time that his companion shot, but that he fired into the ground, which gives rise to the contention here that the State having introduced this declaration is bound by it; but the rule applicable is that the State is only bound when there is no other evidence upon which the jury may base their rejection of any part of such statement. In this case the proof shows that two pistols were used, and appellant so states in his statement above, and also he therein says that the pistol he used was a 38-calibre and the one used by his companion was a 45-calibre. It was conclusively shown by the other evidence that the bullet which killed deceased at the front end of the moving train, and also the one which entered the caboose at the rear of the same train were 38-calibre bullets. This evidence negatives the fact that the fatal shot was fired by appellant's companion and fully justified the jury in concluding that the portion of appellant's statement in which he says that he fired into the ground, was untrue, and also fully sustained the conclusion of the jury that his were the shots which took the life of deceased. Nor can we see that the jury was not justified in assessing the extreme penalty of the law. That man who can coolly shoot into a moving train, or automobile, or other vehicle in which are persons guiltless of any wrongdoing toward him or provocation for such attack, is, if possible, worse than the man who endures insult or broods over a wrong, real or fancied, and then waylays and kills his personal enemy. The shame of the world recently has been the unwarranted killing of persons who were noncombatants and who were doing nothing and were not capable of inflicting injury upon their slayers. Of kindred spirit is he who can shoot in the darkness into houses, crowds or trains and recklessly send into enternity those whom he does not know and against whom he has no sort of reason for directing his malevolence.

The only contention here being that the evidence does not support the verdict, with which we are unable to agree, and there being no errors shown in the charge of the court, or otherwise, we direct that the judgment of the lower court be affirmed.

The judgment of the lower court is affirmed.[1]

Affirmed.

[1]. Cf. State v. Capps, 134 N.C. 622, 46 S.E. 730 (1904).

PEOPLE v. PULLEY

District Court of Appeal, Fourth District, California, 1964.
225 Cal.App.2d 366, 37 Cal.Rptr. 376.

[Defendants, operating another's car without consent, were attempting to outrun a police car after they had been signaled to stop. In their effort they drove through an intersection against the red signal, at from 70 to 80 miles an hour, causing a fatal traffic accident. They appealed from a judgment of conviction of second-degree murder.]

GRIFFIN, PRESIDING JUSTICE. The main and basic contentions of defendants on this appeal are that:

(1) A conviction of murder, under the felony-murder doctrine, cannot be sustained in this case because a violation of Vehicle Code, § 10851 is not a common law felony and is not an offense which can be classified as violent or dangerous to human life.

(2) The trial court erred in instructing the jury that if the death occurred while violating Vehicle Code, § 10851, it is murder in the second degree, even though the death is unintentional or accidental. . . .

Vehicle Code, § 10851 provides that: "Any person who drives or takes a vehicle not his own, without the consent of the owner thereof, and with intent either permanently or temporarily to deprive the owner thereof of his title to or possession of the vehicle, whether with or without intent to steal the same, or any person who is a party or accessory to or an accomplice in the driving or unauthorized taking or stealing is guilty of a felony. . . ." . . .

It has been stated that the felony-murder doctrine applies both in first and second degree murders. If the unlawful killing occurs in the perpetration of one of the serious felonies listed in section 189, Penal Code, it is first degree murder. (People v. Doyell, 48 Cal. 85, 94; 1 Witkin, California Crimes, § 325, p. 295.) In People v. Balkwell, 143 Cal. 259, 76 P. 1017, it was held that where the killing results from a criminal abortion (not an offense mentioned in Penal Code § 189), the felony-murder doctrine applies. . . .

Therefore, a violation of Vehicle Code, section 10851, may come within this rule unless, when defendant committed the felonious act, the chance of death resulting therefrom was so remote that no reasonable man would have taken it into consideration. It is necessary to show that the death ensued in consequence of the felony and it is felony-murder if the homicide is within the *res gestae* of the initial felony. . . . See also 108 A.L.R. 847, where it is said that:
"The weight of authority is that if a number of persons enter upon the commission of a felony, all are criminally responsible for the death of a person that ensues as a natural consequence of the common felonious purpose, although the one accused may not have done

the actual killing. This rule has been deemed broad enough to include homicides committed in attempts to escape from the scene of the crime, or 'where the killing is done immediately after the conclusion of the project, for the purpose of preventing detection.'"

It is defendants' contention that the rule should be qualified and limited with respect to felonies that are not dangerous to human life.

Perkins on Criminal Law, Foundation Press (1957), page 36, expresses what he believes to be a modern viewpoint and concludes that there must be an element of human risk in the felony for the felony-murder rule to apply, but he appears to qualify the degree of human risk necessary. He puts the rule this way:

"Homicide is murder if the death ensues in consequence of the perpetration or attempted perpetration of some other felony unless such other felony was not dangerous of itself and the method of its perpetration or attempt did not appear to involve any appreciable human risk."

To this may be added the explanation, previously suggested, that the danger here referred to may fall considerably short of a plain and strong likelihood that death or great bodily injury will result, but must not be so remote that no reasonable man would have taken it into consideration.

By any reasonable standard, stealing and driving a stolen car and endeavoring to escape pursuing officers with the stolen car, entering an intersection against all rules of the road at 70 to 80 miles per hour and crashing with other cars lawfully proceeding therein, is highly dangerous. Violence in evading the police is within the ambit of risk. Death here was not a freak coincidence, but an expectable incident of the felony, part of the risk that is set in motion by the original crime.

. . .

While the instructions given by the trial court did not fully qualify the rule to the effect that this rule applies unless such other felony was not dangerous of itself and the method of its perpetration or attempt did not appear to involve any appreciable human risk, as suggested in Perkins on Criminal Law, supra, page 36, we conclude that no prejudicial error resulted in view of the other instructions given and the evidence presented in this case. . . .

Judgment affirmed.[1]

COUGHLIN and GERALD BROWN, JJ., concur.

---

[1]. The furnishing, selling or administering narcotics to a minor is a dangerous felony, hence death resulting therefrom is murder in the second degree. People v. Poindexter, 51 Cal.2d 142, 330 P.2d 763 (1958).

Companion to the felony-murder rule was the rule that death resulting from knowingly resisting a lawful arrest was murder. The tendency has been to modify this position also. Thus a conviction of second-degree murder was reversed because it was tried on the theory that such a homicide could not be less. State v. Weisengoff, 85 W. Va. 271, 101 S.E. 450 (1919). The court cited The Queen v. Porter, 12 Cox C.C. 444 (1873). In that case D,

PEOPLE v. HARRIS

Supreme Court of Illinois, 1956.
8 Ill.2d 431, 134 N.E.2d 315.

DAILY, JUSTICE. Defendant, Robert Harris, was indicted in the criminal court of Cook County for the crime of murder. However, at the jury trial which followed, he was convicted of voluntary manslaughter and sentenced to the penitentiary for a term of 14 years. On writ of error, he now contends (1) that the trial court erred in submitting manslaughter instructions for jury consideration; (2) . . . .

The record discloses that on the night of September 18, 1954, James Ellis, the deceased, was employed as a "bouncer" by the Tan Club Tavern, which was located at 2922 West Madison Street in the city of Chicago, and, as such, was wearing a blue uniform and star similar to those of a police officer, and was carrying both a night stick and a holstered gun. Sometime around midnight, the defendant entered the tavern, walked to the rear, and commenced talking with some friends. For some unexplained reason, he was almost immediately accosted by Ellis and ordered to leave the premises, and when he refused to do so, he was severely beaten with the night stick and forcibly evicted. After a lapse of time, the duration of which is in dispute, defendant reappeared at the tavern entrance and fired one shot from a .32 caliber automatic which struck Ellis in the back, resulting in his almost immediate death. Thereupon, the defendant fled from the scene on foot but was pursued and apprehended a few blocks away.

Although all the witnesses agreed that the shooting took place at approximately 12:30 A.M., they were in disagreement as to the time of the prior incident. The testimony of the People's witnesses indicated that the beating occurred around 11:45 P.M. while the witnesses for the defense stated that it took place almost thirty minutes later. The defendant himself testified that he entered the tavern at approximately 12:15 A.M. on the morning of September 19 and was attacked by the deceased without reason. Upon being evicted from the tavern, he walked a short distance down the street and sat on the fender of a parked automobile, where he was found by an acquaintance known only as George Jones who suggested that they return to the tavern to see why he had been beaten. The defendant agreed, and as they approached the tavern entrance, Jones handed him a gun, whereupon the defendant then stepped into the doorway and beckoned for Ellis to

---

who had been lawfully arrested objected to being put in a vehicle which was to take him to jail. As he was being forced inside, his foot came in contact with the head of one of his arrestors and caused his death. The court took the position that if the kick was intentional D was guilty of murder, but that if it was an accidental contact during his unlawful resistance he was guilty of manslaughter.

come outside. According to the defendant's testimony, Ellis turned to face the door, took one or two steps towards the defendant, and then reached for his gun. At that instant, defendant fired the fatal shot. Although an eyewitness swore that Ellis was shot in the back while standing at the bar talking to friends, the defendant describes the shooting as follows: "When he reached for his gun, that is when my gun went off. That was when I fired one shot . . .. When I brought this gun up I did not know I was pulling the trigger. When I went to the Tan Club entrance I did not intend to shoot anybody. I went there to find out why he hit me." Based upon this testimony, instructions as to both accidental shooting and the right of self-defense were given at the request of the defendant. It is now contended, however, that the court erred in giving manslaughter instructions which were tendered by the State.

We have long held that if there is any evidence in the record which, if believed by the jury, would reduce a charge of murder to manslaughter, an instruction defining that crime should be given. . . . In cases of voluntary manslaughter, this evidence must consist of facts which would indicate that a serious and highly provoking injury was inflicted upon the defendant which would be sufficient to excite an irresistible passion in a reasonable man, or that an attempt was made by the deceased to inflict a personal injury, and that the killing resulted from the violent passion before sufficient time had elapsed for the voice of reason to return. What constitutes a sufficient "cooling-off period" depends upon the extent to which the passions have been aroused and the nature of the act which caused the provocation, and, for that reason, no yardstick of time can be used by the court to measure a reasonable period of passion but it must vary as do the facts of every case. Humans react violently to the infliction of a serious injury, and the degree of pain which results therefrom not only governs the passion itself but also influences the duration of the cooling period. . . . In view of the evidence of the severe beating and other provocatory circumstances which so closely preceded the shooting, it is our opinion the trial court was justified in submitting to the jurors' consideration, the question of whether the killing resulted from an irresistible impulse before defendant's passion had cooled and before his voice of reason had returned. Accordingly, we hold that the court did not err in giving the manslaughter instructions now complained of.

Neither do we believe the verdict was contrary to the evidence presented. Although there were facts in the record which might indicate that the defendant was guilty of murder, there was also evidence to support the manslaughter theory. The jury and trial judge observed the witnesses, heard them testify, and were in a much better position to determine their credibility than a court of review. This court will reverse because of insufficient evidence only where that evidence is so palpably contrary to the verdict, or is so unreasonable, improbable, or unsatisfactory as to raise a reasonable doubt of the defendant's guilt. People v. Smith, 404 Ill. 125, 88 N.E.2d 444. This is not true of the present case. . . .

The judgment of the criminal court of Cook County is affirmed.[1]

Judgment affirmed.

STATE v. GRUGIN

Supreme Court of Missouri, Division Two, 1898.
147 Mo. 39, 47 S.W. 1058.

SHERWOOD, J. The appeal in this instance is taken by defendant from the judgment of the trial court, which, based on the verdict of the jury, adjudged and sentenced him to the penitentiary for the term of fifteen years as punishment for the crime of murder in the second degree.

The indictment was for murder in the first degree. . . .

2. The second interrogatory is next for consideration. It embodies and comprehends the question whether *words* constitute a sufficient or reasonable provocation in law? Of course the books abound in utterance of the platitude that words however opprobrious constitute no provocation in law. Speaking as the organ of this court I have often uttered this platitude myself, but the statement is subject to many qualifications. The general good sense of mankind has in some instances so far qualified the rigor of what is termed the ancient rule that a statute has been passed in Texas which reduces a homicide to manslaughter where insulting words are used to or concerning a female relative, the killing is reduced to manslaughter where it occurs as soon as the parties meet after the knowledge of the insult.

In Alabama, a statute provides that opprobrious words shall in some circumstances justify an assault and battery. And in that State, without any statutory provision on the subject, it has been determined that *"insult by mere words,"* when the defendant acts on them and he has not provoked them, may be weighed by the jury with other evidence in determining whether the killing was murder in the first or second degree. [Watson v. State, 82 Ala. 10, 2 So. 455.]

---

[1]. It was held to be reversible error to give an instruction telling the jury in substance that an intentional killing without justification or excuse is murder and that a killing under great provocation can not be held to be manslaughter unless the slayer's mind was so disturbed that he was not really aware of what he was doing. A killing in the sudden heat of passion engendered by great provocation is manslaughter, "not because the law supposes that this passion made him unconscious of what he was about to do, and stripped the act of killing of an intent to commit it, but because it presumes that passion disturbed the sway of reason, and made him regardless of her admonitions". It is an "indulgence which the law accords to human infirmity suddenly provoked into passion". State v. Hill, 20 N.C. 629 (1839).

After speaking of Morley's Case, Hale says: "Many, who were of opinion, that bare words of slighting, disdain, or contumely would not of themselves make such a provocation as to lessen the crime into manslaughter, yet were of this opinion, that if A. gives indecent language to B., and B. thereupon strikes A., but not mortally; and then A. strikes B. again, and then B. kills A. that this is but manslaughter. For the second stroke made a new provocation, and so it was but a sudden falling out; and though B. gave the first stroke, and after a blow received from A., B. gives him a mortal stroke, this is but manslaughter, according to the proverb, the second blow makes the affray. And this was the opinion of myself and some others." [1 Hale, P.C. 456.]

Now in the case Hale supposes, it is as he says the second stroke that made a *"new provocation,"* but the second stroke was given by A. Then what made the *old* provocation? Evidently, the *"indecent words"* of A. which, given by A. to B., prompted the latter to give the *first* stroke. So in Morley's Case, it was agreed that "if upon ill words both of the parties suddenly fight, and one kill the other, this is but manslaughter; for it is a combat betwixt two upon a sudden heat, which is the legal description of manslaughter." [6 How.St.Tr. 771.] In that instance, also, it must be noted that "ill words" were the provocation that made the hot blood which resulted only in manslaughter: To test this matter further, suppose no "ill words" used, what then the crime? Evidently *murder.*

It is said in the books that though an *insufficient* assault or demonstration do not import coming violence, still it and *insulting words combined,* may so excite the passions as to reduce the killing to manslaughter. [2 Bishop's New Cr.Law, sec. 704.]

If the inchoate assault be *naught* as provocation, and the approbrious [sic] words be *naught* as provocation, I am unable to see how the addition of these *two ciphers* can make a *unit.* "The moment, however, the person is touched with apparent insolence, then the provocation is one which, ordinarily speaking, reduces the offense to manslaughter." [1 Whart.Cr.Law (10 Ed.), sec. 456.] And it is held that such *"apparent insolence"* may be manifested in a variety of ways, as for instance, by a contemptuous jostling on the street, by tweaking the nose, by filliping on the forehead, or by spitting in the face. In most of these instances and illustrations there is no *physical pain or injury inflicted,* the "sudden *heat*" springs from the *indignity* the *insult* offered, and from nothing else. [Kelly Cr.Law, sec. 518.] This being true the law should not be so unreasonable as to deny to an *insult* offered *in words* the same force and effect which all men recognize that it has as a matter *of fact.* If it "so excite the passions of the mass of men as to enthrall their reason, the law should hold it adequate cause" for the reduction of the grade of the offense, resulting from the use of the insulting words. No sound distinction can, it seems, be taken in principle between insult offered by acts and that offered by foul and opprobrious words.

I will now refer to some adjudications where insulting words have been held a sufficient basis for a charge or an instruction on the offense of manslaughter. Where the prisoner was indicted for the willful murder of his wife, Blackburn, J., in summing up, said: "As a general rule of law, no provocation of words will reduce the crime murder to that of manslaughter, but under special circumstances there may be such a provocation of words as will have that effect; for instance if a husband suddenly hearing from his wife that she had committed adultery, and he, having no idea of such a thing before, were thereupon to kill his wife, it might be manslaughter. Now, in this case, words spoken by the deceased just previous to the blows inflicted by the prisoner were these: 'Aye; but I'll take no more for thee, for I will have no more children of thee. I have done it once, and I'll do it again.' Now, what you will have to consider is, would these words, which were spoken just previous to the blows, amount to such a provocation as would in an ordinary man, not in a man of violent or passionate disposition, provoke him in such a way as to justify him in striking her as the prisoner did?" [Reg. v. Rothwell, 12 Cox C.C. 145.] In that case (tried in 1871) the husband seized a pair of tongs, close at hand, and struck his wife three violent blows on the head from which she died within a week, and the verdict was for manslaughter.

In Reg. v. Smith, tried in 1866, a woman had left her husband and gone off and lived in adultery with one Langley. He having died, she returned to her home, and her husband forgave her, but she did not prize this forgiveness, because on the next night after her return she violently abused him, taunting him with her preference for Langley and declaring had he not died, she had not returned. Whilst this was going on, she was so violent as to have to be held by two other women who were present; her husband sat by her on the seat trying to pacify her. Finally she broke from the women who were holding her and repeating with much foul language her preference for Langley, spat towards her husband, whereupon he, who was then standing up within a yard of her, gave her a blow in the neck with a sharp pointed pocket knife, which caused her immediate death. And the jury were in substance charged: An assault, too slight in itself to be sufficient provocation to reduce murder to manslaughter, may become sufficient for that purpose, when coupled with words of *great insult*. [4 F. & F. 1066.] A verdict of guilty of manslaughter was returned. . . .

So it will be seen that there *are* circumstances where *words do amount to a provocation in law*, i. e., a reasonable provocation to be submitted to the determination of the jury, and if found by them to exist, then the crime is lowered to the grade of manslaughter. If there ever was a case to which this principle should be applied, it would seem it should be applied to the case at bar. A father is informed that his young daughter just budding into womanhood has been ravished by his son-in-law, while under the supposed protection of his roof. Arriving where the son-in-law is, and making inquiry of him why he had done the foul deed, the father receives the answer, *"I'll do as I damn please about it."* This insolent and defiant reply amounted to an affirmation of Hadley's guilt! So long as human nature remains as God made it, such audacious and atrocious avowals will be met as met by defendant. It should be held, therefore, that the words in question should have been left to the jury to say whether, in the circumstances detailed in evidence, they constituted a reasonable provocation, and if so found, that then defendant was guilty of no higher offense than manslaughter in the fourth degree. . . .

The judgment should be reversed and the cause remanded. BURGESS, J., concurs *in toto*; GANTT, P. J., does not concur as to that portion of paragraph 2 in reference to words being regarded as a reasonable provocation by either court or jury.[1]

PEOPLE v. BORCHERS

Supreme Court of California, In Bank, 1958.
50 Cal.2d 321, 325 P.2d 97.

SCHAUER, JUSTICE. The People appeal "from an Order of the Superior Court . . . modifying the verdict in the above entitled cause by reducing the punishment imposed." (Pen.Code, § 1238(6).) Defendant does not appeal. A jury found defendant guilty of murder of the second degree and found that he was sane at the time of the commission of the offense. The trial judge denied defendant's motion for a new trial on the issue of sanity and ordered that "Defendant's motion for new trial on the case in chief is ruled upon as follows: In lieu of granting a new trial, the verdict of second degree Murder is reduced to Voluntary Manslaughter." The People argue that the evidence was sufficient to justify the implied finding of malice aforethought, that the evidence did not show that defendant was guilty of voluntary manslaughter, and that the trial court erred in reducing the class of crime found by the jury. We have concluded that no ground for reversal is shown.

Defendant, a Pasadena insurance broker, aged 45, met deceased, referred to throughout the testimony as "Dotty," aged 29, at a zoo on May 13, 1956. With Dotty was Tony, an illegitimate child of four whom Dotty had cared for since 16 days after his birth. Defendant

---

[1] "The rule in this State is, as it was at common law, that the law regards no mere epithet or language, however violent or offensive, as sufficient provocation for taking life. Williams v. State, 3 Heisk. 376, 292; Wharton on Homicide (3d Ed.) sec. 173.

"Courts have often had under consideration, in connection with the existence of adequate cause, the use of the vile epithet used by deceased just before he was killed, 'son of a bitch,' and quite without exception have held these words not to constitute adequate cause of provocation." Freddo v. State, 127 Tenn. 376, 155 S.W. 170 (1912).

was attracted by the "warmth," "kindness," and "sweetness" with which Dotty spoke to the child. Defendant spoke to the boy and thus became acquainted with Dotty. They had dinner together that night and thereafter, according to defendant's testimony, "went together steadily from then on" until he killed her on October 9, 1956. From May 13 until October 9 "excepting the days that I was away on a business trip to Mexico and one other day . . . there was not a day that went by but what Tony and Dotty and I saw each other". . . .

[Although defendant was married (divorce proceedings had been started) he and Dotty became "engaged" nine days after they first met. He provided an apartment for her and Tony, and took her on a trip to Las Vegas. There they recited a "common-law marriage ceremony". After they returned to Pasadena he learned that Marvin Prestidge and another man were "hanging around" Dotty and using her automobile. As these men had criminal records, defendant employed Fagg, a private detective, to investigate. Fagg reported that Prestidge had a police record as a pimp, that he was having sexual relations with Dotty, and that she was taking money from defendant and giving it to Prestidge. Defendant believed she was acting because of fear of Prestidge although Fagg assured him that fear was not the reason.

On October 5, 1956, while returning from a trip to San Diego, she said she wished she were dead and tried to jump from the moving car. A few nights later, while they were riding, she repeatedly suggested suicide. She took a pistol from the glove compartment, saying she was going to shoot him, but permitted him to take the weapon. She said he should kill her, Tony and himself. Then she turned to him and said: "Go ahead and shoot. What is the matter—are you chicken?" And as defendant told it, "he heard the explosion of the gun as he shot Dotty in the back of the head."]

Section 1181, paragraph 6 of the Penal Code provides that the trial court may grant a new trial "When the verdict is contrary to law or evidence, but if the evidence shows the defendant to be not guilty of the degree of the crime of which he was convicted, but guilty of a lesser degree thereof, or of a lesser crime included therein, the court may modify the verdict, finding or judgment accordingly without granting or ordering a new trial . . ."

The trial court in ruling on the question of reducing the class of the crime stated that in its opinion there was "a duty fixed on the trial court to independently weigh and consider the testimony and all of the ramifications of it and determine in his own mind if he is satisfied that the evidence beyond a reasonable doubt shows guilt of second degree murder. Tested in that light and tested further in the light of the evidence of the psychiatrists on the mental condition of this defendant, I am not satisfied that the evidence is sufficient to sustain the finding of malice to make this second degree murder; hence, the Court in lieu of granting a new trial will reduce the degree to that of voluntary manslaughter."

In passing on a motion for new trial it is not only the power but also the duty of the trial court to consider the weight of the evidence. The power and duty of the trial court in considering the question of the reduction of the class or degree of the crime are the same.

In a criminal trial the burden is upon the prosecution to prove beyond any reasonable doubt every essential element of the crime of which a defendant is to be convicted. Here, from the evidence viewed as a whole, the trial judge was amply justified in concluding that defendant did not possess the state of mind known as "malice aforethought" which is an essential ingredient of murder. (Pen.Code, § 187.) "Such malice may be express or implied. It is express when there is manifested a deliberate intention unlawfully to take away the life of a fellow-creature. It is implied, when no considerable provocation appears, or when the circumstances attending the killing show an abandoned and malignant heart." (Pen.Code, § 188.) Voluntary manslaughter is "the unlawful killing of a human being, without malice . . . upon a sudden quarrel or heat of passion." (Pen. Code, § 192.)

From the evidence viewed as a whole the trial judge could well have concluded that defendant was roused to a heat of "passion" by a series of events over a considerable period of time: Dotty's admitted infidelity, her statements that she wished she were dead, her attempt to jump from the car on the trip to San Diego, her repeated urging that defendant shoot her, Tony, and himself on the night of the homicide, and her taunt, "are you chicken." As defendant argues persuasively, "passion" need not mean "rage" or "anger". According to dictionary definition, "passion" may be any "violent, intense, high-wrought, or enthusiastic emotion." (Webster's New International Dictionary, 2d ed.) As stated in People v. Logan (1917), 175 Cal. 45, 49, 164 P. 1121, "the fundamental of the inquiry (in determining whether a homicide is voluntary manslaughter) is whether or not the defendant's reason was, at the time of his act, so disturbed or obscured by some passion—not necessarily fear and never, of course, the passion for revenge—to such an extent as would render ordinary men of average disposition liable to act rashly or without due deliberation and reflection, and from this passion rather than from judgment." It may fairly be concluded that the evidence on the issue of not guilty supports a finding that defendant killed in wild desperation induced by Dotty's long continued provocatory conduct. . . .

The trial judge here is to be commended for his diligent alertness to the power and duty, reposed *only in trial courts*, to reappraise the weight of the evidence on motion for new trial. He very properly showed no hesitance in reducing the class of the homicide in the light of his determination, supported by a reasonable view of the evidence, that there was no sufficient showing of malice aforethought. Such unhesitant exercise of this power by the trial judge, when he is satisfied that the action is indicated by the evidence, not only makes for justice in the individual case but tends also to lighten the burden of reviewing courts and to expedite the finality of judgments.

For the reasons above stated the order appealed from is affirmed.[1]

GIBSON, C. J., and SHENK, CARTER, TRAYNOR, SPENCE and MCCOMB, JJ., concur.

STATE v. MATTHEWS

Supreme Court of Missouri, Division Two, 1899.
148 Mo. 185, 49 S.W. 1085.

SHERWOOD, J. Indicted for murder in the first degree for killing one R. H. Morgan with a shotgun on the seventeenth of April, 1896, defendant being put upon his trial was found guilty of the second degree of that offense, and his punishment assessed at fourteen years in the penitentiary.

This homicide grows out of a disputed line, and a portion of a disputed rock fence, which, if removed would open defendant's field and leave it uninclosed, and besides, would admit the water from the hillside to sweep over defendant's field. A lane running north and south divided the two fences of defendant and of Hammond, that of defendant lying on the west and Hammond's on the east of that lane which, at its north end, opened into a public road which at this point ran west on the north side of defendant's field. The north end of the lane terminated at the foot of a steep hill, which was the watershed of that immediate locality. The disputed boundary and rock lay between the northeast and the northwest corners of the respective fields. Hammond had lived on his farm about nineteen years and had never, so far as it appears, had any difference or difficulty with his vis-à-vis neighbor.

Defendant, forty-five years of age, had lived on his farm some fifteen years, in the county some thirty years, had been constable and

---

[1]. It has been pointed out, very properly, that in cases of voluntary homicide there may be recognized mitigation other than the "rule of provocation" because there is an intermediate zone which falls short of justification or excuse without going to the other extreme of malice aforethought. Allison v. State, 74 Ark. 444, 86 S.W. 409 (1905). By way of illustration the Court said: "The mere fact that a man believes that he is in great and immediate danger of life or great bodily harm does not of itself justify him in taking life. There must be some reasonable grounds for such belief, or the law will not excuse him for taking the life of another. But if the slayer acts from an honest belief that it is necessary to protect himself, and not from malice or revenge, even though he formed such conclusion hastily and without due care, and when the facts did not justify it, still under such a case, although such a belief on his part will not justify him, it may go in mitigation of the crime, and reduce the homicide from murder to manslaughter."

justice of the peace some ten or twelve years, and bore an excellent reputation for being a peaceable and law-abiding citizen. On the other hand, Morgan, who had lived on the farm of Hammond, his step-father, for about the space of a year and had rented it, it seems, for the year 1896, had the reputation, as some of the testimony tends to show, of being of a rash, quarrelsome, turbulent and dangerous disposition, of which defendant was informed prior to the fatal occurrence, and he had been warned by some of his neighbors to be on his guard against Morgan. Indeed, it seems Morgan had conceived a strong dislike against defendant, and had made serious threats against him, and of these threats defendant had been told. About two weeks before the homicide, Morgan had gotten into an altercation with defendant's youngest son; had thrown rocks at him, and when remonstrated with by defendant on that occasion had invited defendant out of his field in order to beat him, saying to the latter that he had it laid up for him and intended to do him up.

Morgan was a large stout man weighing one hundred and seventy-five to one hundred and ninety pounds, and was about thirty-eight years old. Defendant had been prosecuted for obstructing the public road at the northeast corner of his field, and was convicted of that offense. On termination of this prosecution, defendant under the direction of the prosecuting attorney and sheriff as to where his fence should be erected, had set his fence back on his line as it was ascertained to be on the trial aforesaid, and he built this portion of the fence of rock in order to prevent his field from being flooded. After this building of his fence back on his line, defendant was repeatedly annoyed by Morgan throwing this fence down, when defendant would rebuild it. This process of rebuilding had just been completed just after noon of the day of the homicide, by defendant and two or three of his nearest neighbors. In the afternoon, a passing neighbor, having informed Morgan, who was at work in his field plowing, of the fence being replaced, he immediately quit his work, sent his team around by the bottom road, went by his house for his ax and pistol, and with Hammond, his step-father, and Mrs. Hammond, his mother, he went to where the rock wall had been replaced, taking with him two chains. The others of the family, two grown women, and two boys, one twelve years and the other younger, all went to what was termed the "rock pile," as the rock wall at the *locus in quo* was called. Arriving there, they all went to work tearing down defendant's fence and placing the rock thus obtained on that of Hammond. Defendant was in his field cutting sprouts; his son who was in the field also and plowing, but somewhat nearer to the rock wall than his father, saw Morgan and called his father's attention to it, whereupon defendant looking up, saw Morgan coming down the hill towards the rock wall, at a brisk walk or run. He had on his arm an ax and defendant thought he saw him have also a pistol. Behind Morgan were his step-father and mother. Defendant also noticed the others of the party proceeding to the same point with horses, etc. Thinking it prudent to do so, defendant went to his house and got a shotgun and returned to the field and went towards where Morgan and the others were tearing defendant's fence down, and when defendant got within about thirty steps of him where they were tearing the fence down, Morgan said to him: "Don't come any closer." Defendant told him to go away and not disturb his fence, when Morgan replied with foul and abusive language.

Whether defendant had his gun presented at Morgan at the time or not is the subject of conflicting evidence. Some of the testimony shows it was thus carried; other that defendant merely carried it in his hands, and other still, that it was on his shoulder. After testifying as above stated, with regard to what Morgan said to him, defendant continued: "I kept insisting that Morgan get away, that I didn't want any trouble with him, and that that was my fence, and he very well knew the court had so decided, and if he thought it wasn't, to go into court, and when the court decided it was his, he should have it, and not until then. He kept on abusing me, and then he had a pistol, the first I saw of it he was behind the wall from me, and he kind o' scooted down by the side of the tree, and I could just see the pistol and a little side of his face, and when he did that I turned and walked a few steps right around towards the lane; I was out from the lane a little ways, and about that time his mother came out and commenced quarreling at me, and I said to the old lady, 'I didn't come over here to quarrel with women, it would look better if you were at the house.' I told her I didn't come to quarrel with the old lady, and it would look better if she was at the house, and I happened to think of myself again, that it was perhaps done to draw my attention, and when I noticed Morgan again he was up and a few feet from the tree, and I says again, 'Go away and don't tear my fence down, and don't abuse me any more. I mean what I say.' I don't think I can repeat the language exactly that I used, and he stooped down and threw some rock from the wall and whirled around in that position (indicating), and that was the time the gun, I guess, fired very quickly. I was a southwest direction from Mr. Morgan, and he reached over just in this position and jerked some rock on, and as he raised up he threw himself in that position, and I thought he was going to draw his pistol, then I fired. I thought he was going to draw his pistol. He was not over four or five feet from where he presented the pistol at me."

There was other testimony tending to show that defendant threatened to shoot Morgan in case he did not quit removing the rock, and that Morgan had his team attached to a stone and had just started to drive the team off, when defendant fired; that the exact words used by defendant to Morgan at that moment, were: "Damn you, if you move that I will shoot you," and Morgan answered: "You kiss my a——, you cowardly son of a b——," and started his team, and that witness did not see Morgan have a pistol. The testimony of some of the witnesses corroborates that of defendant, and that of others is of a contrary effect. . . .

Bishop, when speaking of cases represented by Com. v. Drew, 4 Mass. 391, says: "The doctrine that passion excited by trespass to property can never reduce the killing with a deadly weapon to manslaughter, is too hard for human nature; and though stated many times in the books, is not sufficiently founded in actual adjudication to be received without further examination. For surely, though a man is not so quickly excited by an attack on his property as on his person, and therefore the two cases are not on precisely the same foundation, yet since he has the right to defend his property by all means short of taking human life, if in the heat of passion arising in a lawful defense he seizes a deadly weapon and with it unfortunately kills the aggressor, every principle which in other cases dictates the reduction of the crime to the mitigated form requires the same in this case." [2 Bishop, New Cr.Law, note, sec. 706.]

From these premises it should be concluded that instructions 15 and 23 given of the court's own motion were erroneous. They are the following:

15. "Although you may believe from the evidence that deceased was removing a stone fence belonging to defendant at the time he was shot, that would not justify or excuse him" (defendant).

23. "The defendant had a right to arm himself and go to any part of his own premises and forbid trespass thereon, but as before instructed, had no right to shoot deceased merely for removing stone defendant claimed to be his or on his premises."

The error in these instructions consists in this: That they do not go far enough, and are therefore to that extent erroneous and misleading. Because while it was true that defendant was not *excused* or *justified* in shooting Morgan for taking away stone which inclosed defendant's field or which belonged to defendant, and were used by him to prevent his field from being flooded, yet it was also true that if hot blood was engendered in defendant by seeing his fence or wall thus removed, he was not guilty of a higher grade of offense than manslaughter in the fourth degree; and these instructions should have been enlarged so as to embrace that point. And it is not the law that self-defense may not coexist with a right to have an instruction given, based upon manslaughter in the fourth degree.

Therefore judgment reversed and cause remanded. All concur.

STATE v. HARDIE

Supreme Court of Iowa, 1878.
47 Iowa 647.

ROTHROCK, CH. J. I. It appears from the evidence that the defendant was a boarder in the family of one Gantz, who is his brother-in-law. On the day of the homicide defendant was engaged in varnishing furniture. Mrs. Sutfen, a neighbor, called at the house, and after some friendly conversation she went into the kitchen. When she came back defendant picked up a tack hammer and struck on the door. She said, "My God, I thought it was a revolver." A short time afterwards she went into the yard to get a kitten. Defendant said he would frighten her with the revolver as she came in. He took a revolver from a stand drawer and went out of the room, and was in the kitchen when the revolver was discharged. He immediately came in and said to Mrs. Gantz, his sister, "My God, Hannah, come and see what I have done." His sister went out and found Mrs. Sutfen lying on the sidewalk at the side of the house, with a gunshot wound in the head, and in a dying condition. A physician was immediately called and made an examination of the deceased, took the revolver from the defendant, and informed him that nothing could be done for the deceased, whereupon the defendant became violent, said the shot was accidental, and exclaimed several times that he would kill himself. It became necessary to secure him, which was done by tying him with ropes.

The revolver had been in the house for about five years. It was found by Gantz in the road. There was one load in it when found. Some six months after it was found Gantz tried to shoot the load from it and it would not go off. He tried to punch the load out, but could not move it. He then laid it away, thinking it was harmless. The defendant was about the house and knew the condition of the revolver. Upon one occasion Gantz said he would try to kill a cat with the revolver. Defendant being present said he would not be afraid to allow it to be snapped at him all day. The revolver remained in the same condition that it was when found, no other load having been put into it, and it was considered by the family as well as defendant as entirely harmless.

The foregoing is the substance of all the evidence.

The State did not claim that the defendant was guilty of murder, but that he was guilty of manslaughter because of criminal carelessness. The defendant insisted that there was no such carelessness as to render the act criminal, and that it was homicide by misadventure, and therefore excusable.

The court instructed the jury as follows: "5. And on the charge of manslaughter, I instruct you that if the defendant used a dangerous and deadly weapon, in a careless and reckless manner, by reason of which instrument so used he killed the deceased, then he is guilty of manslaughter, although no harm was in fact intended."

Other instructions of like import were given, and the question of criminal carelessness was submitted to the jury, as follows: "8th. And in this case I submit to you to find the facts of recklessness and carelessness under the evidence, and if you find that the death of the party was occasioned through recklessness and carelessness of the defendant then you should convict him, and if not you should acquit.

And by this I do not mean that defendant is to be held to the highest degree of care and prudence in handling a dangerous and deadly weapon, but only such care as a reasonably prudent man should and ought to use under like circumstances, and if he did not use such care he should be convicted, otherwise he should be acquitted."

There can be no doubt that the instructions given by the court embody the correct rule as to criminal carelessness in the use of a deadly weapon. Counsel for defendant insist that the instructions of the court do not go far enough, and upon the trial asked that the court give to the jury the following instruction:

"3. Although the deceased came to her death from the discharge of a pistol in the hands of the defendant, yet if the defendant had good reason to believe, and did believe, that the pistol which caused her death was not in any manner dangerous, but was entirely harmless, and if he did nothing more than a man of ordinary prudence and caution might have done under like circumstances, then the jury should find him not criminally liable and should acquit."

This instruction and others of like import were refused by the court, and we think the ruling was correct. That the revolver was in fact a deadly weapon is conclusively shown by the terrible tragedy consequent upon defendant's act in firing it off. If it had been in fact unloaded no homicide would have resulted, but the defendant would have been justly censurable for a most reckless and imprudent act in frightening a woman by pretending that it was loaded, and that he was about to discharge it at her. No jury would be warranted in finding that men of ordinary prudence so conduct themselves. On the contrary, such conduct is grossly reckless and reprehensible, and without palliation or excuse. Human life is not to be sported with by the use of firearms, even though the person using them may have good reason to believe that the weapon used is not loaded, or that being loaded it will do no injury. When persons engage in such reckless sport they should be held liable for the consequences of their acts.

II. It is argued that the evidence does not show the defendant guilty of criminal carelessness, because it does not appear that the defendant pointed the pistol at the deceased, or how it happened to be discharged. The fact that defendant took the weapon from the drawer with the avowed purpose of frightening the deceased, and while in his hands it was discharged with fatal effect, together with his admission that he did the act, fully warranted the jury in finding that he purposely pointed the pistol and discharged it at the deceased.

Affirmed.[1]

---

1. Two friends had a revolver. There was one cartridge in the chamber, so placed that they thought it would not fire until the trigger had been pulled about five times. One playfully put the weapon against the side of the other and pulled the trigger three times. The third pull resulted in a fatal shot. A conviction of second-degree murder was affirmed. Commonwealth v. Malone, 354 Pa. 180, 47 A.2d 445 (1946).

PEOPLE v. RODRIGUEZ

District Court of Appeal, Second District,
Division 3, California, 1961.
186 Cal.App.2d 433, 8 Cal.Rptr. 863.

VALLÉE, JUSTICE. By information defendant was accused of manslaughter in that on November 8, 1959 she did wilfully, unlawfully, feloniously, and without malice kill Carlos Quinones. In a nonjury trial she was found guilty of involuntary manslaughter. A new trial was denied. She appeals from the judgment and the order denying a new trial.

In November 1959 defendant was living with her four children in a single-family residence at 130 South Clarence Street, Los Angeles. The oldest child was 6 years of age. Carlos Quinones was the youngest, either 2 or 3 years of age.

Olive Faison lived across the street from defendant. About 10:45 p. m. on November 8, 1959 Miss Faison heard some children calling, "Mommy, mommy." For about 15 or 20 minutes she did not "pay too much attention." She noticed the cries became more shrill. She went to the front window and saw smoke coming from defendant's house. She "ran across the street and commenced to knock the door in and started pulling the children out." There was a screen door on the outside and a wooden door inside the screen door. The screen door was padlocked on the outside. The other door was open. She broke the screen door and with the help of neighbors pulled three of the children out of the house. She tried to get into the house through the front door but could not because of the flames. A neighbor entered through the back door but could not go far because of the flames. Miss Faison took the three children to her apartment and shortly thereafter returned to the scene of the fire. . . .

Maria Lucero, defendant's sister, went to defendant's home about 12 p. m. on November 8, 1959. She went looking for defendant. She found her about 2 or 2:30 a. m. in the same block as "Johnny's Place." Defendant was nervous and frightened, said she knew about the fire and that she went over to tell Johnny Powers about it. Defendant had not been drinking.

Carlos Quinones died from "thermal burns, second and third degree involving 50 to 60 per cent of the body surface." Defendant did not testify. . . .

"Manslaughter is the unlawful killing of a human being without malice. It is of three kinds: . . . 2. Involuntary—in the commission of an unlawful act, not amounting to felony; or in the commission of a lawful act which might produce death, in an unlawful manner, or without due caution and circumspection . . .." Pen. Code, § 192. "In every crime or public offense there must exist a union, or joint operation of act and intent, or criminal negligence."

Pen.Code, § 20. Section 20 of the Penal Code makes the union of act and wrongful intent or criminal negligence an invariable element of every crime unless it is excluded expressly or by necessary implication. People v. Stuart, 47 Cal.2d 167, 171, 302 P.2d 5, 55 A.L.R.2d 705. Section 26 of the Penal Code lists, among the persons incapable of committing crimes, "[p]ersons who committed the act or made the omission charged through misfortune or by accident, when it appears that there was no evil design, intention, or culpable negligence." Thus the question is: Was there any evidence of criminal intent or criminal negligence? . . .

It appears from the record that guilt was predicated on the alleged "commission of a lawful act which might produce death, in an unlawful manner, or without due caution and circumspection." Pen. Code, § 192.

In People v. Penny, 44 Cal.2d 861, 285 P.2d 926, the defendant was convicted of involuntary manslaughter. While engaged in the practice of "face rejuvenation" she applied a formula containing phenol to the skin. Death was caused by phenol poisoning. The trial court charged the jury that ordinary negligence was sufficient to constitute lack of "due caution and circumspection" under Penal Code, § 192. The court said (44 Cal.2d at page 869, 285 P.2d at page 931): "It has been held that without 'due caution and circumspection' is the equivalent of 'criminal negligence.'" After reviewing numerous California authorities, the court continued (44 Cal.2d at page 876, 285 P. 2d at page 935):

"So far as the latest cases are concerned, it appears that mere negligence is sufficient to constitute a lack of due caution and circumspection under the manslaughter statute. Pen.Code, § 192, subd. 2. This does not appear to be a correct rule. Something more, in our opinion, is needed to constitute the criminal negligence required for a conviction of manslaughter." . . .

"We hold, therefore, that the general rule just quoted, sets forth the standard to be used in California for negligent homicide, Pen. Code, § 192, subd. 2, in other than vehicle cases. Defendant here was charged with a violation of section 192, subdivision 2, of the Penal Code."

See 8 Stan.Law Rev. 463.

It is generally held that an act is criminally negligent when a man of ordinary prudence would foresee that the act would cause a high degree of risk of death or great bodily harm. The risk of death or great bodily harm must be great. Whether the conduct of defendant was wanton or reckless so as to warrant conviction of manslaughter must be determined from the conduct itself and not from the resultant harm. Criminal liability cannot be predicated on every careless act merely because its carelessness results in injury to another. The act must be one which has knowable and apparent potentialities for resulting in death. Mere inattention or mistake in judgment resulting even in death of another is not criminal unless the quality of the act makes it so. The fundamental requirement fixing criminal responsibility is knowledge, actual or imputed, that the act of the accused tended to endanger life.

In a case of involuntary manslaughter the criminal negligence of the accused must be the proximate cause of the death. . . .

It clearly appears from the definition of criminal negligence stated in People v. Penny, supra, 44 Cal.2d 861, 285 P.2d 926, that knowledge, actual or imputed, that the act of the slayer tended to endanger life and that the fatal consequences of the negligent act could reasonably have been foreseen are necessary for negligence to be criminal at all. Must a parent never leave a young child alone in the house on risk of being adjudged guilty of manslaughter if some unforeseeable occurrence causes the death of the child? The only reasonable view of the evidence is that the death of Carlos was the result of misadventure and not the natural and probable result of a criminally negligent act. There was no evidence from which it can be inferred that defendant realized her conduct would in all probability produce death. There was no evidence as to the cause of the fire, as to how or where it started. There was no evidence connecting defendant in any way with the fire. There was no evidence that defendant could reasonably have foreseen there was a probability that fire would ignite in the house and that Carlos would be burned to death. The most that can be said is that defendant may have been negligent; but mere negligence is not sufficient to authorize a conviction of involuntary manslaughter. . . .

The judgment and order denying a new trial are reversed.[1]

SHINN, P. J., concurs.

FORD, J., did not participate.

STATE v. DAVIS
Supreme Court of Oregon, 1956.
207 Or. 525, 296 P.2d 240.

BRAND, JUSTICE. On the 15th day of April, 1954, the grand jury of Lane county returned an indictment against defendant Joseph A. Davis, which reads as follows:

"The above named Joseph A. Davis is accused by the Grand Jury of the County of Lane, State of Oregon, by this Indictment, of the crime of Manslaughter committed as follows: . . .

On the 20th of April, 1954 defendant entered his plea of "Not guilty to the crime of manslaughter." On 15 July, 1954 defendant demurred to the indictment on the following grounds: . . .

"(3) The facts stated do not constitute a crime. . . . "

[1]. Accord: People v. Angelo, 246 N.Y. 451, 159 N.E. 394 (1927).

On 11 May judgment on the demurrer was entered for the defendant. The State of Oregon appeals. . . .

The prosecution contends that the indictment states a crime under the general manslaughter act and should be held good under that act, even if it is not good under ORS 483.992(2) (b). The manslaughter act provides that:

"Any person who, in the commission of any unlawful act, or a lawful act without due caution or circumspection, involuntarily kills another, is guilty of manslaughter. The provisions of this subsection shall not apply to the killing of any person where the proximate cause of such killing is an act or omission defined as negligent homicide in ORS 163.090." ORS 163.040(2).

The indictment charges that the defendant was engaged in the unlawful act of reckless driving which is a crime under ORS 483.992 (1). It also alleges that defendant was engaged in the unlawful act of driving a car while under the influence of intoxicating liquor, which is a crime under ORS 483.992(2) (a). The indictment also charges that defendant while in the commission of said unlawful acts killed another person. It would appear then that the indictment comes squarely within the provisions of ORS 163.040(2) unless his act was one which is defined as negligent homicide. The statute defining that crime is as follows:

"When the death of any person ensues within one year as the proximate result of injuries caused by the driving of any motor vehicle in a negligent manner, or by the driving of a vehicle or combination of vehicles which is defectively equipped or loaded, the driver knowing the vehicle or combination of vehicles to be defectively equipped or loaded, the person so driving such vehicle or combination of vehicles is guilty of negligent homicide, and, upon conviction, shall be punished by imprisonment in the county jail for not more than one year, or in the state penitentiary for not more than three years, or by a fine of not to exceed $2,500, or by both fine and imprisonment." ORS 163.090.

Under ORS 163.040(2) the involuntary killing of another is punishable as manslaughter if the killing was done either (1) in the commission of an unlawful act, or (2) in the commission of a lawful act without due caution or circumspection. The exception contained in the manslaughter act, ORS 163.040(2), excludes from the scope of the more serious crime, acts defined as negligent homicide. Thus the negligent homicide statute serves a double purpose. It defines a lesser crime and provides punishment therefor. But it also carves out of the manslaughter statute certain conduct by a limited class of persons guilty of driving in a negligent manner or driving a defective vehicle with fatal results. We should not enlarge the scope or applicability of the negligent homicide statute for two reasons: first, because it is a criminal statute, and second, because to enlarge it by construction would narrow the clearly defined scope of the manslaughter act.

Examination of the negligent homicide statute discloses that the elements of the crime are driving a vehicle in a negligent manner and thereby causing the death of a person within one year. There is in that statute no reference to driving "in the commission of any unlawful act" or driving under the influence of intoxicating liquor. There is certainly no intimation that driving in wilful and wanton disregard of the safety of others is negligent homicide.

A person who drives while under the influence of intoxicating liquor commits an unlawful act. The manslaughter statute makes an express distinction between (1) killing while in the commission of an unlawful act, and (2) killing while doing a lawful act without due caution or circumspection, which is the virtual equivalent of acting in a "negligent manner." State v. Wojahn, 204 Or. 84, 282 P.2d 675. Thus, the negligent homicide statute excludes from the manslaughter act the case of drivers who kill another while driving a motor vehicle in a negligent manner, that is, without due caution and circumspection, but it does not exclude from the manslaughter statute a person who, as operator of a motor vehicle, kills a person while in the commission of an unlawful act, namely, driving under the influence of intoxicating liquor. Nor does it exclude from the manslaughter act a person who, as an operator of a motor vehicle, kills a person while in the performance of the unlawful act of reckless driving, as defined by statute. ORS 483.992(1). . . .

In conclusion we hold that the indictment does not charge negligent homicide. It sufficiently sets forth the commission of two unlawful acts; reckless driving and driving while under the influence of intoxicating liquor. It sufficiently alleges that while in the commission of said acts the defendant killed Wilmer T. Rowley. It thereby charges the crime of manslaughter in violation of ORS 163.040(2). . . .

The trial court erred in sustaining the demurrer. The judgment is reversed and the cause remanded for further proceedings conformable to this opinion.[1]

HARRIS v. STATE

Court of Appeals of Georgia, 1937.
55 Ga.App. 189, 189 S.E. 680.

MacINTYRE, J. W. J. Harris was convicted of voluntary manslaughter, and his punishment was fixed by the verdict at not less than ten nor more than fifteen years. His motion for a new trial was overruled, and he excepted.

[1.] For the statutory offense known as "automobile homicide"—causing a fatal traffic accident by driving carelessly while under the influence of liquor or drug, see State v. Twitchell, 8 Utah 2d 314, 333 P.2d 1075 (1959).

1. Taking the view of the evidence which is most unfavorable to the accused, which we do in passing on a motion for new trial, it in effect shows that the defendant, who was somewhat drawn with rheumatism, was smaller in size than the deceased; that, after an argument about a certain jug which had been left with the defendant at his place of business by the deceased, the defendant not only called the deceased a liar, but also a God damn liar; that the deceased, an able-bodied, strong, and robust man, thereupon struck the defendant two hard blows with his fists, and that the defendant killed the deceased by shooting him three times, once in the thigh, once in the stomach above the navel, and once in the shoulder. A witness testified: "The first shot hit him in the leg. I know, 'cause I seen him give. He just kept right on going down. The second shot missed him. I seen it dig dirt up by him. Harris [the defendant] was shooting somewhere 'bout his legs along about here" (indicating). On the other hand, the effect of the defendant's statement and one of his witness's testimony was that the deceased, after hitting the defendant twice with his fists, hit him a third time over the head with the stick, which knocked him down, and that the deceased thereupon picked up his small goat-cart, or wagon, and was trying to advance on the defendant with that weapon when the defendant shot him. The wagon, or goat-cart, and stick were introduced in evidence by the defendant, without objection. We think the jury were authorized to render a verdict of voluntary manslaughter. . . .

3. The defendant assigns error on the failure of the court to charge the law on involuntary manslaughter. This assignment is based on the evidence of two witnesses, one of whom testified as follows: "Mr. Harris [the defendant] was not shooting up in the body. He was shooting down in his legs, shooting at his feet, yes." The other testified, "Mr. Harris was shooting somewhere about his legs along here" (indicating). The defendant contends that this evidence shows conclusively "that Harris in shooting Pittman down in his legs, at his feet, somewhere about his legs along here (indicating), was the act of a man trying to keep Pittman from unmercifully beating him, and disproves clearly that Harris had any intention at the time to kill Pittman." We can not agree to this contention of the defendant. "Where one voluntarily fires a loaded pistol at another, without excuse and not under circumstances of justification, and kills the person at whom he shot, the law will hold the slayer responsible for the consequences of his act. It conclusively presumes malice on the part of the slayer; and the grade of the homicide, so committed, will not be reduced to involuntary manslaughter, even if the intent of the slayer, under such circumstances, was to wound or cripple the deceased, and not to kill." . . . [1]

Judgment affirmed. BROYLES, C. J., and GUERRY, J., concur.

[1] "We think, however, that an instruction should have been given whereunder Vires could have been found guilty of voluntary manslaughter if the jury believe that the shooting was the result of reckless, wanton and

COLLUM v. STATE

Court of Appeals of Georgia, 1941.
65 Ga.App. 740, 16 S.E.2d 483.

GARDNER, J. The defendant was tried on a charge of murder and convicted of involuntary manslaughter in the commission of an unlawful act. He made a motion for a new trial, based on the usual general grounds, which the court overruled, and he excepted.

The only question for the court to decide is, does the record show sufficient evidence to support the verdict? Briefly the evidence shows as follows: The defendant, the deceased, and two other companions traveling in an automobile, arrived from Colquitt, Georgia, in the City of Americus. All had been drinking to some extent. They went into an eating place, ordered sandwiches, and up to this time they were peaceful. The defendant remarked that he did not know that he wanted a sandwich. The deceased replied: "Go ahead and eat it, you son of a bitch." The defendant retorted: "Don't say that any more." The deceased repeated the opprobrious words. The defendant, according to some of the State's witnesses, facing Jordan, struck him one severe blow with his fist in the face and knocked him back and onto the concrete floor. Jordan was rendered unconscious and was carried to a hospital for treatment. An examination was made of Jordan by Dr. Primrose, on his arrival at the hospital. This occurred about eight o'clock in the evening. The next morning Jordan was removed from the hospital by his family and the family physician, Dr. Smith. The injuries caused the subsequent death of Jordan. . . .

The indictment charged, and the evidence was sufficient to show, that Jordan was struck by a blunt instrument or other means used in a manner and to an extent unjustified under the law. This was peculiarly a jury question. This court is without authority to interfere with its finding. No one will dispute the right of the defendant to assault and beat another for such opprobrious words as Jordan used towards the defendant in the instant case. Code, § 26–1409, announces this right. It provides: "On the trial of an indictment for

felonious disregard of the safety of human life. Also there should have been an instruction authorizing the jury to find Vires guilty of involuntary manslaughter if he was found to be guilty of the reckless use of firearms, though the shooting was not done wantonly and feloniously." Vires v. Commonwealth, 308 Ky. 707, 215 S.W.2d 837 (1948).

"[I]n cases of voluntary manslaughter, although the elements of malice and premeditation are wanting, an intent to kill must exist, and the question of its presence becomes one of fact for the jury to determine from all the circumstances under which the homicide was committed." People v. Forbes, 39 Cal.Rptr. 171, 176 (Cal.App.1964).

An assailant who commits an unlawful assault and battery on another without malice, resulting in death, is guilty of manslaughter although the death was not intended and the assault was not of a character likely to result fatally. State v. Black, 360 Mo. 261, 227 S.W.2d 1006 (1950).

an assault, or an assault and battery, the defendant may give in evidence to the jury any opprobrious words, or abusive language, used by the prosecutor, or person assaulted or beaten; and such words and language may or may not amount to a justification, according to the nature and extent of the battery, all of which shall be determined by the jury." But the law also says, inferentially at least, that the battery can not be disproportionate to the opprobrious words used, and never to the extent of taking life, intentionally or unintentionally, where the battery is excessive. Any step beyond proportionate resentment carries one into the mire of unlawfulness, whether there be one or many blows and the Code section quoted provides the means by which this question is determined, as follows: "And such words and language may or may not amount to a justification, according to the nature and extent of the battery, all of which shall be determined by the jury." It will be seen that this is always a question for the jury in each case under all the facts and circumstances adduced on the trial. The jury heard all the testimony and were correctly informed as to the law applicable thereto. Even though the State's evidence may in part have been in conflict, on the whole evidence the jury determined that the blow inflicted by the defendant was disproportionate to the opprobrious words used and was therefore unlawful whether inflicted with the fist or other instrument causing Jordan's death. . . .

Judgment affirmed. BROYLES, C. J., and MACINTYRE, J., concur.

COMMONWEALTH v. DRUM

Supreme Court of Pennsylvania, 1868.
58 Pa. 9.

William Drum was charged in the Court of Quarter Sessions of Westmoreland County for the murder of David Mohigan. A true bill having been found by the grand jury of that court, it was certified into the Court of Oyer and Terminer of the same county. . . .

JUSTICE AGNEW charged the jury as follows: . . .

A life has been taken. The unfortunate David Mohigan has fallen into an untimely grave; struck down by the hand of violence; and it is for you to determine whose was that hand, and what its guilt. The prisoner is in the morning of life; as yet so fresh and fair. As you sat and gazed into his youthful face, you have thought, no doubt, most anxiously thought, is his that hand? Can he, indeed, be a murderer? This, gentlemen, is the solemn question you must determine upon the law and the evidence.

At the common law murder is described to be, when a person of sound memory and discretion unlawfully kills any reasonable creature in being and under the peace of the Commonwealth, with malice aforethought, express or implied. The distinguishing criterion of murder is malice aforethought. But it is not malice in its ordinary understanding alone, a particular ill-will, a spite or a grudge. Malice is a legal term, implying much more. It comprehends not only a particular ill-will, but every case where there is wickedness of disposition, hardness of heart, cruelty, recklessness of consequences, and a mind regardless of social duty, although a particular person may not be intended to be injured. Murder, therefore, at common law embraces cases where no intent to kill existed, but where the state or frame of mind termed malice, in its legal sense, prevailed.

In Pennsylvania, the legislature, considering that there is a manifest difference in the degree of guilt, where a deliberate intention to kill exists, and where none appears, distinguished murder into two grades—murder of the first and murder of the second degree; and provided that the jury before whom any person indicted for murder should be tried, shall, if they find him guilty thereof, ascertain in their verdict whether it be murder of the first or murder of the second degree. By the Act of 31st March 1860, "all murder which shall be perpetrated by means of poison, or by lying in wait, or by any other kind of wilful, deliberate and premeditated killing, or which shall be committed in the perpetration of, or attempt to perpetrate any arson, rape, robbery or burglary, shall be deemed murder of the first degree; and all other kinds of murder shall be deemed murder of the second degree."

In this case we have to deal only with that kind of murder in the first degree described as "wilful, deliberate, and premeditated." Many cases have been decided under this clause, in all of which it has been held that the *intention* to kill is the essence of the offence. Therefore, if an intention to kill exists, it is wilful; if this intention be accompanied by such circumstances as evidence a mind fully conscious of its own purpose and design, it is deliberate; and if sufficient time be afforded to enable the mind fully to frame the design to kill, and to select the instrument, or to frame the plan to carry this design into execution, it is premeditated. The law fixes upon no length of time as necessary to form the intention to kill, but leaves the existence of a fully formed intent as a fact to be determined by the jury, from all the facts and circumstances in the evidence. . . . [1]

---

1. "No specific period of time is required but if the time is sufficient to fully and clearly conceive the design to kill and purposely and deliberately execute it, the requirements of the statute are satisfied." State v. Pierce, 4 N.J. 252, 267–8, 72 A.2d 305, 313 (1950).

"'When a design to kill another person is once formed, the haste with which it is put into execution in no way affects or modifies the degree of guilt incurred.'" State v. Gregory, 66 Nev. 423, 427, 212 P.2d 701, 703–4 (1949).

A wilful, deliberate and premeditated killing requires "not a general malice, but a special malice that aims at the life of a person." Keenan v. Commonwealth, 44 Pa. 55, 57 (1862).

A killing by "lying in wait" is a killing resulting from ambush for the purpose of killing. State v. Olds, 19 Or. 397, 24 P. 394 (1890). In other words it is a particular kind of wilful, deliberate

Sec. 1   *HOMICIDE*   63

The proof of the intention to kill, and of the disposition of mind constituting murder in the first degree, under the Act of Assembly, lies on the Commonwealth. But this proof need not be express or positive. It may be inferred from the circumstances. If, from all the facts attending the killing, the jury can fully, reasonably, and satisfactorily infer the existence of the intention to kill, and the malice of heart with which it was done, they will be warranted in so doing. He who uses upon the body of another, at some vital part, with a manifest intention to use it upon him, a deadly weapon, as an axe, a gun, a knife or a pistol, must, in the absence of qualifying facts, be presumed to know that his blow is likely to kill; and, knowing this, must be presumed to intend the death which is the probable and ordinary consequence of such an act. He who so uses a deadly weapon without a sufficient cause of provocation, must be presumed to do it wickedly, or from a bad heart. Therefore, he who takes the life of another with a deadly weapon, and with a manifest design thus to use it upon him, with sufficient time to deliberate, and fully to form the conscious purpose of killing, and without any sufficient reason or cause of extenuation, is guilty of murder in the first degree.

All murder not of the first degree, is necessarily of the second degree, and includes all unlawful killing under circumstances of depravity of heart, and a disposition of mind regardless of social duty; but where no intention to kill exists or can be reasonably and fully inferred. Therefore, in all cases of murder, if no intention to kill can be inferred or collected from the circumstances, the verdict must be murder in the second degree.

Manslaughter is defined to be the unlawful killing of another without malice expressed or implied; which may be voluntarily in a sudden heat, or involuntarily, but in the commission of an unlawful act. . . .

You will now take the case and render such a verdict as the evidence warrants; one which will do justice to the Commonwealth and to the prisoner.

and premeditated killing. Accord: State v. Gause, 227 N.C. 26, 40 S.E.2d 463 (1946); Commonwealth v. Mondollo, 247 Pa. 526, 93 A. 612 (1915); Burgess v. Commonwealth, 4 Va. 483 (1825). But the California court held that murder by "lying in wait" does **not** require a deliberate and premeditated plan to kill, but may be perpetrated by killing from ambush as a result of the intentional inflicting of bodily injury under circumstances likely to cause death. People v. Mason, 54 Cal.2d 164, 4 Cal.Rptr. 841, 351 P.2d 1025 (1960).

PEOPLE v. CORNETT
Supreme Court of California, In Bank, 1948.
33 Cal.2d 33, 198 P.2d 877.

TRAYNOR, J. Defendant was charged with the murder of Fred Weaver Cole, the stepfather of his divorced wife. A jury found him guilty of murder in the first degree and made no recommendation as to penalty. The trial court denied his motion for a new trial and sentenced him to death. This is an automatic appeal from the judgment imposing the death penalty. (Pen.Code, § 1239(b).) . . .

The trial court also erred in giving the following instruction: "There must be an intent to kill, but there need be, however, no appreciable space of time between the forming of the intent to kill and the overt act—they may be as instantaneous as successive thoughts of the mind. A man may do a thing wilfully, deliberately and intentionally from a moment's reflection as well as after pondering over the subject for a month or a year. He can premeditate, that is, think before doing the act, the moment he conceives the purpose, as well as if the act was the result of long preconcert or preparation." As held in People v. Bender, 27 Cal.2d 164, 182, 163 P.2d 8, and People v. Valentine, 28 Cal.2d 121, 134, 169 P.2d 1, such a combination of instructions is wholly erroneous. "Of course the instruction that there need be 'no appreciable space of time between the intention to kill and the act of killing . . .' is abstractly a correct statement of the law. It will be properly understood (at least upon *deliberation*) by those learned in the law as referring only to the interval between the fully formulated intent and its execution, *and as necessarily presupposing that true deliberation and premeditation characterized the process of, and preceded ultimate, formulation of such intent* . . . But holding that such declaration is a correct statement of the abstract principle of law is not a holding that the same declaration made to a jury without explanation is not error. Particularly is it misleading when read in the context in which it was used. It excludes from the required showing any deliberation and premeditation between the intent and the act of killing and since other portions of the instructions eliminate any necessity for deliberation or premeditation in forming the intent ('He can premeditate . . . the moment he conceives the purpose . . .,' etc.), we find that the court has wholly deleted the only difference, in this type of case, between first and second degree murder." (People v. Bender, supra, 27 Cal.2d 164, 182–183, 163 P.2d 8.) To say that the defendant "can premeditate . . . the moment he conceives the purpose" precludes the meaning of careful thought and the weighing of considerations embodied in the ordinary dictionary meaning of "deliberation" and "premeditation."

The trial court, however, gave other instructions relating to the meaning of "deliberation and premeditation" essential for murder

Sec. 1   HOMICIDE   65

in the first degree: "The law does not undertake to measure in units of time the length of the period during which the thought must be pondered before it can ripen into an intent to kill which is truly deliberate and premeditated. The time will vary with different individuals and under varying circumstances. The true test is not the duration of time, but rather the extent of the reflection. A cold, calculated judgment and decision may be arrived at in a short period of time, but a mere unconsidered and rash impulse, even though it includes an intent to kill, is not such deliberation and premeditation as will fix an unlawful killing as murder of the first degree. To constitute a deliberate and premeditated killing, the slayer must weigh and consider the question of killing and the reasons for and against such a choice and, having in mind the consequences, decide to and commit the unlawful act causing death." Although the foregoing instruction states the proper meaning of the deliberation and premeditation required to establish the offense of murder in the first degree, it did not cure the error, but instead created a serious conflict in the instructions. Where it is impossible to determine which of inconsistent instructions were followed by the jury, conflicting instructions have been held to constitute reversible error. It cannot reasonably be said that the jury, even though given the proper instruction, was not misled by the further instruction that "a man may do a thing . . . deliberately and intentionally from a moment's reflection. . . . He can premeditate, that is, think before doing the act, the moment he conceives the purpose. . . ." The jury could find defendant guilty of murder in the first degree only by finding that the murder was the result of deliberation and premeditation, since the killing did not take place during the commission of the felonies enumerated in section 189 of the Penal Code. The evidence is without conflict that defendant fired at the decedent after whirling around from a position in which he was looking behind a bed or screen. The jury could have found defendant guilty of murder in the first degree on the basis of either of the following findings: (1) Following the correct instruction it may have found that the defendant had formed an intent to kill after carefully weighing and considering the question of killing, or that the killing may have even been deliberated before his arrival at the home of the decedent; (2) it may have found that defendant entered the upstairs room without previously considering the question of shooting the decedent but that he conceived the thought "upon a moment's reflection" as he whirled around. In view of the evidence it is impossible to determine, therefore, whether or not the jury reached its verdict on the basis of the correct instructions. Clearly the evidence under proper instructions would have supported a verdict of murder in the first degree; it is also clear, however, that it is reasonably probable that the jury, if it was properly and unambiguously instructed, could find defendant guilty of murder of lesser degree, since it could have concluded that he shot the decedent as the result of a sudden impulse engendered by an argument that had taken place between the two men, or by defendant's fear of his own life caused by the tense relationship between them at that time. . . .

After a consideration of the entire record it is clear that the giving of this erroneous instruction, particularly when considered with the other erroneous instructions, has resulted in a miscarriage of justice.

The judgment and the order denying the motion for new trial are reversed.[1]

GIBSON, C. J., CARTER, J., SCHAUER, J., and SPENCE, J., concurred.

PEOPLE v. HÜTER

Court of Appeals of New York, 1906.
184 N.Y. 237, 77 N.E. 6.

HAIGHT, J. Between four and five o'clock on the morning of March 20th, 1905, the defendant broke into the bake-shop of Paul Scheel, located in the basement of premises No. 901 Third avenue, between Fifty-fourth and Fifty-fifth streets in the city of New York. At the time, he had a horse and wagon, stationed in front of the premises, in the care of one Joseph Pesce. He had removed from the bake-shop a crate of eggs and placed it in the wagon, and had returned to the shop to get another crate, when he was discovered by a private watchman. The defendant on discovery, ran out of the premises and told Pesce to run, and they both abandoned the property stolen as well as the horse and wagon, and ran northwardly along the east side of Third avenue to the corner of Fifty-fifth street, pursued by the watchman. The watchman had a night stick, and as he started to pursue the defendant he called for help, sounding his stick upon the walk, and then seeing Police Officer Enright upon the opposite corner of Fifty-fifth street, called to him to arrest the burglar. At the corner of Third avenue and Fifty-fifth street the defendant and Pesce separated, Pesce going westerly along Fifty-fifth street, while the defendant ran easterly. But by this time Police Officer Enright and a private citizen named Felix Stegman took up the pursuit of the defendant, the policeman calling upon him to stop or he would shoot. After running about three hundred feet upon Fifty-fifth street the

---

1. "'Premeditation means thought of beforehand' for some length of time, however short." State v. Chavis, 231 N.C. 307, 311, 56 S.E.2d 678, 681 (1949). An act cannot be both impulsive and premeditated, or both hasty and deliberate. People v. Deloney, 41 Cal. 2d 832, 264 P.2d 532 (1953).

To establish a wilful, deliberate and premeditated murder "the state must prove (a) premeditation, which is the conception of the design to kill, (b) deliberation, which is a reconsideration of the design to kill, a weighing of the pros and cons with respect to it, and (c) wilfulness, which means an intentional execution of the plan to kill which had been conceived and deliberated upon; . . ." State v. Anderson, 35 N.J. 472, 173 A.2d 377, 379 (1961).

Sec. 1 HOMICIDE 67

policeman had so gained upon the defendant that he was but a few feet distant from him when the defendant suddenly drew his revolver and shot the policeman, producing a wound from which he died within a few hours.

In submitting the case to the jury the trial judge called the attention of the jurors to the definition of murder in the first degree, and after instructing them that in case they found that it was the deliberate and premeditated design of the defendant to kill Officer Enright in shooting him in the manner described that it constituted murder in the first degree; but that in case the defendant did not intend to kill Officer Enright, and that the killing was without premeditation or deliberation, yet if the jurors find that he fired the shot at Enright which proved fatal after he had attempted to or had burglarized the premises of Scheel and was attempting to escape from the premises in the manner described by the witnesses, then their verdict ought to be for murder in the first degree. The defendant's counsel took an exception to the instruction of the court with reference to their right to convict if they found that the killing took place while he was engaged in the commission of a felony. This presents the only question which we are called upon to review.

Under the provisions of section 183 of the Penal Code it is murder in the first degree if the killing of a person is not excusable or justifiable when committed from a deliberate and premeditated design to effect the death of the person killed, or of another; or without a design to effect death, by a person engaged in the commission of, or in an attempt to commit a felony, either upon or affecting the person killed or otherwise. The evidence in the case amply warranted the trial court in submitting to the jury the question of the defendant's guilt under the first subdivision of the section referred to; for, it distinctly appears that before the defendant undertook the burglary upon Scheel's premises he provided himself with a loaded revolver and carried it upon his person. It was not an implement which would aid him in breaking into the premises, or in securing the property therein. The only use to which he could have well devoted it was to aid him in escaping in case he was discovered, and it is apparent that that was the use for which he designed it. I think, therefore, that the jury, under the circumstances of this case, would have been justified in finding the deliberate and premeditated design of the defendant to effect the death of any person who should attempt to prevent his escape from the premises in which the burglary was committed, and, in so far as the court charged upon this provision of the Code, no question is now raised as to its correctness. But, as we have seen, the trial court also submitted another provision of the Code to the jury, and instructed them to determine whether or not the defendant was guilty under that provision. The defendant had committed a burglary, and if the death of Enright had been caused by him while engaged in the commission of that crime it would, undoubtedly, have been murder in the first degree; but, as we have seen, after he was discovered by the watchman he immediately ran from the premises, abandoning all of the property which he had stolen, and attempted to escape arrest. It is true that he was immediately pursued by the watchman and by Officer Enright, but we incline to the view that this did not operate to continue the burglary after the defendant had abandoned the property that he undertook to carry away and had escaped from the premises burglarized. In all of the cases to which our attention has been called, in which persons have been convicted of murder in the first degree by reason of the killing of a person while the accused was engaged in the commission of a burglary, the killing took place upon the premises. . . .

A person who attempts or engages in the commission of a felony, is not only chargeable with express malice, but also with being perversely wicked, evincing a depraved mind and a disregard of human life, and if, while so engaged, he causes the death of a person, although unintentional, the legislature has seen fit to enlarge the crime and make it murder in the first degree, so that, if a person engaged in the commission of a rape and in order to accomplish the act resorts to violence, from which death is unintentionally produced and which would be only manslaughter were it not for the malice, wickedness and intent to rape, yet by reason thereof it is made murder in the first degree. The same is true with reference to the unintentional killing of a person while engaged in the commission of a robbery, a burglary or an attempt to escape from imprisonment. There may be no intent to kill, but the violence having been perpetrated while engaged in the robbery, burglary or attempt to escape imprisonment, it is murder in the first degree. . . .

The judgment and conviction should be reversed and a new trial granted.

CULLEN, CH. J., WERNER, WILLARD BARTLETT and HISCOCK, JJ., concur; O'BRIEN and VANN, JJ., concur, except as to the point last discussed in the opinion, as to which they express no opinion.

Judgment of conviction reversed, etc.

CONRAD v. STATE

Supreme Court of Ohio, 1906.
75 Ohio St. 52, 78 N.E. 957.

DAVIS, J. It was charged in the indictment that the plaintiff in error broke into a dwelling-house at night with intent to take and carry away personal property which was in the dwelling; and that while in the perpetration of such burglary, he, the plaintiff in error, shot and killed one Daniel E. Davis. . . .

In substance, the argument in this case is that the perpetration of the burglary was complete when the house was entered, or at least while the burglars were within the house, and that as they carried nothing away in their flight the crime of burglary was complete when they left the house. The body of Officer Davis was found twenty-five or thirty feet from the house and on another lot. Therefore, it is argued, the killing was not in the perpetration of a burglary.

We will pause here to emphasize a distinction which will be apparent to any one on reflection. It is the distinction between the definition of a burglary and a statement of the circumstances which may have occurred "in the perpetration" of a burglary. The former is invariable. The latter varies with each case. The definition of a burglary is the breaking into a house in the night season, with intent to commit a felony; and if a house be so entered it is a burglary whether the felony be executed or not, and regardless of the kind of felony intended, or the manner of its execution, or the manner in which the felony may be frustrated, or the value of the property taken, or any other circumstance which is not intrinsic. On the other hand, while the circumstances which differentiate the crime may be a small part of the transaction, and must always be the same, the things which occur "in the perpetration" of a crime change with every case, and may be numerous.

For example, when a burglary has been planned, in order to carry it out, or, in other words, to perpetrate it, the burglar must go to the building, he must break and enter it; he may effect his purpose or attempt it, and he must come away; for the very nature of the transaction implies that the burglar will not remain in the building. An infinite variety of things may happen in carrying out the crime. The perpetrator may kill a man while going to or trying to enter the building, he may kill a man after he has broken and entered the house, and he may kill a man while trying to escape, either in the house or outside of it. Can any sound reason be suggested why the killing in any one of these instances might be in the perpetration of or attempt to perpetrate a burglary, and not so in the others? The crime of murder in the first degree as defined by the statute (Section 6808, Revised Statutes) certainly can not by any reasonable construction be confined to the moment of breaking and entering the house, the crucial point of the definition of burglary; and it should be noted here again that it is not burglary which we are to define in this case, but murder in the first degree.

Let us suppose a case. Two confederates intending to break and enter a dwelling for a felonious purpose are met by the owner at the door or window which they are forcing and they kill him. Would anybody question that such a killing was in the perpetration, or attempt to perpetrate, a burglary? Surely not. Then let us go further back in the order of time. Suppose that while these confederates are watching the house and waiting for the opportune time, they see the owner of the dwelling come out with a lantern and go across the road to his barn, and they there set upon him and inflict injuries from which he dies, but they take no money or property. They afterwards go across the road towards the house, and, getting inside the yard, are frightened by somebody approaching and hurry away. Would that be murder in an attempt to commit a burglary? It was argued that it was not; but the Supreme Court of Pennsylvania held that it was. Commonwealth v. Eagan, 190 Pa. 10, 42 A. 374.

Suppose another case. The confederates so far succeed as to break and enter the building. A technical burglary has been completed; but afterwards and while yet in the building they shoot and kill somebody. Is that a killing "in the perpetration" of a burglary within the meaning of the statute defining murder in the first degree? It was vigorously contended in the Court of Appeals of New York and also in the Supreme Court of Indiana, that such a killing is not murder in the first degree, but a killing after the crime of burglary had been completed. Both courts hold that the crime in such case is murder in the first degree, notwithstanding that the killing and the breaking and entering are not coincident. Dolan v. People, 64 N.Y. 485; Bissot v. State, 53 Ind. 408.

Now, if the taking of life before reaching the building, and also after breaking and entering the building and before leaving it, is a taking of life in the perpetration, or attempt to perpetrate, a burglary, at what point after the breaking and entering is the line of distinction to be drawn? At what point can it be drawn, short of the absolute completion or abandonment of the whole enterprise? It seems to us that logically there can be no such intermediate point; and we know of no case which holds otherwise. The case of Lamb v. People, 96 Ill. 73, cited by counsel for plaintiff in error is not pertinent here. There the burglars got away with the plunder. They were in undisturbed possession of the goods. Lamb left the party and some time thereafter the others were detected in unloading the goods at a pawnbroker's. Then the shooting occurred.

Take another case. Three men entered a pawnshop, locked the door behind them, beat the proprietor into insensibility, took from the safe certain articles of value and escaped through back windows. They were pursued by a constable who chased them for the distance of four blocks and across two streets. They then turned and fired at the constable and a pistol ball missing him struck a tree and glanced off, killing a boy. The men were indicted for murder while engaged in committing a robbery. A conviction of murder in the first degree resulted as to one of the defendants; and the Supreme Court, in State v. Brown, 7 Or. 186 said:

"The defendant admits that he committed a robbery in the pawnshop of O'Shea, but insists that the crime was completed when he and his co-defendants forcibly seized the property described in the indictment, and, being completed, he denies that the killing of Joseph was done in the commission of the robbery. We do not assent to the correctness of this conclusion. . . . When a person takes with

Sec. 1　　　　　　　　　　HOMICIDE　　　　　　　　　　71

force and violence the goods of another from his person or presence and against his will, he has committed robbery . . . but *it does not necessarily complete the crime*. It constitutes robbery so far as to render the perpetrator liable to conviction for it; but the *act of robbery itself may be prolonged beyond the time when that liability is fixed*. When Brown and his co-defendants took the property by force . . . they committed the crime of robbery so far as to render themselves liable to punishment for it, but the robbery in contemplation of law was not completed until the taking and carrying away was ended. . . . And while anything remains to be done by the robbers to secure complete control over the property taken, the robbery is incomplete. The act of taking and carrying away in the case of Brown and his co-defendants commenced when the seizure was made in the pawnshop of O'Shea, and continued until they had *unmolested dominion* over the property which they had taken. When they first acquired that control the robbery was ended and not before" (pp. 208, 209). . . .

Thus it appears that in all these cases which we have reviewed, cases of killing before, during and after the technical perfection of the collateral crime, the courts practically concur in the view expressed by the Court of Appeals of New York, that, "If, while there engaged in securing his plunder, or *in any of the acts immediately connected with his crime*, he kills any one resisting him, he is guilty of murder under the statute" (Dolan v. People, supra); and by the Supreme Court of Indiana as follows: "In our opinion when the homicide is committed within the *res gestae* of the felony charged, it is committed in the perpetration of, or attempt to perpetrate, the felony, within the meaning of the statute" (Bissot v. State, supra). For the reasons which we have endeavored to make clear, we believe that this construction of the statute is not only reasonable, consistent, conservative and just, but that it exactly conforms to the legislative intent as expressed. . . .

The judgment of the circuit court is Affirmed.

SHAUCK, C. J., SUMMERS and SPEAR, JJ., concur.[1]

(PRICE and CREW, JJ., dissented.)

---

[1] "The res gestae embraces not only the actual facts of the transaction and the circumstances surrounding it, but the matters immediately antecedent to and having a direct causal connection with it, as well as acts immediately following it and so closely connected with it as to form in reality a part of the occurrence." State v. Fouquette, 67 Nev. 505, 221 P.2d 404, 417 (1950).

Kidnaping after the perpetration of robbery may be a kidnaping for the purpose of robbery if it is to effect the escape of the robber or remove the victim to another place where he might less easily sound an alarm. People v. Randazzo, 48 Cal.2d 484, 310 P.2d 413 (1957), certiorari denied 355 U.S. 865, 78 S.Ct. 98, 2 L.Ed.2d 70 (1957).

It is in the perpetration of the crime during flight from the scene thereof, even after abandonment of the plan. Commonwealth v. Devlin, 335 Mass. 555, 141 N.E.2d 269 (1957).

MODEL PENAL CODE
Article 210. Criminal Homicide

Section 210.0. Definitions.

In Articles 210–213, unless a different meaning plainly is required:

(1) "human being" means a person who has been born and is alive;

(2) "bodily injury" means physical pain, illness or any impairment of physical condition;

(3) "serious bodily injury" means bodily injury which creates a substantial risk of death or which causes serious, permanent disfigurement, or protracted loss or impairment of the function of any bodily member or organ;

(4) "deadly weapon" means any firearm, or other weapon, device, instrument, material or substance, whether animate or inanimate, which in the manner it is used or is intended to be used is known to be capable of producing death or serious bodily injury.

Section 210.1. Criminal Homicide.

(1) A person is guilty of criminal homicide if he purposely, knowingly, recklessly [1] or negligently [2] causes the death of another human being.

(2) Criminal homicide is murder, manslaughter or negligent homicide.

Section 210.2. Murder.

(1) Except as provided in Section 210.3(1) (b), criminal homicide constitutes murder when:

(a) it is committed purposely or knowingly; or

(b) it is committed recklessly under circumstances manifesting extreme indifference to the value of human life. Such recklessness and indifference are presumed if the actor is engaged or is an accomplice in the commission of, or an attempt to commit, or flight after committing or attempting to commit robbery, rape or deviate sexual intercourse by force or threat of force, arson, burglary, kidnapping or felonious escape.

(2) Murder is a felony of the first degree [but a person convicted of murder may be sentenced to death, as provided in Section 210.6].

Section 210.3. Manslaughter.

(1) Criminal homicide constitutes manslaughter when:

(a) it is committed recklessly; or

(b) a homicide which would otherwise be murder is committed under the influence of extreme mental or emotional disturbance for

---

In a case of immediate pursuit, with shots being exchanged between the police and the fleeing robbers, a fatal traffic accident 3.2 miles from, and 8 minutes after, a robbery was held to be within the perpetration thereof. People v. Ulsh, 211 Cal.App.2d 258, 27 Cal.Rptr. 408 (1962).

1. "Recklessly" is defined elsewhere in the Code to mean that the actor consciously disregards a substantial and unjustifiable risk amounting to a "gross deviation" from due care. Section 2.02(2) (c).

2. "Negligently" is defined elsewhere in the code in terms equivalent to "inadvertent criminal negligence". Section 2.02(2) (d).

which there is reasonable explanation or excuse. The reasonableness of such explanation or excuse shall be determined from the viewpoint of a person in the actor's situation under the circumstances as he believes them to be.

(2) Manslaughter is a felony of the second degree.

Section 210.4. Negligent Homicide.

(1) Criminal homicide constitutes negligent homicide when it is committed negligently.

(2) Negligent homicide is a felony of the third degree.

Section 210.5. Causing or Aiding Suicide.

(1) Causing Suicide as Criminal Homicide. A person may be convicted of criminal homicide for causing another to commit suicide only if he purposely causes such suicide by force, duress or deception.

(2) Aiding or Soliciting Suicide as an Independent Offense. A person who purposely aids or solicits another to commit suicide is guilty of a felony of the second degree if his conduct causes such suicide or an attempted suicide, and otherwise of a misdemeanor.

(Since a few states do not have capital punishment, provisions for such a penalty in the Code are bracketed, since they would not be needed in such states. A sentence for a felony of the first degree would mean that the maximum would be life imprisonment.)

Section 210.6. Sentence of Death for Murder; Further Proceedings to Determine Sentence.

(1) Death Sentence Excluded. When a defendant is found guilty of murder, the Court shall impose sentence for a felony of the first degree if it is satisfied that:

(a) none of the aggravating circumstances enumerated in Subsection (3) of this Section was established by the evidence at the trial or will be established if further proceedings are initiated under Subsection (2) of this Section; or

(b) substantial mitigating circumstances, established by the evidence at the trial, call for leniency; or

(c) the defendant, with the consent of the prosecuting attorney and the approval of the Court, pleaded guilty to murder as a felony of the first degree; or

(d) the defendant was under 18 years of age at the time of the commission of the crime; or

(e) the defendant's physical or mental condition calls for leniency; or

(f) although the evidence suffices to sustain the verdict, it does not foreclose all doubts respecting the defendant's guilt.

. . .

(If the penalty may be death the Code provides that this shall be determined in a separate proceeding after guilt has been established. The sentence may not be death unless (a) there is found one of the aggravating circumstances enumerated in subsection (3) *and* (b) *no* "mitigating circumstances sufficient to call for leniency".)

(3) Aggravating Circumstances.

(a) The murder was committed by a convict under sentence of imprisonment.

(b) The defendant was previously convicted of another murder or of a felony involving the use or threat of violence to the person.

(c) At the time the murder was committed the defendant also committed another murder.

(d) The defendant knowingly created a great risk of death to many persons.

(e) The murder was committed while the defendant was engaged or was an accomplice in the commission of, or an attempt to commit, or flight after committing or attempting to commit robbery, rape or deviate sexual intercourse by force or threat of force, arson, burglary or kidnapping.

(f) The murder was committed for the purpose of avoiding or preventing a lawful arrest or effecting an escape from lawful custody.

(g) The murder was committed for pecuniary gain.

(h) The murder was especially heinous, atrocious or cruel, manifesting exceptional depravity.

(4) Mitigating Circumstances.

(a) The defendant has no significant history of prior criminal activity.

(b) The murder was committed while the defendant was under the influence of extreme mental or emotional disturbance.

(c) The victim was a participant in the defendant's homicidal conduct or consented to the homicidal act.

(d) The murder was committed under circumstances which the defendant believed to provide a moral justification or extenuation for his conduct.

(e) The defendant was an accomplice in a murder committed by another person and his participation in the homicidal act was relatively minor.

(f) The defendant acted under duress or under the domination of another person.

(g) At the time of the murder, the capacity of the defendant to appreciate the criminality [wrongfulness] of his conduct or to conform his conduct to the requirements of law was impaired as a result of mental disease or defect or intoxication.

(h) The youth of the defendant at the time of the crime.

SECTION 2. ASSAULT AND BATTERY

PEOPLE v. MOORE

Supreme Court of New York, Third Department, 1888.
50 Hun 356, 3 N.Y.S. 159.

LANDON, J. The material facts are not in dispute. The main questions are whether the conceded facts show that the defendant committed an assault[1] upon the complainant, and if so, whether the assault was justifiable.

The defendant was in the employ of the Burden Ore and Iron Company. This company owns a large tract of land in Livingston, Columbia county, and has, in the development of its business, created upon its lands the so-called village of Burden. This consists of the company's offices, shops, sixty or seventy tenement-houses, occupied by its servants and their families, a public store, school-house and chapel. A post-office is established there. An open road or street, wholly upon the company's lands, leads from the public highway to the village. The tenement-houses of the village are in rows upon both sides of the village streets. All these streets and roads are open and to every appearance are public highways. The company, however, retains title to the land, and the public authorities have not claimed or assumed any authority over them.

The complainant Snyder was a peddler of milk and vegetables and had customers for his supplies in this village. The company desired him to discontinue his traffic in the village, and to give it to another person. It notified him that the village and its streets were its private property, and that he must not sell milk there any more. He refused to discontinue. The company directed the defendant to keep him out of the village, but to use no more force than was necessary for the purpose, and to be careful not to do him personal injury. The defendant, in pursuance of this direction, assisted by one Ahlers, on the 14th day of March, 1887, intercepted Snyder upon the road leading from the public highway to the village. Snyder was alone, was seated in his sleigh driving his team of horses on his way to deliver milk to his customers, and especially some apples which had been ordered by one of them. The defendant told Snyder he was trespassing and that he had orders to stop him. Snyder attempted to drive on. The defendant then seized the lines in front of Snyder's

---

1. "An assault is a necessary element of battery, and it is impossible to commit battery without assaulting the victim. The assault, to adopt the statutory language, is 'necessarily included therein'". (Quoting from an earlier decision.) Gomez v. Superior Court, 50 Cal.2d 640, 648, 328 P.2d 976, 981 (1958).

hands, told Ahlers to take the horses by the heads and turn them around, which Ahlers immediately did, the defendant at the same time remarking that "the easiest way is the best way." When the team and sleigh, with Snyder in it, had been turned around, defendant barred the passage towards the village with an iron pipe. Snyder thereupon drove away.

Defendant urges that this was no assault, for the reason that there was no intention to hurt Snyder; and that he did not lay his hands upon him. It is plain, however, that the force which he applied to the horses and sleigh just as effectually touched the person of Snyder, as if he had taken him by his ears or shoulders and turned him right about face. The horses and sleigh were the instruments with which he directed and augmented his personal and physical force against, and upon the body of Snyder. Snyder did receive bodily harm. One receives bodily harm, in a legal sense, when another touches his person against his will with physical force, intentionally hostile and aggressive, or projects such force against his person. Here, for the moment, Snyder was deprived by the defendant of his own control of his own person; and he was controlled, intimidated and coerced by the hostile, aggressive physical force of the defendant. The offer to prove that bodily harm was not intended was made in the face of the defendant's testimony that he intended to do just what he did do. The obvious purpose was to prove that there was no intention to wound or bruise the defendant, or cause him physical pain. So long as this was not claimed or proved on the part of the prosecution, disproof of it was properly rejected for the reason that such disproof would have raised or suggested a false and immaterial issue, tending possibly to the miscarriage of justice.

We assume that if Snyder was a trespasser the assault was justifiable, for no more force was used than was reasonably necessary to eject him from the premises; but he was not a trespasser. The streets leading to and about this village were made and opened by the Burden Iron and Ore Company for such public use as was incident to the wants, convenience and happiness of the people residing there. To the extent of this public use the company subjected its private property to the law which regulates public rights. (Munn v. Illinois, 94 U.S. 113.) No doubt it can depopulate its village and restore its lands to the solitude of its exclusive private dominion; but as long as it enjoys the benefits of public association and communication it must accept the burdens necessarily and properly incident to them. By reserving the legal title to the thoroughfares of its village, it does not reserve autocratic powers over the people residing along them. To prevent the members of its community from buying supplies of Snyder, or of any tradesman not nominated by the company, would be to introduce a condition of vassalage inconsistent with our free institutions. If these families may buy of Snyder, then he may deliver his wares to them, and use for the purpose the appropriate thoroughfares. The assault was, therefore, not justifiable. . . .

The judgment of the Court of Sessions should be affirmed.[1]

LEARNED, P. J., and INGALLS, J., concurred.

Judgment affirmed, with costs.

STATE v. HEMPHILL

Supreme Court of North Carolina, 1913.
162 N.C. 632, 78 S.E. 167.

WALKER, J. It may be that the defendant should have been convicted upon the testimony of the State, but this was not submitted to the jury. The instruction of the court confined the jury to a consideration of the defendant's evidence. We do not think that this evidence was susceptible of only one construction or was so conclusively against the defendant as to warrant a direction to return a verdict of guilty, if the jury believed it. The jury might well have found from the circumstances surrounding the parties at the time, if left untrammeled by this peremptory instruction, but [that][2] the prosecutrix was about to be led astray, and defendant intervened, at the request of her grandmother, her natural guardian and protector, for the innocent and laudable purpose of leading her away from the danger which threatened her, and that he placed his hand upon her, not with the intent of committing an assault upon her, and not in anger, but in kindness, for the purpose of protecting her. It may be true that every touching of the person of another, however, slight or trifling the force may be, if done in an angry, rude, or hostile manner, will constitute an assault and battery; but not so if there was no intention to hurt or injure, and it was so understood by the other party, and there was in fact no injury. Whether it was done in anger or against the consent of the prosecutrix, was a question for the jury. There must be an intent to injure, though this intent may be inferred by the jury from the act, and when the act itself is unlawful, the intent is immaterial or will be presumed. Judge Gaston said in State v. Davis, 23 N.C. 125, 126, that "an assault is an intentional attempt, by violence, to do an injury to the person of another. It must be *intentional*, for if it can be collected, notwithstanding appearances to the contrary, that there is not a present purpose to do an injury,

---

1. It is a battery to spit in another's face, Regina v. Cotesworth, 6 Mod. 172, 87 Eng.Rep. 928 (1705), or to cut the clothes he is wearing, Regina v. Day, 1 Cox C.C. 207 (1845). It is also a battery for a man to kiss a woman against her will, or to lay hands on her for this purpose. Moreland v. State, 125 Ark. 24, 188 S.W. 1 (1916). But it is not an assault (battery) for a man to kiss an intimate friend when he has good reason to believe this will be agreeable to her. Weaver v. State, 66 Tex.Cr.R. 366, 146 S.W. 927 (1912).

2. The word is "but" in the official report and "that" in the Southeastern. The former is obviously a misprint.

there is no assault." And again: "The intention as well as the act makes an assault." If we are restricted to the defendant's testimony, it would appear, or at least there is reason for saying, that he did not intend to injure the prosecutrix, or to do any violence to her person, or to restrain her of her liberty against her will. The jury may reasonably conclude that his object was one of persuasion rather than coercion. He saw her plight—perhaps had been informed of it by her grandmother—and wished to relieve her of its evil consequences. If so, it was an act of kindness and mercy to her, rather than one of hostility. If he laid his hand upon her gently for the purpose of inducing her to return to her home and quit the company or association of designing men, and did not seize her with anger or rudeness, it surely would not be an assault in law. This might have been fairly deduced from his testimony. When she refused to go with him, he did not persist in his effort to persuade her, nor did he offer her any violence or utter any threat. He simply desisted, returned to the house, told her grandmother what had occurred, and she cried, presumably because she knew that the safety of her child was imperiled. This made no more than a case for the jury upon the question whether there had been an assault.

New trial.

HILL v. STATE

Supreme Court of Georgia, 1879.
63 Ga. 578.

BLECKLEY, JUSTICE. According to the evidence, a company of boys attending school were all out in the yard and most of them were engaged in playing. One (Willie Love by name) did not wish to play. An attempt was made by some of his fellows to force him into the sport, as was customary in dealing with a reluctant boy. One Richardson pulled him away from the fence. Love shoved Richardson off. The latter then threw a rock and Love dodged it. Whilst Love was in the act of rising from the position which he had taken to evade this blow, Willie Hill, the accused, threw a rock, and Love, not seeing it, was hit in the mouth. If he had seen it in time he could have dodged it too. It was a way of playing among the boys, to throw rocks at one another, and the evidence indicates that dodging was generally expected. Love and Hill were relatives, and were perfectly friendly. There was no quarrel or cause of quarrel between them, and never had been. The blow with the rock split Love's lip and broke one of his teeth.

1. There is no suggestion that the accused was wanting in age or development, so as to be incapable of committing crime, nor that the throwing of the stone was involuntary. The sole defense is, that he threw in sport, without ill-will or anger, and with no intention to hurt or even hit, relying upon the expertness of his school-fellow in

dodging. It is not shown, however, that he did not throw *at* the latter, or that he gave any notice or warning so as to put him upon guard. Grant that he desired and expected a successful "dodge," yet he did not get it, and the other boy was in no fault in not responding with the anticipated maneuver; he did not see the danger. Throwing stones at others for amusement is a dangerous sport, because the tendency of it is to wound or bruise, and there is no certainty that in a given case the injury will be slight rather than serious. When one has hurled a stone and parted with all power over it, the mischief it may do where it strikes is not matter of calculation, but in a great degree of mere chance. Life itself is not safe where stones are flying about, even though they be thrown by a boy. In the present case, if death had ensued the offense would have been manslaughter at the least. "So, throwing stones at another wantonly in play, being a dangerous sport, without the least appearance of any good intent, or doing any other such idle action as cannot but endanger the bodily hurt of some one or other, and by such means killing a person, is manslaughter." Whar.Hon., § 162. "Where unsuitable and deadly weapons are used in lawful games, the act itself becomes unlawful." Ib., § 479; 1 Hale P.C., 472, 473. "If when engaged in an unlawful or dangerous sport, a man kill another by accident, it is manslaughter. . . . Death produced by practical joking is manslaughter." 2 Whar.Cr.Law, § 1012. In Studstill v. The State, 7 Ga. 2, a boy was shot at the distance of two hundred yards, with an old gun which some of the sporting party said would not hit him at fifteen steps, and the shooting was done when "they were all in a laugh." This court said, on page 13, "Nor can we sanction the position assumed by counsel, that owing to the distance, it was improbable that the ball would reach its object; and that, consequently, the killing is reduced to involuntary manslaughter. Can he who takes deliberate aim at another with a rifle, and kills him, be said not to have intended it? We think not. He might, it is true, suppose the chances to be against it; still he puts forth all his skill to reach the mark and he succeeds. It is enough, as the act itself was unlawful, if the killing was the possible consequence of the act. To hold otherwise would be to trifle with human life." For boys to throw at one another stones of a size and weight to lacerate lips and break teeth, is not innocent play, but wild and wanton mischief, and if they are of responsible age and average mental capacity, they must answer for the consequences of their reckless conduct. It is good for the young to engage in rough and hardy sports, but the state cannot permit her children to beat and batter one another, even at school, with stones or other dangerous missiles. Bad boys should be made to understand that they are accountable to the law, as well as to parents and teachers, for throwing rocks and thereby inflicting personal injuries. . . .[1]

Judgment affirmed.

---

1. "An assault and battery may be committed with a motor vehicle by striking a person, or a vehicle in which he is riding, either intentional-

SMITH v. STATE

High Court of Errors and Appeals of Mississippi, 1860.
39 Miss. 521.

SMITH, C. J., delivered the opinion of the court.

This was a conviction for an assault, in the Circuit Court, Yalobusha county.

The defendant pleaded not guilty; and, on the trial, it was proved by the only witness examined in the cause that he went to defendant's house to levy an execution, and when he arrived there that he found defendant at the grindstone grinding his knife. When the witness made known the purpose of his visit, the defendant swore he should not levy the execution, and threatened, if he did, to cut his throat. Witness leaned up against the fence in a careless manner, and defendant walked up to witness in an angry manner. In talking to witness defendant kept his knife open, speaking in an angry and excited manner, and flourishing his knife, which sometimes passed within six inches of witness's throat. Witness stood motionless, and shamed defendant and told him that he was a better man than witness, and that defendant put up his knife, but soon took it out again. Witness for the time was prevented from making the levy; but defendant's anger subsided after a while, and he made the levy, and defendant rode off with him to a neighbor's house. Witness did nothing to prevent defendant from striking him if he desired to do so. Witness did nothing but talk to defendant. Defendant and witness were the only persons present. Defendant did not touch witness, who did not retreat, but stood still.

The errors assigned arise upon the instructions granted, with reference to the foregoing evidence, in behalf of the prosecution, and upon those which were requested by the defendant and refused by the court.

For the prosecution, the court charged, first, that "If the jury believe from the evidence that the defendant, in an angry manner, drew a deadly weapon and approached Wilson, and, while in reach of him, threatened to do him damage if he did not desist from doing a

---

ly or by driving so negligently as to constitute a reckless disregard of human life and safety. . . .

"Of course, mere negligence would not impute an intent. If negligence be relied on, then it must amount to reckless, willful, and wanton disregard of the rights of others, in which state of case the intent is imputed to the accused." Woodward v. State, 164 Miss. 468, 144 So. 895 (1932).

Cf. State v. Hamburg, 34 Del. 62, 143 A. 47 (1928). An inexperienced driver, who drove his car on the sidewalk and hit two persons while he was attempting to dodge a child who suddenly ran into the street, was held not guilty of assault and battery. People v. Waxman, 232 App.Div. 90, 249 N.Y.S. 180 (1931).

lawful act, and that Wilson did desist, for the time, in consequence of such threat, the defendant being armed with and exhibiting such weapon, then the defendant is guilty of an assault;" and, second, "That to constitute an assault it is not necessary that any damage be done, or that any blow be struck."

And refused in behalf of the defendant to instruct the jury, first, that "If it was not the intention of the defendant to strike, then no assault was committed;" second, "If it was in the power of the defendant to strike, and he did not strike, nor make any attempt to strike, these are circumstances to be considered by the jury to determine whether there was any intention to strike;" and, third, "No threat of words or act can constitute an assault, if the jury believe there was no intention to strike."

These latter instructions are the converse of those given at the instance of the prosecuting attorney; and, in effect, present the question whether a present purpose or intention to do harm to another is necessary to the constitution of an assault.

An assault is said to be "any attempt or offer, with force or violence, to do a corporal hurt to another, whether from malice or wantonness." Roscoe Ev. 257. The offer or attempt must be intentional; for if, notwithstanding appearances to the contrary, it can be collected that there is not a present purpose to do an injury, it is not an assault. Wharton Am.Crim.Law, 1244, 4th ed. And it is said that a mere purpose to commit violence, however plainly declared, if not accompanied by an effort to carry it into immediate execution, falls short of an actual assault. Hence no words of themselves, can amount to an assault. As no words of themselves, or a declared purpose to do an injury to the person of another, unaccompanied with an effort to carry such purpose into immediate effect, amounts to an actual assault, it is not always easy, in practice, to draw a dividing line between violence threatened and violence begun to be executed. But we think it may safely be laid down "that when an unequivocal purpose of violence is accompanied by any act, which, if not stopped or diverted, will be followed by personal injury, the execution of the purpose is then begun—the battery is attempted."

Tested by these rules it seems very clear that the rulings of the court were erroneous. The acts or gestures of the defendant were not an evident attempt to commit violence upon the person of Wilson. It appears certain that he did not so regard them, as he leaned carelessly against the fence, offered no resistance and did not retreat, when it was completely in the power of the defendant to have executed his purpose if he intended to assail him. Under the circumstances in proof before the jury, it was indispensable that they should ascertain what was the intention of the accused. If the proof was clear, or the jury had been satisfied, that the accused, at the time, meditated violence upon the person of Wilson, they would have been justified in finding that his acts amounted to an assault. But the instructions excluded from their consideration all of the facts and circumstances, in proof before them, and which were relied upon to show that the accused did not intend to commit an injury upon the person of Wilson; and hence that he was not guilty as charged.

Judgment reversed, and cause remanded for a new trial.[1]

HANDY, J., dissented, as follows:

I do not concur in the doctrine stated in the opinion of the court.

I am of opinion that if a party make an advance upon another, armed with a dangerous weapon likely to produce great bodily injury, and in a hostile attitude, to all appearance indicating an intention to do the other party great bodily harm, that it is in law an assault, though the party did not intend to do the party any bodily injury.

COMMONWEALTH v. WHITE

Supreme Judicial Court of Massachusetts, 1872.
110 Mass. 407.

COMPLAINT to a trial justice, alleging that the defendant "with force and arms in and upon the body of Timothy Harrington an assault did make, and him did then and there threaten to shoot with a gun, which he then and there pointed and aimed at said Harrington."

At the trial, on appeal, in the Superior Court, before Pitman, J., the Commonwealth introduced evidence tending to show that the defendant was driving in a wagon along a highway which Harrington, one Sullivan and others were repairing; that Sullivan called out to the defendant to drive in the middle of the road; that the defendant made an offensive reply; that thereupon Sullivan came towards the defendant and asked him what he meant; that Sullivan and Harrington were about fifteen feet from the defendant, who was moving

---

1. D raised his drawn sword within striking distance of X and said: "If it were not assize time, I would not take such language from you." This did not constitute an assault. Tuberville v. Savage, 1 Mod. 3, 86 Eng.Rep. 684 (1669).

D doubled up his fist and menaced X, saying: "If you say so again I will knock you down." This was an assault. United States v. Myers, 1 Cranch C.C. 310, 27 Fed.Cas. 43, No. 15,845 (1806).

D, while unlawfully driving away X's cow, faced X with a gun in his hand, cocked but not pointed at X, and declared he would kill anyone who interfered and laid hands on the cow. This was an assault. State v. Horne, 92 N.C. 805 (1885).

While X was where he had a right to be, D drew a pistol and drove X from the place by threatening to shoot if he did not leave. This was held to be an assault although the pistol was not cocked and pointed. State v. Church, 63 N.C. 15 (1868).

Picking up a rock and holding it in a threatening position, with no effort to throw it, was held not sufficient for an assault. Bowden v. State, 27 Ga.App. 768, 109 S.E. 915 (1921).

along all the time; that the defendant took up a double-barrel gun which he had in the wagon, pointed it towards Sullivan and Harrington, took aim at them, and said, "I have got something here that will pick the eyes of you." This was all the evidence of declarations or threats of the defendant at the time of the alleged assault.

Sullivan testifed that he had no fear and did not suppose the defendant was going to do any harm; but there was evidence tending to show that Harrington was put in fear. The defendant testified that the gun was not loaded.

The defendant asked the judge to rule that the complaint could not be sustained, because the Commonwealth had failed to prove the offence as alleged in the complaint; but the judge refused so to rule, and ruled that it was not necessary to prove a threat to shoot as set forth in the complaint.

The defendant also asked the judge to instruct the jury "that the facts testified to did not constitute an assault; that at the time, the defendant must have had an intention to do some bodily harm to Harrington, and the present ability to carry his intention into execution; and that the whole evidence would not warrant the jury in finding a verdict against the defendant." But the judge refused so to instruct the jury, and instructed them "that an assault is any unlawful physical force partly or fully put in motion, which creates a reasonable apprehension of immediate physical injury; and that if the defendant, within shooting distance, menacingly pointed at Harrington a gun, which Harrington had reasonable cause to believe was loaded, and Harrington was actually put in fear of immediate bodily injury therefrom, and the circumstances of the case were such as ordinarily to induce such fear in the mind of a reasonable man, that then an assault was committed, whether the gun was in fact loaded or not." The jury returned a verdict of guilty, and the defendant alleged exceptions. . . .

WELLS, J. . . . The instructions required the jury to find that the acts of the defendant were done "menacingly;" that Harrington had reasonable cause to believe the gun pointed at him was loaded, and was actually put in fear of immediate bodily injury therefrom; and that the circumstances were such as ordinarily to induce such fear in the mind of a reasonable man.

Instructions in accordance with the second ruling prayed for would have required the jury also to find that the defendant had an intention to do some bodily harm, and the present ability to carry his intention into execution. Taking both these conditions literally, it is difficult to see how an assault could be committed without a battery resulting.

It is not the secret intent of the assaulting party, nor the undisclosed fact of his ability or inability to commit a battery, that is material; but what his conduct and the attending circumstances denote at the time to the party assaulted. If to him they indicate an attack, he is justified in resorting to defensive action. The same rule applies to the proof necessary to sustain a criminal complaint for an assault. It is the outward demonstration that constitutes the mischief which is punished as a breach of the peace.

The authorities cited for the Commonwealth amply support the rulings and instructions to the jury at the trial.[1]

Exceptions overruled.

MODEL PENAL CODE

Article 211. Assault; Reckless Endangering; Threats

Section 211.0. Definitions.

In this Article, the definitions given in Section 210.0 apply unless a different meaning plainly is required.

Section 211.1. Assault.

(1) Simple Assault. A person is guilty of assault if he:

(a) attempts to cause or purposely, knowingly or recklessly causes bodily injury to another; or

(b) negligently causes bodily injury to another with a deadly weapon; or

(c) attempts by physical menace to put another in fear of imminent serious bodily injury.

Simple assault is a misdemeanor unless committed in a fight or scuffle entered into by mutual consent, in which case it is a petty misdemeanor.

---

1. May a criminal assault be committed by pointing an unloaded firearm at another within shooting distance but not within striking distance (as a club)?

It was held "yes" under a statute defining assault as a wilful and unlawful attempt or offer, with force or violence, to do a corporal hurt to another. State v. Wiley, 52 S.D. 110, 216 N.W. 866 (1927).

It was held "no" under a statute defining assault as an unlawful attempt, coupled with present ability, to commit violent injury. Klein v. State, 9 Ind.App. 365, 36 N.E. 763 (1894).

Without basing the decision on the wording of the statute it was held that while such a menace is sufficient for a civil action it does not constitute a criminal assault. Chapman v. State, 78 Ala. 463 (1885). A contrary view was expressed in State v. Deso, 110 Vt. 1, 1 A.2d 710 (1938).

While siding with the view that a criminal assault is possible under such circumstances, the court reversed a conviction because the evidence disclosed that the intended victim did not see the weapon and knew nothing about the threat until afterwards. State v. Barry, 45 Mont. 598, 124 P. 775 (1912).

D thrust his hand against X, said "stick 'em up", and began to go through X's pockets until X noticed that D did not have a gun and pushed him away. This was held to be an assault with intent to rob. People v. Rockwood, 358 Ill. 422, 193 N.E. 449 (1934).

Exposing a child to the weather was held not to constitute an assault where the child was rescued before suffering any injury. Regina v. Renshaw, 2 Cox C.C. 285 (1847).

(2) **Aggravated Assault.** A person is guilty of aggravated assault if he:

(a) attempts to cause serious bodily injury to another, or causes such injury purposely, knowingly or recklessly under circumstances manifesting extreme indifference to the value of human life: or

(b) attempts to cause or purposely or knowingly causes bodily injury to another with a deadly weapon.

Aggravated assault under paragraph (a) is a felony of the second degree; aggravated assault under paragraph (b) is a felony of the third degree.

Section 211.2. **Recklessly Endangering Another Person.**

A person commits a misdemeanor if he recklessly engages in conduct which places or may place another person in danger of death or serious bodily injury. Recklessness and danger shall be presumed where a person knowingly points a firearm at or in the direction of another, whether or not the actor believed the firearm to be loaded.

Section 211.3. **Terroristic Threats.**

A person is guilty of a felony of the third degree if he threatens to commit any crime of violence with purpose to terrorize another or to cause evacuation of a building, place of assembly, or facility of public transportation, or otherwise to cause serious public inconvenience, or in reckless disregard of the risk of causing such terror or inconvenience.

SECTION 3. OTHER OFFENSES AGAINST THE PERSON

(A) ABDUCTION

The social interest in the personal security of the individual member of the community goes far beyond the effort to safeguard his life and to protect him against an ordinary attack. Viewed in the most primitive light, the state must undertake to deal with various other types of personal harm in order to have any adequate check upon violent acts of private retaliation. It must do so, furthermore, if the organized group is to continue to strive for an ever higher level of cultural development, and "a more abundant" life, intellectually and morally, as well as physically.

There was no such crime as abduction known to the English common law, but a statute, passed a few years before Columbus discovered America, created a felony which is the forerunner of all the present statutes on abduction. This early statute was designed primarily to protect young heiresses from designing fortune hunters, although its wording was not so limited. It provided in substance that if any person should take any woman ("maid, widow or wife") against her will, unlawfully, and such woman had substance in the form of lands or goods or was the heir apparent of her ancestor, such person should be guilty of felony. It was stated in an introduction to the statute that a woman, so taken, was often thereafter married to or defiled by the misdoer, or to or by another with his consent, but this was not made an element of the original crime itself. This element, however, has been included in many of the modern statutes. Some jurisdictions also have statutes making it a crime for any person to take or entice any unmarried female under a certain age for the purpose of prostitution (or for the purpose of sexual intercourse, concubinage or prostitution). This general field, often involving two or more statutes which may be in different parts of the code, has come to be referred to as *abduction*.

Some statutes prohibit the unlawful taking (perhaps adding enticing or detaining) of a girl under a specified age from her parent or guardian for the purpose of depriving the parent or guardian of his lawful custody; and some make a similar provision with reference to such taking of "any child," and hence extend the protection to boys as well as girls. Such a statute goes beyond the scope of "abduction" as it is ordinarily understood and carries over into the field of kidnaping. The word "abduction," meaning literally a taking or drawing away, was employed by Blackstone in his definition of kidnaping, and "child stealing" is frequently included as a special form of that offense.

(B) ABORTION AND CONTRACEPTIVISM

(i) ABORTION

Abortion literally means miscarriage. It was a misdemeanor at common law to cause the miscarriage of a woman after the foetus had quickened unless necessary or reasonably believed to be necessary to save her life, and the word "abortion" came to be applied to this offense. Most of the statutes in this country have no requirement that the foetus must have quickened, and do not make actual miscarriage essential to guilt. Many do not even require that the woman be actually pregnant at the time, belief in such pregnancy being sufficient. Such an offense is frequently, and more properly, called "attempt to procure an abortion," and consists of the administration of a drug, use of an instrument, or employment of other means with intent to cause a miscarriage not necessary, or reasonably supposed to be necessary, to save the life of the woman.

Some states have made it a statutory offense for a woman to solicit medicine, drugs or substances and use the same herself, or to submit to any operation or treatment, with intent to procure her miscarriage unless necessary to preserve her life. And in at least a dozen states the crime of manslaughter has been extended to include certain types of foeticide.

Therapeutic abortion, an operation necessary or reasonably believed to be necessary to save the life of the woman, is not a common-law offense and is expressly mentioned as an exception under many of the statutes.

Any medicine or means for producing a miscarriage is known as an abortifacient, and statutes punishing the unauthorized sale thereof are not uncommon.

(ii) Contraceptivism

Contraceptivism is unlawful trafficking in contraceptives. It is not a common-law offense, and has not received widespread adoption as a statutory crime although it is to be found in a number of the codes.

(iii) Indecent Advertising

Statutes punishing "indecent advertising" often include advertising the sale of contraceptives and abortifacients.

(iv) Federal Offenses

Contraceptives and abortifacients have been grouped with a number of other things such as obscene books and pictures and declared "non-mailable" by Act of Congress. Knowingly to deposit any such article for mailing or to take from the mails for the purpose of disposition is a federal felony. It is also a federal felony to deposit such an article with a common carrier for interstate transportation or to import it into the United States from a foreign country.

(C) RAPE

Rape, at common law, is unlawful carnal knowledge of a woman without her consent. Any sexual penetration, however slight, is sufficient to complete the crime if the other elements are present.

"By force and against her will" is the phrase often used in the definitions, but as unlawful carnal knowledge of a woman who is insensibly drunk at the time is held to be rape unless she had consented in advance, it is obvious that no more is required than that the deed be done without her consent. Sexual intercourse by a man with his lawful wife is not unlawful and hence is not rape even if she does not consent. But while a husband cannot rape his wife he can be guilty of the crime of rape committed upon her. That is, if A should aid B in having sexual intercourse with A's wife without her consent, both A and B would be guilty of rape.

Statutory rape. It is commonly provided by statute that unlawful carnal knowledge is a crime committed upon a girl under a certain age (called the age of consent) even if she consents. To distinguish between this and the other type of rape, the first is often called "statutory rape" or "carnal knowledge of a child" and the other "common-law rape."

The so-called "age of consent" varies in the different jurisdictions. An early English statute fixed the age at twelve. Modern statutes usually provide a substantially higher age,—not infrequently eighteen.

(D) FALSE IMPRISONMENT

False imprisonment is the unlawful confinement of a person and is an indictable misdemeanor at common law. One may be *imprisoned* not only in the public jail or a private house or in the stocks but even by being detained against his will on the public street. And *imprisonment* may be accomplished by physical barriers or physical force, or it may be by threat of force or assertion of authority which results in submission. One is not imprisoned merely because he is prevented from going in one certain direction, or in several directions, so long as there is an obvious way open for his departure. On the other hand imprisonment is not necessarily stationary. One may be locked in

Sec. 3 OTHER OFFENSES 89

a moving ship or car or may be *imprisoned* by being forcibly taken from one place to another.[a]

Imprisonment is not *false* if it is lawful, as where an officer makes a lawful arrest or a parent in a proper manner confines a little child. On the other hand an arrest made under circumstances in which there is no lawful authority to take the prisoner into custody constitutes false imprisonment.

Some of the modern statutes expressly provide for the punishment of false imprisonment; others do not include this crime as such, although the aggravated features may be included in some other offense such as abduction or kidnaping.

(E) KIDNAPING

Kidnaping is aggravated false imprsonment.

(i) SIMPLE KIDNAPING

There is some disagreement among the different jurisdictions as to the exact ingredients needed to place this type of misconduct in the category of the graver crime. At common law kidnaping was defined as the forcible abduction or stealing away of a man, woman or child from his own country and sending him into another. In other words it was false imprisonment aggravated by conveying the victim out of the country. This would be kidnaping anywhere today but the statutes go beyond this, the most common addition being false imprisonment with intent to cause the victim to be imprisoned secretly within the state.[1] Some enactments go even further, such as including within the offense the forcible or fraudulent taking of a person from his place of residence without authority of law.

---

[a] Forcing one to change seats in a car and to remain in the car is false imprisonment. People v. Zilbauer, 44 Cal.2d 43, 279 P.2d 534 (1955). But locking a person *out of* a particular room is not. Martin v. Lincoln Park West Corp., 219 F.2d 622 (7th Cir. 1955).

1. One type of statute includes imprisonment with intent, (1) to send the victim out of the state, or (2) to confine him secretly within the state. Vandiver v. State, 97 Okl.Cr. 217, 261 P.2d 617 (1953).

Where the victim of robbery was forced to move about through several rooms of the building under force and fear, the offender was guilty of kidnaping for the purpose of robbery as well as robbery. People v. O'Farrell, 161 Cal. App.2d 13, 325 P.2d 1002 (1958).

(ii) Kidnaping for Ransom

Kidnaping was a misdemeanor at common law, punished by fine, imprisonment and pillory. Under modern statutes it is a felony, and the special form of the offense known as "kidnaping for ransom" is regarded as one of the gravest of crimes, not infrequently made a capital offense. A wrongdoer is guilty of kidnaping for ransom if he participates in any of the three elements of the offense,—(1) unlawful seizure, (2) secret confinement, or (3) extortion of ransom. This includes one who acts as a go-between to collect the ransom for the actual abductors.

(iii) Child Stealing

The "child-stealing" statutes commonly provide a penalty for anyone who shall lead, take, entice or detain a child under a specified age with intent to keep or conceal it from its parent, guardian, or other person having lawful care or control thereof. Great variation is found in the age used for this purpose, such as any child under the age of 12, 14 or 16,—or any minor child.

(iv) Consent

There has been no kidnaping if the person who was confined or transported freely consented thereto, without being under any legal, physical or mental disability at the time, or being subjected to any coercion, threats or fraud. A child under the age specified in a child-stealing statute is incapable of giving a legally-recognized consent.

(v) The Federal Kidnaping Act (The Lindbergh Law)

It is a federal felony to take a kidnaped person from one state to another if the captive was "held for ransom or reward or otherwise," and the punishment may be death unless the victim has been liberated unharmed.

(F) MAYHEM

Mayhem, according to the English common law, is maliciously depriving another of the use of such of his members as may render him less able, in fighting, either to defend himself or to annoy his adversary. To cut off a hand or a finger or to put out an eye or knock out a front tooth were all mayhems at common law, if done maliciously, because they rendered the victim less efficient as a fighting man (for the king's army). But to cut off an ear or to slit the nose was not mayhem because it merely disfigured the person. This distinction whereby the penalty for maiming was much more severe than for disfiguring (a mere battery), may have seemed quite appropriate in very ancient times but was not viewed with approval in the seventeenth century when malefactors intentionally slit the nose of a member of Parliament. A statute in 1670, prompted by the facts of that atrocity, provided the death penalty for maliciously intentional disfigurement,—and since such an injury should not be punished more severely than that of the other type the same penalty was provided for mayhem if intentionally perpetrated. This statutory offense, known as mayhem, did not displace the common-law crime of that name but was in addition to it. Thus the definition in terms of English law of the time was required to be in some such form as this: Mayhem is maliciously maiming or maliciously and intentionally disfiguring another,—with the explanation that the penalty for maiming was more severe if it was intentional as well as malicious than if malicious but not actually intentional (such as a wrongful act done in wanton and wilful disregard of the likelihood of maiming but without a specific intent to maim).

This distinction between the two types of injury, traceable to historical accident, has not met with general approval here. Our statutes commonly include both but whereas some follow the common law otherwise and say only "maliciously," others adopt the addition of the English statute and require the injury to be inflicted maliciously and intentionally. Hence mayhem under American statutes is maliciously maiming or disfiguring another, except that in a number of states a specific intent to maim or disfigure is required.

(G) DUELING

Dueling is fighting by previous agreement with deadly weapons. It is usually under a so-called "code of honor" which establishes rules for the conduct of the fight as well as for the preliminary arrangements.

The social interest in the life and security of the individual member of the community is too great to permit the settlement of private disputes and grudges by deadly combat. Hence the law does not permit persons to consent to such an encounter, and no justification or excuse can be established by the fact that such consent was given. Furthermore, since the combat is deliberately arranged the law does not even take notice of whatever provocation there may have been, and which might have been recognized as a mitigating circumstance had the conflict flared up in the heat of passion on the spur of the moment. Because of these facts, one who kills another in a duel is guilty of murder. And since the duel probably would not have been fought if no persons had been found willing to serve as seconds, the seconds are held to have aided and abetted in the killing and hence are also guilty of the murder. This applies to the second for the deceased as well as to the second for the victor. If the duel does not result in death, the participants are guilty of an attempt to commit murder at common law (and usually of some aggravated assault under modern statutes,—such as assault with intent to murder, or assault with a deadly weapon).

The duel is itself a common-law misdemeanor; and parties may be guilty of a misdemeanor even if the duel does not actually take place. One is guilty who challenges another to fight a duel, whether the challenge is accepted or not. One is guilty who is knowingly the bearer of such a challenge, whether it is accepted or not. One is guilty who intentionally provokes such a challenge. In this case, while guilt does not depend upon the actual fighting of the duel, it is necessary that the intentional provocation actually result in the issuance of a challenge.

Dueling is quite generally prohibited by statute, and in many of the states the offense is made a felony. The various provisions differ widely. For example, one who causes the death of another in a duel is guilty of murder in the first degree in Iowa, but is guilty of a special offense punished less severely than murder in the second degree, in California.

Chapter 3

OFFENSES AGAINST THE HABITATION

SECTION 1. BURGLARY

WOODS v. STATE

Supreme Court of Mississippi, Division A, 1939.
186 Miss. 463, 191 So. 283.

GRIFFITH, J., delivered the opinion of the court.

Appellant was indicted and convicted under the charge of the burglary of a dwelling house. The undisputed proof showed that the house in question, although intended for a dwelling house, had been only recently erected and had not yet been occupied as a dwelling. It was vacant.

Appellant relies on Haynes v. State, 180 Miss. 291, 177 So. 360, wherein the court held that a house from which the occupants had permanently removed on the day before the night of the burglary was not a dwelling at the time of the commission of the alleged crime; and that proof of the burglary of such a house would not sustain the conviction under an indictment charging the burglary of a dwelling. Appellant submits that if a house from which the occupants have permanently removed is not a dwelling house within the statutes on burglary, then, upon the same reasoning, a house into which no dwellers have ever yet moved is not a dwelling house; and in this contention appellant is clearly correct. . . .

Reversed and remanded.[1]

STATE v. NEFF

Supreme Court of Appeals of West Virginia, 1940.
122 W.Va. 549, 11 S.E.2d 171.

HATCHER, JUDGE. The two Neffs were charged with burglariously breaking and entering in the night time a chicken house, an outhouse adjoining the dwelling house of J. A. Trent and belonging to

---

[1] The room of a transient guest at an inn should be laid as the dwelling house of the innkeeper, not of the guest, whether the innkeeper lives in the inn or elsewhere. Rogers v. People, 86 N.Y. 360 (1881). Cf. Russell v. State, 36 Ala.App. 19, 52 So.2d 230 (1951), certiorari denied 255 Ala. 581, 52 So.2d 237.

him, and stealing from the chicken house his chickens valued at $30.00. The Neffs were found guilty of burglary and sentenced to the penitentiary.

The evidence is incomplete as to the size of the alleged chicken house and its proximity to the Trent dwelling. The former is described as a "small house", having a floor space of four and a half by five feet; but neither its height, nor evidence from which the height might be estimated, is shown. It had a hinged door fastened by a chain drawn through holes bored in the door and "the building face", respectively. The dwelling "sets back about" seventy-five feet from a public road; the chicken house is "out across" the road somewhere, but its distance from the road or the dwelling is not shown.

At common law burglary was "an offense against the habitation not against the property." 9 C.J. 1009. But burglary could be committed on uninhabited structures, provided they were "parcel of" and within the same common fence as the mansion-house, though not contiguous to it. The Virginia Assembly, Acts 1847–8, Ch. IV, Sec. 13, modified the common law by restricting the burglary of a building other than the dwelling house to "an outhouse adjoining thereto and occupied therewith." That restriction remained in the Virginia statute until this state was formed and then we adopted it. West Virginia Acts, 1882, Ch. 148, Sec. 11, substituted the alternative "or" for the connective "and", so that the phrase read "outhouse adjoining thereto (the dwelling-house) or occupied therewith." There has been no further change. See Code, 61–3–11.

All the words in the phrase are plain and well understood. No reason appears for not holding that they are used in their ordinary sense. We held in State v. Crites, 110 W.Va. 36, 156 S.E. 847, that the word "outhouse" was so used, and, in effect, that it meant a building constructed at least large enough for an adult to enter erect and to turn around comfortably within. The State, failing to show the height of the structure in question, did not prove it to be a house at all. But if we should concede that because the Trents called it a house, it should be taken as such, the State has still failed to make a case because the so-called house, being across the public road one hundred feet or more from the dwelling house, can not, under any fair construction, be said to adjoin it. Since the statute limits the burglary of an outhouse not occupied in connection with the dwelling house, to one "adjoining" it, such contiguity must be proven. We are not advised of any decision on a statute like ours. But the statute, as amended in 1882, differs from the common law more in words than substance. And under the common law an outhouse across a public road from its owner's dwelling house is held to be not parcel thereof and not the subject of burglary.

Sec. 1 BURGLARY 95

The judgment is reversed, the verdict set aside and a new trial awarded defendants.[1]

Reversed and remanded.

CLARKE v. COMMONWEALTH

Supreme Court of Appeals of Virginia, 1874.
25 Grat. 908.

MONCURE, P. . . . The first bill of exceptions states, that on the trial of the cause it was proved, on the part of the commonwealth, that Joseph Dabney and Edward Henderson jointly rented and occupied a room in the house of one Fannie Straus, in the city of Richmond; that each of them had and kept a key to the door of the said room; that the prisoner, Clarke, at the same time rented and occupied an adjoining room up stairs in the same house, the doors of the two rooms opening near each other on the same porch, and Dabney and Henderson and Clarke frequently interchanged visits from one room to the other; that on the night of the 11th day of March 1874 Dabney locked his door and took his key with him, and in going to church met Henderson, who said he was going back to their room, and would join him (Dabney) at church soon; that the windows were nailed, and Dabney left in the room a trunk, which contained nearly all his clothes, and several other articles enumerated in the indictment and exhibited in court; that when he returned to his room he found the door locked and the windows nailed as he had left them, and there

---

[1] "2. The section of the statute upon which the foregoing indictment is framed is as follows: 'Every person who shall be convicted of breaking and entering: *First*, any building within the curtilage of a dwelling house, but not forming a part thereof; or, *second*, any shop, store, booth, tent, warehouse or other building, or any boat or vessel, or any railroad car in which there shall be at the time some human being, or any goods, wares, merchandise, or other valuable thing kept or deposited, with intent to steal or commit any felony therein, shall, on conviction, be adjudged guilty of burglary in the second degree.' R.S. 1889, sec. 3526. . . .

"If the indictment be based on the second clause of the section, then it is bad because the rule as to matters *ejusdem generis* applies—that good rule of construction which requires that 'where a particular class . . . is spoken of, and general words follow, the class first mentioned is to be taken as the most comprehensive, and the general words treated as referring to matters *ejusdem generis* with such class.' Broom, Leg.Max. (6 Ed.) *625.

"Here the term 'chicken house building' is not of the same kind of class as those previously mentioned and therefore can not fall within the definition of the term 'other buildings.'" State v. Bryant, 90 Mo. 534, 2 S.W. 836, and cases cited. See, also, State ex rel. v. Seibert, 123 Mo. loc. cit. 424, 438, 27 S.W. 626." State v. Schuchman, 133 Mo. 111, 34 S.W. 842 (1896). Cf. State v. Thompson, 38 Wash.2d 774, 232 P.2d 87 (1951).

A gasoline tank sunk in the ground is a "storehouse" within the meaning of the statute. Moss v. Commonwealth, 271 Ky. 283, 111 S.W.2d 628 (1937). As to a "dwelling" or a "store building" on wheels see Luce v. State, 128 Tex.Cr.R. 287, 81 S.W.2d 93 (1935); People v. Burley, 26 Cal.App.2d 213, 79 P.2d 148 (1938); State v. Ebel, 92 Mont. 413, 15 P.2d 233 (1932).

was no appearance of any breaking of the premises in doors, windows or elsewhere, but his trunk and its contents were missing, and after search for it the next day, in the evening, he found it at a room (in another house) which was rented by Clarke that day; that Clarke disappeared from the city of Richmond, and, when he was afterwards arrested, he confessed, freely and voluntarily, after but little hesitation, that Henderson led him into the act; agreed with him to take Dabney's trunk; that they went to the room together and unlocked the door, and they entered and took the trunk with intent to take it way and steal it, and it was removed to a place whence it was taken to Clarke's room, the place where it was found, the said Henderson having assisted him in the removal of the trunk from the room into the yard, and put it upon prisoner's shoulder, who carried it off. On the part of the defence it was proved that the trunk and all its contents would not bring twenty-five dollars at auction. This was all the material evidence in the case. Whereupon the prisoner moved the court to instruct the jury as follows, to wit:

"If the jury believe from the evidence that Edward Henderson was a renter, in part, of the room charged to have been broken and entered, occupied by him and Joseph Dabney in common, and that the said Henderson, as one of the legal tenants of that room, had one key and Dabney another key to the same door thereof, and that he, Henderson, voluntarily opened the door of the room, in the exercise of his right as tenant to open the door, then there was no breaking of the same; and to constitute burglary there must be a breaking as well as an entering with the intent charged in the indictment."

Which instruction the court refused to give as offered, but gave with an addition in these words: "But if the jury believe that the prisoner and Henderson agreed together that Henderson should open the door with his key, for the purpose and with the intent of stealing the property alleged to be stolen in the indictment; and that Henderson, the prisoner, being present and consenting, did so open the door in the night time; and that in pursuance of said agreement they entered the room and stole the said property, then the prisoner is guilty of burglary." To which ruling of the court the prisoner excepted. . . .

If the case now under consideration be a case of constructive breaking, it must come under one of the three heads into which that subject is divided by Russell as above set forth. It cannot come under the first or the second, as the entrance was certainly not obtained by threats or fraud. If it comes under any of them, it can only be the third, and on the ground that the entrance was obtained by a conspiracy. Was it obtained by a conspiracy, so as to be a constructive breaking within the meaning of the law in regard to burglary?

The conspiracy, if any, was between the prisoner Clarke and Henderson, who, with Dabney, jointly rented and occupied a room in the house of Fannie Straus, in which room was the trunk of Dabney, which, with its contents, was charged to have been stolen. If there were any such conspiracy what was its object? Could it have been to break and enter the room of which Henderson and Dabney were joint tenants and occupants, of which, each kept a key, and which, of course, each had, at all times, either by day or by night a right to enter at pleasure? or must it not have been only to steal the trunk of Dabney and its contents, which were in the room, and which were actually stolen, as charged in the indictment? They had no occasion to form a conspiracy to break and enter the room. They had a ready and a lawful mode of entering that through the door, which Henderson could at any time unlock. Dabney and Henderson and Clarke had rooms in the same house, the doors of the two rooms opening near each other on the same porch, and they frequently interchanged visits from one room to the other. Suppose Clarke had visited Henderson and Dabney's room in the latter's absence, and in the night time, and that Clarke and Henderson had then agreed to steal Dabney's trunk, and had stolen it accordingly. Of course there would have been no burglary in that case. Can it make any difference that the agreement to steal was made before they unlocked the door and entered the room? Suppose it had been, as it may have been, made in Clarke's room, and the parties had then, immediately, stepped from Clarke's room into Henderson and Dabney's room and stolen the trunk of Dabney. Would the unlocking of the door of the latter room by Henderson, in that case, be a breaking of the room within the meaning of the law in regard to burglary, either as to Clarke or as to Henderson? The case stands upon the same ground on which it would have stood, in this respect, if Henderson had been the sole renter and occupier of the room jointly rented and occupied by himself and Dabney. Each joint tenant had the same right of entry, at pleasure, into the joint room. as he would have had into his several room.

Then, can a man commit burglary by breaking his own house, even by actually breaking it by violence, much less by unlocking the door and entering in the usual way? Can he break it by mere construction of law?

We see nothing in any of the books to warrant the opinion that he can; and it would be contrary to principle, and the very definition of the offence to say that he can. That definition is, "A breaking and entering the mansion house of *another*," &c., not of one's own house. The offence is aimed at the dwelling house of another, which is his castle, and which the law protects both against civil and criminal injuries. Here the offence was aimed, not at the dwelling house of Henderson, that was thrown open to Clarke by the owner or the occupant, but at the trunk of Dabney. It may be said that the joint room was the dwelling house of Dabney as well as of Henderson, and so it was, but that, as before said, can make no difference. Dabney consented to rent a room jointly with Henderson, and thus consented that it should be the dwelling house of Henderson, with all the right of entry possessed by a sole occupant.

The cases of constructive breaking by conspiracy are cases in which one of the conspirators is not the owner of the house, but a servant of the owner, or one having a bare charge and not actual possession thereof; where there is a bare charge, the person having such charge may open the door and enter at pleasure, so long as he is acting in pursuance of such charge, and of the powers and duties which it confers or imposes. But whenever he conspires with another wrongdoer to open the door and let him in to commit a felony, and the opening and entering are accordingly done, both parties are guilty of burglary. There has been in that case a breaking and entering of the mansion house of *another*, in strict pursuance of the definition of the offence. The house is in no sense the house of the servant, who had only a bare charge in regard to it, and the power conferred by that charge ceased to exist when the servant sought to pervert it to the injury of his employer by opening an entrance into his dwelling house to a felon by night. Henderson stood in no relation of a servant to Dabney in regard to the room which they jointly occupied, but had the actual possession and legal right of possession of that room jointly with Dabney. . . .

Judgment reversed.

DAVIS v. COMMONWEALTH

Supreme Court of Appeals of Virginia, 1922.
132 Va. 521, 110 S.E. 356.

KELLY, P., delivered the opinion of the court.

The defendant, Annie Davis, under indictment for burglary was convicted and sentenced to confinement in the penitentiary for a term of five years.

The indictment charged that in the nighttime she broke and entered the dwelling house of one E. P. Fowlkes, and "feloniously and burglariously" stole and carried away therefrom the sum of $412.50 belonging to one Dolly Wingfield.

The case is before us for review, and the sole assignment of error is that the court refused to set aside the verdict as being contrary to the law and the evidence.

It is insisted that the evidence failed to show that the alleged theft was committed in a house owned by E. P. Fowlkes, and also failed to show that the defendant was the thief. As to this contention we express no opinion, because the judgment will have to be reversed and a new trial awarded upon another ground, namely, that there was no "breaking" within the meaning of the familiar definition of burglary.

The evidence tends to show that, as contended by the Commonwealth, the theft was committed in a house owned by Fowlkes, and in a room therein occupied and controlled by Dolly Wingfield, the owner of the stolen money. The testimony of Fowlkes and Dolly Wingfield conclusively shows that the defendant was and long had been their intimate associate and friend, and that with their consent and encouragement she carried a key to the house, was "just the same as at home there," was "over there day and night, and anything she wanted there she came and got it." She was not in any sense a servant or employee of the owners, nor a care keeper or custodian of the property. Her relationship was that of a companion and friend, her right to enter the premises up to the time of the alleged theft being as free and unlimited as that of Dolly Wingfield herself. She came and went at will; she ate and slept there whenever she pleased; and, in short, as expressed by Fowlkes, she was "treated the same as homefolks."

Breaking, as an element of the crime of burglary, may be either actual or constructive. There is a constructive breaking when an entrance has been obtained by threat of violence, by fraud, or by conspiracy. Min.Syn.Cr.Law, page 92; Clarke v. Commonwealth, 25 Grat. (66 Va.) 908, 912. The entrance to the premises in the instant case was not obtained by either of these means, and cannot be classed as a constructive breaking.

Actual breaking involves the application of some force, slight though it may be, whereby the entrance is effected. Merely pushing open a door, turning the key, lifting the latch, or resort to other slight physical force is sufficient to constitute this element of the crime.[1] See the authorities cited, supra. But a breaking, either actual or constructive, to support a conviction of burglary, must have resulted in an entrance contrary to the will of the occupier of the house. . . .

But in the instant case the right of the defendant to enter the premises as freely and unrestrictedly as either Fowlkes or Dolly Wingfield is undisputed, and it follows that she did not "break" and enter the house, and therefore cannot be convicted of the alleged burglary.

The following language of Judge Moncure, who delivered the opinion of the court in Clarke's Case, supra, may well be applied here:

---

[1]. The pushing open of a screen door held shut only by springs is sufficient for a "breaking". State v. Gendusa, 193 La. 59, 190 So. 332 (1939).

Any "act of force, however slight, by which an obstruction to entrance is removed . . . is sufficient . . . where the entry is unlawful". Byington v. State, 363 P.2d 301, 303 (Okl. Cr.1961).

"We have seen no case, and think there has been none, in which the entry was by the voluntary act and consent of the owner or occupier of the house, which has been held to be burglary. And were we to affirm the judgment in this case, we would establish a doctrine of constructive burglary which would not only be new, but contrary to the well known definition of that offense. While the legislature might make such a change, we think it would be judicial legislation in us to do so. If the question, upon principle, were more doubtful than it is, we would be inclined *in favorem vitae*, not to apply the doctrine of constructive burglary to this new case. The offense of burglary may be punished with death."

It is only fair and proper to say that the point upon which we are reversing the judgment does not seem to have been raised in the lower court. The point is one, however, which goes to the substance of the Commonwealth's case, and the failure to raise it at an earlier stage does not deprive the accused of the right to take advantage of it here.

Reversed.

STOWELL v. PEOPLE

Supreme Court of Colorado, en Banc, 1939.
104 Colo. 255, 90 P.2d 520.

BURKE, JUSTICE. . . . Defendant was a freight conductor employed by the Rock Island railway. As such he was furnished with a "switch key" which he used in his work. It opened all switches and all depot and freight room doors on his division. There were no regulations governing its use. By means of it he entered the company's freight warehouse at Genoa and had taken therefrom two parcels of the value of $10, when he was arrested. The question here presented was raised by an instruction tendered and refused and by motion for a directed verdict at the close of all the evidence.

Had the switch key not been furnished defendant by the company, nor any authority given him under the terms of his employment to enter the building at the time and place in question, the evidence would have supported a conviction of burglary under the statute. For present purposes we assume, without deciding, that it would also have supported a conviction under this information. From the record it appears that defendant had a right to enter this warehouse at the time and in the manner he did, provided his intent in so doing was lawful. Hence this offense, if burglary, is raised to that grade solely by his unlawful intent. But intent alone is not always sufficient for that purpose. There is "no burglary, if the person entering has a right so to do, although he may intend to commit, and may actually commit, a felony, and although he may enter in such a way that there would be a breaking if he had no right to enter." 9 C.J. sec. 20, p. 1016. Considering the history of the crime of burglary, and its evolution, this rule appears reasonable and necessary. The common law crime was an offense against habitation. Its purpose was to give security to the home when it was presumably least protected. Essential elements thereof were an actual *breaking*, in the *night time*, with intent to commit a *felony*. It has been extended by statute in most states to entry in any way, into any kind of building, at any time, for any unlawful purpose. Under the rule of strict construction of statutes in derogation of the common law courts must necessarily be careful not to extend such acts beyond the clear intent of the Legislature. For instance, among the buildings enumerated in our statute are "schoolhouses". Hence, but for the rule above stated, a school teacher, using the key furnished her by the district to re-open the schoolhouse door immediately after locking it in the evening, for the purpose of taking (but not finding) a pencil belonging to one of her pupils, could be sent to the penitentiary. . . .

The judgment is accordingly reversed.[1]

PEOPLE v. DUPREE

Supreme Court of Michigan, 1893.
98 Mich. 26, 56 N.W. 1046.

GRANT, J. The respondent was convicted of burglary under section 9132, How.St. The evidence on the part of the people tended to show that the owner of the dwelling house occupied the front room for a shoe shop, and the rear and overhead part as a dwelling. The shop was upon the ground floor, and had two windows, each about four feet from the ground. These windows had double sash; were without pulley weights; were fastened when raised, and bolted when down, by stops operated by springs. When the windows were closed, the springs threw the bolts into the slots in the cases, so that the window could not be raised without drawing the bolt. One of these windows was opened during the night of October 8th, and three pairs of shoes were stolen. The owner closed the shades on the night of the 6th, and did not notice that the window was raised even an eighth of an inch. On the morning of the 9th, on opening his shop, he found the window raised about 1½ feet. The respondent called at the house on October 6th, between noon and 2 P.M., and asked for dinner. He asked permission to step into the shoe shop for the purpose of changing his pantaloons. This request was granted. The window was

---

1. Cf. State v. Corcoran, 82 Wash. 44, 143 P. 453 (1914). The California statute reads: "Every person who enters any house . . . store . . . or other building . . . with intent to commit grand or petit larceny or any felony is guilty of burglary". West's Ann.Cal.Penal Code, § 459. Under this statute, which does not require a breaking, it was held that an entry into a store with intent to steal constituted burglary although it was during business hours when the store was open to the public. People v. Brittain, 142 Cal. 8, 75 P. 314 (1904); People v. Wilson, 160 Cal.App.2d 606, 325 P.2d 106 (1958).

not broken. If the bolt was in the slot, the window could have been raised from the inside only. On Monday following the burglary, respondent had in his possession, and offered for sale, a pair of shoes alleged to have been taken upon the night of October 8th. On the following Wednesday, he sold a pair of shoes which were identified as one of the three pairs stolen on October 8th. The complaining witness testified that he believed that the window was unfastened and raised on October 6th from the inside, and something placed under the sash so as to keep the bolt from entering the slot. The owner left the shop about the time it was necessary to light the lamps to see, and did not return to it till the next morning. No testimony was introduced on the part of the respondent. His counsel moved the court to discharge the respondent for the reason that the crime was not established against him. This the court refused.

It is contended on behalf of the respondent (1) that no breaking or entering in the nighttime was established; (2) that this shop was not a part of the dwelling house; (3) that if the window was partially raised on October 6th, and was further raised on the night of the 8th, the crime was not established. We think the motion was properly overruled, and the case properly submitted to the jury. . . .

3. The theory of the prosecution was that the respondent, when in the shop, either on the 6th or 7th of October, (the court, in its charge, referred to the date as Friday, October 7th,) raised the window just enough to prevent the bolt from entering the slot, and there was evidence to sustain it. It is insisted that even if this was so, and the respondent raised the window on the following night, it did not establish the crime of burglary. We cannot agree with this contention. It is said in Dennis v. People, 27 Mich. 151: "If an entry is effected by raising a trapdoor which is kept down merely by its own weight, or by raising a window kept in its place only by pulley weight, instead of its own, or by descending an open chimney, it is admitted to be enough to support the charge of breaking; and I am unable to see any substantial distinction between such cases and one where an entry is effected through a hanging window over a shop door, and which is only designed for light above, and for ventilation, and is down, and kept down by its own weight, and so firmly as to be opened only by the use of some force, and so situated as to make a ladder, or something of the kind, necessary to reach it for the purpose of passing through it." We think the doctrine there enunciated covers the present case. If there had been no bolt, and respondent had raised the window and entered in the nighttime, under all the authorities, he would have been guilty of burglary. Upon what reason can it be said that his removal of the bolt, or his raising the window a fraction of an inch, in the daytime, changes the character of his offense? If the owner had failed to see that the bolts were in place, or if something had been accidentally placed upon the window sill, which was

of slight thickness, but sufficient to prevent the bolts from entering the slots, the raising of the window would have been sufficient breaking to support the charge. How can the act be relieved of criminality by secretly fixing the window in the daytime so that the bolt or lock will not be effective, and thus render the perpetration of the crime more easy and certain? There is no reason in such a rule. In Lyons v. People, the door was left unlocked, and the court was requested to instruct the jury that, in order to constitute the crime, it must appear that the door was secured in the ordinary way. The supreme court, in determining the question, said: "We are not aware of any authority which goes to the extent of these instructions. To hold that the carelessness of the owner in securing and guarding his property shall be a justification to the burglar or thief would leave communities very much to the mercy of this class of felons. It would in effect be a premium offered for their depredations, by the removal of the apprehension of punishment. Whether property is guarded or not, it is larceny in the thief who steals it. When a door is closed, it is burglary for any one, with a felonious intent, to open it, and enter the house, in the nighttime, without the owner's consent; and it makes no difference how many bolts and bars might have been used to secure it, but which were neglected." The language of the court was perhaps too broad, in stating that if the window was raised any distance, but was not sufficient to permit the defendant to enter, and he raised it further, it would be breaking, in the meaning of the law;[1] but the entire evidence was to the effect that it was raised so little as not to attract the notice of the occupant. We therefore think that the jury could not have been misled by the language. . . .

Conviction affirmed. The other justices concurred.

NICHOLLS v. STATE

Supreme Court of Wisconsin, 1887.
68 Wis. 416, 32 N.W. 543.

CASSODAY, J. There is undisputed testimony on the part of the state to the effect that Saturday, July 25, 1885, the plaintiff in error was stopping at a hotel in Black River Falls, having his name registered as W. H. Eldredge, and a room assigned him opposite thereto. He had then been there about three days. In the afternoon of the day named he had a box or chest taken from the depot to his room, weighing about 150 pounds. No evidence was given as to what was in it. About three o'clock in the afternoon of the same day he arranged with the local express agent for the sending of a box to Chi-

---

[1] Accord: People v. White, 153 Mich. 617, 117 N.W. 161 (1908); State v. Rosencrans, 24 Wash.2d 775, 167 P.2d 170 (1946). Contra: Rose v. Commonwealth, 40 S.W. 245, 19 Ky.L.Rep. 272 (1897); Commonwealth v. Strupney, 105 Mass. 588 (1870).

cago, then at the hotel, and represented by him as weighing about 225 pounds. By his prearrangement, the box was brought to the depot just in time for the 7:50 P.M. Chicago train, and was shipped in the express car thereon by the local agent, as directed. Soon after the starting of the train, there seems to have been a suspicion as to the contents of the box. This suspicion was increased as telegrams were received at different stations from Black River Falls respecting the box. Finally, being convinced by such dispatches that there was a man in the box, the train-men telegraphed forward to Elroy to secure the presence of an officer on the approach of the train to make the arrest. On reaching Elroy, in the night, this box in the express car was opened, and the plaintiff in error was found therein, with a revolver, billy, razor, knife, rope, gimlet, and a bottle of chloroform. There was also evidence tending to show that there were packages of money in the custody of the express agent on the car; that such agent had an assistant as far as Elroy; that from there to Chicago such car was usually in charge of only one man; that after the arrest, and when asked his object in being thus shipped in the box, the prisoner voluntarily admitted, in effect, that he had considered his chances carefully; that he went into the thing as a matter of speculation; that he needed money, and needed it quickly; that he expected to get fully $50,000; that had he passed out of Elroy he would have got off with the money; that, in a case of that kind, if a human life stood in his way, it did not amount to a snap of the finger. . . .

2. The question recurs whether the proofs show that there was a breaking in fact, within the meaning of the statute. Certainly not in the sense of picking a lock, or opening it with a key, or lifting a latch, or severing or mutilating the door, or doing violence to any portion of the car. On the contrary, the box was placed in the express car with the knowledge, and even by the assistance, of those in charge of the car. But it was not a passenger car, and the plaintiff in error was in no sense a passenger. The railroad company was a common carrier of passengers as well as freight. But the express company was exclusively a common carrier of freight, that is to say, goods, wares and merchandise. As such carrier, it may have at times transported animals, birds, etc., but it may be safely assumed that it never knowingly undertook to transport men in packages or boxes for special delivery. True, the plaintiff in error contracted with the local express agent for the carriage and delivery of such box, but neither he nor any one connected with the express car or the train had any knowledge or expectation of a man being concealed within it. On the contrary, they each and all had the right to assume that the box contained nothing but inanimate substance,—goods, wares, or merchandise of some description. The plaintiff in error knew that he had no right to enter the express car at all without the consent of those in charge. The evidence was sufficient to justify the

Sec. 1 BURGLARY 105

conclusion that he unlawfully gained an entrance without the knowledge or consent of those in charge of the car, by false pretenses, fraud, gross imposition, and circumvention, with intent to commit the crime of robbery or larceny, and, in doing so, if necessary, the crime of murder. This would seem to have been sufficient to constitute a constructive breaking at common law, as defined by Blackstone, thus: "To come down a chimney is held a burglarious entry; for that is as much closed as the nature of things will permit. So, also, to knock at the door, and, upon opening it, to rush in with a felonious intent; or, under pretense of taking lodgings, to fall upon the landlord and rob him; or to procure a constable to gain admittance in order to search for traitors, and then to bind the constable and rob the house. All these entries have been adjudged burglarious, though there was no actual breaking, for the law will not suffer itself to be trifled with by such evasions, especially under the cloak of legal process. And so, if a servant opens and enters his master's chamber door with a felonious design; or if any other person, lodging in the same house or in a public inn, opens and enters another's door with such evil intent, it is burglary. Nay, if the servant conspires with a robber and lets him into the house by night, this is burglary in both; for the servant is doing an unlawful act, and the opportunity afforded him of doing it with greater ease rather aggravates than extenuates the guilt." 4 Bl.Comm. 226, 227.

So it has frequently been held in this country that, "to obtain admission to a dwelling-house at night, with the intent to commit a felony, by means of artifice or fraud or upon a pretense of business or social intercourse, is a constructive breaking, and will sustain an indictment charging a burglary by breaking and entering." The same was held in Ohio under a statute against "forcible" breaking and entering. But it is claimed that in this state the common-law doctrine of constructive breaking has no application to a case of this kind, and in fact is superseded by statute, except in so far as it is re-affirmed. Thus: "*Any unlawful entry of* a dwelling-house or other building with intent to commit a felony, shall *be deemed* a breaking and entering of such dwelling-house or other building, within the meaning of the last four sections." Sec. 4411, R.S. This section merely establishes a rule of evidence whereby the scope of constructive breaking is enlarged so as to take in "*any* unlawful entry of a dwelling-house or other building with intent to commit a felony." It in no way narrows the scope of constructive breaking, as understood at common law, but merely enlarges it in the particulars named. In all other respects such constructive breaking signifies the same as at common law. It necessarily follows that as the word "break," used in sec. 4410, had obtained a fixed and definite meaning at common law when applied to a dwelling-house proper or other buildings within the curtilage, the legislature must be presumed to have used it in the same sense when therein applied to other statutory breakings. That is to say, they must be deemed to have used the word as understood at common law in relation to the same or a like subject matter. We must hold the evidence sufficient to support the charge of breaking. . . .

By the Court. The judgment of the circuit court is affirmed.[1]

DANIELS v. STATE

Supreme Court of Georgia, 1886.
78 Ga. 98.

HALL, JUSTICE. 1. The indictment charges the defendant with breaking and entering the depot building of the Western and Atlantic Railroad Company, where valuable goods were contained, with intent to steal, etc. The proof showed that the outer door was left open, but that after getting into the building, which had numerous apartments, the doors to each of these, in which the postage stamps belonging to the company were deposited, were broken and entered and they were stolen and carried away by the defendant. It is now insisted that neither the charge in the indictment nor the facts in proof made out the offence of burglary against the defendant; that in order to fix legal guilt upon him, it should have been alleged and proved that he effected his entrance by breaking the door through which he got into the house, and not by showing that, after entering it, he broke either of the doors of the departments in it, where the valuables in question were found. Such, however, is not our apprehension of the law. It is well-settled, by a number of cases, that where a party is indicted for breaking and entering an out-house within the curtilage or protection of a mansion or dwelling, the burglary should be laid as having been done in the dwelling-house. 1 Wharton's Cr.L. § 815, and citations. If this be true as to an out-house within the protection of the mansion or dwelling-house, *a fortiori* would it be so as to an apartment in the house, a party's place of business in which his goods, wares, etc., were stored or contained, and which was broken and entered with an intent to commit a larceny upon the articles of value therein contained. This indictment does not allege in terms that the depot was the place of business of the railroad company, but no specific objection was taken to it on this account, and had there been one, we are not prepared to hold that it was tenable, as the offence, though not charged in the terms and language of the code, is so plainly set forth that its nature could be easily understood by the jury. It is always best, however, to avoid cavil or dispute, to conform

---

[1] Compare State v. Pierce, 14 Utah 2d 177, 380 P.2d 725 (1963).

to the very words of the statute on which the accusation is based. On this point, there was no error in the instruction given by the court.

. . .

Judgment affirmed.[1]

REX v. DAVIS

Court for Crown Cases Reserved, 1823.
Russ. & Ry. 499, 168 Eng.Rep. 917.

The prisoner was tried at the Old Bailey sessions, in January, 1823, before the Chief Baron Richards, for burglary, in the dwelling-house of Montague Levyson.

The prosecutor Levyson, who dealt in watches and some jewellery, stated, that on the 2d of January, about six o'clock in the evening, as he was standing in Pall Mall opposite his shop, he watched the prisoner, a little boy, standing by the window of the shop which was part of the prosecutor's dwelling-house, and presently observed the prisoner push his finger against a pane of the glass in the corner of the window. The glass fell inside by the force of his finger. The prosecutor added, that, standing as he did in the street, he saw the forepart of the prisoner's finger on the shop side of the glass, and he instantly apprehended him.

The jury convicted the prisoner; but the learned judge having some doubt whether this was an entry sufficient to make the offence a burglary, submitted the case to the consideration of the judges.

In Hilary term, 1823, the case was taken into consideration by the judges; who held, that there was a sufficient entry to constitute burglary.

WALKER v. STATE

Supreme Court of Alabama, 1879.
63 Ala. 49.

BRICKELL, C. J. The statute (Code of 1876, § 4343) provides, that "any person, who, either in the night or day time, with intent to steal, or to commit a felony, breaks into and enters a dwelling-house, or any building, structure or inclosure within the curtilage of a dwelling-house, though not forming a part thereof, or into any shop, store, warehouse, or other building, structure or inclosure in which any goods, merchandise, or other valuable thing is kept for use, sale, or deposit, *provided* such structure, other than a shop, store, ware-house

---

[1] Although the English common law required a "breaking into" the building, a prohibited entry followed by a breaking out is sufficient under the Kentucky statute. Lawson v. Commonwealth, 160 Ky. 180, 169 S.W. 587 (1914).

or building, is specially constructed or made to keep such goods, merchandise, or other valuable thing, is guilty of burglary," &c.

The defendant was indicted for breaking into and entering "a corncrib of Noadiah Woodruff and Robert R. Peeples, a building in which corn, a thing of value, was at the time kept for use, sale, or deposit, with intent to steal," &c. He was convicted; and the case is now presented on exceptions taken to instructions given, and the refusal of instructions requested, as to what facts will constitute a breaking into and entry, material constituents of the offense charged in the indictment. The facts, on which the instructions were founded, are: that in the crib was a quantity of shelled corn, piled on the floor; in April, or May, 1878, the crib had been broken into, and corn taken therefrom, without the consent of the owners, who had the crib watched; and thereafter the defendant was caught under it, and, on coming out, voluntarily confessed that, about three weeks before, he had taken a large auger, and, going under the crib, had bored a hole through the floor, from which the corn, being shelled, ran into a sack he held under it; that he then got about three pecks of corn, and with a cob closed the hole. On these facts, the City Court was of opinion, and so instructed the jury, that there was such a breaking and entry of the crib, as would constitute the offense, and refused instructions requested asserting the converse of the proposition. . . .

The boring the hole through the floor of the crib, was a sufficient breaking; but with it there must have been an entry. Proof of a breaking, though it may be with an intent to steal, or the intent to commit a felony, is proof of one only of the facts making up the offense, and is as insufficient as proof of an entry through an open door, without breaking. If the hand, or any part of the body, is intruded within the house, the entry is complete. The entry may also be completed by the intrusion of a tool, or instrument, within the house, though no part of the body be introduced. Thus, "if A. breaks the house of B. in the night time, with intent to steal goods, and breaks the window, and puts his hand, or puts in a hook, or other engine, to reach out goods; or puts a pistol in at the window, with an intent to kill, though his hand be not within the window, this is burglary."— 1 Hale, 555. When no part of the body is introduced—when the only entry is of a tool, or instrument, introduced by the force and agency of the party accused, the inquiry is, whether the tool or instrument was employed solely for the purpose of *breaking*, and thereby effecting an *entry*; or whether it was employed not only to *break and enter*, but also to aid in the consummation of the criminal intent, and its capacity to aid in such consummation. Until there is a *breaking* and *entry*, the offense is not consummated. The offense rests largely in intention; and though there may be sufficient evidence of an attempt to commit it, which, of itself, is a crime, the attempt may be abandoned—of it there may be repentance, before the consummation of the offense intended. The *breaking* may be at one time, and the *entry* at another. The *breaking* may be complete, and yet an *entry* never effected. From whatever cause an *entry* is not effected, burglary has not been committed. When one instrument is employed to *break*, and is without capacity to aid otherwise than by opening a way of *entry*, and another instrument must be used, or the instrument used in the breaking must be used in some other way or manner to consummate the criminal intent, the intrusion of the instrument is not, of itself, an *entry*. But when, as in this case, the instrument is employed, not only to *break*, but to effect the only *entry* contemplated, and necessary to the consummation of the criminal intent; when it is intruded within the house, *breaking* it, effecting an *entry*, enabling the person introducing it to consummate his intent, the offense is complete. The instrument was employed, not only for the purpose of *breaking* the house, but to effect the larceny intended. When it was intruded into the crib, the burglar acquired dominion over the corn intended to be stolen. Such dominion did not require any other act on his part. When the auger was withdrawn from the aperture made with it, the corn ran into the sack he used in its asportation. There was a *breaking* and *entry*, enabling him to effect his criminal intent, without the use of any other means, and this satisfies the requirements of the law.

Let the judgment be affirmed.[1]

GRAY v. STATE

Supreme Court of Wisconsin, 1943.
243 Wis. 57, 9 N.W.2d 68.

MARTIN, J. The dwelling of Edmund Feldner, located on Highway 38, about three fourths of a mile west of the village of Rosendale in the town of Fond du Lac, Fond du Lac county, Wisconsin, was burglarized on the night of June 19, 1941. Mr. Feldner and members of his family retired at about 8:30 p. m. When he retired his overalls and two suits of clothing were hanging on a hook in his bedroom. His winter overcoat was in a room next to his bedroom. When Mr. Feldner arose at 5:30 a. m. the following morning he noticed that his overalls, his two suits, and overcoat were missing and that some of the rooms of his residence had been ransacked. He found his overalls and the vest and coat of one suit lying outside. One suit, the overcoat, and trousers of the other suit were missing.

At about 1 a. m., on June 20, 1941, George Habeck, a truck driver, left the city of Fond du Lac for Ripon and Berlin via Highway 38. When he reached a point on said highway about three fourths of a

---

[1] Boring a hole through the door, near the bolt, is not an entry in the law of burglary even if the point of the bit penetrates into the interior of the building. The King v. Hughes, 1 Leach 406, 168 Eng.Rep. 305 (1785).

mile west of Rosendale, in the immediate vicinity of the Feldner residence, he saw three Negroes, whom he later identified as the defendants, with their car parked alongside the road. Defendants followed Habeck to Ripon. At Ripon they inquired of Habeck as to the direction to Fond du Lac. He gave them the proper direction, whereupon defendants left but did not go in the direction which had been given them. The facts here related took place between 1 and 2:30 a. m. on June 20th. . . .

To the information charging burglary of a dwelling in the nighttime with intent to commit larceny, defendants entered a plea of not guilty. The jury found defendants guilty in the manner and form as charged in the information. Defendants contend that the evidence did not establish beyond a reasonable doubt that the Feldner dwelling was burglarized in the nighttime. Sec. 352.32, Stats., defines the term "nighttime" as follows:

"The term 'nighttime,' when used in any statute, ordinance, indictment or information shall be construed to mean the time between one hour after the setting of the sun on one day and one hour before the rising of the same on the following day; and the time of sunset and sunrise shall be ascertained according to the mean solar time of the ninetieth meridian west from Greenwich, commonly known as central time, as given in any published almanac."

Sunset on the evening of June 19th was at 7:39 p. m., and sunrise on the morning of June 20th was at 4:23 a. m. Thus, nighttime, within the meaning of the statute, on the night in question, was from 8:39 p. m., June 19th, to 3:23 a. m., June 20th. Defendants argue that since Feldner testified that he retired about 8:30 p. m. on June 19th, and that he arose at about 5:30 a. m. the following morning, his dwelling may have been burglarized either in the daytime or in the nighttime, and that therefore the state failed to establish that the crime had been committed in the nighttime as alleged in the information. It is definitely established that the crime was committed sometime between 8:30 p. m., June 19th, and 5:30 a. m., June 20th. The witness Habeck testified that he left the city of Fond du Lac at about 1 a. m. on June 20th. Rosendale is about eleven miles west of the city of Fond du Lac. According to Habeck's testimony, he would, with normal driving, have arrived at the place where he saw the three defendants and their parked car in the immediate vicinity of the Feldner residence at about 1:30 a. m. The circumstance of defendants having been seen in the immediate vicinity of the burglarized residence at the time fixed by Habeck, well warranted the jury in concluding that the burglary had been committed in the nighttime. See Simon v. State, 125 Wis. 439, 103 N.W. 1100; Winsky v. State, 126 Wis. 99, 102, 105 N.W. 480. In the latter case, referring to State v. Bancroft, 10 N.H. 105, it is said:

"There was no direct proof that the burglary was committed in the nighttime, other than the fact that the property was in the house after dark and was missing the next morning when the witness arose; and the court said that this evidence 'led very strongly to the conclusion that it was taken in the course of the night, although the precise hour when the witness called it dark did not appear, and the time when she arose in the morning was not stated. At whatever time in the morning the loss was discovered, the jury might well weigh the probability whether the article would have been taken from the house in the daytime, in connection with the other evidence. It was sufficient that, upon the whole case, they had no reasonable doubt that the act was done in the nighttime.' Sufficient appears from the evidence in the case before us to warrant the jury in finding that the entry was made in the nighttime. Simon v. State, supra."

. . .

By the Court—Judgment affirmed.[1]

PEOPLE v. ROBLES

District Court of Appeal, Fifth District, California, 1962.
207 Cal.App.2d 891, 24 Cal.Rptr. 708.

STONE, JUSTICE. Appellant and his co-defendant, Rocha, were charged in a three-count indictment with: Count I, violation of section 261, subd. 4 of the Penal Code, rape by means of force and fear; Count II, violation of section 459 of the Penal Code, burglary by entering a dwelling house with intent to commit rape; Count III, violation of section 207 of the Penal Code, kidnaping. A jury found defendant guilty of the burglary, Count II, but failed to reach a verdict as to Count I, rape by force and violence. They acquitted defendant of Count III, kidnaping. Subsequently the court, upon motion of the District Attorney, dismissed Count I "in the interests of justice," and appellant was sentenced to the state prison pursuant to the judgment of convicion of burglary, first degree. Appellant has appealed from the judgment of conviction. . . .

The greater part of appellant's brief is predicated upon a misconception of the law. Appellant asserts that he could not be convicted of burglary charging him with wilfully and unlawfully entering a dwelling house with intent to commit rape, because the jury was unable to agree as to Count I, charging him with rape. He emphasizes that Count I, the charge of rape, was dismissed by the court. Appellant states in his brief, "To constitute burglary, the charge of rape (count I) had to be proven first." Thus appellant argues that the intent to commit rape was not proved because the rape itself was not

---

[1]. Where the uncontradicted evidence showed that if D committed the burglary he did so at night it was proper to instruct the jury that they must either find the defendant not guilty or guilty of the offense charged. There was no need to instruct the jury in regard to the lesser included offense of burglary in the daytime. People v. White, 218 Cal.App.2d 267, 32 Cal.Rptr. 322 (1963).

proved. However, the gist of the offense of burglary is defendant's intent to commit a felony *at the time he enters the building*. Section 459 of the Penal Code, in pertinent part, provides:

"Every person who enters any house . . . with intent to commit grand or petit larceny or any felony is guilty of burglary." [1]

Proof of intent at the time of entry does not depend upon the subsequent commission of the felony or even an attempt to commit it. This is borne out by People v. Guarino, 132 Cal.App.2d 554, at page 559, 282 P.2d 538, at page 541, where it is said:

"The crime of burglary is complete on the entering of the building with intent to commit a felony, though the intended felony be not committed."

In the case of People v. Murphy, 173 Cal.App.2d 367, 373, 343 P.2d 273, 277, the court, in affirming a conviction of burglary predicated upon an entry with intent to commit theft, used the following language:

". . . it is unnecessary to prove a theft under an accusation of burglary. The statute requires evidence only that the entry be effected with the intent to steal or to commit any felony."

Thus appellant's contention that the failure of the jury to find him guilty of Count I, the charge of rape, negatives his conviction of burglary, that is, entering the dwelling of Mrs. Moreno with intent to commit rape, is based upon an erroneous concept of the law of burglary. . . .

The judgment is affirmed.

CONLEY, P. J., and BROWN, J., concur.

PEOPLE v. WRIGHT

District Court of Appeal, Second District
Division 2, California, 1962.
206 Cal.App.2d 184, 23 Cal.Rptr. 734.

[Appellant was informed against for burglarizing a building occupied by a named individual. The evidence established that he broke into that building, not to commit any offense therein, but merely to gain access to another place wherein he intended to commit larceny. It was assumed that the second place was not a building within the meaning of the burglary statute. For that reason the information had been amended by striking out the word "therein". Appellant claims

---

[1]. To convict under the habitual criminal act, prior convictions of burglary in another jurisdiction may be shown if the misdeed would have constituted burglary if committed here. But the mere proof of a burglary conviction in Oklahoma, without more, is not sufficient because an intent to commit any misdemeanor is sufficient for the burglarious intent there while in California petty larceny is the only misdemeanor included in such category. People v. Stanphill, 166 Cal.App.2d 467, 333 P.2d 270 (1958).

that the information, without the stricken word, does not state an offense, and that the evidence does not support a conviction of burglary.]

ASHBURN, JUSTICE. The questions whether the information as amended states an offense and whether the evidence supports the conviction may be answered together. Counsel have proceeded upon the assumption that the "shed" is not a structure that may be burglarized under § 459 of the Penal Code. That section reads: "Every person who enters any house [and numerous other structures and enclosures], with intent to commit grand or petit larceny or any felony is guilty of burglary." The statute does not require that the larceny or felony take place "therein." It is appellant's contention that that word should be read into the statute, otherwise absurd results would obtain from a literal reading. Examples are set forth: One wishes to steal an object from an unlocked automobile (which must be locked under § 459) and toward that end enters a hardware store to buy rubber gloves and a screw driver; one passes through a building to steal an object on the other side. Appellant contends that unless the word "therein" is read into the statute, the crime of burglary will have been committed in those instances. The People argue that it is sufficient to show that the accused intended to commit a theft or other felony in a nearby place and that he entered the building for the purpose of gaining access to that place; or phrased differently, there need be only a direct causal connection between the entry and the theft or felony.

The question has not arisen frequently. Professor Perkins, in his treatise on Criminal Law, has this to say: "Some definitions of burglary, after listing the elements mentioned above, add with intent and so forth 'therein.' This wording emphasizes the necessary causal relation between the burglarious intent and the forced entrance, but seems to inject an unnecessary limitation. While it would not be burglary to break into another's dwelling at night merely to rest in preparation for a felony to be perpetrated elsewhere, it would be burglary, if the purpose was to use the building as a place of concealment from which to shoot an enemy as he passed by on the street, although under well-recognized rules the situs of such a murder would be in the street at the point where the bullet hit the victim, and not the place inside the house from which the shot was fired." (Perkins, Criminal Law, 168 (1957).)

In People v. Shields, 70 Cal.App.2d 628, 161 P.2d 475, the court dealt with the problem presented at bar. Defendant entered a building with a small child, went to the roof, and there violated § 288 of the Penal Code.[1] There was no evidence that he intended at any time to commit the crime within the building. Although the opinion did not analyze the problem presented, it concluded that the evidence never-

---

[1] Lewd or lascivious acts with children—a felony under the statute.

theless supported the verdict of burglary. 70 Cal.App.2d Page 637, 161 P.2d Page 479: "Counsel argues that, 'The assault, if any was committed, occurred on the roof of the apartment house. . . . The house or building within the meaning of the burglary statute must be a structure with walls on all sides and covered by a roof. People v. Stickman (1867), 34 Cal. 242. Therefore, an assault committed upon a roof would not be an assault while in the commission of a burglary, a roof not being covered by a roof and bounded by four walls.' *A sufficient answer to this argument lies in the statute itself.* The Bellevue Apartments is a building. Moreover, it has walls on all sides and is covered by a roof. Appellant entered it. Did he at that time have the intent to commit a felony? From the fact that the jury found him guilty of violating section 288 of the Penal Code it is apparent that they also found that he had the intent to commit that crime when he entered the building." (Emphasis added.) This decision appears to be sound and the Supreme Court denied a hearing. Here we have an unlawful entry of a structure within the statute, made for the purpose of gaining access to an adjacent place in order to commit larceny at the second location. These acts appear to be within the legislative meaning of § 459. . . .

We consider the true rule to be that within the purview of § 459, Penal Code, the intent to commit larceny or any felony is not confined to an intent to commit the crime in the building which is entered if the intent at the time of entry is to commit the offense in the immediate vicinity of the place entered by defendant; if the entry is made as a means of facilitating the commission of the theft or felony; and if the two places are so closely connected that intent and consummation of the crime would constitute a single and practically continuous transaction. Here the entry was made in a building to which the entire shed was physically attached and with intent to steal immediately the tires in the vicinity of the place of entry. That is enough to constitute burglary. . . .[2]

The judgment and order denying new trial are affirmed.

Fox, P. J., and Herndon, J., concur.

UNITED STATES v. BRANDENBURG

United States Court of Appeals, Third Circuit, 1944.
144 F.2d 656.

[In North Carolina Pitts broke into a storehouse and attempted to blow open a safe with dynamite. This constituted the statutory offense of burglary by explosives. To avoid prosecution he left the

---

2. Where the entrance was through an open outside door, a breaking into an inside room in furtherance of a design to commit a felony in the house was sufficient even if the felony was to be committed in another room. Rolland v. Commonwealth, 85 Pa. 66 (1877).

state, and because of information he had received in prison, went to New Jersey to have his appearance altered and his fingerprints removed by Dr. Brandenburg, explaining why it was important. This was accomplished by reducing the area of a large scar and removing most of the fingerprints. It resulted in a conviction of misprision of felony [1]—the felony charged being a violation of the Federal Fugitive Felon Act [2] by Pitts.]

BIGGS, CIRCUIT JUDGE. . . .

The purpose of the Fugitive Felon Act was stated by Congressman Sumners, Chairman of the Committee on the Judiciary of the House of Representatives, quoting the comments of the Attorney General of the United States on the bill as follows: "One of the most difficult problems which local law-enforcement agencies have to deal

---

[Numbered footnotes by the court.]

1. Section 146 of the Criminal Code, R. S. § 5390, 18 U.S.C.A. § 251, creating the federal offense of misprision of felony, provides:

"Whoever, having knowledge of the actual commission of the crime of murder or other felony cognizable by the courts of the United States, conceals and does not as soon as may be disclose and make known the same to some one of the judges or other persons in civil or military authority under the United States, shall be fined not more than $500, or imprisoned not more than three years, or both."

2. The Act of May 18, 1934, c. 302, 48 Stat. 782, 18 U.S.C.A. § 408e, commonly known as the Fugitive Felon Act, provides:

"It shall be unlawful for any person to move or travel in interstate or foreign commerce from any State . . . with intent either (1) to avoid prosecution for murder, kidnaping, burglary, robbery, mayhem, rape, assault with a dangerous weapon, or extortion accompanied by threats of violence, or attempt to commit any of the foregoing, under the laws of the place from which he flees, or (2) to avoid giving testimony in any criminal proceedings in such place in which the commission of a felony is charged. Any person who violates the provision of this section shall, upon conviction thereof, be punished by a fine of not more than $5,000 or by imprisonment for not longer than five years, or by both such fine and imprisonment. Violations of this section may be prosecuted only in the Federal judicial district in which the original crime was alleged to have been committed."

Section 335 of the Criminal Code, 18 U. S.C.A. § 541 provides: "All offenses which may be punished by death or imprisonment for a term exceeding one year shall be deemed felonies. . . ."

The indictment in the case at bar charges that the defendant, Brandenburg, ". . . well knew that . . . Pitts, on . . . May 16, 1941 . . . had unlawfully . . . travelled . . . in interstate commerce from the State of North Carolina . . . to and into the District of New Jersey, with intent to avoid prosecution by the . . . State of North Carolina for two certain burglaries committed by . . . Pitts . . . in . . . the State of North Carolina [and] did wilfully and unlawfully and feloniously conceal the commission of the aforesaid offense against the United States, and did not as soon as he might have, disclose and make known the same to any of the Judges or any other person in Civil authority of the United States, ..."

[Added by the Compiler.]

The Fugitive Felon Act has since been amended to omit any reference to crimes by name. 18 U.S.C.A. § 1073. The relevant words are "a crime, or an attempt to commit a crime, punishable by death or which is a felony under the laws of the place from which the fugitive flees, or which, in the case of New Jersey, is a high misdemeanor under the laws of said State, ..."

with today is the ease with which criminals are able to flee from the State to avoid prosecution . . .. The above bill is considered the most satisfactory solution of this problem, which the States have never been able to solve effectively. This bill will not prevent the States from obtaining extradition of roving criminals, but the complicated process of extradition has proved to be very inefficient. The ability of Federal officers to follow a criminal from one State to any other State or States, as provided in the above bill, should furnish the desired relief from this class of law evaders. . . ." Report No. 1458 of the House Committee on the Judiciary, to accompany S. 2253, May 3, 1934, 73rd Congress, 2nd Session. The same report shows that the word "burglary" and the other specific offenses named in the Act were substituted for the words "a felony" used in the original bill. The general purpose of the Act was to assist in the enforcement of state laws. Compare Jerome v. United States. 318 U.S. 101, 63 S.Ct. 483, 87 L.Ed. 640.

The appellee takes the position, citing Benson v. McMahon, 127 U.S. 457, 464, 8 S.Ct. 1240, 32 L.Ed. 234, that Congress could not have had the common law offenses in mind when it named specific crimes in the Fugitive Felon Act. The appellant contends to the contrary. This court stated in United States v. Patton, 3 Cir., 120 F.2d 73, 75, "It is . . . well settled that when a federal statute uses a term known to the common law to designate a common law offense and does not define that term, courts called upon to construe it should apply the common law meaning," . . .

Cogent arguments can be made in support of both contentions. We shall discuss some of them. The congressional report from which we have quoted shows that the aim of the Act was to impose penalties on a "class of law evaders," viz., "roving criminals" who would be subject to extradition. But seven States do not denominate the offense of burglary as "burglary." [6] New Jersey is an example. If an offender broke into the dwelling house of another in New Jersey in the nighttime with the intent to commit a felony therein and thereby committed "burglary" as that offense is defined at the common law, he would not be guilty of a crime designated as "burglary" under the law of New Jersey but would be guilty of a "high misdemeanor." If the phrase "under the laws of the place from which he flees" is deemed to modify the word "burglary" instead of the word "prosecution," an offender, who had committed in New Jersey (or

---

6. See: Burglary

Florida Stats. Ann.............. Sec. 810.01
Massachusetts Ann. Laws ch. 266, Sec. 14 New Hampshire Rev. Laws 1942 .... c. 453, Sec. 1
Page's Ohio Gen. Code............... Vol. 10, Sec. 12441
New Jersey Stats. Ann............. Title 2:115-1
Vermont Pub. Laws 1933.......... Sec. 8436
Wisconsin Stats. 1943............ Sec. 343.09

in any of the other six States indicated in footnote 6) acts which would constitute common law burglary, would not be within the purview of the Fugitive Felon Act upon fleeing the State, even though he entered that "class of law evaders" which the congressional report refers to as "roving criminals" subject to extradition. A criminal, therefore, would escape the penalty of the Act simply because he had committed his offense in a State which did not make use of the word "burglary" in its statute. We think that such a result was not intended by Congress. . . .

It is our duty to reconcile the provisions of the Act and to hold the Statute constitutional if its provisions can be construed so as to afford an adequate and certain definition of the crime which it purports to create. We think these ends may be accomplished as follows. We conclude that it was the manifest intention of Congress to cause the Act to have universal application throughout the States since this is the purpose expressed in the congressional report. Restricting ourselves solely to the crime of "burglary" named in the Fugitive Felon Act, we say that there is no State in which acts constituting burglary as defined at common law would not be within the purview of an applicable criminal statute. In other words there is no State in which the offense of breaking into the dwelling house of another in the nighttime with the intent to commit a felony therein would not be a crime cognizable under an appropriate state statute. Each State has created numerous statutory offenses which include such crimes as breaking into a dwelling house, a warehouse, a shop, an office, a freight car, or even a boat with the intent to commit a felony therein. These are variously denominated as burglaries, felonies, or high misdemeanors, and in our opinion were not intended by Congress to fall within the crime of "burglary" named in the Fugitive Felon Act. If we boil the Act down and leave in it only those words which create and define the crime, it will read, "It shall be unlawful for any person to move in interstate commerce with intent to avoid prosecution for burglary under the law of the State from which he flees." The statute thus simplified without rearranging any of its component parts, makes good sense, meets the test which we have imposed and provides that if a person who has committed acts which would constitute the crime of burglary at common law flees from a State to avoid prosecution under the law of that State, he has violated the Fugitive Felon Act. The crime which it creates is defined with sufficient certainty to meet the requirements of the Fifth Amendment. Our conclusion is that the qualifying clause must be deemed to modify the word "prosecution" and that the crime of "burglary" referred to in the Act is burglary as defined at common law.

It is obvious that Pitts fled from North Carolina to escape prosecution for the crimes which he had committed. Section 4232 of the North Carolina Code (Consolidated Statutes of 1939) provides that: "There shall be two degrees in the crime of burglary as defined at the common law. If the crime be committed in a dwelling-house, or in a room used as a sleeping apartment in any building, and any person is in the actual occupation of any part of said dwelling-house or sleeping apartment at the time of the commission of such crime, it shall be burglary in the first degree. If such crime be committed in a dwelling house or sleeping apartment not actually occupied by any one at the time of the commission of the crime, or if it be committed in any house within the curtilage of a dwelling-house or in any building not a dwelling-house, but in which is a room used as a sleeping apartment and not actually occupied as such at the time of the commission of the crime, it shall be burglary in the second degree."

We conclude that Pitts did not commit burglary in either the first or the second degree as defined by Section 4232 of the North Carolina Code. While evidence was offered to show that the store of C. A. Lowe & Sons contained a room in which there was a cot occasionally occupied at night by a member of the firm serving as a guard, it is clear that this cannot be considered to be a sleeping apartment within the terms of the statute. The room was unoccupied on the night of the crime. The Supreme Court of North Carolina has held that the sleeping apartment referred to in the statute must be one in which a person regularly sleeps. State v. Foster, 129 N.C. 704, 40 S.E. 209. The offense which Pitts committed bears little resemblance to the crime of burlary as defined at common law.

What was the crime which Pitts committed? Section 4237(a) of the North Carolina Code (Consolidated Statutes of 1939) provides as follows: "Burglary with explosives.—Any person who, with intent to commit crime, breaks and enters, either by day or by night, any building, whether inhabited or not, and opens or attempts to open any vault, safe, or other secure place by use of nitro-glycerine, dynamite, gunpowder, or by any other explosive, or acetylene torch, shall be deemed guilty of burglary with explosives." It is upon this statute that the United States rests this phase of its case. Was Pitts guilty of burglary with explosives? From his own testimony it is clear that he broke into the warehouse bringing explosives with him with the intent of using them to blow open the safe. By removing the dial on the safe Pitts committed an affirmative act sufficient to demonstrate his intent within the meaning of the statute. There was sufficient evidence from which a jury could have found that Pitts was guilty of burglary with explosives committed in North Carolina. This was his crime.

The crime of "burglary with explosives" was unknown to the common law. It follows that when Pitts fled from North Carolina to avoid prosecution for "burglary with explosives" he did not commit an offense within the purview of the Fugitive Felon Act. From this we must conclude that Brandenburg did not commit the crime of misprision of felony within the purview of Section 146 of the Criminal Code.

The judgment of conviction is reversed.[a]

MODEL PENAL CODE

Article 221. Burglary and Other Criminal Intrusion

Section 221.0. Definitions.

In this Article, unless a different meaning plainly is required:

(1) "occupied structure" means any structure, vehicle or place adapted for overnight accommodation of persons, or for carrying on business therein, whether or not a person is actually present.

(2) "night" means the period between thirty minutes past sunset and thirty minutes before sunrise.

Section 221.1. Burglary.

(1) Burglary Defined. A person is guilty of burglary if he enters a building or occupied structure, or separately secured or occupied portion thereof, with purpose to commit a crime therein, unless the premises are at the time open to the public or the actor is licensed or privileged to enter. It is an affirmative defense to prosecution for burglary that the building or structure was abandoned.

(2) Grading. Burglary is a felony of the second degree if it is perpetrated in the dwelling of another at night, or if, in the course of committing the offense, the actor:

(a) purposely, knowingly or recklessly inflicts or attempts to inflict bodily injury on anyone; or

(b) is armed with explosives or a deadly weapon. Otherwise, burglary is a felony of the third degree. An act shall be deemed "in the course of committing" an offense if it occurs in an attempt to commit the offense or in flight after the attempt or commission.

(3) Multiple Convictions. A person may not be convicted both for burglary and for the offense which it was his purpose to commit after the burglarious entry or for an attempt to commit that offense, unless the additional offense constitutes a felony of the first or second degree.

Section 221.2. Criminal Trespass.

(1) Buildings and Occupied Structures. A person commits an offense if, knowing that he is not licensed or privileged to do so, he enters or surreptitiously remains in any building or occupied structure, or separately secured or occupied portion thereof. An offense under this Subsection is a

---

[a.] In holding that "robbery" in the Hobbs Act, proscribing the interference of interstate commerce by robbery, means common-law robbery, the court said:

"To the same effect see United States v. Turley, 1957, 352 U.S. 407, 77 S.Ct. 397, 1 L.Ed.2d 430. It was there said (352 U.S. at page 411, 77 S.Ct. at page 399):

" 'We recognize that where a federal criminal statute uses a common-law term of established meaning without defining it, the general practice is to give that term its common-law meaning.' " United States v. Nedley, 255 F.2d 350, 357 (3d Cir. 1958).

misdemeanor if it is committed in a dwelling at night. Otherwise it is a petty misdemeanor.

(2) *Defiant Trespasser.* A person commits an offense if, knowing that he is not licensed or privileged to do so, he enters or remains in any place as to which notice against trespass is given by:

    (a) actual communication to the actor; or

    (b) posting in a manner prescribed by law or reasonably likely to come to the attention of intruders; or

    (c) fencing or other enclosure manifestly designed to exclude intruders.

An offense under this Subsection constitutes a petty misdemeanor if the offender defies an order to leave personally communicated to him by the owner of the premises or other authorized person. Otherwise it is a violation.

(3) *Defenses.* It is an affirmative defense to prosecution under this Section that:

    (a) a building or occupied structure involved in an offense under Subsection (1) was abandoned; or

    (b) the premises were at the time open to members of the public and the actor complied with all lawful conditions imposed on access to or remaining in the premises; or

    (c) the actor reasonably believed that the owner of the premises, or other person empowered to license access thereto, would have licensed him to enter or remain.

SECTION 2. ARSON

Common-law arson is the malicious burning of the dwelling house of another.

This crime is usually the result of a deliberate intent and this may anciently have been assumed to be requisite. It has been rather common, for example, to give the definition in this form: Arson is the wilful (or voluntary) and malicious burning of the dwelling house of another. The addition of either word, however, lost all meaning when it became established that an intent to burn might be implied by law when it did not exist in fact. Thus, if without justification, excuse or mitigation, one sets a fire which obviously creates an unreasonable fire hazard for another's dwelling, which is actually burned thereby, the result is common-law arson even if this was not an intended consequence but there was hope that it would not happen. The ancient explanation that an intent to burn is implied under such circumstances is quite outmoded. The true explanation is that the law does not require the burning to be intentional but only that it be malicious, and that such a burning of the dwelling house of another *is malicious*.

Common-law arson was a felony and in point of gravity ranked only a little less than the crime of murder. It was very distinctly not regarded as a mere violation of property rights. The harm done to the habitation was the primary consideration. Every man's house was his "castle" no matter how humble it might be, and the essence of this crime was the violation of the "castle." Hence one might be guilty of arson for burning a building which he himself *owned*, if someone else was the actual dweller therein; but he could not commit this offense (at common law) by burning his own habitation, if he did not also burn the habitation of another, even if another held the title and hence would suffer the financial loss. The terror caused by seeing one's abode in flames, and the grave risk to human life, were also taken into consideration. This was not only a capital crime at common law, but in the reign of Edward the First the execution was by burning.

Arson had four requisites at common law:

1. There must be some actual burning (but the requirement does not include a destruction of the building or of any substantial part of the building).

2. The burning must be malicious.

3. The object burned must be a dwelling house (but as in burglary any out-house "within the curtilage," was regarded as "parcel of the dwelling house").

4. The house burned must be the habitation of another.

An actual burning of some part of the house is essential but it is not necessary that the building should be destroyed. A blackening by smoke or blistering of the paint by heat is not enough. On the other hand, if any of fiber of the wood is actually consumed by fire, this is a *burning* even if it does not actually burst into flame.

A negligent burning of the dwelling of another does not constitute arson. The burning must be malicious. An intentional burning of such a building will be malicious unless there is some justification, excuse or mitigation for the deed. In fact, as mentioned above, an obvious fire hazard may be created under circumstances which will amount to a malicious burning if fire does result, even without an actual intent to cause the particular harm which ensues. One, for example, who set fire to his own dwelling to defraud the insurer was held guilty of arson for the burning of his neighbor's house because he had wantonly and wilfully exposed the other building to this hazard, even though he hoped the fire would not spread to the other building.

Although it is not common-law arson for one to burn his own dwelling if no other is burned by this fire, it is a common-law misdemeanor if the burning is intentional and the house is situated in a city or town, or is beyond those limits but so near to other houses as to create a danger to them. Some statutes on arson have eliminated the requirement that the building be the dwelling "of another," thereby including under this offense the wilful burning of one's own dwelling (for the purpose of collecting insurance or otherwise). Other enactments have expressly prohibited this very type of burning—sometimes without using the label "arson." Burning personal property to defraud the insurer has also been made a statutory crime.

It has also been common for statutes to provide a penalty (under the name of arson or otherwise) for the malicious burning of buildings other than dwellings, such as stores, shops, warehouses and so forth. The term "statutory arson" is employed to designate the entire area of statutory proscription which is analogous to, but not included in, common-law arson.

MODEL PENAL CODE

OFFENSES AGAINST PROPERTY

Article 220. Arson, Criminal Mischief and other Property Destruction
Section 220.1. Arson and Related Offenses.

(1) Arson. A person is guilty of arson, a felony of the second degree, if he starts a fire or causes an explosion with the purpose of:

(a) destroying a building or occupied structure of another; or

(b) destroying or damaging any property, whether his own or another's, to collect insurance for such loss. It shall be an affirmative defense to prosecution under this paragraph that the actor's conduct did not recklessly endanger any building or occupied structure of another or place any other person in danger of death or bodily injury.

(2) Reckless Burning or Exploding. A person commits a felony of the third degree if he purposely starts a fire or causes an explosion, whether on his own property or another's, and thereby recklessly:

(a) places another person in danger of death or bodily injury; or

(b) places a building or occupied structure of another in danger of damage or destruction.

(3) Failure to Control or Report Dangerous Fire. A person who knows that a fire is endangering life or a substantial amount of property of another and fails to take reasonable measures to put out or control the fire, when he can do so without substantial risk to himself, or to give a prompt fire alarm, commits a misdemeanor if:

(a) he knows that he is under an official, contractual, or other legal duty to prevent or combat the fire; or

(b) the fire was started, albeit lawfully, by him or with his assent, or on property in his custody or control.

(4) Definitions. "Occupied structure" means any structure, vehicle, or place adapted for overnight accommodation of persons or for carrying on business therein, whether or not a person is actually present. Property is that of another, for the purposes of this section, if anyone other than the actor has a possessory or proprietary interest therein. If a building or struc-

ture is divided into separately occupied units, any unit not occupied by the actor is an occupied structure of another.

Section 220.2. Causing or Risking Catastrophe.

(1) Causing Catastrophe. A person who causes a catastrophe by explosion, fire, flood, avalanche, collapse of building, release of poison gas, radioactive material or other harmful or destructive force or substance, or by any other means of causing potentially widespread injury or damage, commits a felony of the second degree if he does so purposely or knowingly, or a felony of the third degree if he does so recklessly.

(2) Risking Catastrophe. A person is guilty of a misdemeanor if he recklessly creates a risk of catastrophe in the employment of fire, explosives or other dangerous means listed in Subsection (1).

(3) Failure to Prevent Catastrophe. A person who knowingly or recklessly fails to take reasonable measures to prevent or mitigate a catastrophe commits a misdemeanor if:

(a) he knows that he is under an official, contractual or other legal duty to take such measures; or

(b) he did or assented to the act causing or threatening the catastrophe.

Section 220.3. Criminal Mischief.

(1) Offense Defined. A person is guilty of criminal mischief if he:

(a) damages tangible property of another purposely, recklessly, or by negligence in the employment of fire, explosives, or other dangerous means listed in Section 220.2(1); or

(b) purposely or recklessly tampers with tangible property of another so as to endanger person or property; or

(c) purposely or recklessly causes another to suffer pecuniary loss by deception or threat.

(2) Grading. Criminal mischief is a felony of the third degree if the actor purposely causes pecuniary loss in excess of $5,000, or a substantial interruption or impairment of public communication, transportation, supply of water, gas or power, or other public service. It is a misdemeanor if the actor purposely causes pecuniary loss in excess of $100, or a petty misdemeanor if he purposely or recklessly causes pecuniary loss in excess of $25. Otherwise criminal mischief is a violation.

Chapter 4

LARCENY AND KINDRED OFFENSES

(Larceny, Embezzlement, False Pretenses, Robbery, Receiving)

SECTION 1. THE SUBJECT OF LARCENY

Larceny was one of the common-law felonies, punishable anciently by total forfeiture—the loss of life and lands and goods. Had it not been for this drastic penalty the courts would probably have recognized, as a possible subject of larceny, any property capable of being taken into possession and removed to another place. As it was, many such things were held not to be the subject of larceny. This applied to animals of a "base nature". Thus it was larceny to steal a horse, cow, pig or chicken, but not to steal a cat, monkey or fox. Many instruments or documents were excluded. The paper or parchment was no longer the subject of larceny, as such, because it was deemed to have been completely merged in the legal instrument or document written upon it. The latter, in turn, was deemed to be merged in whatever was represented by it. As real estate was not the subject of larceny, so neither was a deed to land. A contract represented an intangible right which could not be stolen and hence the wrongful taking of the written evidence of a contract was not larceny. Even negotiable notes and bills were held to be outside the larceny field. A pawn ticket, on the other hand, was the subject of larceny because it represented a specific chattel which could be stolen. Natural gas was the subject of larceny because it can be taken and carried away although not so easily handled as many other things. Electric current, by the prevailing view, was not, on the theory that it is not a substance but comparable to water power which may be used but not "taken and carried away".

These arbitrary exclusions from the scope of larceny have been almost entirely eliminated today, to a considerable extent as a result of legislation.[1]

---

[1]. The wrongful use of another's machinery to spin 20,000 pounds of raw wool into yarn does not constitute larceny. People v. Ashworth, 220 App. Div. 498, 222 N.Y.S. 24 (1927). The court said:

"Personal property has been variously defined. That which may be the subject of larceny is well comprehended in the following statement (36 Corpus Juris, 737): It 'should have corporeal existence, that is, be something the

PEOPLE v. CARIDIS

Court of Appeals of California, First Appellate District, 1915.
29 Cal.App. 166, 154 P. 1061.

LENNON, P. J. The defendant in this case was, by an information filed in the superior court of the city and county of San Francisco, charged with the crime of grand larceny, alleged to have been committed as follows:

"The said Antonio Caridis on the 29th day of July, A.D.1914, at the said City and County of San Francisco, State of California, did then and there willfully, unlawfully and feloniously steal, take and carry away one lottery ticket of the Original Nacional Company, No. 16235, that theretofore and on the 27th day of July, 1914, the said ticket was, after a drawing held by said Original Nacional Company, and its officers, representatives and agents, declared by said Original Nacional Company and its officers, representatives and agents, to be one of the winning tickets of the said Original Nacional Company, and its officers, representatives and agents, after said drawing aforesaid, did become liable for and did promise to pay to the holder of said ticket the sum of twelve hundred and fifty ($1250.00) dollars in gold coin of the United States of America and did then and there promise to pay to the holder of said ticket the sum of twelve hundred and fifty ($1250.00) dollars in gold coin of the United States of America;

"That thereafter, and on the 30th day of July, 1914, the said Antonio Caridis did present said ticket to said Original Nacional Company and to its officers, representatives and agents, and did receive from said Original Nacional Company, and its officers, representatives and agents, the sum of twelve hundred and fifty ($1250) dollars in gold coin of the United States of America therefor;

"That at all of said times the said lottery ticket was the personal property of Jim Papas and was of the value of twelve hundred and fifty ($1250.00) dollars in gold coin of the United States of America."

A demurrer to the information was allowed upon the ground that the facts stated did not constitute a public offense, in the particular that it affirmatively appeared that the subject matter of the alleged larceny had no legitimate value. The action was thereupon dismissed and the people have appealed from the order allowing the demurrer.

The ruling of the court below was correct. It is essential to the commission of the crime of larceny that the property alleged to have been stolen have some value—intrinsic or relative—which, where grand larceny is charged and the property was not taken from the person of another, must exceed the sum of fifty dollars.

physical presence, quantity, or quality of which is detectable or measurable by the senses or by some mechanical contrivance; for a naked right existing merely in contemplation of law, although it may be very valuable to the person who is entitled to exercise it, is not a subject of larceny.'"

Evidently the information in the present case was framed to fit the requirements of section 492 of the Penal Code, which fixes the value in cases of the larceny of written instruments by providing that "If the thing stolen consists of any evidence of debt, or other written instrument, the amount of money due thereupon, or secured to be paid thereby and remaining unsatisfied, or which in any contingency might be collected thereon or the value of the property the title to which is shown thereby, or the sum which might be recovered in the absence thereof, is the value of the thing stolen." Clearly this section contemplates and controls the value to be placed only upon written instruments which create some legal right and constitute a subsisting and an enforceable evidence of a debt.

The lottery ticket which was the subject matter of the larceny charged in the present case had no relative value save, as affirmatively alleged in the information, as the evidence of a debt due from an enterprise which was denounced by law and which apparently existed and was conducted by its promoters in defiance of the law. (Pen.Code, sec. 319 et seq.) It is a well-settled principle that an obligation which exists in defiance of a law which denounces it has, in the eye of the law, neither validity nor value. An instance of the application of this principle is to be found in the analogous case of Culp v. State, 1 Port. (Ala.) 33, 26 Am.Dec. 357, where the court held that an indictment charging the larceny of several "bills of credit of the United States Bank," which were alleged to be of the aggregate value of $310, could not be sustained because each of the bills was for a sum less than the bank was authorized by its charter to issue, and consequently could not, in contemplation of law, be the subject matter of a larceny.

The fact as alleged in the information, that the drawing had taken place prior to the alleged larceny of the ticket, and that the defendant ultimately collected thereon the sum of $1,250 from the lottery company, added nothing to the validity or value of the ticket. Being a void and valueless obligation in the eye of the law from its very inception, it could not be transformed into a legitimate and valuable thing by a voluntary payment, which in itself was a contravention of the law. Moreover, the sufficiency of the information must be determined by the facts as they existed at the time of the alleged taking, and not by anything that may have occurred subsequently.

Considered as a mere piece of paper, the lottery ticket in question possessed perhaps some slight intrinsic value, which, however small, would have sufficed to make the wrongful taking of it petit larceny, and if that had been the charge preferred against the defendant, it doubtless would have stood the test of demurrer. (1 McClain on Criminal Law, sec. 543.)

The order appealed from is affirmed.

PEOPLE ex rel. KOONS v. ELLING, Sheriff

Supreme Court, Special Term, Ontario County, New York, 1948.
190 Misc. 998, 77 N.Y.S.2d 103.

CRIBB, JUSTICE. The relator, Walter Koons, by this habeas corpus proceeding, seeks his release from the sentence of imprisonment under which he is confined in the Ontario County jail. . . .

It is conceded that the money with the larceny of which relator was charged was removed by him and his confederates from slot machines, commonly referred to as "one armed bandits", located in a room of the Moose Club, by the drilling of a small hole in the machine, through which, by means of an inserted wire, the mechanism was tripped allowing moneys inside to drop down into an exposed receptacle in the same manner as if the machine had been operated in the usual way and had paid out in some amount. The information charged the relator with committing the crime of petit larceny against the property of the named club; the relator plead guilty to the charge. However, if the moneys could not be the subject of larceny, and, as he contends, he therefore committed no crime, his plea of guilty was a nullity. A plea of guilty may not be substituted for the crime itself. Relator maintains that his plea of guilty was a nullity because the moneys were taken from unlawful slot machines in which, as well as in their contents, no person had or could have any title or possessory rights, and that therefore there was no larceny from the "true owner" as contemplated by section 1290 of the Penal Law. The question is therefore presented as to whether money in an unlawful slot machine may be the subject of larceny. Counsel have cited no cases, and the independent search of this Court has discovered none, determinative of the question.

In this case relator was not convicted of stealing the slot machines, which concededly were gambling devices and unlawful under the provisions of section 982 of the Penal Law but rather of stealing moneys contained in them. He was convicted of petit larceny. It is the opinion of this Court that the reasoning adopted by the Court in People v. Otis, 235 N.Y. 421, 139 N.E. 562, is equally applicable in the instant case. In that case the defendant having been indicted for stealing a quantity of whiskey, was convicted of petit larceny. The whiskey was unlawfully possessed under the provisions of the National Prohibition Act, 27 U.S.C.A. § 1 et seq. The question presented was whether the conviction could be sustained under such circumstances. The Court said: "The possessor not being able to make any legal use of it, it is said the liquor itself has no value. This is, however, to make the value of a chattel to its possessor the test as to whether it is the subject of larceny. Such is not the rule. It is enough if the object taken has inherent value. No one can doubt that whiskey has such value. It may be sold by the government and the proceeds covered into the treasury. It may be sold by druggists. That it is held illegally is immaterial."[1] Although the statute, 27 U. S.C.A. § 39, under discussion in that case specifically provided that "no property rights shall exist" in liquor illegally possessed, the Court held that such liquor could be the subject of larceny, and after referring to the statutory provisions for the issuance of search warrants, the seizure and final disposition by the courts of liquor so illegally possessed, and the prohibitory provision as to property rights in such liquor, the Court further said: "Property rights in such liquor are not forever ended. They pass to the government." . . .

An order may be issued dismissing the writ of habeas corpus heretofore granted in this proceeding and remanding relator to the custody of the sheriff of Ontario County to serve the remainder of his sentence in accordance with the provisions of law applicable thereto.

COWAN v. STATE

Supreme Court of Arkansas, 1926.
171 Ark. 1018, 287 S.W. 201.

WOOD, J. Bert Cowan was indicted in the Crawford Circuit Court for the crime of grand larceny. The indictment, in apt language charged him with the crime of grand larceny in the stealing of two automobile license plates, of the total value of $16, the personal property of Paul W. Sheridan.

One of the witnesses introduced by the State testified that he worked for the Paul Sheridan Motor Company, in Van Buren, Crawford County, Arkansas, and that he saw Cowan, on or about the 31st day of May, 1926, in Crawford County, Arkansas, trying to get a license tag off of a Ford car which belonged to Paul Sheridan. Witness went for the sheriff.

The sheriff testified that he saw the defendant take a license tag off of a Ford touring car and stick it under the bib of his overalls, and witness arrested him. The law fixes as the regular price of license for a Ford touring car the sum of $16 from the 1st of January to the 21st of June.

The defendant offered to prove by the sheriff and other witnesses that the replacement cost of the license tags is $1. The court refused to allow the witness to so testify, to which ruling the defendant duly excepted.

The defendant was convicted and sentenced by judgment of the court to imprisonment in the State Penitentiary for a period of one year, from which judgment he duly prosecutes this appeal.

---

[1]. Accord, People v. Odenwald, 104 Cal. App. 203, 285 P. 406 (1930), overruling People v. Spencer, 54 Cal.App. 54, 201 P. 130 (1921), which had held such liquor was not the subject of larceny, because the statute provided that "no property right shall exist in any such liquor".

The law requires every person who owns and desires to operate an automobile in this State to pay a fee for the registration and licensing of such automobile, a minimum of $15 per annum. See § 36, subdiv. (f), act No. 5, approved October 10, 1923, commonly known as the Harrelson law. It is made the duty of the Commissioner of State Lands, Highways and Improvements, when the automobile has been duly registered and the license fee duly paid, to issue to the applicant a registration card and a set of registration plates bearing the number that has been assigned to such motor vehicle. The possession of these registration cards and license plates is evidence of the fact that the owner and operator of the car has complied with the law requiring registration and payment of the license fee. It is unlawful for the owner of any automobile to display any registration plate or plates that are not furnished by the State Highway Commissioner, and the owner of any motor vehicle subject to the payment of a license fee, who fails to pay the same when due, in addition to the license fee, is subject to a penalty for the operation of the car without paying a license.

Under the above and other provisions of act No. 5, supra, and the testimony in this case, it is obvious that the stealing of automobile license plates evidencing the right to own and operate an automobile from Jan. 1 to June 21 constituted grand larceny. The only method by which the appellant could lawfully obtain a license plate to operate his car in this State was by complying with the provisions of act No. 5, supra, and, in order to obtain such license plates, it would be necessary for him to pay not less than the sum of $15. Registration cards and license plates, under the law, are not the subject of barter and sale. They evidence the right of the owner of the particular car that has been registered, and for which license plates have been issued, to operate that car. These original license plates cannot be obtained by any one lawfully without the payment of the license fee. Intrinsically, to be sure, the metal license plates were worth but little or nothing, merely the cost of the metal and the manufacture thereof into plates, but, as an evidence of the right to own and operate a car, they were worth the sum of $16. The effect of the provisions of the Harrelson law is to fix the value of license plates at not less than $15. The value of the license plates stolen by appellant was $16, as shown by the undisputed evidence in this case. It is not a question of what the owner of the automobile would have to pay in order to replace them; the question is, what was the value of the plates to the owner when he obtained them?[1]—that is, what he had to pay for same in order to obtain

---

[1] Whether goods stolen from a store constitute grand or petit larceny is not dependent upon the cost to the store. Defendant was tried by jury for the larceny of a Winchester carbine from Sears Roebuck and Company. The evidence was that the cost price to the store was $44.05 and the retail price asked by the store was $69. The jury returned a verdict finding the defendant guilty and fixing the value of the property at $60. A judgment of conviction of grand larceny was affirmed because there was ample evidence to support the verdict on the question of value. Lee v. People, 137 Colo. 465, 326 P.2d 660 (1958).

them as an evidence of the right to operate his car in this State. The value of these particular plates should be measured by what these particular plates cost, and not by what replacement plates would cost, for appellant was not charged and was not convicted of stealing license plates which had been replaced. He was charged and convicted of stealing automobile license plates of the value of $16. To obtain these license plates the owner had to pay $16, and if appellant, as before stated, had lawfully obtained the same, he would have had to pay the sum of $16 therefor. When motor vehicle license plates are stolen, the thief intends not only to deprive the owner of the car of the evidence of his right to operate such car on the highways of this State, but he also intends to deprive the State of the license fee which he would have to pay as an evidence of his right to operate a motor vehicle. He therefore intends to steal the property of another and to convert the same permanently to his own use, of more than the value of $10. In such case the *lucri causa* is complete, and, under the law, the offender is guilty of grand larceny.

The trial court ruled correctly in holding that the offered testimony was inadmissible, and its judgment is therefore affirmed.[2]

McCulloch, C. J. (dissenting). The offense of larceny consists of stealing, taking and carrying away the property of another, and the degree of the offense is fixed according to the value of the property stolen. The extent of the value is unimportant further than it fixes the degree of the offense, but the property stolen must be of some value. It is not contended in the present case that the two automobile license tags which were stolen were entirely without value, however trifling it may have been, but the contention is that it is limited to the intrinsic value of the tags themselves, and not the value of the privilege, of which the tags constitute mere evidence. I think that counsel for appellant is right in this contention, and that the offense made out is only that of petty larceny. . . .

Two suits of clothes which had been stolen were shown to have been old stock which had been on the shelves of the store three and a half years. For purposes of grand larceny it was held that "the proof must show the fair, cash market value at the time and place of the theft". People v. Fognini, 374 Ill. 161, 165, 28 N.E.2d 95, 97 (1940).

A federal statute making the embezzlement or theft of government property a felony if the value is over $100.00, and otherwise a misdemeanor provides: "The word 'value' means face, par, or market value, or cost price, either wholesale or retail, whichever is greater". 18 U.S.C.A. § 641.

2. It is larceny to steal the clothing from a buried corpse. Haynes's Case, 12 Co.Rep. 113, 77 Eng.Rep. 1389 (1614).

SECTION 2. PROPERTY "OF ANOTHER"

STATE v. COHEN

Supreme Court of Minnesota, 1935.
196 Minn. 39, 263 N.W. 922.

(The defendant, having had her fur coat repaired by a furrier, regained control of it by the pretense of trying it on, after which she concealed it and refused either to return it or to pay for the work done. She appealed from a conviction of the crime of grand larceny in the second degree.)

HOLT, JUSTICE. . . . The verdict is not contrary to law. A person may be guilty of larceny of his own property if taken from the possession of one who has a lien thereon under which possession may lawfully be retained until the lien is discharged. Sections 8507 and 8508, 2 Mason Minn.St.1927, gave a possessory lien to Mellon, and the way defendant procured the coat to see how it looked on her person does not, as a matter of law, bring her within the protection of 2 Mason Minn.St.1927, § 10372. On the contrary, the jury had warrant for finding that defendant's scheme of trying on the coat and disappearing with it was with the felonious intent of depriving Mellon of his lien and his right of possession until the lien was discharged. An owner of personal property may be found guilty of larceny thereof when he wrongfully takes it from a pledgee or from one whom he has given possession for the purpose of having it cared for or repaired under statutes such as ours giving a lien therefor and the right to retain possession until the lien is paid. State v. Hubbard, 126 Kan. 129, 266 P. 939, annotated in 58 A.L.R. 327, 330, 331, where the authorities are cited and this conclusion therefrom is stated:

"If personal property in the possession of one other than the general owner by virtue of some special right or title is taken from him by the general owner, such taking is larceny if it is done with the felonious intent of depriving such person of his rights, or of charging him with the value of the property." . . .

Defendant complains of the ruling excluding evidence of an expert that the material and labor which Mellon expended in making the agreed alterations and repairs on the coat did not enhance its value. We think the ruling right. Defendant was permitted to testify as to her opinion of Mellon's work; that it ruined the coat instead of enhancing its value; that she thought he had substituted inferior fur for that which was in the coat when delivered to him; and that she took possession because she was afraid the value of the coat would be utterly destroyed. All this properly went to disprove felonious intent. But we think the amount of Mellon's lien was not an issue that could be litigated in this case. It was not between the proper parties.

The quantum of proof is not the same in this criminal case as it would be in an action between Mellon and defendant either to establish or defeat a lien. We take it that in this prosecution the only value in issue was the value of the coat which defendant feloniously took and concealed.[1] Mellon was entitled to the possession of the entire coat until his lien was determined in a lawful manner. And defendant was not entitled to have the amount of Mellon's possessory lien determined in this criminal case. It was conceded that possession of the coat had been given by her to Mellon in order that he might alter and repair it at an agreed price.

Other assignments of error are made. They have been examined, but we do not consider them of sufficient merit to note in this opinion.

The conviction is affirmed.[2]

SECTION 3. THE CAPTION AND ASPORTATION

THOMPSON v. STATE

Supreme Court of Alabama, 1891.
94 Ala. 535, 10 So. 520.

Indictment for larceny from the person. The opinion states the material facts. Charge No. 1, asked and refused, was in these words: "The jury must believe, beyond a reasonable doubt, that the defendant got the money into his hand, or actual possession of it, before they can convict him of larceny."

WALKER, J. The witness for the State testified that he held out his open hand with two silver dollars therein, showing the money to the defendant; that the defendant struck witness' hand, and the money was either knocked out of his hand or was taken by the defendant, he could not tell positively which. It was after twelve o'clock at night, and the witness did not see the money, either in defendant's possession or on the ground. The court charged the jury: "If the jury find from the evidence that the defendant, with a felonious intent, grabbed

---

1. If the thief gave consideration for, or had a legal interest in, the stolen property, the amount of such consideration or value shall be deducted from the total value of the property. W.S.A. 943.20.

2. It was held not to be larceny for a wife to appropriate money belonging to 30 people, one of whom was her husband. Rex v. Willis, 1 Moody 375, 168 Eng.Rep. 1309 (1833). It was held otherwise under a statute authorizing a married woman to acquire, hold and transfer property as freely as if she were single. Fugate v. Commonwealth, 308 Ky. 815, 215 S.W.2d 1004 (1948).

One partner does not commit larceny by wrongfully appropriating partnership property since each partner has an individual interest therein. State v. Elsbury, 63 Nev. 463, 175 P.2d 430 (1946).

for the money, but did not get it, but only knocked it from the owner's hand with a felonious intent, this would be a sufficient carrying away of the money, although defendant never got possession at any time of said money." This charge was erroneous. To constitute larceny, there must be a felonious taking and carrying away of personal property. There must be such a caption that the accused acquires dominion over the property, followed by such an asportation or carrying away as to supersede the possession of the owner for an appreciable period of time. Though the owner's possession is disturbed, yet the offense is not complete if the accused fails to acquire such dominion over the property as to enable him to take actual custody or control. It is not enough that the money was knocked out of the owner's hand, if it fell to the ground and the defendant never got possession of it. The defendant was not guilty of larceny, if he did not get the money under his control. If the attempt merely caused the money to fall from the owner's hand to the ground, and the defendant ran off without getting it, the larceny was not consummated, as the dominion of the trespasser was not complete. Charge No. 1 was a proper statement of the law as applicable to the evidence above referred to, and it should have been given.

Reversed and remanded.

REX v. WALSH

Court for Crown Cases Reserved, 1824.
1 Moody 14, 168 Eng.Rep. 1166.

The prisoner was tried before Thomas Denman Esquire, Common Serjeant, at the Old Bailey Sessions, January 1824, on an indictment for stealing a leathern bag containing small parcels, the property of William Ray, the guard to the Exeter mail.

At the trial it appeared that the bag was placed in the front boot, and the prisoner, sitting on the box, took hold of the upper end of the bag, and lifted it up from the bottom of the boot on which it rested. He handed the upper part of the bag to a person who stood beside the wheel on the pavement, and both had hold of it together, endeavouring to pull it out of the boot, with a common intent to steal it. Before they were able to obtain complete possession of the bag, and while they were so engaged in trying to draw it out, they were interrupted by the guard, and dropt the bag.

The prisoner was found guilty, but the facts above stated were specially found by the jury, in answer to questions put to them by the Common Serjeant.

The Common Serjeant, entertaining some doubts, whether the prisoner could be truly said to have "stolen, taken, and carried away" the bag, he respited the judgment, in order that the opinion of the Judges might be taken on the case.

In Easter Term 1824. The Judges met and considered this case. They held the conviction right, being of opinion that there was a complete asportation of the bag. (*Vide* East, P.C. 555, 556, 557; 1 Hale, 508, 527.) [a]

CUMMINS v. COMMONWEALTH

Kentucky Court of Appeals, 1883.
5 Ky.L.Rep. 200.

The appellant, Cummins, according to the evidence, told Sweet he wished to sell him a sow and pigs, and after agreement on the price, went to where a sow and pigs were lying down on the commons and pointed them out as his, and Sweet paid him $7 in money for them and then drove them off. The sow and pigs belonged to John Flauher, who lived near by.

The appellant seems to have been out of money and resorted to this means of obtaining some to supply his wants, and then proceeded to the fair.

Having been convicted of the offense of larceny or hog stealing under the statute, the appellant has appealed, and his counsel contend that his offense was not larceny because there was no asportation *by him*, but it was obtaining money by false pretenses if anything.

He was not indicted for obtaining the $7 for the sow and pigs, but for stealing the sow and pigs. Whether his acts constituted both offenses of larceny of the hogs and obtaining money by false pretenses, for which he might be punished, need not be determined, as there has been no attempt to try him twice for the same acts.

The owner of the sow and pigs never parted with the possession or the property in them. The asportation was by the hand or physical act of Sweet, but the act of felonious taking was that of the appellant committed through Sweet, who was his instrument in committing the trespass upon the property of Flauher.

East, Hale and Hawkins, who are approved by Archbold, say that if the taking be by the hand of another, it is the same as if by the hand of the thief himself. For instance, if the thief procure a child within the age of discretion, or an idiot, to steal goods for him, such taking must be charged to him. . . .

The judgment is therefore affirmed.[1]

---

[a] See People v. Bradovich, 305 Mich. 329, 9 N.W.2d 560 (1943); Adams v. Commonwealth, 153 Ky. 88, 154 S.W. 381 (1913); Rex v. Coslet, 1 Leach C.C. 236 (1782).

[1] Accord: Smith v. State, 11 Ga.App. 197, 74 S.E. 1093 (1912); State v. Hunt, 45 Iowa 673 (1877). Contra: State v. Laborde, 202 La. 59, 11 So.2d 404 (1942). The court said: "Since the defendant at no time had the actual or constructive possession of the animal, the act of the purchaser in carrying it away for his own account cannot be said in legal contemplation to have been the act of the seller. The facts of the case repel any idea of

WILLIAMS v. STATE

Supreme Court of Mississippi, 1885.
63 Miss. 58.

Williams was indicted for the larceny of a hog. The evidence was that he shot and killed a hog, went to it, turned it on its back, stabbed it with a knife and left it there to bleed. When he returned later the owner was there. He was convicted of larceny and appealed.

CAMPBELL, J., delivered the opinion of the court.

Were every fact in evidence embodied in a special verdict the sentence of the law would be that the accused is not guilty of larceny, because there was not a *"carrying away"* of the hog; and while the definition by the court of *asportation* is abstractly correct, it was not applicable to the facts in evidence, on which the court should have instructed the jury not to find the defendant guilty of larceny, but to consider whether he was guilty of an attempt to steal. Cherry's Case, 2 East C.L. 556; State v. Jones, 65 N.C. 395.

Reversed.[1]

HERMANN v. STATE

Supreme Court of Mississippi, 1960.
239 Miss. 523, 123 So.2d 846.

[Appellants, who had less than a dollar in their possession and were nearly out of gas, parked their car at a filling station late at night and remained there until the attendant appeared next morning. After he had filled the tank at their request, and was about to ask for payment, they stopped him at gunpoint to prevent any interference by him as they drove away.]

McGEHEE, CHIEF JUSTICE. The appellants, Richard Hermann and Miss Jane Demuth, were jointly indicted, tried and convicted of the crime of armed robbery in Warren County, Mississippi and the former was sentenced to served [sic] a term of six years in the state penitentiary and the latter a term of three years. From these convictions and sentences, they prosecute this appeal. . . .

Thus, it will be seen from the foregoing that the crime of stealthily obtaining the gasoline was completed before Richard Hermann

---

implied agency, because Jeansonne unquestionably acted as a bona fide purchaser for himself."

1. Accord: McKenzie v. State, 111 Miss. 780, 72 So. 198 (1916); State v. Alexander, 74 N.C. 232 (1876). Contra: Lundy v. State, 60 Ga. 143 (1878). In the Georgia case the evidence was that defendants had shot and killed a cow but were frightened away when they had the animal half skinned. The court said that in the skinning process the men must have moved the carcass about somewhat.

pointed the rifle at James Roy Dewease, with the exception that there had been no asportation of the gasoline from the place of business of W. O. Dewease at that time. The appellants were able to make their getaway with the gasoline by placing the gasoline station attendant in fear by the exhibition of the deadly weapon, telling him not to start anything, and that "if you try to follow me, I will hurt you." The car was driven away while the gasoline station attendant was still standing with his arms and hands raised in the air. At that time Wiley Tyson, father-in-law of W. O. Dewease, was on the inside of the restaurant where he could and did see Roy Dewease holding up his hands as the appellants drove the car away, but was unable to see the car or either of the appellants from the place where he was standing in the cafe or restaurant at that time. . . .

The appellants rely almost entirely on Register v. State, decided by this Court on November 18, 1957 and reported in 232 Miss. 128, 97 So.2d 919. The decision in that case followed the general rule as to what was necessary to constitute the crime of armed robbery, this being the offense of which the appellants were convicted in the case at bar. But that which distinguishes the Register case from the case at bar is the fact that in the instant case it was clearly shown, according to the testimony on behalf of the State, that there was no asportation of the gasoline until after the appellant, Richard Hermann, had drawn the deadly weapon on the gasoline station attendant and put him in fear whereas in the Register case there was no proof at all as to whether the intruder in the room of Miss June Flowers took her money out of her billfold prior or subsequent to the time that he choked her and put her in fear.

It is stated in Wharton's Criminal Law and Procedure, Anderson, Volume 2, page 243 that "In the absence of statutory modification, the constituent elements of the offense of robbery are (1) a felonious taking, (2) accompanied by an asportation, of (3) personal property of value (4) from the person of another or in his presence, (5) against his will, (6) by violence or by putting him in fear, (7) animo furandi." Again at page 252 of the same text it is stated: "The actual taking *and asportation* of some of the victim's personal property is an essential element of robbery." (Italics ours.) Again at page 253 in this same text it is stated: "As in larceny, there must also be an asportation or carrying away of the goods." In the instant case the appellant, Richard Hermann, did not take complete control and dominion over the property of W. O. Dewease until he pointed the rifle on the gasoline station attendant, James Roy Dewease, and placed him in fear by telling him, "Don't start anything," and "If you try to follow me, I will hurt you." This occurred after the obtaining of conditional possession of the gasoline (on the assumption that the occupants of the car would pay for the gasoline) but prior to any attempt to asport the same. They resorted to the means of drawing the rifle in a threatening manner to make good their intention of removing the gasoline from the presence of the gasoline service station attendant *and of making good their escape.*

Again at page 263, Wharton's Criminal Law and Procedure, Anderson, Volume 2, it is said: "The act of the defendant may either precede or be concurrent with the taking of the victim's property." We think that the taking away of the gasoline was contemporaneous with the pointing of the rifle at the gasoline station attendant, and that the commission of this act was essential to the completion of the crime of robbery. . . .

From the foregoing views, it follows that we are of the opinion that this case is distinguishable from the case of Register v. State, supra, principally relied on by appellants, in that the drawing of the rifle on the gasoline station attendant in the case at bar was the means employed to enable them to asport the gasoline from the premises and to enable them to make good their escape.

Affirmed.[1]

ARRINGTON, ETHRIDGE, GILLESPIE and McELROY, JJ., concur.

SECTION 4. THE TRESPASS

(A) THE NECESSITY OF TRESPASS (AND THE MEANING OF THE WORD "TRESPASS" IN LARCENY)

MASTERS v. STATE

Supreme Court of Florida, Special Division B, 1947.
159 Fla. 617, 32 So.2d 276.

BARNES, J. It appears that appellant-defendant found a heifer in his pasture which was not his; that he inquired of one Brannon if he had lost a heifer—Brannon replied that he had and promised to come to Masters' pasture and ascertain if the heifer was his. Brannon did not do so promptly and Masters inquired further of Brannon on occasions and each time Brannon promised to go and see if it was his heifer. Doubtless it was Brannon's heifer.

---

[1]. For robbery the violence or putting in fear must precede, or be concomitant with, the taking of the property. No violence or excitation of fear resorted to merely for the purpose of retaining a possession already acquired, or to effect an escape, is sufficient. Mason v. Commonwealth, 200 Va. 253, 105 S.E.2d 149 (1958). But if one snatches property from the hand of another and uses force to prevent an immediate retaking by the other, this is all one transaction and constitutes robbery. People v. Reade, 197 Cal. App.2d 509, 17 Cal.Rptr. 328 (1961).

There is substantial evidence showing that Masters on several occasions had the heifer put out of his pasture but that she would later be found to have returned to the pasture; that Masters sold the heifer but that Masters was not present when the buyer came and took her away.

Without further elaboration it appears to us that under the circumstances of this case there was no larceny.

As the Judge correctly charged the jury the offense of larceny has been defined:

"Larceny is the stealing, taking and carrying away of the personal property of another with intent to deprive the owner thereof of his property permanently, or to convert it to the taker's or some one else's use. And in order for a conviction to be had on the charge of larceny, there must have been a felonious intent, that is, a conscious purpose to steal that which did not belong to the taker, the felonious intent to steal and take, and there must have been a taking and there must have been a carrying away, some times referred to as asportation."

Under other circumstances the selling of the heifer of another might be larceny but here the possession of the heifer by Masters was not acquired by a felonious act. Had not the means by which Masters became possessed been established the sale might have established larceny.

The evidence is sufficient to establish a wrongful conversion of the heifer but insufficient to establish an intent to *steal* as defined in law.

The judgment appealed is reversed.

TERRELL, ACTING CHIEF JUSTICE, BUFORD, and ADAMS, JJ., concur.

THE QUEEN v. TOWNLEY

Court for Crown Cases Reserved, 1871.
L.R. 1 C.C. 315, 12 Cox C.C. 59.

BOVILL, C. J. The prisoner in this case has been convicted of felony in stealing rabbits, and the question is, whether he has been properly convicted. The facts are, that the rabbits, 126 in number, were taken and killed upon land the property of the Crown. The rabbits were then, together with 400 yards of net, placed in a ditch on the same land on which they had been taken; some of them being in bags, and some in bundles strapped together by the legs. They were placed there by the poachers, who in so placing them had no intention to abandon the wrongful possession which they had acquired by taking them, but placed them in the ditch as a place of deposit till they could conveniently remove them. Here they were found by the keep-

Sec. 4 THE TRESPASS 139

ers at about eight in the morning. At about a quarter to eleven the prisoner arrived, went straight to the place where the rabbits were concealed, and began to remove them.

Now, the first question is as to the nature of the property in these rabbits. In animals ferae naturae there is no absolute property. There is only a special or qualified right of property—a right ratione soli to take and kill them. When killed upon the soil they become the absolute property of the owner of the soil. This was decided in the case of rabbits by the House of Lords in Blade v. Higgs.[1] And the same principle was applied in the case of grouse in Lord Lonsdale v. Rigg.[2] In this case therefore the rabbits, being started and killed on land belonging to the Crown, might, if there were no other circumstance in the case, become the property of the Crown. But before there can be a conviction for larceny for taking anything not capable in its original state of being the subject of larceny, as for instance, things fixed to the soil, it is necessary that the act of taking away should not be one continuous act with the act of severance or other act by which the thing becomes a chattel, and so is brought within the law of larceny. This doctrine has been applied to stripping lead from the roof of a church, and in other cases of things affixed to the soil. And the present case must be governed by the same principle. It is not stated in the case whether or not the prisoner was one of the poachers who killed the rabbits. But my Brother Blackburn says that such must be taken to be the fact. Under all the circumstances of the case I think a jury ought to have found that the whole transaction was a continuous one; and the conviction must be quashed.

. . .

(MARTIN, B., BRAMWELL, B., BYLES, J., and BLACKBURN, J., were of the same opinion, and the conviction was quashed.)

BELL v. STATE

Supreme Court of Tennessee, 1874.
63 Tenn. 426.

DEADERICK, J., delivered the opinion of the Court.

The plaintiff in error was convicted at the November Term, 1874, of the Criminal Court of Montgomery County, of petit larceny, for stealing as charged, cabbage and sweet potatoes, the goods and chattels of G. B. White, the prosecutor, and sentenced to the penitentiary for one year.

It is insisted that the charge of the Judge was erroneous in its definition of the offence charged.

[Footnotes by the Court.]
1. 11 H.L.C. 621; 34 L.J.(C.P.) 286.
2. 1 H. & N. 923; 26 L.J.(Ex.) 196.

In the beginning of his charge the Judge gives a full and accurate definition of the offence, and correctly instructs the jury as to the difference between grand and petit larceny, and the punishment annexed to each.

It is true, in a subsequent part of his instructions, as introductory to the definition of "personal property," he says: "The jury will observe that larceny is the felonious taking away of personal property." He then proceeds to state to the jury when vegetables, etc., growing in or upon the ground, may become "personal property," and the subject of larceny, and uses this language: "If defendant went at night into the garden of another, intending to steal, and dug a lot of sweet potatoes, laying them on the ground, or cut a lot of cabbage, severing them from the earth, and afterwards picked up the vegetables, put them in a bag, and carried them off, that would be larceny."

This latter part of the charge is not strictly accurate, according to the rule of the common law. In 3 Greenleaf on Ev., § 163, it is said: "If the severance and asportation were one continued act of the prisoner, it is only a trespass; but if the severance were the act of another person, or if, after the severance by the prisoner, any interval of time elapsed, after which he returned and took the article away, the severance and asportation being two distinct acts, it is larceny," citing 1 E. Hale P.C., 510; 2 East P.C., 587. . . .

The principle is, that when the severance and asportation constitute one continuous act, then it is a trespass only, but if the severance is a distinct act, and not immediately connected with or followed by the asportation it is a larceny.

To dig potatoes, whereby they are cast upon the surface of the earth, and then immediately to pick them up, and put them in a bag, and carry them away, would be one continuous act, although the picking up, necessarily, was after the digging, and after they had lain upon the ground. The act would be continuous, without cessation, until the asportation, as well as the severance, was completed, and thus a trespass only. And so, also, of cutting a "lot of cabbages," "severing them from the earth," the "severing" necessarily precedes the taking away, yet, when the taking away immediately follows, it is a "continuous act," and is trespass only.

It is argued by the Attorney-General, that the taking of vegetables severed from the ground, and the carrying of stolen goods into another county, seem to stand upon the same footing, although it is conceded that the authorities hold, as to the first mentioned, that the possession is not in the owner as personalty, and in the latter, that the legal possession still remains in him.

The trespasser holds the severed property, as personalty, but he cannot be convicted of a larceny, for he did not obtain that possession feloniously. No felony was committed in the taking and carrying away from the owner, but a trespass only.

In the case of an original felonious taking and carrying away, every moment's continuance of the trespass and felony amounts to a new caption and asportation, (2 Arch.Cr.Pr. & Pl., 343, note 1,) and the offence is considered as committed in every county or jurisdiction into which the thief carries the goods. Ibid. It is difficult to see any difference in the moral guilt of one who takes and carries away immediately upon the severance from the freehold and one who severs at one time and takes away at another, but the Legislature has not altered the distinction made by the common law, and it is still in force in Tennessee.[1]

The judgment of the Criminal Court will be reversed.[2]

(B). APPROPRIATION OF DELIVERED GOODS

(i) IN GENERAL

RAVEN'S CASE

Newgate Sessions, 1662.
J. Kelyng 24, 84 Eng.Rep. 1065.

Mary Raven, *alias* Aston, was indicted for stealing two blankets, three pair of sheets, three pillow-biers, and other goods of William Cannon. And upon the evidence it appeared, that she had hired lodgings and furniture with them for three months, and during that time, conveyed away the goods which she had hired with her lodgings, and she herself ran away at the same time. And it was agreed by my Lord Bridgeman, myself, and my brother Wylde, Recorder of London, then present, that this was no felony, because she had a special property in them by her contract, and so there could be no trespass; and there can be no felony where there is no trespass, as it was resolved in the case of Holmes, who set fire on his own house in London, which was quenched before it went further.

---

1. The legislature made the change later. Williams v. State, 186 Tenn. 252, 257, 209 S.W.2d 29, 31 (1948).

2. Since the *statutory* offense of "theft" includes the taking of anything of value the fact that what was taken was severed from the realty is unimportant. State v. Mills, 214 La. 979, 39 So.2d 439 (1949). Some courts reached a similar result in regard to larceny without the aid of statute. Ex parte Willke, 34 Tex. 155 (1870); Stephens v. Commonwealth, 304 Ky. 38, 199 S. W.2d 719 (1947). The wrongful severance of a part of the realty and its appropriation is expressly made larceny in some of the statutes. More frequently it is punished as some other offense, such as malicious mischief and trespass.

REX v. BANKS

Court for Crown Cases Reserved, 1821.
Russ. & Ry. 441, 168 Eng.Rep. 887.

The prisoner was tried and convicted before Mr. Justice Baylay, at the Lancaster Lent assizes, in the year 1821, for horse-stealing.

It appeared that the prisoner borrowed a horse, under pretence of carrying a child to a neighbouring surgeon. Whether he carried the child thither did not appear; but the day following, after the purpose for which he borrowed the horse was over, he took the horse in a different direction and sold it.

The prisoner did not offer the horse for sale, but was applied to to sell it, so that it was possible he might have had no felonious intention till that application was made.

The jury thought the prisoner had no felonious intention when he took the horse; but as it was borrowed for a special purpose, and that purpose was over when the prisoner took the horse to the place where he sold it, the learned judge thought it right upon the authority of 2 East, P.C. 690, 694, and 2 Russ. 1089, 1090[a], to submit to the consideration of the judges, whether the subsequent disposing of the horse, when the purpose for which it was borrowed was no longer in view, did not in law include in it a felonious taking?

In Easter term, 1821, the judges met and considered this case. They were of opinion that the doctrine laid down on this subject in 2 East, P.C. 690 & 694, and 2 Russell, 1089 & 1090 was not correct. They held that if the prisoner had not a felonious intention when he originally took the horse, his subsequent withholding and disposing of it did not constitute a new felonious taking, or make him guilty of felony; consequently the conviction could not be supported.[1]

[a]. In 2 Russ. 1089, it is said that, "In the case of a delivery of a horse upon hire or loan, if such delivery were obtained *bona fide*, no subsequent wrongful conversion pending the contract will amount to felony; and so of other goods. But when the purpose of the hiring, or loan, for which the delivery was made, has been ended, felony may be committed by a conversion of the goods."

[Note by Compiler.]

1. This case repudiates the theory of the trial court in Tunnard's Case, 1 Leach 214 note, 168 Eng.Rep. 209 note (1729).

(ii) Distinction Between Custody and Possession

THE KING v. BAZELEY

Court for Crown Cases Reserved, 1799.
2 Leach 835, 168 Eng.Rep. 517.

At the Old Bailey in February Session 1799, Joseph Bazeley was tried before John Silvester, Esq. Common Serjeant of the city of London, for feloniously stealing on the 18th January preceding, a Banknote of the value of one hundred pounds, the property of Peter Esdaile, Sir Benjamin Hammett, William Esdaile, and John Hammett.

The following facts appeared in evidence. The prisoner, Joseph Bazeley, was the principal teller at the house of Messrs. Esdaile's and Hammett's bankers, in Lombard-street, at the salary of £100 a year, and his duty was to receive and pay money, notes, and bills, at the counter. The manner of conducting the business of this banking-house is as follows: There are four tellers, each of whom has a separate money-book, a separate money-drawer, and a separate bag. The prisoner being the chief teller, the total of the receipts and payments of all the other money-books were every evening copied into his, and the total balance or rest, as it is technically called, struck in his book, and the balances of the other money-books paid, by the other tellers, over to him. When any monies, whether in cash or notes, are brought by customers to the counter to be paid in, the teller who receives it counts it over, then enters the Bank-notes or drafts, and afterwards the cash, under the customer's name, in his book; and then, after casting up the total, it is entered in the customer's book. The money is then put into the teller's bag, and the Bank-notes or other papers, if any, put into a box which stands on a desk behind the counter, directly before another clerk, who is called the cash bookkeeper, who makes an entry of it in the received cash-book in the name of the person who has paid it in, and which he finds written by the receiving teller on the back of the bill or note so placed in the drawer. The prisoner was treasurer to an association called "The Ding Dong Mining Company"; and in the course of the year had many bills drawn on him by the Company, and many bills drawn on other persons remitted to him by the Company. In the month of January 1799, the prisoner had accepted bills on account of the Company, to the amount of £112, 4s. 1d. and had in his possession a bill of £166, 7s. 3d. belonging to the Company, but which was not due until the 9th February. One of the bills, amounting to £100, which the prisoner had accepted, became due on 18th January. Mr. William Gilbert, a grocer, in the Surry-road, Black-friars, kept his cash at the banking-house of the prosecutors, and on the 18th January 1799, he sent his servant, George Cock, to pay in £137. This sum consisted of £122 in Bank-notes, and the rest in cash. One of these Bank-notes was the note which the prisoner was indicted for stealing. The prisoner received this money from George

Cock, and after entering the £137 in Mr. Gilbert's Bank-book, entered the £15 cash in his own money-book, and put over the £22 in Bank-notes into the drawer behind him, keeping back the £100 Bank-note, which he put into his pocket, and afterwards paid to a banker's clerk the same day at a clearing-house in Lombard-street, in discharge of the £100 bill which he had accepted on account of the Ding Dong Mining Company. To make the sum in Mr. Gilbert's Bank-book, and the sum in the book of the banking-house agree, it appeared that a unit had been added to the entry of £37 to the credit of Mr. Gilbert, in the book of the banking-house, but it did not appear by any direct proof that this alteration had been made by the prisoner; it appeared however that he had made a confession, but the confession having been obtained under a promise of favour it was not given in evidence.

Const and Jackson, the prisoner's Counsel, submitted to the Court, that to constitute a larceny, it was necessary in point of law that the property should be taken from the possession of the prosecutor, but that it was clear from the evidence in this case, that the Bank-note charged to have been stolen, never was either in the actual or the constructive possession of Esdaile and Hammett, and that even if it had been in their possession, yet that from the manner in which it had been secreted by the prisoner, it amounted only to a breach of trust.

The Court left the facts of the case to the consideration of the Jury, and on their finding the prisoner Guilty, the case was reserved for the opinion of the Twelve Judges on a question, whether under the circumstances above stated, the taking of the Bank-note was in law a felonious taking, or only a fraudulent breach of trust.

The case was accordingly argued before nine of the Judges (Lord Kenyon, L. C. J.; C. J. Eyre, C. B. Macdonald, Mr. Baron Hotham, Mr. B. Perryn, Mr. Baron Thompson, Mr. J. Grose, Mr. J. Lawrence, Mr. J. Rooke) in the Exchequer Chamber, on Saturday, 27th April 1799, by Const for the prisoner, and by Fielding for the Crown. . . .

The Judges, it is said, were of opinion, upon the authority of Rex v. Waite, that this Bank-note never was in the legal custody or possession of the prosecutors, Messrs. Esdailes and Hammett; but no opinion was ever publicly delivered [a]; and the prisoner was included in the Secretary of State's letter as a proper object for a pardon.

---

a. On consultation among the Judges, some doubt was at first entertained but at last all assembled agreed that it was not felony, inasmuch as the note was never in the possession of the bankers, distinct from the possession of the prisoner: though it would have been otherwise if the prisoner had deposited it in the drawer, and had afterwards taken it. (Vide Chipchase's case, ante, p. 699.) And they thought that this was not to be differed from the cases of Rex v. Waite, ante, p. 28, and Rex v. Bull, ante, p. 841, which turned on this consideration, that the thing was not taken by the prisoner out of the possession of the owner: and here it was delivered into the possession of the prisoner. That although to many purposes the note was in the actual possession of the masters, yet it was also in the actual possession of the servant, and that possession not to be impeached; for it was a lawful one. Eyre, C. J. also observed that the cases ran into

(In consequence of this case the statute 39 Geo. III, c. 85 was passed, entitled: "An Act to protect Masters and others against Embezzlement, by their Clerks or Servants." The scope of embezzlement has been greatly enlarged by subsequent enactments—both in England and in this country.)

MORGAN v. COMMONWEALTH

Court of Appeals of Kentucky, 1932.
242 Ky. 713, 47 S.W.2d 543.

DIETZMAN, C. J. Appellant was convicted of the offense of grand larceny, sentenced to serve two years in the penitentiary, and appeals.

The undisputed facts in this case are these: The Western Union Telegraph Company has for a number of years maintained a local office in Irvine, Ky. In February, 1930, the appellant was put in full charge of this office. It is not clear how many employees were under him, but at least it is shown that there were a porter and a young lady employee who worked under his direction. The office was equipped with a safe. At the time appellant was put in charge of the office, the combination on this safe was reset and he was given a copy of it. Another copy of the combination was sealed in an envelope and sent to the main office of the company in Nashville, where it was placed among the archives not to be opened unless the appellant severed his connection with the company and it became necessary to ascertain what the combination was in order to get into the safe. Thus although the company could, by opening this sealed envelope, apprise itself of what the combination was, yet so long as appellant continued in its employ it remained in actual ignorance of the combination to the safe and the appellant was the only one who had actual access to the safe. Inside of the safe was a small portable steel vault or box, the keys to which were intrusted to appellant. In this steel vault or box appellant placed at night the funds which came into the office during the day, and in the morning took them out either for use as change, for deposit in bank, or to be forwarded to the company. On the morning of July 5, 1930, the safe was discovered open. Its handle and dial were broken off, and the steel vault or box which had in it approximately $90 of the funds of the company was missing. It was later discovered empty in a field near by appellant's boarding house. We shall assume for the purpose of the decision of this case, and without detailing the facts at length, that the commonwealth's proof made out a case to go to the jury that the abstraction of the steel vault from the safe and the conversion of the funds that it contained were done by

---

one another very much, and were hardly to be distinguished: That in the case of Rex v. Spears, ante, p. 825, the corn was in the possession of the master under the care of the servant: and Lord Kenyon said that he relied much on the Act of Parliament respecting the Bank not going further than to protect the Bank. 2 East, C.L. 574.

the appellant. Appellant was indicted, as stated, for the offense of grand larceny, and he insists on this appeal that his motion for a peremptory instruction should have been sustained because the proof shows that if any offense was committed it was that of embezzlement and not larceny.

The main distinction between embezzlement and larceny in cases like the instant one turns on the distinction between custody and possession. We quote from the case of Warmoth v. Commonwealth, 81 Ky. 135:

"A distinction exists where a servant has merely the custody and where he has the possession of the goods. In the former case the felonious appropriation of the goods is larceny; in the latter it is not larceny, but embezzlement. . . ."

In 20 C.J. 410, it is said: "Embezzlement differs from larceny in that it is the wrongful appropriation or conversion of property where the original taking was lawful, or with the consent of the owner, while in larceny the taking involves a trespass, and the felonious intent must exist at the time of such taking. Thus, a bailee who obtains possession of property without fraudulent intent is not guilty of larceny where he subsequently converts it. So long as he has lawful possession he cannot commit a trespass with respect to the property. But where a person enters into a contract of bailment and obtains possession of the property with felonious intent, existing at the time, to appropriate or apply the property to his own use, he is guilty of a trespass and larceny, and not embezzlement, and if one enters into a contract of bailment fraudulently, but without felonious intent, and afterward converts the property, his offense is larceny and not embezzlement. . . . Since, therefore, larceny at common law involves the element of an original wrongful taking or trespass, it cannot apply to the stealing or wrongful conversion of property by an agent or bailee, or by a servant having the possession, as distinguished from the mere custody, or by anyone else intrusted with the possession of the property; and to remedy this defect and prevent an evasion of justice in such cases, statutes of embezzlement were passed."

Under the peculiar facts of this case, we are constrained to the view that at the time the appellant converted the funds here involved (as we have assumed the evidence so establishes) he had the possession as distinguished from the custody of such funds. They were in the safe, the combination of which was known actually only by him. It was intended, in the absence of some untoward circumstance, that at least until he forwarded these funds to the company they should be in his possession. They came into his possession as the servant of the Western Union. He was in full charge of the office. It was he who locked the safe at night and it was only he who could open it in the morning. Although the company had the right to demand the funds of him at any time, and although the company could potentially enter the safe by opening the sealed envelope and apprising itself of the

Sec. 4 THE TRESPASS 147

combination, yet it was not intended by the company that it should interfere with appellant's control and possession of the contents of this safe and the funds of the company unless and until some condition which had not occurred in this case at the time of the conversion had come to pass. It is quite manifest that the possession of these funds at the time they were converted was in the appellant and that it had not yet become that of the Western Union. This being true, the conversion amounted to an embezzlement and not larceny. Warmoth v. Commonwealth, supra. The two offenses are not degrees of one another. They are distinct offenses. Hence appellant could not be convicted of the offense of larceny when it was shown that what he did constituted embezzlement and not larceny. It follows that appellant's motion for a peremptory instruction should have been sustained. Judgment reversed, with instructions to grant the appellant a new trial in conformity with this opinion.

Whole court sitting.[1]

REX v. SULLENS

Court for Crown Cases Reserved, 1826.
1 Moody 129, 168 Eng.Rep. 1212.

The prisoner was tried before Alexander C. B., at the Spring Assizes for the county of Essex, in the year 1826, on an indictment at common law: the first count of which charged the prisoner with stealing at Doddinghurst, on the 25th September, 1825, one promissory note, value £5, the property of Thomas Nevill and George Nevill, his master; the second count with stealing silver coin, the property of Thomas Nevill and George Nevill.

It appeared in evidence that Thomas Nevill, the prisoner's master, gave him a £5 country note, to get change, on the said 25th of September; that he got change, all in silver, and on his obtaining the change he said it was for his master, and that his master sent him. The prisoner never returned.

The jury found the prisoner not guilty on the first count, but guilty on the second count.

The question reserved for the consideration of the Judges was, whether the conviction was proper, or whether the indictment should not have been on the statute 39 Geo. III. c. 85, for embezzlement?

In Easter Term, 1826, the Judges met and considered this case, and held that the conviction was wrong, because as the masters never

---

[1]. A member of a maintenance crew who had a key to the room in which Prestone was kept, to enable him to enter for other purposes, but who had no authority to remove any Prestone without a requisition from the chief engineer, did not have possession of the Prestone and was guilty of larceny by wrongfully taking it to sell for himself. Warren v. State, 223 Ind. 552, 62 N.E.2d 624 (1945).

had possession of the change, except by the hands of the prisoner, he was only amenable under the statute 39 Geo. III. c. 85. (Rex v. Headge, Russ & Ry. C. C. R. 160; Rex v. Walsh, ib. 215.)

COMMONWEALTH v. RYAN

Supreme Judicial Court of Massachusetts, 1892.
155 Mass. 523, 30 N.E. 364.

HOLMES, J. This is a complaint for embezzlement of money. The case for the government is as follows. The defendant was employed by one Sullivan to sell liquor for him in his store. Sullivan sent two detectives to the store, with marked money of Sullivan's, to make a feigned purchase from the defendant. One detective did so. The defendant dropped the money into the money drawer of a cash register, which happened to be open in connection with another sale made and registered by the defendant, but he did not register this sale, as was customary, and afterward—it would seem within a minute or two—he took the money from the drawer. The question presented is whether it appears, as matter of law, that the defendant was not guilty of embezzlement, but was guilty of larceny, if of anything. The defendant asked rulings to that effect on two grounds: first, that after the money was put into the drawer it was in Sullivan's possession, and therefore the removal of it was a trespass and larceny; . . .

We must take it as settled that it is not larceny for a servant to convert property delivered to him by a third person for his master, provided he does so before the goods have reached their destination, or something more has happened to reduce him to a mere custodian; while, on the other hand, if the property is delivered to the servant by his master, the conversion is larceny.

This distinction is not very satisfactory, but it is due to historical accidents in the development of the criminal law, coupled, perhaps with an unwillingness on the part of the judges to enlarge the limits of a capital offence. . . .

. . . It was settled by St. 21 Hen. VIII. c. 7, that the conversion of goods delivered to a servant by his master was felony, and this statute has been thought to be only declaratory of the common law in later times, since the distinction between the possession of a bailee and the custody of a servant has been developed more fully, on the ground that the custody of the servant is the possession of the master. . . . But probably when the act was passed it confirmed the above mentioned doubt as to the master's possession where the servant was intrusted with property at a distance from his master's house in cases outside the statute, that is, when the chattels were delivered by a third person. In Dyer, 5a, 5b, it was said that it was not within the statute if an apprentice ran off with the money received from a third person for his master's goods at a fair, because he had it not by the delivery of his master. This, very likely, was correct, because the statute only dealt with delivery by the master; but the case was taken before long as authority for the broader proposition that the act is not a felony, and the reason was invented to account for it that the servant has possession, because the money is delivered to him. 1 Hale, P.C. 667, 668. This phrase about delivery seems to have been used first in an attempt to distinguish between servants and bailees; Y.B. 13 Edw. IV. 10, pl. 5; Moore, 248; but as used here it is a perverted remnant of the old and now exploded notion that a servant away from his master's house always has possession. The old case of the servant converting a horse with which his master had intrusted him to go to market was stated and explained in the same way, on the ground that the horse was delivered to the servant. Crompton, Just. 35b, pl. 7. See The King v. Bass, 1 Leach, (4th ed.) 251. Yet the emptiness of the explanation was shown by the fact that it still was held felony when the master delivered property for service in his own house. Kelyng 35. The last step was for the principle thus qualified and explained to be applied to a delivery by a third person to a servant in his master's shop, although it is possible at least that the case would have been decided differently in the time of the Year Books; Y.B. 2 Edw. IV. 15, pl. 7; Fitzh.Nat.Brev. 91 E; and although it is questionable whether on sound theory the possession is not as much in the master as if he had delivered the property himself. . . .

The last mentioned decisions made it necessary to consider with care what more was necessary, and what was sufficient, to reduce the servant to the position of a mere custodian. An obvious case was when the property was finally deposited in the place of deposit provided by the master, and subject to his control, although there was some nice discussion as to what constituted such a place. . . . But it is plain that the mere physical presence of the money there for a moment is not conclusive while the servant is on the spot and has not lost his power over it; as, for instance, if the servant drops it, and instantly picks it up again. Such cases are among the few in which the actual intent of the party is legally important; for, apart from other considerations, the character in which he exercises his control depends entirely upon himself. . . .

It follows from what we have said, that the defendant's first position cannot be maintained, and that the judge was right in charging the jury that, if the defendant before he placed the money in the drawer intended to appropriate it, and with that intent simply put it in the drawer for his own convenience in keeping it for himself, that would not make his appropriation of it just afterwards larceny. The distinction may be arbitrary, but, as it does not affect the defendant otherwise than by giving him an opportunity, whichever offence he was convicted of, to contend that he should have been convicted of the other, we have the less uneasiness in applying it. . . .

Exceptions overruled.

(iii) The Breaking Bulk Doctrine

In 1473 one who had bargained to take certain bales to Southampton wrongfully took them to another place where he broke open the bales and appropriated the contents. Whether or not this was larceny was debated in the Star Chamber. A motion to transfer the case to the common-law court was rejected because "the complainant was a merchant stranger, whose case ought to be judged by the law of nature in Chancery, and without the delay of a trial by jury". Hence it was disposed of in the Exchequer Chamber where most of the judges held that it was larceny, but for different reasons.[1] The reason offered by one was that the carrier had possession of the bales but not the contents so that he committed trespass by removing the contents from the bales. This was later adopted as the holding of the case and resulted in this anomalous rule: If a bailee having lawful possession of a bale wrongfully appropriates it, bale and all, it is not larceny; but if he wrongfully breaks it open and appropriates part or all[2] of the contents this is larceny. In the course of time the doctrine of "breaking bale" seems to have changed to one of "breaking bulk", which was even more peculiar. Under this notion if property such as wheat was delivered in bulk to the bailee's own vehicle it was not larceny if the bailee converted it all, but was larceny if he separated a portion from the mass and converted only that portion.[3] The whole doctrine has been largely, if not entirely, wiped out by legislation.

(iv) Goods Delivered by Mistake

COOPER v. COMMONWEALTH

Court of Appeals of Kentucky, 1901.
110 Ky. 123, 60 S.W. 938.

Opinion of the Court by JUDGE O'REAR. Reversing.

Appellants, Grant Cooper, Fred Cooper, Thomas Harris and Sandy Waggener, were convicted in the Union Circuit Court of the crime of grand larceny, under the following state of facts: The four named had been shucking corn, and were paid $6 for their

---

1. Carrier's Case, Year Book, 13 Ed. IV, 9, pl. 5 (1473).

2. A bailee who wrongfully opens up a bag and takes all of the contents is just as much guilty of larceny as if he had taken only a part. Rex v. Brazier, Russ. and Ry. 337, 168 Eng.Rep. 833 (1817).

3. Commonwealth v. Brown, 4 Mass. 580 (1808); Nichols v. People, 17 N.Y. 114 (1858); Rex v. Howell, 7 Car. and P. 325, 173 Eng.Rep. 145 (1836); Rex v. Pratley, 5 Car. and P. 533, 172 Eng. Rep. 1086 (1833). Contra: Rex v. Madox, Russ. and Ry. 92, 168 Eng.Rep. 700 (1805).

services. In order to divide the money equally among themselves, they went to the Bank of Uniontown to have $2 of the money changed into smaller denominations. Appellant, Sandy Waggener, went into the bank and to the cashier's counter, handed him the $2 and asked for the change. The cashier handed him two half dollars and a roll of small-sized coin wrapped in paper saying, "There are twenty nickels." Waggener, without unwrapping the coins, and not knowing what was in the paper, except from the statement of the cashier, rejoined his companions; and the four together went a distance of some four squares, to a more secluded spot, to divide their money. On opening the package they discovered it contained twenty 5-dollar gold coins, instead of nickels. Waggener remarked, "Boys, banks don't correct mistakes," and the money was divided among the four and appropriated by them. Upon this evidence the court gave the jury the following instruction: "If you believe from the evidence, to the exclusion of a reasonable doubt, that in this county, and prior to the finding of the indictment herein, the defendants, Grant Cooper, Fred Cooper and Thos. Harris and Sandy Waggener, sought to have some money changed at the Bank of Uniontown in order to get twenty nickels, or some small change, and that Chas. Kelleners, the assistant cashier of said bank, in making said change delivered by mistake to the defendants twenty five-dollar gold pieces, wrapped in a paper, believing at the time that he was giving them twenty nickels, and that the defendants, sharing in that belief, shortly thereafter opened said paper, and found therein twenty five-dollar gold pieces, and failed to return said gold pieces to said bank—now, if you further believe from the evidence, to the exclusion of a reasonable doubt, that when said defendants unwrapped said paper, and found therein, and in their possession, the said five-dollar gold pieces, they knew that same had been delivered to them by said Kelleners through mistake, and knew or had the means of ascertaining that the bank was the owner of said gold pieces, but thereupon nevertheless feloniously converted the same to their own use, intending to premanently [sic] deprive the owner thereof, you will find them guilty as charged; and in your verdict you will fix their punishment at confinement in the penitentiary for not less than one nor more than five years." Appellants objected to the foregoing, and asked the court to give the jury these instructions: "(a) The court instructs the jury that, to find the defendants guilty of larceny, they must believe that at the time they received the money from Chas. Kelleners they must have then had the purpose and intent to convert the excess which they received over and above what was justly due them as change to their own use and benefit, and to deprive the bank of its money feloniously; that, unless the felonious intent was proven at the time of receiving the money, the law is for the defendants, and the jury will so find. (b) The court instructs the jury that the felonious intent must exist at the time of receiving the money, and that no felonious intent, subsequent or wrongful conversion, will amount to a felony"—which were rejected by the court.

It was held in Elliott v. Com., 12 Bush 176, that where the possession of the goods was obtained by the accused for a particular purpose, with the intent then, however, on the part of the accused, to convert them to his own use, which he subsequently did, it would constitute larceny. In Snapp v. Com., 82 Ky. 173, we held that, where money came into the hands of the accused lawfully, his subsequent felonious conversion would not be larceny. In the last-named case the court said it devolved upon the Commonwealth to show an unlawful taking of this money from the city (the owner) by the accused with a felonious intent, and that "the money had been received without fraud and as a matter of right, and in such a case, although he may have the *animus furandi* afterwards, and convert it to his own use, he was not guilty of larceny." In Smith v. Com., 96 Ky. 85, 87, 27 S.W. 852, this court announced, "The general and common-law rule is that when property comes lawfully into the possession of a person, either as agent, bailee, part owner, or otherwise, a subsequent appropriation of it is not larceny, unless the intent to appropriate it existed in the mind of the taker at the time it came into his hands." Whart.Cr.Law, section 958, says, "To constitute larceny in receiving an overpayment, the defendant must know at the time of the overpayment, and must intend to steal." The authorities seem to be agreed that, to constitute the crime of larceny, there must be a simultaneous combination of an unlawful taking, an asportation, and a felonious intent.

We conclude that the instructions asked by appellants should have been given to the jury, and that the idea expressed in the first instruction given—that if appellants received the money under a mutual mistake, and after discovering it feloniously converted it—should not have been given. Judgment reversed and cause remanded for a new trial, and for proceedings consistent herewith.[1]

---

[1]. The purchaser of a supposedly empty trunk converted a coat and vest which he found therein. This was held to be larceny. Robinson v. State, 11 Tex. App. 403 (1882). The court said: "The owner, or rather his clerk, whilst selling and delivering the trunk never intended to convey and did not convey either the title or possession of its contents; for he was wholly ignorant of its contents. So was defendant, when he purchased and became possessed of the trunk. The goods, so far as these parties were concerned, were lost, because they neither knew anything of their existence or their whereabouts. When defendant opened, examined and came across them in the trunk, they were in every sense lost goods which he found; as much so as if he had come across them upon the public highway or any other place where the owner had dropped, mislaid, left them by mistake, or lost them." Accord: Merry v. Green, 7 Mees. and W. 623, 151 Eng.Rep. 916 (1841).

BAILEY v. STATE

Supreme Court of Alabama, 1877.
58 Ala. 414.

Defendant, William Bailey, was indicted at the spring term, 1877, of said court, for larceny, the indictment being in the usual form.

The State introduced as a witness the prosecutor, one G. Fuller, who testified that he was indebted to defendant in the sum of two dollars, and upon going to pay said debt, and intending to pay only the two dollars, he paid defendant two bills; that the room where he paid defendant was rather dark, it being cloudy without, and he could not see distinctly, and he made a mistake and gave the defendant a ten dollar instead of a one dollar bill; that next day witness missed a ten dollar bill which he remembered having had before the payment to defendant, so, he went and asked defendant if he did not make a mistake and pay him a ten dollar bill instead of a one dollar bill; and the defendant denied that he was so paid. One Jesse Farmer, another witness for the State, swore that on a certain Sunday before the indictment, he was with defendant and defendant remarked that "he had a secret that he would tell witness," and asked witness "if he noticed Fuller when he paid him (defendant), some money on the day before," to which witness replied that he saw no mistake; defendant then said that Fuller had made a mistake, and had paid him a ten dollar bill instead of a one dollar bill. Witness then asked defendant "what he intended to do about it?" Defendant replied that "Fuller had so much money he would never detect the loss, but if he missed the ten dollar bill, he would make it all right with him." Afterwards, defendant told witness he had spent the ten dollar bill. This being all the evidence, the defendant's counsel asked the court, in writing, to charge the jury that "if they believe from the evidence that Fuller, in paying out the money to defendant, made a mistake and paid him a ten dollar bill, then, before the defendant can be convicted of petit larceny, the evidence must satisfy the jury, beyond a reasonable doubt, that, at the time the mistake was made, the defendant knew of the mistake, and with the knowledge received the ten dollar bill, and that any subsequent appropriation of the money by defendant, without a knowledge of the mistake at the time it was made, will not constitute the offense of petit larceny." The court refused to give the charge, and defendant's counsel excepted.

The defendant now appeals, upon the record, to this court.

. . .

STONE, J. Larceny is the felonious taking and carrying away of the personal goods of another. To constitute larceny under the undisputed facts of this case, the defendant must have known, at the very time he received the money, that he was receiving too much, and more than was intended for him, and must then have intended to convert the money to his own use. This would constitute the taking such a fraud, as would amount to larceny.

On the other hand, if the testimony and circumstances fail to establish the facts and intent as above supposed, with such full measure of proof as to leave in the minds of the jury no reasonable doubt of the defendant's guilty knowledge and intent, at the time he received the money, then he is guilty of no crime, but only of a civil tort, known as trover and conversion.

The Circuit Court erred in the charge given, and in the refusal to charge as asked. Let the judgment be reversed, and the cause remanded. The defendant will remain in custody until discharged by due course of law.

COMMONWEALTH v. HAYS

Supreme Judicial Court of Massachusetts, 1859.
14 Gray 62.

Indictment on St.1857, c. 233, which declares that "if any person, to whom any money, goods or other property, which may be the subject of larceny, shall have been delivered, shall embezzle, or fraudulently convert to his own use, or shall secrete, with intent to embezzle or fraudulently convert to his own use, such money, goods, or property, or any part thereof, he shall be deemed, by so doing, to have committed the crime of simple larceny." The indictment contained two counts, one for embezzlement, and one for simple larceny.

At the trial in the court of common pleas in Middlesex, at October term 1858, before Aiken, J., Amos Stone, called as a witness by the Commonwealth, testified as follows: "I am treasurer of the Charlestown Five Cent Savings Bank. On the 17th day of October 1857, the defendant came into the bank, and asked to draw his deposit, and presented his deposit book. I took his book, balanced it, and handed it back to him. It was for one hundred and thirty dollars in one item. I then counted out to him two hundred and thirty dollars, and said, 'There are two hundred and thirty dollars.' The defendant took the money to the end of the counter, and counted it, and then left the room. Soon after the defendant had left, I discovered that I had paid him one hundred dollars too much. After the close of bank hours I went in search of the defendant, and told him that I had paid him one hundred dollars too much, and asked him to adjust the matter. The defendant asked me how I knew it. He asked me if I could read. I said 'Yes.' He then showed me his book, and said, 'What does that say?' I took it, and read in it one hundred and thirty dollars. The defendant then said, 'That is what I got.' He exhibited two fifties, two tens, and a ten dollar gold piece, and said, 'That is what I got.' I then said to him, 'Do you say that is all and precisely what I gave you?' He replied, 'That is what I got.' I then said to him, 'I can prove that you got two hundred and thirty dollars.' He replied, 'That is what I want; if you can prove it, you will get it; otherwise you wont.' I intended to pay the defendant the sum of two hundred and thirty dollars and did so pay him. I then supposed that the book called for two hundred and thirty dollars. Books are kept at the bank containing an account with depositors, wherein all sums deposited are credited to them, and all sums paid out are charged to them."

The defendant asked the court to instruct the jury that the above facts did not establish such a delivery or embezzlement as subjected the defendant to a prosecution under the St. of 1857, c. 233, and did not constitute the crime of larceny.

The court refused so to instruct the jury; and instructed them "that if the sum of two hundred and thirty dollars was so delivered to the defendant, as testified, and one hundred dollars, parcel of the same, was so delivered by mistake of the treasurer, as testified, and the defendant knew that it was so delivered by mistake, and knew he was not entitled to it, and afterwards the money so delivered by mistake was demanded of him by the treasurer, and the defendant, having such knowledge, did fraudulently, and with a felonious intent to deprive the bank of the money, convert the same to his own use, he would be liable under this indictment." The jury returned a verdict of guilty, and the defendant alleged exceptions.

BIGELOW, J. The statute under which this indictment is found is certainly expressed in very general terms, which leave room for doubt as to its true construction. But interpreting its language according to the subject matter to which it relates, and in the light of the existing state of the law, which the statute was intended to alter and enlarge, we think its true meaning can be readily ascertained.

The statutes relating to embezzlement, both in this country and in England, had their origin in a design to supply a defect which was found to exist in the criminal law. By reason of nice and subtle distinctions, which the courts of law had recognized and sanctioned, it was difficult to reach and punish the fraudulent taking and appropriation of money and chattels by persons exercising certain trades and occupations, by virtue of which they held a relation of confidence or trust towards their employers or principals, and thereby became possessed of their property. In such cases the moral guilt was the same as if the offender had been guilty of an actual felonious taking; but in many cases he could not be convicted of larceny, because the property which had been fraudulently converted was lawfully in his possession by virtue of his employment, and there was not that technical taking or asportation which is essential to the proof of the crime of larceny. The King v. Bazeley, 2 Leach, (4th ed.) 835. 2 East P.C. 568.

The statutes relating to embezzlement were intended to embrace this class of offences; and it may be said generally that they do not apply to cases where the element of a breach of trust or confidence in the fraudulent conversion of money or chattels is not shown to exist. This is the distinguishing feature of the provisions in the Rev.Sts. c. 126, §§ 27–30, creating and punishing the crime of embezzlement, which carefully enumerate the classes of persons that may be subject to the penalties therein provided. Those provisions have been strictly construed, and the operation of the statute has been carefully confined to persons having in their possession, by virtue of their occupation or employment, the money or property of another, which has been fraudulently converted in violation of a trust reposed in them. Commonwealth v. Williams, 3 Gray 461. In the last named case it was held, that a person was not guilty of embezzlement, under Rev.Sts. c. 126, § 30 who had converted to his own use money which had been delivered to him by another for safe keeping.

The St. of 1857, c. 233, was probably enacted to supply the defect which was shown to exist in the criminal law by this decision, and was intended to embrace cases where property had been designedly delivered to a person as a bailee or keeper, and had been fraudulently converted by him. But in this class of cases there exists the element of a trust or confidence reposed in a person by reason of the delivery of property to him, which he voluntarily takes for safe keeping, and which trust or confidence he has violated by the wrongful conversion of the property. Beyond this the statute was not intended to go. Where money paid or property delivered through mistake has been misappropriated or converted by the party receiving it, there is no breach of a trust or violation of a confidence intentionally reposed by one party and voluntarily assumed by the other. The moral turpitude is therefore not so great as in those cases usually comprehended within the offence of embezzlement, and we cannot think that the legislature intended to place them on the same footing. We are therefore of opinion that the facts proved in this case did not bring it within the statute, and that the defendant was wrongly convicted.

Exceptions sustained.[1]

---

[1]. It was held to be larceny for the holder of a check for $36.00 to appropriate over $4,000.00 which was handed to him by the bank teller who misread the check. Sapp v. State, 157 Fla. 605, 26 So.2d 646 (1946).

(v) Goods Obtained by Fraud

THE KING v. PEAR

Court for Crown Cases Reserved, 1779.
1 Leach 212, 168 Eng.Rep. 208.

The prisoner was indicted for stealing a black horse, the property of Samuel Finch. It appeared in evidence that Samuel Finch was a Livery-Stable-keeper in the Borough; and that the prisoner, on the 2d of July 1779, hired the horse of him to go to Sutton, in the county of Surry, and back again, saying on being asked where he lived, that he lodged at No. 25 in King-street, and should return about eight o'clock the same evening. He did not return; and it was proved that he had sold the horse on the very day he had hired it, to one William Hollist, in Smithfield Market; and that he had no lodging at the place to which he had given the prosecutor directions.

The learned Judge said: There had been different opinions on the law of this class of cases; that the general doctrine then was that if a horse be let for a particular portion of time, and after that time is expired, the party hiring, instead of returning the horse to its owner, sell it and convert the money to his own use, it is felony, because there is then no privity of contract subsisting between the parties; that in the present case the horse was hired to take a journey into Surry, and the prisoner sold him the same day, without taking any such journey; that there were also other circumstances which imported that at the time of the hiring the prisoner had it in intention to sell the horse, as his saying that he lodged at a place where in fact he was not known. He therefore left it with the Jury to consider, Whether the prisoner meant at the time of the hiring to take such journey, but was afterwards tempted to sell the horse? for if so he must be acquitted; but that if they were of opinion that at the time of the hiring the journey was a mere pretence to get the horse into his possession, and he had no intention to take such journey but intended to sell the horse, they would find that fact specially for the opinion of the Judges.

The Jury found that the facts above stated were true; and also that the prisoner had hired the horse with a fraudulent view and intention of selling it immediately.

The question was referred to the Judges, Whether the delivery of the horse by the prosecutor to the prisoner, had so far changed the possession of the property, as to render the subsequent conversion of it a mere breach of trust, or whether the conversion was felonious? (see the case of Sharpless and Another, ante, page 92, case 52).

The Judges differed greatly in opinion on this case; and delivered their opinions *seriatim* upon it at Lord Chief Justice De Gray's house on 4th February 1780 and on the 22nd of the same month Mr.

Baron Perryn delivered their opinion on it. The majority of them thought, That the question, as to the original intention of the prisoner in hiring the horse, had been properly left to the jury; and as they had found, that his view in so doing was fraudulent, the parting with the property had not changed the nature of the possession, but that it remained unaltered in the prosecutor at the time of the conversion; and that the prisoner was therefore guilty of felony.[1]

THE QUEEN v. PRINCE

Court for Crown Cases Reserved, 1868.
L.R. 1 C.C. 150.

(Mrs. Allen forged her husband's signature and thereby obtained money equal to his entire deposit in the bank. She then left Allen and ran away with Prince. She gave some of this money to Prince who was convicted of knowingly receiving money stolen from the bank.)

BOVILL, C. J. I am of opinion that this conviction cannot be sustained. The distinction between larceny and false pretences is material. In larceny the taking must be against the will of the owner. That is of the essence of the offence. The cases cited by Mr. Collins on behalf of the prisoner are clear and distinct upon this point, shewing that the obtaining of property from its owner, or his servant absolutely authorized to deal with it, by false pretences will not amount to larceny. The cases cited on the other side are cases where the servant had only a limited authority from his master. Here, however, it seems to me that the bank clerk had a general authority to part with both the property in and possession of his master's money on receiving what he believed to be a genuine order, and that as he did so part with both the property in and possession of the note in question the offence committed by Mrs. Allen falls within the cases which make it a false pretence, and not a larceny, and therefore the prisoner cannot be convicted of knowingly receiving a stolen note.

CHANNELL, B. I am of the same opinion. . . .

BYLES, J. I am of the same opinion. I would merely say that I ground my judgment purely on authority.

BLACKBURN, J. I also am of the same opinion. I must say I cannot but lament that the law now stands as it does. The distinction drawn between larceny and false pretences, one being made a felony and the other a misdemeanour—and yet the same punishment attached to each—seems to me, I must confess, unmeaning and mischievous. The distinction arose in former times, and I take it that

---

[1] The majority held that this was "such a taking as would have made the prisoner liable to an action of trespass at the suit of the owner, . . ." 2 East P.C. 688.

it was then held in favour of life that in larceny the taking must be against the will of the owner, larceny then being a capital offence. However, as the law now stands, if the owner intended the property to pass, though he would not so have intended had he known the real facts, that is sufficient to prevent the offence of obtaining another's property from amounting to larceny; and where the servant has an authority co-equal with his master's, and parts with his master's property, such property cannot be said to be stolen, inasmuch as the servant intends to part with the property in it. If, however, the servant's authority is limited, then he can only part with the possession, and not with the property; if he is tricked out of the possession, the offence so committed will be larceny. In Reg. v. Longstreeth[1], the carrier's servant had no authority to part with the goods, except to the right consignee. His authority was not generally to act in his master's business, but limited in that way. The offence was in that case held to be larceny on that ground, and this distinguishes it from the pawnbroker's case[2], which the same judges, or at any rate some of them, had shortly before decided. There the servant, from whom the goods were obtained, had a general authority to act for his master, and the person who obtained the goods was held not to be guilty of larceny. So, in the present case, the cashier holds the money of the bank with a general authority from the bank to deal with it. He has authority to part with it on receiving what he believes to be a genuine order. Of the genuineness he is the judge; and if under a mistake he parts with money, he none the less intends to part with the property in it, and thus the offence is not, according to the cases, larceny, but an obtaining by false pretences. The distinction is inscrutable to my mind, but it exists in the cases. There is no statute enabling a count for larceny to be joined with one for false pretences; and as the prisoner was indicted for the felony, the conviction must be quashed.

LUSH, J. I also agree that the conviction must be quashed. . . .[a]

[Numbered footnotes by the Court.]

1. 1 Moo.C.C. 137.

2. Reg. v. Jackson, 1 Mood.C.C. 119.

a. See Anderson v. State, 33 Ala.App. 531, 36 So.2d 242 (1948). It was held to be larceny if the title did not actually pass although the intention had been to pass both title and possession. English v. State, 80 Fla. 70, 85 So. 150 (1920). Contra: Rex v. Adams, Russ. & Ry. 225, 168 Eng. Rep. 773 (1812); Rex v. Atkinson, 2 East P.C. 673 (1799).

THE QUEEN v. KILHAM

Court for Crown Cases Reserved, 1870.
L.R. 1 C.C. 261.

Case stated by the Recorder of York.

Indictment under 24 & 25 Vict. c. 96, s. 88, for obtaining goods by false pretences.

The prisoner was tried at the last Easter quarter sessions for York. The prisoner, on the 19th of March last, called at the livery stables of Messrs. Thackray, who let out horses for hire, and stated that he was sent by a Mr. Gibson Hartley to order a horse to be ready the next morning for the use of a son of Mr. Gibson Hartley, who was a customer of the Messrs. Thackray. Accordingly, the next morning the prisoner called for the horse, which was delivered to him by the ostler. The prisoner was seen, in the course of the same day, driving the horse, which he returned to Messrs. Thackray's stables in the evening. The hire for the horse, amounting to 7s., was never paid by the prisoner.

The prisoner was found guilty.

The question was, whether the prisoner could properly be found guilty of obtaining a chattel by false pretences within the meaning of 24 & 2 Vict. c. 96, s. 88.[1] . . .

June 4. The judgment of the Court (Bovill, C. J., Willes, Byles, and Hannen, JJ., and Cleasby, B.) was delivered by

BOVILL, C. J. We are of opinion that the conviction in this case cannot be supported. The statute 24 & 25 Vict. c. 96, s. 88, enacts that, "whosoever shall, by any false pretence, obtain from any other person any chattel, money, or valuable security, with intent to defraud, shall be guilty of misdemeanour." The word "obtain" in this section does not mean obtain the loan of, but obtain the property in, any chattel, &c. This is, to some extent, indicated by the proviso, that if it be proved that the person indicted obtained the property in such manner as to amount in law to larceny, he shall not, by reason thereof, be entitled to be acquitted; but, it is made more clear by referring to the earlier statute from which the language of s. 88 is adopted. 7 & 8 Geo. 4, c. 29, s. 53, recites that "a failure of justice frequently arises from the subtle distinction between 'larceny and fraud,'" and, for remedy thereof, enacts that "if any person shall, by any false pretence, obtain," &c. The subtle distinction which the statute was intended to remedy was this: that if a person, by fraud, induced another to part with the possession only of goods and con-

---

[Numbered footnotes by the Court.]

1. 24 & 25 Vict. c. 96, s. 88, enacts that, "whosoever shall, by any false pretence, obtain from any other person any chattel, money, or valuable security, with intent to defraud, shall be guilty of a misdemeanour."

verted them to his own use, this was larceny; while, if he induced another by fraud to part with the property in the goods as well as the possession, this was not larceny.[2]

But to constitute an obtaining by false pretences it is equally essential, as in larceny, that there shall be an intention to deprive the owner wholly of his property, and this intention did not exist in the case before us. In support of the conviction the case of Reg. v. Boulton[3] was referred to. There the prisoner was indicted for obtaining, by false pretences, a railway ticket with intent to defraud the company. It was held that the prisoner was rightly convicted, though the ticket had to be given up at the end of the journey. The reasons for this decision do not very clearly appear, but it may be distinguished from the present case in this respect: that the prisoner, by using the ticket for the purpose of travelling on the railway, entirely converted it to his own use for the only purpose for which it was capable of being applied. In this case the prisoner never intended to deprive the prosecutor of the horse or the property in it, or to appropriate it to himself, but only intended to obtain the use of the horse for a limited time. The conviction must, therefore, be quashed.

Conviction quashed.[a]

WILKINSON v. STATE

Supreme Court of Mississippi, 1952.
215 Miss. 327, 60 So.2d 786.

ETHRIDGE, JUSTICE. Appellant, Fred Wilkinson, was indicted and convicted at the January 1952 term of the Circuit Court of Franklin County of grand larceny, consisting of the theft of three head of cattle. He argues here that the conviction was against the great weight of the evidence, was based upon the uncorroborated testimony of an accomplice, and that he was indicted and convicted under the wrong statute.

The state's case, which the jury manifestly accepted, is in summary as follows: The three head of cattle which were stolen belonged to Douglas Leonard, who at that time was away at college. The cattle

---

[2]. See the cases on this subject; 2 Russ. on Crimes, 200, 4th ed., and note (d) p. 664. Vol. 1.

[3]. 1 Den.C.C. 508; 19 L.J. (M.C.) 67.

[By the Compiler.]

[a]. Anonymous, 6 Mod. 105, 87 Eng.Rep. 863 (1704).

A. was indicted for *deceitfully* coming to B. as sent from C. to whom B. owed money, to call for and receive the money, and receiving the money, *ubi revera* C. never did send him.

Per Curiam. If he had come with a *false token* it had been criminal, and therefore indictable; but the question is, whether this be such a cheat as is indictable? as playing with false dice is, for that is such a cheat as a person of an ordinary capacity cannot discover; but this is an indictment to punish one man because another is a fool.

Per Curiam. Let it stay.

had drifted away from their home place, so Lee Leonard, father of Douglas, went out and got them for his son in September, 1950, and put them in Sullivan's pasture. The three cattle escaped in November 1950 from this enclosure, and strayed away, turning up in about January, 1951, on the place of Lee Ferguson, who held them as estrays for the true owner, whoever he might be. Whittington lived in that area, and had from time to time owned around thirty head of cattle himself, several of which had strayed away. Appellant Wilkinson lived in Whittington's house and worked on his place as a hired hand. Whittington learned that Ferguson was holding some estrays for the owner, so he and appellant went to Ferguson's place on a Saturday in early March, 1951 to look at them. Whittington told Ferguson that he was looking for some cattle which he had missing, and upon Whittington's request, assented to by Ferguson, Whittington and appellant went down into Ferguson's pasture to look at the estrays. Whittington determined that they were not his cattle, but upon the suggestion and urging of Wilkinson, he pretended that they were and so advised Ferguson. Whittington had an agreement with appellant that he and appellant would sell the cattle, appellant would get $85 and Whittington the balance. Whittington paid Ferguson $10 for taking care of the cattle and advised him that they would come back the following Thursday morning to get them.

Ferguson believed Whittington's story, and transferred the possession of the cattle to him and appellant when they returned on the next Thursday to get them. He apparently knew both Whittington and appellant prior to this encounter. Whittington carried on the conversations with Ferguson, but Wilkinson was present when the false representations were made. Upon obtaining the cattle from Ferguson, Whittington and appellant took them to a cattle sales lot and sold them. Whittington paid appellant $85 and retained the balance of the sale price for himself. The check of the cattle dealer to Whittington for the sale price of the cattle was cashed by him in a store operated by Ransom in the Town of Summit. Whittington and appellant came in together to get Ransom to cash the check. Ransom observed Whittington giving appellant some of the proceeds of it. He heard him ask appellant if he was satisfied. Whittington testified to the same effect. Both Whittington and his wife testified that appellant went with him to look at the cows and helped to build a wire pen to fence them in. Ferguson testified to the circumstances under which he transferred possession of the cattle to Whittington, as did Farmer, Bowlin and Moore, who were present and assisted in loading the cattle on a truck. Bowlin and Moore testified for appellant that they went along with Whittington to help him load the cattle on the truck and that they never heard appellant claim to own the cows, that they understood the cattle belonged to Whittington. Prior to the trial, Whittington had been indicted and convicted of the theft of the cattle in question, and at the time of the trial was serving a term in the state penitentiary. . . .

Secondly, the indictment was properly found under the grand larceny statute, Sec. 2240. The general rule is set forth in 32 Am. Jur., Larceny, Sec. 33: "Although there is some authority to the contrary, the better rule is that one who falsely personates another and in such assumed character receives property intended for such other person is guilty of larceny if he does so with the requisite felonious intent, provided the transaction does not involve the passing of title to the property from the owner to him. Although express statutes to this effect exist in some jurisdictions, it is larceny at common law for a person to pretend that he is the owner or person entitled to personal property in order to obtain possession thereof with the felonious intent of converting it to his own use and depriving the owner of it. Subject to this rule, one who fraudulently claims an estray from the person taking it up or lost property from the finder may be convicted of larceny."

The distinction, a rather fine one, between the crimes of obtaining property by false pretenses and that of larceny through obtaining possession by fraud seems to rest in the intention with which the owner parts with possession. Thus if the possession is obtained by fraud and the owner intends to part with his title as well as his possession, the crime is that of obtaining property by false pretenses, provided the means by which it is acquired comply therewith. But if the possession is fraudulently obtained with a present intent on the part of the person obtaining it to convert the property to his own use, and the owner intends to part with his possession merely and not with the title, the offense is larceny. . . .

At common law, for a person to pretend that he was the owner of the property in order to get possession of it with the felonious intent of converting it to his own use constituted larceny. Accordingly convictions of larceny have been sustained where a person has fraudulently claimed an estray from the person taking it up, and where a person has claimed to be the owner of lost property from the finder. . . .

The foregoing authorities support the conviction under the general grand larceny statute, Sec. 2240. The distinction rests upon the intention with which the owner or possessor parts with possession. Here the possessor of the estrays, Ferguson, obviously had no intent to part with any title to the estrays. Like Sims in the Atterberry case, Ferguson thought he was transferring simply the possession back to the true owner. This accords with the principle that if possession is fraudulently obtained, with present intent on the part of the person obtaining it, to convert the property to his own use, and the owner or possessor intends to part with his possession merely and not with the title, the offense is larceny. The crime for which appellant was convicted constitutes grand larceny both at common law and under Code Sec. 2240. . . .

McGehee, C. J., and Lee, Kyle and Arrington, JJ., concur.

PEOPLE v. KARP

The Court of Appeals of New York, 1948.
298 N.Y. 213, 81 N.E.2d 817.

Appeal, by permission of an Associate Judge of the Court of Appeals, from a judgment of the Appellate Division of the Supreme Court in the second judicial department, entered December 8, 1947, which unanimously affirmed a judgment of the Queens County Court (Downs, J.) convicting defendant of the crimes of grand larceny in the second degree and petit larceny. Chapter 732 of the Laws of 1942 provides, in part, as follows: "Section 1. . . . It is hereby declared as the public policy of the state that the best interests of the people of the state will be served, and confusion and injustice avoided, by eliminating and abolishing the distinctions which have hitherto differentiated one sort of theft from another, each of which, under section twelve hundred and ninety of the penal law, was denominated a larceny, to wit: common law larceny by asportation, common law larceny by trick and device, obtaining property by false pretenses, and embezzlement. . . ."

PER CURIAM. The indictment upon which defendant has been convicted contains thirty counts, fifteen charging theft as bailee and agent, the balance, that sort of theft labeled and prosecuted prior to 1942, as obtaining property by false pretenses. It is with these latter counts that we are concerned.

In this State, before the 1942 amendment of section 1290 of the Penal Law—as at the common law—the crime of obtaining property by false pretenses could not be predicated upon a promise or upon an expression of intention not meant to be fulfilled.[1] The new larceny law (Penal Law, §§ 1290, 1290–a; L.1942, ch. 732), it is true, as the district attorney observes, was aimed at eliminating the subtle and con-

---

1. Accord: Chaplin v. United States, 81 U.S.App.D.C. 80, 157 F.2d 697 (1946); Commonwealth v. Althause, 207 Mass. 32, 93 N.E. 202 (1910); State v. Allison, 186 S.W. 958 (Mo.App.1916).

In reversing a conviction of false pretenses based upon promissory fraud the court said: "We recognize there is authority for the view contended for by appellee that misrepresentation of intention is a misrepresentation of an existing fact. We are not persuaded by that argument and hold with the majority opinion that such is not the correct construction. Many cases could be cited. . . ." Bonney v. United States, 254 F.2d 392, 394 (9th Cir. 1958).

To obtain payment for a lease in advance is not larceny even if there is no intention of turning over possession of the premises to the lessee because it is merely a false promise. People v. Noblett, 244 N.Y. 355, 155 N.E. 670 (1927).

A selection from the whole truth so partial and fragmentary as to give a misleading impression may be ground for criminal liability despite the literal truth of every statement made. Rex v. Kylsant, 48 T.L.R. 62 (1931).

The A.L.I. Model Penal Code takes the position that a false promise (made without the intention of performance) should be sufficient for conviction but adds that "a majority of the American states adhere to a rule of non-liability in false pretense prosecutions". Tentative Draft No. 2, § 206.2 (2), and comment 7 (1954).

fusing distinctions that had previously differentiated the various types of theft. It was not, however, designed to, and did not, broaden the scope of the crime of larceny or designate as criminal that which was previously innocent. Consequently, upon the facts here presented, the trial court should have charged, as requested, that a conviction could not be based upon "intention" or upon "a state of facts not then in existence", and that, to convict, the jury must find that "defendant falsely misrepresented an existing fact"—for, as instructed, the jury was free to return a verdict of guilt based upon evidence of conduct never regarded as criminal in this State.

There must, therefore, be a new trial, and since that is so, we call attention to section 1290-a of the Penal Law which permits proof of false representation or pretense only if there is allegation thereof in the indictment.

The judgments should be reversed, and a new trial ordered.

LOUGHRAN, C. J., and LEWIS, CONWAY, DESMOND, THACHER, DYE and FULD, JJ., concur.

Judgments reversed, etc.

PEOPLE v. ASHLEY

Supreme Court of California, In Bank, 1954.
42 Cal.2d 246, 267 P.2d 271.

TRAYNOR, JUSTICE. Defendant was convicted of four counts of grand theft under section 484 of the Penal Code. He "appeals from the verdicts and judgments as to each count," and from the order denying his motion for a new trial. . . .

Although the crimes of larceny by trick and device and obtaining property by false pretenses are much alike, they are aimed at different criminal acquisitive techniques. Larceny by trick and device is the appropriation of property, the possession of which was fraudulently acquired; obtaining property by false pretenses is the fraudulent or deceitful acquisition of both title and possession. In this state, these two offenses, with other larcenous crimes, have been consolidated into the single crime of theft, Pen.Code, § 484, but their elements have not been changed thereby. The purpose of the consolidation was to remove the technicalities that existed in the pleading and proof of these crimes at common law. Indictments and informations charging the crime of "theft" can now simply allege an "unlawful taking." Pen.Code, §§ 951, 952. Juries need no longer be concerned with the technical differences between the several types of theft, and can return a general verdict of guilty if they find that an "unlawful taking" has been proved. The elements of the several types of theft included within section 484 have not been changed, however, and a judgment of conviction of theft, based on a general verdict of guilty, can be sustained only if the evidence discloses the elements of one of the consolidated offenses. In the present case, it is clear from the record that each of the prosecuting witnesses intended to pass both title and possession, and that the type of theft, if any, in each case, was that of obtaining property by false pretenses. Defendant was not prejudiced by the instruction to the jury relating to larceny by trick and device. Indeed, he requested instructions relating to both larceny by trick and device and obtaining property by false pretenses. Moreover, his defense was not based on distinctions between title and possession, but rather he contends that there was no unlawful taking of any sort.

To support a conviction of theft for obtaining property by false pretenses, it must be shown that the defendant made a false pretense or representation with intent to defraud the owner of his property, and that the owner was in fact defrauded. It is unnecessary to prove that the defendant benefitted personally from the fraudulent acquisition. The false pretense or representation must have materially influenced the owner to part with his property, but the false pretense need not be the sole inducing cause. If the conviction rests primarily on the testimony of a single witness that the false pretense was made, the making of the pretense must be corroborated. Pen. Code, § 1110.

The crime of obtaining property by false pretenses was unknown in the early common law, see Young v. The King, 3 T.R. 98, 102 [1789], and our statute, like those of most American states, is directly traceable to 30 Geo. II, ch. 24, section 1 (22 Statutes-at-Large 114 [1757]). In an early Crown Case Reserved, Rex v. Goodhall, Russ. & Ry. 461 (1821), the defendant obtained a quantity of meat from a merchant by promising to pay at a future day. The jury found that the promise was made without intention to perform. The judges concluded, however, that the defendant's conviction was erroneous because the pretense "was merely a promise of future conduct, and common prudence and caution would have prevented any injury arising from it." Russ. & Ry. at 463. The correctness of this decision is questionable in light of the reasoning in an earlier decision of the King's Bench, Young v. The King, supra—not mentioned in Rex v. Goodhall. By stating that the "promise of future conduct" was such that "common prudence and caution" could prevent any injury arising therefrom, the new offense was confused with the old common law "cheat." The decision also seems contrary to the plain meaning of the statute, and was so interpreted by two English writers on the law of crimes. Archbold, Pleading and Evidence in Criminal Cases 183 [3rd ed., 1828]; Roscoe, Digest of the Law of Evidence in Criminal Cases 418 [2d Amer. ed., 1840]. The opinion in Rex v. Goodhall, supra, was completely misinterpreted in the case of Commonwealth v. Drew, 1837, 19 Pick. 179, at page 185, 36 Mass. 179, at page 185, in which the Supreme Judicial Court of Massachusetts declared by way of dictum, that under the statute "naked lies" could not be regarded as "false pretences." On the basis of these two questionable decisions, Wharton formulated the following generalization: ". . . the false pretense to be within the statute, must relate to a state of things averred to be at the time existing, and not to a state of things thereafter to exist." Wharton, American Criminal Law 542 [1st ed., 1846]. This generalization has been followed in the majority of American cases, almost all of which can be traced to reliance on Wharton or the two cases mentioned above. . . .

In California, the precedents are conflicting. Early decisions of the district courts of appeal follow the general rule as originally formulated by Wharton, . . . but more recently it has been held, and the holdings were approved by this court in People v. Jones, 36 Cal.2d 373, 377, 224 P.2d 353 that a promise made without intention to perform is a misrepresentation of a state of mind, and thus a misrepresentation of existing fact, and is a false pretense within the meaning of section 484 of the Penal Code. . . . These decisions, like those following the majority rule, were made with little explanation of the reasons for the rule. The Court of Appeals for the District of Columbia has, however, advanced the following reasons in defense of the majority rule: "It is of course true that then, [at the time of the early English cases cited by Wharton, supra] as now, the intention to commit certain crimes was ascertained by looking backward from the act and finding that the accused intended to do what he did do. However, where, as here, the act complained of—namely, failure to repay money or use it as specified at the time of borrowing—is as consonant with ordinary commercial default as with criminal conduct, the danger of applying this technique to prove the crime is quite apparent. Business affairs would be materially incumbered by the ever present threat that a debtor might be subjected to criminal penalties if the prosecutor and jury were of the view that at the time of borrowing he was mentally a cheat. The risk of prosecuting one who is guilty of nothing more than a failure or inability to pay his debts is a very real consideration. . . .

"If we were to accept the government's position the way would be open for every victim of a bad bargain to resort to criminal proceedings to even the score with a judgment proof adversary. No doubt in the development of our criminal law the zeal with which the innocent are protected has provided a measure of shelter for the guilty. However, we do not think it wise to increase the possibility of conviction by broadening the accepted theory of the weight to be attached to the mental attitude of the accused." Chaplin v. United States, 81 U.S.App.D.C. 80, 157 F.2d 697, 698–699, 168 A.L.R. 828; but see the dissenting opinion of Edgerton, J., 157 F.2d at pages 699–701. We do not find this reasoning persuasive. In this state, and in the majority of American states as well as in England, false promises can provide the foundation of a civil action for deceit. Civ.Code,

§§ 1572, subd. 4, 1710, subd. 4; see 125 A.L.R. 881–882. In such actions something more than nonperformance is required to prove the defendant's intent not to perform his promise. Nor is proof of nonperformance alone sufficient in criminal prosecutions based on false promises. . . . In such prosecutions the People must, as in all criminal prosecutions, prove their case beyond a reasonable doubt. Any danger, through the instigation of criminal proceedings by disgruntled creditors, to those who have blamelessly encountered "commercial defaults" must, therefore, be predicated upon the idea that trial juries are incapable of weighing the evidence and understanding the instruction that they must be convinced of the defendant's fraudulent intent beyond a reasonable doubt, or that appellate courts will be derelict in discharging their duty to ascertain that there is sufficient evidence to support a conviction.

The problem of proving intent when the false pretense is a false promise is no more difficult than when the false pretense is a misrepresentation of existing fact, and the intent not to perform a promise is regularly proved in civil actions for deceit. Specific intent is also an essential element of many crimes. Moreover, in cases of obtaining property by false pretenses, it must be proved that any misrepresentations of fact alleged by the People were made knowingly and with intent to deceive. If such misrepresentations are made innocently or inadvertently, they can no more form the basis for a prosecution for obtaining property by false pretenses than can an innocent breach of contract. Whether the pretense is a false promise or a misrepresentation of fact, the defendant's intent must be proved in both instances by something more than mere proof of nonperformance or actual falsity. Cf. U. S. v. Ballard, 322 U.S. 78, 64 S.Ct. 882, 88 L.Ed. 1148, and the defendant is entitled to have the jury instructed to that effect. "[T]he accepted theory of the weight to be attached to the mental attitude of the accused" is, therefore, not "broadened," but remains substantially the same. Cf. Chaplin v. United States, supra, 157 F.2d 697, 699. . . .

The purported appeals from the verdicts are dismissed as nonappealable. The judgment and the order denying the motion for a new trial are affirmed.

GIBSON, C. J., and SHENK, EDMONDS and SPENCE, JJ., concur.

SCHAUER, JUSTICE. I concur in the judgment solely on the ground that the evidence establishes, with ample corroboration, the making by the defendant of false representations as to existing facts. On that evidence the convictions should be sustained pursuant to long accepted theories of law.

It is unnecessary on the record to make of this rather simple case a vehicle for the revolutionary holding, contrary to the weight of authority in this state and elsewhere, that a promise to pay or perform at a future date, if unfulfilled, can become the basis for a criminal prosecution on the theory that it was a promise made without a present intention to perform it and that, therefore, whatever of value was received for the promise was property procured by a false representation. Accordingly, I dissent from all that portion of the opinion which discusses and pronounces upon the theories which in my view are extraneous to the proper disposition of any issue actually before us. . . .

CARTER, J., concurs.[1]

Rehearing denied; CARTER and SCHAUER, JJ., dissenting.

ALLEN v. STATE

Court of Appeals of Ohio, Lucas County, 1926.
21 Ohio App. 403, 153 N.E. 218.

RICHARDS, J. The plaintiff in error was convicted of obtaining $400 in money by false pretenses. . . .

On Application for Rehearing

RICHARDS, J. The judgment finding the plaintiff in error guilty of obtaining money under false pretenses was affirmed on February 23, 1926. The money which he was convicted of obtaining under false pretenses was in his possession as agent of the owner. It is now urged that the trial court erred in charging the jury as follows:

"It is not a matter of concern as to whether she paid him the money out of her own pocket, or whether it was money which he had collected and held for her as her agent."

As the statute provides for punishing whoever "obtains" anything of value by false and fraudulent pretenses, it is insisted that the conviction could not be had for obtaining money of which the accused already had the possession, and, no doubt, as a general proposition, that is true; but the rule can have no application where the delivery of the money is not necessary in order to obtain dominion

---

[1]. In a prosecution for cheating an intention not to meet a future obligation is a question of fact and a misrepresentation of a present state of mind as to such intention is a false statement as to an existing fact. State v. McMahon, 49 R.I. 107, 140 A. 359 (1928). "Promises, if made without intent to perform, have long been regarded as frauds" in prosecutions for conspiracy to violate the federal statute prohibiting the use of the mails to defraud. United States v. Rowe, 56 F.2d 747, 749 (2d Cir. 1932).

A misstatement of a state of mind or of the buyer's intention may be a misstatement of "fact" authorizing the rescission of a contract of sale. Ripka v. Philco Corp., 65 F.Supp. 21 (D.C. N.Y.1946).

A Maryland statute makes it a misdemeanor to obtain services of another with intent to defraud, on a promise of payment of wages, and to fail to pay such wages. Noted in 53 Harv.L. Rev. 893 (1940). Cf. Pollock v. Williams, 322 U.S. 4, 64 S.Ct. 792, 88 L. Ed. 1095 (1944).

A misstatement of law will not support a conviction of false pretenses. State v. Edwards, 178 Minn. 446, 227 N.W. 495 (1929).

over it. If the defendant had possession of the money as agent, and obtained the title to it by false and fraudulent pretenses, that would be a sufficient obtaining of the property within the meaning of the statute. The principal [sic] was directly decided in Commonwealth v. Schwartz, 92 Ky. 510, 18 S.W. 775, 36 Am.St.Rep. 609. I quote the third proposition of the syllabus:

"Where one who is in possession of money belonging to another obtains the title by false pretenses, he is guilty of the statutory offense of obtaining money by false pretenses. In such a case it is not necessary to constitute the offense that the possession should have been obtained by false pretenses."

In that case a banker had the money in his possession, which he had collected for the owner, and he thereafter obtained the title to it by false and fraudulent pretenses. He was held to be rightly convicted; the court deciding that the general rule requiring that both the property and the title should be obtained by false pretenses only applies where it takes delivery of the possession to complete the transfer of the title.

Rehearing denied.[1]

WILLIAMS and YOUNG, JJ., concur.

WHITMORE v. STATE

Supreme Court of Wisconsin, 1941.
238 Wis. 79, 298 N.W. 194.

WICKHEM, J. On April 20, 1940, plaintiff in error purchased a 1933 Ford automobile upon a conditional sales contract. The purchase price was $80. By the terms of the conditional sales contract title was reserved in the vendor until the full purchase price was paid. Plaintiff in error gave to the vendor as a down payment a check on the Footville State Bank in the sum of $45. Upon execution of the contract and delivery of the check, plaintiff in error was put in possession of the car. The check failed to clear the bank because plaintiff in error did not have sufficient funds to cover it. The vendor would not have parted with possession of the automobile solely upon the down payment but the conditional sales contract was an essential part of the transaction. The statute which is claimed to have been violated is sec. 343.25, Stats., which reads as follows:

"Any person who shall designedly, by any false pretenses or by any privy or false token and with intent to defraud, obtain from any other person any money, goods, wares, merchandise, or other property, or shall obtain with such intent the signature of any person to

---

1. One who obtained title to property by false pretenses, but did not have possession and never succeeded in getting possession away from the other, was not guilty of false pretenses. Commonwealth v. Randle, 119 Pa. Super. 217, 180 A. 720 (1935).

any written instrument, the false making whereof would be punishable as forgery, shall if the amount of money or other property so received or the face value of such written instrument shall exceed the sum of one hundred dollars, be punished by imprisonment in the state prison not more than five years nor less than one year, or by imprisonment in the county jail not more than one year, or by fine not exceeding one thousand dollars or less than two hundred dollars, and if the amount of money or property so received or face value of such written instrument so procured, shall not exceed the sum of one hundred dollars, he shall be punished by imprisonment in the state prison or county jail not more than one year, or by a fine not exceeding two hundred dollars."

Plaintiff in error first contends that the offense of obtaining money by false pretenses in violation of this section is not established because the evidence fails to show that the vendor delivered the car in sole reliance upon the worthless check. Corscot v. State, 178 Wis. 661, 190 N.W. 465, and Palotta v. State, 184 Wis. 290, 199 N.W. 72, are cited as holding that one of the requisites of obtaining money by false pretenses is reliance by the defrauded person upon the false pretenses or token. We see no merit to this contention. The defrauded vendor relied both upon the down payment and the conditional sales contract, the first to establish a margin of safety for the latter. It cannot be the law that merely because the pretenses constituted only one of several matters relied upon that there can be no offense of obtaining money by false pretenses. If the pretense was one of the material matters relied upon, that is sufficient. There is nothing in the cases cited contrary to this doctrine, and an instruction embodying it was approved in Baker v. State, 120 Wis. 135, 97 N.W. 566, although some of the language of the opinion impairs its usefulness as an authority on the point.

It is next claimed that reservation of title in the vendor compels the conclusion that only possession of the car was obtained, whereas both title and possession must have been obtained by fraud to answer the calls of the statute. Reliance is had upon the statement in Bates v. State, 124 Wis. 612, 617, 103 N.W. 251, 253, "that so long as the defrauded party retains either title or control over the property the crime of obtaining is not consummated." See also State v. Burke, 189 Wis. 641, 207 N.W. 406.

The rule stated in the Bates and Burke Cases is not founded upon a specific requirement in the statute that title pass, but is for the purpose of preserving a distinction between the crime of larceny by bailee and that of obtaining money by false pretenses. The mere delivery of property into the possession of a bailee and his subsequent conversion of it to his own use constitutes larceny by bailee and not the crime of obtaining money by false pretenses. Where, however, goods are sold under a conditional sales contract and the legal title is merely retained for purposes of security, the vendee gets a sufficient property interest to support a conviction of obtaining money by false pretenses provided the other requisites of the offense are present. As pointed out in Chappell v. State, 216 Ind. 666, 25 N.E.2d 999, the doctrine that one must obtain title and possession in order to be guilty of the crime of false pretenses cannot mean an absolute title because any title obtained by fraud is voidable and the requirement would make it impossible for the crime to be consummated. In La Porte Motor Co. v. Firemen's Ins. Co., 209 Wis. 397, 245 N.W. 105, it was held that the purchaser of an automobile by conditional sales contract cannot be guilty of larceny of the automobile even though in default under the contract of conditional sale. Such a vendee is regarded for most purposes as owner of the property covered by the conditional sales contract. He is variously referred to as beneficial, equitable or substantial owner, there being outstanding in the vendor only the naked legal title and this temporarily and for security solely. See Hansen v. Kuhn, 226 Iowa 794, 285 N.W. 249. It is our conclusion that the property interest which accompanied delivery of possession to plaintiff in error is sufficient to satisfy the calls of the statute.[1]

By the Court.—Judgment affirmed.

PEOPLE v. BARNETT

Second Appellate District, Division Two, California, 1939.
31 Cal.App.2d 173, 88 P.2d 172.

CRAIL, P. J. This is an appeal from a conviction of William D. Barnett on each of two counts of an information which charged grand theft.

It is the contention of the appellant that the theory upon which the prosecution proceeded and the only one which its evidence tended at all to support was that the money of the complaining witness, Mary Hill, was obtained by false pretenses; that the only evidence of the false pretenses was the testimony of Mrs. Hill, and that there was no corroboration such as is required under section 1110 of the Penal Code.

It is the contention of the attorney-general, however, that the defendant was convicted of the crime of larceny by trick and device, a crime for the conviction of which no corroboration was necessary.

---

[1]. Accord: Chappell v. State, 216 Ind. 666, 25 N.E.2d 999 (1939).

Where a seller of a chattel has been induced to part with it without receiving full payment by false and fraudulent statements of fact by the buyer, the fact that the seller took a mortgage from the buyer as security will not prevent the latter's conviction of false pretenses. Hite v. United States, 168 F.2d 973 (10th Cir. 1948).

One who executed a worthless check as down payment on a car and executed a conditional sales contract for the balance and received possession of the car, was guilty of larceny by trick since he obtained possession, but not title, by fraud. State v. Thompson, — Or. —, 402 P.2d 243 (1965).

Sec. 4　　　　　　　　*THE TRESPASS*　　　　　　　　173

The law of this state is (1) that where a person parts with the possession of his money to the defendant with the intent that it shall be used by the defendant for a specific and limited purpose, and at the time the defendant receives the possession of said money he intends to convert said money to his own use, he is guilty of larceny by trick and device; and that (2) when a person parts with both the title and possession of his money to the defendant and said party has been induced by the defendant through false pretenses to so part with both his title and possession, then he is guilty of obtaining money by false pretenses. (26 A.L.R. 381(n), and California cases cited on page 382.)

In the case of People v. Curran, 24 Cal.App.2d 673, 75 P.2d 1090, this court said, "The distinction between the offenses of larceny and of obtaining money by false pretenses depends upon the intention with which the owner of the property parted with it to the person taking it. 'In larceny the owner of the thing has no intention to part with his property therein to the person taking it, although he may intend to part with the possession. In false pretenses the owner does intend to part with his property in the money or chattel, but it is obtained from him by fraud.' (People v. Delbos, 146 Cal. 734, 736, 81 P. 131.)"

Adapting the law to this case, then if Mary Hill parted with the money to the defendant with the intention that the money was not to be his personally, but was to be used by him for her to purchase certain oil leases, and the money or a large part of it was not so used by the defendant, but was converted to his own uses, then he is guilty of larceny by trick and device; but if Mary Hill, at the time she turned the money over to the defendant, intended to part both with the title and possession of the money to the defendant and she had been induced by the defendant through false pretenses to so part with both her title and possession, then the defendant would be guilty of obtaining money under false pretenses.

It is the duty of this court to view the evidence in the light most favorable to the People. Mrs. Hill was a widow and met the defendant in his capacity as a salesman selling land located in New Mexico. Four days after their meeting the defendant and his codefendant Amigo came to her home, at which time defendant stated that Amigo was a mining man and down here to buy up some oil leases and make some money out of them; that the defendant, Mrs. Hill and Amigo could get forty acres of land in McKinley County for $1,000; that the defendant would put up $333 and Mrs. Hill and Amigo would each put up a like amount to buy said forty-acre lease. Mrs. Hill said she would consider it. Two days later defendant called at her home again in connection with their joint purchase of said forty-acre lease, at which time she delivered to the defendant $5 to apply toward her share and agreed to deliver the balance of $328 later. The forty-acre lease was to be purchased in the name of Mrs. Hill and Amigo and a separate agreement was to be executed evidencing defendant's one-third interest in said lease. On April 2, 1936, defendant and Amigo called on Mrs. Hill at her home, at which time she delivered to defendant $328 in cash, representing the balance due from her on the purchase price of said McKinley County lease. On April 9th, defendant and Amigo again called on Mrs. Hill at her home, at which time defendant presented to her three copies of a document, all three copies of which were signed by Mrs. Hill and codefendant Amigo, transferring to defendant a fully paid up one-third undivided interest in said forty acres. Mrs. Hill intended and the defendant and Amigo each understood the money was delivered to them and was to be used by them as the joint purchase price of the lease from a third party. Mrs. Hill specifically testified that she did not intend to part with the title to her money to the defendant. Defendant had previous to his meeting Mrs. Hill purchased said forty-acre lease from one Leona Douglas for the sum of $40, and had caused the title to said lease to appear in the name of the witness Starr without Starr's knowledge or consent, and on April 7th defendant secured Starr's signature to an assignment in blank to said forty-acre lease and later filled in the names of Mrs. Hill and Amigo, as assignees, thus making it appear as though said assignment of lease had been purchased from a man by the name of Starr, when in truth and in fact neither of the defendants had paid Starr anything for said assignment. The defendant and his codefendant represented that each of them was investing the sum of $333 together with Mrs. Hill as part of the purchase price of said lease, when in truth and in fact they already owned said lease, and instead of the purchase price being $1,000, it was only $40. From a statement of the evidence which we have set forth it is clear and unequivocal that Mrs. Hill parted with the possession of the money to the defendant with the understanding that he would use her money in connection with money advanced by himself and his codefendant for the purchase from some third person of the oil lease. She did not purchase the lease from the defendant or Amigo and therefore never passed title of such money to the defendant or to Amigo. The same situation exists and is true with regard to count two of the information.

In our view, therefore, there is substantial evidence to sustain the implied findings of the trial court that the defendant was guilty of larceny by trick and device. . . .

Judgment affirmed.[2]

2. If one of the consolidated offenses is excluded from the statute of limitations this does not apply to the others despite the consolidation. People v. Darling, 230 Cal.App.2d 615, **41 Cal.** Rptr. 219 (1964).

REGINA v. HANDS

Court for Crown Cases Reserved, 1887.
16 Cox C.C. 188, 56 L.T. 370.

LORD COLERIDGE, C. J. In this case a person was indicted for committing a larceny from what is known as an "automatic box," which was so constructed that, if you put a penny into it and pushed a knob in accordance with the directions on the box, a cigarette was ejected on to a bracket and presented to the giver of the penny. Under these circumstances there is no doubt that the prisoners put in the box a piece of metal which was of no value, but which produced the same effect as the placing a penny in the box produced. A cigarette was ejected which the prisoners appropriated; and in a case of that class it appears to me there clearly was larceny. The means by which the cigarette was made to come out of the box were fraudulent, and the cigarette so made to come out was appropriated. . . .

UNITED STATES v. TURLEY

Supreme Court of the United States, 1957.
352 U.S. 407, 77 S.Ct. 397.

MR. JUSTICE BURTON delivered the opinion of the Court.

This case concerns the meaning of the word "stolen" in the following provision of the National Motor Vehicle Theft Act, commonly known as the Dyer Act:

"Whoever transports in interstate or foreign commerce a motor vehicle or aircraft, knowing the same to have been stolen, shall be fined not more than $5,000 or imprisoned not more than five years, or both."

The issue before us is whether the meaning of the word "stolen," as used in this provision, is limited to a taking which amounts to common-law larceny, or whether it includes an embezzlement or other felonious taking with intent to deprive the owner of the rights and benefits of ownership. For the reasons hereafter stated, we accept the broader interpretation.

In 1956, an information based on this section was filed against James Vernon Turley in the United States District Court for the District of Maryland. It charged that Turley, in South Carolina, lawfully obtained possession of an automobile from its owner for the purpose of driving certain of their friends to the homes of the latter in South Carolina, but that, without permission of the owner and with intent to steal the automobile, Turley converted it to his own use and unlawfully transported it in interstate commerce to Baltimore, Maryland, where he sold it without permission of the owner. The information thus charged Turley with transporting the automobile in interstate commerce knowing it to have been obtained by embezzlement rather than by common-law larceny.

Counsel appointed for Turley moved to dismiss the information on the ground that it did not state facts sufficient to constitute an offense against the United States. He contended that the word "stolen" as used in the Act referred only to takings which constitute common-law larceny and that the acts charged did not. The District Court agreed and dismissed the information. 141 F.Supp. 527. The United States concedes that the facts alleged in the information do not constitute common-law larceny, but disputes the holding that a motor vehicle obtained by embezzlement is not "stolen" within the meaning of the Act. The Government appealed directly to this Court under 18 U.S.C. § 3731, 18 U.S.C.A. § 3731 because the dismissal was based upon a construction of the statute upon which the information was founded. We noted probable jurisdiction. 352 U.S. 816, 77 S.Ct. 65, 1 L.Ed.2d 44.

Decisions involving the meaning of "stolen" as used in the National Motor Vehicle Theft Act did not arise frequently until comparatively recently. Two of the earlier cases interpreted "stolen" as meaning statutory larceny as defined by the State in which the taking occurred. The later decisions rejected that interpretation but divided on whether to give "stolen" a uniformly narrow meaning restricted to common-law larceny, or a uniformly broader meaning inclusive of embezzlement and other felonious takings with intent to deprive the owner of the rights and benefits of ownership.[4] The Fifth, Eighth and Tenth Circuits favored the narrow definition, while the Fourth, Sixth and Ninth Circuits favored the broader one. We agree that in the absence of a plain indication of an intent to incorporate diverse state laws into a federal criminal statute, the meaning of the federal statute should not be dependent on state law.

We recognize that where a federal criminal statute uses a common-law term of established meaning without otherwise defining it, the general practice is to give that term its common-law meaning. But "stolen" (or "stealing") has no accepted common-law meaning. On this point the Court of Appeals for the Fourth Circuit recently said:

"But while 'stolen' is constantly identified with larceny, the term was never at common law equated or exclusively dedicated to larceny. 'Steal' (originally 'stale') at first denoted in general usage a taking through secrecy, as implied in 'stealth,' or through stratagem, according to the Oxford English Dictionary. Expanded through the years, it became the generic designation for dishonest acquisition, but it never lost its initial connotation. Nor in law is 'steal' or 'stolen' a

---

4. In this opinion felonious is used in the sense of having criminal intent rather than with reference to any distinction between felonies and misdemeanors.

word of art. Blackstone does not mention 'steal' in defining larceny —'the felonious taking and carrying away of the personal goods of another'—or in expounding its several elements. IV Commentaries 229 et seq." Boone v. United States, 4 Cir., 1956, 235 F.2d 939, 940.

Webster's New International Dictionary (2d ed., 1953) likewise defined "stolen" as "Obtained or accomplished by theft, stealth, or craft . . .." Black's Law Dictionary (4th ed., 1951) states that "steal" "may denote the criminal taking of personal property either by larceny, embezzlement, or false pretenses." Furthermore, "stolen" and "steal" have been used in federal criminal statutes, and the courts interpreting those words have declared that they do not have a necessary common-law meaning coterminous with larceny and exclusive of other theft crimes. Freed from a common-law meaning, we should give "stolen" the meaning consistent with the context in which it appears. . . .

We conclude that the Act requires an interpretation of "stolen" which does not limit it to situations which at common law would be considered larceny. The refinements of that crime are not related to the primary congressional purpose of eliminating the interstate traffic in unlawfully obtained motor vehicles. The Government's interpretation is neither unclear nor vague. "Stolen" as used in 18 U.S.C. § 2312, 18 U.S.C.A. § 2312 includes all felonious takings of motor vehicles with intent to deprive the owner of the rights and benefits of ownership, regardless of whether or not the theft constitutes common-law larceny.

Reversed and remanded.

MR. JUSTICE FRANKFURTER, whom MR. JUSTICE BLACK and MR. JUSTICE DOUGLAS join, dissenting.

If Congress desires to make cheating, in all its myriad varieties, a federal offense when employed to obtain an automobile that is then taken across a state line, it should express itself with less ambiguity than by language that leads three Courts of Appeals to decide that it has not said so and three that it has. If "stealing" (describing a thing as "stolen") be not a term of art, it must be deemed a colloquial, everyday term. As such, it would hardly be used, even loosely, by the man in the street to cover "cheating." Legislative drafting is dependent on treacherous words to convey, as often as not, complicated ideas, and courts should not be pedantically exacting in construing legislation. But to sweep into the jurisdiction of the federal courts the transportation of cars obtained not only by theft but also by trickery does not present a problem so complicated that the Court should search for hints to find a command. When Congress has wanted to deal with many different ways of despoiling another of his property and not merely with larceny, it has found it easy enough to do so, as a number of federal enactments attest. See, e. g., 18 U.S.C. §§ 641, 655, 659, 1707, 18 U.S.C.A. §§ 641, 655, 659, 1707. No doubt, penal legislation should not be artificially restricted so as to allow escape for those for whom it was with fair intendment designed. But the principle of lenity which should guide construction of criminal statutes, Bell v. United States, 349 U.S. 81, 83–84, 75 S.Ct. 620, 622, 99 L.Ed. 905, precludes extending the term "stolen" to include every form of dishonest acquisition. This conclusion is encouraged not only by the general consideration governing the construction of penal laws; it also has regard for not bringing to the federal courts a mass of minor offenses that are local in origin until Congress expresses, if not an explicit, at least an unequivocal, desire to do so.

I would affirm the judgment.

(C) APPROPRIATION OF LOST OR MISLAID GOODS

BROOKS v. STATE

Supreme Court of Ohio, 1878.
35 Ohio St. 46.

(Charles B. Newton lost a $200 roll of bank bills. Notice of the loss was published in a newspaper. Nearly a month later George Brooks found the money in the street. There is no evidence that he had seen the published notice or knew of Newton's loss, but he was with other workmen at the time and took pains not to let them know of his find. He appropriated the money shortly thereafter. He was convicted of larceny.)

WHITE, J. We find no ground in the record for reversing the judgment.

The first instruction asked was properly refused. It was not necessary to the conviction of the accused that he should, at the time of taking possession of the property, have known, or have had reason to believe he knew, the *particular person* who owned it, or have had the means of identifying him *instanter*. The charge asked was liable to this construction, and there was no error in its refusal.

The second instruction asked was substantially given in the general charge.

Larceny may be committed of property that is casually lost as well as of that which is not. The title to the property, and its constructive possession, still remains in the owner; and the finder, if he takes possession of it for his own use, and not for the benefit of the owner, would be guilty of trespass, unless the circumstances were such as to show that it had been abandoned by the owner.

The question is, under what circumstances does such property become the subject of larceny by the finder?

In Baker v. The State, 29 Ohio St. 184, the rule stated by Baron Park, in Thurborn's case, was adopted. It was there laid down, that "when a person finds goods that have actually been lost, and takes possession with intent to appropriate them to his own use, really believing, at the time, or having good ground to believe, that the owner can be found, it is larceny."

It must not be understood from the rule, as thus stated, that the finder is bound to use diligence or to take pains in making search for the owner.[1] His belief, or grounds of belief, in regard to finding the owner, is not to be determined by the degree of diligence that he might be able to use to accomplish that purpose, but by the circumstances apparent to him at the time of finding the property. If the property has not been abandoned by the owner, it is the subject of larceny by the finder, when, at the time he finds it, he has reasonable ground to believe, from the nature of the property, or the circumstances under which it is found, that if he does not conceal but deals honestly with it, the owner will appear or be ascertained. But before the finder can be guilty of larceny, the intent to steal the property must have existed at the time he took it into his possession. . . .[2]

Judgment affirmed.

OKEY, J. I do not think the plaintiff was properly convicted. A scavenger, while in the performance of his duties in cleaning the streets, picked up from the mud and water in the gutter, a roll of money, consisting of bank bills of the denominations of five, ten, and twenty dollars, and amounting, in the aggregate, to two hundred dollars. It had lain there several weeks, and the owner had ceased to make search for it. The evidence fails to show that the plaintiff had any information of a loss previous to the finding, and in his testimony he denied such notice. There was no mark on the money to indicate the owner, nor was there any thing in the attending circumstances pointing to one owner more than another. He put the money in his pocket, without calling the attention of his fellow-workmen to the discovery, and afterward, on the same day, commenced applying it to his own use.

No doubt the plaintiff was morally bound to take steps to find the owner. An honest man would not thus appropriate money, before he had made the finding public, and endeavored to find the owner. But in violating the moral obligation, I do not think the plaintiff incurred criminal liability. . . .

GILMORE, C. J., concurs in the dissenting opinion.

---

1. Some of the statutes require diligence on the part of the finder if the circumstances of the finding suggest a means of inquiry. See West's Ann. Cal.Pen.Code § 485 (1949).

2. Regina v. Shea, 7 Cox C.C. 147 (1856).

REGINA v. THURBORN

Court for Crown Cases Reserved, 1848.
1 Den. 387, 169 Eng.Rep. 293.

The prisoner was tried before PARKE, B., at the Summer Assizes for Huntingdon, 1848, for stealing a bank note.

He found the note, which had been accidentally dropped on the high road. There was no name or mark on it, indicating who was the owner, nor were there any circumstances attending the finding which would enable him to discover to whom the note belonged when he picked it up; nor had he any reason to believe that the owner knew where to find it again. The prisoner meant to appropriate it to his own use, when he picked it up. The day after, and before he had disposed of it, he was informed that the prosecutor was the owner, and had dropped it accidentally; he then changed it, and appropriated the money taken to his own use. The jury found that he had reason to believe, and did believe it to be the prosecutor's property, before he thus changed the note.

The learned Baron directed a verdict of guilty, intimating that he should reserve the case for further consideration. Upon conferring with Maule J., the learned Baron was of opinion that the original taking was not felonious, and that in the subsequent disposal of it, there was no taking, and he therefore declined to pass sentence, and ordered the prisoner to be discharged, on entering into his own recognizance to appear when called upon.

On the 30th of April, A.D. 1849, the following judgment was read by Parke B.

A case was reserved by Parke B. at the last Huntingdon Assizes. It was not argued by counsel, but the Judges who attended the sitting of the Court after Michaelmas Term, 1848, namely, the L. C. Baron, Patteson J., Rolfe B., Cresswell J., Williams J., Coltman J., and Parke B., gave it much consideration on account of its importance, and the frequency of the occurrence of cases in some degree similar, in the administration of the criminal law, and the somewhat obscure state of the authorities upon it. [The learned Baron here stated the case.] . . .

The result of these authorities is, that the rule of law on this subject seems to be, that if a man find goods that have been actually lost, or are reasonably supposed by him to have been lost, and appropriates them, with intent to take the entire dominion over them, really believing when he takes them, that the owner cannot be found, it is not larceny. But if he takes them with the like intent, though lost, or reasonably supposed to be lost, but reasonably believing that the owner can be found, it is larceny.

In applying this rule, as indeed in the application of all fixed rules, questions of some nicety may arise, but it will generally be ascertained whether the person accused had reasonable belief that the owner could be found, by evidence of his previous acquaintance with the ownership of the particular chattel, the place where it is found, or the nature of the marks upon it. In some cases it would be apparent, in others appear only after examination.

It would probably be presumed that the taker would examine the chattel as an honest man ought to do, at the time of taking it, and if he did not restore it to the owner, the jury might conclude that he took it, when he took complete possession of it, *animo furandi*. The mere taking it up to look at it, would not be a taking possession of the chattel.

To apply these rules to the present case; the first taking did not amount to larceny, because the note was really lost, and there was no mark on it or other circumstance to indicate then who was the owner, or that he might be found, nor any evidence to rebut the presumption that would arise from the finding of the note as proved, that he believed the owner could not be found, and therefore the original taking was not felonious; and if the prisoner had changed the note or otherwise disposed of it, before notice of the title of the real owner, he clearly would not have been punishable; but after the prisoner was in possession of the note, the owner became known to him, and he then appropriated it, *animo furandi*, and the point to be decided is whether that was a felony.

Upon this question we have felt considerable doubt.

If he had taken the chattel innocently, and afterwards appropriated it without knowledge of the ownership, it would not have been larceny, nor would it, we think, if he had done so, knowing who was the owner, for he had the lawful possession in both cases, and the conversion would not have been a trespass in either. But here the original taking was not innocent in one sense, and the question is, does that make a difference? We think not, it was dispunishable as we have already decided, and though the possession was accompanied by a dishonest intent, it was still a lawful possession and good against all but the real owner, and the subsequent conversion was not therefore a trespass in this case more than the others, and consequently no larceny.

We therefore think that the conviction was wrong.[1]

---

[1]. One who appropriated a coat he found on a bench is not guilty of larceny if the original taking was with intent to restore it to the owner. Milburne's Case, 1 Lewin 251, 168 Eng. Rep. 1030 (1829).

CALHOUN v. STATE

Supreme Court of Mississippi, in Banc, 1941.
191 Miss. 82, 2 So.2d 802.

McGehee, J., delivered the opinion of the court.

Upon an indictment charging him with the larceny of one diamond bar pin of the value of $85, the property of Mrs. E. O. Catledge, the appellant was convicted and sentenced to serve a term of two years in the state penitentiary, and he prosecutes this appeal.

Mrs. Catledge, who lived at Tutwiler, Mississippi, was asked, as a witness for the state upon the trial, to "tell the jury whether or not at any time during this year (1940) you lost a diamond bar pin?" Her reply was: "Well, I didn't exactly lose it. It was either taken or misplaced. I wore the pin the 4th or 5th of April the last time. I remember pulling it off and dropping the safety catch. I picked up the safety catch, put it on the pin and dropped it in the handkerchief case where I kept it. The next day we moved on the other side of town and I didn't wear it any more. I started to dress on the 26th of April and started to get the pin and it was gone. We bought it from Mr. Weiler and he sent me a description of it. I didn't see it any more until they sent for me to identify it in Drew." She further testified as to the value of the pin, and of having identified it after its recovery from a pawn shop in Memphis, Tennessee, during the month of August of the same year.

At the time the pin was taken or misplaced, the appellant was employed at Ruscoe's Pressing Shop at Drew, Mississippi, and was so employed at the time it was later found. Clothing was received at this pressing shop from customers at Tutwiler and other nearby towns to be cleaned and pressed, but the appellant had no part in taking up the clothing or in transporting it to the shop. In fact, he was not shown to have been seen in Tutwiler at any time during the period from April to August, inclusive. Moreover, the proof disclosed without dispute that Mrs. Catledge did not send any clothing to this shop at any time during the month of April, 1940, but that she did so subsequent to the month of April and on through the month of August of that year. The appellant testified that some two or three weeks before this pin was recovered by the owner as aforesaid, he found it in the bottom of a large basket in which suits and dresses were placed when put in the truck to be carried to the shop to be cleaned and pressed, and that it was lying loose in the bottom of the basket when he was preparing to empty some paper from the basket after the clothing had been removed therefrom.

It was also shown that it was the duty of the appellant to search the clothing for money and other articles of value in order that they might be returned to the owner. When anything was thus found, he was supposed to carry the same to the office and identify the article with the name of the owner of the garment from which it had been removed and place it in a desk provided for that purpose. It appears that he had always performed this duty faithfully in regard to all articles found in clothing, as he knew the owner or had the means of ascertaining the owner by reason of the ownership of the garment from which the same had been removed. But, on the occasion in question, it is shown that not knowing who owned this bar pin, and not having any immediate means of ascertaining the true owner, he laid it aside in some place other than in the desk in the office, and let it remain there, without the knowledge of his employer, for two or three weeks awaiting its being claimed; and that no claim therefor having then been made, he sent it to a pawn shop in Memphis by one Will Bibb, who frequently drove a truck to and from Memphis, and requested Bibb to ascertain its value at the pawn shop and try to obtain some money on it. When Bibb carried it to the pawn shop, he was arrested and placed in jail, and with the result that the pin was soon recovered by Mrs. Catledge. . . .

Assuming that the bar pin in question was found by the appellant under the circumstances related by him, since his version of the matter is entirely reasonable, and that he did not relinquish the custody and control of it while it remained in the pressing shop, it would appear that a different case is presented under the law than if he had placed it in the drawer of the desk in the office of his employer, and had later committed a trespass in removing the same from this place after his employer had become the bailee thereof for the benefit of whoever should call for it. In retaining it in his own custody, and under his control, under the circumstances testified to, it cannot be said from the testimony that he either knew the owner or had any immediate means of ascertaining who the owner was with any reasonable degree of certainty at the time he found it, or at the time he later converted it to his own use.

We are, therefore, of the opinion that the peremptory instruction requested by the appellant should have been granted.[1]

Reversed and judgment here for the appellant.

1. See Harris v. State, 207 Miss. 241, 42 So.2d 183 (1949); Long v. State, 33 Ala.App. 334, 33 So.2d 382 (1949).

(D) THE DOCTRINE OF CONTINUING TRESPASS

REGINA v. RILEY

Court of Criminal Appeal, 1853.
6 Cox C.C. 88, Dearsly 149, 169 Eng.Rep. 674.

At the General Quarter Sessions of the Peace for the county of Durham, held at the city of Durham (before Rowland Burdon, Esq., Chairman), on the 18th of October, in the year of our Lord 1852, the prisoner was indicted for having, on the 5th day of October, 1852, stolen a lamb, the property of John Burnside. The prisoner pleaded Not Guilty. On the trial it was proved that on Friday, the 1st day of October, in the year of our Lord 1852, John Burnside, the prosecutor, put ten white-faced lambs into a field in the occupation of John Clarke, situated near to the town of Darlington. On Monday, the 4th day of October, the prisoner went with a flock of twenty-nine black-faced lambs to John Clarke, and asked if he might put them into Clarke's field for a night's keep, and upon Clarke agreeing to allow him to do so for one penny per head, the prisoner put his twenty-nine lambs into the same field with the prosecutor's lambs. At half-past seven o'clock in the morning of Tuesday, the 5th of October, the prosecutor went to Clarke's field, and in counting his lambs he missed one, and the prisoner's lambs were gone from the field also. Between eight and nine o'clock in the morning of the same day, the prisoner came to the farm of John Calvert, at Middleton St. George, six miles east from Darlington, and asked him to buy twenty-nine lambs. Calvert agreed to do so, and to give 8s. a-piece for them. Calvert then proceeded to count the lambs, and informed the prisoner that there were thirty instead of twenty-nine in the flock, and pointed out to him a white-faced lamb; upon which the prisoner said, "If you object to take thirty, I will draw one." Calvert however bought the whole, and paid the prisoner 12l. for them. One of the lambs sold to Calvert was identified by the prosecutor as his property, and as the lamb missed by him from Clarke's field. It was a half-bred white-faced lamb, marked with the letter "T.," and similar to the other nine of the prosecutor's lambs. The twenty-nine lambs belonging to the prisoner were black-faced lambs. On the 5th October, in the afternoon, the prisoner stated to two of the witnesses that he never had put his lambs into Clarke's field, and had sold them on the previous afternoon, for 11l. 12s., to a person on the Barnard Castle-road, which road leads west from Darlington.

There was evidence in the case to show that the prisoner must have taken the lambs from Clarke's field early in the morning, which was thick and rainy.

It was argued by the counsel for the prisoner, in his address to the jury, that the facts showed that the original taking from Clarke's field was by mistake; and if the jury were of that opinion, then, as the original taking was not done *animo furandi*, the subsequent appropriation would not make it a larceny, and the prisoner must be acquitted. The chairman, in summing up, told the jury, that though they might be of opinion that the prisoner did not know that the lamb was in his flock, until it was pointed out to him by Calvert, he should rule that, in point of law, the taking occurred when it was so pointed out to the prisoner and sold by him to Calvert, and not at the time of leaving the field. The jury returned the following verdict: The jury say that at the time of leaving the field the prisoner did not know that the lamb was in his flock, and that he was guilty of felony at the time it was pointed out to him.

The prisoner was then sentenced to six months' hard labour in the house of correction at Durham; and being unable to find bail, was thereupon committed to prison until the opinion of this court could be taken upon the question, whether Charles Riley was properly convicted of larceny. . . .

POLLOCK, C. B. We are all of opinion that the conviction is right. The case is distinguishable from those cited. R. v. Thristle decides only that if a man once gets into rightful possession, he cannot, by a subsequent fraudulent appropriation, convert it into a felony. So in R. v. Thurborn, in the elaborate judgment delivered by my brother Parke on behalf of the court of which I was a member, the same rule is laid down. It is there said that the mere taking up of a lost chattel to look at it, would not be a taking possession of it; and no doubt that may be done without violating any social duty. A man may take up a lost chattel and carry it home, with the proper object of endeavouring to find the owner; and then afterwards, if he yields to the temptation of appropriating it to his own use, he is not guilty of felony. In Leigh's Case, also, the original taking was rightful, but here the original taking was wrongful. I am not desirous of calling in aid the technicality of a continuing trespass; and I think this case may be decided upon the ground either that there was no taking at all by the prisoner in the first instance, or a wrongful taking, and, in either case, as soon as he appropriates the property, the evidence of felony is complete.

PARKE, B. I think that this case may be disposed of on a short ground. The original taking was not lawful, but a trespass, upon which an action in that form might have been founded; but it was not felony, because there was no intention to appropriate. There was, however, a continuing trespass up to the time of appropriation, and at that time, therefore, the felony was committed. Where goods are carried from one county to another, they may be laid as taken in the second county, and the difference between this and Leigh's Case, as well as the others cited, is that the original taking was no trespass. It was by the implied licence of the owner, and the same thing as if he had been entrusted by the prosecutor with the possession of the goods.

WILLIAMS, TALFOURD, and CROMPTON, JJ., concurred.

Conviction affirmed.[1]

STATE v. COOMBS

Supreme Judicial Court of Maine, 1868
55 Me. 477.

DICKERSON, J. Exceptions. The prisoner was indicted for the larceny of a horse, sleigh and buffalo robes. The jury were instructed that, if the prisoner obtained possession of the team by falsely and fraudulently pretending that he wanted it to drive to a certain place, and to be gone a specified time, when in fact he did not intend to go to such place, but to a more distant one, and to be absent a longer time, without intending at the time to steal the property, the team was not lawfully in his possession, and that a subsequent conversion of it to his own use, with a felonious intent while thus using it, would be larceny.

It is well settled that where one comes lawfully into possession of the goods of another, with his consent, a subsequent felonious conversion of them to his own use, without the owner's consent, does not constitute larceny, because the felonious intent is wanting at the time of the taking.

But how is it when the taking is fraudulent or tortious, and the property is subsequently converted to the use of the taker with a felonious intent? Suppose one takes his neighbor's horse from the stable, without consent, to ride him to a neighboring town, with the intention to return him, but subsequently sells him and converts the money to his own use, without his neighbor's consent, is he a mere trespasser, or is he guilty of larceny? In other words, must the felonious intent exist at the time of the original taking, when that is fraudulent or tortious, to constitute larceny?

When property is thus obtained, the taking or trespass is continuous. The wrongdoer holds it all the while without right, and against the right and without the consent of the owner. If at this point no other element is added, there is no larceny. But, if to such taking there be subsequently superadded a felonious intent, that is, an intent to deprive the owner of his property permanently without color of

---

[1]. One who took another's bull from the range, thinking it was his own, and sold it under such claim, was not guilty of larceny even if the owner had laid claim to the bull before the sale was made. Wilson v. State, 96 Ark. 148, 131 S.W. 336 (1910).

Sec. 5   THE INTENT   187

right, or excuse, and to make it the property of the taker without the owner's consent, the crime of larceny is complete. . . .[1]

Exceptions overruled.

Judgment for the State.

SECTION 5. THE INTENT *Mens Rea*

PEOPLE v. BROWN

Supreme Court of California, 1894.
105 Cal. 66, 38 P. 518.

GAROUTTE, J. The appellant was convicted of the crime of burglary, alleged by the information to have been committed in entering a certain house with intent to commit grand larceny. The entry is conceded, and also it is conceded that appellant took therefrom a certain bicycle, the property of the party named in the information, and of such a value as to constitute grand larceny. The appellant is a boy of 17 years of age, and, for a few days immediately prior to the taking of the bicycle, was staying at the place from which the machine was taken, working for his board. He took the stand as a witness, and testified: "I took the wheel to get even with the boy, and, of course, I didn't intend to keep it. I just wanted to get even with him. The boy was throwing oranges at me in the evening, and he would not stop when I told him to, and it made me mad, and I left Yount's house Saturday morning. I thought I would go back and take the boy's wheel. He had a wheel, the one I had the fuss with. Instead of getting hold of his, I got Frank's, but I intended to take it back Sunday night; but, before I got back, they caught me. I took it down by the grove, and put it on the ground, and covered it with brush, and crawled in, and Frank came and hauled off the brush, and said: 'What are you doing here?' Then I told him . . . I covered myself up in the brush so that they could not find me until evening, until I could take it back. I did not want them to find me. I expected to remain there during the day, and not go back until evening." Upon the foregoing state of facts, the court gave the jury the following instruction: "I think it is not necessary to say very much to you in this case. I may say, generally, that I think counsel for the defense here stated to you in his argument very fairly the principles of law governing this case, except in one particular. In defining to you the crime of grand larceny, he says it is essential that the taking of it must be felonious. That is true; the taking with the intent to deprive the owner of it; but he

---

[1]. Accord: Commonwealth v. White, 11 Cush. 483 (Mass.1853).

adds the conclusion that you must find that the taker intended to deprive him of it permanently. I do not think that is the law. I think in this case, for example, if the defendant took this bicycle, we will say for the purpose of riding twenty-five miles, for the purpose of enabling him to get away, and then left it for another to get it, and intended to do nothing else except to help himself away for a certain distance, it would be larceny, just as much as though he intended to take it all the while. A man may take a horse, for instance, not with the intent to convert it wholly and permanently to his own use, but to ride it to a certain distance, for a certain purpose he may have, and then leave it. He converts it to that extent to his own use and purpose feloniously." This instruction is erroneous, and demands a reversal of the judgment. If the boy's story be true, he is not guilty of larceny in taking the machine; yet, under the instruction of the court, the words from his own mouth convicted him. The court told the jury that larceny may be committed, even though it was only the intent of the party taking the property to deprive the owner of it temporarily. We think the authorities form an unbroken line to the effect that the felonious intent must be to deprive the owner of the property permanently. The illustration contained in the instruction as to the man taking the horse is too broad in its terms as stating a correct principle of law. Under the circumstances depicted by the illustration, the man might, and again he might not, be guilty of larceny. It would be a pure question of fact for the jury, and dependent for its true solution upon all the circumstances surrounding the transaction. But the test of law to be applied to these circumstances for the purpose of determining the ultimate fact as to the man's guilt or innocence is, did he intend to permanently deprive the owner of his property? If he did not intend so to do, there is no felonious intent, and his acts constitute but a trespass. While the felonious intent of the party taking need not necessarily be an intention to convert the property to his own use, still it must in all cases be an intent to wholly and permanently deprive the owner thereof. . . . For the foregoing reasons, it is ordered that the judgment and order be reversed, and the cause remanded for a new trial.[1]

We concur: MCFARLAND, J.; HARRISON, J.; VAN FLEET, J.; FITZGERALD, J.; DE HAVEN, J.

[1]. A truck containing a gravity meter was driven onto private land by mistake, since it had once been a public road. The act of the landowner in wrongfully detaining the truck and meter for four days while a claim was being settled was not "theft" of the meter even if the result was that the owner was out of pocket to the extent of $455. Home Fire & Marine Ins. Co. v. E. V. McCollum & Co., 201 Okl. 595, 207 P.2d 1094 (1949). For a servant wrongfully to take and carry away the master's oats is larceny even if the intent is to feed them to the master's horses. The Queen v. Privett, 1 Den. 193, 169 Eng.Rep. 207 (1846).

STATE v. SAVAGE

Court of General Sessions for Sussex County, Delaware. 1936.
37 Del. 509, 186 A. 738.

LAYTON, C. J., sitting. The indictment was for larceny. The evidence on the part of the State was that the defendant took from the unattended automobile of the prosecuting witness a metal can and three gallons of gasoline contained therein; that after taking the property he drove away and at a place about one mile distant he poured the gasoline into the tank of his car and threw the can into a nearby branch, and that he made no effort to inform the owner of his act, or to restore the property or pay for it.

The defendant was allowed to testify that while driving his automobile he ran out of gasoline and seeing the car of the prosecuting witness nearby, went to it and there found the can and gasoline; that he then and there poured the gasoline in his own car and drove off; that he left the can near the branch instructing a companion to return the can to the prosecuting witness and to inform him that he would return a like amount of gasoline. This was denied by the companion.

LAYTON, C. J., charged the jury, in part, as follows:

Larceny has been defined to be the taking and carrying away of the personal property of another with felonious intent to convert it to his own use without the owner's consent.

It is incumbent upon the State to prove to the satisfaction of the jury beyond a reasonable doubt every material element of the crime charged. So, the State must prove that the taking of the property occurred in Sussex County; that the property was of some value; that the person alleged to be the owner had a general or special property in the goods taken; that the defendant took and carried away the property, or some part of it, against the consent of the owner; and that the taker at the time of the taking had the felonious intent to convert the property to his own use.

The word "felonious," as applied to an act, simply means wrongful, in that there was no color of right or excuse for the act.

The issue in this case is within a narrow compass. The defendant admits the taking in Sussex County. There is no denial that the property was of some value. It is not pretended that the taking was with the consent of the owner. That the person named in the indictment as the owner had such a special property in the goods as would support the indictment was sufficiently proved.

The defendant does deny that he took the property with felonious intent to convert it to his own use. He contends that he took it for a temporary purpose, then and there intending to restore that property which was capable of being restored in specie, and a like quantity of gasoline.

It is not every taking of the property of another without his knowledge or consent that amounts to larceny. To constitute the crime the intent must be wholly to deprive the owner of the property. The general rule may be said to be that a taking of property for a temporary purpose with the bona fide intention to return the property to the owner does not amount to larceny, however liable the taker may be in a civil action of trespass. So, a borrowing of property, even though it be wrongful as being without the owner's knowledge or consent, with the intention of returning the property to its owner, is not larceny.

The property here is of two kinds, the can which could be restored, and the gasoline which admittedly was consumed, but exactly the same thing in quantity and quality could be restored, and, on principle, it would seem that if the defendant took the gasoline intending then and there to return a like quantity, the taking would not amount to larceny. It would be a different matter, perhaps, if the property taken were of some particular kind or quality which the owner reasonably might desire to be returned in specie.

It must be kept in mind, however, another principle, that if the defendant, at the time he took the property, had no intention of restoring it to the owner, but took it with the intention of converting it to his own use, the fact that he later repented, and desired or attempted to restore the goods would not purge him of guilt. The taking in such circumstances would be larceny.

You must find the intent with which the defendant took the property from all the facts and circumstances. You, of course, may, and should, consider the testimony of the defendant, and, like all other testimony, you should give to it that degree of credit which you think it ought to have. You may also consider the manner and place of the taking, the conduct of the defendant thereafter, and his effort or attempt, if any, to restore the property or to account to the owner for it.

If you shall find from the evidence that the defendant took the property for a temporary purpose, and with the intention, then and there, to restore the can to the owner, and to account to the owner for the gasoline taken, or if you shall entertain a reasonable doubt of the felonious intent with which the defendant is charged, your verdict should be not guilty.[1]

On the other hand, if you shall find beyond a reasonable doubt that the defendant took the goods and chattels with no intention of

---

1. Compare Mason v. State, 32 Ark. 238 (1877). One who obtained $110,000.00 from a bank by wrongfully having an assistant cashier "juggle" the books and accounts over a period of months cannot defend on the theory that he intended sometime to repay the money. People v. Colton, 92 Cal. App.2d 704, 207 P.2d 890 (1949). One who obtained goods on credit by falsely and fraudulently representing that he had $12,000.00 cash and owed nothing, when he had only $4,500.00 and owed $10,000.00, is guilty of false pretenses even if he intended to pay for the goods. People v. Wieger, 100 Cal. 352, 34 P. 826 (1893).

making restoration, but with the intention of converting the property to his own use, your verdict should be guilty.

REGINA v. HALL

Court for Crown Cases Reserved, 1849.
3 Cox C.C. 245, 1 Den. 382, 169 Eng.Rep. 291.

The following case was reserved by the Recorder of Hull:

John Hall was tried at the last Epiphany Quarter Sessions for the borough of Hull on an indictment charging him with stealing fat and tallow, the property of John Atkin.

John Atkin, the prosecutor, is a tallow-chandler, and the prisoner at the time of the alleged offence was a servant in his employment. On the morning of the 6th of December last, the prosecutor, in consequence of something that had occurred to excite his suspicions, marked a quantity of butcher's fat, which was deposited in a room immediately above the candle-room in his warehouse. In the latter room was a pair of scales used in weighing the fat, which the prosecutor bought for the purposes of his trade. At noon, the foreman and the prisoner left the warehouse to go to dinner, when the former locked the doors and carried the keys to the prosecutor. At that time there was no fat in the scales. In about ten minutes, the prisoner came back and asked for the keys, which the prosecutor let him have. The prosecutor watched him into the warehouse, and saw that he took nothing in with him. In a short time he returned the keys, to the prosecutor, and went away. The prosecutor then went into the candle-room, and found that all the fat which he had marked had been removed from the upper room, and after having been put into a bag, had been placed in the scales in the candle-room. The prosecutor then went into the street, and waited until a man of the name of Wilson came up, who was shortly followed by the prisoner. The latter, on being asked where the fat came from that was in the scales, said it belonged to a butcher of the name of Robinson; and Wilson, in the prisoner's presence, stated that he had come to weigh the fat which he had brought from Mr. Robinson's. The prosecutor told Wilson that he would not pay him for the fat until he had seen Mr. Robinson, and left the warehouse for that purpose. Wilson immediately ran away, and the prisoner, after offering, to the prosecutor's wife if he was forgiven, to tell all, ran away too, and was not apprehended until some time afterwards, at some distance from Hull.

I told the jury that if they were satisfied that the prisoner removed the fat from the upper room to the candle-room, and placed it in the scales with the intention of selling it to the prosecutor as fat belonging to Mr. Robinson, and with the intention of appropriating the proceeds to his own use, the offence amounted to larceny.

The jury found the prisoner guilty.

Dearsley for the prisoner. There was no larceny in this case. The offence was an attempt to commit a statutable misdemeanor, and only punishable as such. The case of R. v. Holloway, supra, p. 241, decides it. There was an asportation; but no intention to dispose of the property, for it was part of the very scheme that the owner should not be deprived of his property in the fat. There must to constitute larceny, be a taking, with intention of gain, and of depriving the owner of the property for ever. The last ingredient is wanting here:

ALDERSON, B. If a man takes my bank note from me, and then brings it to me to change, does he not commit a larceny?

Dearsley. A bank note is a thing unknown to the common law, and therefore the case put could not be larceny at common law.

LORD DENMAN, C. J. The taking is admitted. The question is whether there was an intention to deprive the owner entirely of his property; how could he deprive the owner of it more effectually than by selling it? to whom he sells it cannot matter. The case put of the bank note would be an ingenious larceny, but no case can be more extreme than this.

PARKE, B. In this case there is the intent to deprive the owner of the dominion over his property, for it is put into the hands of an intended vendor, who is to offer it for sale to the owner, and if the owner will not buy it, to take it away again. The case is distinguishable from that of R. v. Holloway by the existence of this intent, and, further, by the additional impudence of the fraud.

ALDERSON, B. I think that he who takes property from another intends wholly to deprive him of it, if he intend that he shall get it back again under a contract by which he pays the full value for it.

COLERIDGE, J., and COLTMAN, J., concurred.

Conviction affirmed.

REGINA v. HOLLOWAY

Court for Crown Cases Reserved, 1849.
3 Cox C.C. 241, 2 Car. and K. 942, 175 Eng.Rep. 395.

The prisoner, William Holloway, was indicted at the General Quarter Sessions, holden in and for the borough of Liverpool, on December 4th, 1848, for stealing within the jurisdiction of the court 120 skins of leather, the property of Thomas Barton and another.

Thomas Barton and another were tanners, and the prisoner was one of many workmen employed by them at their tannery, in Liverpool, to dress skins of leather. Skins when dressed were delivered to the foreman, and every workman was paid in proportion to, and on account of the work done by himself. The skins of leather were afterwards stored in a warehouse adjoining to the workshop. The prisoner, by opening a window and removing an iron bar, got access clandestinely to the warehouse, and carried away the skins of leather mentioned in the indictment, and which had been dressed by other workmen. The prisoner did not remove these skins from the tannery; but they were seen and recognized the following day at the porch or place where he usually worked in the workshop. It was proved to be a common practice at the tannery for one workman to lend work, that is to say, skins of leather dressed by him, to another workman, and for the borrower in such case to deliver the work to the foreman, and get paid for it on his own account, and as if it were his own work.

A question of fact arose as to the intention of the prisoner in taking the skins from the warehouse. The jury found that the prisoner did not intend to remove the skins from the tannery and dispose of them elsewhere, but that his intention in taking them was to deliver them to the foreman and to get paid for them as if they were his own work; and in this way he intended the skins to be restored to the possession of his masters.

The jury under direction of the court found the prisoner guilty, and a point of law raised on behalf of the prisoner was reserved, and is now submitted for the consideration of the justices of either Bench and barons of the Exchequer.

"The question is, whether on the finding of the jury, the prisoner ought to have been convicted of larceny?

"Judgment was postponed, and the prisoner was liberated on bail taken for his appearance at the next or some subsequent Court of Quarter Sessions to receive judgment, or some final order of the court." . . .

PARKE, B. I am of the same opinion. We are bound by the authorities to say that this is not larceny. There is no clear definition of larceny applicable to every case; but the definitions that have been given, as explained by subsequent decisions, are sufficient for this case. The definition in East's Pleas of the Crown is on the whole the best; but it requires explanation, for what is the meaning of the phrase "wrongful and fraudulent?" It probably means "without claim of right." All the cases, however, show that, if the intent was not at the moment of taking to usurp the entire dominion over the property, and make it the taker's own, there was no larceny. If, therefore, a man takes the horse of another with intent to ride it to a distance, and not return it, but quit possession of it, he is not guilty of larceny. So in R. v. Webb, in which the intent was to get a higher reward for work from the owner of the property. If the intent must be to usurp the entire dominion over the property, and to deprive the owner wholly of it, I think that that essential part of the offence is not found in this case.

ALDERSON, B. I cannot distinguish this case from R. v. Webb.

COLERIDGE, J., concurred.

COLTMAN, J. We must not look so much to definitions, which it is impossible *a priori* so to frame that they shall include every case, as to the cases in which the ingredients that are necessary to constitute the offence are stated. If we look at the cases which have been decided, we shall find that in this case one necessary ingredient, the intent to deprive entirely and permanently, is wanting.[1]

Conviction reversed.

REGINA v. PHETHEON
Central Criminal Court, 1840.
9 Car. and P. 552, 173 Eng.Rep. 952.

The prisoner was indicted for stealing, on the 26th of February, 1840, four salt cellars and other articles of silver plate of the value altogether of £18, 5s., the goods of Thomas Robert Baron Hay, his master, in his dwelling-house.

It appeared that the prisoner was under butler to Lord Hay, and while he was in the service pledged the articles mentioned in the indictment.

The jury found the prisoner guilty; but recommended him to mercy, on the ground that they believed he intended to replace the property.

C. C. Jones, for the prisoner, submitted that this finding amounted in law to a verdict of not guilty.

GURNEY, B., without expressing any opinion upon the point, directed that the prisoner should be tried upon another indictment which had been preferred against him.

The prisoner was accordingly charged with stealing on the 6th of November, 1839, one silver saucepan of the value of £2, 10s., the goods of the same prosecutor.

It appeared from the testimony of a servant of Lord Hay, who was more generally known by his Scotch title of Earl of Kinnoul, that the saucepan mentioned in the indictment, was last seen by him upwards of two years previous at Duplin Castle, in Perthshire, where it was in use in Lady Kinnoul's apartment.

A witness proved, that, on the 16th of July, 1840, the prisoner called upon him, and left a parcel with him, which, on being opened,

---

1. Cf. Fort v. State, 82 Ala. 50, 2 So. 477 (1886).

was found to contain ten pawnbroker's duplicates, from one of which it appeared that the silver saucepan was pledged at the shop of a pawnbroker, named Mills, in the Edgeware Road, for £2, 10s., by a young woman.

The prisoner was in the service of Lord Kinnoul, at Duplin Castle, at the time the saucepan was in use there, and followed the family to England, in the month of April, 1838; and a witness stated that, in the natural course of things, the saucepan would come to England with the other property.

C. C. Jones, in his address to the jury for the prisoner, asked them to consider whether the prisoner took the article in question feloniously, or whether he took it, intending at the time he sent it to the pawnbroker's, to redeem it as soon as he could. He argued, that the fact of the prisoner's having kept the duplicate was a strong circumstance to shew that he intended to redeem the property.

GURNEY, B., in his summing up, after stating the facts, observed: You will say whether the prisoner stole this property or not. I confess I think, that if this doctrine of an intention to redeem property is to prevail, Courts of Justice will be of very little use. A more glorious doctrine for thieves it would be difficult to discover, but a more injurious doctrine for honest men cannot well be imagined.

The jury found the prisoner guilty, and he was sentenced to be transported for fourteen years.*

---

* In Carrington's Supplement to the Criminal Law, p. 278, 3rd edition, the following case is reported:—On an indictment for larceny by a servant in stealing his master's plate, it appeared, that, after the plate in question was missed, but before complaint made to the magistrate, the prisoner replaced it; and it was proved by a pawnbroker, that the plate had been pawned by the prisoner who had redeemed it; and, the pawnbroker also stated, that the prisoner had on previous occasions pawned plate and afterwards redeemed it. Hullock, B. (Holroyd, J., being present) left it to the jury to say whether the prisoner took the plate with intent to steal it, or whether he merely took it to raise money on it for a time, and then return it; for that in the latter case it was no larceny. The jury acquitted the prisoner: R. v. Wright, O. B., 1828, MS.

This decision has given rise to much discussion in various cases; and much difficulty has been found in applying the doctrine it lays down, to the facts of particular transactions. In some instances, where it has appeared clearly that the party only intended to raise money on the property for a temporary purpose, and, at the time of pledging the article, had a reasonable and fair expectation of being able shortly, by the receipt of money, to take it out of pawn, juries under the advice of the Judge have acted upon the doctrine and acquitted. But in other instances, where they could not discover any reasonable prospect which the party had at the time of pledging of being able soon to redeem the article, they have considered the doctrine as inapplicable and have convicted.

[Added by the Compiler.]
As to retaking a pledged chattel under the belief that the debt has been fully paid, see People v. Eastman, 77 Cal. 171, 19 P. 266 (1888).

STATE v. MILLS

Supreme Court of Arizona, 1964.
96 Ariz. 377, 396 P.2d 5.

LOCKWOOD, Vice Chief Justice: Defendants appeal from a conviction on two counts of obtaining money by false pretenses in violation of A.R.S. §§ 13–661.A.3. and 13–663.A.1.[1]

The material facts, viewed " . . . in the light most favorable to sustaining the conviction," are as follows: Defendant William Mills was a builder and owned approximately 150 homes in Tucson in December, 1960. Mills conducted his business in his home. In 1960 defendant Winifred Mills, his wife, participated in the business generally by answering the telephone, typing, and receiving clients who came to the office.

In December 1960, Mills showed the complainant, Nathan Pivowar, a house at 1155 Knox Drive and another at 1210 Easy Street, and asked Pivowar if he would loan money on the Knox Drive house. Pivowar did not indicate at that time whether he would agree to such a transaction. Later in the same month Nathan Pivowar told the defendants that he and his brother, Joe Pivowar, would loan $5,000 and $4,000 on the two houses. Three or four days later Mrs. Mills, at Pivowar's request, showed him these homes again.

Mills had prepared two typed mortgages for Pivowar. Pivowar objected to the wording, so in Mills' office Mrs. Mills re-typed the mortgages under Pivowar's dictation. After the mortgages had been recorded on December 31, 1960, Pivowar gave Mills a bank check for $5,791.87, some cash, and a second mortgage formerly obtained from Mills in the approximate sum of $3,000. In exchange Mills gave Pivowar two personal notes in the sums of $5,250.00 and $4,200.00 and the two mortgages as security for the loan.

Although the due date for Mills' personal notes passed without payment being made, the complainant did not present the notes for payment, did not demand that they be paid, and did not sue upon them. In 1962 the complainant learned that the mortgages which he had taken as security in the transaction were not first mortgages on the Knox Drive and Easy Street properties. These mortgages actually covered two vacant lots on which there were outstanding senior mortgages. On learning this, Pivowar signed a complaint charging the defendants with the crime of theft by false pretenses.

On appeal defendants contend that the trial court erred in denying their motion to dismiss the information. They urge that a per-

---

[Footnotes by the Court.]

1. A.R.S. § 13–661.A. (1956) defines "theft" to include:
"3. Knowingly and designingly, by any false or fraudulent representation or pretense, defrauding any other person of money, labor or property, whether real or personal."

manent taking of property must be proved in order to establish the crime of theft by false pretenses. Since the complainant had the right to sue on the defendants' notes, the defendants assert that complainant cannot be said to have been deprived of his property permanently.

Defendants misconceive the elements of the crime of theft by false pretenses. Stated in a different form, their argument is that although the complainant has parted with his cash, a bank check, and a second mortgage, the defendants intend to repay the loan.

Defendants admit that the proposition of law which they assert is a novel one in this jurisdiction. Respectable authority in other states persuades us that their contention is without merit. A creditor has a right to determine for himself whether he wishes to be a secured or an unsecured creditor. In the former case, he has a right to know about the security. If he extends credit in reliance upon security which is falsely represented to be adequate, he has been defrauded even if the debtor intends to repay the debt. His position is now that of an unsecured creditor; at the very least, an unreasonable risk of loss has been forced upon him by reason of the deceit. This risk which he did not intend to assume has been imposed upon him by the intentional act of the debtor, and such action constitutes an intent to defraud.[2] . . .

The cases cited by defendants in support of their contention are distinguishable from the instant case in that they involved theft by larceny. Since the crime of larceny is designed to protect a person's possessory interest in property whereas the crime of false pretenses protects one's title interest, the requirement of a permanent deprivation is appropriate to the former. Accordingly, we hold that an intent to repay a loan obtained on the basis of a false representation of the security for the loan is no defense. . . .

Since we are remanding the case for resentencing on only one count of theft by false pretenses, it is unnecessary to discuss appellants' contention that their sentences were excessive.

Affirmed in part, reversed in part, and remanded for resentencing.

UDALL, C. J., STRUCKMEYER and BERNSTEIN, JJ., and JENNINGS, J. (Retired), concurring.

NOTE: Justice EDWARD W. SCRUGGS having disqualified himself, the Honorable RENZ L. JENNINGS, Retired Justice, was called to sit in his stead and participate in the determination of this appeal.

2. See Perkins Criminal Law 266 (1957).

HENDERSON v. STATE

Court of Criminal Appeals of Texas, 1946.
149 Tex.Cr.R. 167, 192 S.W.2d 446.

KRUEGER, JUDGE. The offense is robbery. The punishment assessed is confinement in the state penitentiary for a term of five years.

The record discloses that on the night of March 25, 1945, appellant, who was accompanied in his automobile by one R. E. Brown, and two ladies, collided with that of James M. Condon who, at the time, was riding in his car in company with two ladies. Immediately after the collision, Condon stopped his car and got out of it to investigate the damage to it, while appellant drove on some distance, then turned around, came back to where Condon was and demanded that he pay him $15.00 or he would "beat hell" out of him. Condon declined to pay him, whereupon appellant struck him, knocked him down and kicked him. When Condon was finally permitted to arise, he told appellant that he did not have $15.00, and in order to convince appellant of the truthfulness of his statement, he pulled his billfold out of his pocket and opened it. Appellant grabbed it and took therefrom five one-dollar bills. He then tore the billfold in two and handed it back to Condon.

Appellant did not testify. However, he proved by two ladies who were with him at the time and place of the occasion in question, that Condon voluntarily gave him the money after they had engaged in a fist fight.

It will be noted from the foregoing brief statement of the facts that whether Condon voluntarily gave the money to appellant, or did so to avoid further punishment at the hands of appellant, was an issue which the jury decided adversely to him. . . .

The court, in his main charge to the jury, instructed them as to the law applicable to the case, and included therein the following instruction:

"The fact that the defendant claimed that said Condon was to blame in damaging his car would not give the defendant the right to extort money in payment thereof by assault or by putting said Condon in fear of life or bodily injury."

Appellant objected thereto on the ground that it was not the law applicable to the case; that it was an undue comment on the weight of the evidence; that it calls the jury's attention to the fact that the defendant attempted to and did extort money for damages by putting Condon in fear of life or bodily injury. The court overruled the objection with the explanation that appellant's attorney claimed that he had a right to assess the damages to his car and to collect the money by force, and that the court deemed it proper to advise the jury of what the law was on the subject, to which ruling appellant excepted. The trial court no doubt followed the instruction in the case of Fannin v. State, 100 S.W. 916, 51 Tex.Cr.R. 41, which is almost in identical language as the one here complained of. The objection in that case, as in the present instance, was that it did not state the law; that the contrary is the law. The trial court evidently deemed it necessary to advise the jury what the law was under the particular facts of this case. Whether or not the injured party ran his automobile into that of the appellant and injured it is not of any moment, since appellant was not legally justified in collecting unliquidated damages by assault or violence or by putting Condon in fear of life or bodily injury. To hold otherwise would be establishing a dangerous doctrine, since it would authorize the accused not only to decide his own injury or damage but to enforce the collection thereof by force and violence. This is contrary to the policy of our form of government. We do not think that the charge in question is any comment on the evidence but is the pronouncement of the law pertaining to the particular facts of this case.

From what we have said it follows that the judgment of the trial court should be affirmed, and it is so ordered.

The foregoing opinion of the Commission of Appeals has been examined by the Judges of the Court of Criminal Appeals and approved by the Court.[1]

MODEL PENAL CODE

Article 223. Theft and Related Offenses

Section 223.0. Definitions.

In this Article, unless a different meaning plainly is required:

(1) "deprive" means: (a) to withhold property of another permanently or for so extended a period as to appropriate a major portion of its economic value, or with intent to restore only upon payment of reward or other compensation; or (b) to dispose of the property so as to make it unlikely that the owner will recover it.

(2) "financial institution" means . . .

(3) "government" means . . .

---

[1]. Compare Moyers v. State, 186 Ga. 446, 197 S.E. 846 (1938); The King v. Bernhard, [1938] 2 K.B.D. 264.

It is larceny to take property wrongfully with intent to conceal it until a reward is offered. Commonwealth v. Mason, 105 Mass. 163 (1870).

One who borrowed a shotgun on his promise to return it the same day, and who had not returned it eight months later, was convicted of embezzlement. This conviction was reversed because there was no showing of any demand upon him for the return of the gun, and no evidence that he had sold, secreted or otherwise disposed of it. In other words, there was no evidence, direct or circumstantial, to show that he ceased to be a borrower and became an embezzler. State v. Britt, 278 Mo. 510, 213 S.W. 425 (1919).

(4) "movable property" means property the location of which can be changed, including things growing on, affixed to, or found in land, and documents although the rights represented thereby have no physical location. "Immovable property" is all other property.

(5) "obtain" means: (a) in relation to property, to bring about a transfer or purported transfer of a legal interest in the property, whether to the obtainer or another; or (b) in relation to labor or service, to secure performance thereof.

(6) "property" means anything of value, including real estate, tangible and intangible personal property, contract rights, choses-in-action and other interests in or claims to wealth, admission or transportation tickets, captured or domestic animals, food and drink, electric or other power.

(7) "property of another" includes property in which any person other than the actor has an interest which the actor is not privileged to infringe, regardless of the fact that the actor also has an interest in the property and regardless of the fact that the other person might be precluded from civil recovery because the property was used in an unlawful transaction or was subject to forfeiture as contraband. Property in possession of the actor shall not be deemed property of another who has only a security interest therein, even if legal title is in the creditor pursuant to a conditional sales contract or other security agreement.

Section 223.1. Consolidation of Theft Offenses; Grading; Provisions Applicable to Theft Generally.

(1) Consolidation of Theft Offenses. Conduct denominated theft in this Article constitutes a single offense. An accusation of theft may be supported by evidence that it was committed in any manner that would be theft under this Article, notwithstanding the specification of a different manner in the indictment or information, subject only to the power of the Court to ensure fair trial by granting a continuance or other appropriate relief where the conduct of the defense would be prejudiced by lack of fair notice or by surprise.

(2) Grading of Theft Offenses.

(a) Theft constitutes a felony of the third degree if the amount involved exceeds $500, or if the property stolen is a firearm, automobile, airplane, motor cycle, motor boat or other motor-propelled vehicle, or in the case of theft by receiving stolen property, if the receiver is in the business of buying or selling stolen property.

(b) Theft not within the preceding paragraph constitutes a misdemeanor, except that if the property was not taken from the person or by threat, or in breach of a fiduciary obligation, and the actor proves by a preponderance of the evidence that the amount involved was less than $50, the offense constitutes a petty misdemeanor.

(c) The amount involved in a theft shall be deemed to be the highest value, by any reasonable standard, of the property or services which the actor stole or attempted to steal. Amounts involved in thefts committed pursuant to one scheme or course of conduct, whether from the same person or several persons, may be aggregated in determining the grade of the offense.

(3) Claim of Right. It is an affirmative defense to prosecution for theft that the actor:

(a) was unaware that the property or service was that of another; or

(b) acted under an honest claim of right to the property or service involved or that he had a right to acquire or dispose of it as he did; or

(c) took property exposed for sale, intending to purchase and pay for it promptly, or reasonably believing that the owner, if present, would have consented.

(4) Theft from Spouse. It is no defense that theft was from the actor's spouse, except that misappropriation of household and personal effects, or other property normally accessible to both spouses, is theft only if it occurs after the parties have ceased living together.

Section 223.2. Theft by Unlawful Taking or Disposition.

(1) Movable Property. A person is guilty of theft if he unlawfully takes, or exercises unlawful control over, movable property of another with purpose to deprive him thereof.

(2) Immovable Property. A person is guilty of theft if he unlawfully transfers immovable property of another or any interest therein with purpose to benefit himself or another not entitled thereto.

Section 223.3. Theft by Deception.

A person is guilty of theft if he purposely obtains property of another by deception. A person deceives if he purposely:

(1) creates or reinforces a false impression, including false impressions as to law, value, intention or other state of mind; but deception as to a person's intention to perform a promise shall not be inferred from the fact alone that he did not subsequently perform the promise; or

(2) prevents another from acquiring information which would affect his judgment of a transaction; or

(3) fails to correct a false impression which the deceiver previously created or reinforced, or which the deceiver knows to be influencing another to whom he stands in a fiduciary or confidential relationship; or

(4) fails to disclose a known lien, adverse claim or other legal impediment to the enjoyment of property which he transfers or encumbers in consideration for the property obtained, whether such impediment is or is not valid, or is or is not a matter of official record.

The term "deceive" does not, however, include falsity as to matters having no pecuniary significance, or puffing by statements unlikely to deceive ordinary persons in the group addressed.

Section 223.4. Theft by Extortion.

A person is guilty of theft if he purposely obtains property of another by threatening to:

(1) inflict bodily injury on anyone or commit any other criminal offense; or

(2) accuse anyone of a criminal offense; or

(3) expose any secret tending to subject any person to hatred, contempt or ridicule, or to impair his credit or business repute; or

(4) take or withhold action as an official, or cause an official to take or withhold action; or

(5) bring about or continue a strike, boycott or other collective unofficial action, if the property is not demanded or received for the benefit of the group in whose interest the actor purports to act; or

(6) testify or provide information or withhold testimony or information with respect to another's legal claim or defense; or

(7) inflict any other harm which would not benefit the actor.

It is an affirmative defense to prosecution based on paragraphs (2), (3) or (4) that the property obtained by threat of accusation, exposure, lawsuit or other invocation of official action was honestly claimed as restitution or indemnification for harm done in the circumstances to which such accusation, exposure, lawsuit or other official action relates, or as compensation for property or lawful services.

Section 223.5. Theft of Property Lost, Mislaid, or Delivered by Mistake.

A person who comes into control of property of another that he knows to have been lost, mislaid, or delivered under a mistake as to the nature or amount of the property or the identity of the recipient is guilty of theft if, with purpose to deprive the owner thereof, he fails to take reasonable measures to restore the property to a person entitled to have it.

Section 223.6. Receiving Stolen Property.

(1) Receiving. A person is guilty of theft if he purposely receives, retains, or disposes of movable property of another knowing that it has been stolen, or believing that it has probably been stolen, unless the property is received, retained, or disposed with purpose to restore it to the owner. "Receiving" means acquiring possession, control or title, or lending on the security of the property.

(2) Presumption of Knowledge. The requisite knowledge or belief is presumed in the case of a dealer who:

(a) is found in possession or control of property stolen from two or more persons on separate occasions; or

(b) has received stolen property in another transaction within the year preceding the transaction charged; or

(c) being a dealer in property of the sort received, acquires it for a consideration which he knows is far below its reasonable value.

"Dealer" means a person in the business of buying or selling goods, or a pawnbroker.

Section 223.7. Theft of Services.

(1) A person is guilty of theft if he purposely obtains services which he knows are available only for compensation, by deception or threat, or by false token or other means to avoid payment for the service. "Services" includes labor, professional service, transportation, telephone or other public service, accommodation in hotels, restaurants or elsewhere, admission to exhibitions, use of vehicles or other movable property. Where compensation for service is ordinarily paid immediately upon the rendering of such service,

as in the case of hotels and restaurants, refusal to pay or absconding without payment or offer to pay gives rise to a presumption that the service was obtained by deception as to intention to pay.

(2) A person commits theft if, having control over the disposition of services of others, to which he is not entitled, he knowingly diverts such services to his own benefit or to the benefit of another not entitled thereto.

Section 223.8. Theft by Failure to Make Required Disposition of Funds Received.

A person who purposely obtains property upon agreement, or subject to a known legal obligation, to make specified payment or other disposition, whether from such property or its proceeds or from his own property to be reserved in equivalent amount, is guilty of theft if he deals with the property obtained as his own and fails to make the required payment or disposition. The foregoing applies notwithstanding that it may be impossible to identify particular property as belonging to the victim at the time of the actor's failure to make the required payment or disposition. An officer or employee of the government or of a financial institution is presumed: (i) to know any legal obligation relevant to his criminal liability under this Section, and (ii) to have dealt with the property as his own if he fails to pay or account upon lawful demand, or if an audit reveals a shortage or falsification of accounts.

Section 223.9. Unauthorized Use of Automobiles and Other Vehicles.

A person commits a misdemeanor if he operates another's automobile, airplane, motorcycle, motorboat, or other motor-propelled vehicle without consent of the owner. It is an affirmative defense to prosecution under this Section that the actor reasonably believed that the owner would have consented to the operation had he known of it.

Chapter 5

OTHER OFFENSES

SECTION 1. OFFENSES AGAINST MORALITY AND DECENCY

The whole field of substantive criminal law constitutes a rather stern moral code. It is not exhaustive in this respect but represents the points at which conduct is deemed so offensive to the moral judgment of the community as to call for punishment. This frequently leads to the question: Why are certain crimes spoken of as offenses against morality?

There is reason to believe that at a very early day the Church pre-empted jurisdiction over certain types of misconduct. It is known that the starting point of benefit of clergy was the Church's refusal to permit members of the clergy to be tried for crime in lay courts. The time came when benefit of clergy could be claimed only after guilt had been established, by verdict or plea, but this was after a very substantial change in the relative power of Church and State. Much earlier the Church had said to the common-law judges, in effect: "If a charge of misconduct is brought against a clergyman, that is none of your business. That is our business; send him to us and we shall handle the matter." And for generations this is exactly what happened.

In like manner it is more than probable that at the peak of its power the Church made it known to the common-law judges that jurisdiction over certain types of misconduct belonged exclusively to the ecclesiastical court. In any event the Church did take jurisdiction over those offenses and the common-law judges did not do so for many years—not in fact until they had been made punishable by acts of Parliament. Prior to that time they were no doubt referred to as "offenses only against morality".

(A) ADULTERY, FORNICATION AND ILLICIT COHABITATION

Adultery is punished as a crime under many of the modern statutes, some of which provide that both parties to the illicit intercourse are guilty of this offense if either is married to a third person.

Fornication—illicit intercourse which is not adultery—is punished in a few states.

Illicit cohabitation is living together in a relation of either adultery or fornication. This is an offense under many of the statutes.

None of the three was a common-law crime except that if illicit cohabitation was so open and notorious as to create a public scandal it was punishable.

(B) BIGAMY

Bigamy is contracting a second marriage during the existence of a prior marital relation or the marrying of more than one spouse at the same time. It was not a common-law crime but is punished under modern statutes.

(C) INCEST

In its broadest scope, incest is either marriage, or sexual intercourse without marrriage, between persons related within the degrees in which marriage is prohibited by law. Originally it was only an ecclesiastical offense but has very generally been made a crime by statute.

(D) SEDUCTION

Although a statutory crime is most states, seduction was not punished by the common law. The statutes are not uniform, but in general seduction may be said to be illicit sexual intercourse obtained by a man with a woman whom he has induced to surrender her chastity by a promise of marriage, or in some states either by such a promise or some other seductive art.

(E) SODOMY

Sodomy is a generic term which includes both "bestiality" and "buggery".

Bestiality is carnal copulation with a beast.

Buggery is copulation per anum—sometimes enlarged by statute to include the case where the act is in the mouth.

Sodomy was not a crime according to the common law of England, being left to the jurisdiction of the ecclesiastical courts. It was made a felony there by early statutes generally assumed to be part of the American common law. Sodomy is usually included in the penal code although some of the statutes refer to it only as the "crime against nature".

(F) PROSTITUTION, OBSCENITY AND INDECENCY

Prostitution is the common lewdness of a woman for gain. It was only an ecclesiastical offense in itself but the keeping of a bawdy house, or house of prostitution, was a common-law nuisance.

Pandering is the paid procurement of a female as an inmate of a house of prostitution. The procurer is often referred to as a "pimp".

The Mann Act, or white slave traffic law, is a federal statute which provides a penalty for the interstate transportation of a female for prostitution or other immoral purpose.

Obscenity is that which is offensive to chastity. It is material which deals with sex in a manner appealing to prurient interest.

Indecency is often used with the same meaning, but may also include anything which is outrageously disgusting. These were not the names of common-law crimes, but were words used in describing or identifying certain deeds which were.

An obscene libel is a writing, book or picture of such an obscene nature as to shock the public sense of decency. It is a misdemeanor at common law to publish such a libel.

Indecent exposure of the person in public is a common-law nuisance, as is also the public utterance of obscene or profane language in such a manner as to annoy the public.

The Model Penal Code suggests something of a return to the original position. It does not penalize nonviolent, uncommercialized sexual sins—fornication, adultery, sodomy or other consensual illicit sexual activity not involving imposition upon children, mental incompetents, wards or other dependents. The position taken is that such matters are best left to religious, educational or other social influences. It does penalize open lewdness, by which others are likely to be affronted or alarmed (Section 251.1), professional prostitution (Section 251.2), and commercialized obscenity (Section 251.4). Also forbidden under penalty are bigamy and polygamy (Section 230.1), incest (Section 230.2) and unjustified abortion (Section 230.3).[1]

SECTION 2. OFFENSES AGAINST THE PUBLIC PEACE

(A) BREACH OF THE PEACE

Misconduct which disturbs the peace and tranquillity of the community may have a special name, such as affray. If not, it is called "breach of the peace", "disturbing the peace" or "public disturbance".

(B) FIGHTING

There is no common-law crime known as "fighting" but a fight (other than a friendly contest of strength or skill) usually constitutes a crime. It may be only an assault and battery—by one, if the other is not exceeding his privilege of self-defense—otherwise by both.

---

[1]. For presentations of the Code's position on these matters see the Model Penal Code, Tent. Draft No. 4 pp. 204–238; Tent. Draft No. 6 pp. 5–95; Tent. Draft No. 9 pp. 146–162. And for a scholarly discussion see Schwartz, Morals Offenses and the Model Penal Code, 63 Colum.L.Rev. 669 (1963).

An *affray* is a mutual fight in a public place to the terror or alarm of the public. It is a common-law misdemeanor. Prize-fighting was not punishable at common law unless held in a public place. In some states it is prohibited, in some it is an offense unless licensed by public authority.

(C) UNLAWFUL ASSEMBLY, ROUT AND RIOT

Each of these was a misdemeanor at common law.

An *unlawful assembly* is a meeting of three or more persons with intent to—

    (a) commit a crime by force or violence, or

    (b) execute a common design, lawful or unlawful, in a manner likely to cause courageous persons to apprehend a breach of the peace.

A *rout* is the movement of unlawful assemblers on the way to carry out their common design.

A *riot* is a tumultuous disturbance by unlawful assemblers in the execution of their plan.

Three or more persons who happen to be together for some other purpose could suddenly engage in a riot. On the other hand they might gather at one place to make plans, go to another place and there accomplish their purpose. If so, they have committed three offenses at common law. Under some statutes a riot may be a felony, and under some no more than two persons are required for any of these three offenses. Rout has frequently been omitted from the codes.

(D) DISTURBANCE OF PUBLIC ASSEMBLY

Any unauthorized disturbance of a public assembly is a misdemeanor at common law, except that it would be excused if quite unintentional.

(E) DISORDERLY HOUSE

Any house in which disorderly persons are permitted to congregate, and to disturb the tranquillity of the neighborhood by fighting, quarreling, swearing or other type of disorder, is a disorderly house; and the keeping thereof is a misdemeanor at common law.

(F) FORCIBLE ENTRY AND DETAINER

A mere trespass upon the land of another is not a crime, but if an entry is accomplished by force or intimidation; or if such methods are employed for detention after peaceable entry, there is a crime according to English law known as forcible entry and detainer. Whether it was punishable by the English common law or not it was made a crime by English statutes old enough to be common law in this country.

Any unlawful act of forcible entry or detainer will involve some other crime, such as an assault. For this reason it is omitted from some penal codes.

(G) LIBEL

Libel is the malicious publication of durable defamation. A common explanation is that the malicious publication of defamation is slander if oral and libel if written. This gives the idea in a general way but libel may be committed without writing, as by hanging a man in effigy. In law "publication" means to make known, and showing the defamatory matter is sufficient. Any intentional publication of defamation is malicious in the absence of some justification or excuse.

SECTION 3. OFFENSES AFFECTING SOVEREIGNTY OR THE ADMINISTRATION OF GOVERNMENTAL FUNCTIONS

(A) TREASON

Treason against the United States is defined by the Constitution and consists only "in levying war against them, or in adhering to their enemies, giving them aid and comfort". Breach of allegiance is the essence of treason and hence this offense cannot be committed by a non-resident foreigner.

(B) PERJURY AND SUBORNATION

The common law had two similar offenses, both misdemeanors. Perjury is a false oath in a judicial proceeding in regard to a material matter. A false oath is a wilful and corrupt sworn statement without sincere belief in its truthfulness. False swearing is what would be perjury except that it is not in a judicial proceeding but in some other proceeding or matter in which an oath is required by law. Many of the statutes combine the two under the name of perjury, which is now usually a felony. An affirmation is now generally recognized as the legal equivalent of an oath. And constructive perjury does not require either oath or affirmation, being a signature attached "under the penalties of perjury".

Subornation of perjury is the procurement of perjury by another.

(C) BRIBERY

Bribery is the corrupt conveyance or receipt of a private price for official action. It was a common-law misdemeanor and is frequently a felony under modern statutes. There has been a tendency for legislation to extend the offense beyond the original field of official bribery. Such enactments may provide a penalty for quasi-official bribery (such as bribery of employees of public institutions), commercial bribery (as where a wholesaler bribes an agent of a retailer), or bribery in sports.

(D) MISCONDUCT IN OFFICE (OFFICIAL MISCONDUCT)

Misconduct in office is corrupt misbehavior by an officer in the exercise of the duties of his office or while acting under color of his office.

Common-law extortion is the corrupt collection of an unlawful fee by an officer under color of his office. (Statutory extortion is what is popularly known as blackmail.)

If the illegal act of the officer, done corruptly to the harm of another and under color of his office, takes some form other than extortion the offense is known as oppression. If the illegal and corrupt act of the officer takes the form of a fraud or breach of trust affecting the public it is known as fraud by an officer or breach of trust by an officer. If it takes the form of wilful forbearance to perform a duty of his office it is called neglect of official duty.

(E) EMBRACERY

Embracery is an attempt, by corrupt and wrongful means, to influence a juror in regard to a verdict to be found.

(F) COUNTERFEITING

Counterfeiting is the unlawful making of false money in the similitude of the genuine.

(G) OBSTRUCTION OF JUSTICE

Any wilful act of corruption, intimidation or force which tends to distort or impede the administration of law, either civil or criminal, is an offense usually known as obstruction of justice, unless it has been given a special name, such as bribery or embracery. One of the common forms of this offense involves an interference with a public officer in the discharge of his official duty.

(H) ESCAPE AND KINDRED OFFENSES

Escape is unauthorized departure of a prisoner from legal custody without the use of force. If the escape is by use of force the offense is *prison breach,* or breach of prison. These two common-law offenses are frequently combined under the name of "escape" in modern statutes.

If the officer in charge of a prisoner permits him to escape the officer is guilty of the offense of *permitting escape,* which is usually punishable more severely if intentional than if merely negligent.

Rescue is forcibly freeing a prisoner from lawful custody.

Violation of parole is commonly made an offense by statute.

(I) MISPRISION OF FELONY

It may be that in very ancient times one who knew of a felony committed by another was guilty of a misdemeanor known as misprision of felony if he did not promptly disclose the matter to an officer. If there ever was such an offense in England it has become obsolete there and has not been recognized as common law here. Misprision of felony is found in some of the modern statutes but not with what is supposed to be the ancient signification. The essence there, in theory at least, was nondisclosure; where found in modern statutes the essence is concealment.[1]

---

1. Recently misprision of felony has been reestablished in England at least to a limited extent. Sykes v. Director of Public Prosecutions, [1961] All Eng. L.R. 33. It was held that active concealment was not essential.

(J) COMPOUNDING CRIME

Following the lead of an English statute in the 1500s it has been common to authorize the compromise of certain crimes, usually with the court's consent as a requirement. It is an offense known as compounding crime to accept anything of value under an agreement not to prosecute a known offender for any offense unless the compromise is authorized by law.

(K) MAINTENANCE, CHAMPERTY AND BARRATRY

In the early days in England, when the administration of the law was in a very insecure position, one form of "racket" was an officious intermeddling in a lawsuit in which the meddler had no interest, by assisting one of the parties with means to prosecute or to defend the suit. There is reason to believe that the mere fact that one of the barons or other person of great power was connected with the case (in which he had no proper interest) exerted a very unwholesome influence upon the outcome of the suit. And this practice became so intolerable that it was made a crime under the name of *"maintenance."* No doubt the meddler charged a price for his improper assistance in any case, but if this price was a share of the matter in suit in case of success the offense was called *"champerty."* An habitual offender in this field was guilty of still another offense, known as *"barratry,"* or "common barratry." Guilt of either maintenance or champerty could be established by proof of a single act, but a series of such acts— three or more—was necessary for conviction of barratry.

The conditions which gave rise to these offenses disappeared long ago and they have become entirely obsolete.[1] Confusion has resulted, however, because in a particular jurisdiction one or more of these words may be found as the name of a crime, though not with the original signification. At present it is not unlawful for one, who has no interest of his own in the litigation, to give help by money or otherwise to either the plaintiff or the defendant, present or prospective, if the suit or the defense for which it is given is just or is reasonably believed to be so, and there is no impropriety in the manner in which, or the motive with which, the assistance is given. As it is improper to stir up litigation known to be unfounded or unjust, any wilful mis-

---

1. The common-law doctrines of champerty and maintenance were never adopted in California. The statute forbidding fee-splitting applies only to the attorney and not to the layman. Cain v. Burns, 131 Cal.App.2d 439, 280 P.2d 888 (1955).

conduct of this nature may be made punishable by statute, perhaps under the name of "maintenance," and the practice of doing so (three or more instances) may constitute an offense called "barratry" which is actually more often included in the modern codes.

Misconduct under the name of "champerty" (or sometimes "maintenance") is much more likely to be encountered today as a defense to a civil action than as a criminal offense. Statutes prohibiting "stirring up quarrels and suits" are not uncommon, the following (Iowa Code Ann. § 740.6) being an example:

"If any judge, justice of the peace, clerk of any court, sheriff, coroner, constable, attorney, or counselor at law, encourage, excite or stir up any action, quarrel or controversy between two or more persons, with intent to injure such persons, he shall be fined not exceeding five hundred dollars, and shall be answerable to the party injured in treble damages."

(L) CONTEMPT

Misconduct adversely affecting the administration of a governmental function may take the form of improper interference with the work of the legislative body or of the court. In England either house of Parliament could commit for contempt of itself, and in this country the power to commit for contempt extends to the Senate and House of Representatives of the United States and to the corresponding bodies of the respective states. Such contempt includes any insult to the legislative body in the form of disrespectful or disorderly conduct in its presence and also any wilful obstruction of the performance of a legislative function. Such misconduct, it is to be noted, is not indictable but is punished by the legislative body itself. Contempt of Congress, or its committees, has been made a misdemeanor by statute and hence such misbehavior may now be dealt with the same as any other offense of corresponding grade.

Under the common law of England courts had the inherent power to punish for contempt and this has been accepted as a part of our common law at least so far as courts of record are concerned. Contempt of court has been classified in two different ways: (a) depending upon the purpose of the proceeding, into (1) civil contempt and (2) criminal contempt, and (b) depending upon the factor of proximity or remoteness, into (1) direct contempt and (2) constructive (indirect or consequential) contempt. Civil contempt is misconduct in the form of disobedience to an order or direction of the court by one party to a judicial proceeding to the prejudice of the other litigant. The harm is to the injured litigant rather than to the public and the "penalty" imposed, being purely coercive in purpose, can be avoided by compliance with the court's order. Thus a person who had wrongfully taken a child from its lawful guardian and disobeyed the order of the judge to bring the child into court or disclose its whereabouts was ordered committed to jail until she should obey the court's order.

A criminal contempt [1] on the other hand is misconduct which is disrespectful to the court, calculated to bring the court into disrepute, or of a nature which tends to obstruct the administration of justice, and the purpose of convicting for such contempt is vindication of the public interest by punishment of contemptuous conduct. The same misdeed may constitute both a civil contempt and a criminal contempt and in one such case the judgment was that the contemnor be imprisoned for one day (punishment for his criminal contempt) and that after the expiration of the first day he remain in prison until he complied with the order of the court (coercive and avoidable by prompt compliance).

A direct contempt is one committed in the presence of the court, or of a judge at chambers, or so near thereto as to interrupt or hinder judicial proceedings. Illustrations include an assault on the marshal in open court or a vindictive and uncalled for remark to the court. A constructive, or indirect contempt is an act done, not in the presence of the court or a judge acting judicially, but at a distance under circumstances that reasonably tend to degrade the court or the judge as a judicial officer, or to obstruct, prevent, or embarrass the administration of justice by the court or judge. It may be committed in many ways, such for example, as by violating the judge's instructions to jurors not to separate or make contact with outsiders during trial, or by published criticism of the judicial proceedings of a nature tending to "scandalize the court" to use the familiar phrase. Insofar as a constructive contempt is in the form of a wilful violation of an order of the court, or other direct obstruction of the judicial proceedings, no difficulty is encountered; but so great and so important is the public interest in a public trial that out-of-court discussions and publications in regard to such a proceeding are protected by constitutional privilege even if they tend to cast discredit upon the court or the judge unless carried to such an extreme as to create a "clear and present danger" to the administration of justice.

1. A "criminal contempt" is not a crime and proceedings for the punishment thereof are not subject to the requirements of a criminal trial. Hence the contemner is not entitled to a jury trial. United States v. Barnett, 376 U.S. 681, 84 S.Ct. 984, 12 L.Ed.2d 23 (1964).

(M) OTHER OFFENSES

If space permitted, numerous other offenses might be considered in this connection. An important governmental function of a democracy is the holding of elections to fill public offices and to determine certain public questions; hence penalties are provided for unlawful registration as a voter, illegal voting, and various other election offenses. Another such function is the raising of public funds; wherefore penalties are provided for failure to file a required income tax return and various other taxation offenses. Most of the states have undertaken to regulate the manufacture and sale of intoxicating liquor, and the results are certain liquor offenses. To this list might be added countless offenses connected with the regulations of trades, occupations, monopolies, banking and finance, the sale of securities and other matters of a similar nature. Only one sample will be used from this list.

Fraudulent banking. This phrase, which might be applied to other misdeeds in the banking field, is usually used only to refer to the following offense. In many states it is made a crime for an officer of a bank to accept a deposit when his bank is insolvent, to his knowledge. A few of the jurisdictions have made a more severe requirement, making it an offense for the officer of a bank, which is in fact insolvent, to accept a deposit when he knows *or has reason to believe* that it is insolvent. Although the distinction between these two types of legislation was overlooked in one case, the proper interpretation is this: Under the first type the banker who accepts a deposit while his bank is insolvent is excused from guilt if he believes in good faith that his bank is solvent, even if he is at fault in not being aware of the insolvency. Under the second type, the banker is not excused unless the insolvency has occurred under such unusual circumstances that he not only does not know of this fact, but is free from criminal negligence in not knowing. Some of the banking laws do not include any such provision, on the ground that whether a bank is or is not insolvent at a certain critical moment in a depression may be difficult to ascertain, and thus the threat of such a penalty may force the closing of banks which it would be in the public interest to have kept open.

Chapter 6

IMPUTABILITY

SECTION 1. THE NECESSITY OF AN ACT

4 Blackstone, Commentaries on the Laws of England, 78–79. Let us next see what is a *compassing* or *imagining* of the death of the king &c. These are synonymous terms, the word *compass* signifying the purpose or design of the mind or will, and not, as in common speech, the carrying such design to effect. . . . But, as this compassing or imagining is an act of the mind, it cannot possibly fall under any judicial cognizance, unless it be demonstrated by some open or *overt* act. . . . There is no question, also, but that taking any measures to render such treasonable purposes effectual, as assembling and consulting on the means to kill the king, is a sufficient overt act of high treason.

STATE v. QUICK
Supreme Court of South Carolina, 1942.
199 S.C. 256, 19 S.E.2d 101.

FISHBURNE, JUSTICE. The defendant was convicted of the unlawful manufacture of intoxicating liquor under Section 1829, Code 1932, and amendments thereto. The main question in the case, as we see it, is whether the lower Court erred in refusing to direct a verdict of acquittal, a motion therefor having been made at the close of the evidence offered by the State. . . .

We think there can be no doubt but that the evidence overwhelmingly tends to show an intention on the part of the appellant to manufacture liquor; certainly such inference may reasonably be drawn. But intent alone, not coupled with some overt act toward putting the intent into effect, is not cognizable by the Courts. The law does not concern itself with mere guilty intention, unconnected with any overt act. State v. Kelly, 114 S.C. 336, 103 S.E. 511; 14 Am.Jur., Sec. 25, Page 786. . . .

In our opinion the defendant is entitled to a new trial in any event. But because of the error in overruling his motion for a directed verdict the judgment is reversed, with direction to enter a verdict of not guilty.

BONHAM, C. J., BAKER and STUKES, JJ., and WM. H. GRIMBALL, A A. J., concur.

REX v. MARTIN

Stafford Assizes, 1827.
3 Car. & P. 211, 172 Eng.Rep. 390.

Manslaughter. The indictment charged the prisoner with giving a quarter of gin to Joseph Sweet, a child of tender age, to wit, of the age of four years, which caused his death. The indictment averred the quantity of gin to be excessive for a child of that age. It appeared that the father of the deceased kept a public-house at Wolverhampton, and that the prisoner went there to drink, and having ordered a quartern of gin, he asked the child if he would have a drop; and that, on his putting the glass to the child's mouth, with his left hand, as he held the child with his right, the child twisted the glass out of his hand, and immediately swallowed nearly the whole of the quartern of gin, which caused his death a few hours after.

VAUGHAN, B. As it appears clearly that the drinking of the gin in this quantity was the act of the child, the prisoner must be acquitted; but if it had appeared that the prisoner had willingly given a child of this tender age a quartern of gin, out of a sort of brutal fun, and had thereby caused its death, I should most decidedly have held that to be manslaughter, because I have no doubt that the causing the death of a child by giving it spirituous liquors, in a quantity quite unfit for its tender age, amounts, in point of law, to that offence.

Verdict—Not guilty.

STATE v. RIDER

Supreme Court of Missouri, 1886.
90 Mo. 54, 1 S.W. 825.

HENRY, C. J. At the September term, 1885, of the Saline criminal court the defendant was indicted for murder for killing one R. P. Tallent, and was tried at the November term of said court, 1885, and convicted of murder in the first degree. From that judgment he has appealed to this court.

The evidence for the state proved that he killed the deceased, and of that fact there is no question. It also tended to prove that he armed himself with a gun, and sought the deceased with the intent to kill him. The evidence tended to prove that the relations between the defendant and his wife were not of the most agreeable character, and that the deceased was criminally intimate with her, and on the day of the homicide had taken her off in a skiff to Brunswick. That defendant went in search of his wife to the residence of the deceased, armed with a shot gun, and met the latter near his residence. What then occurred no one witnessed, except the parties engaged, but defendant testified as follows: "Well, me and Mr. Merrill went to this path that was leading toward the river. When we come to that path

Mr. Merrill stopped, and I went on in the direction of Mr. Tallent's house, to see if I could learn anything about where my wife was, and I discovered no sign of her there, and I started back north on this path, going down on the slough bank; after going down some distance from the bank I meets Mr. Tallent; I spoke to Mr. Tallent and asked him if he knew where my wife was, and he made this remark: 'I have taken her where you won't find her;' and he says, 'God damn you, we will settle this right here.' He started at me with his axe in a striking position, and I bid Mr. Tallent to stop; then he advanced a few feet, and I fired. I fired one time." The axe of deceased, found on the ground, had a shot in the handle near the end farthest from the blade, and on the same side as the blade, and this evidence had a tendency to corroborate the testimony of the accused, showing that the axe was pointing in the direction from which the shot came, and was held in an upright position.

The court, for the state, instructed the jury as follows:

"The court instructs the jury, that if they believe from the evidence that prior to the killing of the deceased, the defendant prepared and armed himself with a gun, and went in search of, and sought out, deceased, with the intention of killing him, or shooting him, or doing him some great bodily harm, and that he did find, overtake, or intercept, deceased, and did shoot and kill deceased while he was returning from the river to his home, then it makes no difference who commenced the assault, and the jury shall not acquit the defendant; and the jury are further instructed that in such case they shall disregard any and all testimony tending to show that the character or reputation of deceased for turbulency, violence, peace and quiet was bad, and they shall further disregard any and all evidence of threats made by deceased against the defendant."

The mere intent to commit a crime is not a crime. An attempt to perpetrate it is necessary to constitute guilt in law. One may arm himself with the purpose of seeking and killing an adversary, and may seek and find him, yet, if guilty of no overt act, commits no crime. It has been repeatedly held in this and nearly every state in the Union, that one against whom threats have been made by another is not justifiable in assaulting him unless the threatener makes some attempt to execute his threats. A threat to kill but indicates an intent or purpose to kill; and the unexpressed purpose or intent certainly affords no better excuse for an assault by the person against whom it exists than such an intent accompanied with a threat to accomplish it. The above instruction authorized the jury to convict the defendant even though he had abandoned the purpose to kill the deceased when he met him, and was assaulted by deceased and had to kill him to save his own life. . . .

For the errors above noted the judgment is reversed and cause remanded. All concur.[1]

[1]. Rider was tried again under proper instructions and again convicted. This conviction was affirmed. State v. Rider, 95 Mo. 474, 8 S.W. 723 (1888).

SECTION 2. WHAT CONSTITUTES AN ACT

STATE v. TAFT

Supreme Court of Appeals of West Virginia, 1958.
143 W.Va. 365, 102 S.E.2d 152.

GIVEN, JUDGE. . . . The indictment in the instant case is in two counts. The first count charges defendant with having driven an automobile while "under the influence of intoxicating liquor". . . . On the verdict of the jury, the judgment was that defendant serve six months in the county jail, the sentence to run consecutively to the sentence mentioned in case No. 10907. . . .

After the jury had considered of a verdict for some time, the foreman requested the trial court to answer the question, "Is there a legal definition for what constitutes driving a car?" Whereupon, over objection of defendant, the court instructed the jury "that the term 'driving' has been defined and construed as requiring that a vehicle be in motion in order for the offense to be committed". Defendant then offered, in writing, an instruction which would have told the jury "that if they believe from the evidence that defendant got in his parked car for the purpose of waiting for someone else, and that the brakes of his car accidentally released and the car drifted some two to three feet into the rear end of a car parked in front of said Taft car, and that the movement of said car was accidental, and not the act and intent of the defendant, then you are authorized to find and determine that the defendant was not then and there driving his said car, and if you so find that the defendant was not then and there driving his said car, you may find the defendant not guilty."

The statute on which the indictment is based makes it a criminal offense for a person "to drive any vehicle on any highway of this state" while "under the influence of intoxicating liquor"; or "under the influence of any narcotic drug". The question posed by the action of the court, as related to the instructions mentioned above, is whether the mere motion of the vehicle constituted "driving" of the vehicle, within the meaning of the statute. We think that it does not.

Though movement of a vehicle is an essential element of the statutory requirement, the mere movement of a vehicle does not necessarily, in every circumstance, constitute a "driving" of the vehicle. To "drive" a vehicle necessarily implies a driver or operator and an affirmative or positive action on the part of the driver. A mere movement of the vehicle might occur without any affirmative act by a driver, or, in fact by any person. If a vehicle is moved by some power beyond the control of the driver, or by accident, it is not such an affirmative or positive action on the part of the driver, as will constitute a driving of a vehicle within the meaning of the statute. This being true, the instruction telling the jury that the vehicle must "be in motion in order for an offense to be committed" necessarily, in view of the evidence before the jury, had the effect of telling them that any accidental movement of the vehicle was sufficient to constitute a driving of the vehicle within the meaning of the statute, and constituted prejudicial error. What is said in this respect also indicates prejudicial error in the refusal to give to the jury the instruction offered by defendant, quoted above, after the giving of the instruction first mentioned. . . .

For the reasons indicated, the judgment of the circuit court is reversed, the verdict of the jury set aside, and defendant is awarded a new trial.

Reversed; verdict set aside; new trial awarded.

PEOPLE v. DECINA

Court of Appeals of New York, 1956.
2 N.Y.2d 133, 157 N.Y.S.2d 558, 138 N.E.2d 799.

[Defendant was convicted of the statutory offense known as "criminal negligence in the operation of a vehicle resulting in death". He appealed, insisting that the court erred (1) in overruling his demurrer to the indictment and (2) in the admission of incompetent testimony. The Appellate Division held that the demurrer was properly overruled but reversed and granted a new trial on the second ground. From this determination both parties appealed.]

FROESSEL, JUDGE. . . . We turn first to the subject of defendant's cross appeal, namely, that his demurrer should have been sustained, since the *indictment* here does not charge a crime. The indictment states essentially that defendant, *knowing* "that he was subject to epileptic attacks or other disorder rendering him likely to lose consciousness for a considerable period of time", was culpably negligent "in that he *consciously* undertook to and *did operate* his Buick sedan on a public highway" (emphasis supplied) and "while so doing" suffered such an attack which caused said automobile "to travel at a fast and reckless rate of speed, jumping the curb and driving over the sidewalk" causing the death of 4 persons. In our opinion, this clearly states a violation of section 1053–a of the Penal Law. The statute does not require that a defendant must deliberately intend to kill a human being, for that would be murder. Nor does the statute require that he knowingly and consciously follow the precise path that leads to death and destruction. It is sufficient, we have said, when his conduct manifests a "disregard of the consequences which may ensue from the act, and indifference to the rights of others. No clearer definition, applicable to the hundreds of varying circumstances that may arise, can be given. Under a given state of facts, whether negligence is culpable is a question of judgment." People v. Angelo, 246 N.Y. 451, 457, 159 N.E. 394, 396.

Assuming the truth of the indictment, as we must on a demurrer, this defendant knew he was subject to epileptic attacks and seizures that might strike *at any time*. He also knew that a moving motor vehicle uncontrolled on a public highway is a highly dangerous instrumentality capable of unrestrained destruction. With this *knowledge*, and without anyone accompanying him, he deliberately took a chance by making a conscious choice of a course of action, in disregard of the consequences which he knew might follow from his conscious act, and which in this case did ensue. How can we say as a matter of law that this did not amount to culpable negligence within the meaning of section 1053–a?

To hold otherwise would be to say that a man may freely indulge himself in liquor in the same hope that it will not affect his driving, and if it later develops that ensuing intoxication causes dangerous and reckless driving resulting in death, his unconsciousness or involuntariness at that time would relieve him from prosecution under the statute. His awareness of a condition which he knows may produce such consequences as here, and his disregard of the consequences, renders him liable for culpable negligence, as the courts below have properly held. To have a sudden sleeping spell, an unexpected heart or other disabling attack, without any prior knowledge or warning thereof, is an altogether different situation, and there is simply no basis for comparing such cases with the flagrant disregard manifested here. . . .

Accordingly, the Appellate Division properly sustained the lower court's order overruling the demurrer, as well as its denial of the motion in arrest of judgment on the same ground. . . .

[The court agreed with the Appellate Division that reversible error had been committed in the admission of evidence.]

Accordingly, the order of the Appellate Division should be affirmed.[1]

---

1. A count for having possession of obscene prints with intent to sell cannot be supported because possession is not an act and the law will not take notice of an intent without an act. Dugdale v. Regina, 1 El. & Bl. 435, 118 Eng.Rep. 499 (1853).

D was convicted under a federal statute which declared that "whoever, without authority, shall have in his possession" any die in the likeness of a die designed for making genuine coin of the United States should be punished. D claimed that the statute was invalid because it would cover unwitting possession. The conviction was affirmed on the ground that the statute must be construed to mean "a willing and conscious possession". Baender v. Barnett, 255 U.S. 224, 41 S.Ct. 271, 65 L.Ed. 597 (1921).

D, who had been awakened with great difficulty from a very deep sleep, almost at once killed the one who had awakened him, a complete stranger. A conviction of manslaughter was reversed because the trial judge had excluded evidence offered to prove that D had been a sleep-walker from infancy, that frequently when aroused from sleep he seemed frightened and attempted violence as if resisting an assault, and for some minutes seemed unconscious of what he did or what went on around him. Fain v. Commonwealth, 78 Ky. 183 (1879).

DESMOND, JUDGE (concurring in part and dissenting in part).

I agree that the judgment of conviction cannot stand but I think the indictment should be dismissed because it alleges no crime. Defendant's demurrer should have been sustained. . . .

Just what is the court holding here? No less than this: that a driver whose brief blackout lets his car run amuck and kill another has killed that other by reckless driving. But any such "recklessness" consists necessarily not of the erratic behavior of the automobile while its driver is unconscious, but of his driving at all when he knew he was subject to such attacks. Thus, it must be that such a black-out-prone driver is guilty of reckless driving, Vehicle and Traffic Law, Consol.Laws, c. 71, § 58, whenever and as soon as he steps into the driver's seat of a vehicle. Every time he drives, accident or no accident, he is subject to criminal prosecution for reckless driving or to revocation of his operator's license, Vehicle and Traffic Law, § 71, subd. 3. And how many of this State's 5,000,000 licensed operators are subject to such penalties for merely driving the cars they are licensed to drive? No one knows how many citizens or how many or what kind of physical conditions will be gathered in under this practically limitless coverage of section 1053–a of the Penal Law and section 58 and subdivision 3 of section 71 of the Vehicle and Traffic Law. It is no answer that prosecutors and juries will be reasonable or compassionate. A criminal statute whose reach is so unpredictable violates constitutional rights, as we shall now show. . . .

CONWAY, Ch. J., DYE and BURKE, JJ., concur with FROESSEL, J.; DESMOND, J., concurs in part and dissents in part in an opinion in which FULD and VAN VOORHIS, JJ., concur.

Order affirmed.

MODEL PENAL CODE
Article 2. General Principles of Liability

Section 2.01. Requirement of Voluntary Act; (Omission as Basis of Liability;) Possession as an Act.

(1) A person is not guilty of an offense unless his liability is based on conduct which includes a voluntary act or the omission to perform an act of which he is physically capable.

(2) The following are not voluntary acts within the meaning of this Section:

    (a) a reflex or convulsion;

    (b) a bodily movement during unconsciousness or sleep;

    (c) conduct during hypnosis or resulting from hypnotic suggestion;

    (d) a bodily movement that otherwise is not a product of the effort or determination of the actor, either conscious or habitual.

. . .

(4) Possession is an act, within the meaning of this Section, if the possessor knowingly procured or received the thing possessed or was aware of his control thereof for a sufficient period to have been able to terminate his possession.

SECTION 3. ATTEMPT AND KINDRED PROBLEMS

(A). ATTEMPT

(i) IN GENERAL

REX v. SCOFIELD

King's Bench, 1784.
Caldecott 397.

(The defendant, in an indictment which purported to be for arson, was charged with having placed a lighted candle in a closet under the stairs of a house, belonging to James Ramsey of which the defendant was in possession for a term of years, with the malicious intention of burning the house. There was neither allegation nor proof of any burning of the house. The jury found the defendant guilty. Several objections had been taken at the trial, but Lord Mansfield declined giving any opinion upon them, declaring at the time to the prisoner's counsel, that they would have the full benefit of them before the court.)

And now LORD MANSFIELD delivered the judgment of the court.

. . .

The next question is, Whether an act done in pursuance of an intent to commit an act, which, if compleated, would be a misdemeanor only, can itself be a misdemeanor? It was objected, that an attempt to commit a misdemeanor was no offence: but no authority for this is cited; and there are many on the other side: as the case cited; of the King v. Johnson, the King v. Sutton, which [b] was an indictment for having in custody and possession stamps *with intent* to impress sceptres on sixpences, &c. And there the court say "lading wool is lawful; but, if it be with *an intent* to transport it, that makes it an offence. Here the intent is the offence; and the having in his custody, an act that is the evidence of that intent." But in the case of the wool, the transporting of it was only a misdemeanor, yet an act done to that end was holden indictable. In the King v. Taylor, the Court [c] granted an information as for a nuisance for keeping great

[b] E. 10 G. 2. 2 Str. 1074.   [c] Tr. 15 G. 2. 2 Str. 1167.

quantities of gunpowder to the endangering of the church and houses where the defendant lived. There is also the case cited of the King v. Samuel Vaughan, which is founded upon the same principle as that of [d] the King v. Plympton; where it was holden that to bribe a corporator by money or promises to vote at corporation elections is an offence, for which an information will lie: the case of Vaughan was that of offering a bribe for an office, and if received, and the office procured, neither party would have been guilty of more than a misdemeanor: and it is laid down by the Court in the case of [e] the King v. Langley that words directly tending to a breach of the peace, are indictable.

There was a distinction made at the bar between an act done with an intent to commit a felony and an act done with an intent to commit a misdemeanor. In the degrees of guilt there is great difference in the eye of the law, but not in the description of the offence. So long as an act rests in bare intention, it is not punishable by our laws: but immediately when an act is done, the law judges, not only of the act done, but of the intent with which it is done; and, if it is coupled with an unlawful and malicious intent, though the act itself would otherwise have been innocent, the intent being criminal, the act becomes criminal and punishable. The case cited of the King v. Sutton is an express authority. We are therefore of opinion that the indictment is good.[1]

Rule discharged.

LORD MANSFIELD then reported, the evidence: and WILLES, J., pronounced the judgment of the court, which was, that the prisoner pay a fine of 300*l.*, be imprisoned in Newgate one year and till his fine be paid; and that he give security for his good behaviour for 7 years, himself in 200*l.* and two sureties in 100*l.* each.

(ii) PERPETRATING ACT

WILSON v. STATE

Supreme Court of Mississippi, 1904.
85 Miss. 687, 38 So. 46.

CALHOON, J., delivered the opinion of the court.

Wilson was convicted of an attempt to commit forgery, the court below properly charging the jury that it could not convict of the crime itself. The instrument of which attempt to commit forgery is predi-

---

[d]. M. 11 G. 2. 1724. 2 Ld.Raym. 1377.

[e]. H. 2 Ann. 2 Salk. 697.

[1]. ". . . an attempt to commit a misdemeanor is a misdemeanor, whether the offence is created by statute or was an offence at common law." Rex v. Roderick, 7 Car. and P. 795 (1837).

cated is a draft for "two and 50–100 dollars," as written out in the body of it, having in the upper right-hand corner the figures "$2.50–100," as is customary in checks, drafts, and notes, and having plainly printed and stamped on the face of the instrument the words "Ten Dollars or Less." Wilson, with a pen, put the figure "1" before the figure "2" in the upper right-hand corner, making these immaterial figures appear "$12.50" instead of "$2.50," and undertook to negotiate it as $12.50. This was not forgery, because it was an immaterial part of the paper, and because it could not possibly have injured anybody. In order to constitute the crime, there must be not only the intent to commit it, but also an act of alteration done to a material part, so that injury might result. . . . These authorities might be numerously added to, but it is enough to say now that they sustain what we have said, and establish also that an instrument void on its face is not the subject of forgery, and that, in order to be so subject, it must have been capable of working injury if it had been genuine, and that the marginal numbers and figures are not part of the instrument, and their alteration is not forgery.

This being true, can the conviction of an attempt to commit forgery be sustained in the case before us? We think not. No purpose appears to change anything on the paper except the figures in the margin, and this could not have done any hurt. Our statute (Code 1892, § 1106) confines the crime of forgery to instances where "any person may be affected, bound, or in any way injured in his person or property." This is not such a case, and sec. 974 forbids convicting of an attempt "when it shall appear that the crime intended or the offense attempted was perpetrated." In this record the innocuous prefix of the figure "1" on the margin was fully accomplished, and no other effort appears, and, if genuine, could have done no harm; and so the appellant is guiltless, in law, of the crime of which he was convicted.

Reversed and remanded.

COMMONWEALTH v. KENNEDY

Supreme Judicial Court of Massachusetts, 1897.
170 Mass. 18, 48 N.E. 770.

HOLMES, J. . . . The second count alleges in substance that the defendant feloniously, wilfully, and maliciously attempted to murder Learoyd by placing a quantity of deadly poison known as "rough on rats," known to the defendant to be a deadly poison, upon, and causing it to adhere to the under side of the crossbar of a cup of Learoyd's known as a mustache cup, the cup being then empty, with the intent that Learoyd should thereafter use the cup for drinking while the poison was there, and should swallow the poison. The motion to quash was argued largely on the strength of some cases as to what

Sec. 3   ATTEMPT AND KINDRED PROBLEMS   227

constitutes an "administering" of poison, which have no application, but the argument also touched another question, which always is present in cases of attempts, and which requires a few words, namely, how nearly the overt acts alleged approached to the achievement of the substantive crime attempted.

Notwithstanding Pub.Sts. c. 210, § 8, we assume that an act may be done which is expected and intended to accomplish a crime, which is not near enough to the result to constitute an attempt to commit it, as in the classic instance of shooting at a post supposed to be a man. As the aim of the law is not to punish sins, but is to prevent certain external results, the act done must come pretty near to accomplishing that result before the law will notice it. But, on the other hand, irrespective of the statute, it is not necessary that the act should be such as inevitably to accomplish the crime by the operation of natural forces, but for some casual and unexpected interference. It is none the less an attempt to shoot a man that the pistol which is fired at his head is not aimed straight, and therefore in the course of nature cannot hit him. Usually acts which are expected to bring about the end without further interference on the part of the criminal are near enough, unless the expectation is very absurd. In this case the acts are alleged to have been done with intent that Learoyd should swallow the poison, and, by implication, with intent to kill him. Intent imports contemplation, and more or less expectation, of the intended end as the result of the act alleged. If it appeared in the count, as it did in the evidence, that the habits of Learoyd and the other circumstances were such that the defendant's expectation that he would use the cup and swallow the poison was well grounded, there could be no doubt that the defendant's acts were near enough to the intended swallowing of the poison, and, if the dose was large enough to kill, that they were near enough to the accomplishment of the murder. But the grounds of the defendant's expectation are not alleged, and the strongest argument for the defence, as it seems to us, would be that, so far as this count goes, his expectation may have been unfounded and unreasonable. But in view of the nature of the crime and the ordinary course of events, we are of opinion that enough is alleged when the defendant's intent is shown. The cup belonged to Learoyd, and the defendant expected that he would use it. To allow him immunity, on the ground that this part of his expectation was ill-grounded, would be as unreasonable as to let a culprit off because he was not warranted in thinking that his pistol was pointed at the man he tried to shoot. A more important point is that it is not alleged in terms that the dose was large enough to kill, unless we take judicial notice of the probable effect of a teaspoonful of "rough on rats"; and this may be likened to the case of firing a pistol supposed to be loaded with ball, but in fact not so, or to administering an innocent substance supposing it to be poison. There is a difference between the case of an attempt and a murder. In the latter case the event shows the dose to have been sufficient, without an express allegation. But we are of opinion that this objection cannot be maintained. Every question of proximity must be determined by its own circumstances, and analogy is too imperfect to give much help. Any unlawful application of poison is an evil which threatens death, according to common apprehension, and the gravity of the crime, the uncertainty of the result, and the seriousness of the apprehension, coupled with the great harm likely to result from poison even if not enough to kill, would warrant holding the liability for an attempt to begin at a point more remote from the possibility of accomplishing what is excepted than might be the case with lighter crimes. But analogy does not require this consideration. The case cited as to firing a pistol not loaded with ball has been qualified at least by a later decision, Kunkle v. State, 32 Ind. 220, 229, a case of shooting with shot too small to kill. . . .

Exceptions overruled.

PEOPLE v. RIZZO

Court of Appeals of New York, 1927.
246 N.Y. 334, 158 N.E. 888.

CRANE, J. The police of the city of New York did excellent work in this case by preventing the commission of a serious crime. It is a great satisfaction to realize that we have such wide-awake guardians of our peace. Whether or not the steps which the defendant had taken up to the time of his arrest amounted to the commission of a crime, as defined by our law, is, however, another matter. He has been convicted of an attempt to commit the crime of robbery in the first degree and sentenced to State's prison. There is no doubt that he had the intention to commit robbery if he got the chance. An examination, however, of the facts is necessary to determine whether his acts were in preparation to commit the crime if the opportunity offered, or constituted a crime in itself, known to our law as an attempt to commit robbery in the first degree. Charles Rizzo, the defendant, appellant, with three others, Anthony J. Dorio, Thomas Milo and John Thomasello, on January 14th planned to rob one Charles Rao of a payroll valued at about $1,200 which he was to carry from the bank for the United Lathing Company. These defendants, two of whom had firearms, started out in an automobile, looking for Rao or the man who had the payroll on that day. Rizzo claimed to be able to identify the man and was to point him out to the others who were to do the actual holding up. The four rode about in their car looking for Rao. They went to the bank from which he was supposed to get the money and to various buildings being constructed by the United Lathing Company. At last they came to One Hundred and Eightieth street and Morris Park avenue. By this time they were watched and followed by two police officers. As Rizzo jumped out of the car and ran into the building all four were arrested. The defendant was taken out from the building in which he was hiding. Neither Rao nor a man named Previti, who was also supposed to carry a payroll, were at the place at the time of the arrest. The defendants had not found or seen the man they intended to rob; no person with a payroll was at any of the places where they had stopped and no one had been pointed out or identified by Rizzo. The four men intended to rob the payroll man, whoever he was; they were looking for him, but they had not seen or discovered him up to the time they were arrested.

Does this constitute the crime of an attempt to commit robbery in the first degree? The Penal Law, section 2, prescribes, "An act, done with intent to commit a crime, and tending but failing to effect its commission, is 'an attempt to commit that crime.'" The word *"tending"* is very indefinite. It is perfectly evident that there will arise differences of opinion as to whether an act in a given case is one *tending* to commit a crime. "Tending" means to exert activity in a particular direction. Any act in preparation to commit a crime may be said to have a tendency towards its accomplishment. The procuring of the automobile, searching the streets looking for the desired victim, were in reality acts tending toward the commission of the proposed crime. The law, however, has recognized that many acts in the way of preparation are too remote to constitute the crime of attempt. The line has been drawn between those acts which are remote and those which are proximate and near to the consummation. The law must be practical, and, therefore, considers those acts only as tending to the commission of the crime which are so near to its accomplishment that in all reasonable probability the crime itself would have been committed but for timely interference. The cases which have been before the courts express this idea in different language, but the idea remains the same. The act or acts must come or advance very near to the accomplishment of the intended crime. In People v. Mills, 178 N.Y. 274, 284, 70 N.E. 786, it was said: "Felonious intent alone is not enough, but there must be an overt act shown in order to establish even an attempt. An overt act is one done to carry out the intention, and it must be such as would naturally effect that result, unless prevented by some extraneous cause." In Hyde v. U. S., 225 U.S. 347, 32 S.Ct. 793, 56 L.Ed. 1114, it was stated that the act amounts to an attempt when it is so near to the result that the danger of success is very great. "There must be dangerous proximity to success." Halsbury in his "Laws of England" (Vol. IX, p. 259) says: "An act, in order to be a criminal attempt, must be immediately, and not remotely, connected with and directly tending to the commission of an offence." Commonwealth v. Peaslee, 177 Mass. 267, 59 N.E. 55, refers to the acts constituting an attempt as coming *very near* to the accomplishment of the crime.

The method of committing or attempting crime varies in each case so that the difficulty, if any, is not with this rule of law regarding an attempt, which is well understood, but with its application to the facts. As I have said before, minds differ over proximity and the nearness of the approach.

How shall we apply this rule of immediate nearness to this case? The defendants were looking for the payroll man to rob him of his money. This is the charge in the indictment. Robbery is defined in section 2120 of the Penal Law as "the unlawful taking of personal property, from the person or in the presence of another against his will, by means of force, or violence, or fear of injury, immediate or future, to his person;" and it is made robbery in the first degree by section 2124 when committed by a person aided by accomplices actually present. To constitute the crime of robbery the money must have been taken from Rao by means of force or violence, or through fear. The crime of attempt to commit robbery was committed if these defendants did an act tending to the commission of this robbery. Did the acts above described come dangerously near to the taking of Rao's property? Did the acts come so near the commission of robbery that there was reasonable likelihood of its accomplishment but for the interference? Rao was not found; the defendants were still looking for him; no attempt to rob him could be made, at least until he came in sight; he was not in the building at One Hundred and Eightieth street and Morris Park avenue. There was no man there with the payroll for the United Lathing Company whom these defendants could rob. Apparently no money had been drawn from the bank for the payroll by anybody at the time of the arrest. In a word, these defendants had planned to commit a crime and were looking around the city for an opportunity to commit it, but the opportunity fortunately never came. Men would not be guilty of an attempt at burglary if they had planned to break into a building and were arrested while they were hunting about the streets for the building not knowing where it was. Neither would a man be guilty of an attempt to commit murder if he armed himself and started out to find the person whom he had planned to kill but could not find him. So here these defendants were not guilty of an attempt to commit robbery in the first degree when they had not found or reached the presence of the person they intended to rob.

For these reasons, the judgment of conviction of this defendant, appellant, must be reversed and a new trial granted. . . . [1]

---

1. Two men planned to rob a payroll clerk of his payroll. They went to the bank where he was to receive the payroll and stationed themselves to waylay him, but were arrested just before the clerk arrived. This was held to be an attempt to rob. People v. Gormley, 222 App.Div. 256, 225 N.Y.S. 653 (1927).

Two men planned to rob a third. They made inquiries about him, procured masks, and hired a taxi to hunt for him. This was held to be preparation

(iii) IMPOSSIBILITY

STATE v. MITCHELL

Supreme Court of Missouri, Division Two, 1902.
170 Mo. 633, 71 S.W. 175.

GANTT, J. Defendant was tried upon an information filed by the prosecuting attorney of Clinton county at the May term, 1901, and convicted of an attempt to murder John O. Warren. His punishment was assessed at five years in the penitentiary. . . .

I. The first insistence is that the first count in the information is so defective that it will not sustain the sentence. Whether the objection is well taken or not, depends upon what constitutes the offense and what is essential to be proven. The statute provides that "every person who shall attempt to commit an offense prohibited by law, and in such an attempt shall do any act towards the commission of such offense, but shall fail in the perpetration thereof, or be intercepted or prevented from executing the same," etc., shall be punished as therein provided. Murder is an offense prohibited. When the defendant armed himself with a loaded revolver and went to the window of the room in which he believed John O. Warren was sleeping, from his knowledge acquired by visiting his family, and fired his pistol at the place where he thought Warren was lying, he was attempting to assassinate and murder him. The fact that Warren was not there as he believed him to be, did not make it any the less an attempt to murder. Our statute on this subject is substantially like that of Massachusetts, construed in Com. v. McDonald, 5 Cush. 365, and Com. v. Sherman, 105 Mass. 169, in which it was held "that neither allegation nor proof was necessary, that there was any property, capable of being stolen, in the pocket or upon the person of the one against whom the attempt to commit larceny was made." . . . [1]

only. Groves v. State, 116 Ga. 516, 42 S.E. 755 (1902).

Two men planned to rob the persons in a saloon. They procured arms and masks. They went to the saloon, pushed open the door and started to enter, but withdrew hastily when they saw a large crowd inside. This was held to be an attempt to rob. People v. Moran, 18 Cal.App. 209, 122 P. 969 (1912).

D planned to kill his wife with the aid of an accomplice. The "accomplice," who pretended to agree but had no intention of doing so, was to gain access to the house as a pretended buyer so that D could get in and kill her. After the accomplice had been sent in, D was arrested in a car in front of the house, with a rifle in the rear of the car. A conviction of attempted murder was affirmed. People v. Parrish, 87 Cal.App.2d 853, 197 P.2d 804 (1948).

In what seems to have been a plan to swindle a depositor, he was persuaded to withdraw $400.00 from the bank. A former victim of the swindler recognized him while the check was being drawn and the depositor did not withdraw the money. A conviction of attempted larceny by trick was reversed. Commonwealth v. Kelley, 162 Pa.Super. 526, 58 A.2d 375 (1948).

[1]. Accord: People v. Moran, 123 N.Y. 254, 25 N.E. 412 (1890).

An English case held, contra, that larceny cannot be attempted by reaching

So in this case the intent evidenced by the firing into the bedroom with a deadly weapon accompanied by a present capacity in defendant to murder Warren if he were in the room, and the failure to do so only because Warren haply retired upstairs instead of in the bed into which defendant fired, made out a perfect case of an attempt within the meaning of the statute, and the information is sufficient. The evidence conclusively supported the information. It discloses a deliberate and dastardly attempt at assassination, which was only averted by the intended victim's going upstairs to bed that night. . . .

We find no error in the record, and affirm the judgment. All concur.

PEOPLE v. ROJAS

Supreme Court of California, In Bank, 1961.
55 Cal.2d 252, 10 Cal.Rptr. 465, 358 P.2d 921.

[Hall, who had stolen $4,500 worth of electrical conduit, was arrested while in possession of the stolen property and taken to the police station. He said he had an arrangement with one of the defendants to sell him any and all electrical materials obtained. From the police station Hall made three phone calls, monitored by the police, which resulted in a plan by which Hall left a truck, containing the conduit, at a place designated by the defendants. Later one of the defendants came and drove away the truck to a lot near his place of business. He was arrested next morning when he began to unload the truck.]

SCHAUER, JUSTICE. In a trial by the court, after proper waiver of jury, defendants Rojas and Hidalgo were found guilty of a charge of receiving stolen property. Defendants' motions for new trial were denied. Rojas was granted probation without imposition of sentence and Hidalgo was sentenced to state prison. They appeal, respectively, from the order granting probation, the judgment, and the orders denying the motions for new trial.

Defendants urge that they were guilty of no crime (or, at most, of an attempt to receive stolen property) because when they received the property it had been recovered by the police and was no longer in a stolen condition. The attorney general argues that because the thief stole the property pursuant to prearrangement with defendants he took it as their agent, and the crime of receiving stolen property was complete when the thief began its asportation toward defendants and before the police intercepted him and recovered the property. We have concluded that defendants are guilty of attempting to receive stolen goods; that other matters of which they complain

---

into an empty pocket. Regina v. Collins, 9 Cox C.C. 497 (1864). This case was later overruled. See Regina v. Ring, 17 Cox C.C. 491 (1892).

do not require a new trial; and that the appeal should be disposed of by modifying the finding that defendants are guilty as charged to a determination that they are guilty of attempting to receive stolen property, and by reversing with directions to the trial court to enter such judgments or probation orders as it deems appropriate based upon the modified finding. . . .

The offense with which defendants were charged and of which they were convicted was receiving "property which has been *stolen* . . ., *knowing the same to be so stolen.*" Pen.Code, § 496, subd. 1; italics added. Defendants, relying particularly upon People v. Jaffe (1906), 185 N.Y. 497, 501 [78 N.E. 169, 9 L.R.A.,N.S., 263, 266], urge that they neither received stolen goods nor criminally attempted to do so because the conduit, when defendants received it, was not in a stolen condition but had been recovered by the police. In the Jaffe case the stolen property was recovered by the owner while it was en route to the would-be receiver and, by arrangement with the police, was delivered to such receiver as a decoy, not as property in a stolen condition. The New York Court of Appeals held that there was no attempt to receive stolen goods "because neither [defendant] nor anyone else in the world could know that the property was stolen property inasmuch as it was not in fact stolen property. . . . If all which an accused person intends to do would if done constitute no crime it cannot be a crime to attempt to do with the same purpose a part of the thing intended."

Defendants also cite People v. Zimmerman (1909), 11 Cal.App. 115, 118, 104 P. 590, which contains the following dictum concerning a state of facts like that in the Jaffe case: "The circumstances of the transaction . . . did not constitute an offense, as the goods were taken to the defendant's house with the consent and at the request of the owner."

As pointed out by the District Court of Appeal in Faustina v. Superior Court (1959), 174 Cal.App.2d 830, 833 [1], 345 P.2d 543, "The rule of the Jaffe case has been the subject of much criticism and discussion." . . .

In the case at bench the criminality of the attempt is not destroyed by the fact that the goods, having been recovered by the commendably alert and efficient action of the Los Angeles police, had, unknown to defendants, lost their "stolen" status, any more than the criminality of the attempt in the case of In re Magidson (1917), 32 Cal.App. 566, 568, 163 P. 689, was destroyed by impossibility caused by the fact that the police had recovered the goods and taken them from the place where the would-be receiver went to get them. In our opinion the consequences of intent and acts such as those of defendants here should be more serious than pleased amazement that because of the timeliness of the police the projected criminality was not merely detected but also wiped out. . . .

The orders denying defendants' motions for new trial are affirmed. The trial court's finding that defendants are guilty as charged is modified to find them guilty of the offense of attempting to receive stolen property. The judgment and probation order are reversed and the cause is remanded to the trial court for further proceedings not inconsistent with the views hereinabove expressed, and with directions to enter such lawful judgment or order against each defendant, based on the modified finding, as the court deems appropriate.[1]

GIBSON, C. J., and TRAYNOR, McCOMB, PETERS, WHITE and DOOLING, JJ., concur.

---

1. The fact that the intended victim of false pretenses was not deceived is not a bar to conviction for an attempt to commit the offense. State v. Visco, 183 Kan. 562, 331 P.2d 318 (1958). A, the keeper of a house of prostitution, was acting as a decoy for the police. G approached A and agreed not to accuse her of being a keeper of a house of prostitution if she would pay him $150. She paid him this sum. From a conviction of attempted extortion, G appealed. In reversing the conviction the General Term of the Supreme Court said:

"It is plain that a conviction cannot be sustained under section 685 of the Penal Code, and that the district attorney acted wisely in not presenting an indictment for the crime of extortion.

"The crucial question in this case is whether a conviction for an attempt to commit the crime of extortion can be sustained where the evidence conclusively shows the absence, on the part of the person against whom the crime is attempted, of a state of mind necessary to make possible the perpetration of the crime attempted.

"We take it to be a general rule, having few, if any, exceptions, that unless the completed act, accomplished as intended and attempted, will constitute a crime, no step or steps taken to perpetrate the act will amount to a criminal attempt. . . .

"A boy so young that he is deemed incapable of perpetrating a rape cannot be convicted of an attempt to commit that offense, nor of an assault with attempt to ravish, but he may be convicted of an assault and battery. (People v. Randolph, 2 Park. 213; 1 Bish.Cr.L. 8th ed. § 746, and cases cited.)

"At common law, if a person intending to steal an article take it with the owner's consent it is not larceny. (Thorne v. Turck, 94 N.Y. 90–95; 2 Bish.Cr.L. 8th ed. § 811; 1 Whart. Cr.L. 8th ed. § 915.) In such a case the completed act, accomplished as intended, not being a crime, none of the steps taken being ingredients of the offense, would constitute a crime, and the taker could not be convicted of an attempt to commit the crime of larceny.

"If an assault should be made on a man dressed as a woman with intent to ravish, the assailant believing the person assaulted to be a woman, he could not be convicted of an intent to ravish, because in such a cause the commission of the crime of rape would be a legal impossibility. So, in the case at bar it was a legal impossibility to commit the crime of extortion as against the woman Amos, because she inveigled the defendant to commit the act and was not put in fear by him." People v. Gardner, 73 Hun 66, 70–1, 25 N.Y.S. 1072, 1075–6 (1893).

This reversal was held to be error, the Court of Appeals saying:

"The threat of the defendant was plainly an act done with intent to commit the crime of extortion, and it tended, but failed, to effect its commission, and therefore, the act was plainly within the statute an attempt to commit the crime. The condition of Mrs. Amos' mind was unknown to the defendant. If it had been as he supposed, the crime could have been and probably would have been consummated. His guilt was just as great as if he had actually succeeded in his purpose. His wicked purpose was the same, and he had brought himself fully and precisely within the letter and policy of the law. The crime as defined in the statute depends upon the mind and intent of the wrongdoer,

BOOTH v. STATE

Court of Criminal Appeals of Oklahoma, 1964.
398 P.2d 863.

[Having stolen a coat, the thief telephoned to Booth saying he had it and would let Booth have it for $20.00. It was arranged that Booth would meet the thief at the latter's house at 11:00 A.M. to effect the transfer. In the meantime the thief was arrested and confessed. The police recovered the coat and called in the owner who identified it. It was then returned to the thief to carry out the original plan which was done, after which Booth was arrested. From a conviction of attempting to receive stolen property an appeal was taken.]

NIX, JUDGE. . . . In People v. Finkelstein, 21 Misc.2d 723, 197 N.Y.S.2d 31 (1960) the court said:

"A defendant may not be convicted for receiving stolen property if property is no longer in category of stolen property when he receives it."

The law seems to be clear on this point, leaving the only question to be decided as whether or not the defendant could be convicted of an attempt to receive stolen property in such cases. It is the defendant's contention that if he could not be convicted of the substantive charge, because the coat had lost its character as stolen property; neither could he be convicted of an attempt because the coat was not in the category of stolen property at the time he received it.

The briefs filed in the case, and extensive research has revealed that two states have passed squarely on the question—New York and California. It is definitely one of first impression in Oklahoma.

The New York Court, in passing upon the question, laid down the following rule in the case of People v. Jaffe, 185 N.Y. 497, 78 N.E. 169, 6 L.R.A.,N.S., 263, on the following facts:

"A clerk stole goods from his employer under an agreement to sell them to accused, but before delivery of the goods the theft was discovered and the goods were recovered. Later the employer redelivered the goods to the clerk to sell to accused, who purchased them for about one-half of their value, believing them to have been stolen.

---

and not on the effect or result upon the person sought to be coerced." People v. Gardner, 144 N.Y. 119, 124, 38 N.E. 1003 (1894).

It is not an essential element of the offense under the statute penalizing every person who uses or deals with, or wins money by any game commonly known as a confidence game, or bunco, that the player of the game shall have reposed confidence in the operator of the game. Hence the fact that the player was an officer seeking evidence will not be a bar to conviction. State v. Hale, 134 Mont. 131, 328 P.2d 930 (1958). There cannot be a conviction for an attempt to commit a crime unless the attempt if successful would have constituted a crime. State v. Weleck, 10 N.J. 355, 91 A.2d 751 (1952).

"Held, that the goods had lost their character as stolen goods at the time defendant purchased them, and that his criminal intent was insufficient to sustain a conviction for an attempt to receive stolen property, knowing it to have been stolen."

The Jaffe case, supra, was handed down in 1906, and has prevailed as the law in New York state 58 years without modification—being affirmed in People v. Finklestein, supra; . . . and finally in the case of People v. Rollino (1962), 37 Misc.2d 14, 233 N.Y.S.2d 580.

The State of California has passed upon the question several times and up until 1959, they followed the rule laid down in the Jaffe case, supra.

In 1959, in the case of People v. Camodeca, 52 Cal.2d 142, 338 P.2d 903, the California Court abandoned the Jaffe rationale that a person accepting goods which he believes to have been stolen, but which was not in fact stolen goods, is not guilty of an attempt to receive stolen goods, and imposed a liability for the attempt, overruling its previous holding to the contrary in the above cited cases. The Camodeca case, supra, was affirmed in People v. Rojas, 55 Cal.2d 252, 10 Cal.Rptr. 465, 358 P.2d 921, 85 A.L.R.2d 252, 1961.

Though the instant case, insofar as it pertains to the specific crime of attempting to receive stolen property is one of first impression in Oklahoma. This Court held in the Nemecek v. State, 72 Okl.Cr. 195, 114 P.2d 492, 135 A.L.R. 1149, involving attempting to receive money by false pretenses:

"An accused cannot be convicted of an attempt to commit a crime unless he could have been convicted of the crime itself if his attempt had been successful. Where the act, if accomplished, would not constitute the crime intended, there is no indictable attempt."

In the Nemecek case, supra, the Court quotes with approval, In re Schurman, 40 Kan. 533, 20 P. 277; wherein the Kansas Court said:

"With reference to attempt, it has also been said that 'if all which the accused person intended would, had it been done, constitute no substantive crime, it cannot be a crime, under the name "attempt," to do, with the same purpose, a part of this thing.'"

The two paramount cases of latest date; Rojas of Calif.1961, supra, and Rollino of New York 1962, supra; present two rationales directly contrary to each other relative to an attempt to receive stolen property after it had been recovered by the police. . . .

The authorities in the various states and the text-writers are in general agreement that where there is a "legal impossibility" of completing the substantive crime, the accused cannot be successfully charged with an attempt, whereas in those cases in which the "factual impossibility" situation is involved, the accused may be convicted of an attempt. Detailed discussion of the subject is unnecessary to make it clear that it is frequently most difficult to compartmentalize a particular set of facts as coming within one of the categories rather than the other. . . . Your writer is of the opinion that the confusion that exists as a result of the two diverse rationales laid down in the Rollino case (NY) supra, and the Rojas case (Calif) supra, was brought about by the failure to recognize the distinction between a factual and a legal impossibility to accomplish the crime. In the Camodeca case (Calif) supra, the facts revealed a prevention of the crime because of a factual situation as stated on page 906, 338 P.2d:

"In the present case there was not a legal but only a factual impossibility of consummating the intended offense . . .."

In the Rojas case, supra, wherein was adopted the departure from the Jaffe case, by saying:

"The situation here is materially like those considered in People v. Camodeca."

The Rojas case was definitely not materially the same. In the Rojas case the facts reveal a legal and not factual impossibility.

In the case at bar the stolen coat had been recovered by the police for the owner and consequently had, according to the well-established law in this country, lost its character as stolen property. Therefore, a legal impossibility precluded defendant from being prosecuted for the crime of Knowingly Receiving Stolen Property. . . . Sayre, 41 Harvard Law Review 821, 853–54 (1928) states the rationale in this manner:

"It seems clear that cases (where none of the intended consequences is in fact criminal) cannot constitute criminal attempts. If none of the consequences which the defendant sought to achieve constitute a crime, surely his unsuccessful efforts to achieve his object cannot constitute a criminal attempt. The partial fulfillment of an object not criminal cannot itself be criminal. If the whole is not criminal, the part cannot be."

The defendant in the instant case leaves little doubt as to his moral guilt. The evidence, as related by the self-admitted and perpetual law violator indicates defendant fully intended to do the act with which he was charged. However, it is fundamental to our law that a man is not punished merely because he has a criminal mind. It must be shown that he has, with that criminal mind, done an act which is forbidden by the criminal law.

Adhering to this principle, the following example would further illustrate the point.

A fine horse is offered to A at a ridiculously low price by B, who is a known horse thief. A, believing the horse to be stolen buys the same without inquiry. In fact, the horse had been raised from a colt by B and was not stolen. It would be bordering on absurdity to suggest that A's frame of mind, if proven, would support a conviction of an attempt. It would be a "legal impossibility". . . .

In view of our statutory law, and the decisions herein related, it is our duty to Reverse this case, with orders to Dismiss, and it is so ordered. However, there are other avenues open to the County Attorney which should be explored.

JOHNSON, P. J., and BUSSEY, J., concur.

[Rehearing denied Feb. 17, 1965.]

PREDDY v. COMMONWEALTH

Supreme Court of Appeals of Virginia, 1946.
184 Va. 765, 36 S.E.2d 549.

[From a judgment of conviction of the crime of attempted rape, the elderly defendant appealed. He had offered evidence tending to show impotency, and claimed that error had been committed by an instruction which told the jury that impotence is not a defense to the crime of attempted rape. Reliance was placed upon a case which had held that since (under Virginia law) a boy under 14 years of age is incapable of committing rape he is "also incapable in law of an attempt to commit it".]

CAMPBELL, CHIEF JUSTICE. . . . The question whether or not an adult who claims to be impotent is incapable of committing the crime of attempt to rape is one of first impression. . . .

In Wharton's Criminal Law, 12th Ed., sec. 223, it is said: "If there be juridical incapacity for the consummated offense (e. g., infancy) there can be no conviction of the attempt; and therefore a boy under fourteen (14) cannot, according to the prevalent opinion, be convicted of an attempt to commit rape as a principal in the first degree. It is otherwise, where the incapacity is merely nervous or physical. A man may fail in consummating a rape for some nervous or physical incapacity intervening between attempt and execution. But this failure would be no defense to the indictment for an attempt. At the same time there must be apparent capacity."

In the case at bar, we are dealing with the question of alleged physical incapacity. Neither at common law nor by statute is an adult clothed with the presumption that he is incapable of committing the crime of rape, or an attempt to rape.

"According to the decided weight of authority, both in England and in this country, an apparent possibility to commit the crime is enough." Clark and Marshall, Crimes, sec. 123.

In Wharton's Criminal Law, 10th Ed., section 552, it is said: "Impotency is a sufficient defense for the consummated offence, though not for an assault with intent." See Wharton & St. Med. Jur., sec. 20.

In an illuminating article in 78 Penn.Law Review, p. 971, it is stated: "When a defendant, with rape in mind, and with the expectation of accomplishing penetration, seizes his female victim in the customary manner in order to achieve his purpose and finds penetration impossible, because of impotency the authorities agree that he is guilty of a real criminal attempt to rape, and his impotency has no bearing on the case except possibly negativing the specific intention to accomplish penetration." . . .

We are of opinion that there is no error in the judgment of the circuit court and that it must be affirmed.

Affirmed.

BROWNING, JUSTICE (dissenting). I do not think that the Commonwealth has proven the case against the defendant beyond a reasonable doubt and this, notwithstanding the verdict of the jury. I think that the testimony of Dr. Mason, who is a distinguished physician, if there were nothing more, casts grave doubt upon the guilt of the accused. Of this, of course, he should have the benefit.

(iv) INTENT

MERRITT v. COMMONWEALTH

Supreme Court of Appeals of Virginia, 1935.
164 Va. 653, 180 S.E. 395.

[Defendant demurred to an indictment charging him with an attempt to commit murder. He took the case to the upper court claiming that the trial court committed error by overruling his demurrer.]

HUDGINS, JUSTICE. . . . In the case at bar, the indictment alleged that the accused did "attempt to commit murder." This part of the indictment does not state against whom the attempt was directed. The indictment proceeds to tell how the commonwealth claims the attempt to commit murder was accomplished, i. e., "by then and there" feloniously and maliciously pointing a loaded pistol at Trull, who was in gunshot range. Even if the jury had believed that the accused pointed a loaded gun at Trull, they would not have been justified in finding him guilty of an attempted murder, unless they believed that at the time he pointed the pistol he had formed the purpose, the intent, to murder, and the act was done in furtherance of that specific intent.

The indictment concludes by stating that the accused "then and there, in the manner and form above stated," i. e., by pointing a loaded pistol, "did attempt to kill and murder." The conclusion is unescapable that the only crime charged in the indictment is an assault, with no specific intent to kill and murder alleged. If the facts alleged in the indictment constitute a misdemeanor, the crime cannot be elevated to a felony simply by being so called by the pleader. The acts here alleged constitute an assault at common law, and there has been no statutory change of the crime in this jurisdiction. . . .

In Fields v. Commonwealth, 129 Va. 774, 106 S.E. 333, the indictment was similar in many respects to the one here in question. There it was alleged that the accused "did discharge and shoot off at and towards one David Tabb" a pistol, "she [the accused] . . . being close enough to the said David Tabb to be within carrying distance of said pistol." One of the objections raised to the indictment was that it "does not allege that the intent existed to kill him." The court in discussing the question thus raised, said:

"It is the settled law of this state that an indictment for murder need not expressly allege the intent to kill, and that an indictment for murder at common law (which does not expressly charge the intent to kill) is valid and sufficient to support a verdict of murder in the first degree, if the evidence introduced on the trial is sufficient to establish that the murder was of that degree. On the same principle we are of opinion that an indictment for an attempt to commit murder at common law is valid and sufficient to support a verdict, such as that rendered in the instant case, convicting the accused of an attempt to commit murder in the first degree, if the evidence was sufficient to prove the commission of that crime."

The fallacy in this statement is that while a person may be guilty of murder though there was no actual intent to kill, he cannot be guilty of an attempt to commit murder unless he has a specific intent to kill. A common example illustrating this principle is: "If one from a house-top recklessly throw a billet of wood upon the sidewalk where persons are constantly passing, and it fall upon a person passing by and kill him, this would be by the common law murder. But if, instead of killing, it inflicts only a slight injury, the party could not be convicted of an assault with intent to commit murder." Moore v. State, 18 Ala. 532.

"Where the substantive crime intended requires a specific intent, though this intent does not in the same sense as in the other case aggravate what is done, still it adds a culpability which mere general malevolence could not give. So that the indictable attempt exists only when the act, short of the substantive crime, proceeds from the specific intent to do the entire evil thing, thus imparting to so much as is done a special culpability. When we say that a man attempted to do a given wrong, we mean that he intended to do it specifically; and proceeded a certain way in the doing. The intent in the mind covers the thing in full; the act covers it only in part.

". . . To commit murder, one need not intend to take life; but to be guilty of an attempt to murder, he must so intend. It is not sufficient that his act, had it proved fatal, would have been murder." Bishop On Criminal Law (9th Ed.) vol. 1, pp. 521, 522. . . .

The intent is the purpose formed in a man's mind, and is usually proved by his conduct, sometimes by his statements; the necessary intent constituting one element in an attempt is the intent in fact, as distinguished from an intent in law. From the act alleged, the law infers a general evil intent, on the principle that a man intends the probable and necessary consequences of his act. The act charged here is an assault. In order to raise this assault to a more substantive crime, it must be done with a specific intent to take life. This intent cannot be inferred from the act alleged. . . .

For the reasons stated, the judgment of the trial court is reversed, the verdict of the jury set aside, and the case remanded for such further proceedings as the commonwealth may be advised.

Reversed and remanded.[1]

(B) AGGRAVATED ASSAULT

STATE v. WILSON

Supreme Court of Oregon, 1959.
218 Or. 575, 346 P.2d 115.

O'CONNELL, JUSTICE. The defendant appeals from a judgment of the circuit court for Multnomah county entered on a verdict pronouncing him guilty of the crime of attempted assault with a dangerous weapon under Count I of the indictment, . . .

---

1. In upholding a conviction of burglary under an indictment charging that the dwelling had been broken into "with intent to commit larceny", the court said (referring to State v. Van Gilder, 140 Kan. 66, 33 P.2d 936 (1934)): "In the opinion we cited State v. Woodruff, 208 Iowa 236, 225 N.W. 254. Numerous cases are cited in a well considered opinion in the Iowa case holding the clear weight of authority to be that an unexplained breaking and entering of a dwelling house in the nighttime is in itself sufficient to sustain a verdict that the breaking and entering was done with the intent to commit *larceny* rather than some other felony. The Iowa case contains quotations from some of the many cases so holding, which need not be repeated here. The fundamental theory upon which the inference of intent to commit larceny is based, absent evidence of other intent or an explanation for the breaking and entering, is that the usual object or purpose of burglarizing a dwelling house at night is theft." State v. Gatewood, 169 Kan. 679, 684, 221 P.2d 392, 396–7 (1950). Accord: State v. Walker, 109 W.Va. 351, 154 S.E. 866 (1930).

An indictment for attempted rape which charges that D, with intent to rape, chased Mrs. X in a secluded spot until she was rescued by a friend is demurrable because the chasing may have been with intent to rob or murder. State v. Lindsey, 202 Miss. 896, 32 So.2d 876 (1947).

D was convicted of an assault with intent to commit mayhem on evidence that she threw red pepper at X, apparently intended for his face. There was no evidence tending to show that she thought red pepper would produce blindness. The conviction was reversed. Dahlberg v. People, 225 Ill. 485, 80 N.E. 310 (1907).

[The evidence showed that defendant had confronted and threatened his estranged wife in her place of employment, after which he procured a loaded shotgun from his car just outside to carry out his threat. He was unable to reach his wife the second time, however, because she was then safely behind locked doors.]

The crime of assault with a dangerous weapon is defined in ORS 163.250 as follows:

"Any person, who is armed with a dangerous weapon and assaults another with such weapon, shall be punished upon conviction by imprisonment in the penitentiary for not more than 10 years, or by imprisonment in the county jail not less than one month nor more than one year, or by a fine of not less than $100 nor more than $1,000."

There is no statute dealing specifically with an attempt to commit assault with a dangerous weapon. The state relies upon the general attempt statute, ORS 161.090, which reads in part as follows:

"Any person who attempts to commit a crime, and in the attempt does any act towards the commission of the crime but fails or is prevented or intercepted in the perpetration thereof, shall be punished upon conviction, when no other provision is made by law for the punishment of such attempt, as follows: . . ."

The defendant attacks Count I of the indictment on the ground that it does not state a crime under the laws of this state. Defendant argues that there is no such crime as an attempted assault with a dangerous weapon. In stating his grounds for objecting to the introduction of evidence in proof of the first count counsel for defendant said " . . . it is the contention of the defendant that there is no such thing as an attempted assault; it is no more than an attempt to inflict an injury or battery, . . . If then, there is such a crime as attempted assault, the one so attempting must have intent to commit an assault. Does he then intend to commit a battery?" To answer this rhetorical question defendant relies upon the following language in Wilson v. State, 1874, 53 Ga. 205, 206:

" . . . Plainly and in terms, they say they find him guilty of attempt to make an assault. The question is, can any judgment be entered upon such a verdict? Is it a legal verdict? Is there any such crime? . . . As an assault is itself an attempt to commit a crime, an attempt to make an assault can only be an attempt to attempt to do it, or to state the matter still more definitely, it is to do any act towards doing an act towards the commission of the offense. This is simply absurd. . . . "

The charge that an attempt to attempt to do an act is beyond understanding, seems at first blush to be justified. It could be interpreted to be the equivalent of a statement that one is guilty of a crime if he proceeds to act in such a way that, if not interrupted, his conduct would result in the commission of an act which if not interrupted would result in a substantive crime.

The bulk of the Oregon cases defining criminal assault, however, do so in terms of attempted battery and limit the crime to acts which are intended to cause corporal injury under circumstances in which the actor has the present ability to carry out his intent. Typical of such definitions is that found in Smallman v. Gladden, 1956, 206 Or. 262, 272, 291 P.2d 749, 754, where the court said:

". . . An assault is an intentional attempt by one person by force or violence to do an injury to the person of another, coupled with present ability to carry the intention into effect. . . ."

Under the latter definition, apprehension of injury on the part of the victim need not be shown to make out the crime. Further, it seems clear that an act done with the intention to place one in apprehension of injury only and not to inflict corporal injury would not constitute the crime of assault in this state. And too, according to the definition, an act done with the intention to inflict corporal injury, but where the actor did not have the present ability to inflict corporal injury would not be a criminal assault . . . We are of the opinion that criminal assault, even as defined by this court, should be regarded as a distinct crime rather than as an uncompleted battery.

If we should regard assault as an attempted battery, is it reasonable to recognize the crime of attempted assault? It has been categorically asserted that there can be no attempt to commit a crime which is itself merely an attempt. 1 Wharton, Criminal Law & Procedure (Anderson ed.). Upon the basis of this premise it is said that there can be no such offense as an attempted assault. 1 Wharton, op. cit. supra, § 72 at 154, states that "as an assault is an attempt to commit a battery there can be no attempt to commit an assault." The same idea is found in Clark & Marshall, Crimes (6th ed.) § 4.07, p. 218, where it is said:

"Since a simple assault is nothing more than attempt to commit a battery, and aggravated assaults are nothing more than attempts to commit murder, rape, or robbery, an attempt to commit an assault, whether simple or aggravated is not a crime."

. . . The mere fact that assault is viewed as preceding a battery should not preclude us from drawing a line on one side of which we require the present ability to inflict corporal injury, denominating this an assault, and on the other side conduct which falls short of a present ability, yet so advanced toward the assault that it is more than mere preparation and which we denominate an attempt. . . . The acts of the defendant after obtaining the gun from his automobile may not have been sufficient to establish that he had the present ability to inflict corporal injury upon his wife who was behind a locked door, but he had proceeded far beyond the stage of preparation and it is reasonable to treat his conduct as an attempt within the meaning of ORS 161.090. It is the function of the law of criminal attempt to permit the courts to adjust the penalty in cases where the conduct falls short of a completed crime. 40 Yale L.J. 53, 74, 75. Our legislature has provided that assault with a dangerous weapon is a crime. ORS 161.090 permits the courts of this state to treat conduct which is short of statutory crimes as a crime, and we regard an attempt to commit an assault as within the intendment of this statute. . . .

The judgment of the lower court is affirmed.[1]

McALLISTER, C. J., dissents.

(C) SOLICITATION

STATE v. BLECHMAN

New Jersey Supreme Court, 1946.
135 N.J.L. 99, 50 A.2d 152.

HEHER, J. . . . Although we have but a meager description of the content of the indictment, it would seem, as said, that it accuses plaintiff in error merely of counseling another to set fire to the dwelling house; and it is urged at the outset that such is not an offense denounced by the cited statute unless the wrongful act thus counseled is done, and the insured property is actually burned. We do not so read the statute. It plainly classifies as a high misdemeanor the counseling or solicitation of another to set fire to or burn any insured building, ship or vessel, or goods, wares, merchandise or other chattels, with intent to prejudice or defraud the insurer; and in this regard the statute is primarily declaratory of the common law.

At common law, it is a misdemeanor for one to counsel, incite or solicit another to commit either a felony or a misdemeanor, certainly so if the misdemeanor is of an aggravated character, even though the solicitation is of no effect, and the crime counseled is not in fact committed. The gist of the offense is the solicitation. It is not requisite that some act should be laid to have been done in pursuance of the incitement. While the bare intention to commit evil is not indictable, without an act done, the solicitation, itself, is an act done toward the execution of the evil intent and therefore indictable. An act done

---

1. "There is no such offense known to the law as 'an attempt to commit an assault with intent to murder'". White v. State, 22 Tex. 608, 609 (1858). A verdict finding defendant guilty of an "attempt to commit an assault with intent to rape" is in legal effect a verdict of guilty of an attempt to rape.

Burton v. State, 8 Ala.App. 295, 62 So. 394 (1913).

Shooting through the roof in an effort to kill a policeman is an assault with intent to murder although the officer was on a different part of the roof at the moment. People v. Lee Kong, 95 Cal. 666, 30 P. 800 (1892).

Sec. 3   ATTEMPT AND KINDRED PROBLEMS   245

with a criminal intent is punishable by indictment. It was said by an eminent common law judge (Lawrence, J., in Rex. v. Higgins, infra) that under the common law all offenses of a public nature, *i.e.*, "all such acts or attempts as tend to the prejudice of the community," are indictable; and it goes without saying that an attempt to incite another to commit arson or a kindred offense is prejudicial to the community and public in its nature. . . . In the case of State v. Brand, 76 N.J.L. 267, 69 A. 1092, affirmed 77 N.J.L. 486, 72 A. 131, this court construed the statute as denouncing two separate and distinct offenses, *i.e.*, the willful or malicious setting fire to or burning of insured property, with intent to prejudice the underwriter, and aiding, counseling, procuring or consenting to the setting fire to or burning of such property; but our court of last resort found it unnecessary to consider the question, for there the indictment used the statutory terms in the conjunctive and thus charged that the merchandise was in fact burned.

The solicitation constitutes a substantive crime in itself,[1] and not an abortive attempt to perpetrate the crime solicited. It falls short of an attempt, in the legal sense, to commit the offense solicited.[2] An attempt to commit a crime consists of a direct ineffectual overt act toward the consummation of the crime, done with an intent to commit the crime. Neither intention alone nor acts in mere preparation will suffice. There must be an overt act directly moving toward the commission of the designed offense—such as will apparently result, in the usual and natural course of events, if not hindered by extraneous causes, in the commission of the crime itself.

Of course, at common law one who counsels, incites or solicits another to commit a felony, is indictable as a principal or an accessory before the fact, if the designed felony is accomplished, depending upon his presence and participation or absence at the time of its commission.

Plaintiff in error sets great store upon the case of Wimpling v. State, 171 Md. 362, 189 A. 248. But it is not in point. The statute there under review was substantially different; it defined the offense of "arson" in terms that clearly signified an actual burning of the property as an indispensible [sic] ingredient of the crime.

We think that, apart from the statutory recognition of a subsisting common law offense, the prime, if not the exclusive, purpose of the legislative act in question was the classification as a high misdemeanor of what would otherwise be a misdemeanor. . . .

Let the judgment be affirmed.[3]

1. "It is complete when the solicitation is made, and it is immaterial that the object of the solicitation is never consummated, or that no steps are taken towards its consummation". People v. Burt, 45 Cal.2d 311, 314, 288 P.2d 503, 505 (1955).

2. Accord: Commonwealth v. Peaslee, 177 Mass. 267, 59 N.E. 55 (1901). Contra, it is an attempt. People v. Bush, 4 Hill 133 (N.Y.1843).

3. Orally addressing a crowd and urging them to kill and rob and commit

(D) ABANDONMENT

GLOVER v. COMMONWEALTH

Supreme Court of Appeals of Virginia, 1889.
86 Va. 382, 10 S.E. 420.

Lewis, P., delivered the opinion of the court.

Among the exceptions taken by the prisoner at the trial was one to the refusal of the court to instruct the jury as follows: "If the jury believe from the evidence that the prisoner at the bar intended to commit a rape on the prosecutrix, Berta Wright, but before the act was finally executed, he voluntarily and freely abandoned it, they are to find a verdict of not guilty."

This exception is not well taken. . . .

Hence, when the prisoner took the prosecutrix into the stable, and there did the acts above mentioned, the attempt to commit a rape was complete; for there was the unlawful intent accompanied by acts done towards the commission of the intended crime, but falling short of its commission. Indeed, it is not denied that there was such attempt, but it is contended—and such was the main defence at the trial—that the subsequent voluntary abandonment of the criminal purpose cleansed the prisoner of all crime, so far as the attempt was concerned. But this is a mistaken view. For on the contrary, it is a rule, founded in reason and supported by authority, that if a man resolves on a criminal enterprise, and proceeds so far in it that his act amounts to an indictable attempt, it does not cease to be such, though he voluntarily abandons the evil purpose.

In Lewis v. The State, 35 Ala. 380, which was an indictment for an attempt to commit a rape, it was ruled by the supreme court of Alabama that if the attempt was in fact made, and had progressed far enough to put the prosecutrix in terror, and render it necessary for her to save herself from the consummation of the attempted outrage by flight, then the attempt was complete, though the prisoner had not in fact touched her; and that an after-abandonment by the prisoner of his wicked purpose, could not purge the crime. And there are many other authorities to the same effect. See 1 Bish.Crim.Law, (6th ed.) sec. 732, and cases cited. . . .

Judgment affirmed.

other acts of violence, is an offense. State v. Schleifer, 99 Conn. 432, 121 A. 805 (1923).

One who asks a woman to have sexual intercourse with him is not guilty of solicitation for prostitution under the Iowa statute. State v. Oge, 227 Iowa 1094, 290 N.W. 1 (1940).

STATE v. PETERSON

Supreme Court of Minnesota, 1942.
213 Minn. 56, 4 N.W.2d 826.

PETERSON, JUSTICE. Defendant was convicted of arson in the second degree, and appeals.

The indictment charges her with burning her dwelling house on October 30, 1940. The house was at Lake Minnetonka in Hennepin county.

The state claimed, and its evidence was to the effect, that she did not personally set the fire, but caused it to be set by an accomplice, one August Anderson. There was no dispute as to Anderson's having set the fire. Defendant stoutly maintained that she did not have anything to do with the burning of her house and that she not only directed Anderson not to go to the house on the occasion when the fire was set, but that she tried to persuade him before he set the fire to leave the premises to which he had gone contrary to her directions. . . .

Numerous errors are assigned to the effect . . . and (4) that, assuming the truth of the state's evidence that Anderson and defendant were accomplices, defendant is not liable because she withdrew before the fire was set. Since it is decisive, only the last point need be discussed.

It is important to bear in mind that defendant is not charged with the crime of conspiracy.[1] A conspiracy to commit arson is a misdemeanor. Mason St.1927, §§ 10055, 10056. Arson is a felony. Id. §§ 10309–10310; Id. 1940 Supp. § 10311. A conspiracy to commit a crime is a separate offense from the crime which is the object of the conspiracy.

One who has procured, counseled, or commanded another to commit a crime may withdraw before the act is done and avoid criminal responsibility by communicating the fact of his withdrawal to the party who is to commit the crime. . . .

By her efforts through Carlson to induce Anderson to leave the premises before he set the fire and to go immediately to her in the hospital where she was then confined, the defendant in the instant case took the most effective measures within her power to arrest the execution of the plan, if there was one, to burn the house. Anderson must have known that if she wanted him to comply with her request to leave the premises before he set the fire she did not want him to

---

[1.] "In the Bridgewater Case [unreported], referred to at the bar, and in which I was counsel, nothing was done in fact; yet a gentleman was convicted because he had entered into an unlawful combination from which almost on the spot he withdrew altogether. No one was harmed, but the public offence was complete." Per Lord Coleridge in Mogul S. S. Co. v. McGregor, Gow & Co., 21 Q.B.D. 544, 549 (1888).

burn the house. She not only withdrew in ample time from any plan to burn the house, but made that fact known to Anderson in an unmistakable manner. By withdrawing, defendant avoided criminal responsibility. Anderson was solely criminally responsible for the fire which he set. The facts being undisputed on this point, the verdict cannot stand.

Reversed.[2]

Mr. JUSTICE STONE, absent because of illness, took no part in the consideration or decision of this case.

MODEL PENAL CODE
Article 5. Inchoate Crimes

Section 5.01. Criminal Attempt.

(1) *Definition of Attempt.* A person is guilty of an attempt to commit a crime if, acting with the kind of culpability otherwise required for commission of the crime, he:

(a) purposely engages in conduct which would constitute the crime if the attendant circumstances were as he believes them to be; or

(b) when causing a particular result is an element of the crime, does or omits to do anything with the purpose of causing or with the belief that it will cause such result without further conduct on his part; or

(c) purposely does or omits to do anything which, under the circumstances as he believes them to be, is an act or omission constituting a substantial step in a course of conduct planned to culminate in his commission of the crime.

(2) *Conduct Which May Be Held Substantial Step Under Subsection (1) (c).* Conduct shall not be held to constitute a substantial step under Subsection (1) (c) of this Section unless it is strongly corroborative of the actor's criminal purpose. Without negativing the sufficiency of other conduct, the following, if strongly corroborative of the actor's criminal purpose, shall not be held insufficient as a matter of law:

(a) lying in wait, searching for or following the contemplated victim of the crime;

(b) enticing or seeking to entice the contemplated victim of the crime to go to the place contemplated for its commission;

(c) reconnoitering the place contemplated for the commission of the crime;

(d) unlawful entry of a structure, vehicle or enclosure in which it is contemplated that the crime will be committed;

(e) possession of materials to be employed in the commission of the crime, which are specially designed for such unlawful use or which can serve no lawful purpose of the actor under the circumstances;

---

[2] The effect of this judgment was that the case was remanded for a new trial. State v. Peterson, 214 Minn. 204, 7 N.W.2d 408 (1943).

(f) possession, collection or fabrication of materials to be employed in the commission of the crime, at or near the place contemplated for its commission, where such possession, collection or fabrication serves no lawful purpose of the actor under the circumstances;

(g) soliciting an innocent agent to engage in conduct constituting an element of the crime.

(3) Conduct Designed to Aid Another in Commission of a Crime. A person who engages in conduct designed to aid another to commit a crime which would establish his complicity under Section 2.06 if the crime were committed by such other person, is guilty of an attempt to commit the crime, although the crime is not committed or attempted by such other person.

(4) Renunciation of Criminal Purpose. When the actor's conduct would otherwise constitute an attempt under Subsection (1) (b) or (1) (c) of this Section, it is an affirmative defense that he abandoned his effort to commit the crime or otherwise prevented its commission, under circumstances manifesting a complete and voluntary renunciation of his criminal purpose. The establishment of such defense does not, however, affect the liability of an accomplice who did not join in such abandonment or prevention.

Within the meaning of this Article, renunciation of criminal purpose is not voluntary if it is motivated, in whole or in part, by circumstances, not present or apparent at the inception of the actor's course of conduct, which increase the probability of detection or apprehension or which make more difficult the accomplishment of the criminal purpose. Renunciation is not complete if it is motivated by a decision to postpone the criminal conduct until a more advantageous time or to transfer the criminal effort to another but similar objective or victim.

Section 5.02. Criminal Solicitation.

(1) Definition of Solicitation. A person is guilty of solicitation to commit a crime if with the purpose of promoting or facilitating its commission he commands, encourages or requests another person to engage in specific conduct which would constitute such crime or an attempt to commit such crime or which would establish his complicity in its commission or attempted commission.

(2) Uncommunicated Solicitation. It is immaterial under Subsection (1) of this Section that the actor fails to communicate with the person he solicits to commit a crime if his conduct was designed to effect such communication.

(3) Renunciation of Criminal Purpose. It is an affirmative defense that the actor, after soliciting another person to commit a crime, persuaded him not to do so or otherwise prevented the commission of the crime, under circumstances manifesting a complete and voluntary renunciation of his criminal purpose.

Section 5.04. Incapacity, Irresponsibility or Immunity of Party to Solicitation or Conspiracy.

(1) Except as provided in Subsection (2) of this Section, it is immaterial to the liability of a person who solicits or conspires with another to commit a crime that:

(a) he or the person whom he solicits or with whom he conspires does not occupy a particular position or have a particular characteristic which is an element of such crime, if he believes that one of them does; or

    (b) the person whom he solicits or with whom he conspires is irresponsibile or has an immunity to prosecution or conviction for the commission of the crime.

(2) It is a defense to a charge of solicitation or conspiracy to commit a crime that if the criminal object were achieved, the actor would not be guilty of a crime under the law defining the offense or as an accomplice under Section 2.06(5) or 2.06(6) (a) or (b).

Section 5.05. Grading of Criminal Attempt, Solicitation and Conspiracy; Mitigation in Cases of Lesser Danger; Multiple Convictions Barred.

(1) Grading. Except as otherwise provided in this Section, attempt, solicitation and conspiracy are crimes of the same grade and degree as the most serious offense which is attempted or solicited or is an object of the conspiracy. An attempt, solicitation or conspiracy to commit a [capital crime or a] felony of the first degree is a felony of the second degree.

(2) Mitigation. If the particular conduct charged to constitute a criminal attempt, solicitation or conspiracy is so inherently unlikely to result or culminate in the commission of a crime that neither such conduct nor the actor presents a public danger warranting the grading of such offense under this Section, the Court shall exercise its power under Section 6.12 [1] to enter judgment and impose sentence for a crime of lower grade or degree or, in extreme cases, may dismiss the prosecution.

(3) Multiple Convictions. A person may not be convicted of more than one offense defined by this Article for conduct designed to commit or to culminate in the commission of the same crime.

SECTION 4. NEGATIVE ACTS

REGINA v. CONDE
Central Criminal Court, 1867.
10 Cox C.C. 547.

(A man and his wife were indicted for the murder of their little son who died from starvation.)

CHANNELL, B., in summing up the case to the jury, directed them as follows: If the prisoners or either of them wilfully withheld necessary food from the deceased, with a wilful determination by with-

---

[1]. Section 6.12 provides: "If, when a person, having been convicted of a felony, the Court having regard to the nature and circumstances of the crime and to the history and character of the defendant, is of the view that it would be unduly harsh to sentence the offender in accordance with the Code, the Court may enter judgment of conviction for a lesser degree of felony or for a misdemeanor and impose sentence accordingly."

holding sustenance which was requisite to cause his death, then the party so withholding such food is guilty of murder. If, however, the prisoners had the means to supply necessaries, the want of which had led to the death of the deceased, and having the means to supply such necessaries, negligently, though not wilfully, withheld food which, if administered, would have sustained life, and so caused the death of the deceased, then that would amount to the crime of manslaughter in the person so withholding the food.

Mary Conde guilty of manslaughter.

John George Conde not guilty.

REGINA v. HOGAN

Court of Criminal Appeal, 1851.
5 Cox C.C. 255.

(An indictment charged Mary Hogan with unlawfully abandoning her bastard child of tender age without having provided means for its support and with the unlawful intent of burdening the parish with its care.)

POLLOCK, C. B. We are all of opinion that this indictment cannot be sustained. No doubt, to neglect a child so as to injure its health is an offence in the person whose duty it is to take care of it; but here there is no allegation of any injury to the child, nor that the mother had the means of supporting it. As to the supposed injury to the parish, we are not disposed to go beyond the authorities, and there is no authority for saying that any person is indictable who occasions loss to a parish by throwing upon it the maintenance of a child as casual poor. It is quite consistent with every allegation in this indictment, that the mother, being unable to maintain the child, left it for a moment, so that it might fall into the hands of those who could, and were bound to, take care of it.

PARKE, B. I am entirely of the same opinion. Irrespectively of the intention to burthen the parish, it is quite clear that the mere act of deserting a child unable to take care of itself is not an indictable offence, unless it be followed by some injury to the health of the child. Then, as to the intention to burthen the parish, the indictment is defective, because there is no averment that the mother had any means of supplying it with nourishment; and if she was unable to carry it to its place of settlement, as might well be, it would be quite consistent with her duty to leave it to be maintained by the parish as casual poor; and any allegation in the indictment is consistent with such a state of facts.

PATTESON, J. Mr. Phinn puts the case upon the abandonment of the child; but what can that signify to the parish? If the mother had not the means of supporting it, the parish must have maintained it as casual poor for the time, whether it was abandoned or not.[1]

WIGHTMAN, J., and MARTIN, B., concurred. . . .

Conviction quashed.

REGINA v. DOWNES

Court of Criminal Appeal, 1875.
13 Cox C.C. 111.

Case reserved for the opinion of this Court by BLACKBURN, J.

1. The prisoner was indicted at the Center Criminal Court for the manslaughter of Charles Downes.

2. It appeared on the trial before me by the evidence that Charles Downes was an infant who, at the time of his death, was a little more than two years old. The child had been ill, and wasting away for eight or nine months, before its death. The prisoner, who resided at Woolwich, was the father of the deceased, and had during the whole of this time the custody of the child.

3. The prisoner was one of a sect who call themselves "The Peculiar People."

4. During the whole period of the child's illness he did not procure any skilled advice as to the treatment of the child, but left it to the charge of women who belonged to his sect, and called in at intervals George Hurry, an engine driver, who prayed over the child, and anointed it with oil.

5. The reason of this course of conduct was explained by George Hurry, who was called as a witness.

6. He stated that the Peculiar People never call in medical advice or give medicines in case of sickness. They had religious objections to doing so. They called in the elders of the church who prayed over the sick person, anointing him with oil in the name of the Lord. This he said they did in literal compliance with the directions in the 14th and 15th verses of the fifth chapter of the Epistle of St. James, and in hope that the cure would follow.

7. This course was pursued with regard to the deceased infant during its illness. The prisoner consulted the witness Hurry as to what was the matter with the child, and as to what should be given to it. They thought it was suffering from teething; and he advised the parents to give it port wine, eggs, arrowroot, and other articles of diet which he thought suitable for a child suffering from such a complaint, all of which were supplied accordingly. There was no

---

1. Compare Pallis v. State, 123 Ala. 12, 26 So. 339 (1898), with Regina v. Renshaw, 2 Cox C.C. 285 (1847).

evidence that this treatment was mischievous, and though this was probably not logically consistent with the doctrines of his sect as described by him, I saw no reason to doubt that it was all done in perfect sincerity.

8. He was asked by the counsel for the prosecution whether if one of their sect met with an accident, such as a broken bone, their principles would prevent their calling in a surgeon to set it, and he answered that he thought they probably would call in a surgeon in such a case, but it had never yet arisen. He was asked whether they trusted to nature in cases of childbirth. He said they did not call in midwives, which would be against their principles, but that several sisters of their persuasion were as skilful as any midwives, and that they assisted the woman in labour.

9. He was further asked whether he had not himself on the trial of Hurry before Mr. Justice Byles promised that in future medical advice should be called in when necessary. He explained that in that case the disease was infectious, and that he understood the judge to say that the law forbade them to endanger the lives of others; and as it was one of their principles to obey the law, he had given a pledge that they would call in medical advice where the disease was infectious, which pledge they had kept. . . .

COLERIDGE, C. J. I think that this conviction should be affirmed. For my own part, but for the statute 31 & 32 Vict. c. 122, s. 37, I should have much doubt about this case, and should have desired it to be further argued and considered. Perhaps it is enough to say that the opinions of Willes, J., and Pigott, B., are deserving of grave consideration. The statute 31 & 32 Vict. c. 122, s. 37, however, is a strong argument in favour of the conviction. By that enactment it is made an offence punishable summarily if any parent wilfully neglects to provide (*inter alia*) medical aid for his child being in his custody under the age of fourteen years, whereby the health of such child shall have been or shall be likely to be seriously injured. That enactment I understand to mean that if any parent intentionally, *i.e.*, with the knowledge that medical aid is to be obtained, and with a deliberate intention abstains from providing it, he is guilty of an offence. Under that enactment upon these facts the prisoner would clearly have been guilty of the offence created by it. If the death of a person results from the culpable omission of a breach of duty created by the law, the death so caused is the subject of manslaughter. In this case there was a duty imposed by the statute on the prisoner to provide medical aid for his infant child, and there was the deliberate intention not to obey the law—whether proceeding from a good or bad motive is not material. The necessary ingredient to constitute the crime of manslaughter existed, therefore, in this case, and for that reason this conviction ought to be affirmed.

BRAMWELL, B. I am of the same opinion. The 31 & 32 Vict. c. 122, s. 37, has imposed a positive and absolute duty on parents, whatever their conscientious or superstitious opinions may be, to provide medical aid for their infant children in their custody. The facts show that the prisoner thought it was irreligious to call in medical aid, but that is no excuse for not obeying the law.

MELLOR, J. I am of the same opinion. The 31 & 32 Vict. c. 122, s. 37, does not seem to have been called to the attention of Pigott, B., in Reg. v. Hines, or my brother Blackburn upon the trial of the present case. Otherwise it may be that Pigott, B., would have summed up differently to the jury.

GROVE, J., and POLLOCK, B., concurred.

Conviction affirmed.[1]

JONES v. UNITED STATES

United States Court of Appeals, District of Columbia Circuit, 1962.
113 U.S.App.D.C. 352, 308 F.2d 307.

[Shirley Green was the mother of the two children mentioned. Because she was not married and was living with her parents at the time, she arranged to have appellant take Robert from the hospital to appellant's home and agreed to pay appellant $72 a month for his care. There was a dispute in the evidence as to whether these payments were continued beyond five months. When Anthony was born, and was ready to leave the hospital, he also was taken to appellant's home. There seems to have been no specific monetary agreement covering his support, but he remained at appellant's home. Shirley also lived there for at least three weeks, there was a dispute in the evidence as to where she was living later.]

WRIGHT, CIRCUIT JUDGE. Appellant, together with one Shirley Green, was tried on a three-count indictment charging them jointly with (1) abusing and maltreating Robert Lee Green, (2) abusing and maltreating Anthony Lee Green, and (3) involuntary manslaughter through failure to perform their legal duty of care for Anthony Lee Green, which failure resulted in his death. At the close of evidence, after trial to a jury, the first two counts were dismissed as to both

---

1. Cf. Regina v. Wagstaffe, 10 Cox C.C. 530 (1868); People v. Pierson, 176 N.Y. 201, 68 N.E. 243 (1903). A woman, entrusted with her grandchild, who became so intoxicated that she allowed it to be suffocated although its screams could be heard throughout the neighborhood, is guilty of manslaughter. Cornell v. State, 159 Fla. 687, 32 So.2d 610 (1947). A guard at a railroad crossing, who did not see an approaching train because he was looking the other way and hence did not operate the safety devices, with the result that a motorist was killed, is guilty of manslaughter. State v. Benton, 38 Del. 1, 187 A. 609 (1936). Compare Regina v. Smith, 11 Cox C.C. 210 (1869) with Rex v. Pittwood, 19 Times Law Rep. 37 (1902) and State v. Harrison, 107 N.J.L. 213, 152 A. 867 (1930).

defendants. On the third count, appellant was convicted of involuntary manslaughter. Shirley Green was found not guilty. . . .

Appellant also takes exception to the failure of the trial court to charge that the jury must find beyond a reasonable doubt, as an element of the crime, that appellant was under a legal duty to supply food and necessities to Anthony Lee. Appellant's attorney did not object to the failure to give this instruction, but urges here the application of Rule 52(b).

The problem of establishing the duty to take action which would preserve the life of another has not often arisen in the case law of this country. The most commonly cited statement of the rule is found in People v. Beardsley, 150 Mich. 206, 113 N.W. 1128, 1129, 13 L.R.A., N.S., 1020:

"The law recognizes that under some circumstances the omission of a duty owed by one individual to another, where such omission results in the death of the one to whom the duty is owing, will make the other chargeable with manslaughter. . . . This rule of law is always based upon the proposition that the duty neglected must be a legal duty, and not a mere moral obligation. It must be a duty imposed by law or by contract, and the omission to perform the duty must be the immediate and direct cause of death. . . ."

There are at least four situations in which the failure to act may constitute breach of a legal duty. One can be held criminally liable: first, where a statute imposes a duty to care for another; second, where one stands in a certain status relationship to another; third, where one has assumed a contractual duty to care for another; and fourth, where one has voluntarily assumed the care of another and so secluded the helpless person as to prevent others from rendering aid.

It is the contention of the Government that either the third or the fourth ground is applicable here. However, it is obvious that in any of the four situations, there are critical issues of fact which must be passed on by the jury—specifically in this case, whether appellant had entered into a contract with the mother for the care of Anthony Lee or, alternatively, whether she assumed the care of the child and secluded him from the care of his mother, his natural protector. On both of these issues, the evidence is in direct conflict, appellant insisting that the mother was actually living with appellant and Anthony Lee, and hence should have been taking care of the child herself, while Shirley Green testified she was living with her parents and was paying appellant to care for both children.

In spite of this conflict, the instructions given in the case failed even to suggest the necessity for finding a legal duty of care. The only reference to duty in the instructions was the reading of the indictment which charged, inter alia, that the defendants "failed to perform their legal duty." A finding of legal duty is the critical element of the crime charged and failure to instruct the jury concerning it was plain error. . . .

Reversed and remanded.[a]

THE QUEEN v. WHITE

Court for Crown Cases Reserved, 1871.
L.R. 1 C.C. 311.

Case stated by the Chairman of the Hants Quarter Sessions.

Indictment under 24 & 25 Vict. c. 100, s. 27 [1] for unlawfully and wilfully abandoning and exposing a child under the age of two years, whereby the life of the child was endangered.

At the trial at Winchester, it appeared from the evidence that Emily White (the wife of William White), who was not included in the indictment, was the mother of the child, which was about nine months old at the time mentioned in the indictment. On the 19th of October, 1870, she had an interview with her husband, from whom she had been living apart since the 11th of August of the same year, and asked him if he intended to give her money or victuals; he passed by her without answering, and went into his house; this was about 7 P.M. His mother, the prisoner Maria White, shut the wicket of the garden, and forbade his wife from coming in; the wife then went to the door of the house, laid the child down close to the door, and called out, "Bill, here's your child, I can't keep it—I am gone." She left, and was seen no more that night. Shortly after William White came out of the house, stepped over the child, and went away. About 8:30 P.M. two witnesses found the child lying in the road outside the wicket of the garden, which was a few yards from the house-door; it was dressed in short clothes, with nothing on its head; they remained at the spot till about 10 P.M., when William White came home. They told him that his child was lying in the road; his answer was, "It must bide there for what he knew, and then the mother ought to be taken up for the murder of it." Another witness, Maria Thorn (the mother of his wife), deposed also to the fact that about the same time, in answer to her observation that he ought to take the child in, he said, "He should not touch it—those that put it there must come and take it." She then went into the house. About 11 P.

---

[a]. A conviction of murder was affirmed in a case in which the jury could have found that an unmarried mother placed her infant child in the attic and left it there unattended until it died. Commonwealth v. Hall, 322 Mass. 523, 78 N.E.2d 644 (1948).

If lives were lost by drowning, when a ship was lost at sea, because the life preservers were unsafe and unsuitable, and the crew untrained and undisciplined, the master is guilty of manslaughter. United States v. Van Schaick, 134 F. 592 (2d Cir. 1904).

1. 24 & 25 Vict. c. 100, s. 27, enacts that, "Whosoever shall unlawfully abandon or expose any child, being under the age of two years, whereby the life of such child shall be endangered, . . . shall be guilty of a misdemeanour." . . .

M., one of the two witnesses went for a police constable, and returned with him to the place about 1 A.M., when the child was found lying on its face in the road, with its clothes blown over its waist, and cold and stiff. The constable took charge of it, and by his care it was restored to animation. At 4.30 A.M. the constable went to the house, and asked William White if he knew where his child was; he said, "No." On being asked if he knew it was in the road, he answered, "Yes." It appeared that, during the time which elapsed between William White leaving his house, about 7 P.M., and his return, about 10 P.M., he had been to the police constable stationed at Beaulieu, and told him that there had been a disturbance between him and his wife, and wished him to come up and settle it, but he did not say anything about the child.

The prisoner's counsel objected that upon these facts there was no evidence of abandonment or exposure, under the Act, by William White.

He also objected that there was no evidence against John White and Maria White.

The Court were of opinion that there was no evidence against the two last-named prisoners, but overruled the objection as to William White, as to whom the case was left to the jury, who found him guilty.

The question for the Court was, whether the prisoner, William White, was properly convicted upon the facts as above stated.

April 29. No counsel appeared.

Cur. adv. vult.

May 6. BOVILL, C. J. We have considered this case, and we are of opinion that the conviction was right, and ought to be affirmed. The prisoner was indicted, under 24 & 25 Vict. c. 100, s. 27, for unlawfully abandoning and exposing a child, under the age of two years, whereby its life was endangered. On the facts stated in the case the objection was taken that there was no evidence of abandonment or exposure. Now, the prisoner was the father of the child, and as such was entitled to the custody and control of it, and was not only morally but legally bound to provide for it. Then it appears that when the child was lying at the door he saw it, stepped over it, and left it there. Afterwards, when the child was in the road, he knew it was there. I am clearly of opinion that there was evidence here upon which the jury might and ought to convict the prisoner. Instead of protecting and providing for the child, as it was his duty to do, he allowed it to remain lying, first at his door, and afterwards in the road, insufficiently clothed, and at a time of year when the result was likely to be the child's death. I think, therefore, he was guilty both of abandonment and exposure.

MARTIN, B. I am of the same opinion, though I have entertained some doubt upon the question. The statute makes it an offence unlawfully to abandon or expose a child, and, construing these words according to their natural meaning, I thought at first that they could only apply to persons who had had the actual custody and possession of the child. But as the prisoner here was the father of the child, entitled to its custody and legally bound to its protection, I do not differ from the rest of the Court.

BRAMWELL, B. I am of the same opinion. If the person who had had the actual custody of the child, and who left it at its father's door, had been a stranger with whom it had been left at nurse, there could, I think, have been no doubt about the case; and I do not think the fact that it was the mother makes any difference.

BLACKBURN, J. I am of the same opinion. The question turns upon the meaning of the words "abandon or expose" in the statute. The Court before whom the prisoner was tried were right in directing the acquittal of the two other persons accused, because there was no legal duty upon them to protect the child, but only a duty of imperfect obligation. But the father's case is different; for upon him there is a strict legal duty to protect the child. And when the child is left in a position of danger of which he knows, and from which he has full power to remove it, and he neglects his duty of protection, and lets the child remain in danger, I think this is an exposure and abandonment by him. If the child had died, the facts were such that a jury might have convicted him of murder, though they might have taken a more merciful view, and found him guilty only of manslaughter; and as the child, though its life was endangered, did not die, the case is within the section.

CHANNELL, B. My Brother Byles, who was a member of the Court when the case was first before the Court, concurs in the judgment; and, having had an opportunity of considering the case this morning, I am of the same opinion.

Conviction affirmed.

REX v. RUSSELL

Supreme Court of Victoria, 1932.
[1933] Vict.L.R. 59.

(Russell was charged with murder in three counts, (1) for the murder of his wife, (2) for the murder of his son Harold, and (3) for the murder of his son Eric. Harold was three and a half years old and Eric one and one-half. There was evidence which seems to have led the jury to believe that the wife drowned herself and the children while defendant stood by without either encouraging her or trying to stop her. And in reply to a question the judge charged the jury that under such facts the defendant would be guilty of manslaughter. Defendant was convicted of manslaughter on all three counts and applies for leave to appeal.)

MANN, J. It was with some doubt as to the principles of law applicable to the case that I answered the question propounded by the jury, and I therefore postponed judgment and intimated my intention of reserving a case for the Full Court. This became unnecessary when the prisoner decided to appeal against the verdict. The appeal attacks the verdict on all three counts, while a case reserved would have dealt with the second and third counts only.

The question of the jury was: "Assuming that the woman took the children into the water without the assistance of putting them in the water by the man, but that he stood by, conniving to the act, what is the position from the standpoint of the law?"[1] This question, heard with knowledge of the course of the trial, including the addresses of counsel and my own charge to the jury, was clearly directed, as I thought and still think, to the second and third counts only, which charged the accused with murder of his two children.

Upon the further consideration given to the matter upon this appeal, I am of opinion that the proper answer for me to have given to the question was that in the case supposed the accused would be guilty of murder.

But apart altogether from the question of murder or manslaughter, it is important that a decision as to the criminal liability of the accused in given circumstances should be referred to the right legal principles. I rested my answer to the jury in effect upon the principles of such cases as R. v. Instan,[e] R. v. Gibbins and Proctor[f] and R. v. Bubb.[g] These cases may be regarded as defining the legal sanctions which the law attaches to the moral duty of a parent to protect his children of tender years from physical harm. If applicable to the present case, those authorities would point to the accused's being guilty of what I may call an independent crime of murder. The outstanding difference between the facts of such cases as I have cited and the facts of the present case is the interposition in the latter of a criminal act of a third person which is the immediate cause of death; and the difficulty in such a case is in saying, in the absence of express authority, that the inaction of the accused has caused the death of the children, within the meaning of the criminal law.

I think the more correct view in the present case is that the prisoner on the facts supposed, while perhaps guilty of an independent

[1]. N.B. When the jury asked the question quoted above the judge asked: "Are you supposing a case where he is offering no encouragement or persuasion to her to do it, but simply standing by and watching the wife drown the children? Is that the Case?" The Foreman: "That is the position."

[e]. [1893] 1 Q.B. 450.

[f]. [1918] 13 Cr.App.R. 134.

[g]. [1850] 4 Cox C.C. 455.

crime, was certainly guilty as participator in the murder committed by his wife. The moral duty of the accused to save his children, the control which by law he has over his wife, and his moral duty to exercise that control, do not in this view cease to be elements in his crime. On the contrary, it is these elements which as a matter of law give to the acquiescence of the father in the acts of the mother committed in his presence the quality of participation. The control which the law recognizes as exercisable by a husband over his wife is well illustrated in the doctrine that the mere presence of the husband at the commission by his wife of a felony, other than murder, is generally enough to exempt the wife altogether from criminal liability. The physical presence and the "connivance" of a parent in the position of the accused has in law, in my opinion, a criminal significance not attaching to the presence and connivance of the mere "passerby" referred to in some of the cases.

It follows that the case put by me to the jury by way of contrast, though based upon a sound theoretical distinction, was not applicable to the special facts. The facts necessary to constitute aiding and abetting were too narrowly conceived, since no legal distinction can be made between tacit and oral concurrence, and a correct direction would be that not only was the accused morally bound to take active steps to save his children from destruction, but by his deliberate abstention from so doing, and by giving the encouragement and authority of his presence and approval to his wife's act, he became an aider and abetter and liable as a principal offender in the second degree. . . .

With regard to the first count, my brother Cussen's view is that the verdict shows a belief in the mind of the jury that in answering the question submitted to me I was also directing them as to the law applicable to the first count; and he thinks that with regard to this count also the prisoner was criminally liable as aiding and abetting in the suicide of his wife. I do not take this view of the matter. I can find no reason, having regard to the various hypotheses put forward at the trial, for saying with certainty that the jury thought the wife committed suicide at all. I think that, the verdict upon the first count being one which was legally open to the jury upon the evidence and no misdirection being established with regard to it, it is unnecessary and unwise to enter upon what seems to me a speculative enquiry as to the process, or perhaps the different processes, of thought by which the jury arrived at that verdict.

I think the appeal fails as to all three counts. . . .

The opinions of CUSSEN, A. C. J., and McARTHUR, J., are omitted. (McARTHUR, J., thought the conviction on the first count should be quashed.)

Application refused.

MORELAND v. STATE

Supreme Court of Georgia, 1927.
164 Ga. 467, 139 S.E. 77.

(The owner of a car and his chauffeur were jointly indicted for murder, based upon a fatal accident. The owner alone was tried (the chauffeur not having been apprehended) and was convicted of involuntary manslaughter in the commission of an unlawful act.)

HILL, J. . . . The Penal Code of 1910, § 67, provides that "Involuntary manslaughter shall consist in the killing of a human being without any intention to do so, but in the commission of an unlawful act, or a lawful act, which probably might produce such a consequence, in an unlawful manner: provided, that where such involuntary killing shall happen in the commission of an unlawful act which, in its consequences, naturally tends to destroy the life of a human being, or is committed in the prosecution of a riotous intent, or of a crime punishable by death or confinement in the penitentiary, the offense shall be deemed and adjudged to be murder." . . . Under the above definition of what constitutes involuntary manslaughter in the commission of an unlawful act, there can be no question that that offense was committed by whomever was responsible for the operation of the automobile in question at the time of the unfortunate homicide. Whoever was responsible, it can not be questioned under the facts as stated by the Court of Appeals that the automobile of Moreland was being operated in violation of the law of this State. It was being run at a rate of fifty miles per hour, when the law says that it could be run upon the public highway at a rate not exceeding thirty miles per hour. It was in violation of the law which prevents one vehicle passing another on the wrong side of the road. It was violating the law in running at a rate of speed in violation of a penal statute which provides that on a sharp curve an automobile shall not exceed the speed of ten miles per hour. And the sole question to be decided is, is Moreland, the owner of the automobile, liable for the acts of his chauffeur done in his presence. He was present, and there is nothing to indicate that he remonstrated with the chauffeur, or attempted to prevent him from running at the high rate of speed of fifty miles per hour, around a curve, while it was raining. Under these circumstances we are of the opinion that the owner of the car was in control thereof, and that he should have seen to it that his chauffeur did not operate the car in such a manner contrary to law as might produce such a consequence in an unlawful manner as that which happened on this fateful occasion. It must be held, therefore, that the owner of the car must have known, and did know, that it was being operated contrary to law, and that he consented and agreed to the running of the car at such a high rate of speed; and that being true, he is responsible for what happened in consequence of such violation of the law. It would be the owner's duty, when he saw that the law was being violated and that his machine was being operated in such a way as to be dangerous to the life and property of others on the highway, to curb and restrain one in his employment and under his control, and prevent him from violating the law with his own property. The owner of the automobile was bound to know that it was very dangerous for his chauffeur to run and operate the car at fifty miles per hour during a rainstorm along a public highway and at a dangerous curve. He was bound to know that a car operated at such a place and in such a manner was liable to come in collision and injure occupants of other automobiles upon the highway; and that being so, he was equally guilty with his employee in causing the homicide in question, although he may have had no intention of injuring or killing the woman in question. It is not insisted that the operator of the car, or the owner, wilfully intended to kill the party named in the indictment. As already stated, it is a question of intentional neglect not to curb the operator of the car when he was violating the highway law of the State. Nor is it a question here that the owner and operator of the car entered into a conspiracy to kill the party so killed, or any one else. The question of conspiracy is not involved.

So we reach the conclusion that the question propounded by the Court of Appeals must be answered in the affirmative.

All the Justices concur.

BECK, P. J., and GILBERT, J., concurred specially.

COMMONWEALTH v. PUTCH

County Court, Allegheny County, Pennsylvania, 1932.
18 Pa.D. & C. 680.

MUSMANNO, J., October 22, 1932. When the owner of an automobile knows that his car, in which he is riding, has struck a dog, even though he is not driving, and he makes no effort to have the car stopped to give aid to the suffering beast, he is guilty of the offense charged under the Act of March 29, 1869, P.L. 22, which provides:

"Any person who shall . . . wantonly or cruelly ill-treat . . . or otherwise abuse any animal . . . and every person who shall encourage, aid or assist therein, . . . " shall be subject to fine or imprisonment.

Such a person certainly wantonly and cruelly abuses an animal in a common-sense and humane interpretation of the act. Ill-treatment and abuse does not need to be active; it may be passive. It does not need to be the commission of an act; it may be the omission to do what the circumstances require.

In the case at bar the evidence shows that on May 2, 1932, in the early evening, the defendant, Samuel F. Putch, in his own car driven by an employe, was proceeding eastward along California Avenue between Whitmer Street and Benton Avenue, traveling on the right-hand side of the street between car track and curb, when a large collie dog belonging to J. W. Connolly, of No. 3911 California Avenue, came upon the street in full view of the driver of the automobile and some distance ahead. The wheel or some other part of the right front of the car struck the dog on its left flank, knocking it to the ground, and in its effort to escape or being thrown about by reason of the force of the collision, it fell upon the street and the car proceeding ran over its tail. Two witnesses, one upon a lawn abutting the scene of the accident and just across the sidewalk from the car and the other upon an adjoining lawn, hearing the cries, endeavored with call and gesture to halt the car of the defendant, but without avail. It passed on, leaving the dog lying at the curb, nor did the defendant or his driver offer any assistance or call to evidence any interest in their victim. The dog was carried into the house by the owner, where it lay about for several days, when it was taken to a veterinary, who pronounced its injuries such that it should be put out of its misery, and, under instructions from the owner, he ended its life humanely.

The evidence shows that the injured animal cried out so loudly as to be heard within one of the neighboring houses; that after striking the dog the driver slowed up his car, hesitated, turned to one side and went on; and that at least two neighbors, one opposite the car and but a few feet distant across the sidewalk, called and gestured in an effort to halt the car, and all this on the side of the car on which defendant sat in the front seat.

We do not know as a positive fact whether the defendant heard and saw what transpired at the time the poor beast was injured, but common experience would establish that he could not avoid knowing what had taken place.

We cannot find the defendant guilty, however, because the information is defective. It charges that on May 2, 1932, the defendant, "after having struck a female collie dog with a certain automobile on a public highway in the said City of Pittsburgh, to wit, California avenue near residence number 3911, did then and there wilfully and unlawfully fail and neglect to stop and render assistance, said dog being the property of a certain W. J. Connolly and the said defendant was operating the said machine on a public highway in the said city in a reckless and careless manner and at an excessive rate of speed."

The evidence clearly shows that it was not the defendant who was driving the car, and the Commonwealth admits this. With the record in the shape that it is, the summary conviction rendered by the alderman must be reversed and the defendant discharged.

MODEL PENAL CODE

Section 2.01. (Requirement of Voluntary Act;) Omission as Basis of Liability; (Possession as an Act.)

. . .

(3) Liability for the commission of an offense may not be based on an omission unaccompanied by action unless:

    (a) the omission is expressly made sufficient by the law defining the offense; or

    (b) a duty to perform the omitted act is otherwise imposed by law.

. . .

SECTION 5. CONSPIRACY [1]

COMMONWEALTH v. DONOGHUE

Court of Appeals of Kentucky, 1933.
250 Ky. 343, 63 S.W.2d 3.

[Defendant combined with two other persons to lend small amounts of money to poor people and charge exorbitant rates of interest. He was indicted for conspiracy. A demurrer to the indictment was sustained and the Commonwealth appealed. A majority of the court concluded that the indictment charged more than that defendant conspired to collect usury, although apparently they would have upheld the indictment had it charged only that. Usury was not itself a criminal offense.]

STANLEY, COMMISSIONER. . . .

3. The comprehensiveness and indefiniteness of the offense of conspiracy has made an exact definition a very difficult one, as has been often stated. But the broad definition or description everywhere accepted is that conspiracy is a combination between two or more persons to do or accomplish a criminal or unlawful act, or to do a lawful act by criminal or unlawful means. . . .

According to the overwhelming weight of authority the objects [sic] of the conspiracy need not be an offense against the criminal law for which an individual could be indicted or convicted, but it is sufficient if the purpose be unlawful. That term "unlawful" in this connection has been expanded beyond its original limits of being only some act

---

[1]. Aiding, abetting and counseling are not terms which presuppose the existence of an agreement. Hence a charge of conspiracy requires proof not essential to conviction of the substantive offense. Pereira v. United States, 347 U.S. 1, 74 S.Ct. 358, 98 L.Ed. 435 (1954). The wrongdoers may be convicted of both the substantive offense and the conspiracy to commit it. Ibid.; People v. Miller, 129 Cal. App.2d 305, 276 P.2d 846 (1954).

punishable as a crime. It is now understood and regarded as covering an act not embraced in the crime of conspiracy as it originally existed. It cannot be said, however—and care must ever be exercised in the application, as all courts recognize—that the term "unlawful" includes every act which violates legal rights of another or such as may create a right of action. . . .

So it may be said that within the contemplation of the offense of criminal conspiracy are the acts which by reason of the combination have a tendency to injure the public, to violate public policy, or to injure, oppress, or wrongfully prejudice individuals collectively or the public generally. . . .

With this abstract understanding as to what may be the subject-matter of a criminal conspiracy, we may direct our consideration to the subject of usurious demands and collections.

Now, the occupation of a usurer has been bitterly denounced in all ages of the civilized world, and in most Christian countries there have been laws to suppress it. The implications and inferences to be drawn from the indictment, coupled with general knowledge of the rapaciousness, the audacious and unconscionable practices of this class of usurious money lenders to be found in every city, suggest the application of the following extravagant phillippic of St. Basil, one of the most learned theologians and illustrious orators of the early Christian church, spoken in the fourth century: "The griping usurer sees, unmoved, his necessitous borrower at his feet, condescending to every humiliation, professing everything that is villifying; he feels no compassion for his fellow-creatures; though reduced to this abject state of supplication, he yields not to his humble prayer; he is inexorable to his entreaties; he melts not at his tears; . . ."

4. Measuring the indictment by the foregoing considerations, the court is of the opinion that it states a public offense.

Wherefore, the judgment is reversed.

Whole court sitting.

CLAY, JUSTICE (dissenting). I am unable to concur in the majority opinion. However indefensible the exaction of usury may be, it is a matter that should be regulated by the Legislature and not by the courts. Already the conspiracy doctrine has been worked overtime, and should not be extended unless plainly required. When a court on the theory of conpiracy declares an act to be a crime, which was not recognized as a crime at the time it was done, its decision savors strongly of an ex post facto law. . . .

The decision not only presents a strained application of the conspiracy doctrine, but its chief danger lies in the fact that for all time to come it will be the basis for the creation of new crimes never dreamed of by the people.

I am authorized to say that Judge DIETZMAN concurs in this dissent.

UNITED STATES v. SANTA RITA STORE CO. AND SANTA RITA MINING CO.

Supreme Court of New Mexico, 1911.
16 N.M. 3, 113 P. 620.

Opinion of the Court

MECHEM, J. 1. The appellants, the Santa Rita Mining Company and the Santa Rita Store Company, were jointly indicted with one John Deegan and one William Young for a violation of Section 3, Act of Congress, approved July 2, 1890, Chapter 647, 26 Stat. at Large 209. . . .

. . . There was no evidence that any officer or agent of either of appellants, (other than Deegan) participated in or had knowledge of the acts of which complaint is made.

Undoubtedly, a conspiracy might be formed by two corporations acting through agents, yet there must be more than one agent or more than one person actually engaged in the formation of the conspiracy. In this case a conspiracy was not formed because of a lack of persons. Deegan could not conspire with himself; neither could two or more corporations conspire alone by means of Deegan. Had some other officer or agent of either corporation participated in, or had knowledge of, the scheme, then a conspiracy might have been formed between the two defendant corporations. "The union of two or more persons, the conscious participation in the scheme of two or more minds, is indispensible [sic] to an unlawful combination, and it cannot be created by the action of one man alone." per Sanborn, J., in Union Pacific Coal Company v. United States, 173 F. 737.

The trial court should have sustained the motion made by appellants for an instructed verdict. For the foregoing reasons the judgment of the lower court is reversed and the case remanded.[1]

ROBERTS, A. J., who was not a member of the Court when the case was submitted, did not participate in this decision.

---

[1]. The common-law theory, that husband and wife are one, made it impossible for them to be guilty of conspiracy if no third person was involved. Dawson v. United States, 10 F.2d 106 (9th Cir. 1926); People v. Miller, 82 Cal. 107, 22 P. 934 (1889). But the tendency is to abandon this theory and hold that they can be guilty of conspiracy even without the cooperation of anyone else. For example, Dawson and Miller have both been overruled. United States v. Dege, 364 U.S. 51, 80 S.Ct. 1589, 4 L.Ed.2d 1563 (1960); People v. Pierce, 61 Cal.2d 879, 40 Cal. Rptr. 845, 395 P.2d 893 (1964).

NORRIS v. UNITED STATES

United States Circuit Court of Appeals, Third Circuit, 1929.
34 F.2d 839.

THOMPSON, DISTRICT JUDGE. . . . First. It is conceded that, under the Eighteenth Amendment, and the Volstead Act passed to carry it into effect, the purchase of liquor is not made an offense. It follows that the purchase, as such, does not subject the buyer to punishment. This is perfectly clear from the act itself. Not only did Congress carefully exclude the purchaser from the penal provisions of the act as originally passed, but has taken no step to extend its provisions to the purchaser, in the 10 years of legislation which have since intervened. That the intention and purpose of Congress is in harmony with the act, as drawn, is thus made perfectly manifest.

Second. While the seller of liquor, who delivers it to the purchaser, is liable under the law both for the sale and transportation, the purchaser to whom the goods are delivered is chargeable with neither the purchase nor the transportation. It thus appears that while the legislative department of the government has deliberately and intentionally made the purchaser of liquor guiltless of any offense under the Prohibition Law, the executive department of the government seeks here, by indirection, to make of the same fact, namely, the purchase, a crime subjecting the purchaser to a maximum fine of $10,000 and imprisonment for a term of two years. Such a situation is scarcely conceivable, and yet that is the position of the government.

Third. Concerning the crime of conspiracy, it is a well-established principle that, where an offense is such that a concert of action between two persons is logically necessary to the completion of the crime, that is to say, the crime cannot take place without concert, a charge of conspiracy against the two persons to commit that crime does not lie.[2] This is the language of Judge Thompson in the case of United States v. Katz, (D.C.) 5 F.2d 527.

On appeal, the Supreme Court affirmed the soundness of this rule in United States v. Katz, 271 U.S. 354, 46 S.Ct. 513, 70 L.Ed. 986. Justice Stone, speaking for the court, said: "The overt act charged in each indictment was the sale of whisky by one defendant to the other. This is an offense under the National Prohibition Act; but as the defendants in each case were only one buyer and one seller, and as the agreement of the parties was an essential element in the sale, an indictment of the buyer and seller for a conspiracy to make the sale would have been of doubtful validity [citing a number of cases]. This embarrassment could be avoided in an indictment for a

---

2. A charge of conspiracy to gamble will not lie if only two persons are alleged to have participated. People v. Purcell, 304 Ill.App. 215, 26 N.E.2d 153 (1940). To illustrate the rule that if an offense requires concert of action a conspiracy to perpetrate it cannot be committed by two alone, the court mentioned such offenses as adultery, bigamy, bribery, dueling and incest.

criminal conspiracy only if the buyer and seller were charged with conspiring to commit a substantive offense having an ingredient in addition to the sale, not requiring the agreement of two persons for its completion."

In La Rosa v. U. S. (C.C.A.) 15 F.2d 479, La Rosa was indicted with Martin and Belman for conspiring to sell, barter, transport, deliver, furnish, possess, and manufacture intoxicating liquor. It appears that the only understanding La Rosa had with Martin and Belman was that he would buy certain whisky from them and show them how to get it to his garage. The judgment of conviction for conspiracy was reversed on the appeal. Notwithstanding, there was evidence in the case from which it could be fairly said that La Rosa aided and abetted the transportation, yet Judge Rose, speaking for the Circuit Court of Appeals, declined to consider the question of conspiracy to transport, in effect holding that it was too unsubstantial to merit serious consideration.

In Becher v. U. S. (C.C.A.) 5 F.2d 45, 50, there was a charge of conspiracy against several defendants to commit different offenses. Liquor was found in the cellar of one of the defendants, Birnbaum, which had been delivered there, and he contended that he was merely a buyer, and that there was no proof that he was a conspirator with the others. Speaking for a unanimous court, Judge Learned Hand said: "We concede at once that merely as buyer he was not a party to the scheme in any criminal sense; that, on the contrary, the prosecution was bound to involve him in the plan as a whole in some other sense."

Fourth. In the case of seller and buyer, transportation by the seller is a mere incident in the sale, and necessary to its completion by delivery to the purchaser. It is an inherent feature, an essential element, of the sale, which the seller had, on his part, to perform. The sale necessarily involves an agreement, a concert of action, between buyer and seller to effect the purchase, and it could not, with any reason, be said that a conspiracy would lie to do something which was an essential element of the sale. . . .

From the foregoing considerations we are of opinion that a sale of liquor, involving such transportation as is necessary to effect the delivery to the purchaser, does not subject the purchaser and seller to an indictment for conspiracy to transport. The judgment is therefore reversed.

BUFFINGTON, CIRCUIT JUDGE, dissents.

(Reversed on another point 281 U.S. 619, 50 S.Ct. 424, 74 L.Ed. 1076.)

GEBARDI v. UNITED STATES

Supreme Court of the United States, 1932.
287 U.S. 112, 77 L.Ed. 206, 53 S.Ct. 35.

Mr. Justice Stone delivered the opinion of the Court.

This case is here on certiorari, 286 U.S. 539, 52 S.Ct. 648, 76 L.Ed. 1278, to review a judgment of conviction for conspiracy to violate the Mann Act (36 Stat. 825; 18 U.S.C., § 397 *et seq.*). Petitioners, a man and a woman, not then husband and wife, were indicted in the District Court for Northern Illinois, for conspiring together, and with others not named, to transport the woman from one state to another for the purpose of engaging in sexual intercourse with the man. At the trial without a jury there was evidence from which the court could have found that the petitioners had engaged in illicit sexual relations in the course of each of the journeys alleged; that the man purchased the railway tickets for both petitioners for at least one journey, and that in each instance the woman, in advance of the purchase of the tickets, consented to go on the journey and did go on it voluntarily for the specified immoral purpose. There was no evidence supporting the allegation that any other person had conspired. The trial court overruled motions for a finding for the defendants, and in arrest of judgment, and gave judgment of conviction, which the Court of Appeals for the Seventh Circuit affirmed 57 F.2d 617, on the authority of United States v. Holte, 236 U.S. 140, 35 S.Ct. 271, 59 L.Ed. 504. . . .

Section 2 of the Mann Act (18 U.S.C. § 398), violation of which is charged by the indictment here as the object of the conspiracy, imposes the penalty upon "Any person who shall knowingly transport or cause to be transported, or aid or assist in obtaining transportation for, or in transporting in interstate or foreign commerce . . . any woman or girl for the purpose of prostitution or debauchery or for any other immoral purpose . . ." Transportation of a woman or girl whether with or without her consent, or causing or aiding it, or furthering it in any of the specified ways, are the acts punished, when done with a purpose which is immoral within the meaning of the law.

The Act does not punish the woman for transporting herself; it contemplates two persons—one to transport and the woman or girl to be transported. For the woman to fall within the ban of the statute she must, at the least, "aid or assist" someone else in transporting or in procuring transportation for herself. But such aid and assistance must, as in the case supposed in United States v. Holte, supra 236 U.S. 145, 35 S.Ct. 271, 59 L.Ed. 504, be more active than mere agreement on her part to the transportation and its immoral purpose. For the statute is drawn to include those cases in which the woman consents to her own transportation. Yet it does not specifically impose any penalty upon her, although it deals in detail with the person by whom she is transported. In applying this criminal statute we cannot infer that the mere acquiescence of the woman transported was intended to be condemned by the general language punishing those who aid and assist the transporter, any more than it has been inferred that the purchaser of liquor was to be regarded as an abettor of the illegal sale. The penalties of the statute are too clearly directed against the acts of the transporter as distinguished from the consent of the subject of the transportation. So it was intimated in United States v. Holte, supra, and this conclusion is not disputed by the Government here, which contends only that the conspiracy charge will lie though the woman could not commit the substantive offense.

We come thus to the main question in the case, whether, admitting that the woman, by consenting, has not violated the Mann Act, she may be convicted of a conspiracy with the man to violate it. Section 37 of the Criminal Code (18 U.S.C., § 88), punishes a conspiracy by two or more persons "to commit any offense against the United States." The offense which she is charged with conspiring to commit is that perpetrated by the man, for it is not questioned that in transporting her he contravened § 2 of the Mann Act. Hence we must decide whether her concurrence, which was not criminal before the Mann Act, nor punished by it, may, without more, support a conviction under the conspiracy section, enacted many years before.

As was said in the Holte Case (p. 144 of 236 U.S., 35 S.Ct. 271, 272), an agreement to commit an offense may be criminal, though its purpose is to do what some of the conspirators may be free to do alone. Incapacity of one to commit the substantive offense does not necessarily imply that he may with impunity conspire with others who are able to commit it. For it is the collective planning of criminal conduct at which the statute aims. The plan is itself a wrong which, if any act be done to effect its object, the state has elected to treat as criminal, Clune v. United States, 159 U.S. 590, 595, 16 S.Ct. 125, 40 L.Ed. 269. And one may plan that others shall do what he cannot do himself.

But in this case we are concerned with something more than an agreement between two persons for one of them to commit an offense which the other cannot commit. There is the added element that the offense planned, the criminal object of the conspiracy, involves the agreement of the woman to her transportation by the man, which is the very conspiracy charged.

Congress set out in the Mann Act to deal with cases which frequently, if not normally, involve consent and agreement on the part of the woman to the forbidden transportation. In every case in which she is not intimidated or forced into the transportation, the statute necessarily contemplates her acquiescence. Yet this acquiescence, though an incident of a type of transportation specifically dealt with by the statute, was not made a crime under the Mann Act itself. Of this class of cases we say that the substantive offense contemplated by the statute itself involves the same combination or community of purpose of two persons only which is prosecuted here as conspiracy. If this were the only case covered by the Act, it would be within those decisions which hold, consistently with the theory upon which conspiracies are punished, that where it is impossible under any circumstances to commit the substantive offense without coöperative action, the preliminary agreement between the same parties to commit the offense is not an indictable conspiracy either at common law, or under the federal statute. But criminal transportation under the Mann Act may be effected without the woman's consent, as in cases of intimidation or force (with which we are not now concerned). We assume therefore, for present purposes, as was suggested in the Holte case, supra, 145 of 236 U.S., 35 S.Ct. 271, 272, that the decisions last mentioned do not in all strictness apply. We do not rest our decision upon the theory of those cases, nor upon the related one that the attempt is to prosecute as conspiracy acts identical with the substantive offense. United States v. Dietrich, 126 F. 664. We place it rather upon the ground that we perceive in the failure of the Mann Act to condemn the woman's participation in those transportations which are effected with her mere consent, evidence of an affirmative legislative policy to leave her acquiescence unpunished. We think it a necessary implication of that policy that when the Mann Act and the conspiracy statute came to be construed together, as they necessarily would be, the same participation which the former contemplates as an inseparable incident of all cases in which the woman is a voluntary agent at all, but does not punish, was not automatically to be made punishable under the latter. It would contravene that policy to hold that the very passage of the Mann Act effected a withdrawal by the conspiracy statute of that immunity which the Mann Act itself confers.

It is not to be supposed that the consent of an unmarried person to adultery with a married person, where the latter alone is guilty of the substantive offense, would render the former an abettor or a conspirator, compare In re Cooper, 162 Cal. 81, 85, 121 P. 318, or that the acquiescence of a woman under the age of consent would make her a co-conspirator with the man to commit statutory rape upon herself. The principle, determinative of this case, is the same.

On the evidence before us the woman petitioner has not violated the Mann Act and, we hold, is not guilty of a conspiracy to do so. As there is no proof that the man conspired with anyone else to bring about the transportation, the convictions of both petitioners must be

Reversed.

MR. JUSTICE CARDOZO concurs in the result.

UNITED STATES v. FALCONE

United States Circuit Court of Appeals, Second Circuit, 1940.
109 F.2d 579.

L. HAND, CIRCUIT JUDGE. . . . In the light of all this, it is apparent that the first question is whether the seller of goods, in themselves innocent, becomes a conspirator with—or, what is in substance the same thing, an abettor of—the buyer because he knows that the buyer means to use the goods to commit a crime. That came up a number of times in circuit courts of appeal while the Eighteenth Amendment was in force, and the answer was not entirely uniform. The first case we have found is Pattis v. United States, 9 Cir., 17 F.2d 562, where, although the accused appears to have been in fact more closely connected with the buyer's crime than merely as a seller, the court affirmed a charge to the jury that he was guilty if he merely had notice of the future destination of the goods. That appears to be the settled doctrine in that circuit. The same is true of the Seventh Circuit. And of the Sixth. The Fifth has, however, held otherwise, though by a divided court, Young v. United States, 5 Cir., 48 F.2d 26. In that case the judges differed because of their interpretation of Edenfield v. United States, 273 U.S. 660, 47 S.Ct. 345, 71 L.Ed. 827, which, on the authority of United States v. Katz, 271 U.S. 354, 46 S.Ct. 513, 70 L.Ed. 986, reversed a conviction upon a count for conspiracy to manufacture liquor without a license. The indictment also contained a count for conspiracy to manufacture liquor contrary to the National Prohibition Law, 41 Stat. 305, and the conviction on this the court did not disturb; the question was whether in doing so it had held that the mere sale of materials for making a still, and of sugar and meal to make liquor, was enough to convict. The opinion below (Edenfield v. United States, 5 Cir., 8 F.2d 614) indicated that there had been nothing more to hold the seller, but when the same court in Young v. United States, supra (5 Cir., 48 F.2d 26), came to consider the effect of the reversal, the majority said that there had in fact been much more; i. e., that the accused had taken part in setting up the stills, and in selling the liquor after it was made. We do not think, therefore, that Edenfield v. United States, supra, 273 U.S. 660, 47 S.Ct. 345, 71 L.Ed. 827, should be regarded as passing upon the point. We are ourselves committed to the view of the Fifth Circuit. United States v. Peoni, 2 Cir., 100 F.2d 401. In that case we tried to trace down the doctrine as to abetting and conspiracy, as it exists in our criminal law, and concluded that the seller's knowledge was not alone enough. Civilly, a man's liability extends to any injuries which he should have apprehended to be likely to follow from his acts. If they do, he must excuse his conduct by showing that the interest which he was promoting outweighed the dangers which its protection imposed upon others; but in civil cases there has been a loss, and the only question is whether the law shall transfer it from the sufferer to another. There are indeed instances of criminal liability of the same kind, where the law imposes punishment merely because the accused did not forbear to do that from which the wrong was likely to follow; but in prosecutions for conspiracy or abetting, his attitude towards the forbidden undertaking must be more positive. It is not enough that he does not forego a normally lawful activity, of the fruits of which he knows that others will make an unlawful use; he must in some sense promote their venture himself, make it his own, have a stake in its outcome. The distinction is especially important today when so many prosecutors seek to sweep within the drag-net of conspiracy all those who have been associated in any degree whatever with the main offenders. That there are opportunities of great oppression in such a doctrine is very plain, and it is only by circumscribing the scope of such all comprehensive indictments that they can be avoided. We may agree that morally the defendants at bar should have refused to sell to illicit distillers; but, both morally and legally, to do so was toto coelo different from joining with them in running the stills.

For these reasons the prosecution did not make out a case against either of the Falcones, Alberico, or John Nole; and this is especially true of Salvatore Falcone. As to Nicholas Nole the question is closer, for when he began to do business as the "Acme Yeast Company", he hid behind the name of a cousin, whom he caused to swear falsely that the affiant was to do the business. Yet it seems to us that this was as likely to have come from a belief that it was a crime to sell the yeast and the cans to distillers as from being in fact any further involved in their business. It showed a desire to escape detection and that was evidence of a consciousness of guilt, but the consciousness may have as well arisen from a mistake of law as from a purpose to do what the law in fact forbade. We think therefore that even as to him no case was made out. . . .

The convictions of Salvatore and Joseph Falcone, of Alberico and of Nicholas and John Nole are reversed. . . .[1]
(Affirmed 311 U.S. 205, 61 S.Ct. 204, 85 L.Ed. 128.)

1. If the commodities involved in the sale are not articles of free commerce such as sugar and cans, but restricted commodities such as narcotic drugs which can be sold only by compliance with order forms and registration and are incapable of further legal use without compliance with rigid regulations, the seller's knowledge of the buyer's extensive illegal use of the drugs over an extended period of time may be sufficient to establish a conspiracy. Direct Sales Co. v. United States, 319 U.S. 703, 63 S.Ct. 1265, 87 L.Ed. 1674 (1943).

C sold a gun to D under such circumstances that it was criminally negligent for him to do so because of the likelihood that D would use it to kill X, which D did. D was convicted of first-degree murder and C was convicted of involuntary manslaughter. People v. Howk, 56 Cal.2d 687, 16 Cal.Rptr. 370, 565 P.2d 426 (1961).

"One who sells a gun to another knowing that he is buying it to commit a murder, would hardly escape conviction as an accessory to the murder by showing that he received full price for the gun." Backun v. United States, 112 F.2d 635, 637 (4th Cir. 1940).

PEOPLE v. CREEKS

Supreme Court of California, in Bank, 1915.
170 Cal. 368, 149 P. 821.

ANGELLOTTI, C. J. The defendant was convicted of murder in the first degree upon an information charging him with the murder of one J. P. Drewry, in October, 1914, in Sacramento County. This is an appeal from the judgment of death given upon such conviction, and from an order denying defendant's motion for a new trial. . . .

It may be assumed for the purposes of this decision that the evidence fails to sufficiently show that defendant personally inflicted any wound on Captain Drewry or personally assaulted him in the conflict near the inside gate, and that in such conflict he devoted his efforts exclusively to Kerr; and further that it fails to show any express specific agreement between Phelps and himself to *kill* anybody in their previously conceived and concerted plan to escape from the prison. This is a matter of no moment in this case. The evidence does clearly show that defendant and Phelps had conspired and combined together to commit an unlawful act, viz.: to accomplish *their* escape, the escape of both Phelps and defendant, from the state prison, and in the accomplishment of that purpose to use such force as was found to be necessary. It was such that a jury could not reasonably conclude otherwise. The law made it a felony on the part of Phelps, a prisoner confined in a state prison for a term less than for life, to escape or to attempt to escape therefrom (Pen.Code, secs. 105 and 106), and any person aiding and abetting him in the commission of this felony would be a principal therein. (Pen.Code, sec. 31.) So that it is immaterial here that the law does not make it a crime for one undergoing a life sentence in a state prison to himself escape or attempt to escape. The conspiracy included as a part of the joint purpose the accomplishment of something admittedly unlawful and a felony,—namely, the escape of Phelps. Of course there is no force whatever in the suggestion that defendant could not, by reason of his *status* as a prisoner for life in a state prison, be held as a principal under the provisions of section 31 of the Penal Code. The conspiracy likewise included the commission by defendant of the felony defined by section 109 of the Penal Code, which provides that "any person who willfully assists . . . any prisoner confined in any prison or jail . . . to escape, or in an attempt to escape from such prison or jail . . . is punishable as provided in section 108 of the Penal Code," viz.: by imprisonment in the state prison not exceeding ten years and by a fine. The willful killing of any person standing between defendant and Phelps and the consummation of their escape was an ordinary, probable, and natural consequence of the execution of their common design.

Sec. 5 CONSPIRACY 275

The law applicable in such cases is well stated in People v. Kauffman, 152 Cal. 331, 334, 92 P. 861, where it is substantially said that under the well-settled rule of law governing the criminal liability of each of several engaging in an unlawful conspiracy or combination, if several parties conspire or combine together to commit any unlawful act, each is criminally responsible for the acts of his associates or confederates committed in furtherance of any prosecution of the common design for which they combine. It was further said: "In contemplation of law the act of one is the act of all. Each is responsible for everything done by his confederates, which follows incidentally in the execution of the common design as one of its probable and natural consequences, even though it was not intended as a part of the common design for which they combine." Of course, as said in the case just referred to, if one member of the party departs from the original design as agreed on by all the members and does an act which was not only not contemplated by those who entered into the common purpose, "but was not in furtherance thereof, and not the natural or legitimate consequence of anything connected therewith, the person guilty of such act, if it was itself unlawful, would alone be responsible therefor." But there is no reasonable basis in the evidence for the application of this doctrine here. Not only was the killing of *any* officer or guard standing between defendant and Phelps and their escape a probable and natural consequence of their plan to escape, as that plan is shown by their acts and conduct, but the evidence shows quite clearly that their plan contemplated the overcoming of Drewry and Kerr by such force and to such an extent as was necessary at the very place where they attacked them, and these men having been rendered powerless to resist them or impede their movements, their subsequent escape through the gates into the yard. Under such circumstances, Creeks would be equally guilty with Phelps of the murder of Drewry, even if he did not personally inflict any wound on him, for under the law the acts of Phelps in the matter were the acts of the defendant also.[1] The verdict of the jury in this regard is not only sufficiently sustained by the evidence, but we do not see how any other verdict could have been given. . . .

We find no other matters requiring notice.

The judgment and order denying a new trial are affirmed.

SHAW, J., LORIGAN, J., MELVIN, J., SLOSS, J., and LAWLOR, J., concurred.

---

1. "We have here a continuous conspiracy. . . . And so long as the partnership in crime continues, the partners act for each other in carrying it forward. It is settled that 'an overt act of one partner may be the act of all without any new agreement specifically directed to that act'. . . . A different case would arise if the substantive offense committed by one of the conspirators was not in fact done in furtherance of the conspiracy, . . ." Pinkerton v. United States, 328 U.S. 640, 646-47, 66 S.Ct. 1180, 1183-84, 90 L.Ed. 1489 (1946).

UNITED STATES v. FOX

United States Circuit Court of Appeals, Third Circuit, 1942.
130 F.2d 56.

GOODRICH, CIRCUIT JUDGE. The appellant William Fox, was indicted with two other persons, J. Warren Davis and Morgan S. Kaufman, charged with conspiracy to obstruct justice and to defraud the United States. The indictment contained the usual residuary clause charging conspiracy of the named conspirators "with divers other persons whose names are to the Grand Jurors unknown, ..." The appellant entered a guilty plea and became a witness for the United States at the trial. The first jury, being unable to agree, was discharged without a verdict. Subsequently, a second trial was had which again resulted in a disagreement and this jury was likewise discharged without a verdict. The appellant was a witness for the government in the second trial also. Sometime thereafter a nolle prosequi was entered upon the application of the government as to the defendants, Davis and Kaufman. The appellant both before and subsequent to the nolle prosequi moved for leave to withdraw his plea of guilty. He also moved, subsequently to the nolle prosequi for a vacation or modification of the sentence which had been imposed prior to entry of judgment of the nolle prosequi. The District Judge refused both requests and his action is assigned as error upon this appeal.

The case for the appellant in this court rests on two grounds. One concerns the doctrines of the law relating to conspiracy to the facts of his case. The other is whether the trial judge went beyond his discretion in refusing the appellant permission to withdraw his guilty plea.

The law of conspiracy has been nearly as proliferative as that of larceny in its development of technical doctrine. The question in this case is limited, however, to the growth of one branch. By definition conspiracy is a group offense; therefore, two or more people must participate to create the crime. Then it is held that where an indictment for conspiracy names only two, an acquittal or reversal as to one is an acquittal or reversal as to the other. This is no doubt the law announced by the majority of the decisions including the federal courts, although as the New York court says the "contrary view is arguable". This result, however, is not to be expanded into a general "all or none" rule. The conviction of some alleged conspirators does not fall because others named are acquitted, even though the conviction of the others is logically required for the finding of guilty of those held. Nor is the conviction of one alleged conspirator vitiated because of the possible later acquittal of co-defendants not yet tried or even apprehended. Furthermore, one may be convicted and punished for a conspiracy even though his fellow conspirators may be immune from prosecution because of the immunity attaching to representatives of foreign governments, the Fifth Circuit declaring that "The rule that the acquittal of all save one of alleged conspirators results in the acquittal of all applies to acquittals on the merits".

The appellant does not contend that his alleged fellow conspirators were acquitted, but does argue that the nolle prosequi puts an end to charges made by this indictment and so should be treated as having the same effect as an acquittal. This point will be taken up later.
. . .

We think that to treat a convicted conspirator whose fellow conspirator's case has ended by a nolle prosequi like the case where one is convicted and the other is acquitted goes too far. The analogy overlooks the difference between an acquittal and a nolle prosequi. The courts seem to have treated the acquittal in this connection as though the jury had expressly found that the defendant did not participate in the conspiracy charged. Therefore, the defendant who is convicted stands in the situation of having been found to conspire by himself, a manifest impossibility by the definition of conspiracy. One may criticize that rule as being founded upon a false premise, for a not guilty verdict is not necessarily a declaration of innocence by the jury, but simply an indication of lack of proof of guilt beyond reasonable doubt. Be that as it may, the acquittal of the alleged conspirator does free the accused from further prosecution for the offense charged. The nolle prosequi does not. As in the case of disagreement of a jury, "The prisoner has not been convicted or acquitted, and may again be put upon his defence." It is not a bar to a second indictment covering the same matter, although it does terminate the proceedings in which the nolle prosequi occurs. It is a very considerable step which has to be taken to apply the rule as to acquittal to the termination of proceedings by a nolle prosequi. We are not called upon to take it either by reason or by authority. . . .

The Judgment of the District Court is affirmed.[1]

(Certiorari denied 317 U.S. 666, 63 S.Ct. 74, 87 L.Ed. 535.)

[1]. Contra, State v. Jackson, 7 S.C. 283 (1876). No overt act was required by common law for conviction of conspiracy. As to the effect of statutes requiring such an act, see Hyde v. United States, 225 U.S. 347, 32 S.Ct. 793, 56 L.Ed. 1114 (1912). Where an overt act is required by statute for conviction of conspiracy the required act need not be sufficient to constitute an attempt. People v. George, 74 Cal.App. 440, 241 P. 97 (1925).

SCALES v. UNITED STATES

Supreme Court of the United States, 1961.
367 U.S. 203, 81 S.Ct. 1469.

Mr. Justice Harlan delivered the opinion of the Court.

Our writ issued in this case (358 U.S. 917, 79 S.Ct. 289, 3 L.Ed.2d 237) to review a judgment of the Court of Appeals (4 Cir., 260 F.2d 21) affirming petitioner's conviction under the so-called membership clause of the Smith Act. 18 U.S.C. § 2385, 18 U.S.C.A. § 2385. The Act, among other things, makes a felony the acquisition or holding of knowing membership in any organization which advocates the overthrow of the Government of the United States by force or violence. The indictment charged that from January 1946 to the date of its filing (November 18, 1954) the Communist Party of the United States was such an organization, and that petitioner throughout that period was a member thereof, with knowledge of the Party's illegal purpose and a specific intent to accomplish overthrow "as speedily as circumstances would permit." . . .

II.

Constitutional Challenge to the Membership Clause on its Face.

Petitioner's constitutional attack goes both to the statute on its face and as applied. At this point we deal with the first aspect of the challenge and with one part of its second aspect. The balance of the latter, which essentially concerns the sufficiency of the evidence, is discussed in the next section of this opinion.

It will bring the constitutional issues into clearer focus to notice first the premises on which the case was submitted to the jury. The jury was instructed that in order to convict it must find that within the three-year limitations period (1) the Communist Party advocated the violent overthrow of the Government, in the sense of present "advocacy of action" to accomplish that end as soon as circumstances were propitious; and (2) petitioner was an "active" member of the Party, and not merely "a nominal, passive, inactive or purely technical" member, with knowledge of the Party's illegal advocacy and a specific intent to bring about violent overthrow "as speedily as circumstances would permit." . . .

We hold that the statute was correctly interpreted by the two lower courts, and now turn to petitioner's basic constitutional challenge.

2. Fifth Amendment.

In our jurisprudence guilt is personal, and when the imposition of punishment on a status or on conduct can only be justified by reference to the relationship of that status or conduct to other concededly criminal activity (here advocacy of violent overthrow), that relationship must be sufficiently substantial to satisfy the concept of personal guilt in order to withstand attack under the Due Process Clause of the Fifth Amendment. Membership, without more, in an organization engaged in illegal advocacy, it is now said, has not heretofore been recognized by this Court to be such a relationship. This claim stands, and we shall examine it, independently of the claim made under the First Amendment.

Any thought that due process puts beyond the reach of the criminal law all individual associational relationships, unless accompanied by the commission of specific acts of criminality, is dispelled by familiar concepts of the law of conspiracy and complicity. While both are commonplace in the landscape of the criminal law, they are not natural features. Rather they are particular legal concepts manifesting the more general principle that society, having the power to punish dangerous behavior, cannot be powerless against those who work to bring about that behavior. The fact that Congress has not resorted to either of these familiar concepts means only that the enquiry here must direct itself to an analysis of the relationship between the fact of membership and the underlying substantive illegal conduct, in order to determine whether that relationship is indeed too tenuous to permit its use as the basis of criminal liability. In this instance it is an organization which engages in criminal activity,[18] and we can perceive no reason why one who actively and knowingly works in the ranks of that organization, intending to contribute to the success of those specifically illegal activities, should be any more immune from prosecution than he to whom the organization has assigned the task of carrying out the substantive criminal act. Nor should the fact that Congress has focussed here on "membership," the characteristic relationship between an individual and the type of conspiratorial quasi-political associations with the criminal aspect of whose activities Congress was concerned, of itself require the conclusion that the legislature has traveled outside the familiar and permissible bounds of criminal imputability. In truth, the specificity of the proscribed re-

18. [Footnotes by the Court.] The problems in attributing criminal behavior to an abstract entity rather than to specified individuals, though perhaps difficult theoretically, as a practical matter resolve themselves into problems of proof. Whether it has been successfully shown that a particular group engages in forbidden advocacy must depend on the nature of the organization, the occasions on which such advocacy took place, the frequency of such occasions, and the position within the group of the persons engaging in the advocacy. (See pages 253–254 of 367 U.S., pages 1498–1499 of 81 S.Ct., infra.) Understood in this way, there is no great difference between a charge of being a member in a group which engages in criminal conduct and being a member of a large conspiracy, many of whose participants are unknown or not before the court. Whatever difficulties might be thought to inhere in ascribing a course of criminal conduct to an abstract entity are certainly cured, so far as any particular defendant is concerned, by the requirement of proof that he knew that the *organization* engages in criminal advocacy, and that it was his purpose to further that criminal advocacy.

lationship is not necessarily a vice; it provides instruction and warning.[19]

What must be met, then, is the argument that membership, even when accompanied by the elements of knowledge and specific intent, affords an insufficient quantum of participation in the organization's alleged criminal activity, that is, an insufficiently significant form of aid and encouragement to permit the imposition of criminal sanctions on that basis. It must indeed be recognized that a person who merely becomes a member of an illegal organization, by that "act" alone need be doing nothing more than signifying his assent to its purposes and activities on one hand, and providing, on the other, only the sort of moral encouragement which comes from the knowledge that others believe in what the organization is doing. It may indeed be argued that such assent and encouragement do fall short of the concrete, practical impetus given to a criminal enterprise which is lent for instance by a commitment on the part of a conspirator to act in furtherance of that enterprise. A member, as distinguished from a conspirator, may indicate his approval of a criminal enterprise by the very fact of his membership without thereby necessarily committing himself to further it by any act or course of conduct whatever.

In an area of the criminal law which this Court has indicated more than once demands its watchful scrutiny these factors have weight and must be found to be overborne in a total constitutional assessment of the statute. We think, however, they are duly met when the statute is found to reach only "active" members having also a guilty knowledge and intent, and which therefore prevents a conviction on what otherwise might be regarded as merely an expression of sympathy with the alleged criminal enterprise, unaccompanied by any significant action in its support or any commitment to undertake such action.

Thus, given the construction of the membership clause already discussed, we think the factors called for in rendering members criminally responsible for the illegal advocacy of the organization fall within established, and therefore presumably constitutional, standards of criminal imputability. . . .

The judgment of the Court of Appeals must be
Affirmed.

[The CHIEF JUSTICE, and JUSTICES BLACK, BRENNAN and DOUGLAS, dissented.]

---

19. See generally Hart, The Aims of the Criminal Law, 23 Law & Contemp. Prob. 401 (1958).

MODEL PENAL CODE

Section 5.03. Criminal Conspiracy.

(1) Definition of Conspiracy. A person is guilty of conspiracy with another person or persons to commit a crime if with the purpose of promoting or facilitating its commission he:

> (a) agrees with such other person or persons that they or one or more of them will engage in conduct which constitutes such crime or an attempt or solicitation to commit such crime; or

> (b) agrees to aid such other person or persons in the planning or commission of such crime or of an attempt or solicitation to commit such crime.

(2) Scope of Conspiratorial Relationship. If a person guilty of conspiracy, as defined by Subsection (1) of this Section, knows that a person with whom he conspires to commit a crime has conspired with another person or persons to commit the same crime, he is guilty of conspiring with such other person or persons, whether or not he knows their identity, to commit such crime.

(3) Conspiracy With Multiple Criminal Objectives. If a person conspires to commit a number of crimes, he is guilty of only one conspiracy so long as such multiple crimes are the object of the same agreement or continuous conspiratorial relationship.

(4) Joinder and Venue in Conspiracy Prosecutions.

> (a) Subject to the provisions of paragraph (b) of this Subsection, two or more persons charged with criminal conspiracy may be prosecuted jointly if:

>> (i) they are charged with conspiring with one another; or

>> (ii) the conspiracies alleged, whether they have the same or different parties, are so related that they constitute different aspects of a scheme of organized criminal conduct.

> (b) In any joint prosecution under paragraph (a) of this Subsection:

>> (i) no defendant shall be charged with a conspiracy in any county [parish or district] other than one in which he entered into such conspiracy or in which an overt act pursuant to such conspiracy was done by him or by a person with whom he conspired; and

>> (ii) neither the liability of any defendant nor the admissibility against him of evidence of acts or declarations of another shall be enlarged by such joinder; and

>> (iii) the Court shall order a severance or take a special verdict as to any defendant who so requests, if it deems it necessary or appropriate to promote the fair determination of his guilt or innocence, and shall take any other proper measures to protect the fairness of the trial.

(5) Overt Act. No person may be convicted of conspiracy to commit a crime, other than a felony of the first or second degree, unless an overt act

in pursuance of such conspiracy is alleged and proved to have been done by him or by a person with whom he conspired.

(6) Renunciation of Criminal Purpose. It is an affirmative defense that the actor, after conspiring to commit a crime, thwarted the success of the conspiracy, under circumstances manifesting a complete and voluntary renunciation of his criminal purpose.

(7) Duration of Conspiracy. For purposes of Section 1.06(4):

(a) conspiracy is a continuing course of conduct which terminates when the crime or crimes which are its object are committed or the agreement that they be committed is abandoned by the defendant and by those with whom he conspired; and

(b) such abandonment is presumed if neither the defendant nor anyone with whom he conspired does any overt act in pursuance of the conspiracy during the applicable period of limitation; and

(c) if an individual abandons the agreement, the conspiracy is terminated as to him only if and when he advises those with whom he conspired of his abandonment or he informs the law enforcement authorities of the existence of the conspiracy and of his participation therein.

Section 5.05. Grading of Criminal Attempt, Solicitation and Conspiracy; Mitigation in Cases of Lesser Danger; Multiple Convictions Barred.

(1) Grading. Except as otherwise provided in this Section, attempt, solicitation and conspiracy are crimes of the same grade and degree as the most serious offense which is attempted or solicited or is an object of the conspiracy. An attempt, solicitation or conspiracy to commit a [capital crime or a] felony of the first degree is a felony of the second degree.

(2) Mitigation. If the particular conduct charged to constitute a criminal attempt, solicitation or conspiracy is so inherently unlikely to result or culminate in the commission of a crime that neither such conduct nor the actor presents a public danger warranting the grading of such offense under this Section, the Court shall exercise its power under Section 6.12 to enter judgment and impose sentence for a crime of lower grade or degree or, in extreme cases, may dismiss the prosecution.

(3) Multiple Convictions. A person may not be convicted of more than one offense defined by this Article for conduct designed to commit or to culminate in the commission of the same crime.

[Section 5.04. Incapacity, Irresponsibility or Immunity of Party to Solicitation or Conspiracy, was quoted at the end of Section 3.]

SECTION 6. AGENCY

REX v. HUGGINS

King's Bench, 1730.
2 Ld.Raym. 1574, 92 Eng.Rep. 518.

(An indictment charged the warden of a prison, and his deputy, with the murder of a prisoner, by keeping him in an unwholesome place, and so forth, until he died. The jury returned a special verdict. The LORD CHIEF JUSTICE—RAYMOND—delivered the opinion of the justices.)

In this case two questions have been made. 1. What crime the facts found upon Barnes in the special verdict will amount to? 2. Whether the prisoner at the Bar is found guilty of the same offence with Barnes?

1. As to the first question, it is very plain that the facts found upon Barnes do amount to murder in him. Murder may be committed without any stroke. The law has not confined the offence to any particular circumstances or manner of killing; but there are as many ways to commit murder, as there are to destroy a man, provided the act be done with malice, either express or implied. Hale P.C. 46. 3 Inst. 52. Murder is, where a person kills another of malice, so he dies within a year and a day. Hale P.C. 43. And malice may be either expressed or implied. In this case the jury have found the malice express: for the facts charged on Barnes are laid in the indictment to be ex malitia sua praecogitata, to wit, that he having the custody of Arne assaulted him, and carried him to this unwholesome room, and confined him there by force against his will, and without his consent, and without proper support, ex malitia sua praecogitata; by means of which he languished and died. And the jury have found that Barnes did all these facts, modo et forma prout in indictamento praedicto specificatur. . . .

The Judges are all unanimously of opinion, that the facts found in this special verdict do not amount to murder in the prisoner at the Bar; but as this special verdict is found, they are of opinion, that he is not guilty. Though he was warden, yet it being found, that there was a deputy; he is not, as warden, guilty of the facts committed under the authority of his deputy. He shall answer as superior for his deputy civilly,[1] but not criminally. It has been settled, that though a sheriff must answer for the offences of his gaoler civilly, that is, he is subject in an action, to make satisfaction to the party injured; yet he is not to answer criminally for the offences of his under-officer. He only is criminally punishable, who immediately does the act, or per-

---

[1] But see Oppenheimer v. Los Angeles, 104 Cal.App.2d 545, 232 P.2d 26 (1951).

mits it to be done. Hale's P.C. 114. So that if an act be done by an under-officer, unless it is done by the command or direction, or with the consent of the principal, the principal is not criminally punishable for it. In this case the fact was done by Barnes; and it no where appears in the special verdict, that the prisoner at the Bar ever commanded, or directed, or consented to this duress of imprisonment, which was the cause of Arne's death. 1. No command or direction is found. And 2. It is not found, that Huggins knew of it. That which made the duress in this case was, 1. Barnes's carrying, and putting, and confining Arne in this room by force and against his consent. 2. The situation and condition of this room. Now it is not found that Huggins knew these several circumstances, which made the duress. 1. It is not found, that he knew any thing of Barnes's carrying Arne thither. 2. Nor that he was there without his consent, or without proper support. 3. As to the room, it is found by the verdict, 1. That the room was built of brick and mortar. 2. That the walls were valde humidae. 3. That the room was situate on the common sewer of the prison, and near the place where the filth of the prison and excrement of the prisoners were usually laid, ratione quorum the room was very unwholesome, and the life of any man kept there was in great danger. But all that is found with respect to the prisoner's knowledge is, that for fifteen days before Arne's death he knew that the room was then lately built, recenter, that the walls were made of brick and mortar, and were then damp. But it is not found, nor does it appear, that he knew, they were dangerous to a man's life, or that there was a want of necessary support. Nor is it found, that he directed, or consented, that Arne should be kept or continued there. . . .

Upon the whole, there is no authority against the Court's giving judgment of acquittal, upon a verdict that is not sufficient to convict; and therefore this verdict, not finding facts sufficient to make the prisoner guilty of murder, he must be adjudged not guilty. And he was discharged.

REGINA v. BLEASDALE

Liverpool Assizes, 1848.
2 Car. & K. 765, 175 Eng.Rep. 321.

The prisoner was indicted under 7 & 8 Geo. 4, c. 10, s. 37, for stealing from the mine of one Henry John Gunning coal, the property of the said H. J. Gunning: and, in the same count, he was charged with stealing from the mines of thirty other proprietors other coal, the property of each of such proprietors. There were also counts charging him with the severing of coal with intent to steal, and with common larceny; and in each count the coal was charged as being the property of the said H. J. Gunning; and also as being the property of the said thirty other separate and distinct owners. . . .

Sec. 6 AGENCY 285

ERLE, J., in summing up, said: The remarkable part of this case is, the extent of the property taken; and it has been urged that the taking of each day was a separate felony, and that only one felony could be inquired into by you on this indictment. But I should say, that, as long as coal was gotten from one shaft, it was one continuous taking, though the working was carried on by means of different levels and cuttings, and into the lands of different people. As, however, complaint was made by the counsel for the prisoner, I have thought it better that your attention should be confined to the charge of taking the coal of one owner. But, in order to shew that, when the prisoner took the coal of Mr. Gunning in No. 10 Drift, he knew he was out of his boundary, I have permitted it to be proved, that he has gone out of his boundary in many other instances, and into the property of many other persons, taking in all 15,000 yards of coal. The prisoner did not, by his own hand, pick or remove the coal: but if a man does, by means of an innocent agent, an act which amounts to a felony, the employer, and not the innocent agent, is the person accountable for that act.[1]

The prisoner was convicted.

REGINA v. HOLBROOK

Queen's Bench Division, 1877.
13 Cox C.C. 650.

This was a criminal information for libel, tried at Winchester before Lindley, J., and a special jury, a verdict of guilty having been found against the defendants, who are the proprietors and publishers of the *Portsmouth Times and Naval Gazette.*

The information had been granted at the instance of Mr. John Howard, the clerk of the peace for the borough of Portsmouth, who in effect, had been charged by an article in that newspaper with having packed a grand jury at the borough quarter sessions, for the purpose of improperly dealing with an indictment for personation at a municipal election.

The defendants, who pleaded Not Guilty only, were proved to be the publishers of the paper and to be actively engaged in the management. It appeared, however, that they employed a competent editor to superintend that part of the paper in which the libel appeared, and he had general authority to publish whatever he thought proper. The defendants then tendered evidence to show their exemption from liability under the 7th section of Lord Campbell's Act (6 & 7 Vict. c. 96). This evidence the learned judge refused to admit, and he directed the jury that the defendants were not in a position to avail themselves of that section. . . .

---

[1] Davis v. United States, 55 F.2d 550 (5th Cir. 1932), certiorari denied 286 U.S. 564, 52 S.Ct. 646, 76 L.Ed. 1296 (1932).

COCKBURN, C. J. I am of opinion that this rule must be made absolute. The facts, as I understand them, show that the defendants are the three joint proprietors of this newspaper; but it appears that, when not absent from Portsmouth, the duties of conducting the paper are divided between four persons, viz., the three defendants and an editor appointed by them to manage the literary department. The defendants undertake respectively the commercial, the advertising, and the publishing duties. At the time of the publication of this libel one of the defendants was absent in Somerset on account of his health, and he clearly was not cognisant of the publication. The others were present, and discharging their ordinary duties; but, as the editor had full discretion to publish whatever he thought proper in that department which issued the libellous publication without consulting them, all the defendants must be taken, for the purpose of this rule, to have known nothing of the insertion of the article complained of. The question is whether the defendants, or either of them, are criminally responsible. It is an undoubted principle of law that a man is responsible criminally only for his own acts, or those authorised expressly by him through his appointed agent. It is not to be implied or inferred from the fact that the defendants gave their editor a general authority to manage the paper as he thought proper, that they authorised him to do what was unlawful in the conduct of his ordinary business. Although this is the rule of law, there seems to have been introduced an exception with respect to libel. Lord Tenterden, at Nisi Prius in 1829, following a previous direction of Lord Kenyon, and a statement of the law in Hawkins' Pleas of the Crown, laid down that a proprietor of a newspaper was criminally responsible for a libel, although he took no part in the publication of the newspaper, nor of the libel in question. He further proceeded to justify this ruling, and expatiated upon the danger to the public which its modification might cause. It is not necessary to say how far we dissent from that doctrine; it was considered an anomaly by high authority at the time, and I cannot doubt that the 7th section of Lord Campbell's Act was passed to put an end to it. It has been suggested that the object of this legislation was only to get rid of the presumption from particular evidence created by previous statute, or to apply to a case where the libel has been inserted by some one who had no authority to interfere at all with the publication. The answer to both these suggestions is that the section was unnecessary for the accomplishment of either of these objects; and I can come to no other conclusion than that it was intended by these words to reverse this anomaly, and to render libel subject to the general law. If then, as I think, this provision was designed to protect the proprietor of a newspaper from criminal responsibility for the act of another person, committed through no fault of his and without his authority, does not the case here come within its application? As to the defendant who was absent, he clearly is protected unless the prosecution can show that his general authority to the editor expressly included power to publish libels. As to the other two defendants, the section provides protection from liability for a publication made without a publisher's authority, consent, or knowledge, if he has exercised due care and caution: it would then be a question for the jury looking at all the circumstances, whether those defendants can show themselves entitled to that protection. If the jury should be in the defendants' favour on these points they can neither of them be criminally liable. I say nothing about their position civilly, but it seems to me that the section can have no application at all if it does not apply to this case. It is not for us to say whether it is expedient or desirable that proprietors of newspapers should be freed from liability under such circumstances; and I do not consider that question. Simply this section is, in my opinion, applicable to the facts upon which this rule has been granted; I think it must be made absolute, and the case must go back for a new trial.

MELLOR, J. I regret much that I am unable to concur with the Lord Chief Justice and my brother Lush in their view of this matter. I dissent with the greatest diffidence, but I cannot think that the Legislature intended to apply sect. 7 of this Act to persons situated as these defendants are. They do not in the ordinary way live at any distance from the publishing office, they do not keep away from the general management of the paper, and the whole business is conducted for their profit and by their authority. The editor might by inadvertence have published this libel, but the want of care would then deprive the publication of the protection given in the Act. I think, too, that the absent partner is in the same position as the other two; they all gave their editor a general authority to do what he liked; they vested their discretion in him, they put themselves in his hands, and they must be taken to have authorized whatever he has done. The 7th section requires not only the absence of authority, consent, and knowledge, but also the presence of care and caution. . . .

Rule absolute for a new trial.[1]

MODEL PENAL CODE

Section 2.06. Liability for Conduct of Another; Complicity.

(1) A person is guilty of an offense if it is committed by his own conduct or by the conduct of another person for which he is legally accountable, or both.

---

[1]. One cannot commit a crime by ratifying what is already done. The rule that subsequent ratification is equivalent to prior authorization cannot be applied to criminal cases. Cook v. Commonwealth. 141 Ky. 439, 132 S.W. 1032 (1911).

SECTION 7. INCORPORATION

"A corporation is not indictable, but the particular members are." This statement of Chief Justice Holt [1] represents the original position of the common law which held firm for many years. It was repeated in substance by Blackstone [2] and in judicial opinion in this country.[3] Now, however, it represents little more than an echo from a bygone day. The change from this position originated in the area where the proceeding is criminal in form but civil in substance,—the so-called "civil offense." And the first step was unavoidable. To insure proper maintenance of roads and bridges a statutory fine was provided for those who, having the duty to make needed repairs thereof, failed to do so. If a corporation had such a duty, which it neglected to perform, no sound reason against its conviction was available. And it was but a short step from recognition of corporate guilt of a civil offense based on nonfeasance to such guilt based on misfeasance. Since such an offense does not have the normal mens rea requirement for criminal guilt, and conviction may be supported on the basis of *respondeat superior*, the possibility of convicting a corporation of a civil offense became firmly established.[4] For years it seemed that the change from the original position would stop at this point and that a corporation would be held incapable of committing a true crime on the ground that the corporation could not have mens rea. "[C]orporations are not properly indictable for crimes involving a criminal state of mind, . . ." said a writer [5] as late as 1914. And ten years later another writer pointed out that the numerous statements in regard to convicting a corporation were chiefly *dicta* except in the civil offense field.[6] Gradually, however, the change moved forward into the area of true crime. On the one hand it was urged that the punishment,—a fine imposed on the corporation, falls upon those who are entirely free from fault as well as upon others who are blameworthy, and hence is unjust.[7] Others urged that nothing less would suffice to keep corporate activities in proper hands.[8] No one seriously urged that it would withhold the

---

1. Anonymous, 12 Mod. 559, 88 Eng. Rep. 1518 (K.B. 1701).

2. 1 Bl.Comm. *476.

3. State v. Great Works Milling & Manufacturing Co., 20 Me. 41 (1841).

4. Overland Cotton Mill Co. v. People, 32 Colo. 263, 75 P. 924 (1904).

5. Canfield, Corporate Responsibility for Crime, 14 Col.L.Rev. 469, 480 (1914).

6. Francis, Criminal Responsibility of the Corporation, 18 Ill.L.Rev. 305 (1924). "Punishment falls on the individual members alone. Such being the case, the punishment is awkward, unscientific, and uncertain." Id. at 322.

7. See the articles in notes 5 and 6.

8. Edgerton, Corporate Criminal Responsibility, 36 Yale L.Jour. 827 (1927).

hand of the law from the guilty individuals because conviction of the corporation would be no bar to a prosecution of those persons who actually caused the harm.

If a truck driver has a fatal traffic accident, as a result of his criminal negligence in driving the vehicle, he is guilty of manslaughter. This will not of itself be sufficient to taint his employer with criminal guilt, but the employer might have sent out the driver with such instructions as to speed, or with a vehicle known to him to be so unsafe, that the employer also acted with criminal negligence. If so, the employer also is guilty of manslaughter if he is an individual. Would a corporate employer be guilty of manslaughter in such a case? The New Jersey court said yes.[9] The New York court said no.[10] In the latter case, however, it was recognized that a corporation can be guilty of a true crime and the reversal of this conviction was based entirely upon the definition of the particular offense. The court pointed out that manslaughter requires homicide and that homicide is defined by its statute (as at common law) as the killing of one human being "by another." This was held, quite properly, to mean the killing by another human being. The court then concluded that a corporation cannot be guilty of manslaughter, overlooking entirely that the corporation can do nothing except by aid of human beings. There could never be a case in which a corporation has killed a human being who was not killed by a human being. Under certain circumstances the act of the employee is imputed to the employer. The difficult problem is to determine whose criminal negligence (or knowledge or intent and so forth) shall be held to be the criminal negligence of the corporation as distinguished from that of an agent of the corporation.[11]

UNITED STATES v. GEORGE F. FISH, INC.

United States Circuit Court of Appeals, Second Circuit, 1946.
154 F.2d 798.

CLARK, CIRCUIT JUDGE. An information filed in the District Court charged the defendants George F. Fish, Inc., a wholesale dealer in fruits and vegetables, and Michael Simon, its salesman, with "unlawfully, wilfully and knowingly" evading the provisions of Revised Maximum Price Regulation No. 426, issued under the authority of § 2, Emergency Price Control Act of 1942, 50 U.S.C.A.Appendix, § 902. After a jury verdict of guilt, the court entered judgment of a fine

---

9. State v. Lehigh Valley R. Co., 90 N.J.L. 372, 103 A. 685 (1917).

10. People v. Rochester Railway & Light Co., 195 N.Y. 102, 88 N.E. 22 (1909).

11. "In all cases where a corporation is convicted of an offense for the commission of which a natural person would be punishable with imprisonment, as for a felony, such corporation is punishable by a fine of not more than five thousand dollars." N.Y.Pen.Laws 1932.

against the corporate defendant, and imprisonment against the individual defendant. 50 U.S.C.A.Appendix, §§ 904, 925(b). Defendants appeal from the conviction, urging the invalidity of the regulation, the failure of the information to allege a crime, the insufficiency of the evidence to support the verdict, and the nonliability of the corporate defendant to criminal prosecution for the acts charged. . . .

The corporate defendant makes a separate contention that the guilt of its salesman is not to be attributed to it. But the Supreme Court has long ago determined that the corporation may be held criminally liable for the acts of an agent within the scope of his employment, and the state and lower federal courts have been consistent in their application of that doctrine. . . .

No distinctions are made in these cases between officers and agents, or between persons holding positions involving varying degrees of responsibility. And this seems the only practical conclusion in any case, but particularly here, where the sales proscribed by the Act will almost invariably be performed by subordinate salesmen, rather than by corporate chiefs, and where the corporate hierarchy does not contemplate separate layers of official dignity, each with separate degrees of responsibility. The purpose of the Act is a deterrent one; and to deny the possibility of corporate responsibility for the acts of minor employees is to immunize the offender who really benefits, and open wide the door for evasion. Here Simon acted knowingly and deliberately and hence "wilfully" within the meaning of the Act, and his wilful act is also that of the corporation. . . .

Judgment affirmed.

(Certiorari denied 328 U.S. 869, 66 S.Ct. 1377, 90 L.Ed. 1639.)

PEOPLE v. CANADIAN FUR TRAPPERS CORPORATION

Court of Appeals of New York, 1928.
248 N.Y. 159, 161 N.E. 455.

CRANE, J. The defendant, a corporation, has been found guilty of grand larceny, second degree, and fined $5,000. The argument presented here is that a corporation cannot commit the crime of larceny as it is impossible for a corporation as such to have intent to steal or misappropriate property.

We think this question has been fairly well settled to the contrary. . . .

It has long been the law that a corporation may be liable criminally for the acts of its agents in doing things prohibited by statute. . . .

This is the law for corporations whose servants violate positive prohibitions or commands of statutes regarding corporate acts. Such offenses do not necessarily embody the element of intent to commit a crime. The corporation would be guilty of the violation in many instances irrespective of intent or knowledge.

When it comes, however, to such crimes as larceny, there enters as a necessary element the intent accompanying the act. There must be the intent to steal, to misappropriate, to apply the property of another to the use of the corporation to constitute the crime. The mere knowledge and intent of the agent of [or] the servant to steal would not be sufficient in and of itself to make the corporation guilty. While a corporation may be guilty of larceny, may be guilty of the intent to steal, the evidence must go further than in the cases involving solely the violation of prohibitive statutes. The intent must be the intent of the corporation and not merely that of the agent. How this intent may be proved or in what cases it becomes evident depends entirely upon the circumstances of each case. Probably no general rule applicable to all situations could be stated. It has been said that the same evidence which in a civil case would be sufficient to prove a specific or malicious intention upon the part of a corporation defendant would be sufficient to show a like intention upon the part of a corporation charged criminally with the doing of an act prohibited by law (U. S. v. Kelso Co., 86 F. 304), and Judge Hough in U. S. v. New York Herald Co., 159 F. 296, said: "To fasten this species of knowledge upon a corporation requires no other or different kind of legal inference than has long been used to justify punitive damages in cases of tort against an incorporated defendant." See, also, People v. Star Co., 135 App.Div. 517, 120 N.Y.S. 498, where the malicious intent of the agents in writing a libel was attributable to the corporation. See, also, Grant Bros. Construction Co. v. U. S., 13 Ariz. 388, 114 P. 955, and State v. Salisbury Ice & Fuel Co., 166 N.C. 366, 81 S.E. 737, involving false pretenses. Also Standard Oil Co. v. State, 117 Tenn. 618, 100 S.W. 705, where the intent of the officers became the intent of the corporation. Sufficient to say that in this case the law was correctly laid down to the jury by the trial judge when he said: "The defendant is liable in a prosecution for larceny only for acts which it authorizes through action of its officers or which is done with the acquiescence of its officers, and unless the jury find beyond a reasonable doubt such authority or acquiescence, there must be an acquittal." This in my judgment was a correct statement of the law for this case. . . .

In this case the able assistant district attorney, Mr. Marcy, recognized the rule and attempted to bring his evidence within it. He sought to prove that one of the officers of the corporation had given instructions to do the acts constituting larceny and he also sought to prove that there had been such a long-continued user of felonious practices as to prove knowledge or intent upon the part of the corporation. In his attempt to substantiate these elements of the crime, he was largely frustrated by the rulings of the trial judge.

At this point it may be well to state the facts in order to elucidate our meaning. The defendant was a domestic corporation known as Canadian Fur Trappers Corporation, carrying on the business of selling fur coats on the installment plan in Buffalo, N. Y., under the name of "Fields." Four brothers, named Dornfeldt, constituted the corporation and were its only officers. It advertised attractive sales during the summer of 1926. The prosecuting witness, Mrs. Ella Stanley, bought a coat at one of these sales for $295, paying a deposit of $25, the coat to be delivered to her upon payment of the balance. There was no time fixed in which the balance was to be paid. The evidence fairly shows that the defendant agreed to keep the coat in storage or on deposit for Mrs. Stanley until the balance was paid. Later in the fall when she paid the balance the coat was gone. It had been disposed of and there was evidence which would justify the jury in believing that some one in the defendant's employ had resold the coat. The defendant's employees and officers attempted to deliver to Mrs. Stanley another coat which they said was the one she had selected. In this they were evidently mistaken, if not willfully falsifying, as the coat was of a different size and make. The evidence is quite conclusive upon this point. There is also evidence to show that the coat which this defendant through its employees attempted to deliver to Mrs. Stanley as the one purchased had been theretofore sold to Vera M. Owen. Whatever became of Mrs. Stanley's coat no one apparently knows. The fact is she did not receive it when she paid the balance of her money, and the coat which was offered to her was not the one she had selected. The evidence sustains this conclusion. Of course upon these facts alone, these two transactions, the defendant could not be found guilty of larceny as defined by our penal law. It is at this point the People, therefore, attempted to prove that the officers of the corporation had instructed the employees to resell the coats held on deposit and that this was the method of doing business. When a coat was purchased and the deposit paid, instead of keeping the coat for the purchaser, as the defendant promised to do, until the balance was paid, the course of business was to resell the coat many times and deliver it to whomever first paid the full purchase price. Such facts, if proved, would no doubt establish larceny by the corporation. The difficulty arises over the failure of this proof. . . .

This leaves the charge against the defendant resting upon the sale to Mrs. Stanley and the evidence of the resale or attempted resale later of Mrs. Owen's coat to Mrs. Stanley. The defendant's officers and employees denied that they had resold Mrs. Stanley's coat or that such was their method of doing business.

Under the law as correctly charged in this case by the trial judge, the defendant corporation was criminally liable only for such felonious acts as it had authorized through the Dornfeldts, the officers of the corporation, or for such acts as through a course of business must have been known to the corporation and its officers, and thus authorized by them. The People failed to prove that the officers or any one acting as manager of the Buffalo store, in the place and stead of the officers had authorized a resale of the complainant's coat; and further, that if the complainant's coat was resold, the resale of purchased coats was a continuous and established practice in the defendant's establishment. . . .

There are other rulings which we think were not quite correct, but it is unnecessary to refer to them, as in view of what is here said the judgment of the Appellate Division and that of the County Court should be reversed and a new trial ordered.

CARDOZO, C. J., POUND, ANDREWS, LEHMAN, KELLOGG and O'BRIEN, JJ., concur.

Judgments reversed, etc.[1]

STATE v. HOLDREN

Supreme Court of Montana, 1963.
143 Mont. 103, 387 P.2d 446.

[Norman G. Holdren was the executive officer of United Businesses, Inc., a corporation doing business as a collecting agency, under the name of Professional Collector's and Personal Budget Service. This corporation collected $285.33 for the Montana Reserve Finance Corporation which never received any part of this sum. The evidence indicated that it and the money of other clients was wrongfully appropriated by the first corporation for its own purposes.]

CASTLES, JUSTICE. The appellant, Norman G. Holdren, hereinafter referred to as defendant, was convicted on two counts on a charge of grand larceny of property held by him as an agent, under R.C.M.1947, § 94–2701, subd. 2. A two year sentence was imposed on each count; said sentences to be served concurrently. This appeal is taken from the judgment of conviction entered on the verdicts. . . .

Defendant makes three specifications of error. The first is "That the Court erred in refusing to dismiss the informations . . . for the reasons that there is a fatal variance between the pleadings and the proof . . . .."

R.C.M.1947, § 94–2701, is denominated as our larceny statute. It is divided into two subsections, and covers both the crimes of lar-

---

1. The president of a corporation is not criminally liable for the acts of his subordinate unless they are authorized or consented to by him. State v. Carmean, 126 Iowa 291, 102 N.W. 97 (1905). But the president of a corporation can be convicted, on proof by circumstantial evidence, that he aided and abetted his subordinates in their criminal activities. Nye & Nissen v. United States, 336 U.S. 613, 69 S.Ct. 766, 93 L.Ed. 919 (1949).

ceny and embezzlement. Defendant has been convicted on both counts of the crime of embezzlement. "The crime of embezzlement is based solely on statute and is designed to penalize those conversions which could not be prosecuted at common law as larceny because there was no trespassory taking. In most jurisdictions, this distinction between embezzlement and larceny has been preserved. In some jurisdictions, however, the definition of larceny has been expanded so as to include embezzlement." II Wharton, Criminal Law, § 514, (Anderson, 1957) pp. 191–192. (Citing Montana as being one of those jurisdictions.)

Such is the case here in Montana. R.C.M.1947, § 94–2701, subd. (1), is the statutory codification of the common-law crime of larceny. Subdivision (2) codifies the crime of embezzlement. These subsections combined now constitute the crime of larceny in Montana. . . .

Now, turning to the second question presented in the first specification of error. Must it have been shown that this defendant individually acted as the agent of Montana Reserve Finance before his conviction can be sustained?

We have already demonstrated that the corporation was an agent under the statute. But in this case, under these facts, should the existence of this corporate entity shield this defendant from individually being held responsible for a criminal act? We think not.

"If any general rule can be laid down . . ., it is that a corporation will be looked upon as a legal entity . . . until sufficient reason to the contrary appears; but, when the notion of legal entity is used to defeat public convenience, justify wrong, protect fraud, or *defend crime*, the law will regard the corporation as an association of persons." Emphasis supplied. United States v. Milwaukee Refrigerator Transit Co., 7 Cir., 142 F. 247, 255. "It [the corporate entity] has also been said to be properly disregarded in criminal prosecutions against the real offender although this may be criticised as circuitous reasoning to hold one responsible for his own crime." 1 Fletcher, Cyclopedia Corporations, § 41 (perm. ed. 1931) p. 139.

There is nothing particularly unusual or startling about "piercing the corporate veil" or as it is sometimes called "disregarding the corporate entity". This has been done in Montana in civil matters on several instances. . . .

We also have State v. Hall, 45 Mont. 498, 125 P. 639, which is a criminal case involving facts somewhat similar to the instant case. . . .

Counsel for defendant, in oral argument, admitted that the Hall case could not be distinguished but said that it was "bad law". The effect of defendant's argument, as applied to the facts of that and this case, standing by itself, would put the business community of this state at the mercy of every collection agency which had the foresight to incorporate. Here, as there, with these facts such cannot be the case. . . .

Therefore, under these facts, the corporate entity does not shield this defendant from individually being held responsible for his criminal act.

For the above reasons we find there was no fatal variance between that which was plead and the facts proved. . . .

The judgment is affirmed.

JAMES T. HARRISON, C. J., and JOHN CONWAY HARRISON, ADAIR, DOYLE, JJ., concur.

MODEL PENAL CODE

Section 2.07. Liability of Corporations, Unincorporated Associations and Persons Acting, or Under a Duty to Act, in Their Behalf.

(1) A corporation may be convicted of the commission of an offense if:

(a) the offense is a violation or the offense is defined by a statute other than the Code in which a legislative purpose to impose liability on corporations plainly appears and the conduct is performed by an agent of the corporation acting in behalf of the corporation within the scope of his office or employment, except that if the law defining the offense designates the agents for whose conduct the corporation is accountable or the circumstances under which it is accountable, such provisions shall apply; or

(b) the offense consists of an omission to discharge a specific duty of affirmative performance imposed on corporations by law; or

(c) the commission of the offense was authorized, requested, commanded, performed or recklessly tolerated by the board of directors or by a high managerial agent acting in behalf of the corporation within the scope of his office or employment.

(2) When absolute liability is imposed for the commission of an offense, a legislative purpose to impose liability on a corporation shall be assumed, unless the contrary plainly appears.

(3) An unincorporated association may be convicted of the commission of an offense if:

(a) the offense is defined by a statute other than the Code which expressly provides for the liability of such an association and the conduct is performed by an agent of the association acting in behalf of the association within the scope of his office or employment, except that if the law defining the offense designates the agents for whose conduct the association is accountable or the circumstances under which it is accountable, such provisions shall apply; or

(b) the offense consists of an omission to discharge a specific duty of affirmative performance imposed on associations by law.

(4) As used in this Section:

(a) "corporation" does not include an entity organized as or by a governmental agency for the execution of a governmental program;

(b) "agent" means any director, officer, servant, employee or other person authorized to act in behalf of the corporation or association and, in the case of an unincorporated association, a member of such association;

(c) "high managerial agent" means an officer of a corporation or an unincorporated association, or, in the case of a partnership, a partner, or any other agent of a corporation or association having duties of such responsibility that his conduct may fairly be assumed to represent the policy of the corporation or association.

(5) In any prosecution of a corporation or an unincorporated association for the commission of an offense included within the terms of Subsection (1) (a) or Subsection (3) (a) of this Section, other than an offense for which absolute liability has been imposed, it shall be a defense if the defendant proves by a preponderance of evidence that the high managerial agent having supervisory responsibility over the subject matter of the offense employed due diligence to prevent its commission. This paragraph shall not apply if it is plainly inconsistent with the legislative purpose in defining the particular offense.

(6) (a) A person is legally accountable for any conduct he performs or causes to be performed in the name of the corporation or an unincorporated association or in its behalf to the same extent as if it were performed in his own name or behalf.

(b) Whenever a duty to act is imposed by law upon a corporation or an unincorporated association, any agent of the corporation or association having primary responsibility for the discharge of the duty is legally accountable for a reckless omission to perform the required act to the same extent as if the duty were imposed by law directly upon himself.

(c) When a person is convicted of an offense by reason of his legal accountability for the conduct of a corporation or an unincorporated association, he is subject to the sentence authorized by law when a natural person is convicted of an offense of the grade and the degree involved.

SECTION 8. PARTIES TO CRIME

The common law applied the label "accessory" to certain parties guilty of crime. This was in felony cases only. There was no accessory to treason or to misdemeanor. This has reference only to the label and not to the question of guilt. With one exception the party who would be called *accessory* in a felony case is a guilty *principal* in case of either treason or misdemeanor.[1] The lone exception is this:

---

1. State v. Scott, 80 Conn. 317, 323, 68 A. 258, 260 (1907).

Sec. 8   *PARTIES TO CRIME*   297

one who would be an accessory *after* the fact in a felony case is not regarded as a guilty party if the offense is a misdemeanor. He is a principal if it is treason.

In felony cases the ancient common law used the word principal to apply only to the perpetrator of the crime. Any other guilty party was an accessory. And based upon the elements of time and place, accessories were classified as (1) accessory before the fact, (2) accessory at the fact, and (3) accessory after the fact.[2] One who was not himself the perpetrator of the felony, but who counseled or commanded it, or encouraged or assisted the perpetrator in any way with guilty knowledge, was an accessory before the fact if not present at the perpetration and an accessory at the fact if present at that time. After the felony had been committed one, not himself the perpetrator[3] but having knowledge of the felony, who gave aid to the perpetrator in order to hinder his apprehension, trial, conviction or punishment, was an accessory after the fact.[4]

At a relatively early day a change was made in one of the labels used. The guilty party who anciently was called accessory at the fact came to be known as a principal in the second degree.[5] Hence the modern common law, in felony cases, recognizes two kinds of guilty parties and two varieties of each. Principals are either in the first degree or the second degree, and accessories are either before the fact or after the fact. The closest resemblance is between the principal in the second degree and the accessory before the fact. Exactly the same kind of guilty counsel, command, encouragement or aid which will make one a principal in the second degree, if present at the moment of perpetration, will make him an accessory before the fact if he is absent,[6]—except that factually more opportunities are available if he is present. This came to be the determining factor at this point of the classification scheme. One so situated as to be in a position to give actual assistance to the perpetrator, at the very moment of perpetration, is held to be present constructively if not actually.[7]

---

2. Ibid.

3. "One who is a principal cannot be an accessory after the fact." People v. Chadwick, 7 Utah 134, 138, 25 P. 737, 738 (1891). One who would have been an accessory before the fact at common law probably may be accessory after the fact also, even if declared to be a principal by statute. Cf. Aaronson v. United States, 175 F.2d 41 (4th Cir. 1949). In order to avoid an absurd result in the interpretation of statutes dealing with the testimony of an accomplice, the California court felt it was necessary to say that a murderer can be accessory after the fact to his own murder. People v. Wallin, 32 Cal.2d 803, 197 P.2d 734 (1948). This is quite out of line with the body of the case law.

4. One who attempts to frustrate the prosecution of a murderer, by telling those present at the time of the crime not to tell what they know, is accessory after the fact. Fields v. State, 213 Ark. 899, 214 S.W.2d 230 (1948).

5. 1 Hale P.C. *437.

6. Id. at p. 435.

7. 4 Bl.Comm. *34. See Skidmore v. State, 80 Neb. 698, 700, 115 N.W. 288, 289 (1908).

Hence if one so situated is a guilty party he is a principal in the second degree even if his guilt consisted in counsel or encouragement given at a previous time. The typical case of a guilty party who is constructively present (and hence a principal in the second degree rather than an accessory before the fact) is the lookout who is posted on the outside of a building while another enters to commit a felony inside.[8] The most extreme example involved the hold-up of a stagecoach. One of the conspirators stationed himself on a mountain top, thirty or forty miles from the intended ambush and signaled the approach of the vehicle by smoke from a controlled fire. Because so situated as to be of assistance at the moment he was held to be a principal in the second degree.[9]

The law of accessories developed at a time when all felonies (except petit larceny) were punishable by death, and when statutes had made felonies out of a multitude of misdeeds not sufficiently grave to merit such a penalty. It was one of several devices employed to reduce the number of capital convictions. These handicaps upon prosecution have been removed for the most part by modern statutes and hence will be stated very briefly. Chiefly they were: (1) Jurisdiction. A principal was triable at the situs of the crime,[10] but an accessory who incited the perpetration of a felony in another jurisdiction was triable only where his act of accessoryship occurred.[11] (2) Pleading. One charged as a principal could not be convicted if the evidence established accessorial guilt,[12] and one charged as accessory could not be convicted on proof showing him to be a principal.[13] (3) Trial. The accessory could not be forced to trial before the trial of the principal.[14] Hence if the principal was never apprehended, or died before conviction, or was acquitted, there was no possibility of convicting the accessory.[15] (4) Degree of guilt. An accessory could not be recognized as guilty of a higher crime than the principal.[16]

The fact that there was no need for such rules (other than to reduce the number of capital convictions) is shown by the fact that no corresponding rules applied to principals in different degrees. (1) Jurisdiction. Since the principal in the second degree is always present at the perpetration, constructively if not actually, his abetment (in legal theory) is always at the same place as the perpetration by

---

8. Clark v. Commonwealth, 269 Ky. 833, 108 S.W.2d 1036 (1937).

9. State v. Hamilton, 13 Nev. 386 (1878).

10. State v. Hall, 114 N.C. 909, 19 S.E. 602 (1894).

11. 1 Hale P.C. *623.

12. Smith v. State, 37 Ark. 274 (1881); Skidmore v. State, 80 Neb. 698, 115 N.W. 288 (1908).

13. Regina v. Brown, 14 Cox C.C. 144 (1878).

14. 1 Hale P.C. *623; 2 Pollock and Maitland, History of English Law 509 (2d ed. 1899).

15. 1 Hale P.C. *625. Commonwealth v. Phillips, 16 Mass. 423, 425 (1820).

16. 4 Bl.Comm. *36; Tomlin v. State, 155 Tex.Cr.R. 207, 233 S.W.2d 303 (1950).

the principal in the first degree. Hence the court having jurisdiction over the case of one principal will also have jurisdiction over that of the other.[17] (2) Pleading. It is not necessary for the indictment or information to disclose whether the defendant is a principal in one degree or the other.[18] (3) Trial. The principal in the second degree may be tried and convicted prior to the trial of the principal in the first degree,[19] or even after his acquittal.[20] (4) Degree of guilt. The principal in the second degree may be convicted of a higher degree of guilt than the principal in the first degree. The former may be convicted of murder, for example, although the latter has been convicted of manslaughter,[21] since an abettor may counsel with malice aforethought what the other perpetrates in the sudden heat of passion.[22] In other words, the designation of a principal as of one degree or the other is merely a factual description without legal significance.[23] The accessory before the fact to a felony is often the "man higher up" who is more of a social menace than the underlings he employs. There is no sound reason why he should not be called a "principal," and treated as such for all purposes, just as he would be if the crime were treason or misdemeanor. And the trend is in this direction.

With reference to the accessory after the fact the problem is somewhat different. Although anciently his punishment was the same as that of the principal,[24] provisions for a milder penalty made their appearance at a very early day.[25] The present trend is to retain the label "accessory after the fact," remove procedural obstacles from the prosecution and conviction of such a party, provide a milder punishment than that established for the principal, and exclude from this type of guilt those who are intimately related to the principal.

17. State v. Hamilton, 13 Nev. 386 (1878).

18. 1 Hale P.C. *437–8; Adkins v. State, 187 Ga. 519, 1 S.E.2d 420 (1939).

19. 1 Hale P.C. *437; Regina v. Griffeth, 1 Pl. 97, 75 Eng.Rep. 152 (1553).

20. Regina v. Wallis, 1 Salk. 334, 91 Eng.Rep. 294 (1703); Rooney v. United States, 203 F. 928, (9th Cir. 1913); People v. Newberry, 20 Cal. 439 (1862); State v. Lee, 91 Iowa 499, 60 N.W. 119 (1894); State v. Phillips, 24 Mo. 475 (1857). And see People v. Blackwood, 35 Cal.App.2d 728, 733, 96 P.2d 982 (1939). Contra: State v. Haines, 51 La.Ann. 731, 25 So. 372 (1899). The trend of the modern statutes is in the direction of permitting an accessory to be convicted after the acquittal of the principal. The guilt of the principal must be shown in order to convict the accessory but the previous acquittal of the principal is not *res judicata* of the principal's innocence as between the commonwealth and the accused. Commonwealth v. Long, 246 Ky. 809, 56 S.W.2d 524 (1933).

21. 1 Hale P.C. *438; Bruce v. State, 99 Ga. 50, 25 S.E. 760 (1896).

22. 1 East P.C. 350 (1803).

23. "[T]he distinction between principals in the first and second degrees is a distinction without a difference." State v. Whitt, 113 N.C. 716, 720, 18 S.E. 715, 719 (1893). Quoting from Wharton on Criminal Law.

24. 4 Bl.Comm. *39.

25. A number of the early statutes denied benefit of clergy to the principal and to the accessory before, without extending such denial to the accessory after. Ibid.

Differences are to be found in the enactments and in their interpretation. And to what extent, if any, the present law of a particular state falls short of the trends mentioned, in regard to one type of accessory or the other, can be determined only by a study of its statutes and decisions.

In outline form the character of the party (1) and the name applied (2) may be indicated as follows:

A. (1) The actual perpetrator of the crime:

    (2) Felony—principal in the first degree. Treason—principal. Misdemeanor—principal.

B. (1) One not the actual perpetrator who, with mens rea, counsels or commands the other to commit the crime, or gives him any encouragement or assistance in doing so, and is present actually or constructively at the moment of perpetration: [26]

    (2) Felony—principal in the second degree. Treason—principal. Misdemeanor—principal.

C. (1) Same, except not present either actually or constructively at the moment of perpetration:

    (2) Felony—accessory before the fact, at common law, with the statutory trend in the direction of applying the label "principal". Treason—principal. Misdemeanor —principal.

D. (1) One not the perpetrator who, with knowledge of the crime, gives aid or comfort to the perpetrator in the effort to hinder his apprehension, trial, conviction or punishment:

    (2) Felony—accessory after the fact. Treason—principal. Misdemeanor—not a guilty party without additional facts.

The word "accomplice" is a broader word than either "principal" or "accessory". There is some authority for using the word accomplice to include all principals and all accessories to a particular crime. The preferred usage, however, is to include all principals and all accessories before the fact, but to exclude accessories after the fact,[27] except that one accessory after the fact might be the accomplice of another accessory after the fact to the same felony.

---

26. The mere fact that a bystander does not interfere in the effort to prevent a murder being committed in his presence does not make him a guilty party to the murder. Connaughty v. State, 1 Wis. 159 (1853). It is otherwise if the bystander owes a duty to protect the victim of the attack. Mobley v. State, 227 Ind. 335, 85 N.E.2d 489 (1949).

27. See Levering v. Commonwealth, 132 Ky. 666, 677, 679, 117 S.W. 253, 257 (1909); People v. Sweeney, 213 N.Y. 37, 46, 106 N.E. 913, 917 (1914); People v. Chadwick, 7 Utah 134, 25 P. 737 (1891).

PEOPLE v. AH GEE

District Court of Appeal, Third Appellate District, California, 1918.
37 Cal.App. 1, 174 P. 371.

HART, J. Defendant and two others, Toy Lee and Foo Kee, were jointly charged, in an information filed by the district attorney of San Joaquin County, with the murder of one Lee Wun, in the city of Stockton, on March 21, 1917. Separate trials of the defendants were had and Ah Gee was convicted of the crime of murder of the first degree and was sentenced to imprisonment in the state prison for the term of his natural life. The appeal is from the judgment and from an order denying defendant's motion for a new trial.

The record discloses that Lee Wun met his death during a tong war. He and the three defendants above named were engaged in the shooting and Foo Kee testified that he was fired upon by one Lim Buck Hee.

There is but one point urged for a reversal and it is this: That the prosecution presented its case upon two distinct and inconsistent theories, to wit: 1. That the defendant aided, abetted, and assisted Toy Lee in the murder of Lee Wun and 2. That Ah Gee himself actually killed and murdered said Lee Wun. In support of this proposition, appellant calls attention to the testimony of the witnesses, C. W. Potter and A. F. Peterson, who testified to having been eyewitnesses to the homicide and who gave testimony for the people. . . .

According to the testimony of Potter, so the argument goes, the defendant, having fired two unavailing shots at the deceased and then ran [sic] away or disappeared from the scene of the homicide, merely aided, abetted, and assisted Toy Lee in the commission of the crime, while, on the other hand, according to the testimony of Peterson, the defendant actually fired the shot which produced the death of Lee Wun. Hence, so the argument proceeds, there were presented by the people two inconsistent theories of the part taken by the defendant in the commission of the crime, and this, it is claimed, is fatal to the result reached by the jury.

The position of the defendant, as above set forth, is not well taken.

Under the common law, a principal in the commission of a crime was of two degrees, viz.: 1. One who was the actual actor or absolute perpetrator of the crime, who was a principal in the first degree; 2. One who was present, actually or constructively, aiding and abetting the fact to be done, who was a principal in the same [sic] degree. (4 Cooley's Blackstone, 4th ed., p. 34.) One who, being absent at the time of the crime committed, procured, counseled, or commanded another to commit the crime, was an accessory before the fact, and under the common law it was necessary to prosecute, try, and punish him as such accessory and not as a principal. (Id., p. 37). The distinction between a principal in the second degree and an accessory before the fact, it will be observed, was founded upon the presence or nonpresence at the commission of the crime of the party aiding and abetting the actual perpetrator of the act which constituted the final consummation of the crime in its commission. . . .

Thus, undoubtedly, our legislature viewed the proposition and, therefore, by express mandate, has abrogated the mere formal distinction (and it was no more than this) existing at common law between principals in the commission of crimes and accessories before the fact, or those participating in their commission without actually perpetrating the acts which, with the intent, constitute the crime. Therefore, whatever may be the law in other jurisdictions, the rule in this state, as laid down by the legislature, is that "all persons concerned in the commission of a crime, whether it be felony or misdemeanor, *and whether they directly commit the act constituting the offense, or aid and abet in its commission, or, not being present, have advised and encouraged its commission,* . . . are principals in any crime so committed." (Pen.Code, sec. 31.) Again, the rule, as promulgated by the legislature, is that "the distinction between an accessory before the fact and a principal, and between principals in the first and second degree, in cases of felony, is abrogated; and all persons concerned in the commission of a felony, *whether they directly commit the act constituting the offense, or aid and abet in its commission, though not present,* shall hereafter be *prosecuted, tried* and punished as principals, and no other facts need be alleged in any indictment or information against such an accessory than are required in an indictment or information against his principal." (Pen. Code, sec. 971.) . . .

Under our code sections, above quoted herein, an accessory is not only to be charged in the accusatory pleading as a principal, but is also to be *tried* as a principal; hence it is immaterial what the proof shows was the nature of the part that the accused took in the commission of the crime—that is, it is not a matter of material importance whether he is shown to have been the actual perpetrator of the criminal act or only aided and abetted in its commission. In either case, he is a principal, and it can make no difference in the proof of the charge what particular act he did or part he took in the execution of the criminal act that made him one.

In the present case, the defendant, jointly with two others, is charged in the information with the murder of Lee Wun. There is but one count in the information and that is the usual or common one by which murder, as defined by the law, is charged. There is no attempt at describing how or in what manner the act was committed or any allegation that the defendant was merely an aider and abettor of the crime, an allegation which is not required under our law. The prosecution was entitled to prove the charge by any testimony which would reveal the defendant's connection therewith. It happened that, while one of the witnesses presented by the people to support the charge testified that he saw the defendant fire a shot into the body of Lee Wun, another witness, likewise presented, testified that the accused fired a couple of shots at the deceased, which apparently failed of their mark, and then disappeared from the scene of the shooting. Even according to the common law, the defendant would be a principal under the testimony of the witness Potter. But the testimony of both witnesses was material, relevant, and competent, and, therefore, clearly admissible in any event as tending to prove the ultimate fact in issue, viz.: That the defendant killed and murdered Lee Wun. Indeed, the objection to the testimony on the ground that it tended to establish two different theories upon which the defendant might have been a participant in the commission of the crime does not go to the proposition that said testimony does not show, or tend to show, the guilt of the accused of the crime charged but to the proposition that he was a party to the commission of the crime in two different ways. As we view the situation, the proposition is no different in principle from a case where one witness for the people had testified that the deceased had been killed by a blow with a club in the hands of and wielded by the defendant, while another witness for the people had testified that the death of the deceased had been produced by the defendant by means of a knife, the particular manner in which death was produced not being alleged in the indictment.

But, as stated, the people had the right to make the proof as it was made and leave to the judgment of the jury the question whether upon the whole the evidence was of sufficient probative force to warrant the conviction in their minds that, beyond a reasonable doubt, the defendant, whatever might have been the nature or extent of the part he might have taken in the commission of the act, was guilty as charged. . . .

The judgment and the order are affirmed.[1]

CHIPMAN, P. J., and BURNETT, J., concurred.

A petition to have the cause heard in the supreme court, after judgment in the district court of appeal, was denied by the supreme court on June 14, 1918.

---

1. One may be convicted of voluntary manslaughter as an accessory before the fact although the perpetrator has been convicted of murder in the first degree. Moore v. Lowe, Sheriff, 116 W.Va. 165, 180 S.E. 1 (1935), certiorari denied 296 U.S. 574, 56 S.Ct. 130, 80 L.Ed. 406. Cf. State v. McVay, 47 R.I. 292, 132 A. 436 (1926).

"In order to sustain the conviction of a defendant who had been charged as an aider or abettor, it is necessary that there be evidence showing an offense to have been committed by a principal and that the principal was aided and abetted by the accused, although it is not necessary that the principal be convicted or even that the identity of the principal be established". Hendrix v. United States, 327 F.2d 971, 975 (5th Cir. 1964).

PEOPLE v. KEEFER

Supreme Court of California, Department One, 1884.
65 Cal. 232, 3 P. 818.

McKINSTRY, J. Counsel for defendant asked the court to charge the jury:

"If you believe from the evidence that the defendant James Keefer was not present when the Chinaman *Lee Yuen* was killed by *Chapman*, and did not aid and abet in the killing, and that defendant, at the time or prior to the killing, had not conspired with *Chapman* to commit the act, and that he had not advised and encouraged *Chapman* therein, and that the killing was not done in pursuance of any conspiracy between this defendant and *Chapman* to rob said Chinaman, and that this defendant only assisted in throwing the dead body of the Chinaman into the creek, then you are instructed that, under the indictment, you must find the defendant not guilty."

It is to be regretted that the foregoing instruction was not given to the jury. Of course, if defendant had done no act which made him responsible for the murder, the mere fact that he aided in concealing the dead body would render him liable only as accessory after the fact—an offense of which he could not be found guilty under an indictment for murder. However incredible the testimony of defendant he was undoubtedly entitled to an instruction based upon the hypothesis that his testimony was entirely true.

Assuming the testimony of defendant to be true, there was evidence tending to show that no robbery was committed or attempted. In robbery, as in larceny, it must appear that the goods were taken *animo furandi*; and there was evidence tending to prove that his property was not taken from deceased *lucri causa*, or with intent to deprive him of it permanently. So also there was evidence tending to prove that defendant was not personally present at the killing, and that the killing was not done in pursuance of any agreement or understanding to which defendant was a party, but that it was done by Chapman without the knowledge, assent, or connivance of the defendant.

The testimony of defendant was to the effect that he did not advise or encourage Chapman to follow and *tie* the deceased. But even if we could be supposed to be justified in deciding the *fact*, in holding that his conduct conclusively proved—notwithstanding his testimony to the contrary—that he did encourage Chapman in his purpose to follow and tie the deceased, such encouragement would not of itself, make him accessory to the killing. An accessory before the fact to a robbery (or any other of the felonies mentioned in section 198 of the Penal Code), although not present when the felony is perpetrated or attempted, is guilty of a murder committed in the perpetration or attempt to perpetrate the felony. This is by reason of the statute, and because the law super-adds the intent to kill to the original felonious intent. One who has only advised or encouraged a misdemeanor, however, is not *necessarily* responsible for a murder committed by his co-conspirator, not in furtherance, but independent of the common design.

In the case at bar, if defendant simply encouraged the *tying* of the deceased—a misdemeanor which did not and probably could not cause death or any serious injury—as the killing by Chapman was neither necessarily nor probably involved in the battery or false imprisonment, nor incidental to it, but was an independent and malicious act with which defendant had no connection, the jury were not authorized to find defendant guilty of the murder, or of manslaughter. If the deceased had been strangled by the cords with which he had been carelessly or recklessly bound by Chapman, or had died in consequence of exposure to the elements while tied, defendant might have been held liable. But, if the testimony of defendant was true—and as we have said, he was entitled to an instruction based upon the assumption that the facts were as he stated them to be—the killing of deceased was an independent act of Chapman, neither aided, advised, nor encouraged by him, and not involved in nor incidental to any act by him aided, advised, or encouraged. The court erred in refusing the instruction. . . .

Judgment and order reversed and cause remanded for a new trial.

Ross, J., concurring. As there was testimony tending to show that defendant was not personally present at the killing, and that the killing was not done in pursuance of any agreement or undertaking to which defendant was a party, I agree that the court below erred in refusing to give the instruction first set out in the opinion of Mr. Justice McKinstry, and therefore concur in the judgment. I also agree with what is said in the opinion upon the last point discussed.

McKee, J., concurred in the opinion of Mr. Justice Ross.[1]

STATE v. WILLIAMS

Supreme Court of North Carolina, 1948.
229 N.C. 348, 49 S.E.2d 617.

The defendants were indicted for being accessories after the fact to the felony of the murder of Thompson Hooker by Bud Hicks. The indictment contained the specific allegation that the aid rendered to the principal offender, Bud Hicks, by the defendants consisted in

---

[1] If an officer is disarmed, and killed with his own weapon, one who had assisted in the disarming is not guilty of murder if he did not know, or have reason to know, that shooting was intended. Lee v. State, 152 Tex.Cr.R. 401, 214 S.W.2d 619 (1948).

transporting him from the scene of his crime for the purpose of enabling him to escape apprehension and punishment.

Testimony was presented at the trial by both the prosecution and the defense. This evidence is stated below in the light most favorable to the State.

On the afternoon of Sunday, June 6, 1948, Bud Hicks deliberately shot and wounded Thompson Hooker without provocation while the latter was standing before his doorstep at 404 Ramseur Street in Sanford. Immediately after the shooting, Hicks fled from Sanford to a rural section of Lee County in an automobile owned by himself and driven by the defendant, Prentiss Watson. Hicks and Watson were accompanied on this flight by the defendants, Annie Williams and Elizabeth Badgett. Peace officers found Hicks and his companions at the home of Annie Williams in a country neighborhood in Lee County at a later hour of the afternoon. Hicks, Watson, and Annie Williams thereupon sought unsuccessfully to dissuade the officers from arresting Hicks by falsely representing that Hicks had not been in Sanford any time that day. After all these events had transpired, namely, on Monday, June 7, 1948, Thompson Hooker died in consequence of his gun-shot wound.

Elizabeth Badgett was acquitted, but the jury found Annie Williams and Prentiss Watson guilty as charged in the bill of indictment. Judgment was pronounced against both of these parties. Watson accepted his sentence, and Annie Williams appealed to this Court, assigning as error the denial of her motion for judgment of nonsuit made when the State rested its case and renewed when all the evidence was concluded.

ERVIN, JUSTICE. When the State prosecutes one upon the charge of being an accessory after the fact to the felony of murder, it assumes the burden of proving the three essential elements of the offense, namely: (1) That the principal felon had actually committed the felony of murder; (2) that the accused knew that such felony had been committed by the principal felon; and (3) that the accused received, relieved, comforted, or assisted the principal felon in some way in order to help him escape, or to hinder his arrest, trial, or punishment. . . .

In the nature of things, one cannot become an accessory after the fact to a felony until such felony has become an accomplished fact. Consequently, it is well established in law that "one cannot be convicted as an accessory after the fact unless the felony be complete, and until such felony has been consummated, any aid or assistance rendered to a party in order to enable him to escape the consequences of his crime will not make the person affording the assistance an accessory after the fact." . . .

Thus, it is held that a person cannot be convicted as an accessory after the fact to a murder because he aided the murderer to escape, when the aid was rendered after the mortal wound was given, but before death ensued, as a murder is not complete until the death results. . . .

Such is the instant case. The evidence disclosed that the assistance, which was alleged to have been rendered by the appellant, Annie Williams, with intent to enable the principal felon, Bud Hicks, to escape, was given after Thompson Hooker had been mortally wounded, but before he died. Hence, the testimony showed that the felony of murder was not an accomplished fact when the assistance was given, and the Court erred in denying the appellant's motion for judgment of involuntary nonsuit. G.S. § 15–173.

The statute provides for punishment for any person becoming an accessory after the fact to any felony, "whether the same be a felony at common law or by virtue of any statute made, or to be made." G.S. § 14–7. Since no such charge is laid in the present indictment, we refrain from expressing any opinion as to whether the evidence made out a case for the jury against the appellant as an accessory after the fact to the statutory felony of a secret assault under G.S. § 14–31 or the statutory felony of an assault with intent to kill under G.S. § 14–32. But it is noted that there are at least two interesting decisions in other States in which similar problems are considered. . . .

For the reasons stated, the judgment pronounced against the appellant, Annie Williams, in the court below is

Reversed.[1]

LAW v. COMMONWEALTH

Supreme Court of Appeals of Virginia, 1881.
75 Va. 885.

STAPLES, J., delivered the opinion of the court.

The accused was indicted in the county court of Franklin as principal in the second degree, for aiding and abetting one John Henry Law in committing the crime of rape. Upon the trial, the Commonwealth proved the offence, and that John H. Law, the principal in the first degree, had been convicted and sentenced to three years' confinement in the penitentiary. It was further proved that the accused, at the time of the commission of the offence, was of the age of eleven years and eleven months. After the testimony was con-

---

[1]. Accord: Baker v. State, 184 Tenn. 503, 201 S.W.2d 667 (1947).

P sold counterfeit bills to R who sold them to D, all three knowing them to be counterfeit. P's knowledge that R probably would sell them to a guilty buyer, rather than attempt to pass them to an innocent taker, does not make P an accessory to the unlawful possession by D. United States v. Peoni, 100 F.2d 401 (2d Cir. 1938).

cluded his counsel asked the court to give the jury the following instructions:

"The court instructs the jury that if they believe, from the evidence, that Nathaniel Thomas Law was under fourteen years of age at the time of the commission of the crime charged, and did not have the capacity to commit it, they must acquit him."

"The court further instructs the jury that if they believe, from the evidence, that John Henry Law, the principal in the first degree, was not guilty of rape, but only of an attempt to commit rape, they cannot find Nathaniel Thomas Law guilty of principal in the second degree; provided, they believe he was under the age of fourteen, but must acquit him."

These instructions were refused by the court, and the accused excepted. Thereupon the jury found him guilty, and fixed his term of confinement in the penitentiary at three years. He then submitted a motion for a new trial upon the ground that the verdict was contrary to the law and the evidence; which motion was overruled and judgment rendered upon the verdict. To that judgment the accused applied for a writ of error to the circuit court, which was refused. He then applied for and obtained a writ of error from one of the judges of this court.

The first question to be considered is, whether the county court erred in refusing the instructions asked for by the accused. The theory of these instructions, so far as we can understand them, is that John Henry Law, the principal in the first degree, was convicted of a mere attempt at rape, and as the accused, by reason of his tender years, was incapable either of the crime of rape or an attempt at its commission, he cannot be convicted of either offence—as principal in the first or principal in the second degree.

It has long been settled in England that an infant under fourteen years of age, by reason of his supposed impotency, cannot be guilty of the crime of rape or of an attempt at its commission, although he may be convicted of an assault with an intent to commit the offence. This doctrine of the English courts has never been fully recognized in this country. In some of the States it has been expressly repudiated. In Virginia it does not appear to have been passed upon by any court of the last resort. The purposes of this case do not require that it be considered now; for here the accused is charged simply as principal in the second degree, with aiding and assisting another in the perpetration of the crime. And although the infant may himself be incapable of committing the specific offence, yet, if of sufficient natural discretion, he may be present, aiding and assisting another in its perpetration. The rule is thus laid down in 2d Archibald Crim.Prac. and Plead. 156: "For though in other felonies, *malitia supplet aetatem*, yet as to this particular species of felony (rape) the law supposes an embecility of body as well as of mind.

But as this doctrine is founded upon the ground of impotency rather than want of discretion, a boy under fourteen who *aids* and *assists* another person in the commission of the offence, is not the less a principal in the second degree, if it appear under all the circumstances that he had a mischievous discretion." And this is the result of all the authorities, without an exception. It is not at all important to inquire whether John H. Law, the principal in the first degree, was convicted of rape or of the mere attempt. Inasmuch as he was sentenced to confinement in the penitentiary for three years only, and as the minimum punishment for rape is ten years' confinement, the inference is inevitable that he was convicted of the lesser offence. The punishment for the attempt is not less than three nor more than eighteen years' imprisonment. The attempt is therefore a felony, and in every case of felony the principal in the second degree is punishable as if he was the principal in the first degree. So that the person who attempts to commit rape and does any act towards its commission, and the person who aids and abets him in that attempt, are equally guilty and alike punishable. It is apparent, therefore, that the county court committed no error in refusing to give the instructions asked for by the counsel for the accused. . . .[1]

(For other reasons the judgment was reversed and the case remanded for a new trial.)

THE KING v. RICHARDSON

Old Bailey, 1785.
1 Leach 387, 168 Eng.Rep. 296.

At the Old Bailey in June Session 1785, Daniel Richardson and Samuel Greenow were indicted before Mr. Justice Buller for a highway robbery on John Billings.

It appeared in evidence, that the two prisoners accosted the prosecutor as he was walking along the street, by asking him, in a peremptory manner, what money he had in his pocket? that upon his replying that he had only two-pence half-penny, one of the prisoners immediately said to the other, "if he really has no more do not take that," and turned as if with an intention to go away; but the other prisoner, stopped the prosecutor, and robbed him of the two-pence half-penny, which was all the money he had about him. But

---

1. A person not a state official may be guilty of the crime of embezzling public funds if he aids and abets an official in this act. People v. Hess, 104 Cal.App.2d 642, 234 P.2d 65 (1951).

The California statute on living together in a state of cohabitation and adultery provides a penalty only for a married person who violates its provisions. Cal.Pen.Code, § 269b (1949). This clear manifestation of legislative intent restricts the finding of guilt as a principal in the second degree. Under this statute, if an unmarried person knowingly so lives with a married person only the latter can be convicted. Re Grace Cooper, 162 Cal. 81, 121 P. 318 (1912).

the prosecutor could not ascertain which of them it was that had used this expression, nor which of them had taken the half-pence from his pocket.

THE COURT. The point of law goes to the acquittal of both the prisoners; for if two men assault another with intent to rob him, and one of them, before any demand of money, or offer to take it be made, repent of what he is doing, and desist from the prosecution of such intent, he cannot be involved in the guilt of his companion who afterwards takes the money; for he changed his evil intention before the act, which completes the offence, was committed. That prisoner therefore, whichever of the two it was who thus desisted, cannot be guilty of the present charge; and the prosecutor cannot ascertain who it was that took the property. One of them is certainly guilty, but which of them personally does not appear. It is like the Ipswich case, where five men were indicted for murder; and it appeared, on a special verdict, that it was murder in one, but not in the other four; but it did not appear which of the five had given the blow which caused the death, and the Court thereupon said, that as the man could not be clearly and positively ascertained, all of them must be discharged.

The two prisoners were accordingly acquitted.[1]

MODEL PENAL CODE

Section 2.06. Liability for Conduct of Another; Complicity.

(1) A person is guilty of an offense if it is committed by his own conduct or by the conduct of another person for which he is legally accountable, or both.

(2) A person is legally accountable for the conduct of another person when:

(a) acting with the kind of culpability that is sufficient for the commission of the offense, he causes an innocent or irresponsible person to engage in such conduct; or

(b) he is made accountable for the conduct of such other person by the Code or by the law defining the offense; or

(c) he is an accomplice of such other person in the commission of the offense.

---

1. If two conspire to commit robbery, and the victim is killed in the prosecution of the common design, both are guilty of murder even if the slayer had assured the other that there would be no killing. Miller v. State, 25 Wis. 384 (1870).

D, desiring to kill his wife, consulted A who advised poison and procured it for D. D poisoned a roasted apple and gave it to his wife who innocently handed it to their little daughter. D tried to persuade the daughter not to eat it but dared not explain why. In D's presence she ate the apple and died. A was held not to be an accessory to the murder of the girl. Regina v. Saunders and Archer, 2 Plow. 473, 75 Eng.Rep. 706 (1575).

A counseled D to murder X. D killed Y, mistaking him for X. A was held to be an accessory to the murder of Y. State v. Kennedy, 85 S.C. 146, 67 S.E. 152 (1909).

(3) A person is an accomplice of another person in the commission of an offense if:

    (a) with the purpose of promoting or facilitating the commission of the offense, he

        (i) solicits such other person to commit it; or

        (ii) aids or agrees or attempts to aid such other person in planning or committing it; or

        (iii) having a legal duty to prevent the commission of the offense, fails to make proper effort so to do; or

    (b) his conduct is expressly declared by law to establish his complicity.

(4) When causing a particular result is an element of an offense, an accomplice in the conduct causing such result is an accomplice in the commission of that offense, if he acts with the kind of culpability, if any, with respect to that result that is sufficient for the commission of the offense.

(5) A person who is legally incapable of committing a particular offense himself may be guilty thereof if it is committed by the conduct of another person for which he is legally accountable, unless such liability is inconsistent with the purpose of the provision establishing his incapacity.

(6) Unless otherwise provided by the Code or by the law defining the offense, a person is not an accomplice in an offense committed by another person if:

    (a) he is a victim of that offense; or

    (b) the offense is so defined that his conduct is inevitably incident to its commission; or

    (c) he terminates his complicity prior to the commission of the offense and

        (i) wholly deprives it of effectiveness in the commission of the offense; or

        (ii) gives timely warning to the law enforcement authorities or otherwise makes proper effort to prevent the commission of the offense.

(7) An accomplice may be convicted on proof of the commission of the offense and of his complicity therein, though the person claimed to have committed the offense has not been prosecuted or convicted or has been convicted of a different offense or degree of offense or has an immunity to prosecution or conviction or has been acquitted.

Section 242.3. Hindering Apprehension or Prosecution.

A person commits an offense if, with purpose to hinder the apprehension, prosecution, conviction or punishment of another for crime, he:

    (1) harbors or conceals the other; or

    (2) provides or aids in providing a weapon, transportation, disguise or other means of avoiding apprehension or effecting escape; or

    (3) conceals or destroys evidence of the crime, or tampers with a witness, informant, document or other source of information, regardless of its admissibility in evidence; or

(4) warns the other of impending discovery or apprehension, except that this paragraph does not apply to a warning given in connection with an effort to bring another into compliance with law; or

(5) volunteers false information to a law enforcement officer.

The offense is a felony of the third degree if the conduct which the actor knows has been charged or is liable to be charged against the person aided would constitute a felony of the first or second degree. Otherwise it is a misdemeanor.

Section 242.4. Aiding Consummation of Crime.

A person commits an offense if he purposely aids another to accomplish an unlawful object of a crime, as by safeguarding the proceeds thereof or converting the proceeds into negotiable funds. The offense is a felony of the third degree if the principal offense was a felony of the first or second degree. Otherwise it is a misdemeanor.

Section 242.5. Compounding.

A person commits a misdemeanor if he accepts or agrees to accept any pecuniary benefit in consideration of refraining from reporting to law enforcement authorities the commission or suspected commission of any offense or information relating to an offense. It is an affirmative defense to prosecution under this Section that the pecuniary benefit did not exceed an amount which the actor believed to be due as restitution or indemnification for harm caused by the offense.

SECTION 9. CAUSATION

"Starting with a human act, we must next find a causal relation between the act and the harmful result; for in our law—and, it is believed, in any civilized law—liability cannot be imputed to a man unless it is in some degree a result of his act." Beale, The Proximate Consequences of An Act, 33 Harv.L.Rev. 633, 637 (1920).

"As the law of evidence excludes much that is evidential, the law of causation excludes much that is consequential." Edgerton, *Legal Cause*, 72 U. of Pa.Law Rev. 343, 344 (1924).

"John Stuart Mill, in his work on logic 9th Eng.Ed. 378–383 says, in substance, that the cause of an event is the sum of all the antecedents, and that we have no right to single out one antecedent and call that the cause. . . . The question is not what philosophers or logicians will say is the cause. The question is what the courts will regard as the cause." Jeremiah Smith, *Legal Cause in Actions of Tort*, 25 Harv.Law Rev. 103, 104 (1911).

"It would seem too clear for argument that considerations of fairness or justice have a bearing." McLaughlin, *Proximate Cause*, 39 Harv.Law Rev. 149, 155 (1925).

"It has been said that an act which in no way contributed to the result in question cannot be a cause of it; but this, of course, does not mean that an event which *might* have happened in the same way though the defendant's act or omission had not occurred, is not a result of it. The question is not what would have happened, but what did happen." Beale, *The Proximate Consequences of An Act*, 33 Harv. Law Rev. 633, 638 (1920).

"Here is the key to the juridical treatment of the problems of causation. We pick out the cause which in our judgment ought to be treated as the dominant one with reference, not merely to the event itself, but to the jural consequences that ought to attach to the event." Cardozo, The Parodoxes of Legal Science, 83 (1928).

The line of demarkation between causes which will be recognized as "proximate" and those disregarded as "remote" "is really a flexible line." I Street, Foundations of Legal Liability, 111 (1906).

"There are no cases where it can be truthfully said that legal cause exists where cause in fact does not though it may happen by reason of relaxation of proof that liability will be imposed in cases where cause in fact is not by the ordinary rules of proof shown to exist." Carpenter, Workable Rules for Determining Proximate Cause, 20 Cal.Law Rev. 396, 407 (1932).

"A primary requisite to either criminal or civil liability is that the act of the defendant be the cause in fact of the injury. This requirement is embodied in the familiar *causa sine qua non* rule, generally called the 'but for' rule. This test generally is satisfactory when applied in negative form, and it is a basic principle that a defendant is not liable unless the injury would not have resulted but for his wrongful act. But as an affirmative test the 'but for' rule provides no infallible standard and does not constitute a fair test of liability in the absence of further qualifications. . . .

"The modern authorities, while agreed that the 'but for' test is inadequate differ materially in their concepts of proximate causation. The theories conveniently may be placed into two groups. One group seeks the necessary connection between the result and the act; the other, between the result and the actor's mind." Focht, Proximate Cause In the Law of Homicide—With Special Reference To California Cases, 12 So.Cal.L.Rev. 19, 20–21 (1938).

"There are three, and only three, tests of proximateness, namely, intention, probability and the non-intervention of an independent cause.

"Any intended consequence of an act is proximate. It would plainly be absurd that a person should be allowed to act with an intention to produce a certain consequence, and then when that very consequence in fact follows his act, to escape liability for it on the plea that it was not proximate.

"Probability . . . is a name for some one's opinion or guess as to whether a consequence will result. . . .

"The person whose opinion is taken is a reasonable and prudent man in the situation of the actor. . . .

"The third test of proximateness is the non-intervention of an independent cause between the original cause and the consequence in question. . . . Therefore it will be convenient to call it an isolating cause." Terry, Proximate Consequences in the Law of Torts, 28 Harv.L.Rev. 10, 17–20 (1914).[1]

STATE v. WOOD

Supreme Court of Vermont, 1881.
53 Vt. 560.

VEAZEY, J. This is an indictment charging the respondents jointly with the murder of one Luman A. Smith. The respondent Alma R. Smith was the wife of Luman A. . . .

III. We think the exception to the charge of the court to the jury in response to the sixth request must be sustained. The evidence on the part of the State showed that Luman A. died from the effects of the wound inflicted by Alma, and not from that inflicted by Wood; and their evidence tended to show that there was no concert between them, but that each acted independently.

The court instructed the jury in substance that although Luman A. died of the wound inflicted by Alma and not from that inflicted by Wood, and although there was no concert between them, and each acted independently, and they were therefore only responsible for their own acts respectively, still if the wound inflicted by Wood was mortal, and would in course of time have killed Luman A., if he had not previously died from the wound inflicted by Alma, and although he did not die of the wound by Wood, yet the latter could be convicted of murder.

The court was in error in the assumption that a man can be convicted of murder although his act does not cause the death. The question does not turn upon the moral aspect of the case. The intent to murder may be never so plain, yet if something intervenes to prevent the consummation of the intent, if death does not follow from the act of the accused, he is not in law a murderer. All of the definitions of murder found in the books involve the idea and fact of a killing. This must have reference, when a man is on trial, to a killing by him. If one inflicts a mortal wound, but before death ensues, another kills the same person by an independent act, without concert with, or procurement of, the first man, how can he be said to have done the killing? The second person could be convicted of murder, if he killed

---

[1] "A cause must be the efficient, commonly called the proximate, cause or it is not a cause at all in law". State v. Osmus, 73 Wyo. 183, 276 P.2d 469, 474 (1954).

with malice aforethought, and to convict the first man would be assuming that he killed the same person at another time. . . .

Verdict set aside, and new trial granted.[1]

GAY v. STATE

Supreme Court of Tennessee, 1891.
90 Tenn. 645, 18 S.W. 260.

LEA, J. The plaintiff in error was indicted and convicted of a nuisance in keeping and maintaining a hog-pen in a filthy condition. There were several witnesses who proved it was a nuisance. There were several who proved that the pen was kept remarkably clean, and was no nuisance; and several proved that, if there was a nuisance, it was caused by a number of hog-pens in the neighborhood.

His Honor, among other things, charged the jury: "If the jury find that the smell created by the defendant's pen was not sufficient within itself to constitute a nuisance, yet it contributed with other pens in the neighborhood to forming a nuisance, the defendant would be guilty."

This was error. The defendant can only be held liable for the consequences which his act produced. The nuisance complained of must be the natural and direct cause of his own act.

PEOPLE v. LEWIS

Supreme Court of California, Department Two, 1899.
124 Cal. 551, 57 P. 470.

TEMPLE, J. The defendant was convicted of manslaughter and appeals from the judgment and from an order refusing a new trial. It is his second appeal. The main facts are stated in the decision of the former appeal, People v. Lewis, 117 Cal. 186, 48 P. 1088, 59 Am. St.Rep. 167. . . .

Defendant and deceased were brothers-in-law, and not altogether friendly, although they were on speaking and visiting terms. On the morning of the homicide the deceased visited the residence of the defendant, was received in a friendly manner, but after a while an altercation arose, as a result of which defendant shot deceased in the abdomen, inflicting a wound that was necessarily mortal. Farrell fell to the ground, stunned for an instant, but soon got up and went into the house, saying: "Shoot me again; I shall die anyway." His

---

1. D inflicted a knife wound on X after which D's son shot X. It was held that if the knife wound contributed to the death of X, D may be convicted of murder even if there was no preconcert between D and his son, and the knife wound was not necessarily fatal. Henderson v. State, 11 Ala.App. 37, 65 So. 721 (1913).

strength soon failed him and he was put to bed. Soon afterwards, about how long does not appear, but within a very few minutes, when no other person was present except a lad about nine years of age, nephew of the deceased and son of the defendant, the deceased procured a knife and cut his throat, inflicting a ghastly wound, from the effect of which, according to the medical evidence, he must necessarily have died in five minutes. The wound inflicted by the defendant severed the mesenteric artery, and medical witnesses testified that under the circumstances it was necessarily mortal, and death would ensue within one hour from the effects of the wound alone. Indeed, the evidence was that usually the effect of such a wound would be to cause death in less time than that, but possibly the omentum may have filled the wound, and thus, by preventing the flow of the blood from the body, have stayed its certain effect for a short period. Internal hemorrhage was still occurring, and, with other effects of the gunshot wound, produced intense pain. The medical witnesses thought that death was accelerated by the knife wound. Perhaps some of them considered it the immediate cause of death.

Now, it is contended that this is a case where one languishing from a mortal wound is killed by an intervening cause, and, therefore, deceased was not killed by Lewis. To constitute manslaughter, the defendant must have killed some one, and if, though mortally wounded by the defendant, Farrell actually died from an independent intervening cause, Lewis, at the most, could only be guilty of a felonious attempt. He was as effectually prevented from killing as he would have been if some obstacle had turned aside the bullet from its course and left Farrell unwounded. And they contend that the intervening act was the cause of death, if it shortened the life of Farrell for any period whatever.

The attorney general does not controvert the general proposition here contended for, but argues that the wound inflicted by the defendant was the direct cause of the throat cutting, and, therefore, defendant is criminally responsible for the death. He illustrates his position by supposing a case of one dangerously wounded and whose wounds had been bandaged by a surgeon. He says, suppose through the fever and pain consequent upon the wound the patient becomes frenzied and tears away the bandage and thus accelerates his own death. Would not the defendant be responsible for a homicide? Undoubtedly he would be, for in the case supposed the deceased died from the wound, aggravated, it is true, by the restlessness of the deceased, but still the wound inflicted by the defendant produced death. Whether such is the case here is the question.

The attorney general seems to admit a fact which I do not concede, that the gunshot wound was not, when Farrell died, then itself directly contributory to the death. I think the jury were warranted in finding that it was. But if the deceased did die from the effect of the knife wound alone, no doubt the defendant would be responsible, if it was made to appear, and the jury could have found from the evidence, that the knife wound was caused by the wound inflicted by the defendant in the natural course of events. If the relation was causal, and the wounded condition of the deceased was not merely the occasion upon which another cause intervened, not produced by the first wound or related to it in other than a casual way, then defendant is guilty of a homicide. But, if the wounded condition only afforded an opportunity for another unconnected person to kill, defendant would not be guilty of a homicide, even though he had inflicted a mortal wound. In such case, I think, it would be true that the defendant was thus prevented from killing.

The case, considered under this view, is further complicated from the fact that it is impossible to determine whether deceased was induced to cut his throat through pain produced by the wound. May it not have been from remorse, or from a desire to shield his brother-in-law? In either case the causal relation between the knife wound and the gunshot wound would seem to be the same. In either case, if defendant had not shot the deceased, the knife wound would not have been inflicted.

Suppose one assaults and wounds another intending to take life, but the wound, though painful, is not even dangerous, and the wounded man knows that it is not mortal, and yet takes his own life to escape pain, would it not be suicide only? Yet, the wound inflicted by the assailant would have the same relation to death which the original wound in this case has to the knife wound. The wound induced the suicide, but the wound was not, in the usual course of things, the cause of the suicide. . . .

This case differs from that in this, that here the intervening cause, which it is alleged hastened death, was not medical treatment, designed to be helpful, and which the deceased was compelled to procure because of the wound, but was an act intended to produce death, and did not result from the first wound in the natural course of events. But we have reached the conclusion by a course of argument unnecessarily prolix, except from a desire to fully consider the earnest and able argument of the defendant, that the test is—or at least one test—whether, when the death occurred, the wound inflicted by the defendant, did contribute to the event. If it did, although other independent causes also contributed, the causal relation between the unlawful acts of the defendant and the death has been made out. Here, when the throat was cut, Farrell was not merely languishing from a mortal wound. He was actually dying—and after the throat was cut he continued to languish from both wounds. Drop by drop the life current went out from both wounds, and at the very instant of death the gunshot wound was contributing to the event. If the throat cutting had been by a third person, unconnected with the defendant, he might be guilty; for although a man cannot be killed twice, two persons, acting independently, may contribute to his death and each be guilty of a homicide. A person dying is still in life, and may be killed, but if he is dying from a wound given by another both may properly be said to have contributed to his death. . . .

The court refused to instruct the jury as follows: "If you believe from the evidence that it is impossible to tell whether Will Farrell died from the wound in the throat, or the wound in the abdomen, you are bound to acquit." The instruction was properly refused. It assumed that death must have resulted wholly from one wound or the other, and ignored the proposition that both might have contributed —as the jury could have found from the evidence.

The other points are relatively trivial. I have examined them and cannot see how injury could have resulted, supposing the rulings to have been erroneous.

The judgment is affirmed.[1]

McFARLAND, J., and HENSHAW, J., concurred.

Hearing in Bank denied.

EX PARTE HEIGHO

Supreme Court of Idaho, 1910.
18 Idaho 566, 110 P. 1029.

AILSHIE, J. Petitioner was held by the probate judge of Washington county to answer the charge of manslaughter, and has applied to this court for his discharge on the ground that the facts of the case do not disclose the commission of a public offense. The evidence produced at the preliminary examination has been attached to the petition. This court cannot weigh the evidence on habeas corpus, but, if it wholly fails to disclose a public offense for which a prisoner may be held on preliminary examination, then the petitioner would be entitled to his discharge. In re Knudtson, 10 Idaho 676, 79 P. 641.

The facts disclosed by the evidence are in substance as follows: On the 4th day of August, 1910, at Weiser, Washington county, the petitioner, Edgar M. Heigho, hearing that one J. W. Barton had made remarks derogatory to petitioner's character, called one of his employes, Frank Miller, and requested him to accompany petitioner to the residence of Barton. Heigho and Miller went to Barton's residence about 7 o'clock in the evening, ascended the front porch, and Heigho rang the doorbell. Mrs. Sylvia Riegleman, the mother-in-law of Barton, was living at the Barton residence, and was in a bedroom at the front of the house, and immediately off from and adjoining the reception room or hallway, at the time the doorbell rang.

---

[1] One who inflicted a mortal wound by a shot fired in privileged self defense, and later fired another shot after all danger to himself had obviously come to an end is guilty of murder if the second shot contributed to the death. People v. Brown, 62 Cal.App. 96, 216 P. 411 (1923).

Barton responded to the call, and, as he passed through the front room and was about to open the front door, Mrs. Riegleman, who was then near him, exclaimed, "Oh, he has a gun." Barton stepped out at the door and found Heigho standing on the front porch with a gun, commonly called a revolver or pistol, hanging in a holster or scabbard which was strapped about his body. Miller stood by the side of Heigho. Heigho asked Barton some questions as to the statements Barton had been making about him, and, upon Barton asserting that he had not told anything that was not true or not common talk in the town, Heigho struck him in the face with his fist, and Barton staggered back, and fell into the wire netting on the screen door. Barton did not rise for a few seconds, and in the meanwhile his wife came and assisted him to arise. Heigho and Miller backed off the porch and stood in front of the doorway. Barton advanced on Heigho and struck him a couple of blows, whereupon they clinched, and the wife interfered and separated them, and ordered Heigho and Miller off the premises. Mrs. Riegleman was at this time at the door crying, and had been heard to say a time or two, "He will kill you," or "He has a gun." Barton and wife immediately mounted the porch where Mrs. Riegleman was on her knees, resting against or over the banister, apparently unable to rise. She remarked to Barton that she was dying, and again repeated something about "him having a gun." She began spitting a bloody froth and rattling in the chest. A physician was called, and was unable to give her any relief, and she died inside of about 30 minutes from the time of the appearance of Heigho on the front porch. The physician who attended her made a post mortem examination, and testified that she had an aneurism of the ascending aorta, and this had ruptured into the superior vena cava and caused her death. He said that excitement was one of three principal causes that will produce such a result. Heigho was thereafter arrested on the charge of manslaughter in causing the death of Mrs. Riegleman by terror and fright while he was engaged in the commission of an unlawful act not amounting to felony.

We are now asked to determine whether under the statute of this state a person can be held for manslaughter where death was caused by fright, fear, or nervous shock, and where the prisoner made no assault or demonstration against the deceased, and neither offered nor threatened any physical force or violence toward the person of the deceased. In the early history of the common law a homicide to be criminal must have resulted from corporal injury. Fright, fear, nervous shock, or producing mental disturbance, it was said, could never be the basis of a prosecution for homicide. East in his Pleas of the Crown, c. 5, § 13, says: "Working upon the fancy of another or treating him harshly or unkindly, by which he dies of grief or fear, is not such a killing as the law takes notice of." An examination of the ancient English authorities fully corroborates and establishes this to have been the early English rule. 1 Hale P.C. 425–29; Steph.

Dig.Cr.Law, art. 221. This rule appears, however, to have been gradually modified and greatly relaxed in modern times by most of the English courts. So in later years we find the court holding a prisoner for manslaughter where his conduct toward his wife caused her death from shock to her nervous system. Reg. v. Murton, 3 F. & F. 492. And in Reg. v. Dugal, 4 Quebec, 492, the Canadian court held the prisoner guilty of manslaughter where with violent words and menaces he had brandished a table knife over his father, and the latter became greatly agitated and weakened from the fright, and died in 20 minutes thereafter of syncope. . . .

As to whether a death caused from fright, grief, or terror, or other mental or nervous shock, can be made the basis for a criminal prosecution, has been touched upon but lightly by the text-writers, and none have ventured to enunciate a modern rule on the subject. Such comments and observations as the text-writers have made are valuable as indicating the personal views of the writers touching this matter. Sir James Stephen in his note to article 221 of his Digest of Criminal Law, commenting on the old rule, says: "Suppose a man were intentionally killed by being kept awake till the nervous irritation of sleeplessness killed him; might not this be murder? Suppose a man kills a sick man, intentionally, by making a loud noise which wakes him when sleep gives him a chance of life, or suppose, knowing that a man has aneurism of the heart, his heir rushes into his room and roars in his ear, 'Your wife is dead,' intending to kill and killing him, why are not these acts murder? They are no more 'secret things belonging to God' than the operation of arsenic. As to the fear that by admitting that such acts are murder people might be rendered liable to prosecution for breaking the hearts of their fathers or wives by bad conduct, the answer is that such an event could never be proved. A long course of conduct gradually 'breaking a man's heart' could never be the 'direct or immediate' cause of death. If it was, and it was intended to have that effect, why should it not be murder?" The author of the text in 21 Am. & Eng.Ency. of Law (2d Ed.) p. 98, speaking of the reason for the old rule and the modern trend of authority, says: "A hint of the reason for this exclusion may be gathered from Lord Hale's assertion that 'secret things belong to God,' upon which Sir James Stephen comments that he suspects the fear of encouraging prosecutions for witchcraft was the real reason. In default of a better explanation it would seem, therefore, that the rule has no firmer foundation than the ignorance and superstition of the time in which it was formulated. Hence the courts have in some later cases shown a tendency to break away from the old rule where substantial justice required it. It will be observed, however, that in all these cases the death has been caused by shock of terror produced by an assault, so that the question in many of its aspects may still be regarded as unsettled. Yet on principle there is no reason why a death from nervous irritation or shock should not be as criminal as any other. It certainly entails greater difficulty in the matter of proof, but this is purely a question of fact, and, if the prosecution is able to establish its case by evidence satisfactory to a jury, there seems to be no sufficient reason why the law should forbid a conviction." Clark & Marshall on the Law of Crimes (2d Ed.) p. 314, says: "It is no doubt very true that the law cannot undertake to punish as for homicide when it is claimed that the death was caused solely by grief or terror, for the death could not be traced to such causes with any degree of certainty. Working upon the feelings and fears of another, however, may be the direct cause of physical or corporeal injury resulting in death, and in such a case the person causing the injury may be as clearly responsible for the death as if he had used a knife." The statute of this state (section 6565, Rev.Codes) defines manslaughter as follows: "Manslaughter is the unlawful killing of a human being without malice. It is of two kinds: (1) Voluntary—upon a sudden quarrel or heat of passion; (2) involuntary—in the commission of an unlawful act, not amounting to felony, or in the commission of a lawful act which might produce death, in an unlawful manner, or without due caution and circumspection." Manslaughter has perhaps in the variety of its circumstances no equal in the catalogue of crimes. An unlawful killing, though unintentional and involuntary, if accomplished by one while engaged in the commission of an unlawful act, is defined by the statute as manslaughter, and this statute does not circumscribe the means or agency causing the death. The law clearly covers and includes any and all means and mediums by or through which a death is caused by one engaged in an unlawful act. The statute has the effect of raising the grade of the offense in which the party is engaged to the rank of manslaughter where it results in the death of a human being.

With such aid as we get from the foregoing authorities and the independent consideration we have been able to give the matter, we reach the conclusion that it would be unsafe, unreasonable, and often unjust for a court to hold as a matter of law that under no state of facts should a prosecution for manslaughter be sustained where death was caused by fright, fear or terror alone, even though no hostile demonstration or overt act was directed at the person of the deceased. Many examples might be called to mind where it would be possible for the death of a person to be accomplished through fright, nervous shock, or terror as effectually as the same could be done with a knife or gun. If the proof in such a case be clear and undoubted, there can be no good reason for denying a conviction. If A. in a spirit of recklessness shoot through B.'s house in which a sick wife or child is confined, and the shock and excitement to the patient cause death, the mere fact that he did not shoot at or hit any one and that he did not intend to shoot any one should not excuse him. It should be enough that he was at the time doing an unlawful act or was acting "without due caution and circumspection." It would seem that in some instances force or violence may be applied to the mind or nervous system as effectually as to the body (1 Russel on Crimes, p. 489). Indeed, it is a well-recognized fact, especially among physicians and metaphysicians, that the application of corporal force or violence often intensifies mentally and nervously the physical effects that flow from the use and application of such force or violence.[1]

We express no opinion whatever and refrain from any comment on the evidence in this case. That is a matter to be passed on by a jury. They should determine from all the facts and circumstances whether the accused was the direct and actual cause of the death of the deceased. As was said by Justice Denman in the Towers Case, it would be "laying down a dangerous precedent for the future" for us to hold as a conclusion of law that manslaughter could not be committed by fright, terror, or nervous shock. The fair and deliberate judgment of a jury of 12 men can generally be relied upon as an ample safeguard for the protection of one who should in fact be acquitted. The dangers of unwarranted prosecutions for such causes are no greater or more imminent than from any other cause, while, on the other hand, the proofs will generally be more difficult. The difficulty of making proofs, however, should never be considered as an argument against the application of a rule of law.

The writ is quashed, and the prisoner is remanded to the custody of the sheriff of Washington county.

SULLIVAN, C. J., concurs.

STATE v. FRAZIER

Supreme Court of Missouri, Division Two, 1936.
339 Mo. 966, 98 S.W.2d 707.

ELLISON, J. The appellant was convicted of manslaughter and his punishment assessed at a fine of $400 and six months in the county jail, for the killing of Daniel I. Gross in Fredericktown in August, 1934. The cause was tried in St. Francois County on change of venue from Madison County. The deceased was a hemophiliac, or "bleeder." The appellant struck him on the jaw once with his fist. A slight laceration on the inside of the mouth resulted which produced a hemorrhage lasting ten days and ending in death. The State's evidence showed the appellant's assault upon the deceased was unprovoked. The evidence for the appellant was that he acted in self-

---

1. Defendant's negligently-parked car on a hillside crashed into a house in which deceased was sleeping. He had high blood pressure and a heart condition and it was claimed his death from heart failure ten days later was due to fright induced by this crash, and defendant was sued by deceased's widow. His motion for summary judgment was denied on the ground that direct physical impact is not essential to a recovery for death from fright. Colla v. Mandella, 1 Wis.2d 594, 85 N.W.2d 345 (1957).

defense; and his theory further was that Gross's death was not caused by the blow struck but by his disease, aforesaid, and the failure to treat it properly. Other assignments in appellant's motion for new trial and brief in this court challenge the information and the overruling of his plea in abatement thereto, the sufficiency of the evidence and the overruling of his demurrers thereto; and complain of the admission of evidence, the giving of instructions, and the failure to instruct the jury properly. . . .

Remembering the appellant was convicted of manslaughter, two questions remain: (1) was it an adequate defense that the appellant did not know the deceased was a hemophiliac, and struck only one moderate blow with his fist, which ordinarily would not have been dangerous to life; (2) is he to be excused because the blow producing the hemorrhage would not have resulted fatally if deceased had not been a hemophiliac? Both these questions must be answered in the negative. Section 3988, Revised Statutes 1929 (Mo.Stat.Ann., p. 2793), provides that "every killing of a human being by the act, procurement or culpable negligence of another, not herein declared to be murder or excusable or justifiable homicide, shall be deemed manslaughter." If one commits an unlawful assault and battery upon another without malice and death results, the assailant is guilty of manslaughter although death was not intended and the assault was not of a character likely to result fatally.

Neither is it an excuse that appellant did not know the deceased was a hemophiliac, and that death would not have resulted but for that affliction. On this point 13 Ruling Case Law, section 55, page 750, says: "The law declares that one who inflicts an injury on another and thereby accelerates his death shall be held criminally responsible therefor, although death would not have resulted from the injury but for the diseased or wounded condition of the person so injured." And the doctrine is more fully set out in 29 Corpus Juris, section 57, page 1082, as follows: "If the deceased was in feeble health and died from the combined effects of the injury and of his disease, or if the injury accelerated the death from the disease, he who inflicted the injury is liable, although the injury alone would not have been fatal. The same rule applies, although the disease itself would probably have been fatal, if the injury accelerated death. It is immaterial that defendant did not know that the deceased was in the feeble condition which facilitated the killing, or that he did not reasonably anticipate that his act would cause death." . . .

Finding no reversible error the judgment and sentence below are affirmed. All concur.

PEOPLE v. COOK

Supreme Court of Michigan, 1878.
39 Mich. 236.

MARSTON, J. The respondent was tried upon an information charging him with having committed the crime of murder and was convicted of manslaughter. The case comes here upon exceptions before sentence. The shooting of the deceased by respondent was not denied on the trial. The defense relied on was:

First. That the death was actually caused by morphine poisoning before the wound had so far affected vitality as to induce a belief that it was or could have been the cause of death; . . .

The ninth request was not given. This request was based upon a theory that where a mortal wound has been given, but the death is actually produced by morphine administered by the hand of another, there must be an acquittal. The State v. Scates, 5 Jones (N.C.) 420, was relied upon as an authority in support of this proposition. In that case the jury was charged that if one person inflicts a mortal wound, and before the assailed person dies, another person kills him by an independent act, the former is guilty of murder, and this was held error.

This case does not, however, come within the principle of that case. Here a mortal wound was given. Physicians were called in who prescribed for and treated the wounded man. Morphine was administered, and it is claimed in such unreasonably large quantities that it caused death. It was not claimed that these physicians were deficient in medical skill, or that morphine in proper quantities, and at proper times, should not have been administered, or that the deceased could under any treatment, or in the absence of all treatment, have survived. Admitting the correctness of the authority relied upon, what application can such a rule have to cases like the present? If death was actually produced by morphine, can it be said in view of the facts, "that another person killed the deceased by an independent act?" Here morphine was administered as a medicine by competent and skillful physicians; it was a proper and appropriate medicine to be given. Was it the independent act of the physicians who prescribed, or of the nurses who administered the morphine? Was it the mortal wound likely to cause death at any moment, or an undue quantity of medicine, unskillfully but honestly given to alleviate suffering, which actually caused death? Were the last powders, which constituted the over-dose, given during the dying man's last moments, or so recently before death that they could not have caused it or materially contributed thereto? How under the conflicting theories and uncertainties, which would inevitably arise in such a case, could it be said which was the real cause? Could it be made to appear with clearness and certainty that not the wound, but the medicines administered, were the sole cause of the death? There are authorities which hold that the burthen of so proving would rest upon the accused, in cases where the wound was not a mortal one. The position which counsel seeks to establish amounts to this: that if a competent physician and surgeon, in the treatment of a mortal wound directly causes death, although hastened by never so short a period, the assailant is excused, even although death would inevitably have resulted from the wound under any or in the absence of all treatment. Such is not the law. Neglect or mistreatment, and beyond such this case does not go, will not excuse, except in cases where doubt exists as to the character of the wound. Where death results in a case like the present, it can in no proper or legal sense be said to be the independent act of a third person. In a case where the wound is not mortal, the injured person may recover, and thus no homicide have been committed. If, however, death do result, the accused will be held responsible, unless it was occasioned, not by the wound, but by grossly erroneous medical treatment. But where the wound is a mortal one, there is no chance for the injured person to recover, and therefore the reason which permits the showing of death from medical treatment does not exist. . . .

It must be certified to the circuit court that the exceptions are not well taken, and that the court proceed to judgment.

The other Justices concurred.[1]

BELK v. PEOPLE

Supreme Court of Illinois, 1888.
125 Ill. 584, 17 N.E. 744.

Mr. Justice Shope delivered the opinion of the Court.

The plaintiffs in error, John Belk, John Hill and George Williams, with George Belk, were jointly indicted, in the Jo Daviess circuit court, for the murder of Ann Reed, the indictment charging in the various counts, in varying forms, that the murder was committed by the defendants, by willfully, recklessly, negligently, wrongfully and feloniously driving a team of horses hitched to a wagon, upon and against a wagon in which the deceased was riding, thereby causing the horses attached to the wagon in which she was so riding, to run away, thereby throwing said Ann Reed upon the ground, whereby she received wounds and injuries from which she died the following day. A trial resulted in an acquittal of said George Belk, and a ver-

---

1. If a gun-shot wound inflicted by D on a pregnant woman caused a miscarriage, and the miscarriage caused septic peritonitis which in turn resulted in death, D has caused the death even if the medical treatment received by the woman in the hospital was not of the best. People v. Kane, 213 N.Y. 260, 107 N.E. 655 (1915).

If pneumonia was the *sole* cause of the death of a wounded man, he who inflicted the wound did not cause the death. Quinn v. State, 106 Miss. 844, 64 So. 738 (1914).

dict of guilty of manslaughter as to plaintiffs in error, and fixing their punishment at confinement in the penitentiary at one year each. Motions for new trial and in arrest were severally overruled, and sentence pronounced by the court upon the verdict. . . .

Some question is made whether the collision was the proximate cause of the team running away, and of the injury and death of Mrs. Reed; but it is enough to say, the evidence was sufficient upon which to base the finding of the jury in that respect. The question was submitted under proper instructions, and there is no ground for disturbing the verdict for that reason. There was direct causal connection between the collision and the death of the deceased. Between the acts of omission or commission of the defendants, by which it is alleged the collision occurred, and the injury of the deceased, there was not an interposition of a human will acting independently of the defendants, or any extraordinary natural phenomena, to break the causal connection. It may be fairly said that what followed the colliding of the defendants' team with the wagon in which the deceased was riding, was the natural and probable effect of the collision, and the collision was in consequence of the manner in which the team of the defendants was controlled. It can make no difference whether the driver of the team after which the deceased was riding, was guilty of negligence in not controlling or failing to control his team after the collision. It may be that persons standing by, or the driver, might, by the exercise of diligence and care, have checked the horses, and thereby prevented the final catastrophe; but because they did not do so, and were derelict in moral or even legal duty in that regard, will not release defendants from the responsibility of their wrongful act or omission of their legal duty. If the driver, instead of being negligent, as is claimed in controlling his team, had done some act contributing to the running away of his horses, or driven upon a bank, whereby the carriage had been overturned and the deceased thrown out, or the like, it might justly be said that it was the act of the driver, and not of the defendants, to which the death of the deceased was legally attributable. Wharton on Crim.Law, 341, *et seq.;* Roscoe on Crim. Ev. 700, *et seq.* . . .

(For other reasons the judgment was reversed.)

LETNER v. STATE

Supreme Court of Tennessee, 1927.
156 Tenn. 68, 299 S.W. 1049.

Mr. Justice McKinney delivered the opinion of the Court.

Plaintiff in error, referred to herein as the defendant, was indicted for murder of Alfred Johnson. The jury found him guilty of involuntary manslaughter and fixed his punishment at two years in the penitentiary.

Alfred Johnson, nineteen years of age, his older brother, Walter Johnson, and Jesse Letner, seventeen years of age, half brother of the defendant, were crossing Emory River in a boat from the west to the east side, at a point known as "Devil's Race Track," this being a dangerous place, of unknown depth, where the water circles and eddies continuously. When in the middle of the river some man on the high bluff above the west bank shot into the water about six feet east of the boat, which caused the water to splash up. A second shot was fired, which hit the water nearer the boat; thereupon Walter Johnson, who was steering the boat, jumped out of same into the river, resulting in its being capsized, and Alfred and Walter were drowned.

The only question of fact is were either of these shots fired by defendant? He did not testify, and offered no evidence in his behalf. . . .

(4) It is also assigned for error that the court improperly charged the jury as follows:

"If you should believe from the evidence, and that beyond a reasonable doubt, that this defendant saw the deceased and other boys in a canoe or boat, and shot into the river near them without any purpose of hitting the deceased, but to play a prank on the deceased, and if the deceased became frightened and jumped into the river and was drowned, then in that event, the defendant would be guilty of involuntary manslaughter."

This was a correct statement of the law, but was inaccurate so far as the facts of this case are concerned. The uncontroverted testimony shows that deceased did not jump out of the boat, but that his brother, Walter, jumped out and, in doing so, capsized the boat and precipitated the deceased into the water. No criticism, however, is made with respect to this feature of the charge.

The act of the defendant, whether he was shooting to kill or only to frighten these boys, was an unlawful one, and comes within the universal rule that every person will be held to contemplate and be responsible for the natural consequences of his own act; but he will not be held criminally responsible for a homicide unless his act can be said to be the cause of death.

(5) When a person unintentionally or accidentally kills another, while engaged in an unlawful act, the authorities all hold that he is guilty of some degree of homicide.

In this case if defendant had accidentally struck the deceased, causing his death, or had capsized the boat and deceased had drowned, unquestionably he would have been guilty of some grade of homicide. . . .

From the foregoing it appears that the defendant is liable even where his act was not the immediate cause of the death, if he was connected with the intervening cause, or if the act or intervention was the natural result of his act.

(7) In other words, the defendant cannot escape the consequences of his wrongful act by relying upon a supervening cause when such cause naturally resulted from his wrongful act.

By firing the gun the defendant caused Walter Johnson to take to the water, resulting in the overturn of the boat and the drowning of Alfred. . . .

The judgment should also provide that the defendant undergo confinement in the penitentiary (in this case) not less than one nor more than two years. As thus modified, the judgment of the trial court will be affirmed.[1]

STATE v. LEOPOLD

Supreme Court of Errors of Connecticut, 1929.
110 Conn. 55, 147 A. 118.

BANKS, J. In the early morning of February 5, 1928, an explosion followed by a fire occurred in a building on Baldwin street in Waterbury, and two boys, the sons of a tenant of the building, were burned to death. The fee of the property was in the name of the wife of the accused, and a portion of the building was used for the storage of furniture by the Waterbury Furniture Company, a corporation of which the accused was a majority stockholder. The accused, jointly with one Shellnitz, was indicted upon a charge of murder in the first degree, and of having caused the death of the two boys by willfully burning the building. The charge against the accused was that he employed Weiss to set fire to the building, for the purpose of collecting insurance upon the building and the furniture stored in it. Weiss was burned to death in the fire. . . .

Error is predicated upon the refusal of the court to charge as requested, upon the charge as given, and upon numerous rulings upon evidence. The accused claimed that the two boys who were burned to death were awake after the fire, and were on their way out of the building, and would not have met their death if they had continued on their way, but that of their own will they remained in the building, or were sent back into a room of the building by their father to recover some money or other property there deposited, and requested the court to charge that, if they had a reasonable opportunity to es-

---

[1]. D made improper advances to a girl in a moving automobile. To avoid him she jumped from the car and was killed by the fall. A conviction of murder was reversed because the judge's charge to the jury permitted conviction of murder without requiring a finding (a) that deceased's fear of a felonious assault was a reasonable one, or (b) that her act in jumping was an act of a reasonably prudent person under the circumstances, or (c) that her act in jumping was one which in its consequences naturally tended to destroy the life of a human being. Patterson v. State, 181 Ga. 698, 184 S.E. 309 (1936). Cf. State v. Myers, 7 N.J. 465, 81 A.2d 710 (1951).

cape from the burning building, and would have escaped but for their own conduct, or the act of their father in directing them to return, the accused could not be found guilty of causing their death. The court did not so charge, but told the jury that the negligence of the victims of a crime did not diminish or nullify the crime, and that, even if they found the claim as to the conduct of these boys to be true, the accused would not thereby be excused. This was a correct statement of the law. . . . Every person is held to be responsible for the natural consequences of his acts, and if he commits a felonious act and death follows, it does not alter its nature or diminish its criminality to prove that other causes co-operated to produce that result. The act of the accused need not be the immediate cause of the death; he is responsible, though the direct cause is an act of the deceased, if such act, not being itself an independent and efficient cause, results naturally from, and is reasonably due to, the unlawful act of the accused. If the death of these boys resulted in a natural sequence from the setting of the building on fire, even though their conduct contributed to, or was the immediate cause of it, the accused would be responsible, and the effort of a person to save property of value which is liable to destruction by fire is such a natural and ordinary course of conduct that it cannot be said to break the sequence of cause and effect. . . .

A careful examination of the entire record fails to disclose any error prejudicial to the accused, and makes it clear that he had a fair trial.

There is no error.

All the Judges concur.[1]

COMMONWEALTH v. MOYER

Supreme Court of Pennsylvania, 1947.
357 Pa. 181, 53 A.2d 736.

Opinion by Mr. Chief Justice Maxey, June 30, 1947.

Charles Frederick Moyer and William Paul Byron were jointly tried for the murder of Harvey Zerbe, which occurred during the perpetration of a robbery. The jury convicted them of murder in the first degree and imposed the death penalty. . . .

The second assignment of error is based on the excerpt from the charge of the court in which the jury was instructed that: "All of the participants in an attempted robbery are guilty of murder in the first degree if someone is killed in the course of the perpetration of the first-named crime. That is the law of the Commonwealth of

---

[1] D maliciously set fire to a store building and a fireman lost his life while fighting the fire. A conviction of first degree murder was affirmed. State v. Glover, 330 Mo. 709, 50 S.W.2d 1049 (1932).

Pennsylvania." The appellants challenge that statement and say that the issue in this case is whether or not the decedent met his death by a wound inflicted by the defendant Moyer or by the garage owner Shank.

This assignment of error poses the question whether or not these defendants can legally be convicted of murder if the bullet which killed Zerbe came from the revolver fired by the latter's employer in an attempt by him to frustrate the attempted robbery. We have no doubt that even under these facts, which facts the Commonwealth does not concede, the complained of conviction was proper.

A man or men engaged in the commission of such a felony as robbery can be convicted of murder in the first degree if the bullet which causes death was fired not by the felon but by the intended victim in repelling the aggressions of the felon or felons. This is a question which apparently has never before arisen in this Commonwealth and has arisen elsewhere only rarely. Our Act of June 24, 1939, P.L. 872, section 701, 18 P.S. 4701, reads as follows: "All murder which shall be . . . committed in the perpetration of, or attempting to perpetrate any arson, rape, robbery, burglary, or kidnapping, shall be murder in the first degree." This section is, with the addition of the word "kidnapping" and with a negligible change in phraseology, a re-enactment of the corresponding provision of the Criminal Code of March 31, 1860, P.L. 382, and of later Acts and of the Act of 1794. . . .

. . . For any individual forcibly to defend himself or his family or his property from criminal aggression is a primal human instinct.[3] It is the right and duty of both individuals and nations to meet criminal aggression with effective countermeasures. Every robber or burglar knows when he attempts to commit his crime that he is inviting dangerous resistance. Any robber or burglar who carries deadly weapons (as most of them do and as these robbers did) thereby reveals that he expects to meet and overcome forcible opposition. What this court said in Commonwealth v. LeGrand, 336 Pa. 511, 518, 9 A.2d 896, about burglars, applies equally to robbers: "Every burglar is a potential assassin and when his felonious purpose encounters human opposition his *intent to steal* becomes an *intent to kill* and any weapon he finds at hand becomes a weapon of murder." Every robber or burglar knows that a likely later act in the chain of events he inaugurates will be the use of deadly force against him on the part of the selected victim. For whatever results follow from that natural and legal use of retaliating force, the felon must be held responsible. For Earl Shank, the proprietor of a gas station in Ridley Township, Delaware County, which at 11 P. M. on July 13, 1946, was being attacked by armed robbers, to return the fire of these rob-

---

3. "Such homicide as is committed for the prevention of any forcible and atrocious crime is justifiable by the law of nature; and also by the law of England." 4 Blackstone, section 181. [Court's footnote.]

bers with a pistol which he had at hand was as proper and as inevitable as it was for the American forces at Pearl Harbor on the morning of December 7, 1941, to return the fire of the Japanese invaders. The Japanese felonious invasion of the Hawaiian Islands on that date was in law and morals the proximate cause of all the resultant fatalities. The Moyer-Byron felonious invasion of the Shank gas station on July 13, 1946, was likewise the proximate cause of the resultant fatality.

If *in fact* one of the bullets fired by Earl Shank in self-defense killed Harvey Zerbe, the responsibility for that killing rests on Moyer and his co-conspirator Byron, who had armed themselves with deadly weapons for the purpose of carrying out their plan to rob Shank and whose murderous attack made Shank's firing at them in self-defense essential to the protection of himself and his employees and his property. If, for example, a father sees his child being kidnapped and opens fire, as any normal father would be expected to do if he had a gun available, and if the bullet which he fires at the kidnapper inadvertently kills the child, the death of the child is properly attributable to the malicious act of the kidnapper. The principle which sustains this conclusion is expressed by Bishop on Criminal Law, 9th Ed., Vol. 2, section 637, page 480, as follows: "It is a rule both of reason and law that whenever one's will contributes to impel a physical force, whether another's, his own, or a combined force proceeding from whatever different sources, he is responsible for the result, the same as if his own unaided hand had produced it. The contribution, however, must be of such magnitude, and so near the result, that sustaining to it the relation of contributory cause to effect, the law takes it within its cognizance."

Stephen's History of the Criminal Law of England, Vol. 3, page 21, says that at common law "murder was homicide with malice aforethought and that the latter consisted of any of the following states of mind: 1. . . . 2. . . . 3. . . . 4. An intent to commit any felony whatever." Blackstone, Book IV, pages 192–193, says: "When an involuntary killing happens in consequence of an unlawful act it would be either murder or manslaughter according to the nature of the act which occasioned it, but in consequences naturally tending to bloodshed it will be murder."

In Keaton v. State, 41 Tex.Cr.R. 621, 57 S.W. 1125, the Court of Criminal Appeals of Texas held that where the defendant and others went to rob a train, and, after stopping it, forced the fireman to the door of the express car, after being warned that some one would probably commence shooting at them from the rear of the car, and persons resisting the attempted robbery, and *intending to kill the robbers, shot and killed the fireman*, the defendant was held guilty of murder. . . .

In Johnson v. Alabama, 142 Ala. 70, 38 So. 182, 2 L.R.A.,N.S., 897, it was held by the Supreme Court of Alabama that one who, by interfering in aid of his insane parent, whom officers are attempting to arrest, frees his hands, and enables him to kill one of the officers, is guilty of murder. "The person who unlawfully sets the means of death in motion . . . is the guilty cause of the death at the time and place at which his unlawful act produces its fatal result; . . . ": Gray, J. in Com. v. Macloon, 101 Mass. 1, 100 Am.Dec. 89. . . .

This same principle is illustrated in the so-called "Squib Case" of Scott v. Shepherd, 2 William Blackstone's Rep. 892. In that case, there was instituted an action of trespass for tossing a lighted squib against the infant plaintiff and striking him on the face and so burning one of his eyes that he lost the sight of it. The facts were that on the 28th of October 1770, defendant threw a lighted squib made of gunpowder from the street into the market house. A large concourse of people were assembled there. One Willis to prevent injury to himself and to the goods of one Yates, grasped the lighted squib and threw it across the market house where it fell upon one Ryal. The latter, to save his own goods from being injured, took up the lighted squib and threw it to another part of the market house and struck the plaintiff in the face, putting out one of his eyes. In that case, Justice Gould said, ". . . the defendant may be considered in the same view as if he himself had personally thrown the squib in the plaintiff's face. The terror impressed upon Willis and Ryal excited self-defense, and deprived them of the power of recollection. What they did therefore was the inevitable consequence of the defendant's unlawful act." Chief Justice Degrey said, "The throwing the squib was an act unlawful and tending to affright the bystanders. So far, mischief was originally intended; not any particular mischief, but mischief indiscriminate and wanton. Whatever mischief therefore follows, he is the author of it; —*Egrediturpersonam*,[1] as the phrase is in criminal cases. And though criminal cases are no rule for civil ones, yet in trespass I think there is an analogy. Every one who does an unlawful act is considered as the doer of all that follows; if done with a deliberate intent, the consequence may amount to murder. . . ." The court held that an action of trespass was maintainable against the defendant Shepherd whose unlawful act started the squib on its journey through two other hands to the eyes of the plaintiff. . . .

The judgments are affirmed and the record is remitted so that the sentences may be executed.[2]

[By the Compiler.]

1. This is written as one word in the state report and two words in the Atlantic Reporter. The former is obviously a misprint.

2. D unlawfully attacked L and during an exchange of shots a bystander was killed. A conviction was reversed because the judge's instruction permitted conviction of D even if the fatal shot was fired by L. State v. Oxendine, 187 N.C. 658, 122 S.E. 568 (1924).

PEOPLE v. WASHINGTON

Supreme Court of California, In Bank, 1965.
62 Cal.2d 777, 44 Cal.Rptr. 442, 402 P.2d 130.

TRAYNOR, CHIEF JUSTICE. Defendant appeals from a judgment of conviction entered upon jury verdicts finding him guilty of first degree robbery (Pen.Code, §§ 211, 211a) and first degree murder and fixing the murder penalty at life imprisonment. (Pen.Code, §§ 187, 189, 190, 190.1.) He was convicted of murder for participating in a robbery in which his accomplice was killed by the victim of the robbery.

Shortly before 10 p. m., October 2, 1962, Johnnie Carpenter prepared to close his gasoline station. He was in his office computing the receipts and disbursements of the day while an attendant in an adjacent storage room deposited money in a vault. Upon hearing someone yell "robbery," Carpenter opened his desk and took out a revolver. A few moments later, James Ball entered the office and pointed a revolver directly at Carpenter, who fired immediately, mortally wounding Ball. Carpenter then hurried to the door and saw an unarmed man he later identified as defendant running from the vault with a moneybag in his right hand. He shouted "Stop." When his warning was not heeded, he fired and hit defendant who fell wounded in front of the station.

The Attorney General, relying on People v. Harrison, 176 Cal. App.2d 330, 1 Cal.Rptr. 414, contends that defendant was properly convicted of first degree murder. In that case defendants initiated a gun battle with an employee in an attempt to rob a cleaning business. In the cross fire, the employee accidentally killed the owner of the business. The court affirmed the judgment convicting defendants of first degree murder, invoking Commonwealth v. Almeida, 362 Pa. 596, 68 A.2d 595, 12 A.L.R.2d 183, and People v. Podolski, 332 Mich. 508, 52 N.W.2d 201, which held that robbers who provoked gunfire were guilty of first degree murder even though the lethal bullet was fired by a policeman.

Defendant would distinguish the Harrison, Almeida, and Podolski cases on the ground that in each instance the person killed was an innocent victim, not one of the felons. He suggests that we limit the rule of the Harrison case just as the Supreme Courts of Pennsylvania and Michigan have limited the Almeida and Podolski cases by holding that surviving felons are not guilty of murder when their accomplices are killed by persons resisting the felony. (Commonwealth v. Redline, 391 Pa. 486, 137 A.2d 472; People v. Austin, 370 Mich. 12, 120 N.W.2d 766; see also People v. Wood, 8 N.Y.2d 48, 201 N.Y.S.2d 328, 167 N.E.2d 736.) A distinction based on the person killed, however, would make the defendant's criminal liability turn upon the marksmanship of victims and policemen. A rule of law cannot reasonably be based on such a fortuitous circumstance. The basic issue therefore is whether a robber can be convicted of murder for the killing of any person by another who is resisting the robbery.

"Murder is the unlawful killing of a human being, with malice aforethought." (Pen.Code, § 187.) Except when the common-law-felony-murder doctrine is applicable, an essential element of murder is an intent to kill or an intent with conscious disregard for life to commit acts likely to kill. The felony-murder doctrine ascribes malice aforethought to the felon who kills in the perpetration of an inherently dangerous felony. That doctrine is incorporated in section 189 of the Penal Code, which provides in part: "All murder . . . committed in the perpetration or attempt to perpetrate . . . robbery . . . is murder of the first degree." Thus, even though section 189 speaks only of degrees of "murder," inadvertent or accidental killings are first degree murders when committed by felons in the perpetration of robbery.

When a killing is not committed by a robber or by his accomplice but by his victim, malice aforethought is not attributable to the robber, for the killing is not committed by him in the perpetration or attempt to perpetrate robbery. It is not enough that the killing was a risk reasonably to be foreseen and that the robbery might therefore be regarded as a proximate cause of the killing. Section 189 requires that the felon or his accomplice commit the killing, for if he does not, the killing is not committed to perpetrate the felony. Indeed, in the present case the killing was committed to thwart a felony. To include such killings within section 189 would expand the meaning of the words "murder . . . which is committed in the perpetration . . . [of] robbery . . . " beyond common understanding.

The purpose of the felony-murder rule is to deter felons from killing negligently or accidentally by holding them strictly responsible for killings they commit. This purpose is not served by punishing them for killings committed by their victims. . . .

A defendant need not do the killing himself, however, to be guilty of murder. He may be vicariously responsible under the rules defining principals and criminal conspiracies. All persons aiding and abetting the commission of a robbery are guilty of first degree murder when one of them kills while acting in furtherance of the common design. Moreover, when the defendant intends to kill or intentionally commits acts that are likely to kill with a conscious disregard for life, he is guilty of murder even though he uses another person to accomplish his objective.

Defendants who initiate gun battles may also be found guilty of murder if their victims resist and kill. Under such circumstances, "the defendant for a base, anti-social motive and with wanton disregard for human life, does an act that involves a high degree of probability that it will result in death", and it is unnecessary to imply malice by invoking the felony-murder doctrine. To invoke the felony-murder doctrine to imply malice in such a case is unnecessary and overlooks the principles of criminal liability that should govern the responsibility of one person for a killing committed by another.

To invoke the felony-murder doctrine when the killing is not committed by the defendant or by his accomplice could lead to absurd results. Thus, two men rob a grocery store and flee in opposite directions. The owner of the store follows one of the robbers and kills him. Neither robber may have fired a shot. Neither robber may have been armed with a deadly weapon. If the felony-murder doctrine applied, however, the surviving robber could be convicted of first degree murder, even though he was captured by a policeman and placed under arrest at the time his accomplice was killed.

The felony-murder rule has been criticized on the grounds that in almost all cases in which it is applied it is unnecessary and that it erodes the relation between criminal liability and moral culpability. . . . Although it is the law in this state (Pen.Code, § 189), it should not be extended beyond any rational function that it is designed to serve. Accordingly, for a defendant to be guilty of murder under the felony-murder rule the act of killing must be committed by the defendant or by his accomplice acting in furtherance of their common design. . . .

The judgment is affirmed as to defendant's conviction of first degree robbery and reversed as to his conviction of first degree murder.

PETERS, TOBRINER, PEEK and *WHITE, JJ., concur.

BURKE, JUSTICE (dissenting).

I dissent. The unfortunate effect of the decision of the majority in this case is to advise felons:

"Henceforth in committing certain crimes, including robbery, rape and burglary, you are free to arm yourselves with a gun and brandish it in the faces of your victims without fear of a murder conviction unless you or your accomplice pulls the trigger. If the menacing effect of your gun causes a victim or policeman to fire and kill an innocent person or a cofelon, you are absolved of responsibility for such killing unless you shoot first."

Obviously this advance judicial absolution removes one of the most meaningful deterrents to the commission of armed felonies.

In the present case defendant's accomplice was killed when the robbery victim fired after the accomplice had pointed a revolver at him. In People v. Harrison (1959) 176 Cal.App.2d 330, 1 Cal.Rptr. 414 (hearing in Supreme Court denied without a dissenting vote), the rationale of which the majority now disapprove, the robbery victim was himself accidentally killed by a shot fired by his employee after defendant robbers had opened fire, and the robbers were held guilty of murder for the killing. The majority now attempt to distinguish Harrison on the ground that there the robbers "initiated" the gun battle; in the present case the victim fired the first shot. As will appear, any such purported distinction is an invitation to further armed crimes of violence. There is no room in the law for sporting considerations and distinctions as to who fired first when dealing with killings which are caused by the actions of felons in deliberately arming themselves to commit any of the heinous crimes listed in Penal Code section 189. If a victim—or someone defending the victim—seizes an opportunity to shoot first when confronted by robbers with a deadly weapon (real or simulated), any "gun battle" *is* initiated by the armed robbers. In such a situation application of the felony-murder rule of section 189 of the Penal Code supports, if not compels, the conclusion that the surviving robbers committed murder even if the lethal bullet did not come from one of their guns, and whether it is an innocent person or an accomplice who dies. . . .

McComb, J., concurs.

PEOPLE v. ROCKWELL

Supreme Court of Michigan, 1878.
39 Mich. 503.

Campbell, C. J. Respondent was convicted of manslaughter for killing one Wilber. The death occurred during a dispute concerning the possession of a horse. Rockwell was shown to have struck Wilber with his fist and knocked him down. It was not shown directly how he was killed, but it appeared distinctly this blow did not kill him. The facts indicated either that Rockwell kicked him after he fell, or else that he was killed by the horse trampling on him. On a first trial the jury disagreed. On a second trial, after being out some time, they came in and asked the court to instruct them "whether the respondent would be guilty if he knocked Wilber down, and the horse jumped on him (Wilber) or kicked him, and thus killed him." To which inquiry the court, as the record shows, reiterated that portion of the charge before given that he would be so guilty. The jury then found him guilty.

The charge before given was unqualified that if the blow was not justifiable and Wilber so fell that the horse jumped and struck Wilber and killed him with his feet, or kicked him, respondent was guilty.

It is impossible to maintain such a charge without making every one liable not only for natural and probable consequences, but for all possible consequences and circumstances which immediately follow a wrongful act. There was no necessary connection between the act of respondent and the conduct of the horse, which he cannot be said from the record to have been responsible for. And the case was not even put as permissive. The liability was laid down as positive.

The conviction cannot be maintained. And inasmuch as it is clear from the record that the jury would not have convicted except upon this instruction, we think the court below should be advised to stop the prosecution.

The other Justices concurred.[1]

STATE v. MONROE

Supreme Court of North Carolina, 1897.
121 N.C. 677, 28 S.E. 547.

Indictment for assault and battery, tried at August Term, 1897, of UNION, before HOKE, J., and a jury.

The defendant was convicted and appealed. The facts sufficiently appear in the opinion.

FAIRCLOTH, C. J. Will Horn administered to Ernest Barrett a dose of croton oil, and the oil had an injurious effect on Barrett. Defendant admits he sold the oil to Horn and at his request dropped it into a piece of candy, but says he did not know that these parties were playing practical jokes on each other and did not know for what purpose Horn wanted the oil. Another witness testified that defendant said that Horn said he wanted the oil "for a fellow." Defendant denied saying this. Another witness testified to the quinine episode and to Barrett's and Horn's tricks with each other. Defendant testified that he knew that, a day or two before, Horn had given Barrett a dose of quinine, as a joke, in lemonade. There were other witnesses on these matters.

Defendant is indicted for an assault on Barrett. If guilty, he must be so as a principal, not as an accessory. His guilt, then, depends upon whether he knew, or had reason to believe, that the dose was intended for Barrett or some other person, as a trick, and not for medicinal purposes.

The whole evidence was submitted to the jury, who rendered a verdict of guilty. His Honor instructed the jury that when the defendant sold the oil, if he "knew or had reason to believe, and did believe, that it was intended for Barrett or some other person by way of a trick or joke, and not for a medicinal purpose, the defendant would be guilty of assault and battery."

He also charged that it was not necessary that it should be a poisonous or deadly dose; that it was sufficient if it was an unusual

---

1. D struck X and left X unconscious by the side of the road on a dark night where he was likely to be run over by a car. X died, either from the blow or from being run over by a car. A conviction of first degree murder was affirmed. People v. Fowler, 178 Cal. 657, 174 P. 892 (1918).

dose, likely to produce serious injury. To this instruction we see no objection, and we think it covers the substance of the defendant's prayers proper to go to the jury. There was no exception to the evidence. For duties of druggists, see Code, sec. 3143–5.

No error.

REGINA v. BENGE AND ANOTHER

Maidstone Crown Court, Kent Summer Assizes, 1865.
4 F. & F. 504, 176 Eng.Rep. 665.

[Benge and Gallimore were indicted for manslaughter, but it was admitted that there was no case against Gallimore and the case proceeded only against Benge. He was foreman of a crew employed to repair rails on a certain portion of the track. He had a book telling exactly when trains were due but looked at the wrong date and as a result ordered certain rails removed from a bridge shortly before a train was due. As was usual he sent one of the crew with a flag to signal if any train should approach while the rails were not in place. This man was to go at least 1000 yards in the direction from which a train would come, but he went only 540 yards. The flag signal could be seen by the engineer at a distance of 500 yards or more but he was inattentive and did not see it until abreast of the flagman. He did all he could to stop the train but it was then too late and a wreck resulted in which many lives were lost. There was evidence showing that the train could easily have been stopped within 1000 yards at any speed.]

PIGOTT, B., said, that assuming culpable negligence on the part of the prisoner which materially contributed to the accident, it would not be material that others also by their negligence contributed to cause it. Therefore he must leave it to the jury whether there was negligence of the prisoner which had been the substantial cause of the accident. In summing up the case to the jury, he said, their verdict must depend upon whether the death was mainly caused by the culpable negligence of the prisoner. Was the accident caused by the taking up of the rails at a time when an express train was about to arrive, was that the act of the prisoner, and was it owing to culpable negligence on his part? . . . Now, here the primary cause was certainly the taking up of the rails at a time when the train was about to arrive, and when it would be impossible to replace them in time to avoid the accident. And this the prisoner admitted was owing to his own mistake. Was that mistake culpable negligence, and did it mainly or substantially cause the accident? Then as to its being the main cause of the accident, it is true that the company had provided other precautions to avoid any impending catastrophe, and that these were not observed upon this particular occasion; but was it not owing to the prisoner's culpable negligence that the accident was impending, and if so, did his negligence the less cause it, because if other persons had not been negligent it might possibly have been avoided?[1]

Verdict—Guilty.

REGINA v. MICHAEL

Court for Crown Cases Reserved, 1840.
2 Moody 120, 169 Eng.Rep. 48.

The prisoner Catherine Michael was tried before MR. BARON ALDERSON at the Central Criminal Court in April 1840 (MR. JUSTICE LITTLEDALE being present), for the wilful murder of George Michael, an infant of the age of nine months, by administering poison.

The indictment alleged that the prisoner contriving and intending to kill and murder George Michael on the 31st of March, in the third year of the reign of her present Majesty, upon the said George Michael feloniously, &c. did make an assault; and that the prisoner a large quantity, to wit half an ounce weight of a certain deadly poison called laudanum, feloniously, &c. did give and administer unto said George Michael, with intent that he should take and swallow the same down into his body (she then and there well knowing the said laudanum to be a deadly poison), and the said laudanum so given and administered unto him by the said Catherine Michael as aforesaid, the said George Michael did take and swallow down into his body, by reason and by means of which said taking and swallowing down the said laudanum into his body as aforesaid, the said George Michael became and was mortally sick and distempered in his body, of which said mortal sickness and distemper the said George Michael from &c. till &c. did languish &c. and died; and concluding in the usual form as in cases of murder.

It appeared in evidence that the prisoner on the 27th day of March last, delivered to one Sarah Stephens, with whom the child was at nurse, a quantity of laudanum about an ounce, telling the said Sarah Stephens that it was proper medicine for the child to take, and directing her to administer to the child every night a teaspoonful thereof. That such a quantity as a teaspoonful was quite sufficient to kill a child; and that the prisoner's intention, as shewn by the finding of the jury in so delivering the laudanum and giving such directions as aforesaid, was to kill the child.

---

[1]. D shot X who was taken to a hospital promptly and in time to have been saved by proper surgical treatment. But he died from hemorrhage because the surgeon neglected for more than ten hours to control the bleeding. A conviction of manslaughter was affirmed on the ground that the surgeon's gross neglect was not superseding. "The factual situation is in legal effect the same, whether the victim bleeds to death because surgical attention is not available, or because, although available, it is delayed by reason of the surgeon's gross neglect or incompetence." People v. McGee, 31 Cal.2d 229, 243, 187 P.2d 706, 715 (1947).

That Sarah Stephens took home with her the laudanum, and thinking the child did not require medicine had no intention of administering it. She however not intending to give it at all, left it on the mantelpiece of her room, which was in a different house from where the prisoner resided, she, the prisoner, then being a wet nurse to a lady; and some days afterwards, that is, on the 31st of March, a little boy of the said Sarah Stephens, of the age of five years, during the accidental absence of Sarah Stephens, who had gone from home for some hours, removed the laudanum from its place and administered to the prisoner's child a much larger dose of it than a teaspoonful, and the child died in consequence.

The jury were directed that if the prisoner delivered to Sarah Stephens the laudanum, with intent that she should administer it to the child and thereby produce its death, the quantity so directed to be administered being sufficient to cause death; and that if the (prisoner's original intention still continuing) the laudanum was afterwards administered by an unconscious agent, the death of the child under such circumstances was murder on the part of the prisoner.

They were directed that if the teaspoonful of laudanum was sufficient to produce death, the administration by the little boy of a much larger quantity would make no difference.

The jury found the prisoner guilty. The judgment was respited, that the opinion of the Judges might be taken, whether the facts above stated constituted an administering of the poison by the prisoner to the deceased child.

This case was considered by all the Judges (except GURNEY, B. and MAULE, J.) in Easter Term, 1840, and they were unanimously of opinion that the conviction was right.

BUSH v. COMMONWEALTH

Court of Appeals of Kentucky, 1880.
78 Ky. 268.

JUDGE HINES delivered the opinion of the court.

For the purpose of testing the correctness of the instructions, we will assume that every deduction that the jury were authorized from the evidence to make, is a fact established by the evidence.

The jury might have found, 1st, that the girl was accidentally shot by appellant in an attempt to shoot, in necessary self-defense, her father; 2d, that the accused had the pistol in his hand for defense from an anticipated assault, and that the shot producing the wound was unintentional, both as to the firing of the pistol and as to the person wounded; 3d, that the killing was deliberate murder. The finding was guilty of murder, and a sentence of death by hanging.

. . .

It is proper, in this connection, to state that the evidence was such as to justify the jury in finding that the wound inflicted by the shot was neither necessarily nor probably mortal, and that the death ensued, not from the wound, but from scarlet fever, negligently communicated by the attending physician.

As said in Commonwealth v. Hackett (2 Allen 136, 141), the rule of the common law would seem to be, that if the wound was a dangerous wound, that is, calculated to endanger or destroy life, and death ensued therefrom, it is sufficient proof of murder or manslaughter; and that the person who inflicted it is responsible, though it may appear that the deceased might have recovered if he had taken proper care of himself, or submitted to a surgical operation, or that unskillful or improper treatment aggravated the wound and contributed to the death, or that death was immediately caused by a surgical operation rendered necessary by the condition of the wound. The principle on which this rule is founded is, that every one is held to contemplate and to be responsible for the natural consequences of his own acts. But if the wound is not dangerous in itself, and death results from improper treatment, or from disease subsequently contracted, not superinduced by or resulting from the wound, the accused is not guilty. When the disease is a consequence of the wound, although the proximate cause of the death, the person inflicting the wound is guilty, because the death can be traced as a result naturally flowing from the wound and coming in the natural order of things; but when there is a supervening cause, not naturally intervening by reason of the wound and not produced by any necessity created by the wound, the death is by the visitation of Providence and not from the act of the party inflicting the wound. In the case under consideration, the fever was not the natural consequence of the wound, nor was it produced by any necessity created by the infliction of the wound. It did not render it necessary to have the wound treated by a physician just recovering from the scarlet fever, even if it be conceded that medical treatment was necessary at all. If the death was not connected with the wound in the regular chain of causes and consequences, there ought not to be any responsibility. If a new and wholly independent instrumentality interposed and produced death, it cannot be said that the wound was the natural or proximate cause of the death. This view of the law was not so presented to the jury as to give the appellant its full benefit. It should have been clearly and definitely presented to the jury that if they believed from the evidence that death would not have resulted from the wound but for the intervention of the disease, they should not find the accused guilty of murder or manslaughter, but that they might find him guilty of wilfully and maliciously shooting and wounding under section 2, article 6, chapter 29, General Statutes; or of shooting and wounding in sudden affray, or in sudden heat and passion, without malice, under section 1, article 17, chapter 29, General Statutes. . . .

We deem it unnecessary to pass in detail upon each of the instructions granted and refused, as the intimation here given will be a sufficient guide in a retrial of the cause.

Judgment reversed, and cause remanded, with directions for further proceedings consistent with this opinion.[1]

MODEL PENAL CODE

Section 2.03. Causal Relationship Between Conduct and Result; Divergence Between Result Designed or Contemplated and Actual Result or Between Probable and Actual Result.

(1) Conduct is the cause of a result when:

(a) it is an antecedent but for which the result in question would not have occurred; and

(b) the relationship between the conduct and result satisfies any additional causal requirements imposed by the Code or by the law defining the offense.

(2) When purposely or knowingly causing a particular result is an element of an offense, the element is not established if the actual result is not within the purpose or the contemplation of the actor unless:

(a) the actual result differs from that designed or contemplated, as the case may be, only in the respect that a different person or different property is injured or affected or that the injury or harm designed or contemplated would have been more serious or more extensive than that caused; or

(b) the actual result involves the same kind of injury or harm as that designed or contemplated and is not too remote or accidental in its occurrence to have a [just] bearing on the actor's liability or on the gravity of his offense.

(3) When recklessly or negligently causing a particular result is an element of an offense, the element is not established if the actual result is not within the risk of which the actor is aware or, in the case of negligence, of which he should be aware unless:

(a) the actual result differs from the probable result only in the respect that a different person or different property is injured or affected or that the probable injury or harm would have been more serious or more extensive than that caused; or

(b) the actual result involves the same kind of injury or harm as the probable result and is not too remote or accidental in its occurrence to have a [just] bearing on the actor's liability or on the gravity of his offense.

(4) When causing a particular result is a material element of an offense for which absolute liability is imposed by law, the element is not established unless the actual result is a probable consequence of the actor's conduct.

---

1. Bush was tried again and convicted. This conviction was reversed by the Supreme Court of the United States on other grounds. Bush v. Kentucky, 107 U.S. 110, 1 S.Ct. 625, 27 L.Ed. 354 (1882).

Chapter 7

RESPONSIBILITY: IN GENERAL

SECTION 1. MENS REA

Responsibility means answerability or accountability. It is used in the criminal law in the sense of "criminal responsibility" and hence means answerability to the criminal law. No one is answerable to the criminal law for consequences not legally imputable to him. The present problem does not arise except in connection with consequences attributable to the one accused within the rules of imputability. On the other hand, consequences properly imputable to a certain person may be very harmful and yet not under such circumstances as to require him to answer criminally for what he has done. Whether they do or do not require him so to answer presents the problem of "responsibility."

Crime is frequently said to require both act and intent. As so used the word "intent" has quite a different meaning than "intention." An effort to avoid this variant use of the word has led to this suggestion: For guilt of crime there must be the union or joint operation of act and intent, or criminal negligence. This is not an improvement. It implies the use of "intent" in the strict sense of "intention," and with this limitation the mere addition of "criminal negligence" is inadequate to give full scope to the mental element involved in crime. Either form of expression, however, emphasizes the existence of the mental element. Leaving aside for the moment (1) the so-called "civil offenses" which are beyond the periphery of true crime, (2) the possibility of change by statute, and (3) difficulties of interpretation in certain situations, we find blameworthiness essential to criminal guilt.

The phrase "criminal intent" often has been used to express this requirement of blameworthiness. At other times "general criminal intent" has been employed to emphasize that the mental element so designated is not limited to actual intention.[1] Hence it is necessary

---

[1] "Criminal intent" in its narrow and proper sense is "nothing more than the intentional doing of 'that which the law declares to be a crime,' . . ." People v. Zerillo, 36 Cal.2d 222, 232, 223 P.2d 223, 230 (1950). "It is the criminal mind and purpose going with the act which distinguishes a criminal trespass from a mere civil injury." State v. Smith, 135 Mont. 18, 334 P.2d 1099, 1102 (1959).

to draw a very sharp line between actual intent (in the strict sense) and the various states of mind included within the very loose label of "general criminal intent."

The requirement of blameworthiness frequently has been couched in law Latin: "*Actus non facit reum, nisi mens sit rea.*" And it has been common to pick two words from this sentence and substitute "*mens rea*" for "guilty mind" or "mind at fault." Hence *mens rea* is essential to criminal guilt (with the qualifications mentioned above as to blameworthiness, which will receive attention under the head of "strict liability" and will be assumed here without further repetition).

Stated in other words, every crime is made up of two constituent parts: (1) the physical part and (2) the mental part. These may be described quite adequately as "the physical part of the crime" and "the mental part of the crime." Shorter labels are needed, however, for discussion purposes. The terms "guilty deed" and "guilty mind" are not entirely satisfactory because the former may be thought to be sufficient for punishment, whereas the union of both parts is required for conviction of crime. Hence it may be well to substitute Latin phrases which have the same meaning. These phrases are *actus reus* and *mens rea*.

If we can prove the existence of the physical part of the crime charged, and that this happening is attributable to the defendant within the legal rules of imputability, we have established his *actus reus*. And if we can prove that in doing what he did the defendant's state of mind was one which satisfies the requirements of the mental element of the crime charged we have established his *mens rea*. Neither one alone is sufficient for conviction; it is the combination of the two which constitutes criminal guilt.

The general mens rea. The mental element of crime is sometimes regarded as a state of mind common to all offenses, and sufficient for some, although an additional mental element may be required for others. Stated as a formula: "State-of-mind-X is common to all crimes and is sufficient for conviction unless the particular offense requires some additional mental element such as state-of-mind-Y or state-of-mind-Z."

Such a formula may have some value if care is taken to limit its application rather narrowly. A person may be so young that nothing can exist in his mind which will meet the juridical requirement of *mens rea*; hence it may be said that for *mens rea* the mind of the person must not be too young. Again, for *mens rea* the mental faculties must not be too greatly disturbed by mental disease; and under many circumstances a sane mind must not be too greatly diverted by a misunderstanding of the relevant facts or constrained by certain types of compulsion. Without going further into detail it is sufficient to point out the need of excluding every mental pattern which contains any factor sufficient in law to exculpate one who has done the particular deed in question. If every such factor is excluded and there is present an intent to do the deed which constitutes the *actus reus* of a certain offense, the result may be said to be the "general *mens rea*." It is necessary to add, however, that for certain crimes it is possible to substitute some other mental factor (such as criminal negligence) for the actual intent to do the *actus reus*.

In brief, while *mens rea* has certain factors which remain constant, these have to do with the general outlines of the mental pattern rather than with the minute details. For *mens rea*: (1) on the negative side there must not be found any factor which is sufficient for exculpation; (2) on the positive side there must be found an intent to do the deed which constitutes the *actus reus* of the offense charged (or some other mental element recognized as a substitute as, for example, criminal negligence in prosecutions for certain crimes). This is the so-called "general *mens rea*" or "general criminal intent" which is common to all true crime. It is indispensable, and is sufficient for guilt of some offenses although some additional mental element is required for others.

The *actus reus* may be the same in two crimes as in murder and manslaughter. For the most part, however, it differs from crime to crime. In burglary the *actus reus* is the nocturnal breaking into the dwelling house of another; in murder it is homicide; in battery it is the unlawful application of force to the person of another. The other constituent part also differs from crime to crime. In common-law burglary the *mens rea* is the intent to commit a felony; in murder it is malice aforethought; in battery no more is needed than the so-called "general criminal intent" which in a particular case may be criminal negligence. Hence in considering whether or not the actual *mens rea* has been established in a particular case, it is necessary to direct attention, not only to the state of mind with which the defendant acted, but also to the particular offense with which he is charged.

STATE v. CHICAGO, MILWAUKEE & ST. PAUL R. CO.

Supreme Court of Iowa, 1903.
122 Iowa 22, 96 N.W. 904.

The defendant's line of road crosses that of the Northwestern Railroad Company at Slater on the level. On the 14th day of February, 1902, the defendant, through its engineer, pulled its freight train over said crossing without stopping, as required by section 2073 of the Code, and in this action recovery of the penalty as therein provided was claimed. Trial to jury resulted in verdict and judgment for the state. The defendant appeals.—Reversed.

LADD, J. The defendant admitted the failure of its train to stop within 800 feet and more than 200 feet from the crossing, and interposed the defense that the engineer in charge did all he could to stop it, but that, owing to the brakes not working in the usual manner, the momentum of the train carried it over the crossing. The court submitted the case to the jury on the theory that the burden of proof was on the defendant, in order to exonerate itself from liability, to show by a preponderance of evidence that the failure to stop was not due to any negligence on the part of its employes in operating the train, or of the company in not having proper appliances, or in keeping those had in proper condition, and that the company might be liable even though the engineer was not. Possibly that should have been the law, but it was not so written by the legislature. The statute in question reads: "All trains run upon any railroad in this state which intersects or crosses any other railroad on the same level shall be brought to a full stop at a distance of not less than two hundred and not more than eight hundred feet from the point of intersection or crossing, before such intersection or crossing is passed, except as otherwise provided in this chapter. Any engineer violating the provisions of this section shall forfeit one hundred dollars for each offense, to be recovered in an action in the name of the state for the benefit of the school fund, and the corporation on whose road the offense is committed shall forfeit the sum of two hundred dollars for each offense to be recovered in like manner." Section 2073, Code. The latter part of the statute is purely penal in character, with the evident object of punishing the offender, rather than afford [sic] a remedy for the wrongful act. In this respect it differs radically from provisions awarding damages flowing from certain acts, such as the setting out of fire. Its meaning, then, cannot be extended beyond the terms employed. But one offense is denounced by it, and that is the omission of the engineer to stop the train as required. The first sentence commands what shall be done—defines a duty; the first clause of the second sentence imposes a penalty on any engineer for "each offense" of omitting such duty; the second clause of the second sentence adds a penalty against the corporation "on whose road such offense is committed." To what do these last words refer? Manifestly, to the offense of which the engineer is guilty. No other is mentioned in the section. The statute cannot be fairly read otherwise. The thought seems to have been that, as the engineer controls the train, the fault in failing to stop as required is primarily his, and secondarily that of the company for which he acts. There is no ground for holding that the company may be liable independent of any fault of the engineer. The forfeiture of the corporation is made to depend upon his guilt of the offense defined, and upon that only.

II. As the statute is purely penal in character, it ought not to be construed as fixing an absolute liability. A failure to stop may sometimes occur, notwithstanding the utmost efforts of the engineer. In such event this omission cannot be regarded as unlawful. The law never designs the infliction of punishment where there is no wrong.

The necessity of intent of purpose is always to be implied in such statutes. An actual and conscious infraction of duty is contemplated. The maxim, "*Actus non facit reum nisi meus* [sic] *sit rea*," obtains in all penal statutes unless excluded by their language. See Regina v. Tolson, 23 Q.B.Div. 168, where it was said, "Crime is not committed where the mind of the person committing the act is innocent." See, also, Sutherland on Statutory Construction, section 354 et seq. No doubt many statutes impose a penalty regardless of the intention of those who violate them, but these ordinarily relate to matters which may be known definitely in advance. In such cases commission of the offense is due to neglect or inadvertence. But even then it can hardly be supposed the offender would be held if the act were committed when in a state of somnambulism or insanity. As it is to be assumed in the exercise of the proper care that the engineer has control of his train at all times, proof of the mere failure to stop makes out a *prima facie* case. But this was open to explanation, and if, from that given, it was made to appear that he made proper preparation, and intended to stop, and put forth every reasonable effort to do so, he should be exonerated. . . .

Reversed.

STATE v. PEERY

Supreme Court of Minnesota, 1947.
224 Minn. 346, 28 N.W.2d 851.

THOMAS GALLAGHER, JUSTICE. Two appeals involving a conviction for indecent exposure, one from an order of the municipal court of St. Paul vacating its prior order granting defendant a new trial, and the other from a subsequent order denying defendant's motion for a new trial on the ground of newly discovered evidence. . . .

The evidence presented at the trial indicates that defendant, 23 years of age, a veteran of four major campaigns of the United States army in the South Pacific and at the time in question a seminar student at Concordia College awaiting the opening of the fall term at the University of Minnesota, occupied a corner ground-floor room in the Men's Dormitory at Concordia. The room has two windows, one opening to the west and the other to the north. About 15 to 20 feet from the west window, a cement sidewalk passes through the college grounds. It is used by the public generally and particularly by employees going to and coming from their work at the Brown & Bigelow plant nearby.

The state's witnesses here, several young ladies employed by Brown & Bigelow, testified in substance that on several occasions in passing by the Men's Dormitory on their way from work about 5 p. m. they had observed defendant unclothed, standing in front of or near the north window of his room, and that he later walked across and stood in the same condition near the west window; that on one such occasion they had observed him raise the west window shade and stand near this window exposed to view, entirely unclothed. There is no evidence that defendant had signaled or called to these witnesses or otherwise endeavored to direct their attention to himself.

In his defense, defendant testified that he returned to his room in the dormitory about 5 p. m. each evening; that it was his custom then to change his work clothing, take a shower in the basement of the dormitory, return to his room, and dress for his evening meal and classes. He denied that he had intentionally exposed himself. He admitted that on some occasions he may have neglected to draw the shades, but testified that he was not conscious of passers-by on the days in question; that he was careful as to his conduct at all times because of his high regard for his classmates who occupied neighboring dormitories. He stated that on at least one of the dates testified to by the state's witnesses he had not worked or changed his clothing at the time such witnesses had testified that they had passed his quarters and observed him.

Dr. Hugo W. Thompson, professor of Religion and Philosophy at Macalester College in St. Paul, testified that he was in charge of the industrial seminar at Concordia College attended by defendant; that the classes therein were held at night; that the students, including defendant, taking such course had been carefully selected from other colleges and were required, as part of the seminar, to be employed during the daytime; that defendant had always conducted himself as a gentleman, and the records of the project so indicated; that he (Dr. Thompson) had often used the walk in front of the Men's Dormitory at about the same time of day the state's witnesses passed defendant's quarters; that on such occasions he had often looked toward the Men's Dormitory, including defendant's room, but at no time had he witnessed any such incidents as testified to by the state's witnesses; that the walk is on college property and not a public street; that west of the walk is a thick hedge; that it is 40 feet from the west wall of the building to said walk; that defendant's room could be seen from his office across the way, but at no time had he seen any conduct on the part of defendant such as testified to by the state's witnesses. A portion of the settled case which the trial court certified as true and correct stated:

"There was no testimony by any of the witnesses either for the Prosecution or the Defense that defendant had waved or signaled to any of the girl witnesses for the Prosecution who claimed to have seen any of the exposures, or that he had in any way attempted to attract their attention or that he had called to or whistled at them or made any sound or done anything else calculated to attract their attention or the attention of anyone; other than the facts hereinbefore specifically recited.

"There was no testimony by any of the witnesses that defendant had committed any lewd or indecent acts other than the claimed exposures." . . .

1. The principle is well established that under either the ordinance or the statute, before the offense of indecent exposure can be established, the evidence must be sufficient to sustain a finding that the misconduct complained of was committed with the deliberate intent of being indecent or lewd. Ordinary acts or conduct involving exposure of the person as the result of carelessness or thoughtlessness do not in themselves establish the offense of indecent exposure. This would seem to be particularly true where the acts complained of take place within the privacy of a lodging removed from public places and where observation thereof is to some extent an invasion of the rights of privacy ordinarily attached to a home, whether it be a dwelling house or a room in a college dormitory. . . .

3. In the instant case, we are far from satisfied that the evidence is sufficient to sustain the trial court's finding that defendant's conduct was wilful and lewd rather than the result of carelessness or thoughtlessness. Defendant has denied the intent. He is a man without a previous blemish against his record. He is a combat veteran of four major campaigns of the South Pacific, honorably discharged as a staff sergeant, seeking a college education, and working part time to help defray his expenses. He concedes that on occasions he may have been careless. His room is small and fairly close to the sidewalk. His ordinary activity therein at about the times in question, when it was his custom to remove his clothing preparatory to bathing, might easily be misinterpreted by passers-by looking into his room.

There is no evidence whatsoever that he endeavored to attract the attention of passers-by by motioning, signaling, or calling to them, unless his act of raising the shade on one occasion might be thus regarded. This would seem rather flimsy evidence upon which to convict a man of the charge specified and to forever blemish his name and character as a result.

The testimony of Dr. Hugo Thompson, professor of Religion and Philosophy at Macalester College, characterizes defendant as a man of good reputation and high standing in the seminar. All the testimony in the case is consistent with defendant's testimony that he may have been careless or heedless, but that he did not intentionally expose himself. In our opinion, the evidence as submitted is insufficient to sustain a finding that defendant wilfully and intentionally indecently exposed himself in violation of either the ordinance or the statute above designated.

Reversed with directions to enter judgment discharging defendant.

PETERSON, JUSTICE (dissenting). Because I think that the evidence was sufficient to justify a finding of intentional indecent exposure, I dissent.

There is no dispute concerning certain facts such as those that defendant was nude in the room in question under such circumstances as to be visible through the windows to casual passers-by on the sidewalk outside; that the room is on the first floor at the northwest corner of the building; that there is a window on the north side opening onto the street lying to the north; that there is a window on the west side opening onto the sidewalk; that the bottom sills of the windows are only knee-high from the floor; that if a man stood nude in front of a window his private parts would be exposed to public view; and that girls employed in the vicinity passed on the sidewalk outside the window in going to and from their work. . . .

The majority holding simply amounts to saying that it is lawful for a man to stand nude in front of a window knowing that passers-by will see him. I cannot subscribe to such a doctrine, because I think it is not the law.

LIMICY v. STATE

Court of Criminal Appeals of Texas, 1945.
148 Tex.Cr.R. 130, 185 S.W.2d 571.

BEAUCHAMP, JUDGE. The appeal is from a conviction on a charge of committing an abortion. The sentence was four years in the penitentiary.

The court in the indictment upon which conviction was had alleges that John Limicy did "willfully and designedly in and upon Lula May Howard, a women [sic] then and there pregnant, did make an assault, and did then and there unlawfully, and designedly without the consent of the said Lula May Howard, procure an abortion by then and there striking, kicking, beating and violently using the person of her, the said Lula May Howard, during her pregnancy." It becomes necessary under the charge to show that appellant "designedly" committed the offense, with the intention to force an abortion. The principal question raised by the appeal is on the sufficiency of the evidence to support a finding in accordance with the indictment.

The prosecuting witness, Lula May Howard, a twenty-year-old girl, had lived with appellant since 1940 without being married to him. They had a child born of this illegitimate cohabitation and, if we properly understand the record, she had a miscarriage at a previous time. Some five months before the date of the alleged offense they had discovered that she was again pregnant and this fact was frequently discussed between them. There is, however, no intimation that any trouble had arisen about it or that appellant was displeased because she was pregnant and the fact of her being pregnant was not mentioned or considered in any way at the time of the fight which gave rise to the prosecution. He used no language that would indicate any intention to force an abortion and the jury had only the facts and circumstances involved in the fight upon which they could find him guilty under the court's charge. The prosecutrix describes the "fight" between her and the appellant as beginning on July 8th. He first beat her with a chair. That was during the night time. After she succeeded in getting the chair away from him he grabbed a rub board and broke it over her head. He also broke the broom handle in striking her. . . . They fussed and fought intermittently until Monday, July 10th, following the Saturday night when she describes the fight as beginning. The wounds were principally on her shoulders and head. When the fighting ceased they went up town together and later returned home after which she began to suffer. The appellant had gone and she sent for a negro woman who was known as being "kind of a granny woman." A doctor was called during the night. Whatever he did and the condition which he found is not in the record. The next day Dr. Wilson was called and he testifies in the case that in his opinion the premature birth of the child, after it had died in the mother's womb, was brought about by the injuries which he found inflicted on the prosecutrix.

The record does not disclose the origin of the trouble between the parties nor is it contended that he alone engaged in the conflict. It was a fight between them in which she was the loser by considerable odds. She testified in behalf of the State and said "we just had a fight that time and he beat me up." They were fussing over the little boy and she told him she was tired of living the way they were. . . . She further says that nothing was said during all of that time about the unborn baby other than that she remarked the way he was doing he did not want her to have the baby. She does not remember what he said about that.

The facts of this case present an aggravated and brutal attack made upon the woman in a delicate condition. That he has subjected himself to a penalty quite as severe as that inflicted by the jury will be conceded. We can, however, find no evidence supporting the conclusion reached by the jury of an intent to commit an abortion. Intent may be presumed from all of the facts and circumstances of a case, as charged by the court, but the mere fact of the premature birth of the child as a result of the things done, considered with all of the circumstances of this case, will not suffice because of the very nature of the fight between them. He struck her on the head and and [sic] the shoulders, and inflicted a slight wound on the leg, all of which were calculated to inflict injuries of a serious nature but none of which were directed in a manner to indicate an intention to bring about the death of the unborn child or to cause a miscarriage. . . . The conflict seems to have arisen as a result of their quarrel in which the prosecutrix took an active part and possibly the lead. If he originated the fight without cause support would be given to the State's contention, at least to some degree. As we find the record we believe it to be insufficient to support the jury's finding.

The judgment of the trial court is reversed and the cause is remanded.

SECTION 2. CRIMINAL NEGLIGENCE

Statements can be found to the effect that "negligence is a state of mind" or on the other hand that it is "not a state of mind." The difference is largely in the use of terms. Thus if negligence is said to be a state of mind it is conceded that to have juridical consequences it must be "manifested." If it is said not to be a state of mind, this is to emphasize that "the state of mind, which is the cause, must be distinguished from the actual negligence, which is its effect." The tendency is to use the word "negligence" as a synonym for "negligent conduct." This implies something done (or not done under circumstances involving a breach of duty to perform) with a state of mind involving this type of blameworthiness.

Intentional harm falls into quite a different category; and an act may be done with such a wanton and wilful disregard of a socially-harmful consequence known to be likely to result, that the attitude of mind will be more blameworthy than is imported by the word "negligence." Hence attention must be directed to risks of harm created by a state of mind different from either of these. Since some element of risk is involved in many kinds of useful conduct, socially-acceptable conduct cannot be limited to acts which involve no risk at all. To distinguish risks not socially acceptable from those regarded as fairly incident to our mode of life, the former are spoken of as "unreasonable." Even an unreasonable risk, (from the standpoint of the one endangered), may have been created without social fault, if the one who created the risk did not know or have reason to know of the existence of such risk under the circumstances. Hence a distinction is made between risks that are "realizable" and those that are not. Conduct, therefore, may be said to fall below the line of social acceptability if it involves a realizable and unreasonable risk of social harm. With this preface the following definition may be offered: Negligence is any conduct, except conduct intentionally harmful or wantonly and wilfully disregardful of an interest of others, which falls below the standard established by law for the protection of others against unreasonable risk of harm.[1]

1. This follows rather closely the definition adopted for torts by the American Law Institute: "In the Restatement of this Subject, negligence is any conduct, which falls below the standard established by law for the protec-

The social purpose underlying the requirement of compensation to the person harmed is not identical with that which forms the basis of punishment. Conceivably, therefore, the standard adopted in the criminal law of negligence might be entirely different from that used in civil cases. This is not exactly the answer since the "measuring stick" here, as well as there, is the conduct of a reasonable man under like circumstances. But whereas the civil law requires conformity to this standard, a very substantial deviation is essential to criminal guilt according to the common law. To express this greater degree of deviational behavior it has been common to modify the word "negligence" with some such epithet as "criminal," "culpable," "gross" or "wicked." Needless to say this is a field not subject to exact measurement. What it amounts to as a practical matter is a caution to the jury not to convict of crime, where other elements of culpability are lacking, except where the conduct causing the harm represents a rather extreme case of negligence. And despite an unfortunate lack of uniformity in expressing the idea, there is a tendency to speak of the types of behavior amounting to criminal negligence in terms of "reckless conduct" or "recklessness." [2]

Under some of the statutes guilt may be established by proof of negligence without showing that the conduct fell so far short of social acceptability as to merit the label "criminal" negligence. And a few jurisdictions seem to have taken this position as a matter of common law. On the other side of the picture, many offenses require something more than negligence of any degree in order to establish the *mens rea*.

COMMONWEALTH v. PIERCE

Supreme Judicial Court of Massachusetts, 1884.
138 Mass. 165.

HOLMES, J. The defendant has been found guilty of manslaughter, on evidence that he publicly practised as a physician, and, being called to attend a sick woman, caused her, with her consent, to be kept in flannels saturated with kerosene for three days, more or less, by rea-

tion of others against unreasonable risk of harm. It does not include conduct recklessly disregardful of an interest of others." Restatement, Second, Torts § 282 (1965).

The torts definition does not include intentional harm. Id. at comment d. For our purposes it seems better to express this exclusion than to leave it to inference. In the criminal law cases there is a tendency to use "recklessness" in connection with conduct amounting to criminal negligence. Hence in this field it is better to word this part of the exclusion in terms of conduct "wantonly and wilfully disregardful of an interest of others."

2. See, for example, State v. Clark, 118 Utah 517, 223 P.2d 184 (1950); Weaver v. State, 185 Tenn. 276, 206 S.W.2d 293 (1947); Radley v. State, 197 Ind. 200, 150 N.E. 97 (1925).

"Criminal negligence" exists where acts show a degree of carelessness amounting to culpable disregard of the rights and safety of others. Crosset v. State, 96 Okl.Cr. 209, 252 P.2d 150 (1952).

son of which she died. There was evidence that he had made similar applications with favorable results in other cases, but that in one the effect had been to blister and burn the flesh as in the present case.

The main questions which have been argued before us are raised by the fifth and sixth rulings requested on behalf of the defendant, but refused by the court, and by the instructions given upon the same matter. The fifth request was, shortly, that the defendant must have "so much knowledge or probable information of the fatal tendency of the prescription that [the death] may be reasonably presumed by the jury to be the effect of obstinate, wilful rashness, and not of an honest intent and expectation to cure." The seventh request assumes the law to be as thus stated. The sixth request was as follows: "If the defendant made the prescription with an honest purpose and intent to cure the deceased, he is not guilty of this offence, however gross his ignorance of the quality and tendency of the remedy prescribed, or of the nature of the disease, or of both." The eleventh request was substantially similar, except that it was confined to this indictment.

The court instructed the jury, that "it is not necessary to show an evil intent;" that, "if by gross and reckless negligence he caused the death, he is guilty of culpable homicide;" that "the question is whether the kerosene (if it was the cause of the death), either in its original application, renewal, or continuance, was applied as the result of foolhardy presumption or gross negligence on the part of the defendant;" and that the defendant was "to be tried by no other or higher standard of skill or learning than that which he necessarily assumed in treating her; that is, that he was able to do so without gross recklessness or foolhardy presumption in undertaking it." In other words, that the defendant's duty was not enhanced by any express or implied contract, but that he was bound at his peril to do no grossly reckless act when in the absence of any emergency or other exceptional circumstances he intermeddled with the person of another.
. . .

If a physician is not less liable for reckless conduct than other people, it is clear, in the light of admitted principle and the later Massachusetts cases, that the recklessness of the criminal no less than that of the civil law must be tested by what we have called an external standard. In dealing with a man who has no special training, the question whether his act would be reckless in a man of ordinary prudence is evidently equivalent to an inquiry into the degree of danger which common experience shows to attend the act under the circumstances known to the actor. The only difference is, that the latter inquiry is still more obviously external to the estimate formed by the actor personally than the former. But it is familiar law that an act causing death may be murder, manslaughter, or misadventure, according to the degree of danger attending it. If the danger is very great, as in the case of an assault with a weapon found by the jury to be deadly, or an assault with hands and feet upon a woman known to be exhausted by illness, it is murder.

The very meaning of the fiction of implied malice in such cases at common law was, that a man might have to answer with his life for consequences which he neither intended nor foresaw. To say that he was presumed to have intended them, is merely to adopt another fiction, and to disguise the truth. The truth was, that his failure or inability to predict them was immaterial, if, under the circumstances known to him, the court or jury, as the case might be, thought them obvious.

As implied malice signifies the highest degree of danger, and makes the act murder; so, if the danger is less, but still not so remote that it can be disregarded, the act will be called reckless, and will be manslaughter, as in the case of an ordinary assault with feet and hands, or a weapon not deadly, upon a well person. Cases of Drew and Fox, ubi supra. Or firing a pistol into the highway, when it does not amount to murder. . . .

If the principle which has thus been established both for murder and manslaughter is adhered to, the defendant's intention to produce the opposite result from that which came to pass leaves him in the same position with regard to the present charge that he would have been in if he had had no intention at all in the matter. We think that the principle must be adhered to, where, as here, the assumption to act as a physician was uncalled for by any sudden emergency, and no exceptional circumstances are shown; and that we cannot recognize a privilege to do acts manifestly endangering human life, on the ground of good intentions alone. . . . [1]

Exceptions overruled.

REGINA v. SALMON

Court for Crown Cases Reserved, 1880.
14 Cox C.C. 494.

Case reserved for the opinion of this Court by LORD COLERIDGE, C. J., at the Summer Assizes at Wells, 1880.

The three prisoners were tried before me on the 27th day of July, 1880, for the manslaughter of William Wells, a little boy of ten years old, under the following circumstances:

George Salmon is a member of the Frome Selwood Rifle Corps. On the 29th day of May he attended the rifle practice. He took his rifle from the armoury, had fourteen ball cartridges served out to him, and fired them all away. After the practice was over, he took away

---

[1] It must be culpable or criminal negligence to support a conviction of manslaughter. Frey v. State, 97 Okl.Cr. 410, 265 P.2d 502 (1953).

with him his rifle, which it was his duty to return to the armoury. He did not take it back, and the drill instructor missed six cartridges from the magazine when he went there about half an hour after the practice was over.

About seven o'clock, that is shortly after the practice was over, the three prisoners came together to the house of a witness (Newport) who was called, and whose evidence, so far as it is material to the point to be determined, was as follows:

"The three prisoners came to my father's house somewhere about seven in the evening on the 29th day of May. George Salmon had a rifle with him and some ball cartridges. All three wanted to fire off one or two shots, and they asked me for something to fire at. I gave them a board from our fowl house. I went with them into a field close by, and the prisoner Hancock climbed into a tree. George Salmon handed up the board to him. Hancock fixed it in the tree about eight feet from the ground. They all went about a hundred yards up the field, and all laid down in the grass. I heard two shots. I cannot tell which of them fired the shots, for I was looking at the board. I am not sure whether the first shot struck the target; the second shot did strike it. I do not know which of them fired it. Two more shots were fired afterwards, when Wells and Knight came running up and told us what had happened." . . .

It was proved that the distance from the spot where the shot was fired to the tree in which the boy was killed was three hundred and ninety-three yards; but the rifle was sighted for nine hundred and fifty yards, and would probably be deadly at a mile. . . .

The jury found all the prisoners guilty of manslaughter, but I allowed them to go out on bail till I could take the opinion of the Court of Criminal Appeal on the case.

I have to request the opinion of the Court whether there was any evidence upon which either or all of the prisoners could be convicted of manslaughter.

(Signed) COLERIDGE

No counsel appeared to argue on behalf of the prisoners.

Norris for the prosecution. The prisoner who fired the fatal shot was clearly guilty of manslaughter, but the evidence of his identity not being clear, the rule that all persons engaged in a common enterprise are jointly liable will apply. All the prisoners went into the field for a common purpose—rifle practice—and it was their duty to take all proper precautions to prevent any danger to other persons. The plan attached to the case shows that they fired across three highways, and that they were firing too near to the neighbouring gardens, in one of which the deceased boy was.

LORD COLERIDGE, C. J. I am of opinion that the conviction was right and ought to be affirmed. If a person does a thing which in itself is dangerous, and without taking proper precautions to prevent danger arising, and if he so does it and kills a person, it is a criminal act as against that person. That would make it clearly manslaughter as regards the prisoner whose shot killed the boy. It follows as the result of the culpable negligence of this one, that each of the prisoners is answerable for the acts of the others, they all being engaged in one common pursuit.

FIELD, J. I am of the same opinion. At first I thought it was necessary to show some duty on the part of the prisoners as regards to the boy, but I am now satisfied that there was a duty on the part of the prisoners towards the public generally not to use an instrument likely to cause death without taking due and proper precautions to prevent injury to the public. Looking at the character of the spot where the firing took place, there was sufficient evidence that all three prisoners were guilty of culpable negligence under the circumstances.

LOPES, J., concurred.

STEPHEN, J. I am of opinion that all three prisoners were guilty of manslaughter. The culpable omission of a duty which tends to preserve life is homicide; and it is the duty of every one to take proper precautions in doing an act which may be dangerous to life. In this case the firing of the rifle was a dangerous act, and all three prisoners were jointly responsible for not taking proper precautions to prevent the danger.

WATKIN WILLIAMS, J., concurred.

Conviction affirmed.

STATE v. BARNETT

Supreme Court of South Carolina, 1951.
218 S.C. 415, 63 S.E.2d 57.

OXNER, JUSTICE. Appellant was convicted of involuntary manslaughter. It was alleged in the indictment that the homicide resulted from criminal negligence in the operation of an automobile. The exceptions on this appeal relate solely to the charge. . . .

Error is assigned in the instructions relating to the degree of negligence necessary to sustain a conviction of involuntary manslaughter. It is said that the Court erred in charging that ordinary negligence is sufficient and that the jury should have been instructed that it was incumbent upon the State to show gross negligence or recklessness.

After defining involuntary manslaughter and distinguishing that offense from voluntary manslaughter, the Court stated that involuntary manslaughter may consist in the "killing of another without malice and unintentionally, but while one is engaged in the commission of some unlawful act not amounting to a felony and not naturally tending to cause death or great bodily harm", or in "the killing of another without malice and unintentionally but while one is negligently engaged in doing a lawful act." The jury was given the usual definition of negligence but was not instructed as to gross negligence, recklessness or wantonness. . . .

The degree of negligence necessary to establish criminal liability has perplexed the courts of England and America for centuries. The subject has at times been the source of much confusion. In the early development of the criminal law in England it was held that ordinary negligence, that is, the failure to exercise due care, was sufficient. Later it was found that this rule was too harsh. A noted English authority observed that an accident brought about by an act of ordinary negligence "may be the lot of even the wisest and best of mankind." The English courts finally concluded that more carelessness was required to create criminal liability than civil but they found it difficult to determine "how much more". They use such words as "gross", "reckless" and "culpable", and hold that it is for the jury to decide, in view of all the circumstances, whether the act was of such character as to be worthy of punishment. . . .

There was a tendency in the early American decisions to follow the rule first adopted in England to the effect that ordinary negligence was sufficient. That standard was soon repudiated, however, by the great majority of the courts in this country and it is now generally held that the negligence of the accused must be "culpable", "gross", or "reckless", that is, the conduct of the accused must be such a departure from what would be the conduct of an ordinarily prudent or careful man under the same circumstances as to be incompatible with a proper regard for human life, or conduct amounting to an indifference to consequences. . . .

Adverting now to homicides resulting from the operation of automobiles, in almost all jurisdictions, either by statute or by application of the rule governing involuntary manslaughter at common law, the rule is that the negligence necessary to convict a motorist of involuntary manslaughter must be of a higher degree than is required to establish negligent default on a mere civil issue and that the proof must show recklessness or such carelessness as is incompatible with proper regard for human life. . . .

There being no statutory definition of involuntary manslaughter, the courts of this State necessarily followed the common law definition. In doing so, as might have been expected from the experience of other courts, there has been some difficulty, and at times confusion, in determining the degree of negligence necessary to establish the offense. . . .

It seems to be thoroughly settled by the foregoing decisions that where the instrument involved is not inherently dangerous, we follow the general rule requiring more than ordinary negligence to support a conviction for involuntary manslaughter, but hold that simple negligence causing the death of another is sufficient if the instrumentality is of such character that its negligent use under the surrounding circumstances is necessarily dangerous to human life or limb. This Court is also committed to the view that firearms and motor vehicles fall within the latter category. We shall not now undertake to develop the rationale of this distinction. It may perhaps be explained upon the theory that want of ordinary care in the handling of a dangerous instrumentality is the equivalent of culpable or gross negligence. . . .

We have reviewed at great length, perhaps too much so, the decisions in this State, as well as the authorities elsewhere, relating to involuntary manslaughter. This has been deemed necessary in deciding whether we should adhere to the rule that an automobile is an instrumentality of such character that simple negligence in its operation is sufficient to support the common law offense of involuntary manslaughter. It must be conceded that only scant support can be found for this rule in other jurisdictions. But public policy requires that due consideration should be given to the principle of stare decisis. The Hanahan case has withstood attack for over a quarter of a century. The rule there announced and followed in a long line of cases was sanctioned, impliedly at least, by the Legislature, when it enacted the offense of reckless homicide. Under all the circumstances mentioned, we think the wisest policy is to adhere to the simple negligence rule in automobile homicide cases. If a change or modification is desirable, it should come from the law-making body.

Mr. Justice Taylor and the writer desire to say that they regard the simple negligence rule in automobile homicide cases as too harsh and if the question were one of original impression, they would not be in favor of adopting it.

All exceptions are overruled and the judgment affirmed.

FISHBURNE, STUKES and TAYLOR, JJ., concur.

BAKER, C. J., not participating.

SECTION 3. SPECIFIC INTENT

Despite the loose phrases "criminal intent" and "general criminal intent" courts have not lost sight of the fact that the word "intent" in its strict sense has the same meaning as "intention." Hence we find them reiterating that intent means purpose or design. The effort to assign the exact meaning has not been free from difficulty. "Intention then," writes Markby, "is the attitude of mind in which the doer of an act adverts to a consequence of the act and desires it to follow. But the doer of an act may advert to a consequence and not desire it: and therefore not intend it."[1] At the other extreme, Austin says that a result is intended if it is contemplated as a probable consequence, whether it is desired or not.[2] Salmond requires the element of desire but gives this word a somewhat forced construction. He says that a man desires not only the end but also the means to the end, and hence desires, although he may "deeply regret" the necessity for, the means.[3]

So far as actual intention is concerned, more is required than an expectation that the consequence is likely to result from the act. On the other hand it is not necessary that the consequence should be "desired" in the usual sense of the word, although this element may become important. If one acts for the purpose of causing a certain result he intends that result whether it is likely to happen or not. On the other hand he intends a consequence which he knows is bound to result from his act whether he desires it, regrets it or is quite indifferent as to it. And to avoid philosophical imponderables as to what is or is not "bound to happen" it is customary to speak of consequences "substantially certain to be produced." Stated in terms of a formula: Intended consequences are those which (a) represent the very purpose for which an act is done (regardless of likelihood of occurrence), or (b) are known to be substantially certain to result (regardless of desire).[4]

Use of the phrases "criminal intent" and "general criminal intent," in the broad sense of blameworthiness, has caused some confusion when actual intention was the idea to be expressed. At times the phrase "specific intent" has been employed for this purpose. In this sense "specific intent" indicates actual intention as distinguished from "general criminal intent" which includes the whole field of blameworthiness. Actual intention, however, can be expressed without the use of this phrase and there is a more important meaning for which "specific intent" should be reserved.

Some crimes require a specified intention in addition to an intended act. For example, the physical part of the crime of larceny is the trespassory taking and carrying away of the personal goods of another. But this may be done intentionally, deliberately, with full knowledge of all the facts and complete understanding of the wrong-

---

1. Markby, Elements of Law, § 220 (4th ed. 1889).

2. 1 Austin, Jurisprudence 424 (5th ed. 1885).

3. Salmond, Jurisprudence 395 (8th ed. 1930).

4. "The word 'intent' is used throughout the Restatement of this Subject to denote that the actor desires to cause the consequences of his act, or that he believes that the consequences are substantially certain to result from it". Restatement, Second, Torts § 8A (1965).

fulness of the act without constituting larceny. If this wilful misuse of another's property is done with the intention of returning it (with no change of mind in this regard) the state of mind needed for larceny is lacking. Such a wrongdoer is answerable in a civil suit, and may be guilty of some special statutory offense, such as operating a motor vehicle without the owner's consent. For guilt of common-law larceny, however, he must not only intentionally take the other's property by trespass, and carry it away; he must also have an additional intention in mind—the intent to steal. Burglary, moreover, cannot be defined as "intentionally breaking and entering the dwelling house of another in the nighttime," because this may be done without committing this felony. For common-law burglary there is required, not only the intentional breaking and entering of the dwelling house of another in the nighttime, but also an additional intent,—which is to commit a felony. This additional requirement is a "specific intent." It is an additional intent specifically required for guilt of the particular offense.

BANOVITCH v. COMMONWEALTH

Supreme Court of Appeals of Virginia, 1954.
196 Va. 210, 83 S.E.2d 369.

[Defendant claimed to be a medical doctor but was not licensed to practice in Virginia. According to his testimony he had studied medicine in Germany and was a graduate of the University of Vienna. He had a "cancer remedy" which consisted of three salves, one of which was a strong corrosive chemical. The medical testimony was that the treatment of cancer by the application of these salves was not approved or recognized in the medical profession. Miss Hazlewood told him she had cancer and he gave her the three salves for the treatment thereof. There is no evidence that she actually had cancer or that this treatment did any good, but also no evidence that it did any harm. Later she visited him saying she had cancer of the nose,—entirely different from the first supposed cancer. His treatment of the nose with the same salves caused her to lose part of the nose. According to a sister the nose was practically gone. During this treatment they became engaged and he was apparently still expecting to marry her at the time of her death several months later from some cause not in any way identified with the treatment.]

BUCHANAN, JUSTICE. An indictment under the maiming statute, § 18–70 of the Code, was returned against the defendant, Joseph E. Banovitch, charging that in July, 1952, he unlawfully made an assault on Lucy L. Hazlewood and by the use of certain salves and medicines unlawfully caused her bodily injury, with the intent to maim and disfigure her. On his trial to a jury he was found guilty of unlawful wounding "as charged in the within indictment," his punishment fixed at five years in the penitentiary and he was sentenced accordingly. On this appeal he alleges that error was committed in the admission of evidence, in the argument of the Commonwealth's attorney and in holding the evidence to be sufficient to sustain the verdict. . . .

Microscopic examination of tissue taken from the nose of Miss Hazlewood after her death disclosed no evidence of any malignancy. Miss Hazlewood's sister testified that when the defendant began the treatment on July 2 there were no marks, discoloring, moles or anything of that nature on her nose or face and nothing to indicate there was anything wrong with her.

At the conclusion of the evidence the court instructed the jury without objection that if the defendant applied the salve to Miss Hazlewood with a corrupt and evil intent of maiming or disfiguring her permanently, and not as a cure for some disease he may have thought she had, then he was guilty of unlawful maiming as charged in the indictment. The jury were also told that the Commonwealth must prove beyond a reasonable doubt that the defendant made an assault upon Miss Hazlewood "with the particular intent to maim or permanently disfigure her before he can be found guilty of unlawful wounding as charged in the indictment."

These instructions became the law of the case and they consist with the law of the land. Thus in Thacker v. Commonwealth, 134 Va. 767, 770, 114 S.E. 504, 505, it is said:

"When a statute makes an offense to consist of an act combined with a particular intent, that intent is just as necessary to be proved as the act itself, and must be found as a matter of fact before a conviction can be had; and no intent in law or mere legal presumption, differing from the intent in fact, can be allowed to supply the place of the latter." [1]

Section 18-70 of the Code, the maiming statute, provides that if any person maliciously or unlawfully shoot, stab, cut or wound another, or by any means cause him bodily injury, with the intent to maim, disfigure, disable or kill him, he shall be punished as the statute prescribes. In Harris v. Commonwealth, 150 Va. 580, 585, 142 S.E. 354, 355, 58 A.L.R. 1316, it is said: "The true purpose and meaning of the statute was doubtless conceived to be to define and punish as felonies those acts which had theretofore been considered misdemeanors only in those cases where it also appeared that there was the felonious intent to maim, disfigure, disable, or kill."

Proof of the specific intent is necessary to a conviction under the statute. "The test of the offense of maliciously or unlawfully causing

---

[1]. "When a specific intent to commit a fraud is a necessary element of the offense, proof of such intent may not be eliminated by the loose generalization that a man is presumed to intend the natural consequences of his acts". Windisch v. United States, 295 F.2d 531, 532 (5th Cir. 1961).

bodily injury is the intent with which the result is accomplished rather than the nature of the means, where the means are specified and established." The indictment must charge the specific intent and the verdict must find its existence either in terms or by necessary implication, Lane v. Commonwealth, 190 Va. 58, 55 S.E.2d 450.

The specific intent may, like any other fact, be shown by circumstances. Intent is a state of mind which can be evidenced only by the words or conduct of the person who is claimed to have entertained it. Thus when a person without any provocation strikes another with a deadly weapon or throws a corrosive acid in his face and thereby maims or disfigures him, he is presumed to have intended to maim or disfigure because that was the natural and probable consequence of his act.

However, an intent to maim or disfigure cannot be presumed from an act which does not naturally bespeak such intent. "The color of the act determines the complexion of the intent only in those situations where common experience has found a reliable correlation between a particular act and a corresponding intent." Hubbard v. United States, 9 Cir., 79 F.2d 850, 853; 22 C.J.S. Criminal Law, § 32, pages 91–92, note 4.

In Merritt v. Commonwealth, supra, the indictment charged the accused with maliciously pointing a loaded gun at Trull, who was in shooting range. It was held that the indictment charged an assault only, and "In order to raise this assault to a more substantive crime, it must be done with a specific intent to take life. This intent cannot be inferred from the act alleged." 164 Va. at pages 662–663, 180 S.E. at page 399.

The Commonwealth states in its brief that it has found no prior case in which a person purporting to practice medicine has been convicted of mayhem for the improper treatment of disease, but cites cases of convictions of manslaughter where death resulted from such treatment, whether the person giving the treatment was a licensed doctor or merely assumed to act as such. It then cites the statement in Harris v. Commonwealth, 134 Va. 688, 693, 114 S.E. 597, 599, that if the accused in that case would have been guilty of manslaughter if he had killed Quick, then he was guilty of unlawful wounding in shooting him. But that case was referring to voluntary manslaughter, an intentional killing, and not to involuntary manslaughter, an accidental killing, of which intent is not an element. . . .

The evidence in this case does not furnish proof beyond a reasonable doubt that the defendant applied the salves to the person of Miss Hazlewood with the specific intent to maim or disfigure her nor does it present facts from which such intent may properly be presumed. For the absence of that proof the judgment of conviction of unlawful wounding must be reversed. . . .

It is generally held, as noted, that if a physician, or a person assuming to act as such, through criminal negligence in the treatment of a patient causes his death he is guilty of manslaughter. If the criminal negligence results only in bodily injury to the patient, instead of death, it follows, we think, that the offense of assault and battery is committed, for the same reason as it was decided in Davis v. Commonwealth, supra, that the defendant there was guilty of assault and battery if he injured another while driving his automobile in a criminally negligent manner.

In Richardson v. Commonwealth, 192 Va. 55, 57, 63 S.E.2d 731, 732, it was said that in order to support a conviction of criminal negligence the Commonwealth "must prove beyond a reasonable doubt that the act, or series of acts, charged are of such reckless, wanton or flagrant nature as to show utter disregard of the safety of others under circumstances likely to cause injury. . . ."

We are, therefore, of opinion to remand this case to permit retrial, limited to the charge of assault and battery. . . .

DOBBS' CASE

Buckingham Assizes, 1770.
2 East, P.C. 513.

Joseph Dobbs was indicted for burglary in breaking and entering the stable of James Bayley, part of his dwelling-house, in the night, with a felonious intent to kill and destroy a gelding of one A. B. there being. It appeared that the gelding was to have run for 40 guineas, and that the prisoner cut the sinews of his fore-leg to prevent his running, in consequence of which he died.

PARKER, CH. B., ordered him to be acquitted; for his intention was not to commit the felony by killing and destroying the horse, but a trespass only to prevent his running; and therefore no burglary. But the prisoner was again indicted for killing the horse, and capitally convicted.[1]

[1]. One charged with having possession of a forged motor vehicle coupon, with intent to deceive, is not guilty if he in fact had no intent to deceive. Brend v. Wood, 62 L.T. 462 (1946). The court indicated *obiter* that the possession of a "deceptive document," such as this, is sufficient to establish a *prima facie* case of intent to deceive.

In an embezzlement case an instruction told the jury that they might infer an intent to defraud from acts which tend to produce that result; that this inference was not conclusive but that it would prevail unless the defendant introduced evidence which showed beyond a reasonable doubt that there was no such intent. This was held to be error. McKnight v. United States, 115 F. 972 (6th Cir. 1902).

Sec. 3   *SPECIFIC INTENT*   365

THACKER v. COMMONWEALTH

Supreme Court of Appeals of Virginia, 1922.
134 Va. 767, 114 S.E. 504.

WEST, J., delivered the opinion of the court.

This writ of error is to a judgment upon the verdict of a jury finding John Thacker, the accused, guilty of attempting to murder Mrs. J. A. Ratrie, and fixing his punishment at two years in the penitentiary.

The only assignment of error is the refusal of the trial court to set aside the verdict as contrary to the law and the evidence.

The accused, in company with two other young men, Doc Campbell and Paul Kelly, was attending a church festival in Alleghany county, at which all three became intoxicated. They left the church between ten and eleven o'clock at night, and walked down the county road about one and one-half miles, when they came to a sharp curve. Located in this curve was a tent in which the said Mrs. J. A. Ratrie, her husband, four children and a servant were camping for the summer. The husband, though absent, was expected home that night, and Mrs. Ratrie, upon retiring, had placed a lighted lamp on a trunk by the head of her bed. After eleven o'clock she was awakened by the shots of a pistol and loud talking in the road near by, and heard a man say, "I am going to shoot that God-damned light out;" and another voice said, "Don't shoot the light out." The accused and his friends then appeared at the back of the tent, where the flaps of the tent were open, and said they were from Bath county and had lost their way, and asked Mrs. Ratrie if she could take care of them all night. She informed them she was camping for the summer and had no room for them. One of the three thanked her, and they turned away, but after passing around the tent the accused used some vulgar language and did some cursing and singing. When they got back in the road, the accused said again he was going to shoot the light out, and fired three shots, two of which went through the tent, one passing through the head of the bed in which Mrs. Ratrie was lying, just missing her head and head of her baby, who was sleeping with her. The accused did not know Mrs. Ratrie and had never seen her before. He testified he did not know any of the parties in the tent and had no ill will against either of them; that he simply shot at the light, without any intent to harm Mrs. Ratrie or anyone else; that he would not have shot had he been sober, and regretted his action.

The foregoing are the admitted facts in the case.

An attempt to commit a crime is composed of two elements: (1) The intent to commit it; and (2) a direct, ineffectual act done towards its commission. The act must reach far enough towards the accomplishment of the desired result to amount to the commencement of the consummation.

The law can presume the intention so far as realized in the act, but not an intention beyond what was so realized. The law does not presume, because an assault was made with a weapon likely to produce death, that it was an assault with the intent to murder. And where it takes a particular intent to constitute a crime, that particular intent must be proved either by direct or circumstantial evidence, which would warrant the inference of the intent with which the act was done.

When a statute makes an offense to consist of an act combined with a particular intent, that intent is just as necessary to be proved as the act itself, and must be found as a matter of fact before a conviction can be had; and no intent in law or mere legal presumption, differing from the intent in fact, can be allowed to supply the place of the latter.

In discussing the law of attempts, Mr. Clark, in his work on criminal law, says, at p. 111: "The act must be done with the specific intent to commit a particular crime. This specific intent at the time the act is done is essential. To do an act from general malevolence is not an attempt to commit a crime, because there is no specific intent, though the act according to its consequences may amount to a substantive crime. To do an act with intent to commit one crime cannot be an attempt to commit another crime though it might result in such other crime. To set fire to a house and burn a human being who is in it, but not to the offender's knowledge, would be murder, though the intent was to burn the house only; but to attempt to set fire to the house under such circumstances would be an attempt to commit arson only and not an attempt to murder. A man actuated by general malevolence may commit murder though there is no actual intention to kill; to be guilty of an attempt to murder there must be a specific intent to kill."

Mr. Bishop, in his Criminal Law, Vol. 1 (8th ed.), at section 729, says: "When the law makes an act, whether more or less evil in itself, punishable, though done simply from general malevolence, if one takes what, were all accomplished, would be a step towards it, yet if he does not mean to do the whole, no court can justly hold him answerable for more than he does. And when the thing done does not constitute a substantive crime, there is no ground for treating it as an attempt. So that necessarily an act prompted by general malevolence, or by a specific design to do something else, is not an attempt to commit a crime not intended. . . . When we say that a man attempted to do a given wrong, we mean that he intended to do, specifically, it; and proceeded a certain way in the doing. The intent in the mind covers the thing in full; the act covers it only in part. Thus (section 730) to commit murder, one need not intend to take life, but to be guilty of an attempt to murder, he must so intend. It is not sufficient that his act, had it proved fatal, would have been murder (section 736). We have seen that the unintended taking of life may be murder, yet there can be no attempt to murder without the specific intent to commit it—a rule the latter branch whereof appears probably in a few of the States to have been interfered with by statutes (citing Texas cases). For example, if one from a housetop recklessly throws down a billet of wood upon the sidewalk where persons are constantly passing, and it falls upon a person passing by and kills him, this would be the common law murder, but if, instead of killing, it inflicts only a slight injury, the party could not be convicted of an assault with attempt to commit murder, since, in fact, the murder was not intended."

The application of the foregoing principles to the facts of the instant case shows clearly, as we think, that the judgment complained of is erroneous. While it might possibly be said that the firing of the shot into the head of Mrs. Ratrie's bed was an act done towards the commission of the offense charged, the evidence falls far short of proving that it was fired with the intent to murder her.

However averse we may be to disturb the verdict of the jury, our obligation to the law compels us to do so.

The judgment complained of will be reversed, the verdict of the jury set aside, and the case remanded for a new trial therein, if the Commonwealth shall be so advised.[1]

Reversed.

PEOPLE v. CONNORS

Supreme Court of Illinois, 1912.
253 Ill. 266, 97 N.E. 643.

MR. JUSTICE VICKERS delivered the opinion of the court: . . .

. . . There is, however, a general agreement among the witnesses that the plaintiffs in error and their associates, through threats of violence and by the presentation of drawn revolvers, sought to compel the members of the International Association to cease work, take off their overalls and go down and join the United Association, threatening that unless this demand was complied with they would shoot or kill the members of the International Association. Morgan H. Bell, upon whom the alleged assault to murder was committed, at the time of the attack was at work on the lower floor. The evidence shows that someone of the attacking party, approaching Bell and Lefevre, said, "Get that big son-of-a-b———." The men walked up to Bell, and plaintiff in error Storgaard pulled a revolver partly out of his pocket, presented the point at Bell and told him to take off

---

1. The jury were instructed that if four were acting together with a common purpose to resist arrest and any one of the four shot an officer, in that effort, with intent to kill, all would be guilty of an assault with that intent. This was held to be error. State v. Taylor, 70 Vt. 1, 39 A. 447 (1896).

his overalls or "they would bore a hole through him." Bell succeeded in getting away at that time and went upstairs, followed by two of his pursuers. Bell gives the following account of what occurred after he got upstairs: "There was some of them got me there and put their guns up to me. One of them held two guns at my stomach and another one at my head, and told me if I didn't quit my fooling and get out of there they would fill me full of holes." Plaintiff in error Connors is identified as one of the men who held a pistol on Bell, accompanied by the threat above stated. This witness states that the revolvers were held against him until he began to remove his overalls. Plaintiff in error Gentleman is also identified as one of the men who made the attack upon Bell. The evidence shows that similar attacks were made upon other workmen, who were commanded to take off their overalls under pain of being shot, and to go down to Burke and get a permit to work. Two of plaintiffs in error, O'Connor and Connors, are shown to have made a similar attack upon one Lettker, commanding him to take off his overalls, and threatening that if he did not do so to bore a hole through him. Lettker complied with the request, as did also Bell and others, to the extent of taking off their overalls. Lettker says in his testimony: "I took the gentlemen at their word. You know they said they were going to bore a hole through me, and I didn't want to be riddled or killed, and I took the man's word." This witness identifies Kane, O'Connor, Connors, Gentleman and Storgaard as being present and participating in the assault. Pistols were also drawn upon Kapritzki, and he was commanded as were the others, and to him it was said, "If you look for trouble I shoot you like a dog;" and again, "If you don't go right away you will get killed." A police station was only a block away. Some of the workmen had apparently escaped unnoticed and notified the police, and about the time that Kapritzki was being assaulted there was a cry of "Jiggers!" and "Coppers!" and at that moment a number of policemen appeared upon the scene. When the police arrived the attacking party made a hasty exit in all directions. Some of them ran down the Illinois Central tracks, some across the coal yards, and some in other directions. As he ran, plaintiff in error Gentleman was seen to throw a revolver away, and another, who went down the Illinois Central tracks, put his revolver by the fence, where it was afterwards picked up by a watchman and taken to the police station. All of the attacking party succeeded in making good their escape except plaintiff in error Storgaard, who was arrested by the police on the lower floor and a loaded revolver taken from him. The presence and participation of Storgaard and Gentleman in this affair is not denied. Connors testifed that he was not present, but he is not corroborated in any substantial particular and the testimony is amply sufficient to justify a finding that he was present. Arthur O'Connor also denied that he was present, claiming that he was confined to his home at the time by illness. There is some evidence tending to corroborate O'Connor's testimony, which will be considered hereafter.

Plaintiffs in error contend that the trial court erred in giving instruction No. 9 on behalf of the prosecution. That instruction is as follows:

"The court instructs you as to the intent to kill alleged in the indictment, that though you must find that there was a specific intent to kill the prosecuting witness, Morgan H. Bell, still, if you believe, from the evidence, beyond a reasonable doubt, that the intention of the defendants was only in the alternative,—that is, if the defendants, or any of them, acting for and with the others, then and there pointed a revolver at the said Bell with the intention of compelling him to take off his overalls and quit work, or to kill him if he did not,—and if that specific intent was formed in the minds of the defendants and the shooting of the said Bell with intent to kill was only prevented by the happening of the alternative,—that is, the compliance of the said Bell with the demand that he take off his overalls and quit work,—then the requirement of the law as to the specific intent is met."

The plaintiffs in error earnestly contend that pointing a loaded revolver at another within shooting distance and threatening to shoot unless some demand made by the assaulting party is complied with cannot be held to be a felonious assault with intent to kill and murder, for the reason that the intent is in the alternative and is coupled with a condition, and for that reason is not a specific intent to kill, which is necessary to sustain a conviction for an assault with an intent to murder. All the authorities agree upon the general proposition that in a prosecution for an assault with intent to murder, or with intent to commit some other felony, the specific intent charged is the gist of the offense and must be proven as charged in the indictment. Upon this and like authorities where the general rule is stated, plaintiffs in error contend that the intent to commit the crime charged must be absolute and unconditional and that if a dangerous weapon is presented in a threatening manner, accompanied with a demand upon the assaulted party and a threat to destroy his life unless such demand is complied with, the offense can not be an assault to murder. It is argued that the condition which accompanies the threat negatives the existence of that positive and specific intent which, under the law, is a necessary element in the offense charged.

No case decided by this court is cited by either party, and we are not aware that any such case exists, that is conclusive of the precise question which is raised here. In support of the view that an assault with a loaded revolver and a threat to shoot unless the party assaulted complies with a demand is not an assault with an intent to murder, plaintiffs in error rely with great confidence upon the case of Hairston v. State, 54 Miss. 689. In that case Hairston, in company with others, attempted to remove the personal effects of a laborer from the plantation of his employer, Richards, to whom said laborer was indebted on account of advances of money or provisions made to said laborer. Hairston was in the act of hauling away the household furniture when Richards attempted to stop the wagon and took hold of Hairston's mules saying that he could not move the household goods until his debt was settled. Thereupon Hairston drew a pistol and pointed it at Richards and said, "I came here to move Charles Johnson and by God I am going to do it, and I will shoot any God damned man who attempts to stop my mules," at the same time urging his mules forward as he spoke. His manner was threatening and angry and his voice loud and boisterous. Other persons who were accompanying Hairston, some of whom were armed with guns, pressed around Richards, as if they intended to aid Hairston if necessary. Richards was deterred by the apparent danger and released the mules and the wagon moved on. Under the above facts Hairston was convicted of an assault with an intent to murder Richards. The conviction was reversed by the Supreme Court of Mississippi. The reasoning of the court in that case is as follows: Richards was in the act of committing a trespass upon Hairston's property by laying his hands upon the mules and forcibly stopping Hairston upon the public highway. Hairston had a right to protect his property from such unlawful trespass, using no more force than was necessary. His threat to shoot was conditioned upon a demand which he had a right to make. In disposing of the case the Supreme Court of Mississippi uses the following language: "Here there was only a conditional offer to shoot, based upon a demand which the party had a right to make. While the law will not excuse the assault actually committed in leveling the pistol within shooting distance, it cannot, from this fact alone, infer an intent to murder. The intent must be actual,—not conditional,—and especially not conditioned upon non-compliance with a proper demand." A careful analysis of that case will show that the court laid special stress on the circumstance that the threat to shoot was coupled with a demand which the prisoner had a lawful right to make. . . .

In McClain's Criminal Law (section 232) the rule applicable to the case at bar is thus stated: "If the threatened injury, coupled with present ability to inflict it, is conditioned upon the party assailed refusing to do something which the assailant has no right to require him to do, it will constitute an assault even though the conditions are complied with and therefore no violence is used." . . .

We find no error in this record requiring a reversal of the judgment below. It is therefore affirmed.

Judgment affirmed.[1]

---

[1]. One who had a right to have her truck loaded first became involved in an argument with another trucker and warned the other that she would kill him if he loaded his truck ahead of hers. It was held that she placed in her threat a condition which she had a right to make and hence the

SECTION 4. OTHER PARTICULAR STATES OF MIND

The phrase "specific intent" has been used, at times, to refer to any special state of mind required for the *mens rea* of a particular offense. The underlying thought is this: Some crimes require only the general *mens rea;* others require a specific intent. Unfortunately, this adds to the confusion attaching to the use of the word "intent." This usage is too common to be ignored. It is well to emphasize, however, that many offenses require some particular state of mind other than a "specific intent" in the strict sense of the phrase.

If guilt of a certain offense requires that an act be done "fraudulently," this means it must be done with an intent to defraud. This is a specific intent in the strict sense of the phrase, but other factors are involved if the *mens rea* requirement is "malice," "knowledge" or "wilfulness."

(A) MALICE

Many statements are to be found to the effect that malice, as it is used in the law, does not imply any feeling of hatred, grudge, anger or ill-will, but requires only an intent to do harm without lawful justification or excuse. The last clause requires some modification in the homicide cases. An intent to kill may be in such sudden heat of passion engendered by adequate provocation as to fall outside of the "malice" label. On the other side, an act may be done with such wanton and wilful disregard of an obvious and extreme risk of causing death that it will be said to be done with malice aforethought (if there was no justification, excuse or mitigation) even if there was no actual intent to kill. To say that the law will "imply" an intent to kill in such a case, or that such a wanton and wilful disregard of an obvious hazard is "equivalent" to an intent to kill, is to indulge in "double-talk." It is quite proper to bring such a killing within the category of murder. The preferable explanation, however, is a frank recognition of the possibility of malice aforethought without an actual intent to kill. This may be illustrated by the case of one who intentionally blows up a building, without justification, excuse or mitigation, hoping the place to be empty but having no way of knowing

threat did not violate the statute. Spencer v. State, 156 Tex.Cr.R. 628, 245 S.W.2d 710 (1952). If one wrongfully bites another's ear, and holds on so tightly that the ear is torn from the head when the two are separated, this was done "on purpose and with intent to disfigure." State v. Skidmore, 87 N.C. 509 (1882).

whether this is the fact or not. The wrongdoer is guilty of murder if there were people in the building who were killed by the explosion. To say he "intended" to take human life is to misuse the word, but to speak of his state of mind as "malicious" is entirely unobjectionable.

If the word as it is used in the phrase "malice aforethought" gives a reasonable clue to its meaning in other than homicide cases, it would seem to be this: "Malice" means an intent to do the very harm done, or harm of a similar nature, or a wanton and wilful disregard of an obvious likelihood of causing such harm, with an implied negation of any justification, excuse or mitigation.

STATE v. LAUGLIN

Supreme Court of North Carolina, 1861.
53 N.C. 354.

Indictment for felonious burning, tried before SAUNDERS, JUDGE, at the spring term, 1861, of Robeson Superior Court.

The indictment charged that the defendant "feloniously, wilfully, and maliciously did set fire to, and burn a certain barn then having corn in the same." The proof was that the prisoner maliciously and wilfully did set fire to a stable with fodder in it, and that a crib with corn and peas in it, which stood within twenty-six feet of the stable, was partially consumed, but by great exertion was saved from total destruction.

The Court charged as to the crib (which he sometimes in the alternative calls a barn), "that if satisfied of the burning of the stable by the prisoner, as it was an unlawful act, the prisoner was responsible for the consequences; and if they (the jury) were satisfied, beyond a reasonable doubt, that the stable was likely to and did communicate to the crib, and it was thereby burnt, they should convict; but they were to be satisfied that by the burning of the stable, the burning of the crib was a reasonable probability to follow; in which case the prisoner would be answerable." The defendant's counsel excepted.

Verdict, "guilty." Sentence was pronounced, and defendant appealed.

BATTLE, JUDGE. The bill of exceptions presents for consideration two questions, both of which are of great importance to the community, as well as to the prisoner. The first is, whether the wilful and malicious setting fire to the house of another, the burning of which is only a misdemeanor, will become a capital felony, if a dwelling-house or barn with grain in it, be thereby burnt, where such burning is the probable consequence of the first illegal act. Upon this question we concur in the opinion given in the Court below: that in such a case, the prisoner is guilty of the felonious burning of the dwelling-

Sec. 4 OTHER PARTICULAR STATES OF MIND 373

house or barn, upon the principle that he is to be held responsible for the natural and probable consequence of his first criminal act. In support of this proposition, the burning of one's own dwelling-house with a malicious and unlawful intent, furnishes a strong argument from analogy. Such burning is, of itself, only a high misdemeanor; but if the dwellings of other persons be situated so near to the one burnt, that they take fire and are consumed, as an immediate and necessary consequence of the first illegal act, it will amount to a felony. . . .[1]

(For other reasons the judgment was reversed.)

TERRELL v. STATE

Supreme Court of Tennessee, 1888.
86 Tenn. 523, 8 S.W. 212.

CALDWELL, J. The plaintiff in error, Ned Terrell, stands convicted of the crime of mayhem, and is under sentence of two years' confinement in the penitentiary. The indictment charges him with having unlawfully, feloniously, willfully, and maliciously made an assault upon the prosecutor, James Wilson, and struck him in one eye with a stone, or some other hard substance, whereby the eye was put out, and the prosecutor was maimed and disfigured. It is shown in the proof, and admitted by the prisoner, that he struck the prosecutor in one eye with "a half of a brick," and that the prosecutor was thereby rendered entirely blind, having previously lost the other eye. On the trial of the case his honor, the circuit judge, quoted to the jury the statute under which the prisoner is presented, and then charged them further, and among other things, that "in order to convict the defendant in this case, it must be shown by the proof that he did put out the eye of the prosecutor, as alleged in the indictment, by willfully and maliciously striking him in the eye with the brick or other hard substance and that it was done unlawfully,—that is, without lawful excuse, . . . " and that if he did this "from feelings of malice toward the prosecutor . . . he would be guilty as charged." The prisoner's counsel requested the court to instruct the jury, in addition, that unless "the defendant did of his malice aforethought inflict the blow, with purpose or intent to put out the eye, or inflict some other mayhem on the prosecutor, then the defendant would not be guilty of mayhem." This request was refused by the court, and that refusal is assigned as error.

Upon this action arises the inquiry, is a specific intent to maim a necessary element of the crime of mayhem? This precise question

---

1. In a prosecution for statutory extortion, based upon a threat to accuse X of arson with intent to extort money from X, evidence that X did in fact burn the building was excluded as immaterial. Commonwealth v. Buckley, 148 Mass. 27, 18 N.E. 577 (1888). One who threatens a thief with criminal prosecution unless he returns the stolen property is guilty of extortion. People v. Beggs, 178 Cal. 79, 172 P. 152 (1918).

never having been decided in this state, its solution can be best arrived at by a brief review of some of the authorities and statutes upon the general subject. "Mayhem, at common law," says Mr. East, "is such a bodily hurt as renders a man less able, in fighting, to defend himself or annoy his adversary; but if the injury be such as disfigures him only, without diminishing his corporal abilities, it does not fall within the crime of mayhem." 1 Whart.Crim.Law, (8th Ed.) § 581. . . .

The words characterizing the forbidden acts are "unlawfully and maliciously." They are used alike with respect to every offense mentioned in the section, and must be given the same significance as applied to each of them. They mean the same thing when applied to mayhem that they do when applied to malicious shooting or stabbing. "Unlawfully" always means without legal justification; but "maliciously" has different meanings, which it is not important now to give in detail. Its signification as used in the fifty-fifth section of the act of 1829 is well stated and illustrated in Wright v. State, 9 Yerg. 343, 344. Wright was indicted and convicted for malicious stabbing under that section, and on appeal in error to this court it was insisted, in his behalf, that the proof did not show that degree of malice necessary to constitute the offense charged. JUDGE TURLEY, delivering the opinion of the court, said: "It is true that the statute requires that this offense shall be committed with malice aforethought, by which is not meant such malice as is required by the third section of the same act to constitute the crime of murder in the first degree, but malice according to its common law signification, which is not confined to a particular animosity to the person injured, but extends to an evil design in general, a wicked and corrupt nature, an intention to do evil." . . . "The question then arises, is the proof in this case of a character to justify the jury in having found the existence of malice according to the definition given? We consider it unnecessary to go into a minute investigation of the testimony on this point. It shows beyond a doubt that the prisoner stabbed Lewis Underwood, the prosecutor. Upon this proof the law presumes malice." With this approved interpolation, applied, as it must be, in reference to each of the offenses enumerated, the use of the word "maliciously" in the statutes is shown to afford no justification for the contention that the crime of mayhem can be committed only when the blow is stricken for the purpose of inflicting that particular injury upon the sufferer. The character of malice necessary to the crime of mayhem has in fact been held by this court to be the same as that defined in the case of malicious stabbing just quoted. Werley v. State, 11 Humph. 175. Werley was convicted for the castration of his slave. In his defense it was shown that the slave was of very lewd character, and that his master's purpose was to reform him. Upon the facts it was argued that the necessary malice was wanting. The decision was that the act was unlawful, and, that being so, malice would be implied unless circumstances of provocation be shown to remove the legal presumption. The conviction was affirmed. . . .

It is next insisted that, even under the charge of the law as given to the jury, the verdict is not supported by the evidence. Upon this contention, the whole of the evidence has been given a very careful consideration by this court, but it is not deemed necessary to enter into a minute statement or discussion of it in this opinion. It is sufficient to say that the prosecutor's testimony makes a strong case of an unexpected, unprovoked, and violent assault upon him in the nighttime, resulting, as already stated, in the destruction of his only eye, and rendering him totally blind. The only countervailing testimony is that of the defendant himself, introduced for the purpose of showing provocation and apprehension of danger from the prosecutor when the blow was stricken. The other testimony in the record is in conflict with his statements, and corroboration of those of the prosecutor.

We are well satisfied with the verdict. Let the judgment be affirmed.

TURNEY, C. J., and SNODGRASS, J., dissent.

STATE v. JOHNSON

Supreme Court of Wyoming, 1898.
7 Wyo. 512, 54 P. 502.

B. A. Johnson was charged with malicious trespass under the statute. There was an agreed statement of the evidence, and the district court reserved four questions for the decision of this court, as follows: . . . (4) Does the information in this case, under the statement of facts as agreed upon, charge any offense under the laws of this state? The facts are, in brief, that the defendant, in driving a band of sheep from a dipping corral to a neighboring railroad station, drove them over and across certain uninclosed, unimproved, and uncultivated land of the prosecuting witness, and that the defendant did not stop to graze them thereon for any greater length of time than sheep do graze while being driven from place to place by the usual and ordinary method of so driving them.

CORN, J. (after stating the facts as above). If this were a civil action for damages, a part of the questions would become important, which in this case, involving only the construction of a criminal statute, it will be unnecessary for us to decide. It is very well settled that the mere roaming of cattle and other domestic animals upon uninclosed private lands in the Western country does not constitute a trespass. A distinction has been insisted upon in the case of sheep, which are not permitted to roam at will, but are herded and directed by a shepherd; and it is maintained that, when they are driven upon such lands for the purpose of pasturage, it constitutes a trespass, for which damages may be recovered by the owner of the land. A decision of the latter question is not required by the facts of this case. The statute invoked by the prosecution is one of a very large class, both in England and this country, and provides that "whoever maliciously or mischievously injures, or causes to be injured, any property of another or any public property, is guilty of malicious trespass." Under similar statutes in England it has been held that in order to constitute the offense the act must be done from malice against the owner. The doctrine has not been carried to that extent in this country, but the authorities are nevertheless substantially agreed that the malice necessary to constitute the offense is something more than the malice which is ordinarily inferred from the willful doing of an unlawful act without excuse. The statutes were not intended to make every willful and wrongful act punishable as a crime, but they were devised to reach that class of cases where the act is done with a deliberate intention to injure. In Com. v. Williams, 110 Mass. 401, which was a prosecution for a willful and malicious injury to a building, the court say: "The jury must be satisfied that the injury was done out of a spirit of cruelty, hostility, or revenge. This element must exist in all those injuries to real or personal property which are enumerated and made criminal in the several statutes. The injury must not only be willful (that is, intentional and by design as distinguished from that which is thoughtless or accidental), but it must, in addition, be malicious, in the sense above given. The willful doing of an unlawful act without excuse, which is ordinarily sufficient to establish criminal malice, is not alone sufficient under these statutes. The act, although intentional and unlawful, is nothing more than a civil injury, unless accompanied with that special malice which the words 'willful and malicious' imply." In Duncan v. State, 49 Miss. 331, which was an indictment for malicious mischief in killing a hog, the jury returned a verdict, "We, the jury, find the accused guilty of the willful and unlawful killing of the hog, but not out of a spirit of mischief, revenge, or wanton cruelty." And this was held to be an acquittal of the accused of the charge of the indictment. So, in Wright v. State, 30 Ga. 325, which was an indictment for malicious mischief in shooting a mule, the court say: "The question to be tried was not whether he was justified in shooting the mule, but whether his motive in shooting was malicious. The question of justification would be the issue in an action for damages against him, but on this indictment the issue was malice or no malice. If he shot from the motive of protecting his crop, and not from either ill will to the owner or cruelty to the animal, his motive was not malicious, whether it was justifiable or not, and his act was not malicious mischief." In a New Jersey case the defendant was indicted for willfully and maliciously tearing down an advertisement of sale set up by the sheriff. His defense was that he took it down for the purpose of showing it to his counsel, and from no bad motive. The court say: "The word 'maliciously,' when used in the definition of a statutory crime, the act forbidden being merely malum prohibitum, has almost always the effect of making a bad intent or evil mind a constituent of the offense. The whole doctrine of that large class of offenses falling under the general denomination of 'malicious mischief' is founded on this theory. For example, it was declared by the supreme court of Massachusetts in the case of Com. v. Walden, 3 Cush. 558, that the word 'maliciously,' as used in the statute relating to malicious mischief, was not sufficiently defined as 'the willful doing of an act prohibited by law, and for which the defendant has no lawful excuse.' But that, to the contrary, in order to justify a conviction under the act referred to, the jury must be satisfied that the injury was done either out of a spirit of wanton cruelty or wicked revenge." Folwell v. State, 49 N.J.Law 31, 6 A. 619. And it seems to be generally held that, in order to bring an offense under the head of malicious mischief, it must appear that the mischief was itself the object of the act, and not that it was incidental to some other act, lawful or unlawful. . . . No answer is made to the first, second, and the third questions, none being necessary, and the fourth is answered in the negative.[1]

POTTER, C. J., and KNIGHT, J., concur.

STATE v. LAMBERT

Supreme Court of Louisiana, 1938.
188 La. 968, 178 So. 508.

ROGERS, JUSTICE. Stark E. Lambert was found guilty of libel and sentenced to pay a fine of $30 and costs and to be imprisoned in

---

1. A veterinarian caused a swelling in a mare's shoulders in order to get money by pretending to cure the animal of a disease. This intentional harm to the animal was held to constitute malicious mischief although inflicted without ill will toward either the owner or the mare. Brown v. State, 26 Ohio St. 176 (1875).

One who was driving from side to side of the road with reckless abandon ran a buggy shaft into another's horse. This wanton and wilful disregard of the obvious danger to persons and property was held sufficient to make him guilty of malicious mischief although the injury was unintentional. Porter v. State, 83 Miss. 23, 35 So. 218 (1903).

The killing of a mare by a forest ranger, in good faith discharge of his duties and in compliance with a regulation of the Secretary of Agriculture, was not malicious mischief even if the regulation was invalid. Fears v. State, 33 Ariz. 432, 265 P. 600 (1928).

During the early days of prohibition in Kansas a militant reformer wrecked a saloon with an ax. Being charged with malicious trespass she insisted that she was merely putting an unlawful establishment out of business, and had "no ill will against the owner or possessor of the property, or design to destroy property merely for the purpose of its destruction", and hence had acted without malice. In upholding her conviction the court held the word "malicious" as found in this statute is employed in "the usual sense in which it is used in criminal statutes". State v. Boies, 68 Kan. 167, 74 P. 630 (1903).

the parish jail for 20 days, and in default of payment of the fine to be imprisoned for an additional period of 50 days. Not having the right of appeal, he applied for writs of certiorari and prohibition. Certiorari issued and the proceedings complained of by relator are now before us for review.

Relator, an uneducated manual laborer, is a resident of the State of Texas. On the death of his wife, Care Farley, he permitted her sister, Mrs. Ethel Farley, wife of William Bailey, to remove his minor children, Olean Lambert and Harold Lambert, to her home in Terrebonne parish, La. Mrs. Lillian Farley, wife of Conrad Morris, known to her family and friends as "Curley," is also a sister of his deceased wife.

On July 19, 1937, relator wrote a letter to Mrs. Ethel Farley Bailey, which letter reads as follows, viz.: . . .

The portion of relator's letter which it is alleged constitutes the libel is in the following words, viz.: "I have objected to Orleen living with Kerley all the time She has been living in Houma for over three years and has lived with Conrad Morris ever since She has been thear and has Been Married abought five monts She might wont Orleen to live with a man a few years Befor She mearried him it Sure woodent suit me."

The record presents two bills of exception. The first exception is to the overruling of defendant's objection to the admission in evidence of his letter to Mrs. Bailey, on the ground that it is a privileged communication, being a private letter from defendant to his deceased wife's sister, protesting that his daughter, eight years of age, should not be permitted to visit Lillian Farley, because of her relation with Conrad Morris, with whom she had been living in adultery. The other exception is taken to the overruling of defendant's motion for a new trial, predicated on the ground that the private letter from defendant to his deceased wife's sister, protesting the residence of his daughter, eight years of age, with Mrs. Morris, was prompted only by paternal concern for the welfare of his daughter and not by any malice that he bore Mrs. Morris, who he sincerely believed was living in adultery; that the letter was a privileged communication and, as such, could not form the basis of a charge of libel.

The trial judge assigns as his reasons for overruling defendant's motion for a new trial that: "The letter referred to above is in the record and speaks for itself. The lady referred to therein is or was also his sister-in-law. The evidence in the case satisfied the Court that the lady, Mrs. Morris, was legally married to her husband, and did not deserve the reflections contained in the letter."

Relator is prosecuted for the violation of sections 804 and 3643 of the Revised Statutes. These sections read as follows, viz.:

"Whoever shall maliciously defame any person by making, writing, publishing, or causing to be published, any manner of libel, shall, on conviction thereof, suffer fine or imprisonment, or both, at the discretion of the court."

Under the express terms of the statute, malice is an ingredient of the crime of libel. Without malice there can be no criminal responsibility. The general rule is, that legal malice, which in law means a wrongful act done intentionally, without just or lawful excuse, is sufficient to support a charge that the publication is libelous. And malice is presumed by the publication. But the rule has its limitations in cases of privileged communications. Where the communication is privileged, malice is not presumed by law. In such communications the privilege can only be destroyed by actual malice, legal malice is not sufficient for the purpose.

Privileged communications are either absolutely privileged or qualifiedly privileged. The qualified privileged exists where the communication complained of is made in good faith on any subject matter in which the party has an interest or in reference to which he has a duty, either legal, moral, or social, if made to a person having a corresponding interest or duty.

The defense of privilege is recognized in criminal as well as civil proceedings for libel or slander.

This case was tried by the judge of the district court without the intervention of a jury. At defendant's request, the trial judge specially charged himself that malice is necessary to convict in a criminal prosecution for libel. From which we must assume the trial judge found that the publication was made maliciously and not for a justifiable purpose, and, therefore, was not protected by the privilege invoked by the defendant.

If the privilege is only qualified the onus lies on the plaintiff in a civil suit or on the State in a criminal prosecution of proving actual malice. This may be done either by extrinsic evidence of personal ill feeling or by intrinsic evidence, such as the exaggerated language, the mode and extent of the publication, and other matters in excess of the privilege.

An examination of the record discloses that the conviction of defendant was not based on any extrinsic proof that he acted through hatred, ill will, and a malicious design to injure the prosecutrix.

As shown by the per curiam attached to the bill of exception taken to the overruling of the motion for a new trial, the trial judge found defendant guilty, because he was convinced that the prosecutrix, defendant's sister-in-law, was legally married and did not deserve the reflections contained in defendant's letter and that the letter itself afforded intrinsic proof of its malicious character. . . .

Defendant's letter was a private communication from a father to the custodian of his minor daughter. The letter was not circulated and published generally. Both defendant, as the father, and the recipient, as the custodian, had an interest in the subject matter. The language of the letter indicates that it was prompted solely by the defendant's solicitude for the welfare of his little daughter, to whom he owed a legal and moral duty. It also indicates that defendant thought the occasion called for his protest and admonition to the person to whom he had temporarily intrusted the custody of his daughter, who likewise owed a legal and moral duty to the child who had been placed in her care.

The trial judge, in his per curiam, shows that the statement concerning the prosecutrix was untrue, but he does not show that defendant knew that it was untrue, and, so knowing, acted with a wanton desire to injure her. On the contrary, the letter indicates that defendant honestly thought the statement was true and that he acted from an honest motive and for a justifiable purpose.

In the absence of a showing of express malice, defendant's communication, without regard to its truth or falsity, was qualifiedly privileged, and his prosecution therefor cannot be sustained.

For the reasons assigned, the conviction and sentence of the relator, Stark E. Lambert, are annulled, and relator is ordered discharged.

(B) KNOWLEDGE

The relation of knowledge to convictability is a variable factor within a wide range. At one extreme is found the type of offense for which knowledge of some particular matter is required for guilt by the very definition of the crime itself; as, uttering a forged instrument with knowledge of the forgery, receipt of deposit by a banker knowing that his bank is insolvent, or transportation of a vehicle in interstate commerce, knowing it to have been stolen. At the other extreme is found the type (which should be restricted to the so-called public torts or civil offenses) in connection with which the element of knowledge or lack of knowledge is so immaterial that conviction may result although the defendant acted under such a mistake that, had the facts been as he reasonably supposed them to be, his conduct would have been acceptable in every respect. Such "offenses" are considered under "strict liability."

Between these two extremes are found offenses, for guilt of which the matter of knowledge cannot be ignored although the definitions themselves contain no specific requirement thereof. This is because knowledge or lack of knowledge may be among the determining factors of some other attitude of mind, which is required, such as intent, wilfulness, malice or criminal negligence.

Sec. 4   *OTHER PARTICULAR STATES OF MIND*   381

From the standpoint of the prosecution (leaving out of consideration those "offenses" which have no normal *mens-rea* requirement) knowledge may be a positive factor or the want of knowledge may be a negative factor. In some prosecutions the state must prove defendant's knowledge of some particular matter to make out even a *prima facie* case of guilt. Such knowledge may be proven, like any other fact, by circumstantial evidence. It may be established from all the facts and circumstances of the case, although denied by the defendant. But the burden is on the State. In other prosecutions the want of knowledge may be peculiarly a matter of defense.

"Absolute knowledge can be had of but few things," said the Massachusetts court, and the philosopher might add "if any." For most practical purposes "knowledge" is not confined to what we have personally observed or to what we have evolved by our own cognitive faculties. Even within the domain of the law itself the word is not always employed with exactly the same signification. Suppose a man has been told that a certain bill of exchange is a forgery and he believes the statement to be true. Does he have *knowledge* of this? Obviously not if the purpose of the inquiry is to determine whether he is qualified to take the witness stand and swear that the instrument is false. But if he passes the bill as genuine he will be uttering a forged instrument with "knowledge" of the forgery if his belief and the fact correspond.

The need, therefore, is to search for the state of mind, or states of mind, which the courts have spoken of as "knowledge" for the purpose of a particular case.

STATE v. GOLDMAN

Supreme Court of New Jersey, 1900.
65 N.J.L. 394, 47 A. 641.

FORT, J. The writ of error in this case brings up the conviction of the defendant in the Quarter Sessions of Mercer county upon an indictment charging him with receiving stolen goods, knowing them to have been stolen. . . .

The only remaining assignment of error is the fourth. It is to the following extract from the charge of the court: "That which a man ought to have suspected, in the position of the defendant, he should have suspected and he must be regarded as having suspected, in order to put himself upon his guard and upon inquiry. The proof in any case is to be inferential."

I am unable to find any authority to sustain the statement of law as the court here makes it.

Guilty knowledge is of the very essence of the crime charged in this indictment, under our statute. The mere receiving stolen goods is no crime under our statute, but receiving goods "stolen from any other person . . . *knowing* the same to have been stolen," is a crime.

In order to convict under this statute or at common law, for the rule was the same there, the defendant must be proven guilty as charged—that is, to have received the goods, *knowing* that they were stolen, and that knowledge must be proven as of the time they were received.

Knowledge in cases of this kind, of course, may be proven either by direct evidence or by facts and circumstances which impute guilty knowledge. Such a method of proving knowledge was sustained by this court in another class of crime in which knowledge was the essential element of the crime.

Guilty knowledge may be found by the jury where the defendant receives the goods under such circumstances as would satisfy a man of ordinary intelligence and caution that they were stolen.

I have read the part of the charge excepted to, in connection with the other parts of the charge, and I am unable to reach the conclusion that the language of the court was justified under the law or that it was not prejudicial to the defendant. The language used clearly cannot be classed as comments or as an expression of opinion by the court.

It was a statement to the jury that they might find knowledge in the defendant—that is, criminal knowledge, intent to receive the goods knowing them to have been stolen, because he ought to have suspected that which the jury might think he should have suspected, and that he must be regarded as having suspected that which the jury might think he should have suspected, and the adding to what the court said upon this subject right in the same connection, the statement that "the proof in any case is to be inferential," intensified the misleading character of this instruction.

The proof must be that the defendant had knowledge, not that he had suspicions. Suspicious circumstances, it is true, may be a part of the circumstances from which knowledge may be inferred, but the jury must be satisfied that these circumstances were of such a character, when taken in connection with the whole transaction, as to lead to the conclusion that the defendant knew that the goods were stolen.

For this error, we think the judgment must be reversed.

STATE v. GARGARE

Court of Errors and Appeals of New Jersey, 1915.
88 N.J.L. 389, 95 A. 625.

On appeal from the Supreme Court, in which court the following *per curiam* was filed:

"The defendant in this case was convicted of the crime of receiving stolen goods, viz., a Ford automobile belonging to Herbert I. Davis. The case comes up under the one hundred and thirty-sixth section of the Criminal Procedure act. . . .

"Next it was claimed that there was error in the following instructions to the jury: 'If you find the circumstances of that purchase, or getting, on the part of the defendant were such as to lead a rational man, a man of ordinary caution and intelligence, to be put on his inquiry, and would compel that man's mind to believe that those goods were stolen; if you find that the circumstances were such as I have described, then such circumstances may be sufficient to justify you in finding a verdict of guilty.' This instruction was justified by our decision in State v. Goldman, 65 N.J.L. 394, 47 A. 641, and our subsequent decision in State v. Di Benedetto, 82 N.J.L. 168, 82 A. 521.

. . .

"The judgment under review will be affirmed."

PER CURIAM. The judgment under review will be affirmed, for the reasons expressed in the per curiam opinion of the Supreme Court.[1]

STATE v. DREW

Supreme Court of Minnesota, 1910.
110 Minn. 247, 124 N.W. 1091.

The defendant was convicted in the district court for Ramsey county upon an indictment under R.L.1905, § 5118, charging him with receiving a deposit in his private bank, the Bank of Hamline, while he well knew that he was insolvent. His motion for a new trial was denied, OLIN B. LEWIS, J. He was then sentenced to two years' im-

---

1. In a trial for receiving stolen property it was error to instruct the jury that defendant was guilty if he received it under such circumstances that he "ought to have known that the property was stolen." Meath v. State, 174 Wis. 80, 182 N.W. 334 (1921).

A junk dealer, after recent and repeated warnings to be on the alert for stolen railroad brass, received a large amount of such brass from a boy. The boy said he had not stolen it but offered no explanation other than that he had found it. This was held sufficient to support a conviction of receiving stolen property. People v. Rife, 382 Ill. 588, 88 N.E.2d 367 (1943).

Defendant's knowledge that property received by him was stolen could be inferred from the fact that he was carrying the stolen cameras in gunny sacks and made evasive answers when questioned about them. Hence the jury's verdict finding him guilty will not be disturbed. People v. Hyde, 51 Cal.2d 152, 331 P.2d 42 (1958).

prisonment at hard labor. From the judgment entered thereon, he appealed. Reversed and new trial granted.

LEWIS, J. . . . The trial court charged the jury that the state was not required to show that the defendant had actual knowledge that he was insolvent; that it was sufficient if the state proved beyond a reasonable doubt that appellant had good reason to know that fact. This raises the question whether the state was not required to prove the offense as charged in the indictment, viz., that appellant knew he was unsafe and insolvent at the time the deposit was received.

It is possible that members of the profession have been misled with reference to the meaning of this statute by certain statements in the opinion in State v. Quackenbush, 98 Minn. 515, 108 N.W. 953, and in State v. Strait, 99 Minn. 327, 109 N.W. 598. An examination discloses that in both of those cases the indictments were identical with the one here under consideration. In the Quackenbush case the court instructed the jury that it was necessary to find from the evidence that the defendant knew he was insolvent at the time of receiving the deposit, and the question now before us was not involved nor considered on the appeal. That part of the opinion in the Quackenbush case, referred to by the state, involved an entirely different matter. The court was discussing the merits of an instruction to the effect that a person doing a banking business was presumed to know that he was insolvent, and the language used should be considered with reference only to the instruction then under consideration. The language used in the opinion in the Strait case may be explained on similar grounds, so that, so far as judicial construction is concerned, we are free to treat the subject as one of first impression.

The statute, for some reason, established degrees of knowledge of insolvency: First, actual knowledge; and, second, good reason to believe it. A banker receiving deposits of money cannot shut his eyes to his own financial status, and he is required to investigate conditions which are suggested by circumstances already known to him. But the failure to discover a condition unknown to him, but which in the exercise of reasonable diligence, might have been discovered, is quite a different thing. The state charged appellant with knowledge of insolvency, and the evidence must be sufficient to warrant the jury in finding such to be the fact. The purpose of an indictment is to notify the defendant upon what issue he will be put to trial, in order that he may make preparation; and, while appellant may have been prepared to meet the issues presented, there was nothing in the indictment to apprise him that he was upon trial for a failure to exercise diligence in acquiring information which he did not have.

It is not intended to intimate that under such an indictment the state is required to prove knowledge by positive, direct evidence of the defendant's state of mind. But the evidence must be sufficient to prove beyond a reasonable doubt that he must have known of his in-

Sec. 4   OTHER PARTICULAR STATES OF MIND   385

solvency; that fact having been established. We are of opinion that it was error to charge the jury that it was sufficient if they should find that he had reason to believe he was insolvent. . . .

Reversed and a new trial granted.[1]

O'BRIEN, J., took no part.

(C) WILFULNESS

The adverb "wilfully" has such extreme differences of meaning that it gives no clue to the *mens rea* requirement to which it refers if it is considered alone. It must be studied with its context and in the light of the particular offense. With reference to its meaning the Supreme Court of the United States has had this to say: "The word often denotes an act which is intentional, or knowing, or voluntary, as distinguished from accidental. But when used in a criminal statute it generally means an act done [1] with a bad purpose . . .; [2] without justifiable excuse . . .; [or 3] stubbornly, obstinately, pereversely . . .. The word is also employed [4] to characterize a thing done without ground for believing it is lawful . . ., or [5] conduct marked by careless disregard whether or not one has the right so to act, . . ."[2]

---

1. In a trial for uttering a forged instrument it is reversible error to charge the jury that they may convict if they find that defendant uttered the instrument having reasonable cause to believe it was forged. Carver v. People, 39 Mich. 786 (1878).

   In a prosecution for false pretenses it is reversible error to instruct that making a statement which is in fact false, recklessly and without information sufficient to justify such a belief, is equivalent to making it knowing it to be false. State v. Pickus, 63 S.D. 209, 257 N.W. 284 (1934).

2. United States v. Murdock, 290 U.S. 389, 394–5, 54 S.Ct. 223, 225, 78 L.Ed. 381 (1933). Brackets added. And see Nabob Oil Co. v. United States, 190 F.2d 478 (10th Cir. 1951).

   The word "wilful" in a criminal statute means no more than that the forbidden act was done deliberately and with knowledge. It does not require an evil intent. McBride v. United States, 225 F.2d 249 (5th Cir. 1955).

   "Wilfulness", as used in the statute proscribing the wilful failure to make timely payment of income taxes, requires a specific wrongful intent. United States v. Palermo, 259 F.2d 872 (3d Cir. 1958). Even gross negligence in the failure to pay the tax does not warrant conviction under this statute. Ibid.

Perkins Cs.Crim.Law & Procedure 3rd Ed.–UCB—25

FIELDS v. UNITED STATES

United States Court of Appeals, District of Columbia, 1947.
164 F.2d 97.

CLARK, ASSOCIATE JUSTICE. Appellant was convicted by the verdict of a jury in the District Court of the United States for the District of Columbia under an indictment charging him with violation of 52 Stat. 942, Act June 22, 1938, 2 U.S.C.A. § 192 which reads as follows: "Every person who having been summoned as a witness by the authority of either House of Congress to give testimony or to produce papers upon any matter under inquiry before either House, or any joint committee established by a joint or concurrent resolution of the two Houses of Congress, or any committee of either House of Congress, willfully makes default, or who, having appeared, refuses to answer any question pertinent to the question under inquiry, shall be deemed guilty of a misdemeanor, punishable by a fine of not more than $1,000 nor less than $100 and imprisoned in a common jail for not less than one month nor more than twelve months." He appeals from the judgment of conviction. . . .

For his failure to produce the records called for by the subpoena appellant was cited by the House of Representatives, upon the recommendation of the committee, for contempt. The indictment returned by the grand jury contained two counts of alleged contempt, similar in substance but referring to the separate days of August 14 and 15, 1946. The lower court granted a motion for acquittal as to the first count but appellant was convicted on the second count. He was sentenced to be confined for a term of three months and to pay a fine of two hundred and fifty dollars.

The Government charged there were at least three documents pertinent to the transaction under investigation by the committee which were available to the appellant at the time of the committee hearing. These documents were produced at the trial. The jury found that one or more of these documents had been willfully withheld from the committee by the appellant.

The principal issues raised on appeal are whether or not the court below erred in failing to direct a judgment of acquittal as to the second count; whether or not the word "willfully", as used in the statute, implies an evil or bad purpose; and the related question of whether or not good faith has any bearing on the issue of willfulness. The last two issues arise from the court's charge to the jury that an evil or bad purpose is immaterial, and the court's refusal to charge that appellant's acts assertedly constituting good faith had a bearing on the issue of willfulness.

As to the first issue we are of the opinion that the evidence presented by the Government was clearly sufficient to warrant submission of the case to the jury.

Appellant contends that the word "willful" has a meaning which includes an evil or bad purpose when used in a criminal statute. We think the term has acquired no such fixed meaning according to the type of statute in which it is employed. The Supreme Court has said, long ago, "In construing a statute, penal as well as others, we must look to the object in view, and never adopt an interpretation that will defeat its own purpose, if it will admit of any other reasonable construction." The Emily and The Caroline, 1824, 9 Wheat. 381, 6 L. Ed. 116. . . .

The apparent objective of the statute involved here would be largely defeated if, as appellant contends, a person could appear before a congressional investigating committee and by professing willingness to comply with its requests for information escape the penalty for subsequent default. This court said, in Townsend v. United States, 1938, 68 App.D.C. 223, 229, 95 F.2d 352, 358: "The meaning of the word [willful] depends in large measure upon the nature of the criminal act and the facts of the particular case. It is only in very few criminal cases that 'willful' means 'done with a bad purpose.' Generally, it means 'no more than that the person charged with the duty knows what he is doing. It does not mean that, in addition, he must suppose that he is breaking the law.'" (Quoting Learned Hand, J., in American Surety Co. v. Sullivan, 2 Cir., 1925, 7 F.2d 605, 606.) At the trial of this case the court said, in its charge to the jury: "The word 'willful' does not mean that the failure or refusal to comply with the order of the committee must necessarily be for an evil or a bad purpose. The reason or the purpose of failure to comply or refusal to comply is immaterial, so long as the refusal was deliberate and intentional and was not a mere inadvertence or an accident." We uphold that differentiation in our view of the purpose of the statute.

Closely related to the issue of willfulness is appellant's assertion of error in the trial court's refusal to charge that appellant's voluntary production of certain records constituted evidence that he acted in good faith and did not "willfully" default. Such an assertion does not penetrate the question whether or not appellant was guilty of deliberately failing to produce subpoenaed records subject to his control, and it was the alleged failure to do so that served as the basis for the contempt citation. That question of fact was properly referred to the jury in the trial below, and the jury returned a verdict against the appellant. . . .

In conclusion, we have carefully examined the record on appeal and find in it no reversible error. Accordingly, the judgment of the trial court is

Affirmed.[1]

(Certiorari denied 332 U.S. 851, 68 S.Ct. 355, 92 L.Ed. 421. Rehearing denied 333 U.S. 839, 68 S.Ct. 607, 92 L.Ed. 1123.)

1. Compare People v. Von Tiedeman, 120 Cal. 128, 52 P. 155 (1898).

SECTION 5. STRICT LIABILITY

It has been necessary to recognize that some *offenses* are not *true crimes*. Parking overtime in a restricted zone is an extreme illustration. In the absence of legislation a properly parked car could be left where it is for three hours as justifiably as for ten minutes. In the exercise of the police power, zones have been established in moderately congested areas in which parking is permitted, but for limited periods only. The length of the period depends upon needs of the particular situation. If the limit established for a certain zone is thirty minutes this is not for the reason that it would be inherently wrong for a car to be left there for a longer period. Nothing but expediency is involved. Penalties are provided as a means of enforcement but no one considers the driver who has parked overtime a criminal. His violation differs from murder or theft by more than degree. It is a different kind of a breach.

To express this difference there has been a tendency to speak of such violations as "civil offenses," "public torts," "public welfare offenses," or "administrative misdemeanors." Since they are not true crimes the normal *mens rea* requirement of crime does not attach.[1] They are enforced on the basis of "strict liability" unless the particular statute or ordinance adds some limitation.

It is necessary to give special attention to three problems: (1) Is the particular offense under consideration a "civil offense" or a true crime? (2) If it is a "civil offense," has the wording of the enactment added a *mens rea* requirement of some nature? (3) If it is a true crime, has the wording of a statute eliminated the *mens rea* requirement (and if so what is the effect)?

THE QUEEN v. STEPHENS

Queen's Bench, 1866.
L.R. 1 Q.B. 702.

INDICTMENT. First count for obstructing the navigation of a public river called the Tivy by casting and throwing, and causing to be cast and thrown, slate stone and rubbish in and upon the soil and bed of the river, and thereby raising and producing great mounds projecting and extending along the stream and waterway of the river.

Second count that the defendant was the owner of large quantities of slate quarried from certain slate quarries near the river Tivy, and that he unlawfully kept, permitted, and suffered to be and remain

---

1. Kenny, Outlines of Criminal Law 44–45 (18th ed. by Turner, 1962).

large quantities of slate sunk in the river, so that the navigation of the river was obstructed.

Plea, not guilty.

The indictment was tried before Blackburn, J., at the last spring assizes for Pembrokeshire, when the following facts were proved:— The Tivy is a public navigable river which flows through Llechryd Bridge, thence by Kilgerran Castle, and from thence past the town of Cardigan to the sea. About twenty years ago the Tivy was navigable to within a quarter of a mile of Llechryd Bridge, from which place a considerable traffic was carried on in limestone and culm by means of lighters.

The defendant is the owner of a slate quarry called the Castle Quarry, situate near the Castle of Kilgerran, which he has extensively worked since 1842. The defendant had no spoil bank at the quarry. The rubbish from the quarry was stacked about five or six yards from the edge of the river. Previous to 1847, the defendant erected a wall to prevent it from falling into the river, but in that year a heavy flood carried away the wall, and with it large quantities of the rubbish. Quantities of additional rubbish were from time to time shot by the defendant's workmen on the same spot, and so slid into the river. By these means the navigation was obstructed, so that even small boats were prevented from coming up to Llechryd Bridge.

The defendant being upwards of eighty years of age was unable personally to superintend the working of the quarry, which was managed for his benefit by his sons. The defendant's counsel was prepared to offer evidence that the workmen at the quarry had been prohibited both by the defendant and his sons from thus depositing the rubbish; and that they had been told to place the rubbish in the old excavations and in a place provided for that purpose. The learned judge intimated that the evidence was immaterial; and he directed the jury that as the defendant was the proprietor of the quarry, the quarrying of which was carried on for his benefit, it was his duty to take all proper precautions to prevent the rubbish from falling into the river, and that if a substantial part of the rubbish went into the river from having been improperly stacked so near the river as to fall into it, the defendant was guilty of having caused a nuisance, although the acts might have been committed by his workmen, without his knowledge and against his general orders. The jury found a verdict of guilty.

A rule having been obtained for a new trial, on the ground that the judge misdirected the jury in telling them that the defendant would be liable for the acts of his workmen in depositing the rubbish from the quarries so as to become a nuisance, though without the defendant's knowledge and against his orders, . . .

MELLOR, J. In this case I am of opinion, and in my opinion my Brother Shee concurs,[1] that the direction of my Brother Blackburn was right. It is quite true that this in point of form is a proceeding of a criminal nature, but in substance I think it is in the nature of a civil proceeding, and I can see no reason why a different rule should prevail with regard to such an act as is charged in this indictment between proceedings which are civil and proceedings which are criminal. I think there may be nuisances of such a character that the rule I am applying here, would not be applicable to them, but here it is perfectly clear that the only reason for proceeding criminally is that the nuisance, instead of being merely a nuisance affecting an individual, or one or two individuals, affects the public at large, and no private individual, without receiving some special injury, could have maintained an action. Then if the contention of those who say the direction is wrong is to prevail, the public would have great difficulty in getting redress. The object of this indictment is to prevent the recurrence of the nuisance. The prosecutor cannot proceed by action, but must proceed by indictment, and if this were strictly a criminal proceeding the prosecution would be met with the objection that there was no mens rea: that the indictment charged the defendant with a criminal offence, when in reality there was no proof that the defendant knew of the act, or that he himself gave orders to his servants to do the particular act he is charged with; still at the same time it is perfectly clear that the defendant finds the capital, and carries on the business which causes the nuisance, and is carried on for his benefit; although from age or infirmity the defendant is unable to go to the premises, the business is carried on for him by his sons, or at all events by his agents. Under these circumstances the defendant must necessarily give to his servants or agents all the authority that is incident to the carrying on of the business. It is not because he had at some time or other given directions that it should be carried on so as not to allow the refuse from the works to fall into the river, and desired his servants to provide some other place for depositing it, that when it has fallen into the river, and has become prejudicial to the public, he can say he is not liable on an indictment for a nuisance caused by the acts of his servants. It appears to me that all it was necessary to prove is, that the nuisance was caused in the carrying on of the works of the quarry. That being so my Brother Blackburn's direction to the jury was quite right.

I agree that the authorities that bear directly upon the case are very few. In the case of Reg. v. Russell,[2] the observations of Lord Campbell might have been justified by the circumstances of that case, though as I understand it the judgment of the other judges did not proceed on the same reasons. It is therefore only the opinion of

[Footnotes 1 and 2 are official.]
1. Shee, J., left the court just before the conclusion of the argument.
2. 3 E. & B. 942; 23 L.J. (M.C.) 173.

Lord Campbell as applied to that case. Whether there is or is not any distinction between that case and the present may be open to question; but if there is no distinction, I should be prepared rather to have acted upon the reasons which influenced the other judges than those which influenced Lord Campbell. Inasmuch as the object of the indictment is not to punish the defendant, but really to prevent the nuisance from being continued, I think that the evidence which would support a civil action would be sufficient to support an indictment.

The rule must be discharged. As I have said, my Brother Shee concurs with me in that opinion.

BLACKBURN, J. I need only add that I see no reason to change the opinion I formed at the trial. I only wish to guard myself against it being supposed that either at the trial or now, the general rule that a principal is not criminally answerable for the act of his agent is infringed. All that is necessary to say is this, that where a person maintains works by his capital, and employs servants, and so carries on the works as in fact to cause a nuisance to a private right, for which an action would lie, if the same nuisance inflicts an injury upon a public right the remedy for which would be by indictment, the evidence which would maintain the action would also support the indictment. That is all that it was necessary to decide and all that is decided.

Rule discharged.[3]

STATE v. KELLY

Supreme Court of Ohio, 1896.
54 Ohio St. 166, 43 N.E. 163.

Exceptions from court of common pleas, Franklin county.

Dennis Kelly was convicted of selling adulterated food, and to a judgment of the common pleas reversing the judgment of conviction the prosecuting attorney files exceptions. Sustained.

Dennis Kelly was tried and convicted in a justice's court of Franklin county for an alleged violation of the act of March 20, 1884, to provide against the adulteration of food and drugs. Kelly, having been adjudged to pay a fine of $100, filed his petition in error in the common pleas court, where the judgment was reversed for the following reasons: (1) "The affidavit upon which said action was predicated is defective, in this: that it fails to allege that said article of food so sold by the defendant below was sold to the purchaser

---

3. One who shot and killed a house pigeon, thinking it was a wild bird, was guilty of unlawfully and wilfully killing a house pigeon. "A person who shoots a pigeon which turns out to be a house pigeon must take the consequences of his act". Had the pigeon been killed by accident he would not be guilty. Horton v. Gwynne, [1921] 2 K.B. 661.

thereof to be used as human food." (2) "That the justice erred in refusing to give to the jury the following instruction requested by the defendant: 'While it is not necessary to charge knowledge in the affidavit, want of knowledge and absence of intent is a valid defense. You will carefully weigh the evidence of all the witnesses; and if the evidence discloses that the defendant bought the molasses, he is here charged with selling, for pure New Orleans molasses, and honestly believed it to be such; that, still believing it to be pure, he sold it as such, without intent to deceive the purchaser thereof as to its true character,—you must acquit the prisoner.'" The substantial part of the affidavit is that Kelly "did unlawfully offer for sale and sell to one D. J. Minton a quantity, to wit, a package of a certain article of human food, namely, New Orleans molasses; that then and there said food was adulterated by having mixed therewith glucose, whereby the quality, strength, and purity thereof was lowered and depreciated; that then and there said package of food was not labeled as a mixture or compound, nor labeled with the name and per cent. of each ingredient therein."

SHAUCK, J. (after stating the facts). The first section of the act of March 20, 1884 (Giauque's Rev. St. § 8805), provides "that no person shall within this state manufacture for sale, offer for sale, or sell any drug or article of food which is adulterated, within the meaning of this act." Other provisions of the statute are devoted to definition of the terms used in the first section, and to prescribing penalties for the violation of the act. It is not doubted that molasses to which glucose has been added is an article of adulterated food, within the meaning of the statute. The act does not, in terms, require, to constitute an offense against its provisions, that the adulterated article of food shall be sold to be used by the purchaser as human food. Nor does it, in terms, require, as an element of the offense, knowledge of the fact that the article is adulterated, or provide that a want of such knowledge shall constitute a defense. Both conclusions stated in the decision of the court of common pleas are therefore wrong, unless they are justifiable inferences from the purpose and indicated policy of the act. The act is not a provision for the punishment of those who sell adulterated food or drugs because of any supposed turpitude prompting such sales, or indicated by them. Its purpose is indicated by its title. It is "An act to provide against the adulteration of food and drugs." It is a plan devised by the general assembly to protect the public against the hurtful consequences of the sales of adulterated food and drugs; those consequences being in no degree increased by the vendor's knowledge, or diminished by his ignorance, of the adulteration of the articles which he offers for sale. The provisions of the act are appropriate to the purpose indicated by its title. It would have been inconsistent with that purpose to provide for the trial of such immaterial issues as the object of the vendor in making a sale, or of the extent of his

Sec. 5   STRICT LIABILITY   393

knowledge touching the quality of the article sold. Those who produce the adulterated articles whose sale is forbidden may live without the state. Purpose and knowledge, except when they are indicated by the character of the forbidden act, are, in most cases, insusceptible of proof. If this statute had imposed upon the state the burden of proving the purpose of the vendor in selling an article of food, or his knowledge of its adulteration, it would thereby have defeated its declared purpose. Since it is the duty of courts to so construe doubtful statutes as to give effect to the purpose of the legislature, they cannot, in case of a statute whose provisions are unambiguous, and whose validity is clear, defeat its purpose by construction. The correct view of statutes of this general nature is stated by the supreme court of Massachusetts in Com. v. Murphy, 42 N.E. 504: "Considering the nature of the offense, the purpose to be accomplished, the practical methods available for the enforcement of the law, and such other matters as throw light upon the meaning of the language, the question, in interpreting a criminal statute, is whether the intention of the legislature was to make knowledge of the facts an essential element of the offense, or to put upon every one the burden of finding out whether his contemplated act is prohibited, and of refraining from it if it is." In Com. v. Farren, 9 Allen, 489, in construing a statute which provides that "whoever sells or keeps or offers for sale adulterated milk, or milk to which water or any foreign substance has been added," shall be punished as provided, it was held that it is not necessary either to allege or prove that the accused knew that the milk he offered for sale was adulterated. With respect to a similar statute, the same conclusion was reached in State v. Smith, 10 R.I. 258. If knowledge of the adulteration were an element of the offense, it would be incumbent upon the state to establish it; but, since it is not, the defendant could derive no advantage from any evidence tending to show the absence of such knowledge. With respect to the absence of the allegation that the adulterated article of food "was sold to be used as human food," it is sufficient that the statute forbids the sale of such article, without any requirement as to the purpose, assuming that it is to be used for that purpose to which it is appropriate. In the enactment of this statute, it was the evident purpose of the general assembly to protect the public against the harmful consequences of the sales of adulterated food and drugs, and, to the end that its purpose might not be defeated, to require the seller, at his peril, to know that the article which he offers for sale is not adulterated, or to demand of those from whom he purchases indemnity against the penalties that may be imposed upon him because of their concealment of the adulteration of the articles. Exceptions sustained.[1]

[1]. In upholding the conviction of a dealer for possessing adulterated tobacco, although he neither knew nor had any reason to suspect the adulteration, it was said that since he knew he was in possession of the tobacco "it is not necessary that he should know that the tobacco was adulterat-

SMITH v. CALIFORNIA

Supreme Court of the United States, 1959.
361 U.S. 147, 80 S.Ct. 215.

[Defendant was convicted of a violation of a Los Angeles ordinance which made it unlawful for a bookseller to have an obscene book in his shop. As interpreted by the California courts, guilt of this offense was not dependent upon awareness of the obscene nature of the book.]

MR. JUSTICE BRENNAN delivered the opinion of the Court. . . .

Almost 30 years ago, Chief Justice Hughes declared for this Court: "It is no longer open to doubt that the liberty of the press and of speech is within the liberty safeguarded by the due process clause of the Fourteenth Amendment from invasion by state action. It was found impossible to conclude that this essential personal liberty of the citizen was left unprotected by the general guaranty of fundamental rights of person and property. . . ." . . . .

California here imposed a strict or absolute criminal responsibility on appellant not to have obscene books in his shop. "The existence of a *mens rea* is the rule of, rather than the exception to, the principles of Anglo-American criminal jurisprudence." Still, it is doubtless competent for the States to create strict criminal liabilities by defining criminal offenses without any element of scienter—though even where no freedom-of-expression question is involved, there is precedent in this Court that this power is not without limitations. See Lambert v. People of State of California, 355 U.S. 225, 78 S.Ct. 240, 2 L.Ed.2d 228. But the question here is as to the validity of this ordinance's elimination of the scienter requirement—an elimination which may tend to work a substantial restriction on the freedom of speech and of the press. . . .

These principles guide us to our decision here. We have held that obscene speech and writings are not protected by the constitutional guarantees of freedom of speech and the press. Roth v. United States, 354 U.S. 476, 77 S.Ct. 1304, 1 L.Ed.2d 1498. The ordinance here in question, to be sure, only imposes criminal sanctions on a bookseller if in fact there is to be found in his shop an obscene book. But our holding in Roth does not recognize any state power to restrict the dissemination of books which are not obscene; and we

---

ed. . . ." Regina v. Woodrow, 15 M. & W. 404, 415, 153 Eng.Rep. 907, 912 (Ex. 1846). A butcher was convicted of selling unsound meat although he was unaware of the unsoundness and could not have discovered it by any examination which he could have been expected to make. Hobbs v. Winchester Corp., [1910] 2 K.B. 471. "It is no defense to a prosecution for driving an overloaded truck in violation of the Vehicle Code that defendant had first obtained a weight certificate from a licensed weightmaster which indicated that the truck was not overloaded". Commonwealth v. Olshefski, 64 Pa.D. & C. 343 (1948).

think this ordinance's strict liability feature would tend seriously to have that effect, by penalizing booksellers, even though they had not the slightest notice of the character of the books they sold. The appellee and the court below analogize this strict-liability penal ordinance to familiar forms of penal statutes which dispense with any element of knowledge on the part of the person charged, food and drug legislation being a principal example. We find the analogy instructive in our examination on the question before us. The usual rationale for such statutes is that the public interest in the purity of its food is so great as to warrant the imposition of the highest standard of care on distributors—in fact an absolute standard which will not hear the distributor's plea as to the amount of care he has used. His ignorance of the character of the food is irrelevant. There is no specific constitutional inhibition against making the distributors of food the strictest censors of their merchandise, but the constitutional guarantees of the freedom of speech and of the press stand in the way of imposing a similar requirement on the bookseller. . . .

We have said: "The fundamental freedoms of speech and press have contributed greatly to the development and well-being of our free society and are indispensable to its continued growth. Ceaseless vigilance is the watchword to prevent their erosion by Congress or by the States. The door barring federal and state intrusion into this area cannot be left ajar; it must be kept tightly closed and opened only the slightest crack necessary to prevent encroachment upon more important interests." Roth v. United States, supra, 354 U.S. at page 488, 77 S.Ct. at page 1311. This ordinance opens that door too far. The existence of the State's power to prevent the distribution of obscene matter does not mean that there can be no constitutional barrier to any form of practical exercise of that power. It is plain to us that the ordinance in question, though aimed at obscene matter, has such a tendency to inhibit constitutionally protected expression that it cannot stand under the Constitution.

Reversed.

MR. JUSTICE FRANKFURTER, concurring. . . .

The Court accepts the settled principle of constitutional law that traffic in obscene literature may be outlawed as a crime. But it holds that one cannot be made amenable to such criminal outlawry unless he is chargeable with knowledge of the obscenity. Obviously the Court is not holding that a bookseller must familiarize himself with the contents of every book in his shop. No less obviously, the Court does not hold that a bookseller who insulates himself against knowledge about an offending book is thereby free to maintain an emporium for smut. How much or how little awareness that a book may be found to be obscene suffices to establish scienter, or what kind of evidence may satisfy the how much or the how little, the Court leaves for another day. . . .

[BLACK, J. and DOUGLAS, J. also wrote concurring opinions. HARLAN, J. wrote an opinion concurring in part and dissenting in part.]

MORISSETTE v. UNITED STATES

Supreme Court of the United States, 1952.
342 U.S. 246, 72 S.Ct. 240.

MR. JUSTICE JACKSON delivered the opinion of the Court.

This would have remained a profoundly insignificant case to all except its immediate parties had it not been so tried and submitted to the jury as to raise questions both fundamental and far-reaching in federal criminal law, for which reason we granted certiorari.

On a large tract of uninhabited and untilled land in a wooded and sparsely populated area of Michigan, the Government established a practice bombing range over which the Air Force dropped simulated bombs at ground targets. These bombs consisted of a metal cylinder about forty inches long and eight inches across, filled with sand and enough black powder to cause a smoke puff by which the strike could be located. At various places about the range signs read "Danger—Keep Out—Bombing Range." Nevertheless, the range was known as good deer country and was extensively hunted.

Spent bomb casings were cleared from the targets and thrown into piles "so that they will be out of the way." They were not stacked or piled in any order but were dumped in heaps, some of which had been accumulating for four years or upwards, were exposed to the weather and rusting away.

Morissette, in December of 1948, went hunting in this area but did not get a deer. He thought to meet expenses of the trip by salvaging some of these casings. He loaded three tons of them on his truck and took them to a nearby farm, where they were flattened by driving a tractor over them. After expending this labor and trucking them to market in Flint, he realized $84.

Morissette, by occupation, is a fruit stand operator in summer and a trucker and scrap iron collector in winter. An honorably discharged veteran of World War II, he enjoys a good name among his neighbors and has had no blemish on his record more disreputable than a conviction for reckless driving.

The loading, crushing and transporting of these casings were all in broad daylight, in full view of passers-by, without the slightest effort at concealment. When an investigation was started, Morissette voluntarily, promptly and candidly told the whole story to the authorities, saying that he had no intention of stealing but thought the property was abandoned, unwanted and considered of no value to the Government. He was indicted, however, on the charge that he "did unlawfully, wilfully and knowingly steal and convert" property of the United States of the value of $84, in violation of 18 U.S.C. § 641, 18 U.S.C.A. § 641, which provides that "whoever embezzles, steals, purloins, or knowingly converts" government property is punishable by fine and imprisonment. Morissette was convicted and sentenced to imprisonment for two months or to pay a fine of $200. The Court of Appeals affirmed, one judge dissenting.

On his trial, Morissette, as he had at all times told investigating officers, testified that from appearances he believed the casings were cast-off and abandoned, that he did not intend to steal the property, and took it with no wrongful or criminal intent. The trial court, however, was unimpressed, and ruled: "[H]e took it because he thought it was abandoned and he knew he was on government property. . . . That is no defense. . . . I don't think anybody can have the defense they thought the property was abandoned on another man's piece of property." The court stated: "I will not permit you to show this man thought it was abandoned. . . . I hold in this case that there is no question of abandoned property." The court refused to submit or to allow counsel to argue to the jury whether Morissette acted with innocent intention. It charged: "And I instruct you that if you believe the testimony of the government in this case, he intended to take it. . . . He had no right to take this property. . . . [A]nd it is no defense to claim that it was abandoned, because it was on private property. . . . And I instruct you to this effect: That if this young man took this property (and he says he did), without any permission (he says he did), that was on the property of the United States Government (he says it was), that it was of the value of one cent or more (and evidently it was), that he is guilty of the offense charged here. If you believe the government, he is guilty. . . . The question on intent is whether or not he intended to take the property. He says he did. Therefore, if you believe either side, he is guilty." Petitioner's counsel contended, "But the taking must have been with a felonious intent." The court ruled, however: "That is presumed by his own act."

The Court of Appeals suggested that "greater restraint in expression should have been exercised", but affirmed the conviction because, "As we have interpreted the statute, appellant was guilty of its violation beyond a shadow of doubt, as evidenced even by his own admissions." Its construction of the statute is that it creates several separate and distinct offenses, one being knowing conversion of government property. The court ruled that this particular offense requires no element of criminal intent. This conclusion was thought to be required by the failure of Congress to express such a requisite and this Court's decisions in United States v. Behrman, 258 U.S. 280, 42 S.Ct. 303, 66 L.Ed. 619, and United States v. Balint, 258 U.S. 250, 42 S.Ct. 301, 66 L.Ed. 604.

In those cases this Court did construe mere omission from a criminal enactment of any mention of criminal intent as dispensing with it. If they be deemed precedents for principles of construction generally applicable to federal penal statutes, they authorize this conviction. Indeed, such adoption of the literal reasoning announced in those cases would do this and more—it would sweep out of all federal crimes, except when expressly preserved, the ancient requirement of a culpable state of mind. We think a résumé of their historical background is convincing that an effect has been ascribed to them more comprehensive than was contemplated and one inconsistent with our philosophy of criminal law. . . . A relation between some mental element and punishment for a harmful act is almost as instinctive as the child's familiar exculpatory "But I didn't mean to," and has afforded the rational basis for a tardy and unfinished substitution of deterrence and reformation in place of retaliation and vengeance as the motivation for public prosecution. Unqualified acceptance of this doctrine by English common law in the Eighteenth Century was indicated by Blackstone's sweeping statement that to constitute any crime there must first be a "vicious will." Common-law commentators of the Nineteenth Century early pronounced the same principle, although a few exceptions not relevant to our present problem came to be recognized.

Crime, as a compound concept, generally constituted only from concurrence of an evil-meaning mind with an evil-doing hand, was congenial to an intense individualism and took deep and early root in American soil. As the states codified the common law of crimes, even if their enactments were silent on the subject, their courts assumed that the omission did not signify disapproval of the principle but merely recognized that intent was so inherent in the idea of the offense that it required no statutory affirmation. Courts, with little hesitation or division, found an implication of the requirement as to offenses that were taken over from the common law. The unanimity with which they have adhered to the central thought that wrongdoing must be conscious to be criminal is emphasized by the variety, disparity and confusion of their definitions of the requisite but elusive mental element. . . .

However, the Balint and Behrman offenses belong to a category of another character, with very different antecedents and origins. The crimes there involved depend on no mental element but consist only of forbidden acts or omissions. This, while not expressed by the Court, is made clear from examination of a century-old but accelerating tendency, discernible both here and in England, to call into existence new duties and crimes which disregard any ingredient of intent. The industrial revolution multiplied the number of workmen exposed to injury from increasingly powerful and complex mechanisms, driven by freshly discovered sources of energy, requiring higher precautions by employers. Traffic of velocities, volumes and varieties unheard of came to subject the wayfarer to intolerable casualty risks, if owners and drivers were not to observe new cares and uniformities of conduct. Congestion of cities and crowding of quarters called for health and welfare regulations undreamed of in simpler times. Wide distribution of goods became an instrument of wide distribution of harm when those who dispersed food, drink, drugs, and even securities, did not comply with reasonable standards of quality, integrity, disclosure and care. Such dangers have engendered increasingly numerous and detailed regulations which heighten the duties of those in control of particular industries, trades, properties or activities that affect public health, safety or welfare.

While many of these duties are sanctioned by a more strict civil liability, lawmakers, whether wisely or not, have sought to make such regulations more effective by invoking criminal sanctions to be applied by the familiar technique of criminal prosecutions and convictions. This has confronted the courts with a multitude of prosecutions, based on statutes or administrative regulations, for what have been aptly called "public welfare offenses." These cases do not fit neatly into any of such accepted classifications of common-law offenses, such as those against the state, the person, property, or public morals. Many of these offenses are not in the nature of positive aggressions or invasions, with which the common law so often dealt, but are in the nature of neglect where the law requires care, or inaction where it imposes a duty. Many violations of such regulations result in no direct or immediate injury to person or property but merely create the danger or probability of it which the law seeks to minimize. While such offenses do not threaten the security of the state in the manner of treason, they may be regarded as offenses against its authority, for their occurrence impairs the efficiency of controls deemed essential to the social order as presently constituted. In this respect, whatever the intent of the violator, the injury is the same, and the consequences are injurious or not according to fortuity. Hence, legislation applicable to such offenses, as a matter of policy, does not specify intent as a necessary element. The accused, if he does not will the violation, usually is in a position to prevent it with no more care than society might reasonably expect and no more exertion than it might reasonably exact from one who assumed his responsibilities. Also, penalties commonly are relatively small, and conviction does no grave damage to an offender's reputation. Under such considerations, courts have turned to construing statutes and regulations which make no mention of intent as dispensing with it and holding that the guilty act alone makes out the crime. This has not, however, been without expressions of misgiving. . . .

Judge Cardozo . . . pointed out, as a basis for penalizing violations whether intentional or not, that they were punishable only by fine "moderate in amount", but cautiously added that in sustaining the power so to fine unintended violations "we are not to be understood as sustaining to a like length the power to imprison. We leave that question open." People ex rel. Price v. Sheffield Farms-Slawson-Decker Co., 1918, 225 N.Y. 25, 32–33, 121 N.E. 474, 476, 477.

Thus, for diverse but reconcilable reasons, state courts converged on the same result, discontinuing inquiry into intent in a limited class of offenses against such statutory regulations.

Before long, similar questions growing out of federal legislation reached this Court. Its judgments were in harmony with this consensus of state judicial opinion, the existence of which may have led the Court to overlook the need for full exposition of their rationale in the context of federal law. In overruling a contention that there can be no conviction on an indictment which makes no charge of criminal intent but alleges only making of a sale of a narcotic forbidden by law, Chief Justice Taft, wrote: "While the general rule at common law was that the *scienter* was a necessary element in the indictment and proof of every crime, and this was followed in regard to statutory crimes even where the statutory definition did not in terms include it . . ., there has been a modification of this view in respect to prosecutions under statutes the purpose of which would be obstructed by such a requirement. It is a question of legislative intent to be construed by the court. . . ." United States v. Balint, supra, 258 U.S. 251–252, 42 S.Ct. 302.

He referred, however, to "regulatory measures in the exercise of what is called the police power where the emphasis of the statute is evidently upon achievement of some social betterment rather than the punishment of the crimes as in cases of *mala in se*," and drew his citation of supporting authority chiefly from state court cases dealing with regulatory offenses. Id., 258 U.S. at page 252, 42 S.Ct. at page 302. . . .

Neither this Court nor, so far as we are aware, any other has undertaken to delineate a precise line or set forth comprehensive criteria for distinguishing between crimes that require a mental element and crimes that do not. We attempt no closed definition, for the law on the subject is neither settled nor static. The conclusion reached in the Balint and Behrman cases has our approval and adherence for the circumstances to which it was there applied. A quite different question here is whether we will expand the doctrine of crimes without intent to include those charged here.

Stealing, larceny, and its variants and equivalents, were among the earliest offenses known to the law that existed before legislation; they are invasions of rights of property which stir a sense of insecurity in the whole community and arouse public demand for retribution, the penalty is high and, when a sufficient amount is involved, the infamy is that of a felony, which, says Maitland, is ". . . as bad a word as you can give to man or thing." State courts of last resort, on whom fall the heaviest burden of interpreting criminal law in this country, have consistently retained the requirement of intent in larceny-type offenses. If any state has deviated, the exception has neither been called to our attention nor disclosed by our research.

Congress, therefore, omitted any express prescription of criminal intent from the enactment before us in the light of an unbroken course of judicial decision in all constituent states of the Union holding intent inherent in this class of offense, even when not expressed in a statute. . . .

The Government asks us by a feat of construction radically to change the weights and balances in the scales of justice. The purpose and obvious effect of doing away with the requirement of a guilty intent is to ease the prosecution's path to conviction, to strip the defendant of such benefit as he derived at common law from innocence of evil purpose, and to circumscribe the freedom heretofore allowed juries. Such a manifest impairment of the immunities of the individual should not be extended to common-law crimes on judicial initiative.

The spirit of the doctrine which denies to the federal judiciary power to create crimes forthrightly admonishes that we should not enlarge the reach of enacted crimes by constituting them from anything less than the incriminating components contemplated by the words used in the statute. And where Congress borrows terms of art in which are accumulated the legal tradition and meaning of centuries of practice, it presumably knows and adopts the cluster of ideas that were attached to each borrowed word in the body of learning from which it was taken and the meaning its use will convey to the judicial mind unless otherwise instructed. In such case, absence of contrary direction may be taken as satisfaction with widely accepted definitions, not as a departure from them.

We hold that mere omission from § 641 of any mention of intent will not be construed as eliminating that element from the crimes denounced. . . .

Congress, by the language of this section, has been at pains to incriminate only "knowing" conversions. But, at common law, there are unwitting acts which constitute conversions. In the civil tort, except for recovery of exemplary damages, the defendant's knowledge, intent, motive, mistake, and good faith are generally irrelevant. If one takes property which turns out to belong to another, his innocent intent will not shield him from making restitution or indemnity, for his well-meaning may not be allowed to deprive another of his own.

Had the statute applied to conversions without qualification, it would have made crimes of all unwitting, inadvertent and unintended conversions. Knowledge, of course, is not identical with intent and may not have been the most apt words [sic] of limitation. But knowing conversion requires more than knowledge that defendant was taking the property into his possession. He must have had knowledge of the facts, though not necessarily the law, that made the taking a conversion. In the case before us, whether the mental element that Congress required be spoken of as knowledge or as intent, would not seem to alter its bearing on guilt. For it is not apparent how Morissette could have knowingly or intentionally converted property that he did not know could be converted, as would be the case if it was in fact abandoned or if he truly believed it to be abandoned and unwanted property. . . .

Of course, the jury, considering Morissette's awareness that these casings were on government property, his failure to seek any permission for their removal and his self-interest as a witness, might have disbelieved his profession of innocent intent and concluded that his assertion of a belief that the casings were abandoned was an afterthought. Had the jury convicted on proper instructions it would be the end of the matter. But juries are not bound by what seems inescapable logic to judges. They might have concluded that the heaps of spent casings left in the hinterland to rust away presented an appearance of unwanted and abandoned junk, and that lack of any conscious deprivation of property or intentional injury was indicated by Morissette's good character, the openness of the taking, crushing and transporting of the casings, and the candor with which it was all admitted. They might have refused to brand Morissette as a thief. Had they done so, that too would have been the end of the matter.

Reversed.

Mr. Justice Douglas concurs in the result.

Mr. Justice Minton took no part in the consideration or decision of this case.

STATE v. PRINCE

Supreme Court of New Mexico, 1948.
52 N.M. 15, 189 P.2d 993.

Compton, Justice. Defendant in error was charged by an information containing two counts, based upon Section 41–4519, New Mexico Statutes, 1941 Compilation, which reads as follows: "Any person being in the possession of the property of another, who shall convert such property to his own use, or dispose of such property in any way not authorized by the owner thereof, or by law, shall be guilty of embezzlement . . ." Sec. 2, Ch. 70, Laws 1923, N.M. Sts.

The information charged:
"That in the county of Bernalillo, State of New Mexico, the said Lewis Prince, being entrusted in the possession of certain monies of

Sec. 5 STRICT LIABILITY 403

Markus and Markus, a partnership, did on the 20th day of March, 1946, fraudulently convert the sum of forty-one dollars and 41/100 ($41.41) to his own use or did dispose of such property in a way not authorized by the owner thereof or by law.

"Count 2. On the 2nd day of August, 1946, in the same county and state, the said Lewis Prince, being entrusted in the possession of certain monies of Markus and Markus, a partnership, did fraudulently convert the sum of Fifty-four and 50/100 ($54.50) dollars to his own use or did dispose of such property in a way not authorized by the owner thereof or by law."

The statute in question expressly repealed a prior statute which read: "If any person who shall be *entrusted* with any property which may be the subject of larceny, shall *embezzle or fraudulently convert* to his own use, or *shall secrete with intent to embezzle or fraudulently convert* to his own use any such property, he shall be deemed guilty of larceny." Section 1543, Code 1915. (Emphasis ours.)

From an order sustaining a motion to quash the information as unconstitutional and void, plaintiff brings the case here for review by writ of error, assigning the following as error:

1. The court erred in making its conclusions of law.

2. The court erred in dismissing the information.

3. The court erred in dismissing the defendant. . . .

The single question for our determination is whether the statute may be sustained when it omits certain essential elements necessary to constitute the crime of embezzlement, viz., entrustment and fraudulent appropriation.

The essential elements of the offense of embezzlement are: (a) That the property belonged to some one other than the accused. (b) That the accused occupied a designated fiduciary relationship and that the property came into his possession by reason of his employment or office. (c) That there was a fraudulent intent to deprive the owner of his property. Section 1543, supra, was before the legislature when Section 41–4519, supra, was enacted. It knew the essential elements necessary to constitute the offense of embezzlement. It expressly repealed that effective statute. . . .

A penal statute should define the act necessary to constitute an offense with such certainty that a person who violates it must know that his act is criminal when he does it. Then can it be said a person having property of another in his possession, which he believes to be his own, could possibly know that he had violated the law when he sells it or otherwise appropriates it to his own use. But it clearly appears from reading the statutes in question, such appropriation is made a crime. Under its terms there is no defense for simple conversion, and to make an act, innocent itself, a crime, and criminals of those who might perchance fall within its interdiction, is inconsistent with law. The statute is uncertain in its meaning, vague and indefinite. A person charged thereunder is deprived of due process of law, in violation of the Fourteenth Amendment of the Constitution of the United States. . . .

Plaintiff also urges that in the exercise of police power the legislature has authority to define embezzlement and declare what constitutes an offense. It must be conceded that such power inheres in the state but in order that a statute may be sustained as an exercise of such power it must appear that the enactment has for its purpose the prevention of certain manifest or anticipated evil, or the preservation of the public health, safety, morals, or general welfare. As defined by Justice Holmes: "It may be said in a general way that the police power extends to all the great public needs. . . . It may be put forth in aid of what is sanctioned by usage, or held by the prevailing morality or strong and preponderant opinion to be greatly and immediately necessary to the public welfare." Nobel State Bank v. Haskell, 219 U.S. 104, 31 S.Ct. 186, 188, 55 L.Ed. 112, 32 L.R.A., N.S., 1062, Ann.Cas.1912A, 487.

The power thus defined, and a prior valid statute having been repealed, we are unable to determine that there existed, or was anticipated, that condition of public health, safety, morals or preponderant opinion making the statute in question immediately necessary for the public welfare. No additional power is conferred by the new statute, unless it has for its purpose to embrace within its ambits the guilty and innocent alike. This would afford no reasonable ascertainable standard of guilt, and is therefore too vague and uncertain to be enforced. The accused, though presumed to be innocent, if proven guilty of simple conversion, nevertheless is a felon under the statute, in violation of the Sixth and Fourteenth Amendments to the Constitution of the United States.[1]

To sustain the statute, we would supply by intendment, words of limitation, and this would be judicial legislation. The statute cannot be extended or sustained as a reasonable exercise of police power. . . .

Our conclusion leaves the state without a statute defining embezzlement unless we determine whether section 1543, supra, has been disturbed by the repealing clause of chapter 70, Laws of 1923, N.M. St. supra.

The public welfare impels us to decide this point. . . .

It is evident that the legislature intended to displace the embezzlement law by substituting a new one. We are not satisfied that the

---

[1]. But this does not invalidate another section of the Act dealing with embezzlement of public funds. State v. Chavez, 58 N.M. 802, 277 P.2d 302 (1954); State v. Nolan, 59 N.M. 437, 285 P.2d 798 (1955). In Nolan the court held that public funds could not be converted to private use without fraud and hence the absence of the word "fraudulently" in the statute is not fatal.

legislature would have repealed the former act if it had not been supposed that the new act adopted in lieu of it was valid.

This being so, under the rule announced, the repealing clause necessarily fails when the purpose of the act fails and no former act is repealed. It follows that the embezzlement law existing prior to the Act of 1923 was not repealed. The judgment of the court was correct in holding that Section 41–4519, supra, did not define embezzlement, but the information having charged a crime under the act sought to be repealed, the court erred in discharging appellant.

The judgment is reversed, with directions to the trial court to reinstate the case upon its docket and proceed in a manner not inconsistent herewith, and it is so ordered.[2]

BRICE, C. J., and LUJAN and MCGHEE, JJ., concur.

SADLER, JUSTICE (dissenting). The prevailing opinion is correct in directing a reversal of the order of the trial court quashing the criminal information filed below. The holding that the statute in question is unconstitutional as denying to an accused due process of law under the Fourteenth Amendment to the Constitution of the United States is plainly erroneous. It convicts the legislature of sheer stupidity to hold that in enacting 1941 Comp. § 41–4519, it intended to authorize punishment of the innocent and well intentioned along with the venal and criminally disposed. . . .

COMMONWEALTH v. KOCZWARA

Supreme Court of Pennsylvania, 1959.
397 Pa. 575, 155 A.2d 825.

COHEN, JUSTICE. This is an appeal from the judgment of the Court of Quarter Sessions of Lackawanna County sentencing the defendant to three months in the Lackawanna County Jail, a fine of five hundred dollars and the costs of prosecution, in a case involving violations of the Pennsylvania Liquor Code. . . .

Defendant raises two contentions, both of which, in effect, question whether the undisputed facts of this case support the judgment and sentence imposed by the Quarter Sessions Court. Judge Hoban

---

2. A New York statute penalizing the receipt of stolen goods by a junk-man without a requirement either of knowledge or lack of diligent inquiry as to the rights of the party selling was held to be invalid. People v. Estreich, 272 App.Div. 698, 75 N.Y.S.2d 267, affirmed 297 N.Y. 910, 79 N.E.2d 742 (1947).

A statute made it an offense for any person, except persons of certain specified classes, to have or possess a hypodermic syringe or needle unless such possession was authorized by prescription or certificate of a physician. Since the statute made no exception in case of possession for a lawful purpose it was held to violate the due process clause of the Fourteenth Amendment. State v. Birdsell, 235 La. 396, 104 So.2d 148 (1958).

found as fact that "in every instance the purchase [by minors] was made from a bartender, not identified by name, and service to the boys was made by the bartender. There was *no* evidence that the defendant was present on any one of the occasions testified to by these witnesses, nor that he had any personal knowledge of the sales to them or to other persons on the premises." We, therefore, must determine the criminal responsibility of a licensee of the Liquor Control Board for acts committed by his employees upon his premises, without his personal knowledge, participation, or presence, which acts violate a valid regulatory statute passed under the Commonwealth's police power.

While an employer in almost all cases is not criminally responsible for the unlawful acts of his employees, unless he consents to, approves, or participates in such acts, courts all over the nation have struggled for years in applying this rule within the framework of "controlling the sale of intoxicating liquor." At common law, any attempt to invoke the doctrine of *respondeat superior* in a criminal case would have run afoul of our deeply ingrained notions of criminal jurisprudence that guilt must be personal and individual.[1] In recent decades, however, many states have enacted detailed regulatory provisions in fields which are essentially noncriminal, e. g., pure food and drug acts, speeding ordinances, building regulations, and child labor, minimum wage and maximum hour legislation. Such statutes are generally enforceable by light penalties, and although violations are labelled crimes, the considerations applicable to them are totally different from those applicable to true crimes, which involve moral delinquency and which are punishable by imprisonment or another serious penalty. Such so-called statutory crimes are in reality an attempt to utilize the machinery of criminal administration as an enforcing arm for social regulations of a purely civil nature, with the punishment totally unrelated to questions of moral wrongdoing or guilt. It is here that the social interest in the general well-being and security of the populace has been held to outweigh the individual interest of the particular defendant. The penalty is imposed despite the defendant's lack of a criminal intent or mens rea. . . .

In the Liquor Code, Section 493, the legislature has set forth twenty-five specific acts which are condemned as unlawful, and for which penalties are provided in Section 494. Subsections (1) and (14) of Section 493 contain the two offenses charged here. In neither of

---

1. The distinction between *respondeat superior* in tort law and its application to the criminal law is obvious. In tort law, the doctrine is employed for the purpose of settling the incidence of loss upon the party who can best bear such loss. But the criminal law is supported by totally different concepts. We impose penal treatment upon those who injure or menace social interests, partly in order to reform, partly to prevent the continuation of the antisocial activity and partly to deter others. If a defendant has personally lived up to the social standards of the criminal law and has not menaced or injured anyone, why impose penal treatment?

these subsections is there any language which would require the prohibited acts to have been done either knowingly, wilfully or intentionally, there being a significant absence of such words as "knowingly, wilfully, etc." That the legislature intended such a requirement in other related sections of the same Code is shown by examining Section 492(15), wherein it is made unlawful to *knowingly* sell any malt beverages to a person engaged in the business of illegally selling such beverages. The omission of any such word in the subsections of Section 494 is highly significant. It indicates a legislative intent to eliminate both knowledge and criminal intent as necessary ingredients of such offenses. To bolster this conclusion, we refer back to Section 491 wherein the Code states, "It shall be unlawful (1) For any person, by himself *or by an employe or agent,* to expose or keep for sale, or directly or *indirectly* . . . to sell or offer to sell any liquor within this Commonwealth, except in accordance with the provisions of this act and the regulations of the board." The Superior Court has long placed such an interpretation on the statute.

As the defendant has pointed out, there is a distinction between the requirement of a mens rea and the imposition of vicarious absolute liability for the acts of another. It may be that the courts below, in relying on prior authority, have failed to make such a distinction. In any case, we fully recognize it. Moreover, we find that the intent of the legislature in enacting this Code was not only to eliminate the common law requirement of a mens rea, but also to place a very high degree of responsibility upon the holder of a liquor license to make certain that neither he nor anyone in his employ commit any of the prohibited acts upon the licensed premises. Such a burden of care is imposed upon the licensee in order to protect the public from the potentially noxious effects of an inherently dangerous business. We, of course, express no opinion as to the *wisdom* of the legislature's imposing vicarious responsibility under certain sections of the Liquor Code. There may or may not be an economic-sociological justification for such liability on a theory of deterrence. Such determination is for the legislature to make, so long as the constitutional requirements are met.

Can the legislature, consistent with the requirements of due process, thus establish absolute criminal liability? Were this the defendant's first violation of the Code, and the penalty solely a minor fine of from $100–$300, we would have no hesitation in upholding such a judgment. Defendant, by accepting a liquor license, must bear this financial risk. Because of a prior conviction for violations of the Code, however, the trial judge felt compelled under the mandatory language of the statute, Section 494(a), to impose not only an increased fine of five hundred dollars, but also a three month sentence of imprisonment. Such sentence of imprisonment in a case where liability is imposed vicariously cannot be sanctioned by this Court consistently with the law of the land clause of Section 9, Article I of the Constitution of the Commonwealth of Pennsylvania., P.S.

The Courts of the Commonwealth have already strained to permit the legislature to carry over the civil doctrine of *respondeat superior* and to apply it as a means of enforcing the regulatory scheme that covers the liquor trade. We have done so on the theory that the Code established petty misdemeanors involving only light monetary fines. It would be unthinkable to impose vicarious criminal responsibility in cases involving true crimes. Although to hold a principal criminally liable might possibly be an effective means of enforcing law and order, it would do violence to our more sophisticated modern-day concepts of justice. Liability for all true crimes, wherein an offense carries with it a jail sentence, must be based exclusively upon personal causation. It can be readily imagined that even a licensee who is meticulously careful in the choice of his employees cannot supervise every single act of the subordinates. A man's liberty cannot rest on so frail a reed as whether his employee will commit a mistake in judgment. See Sayre, Criminal Responsibility For Acts of Another, 43 Harv.L.Rev. 689 (1930). . . . Therefore, we are only holding that so much of the judgment as calls for imprisonment is invalid, and we are leaving intact the five hundred dollar fine imposed by Judge Hoban under the subsequent offense section. . . .

Judgment, as modified, is affirmed.[2]

BELL, MUSMANNO and MCBRIDE, JJ., file separate dissenting opinions.

BELL, JUSTICE (disenting). . . .

I would affirm the judgment and the sentence on the opinion of Judge Hirt, speaking for a unanimous Superior Court.

MUSMANNO, JUSTICE (dissenting). . . .

I conclude by saying that the Majority has been so remiss in affirming the conviction in this case that I myself would be remiss if I did not dissent against a decision which flouts the Constitution, ignores the Bill of Rights and introduces into the temple of the law the Asiatic rite of "vicarious criminal liability."

[Added by the Compiler.]

2. A truck driver whose cargo contained undersized fish was held not guilty of violating the statute if he had no knowledge that the cargo consisted of undersized fish and the cargo was so packed that it would have been unreasonable and impracticable to require him to inspect it. State v. Williams, 94 Ohio App. 249, 115 N.E.2d 36 (1952). Conviction of violating the city ordinance by driving through a flashing red light without stopping was held to be unsupportable in the face of an express finding that the driver was unable to stop because of brake failure, having experienced no prior brake trouble and having no knowledge of the defective condition of the brake. State v. Kremer, 262 Minn. 190, 114 N.W.2d 88 (1962).

MCBRIDE, JUSTICE (dissenting). I would agree that a man who sells liquor to a minor may be punished even if he did not know that the person to whom he sold was a minor. But in my opinion, the statute does not and cannot validly create an indictable misdemeanor under which a liquor licensee is punished by a fine or imprisonment, or both, for the act of an employee in selling to a minor, where, as here, the act itself is done without the licensee's knowledge, consent, or acquiescence. I would reverse the judgment and discharge the defendant.

SECTION 6. UNLAWFUL CONDUCT

It is frequently said that one who is committing an unlawful act has "general *mens rea*" or a "general criminal intent." Care must be taken not to infer too much from such a statement. In the first place the phrase "unlawful act," as used in this connection, has a very restricted meaning. The state of mind of one who is committing such an "unlawful act" may be substituted for criminal negligence in establishing the *mens rea* needed for guilt of certain crimes. This is true of manslaughter and of battery but it is not true of most offenses.

COMMONWEALTH v. MINK

Supreme Judicial Court of Massachusetts, 1877.
123 Mass. 422.

INDICTMENT for the murder of Charles Ricker at Lowell, in the county of Middlesex, on August 31, 1876. Trial before Ames and Morton, JJ., who allowed a bill of exceptions in substance as follows:

It was proved that Charles Ricker came to his death by a shot from a pistol in the hand of the defendant. The defendant introduced evidence tending to show that she had been engaged to be married to Ricker; that an interview was had between them at her room, in the course of which he expressed his intention to break off the engagement and abandon her entirely; that she thereupon went to her trunk, took a pistol from it, and attempted to use it upon herself, with the intention of taking her own life; that Ricker then seized her to prevent her from accomplishing that purpose, and a struggle ensued between them; and that in the struggle the pistol was accidentally discharged, and in that way the fatal wound inflicted upon him.

The jury were instructed on this point as follows: "If you believe the defendant's story, and that she did put the pistol to her head with the intention of committing suicide, she was about to do a criminal and unlawful act, and that which she had no right to do. It is true, undoubtedly, that suicide cannot be punished by any proceeding of the courts, for the reason that the person who kills himself has placed himself beyond the reach of justice, and nothing can be done. But the law, nevertheless, recognizes suicide as a criminal act, and the attempt at suicide is also criminal. It would be the duty of any bystander who saw such an attempt about to be made, as a matter of mere humanity, to interfere and try to prevent it. And the rule is, that if a homicide is produced by the doing of an unlawful act, although the killing was the last thing that the person about to do it had in his mind, it would be an unlawful killing, and the person would incur the responsibility which attaches to the crime of manslaughter. . . .

GRAY, C. J. The life of every human being is under the protection of the law, and cannot be lawfully taken by himself, or by another with his consent, except by legal authority. By the common law of England, suicide was considered a crime against the laws of God and man, the goods and chattels of the criminal were forfeited to the King, his body had an ignominious burial in the highway, and he was deemed a murderer of himself and a felon, *felo de se*. . . .

Suicide has not ceased to be unlawful and criminal in this Commonwealth by the simple repeal of the Colony Act of 1660 by the St. of 1823, c. 143, which (like the corresponding St. of 4 G. IV c. 52, enacted by the British Parliament within a year before) may well have had its origin in consideration for the feelings of innocent surviving relatives; nor by the briefer directions as to the form of coroner's inquests in the Rev.Sts. c. 140, § 8, and the Gen.Sts. c. 175, § 9, which in this, as in most other matters, have not repeated at length the forms of legal proceedings set forth in the statutes codified; nor by the fact that the Legislature, having in the general revisions of the statutes measured the degree of punishment for attempts to commit offences by the punishment prescribed for each offence if actually committed, has, intentionally or inadvertently, left the attempt to commit suicide without punishment, because the completed act would not be punished in any manner. Rev.Sts. c. 133, § 12. Gen.Sts. c. 168, § 8. Commonwealth v. Dennis, 105 Mass. 162. After all these changes in the statutes, the point decided in Bowen's case was ruled in the same way by Chief Justice Bigelow and Justices Dewey, Metcalf and Chapman, in a case which has not been reported.

Since it has been provided by statute that "any crime punishable by death or imprisonment in the state prison is a felony, and no other crime shall be so considered," it may well be that suicide is not technically a felony in this Commonwealth. Gen.Sts. c. 168, § 1. St. 1852, c. 37, § 1. But being unlawful and criminal as *malum in se*, any attempt to commit it is likewise unlawful and criminal. Every one has the same right and duty to interpose to save a life from being so unlawfully and criminally taken, that he would have to defeat an attempt unlawfully to take the life of a third person. And it is not disputed that any person who, in doing or attempting to do an act which is unlawful and criminal, kills another, though not intending his death, is guilty of criminal homicide, and, at the least, of manslaughter.

The only doubt that we have entertained in this case is, whether the act of the defendant, in attempting to kill herself, was not so malicious, in the legal sense, as to make the killing of another person, in the attempt to carry out her purpose, murder, and whether the instructions given to the jury were not therefore too favorable to the defendant.

Exceptions overruled.

STATE v. HORTON

Supreme Court of North Carolina, 1905.
139 N.C. 588, 51 S.E. 945.

HOKE, J., after stating the case: It will be noted that the finding of the jury declares that the act of the defendant was not in itself dangerous to human life and excludes every element of criminal negligence, and rests the guilt or innocence of the defendant on the fact alone that at the time of the homicide the defendant was hunting on another's land without written permission from the owner. The act which applies only in the counties of Orange, Franklin and Scotland, makes the conduct a misdemeanor, and imposes a punishment on conviction, of not less than five nor more than ten dollars.

The statement sometimes appears in works of approved excellence to the effect that an unintentional homicide is a criminal offense when occasioned by a person engaged at the time in an unlawful act. In nearly every instance, however, will be found the qualification that if the act in question is free from negligence, and not in itself of dangerous tendency, and the criminality must arise, if at all, entirely from the fact that it is unlawful, in such case, the unlawful act must be one that is *malum in se* and not merely *malum prohibitum*, and this we hold to be the correct doctrine. In Foster's Crown Law, it is thus stated at page 258: "In order to bring a case within this description (excusable homicide) the act upon which death ensueth must be lawful. For if the act be unlawful, I mean if it be *malum in se*, the case will amount to felony, either murder or manslaughter, as circumstances may vary the nature of it. If it be done in prosecution of a felonious intent, it will be murder; but if the intent went no further than to commit a bare trespass, it will be manslaughter." At page 259, the same author puts an instance with his comments thereon as follows: "A shooteth at the poultry of B and by accident killeth a man; if his intention was to steal the poultry, which must be collected from circumstances, it will be murder by reason of that felonious intent, but if it was done wantonly and without that intention, it will be barely manslaughter. The rule I have laid down supposeth that the act from which death ensued was *malum in se*. For if it was barely *malum prohibitum*, as shooting at game by a person not qualified by statute law to keep or use a gun for that purpose, the case of a person so offending will fall under the same rule as that of a qualified man. For the statutes prohibiting the destruction of the game under certain penalties will not, in a question of this kind, enhance the accident beyond its intrinsic moment."

One of these disqualifying statutes here referred to as an instance of *malum prohibitum* was an act passed (13 Richard II, chap. 13), to prevent certain classes of persons from keeping dogs, nets or engines to destroy game, etc., and the punishment imposed on conviction was one year's imprisonment. There were others imposing a lesser penalty.

1 Bishop, New Criminal Law, sec. 332, treats of the matter as follows: "In these cases of an unintended evil result, the intent whence the act accidentally sprang must probably be, if specific, to do a thing which is *malum in se* and not merely *malum prohibitum*." Thus Archbold says: "When a man in the execution of one act, by misfortune or chance and not designedly, does another act for which if he had willfully committed it, he would be liable to be punished—in that case, if the act he were doing were lawful or merely *malum prohibitum*, he shall not be punishable for the act arising from misfortune or chance, but if it be *malum in se*, it is otherwise. To illustrate: since it is *malum prohibitum*, not *malum in se*, for an unauthorized person to kill game in England contrary to the statutes, if, in unlawfully shooting at game, he accidentally kills a man, it is no more criminal in him than if he were authorized. But, to shoot at another's fowls, wantonly or in sport, an act which is *malum in se*, though a civil trespass, and thereby accidentally to kill a human being is manslaughter If the intent in the shooting were to commit larceny of the fowls, we have seen that it would be murder."

An offense *malum in se* is properly defined as one which is naturally evil as adjudged by the sense of a civilized community, whereas an act *malum prohibitum* is wrong only because made so by statute. For the reason that acts *mala in se* have, as a rule, become criminal offenses by the course and development of the common law, an impression has sometimes obtained that only acts can be so classified which the common law makes criminal, but this is not at all the test. An act can be, and frequently is, *malum in se*, when it amounts only to a civil trespass, provided it has a malicious element or manifests an evil nature, or wrongful disposition to harm or injure another in his person or property.

The distinction between the two classes of acts is well stated in 19 Am. & Eng.Enc. (2d Ed.) at p. 705: "An offense *malum in se* is one which is naturally evil, as murder, theft, and the like. Offenses at common law are generally *malum in se.* An offense *malum prohibitum,* on the contrary, is not naturally an evil, but becomes so in consequence of being forbidden."

We do not hesitate to declare that the offense of the defendant in hunting on the land without written permission of the owner was *malum prohibitum,* and the special verdict having found that the act in which the defendant was engaged was not in itself dangerous to human life, and negatived all idea of negligence, we hold that the case is one of excusable homicide, and the defendant should be declared not guilty. . . .

There was error in holding the defendant guilty, and, on the facts declared, a verdict of not guilty should be directed and the defendant discharged.

Reversed.

WALKER, J., concurs in result only.

STATE v. SEALY

Supreme Court of North Carolina, 1961.
253 N.C. 802, 117 S.E.2d 793.

DENNY, JUSTICE. The defendant assigns as error those portions of the court's charge to the jury hereinafter set out. The court, after having read to the jury G.S. § 20–158 (the statute which requires the driver of a motor vehicle to stop before entering or crossing certain through highways), and G.S. § 20–140 (the statute defining reckless driving), charged: "If you find from the evidence in this case, . . . beyond a reasonable doubt that the defendant intentionally violated one or more of the statutes read to you, designed and intended to protect human life, and . . . that such intentional violation thereof was the proximate cause of the death of the deceased, then it would be your duty to return a verdict of guilty of involuntary manslaughter."

". . . (I)f you are satisfied from the testimony beyond a reasonable doubt that the driver of this car, the defendant in this case, Mr. Howard Franklin Sealy, was operating his motor vehicle in violation of the statute, in respect to stopping at the stop sign, . . . and that such action on his part was the proximate cause of the death of these two men, you would find him guilty of involuntary manslaughter."

The above instructions are conflicting and the State concedes error in the latter. According to the provisions of G.S. § 20–158, a violation thereof is not negligence *per se* in any action at law for injury to person or property, but the failure to stop at a stop sign before entering an intersection with a dominant highway may be considered with other facts in the case in determining whether or not under all the facts and circumstances involved, such driver was guilty of negligence or contributory negligence.

"Culpable negligence in the law of crimes necessarily implies something more than actionable negligence in the law of torts."
. . .

"An intentional, wilful or wanton violation of a statute or ordinance, designed for the protection of human life or limb, which proximately results in injury or death, is culpable negligence." State v. Cope, supra [204 N.C. 28, 167 S.E. 458]. But, where there is an unintentional or inadvertent violation of the statute, such violation standing alone does not constitute culpable negligence. The inadvertent or unintentional violation of the statute must be accompanied by recklessness of probable consequences of a dangerous nature, when tested by the rule of reasonable prevision, amounting altogether to a thoughtless disregard of consequences or of a heedless indifference to the safety of others.

Other assignments of error need not be considered or discussed since they may not arise on another hearing.

The defendant is entitled to a new trial and it is so ordered.

New trial.[1]

PEOPLE v. MULCAHY
Supreme Court of Illinois, 1925.
318 Ill. 332, 149 N.E. 266.

MR. JUSTICE HEARD delivered the opinion of the court.

Plaintiff in error (hereinafter called defendant) was indicted, tried and convicted in the criminal court of Cook county of involuntary manslaughter and sentenced to an indeterminate term in the penitentiary.

---

1. D ran into a boy and knocked him down while D was driving a sleigh in violation of the speed law. This was held not to be sufficient to establish guilt of assault and battery. Commonwealth v. Adams, 114 Mass. 323 (1873).

D fired a shot into the night which injured a woman 216 feet away. It was held that the fact that the shot was in violation of a city ordinance could be considered with other facts on the general question of culpable negligence. Commonwealth v. Hawkins, 157 Mass. 551, 32 N.E. 862 (1893).

Accidental death by one driving a car without a license is manslaughter. Commonwealth v. Romig, 22 Pa.D. & C. 341 (1934). Contra: Commonwealth v. Williams, 133 Pa.Super. 104, 1 A.2d 812 (1938). The mere fact that the act which caused death was a trespass is not sufficient to establish criminal homicide. Regina v. Franklin, 15 Cox C.C. 163 (1883).

An unintentional and nonnegligent violation of the Health and Safety Code which results in death is not manslaughter. People v. Stuart, 47 Cal.2d 167, 302 P.2d 5 (1956). A prescription calling (in part) for sodium citrate was filled with sodium nitrate, but the fault was with someone else who had mislabeled the bottle and not with the pharmacist who filled the prescription.

Defendant was a uniformed police officer of the city of Chicago patrolling a beat on Sixty-third street. On December 31, 1923, he went on patrol duty at eight o'clock in the evening and patrolled his beat until four o'clock A.M., January 1, 1924. In the course of his duty on this night, as upon previous nights, by direction of his superior officer he visited a Chinese-American restaurant or cabaret, at which place the deceased Jennie Plarski, was employed as a checkroom clerk. . . . While they were sitting at the table, talking, some patron of the place who was intoxicated raised a disturbance and the proprietor put him out, but before doing so took a revolver out of the disturber's pocket and placed it on the table back of where defendant was sitting. The deceased noticed the gun upon the table, and exclaimed, "Johnny, be careful! There is a gun behind you!" Thereupon defendant took his police revolver out of his pocket and cocked it, but seeing that the revolver was not in the hand of any person he attempted to ease the hammer down to a position of safety, and his testimony, which is not contradicted, is: "I pulled the trigger and was releasing it and she made a jerk, and she says, 'Johnny! be careful!' and she made a jerk. I don't know whether she touched the revolver. It all happened so quickly I cannot understand it." The revolver was discharged, the bullet entering the body of the deceased, later causing her death. All the witnesses present at the time of the shooting testified that everything appeared to be friendly between defendant and the deceased. Defendant at all times maintained that the shooting was purely accidental, and while a statement of the deceased as to the circumstances of the shooting is in evidence, in her statement she did not claim that the shooting was intentional or grossly negligent on the part of defendant.

It is conceded that defendant fired the shot resulting in the girl's death, and the only question for the jury to determine was whether or not the shot was fired under such circumstances as to constitute the crime of manslaughter. In the brief of defendant in error it is said, "The case is a close one on the facts."

Upon the trial the court allowed the State to prove, over the objection of defendant, that before and at the time of the shooting, in the room in which it took place and in the presence of defendant, an open gambling game of stud poker was being conducted. This evidence did not tend to prove or disprove whether the shooting was accidental or criminal, but it did tend to show that at that time defendant, who was a police officer, was violating the law by not arresting the offenders who were committing the crime of gambling in his presence. The court instructed the jury, in the language of the statute, that "manslaughter is the unlawful killing of a human being without malice, express or implied, and without any mixture of deliberation whatever. It must be voluntary, upon a heat of passion caused by a provocation apparently sufficient to make the passion irresistible or involuntary in the commission of an unlawful act, or a lawful act without due caution or circumspection." The court also gave to the jury the following instruction:

"The court instructs the jury, in the language of the statute, that any intoxicated person found in any street, highway or public place, or so found disturbing the peace of the public, or of his own or any other family in any private building or place, shall for the first offense be fined not more than $5 and upon a subsequent conviction shall be fined not exceeding $25."

The admission of the evidence with reference to gambling and the giving of this instruction are assigned as error. This instruction should not have been given in this case without limiting it to the intoxication of the plaintiff in error. The jury hearing the evidence as to gambling committed in the presence of the officer, and the evidence that a drunken person disturbing the peace in the presence of the officer was not arrested by him, and then hearing these instructions, might easily be led to believe that at the time of the shooting defendant was in the commission of an unlawful act in failing to arrest offenders committing criminal offenses in his presence. While it may be stated generally that a homicide is committed in the perpetration of another crime when the accused, intending to commit some crime other than the homicide, is engaged in any one of the acts which such intent requires for its full execution, and while so engaged, and within the *res gestae* of the intended crime and in consequence thereof, the killing results, to make such homicide unlawful by reason thereof it must appear that there was such legal relation between the killing and the crime committed or attempted that the killing can be said to have occurred as a part of the perpetration of the crime or in furtherance of an attempt or purpose to commit it. To convict one of manslaughter for killing a person while in the commission of an unlawful act the State must show more than a mere coincidence of time and place between the wrongful act and the death. It must also show that the unlawful act was the proximate cause of the killing.

In Jackson v. State, 101 Ohio St. 152, 127 N.E. 870, where it appeared that the killing was occasioned by the violation of a statute forbidding an excessive rate of speed in the operation of a motor vehicle, the court, in holding that the disobedience of the statute must have been the proximate cause of death, said: "The square question is raised here as to whether an accidental, unintentional killing of a person by another engaged in an unlawful act makes that person guilty of manslaughter under the statute, irrespective of any connection between the unlawful act and the unintentional killing and it seems to this court that an analysis of the illogical and absurd results which would necessarily follow the recognition of such a rule will answer the query. For instance, if it be the law, as charged by the trial court in this case, that if the jury find the accused unintentionally struck and killed the decedent while engaged in an unlawful act, to-wit, operating his car at a greater rate of speed than fifteen miles per hour, they must find him guilty of manslaughter without reference to causation, then it must follow that if the accused had been violating any other valid statute, however unconnected with the death at the time of the unintentional killing, he would be guilty of manslaughter. For instance, it is a violation of a valid statute to operate a motor vehicle without having first registered same with the Secretary of State, . . . yet . . . should the driver of an automobile, while driving his car without first having registered it with the Secretary of State, . . . be so unfortunate as to unintentionally run over and kill a person who inadvertently or purposely projected himself in front of the car, he would be guilty of manslaughter for, clearly, it would be an unintentional killing by a person operating a car in the violation of a valid statute, and yet there would be no relationship between the violation of the statute and the death. The accident would have occurred just as surely had the motor vehicle been registered. . . . The proximate cause would have been the same in each case, although the result to the driver of the car would have been the appalling difference between criminal guilt and legal innocence. . . ."

The fact that defendant did not arrest the persons guilty of gaming nor the drunken disturber of the peace was not the proximate cause of the killing and had absolutely no connection therewith, and the admission of this evidence and the giving of the instruction to which exception is taken would have a natural tendency to mislead the jury and prejudice them against the defendant. While errors in the admission of evidence or in the giving of instructions which are not of a prejudicial character will not justify a reversal of a judgment of conviction when the jury, acting reasonably on the competent evidence and under proper instructions, could have reached no other conclusion, where the guilt of the accused is a close question on the facts to sustain a conviction the record must be free from material and substantial error and the jury must be accurately instructed. . . .

For the errors in the admission of evidence and the giving and modification of instructions the judgment of conviction is reversed and the cause remanded to the criminal court of Cook county.

Reversed and remanded.

SECTION 7. "TRANSFERRED INTENT"

A tort concept, which serves a useful purpose in that field [1] but has no proper place in criminal law, because it tends more to confusion than to clarity of thought, is the so-called "doctrine of the transfer of the intent to the unintended act." This is frequently stated in some such form as this: Whenever a man meaning one wrong does another unmeant, he is punishable unless some specific intent is required. The reason sometimes offered is that "the thing done, having proceeded from a corrupt mind, is to be viewed the same whether the corruption was of one particular form or another." [2]

Such a notion results from an imperfect analysis of certain cases. Burglary is the breaking and entering of the dwelling house of another in the nighttime with intent to commit a felony. In other words the intent to commit some *other* crime (which must be a felony at common law) is the very state of mind which constitutes the *mens rea* for burglary. For certain offenses the intent to commit some other offense is not essential to the *mens rea* but may suffice for this purpose. Murder is an excellent example. Certain crimes such as arson, rape, robbery and burglary have been found to involve such an unreasonable element of human risk that he who is perpetrating or attempting one of them is held to have a state of mind which falls within the label "malice aforethought." Hence if homicide is caused thereby it is murder however unintended the killing may be. This is due to the law of homicide and not to any doctrine of "transferred intent."

To test the soundness of such a doctrine it is necessary to consider offenses other than burglary (which requires an intent to commit some other crime) or murder (for which an intent to commit certain other crimes will be sufficient for the *mens rea* requirement). A man who has in his pocket a weapon he has no authority to carry is not guilty of the crime of carrying a concealed weapon if it was put there secretly by others without his knowing or having any reason to know of its presence. And a man who marries a second wife, after the death of the first, is not guilty of bigamy even if he does not know of the death and thinks the first wife is still alive. In the first case we find the *actus reus* but no *mens rea*. In the second, the *mens rea* but no *actus reus*. And if the man who contracted such a marriage happened to be wearing a coat with an unsuspected weapon concealed therein, the intent to commit bigamy could not be coupled with the unintentional carrying of the concealed weapon so as to estab-

---

1. If defendant shoots at A and hits B instead, the "intent is said to be 'transferred' to the victim—which is obviously a fiction, or a legal conclusion, to accomplish the desired result of liability". Prosser, Law of Torts 33 (2d ed. 1955).

2. Bishop, Criminal Law § 327 (8th ed. 1892).

lish guilt of either offense. If he borrowed the coat for the sole purpose of wearing it during the wedding ceremony there would be some connection between the two but the *actus reus* and the *mens rea* still would not match in such a manner as to constitute criminal guilt.

It was stated by Lord Hale, and repeated in substance by Blackstone, that "if A. by malice aforethought strikes at B. and missing him strikes C. whereof he dies, though he never bore any malice to C. yet it is murder, and the law transfers the malice to the party slain." [3] Unquestionably the slayer is guilty of murder in such a case, and if any resort is to be made to a theory of transferred intent it should be limited to this general type of situation. The general mental pattern is the same whether the malicious endeavor was to kill B or to kill C. If the word "malicious" is omitted the statement might not be true. An intent to kill B might represent a very different mental pattern than an intent to kill C. For example, B at the time might be a murderer, fleeing from lawful arrest under such circumstances that A was privileged to kill him. If such was the fact an intent by A to kill B would not be a guilty state of mind. It would not constitute *mens rea*. If at the same time C was obviously an innocent bystander an intent by A to kill C would amount to malice aforethought. Under such circumstances, if A should shoot at B in the proper and prudent exercise of his privilege and should happen quite unexpectedly, by a glance of the bullet, to cause the death of C, A would be free from criminal guilt. This seems to lend support to the theory of "transferred intent." The intent to kill B did not constitute *mens rea* and this innocent intent *seems* to be transferred to the unintended victim.

The hypothetical situation, however, supposes not only the privilege to direct deadly force against B, but also the proper and prudent exercise of this privilege. If, on the other hand, he exercised this privilege so imprudently and improperly as to constitute a criminally negligent disregard of the life of the innocent bystander, C, the killing of C would be manslaughter. The intent is given due consideration, but it is not "transferred."

REX v. LEWIS

Hereford Assizes, 1833.
6 Car. & P. 161, 172 Eng.Rep. 1190.

Indictment on the stat. 9 Geo. IV. c. 31, s. 11 (set forth *ante*, vol. iv. p. 372, n.), for "administering" poison to Elizabeth Davis. There was a second count for "causing it to be taken."

It appeared, that, soon after the prisoner had been at the shop of Mrs. Halford buying salt, the latter found a parcel containing half a pound of moist sugar, and an ounce of tea, on the shop counter.

---

3. 1 Hale, P.C. 466; 4 Bl.Comm. 201.

This parcel was directed "To be left at Mrs. Daws, Fownhope." This parcel was sent by Mrs. Halford to Mrs. Elizabeth Davis, who used some of the sugar, which was found afterwards to contain corrosive sublimate. This caused Mrs. Davis to become very ill, but did not occasion her death.

It further appeared, that, on the day on which the prisoner was committed, she and several others were summoned before the Rev. Charles Bird, and examined on oath touching this poisoning, there being at first no specific charge against any person; but, on the conclusion of the examination, the prisoner was committed for trial on this charge. . . .

GURNEY, B. (in summing up). The question is, whether the prisoner laid this poison on the shop counter intending to kill some one. If it was intended for Mrs. Daws, and finds its way to Mrs. Davis, and she take it, the crime is as much within this Act of Parliament as if it had been intended for Mrs. Davis. If a person sends poison with intent to kill one person, and another person takes that poison, it is just the same as if it had been intended for such other person.[b]

Verdict, Not guilty.

STATE v. MARTIN

Supreme Court of Missouri, Division Two, 1938.
342 Mo. 1089, 119 S.W.2d 298.

ELLISON, J. This case comes to the writer on reassignment. An opinion was written by COOLEY, C., which failed of adoption by the court on a divided vote on a question of law. We have concluded he was right in his conclusions and shall use his statement of the facts.

The appellant, George Martin, and Joe Arvin and Harold Johnson were charged by information in the Circuit Court of Buchanan County with felonious assault with intent to maim Lloyd DeCasnett. A severance was granted and appellant Martin, whom we shall call defendant, was tried alone. He was convicted, sentenced to two years' imprisonment in the penitentiary and has appealed. Among numerous other assignments of error he claims that the evidence did not justify submission of the case to the jury.

The information is based upon Section 4014, Revised Statutes 1929 (Mo.Stat.Ann., p. 2817) making it a felony for any person to shoot at or stab another or "assault or beat another with a deadly weapon, or by any other means or force likely to produce death or

---

[b] "In some cases a man shall be said, in the judgment of the law, to kill one who is in truth actually killed by another, or by himself, as where one lays poison with an intent to kill one man, which is afterwards accidentally taken by another, who dies thereof." 1 Curw.Hawk. 92. See also the case of Rex v. Harley, ante, vol. iv. p. 369.

great bodily harm, with intent to kill, maim, ravish or rob such person. . . ." It charges an assault by defendant and Joe Arvin and Harold Johnson upon Lloyd DeCasnett "with a certain dangerous and deadly substance likely to produce death or great bodily harm, to-wit: a certain glass bulb, then and there containing sulphuric acid," with intent to maim said DeCasnett. . . .

The point upon which the case was decided in the former opinion was this. It will be remembered the State's evidence showed that shortly after midnight someone in the Chevrolet sedan owned and driven by appellant threw an electric light bulb filled with sulphuric acid against the *left* front door of the Terminal Taxicab about six inches above the lower hinge, as the two cars passed at moderate city driving speed about 8 or 10 feet apart. The windows of the taxicab were open. The prosecuting witness, DeCasnett, was riding on the *right* side and Miss Main on the left side of the back seat, and the driver, Stoneburner, on the left side of the front seat. There was nothing in the evidence to show the assailants knew DeCasnett was in the car. The acid splattered over the taxicab and some of it reached the upholstery inside, but none of the occupants was burned. The opinion held these facts failed to make a case for the jury under Sec. 4014, R.S.Mo.1929, Mo.Stat.Ann., p. 2817, on authority of State v. Mulhall, 199 Mo. 202, 214, 97 S.W. 583, 586, 7 L.R.A.,N.S., 630, 8 Ann.Cas. 781; State v. Williamson, 203 Mo. 591, 102 S.W. 519, 120 Am.St.Rep. 678; and State v. Kester, Mo., 201 S.W. 62, 64.

In the Mulhall case the defendant shot with a pistol at R but missed him and hit but did not kill M who was four or five steps away and not in line with the intended victim. The accused was prosecuted for assaulting M with intent to kill. It was ruled the statute requires a charge and proof that the accused assaulted a particular person with specific intent to kill, maim, ravish or rob *that* person; and hence the decision was that a prosecution under the statute would not lie for shooting M by mistake when the assault and felonious intent were directed at R. The gravamen of the offense, says this Mulhall case, is the felonious intent against the person assailed; and doubtless if the information had charged an assault with intent to kill R, the person shot at but missed, instead of M, the person wounded but against whom the accused had no felonious intent, the result should have been different.

In the Williamson case, likewise, the defendant shot at one person and hit another, Dorn. The opinion held the evidence was insufficient to make a case under the statute, saying, "it is clear from the evidence that the defendant did not intend to shoot Dorn, for there is no evidence that he even saw him at the time he fired the shot." In the Kester case the defendant shot from the highway into a darkened dwelling house at night wounding the housewife. There was no evidence that he could have seen her, and the conviction was reversed, Faris, J., concurring in the result with expressed reluctance.

In State v. Wansong, 271 Mo. 50, 61, 195 S.W. 999, 1003, strikers were prosecuted for assaulting with intent to kill a milk wagon driver whom they had set up in the dark. Their defense was that they had no felonious intent against *him*, but thought he was another man against whom they had a grudge. This was held to be no defense since they did intend to assault the identical person they assailed, though mistaken as to his identity. There was a similar holding in State v. Layton, 332 Mo. 216, 58 S.W.2d 454, where the defendant heard a noise behind a closed door and shot, wounding one person whom he believed to be another.

The instant case presents facts different from those in the decisions reviewed above, but the same principle applies. If a man throws a splattering acid bulb or an explosive bomb, or fires a scattering shotgun charge, at a group of persons all within range, he would be liable to prosecution under Section 4014, supra, for felonious assault upon any one of them, and he could not go acquit as to one by saying he harbored a felonious intent only against another of the group. The reasonable and probable consequences of the act being to injure the whole group, he could no more escape them by such a denial than he might by deliberately shooting at one person and disclaiming a felonious intent against that person. While the law in such cases requires a specific intent, it does not require malice in fact in the sense of actual spite or ill will against the person alleged to have been the object of the attack.

On the other hand, the intent will not be imputed, in the sense of being transferred or transposed from the person aimed at and missed to a person out of range and mistakenly hit. If A shoots at B and the bullet wounds C whose presence is unknown all the cases hold there can be no conviction under Section 4014, supra. Neither will the intent be transferred from those known to be in a group to others of whose presence the accused is ignorant. We do not mean that he must know of each individual in the group. If he knows the probable consequence of the assault will be to injure any one or all of the persons he sees or otherwise is bound to believe are before him, he will be liable as to any one of them. But if, without his knowledge there be still another person present concealed, as behind a bush or wall for illustration, he would not be liable as to that person for he could have no specific intent as to him. This, we conceive, is the crucial distinction in this case.

The statement of facts set out above says there was nothing in the evidence to show the assailants knew the prosecuting witness DeCasnett was in the taxicab. We have reexamined the record on that point. The driver, Stoneburner, and Miss Main were on the left side of the front and rear seats, respectively. This was the side next to appellant's automobile as the two cars passed, and presumably the acid throwers saw them. DeCasnett was on the right side of the rear seat, away from appellant. It was past midnight. There is testimony that Eighth Street was "pretty well lighted" right at the intersection with Seneca Street. There is no evidence as to the height and brilliance of the street lights, but some ambiguous testimony developed by appellant's counsel on cross-examination that there were two lights, one on the southeast corner and one on the northwest corner. The taxicab had made a U turn at this intersection before the acid throwing occurred. Miss Main thought it had just got straightened out and was heading back north on Eighth Street at the time. DeCasnett and Stoneburner variously estimated it was from 60 to 100 feet north of the north curb of the intersection, the latter saying it was by a telephone pole about one-third way up the block. At any rate the nearest street light at the northwest corner of the intersection was behind and on the side of the street away from DeCasnett, and the light on his side of the car at the southeast corner of the intersection was further away and almost directly behind him. . . .

. . . We cannot go so far as to extend it to a person not known to be there. Perhaps the prosecutor had some good reason for charging an assault with felonious intent upon DeCasnett, instead of upon Stoneburner or Miss Main both of whom were more directly within view of their assailants. Stoneburner was the driver of the car, sitting by the left front door where the acid bulb hit. And the assailants must have known some person was driving the car even though they could not see him. The car would not run without a driver. Whatever the reasons were for designating DeCasnett as the object of the assault, they do not appear of record. We think the State did not make a case as to him for the reasons stated.

The crime was brutal and deserves commensurate punishment. It would seem to be impossible to throw a missile like an electric light bulb filled with acid from one automobile moving 15 to 25 miles per hour against another with open windows passing in the opposite direction at the same speed so as to hit above the lower door hinges of the latter, without great danger of serious injury to the occupants. In view of the facts and conclusions we have reached, the judgment is reversed and the cause remanded. All concur.[1]

1. Compare: State v. Shanley, 20 S.D. 18, 104 N.W. 522 (1905); State v. Gallagher, 83 N.J.L. 321, 85 A. 207 (1912).

REGINA v. SMITH

Court of Criminal Appeal, 1855.
Dears. 560, 169 Eng.Rep. 845.

The following case was stated for the opinion of the Court of Criminal Appeal by MR. JUSTICE CROMPTON.

The prisoner was convicted before me at the Winchester Summer Assizes, 1855, on an indictment charging him with wounding William Taylor, with intent to murder him.

On the night in question the prisoner was posted as a sentry at Parkhurst, and the prosecutor, Taylor, was posted as a sentry at a neighbouring post.

The prisoner intended to murder one Maloney, and supposing Taylor to be Maloney, shot at and wounded Taylor.

The jury found that the prisoner intended to murder Maloney, not knowing that the party he shot at was Taylor, but supposing him to be Maloney, and the jury found that he intended to murder the individual he shot at supposing him to be Maloney.

I directed sentence of death to be recorded, reserving the question, whether the prisoner could be properly convicted on this state of facts of wounding Taylor with intent to murder him?

CHARLES CROMPTON.

This case was considered on 24th November 1855, by JERVIS, C. J., and PARKE, B., WIGHTMAN, J., CROMPTON, J., and WILLES, J.

No Counsel appeared either for the Crown or for the prisoner.

JERVIS, C. J. There is nothing in the objection. The conviction is good.

PARKE, B. The prisoner did not intend to kill the particular person, but he meant to murder the man at whom he shot.[2]

The other learned Judges concurred.

Conviction affirmed.

REGINA v. PEMBLITON

Court of Criminal Appeal, 1874.
12 Cox C.C. 607.

LORD COLERIDGE, C. J. I am of opinion that this conviction must be quashed. The facts of the case are these. The prisoner and some other persons who had been drinking in a public house were turned

---

[2] D shot at W and hit both W and M. He was indicted for shooting M with intent to commit murder. A conviction was affirmed. The indictment did not say, and under the statute was not required to say, that the intent was to murder M. State v. Thomas, 127 La. 576, 53 So. 868 (1910).

out of it at about 11 p. m. for being disorderly, and then they began to fight in the street near the prosecutor's window. The prisoner separated himself from the others, and went to the other side of the street, and picked up a stone, and threw it at the persons he had been fighting with. The stone passed over their heads and broke a large plate glass window in the prosecutor's house, doing damage to an amount exceeding 5*l*. The jury found that the prisoner threw the stone at the people he had been fighting with, intending to strike one or more of them with it, but not intending to break the window. The question is whether under an indictment for unlawfully and maliciously committing an injury to the window in the house of the prosecutor the proof of these facts alone, coupled with the finding of the jury, will do? Now I think that is not enough. The indictment is framed under the 24 & 25 Vict. c. 97, s. 51. The Act is an Act relating to malicious injuries to property, and sect. 51 enacts that whosoever shall unlawfully and maliciously commit any damage, &c., to or upon any real or personal property whatsoever of a public or a private nature, for which no punishment is hereinbefore provided, to an amount exceeding 5*l*., shall be guilty of a misdemeanor. There is also the 58th section which deserves attention. "Every punishment and forfeiture by this Act imposed on any person maliciously committing any offence, whether the same be punishable upon indictment or upon summary conviction, shall equally apply and be enforced, whether the offence shall be committed from malice conceived against the owner of the property in respect of which it shall be committed, or otherwise." It seems to me on both these sections that what was intended to be provided against by the Act is the wilfully doing an unlawful Act, and that the Act must be wilfully and intentionally done on the part of the person doing it, to render him liable to be convicted. Without saying that, upon these facts, if the jury had found that the prisoner had been guilty of throwing the stone recklessly, knowing that there was a window near which it might probably hit, I should have been disposed to interfere with the conviction, yet as they have found that he threw the stone at the people he had been fighting with intending to strike them and not intending to break the window, I think the conviction must be quashed. I do not intend to throw any doubt on the cases which have been cited and which show what is sufficient to constitute malice in the case of murder. They rest upon the principles of the common law, and have no application to a statutory offence created by an Act in which the words are carefully studied.

BLACKBURN, J. I am of the same opinion, and I quite agree that it is not necessary to consider what constitutes wilful malice aforethought to bring a case within the common law crime of murder, when we are construing this statute, which says that whosoever shall unlawfully and maliciously commit any damage to or upon any real or personal property to an amount exceeding 5*l*., shall be guilty of a misdemeanor. A person may be said to act maliciously when he wilfully does an unlawful act without lawful excuse. The question here is can the prisoner be said, when he not only threw the stone unlawfully, but broke the window unintentionally, to have unlawfully and maliciously broken the window. I think that there was evidence on which the jury might have found that he unlawfully and maliciously broke the window, if they had found that the prisoner was aware that the natural and probable consequence of his throwing the stone was that it might break the glass window, on the principle that a man must be taken to intend what is the natural and probable consequence of his acts. But the jury have not found that the prisoner threw the stone, knowing that, on the other side of the men he was throwing at, there was a glass window and that he was reckless as to whether he did or did not break the window. On the contrary, they have found that he did not intend to break the window. I think therefore that the conviction must be quashed.

PIGOTT, B. I am of the same opinion.

LUSH, J. I also think that on this finding of the jury we have no alternative but to hold that the conviction must be quashed. The word "maliciously" means an act done either actually or constructively with a malicious intention. The jury might have found that he did intend actually to break the window or constructively to do so, as that he knew that the stone might probably break it when he threw it. But they have not so found.

CLEASBY, B., concurred.

Conviction quashed.

REGINA v. FAULKNER

Court of Crown Cases Reserved, Ireland, 1877.
13 Cox C.C. 550.

Case reserved by Lawson, J., at the Cork Summer Assizes, 1876, the prisoner was indicted for setting fire to the ship *Zemindar*, on the high seas, on the 26th day of June, 1876. . . . It was proved that the *Zemindar* was on her voyage home with a cargo of rum, sugar, and cotton, worth 50,000*l*. That the prisoner was a seaman on board, that he went into the forecastle hold, opened the sliding door in the bulk head, and so got into the hold where the rum was stored; he had no business there, and no authority to go there, and went for the purpose of stealing some rum, that he bored a hole in the cask with the gimlet, that the rum ran out, that when trying to put a spile in the hole out of which the rum was running, he had a lighted match in his hand; that the rum caught fire; that the prisoner himself was burned on the arms and neck; and that the ship caught fire and was completely destroyed. At the close of the case for the Crown, counsel for the prisoner asked for a direction of an acquittal on the ground that on the facts proved the indictment was not sustained, nor the allegation that the prisoner had unlawfully and maliciously set fire to the ship proved. The Crown contended that, inasmuch as the prisoner was at the time engaged in the commission of a felony, the indictment was sustained, and the allegation of the intent was immaterial.

At the second hearing of the case before the Court for Crown Cases Reserved, the learned judge made the addition of the following paragraph to the case stated by him for the court.

"It was conceded that the prisoner had no actual intention of burning the vessel, and I was not asked to leave any question to the jury as to the prisoner's knowing the probable consequences of his act, or as to his reckless conduct."

The learned judge told the jury that, although the prisoner had no actual intention of burning the vessel, still if they found he was engaged in stealing the rum, and that the fire took place in the manner above stated, they ought to find him guilty. The jury found the prisoner guilty on both counts, and he was sentenced to seven years' penal servitude. The question for the court was whether the direction of the learned judge was right, if not, the conviction should be quashed. . . .

FITZGERALD, J. I concur in opinion with my brother Barry, and for the reasons he has given, that the direction of the learned judge cannot be sustained in law, and that therefore the conviction should be quashed. I am further of opinion that in order to establish the charge of felony under sect. 42, the intention of the accused forms an element in the crime to the extent that it should appear that the defendant intended to do the very act with which he was charged, or that it was the necessary consequence of some other felonious or criminal act in which he was engaged, or that having a probable result which the defendant foresaw, or ought to have foreseen, he, nevertheless, persevered in such other felonious or criminal act. The prisoner did not intend to set fire to the ship—the fire was not the necessary result of the felony he was attempting; and if it was a probable result, which he ought to have foreseen, of the felonious transaction on which he was engaged, and from which a malicious design to commit the injurious act with which he is charged might have been fairly imputed to him, that view of the case was not submitted to the jury. On the contrary, it was excluded from their consideration on the requisition of the counsel for the prosecution. Counsel for the prosecution in effect insisted that the defendant, being engaged in the commission of, or in an attempt to commit a felony, was criminally responsible for every result that was occasioned thereby, even though it was not a probable consequence of his act or such as he could have reasonably foreseen or intended. No authority has been cited for a proposition so extensive, and I am of opinion that it is not warranted by law. Referring to the statute on which the prisoner is charged, it is to be observed that in several instances the sections creating substantive felonies are followed by others making an attempt to do the same thing also a felony. Now, it is obvious that an attempt to do a particular thing necessarily involves the intention to commit the act. If, in the case before us, the burning rum had been extinguished before the ship took fire, could it be contended that an indictment for a wilful and malicious attempt to set fire to the ship could have been maintained?

FITZGERALD, B. I am of opinion that the direction of the learned judge at the trial was wrong, and that the conviction cannot be sustained. There can, I think, be no doubt that malice or malicious intent (which seems to me to mean the same thing) is an essential part of the character of the felony charged in the indictment. . . .

O'BRIEN, J. I am also of opinion that the conviction should be quashed, . . .

KEOGH, J. I have the misfortune to differ from the other members of the Court. . . . I am, therefore, of opinion, that the conviction should stand, as I consider all questions of intention and malice are closed by the finding of the jury, that the prisoner committed the act with which he was charged whilst engaged in the commission of a substantive felony. . . .

PALLES, C. B. I concur in the opinion of the majority of the Court, and I do so for the reasons already stated by my brother Fitzgerald. I agree with my brother Keogh that from the facts proved the inference might have been legitimately drawn that the setting fire to the ship was malicious within the meaning of the 24 & 25 Vict. c. 97. I am of opinion that that inference was one of fact for the jury, and not a conclusion of law at which we can arrive upon the case before us. . . .

DEASY, B., and LAWSON, J., concurred.

Conviction quashed.

REX v. KELLY

Monaghan Assizes, Ireland, 1832.
1 Craw. & D. 186.

INDICTMENT for maliciously killing a horse. The evidence was that the prisoner had fired at the prosecutor, and killed his horse.

BUSHE, C. J. Under this Act the offence must be proved to have been done maliciously, and malice implies intention. Here the proof negatives the intention of killing the horse. The prisoner must therefore be acquitted.

SECTION 8. MOTIVE

Although sometimes confused, motive and intent are not synonymous terms. Motive has been said to be "that something in the mind, or that condition of the mind, which incites to the action," or the "moving power which impels to action," "induces action," or "gives birth to a purpose." The difference between intent and motive may be emphasized by illustration. If one man has caused the death of another by a pistol shot, his *intent* may have been any one of a number, such as (a) to kill the deceased, (b) to frighten the deceased by shooting near him without hitting him, (c) to intimidate the deceased by pointing the weapon at him without shooting (the trigger having been pulled by accident), (d) to shoot at a target (perhaps without realizing that any other person was present), or (e) to test the "pull" of a trigger of a gun supposed to be unloaded. If in the particular case the intent was to kill the deceased, the *motive* of the shooter may also have been one (or more) of a number of possible motives, such as (a) hatred, (b) revenge, (c) jealousy, (d) avarice, (e) fear or even (f) love (as where a loved one is slain to end the suffering from an incurable disease).

Some writers have advanced the notion that when an act is committed with more than one object in view, only the most immediate intent is called "intent" and any "ulterior intent is called the motive of the act." Stroud, for example, would say that if a burglar breaks and enters the dwelling of another in the nighttime with intent to steal, his mental attitude in regard to the contemplated larceny is not (at the time of breaking into the building) an *intent* but a *motive*.[1] This, however, is quite at variance with juridical usage of these terms. The burglar's design to steal is so far from being no intent at all that it is called a "specific intent." The search for the distinction must go much deeper than this. If in the supposed case the burglar's purpose was to steal food which he wished to eat, his intent to eat would also be an *intent* although one more step removed from his immediate intent at the time of the breaking. But his urge to satisfy his appetite would be, not an *intent*, but a *motive*. This urge might come from the immediate pangs of hunger or from the recollection of such pangs on previous occasions. The burglarious act of another may be prompted by the urge for the feeling of power which money may give, or by any other impulse which may prompt a man to desire that which he does not have.

An emotional urge, unless counteracted by other urges, "leads the mind to desire" a particular result. This desire in turn may—or may not—prompt an intent to bring about that end. If the mental

---

1. Stroud, Mens Rea 114 (1914).

activity continues until such an intent is developed (all of which might occur with lightning speed) the desire is coupled with the intention and may in a sense be a part thereof. Nevertheless it is important to distinguish between the basic urge itself and the intent which resulted in the mind of the particular person, but which might not have been generated in the mind of another. When, for example, it is said that a legatee, who was aware of a large bequest in his favor, had a motive for killing his deceased testator, it is not meant that this fact is sufficient to establish an intent to kill. No more is meant than that this fact was sufficient to generate a primitive urge in that direction, although it might be completely checked by more social impulses.

It is frequently said that "motive is not an essential element of crime." [2] Sometimes the statement is even more positive in form: "Motive is never an essential element of a crime." [3] Such broad generalizations cannot be accepted without some reservation, but with complete assurance we may say: "Proof of motive is never necessary to support a conclusion of guilt otherwise sufficiently established."[4]

The motive with which an *actus reus* was committed is always relevant and material. The presence or absence of a motive on the part of the defendant which might tend to the commission of such a deed may always be considered by the jury on the question of whether he did commit it. But whenever it is clearly established that he committed it, with whatever state of mind is required for the *mens rea* of the particular offense, all the requisites of criminal guilt are present, even if no possible motive for the deed can be shown.[5]

PEOPLE ex rel. HEGEMAN v. CORRIGAN

Court of Appeals of New York, 1909.
195 N.Y. 1, 87 N.E. 792.

CULLEN, CH. J. The perjury with which the relator is charged is the verification under oath of a report to the insurance department of the state, in which, in answer to a question calling for a statement of the loans held by the company secured by the pledge of bonds, stock or other collateral, it was stated that there were none. . . .

---

2. People v. Zammuto, 280 Ill. 225, 227, 117 N.E. 454, 455 (1917).

3. People ex rel. Hegeman v. Corrigan, 195 N.Y. 1, 12, 87 N.E. 792, 796 (1909).

4. State v. Guilfoyle, 109 Conn. 124, 140, 145 A. 761, 767 (1929).

5. A soldier, home on leave to visit a sick child, found that it was suffering and completely neglected by its mother. Just before the expiration of his leave he killed the child because: "I could not see it suffer any longer and have to go away and leave it". An application for leave to appeal was dismissed. Rex v. Simpson, 84 L.J. K.B. 1893 (1915). It is murder to aid in the killing of one's wife even if it is at her request and because of an impulse to end her suffering from an incurable disease. People v. Roberts, 211 Mich. 187, 178 N.W. 690 (1920).

3. Doubtless, to constitute perjury there must be criminal intent, but intent must be distinguished from motive and from ultimate object. As was said by Judge Werner in People v. Molineux (168 N.Y. 264, 297, 61 N.E. 286): "In the popular mind intent and motive are not infrequently regarded as one and the same thing. In law there is a clear distinction between them. Motive is the moving power which impels to action for a definite result. Intent is the purpose to use a particular means to effect such result." "Motive is that which incites or stimulates a person to do an act. . . . Motive is never an essential element of a crime. A good motive does not prevent an act from being a crime." There runs through the criminal law a distinction between offenses that are *mala prohibita* in which no intent to do wrong is necessary to constitute the offense, and offenses that are *mala in se* in which a criminal intent is a necessary ingredient of the crime. While there are to be found both in judicial decisions and in text books elaborate discussions of what is a criminal intent, no attempt has been made to accurately define the term. Very possibly the attempt to make a definition so comprehensive as to be applicable to all cases would be futile, and it has often been doubted whether the term "intent" is an accurate one. However this may be, it is very apparent that the innocence or criminality of the intent in a particular act generally depends on the knowledge or belief of the actor at the time. An honest and reasonable belief in the existence of circumstances which, if true, would make the act for which the defendant is prosecuted innocent, would be a good defense. Thus, if a man killed another under such circumstances as gave proper and reasonable grounds for the belief that the person killed was about to take the life of the slayer, although the person killed was only playing a practical joke, no crime would be committed. But if the facts and circumstances which the person believed to exist were not such as in law to justify his act, then there would be no defense to the act. In other words, it is the knowledge or belief of the actor at the time that stamps identically the same intent as either criminal or innocent, for the intent to take life, unless under circumstances that the law regards as sufficient to justify the taking, is the criminal intent and the only criminal intent that can exist in case of murder (excepting where the killing is done in the commission of an independent felony). So, ordinarily, a criminal intent is an intent to do knowingly and wilfully that which is condemned as wrong by the law and common morality of the country, and if such an intent exists, it is neither justification nor excuse that the actor intended by its commission to accomplish some ultimate good.

To constitute perjury under our law it is not necessary to establish any other intent than that specified in the statute, for by its terms it is not sufficient that the affiant testifies as to what is false, but the testimony must be given willfully and knowingly, and the affiant must know that the testimony is false; if it be given in the honest belief that it is true, or by mistake or inadvertence, the case does not fall within the statute. Therefore, if a person willfully testifies to what he knows to be false, this is the criminal intent and the only criminal intent that can exist in the crime. That the ultimate object to be attained by the perjury may be beneficent or indifferent in no way absolves or qualifies the criminality of the act. One may not commit a crime because he hopes or expects that good will come of it. It is no defense to a charge of intentionally committing an act prohibited by law even that the dictates of his religious belief require one to do the act. In Reynolds v. United States, 98 U.S. 145, 25 L.Ed. 244, the prisoner was indicted for having committed bigamy in Utah, and contended in his defense that polygamy was a duty enjoined on him by his religious belief. The court there said: "This (defense) would be introducing a new element into criminal law. Laws are made for the government of actions, and while they cannot interfere with mere religious belief and opinions, they may with practices. Suppose one believed that human sacrifices were a necessary part of religious worship, would it be seriously contended that the civil government under which he lived could not interfere to prevent a sacrifice?" In People v. Pierson (176 N.Y. 201, 68 N.E. 243) this court upheld a conviction for misdemeanor where the father, acting under the dictates of his religious faith, failed to call a physician to attend his sick child. In that case the defendant, far from intending to injure his child, sought by his conduct to preserve it, and believed that his action would most conduce to that result. . . .

If one may not violate the law with impunity in obedience to the requirements of his religious faith, much less can he justify such violation merely to escape personal inconvenience or annoyance. Therefore, the explanation offered by the relator that his act was impelled solely by the desire to escape the importunities of "Wall street," if true (and the truth of this statement was plainly a question of fact), is entirely immaterial to the charge against him. The sole questions in this prosecution are: 1st. Were the facts stated by the relator in the report true or false? 2nd. If false, did the relator know them to be false when he verified the report? Though the statements made in the return may have been incorrect, if the relator made them in good faith either by inadvertence or mistake, or in the honest belief that the statements were true, then, of course, he did not commit the offense. We think the evidence contained in the affidavits was sufficient to present a question of fact on these issues.

The order of the Appellate Division should be reversed, that of the Special Term affirmed, and the relator remanded to custody. . . .[1]

---

1. One who sends obscene matter through the mails is guilty of a federal offense even if his purpose is to expose, and thereby correct, sexual abuses. United States v. Harmon, 45 F. 414 (D.C.Kan.1891).

The federal obscenity statute punishing the mailing of material that is obscene

Sec. 8   *MOTIVE*   433

LANGFORD v. UNITED STATES

United States Court of Appeals, Ninth Circuit, 1949.
178 F.2d 48.

POPE, CIRCUIT JUDGE. Langford, the appellant, was convicted of violation of the Mann Act, 18 U.S.C.A. § 398 [now § 2421]. The indictment was in two counts. Count One charged the transportation of a woman, one Carol Jones, in foreign commerce, from Los Angeles County, California, to Tiajuana, Mexico, for purposes of prostitution, debauchery and other immoral practices. The second count charged transportation of the same woman, for the same purposes, from Tiajuana to Los Angeles County. Conviction was on Count Two only.

The evidence showed that at the time of the transportation mentioned in Count One, the parties went to Mexico to be married there, and that the transportation charged in Count Two was their return trip. It is urged upon this appeal that notwithstanding the evidence of prior and subsequent prostitution, the entire trip, both going and returning, was an innocent one under the rule of Mortensen v. United States, 322 U.S. 369, 64 S.Ct. 1037, 88 L.Ed. 1331. Therefore, it is said, the verdict is against law, and not supported by the evidence. . . .

Jones, the prosecuting witness, was white and a college graduate, with a degree in sociology and applied psychology. She had been employed as a case worker in Los Angeles. She testified that she met Langford, a Negro, at a Los Angeles night club and that she voluntarily went to his home to live with him in January, 1948. A week or so later, Langford brought four sailors home with him and asked her to perform acts of sexual intercourse with them. She refused at first, but consented when Langford slapped her. At this time there was another girl present whom Jones described as a prostitute for herself and Langford. . . .

Jones testified that, although she was in love with Langford, she left him twice in March. The first time, he saw her in a car with some men and dragged her out of it so she returned to his home. She left him the second time, because he had slapped her and beaten her with a belt. On this occasion she took a room in a private home and did not engage in prostitution for several days. On the evening of April 5, Langford telephoned her and asked permission to come to

---

does not offend constitutional safeguards against convictions based upon protected material since obscenity is not within the area of constitutionally protected speech or press. Roth v. United States, 354 U.S. 476, 77 S.Ct. 1304 (1957). "Obscene material is material which deals with sex in a manner appealing to prurient interest". 354 U.S. at 487, 77 S.Ct. at 1310.

One who carries a concealed pistol is guilty of violating the statute even if his only purpose is to exhibit it as a curiosity. Walls v. State, 7 Blackf. 572 (Ind.1845). The intentional shooting of another was "with intent to do him some grievous bodily harm" even if the only motive was to prevent an arrest. Rex v. Gillow, 1 Moody 85, 168 Eng.Rep. 1195 (1825).

see her. He came very humbly, protesting his love for her, and proposed marriage, a subject Jones had previously broached to him. Jones accepted this proposal although Langford told her she would still have to engage in prostitution for a month or two until his car was paid for. However, at this time there was an anti-miscegenation statute in effect in California [1] so the parties decided to drive to Tiajuana, Mexico, where the law permitted marriage between the races.

. . .

In the Mortensen case, supra, a man and wife, proprietors of a house of ill fame in Nebraska, allowed two of their prostitutes to accompany them on a vacation trip to Salt Lake City, Utah. It was charged that they had violated the Mann Act because they had brought the girls back from Salt Lake City to Nebraska and the girls had resumed their occupation upon their return. The Supreme Court, through Mr. Justice Murphy, held [2] that the language of the Mann Act "is conditioned upon the use of interstate transportation for the purpose of, or as a means of effecting or facilitating, the commission of the illegal acts. Here the interstate round trip had no such purpose and was in no way related to the subsequent immoralities in Grand Island."

The rule is conceded that the dominant motive for the interstate transportation of the victim must be the purpose proscribed by the statute,[3] but we think the jury was justified in finding that this case fell within the rule. In its argument to the jury, the government advanced two theories: (1) that Langford had married Jones primarily for the purpose of causing her to return to him and continue to work for him as a prostitute; and (2) that the dominant purpose of Langford in bringing Jones back from Tiajuana to Los Angeles was to get her back to work immediately earning money for him. In the Mortensen case there was no evidence justifying the inference that, had the Mortensens not taken the girls on the interstate vacation trip, the girls would have refused to perform the proscribed activities for the Mortensens. Here, however, the fact that Langford had used force and threats to keep Jones with him, that she had nevertheless left him again, and that he had put her back to work just a day after the "mar-

---

1. Cal.Civil Code, 1941, Sec. 60. This statute was held unconstitutional on October 1, 1948 in Perez v. Lippold, 32 Cal.2d 711, 198 P.2d 17.

2. 322 U.S. 369, 377, 64 S.Ct. 1037, 1042, 88 L.Ed. 1331.

3. Hansen v. Haff, 291 U.S. 559, 54 S.Ct. 494, 78 L.Ed. 968; Mortensen v. United States, supra. [Footnotes 1-3 are by the Court.]

[Added by Compiler.] It is not necessary that the sole object be for immoral purposes. It suffices if one of the efficient and compelling purposes was illicit conduct. O'Neal v. United States, 240 F.2d 700 (10th Cir. 1957).

"Interstate transportation of the prosecutrix between Arkansas and Oklahoma was conceded, and the only factual issue in the case was whether petitioner's dominant purpose in making the trip was to facilitate her practice of prostitution in Tulsa, Oklahoma", or was merely an accommodation to her in connection with a business trip he was making at the time. Hawkins v. United States, 358 U.S. 74, 79-80, 79 S.Ct. 136, 139 (1958).

Sec. 8   MOTIVE   435

riage", warrant the conclusion that the interstate journey and marriage were nothing but a device to, in the words of the statute, "induce, entice, or compel her to give herself up to the practice of prostitution". The facts here are such that the jury might well disbelieve that the reason for the marriage was the usual one.

The other cases upon which appellant relies are readily distinguishable for the same reason. In Van Pelt v. United States, 4 Cir., 240 F. 346, the object of the interstate transportation was to take defendant's mistress from Virginia to Maryland to stay in the latter state until their child was born. The trip was held to have played no part in inducing the commission of a sexual act in Maryland. In Fisher v. United States, 4 Cir., 266 F. 667, 670, the purpose of the trip was to visit the girl's mother. Although illicit relations were resumed on the return, the court held that ". . . the mere fact that a journey from one state to another is followed by such intercourse, when the journey was not for that purpose, but wholly for other reasons, to which intercourse was not related cannot be regarded as a violation of the statute." Here, in view of the unusual attitude of the appellant towards marriage, we think the jury were warranted in finding that so far as appellant was concerned his dominant motive for the marriage was to get control of Jones and re-establish a relationship of pander and prostitute from which he profited so extensively, and that the trip, marriage and all, had that primary end in view. . . . [4]

Since we find no error in the record, the judgment is affirmed. (Certiorari denied 339 U.S. 938, 70 S.Ct. 669, 94 L.Ed. 589.)

LAWS v. STATE

Court of Appeals of Texas, 1888.
26 Tex.App. 643, 10 S.W. 220.

This conviction was in the second degree for the murder of Hiram Garrison, in Franklin county, Texas, on the twenty-first day of August, 1888. A term of fifteen years in the penitentiary was the penalty imposed by the verdict and judgment. . . .

WILLSON, JUDGE. Homicide is permitted by law when inflicted for the purpose of preventing theft at night, and the homicide in such case is justifiable at any time while the offender is at the place where the theft is committed, or within reach of gunshot from such place. (Penal Code, art. 570.)

---

4. A conviction under the Mann Act was not authorized by proof that defendant took a prostitute from New York to New Jersey for a week-end of recreation and returned her to New York where she again engaged in prostitution. United States v. Ross, 257 F.2d 292 (2d Cir. 1958). When one induces a woman to travel in interstate commerce for the purpose of prostitution the Mann Act has been violated the moment she crosses the state line. Wiley v. United States, 257 F.2d 900 (8th Cir. 1958).

In this case no question is made as to the commission of the homicide by the defendant, but defendant claims that, at the time he shot and killed the deceased, the latter had committed theft of whisky belonging to the former, and was within gunshot of the place where the theft was committed, and that it was nighttime when the theft and homicide were committed, and that he committed the homicide for the purpose of preventing the consequences of the theft. There is evidence tending to support this defense. . . .

In this State, with reference to the crime of burglary, it is provided: "By the term 'day time' is meant any time of the twenty-four hours from thirty minutes before sun rise until thirty minutes after sun set." (Penal Code, art. 710.) Again, it is provided that "words which have their meaning specially defined shall be understood in that sense, though it be contrary to their usual meaning." (Penal Code, art. 10.) It is clear to our minds, in view of the provisions cited, that a "theft by night" is a theft committed at any time between thirty minutes after sun set and thirty minutes before sun rise, and the court should have so instructed the jury; and, having failed to do so, committed a material error calculated to injure the defendant's rights.

Relating to the defense before mentioned, the court among other instructions gave to the jury the following in substance: "If you find that the defendant killed the deceased in the execution of a previously formed intent or plan to take his life, and not to prevent theft then being committed, or to prevent the consequences of the same, such killing would not be justified though done in the night time and whilst deceased was committing or had committed a theft." This instruction was not excepted to, but was urged by defendant as error in his motion for a new trial, and is insisted upon here as error. We are of the opinion that the instruction is not erroneous. If the killing was upon malice, and not to prevent a theft or the consequences of a theft, it would not be justified under the statute, although a theft by night was actually being committed by the deceased at the time he was killed. It is not the intention of the statute to justify *murder*. Such a construction of the statute would to our minds be unreasonable and exceedingly dangerous.

Other questions presented on this appeal are not discussed and determined, because they are not likely to arise on another trial. Because the charge of the court is materially defective in not instructing the jury in the legal meaning of day time and night time, the judgment is reversed and the cause is remanded.

Reversed and remanded.

Opinion delivered December 19, 1888.

TROGDON v. STATE

Supreme Court of Judicature of Indiana, 1892.
133 Ind. 1, 32 N.E. 725.

McBRIDE, J. The appellant was tried on a charge of murder in the first degree. The jury found him guilty of voluntary manslaughter, and fixed his punishment at imprisonment in the State Prison for the period of five years.

He seeks a reversal of the judgment of conviction on this verdict, because of alleged error of the Circuit Court in overruling his motion for a new trial. _ _ _

The accused admitted that he killed the decedent, but insisted that it was done in self-defense. The court instructed the jury very fully relative to the law of self-defense, not only as to the general principles, but specifically applying the law to the facts as they were claimed to be by the defense and by the prosecution respectively. These instructions were full, and, with one exception, to be hereafter noted, were accurate statements of the law. . . .

The appellant contends that the court should have instructed the jury that if there was, in fact, danger that the accused might suffer injury or death at the hands of the deceased, the killing was justifiable, as in self-defense, regardless of any question of apprehension of danger on his part, or of any appearance of danger; that one may kill another when he is in no apparent danger, does not apprehend danger, and may even act from feelings of malice in so doing, and may successfully defend as having acted in self-defense if it can be shown that there was actual danger of which he, at the time, knew nothing.

This is not the law. The law allows one who is himself without fault, and is in a place where he has the right to be, to protect himself from threatened danger, and to use for that purpose such force as may, at the time, reasonably seem necessary and no more. The danger may be actual, or only apparent. As stated by the court, in the instruction given, "The question of apparent necessity, as well as of the amount of force necessary to employ to resist an attack, can only be determined from the standpoint of the defendant at the time, and under all the existing circumstances." Ordinarily, one exercising the right of self-defense is compelled to act upon the instant, and with no time for deliberation or investigation, and under such circumstances a danger which exists only in appearance is to him as real and imminent as if it were actual.

It is, however, not the law that one who is in no apparent danger even, who does not, in fact, apprehend any danger, and who has no reasonable ground for such apprehension, may deliberately and maliciously kill another and successfully interpose the defense of self-defense because it subsequently appears that there was actual danger, of which he was at the time ignorant. . . .[1]

(For other reasons the judgment was reversed and a new trial directed.)

SECTION 9. CONCURRENCE OF MENS REA AND ACTUS REUS

The *mens rea* and the *actus reus* must concur to constitute a crime. The doctrine of trespass *ab initio* does not apply in criminal jurisprudence. The doctrine of continuing trespass is altogether different. *Trespass de bonis asportatis* is deemed to continue, so far as the law of larceny is concerned, as long as the trespasser keeps possession of the property so obtained. But this assumes an original trespass. It does not make a trespass out of what was not a trespass when done by any theory of "relation." And the familiar maxim *"omnis ratihabitio retrotrahitur, et mandato priori equiparatur"* (every ratification relates back, and is equivalent to a prior authorization), does not apply to criminal cases.

Concurrence, it should be emphasized, is something other than mere coincidence. The two elements of the crime must be "brought together" in the sense that the *actus reus* must be attributable to the *mens rea*.

COMMONWEALTH v. CALI

Supreme Judicial Court of Massachusetts, 1923.
247 Mass. 20, 141 N.E. 510.

BRALEY, J. The defendant having been indicted, tried and convicted under G.L. c. 266, § 10, of burning a building in Leominster belonging to Maria Cali, which at the time was insured against loss or damage by fire, with intent to injure the insurer, the case is here on his exceptions to the denial of his motion for a directed verdict, and to rulings at the trial. . . .

1. "One may harbor the most intense hatred toward another; he may court an opportunity to take his life; he may rejoice while he is imbruing his hands in his heart's blood; and yet, if, to save his own life, the facts showed that he was fully justified in slaying his adversary, his malice shall not be taken into account". Golden v. State, 25 Ga. 527 (1858). The fact that the fear of being caught was the sole reason for refraining from criminal conduct is unimportant so far as the law is concerned. "In the eyes of the law, a man is innocent if he did not commit the unlawful act, whatever the explanation may be for his good behavior." Evans v. United States, 257 F.2d 121, 127 (9th Cir. 1958).

Sec. 9 *CONCURRENCE OF MENS REA AND ACTUS REUS* 439

The only evidence as to the origin, extent and progress of the fire were the statements of the defendant to the police inspector, and as a witness. The jury who were to determine his credibility and the weight to be given his testimony could find notwithstanding his explanations of its origin as being purely accidental, that when all the circumstances were reviewed he either set it, or after the fire was under way purposely refrained from any attempt to extinguish it in order to obtain the benefit of the proceeds of the policy, which when recovered, would be applied by the mortgagee on his indebtedness. If they so found, a specific intent to injure the insurer had been proved. The motion, and the defendant's requests in so far as not given were denied rightly.

The instructions to the jury that, "If a man does start an accidental fire what is his conduct in respect to it? A question might arise—as if after the fire has started accidentally, and he then has it within his power and ability to extinguish the fire and he realizes and knows that he can, and then he forms and entertains an intent to injure an insurance company he can be guilty of this offence. It is not necessary that the intent be formed before the fire is started," also show no error of law. It is true as the defendant contends, that, if he merely neglected in the emergency of the moment to act, his negligence was not proof of a purpose to commit the crime charged. The intention, however, to injure could be formed after as well as before the fire started. On his own admissions the jury were to say whether, when considered in connection with all the circumstances, his immediate departure from the premises for his home in Fitchburg, without giving any alarm, warranted the inference of a criminal intent or state of mind, that the building should be consumed. . . .

Exceptions overruled.

JACKSON v. COMMONWEALTH

Court of Appeals of Kentucky, 1896.
100 Ky. 239, 38 S.W. 422, 1091.

JUDGE HAZELRIGG delivered the opinion of the court.

The appellant was jointly indicted with one Alonzo Walling in the Campbell Circuit Court for the murder of Pearl Bryan, and on his separate trial was found guilty and sentenced to be hanged.

It will be necessary to submit only a brief summary of the facts disclosed in the voluminous record before us to render intelligible the various complaints urged on this appeal against the judgment of conviction.

On the morning of Saturday, February 1, 1896, the headless body of a woman was found on the farm of one Locke, near Newport, in Campbell county. Every effort to find the head proved futile, but the shoes the dead girl wore were marked: "Lewis & Hayes, Greencastle, Indiana," and this circumstance led to the identification of the body as that of Pearl Bryan, a young girl of that city. Her clothes were saturated with blood, particularly about the neck, and a large quantity of it was found on the ground near the neck, covering a circular spot some six or seven inches in diameter, and also a spot of similar kind some feet away. Extending near to or over this last named spot there were some privet bushes, the leaves of which were spattered with blood, and drops were discovered pending under the leaves, as though the blood had reached the under side of them by spurting from the neck, which it might do as disclosed by the testimony if the decapitation had taken place or been commenced at the spot near the bushes, and if the victim were alive at the time.

These and other circumstances led the authorities to proceed on the theory that the murder—for such it evidently appeared to be—occurred in Campbell county. . . .

The conclusion is fairly deducible from certain portions of the testimony that an attempt was made to kill the girl by the administration of cocaine while in Cincinnati, and that this was done by the defendant or at his instance, but that she was not thereby killed. It is to be remembered that, according to the testimony of Jackson, he did not see the girl in life after Wednesday, and, according to Walling, he did not see her after that day; but the proof conduces to show that they were both with her Friday night when she was in the cab, and that they brought her over to Campbell county.

If she was then dead, as might be supposed from her making no outcry, a verdict of guilty could not have been rendered; but if she was then alive, though appearing to be dead, and by the cutting of her throat she was killed while in Campbell county, then the jury might find a verdict of guilty, although the cutting off of the head was merely for the purpose of destroying the chances for identification or for any other purpose. At least, the instruction does not authorize a verdict of conviction unless Jackson is shown to have cut off the head of his victim in Campbell county—and whilst she was in fact alive—and if he did this, he was guilty of murder, though believing her already dead, if the act succeeded and was but a part of the felonious attempt to kill her in Cincinnati. . . .

The judgment must be affirmed.

The court delivered the following response to petition for rehearing February 13, 1897:

With great earnestness, force and plausibility two contentions are made by the petitions for rehearing in this case and in the case of Walling v. Commonwealth:

1st. That no facts which occurred in the foreign jurisdiction of Ohio can be tacked on to facts which occurred in Kentucky for the pur-

Sec. 9 CONCURRENCE OF MENS REA AND ACTUS REUS   441

pose of supplying the elements necessary to constitute the crime of murder in Kentucky.

2d. (And this appears to be the point chiefly relied on) That in giving its instructions to the jury the trial court is not authorized to refer to any fact which occurred in the foreign jurisdiction. Other suggestions are made in the petitions, but in our judgment do not require specific response.

These two contentions may be considered together, as the first is necessarily raised and considered in the decision of the second, and so treated in the petition.

Reduced to its lowest terms, the claim of counsel is that an attempt to commit a murder in another State, supposed by the guilty party to have been there successful, but in reality completed in this State, though by an act not by him believed to be the consummation of his purpose, is not in this State punishable.

Such is not nor should it be the law. By the law of this State a crime is punishable in the jurisdiction in which it has effect. Statutes in numbers have been passed by the general assembly of this Commonwealth providing that jurisdiction should be had of crimes in the county in which the crime became effectual. (Chapter 36, article 2, Kentucky Statutes.) Such we believe to have been the common law before such enactments.

Assuming that what the jury found was true, in what State or district could the crime be punished? If not here, where? If we concede the claims of counsel for appellants no serious crime was committed in Ohio. Nothing was there done but an ineffective attempt to murder. None was committed here. What was done in this jurisdiction was only the mutilation of a supposed corpse, and yet the fact, established by overwhelming testimony, remains that the crime has been committed. Not all the refinements of counsel can lead us from the conclusion that, when a crime has been completed the result of which is a death in this Commonwealth, we can take jurisdiction of the offense.

Not for a moment can we admit as law the logical conclusion of counsel's argument, namely, that there is a variety of murder, which, by reason of error in its commission, is not anywhere in any jurisdiction punishable; not in Ohio, for the reason that the attempt there made was not successful; not in Kentucky, for the reason that the act there done, and which accomplished and completed the actual killing, was done upon the supposition that the murder had already been accomplished. . . .

We have carefully examined the immense mass of testimony in the case, and see no error to the prejudice of any substantial right of the appellant.[1]

The petition for rehearing is overruled.

1. Accord, Thabo Meli v. Regina, [1954] All E.R. 373.

MODEL PENAL CODE

Section 2.02. General Requirements of Culpability.

(1) Minimum Requirements of Culpability. Except as provided in Section 2.05, a person is not guilty of an offense unless he acted purposely, knowingly, recklessly or negligently, as the law may require, with respect to each material element of the offense.

(2) Kinds of Culpability Defined.

(a) Purposely.

A person acts purposely with respect to a material element of an offense when:

(i) if the element involves the nature of his conduct or a result thereof, it is his conscious object to engage in conduct of that nature or to cause such a result; and

(ii) if the element involves the attendant circumstances, he is aware of the existence of such circumstances or he believes or hopes that they exist.

(b) Knowingly.

A person acts knowingly with respect to a material element of an offense when:

(i) if the element involves the nature of his conduct or the attendant circumstances, he is aware that his conduct is of that nature or that such circumstances exist; and

(ii) if the element involves a result of his conduct, he is aware that it is practically certain that his conduct will cause such a result.

(c) Recklessly.

A person acts recklessly with respect to a material element of an offense when he consciously disregards a substantial and unjustifiable risk that the material element exists or will result from his conduct. The risk must be of such a nature and degree that, considering the nature and purpose of the actor's conduct and the circumstances known to him, its disregard involves a gross deviation from the standard of conduct that a law-abiding person would observe in the actor's situation.

(d) Negligently.

A person acts negligently with respect to a material element of an offense when he should be aware of a substantial and unjustifiable risk that the material element exists or will result from his conduct. The risk must be of such a nature and degree that the actor's failure to perceive it, considering the nature and purpose of his conduct and the circumstances known to him, involves a gross deviation from the standard of care that a reasonable person would observe in the actor's situation.

(3) Culpability Required Unless Otherwise Provided. When the culpability sufficient to establish a material element of an offense is not prescribed by law, such element is established if a person acts purposely, knowingly or recklessly with respect thereto.

Sec. 9 CONCURRENCE OF MENS REA AND ACTUS REUS 443

(4) *Prescribed Culpability Requirement Applies to All Material Elements.* When the law defining an offense prescribes the kind of culpability that is sufficient for the commission of an offense, without distinguishing among the material elements thereof, such provision shall apply to all the material elements of the offense, unless a contrary purpose plainly appears.

(5) *Substitutes for Negligence, Recklessness and Knowledge.* When the law provides that negligence suffices to establish an element of an offense, such element also is established if a person acts purposely, knowingly or recklessly. When recklessness suffices to establish an element, such element also is established if a person acts purposely or knowingly. When acting knowingly suffices to establish an element, such element also is established if a person acts purposely.

(6) *Requirement of Purpose Satisfied if Purpose Is Conditional.* When a particular purpose is an element of an offense, the element is established although such purpose is conditional, unless the condition negatives the harm or evil sought to be prevented by the law defining the offense.

(7) *Requirement of Knowledge Satisfied by Knowledge of High Probability.* When knowledge of the existence of a particular fact is an element of an offense, such knowledge is established if a person is aware of a high probability of its existence, unless he actually believes that it does not exist.

(8) *Requirement of Wilfulness Satisfied by Acting Knowingly.* A requirement that an offense be committed wilfully is satisfied if a person acts knowingly with respect to the material elements of the offense, unless a purpose to impose further requirements appears.

(9) *Culpability as to Illegality of Conduct.* Neither knowledge nor recklessness or negligence as to whether conduct constitutes an offense or as to the existence, meaning or application of the law determining the elements of an offense is an element of such offense, unless the definition of the offense or the Code so provides.

(10) *Culpability as Determinant of Grade of Offense.* When the grade or degree of an offense depends on whether the offense is committed purposely, knowingly, recklessly or negligently, its grade or degree shall be the lowest for which the determinative kind of culpability is established with respect to any material element of the offense.

Section 2.05. When Culpability Requirements Are Inapplicable to Violations and to Offenses Defined by Other Statutes; Effect of Absolute Liability in Reducing Grade of Offense to Violation.

(1) The requirements of culpability prescribed by Sections 2.01 and 2.02 do not apply to:

(a) offenses which constitute violations, unless the requirement involved is included in the definition of the offense or the Court determines that its application is consistent with effective enforcement of the law defining the offense; or

(b) offenses defined by statutes other than the Code, insofar as a legislative purpose to impose absolute liability for such offenses or with respect to any material element thereof plainly appears.

(2) Notwithstanding any other provision of existing law and unless a subsequent statute otherwise provides:

(a) when absolute liability is imposed with respect to any material element of an offense defined by a statute other than the Code and a conviction is based upon such liability, the offense constitutes a violation; and

(b) although absolute liability is imposed by law with respect to one or more of the material elements of an offense defined by a statute other than the Code, the culpable commission of the offense may be charged and proved, in which event negligence with respect to such elements constitutes sufficient culpability and the classification of the offense and the sentence that may be imposed therefor upon conviction are determined by Section 1.04 and Article 6 of the Code.

Chapter 8

RESPONSIBILITY: LIMITATIONS ON CRIMINAL CAPACITY

SECTION 1. IMMATURITY (INFANCY)

Every civilized society must recognize criminal incapacity based upon extreme immaturity. No matter what harm is caused by one of very tender years the situation must be dealt with by some means other than the machinery established for the administration of criminal justice. This is too clear for any possibility of doubt, although there are differences of opinion as to just what should be regarded as such immaturity as to preclude criminal guilt.

While failing to develop techniques comparable to modern juvenile court and youth correction authority acts, the common law made a very reasonable approach to this problem. Because of wide differences in individuals two ages were emphasized. A child under the age of seven has no criminal capacity. At common law there is an "irrebuttable presumption of incapacity" on the part of one so young, —to use the familiar explanation of the judges. Fourteen is the other age. One who has reached the age of fourteen has criminal capacity unless incapacity is established on some entirely different basis, such as insanity. Furthermore, this means physical age and not so-called "mental age." Between the ages of seven and fourteen there is a rebuttable presumption of criminal incapacity. The common law permits the criminal conviction of a child between these ages, but only upon clear proof of such precocity as to establish a real appreciation of the wrongfulness of the thing done. This presumption is extremely strong at the age of seven and diminishes gradually until it disappears entirely at the age of fourteen.

The words of Blackstone are significant: "The law of England does in some cases privilege an infant under the age of twenty-one, as to common misdemeanors, so as to escape fine, imprisonment, and the like: and particularly in cases of omission, as not repairing a bridge, or a highway, and other similar offences; for, not having the command of his fortune till twenty-one he wants the capacity to do those things which the law requires. But where there is any notorious breach of the peace, a riot, battery, or the like (which infants, when full grown, are at least as liable as others to commit) for these an infant, above the age of fourteen, is equally liable to suffer as a person at the full age of twenty-one.

"With regard to capital crimes, the law is still more minute and circumspect; distinguishing with greater nicety the several degrees of age and discretion. . . . Thus a girl of thirteen has been burned for killing her mistress: and one boy of ten, and another of nine years old, who had killed their companions, have been sentenced to death, and he of ten years actually hanged; because it appeared, upon their trials, that the one hid himself, and the other hid the body he had killed, which hiding manifested a consciousness of guilt, and a discretion to discern between good and evil. And there was an instance in the last century where a boy of eight years old was tried at Abingdon for firing two barns; and, it appearing that he had malice, revenge, and cunning, he was found guilty, condemned, and hanged accordingly. Thus, also, in very modern times, a boy of ten years old was convicted on his own confession of murdering his bedfellow, there appearing in his whole behaviour plain tokens of a mischievous discretion; and, as the sparing this boy merely on account of his tender years might be of dangerous consequence to the public by propagating a notion that children might commit such atrocious crimes with impunity, it was unanimously agreed by all the judges that he was a proper subject of capital punishment. But, in all such cases, the evidence of that malice which is to supply age ought to be strong and clear beyond all doubt and contradiction" (4 Bl.Comm. 22–24).

The age, below which there is complete criminal incapacity, has been raised by statute in some jurisdictions. Thus it has been placed at eight in England, at nine in Texas, at ten in Georgia and at twelve in Arkansas. Furthermore, the net result of some of the juvenile delinquency statutes is to raise it much higher.

Such age is omitted entirely from some of the statutes as, for example, the California section which provides in substance that children under the age of fourteen are incapable of crime "in the absence of clear proof that at the time of committing the act charged against them, they knew its wrongfulness" (Cal.Pen.Code § 26). Any provision of this nature should be read in the light of the common law. It clearly recognizes the existence of a presumption although the word is not used. And it is more logical to assume this means the established presumption of the common law than any other: that is, a presumption which is conclusive below the age of seven, extremely strong at that age, and does not disappear entirely until the age of fourteen.

Whether such a statute does or does not abolish the conclusive part of the common-law presumption is largely academic. This presumption applies only to one *under* the age of seven. Except where the age has been raised by statute it has always been possible, in legal theory, to rebut the presumption of incapacity of a seven-year-old child,—but it has never yet been done.

What has been said has reference to mental incapacity. An additional presumption applies in the rape cases. Under the English common law a boy under the age of fourteen is conclusively presumed to be incapable of committing this offense. If two indictments were found against a thirteen-year-old boy, one charging rape and the other charging murder, the prosecution of the rape case would be stopped the moment his age was established. The murder case would be permitted to go to the jury with an instruction emphasizing the prima-facie presumption of incapacity. Some of the states in this country have adopted the same view. In others the presumption of physical incapacity of a boy under fourteen to commit rape is rebuttable.

What amounts to a limitation of criminal capacity has been established in a few jurisdictions at a much higher age. This is in the form of a provision that no one shall be deprived of life by reason of any act done before attaining a specified age. The age so specified in Texas, for example, is seventeen, and that in California is eighteen.[1]

The problem of criminal incapacity by reason of immaturity has been disguised to some extent by the juvenile delinquency statutes, with particular emphasis upon procedure. These enactments differ widely from state to state. Some of the earlier acts merely provided an alternative procedure which might be used, in the discretion of the judge, in cases of children below a specified age. The more progressive statutes provide that what would be a crime, if committed by an older person, is not a crime but an entirely different type of misbehavior, called "juvenile delinquency," if committed by a "juvenile." Most of these statutes do not remove from the category of crime any act punishable by death or by life imprisonment. The most recent development is to enlarge the scope of "juvenile delinquency" to include even a misdeed which would be capital on the part of an older person.[2] The net result of such a provision is to raise the age of total criminal incapacity.

PEOPLE v. LEWIS

Court of Appeals of New York, 1932.
260 N.Y. 171, 183 N.E. 353.

CROUCH, J. This is a juvenile delinquency proceeding under chapter 393 of the Laws of 1930, known as the Children's Court Act of the State of New York. Its proper title is not "The People of the State of New York against Arthur L. Lewis," as printed on the record and briefs. It was commenced and carried to judgment under the

---

1. West's Ann.Cal.Pen.Code, § 190.1 (as amended in 1957).

2. This is the effect of the 1948 amendment to the New York statutes, subject to a qualification if the act is committed by a child of fifteen. New York Penal Law, § 486 (as amended in 1948); New York Code of Criminal Procedure, §§ 312–c, 312–f (as amended in 1948).

correct title of "In the Matter of Arthur Lewis, a child under the Age of Sixteen Years." (§ 10.) The distinction is not without significance.

Arthur Lewis, fifteen years old, in company with a younger boy, broke into a store in Binghamton and stole twelve dollars. Afterward the two boys, together with two other boys, made their way to Buffalo by means of three automobiles stolen in succession. Brought home, each boy, in separate proceedings, was charged in Children's Court with juvenile delinquency. In this particular case the charge was based upon the theft of the money. No fault is found with the proceedings had prior to the hearing. The hearings in the four cases were held in succession on the same day. Each boy was examined separately in his own proceeding in the presence of his parents, relatives and friends. When so examined the other boys were not in the room. The entire testimony thus taken was apparently deemed evidence in each case. The course of the hearing in this case, then, was as follows: The boy, in company with his mother, sister and the family clergyman, appeared and their appearances were noted. They were advised by the judge that they might have the aid of counsel if they so desired. The boy was then questioned by the judge. The other boys were thereafter examined in the manner above stated. All the testimony thus given appears in the record by question and answer. Each boy told substantially the same story. The testimony sustains the charge beyond any doubt. Indeed, there was full admission and no attempt at denial. The judge then inquired if any one desired to speak on behalf of the boy. There was no answer. The boy was thereupon adjudged a delinquent child and was committed to the State Industrial and Agricultural School at Industry, N. Y.

Upon appeal to the Appellate Division, the judgment was reversed. The decision is placed upon the ground that the specific act upon which the delinquency charge is based would be a felony if committed by an adult and must be proved in substantially the same manner. The judgment, it is said is supported by no evidence received in the boy's presence, and hence rests solely upon his own confession made without a warning against self-incrimination.

Even in a criminal trial the confession which requires corroboration to sustain conviction is only the extra-judicial confession, not the admission made in open court on the witness stand. If the hearing here had been a criminal trial, its sole defect would have been the failure to warn against self-incrimination. But it was not a criminal trial and there was no defect. . . .

The proceeding here is under a widely different statute, which clearly and unmistakably abolishes the distinction referred to above between the two classes of children. The concept of crime and punishment disappears. To the child delinquent through the commission of an act criminal in its nature, the State extends the same aid, care

Sec. 1   IMMATURITY (INFANCY)   449

and training which it had long given to the child who was merely incorrigible, neglected, abandoned, destitute or physically handicapped. All suggestion and taint of criminality was intended to be and has been done away with. The legislative intent is made as plain as language can make it. The statute (§ 45) says: "No adjudication under the provisions of this act shall operate as a disqualification of any child subsequently to hold public office or as a forfeiture of any right or privilege or to receive any license granted by public authority; and no child shall be denominated a criminal by reason of such adjudication, nor shall such adjudication be denominated a conviction. Neither the fact that a child has been before the Children's Court for hearing, nor any confession, admission or statement made by him to the court or to any officer thereof while he is under the age of sixteen years, shall ever be admissible as evidence against him or his interests in any other court."

"All provisions of the penal law or code of criminal procedure or other statutes inconsistent with or repugnant to any of the provisions of this act shall be considered inapplicable to the cases arising under this act."

The final mandate of the statute is that "This act shall be construed to the end that the care, custody and discipline of the children brought before the court shall approximate as nearly as possible that which they should receive from their parents, and that as far as practicable they shall be treated not as criminals but as children in need of aid, encouragement and guidance." . . .

The rights of the child and of the parents are thus amply safeguarded, for the statute provides not only for appeals (§ 43) but it also provides (§ 25) that in delinquency cases, such as this, the court on its own motion or upon application by any interested person may set aside or arrest judgment or grant a new hearing in the exercise of its powers of protection over the child, either before or after final adjudication or commitment. Moreover, though it is not now necessary so to hold, it may be that the Supreme Court has power, under its general chancery jurisdiction, to intervene in any given case.

The judgment of the Appellate Division should be reversed and that of the Children's Court affirmed.[1]

CRANE, J. (dissenting). Do the Constitution of the United States and the Constitution of the State of New York apply to children or

---

1. "One of the principal contentions made by appellant is that he was improperly compelled to answer a question, the answer to which involved self-incrimination, . . . Article I, Section 9 of the Constitution, P.S., provides that 'In all *criminal* prosecutions the accused . . . cannot be compelled to give evidence against himself'. But since, as pointed out, Juvenile Courts *are not criminal* courts, the constitutional rights granted to persons accused of *crime* are not applicable to children brought before them . . ." In re Joseph Holmes, 379 Pa. 599, 604, 109 A.2d 523, 525 (1954), certiorari denied 348 U.S. 973, 75 S.Ct. 535, 99 L.Ed. 757 (1955).

only to adults? By the Fifth Amendment to the Federal Constitution, applicable to Federal courts, no person shall be compelled in a criminal case to be a witness against himself, nor deprived of his liberty, without due process of law. The latter provision, by the Fourteenth Amendment, is made binding on all the States.

. . . If the Legislature can thus wipe out the constitutional protection by changing a name, the substance and reality remaining the same, at what age of an accused does this power begin and end? May the Legislature call forgery, larceny, burglary, assault, "moral delinquency," and send a person twenty years of age to Elmira Reformatory, or some other correctional institution, on his own confession, wrung from him by an inquisitorial process in court, compelling him to be a witness against himself? If this legislative power exists regarding a boy fifteen years of age, why is it not also possible to do the same thing to a young man twenty years of age? At what age do the constitutional safeguards and protection begin? The Constitution of this State and the Federal Constitution, in so far as it is applicable, cannot be nullified by a mere nomenclature, the evil or the thing itself remaining the same. . . .

The judgment of the Appellate Division should be affirmed.[2]

POUND, CH. J., LEHMAN, O'BRIEN and HUBBS, JJ., concur with CROUCH, J.; CRANE, J., dissents in opinion in which KELLOGG, J., concurs.

Judgment accordingly.

(Certiorari denied 289 U.S. 709, 53 S.Ct. 786, 77 L.Ed. 1464.)

2. The Federal Youth Correction Act (18 U.S.C.A. ch. 402) applies to persons under twenty-two at the time of conviction and provides that such a "youth offender" may be sentenced to the custody of the Attorney General "for treatment and supervision". If it is found necessary he may be kept in custody up to four years and under supervision for two more. C, who had committed a federal misdemeanor was sentenced under this Act. As the maximum sentence provided for this misdemeanor was one year, C objected to his sentence to the custody of the Attorney General with its four to six-year provision. He claimed that it imposed cruel and unusual punishment in violation of the Eighth Amendment and also that it violated due process of law guaranteed by the Fifth. The court rejected both claims and upheld the constitutionality of the statute. The Act, it was said, provides "not heavier penalties and punishment than are imposed upon adult offenders, but the opportunity to escape from the physical and psychological shocks and traumas attendant upon serving an ordinary penal sentence while obtaining the benefits of corrective treatment, looking to rehabilitation and social redemption and restoration". Cunningham v. United States, 256 F.2d 467 (5th Cir. 1958).

Failure of the court to explain the difference between a sentence under this Act and an ordinary sentence was held, where prejudicial, sufficient to entitle defendant to withdraw his plea of guilty. Pilkington v. United States, 315 F.2d 204 (4th Cir. 1963). And see Eller v. United States, 327 F.2d 639 (9th Cir. 1964); Freeman v. United States, 350 F.2d 940 (9th Cir. 1965).

PEOPLE v. ROPER

Court of Appeals of New York, 1932.
259 N.Y. 170, 181 N.E. 88.

LEHMAN, J. A little before two o'clock in the morning of January 20th, 1931, two youths or men, with handkerchiefs covering their faces and armed with pistols, entered a negro restaurant on Seventh avenue in New York city. At the point of the pistol, one of them compelled the people in the restaurant to go to the rear and took some money from their persons. The same youth shot and killed William Groce, a customer of the restaurant. The other bandit took money from the cash register. Then both escaped. . . .

The trial was conducted with eminent fairness, and we find no reversible error in the admission or exclusion of evidence or in the charge, if the case was tried and submitted to the jury on the proper theory. Perhaps there may be doubt as to Thorp's identification of the defendant. On that question the defendant has had a fair trial, and none of his substantial rights have been infringed by excess of zeal or fault of police, prosecuting attorney or trial judge. A majority of the court, at least, find that the verdict of the jury is not against the weight of evidence upon the issue presented to the jury. We confine discussion in this opinion to the question whether the jury's finding of guilt on these issues supports the defendant's conviction of the crime of murder in the first degree.

Thorp's testimony establishes that a negro, whom he identified as the defendant on trial, shot and killed William Groce while he and another negro were engaged in taking money at the point of a pistol from the cash register of the restaurant and from the persons of those who were present in the restaurant. The defendant's age at the time of the homicide was not determined in the manner provided by section 817 of the Penal Law. Upon the preliminary examination of the jurors, the assistant district attorney stated to them: "The defendant Louis Roper at the time of the alleged commission of the crime by him was between fifteen and sixteen years of age." Testimony that the defendant was under the age of sixteen was uncontradicted. The case was tried and submitted to the jury upon the assumption that the fact that the defendant was at the time of the homicide under the age of sixteen carries no legal consequences in a trial for murder in the first degree. We are called upon to test the validity of that assumption in this case.

Only a child under the age of seven years is incapable as matter of law of committing a crime (Penal Law, § 816), though a child "of the age of seven years, and under the age of twelve years, is presumed to be incapable of crime, but the presumption may be removed by proof that he had sufficient capacity to understand" (§ 817). Even so, not every act or omission which, if committed by an adult, would be a crime, is a crime when committed by a child, for the Legislature has expressly decreed that "a child of more than seven and less than sixteen years of age, who shall commit any act or omission which, if committed by an adult, would be a crime not punishable by death or life imprisonment, shall not be deemed guilty of any crime, but of juvenile delinquency" (Penal Law, § 2186). Murder in the first degree is punishable by death. Therefore, it is clear that a child of fifteen may be guilty of the crime of murder in the first degree. When guilt of a crime has been established, its penal consequences are the same for child and adult criminal. But guilt cannot be established without proof of every essential element of the crime and, since a felonious intent is an essential element of the crime of murder, guilt of a defendant can never be established without proof of such intent. Thus, the guilt of a defendant charged with murder in the first degree may depend upon his capacity to form the felonious intent. Then the fact that a defendant is under the age of sixteen may carry legal consequences.

"There can be no murder without evidence of malice and of a felonious intent and a depraved mind. The indictment was sufficient in form when it simply accused defendant of having killed the deceased 'willfully, feloniously and with malice aforethought.' On the trial it was necessary to prove such malice and willful and felonious conduct, and this necessity was satisfied in accordance with the provisions of the statute by showing that the homicide occurred while the defendant was engaged in the commission of another felony." (People v. Nichols, 230 N.Y. 221, 226, 129 N.E. 883.)

Here, as in that case, the conviction rests upon a finding of the jury that a human being was killed by a person "engaged in the commission of another felony." True, the evidence is sufficient to support a finding that the homicide was committed by the defendant "from a deliberate and premeditated design to effect the death of the person killed," and a homicide committed in that way also would constitute murder in the first degree (Penal Law, § 1044) and might be proven under an indictment in common-law form. The jury, if such question had been presented to it, might have found that the defendant formed such a deliberate design, though under the age of sixteen; but the jury here made no such finding, for no such question was presented to it. If the trial judge in his charge had left that question to the jury, he would have been bound to charge on the degrees of homicide, and the jury would have been free to find a verdict of guilt in lesser degree than murder in the first degree. He chose to do otherwise. He charged the jurors that they were concerned only with the question of whether a human being was killed during the commission of a felony in which the defendant was a guilty participant, and that their verdict must be either guilty of murder in the first degree or not guilty. . . .

The charge of the trial judge was fair and accurate, if the defendant's participation was with felonious intent. The crime of murder charged in the indictment is a single crime, whether committed by design or during the commission of an independent felony; "the independent felony like the deliberate and premeditated intent, being established solely for the purpose of characterizing the degree of the crime so charged, the evil mind or purpose inherent in the killing." (People v. Lytton, 257 N.Y. 310, 315, 178 N.E. 290.) The defendant may have participated in the robbery; but unless that participation was with felonious intent he was not guilty of the felony, and if he was not guilty of the independent felony, participation does not evince "the evil mind or purpose inherent in the killing." (See People v. Koerber, 244 N.Y. 147, 155 N.E. 79.)

Sometimes a spirit of innocent mischief, sometimes evil associations, not of his own choice but forced upon him by family conditions, impel a child under the age of sixteen to commit acts which constitute felonies as defined by law. The State has adopted a humane policy in its treatment of a child under the age of sixteen who commits such acts. It does not, upon proof of guilt, fasten upon him the ineffaceable stain of conviction of guilt of a felony, nor subject him to imprisonment with adult offenders. For the child's benefit, as well as for the benefit of the State, it treats a child who commits acts which, if committed by an adult would constitute a felony, not punishable by death or life imprisonment, merely as a juvenile delinquent, an unfortunate ward of the State rather than a criminal. The law, in its mercy, demands that a child should be subject to such correction as may tend to remove the causes which have led the child to commit acts inimical to society; where it might demand that an adult committing the same acts should be visited with punishment of deterrent effect.

Doubtless at times the causes which have led a child into "juvenile delinquency" are too deep-seated to be removed by such corrective treatment as the State now offers. Perhaps at times "innate depravity" is more than a fiction. The Penal Law is not concerned with such abstractions. It decrees that the acts of a child shall, in all cases other than acts constituting a felony punishable by death or life imprisonment, be treated as if done without the "evil mind" which characterizes felonious intent, and each child must be given the opportunity to benefit by corrective treatment though he be unable or unwilling to avail himself of the benefit. The law does not say that a criminal under the age of sixteen is not subject to punishment for a crime; it says that proof of acts which would establish guilt of crime if committed by an older person does not establish the guilt of a child under the age of sixteen years, of any crime, but only of juvenile delinquency.

These considerations must lead to a reversal in this case. The defendant can be convicted of murder in the first degree only upon a finding of "felonious intent." The verdict of the jury imports a finding that the defendant participated in the commission of a robbery, as defined by the statute, for the trial judge charged that without such finding the verdict must be not guilty. Upon the trial of a defendant over the age of sixteen years a finding of participation in a robbery, as defined by the statute, would import a finding of "felonious intent;" for robbery, in every degree, is a felony. Upon the trial of a child under the age of sixteen, the participation of a child in a robbery, or at least in a robbery in the second or third degrees, would not establish the guilt of a felony but only of a minor offense characterized as juvenile delinquency. Hence, it is plain that the defendant's conviction rests upon no finding of guilt of a felony and thus no finding of felonious intent, and the judgment must be reversed. (People v. Moran, supra.) That is true even though no exception was taken to the charge which raises such question. A child under sixteen can be guilty of murder in the first or second degrees where he kills a man with felonious intent, but such felonious intent is not established without both proof and finding of intent to kill or of *guilt of an independent felony* during which the homicide occurred. . . .

Thus at the present time, even if not at the time of the original trial, proof that a child under the age of sixteen years participated in a robbery in the first degree cannot establish the child's guilt of a felony. Change in the punishment for that crime has the indirect result of removing the crime of robbery in the first degree from the category of crimes of which a child can be guilty if it ever was within that category. The effect is the same as if the Legislature had expressly declared that no child under the age of sixteen years can be guilty of robbery in any degree, and that upon the trial of such child for murder in the first degree, "felonious intent" may not be predicated upon guilt of robbery. In the absence of a clause excluding from its provisions offenses previously committed, the law as amended applies in all trials held thereafter, even for offenses previously committed.

Upon the new trial this defendant may be tried for murder in the first or second degrees committed through the killing of a human being with intent to effect his death. Such an action may be impelled by "evil mind" and felonious intent as evidenced by the criminal acts of the child, but not by acts which the Legislature has declared are not criminal when committed by a child. A person who with evil mind commits a crime may, in the interests of society, be punished even by death for the undesigned and unforeseen result of the crime. No person, certainly no child under the age of sixteen, is subject to death or life imprisonment because of the calamitous though undesigned result of acts which are not criminal in their inception.

The judgment of conviction should be reversed and a new trial ordered. (See 259 N.Y. 635, 182 N.E. 213.)

POUND, CH. J., CRANE, KELLOGG, O'BRIEN and HUBBS, JJ., concur.

Judgment reversed, etc.[1]

(Reargument denied 259 N.Y. 635, 182 N.E. 213.)

---

[1]. In 1948 an amendment to the New York statutes enlarged the phrase "juvenile delinquency" to include an act, which would be capital on the part

MITCHELL v. GLADDEN

Supreme Court of Oregon, 1961.
229 Or. 192, 366 P.2d 907.

O'CONNELL, JUSTICE. This is a proceeding brought under the Post-Conviction Hearing Act (ORS 138.510–138.670). Petitioner seeks an adjudication declaring invalid a judgment and sentence of the circuit court of Douglas county on October 14, 1955 and a judgment and sentence of the circuit court of Harney county on January 18, 1956. The petition alleges four grounds for relief, two of which have been abandoned on appeal.

The first question presented is whether petitioner was deprived of his constitutional rights in the course of the procedure under which he was sentenced following his conviction after a plea of guilty to the crime of robbery.[1] The petition for post-conviction relief contained the following allegation:

"That at the time of sentencing as alleged above, the plaintiff was eighteen years of age; that the District Attorney furnished the Court with a telegram purporting to be from the Federal Bureau of Investigation, wherein there was alleged information concerning the activities of the plaintiff when he was a juvenile and were not convictions of any crime, and therefore prejudicial to the plaintiff and not proper matters to bring before the Court; that the District Attorney further advised the Court that the plaintiff had holds placed against him from other agencies, and this matter was prejudicial to the plaintiff, as these were not proof of other crimes of which the plaintiff had been properly convicted, but were mere accusations; that the Court then took these matters into consideration when passing sentence upon the plaintiff, and did not consider the plaintiff as a first offender; that said in-

---

of an older person, if committed by one under sixteen,—except that it does not include an act, normally punishable by death or life imprisonment, if committed by a child of fifteen, unless there has been a court order removing the action to the children's court. New York Penal Law, § 486 (as amended in 1948). New York Code of Criminal Procedure, §§ 312–c, 312–f (as amended in 1948).

A statute providing a special penalty for an assault committed by an "adult male," upon a female or a child, refers to one of the "full age of twenty-one years." State v. Henderson, 34 Ariz. 430, 272 P. 97 (1928).

The statute gives exclusive jurisdiction of cases involving noncapital crimes to the juvenile court. If the indictment charges one under 18 with murder the district court had jurisdiction and did not lose jurisdiction by accepting a plea of murder in the second degree. State ex rel. Hinkle v. Skeen, 138 W.Va. 116, 75 S.E.2d 223 (1953), certiorari denied 345 U.S. 967, 73 S.Ct. 954 (1953). And see Hinkle v. Skeen, 117 F.Supp. 846 (1954).

[Footnotes by the Court.]

1. Apparently petitioner relies upon ORS 138.530(1) (a) of the Post-Conviction Hearing Act which provides as follows:

"(a) A substantial denial in the proceedings resulting in petitioner's conviction, or in the appellate review thereof, of petitioner's rights under the constitution of the United States, or under the Constitution of the State of Oregon, or both, and which denial rendered the conviction void."

formation given to the Court was not in conformity to ORS 137.080 and following."

Petitioner contends that in sentencing him for the crime of robbery it was improper to consider any judgment, order or other matter in any juvenile proceedings to which he had been subjected. For this proposition petitioner relies upon ORS 419.572 [2] which provided as follows:

"419.572 The disposition of a minor by any juvenile court of this state, including any order, judgment or decree pertaining thereto, or any testimony or evidence given in any juvenile court hearing in this state, is incompetent evidence against such child in any other proceeding or cause, whether civil, criminal or otherwise, in any court of this state. No such evidence or testimony shall be given by the juvenile court to anyone for use against such child."

It is petitioner's position that the trial judge, in sentencing a mature criminal, is prohibited under ORS 419.572 from examining the criminal's juvenile record. The statute provides that the matters mentioned are incompetent evidence *"against such child"* and that "No such evidence or testimony shall be given by the juvenile court to anyone for use *against such child.*" There is no proscription against the use of such evidence against a person after he has reached his majority. The obvious purpose of the statute is to protect a child from the stigma of his wrongdoing in his effort to rehabilitate himself. When he is no longer a child and when it is demonstrated by his conviction that he has not rehabilitated himself, there is no longer any reason to preclude the use of the evidence in the juvenile proceedings for the purpose of fixing his sentence. We hold that the trial judge properly considered the petitioner's juvenile record and that no constitutional right was invaded.

The second ground relied upon by petitioner in invoking the Post-Conviction Hearing Act is that his sentence was for a fixed period of time (the sentence was for "a term of five years in the Oregon State Penitentiary") and not for an indeterminate period of time with a maximum term as required by ORS 137.120(2).[3] The imposition of a sentence for a specified period is to be construed as fixing the maximum period which is to be served under an indeterminate sentence.

The judgment of the lower court is affirmed.

---

2. ORS 419.572 was in effect at the time petitioner was sentenced. It was later repealed, effective January 1, 1960. Oregon Laws 1959, ch. 432, § 59.

3. Petitioner contends that ORS 138.530 (1) (c) of the Post-Conviction Hearing Act was thus violated. That subsection provides as follows:

"(c) Sentence in excess of, or otherwise not in accordance with, the sentence authorized by law for the crime of which petitioner was convicted; or unconstitutionality of such sentence."

MODEL PENAL CODE

Section 4.10. Immaturity Excluding Criminal Conviction; Transfer of Proceedings to Juvenile Court.

(1) A person shall not be tried for or convicted of an offense if:

(a) at the time of the conduct charged to constitute the offense he was less than sixteen years of age, [in which case the Juvenile Court shall have exclusive jurisdiction *]; or

(b) at the time of the conduct charged to constitute the offense he was sixteen or seventeen years of age, unless:

(1) the Juvenile Court has no jurisdiction over him, or,

(2) the Juvenile Court has entered an order waiving jurisdiction and consenting to the institution of criminal proceedings against him.

(2) No court shall have jurisdiction to try or convict a person of an offense if criminal proceedings against him are barred by subsection (1) of this section. When it appears that a person charged with the commission of an offense may be of such an age that criminal proceedings may be barred under subsection (1) of this section, the Court shall hold a hearing thereon, and the burden shall be on the prosecution to establish to the satisfaction of the Court that the criminal proceeding is not barred upon such grounds. If the Court determines that the proceeding is barred, custody of the person charged shall be surrendered to the Juvenile Court, and the case, including all papers and processes relating thereto, shall be transferred.

Section 6.05. Young Adult Offenders.

(1) Specialized Correctional Treatment. A young adult offender is a person convicted of a crime who, at the time of sentencing, is sixteen but less than twenty-two years of age. A young adult offender who is sentenced to a term of imprisonment which may exceed thirty days [alternatives: (1) ninety days; (2) one year] shall be committed to the custody of the Division of Young Adult Correction of the Department of Correction, and shall receive, as far as practicable, such special and individualized correctional and rehabilitative treatment as may be appropriate to his needs.

(2) Special Term. A young adult offender convicted of a felony may, in lieu of any other sentence of imprisonment authorized by this Article, be sentenced to a special term of imprisonment without a minimum and with a maximum of four years, regardless of the degree of the felony involved, if the Court is of the opinion that such special term is adequate for his correction and rehabilitation and will not jeopardize the protection of the public.

[(3) Removal of Disabilities; Vacation of Conviction.

(a) In sentencing a young adult offender to the special term provided by this Section or to any sentence other than one of imprisonment, the Court may order that so long as he is not convicted of another felony, the judgment shall not constitute a conviction for the purposes of any disqualification or disability imposed by law upon conviction of a crime.

---

*. The bracketed words are unnecessary if the Juvenile Court Act so provides or is amended accordingly.

(b) When any young adult offender is unconditionally discharged from probation or parole before the expiration of the maximum term thereof, the Court may enter an order vacating the judgment of conviction.]

[(4) Commitment for Observation. If, after presentence investigation, the Court desires additional information concerning a young adult offender before imposing sentence, it may order that he be committed, for a period not exceeding ninety days, to the custody of the Division of Young Adult Correction of the Department of Correction for observation and study at an appropriate reception or classification center. Such Division of the Department of Correction and the [Young Adult Division of the] Board of Parole shall advise the Court of their findings and recommendations on or before the expiration of such ninety-day period.]

THE AMERICAN LAW INSTITUTE

YOUTH CORRECTION AUTHORITY ACT [1]

INTRODUCTORY EXPLANATION

Youthful offenders are an especially serious factor in the crime problem of the country. Young people between fifteen and twenty-one years of age constitute only 13 per cent. of our population above fifteen, but their share in the total amount of serious crime committed far exceeds their proportionate representation. Though but 13 per cent. of the population, they are responsible for approximately 26 per cent. of our robberies and thefts; they constitute some 40 per cent. of our apprehended burglars and nearly half of our automobile thieves. Boys from seventeen to twenty are arrested for major crimes in greater numbers than persons of any other four-year group. They come into court, not for petty offenses but for serious crime, twice as often as adults of thirty-five to thirty-nine; three times as often as those of forty-five to forty-nine; five times as often as men of fifty to fifty-nine. Nineteen-year-olds offend more frequently than persons of any other age, with eighteen-year-olds next. Moreover the proportion of youths less than twenty-one in the whole number of persons arrested has increased by 15 per cent. during the past three years; 108,857 not yet old enough to vote were arrested and fingerprinted last year.

But these figures, appalling as they are, paint only a part of the picture. A tremendous proportion of adult criminality has its inception in conviction of crime before the age of twenty-one. Every study that has ever been made indicates that if the known criminals between sixteen and twenty-one years old—those young persons actually convicted and dealt with in the courts—had somehow been prevented by that conviction from continuing a course of crime, the country's total

---

1. Portions of the Introductory Explanation are included here by permission of The American Law Institute and Professor John B. Waite, Reporter.

burden of offenses would be a small fraction of what it is. The criminality of youth is an evil not limited by the boundaries of youth. It projects its social damage far into the years of maturity. If and when we manage to check the criminal propensities of any youth we shall decrease the occurrence of crime now and in the future. Youth is in this sense the focal source of the country's crime burden and is, therefore, the focus upon which crime prevention efforts must wisely be centered.

This peculiar necessity for dealing wisely and effectively with youthful wrongdoers does not of course negative the importance of proper treatment of adult offenders. Concededly the public requires adequate protection from both. And a preventive process that is effective with boys of twenty should have at least a modicum of success with men of twenty-two or forty-two. But changes in established procedures to be feasible under given conditions must often be gradual. In view of certain practical requirements of the processes set up by this proposed Act the wisdom of building slowly will be apparent as the Act is studied. Hence because of the peculiar advantages to be gained through improvement in the treatment of youthful wrongdoers especially, the Act, as a beginning, is confined in its application to youth. The age of twenty-one rather than that of twenty or twenty-two, is admittedly arbitrary, but is chosen because it is the traditional end of the period of minority in the law of this country.

All crime prevention efforts, whether dealing with youth or maturity, are one or the other of two general types. On the one hand they may seek to eliminate, or ameliorate, or redirect the external conditions which impel people toward the commission of crime. Thus one crime prevention agency may strive to reduce the miseries of poverty; another to make less easily obtainable the wherewithal for intoxication. Of the other type are those activities designed to operate directly upon the individual himself and to influence his personal reaction to conditions. This proposed statute will operate upon the individual, not upon external conditions. It is not offered as a substitute for efforts to prevent crime by improvement of conditions. Neither does its advocacy depreciate in any way the activities of other agencies. It is designed to begin operation after other crime prevention activities have failed and to help strengthen resistance to criminal impulses by direct operation upon individuals.

Traditionally the criminal law has relied upon punishment and the threat of punishment as the only method of building up resistance to criminal inclinations. But with increasing knowledge of the causes of human action has come a general realization that reliance upon "punishment" as the only means of control is logically unsound. Moreover, as a practical matter, punishment as the primary method of control is not only logically unsound but obviously ineffective. It is not a satisfactory means of social protection against crime because it does not sufficiently prevent crime.

In the first place the threat of punishment does not notably prevent the commission of first offenses. As a matter of record there is now one man in jail for every 225 men over sixteen years of age who are free. And of course a great many of those who are free have previously been in jail or eventually will be in jail. Hence criminologists estimate that one or two out of every hundred males sooner or later commit a crime serious enough to call for imprisonment, undeterred by threat of punishment. . . .

Reasons for this failure are not difficult to find. Science now recognizes the existence of numerous "psychopathic personalities" whose courses of action cannot conceivably be affected by mere prospect or even experience of consequences such as the criminal law imposes. With some of them, indeed, the possible consequence, perverted in their conceptions, is an inducement rather than a deterrent. Still other people may be driven to crime by physical abnormalities whose impulsive force punishment, as such, makes no pretense of diminishing and cannot effectively counteract. More serious a defect than anything else, "punishment" takes no account whatever of the causal conditions of crime, but eventually returns its victims to social freedom not one whit better equipped than before to cope with the same necessities, incapacities, and desires to whose pressure they previously yielded.

These are negative faults in the punitive method. Even more dangerous are its positive evils. If it merely did not reform, it might be merely useless. But its worst influence is no mere innocuous failure to prevent crime; there is cogent reason to believe that it creates crime. By herding youth with maturity, the novice with the sophisticate, the impressionable with the hardened; by giving opportunity for dissemination of evil not counteracted by the prophylaxis of normal contacts; our penitentiaries actively spread the infection of crime. The penal system fosters, not checks, the plague. Small wonder therefore that punishment alone has so completely failed of its purpose. . . .

It was this unsatisfactory state of affairs which led the Institute to authorize the drafting of model statutes dealing with the treatment of youthful offenders. The Youth Correction Authority Act which is here presented for consideration is the first of two such statutes prepared. It relates only to the treatment of persons after conviction. It leaves the processes of arrest, accusation and trial unaffected. Its operation begins only after conviction and alters only post-conviction procedures.

The proposals of the Act are by no means radical. On the contrary, almost every detail of it is already the accepted law, or the approved practice, in one or more states. The Act as a whole is novel, however, because it frankly and specifically departs from the merely punitive ideas of dealing with convicted criminals and sets up the objective of rehabilitation. It is designed to protect the public from repeated crime; first, by safe segregation of dangerous persons so long as segregation is necessary; second, by such treatment of individual wrongdoers as is calculated to increase the probability that they will refrain from crime thereafter.

To these ends the Act creates a central state commission—called in the Act a Youth Correction Authority—which is invested with carefully limited and safeguarded powers to set up appropriate agencies and to determine the proper treatment for each youth committed to it by the courts. The membership of this commission and the details of its powers are discussed in connection with the various sections of the Act. Judges are left with a wide discretion as to whether they will sentence convicted youths to the custody and control of this commission or not. But no youth can merely be committed to prison. The judge of any court, except a juvenile court, before whom a youth is convicted, unless he discharges the youth or sentences him to payment of a fine only, must commit him to the Correction Authority to be dealt with by it as the statute authorizes. The Authority is given power to decide what treatment he shall be subjected to. And to the end that the treatment shall be most effective and most economically administered the Authority is authorized, within limits, to use, and thereby to bring into co-operative activity, all the facilities of the state. This is one of the most interesting features of the Act. It provides for a unified program of correctional treatment in contrast with the prevailing practice of having a variety of agencies—probation departments, parole departments, county jails and state institutions—concerned at different times in uncoordinated effort to deal with an offender.

This Act does not affect the jurisdiction or authority of existing juvenile courts. The theory upon which those courts are established is essentially the theory of this proposed Act; i. e., that corrective treatment of young persons, with segregation when necessary, is a more effective preventive of repeated crime than any mere punishment could be.

On the other hand, it seems undesirable to extend the scope of juvenile court activity to the older youths who are covered by this Act. Those courts utilize an informality of procedure wholly unsuited to the trial of older youths accused of serious crime. Moreover, there are undeniable physical and mental differences between the children, the "juveniles," with whom juvenile courts are designed to deal and the "youths" between juvenile court age and twenty-one with whose proper treatment this Act is concerned. Treatments which are sufficient when applied to children of fourteen or fifteen might be woefully inadequate for hardened young men of nineteen or twenty. Yet it would be utterly impractical to expect any juvenile court judge to administer, or even to select, treatments needed by the older youths as he selects them for children. Moreover the intermingling of juveniles and older youths which would normally result from a mere extension of juvenile court jurisdiction would be harmful. Hence, though juvenile court procedure and the proposed Act rest upon the same fundamental theories, each has its own appropriate place and the two should not be combined.

The upper age limit of juvenile court jurisdiction varies in different states. However, while in many states juvenile courts deal with delinquents over sixteen, in practice they rarely deal with youths charged with serious offenses over that age. Possibly in some states the upper age limit of the juvenile court is too high and the line of demarcation between the scope of the Act and the powers of the juvenile court will not fall in the wisest place. If this be thought true in any particular state the juvenile court law can be amended by the legislature.

Neither are the provisions of this proposed Act inconsistent with present practices and establishments relating to probation and parole. The Act extends, for reasons which have been already stated, only to persons less than twenty-one years old at the time of their apprehension. The use of probation or parole in respect to persons over twenty-one who commit crime is therefore entirely unaffected. So far as youthful offenders are concerned, the use of probation by order of criminal court judges is terminated, though it is still available to juvenile court judges. But this does not mean that probation will not be used for youths. On the contrary, it is conceivable that its use will be even more frequent; the only difference being that under the Act orders for probation—as well as for the equivalent of parole—will be made by the Correction Authority, instead of by the trial judge or parole board.

In summation, then, this proposed Act is neither a radical departure from existing law, nor even basically novel. On the contrary, it is merely a synthesis of the theories and practices which have already been given widespread acceptance and approval, and is designed to improve public protection against crime by effective utilization of scientific knowledge and modern methods.[1]

John B. Waite,
Reporter.

---

1. See Proposals for the Sentencing and Treatment of the Young Adult Offender under the Model Penal Code: Paul W. Tappan, Tentative **Draft No. 3** (1955). See also Tentative **Draft No.** 7 (1957).

SECTION 2. MENTAL DISEASE OR DEFECT (INSANITY)

The problem of insanity may become important at various points in a criminal case. The *first* is at the time of the alleged crime. Insanity of the defendant at the time of the *actus reus*, if of such character and degree as to negative criminal responsibility, will entitle him to an acquittal. The *second* point is at the time set for arraignment. If the mind of one accused of crime by indictment or information is so disordered by mental disease that he is unable to understand the charge against him, and to plead intelligently thereto, he should not be permitted to plead until his reason is restored. This problem is similar to the next and can be considered therewith. The *third* point is at the time set for trial,—or during the trial.[1] Mental disorder at this time has nothing to do with the issue of guilt or innocence (except to the extent that it may have some tendency to indicate what his mental condition was at the time of the harmful deed). But one whose mental condition is now so disordered that he is unable to understand the charge against him, and possible defenses thereto, and hence is unable properly to advise with his counsel in regard to the conduct of the trial, ought not to be tried now,—whatever his mental condition may have been at the time of the alleged crime. Hence upon such a finding the defendant is committed to some proper hospital. He is to remain there until his reason is restored, at which time he is to be returned to the court for trial.

The *fourth* point is at the time of allocution (when the defendant is asked by the judge, after a verdict or plea of guilty, if he knows of any reason why judgment should not be pronounced against him). In the words of Blackstone: "If, after he be tried and found guilty, he loses his senses before judgment, judgment shall not be pronounced . . .: for peradventure, says the humanity of the English law, had the prisoner been of sound memory, he might have alleged something in stay of judgment . . .." (4 Bl.Comm. 24–25). A finding of insanity at this point requires a commitment of the defendant to a proper hospital until he regains his reason. He is then to be returned for sentence.

The *fifth* point is at the time of execution.[2] At common law this probably was limited to the execution of a sentence of death, but it is

---

1. "One might not be insane in the sense of being incapable of standing trial and yet lack the capacity of standing trial without the benefit of counsel". Massey v. Moore, 348 U.S. 105, 108, 75 S.Ct. 145, 147, 99 L.Ed. 135 (1954).

   An insane person cannot plead to an indictment, be subjected to trial, have judgment pronounced against him or undergo punishment, but a valid indictment may be found against him although no further proceedings can be had at the time. Frye v. Settle, 168 F.Supp. 7 (D.C.Mo.1958).

2. One under sentence of death asked the governor to postpone execution on the ground that he had become insane after conviction. Under authority of a

to be remembered that all felonies were capital at common law. In any event he must not be put to death while out of his mind, for if he had his reason he might be able to allege something in stay of execution.

Quite apart from a criminal case, it may be added, one who is mentally disordered to such an extent as to be a menace to himself, or to others, may be committed to a proper hospital until and unless his reason is restored. This, however, is not our present problem. As a matter of logic this section is concerned only with the first point mentioned although it will be convenient to extend the inquiry somewhat beyond this.

The nature and extent of mental disorder which will entitle the defendant to an acquittal, constitutes the outstanding problem in this branch of the law of insanity. No distinction is made, in this inquiry, between *dementia* and *amentia*. The point here is not whether the person once had a sound mind which has deteriorated as a result of disease or injury, or was mentally deficient from birth. The sole determinant is the nature and extent of the mental abnormality. It must be emphasized that the phrase "mental disease" is employed in a very broad sense in the criminal law. Any serious mental disorder or abnormality resulting from mental disease, physical disease, physical injury or congenital deficiency often will be placed loosely under the label "mental disease." This is because the consequences of all are the same, so far as the law of crimes is concerned. At times some other phrase has been used such as "mental disease or defect." This is more precise, but it is important to keep in mind that the term "mental disease" often is used in the cases to cover the entire field.

Similarly, the phrase "insanity or idiocy" may be more precise, as a label for this department of the law, than the single word "insanity." The essential need is to distinguish deviational mental conditions due to disease, injury or congenital defect, from excitement or stupefaction resulting from intoxicating liquor or drugs. Simple labels are helpful, and the two departments are usually designated respectively as (1) "insanity" and (2) "intoxication." Only the first of these is under consideration here, but before going farther it is necessary to say more about the word "insanity" itself. It has other differences of meaning entitled to attention. At times it is used to refer to the mental condition of one who is "out of his head" from

---

state statute the governor appointed three doctors who examined the convict and declared him sane. In denying relief in habeas corpus proceedings the court held that this procedure was not a denial of due process under the Fourteenth Amendment. Solesbee v. Balkcom, 339 U.S. 9, 70 S.Ct. 457 (1950). In another case in which responsibility for determining the prisoner's sanity was vested in the prison warden rather than the governor, the warden's determination being based on reports of the prison psychiatrists, there was also held to be no denial of due process. Caritativo v. California, 357 U.S. 549, 78 S.Ct. 1263, 2 L.Ed.2d 1531 (1958).

Sec. 2 MENTAL DISEASE OR DEFECT (INSANITY)

whatever cause. Thus "moral insanity"[3] has been used at times to refer to one who wilfully let his passions go until they carried him to a state of fury; and "drunken insanity" has been employed occasionally to indicate an extreme condition of intoxication. Neither of these comes within the scope of this section and it would be wise to substitute some other form of expression for the word "insanity" to convey any such idea. If this is done, and the word is accepted as broad enough to include congenital defect as well as mental disease proper, there are still two different meanings of "insanity." In one sense, any serious mental disease or defect is spoken of as "insanity," as in the sentence: "The kind and degree of insanity available as a defense to crime has many times been defined by the decisions of this court."[4] In the other sense the word "insanity" is used to express that kind and degree of mental disease or defect which establishes criminal incapacity (or contractual incapacity or testamentary incapacity or whatever the particular issue may be). The latter usage, while perhaps unfortunate, cannot be ignored because the word is found frequently in the statutes with that signification. If the two meanings are kept clearly in mind the context usually will indicate which is to be understood in the particular sentence.

While it is accepted that mental disease or defect may be so extreme as to negate criminal responsibility we do not have uniformity as to the type of disorder required for this purpose.

"M'Naghten's Case".[5] Daniel M'Naghten, who had killed Edward Drummond mistaking him for Sir Robert Peel, was found "not guilty by reason of insanity". The case was so clear on the facts that it would have been soon forgotten had it not been for a peculiar aftermath. Since the intended victim had been Sir Robert Peel there was great public excitement and the House of Lords put certain questions to the judges. The answers of the judges, given in the House of Lords, were published in connection with M'Naghten's Case and any mention of that case today has reference not to the trial of M'Naghten but to these answers of the judges. The answer of chief significance was to the effect that a defendant is not entitled to a "defence on the ground of insanity" unless at the time he "was labouring under such a defect of reason, from disease of the mind, as not to know the nature and quality of the act he was doing; or, if he did know it, that he did not know he was doing what was wrong" This is the so-called "right-wrong" test of insanity, or the "M'Naghten rule".

---

3. "Moral insanity" should be reserved for mental disease which affects primarily the conative functions, tending toward certain compulsions with no apparent loss of perception or intelligence.

4. People v. Gilberg, 197 Cal. 306, 313, 240 P. 1000, 1003 (1925). See also:

"Before the jury can acquit the prisoner on the ground of insanity, they must believe . . . that his insanity was of such character . . . ." Fisher v. People, 23 Ill. 283, 285 (1860).

5. 10 Clark & F. 200, 8 Eng.Rep. 718 (H.L.1843).

With reference to a question concerning an insane delusion the judges answered: "To which question the answer must of course depend on the nature of the delusion: but, making the same assumption as we did before, namely, that he labours under such partial delusion only, and is not in other respects insane, we think he must be considered in the same situation as to responsibility as if the facts with respect to which the delusion exists were real." There was also a question as to procedure, but with reference to the substantive law the two answers above are often referred to as the "M'Naghten rules".[6]

FISHER v. UNITED STATES

Supreme Court of the United States, 1946.
328 U.S. 463, 90 L.Ed. 1382, 66 S.Ct. 1318.

MR. JUSTICE REED delivered the opinion of the Court.

This writ of certiorari brings here for review the sentence of death imposed upon petitioner by the District Court of the United States for the District of Columbia after a verdict of guilty on the first count of an indictment which charged petitioner with killing by choking and strangling Catherine Cooper Reardon, with deliberate and premeditated malice. The United States Court of Appeals for the District of Columbia affirmed the judgment and sentence of the District Court. 80 U.S.App.D.C. 96, 149 F.2d 28.

The errors presented by the petition for certiorari and urged at our bar were, in substance, that the trial court refused to instruct the jurors that they should consider the evidence of the accused's psychopathic aggressive tendencies, low emotional response and borderline mental deficiency to determine whether he was guilty of murder in

---

6. The fact that D had been pronounced insane in a separate proceeding did not entitle him to a directed verdict. The question of insanity at the time of the alleged crime is to be determined by the jury from the evidence. Sharp v. Commonwealth, 308 Ky. 765, 215 S.W.2d 983 (1948). There are many different kinds and degrees of insanity and the fact of commitment as an insane person does not necessarily establish the want of criminal capacity. People v. Field, 108 Cal.App.2d 496, 238 P.2d 1052 (1951). One who has been adjudged insane at the time of the trial for crime, and placed under a guardian, is presumed to have been insane at the time of trial. If he was insane he could not properly render assistance to his counsel. The trial therefore violated his constitutional rights. The court had no jurisdiction and the conviction is subject to attack by habeas corpus proceedings. Ashley v. Pescor, 147 F.2d 318 (8th Cir. 1945). One who has been acquitted on the ground of insanity is entitled to be released, if he is sane now, although the evidence shows he has the same mental condition now that he had at the time of the harmful deed. Yankulov v. Bushong, 88 Ohio App. 497, 77 N.E.2d 88 (1945). "If a person indicted for murder or manslaughter is acquitted by the jury by reason of insanity, the court shall order him to be committed to a state hospital or to the Bridgewater state hospital during his natural life. The governor, with the advice and consent of the council, may discharge such a person therefrom when he is satisfied after an investigation by the department that such discharge will not cause dangers to others." M.G.L.A., c. 123 § 101. See also c. 123, § 100A; c. 278 § 13.

Sec. 2   *MENTAL DISEASE OR DEFECT (INSANITY)*   467

the first or in the second degree. The aggregate of these factors admittedly was not enough to support a finding of not guilty by reason of insanity. Deliberation and premeditation are necessary elements of first degree murder.

Considerations as to the exercise of authority by this Court over the courts of the District of Columbia in the interpretation of local criminal statutes induced us to grant the writ in view of the issue presented. Judicial Code, § 240(a).

The homicide took place in the library building on the grounds of the Cathedral of Saint Peter and Saint Paul, Washington, D. C., between eight and nine o'clock, a. m., on March 1, 1944. The victim was the librarian. She had complained to the verger a few days before about petitioner's care of the premises. The petitioner was the janitor. The verger had told him of the complaint. Miss Reardon and Fisher were alone in the library at the time of the homicide. The petitioner testified that Miss Reardon was killed by him immediately following insulting words from her over his care of the premises. After slapping her impulsively, petitioner ran up a flight of steps to reach an exit on a higher level but turned back down, after seizing a convenient stick of firewood, to stop her screaming. He struck her with the stick and when it broke choked her to silence. He then dragged her to a lavatory and left the body to clean up some spots of blood on the floor outside. While Fisher was doing this cleaning up, the victim "started hollering again." Fisher then took out his knife and stuck her in the throat. She was silent. After that he dragged her body down into an adjoining pump pit, where it was found the next morning. The above facts made up petitioner's story to the jury of the killing. . . .

The effort of the defense is to show that the murder was not deliberate and premeditated; that it was not first but second degree murder. A reading of petitioner's own testimony, summarized above, shows clearly to us that there was sufficient evidence to support a verdict of murder in the first degree, if petitioner was a normal man in his mental and emotional characteristics. But the defense takes the position that the petitioner is fairly entitled to be judged as to deliberation and premeditation, not by a theoretical normality but by his own personal traits. In view of the status of the defense of partial responsibility in the District and the nation no contention is or could be made of the denial of due process. It is the contention of the defense that the mental and emotional qualities of petitioner were of such a level at the time of the crime that he was incapable of deliberation and premeditation although he was then sane in the usual legal sense. He knew right from wrong. See M'Naghten's Case, 10 Cl. & Fin. 200, 210. His will was capable of controlling his impulses. Testimony of psychiatrists to support petitioner's contention was introduced. An instruction charging the jury to consider the personality of the petitioner in determining intent, premeditation and deliberation was sought and refused. . . .

Petitioner urges forcefully that mental deficiency which does not show legal irresponsibility should be declared by this Court to be a relevant factor in determining whether an accused is guilty of murder in the first or second degree, upon which an instruction should be given, as requested. It is pointed out that the courts of certain states have adopted this theory. Others have rejected it. It is urged, also, that since evidence of intoxication to a state where one guilty of the crime of murder may not be capable of deliberate premeditation requires in the District of Columbia an instruction to that effect (McAffee v. United States, 72 App.D.C. 60, 111 F.2d 199, 205 r. c.), courts from this must deduce that disease and congenital defects, for which the accused may not be responsible, may also reduce the crime of murder from first to second degree. This Court reversed the Supreme Court of the Territory of Utah for failure to give a partial responsibility charge upon evidence of drunkenness in language which has been said to be broad enough to cover mental deficiency. Hopt v. People, 104 U.S. 631, 634. It should be noted, however, that the Territory of Utah had a statute specifically establishing such a rule.

No one doubts that there are more possible classifications of mentality than the sane and the insane. White, Insanity and the Criminal Law 89. Criminologists and psychologists have weighed the advantages and disadvantages of the adoption of the theory of partial responsibility as a basis of the jury's determination of the degree of crime of which a mentally deficient defendant may be guilty. Congress took a forward step in defining the degrees of murder so that only those guilty of deliberate and premeditated malice could be convicted of the first degree. It may be that psychiatry has now reached a position of certainty in its diagnosis and prognosis which will induce Congress to enact the rule of responsibility for crime for which petitioner contends. For this Court to force the District of Columbia to adopt such a requirement for criminal trials would involve a fundamental change in the common law theory of responsibility. . . .

Matters relating to law enforcement in the District are entrusted to the courts of the District. Our policy is not to interfere with the local rules of law which they fashion, save in exceptional situations where egregious error has been committed.

Where the choice of the Court of Appeals of the District of Columbia in local matters between conflicting legal conclusions seems nicely balanced, we do not interfere. The policy of deferring to the District's courts on local law matters is reinforced here by the fact that the local law now challenged is long established and deeply rooted in the District.

Affirmed.

MR. JUSTICE JACKSON took no part in the consideration or decision of this case. . . .

[MR. JUSTICE MURPHY, MR. JUSTICE FRANKFURTER and MR. JUSTICE RUTLEDGE dissented.]

PEOPLE v. HENDERSON

Supreme Court of California, In Bank, 1963.
60 Cal.2d 482, 35 Cal.Rptr. 77, 386 P.2d 677.

TRAYNOR, JUSTICE. A jury found defendant guilty of murder of the first degree and fixed the penalty at death. This appeal is automatic. . . .

Defendant contends that the trial court erred in failing on its own motion to instruct the jury on the legal significance of the evidence of defendant's mental illness and in refusing to give defendant's proffered instruction on manslaughter.

"It would seem elementary that a plea of not guilty to a charge of murder puts in issue the existence of the particular mental states which are essential elements of the two degrees of murder and of manslaughter . . .. Accordingly, it appears only fair and reasonable that defendant should be allowed to show that in fact subjectively, he did not possess the mental state or states in issue." (People v. Gorshen, 51 Cal.2d 716, 733, 336 P.2d 492, 502; People v. Wells, 33 Cal.2d 330, 343–357, 202 P.2d 53. . . .

It can no longer be doubted that the defense of mental illness not amounting to legal insanity is a "significant issue" in any case in which it is raised by substantial evidence. Its purpose and effect are to ameliorate the law governing criminal responsibility prescribed by the M'Naughton [sic] rule. (See Lindman & McIntyre, The Mentally Disabled and the Law (1961) 355–356.) Under that rule a defendant is not insane in the eyes of the law if at the time of the crime he knew what he was doing and that it was wrong. Under the Wells-Gorshen rule of diminished responsibility even though a defendant be legally sane according to the M'Naughton [sic] test, if he was suffering from a mental illness that prevented his acting with malice aforethought or with premeditation and deliberation, he cannot be convicted of murder of the first degree. This policy is now firmly established in the law of California and where, as here, substantial evidence sufficient to inform the court that defendant is relying upon the defense of diminished responsibility is received, it must on its own motion instruct the jury as to the legal significance of such evidence, for such an instruction is "necessary for the jury to be fully and fairly charged upon the relevant law." (People v. Jackson, 59 Cal.2d 375, 380, 29 Cal.Rptr. 505, 508, 379 P.2d 937, 940, and cases cited therein.) . . .

We agree that in light of such extensive argument on the issue of defendant's responsibility he could not have been harmed by the failure to instruct on that issue if the jury was otherwise properly instructed on intent. The jury, however, was not properly instructed on that issue. It was instructed that to constitute willful, deliberate, and premeditated murder the killing must be accompanied by a clear intent to take life resulting from deliberation and formed upon a pre-existing reflection and not in heat of anger, and that the slayer must weigh and consider the question of killing and the reasons for and against such choice and, having in mind the consequences, decide to and commit the unlawful act causing death. These instructions were proper, but they informed the jury only that a particular intent was necessary. How the jury should discover whether that intent existed was covered by the following instruction: "The intent or intention is manifested by the circumstances connected with the offense and the sound mind and discretion of the accused, and I further instruct you that all persons are of sound mind who are neither idiots nor lunatics nor affected with insanity to such an extent as to be unable to discern right from wrong."

Although counsel argued and the court instructed that defendant's intent was the crucial issue in the case, the only instruction that purported to tell the jury how to determine what that intent was told them to look to the circumstances of the offense and defendant's "sound mind" unless they found him to be an idiot, lunatic or legally insane.

"The prejudicial nature of the instruction appears most clearly in the difficulties that it creates for the jury in the application of the rule . . . that evidence of a mental infirmity, not amounting to legal insanity, is admissible and should be considered by the jury on the questions of premeditation and deliberation. If the defendant has a 'sound mind,' that is, 'a healthy and robust mind, neither diseased nor injured,' it necessarily follows that he would not have a mental infirmity making him incapable of premeditating or deliberating." (People v. Baker, 42 Cal.2d 550, 569, 268 P.2d 705, 716.)

Defendant admitted that he killed and mutilated the deceased. These were the major "circumstances connected with the offense" from which the jury was instructed it could infer defendant's intent. His sole defense was diminished responsibility because of his "unsound" though not insane mind, and this defense was withdrawn from the jury by the court's instruction that defendant was of sound mind if he was not an idiot, lunatic or legally insane. There could be no question of defendant's legal insanity during the trial of his guilt or innocence since that issue was to be determined on the separate proceeding under his plea of not guilty by reason of insanity, which was not withdrawn until the conclusion of the trial on the issue of guilt. Under these circumstances, defendant is "conclusively presumed to have been sane at the time the offense is alleged to have been committed." (Pen.Code, § 1026). There was no evidence that defendant was a lunatic or an idiot within the ordinary meaning of those words. Based on the only criteria it was given, the jury could only have found that defendant was of "sound mind." The effect of the instruction that defendant was of sound mind together with the failure to instruct on the significance of his defense of diminished responsibility was to withdraw from the jury all consideration of the evidence introduced in support of that defense. Such evidence, although disputed, was considerable. . . .

Since defendant was deprived of the right to a jury determination of the only real issue in the case, the conviction must be reversed, for the denial of such a right itself is a miscarriage of justice within the meaning of article VI, section 4½ of the Constitution.[1]

Since the judgment must be reversed, we shall consider other contentions that may arise on retrial. . . .

DAVIS v. STATE

Supreme Court of Tennessee, 1930.
161 Tenn. 23, 28 S.W.2d 993.

MR. CHIEF JUSTICE GREEN delivered the opinion of the Court.

The plaintiff in error was indicted for killing one L. R. Noe and convicted of murder in the second degree. . . .

The case was tried at length and submitted to the jury. After some deliberation, the jury returned to the courtroom and reported in substance that they found that the defendant below was insane on the subject of the relations between his late wife and Noe, but they further found that he knew the difference between right and wrong, and they asked the court what, under such circumstances, they should do.

In response, the court read to the jury a part of his charge previously given them and added some further instructions. The court rejected the contention that, if by reason of mental disease, the will power of the defendant below was so impaired, he was unable to resist the impulse to kill Noe, he would not be guilty, although he could distinguish between right and wrong as to the particular act.

(1) The charge of the court was to the effect that although plaintiff in error acted under an irresistible impulse produced by an insane delusion he would still be guilty if he could distinguish between right and wrong and knew that it was wrong to kill Noe.

Counsel contend that there may be a mental disease destroying the faculty of volition, of choosing, as well as a mental disease destroying the faculty of perception, and that either condition would relieve defendant of criminal accountability.

The court refused to recognize as a defense destroyed volition, even as a result of mental disease, apart from destroyed perception.

---

[1]. Disease of the mind, insufficient for acquittal, can prevent one from truly deliberating and from being capable of a deliberate premeditation necessary for guilt of first-degree murder. State v. Padilla, 66 N.M. 289, 347 P.2d 312 (1959).

This difference between counsel for the defendant below and the trial judge is with respect to a matter upon which the courts of the country are divided. Irresistible impulse, coming from disease, not emotion, moral depravity, or criminal perversion, is regarded in many jurisdictions as a defense in criminal prosecutions. In other jurisdictions the idea is rejected.

The cases are collected and cited in 29 Corpus Juris, 1053. They are too numerous to justify a review, particularly in view of former decisions of this court.

It is insisted by counsel for the plaintiff in error that this court is not so far committed on the doctrine of irresistible impulse but we think that this is a mistake.

In Wilcox v. State, 94 Tenn. 106, it was said by the court that:

"The idea that an irresistible impulse is an excuse for the commission of crime, where the party is capable of knowing right from wrong, has no foundation in our jurisprudence." . . .

(2) So while upon the facts of the case, the plaintiff in error, notwithstanding his delusion, cannot be acquitted of criminal accountability, we do not approve the conviction for murder in the second degree.

We are of opinion that if as a matter of fact the deceased had debauched the wife of plaintiff in error and the plaintiff in error had been apprised of that fact and had become convinced of its truth on the day of the wedding or thereafter, and, with reasonable expedition while under the influence of passion and agitation produced by such information, had killed Noe, he would only have been guilty of voluntary manslaughter.

(3) The right and wrong test above mentioned was authoritatively laid down in McNaughten's [sic] case, 1 C. & K., 130, 8 Eng. Reprint, 718. Under that case and those following it a homicide commmitted under an insane delusion is excusable, if the notion embodied in the delusion and believed to be a fact, if a fact indeed, would have excused the defendant.

(4) "Manslaughter is the unlawful killing of another without malice, either express or implied, which may be either voluntary upon a sudden heat, or involuntary, but in the commission of some unlawful act." Thompson's-Shannon's Code, sec. 6444.

Such being the law, it ensues that plaintiff in error would have been guilty of manslaughter only, if when he was first obsessed by this insane conceit, acting under the passion and agitation thereby produced, he had killed Esquire Noe.

(5) In the case of a normal man who has been apprised of the violation of the chastity of a female member of his family, if sufficient time has elapsed between the receipt of the information and the

homicide so that his passion has had time to cool, the killing of the seducer would be murder. Toler v. State, supra.

Cooling time affects the degree of a defendant's guilt under the law because during such an interval there is opportunity for the voice of reason, the voice of conscience, to be heard. If these voices are ignored, the killing will be attributed to deliberate revenge and punished as murder.

(6) We have before us a man found by the jury to have been insane on the subject of his wife's relations with deceased. How could his status under the law have been affected by a lapse of time between his conception of the provocation and the homicide? Possessed by this insane delusion, deranged on the subject, he remained deaf to the voice of reason and to the voice of conscience. He was beyond reason and conscience in this particular, as the record clearly shows.

It is not necessary that a defendant's reason be dethroned to mitigate a killing to manslaughter. It is error so to instruct a jury. If the excitement and passion adequately aroused obscures the reason of the defendant, the killing will be reduced to manslaughter. A defendant acting under such temporary mental stress is presumed to be incapable of malice, an essential ingredient of murder.

How then can malice be imputed to a defendant when his reason is not merely obscured but has been swept away and kept away by an insane delusion under which he acts? How can such a defendant be guilty of murder while his delusion persists? . . .

Upon the facts for the reasons stated, we conclude that the verdict of murder in the second degree is not sustained by the proof. . . .

Reversed and remanded.

DURHAM v. UNITED STATES

United States Court of Appeals, District of Columbia Circuit, 1954.
94 U.S.App.D.C. 228, 214 F.2d 862.

BAZELON, CIRCUIT JUDGE. Monte Durham was convicted of housebreaking, by the District Court sitting without a jury. The only defense asserted at the trial was that Durham was of unsound mind at the time of the offense. We are now urged to reverse the conviction (1) because the trial court did not correctly apply existing rules governing the burden of proof on the defense of insanity, and (2) because existing tests of criminal responsibility are obsolete and should be superseded. . . .

II

It has been ably argued by counsel for Durham that the existing tests in the District of Columbia for determining criminal responsibility, *i. e.*, the so-called right-wrong test supplemented by the irresistible impulse test, are not satisfactory criteria for determining criminal responsibility. We are urged to adopt a different test to be applied on the retrial of this case. This contention has behind it nearly a century of agitation for reform.

A. The right-wrong test, approved in this jurisdiction in 1882,[13] was the exclusive test of criminal responsibility in the District of Columbia until 1929 when we approved the irresistible impulse test as a supplementary test in Smith v. United States.[14] The right-wrong test has its roots in England. There, by the first quarter of the eighteenth century, an accused escaped punishment if he could not distinguish "good and evil," *i. e.*, if he "doth not know what he is doing, no more than . . . a wild beast."[15] Later in the same century, the "wild beast" test was abandoned and "right and wrong" was substituted for "good and evil."[16] And toward the middle of the nineteenth century, the House of Lords in the famous M'Naghten case[17] restated what had become the accepted "right-wrong" test[18] in a form which has since been followed, not only in England[19] but in most American jurisdictions[20] as an exclusive test of criminal responsibility:

" . . . the jurors ought to be told in all cases that every man is to be presumed to be sane, and to possess a sufficient degree of reason to be responsible for his crimes, until the contrary be proved to their satisfaction; and that, to establish a defence on the ground

---

13. 1882, 12 D.C. 498, 550, 1 Mackey 498, 550. The right-wrong test was reaffirmed in United States v. Lee, 1886, 15 D.C. 489, 496, 4 Mackey, 489, 496.

14. 1929, 59 App.D.C. 144, 36 F.2d 548, 70 A.L.R. 654.

15. Glueck, Mental Disorder and the Criminal Law 138–39 (1925), citing Rex v. Arnold, 16 How.St.Tr. 695, 764 (1724).

16. Id. at 142–52, citing Earl Ferrer's case, 19 How.St.Tr. 886 (1760). One writer has stated that these tests originated in England in the 13th or 14th century, when the law began to define insanity in terms of intellect for purposes of determining capacity to manage feudal estates. Comment, *Lunacy and Idiocy—The Old Law and Its Incubus*, 18 U. of Chi.L.Rev. 361 (1951).

17. 8 Eng.Rep. 718 (1843).

18. Hall, Principles of Criminal Law 480, n. 6 (1947).

19. Royal Commission on Capital Punishment 1949–1953 Report (Cmd. 8932) 79 (1953) (hereinafter cited as Royal Commission Report).

20. Weihofen, *The M'Naghten Rule in Its Present Day Setting*, Federal Probation 8 (Sept. 1953); Weihofen, Insanity as a Defense in Criminal Law 15, 64–68, 109–47 (1933); Leland v. State of Oregon, 1952, 343 U.S. 790, 800, 72 S.Ct. 1002, 96 L.Ed. 1302. . . .

Mentally Defective Offenders, 43 J.Crim. L., Criminology & Police Sci. 312, 314 (1952).

Sec. 2   *MENTAL DISEASE OR DEFECT (INSANITY)*   475

of insanity, it must be clearly proved that, at the time of the committing of the act, the party accused was labouring under such a defect of reason, from disease of the mind, as not to know the nature and quality of the act he was doing, or, if he did not know it, that he did not know he was doing what was wrong." [21]

As early as 1838, Isaac Ray, one of the founders of the American Psychiatric Association, in his now classic Medical Jurisprudence of Insanity, called knowledge of right and wrong a "fallacious" test of criminal responsibility.[22] . . .

We find that as an exclusive criterion the right-wrong test is inadequate in that (a) it does not take sufficient account of psychic realties and scientific knowledge, and (b) it is based upon one symptom and so cannot validly be applied in all circumstances. We find that the "irresistible impulse" test is also inadequate in that it gives no recognition to mental illness characterized by brooding and reflection and so relegates acts caused by such illness to the application of the inadequate right-wrong test. We conclude that a broader test should be adopted.

B. In the District of Columbia, the formulation of tests of criminal responsibility is entrusted to the courts and, in adopting a new test, we invoke our inherent power to make the change prospectively.

The rule we now hold must be applied on the retrial of this case and in future cases is not unlike that followed by the New Hampshire court since 1870.[47] It is simply that an accused is not criminally responsible if his unlawful act was the product of mental disease or mental defect.[48]

We use "disease" in the sense of a condition which is considered capable of either improving or deteriorating. We use "defect" in the sense of a condition which is not considered capable of either improving or deteriorating and which may be either congenital, or the result of injury, or the residual effect of a physical or mental disease.

Whenever there is "some evidence" that the accused suffered from a diseased or defective mental condition at the time the unlawful act was committed, the trial court must provide the jury with guides for determining whether the accused can be held criminally responsible. We do not, and indeed could not, formulate an instruction which would be either appropriate or binding in all cases. But under the rule now announced, any instruction should in some way

---

21. 8 Eng.Rep. 718, 722 (1843). . . .

22. Ray, Medical Jurisprudence of Insanity 47 and 34 et seq. (1st ed. 1838). "That the insane mind is not entirely deprived of this power of moral discernment, but in many subjects is perfectly rational, and displays the exercise of a sound and well balanced mind is one of those facts now so well established, that to question it would only betray the height of ignorance and presumption." Id. at 32.

47. State v. Pike, 1870, 49 N.H. 399.

48. Cf. State v. Jones, 1871, 50 N.H. 369, 398.

convey to the jury the sense and substance of the following: If you the jury believe beyond a reasonable doubt that the accused was not suffering from a diseased or defective mental condition at the time he committed the criminal act charged, you may find him guilty. If you believe he was suffering from a diseased or defective mental condition when he committed the act, but believe beyond a reasonable doubt that the act was not the product of such mental abnormality, you may find him guilty. Unless you believe beyond a reasonable doubt either that he was not suffering from a diseased or defective mental condition, or that the act was not the product of such abnormality, you must find the accused not guilty by reason of insanity. Thus your task would not be completed upon finding, if you did find, that the accused suffered from a mental disease or defect. He would still be responsible for his unlawful act if there was no causal connection between such mental abnormality and the act.[49] These questions must be determined by you from the facts which you find to be fairly deducible from the testimony and the evidence in this case.

* * *

The legal and moral traditions of the western world require that those who, of their own free will and with evil intent (sometimes called *mens rea*), commit acts which violate the law, shall be criminally responsible for those acts. Our traditions also require that where such acts stem from and are the product of a mental disease or defect as those terms are used herein, moral blame shall not attach, and hence there will not be criminal responsibility.[57] The rule we state in this opinion is designed to meet these requirements.[1]

Reversed and remanded for a new trial.

---

49. "There is no *a priori* reason why every person suffering from any form of mental abnormality or disease, or from any particular kind of mental disease, should be treated by the law as not answerable for any criminal offence which he may commit, and be exempted from conviction and punishment. Mental abnormalities vary infinitely in their nature and intensity and in their effects on the character and conduct of those who suffer from them. Where a person suffering from a mental abnormality commits a crime, there must always be some likelihood that the abnormality has played some part in the causation of the crime; and, generally speaking, the graver the abnormality, . . . the more probable it must be that there is a causal connection between them. But the closeness of this connection will be shown by the facts brought in evidence in individual cases and cannot be decided on the basis of any general medical principle." Royal Commission Report 99.

57. An accused person who is acquitted by reason of insanity is presumed to be insane, Orencia v. Overholser, 1947, 82 U.S.App.D.C. 285, 163 F.2d 763; Barry v. White, 1933, 62 App.D.C. 69, 64 F.2d 707, and may be committed for an indefinite period to a "hospital for the insane." D.C.Code § 24–301 (1951).

We think that even where there has been a specific finding that the accused was competent to stand trial and to assist in his own defense, the court would be well advised to invoke this Code provision so that the accused may be confined as long as "the public safety and . . . [his] welfare" require. Barry v. White, 62 App. D.C. at page 71, 64 F.2d at page 709.

1. (Added by Compiler) "This Court has no desire to join the courts of New Hampshire and the District of Columbia in their 'magnificent isolation' of rebellion against M'Naghten, . . ." Andersen v. United States, 237 F.2d

UNITED STATES v. CURRENS

United States Court of Appeals, Third Circuit, 1961.
290 F.2d 751.

[Currens was convicted of a violation of the National Motor Vehicle Theft Act—the so-called "Dyer Act". Instructing on the theory of the defense—insanity—the trial judge charged the jury in terms of the right-wrong test of the "M'Naghten rules" and on irresistible impulse, but refused defendant's request to include an instruction in the terms recommended in Durham. This refusal is claimed to have been error.]

BIGGS, CHIEF JUDGE. . . . The Durham formula has been severely criticized on the ground that it is too vague and indefinite to provide a workable rule for the determination of criminal responsibility. Two of the key words "disease" and "defect" are defined to a limited extent in the opinion. The word "product" was not defined and this led the American Law Institute to reject the Durham formula as a test for its proposed Model Penal Code. See also the excellent opinion of Judge Brosman in United States v. Smith, 5 U.S.C.M.A. 314, which is critical of the Durham formula because of alleged vagueness. . . .

To achieve the necessary foundation to resolve the vital issue of criminal responsibility it is necessary that the entire picture of the defendant be presented to the court and to the jury insofar as the rules of evidence will allow. The defendant's entire relevant symptomatology must be brought before the court and fully explained. Such a course assigns to the medical expert, the psychiatrist, his proper duty in the criminal proceedings. The psychiatrist must make his contribution, from his knowledge, experience and examinations of the accused, in respect to his behavior. Mental illness, resulting in criminal acts, is not a sudden growth, even if the prohibited conduct seems, at first sight, to be of a sudden, explosive nature. The way must be cleared in every case, in which the mental condition of the defendant is at issue, for the psychiatrist to explain the condition of the defendant to the jury in understandable terms. . . .

Were this our only objective the Durham formula might be held to be sufficient. As we have previously pointed out, the psychiatrist, under the Durham formula, may give the jury a complete picture of the defendant's mental condition. It is not enough, however, in a case

118, 127 (9th Cir. 1956. Accord, Sauer v. United States, 241 F.2d 640 (9th Cir. 1957); Howard v. United States, 229 F.2d 602 (5th Cir. 1956).

A man who has sufficient reason to know that the act he is doing is wrong and deserves punishment is legally of sound mind and is criminally responsible for his acts. Revard v. State, 332 P.2d 967 (Okl.Cr.1958).

such as that at bar, to give the jury a complete picture of the defendant's mental condition. The jury must be further provided with a standard or formula by means of which it can translate that mental condition into an answer to the ultimate question of whether the defendant possessed the necessary guilty mind to commit the crime charged. Our second objective is, therefore, to verbalize the relationship between mental disease and the concept of "guilty mind" in a way that will be both meaningful to a jury charged with the duty of determining the issue of criminal responsibility and consistent with the basic aims, purposes and assumptions of the criminal law. See the illuminating concurring opinion of Judge Burger in Blocker v. United States, supra.

The concept of *mens rea*, guilty mind, is based on the assumption that a person has a capacity to control his behavior and to choose between alternative courses of conduct. This assumption, though not unquestioned by theologians, philosophers and scientists, is necessary to the maintenance and administration of social controls. It is only through this assumption that society has found it possible to impose duties and create liabilities designed to safeguard persons and property. . . . It should be made clear to the jury that the fact that a defendant was mentally diseased is not determinative of criminal responsibility in and of itself but is significant only insofar as it indicates the extent to which the particular defendant lacked normal powers of control and choice at the time he committed the criminal conduct with which he is charged. In other words the test must provide the jury with a verbal tool by which it can relate the defendant's mental disease to his total personality and by means of which it can render an ultimate social and moral judgment.

The Durham formula obviously does not meet these requirements. Under that test the prosecution must prove, in substance, that the act committed was not the product of mental disease or defect. The test stresses, to the complete exclusion of all other considerations, a possible causal connection between the mental disease with which the defendant is afflicted and the act which he committed. When considering this test it is natural to think of the mental disease as a distinct vital force in the defendant's mind, producing some acts but not others. Insofar as it has this effect the test is, in much the same way as the M'Naghten Rules are, subject to the criticism that it wrongly assumes that the mind can be broken up into compartments, one part sane and the other insane. . . .

We are of the opinion that the following formula most nearly fulfills the objectives just discussed: The jury must be satisfied that at the time of committing the prohibited act the defendant, as a result of mental disease or defect, lacked substantial capacity to con-

Sec. 2   MENTAL DISEASE OR DEFECT (INSANITY)   479

form his conduct to the requirements of the law which he is alleged to have violated.[1] . . .

The judgment of conviction will be reversed and a new trial ordered, with directions to proceed in accordance with this opinion.

HASTIE, CIRCUIT JUDGE (dissenting in part). . . .

FEGUER v. UNITED STATES

United States Court of Appeals, Eighth Circuit, (1962).
302 F.2d 214.

[Dr. Bartels left his home in Dubuque, Iowa, in response to a telephone call for medical assistance. He did not return and his body was found a few days later in Illinois. He had been shot. Defendant was indicted under the National Kidnaping Act, in that he had knowingly transported the kidnaped person in interstate commerce and the victim had not been liberated unharmed. The trial resulted in a verdict of guilty and the jury recommended death.]

BLACKMUN, CIRCUIT JUDGE. .

4. *Instructions as to the defense of insanity.*

The trial court's instructions to the jury with respect to the issue of the defendant's sanity at the time of the commission of the crime embraced the right and wrong test, which emerged from M'Naghten's Case, 1843, 10 Cl. & Fin. 200, 8 Eng.Rep. 718, *plus* the additional condition of absence of an uncontrollable or irresistible impulse. The refused instructions offered by the defense incorporated respectively (a) the Durham standard in the exact form suggested by the Court of Appeals for the District of Columbia in Durham v. United States, 1954, 94 U.S.App.D.C. 228, 214 F.2d 862, 875, 45 A.L.R.2d 1430; (b) the American Law Institute proposals contained in its Model Penal Code, and (c) a charge, based on § 402(2) of that Code, which would

---

1. "To lack 'substantial capacity to conform his conduct to the requirements of law' is to have an irresistible impulse" ("an almost unusable defense"). Freedman, Guttmacher and Overholser, Mental Disease or Defect Excluding Responsibility. 1961 Wash.U.L.Q. 250, 252.

New Jersey adheres to the M'Naghten rule governing insanity as a defense, but with respect to whether the penalty should be death or imprisonment for life, it will permit evidence of mental disorder unrestrained by the M'Naghten concept. State v. Di Paolo, 34 N.J. 279, 168 A.2d 401 (1961).

By statute, Maine abolished the M'Naghten Rule and adopted the Durham Rule in substance. "An accused is not criminally responsible if his unlawful act was the product of mental disease or mental defect". In holding that mental disease or defect, insufficient to establish innocence, does not compel a reduction of homicide from murder to manslaughter, the court said: "We had no such rule of partial or limited responsibility under the McNaghten (sic) Rule. There is nothing inherent in our Durham Rule requiring the creation of a new zone of uncertain width with changing shadows for the benefit of those charged with crime." State v. Park, 159 Me. 328, 193 A.2d 1 (1963).

require the jury to consider, in determining punishment and in **favor of life imprisonment as distinguished from the death penalty, any impairment of the defendant's capacity because of mental disease or defect.** . . .

(a) So far as the proposed instruction based on the Durham rule is concerned, we need only observe that this court three times, in the last three and one-half years, has refused to follow the Durham case. We adhere to that position and note, as we pass, that it has been said that "Every court which considered Durham has rejected it". Blocker v. United States, supra, concurring opinion, p. 866 of 288 F.2d and cases cited there in footnote 22. . . .

(c) This leaves for consideration the propriety of the trial court's use of the right and wrong test of M'Naghten plus irresistible impulse and the court's alleged refusal to incorporate into its instructions all the features of the Model Penal Code's proposal. We need not at this late date review in detail the origin, history, application, and variations of M'Naghten. This has been done adequately and at length in many places. We note, as we have before in Voss v. United States, supra, pp. 702–703 of 259 F.2d; Dusky v. United States, supra, p. 394 of 271 F.2d; and Dusky v. United States, supra, p. 753 of 295 F.2d, that the Supreme Court of the United States, thus far at least, has approved the use of the M'Naghten right and wrong test. . . .

Neither need we attempt to ascertain in what respects, if any, the Model Penal Code's proposal varies in substance from the instructions actually given by the trial court here, or to formulate a more acceptable variation of it as the Third Circuit has tried to do in United States v. Currens, supra, p. 774, footnote 32, of 290 F.2d.

This court's approach to this issue was set forth in the second Dusky, supra, 295 F.2d 743, decided since the present defendant's trial and conviction. We repeat what was said there, p. 759:

"We might add by way of addendum, . . . that we are fully aware of the controversy presently pending in the federal courts over the respective merits of M'Naghten and its irresistible impulse and other variations, and Durham and of other suggested definitions of insanity as a defense to crime. We are aware specifically not only of Durham itself and of our rejection of it in the first Dusky appeal and in Voss, supra, 259 F.2d 699, to which rejection we continue to adhere, but of the approximately 80 cases, after Durham and occasioned by it, which have come before the Court of Appeals of the District of Columbia. . . .[1]

---

1. "Since its announcement in 1954, the rule of the Durham case has not been adopted in a single state adhering to the M'Naghten Rule, and the most recent decisons expressly reject both the Durham Rule and the proposed American Law Institute rule, and reaffirm M'Naghten, Dare v. State (Okl.1963), 378 P.2d 339; State v. White, (1962), 60 Wash.2d 551, 374 P.2d 942; Chase v. State of Alaska, (Ala.1962), 369 P.2d 997; Newsome v. Commonwealth, (Ky.

Sec. 2   MENTAL DISEASE OR DEFECT (INSANITY)   481

The present case is one where the trial court employed instructions on insanity which this court had theretofore approved in Voss and in the first Dusky. Furthermore, the court's instructions here met the standard of the second Dusky namely, the embracement and requirement of positive findings, as to three elements, the defendant's cognition, his volition, and his capacity to control his behavior. Knowledge, will, and choice are all emphasized in the court's charge as essential constituents of the defendant's legal sanity. We therefore hold, in line with what we said in the second Dusky, that the trial court's definition of insanity as given to the jury in this case is not improper. . . .

Affirmed.

STATE v. WHITE

Supreme Court of Washington, En Banc, 1962.
60 Wash.2d 551, 374 P.2d 942.

DONWORTH, JUDGE. Appellant was charged, by Information, with committing two murders alleged to have been committed at different times and places on the same day (December 24, 1959). . . .

Assignment No. 9. Appellant contends that:
"The court erred in giving instruction No. 33 and further erred in failing to give the appellant's requested instructions on mental irresponsibility, which is the American Law Institute test for mental irresponsibility."

Instruction No. 33 told the jury that:
"You are instructed that the term 'mental irresponsibility', as used alternatively with the term 'insanity' in the further plea of the defendant and elsewhere in these instructions, means what is defined in law as criminal insanity. Therefore, if you find that the defendant was mentally irresponsible under the definition as contained herein, you must find the defendant not guilty by reason of mental irresponsibility.

"If the defendant is to be acquitted upon his plea of mental irresponsibility or insanity, he must convince you by a preponderance of the evidence that, at the time the crime is alleged to have been committed, his mind was diseased to such an extent that he was unable to perceive the moral qualities of the act with which he is charged, and was unable to tell right from wrong with reference to the particular act charged. A person may be sick or diseased in body or mind and

1963), 366 S.W.2d 174; State v. Poulson, 14 Utah 2d 213, 381 P.2d 93. While we are not controlled by the number of court cases of other jurisdictions on the question we do believe that they are most persuasive under present day circumstances." State v. Noble, 142 Mont. 284, 384 P.2d 504 (1963).

yet be able to distinguish right from wrong with respect to a particular act."

Proposed instruction No. 21 (if substituted in place of No. 33) would have stated the rule as follows: . . .

" 'Mental irresponsibility means that the defendant is not responsible for the crimes charged herein if at the time of said crimes, as a result of mental disease or defect, he lacked substantial capacity either to appreciate the criminality of his act, or to conform his conduct to the requirements of law.

" 'The terms "mental disease" or "defect" do not include an abnormality manifested only by repeated criminal or otherwise antisocial conduct.' "

The essential difference between the two instructions is that the instruction which was given to the jury did not allow for an acquittal based on insanity or mental irresponsibility, if the accused had cognition (the ability to understand the nature and quality of his acts) with regard to what he did, even though his volition (his capacity "to conform his conduct to the requirements of the law") may have been substantially impaired by mental disease or defect. In other words, under the given instruction, the defense of "not guilty by reason of mental irresponsibility" is not available to a person who has the ability to understand the nature and quality of his acts, but, because of mental disease or defect, is somehow unable to control his own behavior.

The proposed but rejected instruction was based upon § 4.01 of the Model Penal Code, which test has since been adopted by the American Law Institute, on May 24, 1962. The concept that volitional control is an element of sanity for the purpose of criminal responsibility is accepted in several states. Some recognize "irresistible impulse" as a defense; others use language much like that found in the American Law Institute test.

The instruction which was assigned as error (No. 33) is based on the M'Naghten rule, which is the law in the majority of states.

The question whether the jury was correctly instructed is squarely presented by the facts of this case. There was substantial evidence from which the jury could have found that appellant could not control his own behavior, even though, at the time, he knew the difference between right and wrong. . . .

Before the two tests between which the trial court was compelled to make a choice are discussed, a third test should be mentioned. That third test is the "product" test, often called the Durham rule because of the widespread notoriety it received upon being adopted in the District of Columbia in Durham v. United States, 94 App. D.C. 228, 214 F.2d 862, 45 A.L.R.2d 1430 (1954). In essence, this rule is that a defendant in a criminal case is not responsible if his unlawful act was the product of a mental disease or mental defect.

The rule in New Hampshire has been stated in the same way for over ninety years. State v. Pike, 49 N.H. 399, 6 Am.Rep. 533 (1870), and State v. Jones, 50 N.H. 369, 9 Am.Rep. 242 (1871).

However, very recently the Court of Appeals in the District of Columbia has gone far beyond the original Durham rule as it was first adopted by that court in 1954.

In Campbell v. United States, D.C.Cir., 307 F.2d 597 (March 29, 1962), the conviction of a defendant with an "emotionally unstable personality" (administratively classified by government psychiatrists as a mental disease since 1957) was reversed. It was held by the majority that the instructions of the trial court placed too much emphasis upon the defendant's capacity to control his own behavior, rather than simply instructing the jury that they must determine whether the criminal act was a product of a mental disease. They say that the test is whether he would have committed the act if he had not been the victim of a mental disease, to wit, an emotionally unstable personality. Thus, they hold that the defendant could be found innocent if his motivation was the result of such mental disease, regardless of whether or not the sanctions of the criminal law as a deterrent could have influenced him.

The fallacy in that view, as pointed out by Judge Burger in his very vigorous dissent, is that almost all criminals could come under such a definition of insanity. . . .

What is meant by "criminal insanity" and mental irresponsibility" in our statute? It has consistently been held that both terms mean the same thing for purposes of criminal responsibility. The test is M'Naghten. State v. Maish, 29 Wash.2d 52, 185 P.2d 486, 173 A.L.R. 382 (1947), made it especially clear that Washington has rejected the volitional test as embodied in the so-called "irresistible impulse" rule. . . .[1]

With regard to capacity to control one's behavior, it would appear that there is no more psychiatric certainty today than there was when this court decided State v. Maish, supra.

Finally, M'Naghten is preferable to the American Law Institute test in that the M'Naghten rule better serves the basic purpose of the criminal law—to minimize crime in society. The earlier quotation from Wechsler pointed out that, when M'Naghten is used, all who might possibly be deterred from the commission of criminal acts are included within the sanctions of the criminal law. Sol Rubin points out that the application of the M'Naghten rule can even help in the rehabilitation process:

" . . . The M'Naghten rule declares that one who is so far removed from reality that he does not know the nature of his act does

---

[1]. The irresistible-impulse defense is not recognized. People v. Gorshen, 51 Cal.2d 716, 336 P.2d 492 (1959); Piccott v. State, 116 So.2d 626 (Fla.1960). It is recognized in the federal courts. Pollard v. United States, 282 F.2d 450 (6th Cir. 1960).

not have the mentality to be adjudged responsible. Such a holding is inevitable because of the requirement of *mens rea*. But the Durham rule would exculpate a defendant who does know the nature of his act. For the law to tell such a person that he is not responsible for his act is likely to deter and complicate his rehabilitation, because it contradicts common sense fact. To declare that such a defendant is legally responsible, but, because of his mental illness, is subject to special treatment is more consistent with reality and more likely to support his rehabilitation. . . ." "A New Approach to M'Naghten v. Durham," 45 J.Am.Jud.Soc'y 133, 136 (December, 1961).

Mr. Rubin then continues the discussion of this subject in his article and supports his position with cogent reasoning.

In summary, then, not only would any other rule be difficult to apply, but the M'Naghten rule is, for good reason, the established rule in the State of Washington. There was no error in giving the jury the instruction (No. 33) based on that test, nor in refusing to instruct on the basis of any other test of mental responsibility as requested by appellant. . . .

CONCLUSION

We have carefully considered each of appellant's assignments of error in the light of the record and the law applicable thereto. We are of the opinion that appellant had a fair trial. Finding no reversible error in the record, the judgment and sentence of the trial court entered upon the several verdicts of the jury must be affirmed.

. . .

The judgment and sentence is hereby affirmed.[2]

WEAVER, OTT and ROSELLINI, JJ., concur.

HILL, JUDGE (concurring specially).

I concur in the majority opinion. However, I find myself in accord with some of the views expressed by Chief Justice Weintraub of the Supreme Court of New Jersey, in a concurring opinion in State

---

2. "[Under the original M'Naghten language from which the California rule has been evolved] a mentally ill defendant could be found sane even though his 'knowledge' of the nature or wrongfulness of his act was merely a capacity to verbalize the 'right' (i. e., socially expected) answers to questions put to him relating to that act, without such 'knowledge' having any affective meaning for him as a principle of conduct. Such a narrow, literal reading of the M'Naughton [sic] formula has been repeatedly and justly condemned. Rather, it is urged by many that the word 'know' as used in the formula be given 'a wider definition so that it means the kind of knowing that is relevant, i. e., realization or appreciation of the wrongness of seriously harming a human being'. 'If the word "know" were given this broader interpretation, so as to require knowledge "fused with affect" and assimilated by the whole personality—so that, for example, the killer was capable of identifying with his prospective victim—much of the criticism of the knowledge test would be met.'" People v. Wolff, 61 Cal.2d 795, 800, 40 Cal.Rptr. 271, 273–74, 394 P.2d 959, 961–62 (1964).

Sec. 2   MENTAL DISEASE OR DEFECT (INSANITY)   485

v. Lucas (1959), 30 N.J. 37, 152 A.2d 50; he says (p. 83, 152 A.2d p. 75):

"No one will dispute that society must be protected from the insane as well as the sane. The area of disagreement is whether a civil or a criminal process should be employed when forbidden acts have been committed. If we could think of a conviction simply as a finding that the mortal in question has demonstrated his capacity for anti-social conduct, most of the battle would be decided. What would remain is the employment of such post-conviction techniques as would redeem the offender if he can be redeemed and secure him if he cannot. . . .

[Three judges expressed a preference for the position taken in Currens.]

Petition for writ of habeas corpus dismissed. White v. Rhay, 64 Wash.2d 15, 390 P.2d 535 (1964).

ARGENT v. UNITED STATES

United States Court of Appeals, Fifth Circuit, 1963.
325 F.2d 162.

RIVES, CIRCUIT JUDGE. The indictment charged that the defendant "did, with unlawful and fraudulent intent, cause to be transported in interstate commerce from Pensacola, Florida, to Montgomery, Alabama, a falsely made and forged . . . check . . . in the amount of $20.00, knowing the same to have been falsely made and forged. (18 U.S.C. 2314)"

The defendant never, at any time, denied that he caused the forged check to be transported in interstate commerce. . . .

The test of a knowledge of right and wrong as applied to the particular act was established in the great leading case of McNaghten, [sic] 10 Clark & Finn 200, decided in 1843 before the English House of Lords. "It was decided by the judges in that case that, in order to entitle the accused to acquittal, it must be clearly proved that, at the time of committing the offense, he was laboring under such a defect of reason, from disease of the mind, as not to know the nature and quality of the act he was doing, or, if he did, not to know that what he was doing was wrong."

As to the burden of proof, the Supreme Court of the United States repudiated the rule of the McNaghten [sic] case in Davis v. United States, 1895, 160 U.S. 469, 486, 487, 488, 16 S.Ct. 353, 358, 40 L.Ed. 469,[1] where it was said:

---

1. Oregon formerly required the accused on a plea of insanity to establish that defense beyond a reasonable doubt. This was held not to be a violation of due process. Leland v. Oregon, 343 U.S. 790, 72 S.Ct. 1002, 96 L.Ed. 1302 (1952). Some twenty states place the burden on the accused to establish his insanity by a preponderance of the evidence.

"In a certain sense it may be true that where the defence is insanity, and where the case made by the prosecution discloses nothing whatever in excuse or extenuation of the crime charged, the accused is bound to produce some evidence that will impair or weaken the force of the legal presumption in favor of sanity. But to hold that such presumption must absolutely control the jury until it is overthrown or impaired by evidence sufficient to establish the fact of insanity beyond all reasonable doubt or to the reasonable satisfaction of the jury, is in effect to require him to establish his innocence by proving that he is not guilty of the crime charged.

* * * * * * * *

"Strictly speaking, the burden of proof, as those words are understood in criminal law, is never upon the accused to establish his innocence or to disprove the facts necessary to establish the crime for which he is indicted. It is on the prosecution from the beginning to the end of the trial and applies to every element necessary to constitute the crime. Giving to the prosecution, where the defence is insanity, the benefit in the way of proof of the presumption in favor of sanity, the vital question from the time a plea of not guilty is entered until the return of the verdict, is whether upon all the evidence, by whatever side adduced, guilt is established beyond reasonable doubt. If the whole evidence, including that supplied by the presumption of sanity, does not exclude beyond reasonable doubt the hypothesis of insanity, of which some proof is adduced, the accused is entitled to an acquittal of the specific offence charged. . . ."

Reversed and remanded.[2]

JONES, CIRCUIT JUDGE (dissenting in part). . . .

MODEL PENAL CODE

Article 4. Responsibility

Section 4.01. Mental Disease or Defect Excluding Responsibility.

(1) A person is not responsible for criminal conduct if at the time of such conduct as a result of mental disease or defect he lacks substantial

---

Evidence that a man of 28 has the mind of a normal boy of 11 does not raise a presumption of criminal incapacity. State v. Schilling, 95 N.J.L. 145, 112 A. 400 (1920).

2. A statute withdrawing the defense of insanity from the court and jury and vesting it in a commission is unconstitutional. State v. Lange, 168 La. 958, 123 So. 639, 67 A.L.R. 1447 (1929). An accused has a constitutional right to have a jury pass upon his insanity defense. State v. Strasburg, 60 Wash. 106, 110 P. 1020 (1910). The "bifurcated trial" provided in some jurisdictions has been upheld. Under this procedure, if defendant pleads both not guilty and not guilty by reason of insanity, all other issues are decided in the trial under the general plea, after which if the verdict is guilty the insanity issue is determined under the special plea. See Louisell and Hazard, Insanity as a Defense: The Bifurcated Trial, 49 Cal.L.Rev. 805 (1961).

capacity either to appreciate the criminality [wrongfulness] of his conduct or to conform his conduct to the requirements of law.

(2) As used in this Article, the terms "mental disease or defect" do not include an abnormality manifested only by repeated criminal or otherwise anti-social conduct.

Section 4.02.   Evidence of Mental Disease or Defect Admissible When Relevant to Element of the Offense; [Mental Disease or Defect Impairing Capacity as Ground for Mitigation of Punishment in Capital Cases].

(1) Evidence that the defendant suffered from a mental disease or defect is admissible whenever it is relevant to prove that the defendant did or did not have a state of mind which is an element of the offense.

[(2) Whenever the jury or the Court is authorized to determine or to recommend whether or not the defendant shall be sentenced to death or imprisonment upon conviction, evidence that the capacity of the defendant to appreciate the criminality [wrongfulness] of his conduct or to conform his conduct to the requirements of law was impaired as a result of mental disease or defect is admissible in favor of sentence of imprisonment.]

Section 4.03.   Mental Disease or Defect Excluding Responsibility Is Affirmative Defense; Requirement of Notice; Form of Verdict and Judgment When Finding of Irresponsibility is Made.

(1) Mental disease or defect excluding responsibility is an affirmative defense.

(2) Evidence of mental disease or defect excluding responsibility is not admissible unless the defendant, at the time of entering his plea of not guilty or within ten days thereafter or at such later time as the Court may for good cause permit, files a written notice of his purpose to rely on such defense.

(3) When the defendant is acquitted on the ground of mental disease or defect excluding responsibility, the verdict and the judgment shall so state.

SECTION 3.   DRUNKENNESS (INTOXICATION)

The early common law seems to have ignored the problem of intoxication at the time of the *actus reus*.[1] Coke and Blackstone, in fact, were inclined to urge that intoxication of one who committed a harmful deed should be regarded as a circumstance of aggravation. This suggestion was not adopted, but prior to the nineteenth century drunkenness, to whatever extent, was no defense in a criminal case. Since then there have been some modifications of that strict rule. Three modifications usually are mentioned: (1) Involuntary intoxication may be so extreme as to be exculpating; (2) voluntary intoxica-

1. Under the law of England until the early 19th Century voluntary intoxication was never an excuse for criminal misconduct. Director of Public Prosecutions v. Beard, [1920] App.Cas. 479.

tion may entitle the defendant to an acquittal if the crime charged requires a specific intent and he was too drunk to have such intent; (3) delirium tremens is treated the same as other types of insanity although it results from overindulgence in liquor.

Firmly entrenched in the common law, although the wisdom thereof has been questioned by some, is the rule that voluntary intoxication is never exculpating. It is necessary, however, to draw a clear distinction between lack of excuse, on one hand, and disproof of some essential element of the crime charged, on the other. If the offense charged requires a specific intent, the defendant is not guilty if he was too intoxicated at the time to have any such intent, and had not entertained such an intent prior to his intoxication.[2] In such a case, proof of extreme intoxication (although "voluntary") may result in an acquittal, but it is not on any theory of exculpation. Suppose D has been indicted for burglary, for example. The indictment charges that D broke and entered the dwelling house of X at night with intent to steal. The evidence shows that D opened the front door of X's house late at night, went in and was found in a drunken stupor on the floor. He was searched and it was learned that he had taken nothing. And when he is tried the jury is satisfied that while he managed to stumble into X's house before he lost consciousness, his mind was too befogged with drink to be capable of entertaining any intent. Such a finding will not support a conviction of burglary.[3] This is not on any theory of excusing his conduct. One of the essential elements of the crime charged is missing. If he broke and entered the dwelling house of another at night (however wrongfully), he is still not guilty of burglary unless he did so with the intention of committing some crime therein (which crime must amount to felony at common law). Any evidence which proves the absence of such intent will disprove the charge of burglary.[4]

A man should not be convicted of larceny upon proof that he drank until his mind was so blank that he staggered away from the bar still clutching the glass from which he had been drinking, but unable to realize this fact or to entertain any intent. One who jumps from a bridge into the water below for the purpose of ending his life

---

2. One who drinks to "nerve" himself to commit a crime already decided upon, and who thereupon does commit that crime, is not in a position to maintain that he was too drunk at the time to entertain the intent which he executed. State v. Butner, 66 Nev. 127, 206 P.2d 253 (1949); State v. Robinson, 20 W.Va. 713 (1882).

3. State v. Phillips, 80 W.Va. 748, 93 S.W. 828 (1917). And a fumbling effort to get into a building by one too drunk to be capable of entertaining any intent is not an attempt to commit burglary. People v. Jones, 263 Ill. 564, 105 N.E. 744 (1914).

4. Or any other crime requiring a specific intent, such as larceny. Johnson v. State, 32 Ala.App. 217, 24 So.2d 228 (1945); People v. Walker, 38 Mich. 156 (1878); Jamison v. State, 53 Okl. Cr. 59, 7 P.2d 171 (1932). Or assault with intent to commit rape. Whitten v. State, 115 Ala. 72, 22 So. 483 (1896). Or the "felony-murder" rule. People v. Koerber, 244 N.Y. 147, 155 N.E. 79 (1926).

is punishable for an attempt to commit suicide, in some jurisdictions. But the inebriate who stumbles against the rail and tumbles over after the last spark of intelligence has faded from his mind is not guilty of such an attempt,—because an attempt requires a specific intent.[5] A drunkard (voluntarily drunk) walking with an axe on his shoulder who staggers in such a manner as to bump another with the axe is guilty of battery. This is true however intoxicated he may be because battery requires no more than criminal negligence. But he is not guilty of assault with intent to murder if he had no such intention. And proof that he was too dazed at the time to be capable of entertaining any intent will disprove the aggravated charge.

Provocation. Voluntary homicide is manslaughter rather than murder if it results from heat of passion engendered by adequate provocation and before the lapse of the "cooling time." Whether the provocation received was adequate or inadequate, and whether the time between the provocation and the fatal blow was sufficient or insufficient for passion once inflamed to subside, are both measured by an objective test,—the ordinary reasonable man. Hence the fact of intoxication has no bearing on the adequacy of the provocation or the sufficiency of the time for "cooling."[6] But whether the killing was actually in hot blood or cold blood depends upon the frame of mind of the killer himself. And if the fact of intoxication tends to throw any light upon the frame of mind of the defendant at the moment of the killing, the jury should have the benefit of this evidence with an instruction to consider it on this point only.[7]

Alcoholism. The fact that alcoholism is a disease, not to be cured by frequent periods of incarceration for public drunkenness, or disorderly conduct, has not received due attention in the enforcement of justice.

---

5. In a prosecution for attempted suicide intoxication of the prisoner at the time of the alleged attempt "is a material fact in order to arrive at the conclusion whether or not the prisoner really intended to destroy his life." Regina v. Doody, 6 Cox C.C. 463 (1854).

In a robbery trial there was evidence tending to show that D was too drunk at the time to form an intent to rob. It was reversible error for the judge to refuse to let this issue go to the jury. Womack v. United States, 336 F.2d 959 (D.C.Cir. 1964).

6. Bishop v. United States, 71 App.D.C. 132, 107 F.2d 297 (1939); Keenan v. Commonwealth, 44 Pa. 55 (1862); Willis v. Commonwealth, 73 Va. 929 (1879); Rex v. Carroll, 7 Car. & P. 145, 173 Eng.Rep. 64 (1835).

Some courts have repeated Bishop's suggestion that an intent to drink may supply the malice aforethought needed for guilt of murder. See, for example, Newsome v. State, 214 Ark. 48, 50, 214 S.W.2d 778, 779 (1948); Weakley v. State, 168 Ark. 1087, 1089, 273 S.W. 374, 376 (1925).

7. Rex v. Thomas, 7 Car. & P. 817, 173 Eng.Rep. 356 (1837).

STATE v. BROWN

Supreme Court of Kansas, 1888.
38 Kan. 390, 16 P. 259.

VALENTINE, J. This was a criminal prosecution, brought in the district court of Chase county, wherein the defendant, John Brown, is charged with a violation of the provisions of chapter 104, Laws 1883 (Comp.Laws 1885, c. 31, par. 2223). The statute reads as follows: "Section 1. If any person shall be drunk in any highway, street, or in any public place or building, or if any person shall be drunk in his own house, or any private building or place, disturbing his family or others, he shall be deemed guilty of a misdemeanor, and upon conviction thereof, shall be fined in any sum not exceeding twenty-five dollars, or by imprisonment in the county jail for a period not exceeding thirty days." The information contains two counts,—in the first of which the defendant is charged with the offense of being drunk in a street in the city of Cottonwood Falls; in the second, he is charged with the offense of being drunk in the court-house in said city. A trial was had before the court and a jury, and the defendant was found guilty "as charged in the information," and was sentenced to pay a fine of $10 and the costs of suit, and to stand committed to the county jail until such fine and costs were paid. From this sentence he now appeals to this court. . . .

The next question is a more difficult one. It is whether a person may be guilty of the offense forbidden by the statute, where he innocently drinks the liquor which intoxicates him, without having any knowledge of its intoxicating qualities, and without having any idea that it would make him drunk. The court below, over his objections and exceptions, excluded nearly all the evidence offered by him to show his ignorance of the intoxicating character of the liquor, and its possible power to produce drunkenness; and the court also gave, among others, the following instruction to the jury, to-wit: "The defendant's ignorance of the intoxicating character of liquors drank by him, if he did drink any such, is no excuse for any drunkenness resulting therefrom, if any did so result." It has always been a rule of law that ignorance or mistake of law never excuses, and this, with a kindred rule that all men are conclusively presumed to know the law, is founded upon public policy, and grounded in necessity; but no such rule is invoked in this case. The question in this case is simply whether ignorance or mistake of *fact* will excuse. It is claimed by the prosecution that it will not; and this, on account of the express terms of the statute. The statute provides in express terms, and without any exception, that "if any person shall be drunk," etc., he shall be punished. And it would seem to be contended that there can be no exceptions. But are idiots, insane persons, children under seven years of age, babes, and persons who have been made drunk by force or fraud, and carried into a public place, to be punished under the statute? And if not, why not? And, if these are not to be punished, then no sufficient reason can be given for punishing those who have become drunk through unavoidable accident, or through an honest mistake. . . . Voluntary drunkenness in a public place was always a misdemeanor at common law, and it was always wrong, morally and legally. It is *malum in se*. Therefore, under either the rule enunciated by Mr. Bishop, or the one enunciated by Mr. Greenleaf, this case was erroneously tried in the court below. Whether the latter portion of said section of Mr. Greenleaf's evidence is correct or not it is not necessary for us now to decide. Whether a party, who, through an honest ignorance or mistake of fact, commits an act which is only *malum prohibitum*, may be punished for the act or not, it is not necessary now to determine. Mr. Bishop would say not; Mr. Greenleaf, following the Massachusetts supreme court decisions, would say he should be. Mr. Bishop's views are more in consonance with justice.

Before closing this opinion, it might be well to state that the fact that the defendant became intoxicated through an honest mistake might not constitute a complete defense to the action. If, after becoming drunk, he was still sufficiently in the possession of his faculties to know what he was doing, and to know the character of his acts, and went voluntarily into a public place, he would be guilty.

The judgment of the court below will be reversed, and cause remanded for a new trial.

(All the justices concurring.)

PEOPLE v. PENMAN

Supreme Court of Illinois, 1915.
271 Ill. 82, 110 N.E. 894.

DUNN, J. Augustus Penman, having been convicted in the circuit court of Champaign county of murder and sentenced to imprisonment in the penitentiary for life, has sued out a writ of error to reverse the judgment. . . .

Dr. Norbury made an examination of the plaintiff in error in the jail on September 4, 1913. After describing his physical characteristics and the general effects of cocaine upon a human being, he stated that the effects of the drug upon persons lasted from a few minutes to several days. He was asked, but the court refused to let him give his opinion, as to how long the effect upon the plaintiff in error would last, or whether it would cause a loss of consciousness or memory. Dr. Jesse testified that he was familiar with the effect of delirifacient drugs, and had made a study of cocaine and like drugs. The court refused to permit him to answer what were the symptoms of cocaine poisoning, or to give his opinion, from symptoms testified to and stated in a hypothetical question, as to what the plaintiff in error was suffering from, or to answer whether he had an opinion or not. Dr. Jesse saw the plaintiff in error at the doctor's house about 5 o'clock in the afternoon of Sunday, August 10th, and treated his eyes. He described his appearance and actions at that time. A hypothetical question was put to him, including his condition on Sunday. It was objected to on the ground that it took into consideration facts occurring on the day following the homicide, and he was not allowed to answer. The court should have allowed these questions to be answered. The plaintiff in error should not have been confined to mere opinions that he was suffering from cocaine poisoning and was insane, nor to his condition at the precise time of the events under investigation. Dr. Norbury, having testified that persons might be affected by cocaine from a few minutes to several days, should have been permitted to apply his knowledge directly to the case in hand, and to answer, from his personal examination of the plaintiff in error and the knowledge of his physical characteristics acquired by such examination, how long the plaintiff in error would be affected and whether his consciousness or memory would be affected. The plaintiff in error had a right to submit to the jury the expert's opinion on the concrete case. . . .

The plaintiff in error attempted to prove that the man who gave him the tablets in Danville told him they were breath perfumers, but was not permitted to do so. The testimony should have been received. The defense of insanity [1] was based upon the taking of those tablets and whether the defendant took them voluntarily, knowing what they were, or involuntarily took cocaine, supposing it to be some innocent thing, was a question materially affecting his responsibility. It was proper to show what was said, in order to show that he was deceived into taking the tablets, supposing them to be innocent. . .

The court refused instruction No. 56 asked by the defendant. This instruction is as follows:

"(56) The jury are instructed that if you believe, from the evidence, that the shooting alleged to have been done by the defendant was done at a time when the defendant was affected by and labored under an attack of a brief or temporary madness or insanity, the re-

---

1. "Intoxication" includes excitement or stupefaction induced by drugs as well as by liquor. People v. Lim Dum Dong, 26 Cal.App.2d 135, 78 P.2d 1026 (1938). A drunken frenzy is not insanity despite the fact that it has sometimes been referred to loosely as "delirium tremens". Cheadle v. State, 11 Okl.Cr. 566, 149 P. 919 (1915); State v. Kidwell, 62 W.Va. 466, 59 S.E. 494 (1907). Delirium tremens proper is a form of mental disease and is treated on the same basis as any other form of insanity. State v. Alexander, 215 La. 245, 40 So.2d 232 (1949).

The person suffering from delirium tremens is not free from fault, it is true, but the law takes notice only of the *immediate* condition which is a mental disease, and not of the excessive drinking which is *remote*. United States v. Drew, 25 Fed.Cas.No.14,993 (C.C.D.Mass.1828).

Voluntary intoxication is not an excuse but may be taken into consideration in determining the existence or nonexistence of malice aforethought which distinguishes murder from manslaughter. State v. Hudson, 85 Ariz. 77, 331 P.2d 1092 (1958).

sult of an involuntary taking by the defendant of some drug preceding the act, and that he was thereby rendered unconscious of what he was doing, that would constitute, in law, a complete and entire defense to the whole prosecution, and he should, under such state of the proof, be acquitted."

This instruction stated a correct rule of law which was not included in any other instruction given to the jury. It was error to refuse it.

Objection is made to the giving and refusal of other instructions, but we do not deem it necessary to discuss them.

For the errors indicated the judgment of the circuit court will be reversed, and the cause remanded.

Reversed and remanded.

FARMER, C. J., dissenting.

BURROWS v. STATE

Supreme Court of Arizona, 1931.
38 Ariz. 99, 297 P. 1029.

LOCKWOOD, J. Richard N. Burrows, hereinafter called defendant, on the 7th day of June, 1929, was informed against by the county attorney of Maricopa county for the crime of murder, alleged to have been committed April 26th of that year. He was duly tried on such information, and the jury returned a verdict finding defendant guilty of murder in the first degree, fixing the penalty at death, and, from the judgment rendered on the verdict and the order overruling the motion for a new trial, this appeal has been taken. With the exception of two points, which we shall refer to in the course of this opinion, there is singularly little conflict in the evidence, and we therefor [sic] state the facts as follows:

Defendant, whose home was in Chicago, was a boy of eighteen or nineteen, and during the spring of 1929 was at a military school in Delafield, Wis. His closest friend there was one Milton Drucker. The two boys apparently came to the conclusion they would leave school for the purpose of seeing the country, and, taking a car belonging to the Drucker boy's parents, started west. They were at that time in the possession of some $55 in cash, while Drucker had a small amount of money in bank. After some days' travel they reached Phoenix, and were there detained by the police at the request of Drucker's parents. The latter's mother came on from San Diego, where she had been staying, and took her son back to Chicago. Defendant asked permission to go back with them, but was informed by Mrs. Drucker that his adopted parents had decided it would be a good lesson for him if he had to shift for himself and go to work, and for that reason she would not take him. He was alone in Phoenix, unacquainted with any one except the police who had had him in charge for a few days, and substantially, if not entirely, without money. He determined to try to get back to Chicago, and beat his way by railroad as far as Aguila, Ariz., where he discovered that he was on the way to Los Angeles instead of Chicago. He then decided to try to get back to Phoenix, where he had left a suitcase containing personal effects, and make a new start for Chicago, and seeing one Jack Martin, whom we shall hereafter call deceased, at a filling station in Aguila, and discovering the latter was going to Phoenix, asked if he might ride with him. Deceased answered affirmatively, and the two started to Phoenix in the latter's car.

Deceased was either carrying intoxicating liquor in his car, or secured some along the road, for by the time they reached Morristown, a small town some fifty miles northwest of Phoenix, he was so obviously intoxicated that the service station proprietor there suggested to the two that defendant had better drive, to which deceased assented. They left Morristown, and some few miles beyond it defendant shot and killed deceased, who was at that time sitting slumped down in the car in a drunken stupor. Defendant drove the car off the road to a small arroyo, and after taking what money deceased had on his person, placed the body in the arroyo and partially covered it with dirt, took the car, and went on to Phoenix, where he stopped at the police station and secured his personal effects. He then drove on to Denver, Colo., where he was apprehended and brought back to Phoenix. This statement of the facts is based on defendant's own testimony, and in the absence of anything further unquestionably establishes beyond the peradventure of a doubt a case of murder in the first degree.

The only defense offered at the trial was one of involuntary intoxication. Defendant testified that shortly after they left Aguila deceased began urging him to drink some beer which he was carrying in the car. Defendant had never tasted intoxicating liquor and objected most strenuously, whereupon deceased became very abusive, stating that, if defendant would not drink he would put him out of the car. Defendant, being alone, penniless, and fearing that he might be ejected and left on the desert, did drink three or four bottles of the beer, and since he was unused to intoxicating liquor, and had had little to eat in the preceding twenty-four hours, began to feel very queer.

When the parties reached Wickenburg, deceased procured some whisky, and with increasing vehemence urged defendant to partake of that. At first the latter remonstrated, but finally, as he states, through fear of what deceased might do to him, did drink some whisky. He claimed that its effect was to make him sick at the stomach and dizzy, until he had very little idea of what was happening, and that at the time the shooting occurred he was so dazed that he was unable to realize what was happening until after the fatal shot was fired, when his mind cleared up and he did realize what he had done, and that his conduct thereafter was due to panic at realizing his situation, and an effort to escape from the consequences thereof. . . .

The real issue involved is as to the manner in which involuntary intoxication must be induced, and the extent to which it must go. So far as the last point is concerned, we are of the opinion that the intoxication must be sufficient to affect the reason of a defendant to the extent that he does not understand and appreciate the nature and consequences of his act, or, as is commonly said, that he does not know right from wrong.

The other point is more difficult. It is the contention of defendant that any suggestion or influence which induces another to become intoxicated, when, if he had been left entirely to himself, he would have remained sober, excuses him from the consequences of a crime. It is the theory of the state that the influence must go to the extent of actual coercion and abuse. While this precise point has never been decided by any court, so far as the matter has been called to our attention, we are of the opinion that the true rule is that the influence exercised on the mind of a defendant must be such as to amount to duress or fraud. The law has always jealously guarded the effect of drunkenness as a defense in criminal cases, and, even with all the restrictions surrounding it, the doctrine is a dangerous one, and liable to be abused. In this case there is no suggestion of fraud, and it was for the jury to decide whether or not there was coercion and abuse to the extent of duress. While the instruction was not, perhaps as happily worded as it might have been, we are of the opinion that the jury was correctly informed as to the true rule in regard to a defense of involuntary intoxication; that (1) it must be induced by acts amounting in effect to duress; and that (2) it must go to such an extent that the mind of the defendant was incapable of understanding the criminal nature of his act. . . .

Because of the necessarily prejudicial remarks of the county attorney above discussed, the judgment is reversed, and the case remanded to the superior court of Maricopa county for a new trial.

McAlister, C. J., and Ross, J., concur.[1]

---

1. If a drug taken under a doctor's prescription unexpectedly had such an influence that the patient became incapable of controlling the car he was driving and hit a pedestrian, the patient is not guilty of "assault and battery with an automobile". Burnett v. Commonwealth, 284 S.W.2d 654 (Ky.1955).

One who strikes a woman with a car, and does not stop and give aid, is guilty of not stopping and giving aid even if he did not know he had hit her, if the only reason he did not know was because he was drunk. Martinez v. State, 137 Tex.Cr.R. 434, 128 S.W.2d 398 (1939). The provision of West's Ann.Cal.Pen.Code § 26 exculpating persons "who committed the act charged without being conscious thereof" does not apply to one whose unconsciousness is due to voluntary intoxication. People v. Anderson, 87 Cal.App.2d 857, 197 P.2d 839 (1948).

MODEL PENAL CODE

Section 2.08. Intoxication.

(1) Except as provided in Subsection (4) of this Section, intoxication of the actor is not a defense unless it negatives an element of the offense.

(2) When recklessness establishes an element of the offense, if the actor, due to self-induced intoxication, is unaware of a risk of which he would have been aware had he been sober, such unawareness is immaterial.

(3) Intoxication does not, in itself, constitute mental disease within the meaning of Section 4.01.

(4) Intoxication which (a) is not self-induced or (b) is pathological is an affirmative defense if by reason of such intoxication the actor at the time of his conduct lacks substantial capacity either to appreciate its criminality [wrongfulness] or to conform his conduct to the requirements of law.

(5) Definitions. In this Section unless a different meaning plainly is required:

(a) "intoxication" means a disturbance of mental or physical capacities resulting from the introduction of substances into the body;

(b) "self-induced intoxication" means intoxication caused by substances which the actor knowingly introduces into his body, the tendency of which to cause intoxication he knows or ought to know, unless he introduces them pursuant to medical advice or under such circumstances as would afford a defense to a charge of crime;

(c) "pathological intoxication" means intoxication grossly excessive in degree, given the amount of the intoxicant, to which the actor does not know he is susceptible.

A Massachusetts conviction of driving while "under the influence" was held not to be sufficient to authorize revocation of a chauffeur's license in New York because the New York statute spoke of driving "while intoxicated" and the two are not the same. Cashion v. Harnett, 234 App.D.C. 332, 255 N.Y.S. 169 (1932). "Under the influence" requires more than proof of sufficient alcohol to produce some effect. It requires substantial impairment of driving ability as a result of alcohol. People v. Dingle, 56 Cal.App. 445, 205 P. 705 (1922).

"It will be noticed that it is not essential to the existence of the statutory offense that the driver of the automobile should be so intoxicated that he cannot *safely* drive a car. The expression 'under the influence of intoxicating liquor' covers not only all the well-known and easily recognized conditions and degrees of intoxication, but any abnormal mental or physical condition which is the result of indulging in any degree in intoxicating liquors and which tends to deprive him of that clearness of intellect and control of himself which he would otherwise possess. So one driving an automobile upon a public street while under the influence of intoxicating liquor offends against the Disorderly Persons' act even though he drives so slowly and so skillfully and carefully that the public is not annoyed or endangered; but such a driver is clearly not guilty of a public nuisance. To render him guilty of a public nuisance, facts not within the definition of the offense prohibited by the act of 1913 must be shown. In other words it must appear that the public was inconvenienced or endangered by the driving. This might be shown by proof that the degree of intoxication of the driver was such as to render him incapable of *properly* driving the machine; or by proof that in fact he drove it in such a manner as to endanger those using the street". State v. Rodgers, 91 N.J.L. 212, 215–16, 102 A. 433, 435 (1917).

SECTION 4. COVERTURE

Under rather narrow limitations, to be considered in a subsequent chapter, a harmful deed which would otherwise be a crime will be excused if done under compulsion. Under the common-law "doctrine of coercion" a married woman was excused for an *actus reus* perpetrated by her under the command or coercion of her husband, without being subject to the ordinary limitations of compulsion. In fact, under the "doctrine of coercion," coverture involved a limitation of criminal capacity. The wife "cannot be guilty", says Lord Hale, if her husband is guilty of the same larceny or burglary (1 Hale P.C. 46).

The "doctrine of coercion" did not apply in cases of treason or murder, or in offenses such as keeping a brothel which are assumed to be "generally conducted by the intrigues of the female sex." Except for these offenses (and perhaps robbery) a married woman was entitled to an acquittal if the *actus reus* was perpetrated by her under the coercion, or even the bare command, of her husband. Furthermore, the mere presence of the husband at the time of the harmful deed was sufficient to give rise to a presumption of coercion on his part. This presumption could be rebutted by evidence showing clearly the absence of coercion, but it was a powerful shield in her defense.

There may have been some reason for this doctrine in the ancient law, but there is none today. And it is definitely on the wane. It is no longer true that a married woman cannot be guilty of the very same larceny or burglary of which her husband is convicted. The presumption of coercion arising from the mere presence of the husband is usually not as strong as formerly, even where still recognized. It is a mistake, however, to assume that the "doctrine of coercion" has disappeared entirely.

PEOPLE v. STATLEY

Appellate Department, Superior Court, Los Angeles County, California, 1949.
91 Cal.App.2d Supp. 943, 206 P.2d 76.

BISHOP, J. Convicted on a charge that she had failed to yield the right of way to a pedestrian in a crosswalk, the defendant contends that the judgment of conviction should be reversed because the trial court failed to give her requested instruction that "under the laws of this State, a married woman is not capable of committing a misdemeanor while acting under threats, command or coercion of her husband." In support of her contention the defendant advances three arguments: (a) the instruction embodies a correct principle of law;

(b) it was called for in this case by direct evidence that she was acting under her husband's command; (c) it was made pertinent by the common law presumption that a misdemeanor committed by a married woman in her husband's presence is done under his coercion. We have reached the conclusion that the instruction should have been given. It was a correct statement of the law, and the evidence before the jurors made it applicable. We cannot, however, square the ancient presumption with the facts of modern life. We are not ready to put our stamp of approval on the statement that, when a married woman who is operating a motor vehicle in which her husband is a passenger, neglects to make a boulevard stop, fails to signal before she turns, or commits any other violation of the traffic laws, the probability is that she did so because he made her do so.

There can be no doubt that the requested instruction is a correct statement of the law, for we find in section 26, Penal Code: "All persons are capable of committing crimes except . . .: Seven. Married women (except for felonies) acting under the threats, commands, or coercion of their husbands." One of the two exceptions contained in the language of the section was eliminated in People v. Graff (1922), 59 Cal.App. 706, 708, 211 P. 829, 830, by rephrasing the quoted provision to read: "Married women are persons capable of committing all crimes, except misdemeanors committed by them when acting under the threats, command, or coercion of their husbands." It may quite properly be restated, for the purpose of this misdemeanor case, to eliminate all exceptions: "Married women are persons not capable of committing misdemeanors when acting under the threats, command, or coercion of their husbands." It was this principle of law that the defendant desired to have implanted in the minds of the jurors in order that she might have the benefit of it. The possibility that this code provision has become anachronistic does not justify the courts in disregarding it. A legislative enactment is not repealed by time or changed conditions, but only by further legislation.

The testimony which gave pertinency to this instruction came from the lips of defendant's husband. After relating how the automobile which the defendant was driving, and in which he was riding, had stopped, to permit the traffic to clear up in the lane between them and the crosswalk, defendant's husband continued by repeating the words he had addressed to her, "You have got plenty of clearance, take it." She had begun to move forward just before he spoke these words, and following their utterance she drove on and into the crosswalk, causing a pedestrian to jump back.

We find in this evidence no basis for concluding that the defendant, in driving across the lane of traffic and into the crosswalk, had acted under a threat or under the coercion of her husband, but, had the matter been submitted to the jury, it is possible that it would have been determined that she acted under his command, or at least have entertained a reasonable doubt about the matter. His declara-

Sec. 4 COVERTURE 499

tion to her was couched in the form of a command, and while it must be conceded that the jury might have determined that the defendant paid no attention to what her husband was saying, the question was one of fact, and the defendant was entitled to have the case submitted to the jury on her theory of the facts. Of course, the husband's denial that his words "Take it" constituted a command, no more removed the possibility of a command from the case than did his denial that there was a pedestrian in the crosswalk do away with him.

The defendant contends that the requested instruction was pertinent not only because there was direct evidence of a command but for the further reason that a presumption had arisen that she was acting under the coercion or command of her husband, and she requested, vainly, a further instruction that there was such a presumption. Whether or not such a presumption arises is a question that will be involved in any retrial of this case, and so merits attention. Our determination that there is no such presumption applying in this case is not predicated on any misapprehension about the existence of the presumption at common law. It did exist. It is referred to in O'Donnell v. State (1941), 73 Okl.Cr. 1, 117 P.2d 139, 141, as being: "the rule of the common law that where a crime, with some exceptions, was committed by a married woman conjointly with or in the presence of her husband, prima facie she was not criminally liable, as it was presumed that she acted in obedience to his commands and under his coercion. This doctrine is announced by Blackstone, who says that it is a thousand years old."

"But the foregoing view of the legal relationship of husband and wife is no longer warranted, when by modern conditions and through modern statutory provisions the wife has been emancipated with respect to her personal wages and earnings. Where the reason for a rule of common law which is the spirit and soul of that law, fails, the rule itself fails." [1]

We conclude, then, that the reign of the thousand year old presumption has come to an end. In our society, where almost no bride promises to obey her husband, and where it is not accepted as the usual that a wife does what her husband wishes by way of yielding obedience to a dominant will, the basis for the presumption has disappeared. A presumption that has lost its reason must be confined to a museum; it has no place in the administration of justice. If, therefore, a wife is to escape the consequences of her disobedience of a statute on the ground that she was acting in obedience to her husband, the fact is not established by the mere circumstance that her husband

---

1. Where not hampered by statute some courts have completely repudiated the common-law doctrine of coercion of a married woman by her husband. United States v. Dege, 364 U.S. 51, 80 S.Ct. 1589, 4 L.Ed.2d 1563 (1960); State v. Turnbow, 67 N.M. 341, 354 P.2d 533 (1960).

was present when she offended. The judgment and order appealed from are reversed; the case is remanded for a new trial.

SHAW, P. J., and STEPHENS, J., concurred.[2]

MODEL PENAL CODE

Section 2.09. Duress. . . .

(3) It is not a defense that a woman acted on the command of her husband, unless she acted under such coercion as would establish a defense under this Section. [The presumption that a woman, acting in the presence of her husband, is coerced is abolished.]

2. "Especially since the passage of the married woman's emancipation legislation in this State, the married woman is as capable of and as responsible for crime as if she were single. . . . She is to be regarded, in the contemplation of our criminal statutes, as an independent entity." Johnson v. State, 152 Tenn. 184, 187, 274 S.W. 12 (1925).

Chapter 9

RESPONSIBILITY: MODIFYING CIRCUMSTANCES

SECTION 1. IGNORANCE OR MISTAKE

(A) IGNORANCE OR MISTAKE OF LAW

"Ignorance of the law is no excuse," is one of the most familiar phrases in this branch of jurisprudence. It is not entirely without exception, although the exceptions are rare. What is intended to convey the same general idea in other words is this: "Every person is presumed to know the law." In order to understand either the rule itself, or the exceptions thereto, it is necessary to know what is meant by the word "presumed." And this is complicated by the fact that the words "presumed" and "presumption" are used in three different senses in the law.

One of the senses is to signify a mere inference of fact. If two men are in a small well-lighted room at the same time when no one else is there, and if both are there, fully conscious, for a substantial period of time, it can be inferred ("presumed") that each knew of the other's presence. This is not a rule of law. It is merely a common sense conclusion based upon ordinary experience. It is unfortunate that the words "presumed" and "presumption" were ever used in this sense, and such usage can be ignored for the purposes of this subsection. Nothing could be more absurd than to suggest as a common sense conclusion, based upon ordinary experience, that everyone knows all of the criminal law.[1] The fair inference is that nobody does. Hence attention here may be concentrated upon the other two meanings.

A true presumption is a rule of law which calls for a certain result unless the party adversely affected comes forward with evidence to overcome it. This (although it is the true presumption) often is referred to as a "prima facie presumption" to distinguish it from the so-called "conclusive presumption" which is a legal device in the form of a postulate used for the determination of a particular

---

[1]. A judge thinking of this presumption in terms of an inference of fact would be bound to reject it. "There is no presumption in this country that every person knows the law: it would be contrary to common sense and reason if it were so." Per Maule, J. in Martindale v. Falkner, 2 C.B. 706, 719, 135 Eng.Rep. 1129 (1846). Quoted in Ryan v. State, 104 Ga. 78, 82, 30 S.E. 678, 680 (1898).

case whether it represents the actual facts or not. A typical example is the conclusive presumption of delivery by all prior parties to a negotiable instrument which has reached the hands of a holder in due course. The net result of this "conclusive presumption" is that such a holder in due course can enforce the instrument as effectively against a prior party who did not deliver it as against one who did. It merely disguises a rule of substantive law in the language of a rule of evidence.

If "everyone is presumed to know the law" in this sense, it means that a particular case will be disposed of exactly as if the defendant actually did know the law whether such is the fact or not. And this is exactly the sense in which this word is used ordinarily in this phrase. This is the sense in which it is used in all of those cases in which "ignorance of the law is no excuse." In those rare and exceptional cases in which ignorance of the law is recognized as an excuse in a criminal case the presumption is rebuttable. In other words, while there are exceptions to the rule that "ignorance of the law is no excuse" there are none to the statement that "everyone is presumed to know the law"—except to the extent that the presumption may be overcome by evidence where this is permissible. Stated differently, knowledge of the law is presumed; in most cases this presumption is conclusive but under exceptional circumstances it is disputable.

The most obvious instance in which the presumption of knowledge of the law is rebuttable is in a prosecution for an offense requiring a specific intent. One does not commit larceny, for example, by a trespassory taking and carrying away of the chattel of another if it is done without an intent to steal. Hence one does not commit larceny by such an asportation of another's chattel if he does so under the honest belief that it belongs to him and he has the right to immediate possession of it. And under such circumstances it is immaterial whether the error which led to this bona-fide belief was due to a mistake of fact or a mistake of law. It is to be observed, however, that the ignorance or mistake in such a case concerns some other law and not the law violated. In a larceny case it may be shown that a misunderstanding of property law led to a bona-fide belief that the particular chattel belonged to the defendant and that he had a lawful right to immediate possession thereof, but not that he never heard of the law of larceny or that he mistakenly believed he could take away and appropriate another's property wrongfully without subjecting himself to the penalty of that law under the particular circumstances of the taking. To illustrate further: In a prosecution for malicious trespass based upon removing a fence from a certain path, it could be shown that a mistaken belief with reference to the law of right of way led to the opinion that the fence should not be there, but not that the defendant did not know there was a penalty for wrongfully tearing down another's property.

Problems of particular difficulty in this field are: (1) To what extent does the rule permitting evidence of a misunderstanding of some law, other than the one violated, apply to offenses requiring some particular state of mind which is not "specific intent?" and (2) may circumstances ever be so exceptional as to permit an excuse based upon ignorance or mistake of law (a) in prosecutions for offenses requiring only the "general mens rea," or (b) in prosecutions for a violation of the very law which is claimed to have been misunderstood? [2]

STATE v. CUDE

Supreme Court of Utah, 1963.
14 Utah 2d 287, 383 P.2d 399.

CALLISTER, JUSTICE. Defendant appeals from his conviction and judgment of grand larceny. It appears from the record that the defendant left his automobile at a garage in Ogden, Utah with the request that the same be repaired. The garage owner initially estimated the cost of the necessary work to be in the neighborhood of $180.00. There was evidence, however, that the defendant authorized the garage owner to fix the car, irrespective of the cost. After leaving his automobile at the garage, defendant left the state and returned a few days later. At that time he was presented with a repair bill in the amount of $345.00. Unable to pay this charge (or, for that matter, the estimate of $180.00) the defendant was refused possession of the car by the garageman. Several hours thereafter (after the garage had closed for the night) defendant returned and, using a duplicate key, drove the automobile away.

The automobile was recovered by the police a day or so later while in the possession of a friend of the defendant. It was the contention of the latter that he had taken the car for the purpose of selling the same to realize enough cash to pay off the garage bill.

This court has previously ruled that an owner of personalty in the possession of another by virtue of some special right or title, as bailee or otherwise, is guilty of larceny, if he takes such property from the person in possession *with the fraudulent intention of depriving such person of his rights.*

The defendant requested an instruction regarding his defense, namely, that he could not be found guilty if, at the time of the taking, he honestly believed that he had a right to the possession of the automobile. We are of the opinion that the lower court erred in refusing to give such an instruction.

---

2. Ignorance of the law of arrest was no defense to a charge of unlawfully interfering with the United States Attorney's performance of his official duties by arresting him. Finn v. United States, 219 F.2d 894 (9th Cir. 1955), certiorari denied 349 U.S. 906, 75 S.Ct. 583 (1955).

It is fundamental that an essential element of larceny is the intent to steal the property of another. Consequently, if there is any reasonable basis in the evidence upon which the jury could believe that the accused thought he had a right to take possession of his automobile, or if the evidence in that regard is such that it might raise a reasonable doubt that he had the intent to steal, then that issue should be presented to the jury. The principle is correctly stated in 52 C.J.S. Larceny § 150, p. 999, that if the property was taken under any " . . . circumstances from which the jury might infer that the taking was under a claim of right, [the] accused is entitled to an appropriate charge distinguishing larceny from a mere trespass." . . .

It is held, and we think correctly so, that the general charge that the accused must have the intent to steal does not meet the request to have this particular theory of defense presented to the jury. In a prosecution for stealing sheep, the trial court had given such a general instruction but refused to give the defendant's request, similar to the one submitted here, that if the defendant believed he had a right to take the sheep, he would not be guilty of larceny. Defendant assigned the refusal to give his request as error. After discussing a number of authorities on the subject the court reversed on that ground stating:

"The foregoing authorities would seem to clearly establish that the defendant's requested instruction . . . [as to belief of right to possession] . . . or one similar to it should have been given by the district court, and that it was prejudicial error to refuse it."

It is suggested that the defendant's own evidence shows he had the necessary intent to steal at the time he took the car. This seems to argue the weight of the evidence; that the defense was not made in good faith; and that it could not be believed. This is a jury question. The defendant's position was exactly to the contrary. The testimony of the garageman is that the defendant requested permission to leave his car on the lot while he went to Salt Lake to get money. Defendant gave an explanation of his return to the lot and the removal of the car which could be considered as consistent with his theory of defense. He also testified that, "But since that I was the owner of the automobile I had never in my life believed I was committing any felony by taking the car for just a day or two, and that is what I did." That he thought he had a right to take his own car was the only avenue of defense open to the defendant and the only one he asserted. It is consistent with the testimony just quoted and with his request for the instruction referred to above. We think it inescapable that the refusal of the trial court to submit the case to the jury upon his theory deprived defendant of a fair trial, and for that reason the judgment should be reversed on that ground.

We find no merit to defendant's assignment of error relating to the cross-examination with respect to his felony record.

Reversed and remanded for a new trial.

McDonough, Crockett and Wade, JJ., concur.

Henriod, Chief Justice (dissenting). . . .

CUTTER v. STATE

Supreme Court of New Jersey, 1873.
36 N.J.L. 125.

Beasley, Chief Justice. The defendant was indicted for extortion in taking fees to which he was not entitled, on a criminal complaint before him as a justice of the peace. The defence which he set up, and which was overruled, was that he had taken these moneys innocently, and under a belief that by force of the statute he had a right to exact them.

This subject is regulated by the twenty-eighth section of the act for the punishment of crimes. This clause declares that no justice or other officer of this state shall receive or take any fee or reward, to execute and do his duty and office, but such as is or shall be allowed by the laws of this state, and that "if any justice, &c., shall receive or take, by color of his office, any fee or reward whatsoever, not allowed by the laws of this state, for doing his office, and be thereof convicted, he shall be punished," &c.

On the part of the state it is argued that this statute is explicit in its terms, and makes the mere taking of an illegal fee a criminal act, without regard to the intent of the recipient. Such undoubtedly is the literal force of the language, but then, on the same principle, the officer would be guilty if he took, by mistake or inadvertence, more than the sum coming to him. Nor would the statutory terms, if taken in their exact signification, exclude from their compass, an officer who might be laboring under an insane delusion. Manifestly therefore, the terms of this section are subject to certain practical limitations. This is the case with most statutes couched in comprehensive terms, and especially with those which modify or otherwise regulate common law offences. In such instances the old and the new law are to be construed together; and the former will not be considered to be abolished except so far as the design to produce such effect appears to be clear. In morals it is an evil mind which makes the offence, and this, as a general rule, has been at the root of criminal law. The consequence is that it is not to be intended that this principle is discarded, merely on account of the generality of statutory language. It is highly reasonable to presume that the law makers did not intend to disgrace or to punish a person who should do an act under the belief that it was lawful to do it. And it is this presumption that fully justifies the statement of Mr. Bishop, "that a statute will not generally make an act criminal, however broad may be its language, unless the offender's intent concurred with his act."

This doctrine applies with full force to the present case. If the magistrate received the fees in question without any corrupt intent, and under the conviction that they were lawfully his due, I do not think such act was a crime by force of that statute above recited.

But it is further argued on the part of the prosecution, that as the fees to which the justice was entitled are fixed by law, and as he cannot set up, as an excuse for his conduct his ignorance of the law, his guilty knowledge is undeniable. The argument goes upon the legal maxim *ignorantia legis neminem excusat*. But this rule, in its application to the law of crimes, is subject, as it is sometimes in respect to civil rights, to certain important exceptions. Where the act done is *malum in se*, or where the law which has been infringed was settled and plain, the maxim, in its rigor, will be applied; but where the law is not settled, or is obscure, and where the guilty intention, being a necessary constituent of the particular offense, is dependent on a knowledge of the law, this rule, if enforced, would be misapplied. To give it any force in such instances, would be to turn it aside from its rational and original purpose, and to convert it into an instrument of injustice. The judgments of the courts have confined it to its proper sphere. Whenever a special mental condition constitutes a part of the offence charged, and such condition depends on the question whether or not the culprit had certain knowledge with respect to matters of law, in every such case it has been declared that the subject of the existence of such knowledge is open to inquiry, as a fact to be found by the jury. This doctrine has often been applied to the offence of larceny. The criminal intent, which is an essential part of that crime, involves a knowledge that the property taken belongs to another; but even when all the facts are known to the accused, and so the right to the property is a mere question of law, still he will make good his defence if he can show, in a satisfactory manner, that being under a misapprehension as to his legal rights, he honestly believed the articles in question to be his own.

The adjudications show many other applications of the same principle, and the facts of some of such cases were not substantially dissimilar from those embraced in the present inquiry. In the case of The People v. Whaley, 6 Cow. 661, a justice of the peace had been indicted for taking illegal fees, and the court held that the motives of the defendant, whether they showed corruption or that he acted through a mistake of the law, were a proper question for the jury. The case in The Commonwealth v. Shed, 1 Mass. 228, was put before the jury on the same ground. This was likewise the ground of decision in the case of The Commonwealth v. Bradford, 9 Metc. 268, the charge being for illegal voting, and it being declared that evidence that the defendant had consulted counsel as to his right of suffrage, and had acted on the advice thus obtained, was admissible in his favor. This evidence was only important to show that the defendant in infringing the statute had done so in ignorance of the rule of law upon the subject. Many other cases, resting on the same basis, might be cited; but the foregoing are sufficient to mark clearly the boundaries delineated by the courts to the general rule, that ignorance of law is no defence where the mandates of a statute have been disregarded or a crime has been perpetrated.

That the present case falls within the exceptions to this general rule, appears to me to be plain. There can be no doubt that an opinion very generally prevailed that magistrates had the right to exact the fees which were received by this defendant, and that they could be legally taken under similar circumstances. The prevalence of such an opinion could not, it is true, legalize the act of taking such fees; but its existence might tend to show that the defendant, when he did the act with which he stands charged, was not conscious of doing anything wrong. If a justice of the peace, being called upon to construe a statute with respect to the fees coming to himself, should, exercising due care, form an honest judgment as to his dues, and should act upon such judgment, it would seem palpably unjust, and therefore inconsistent with the ordinary grounds of judicial action, to hold such conduct criminal if it should happen that a higher tribunal should dissent from the view thus taken, and should decide that the statute was not susceptible of the interpretation put upon it. I think the defendant had the right in this case to prove to the jury that the moneys, which it is charged he took extorsively, were received by him under a mistake as to his legal rights, and that as such evidence being offered by him was overruled, the judgment on that account must be reversed.

PEOPLE v. WEISS

Court of Appeals of New York, 1938.
276 N.Y. 384, 12 N.E.2d 514.

[During the investigation of the kidnaping and murder of the Lindbergh baby in New Jersey, one of the suspects was Wendel. In the effort to solve the case, defendants assisted a New Jersey detective in seizing Wendel in New York and there confining him in an effort to extort a confession from him. They offered evidence to show that before they assisted in the arrest they were assured by the detective that he had authority to make the arrest, and power to authorize their assistance, and they believed they were authorized and were doing police work. Most of this evidence was excluded by the trial judge.]

O'BRIEN, JUDGE. . . . Counsel for defendants requested: "That if the defendants, or either of them, acted in the honest belief that his act in seizing and confining Wendel was done with authority of law, even if they were mistaken in such belief, that they cannot be convicted of seizing, confining or kidnapping Wendel, with intent, to cause him without authority of law to be confined or imprisoned within the State, and the jury must acquit such defendants or defendant." To this request the court replied: "I not only decline to charge that but I repeat that the question of good faith is no defense." The jury was also instructed that "even if they [defendants] did believe it, it is no defense in this case." If such interpretation is to prevail, then it must follow that in every instance where a defendant admits the fact that he intended to make the arrest and the courts later declare the arrest to have been made without authority of law, he must necessarily be convicted as a kidnapper, irrespective of his belief or his intentions to conform with the law. A peace officer, in the mistaken belief that he is acting with authority of law, makes an illegal arrest and later, in an effort to extort a confession, puts his prisoner through the third degree. He is guilty of the crime of assault, or of official oppression, but he is certainly not a kidnapper. The question of assault is not in this case. So the trial judge charged.

The intent of defendants to seize and confine Wendel cannot be doubted, but their intent to perform these acts without authority of law depends upon the state of mind of the actors. If in good faith they believed that they were acting within the law, there could have been no intent to act "without authority of law." Their belief or disbelief indicates intent or lack of it, and they were entitled to testify in respect to their intent based upon their belief.

No matter how doubtful the credibility of these defendants may be or how suspicious the circumstances may appear, we cannot say as matter of law that, even in so strong a case as this for the prosecution, the jury was not entitled to consider the question whether defendants in good faith believed that they were acting with authority of law. We are, therefore, constrained to reverse the judgment of conviction and order a new trial for the purpose of submitting that question of fact to the jury.

The judgments should be reversed and a new trial ordered.

CRANE, CHIEF JUDGE (dissenting). I must dissent from the conclusions of Judge O'BRIEN in this case, upon three grounds:

First. I believe that the charge and rulings of the court were correct, and that the law has been well stated by Judge Johnston in the prevailing opinion. The fact that the defendants may have thought they had authority to confine Wendel is no excuse for the criminal act and no defense. The crime of kidnapping is committed when a person seizes and confines another with intent to cause him to be confined or imprisoned within the state, and the act is done without lawful authority. The fact that the person thought he had lawful authority has nothing to do with the matter. The intent applies to the seizing and to the confining. The defendants in this case intended to seize Wendel and to confine him within the state. In fact they confined him, bound, in Schlossman's home. Whether they thought they were acting according to law or not, or had legal authority, is no defense. They had no legal authority, and the judge so charged as matter of law. In this he was correct, for such is the law. In fact, no one claims they had any legal authority. Where, therefore, one is seized, taken away, and secretly confined, and it turns out that the person doing it had no legal authority to do it, the crime of kidnapping is committed. Of course, if there be legal authority, there is no crime, but the fact that the person mistakenly thought that they had authority does not lessen the crime. . . .

LEHMAN, LOUGHRAN, and RIPPEY, JJ., concur with O'BRIEN, J.

CRANE, C. J., dissents in opinion, in which HUBBS and FINCH, JJ., concur.

Judgments reversed, etc.

COMMONWEALTH v. BENESCH

Supreme Judicial Court of Massachusetts, 1935.
290 Mass. 125, 194 N.E. 905.

QUA, J. These two indictments are now before this court on the exceptions of the defendants Benesch, Davison and Tibbetts. . . . The second indictment charges the same persons with conspiring to have registered brokers or salesmen sell securities in accordance with an instalment or partial payment contract which was not approved by the public utilities commission. . . .

2. We now come to the second indictment. It is not disputed that the instalment plan contracts had not been approved by the public utilities commission. Under this indictment, in order to hold any one defendant, it was necessary for the Commonwealth to show as to that defendant that he entered into a combination with others for the purpose of doing the illegal act of selling securities on an instalment plan contract which had not been approved by the commission. In the case of conspiracy, as with other common law crimes, it is necessary that criminal intent be shown. Speaking in general terms, there must be an intent to do wrong. Selling the shares on instalments was not in itself wrong. It need involve no deceit or other element detrimental to the individual purchaser or to the public interest. So long as the contracts had not been approved, sale of the shares was *malum prohibitum* because of the statute, and nothing more. While no decision in this Commonwealth directly in point has been called to our attention, it has been held by excellent authority in other jurisdictions that in order to sustain an indictment for conspiracy to commit an offence which, like that here involved, is *malum prohibitum* only,

belonging to a general type of offences which has been greatly extended by modern legislation in many fields, it must appear that the defendant knew of the illegal element involved in that which the combination was intended to accomplish. We believe this is sound law, where the charge is conspiracy. We do not imply that proof of criminal intent is required to sustain a complaint or indictment for the substantive offence prohibited by the statute. To constitute the criminal intent necessary to establish a conspiracy there must be both knowledge of the existence of the law and knowledge of its actual or intended violation.

The trial judge charged the jury in accordance with these principles, but he left it for the jury to say whether all three of the defendants now before the court had a criminal intent with respect to this second indictment. We think this was error. Perhaps as to Benesch alone there was evidence of the necessary intent. He could be found to have been at the head and front of the whole enterprise. If approval of the contracts had been obtained, it could have been inferred that he would have attended to it or would have known of it and that he must have known approval had not been obtained. He contends that he had no knowledge of the act of 1924 requiring approval, but while actual knowledge cannot be predicated solely upon the maxim that every man is presumed to know the law, yet under many circumstances knowledge of important requirements of law having to do with the kind of business in which a person is engaged may be readily inferable. It appears that Benesch at least knew that there were "Blue Sky Laws," and asked his counsel to look out for them. But one cannot be a conspirator alone. We are of opinion that the evidence is insufficient to support a verdict that any of the other alleged conspirators had the knowledge, both of the existence of the prohibition and of its violation, which is necessary to prove affirmatively a criminal intent. There is no evidence that any of them knew that the contracts had not been approved or that any of them occupied such a position in the Trust that such knowledge could be inferred. It may be doubted whether there is any evidence that Davison knew even that any shares were being sold on the instalment plan. Tibbetts was a subordinate salesman taking orders from his superiors. There is nothing to show that it was his duty to see that the contracts were approved. Whether he might be found guilty, if charged with the substantive offence of making sales, is not before us. We are now concerned with actual criminal intent. Simpson was treasurer and director. He was not a promoter, but was hired by Benesch on a salary. The duties performed by him seem to have been chiefly of a routine character. It would be carrying inferences of fact too far to assume without further evidence that he knew the law and also knew that those who had organized the Trust and put it in working order had failed to obey the law. Mr. Swift was a lawyer and was a director. He testified that he did not know of the statute of 1924 until

November, 1927, and that these matters had been left to one Mr. Burns who had secured the incorporation of the Trust. There was evidence introduced by the Commonwealth that partial payment sales were stopped by September 20, 1927. If it can be inferred that Mr. Swift did know of the law, there was no evidence that he knew before November that it had not been complied with. There was no substantial evidence that partial payment sales were continued after that time. Wells and Robinson stand in much the same position. Both came into the office of the Trust long after it had been organized and was in full operation. There is at most no more than a scintilla of evidence that any of the alleged coconspirators with Benesch consciously and intentionally joined in a conspiracy to sell shares for instalments on unapproved contracts.

Other exceptions not here mentioned have become immaterial.

It follows that the exceptions of the defendants Davison and Tibbetts in the first case are sustained and the exceptions of the defendant Benesch are overruled, and that the exceptions of all three defendants in the second case are sustained.

So ordered.

LAMBERT v. CALIFORNIA

Supreme Court of the United States, 1957.
355 U.S. 225, 78 S.Ct. 240.

MR. JUSTICE DOUGLAS delivered the opinion of the Court.

Section 52.38(a) of the Los Angeles Municipal Code defines "convicted person" as follows:

"Any person who, subsequent to January 1, 1921, has been or hereafter is convicted of an offense punishable as a felony in the State of California, or who has been or who is hereafter convicted of any offense in any place other than the State of California, which offense, if committed in the State of California, would have been punishable as a felony."

Section 52.39 provides that it shall be unlawful for "any convicted person" to be or remain in Los Angeles for a period of more than five days without registering; it requires any person having a place of abode outside the city to register if he comes into the city on five occasions or more during a 30-day period; and it prescribes the information to be furnished the Chief of Police on registering.

Section 52.43(b) makes the failure to register a continuing offense, each day's failure constituting a separate offense.

Appellant, arrested on suspicion of another offense, was charged with a violation of this registration law. The evidence showed that she had been at the time of her arrest a resident of Los Angeles for over seven years. Within that period she had been convicted in Los

Angeles of the crime of forgery, an offense which California punishes as a felony. Though convicted of a crime punishable as a felony, she had not at the time of her arrest registered under the Municipal Code. At the trial, appellant asserted that § 52.39 of the Code denies her due process of law and other rights under the Federal Constitution, unnecessary to enumerate. The trial court denied this objection. The case was tried to a jury which found appellant guilty. The court fined her $250 and placed her on probation for three years. Appellant, renewing her constitutional objection, moved for arrest of judgment and a new trial. This motion was denied. On appeal the constitutionality of the Code was again challenged. The Appellate Department of the Superior Court affirmed the judgment, holding there was no merit to the claim that the ordinance was unconstitutional. The case is here on appeal. 28 U.S.C. § 1257(2), 28 U.S.C.A. § 1257 (2). We noted probable jurisdiction, 352 U.S. 914, 77 S.Ct. 218, 1 L. Ed.2d 121, and designated *amicus curiae* to appear in support of appellant. The case, having been argued and reargued, we now hold that the registration provisions of the Code as sought to be applied here violate the Due Process requirement of the Fourteenth Amendment.

The registration provision, carrying criminal penalties, applies if a person has been convicted "of an offense punishable as a felony in the State of California" or, in case he has been convicted in another State, if the offense "would have been punishable as a felony" had it been committed in California. No element of willfulness is by terms included in the ordinance nor read into it by the California court as a condition necessary for a conviction.

We must assume that appellant had no actual knowledge of the requirement that she register under this ordinance, as she offered proof of this defense which was refused. The question is whether a registration act of this character violates Due Process where it is applied to a person who has no actual knowledge of his duty to register, and where no showing is made of the probability of such knowledge.

We do not go with Blackstone in saying that "a vicious will" is necessary to constitute a crime, 4 Bl.Comm. *21, for conduct alone without regard to the intent of the doer is often sufficient. There is wide latitude on the law-makers to declare an offense and to exclude elements of knowledge and diligence from its definition. But we deal here with conduct that is wholly passive—mere failure to register. It is unlike the commission of acts, or the failure to act under circumstances that should alert the doer to the consequences of his deed. The rule that "ignorance of the law will not excuse" is deep in our law, as is the principle that of all the powers of local government, the police power is "one of the least limitable." On the other hand, Due Process places some limits on its exercise. Engrained in our concept of Due Process is the requirement of notice. Notice is sometimes essential so that the citizen has the chance to defend charges. Notice is required before property interests are disturbed, before assessments are made, before penalties are assessed. Notice is required in a myriad of situations where a penalty or forfeiture might be suffered for mere failure to act. . . . These cases involved only property interests in civil litigation. But the principle is equally appropriate where a person, wholly passive and unaware of any wrongdoing, is brought to the bar of justice for condemnation in a criminal case.

Registration laws are common and their range is wide. Many such laws are akin to licensing statutes in that they pertain to the regulation of business activities. But the present ordinance is entirely different. Violation of its provisions is unaccompanied by any activity whatever, mere presence in the city being the test. Moreover, circumstances which might move one to inquire as to the necessity of registration are completely lacking. At most the ordinance is but a law enforcement technique designed for the convenience of law enforcement agencies through which a list of the names and addresses of felons then residing in a given community is compiled. The disclosure is merely a compilation of former convictions already publicly recorded in the jurisdiction where obtained. Nevertheless, this registrant on first becoming aware of her duty to register was given no opportunity to comply with the law and avoid its penalty, even though her default was entirely innocent. She could but suffer the consequences of the ordinance, namely, conviction with the imposition of heavy criminal penalties thereunder. We believe that actual knowledge of the duty to register or proof of the probability of such knowledge and subsequent failure to comply are necessary before a conviction under the ordinance can stand. As Holmes wrote in The Common Law, "A law which punished conduct which would not be blameworthy in the average member of the community would be too severe for the community to bear." Id., at 50. Its severity lies in the absence of an opportunity either to avoid the consequences of the law or to defend any prosecution brought under it. Where a person did not know of the duty to register and where there was no proof of the probability of such knowledge, he may not be convicted consistently with Due Process. Were it otherwise, the evil would be as great as it is when the law is written in print too fine to read or in a language foreign to the community.

Reversed.[1]

---

[1]. On remand the Municipal Court ordered a new trial. On petition the California Supreme Court issued a writ of prohibition on the ground that the Los Angeles ordinance violated the state constitution, Art. XI, sec. 1, since it is in conflict with state legislation which has preempted this field. Lambert v. Municipal Court, 53 Cal.2d 690, 3 Cal.Rptr. 168, 349 P.2d 984 (1960).

MR. JUSTICE BURTON, dissents because he believes that, as applied to this appellant, the ordinance does not violate her constitutional rights.

MR. JUSTICE FRANKFURTER, whom MR. JUSTICE HARLAN and MR. JUSTICE WHITTAKER join, dissenting. . . .

LONG v. STATE

Supreme Court of Delaware, 1949.
44 Del. 262, 65 A.2d 489.

PEARSON, JUDGE, delivering the opinion of the court:

The defendant Long was married to his first wife in Wilmington, and resided there with her for thirty years prior to their separation in October 1945. On September 21, 1946, he went to Arkansas. He had been pensioned from the police force, and had been in bad health for a number of years. He testified that he went to Arkansas on account of his health because he "thought it would be a better climate"; also that he went there to obtain a divorce; and that he intended "to leave Delaware permanently and take up a permanent domicile in Arkansas". His health improved there. He returned to Wilmington for a few days in November "for business reasons" and spent the Christmas holidays in Wilmington. On December 3, he renewed his Delaware automobile registration for six months ending June 30, 1947. He remained in Arkansas for the statutory period of residence required for divorce in that state, and instituted divorce proceedings against his wife in the Chancery Court of Garland County. On January 7, 1947, that court entered a decree of absolute divorce. The decree recites publication of a notice and the mailing of a registered letter with a copy of the complaint to defendant's wife, a nonresident of Arkansas. She did not appear in the proceeding. She testified before the lower court here that she was not "served with any divorce papers" and did not receive any mail or a registered letter from Arkansas. On the same day the divorce decree was granted, defendant left Arkansas and returned to Wilmington where he has since resided. While in Wilmington during the Christmas holidays of 1946, he had been offered a job in a hospital there. He accepted this job after the divorce decree was granted and began work on January 13, 1947. On January 25, he was married to a second wife in Wilmington. This marriage was the subject of the bigamy prosecution under Rev.Code of Del. Sec. 5254. Defendant contends that the court below was required to recognize the Arkansas decree because of the provisions of a Delaware statute, 45 Laws of Del. Chap. 225, p. 906; that recognition of the decree was required under the full faith and credit clause of the Federal Constitution, article 4, § 1; that even if not required to do so, the court should have recognized the decree on the ground of comity; that the court erred in charging the jury with respect to the

Sec. 1   *IGNORANCE OR MISTAKE*   515

time when domicile of defendant in Arkansas was required in order that the Arkansas decree be recognized as valid; that the court erred in excluding evidence of a reasonable mistake by defendant in the application of law to the facts, and in rejecting other testimony. . . .

The evidence of defendant's consulting an attorney and following his advice was refused on two grounds: (1) that it is "not proper to presume, in view of the bigamy statute and the exceptions thereto that our Legislature intended that other and additional exceptions be extended by the Courts of this State"; and (2) that defendant's mistake was one of law, and is a case "to which the maxim 'ignorantia juris non excusat' applies." Numerous authorities are cited by the court. . . .

We turn now to the ground that this is a case to which the ignorance of law maxim applies. In many crimes involving a *specific* criminal intent, an honest mistake of law constitutes a defense if it negatives the specific intent. State v. Pullen, 3 Pennewill, 184, 50 A. 538 (larceny); State v. Collins, 1 Marv. 536, 41 A. 144 (embezzlement); see list of cases in the Keedy article, supra, at p. 89; also Perkins: Ignorance and Mistake in Criminal Law, 88 Univ. of Pa.Law Rev. 35, 45, 46. As to crimes not involving a specific intent, an honest mistake of law is usually, though not invariably, held not to excuse conduct otherwise criminal. (Perkins article, pp. 41–45 and cases cited.) A mistake of law, where not a defense, may nevertheless negative a general criminal intent as effectively as would an exculpatory mistake of fact. Thus, mistake of law is disallowed as a defense in spite of the fact that it may show an absence of the criminal mind. The reasons for disallowing it are practical considerations dictated by deterrent effects upon the administration and enforcement of the criminal law, which are deemed likely to result if it were allowed as a general defense. As stated in the Perkins article, supra, p. 41: " . . . But if such ignorance were available as a defense in every criminal case, this would be a constant source of confusion to juries, and it would tend to encourage ignorance at a point where it is peculiarly important to the state that knowledge should be as widespread as is reasonably possible. In the language of one of the giants of the profession, this is a point at which 'justice to the individual is rightly outweighed by the larger interests on the other side of the scales.' " Quoting from Holmes: The Common Law, p. 48.

Similar considerations are involved when we disallow ignorance or mistake of law as a defense to a defendant who engages in criminal conduct (even though not obviously immoral or anti-social) where his ignorance or mistake consists merely in (1) unawareness that such conduct is or might be within the ambit of any crime; or (2) although aware of the existence of criminal law relating to the subject of such conduct, or to some of its aspects, the defendant erroneously concludes (in good faith) that his particular conduct is for some reason not subject to the operation of any criminal law. But it seems to us significantly different to disallow mistake of law where (3) together with the circumstances of the second classification, it appears that before engaging in the conduct, the defendant made a bona fide, diligent effort, adopting a course and resorting to sources and means at least as appropriate as any afforded under our legal system, to ascertain and abide by the law, and where he acted in good faith reliance upon the results of such effort. It is inherent in the way our legal system functions that the criminal law consequences of any particular contemplated conduct cannot be determined in advance with certainty. Not until after the event, by final court decision, may the consequences be definitely ascertained. Prior to the event, the ultimate that can be ascertained about the legal consequences consists of predictions of varying degrees of probability of eventuation. Hence, in the sense in which we are concerned with the expression, a "mistake of law" of the second or third classification refers to the failure of predictions of legal consequences to come to pass. No matter how logical, plausible and persuasive may be the bases for a prediction (assumptions, abstract legal rules, reasoning, etc.,) a mistake of law arises if the prediction does not eventuate; and there is no mistake of law if the prediction eventuates. . . .

We find nothing about the crime of bigamy under our statute which calls for a contrary holding. As previously decided, an absence of general criminal intent is a defense to this crime. As to the acts involved in the crime, remarriage is obviously neither immoral nor anti-social in our culture. These aspects lie in the circumstance that the defendant has a spouse living from whom a divorce has not been obtained which our courts will recognize as valid. The matters to which a mistake of law might relate are legal questions concerning marriage and divorce. It is a gross understatement to say that such questions are more frequently perplexing than obvious to a layman. For these reasons, the defense seems appropriate and we hold it available in prosecutions for bigamy.

Here, from the evidence rejected by the lower court, the jury might have found substantially as follows: (1) that prior to his second marriage, defendant consulted a reputable Delaware attorney for the purpose of ascertaining whether such marriage would be lawful or unlawful in Delaware, and so that he might abide by the law; (2) that the attorney advised him that the proposed remarriage would not be unlawful; (3) that he relied on this advice, honestly believing his remarriage lawful; (4) that his efforts to ascertain the law were at all times diligent and in good faith, not by way of subterfuge, and such that there was no better course for ascertaining the law than that which he followed; and hence, that he made a full disclosure to the attorney of the relevant circumstances as well as of what he proposed to do, and that he had no substantial reason to believe that the advice received was ill-founded, such as circumstances reasonably indicating that the attorney was incompetent to give advice about this matter, or had not given the question sufficient consideration, or that the advice was lacking in candor. Assuming that the Arkansas decree be held invalid here, such findings would constitute a defense to the present charge as a mistake of law of the third classification. They would meet the test of bona fide, diligent efforts, as well designed to accomplish ascertainment of the law as any available under our system. The conditions indicated furnish safeguards against pretext and fraud. The defendant would have the burden of demonstrating that his efforts were well nigh exemplary. It would not be enough merely for him to say that he had relied on advice of an attorney, unless the circumstances indicated that his conduct throughout in seeking to ascertain the law and in relying on advice received manifested good faith and diligence beyond reproach. We see no occasion to assume that recognizing such a defense would foster dishonest practices among attorneys. These might well be expected to be deterred by the availability of disciplinary measures for non-professional conduct. Moreover, although erroneous advice might save a defendant from criminal responsibility for acts in reliance on it, the same acts would in many instances incur substantial civil responsibility and financial loss. The risk of possible disingenuous resort to the defense does not seem to us sufficient to warrant withholding it from those acting in good faith. Accordingly, the evidence should have been submitted to the jury under proper instructions.

A new trial should be awarded for the reasons set forth in this opinion.

An order accordingly will be entered.[1]

STATE v. STRIGGLES

Supreme Court of Iowa, 1926.
202 Iowa 1318, 210 N.W. 137.

ALBERT, J. We gather from the record and arguments of counsel the following history of the case at bar: It appears that in the early part of 1923 there was installed in several places of business in the

---

1. Selling securities without a permit is *malum prohibitum*, not *malum in se*. Hence one who was advised by the Corporation Commissioner that no permit was required for certain sales, and who relied upon that advice in good faith, could not properly be convicted for making such sales even if the advice was wrong. People v. Ferguson, 134 Cal.App. 41, 24 P.2d 965 (1933). One who erects and maintains a sign, which in fact violates the law, is guilty even if he acted in good faith reliance upon the advice of the State's Attorney that this sign would not violate the law. Hopkins v. State, 193 Md. 489, 69 A.2d 456 (1949).

Reliance upon advice of counsel is an element of good faith where the applicability of a statute to a factual situation is doubtful. United States v. McMillan, 114 F.Supp. 638 (D.C.D.C. 1953).

city of Des Moines a gum- or mint- vending machine. The machine and its workings are fully set out in the opinion in the case of State v. Ellis, 200 Iowa 1228, 206 N.W. 105. In that opinion it was judicially determined that such machine was a gambling device, within the inhibition of the statute.

On August 1, 1923, in several proceedings then pending in the municipal court of the city of Des Moines, a decision was rendered holding that such machine was not a gambling device. The distributors of the machine in question thereupon secured a certified copy of said decree, and equipped themselves with a letter from the county attorney's office, and also one from the mayor of the city, which stated that such machine was not a gambling device. Thus equipped, they presented themselves to appellant, Striggles, who conducted a restaurant in the city of Des Moines, and induced him to allow them to install a machine in his place of business.

Subsequent thereto, in the early part of 1925, the Polk County grand jury returned an indictment against appellant, in which it charged that he did "willfully and unlawfully keep a house, shop, and place . . . resorted to for the purpose of gambling, and he, . . . did then and there willfully and unlawfully permit and suffer divers persons, . . . in said house, shop, and place . . . to play a certain machine . . . being then and there a gambling device." On entering a plea of not guilty, the appellant was put on trial. He offered in evidence the aforesaid certified copy of the judgment decree of the court, and the letters from the county attorney and the mayor, which were promptly objected to, and the objection sustained. The appellant, while testifying, was permitted by the court to say that the exhibits had been presented to him before he permitted the machine to be installed. He was then asked by his counsel whether he relied on the contents of the papers when he gave his permission for installation of the machine. Objection to this line of testimony was sustained. He was also asked whether he would have permitted the machine to be installed, had he believed it to be a gambling device. He was not permitted to answer this question.

It is first urged in this case that the certified copy of the judgment from the municipal court was admissible in evidence, on the strength of the case of State v. O'Neil, 147 Iowa 513, 126 N.W. 454. A careful reading of the case, however, shows that it has no application to the case at bar. A certain statute of this state was held to be violative of the Constitution of the United States, and therefore void, in State v. Hanaphy, 117 Iowa 15, 90 N.W. 601, and State v. Bernstein, 129 Iowa 520, 105 N.W. 1015. The United States Supreme Court then decided Delamater v. South Dakota, 205 U.S. 93, 27 S.Ct. 447, 51 L.Ed. 724. On the strength of this opinion by the United States Court, we then overruled the Hanaphy and Bernstein cases, in McCollum v. McConaughy, 141 Iowa 172, 119 N.W. 539.

The crime with which O'Neil was charged, was committed by him between the time of the filing of the opinion of this court and the filing of the opinion of the United States Supreme Court. We held in that case that the appellant could not be guilty, because he was entitled to rely on the decision of this court which held the law in question unconstitutional.

Cases cited from other jurisdictions in appellant's argument are in line with the O'Neil case. There is no case cited, nor can we find one, on diligent search, holding that the decision of an inferior court can be relied upon to justify the defendant in a criminal case in the commission of the act which is alleged to be a crime. We are disposed to hold with the O'Neil case, that, when the court of highest jurisdiction passes on any given proposition, all citizens are entitled to rely upon such decision; but we refuse to hold that the decisions of any court below, inferior to the Supreme Court, are available as a defense, under similar circumstances. . . .

The matters of which complaint is made should have been taken into consideration by the district court in passing sentence on a verdict of guilty, and this was apparently done in this case, as the fine assessed was the minimum.—Affirmed.

EVANS, STEVENS, FAVILLE, and MORLING, JJ., concur.[1]

MODEL PENAL CODE

Section 2.04. Ignorance or Mistake.

(1) Ignorance or mistake as to a matter of fact or law is a defense if:

(a) the ignorance or mistake negatives the purpose, knowledge, belief, recklessness or negligence required to establish a material element of the offense; or

(b) the law provides that the state of mind established by such ignorance or mistake constitutes a defense.

(2) Although ignorance or mistake would otherwise afford a defense to the offense charged, the defense is not available if the defendant would be guilty of another offense had the situation been as he supposed. In such case, however, the ignorance or mistake of the defendant shall reduce the grade and degree of the offense of which he may be convicted to those of the offense of which he would be guilty had the situation been as he supposed.

---

1. New York C.P.A. § 1177 (1939). "Whenever, by the decision of the appellate division of the supreme court, a construction is given to a statute, an act done in good faith and in conformity to that construction, after the decision was made and before a reversal thereof by the court of appeals, is so far valid that the party doing it is not liable to any penalty or forfeiture for an act that was adjudged lawful by the court below. This section does not control or affect the decision of the court of appeals upon an appeal actually taken before the reversal."

(3) A belief that conduct does not legally constitute an offense is a defense to a prosecution for that offense based upon such conduct when:

    (a) the statute or other enactment defining the offense is not known to the actor and has not been published or otherwise reasonably made available prior to the conduct alleged; or

    (b) he acts in reasonable reliance upon an official statement of the law, afterward determined to be invalid or erroneous, contained in (i) a statute or other enactment; (ii) a judicial decision, opinion or judgment; (iii) an administrative order or grant of permission; or (iv) an official interpretation of the public officer or body charged by law with responsibility for the interpretation, administration or enforcement of the law defining the offense.

    (4) The defendant must prove a defense arising under Subsection (3) of this Section by a preponderance of evidence.

Section 2.02. (9) Culpability as to Illegality of Conduct. Neither knowledge nor recklessness or negligence as to whether conduct constitutes an offense or as to the existence, meaning or application of the law determining the elements of an offense is an element of such offense, unless the definition of the offense or the Code so provides.

(B) IGNORANCE OR MISTAKE OF FACT

    Ignorance or mistake of fact is very often an excuse for what would otherwise be a crime. A street car conductor, for example, who ejects a passenger from the car (without the use of unreasonable force) under the honest and reasonable, though mistaken, belief that his fare has not been paid, is liable to the passenger in a civil action but not guilty of criminal assault and battery. *"Ignorantia facti excusat,"* however, is too sweeping even for a general statement of law, because it is clear (to mention only one point for the moment) that if a certain deed would constitute exactly the same crime under either of two factual situations, it will be no excuse that one was mistaken for the other.

    A general statement which will apply to the ordinary situation, although it is subject to important qualifications, is this: Mistake of fact will disprove a criminal charge if the mistaken belief is (a) honestly entertained, (b) based upon reasonable grounds, and (c) of such a nature that the conduct would have been lawful had the facts been as they were reasonably supposed to be. This general rule is subject to many exceptions and these exceptions may cut in either direction, so to speak. (1) At times an honest mistake of fact may be exculpating although not based upon reasonable grounds. (2) In other prosecutions a well-grounded belief of a fact which would entitle the defendant to an acquittal if true may not save him from conviction if erroneous.

Sec. 1 IGNORANCE OR MISTAKE 521

Typical instances of the first kind of exception are found in prosecutions of those offenses, such as larceny, requiring a specific intent. There is no such thing in the common law as larceny by negligence. One does not commit this crime by carrying away the chattel of another in the mistaken belief that it is his own, no matter how great may have been the fault leading to this belief, if the belief itself is genuine. And the defendant is entitled to an acquittal in the prosecution for any crime requiring a specific intent or other special mental element, if such intent or other element is lacking,—even if the reason for its absence is a mistaken belief as to some fact. Such a belief must be genuine and sincere but it is not necessary for it to be based upon due care.

Offenses enforced on the basis of strict liability give opportunity for exceptions of the second type. Cases holding that a mistake of fact can never be a defense to a prosecution for a civil offense go too far, but even a well-grounded mistake of fact is not exculpating if the mistake could have been discovered by the use of greater care which it is not unreasonable to require of one in such a situation.

STATE v. NASH

Supreme Court of North Carolina, 1883.
88 N.C. 618.

ASHE, J. The question presented by the record is, was there error in the refusal of the judge to receive the evidence offered by the defendant. We are of the opinion there was error in rejecting so much of the proposed testimony as tended to show, on the part of the defendant, a *reasonable ground of belief* that the trespassers upon his premises had fired into his house and wounded his child.

It may be, as testified by the prosecutor, that the band of young men, who went to the defendant's house on the night in question, only intended innocent amusement; but there is one unusual and rather extraordinary feature in the transaction, that the party, intending a mere serenade, should, on such an occasion, carry guns and pistols; they are certainly very unusual instruments of music in the hands even of a calithumpian band.

They entered the enclosure, twenty in number; marched round his house, blowing horns, ringing bells and firing guns and pistols; which must have greatly frightened the family and the defendant himself, unless he is a man of more than ordinary courage. But whether awed or not by such a display of numbers and lawlessness, yielding to the dictates of prudence, he submitted to the humiliating indignity and remained within doors, until his little daughter, as he proposed to show, ran to him with her face bleeding; and believing, as was natural under the circumstances, that she had been shot, he seized his gun and went to the door, saw the flash of firearms, and shot into the crowd and wounded the prosecutor. We must suppose it was all the work of an instant.

Did the defendant, under these circumstances, have reasonable ground to believe that his daughter had been shot, and the assault upon him and his house was continuing? If he had, then he ought to have been acquitted.

We know this has been a much mooted question, but upon an investigation of the authorities, our conclusion is, that a reasonable belief that a felony is in the act of being committed on one, will excuse the killing of the supposed assailant, though no felony was in fact intended. And whatever will excuse a homicide, will of course, excuse an assault and battery. . . .

The same doctrine was enunciated by Parker, J., afterwards Chief-Justice of the supreme court of Massachusetts, in the famous case of Commonwealth v. Selfridge, Self. Trial, 100, and the principle is thus illustrated: "A, in the peaceful pursuit of his affairs, sees B walking towards him with an outstretched arm and a pistol in his hand, and using violent menaces against his life as he advances. Having approached near enough in the same attitude, A, who has a club in his hand, strikes B over the head before or at the instant the pistol is fired, and of the wound B dies. It turned out that the pistol was in fact loaded with powder only, and that the real design of B was only to terrify A." The judge inquired: "Will any reasonable man say that A is more criminal than he would have been if there had been a ball in the pistol?"

But it may be objected that the defendant acted too rashly: before he resorted to the use of his gun, he should have taken the precaution to ascertain the fact whether his child had been actually shot. But that doctrine is inconsistent with the principle we have announced. If the defendant had reason to believe and did believe in the danger, he had the right to act as though the danger actually existed, and was imminent. Taking, then, the fact to be, that the trespassers had fired into defendant's house and shot his child, and the firing continued, there was no time for delay. The occasion required prompt action. The next shot might strike him or some other member of his family. Under these circumstances, the law would justify the defendant in firing upon his assailants in defence of himself and his family.

But, as we have said, the grounds of belief must be reasonable. The defendant must judge, at the time, of the ground of his apprehension, and he must judge at his peril; for it is the province of the jury on the trial to determine the reasonable ground of his belief. And here, the error is in the court's refusing to receive the proposed evidence, and submitting that question to the consideration of the jury. A *venire de novo* must be awarded.

SMITH, C. J., dissenting. I am unable to concur with the other members of the court, in the conclusion reached, that the testimony of the defendant in explanation of his conduct, if admitted and believed, would be a defence to the charge, or have any other legal effect than to mitigate his offence, and hence, as immaterial upon the issue and tending to mislead, there is no error in rejecting it.

The facts in connection with this proposed statement are summarily as follows: A boisterous and unruly crowd, in what seems to have been a frolick, enter the defendant's premises in the early night with bells, horns and firearms, by the noise of which, as they pass around his dwelling, himself and his family are greatly annoyed and their peace disturbed. As they are about to leave, his little frightened daughter runs up to him with blood upon her face, caused by her striking against a table, but which he then supposed to proceed from a shot wound. Acting upon the impulse produced by this misconception and without stopping to make inquiry as to the cause or extent of the injury, he seizes his gun loaded with shot of large size, hastens to the door and out into the porch, and, seeing the flash of a gun, fires into the retreating body then near the outer gate, some thirty-five yards distant, without a word of warning or remonstrance, and wounds one of the number in the leg.

This was, in my opinion, a hasty and unauthorized act in the use of a deadly weapon, not in defence of himself or family, or premises, but the offspring of a spirit of retaliation for what he erroneously supposed to have been done, and whose error could at once have been corrected. If death had ensued, the circumstances would not have excused the homicide; and as it was not fatal, it cannot be less than an assault.

Human life is too safely guarded by law to allow it to be put in peril upon such provocation; and, however much it may palliate the defendant's impulse and the rash act in which it resulted, it cannot, in my opinion, excuse his use of a deadly instrument in so reckless a manner.

PER CURIAM. *Venire de novo.*

THE KING v. EWART

Court of Appeal of New Zealand, 1905.
25 N.Z.L.R. 709.

(A newspaper vendor sold a copy of a paper containing obscene matter and was indicted for violation of the statute on that subject.)

STOUT, C. J.: The first question that arises in this case is whether the provisions of section 3 of "The Offensive Publications Act, 1892," require that, before a conviction can be affirmed against an accused person, there must be proof that he knew the publication he sold to be indecent, and whether there can be no conviction if the jury believes he did not know that the newspaper he sold was indecent; in fact, whether *mens rea* is required to be proved under this Act. . . .

The sole questions, in my opinion, that the jury had to determine were, 1, whether the prisoner did sell the newspaper, and, 2, whether the newspaper sold was indecent, immoral, or obscene. The jury found both these questions in the affirmative.

I am therefore of opinion that the conviction should be affirmed.

WILLIAMS, J.: . . . Exactly similar considerations apply to subsection 5 of section 82 of "The Post Office Act, 1900." That subsection makes it penal without any qualification to post any postal packet containing indecent or obscene matter. A bishop who was obliging enough to post such a packet for a stranger would have to be convicted if knowledge were immaterial. In my opinion, therefore, honest ignorance is a defence to the charge in the present case. The act forbidden having been done, it lay upon the defendant to show that he did it unwittingly and without a guilty mind. If he knew the publication contained indecent matter, or if he suspected that it contained such matter and abstained from ascertaining whether it did or not, the tainted mind would be present. It would be, however, competent for him to establish its absence, and if the jury were satisfied upon the evidence that it was absent he was entitled to be acquitted, and I think the jury should have been so directed. As to the other questions raised, I agree with His Honour. I think, therefore, the conviction should be quashed, and that there should be a new trial.

EDWARDS, J. . . . There are, therefore, two classes of cases under the statute law—1, those in which, following the common-law rule, a guilty mind must either be necessarily inferred from the nature of the act done or must be established by independent evidence; 2, those in which, either from the language or the scope and object of the enactment to be construed, it is made plain that the Legislature intended to prohibit the act absolutely, and the question of the existence of a guilty mind is only relevant for the purpose of determining the quantum of punishment following the offence. There is also a third class in which, although from the omission from the statute of the words "knowingly" or "wilfully" it is not necessary to aver in the indictment that the offence charged was "knowingly" or "wilfully" committed, or to prove a guilty mind, and the commission of the act in itself *prima facie* imports an offence, yet the person charged may still discharge himself by proving to the satisfaction of the tribunal which tries him that in fact he had not a guilty mind. . . .

The case does, I think, clearly come within the third class of cases to which I have referred. The act charged is, I think, clearly an act which, upon the true construction of the statute, is made in itself *prima facie* to import a guilty mind, but as to which the presumption arising from the doing of the act may be rebutted by evidence adduced by the person charged. This, I think, is the result of the authorities, and it is one which will insure justice being done in all such cases.

I desire to guard myself from appearing to suggest that a person charged with this offence can in all cases discharge himself from the consequences simply by swearing that he did not know the contents of what he was selling. In any case it will be for the jury to decide whether they will believe the prisoner's evidence upon that point or not. Further, I think that if the prosecution can in any such case establish that any particular newspaper or serial publication has acquired the reputation of publishing indecent, immoral, or obscene matter, and that nevertheless the person charged has sold any issue of that paper or serial publication which does contain indecent, immoral, or obscene matter, the jury would be justified in inferring, and indeed ought to infer, that if the person charged did not take the precaution to see that what he sold did not contain such matter, it was because he wilfully abstained from making an inquiry which it was his duty to make. It may, I think, be safely laid down that it is the duty of a news-vendor to know at least the general character of the newspapers and serial publications which he sells, and either to abstain altogether from selling those which in their previous issues have acquired a doubtful character or to ascertain with respect to each copy that he sells that it contains nothing indecent, immoral, or obscene.

In my opinion the case, as it stood, ought to have been left to the jury, with the direction that if they believed that the prisoner was honestly ignorant of the contents of the newspaper in question then they should acquit him. The prisone[r] is therefore, in my opinion, entitled to a new trial, and there should be an order accordingly.

. . .

New Trial Ordered.

(COOPER, J., wrote an opinion in favor of upholding the conviction. CHAPMAN, J., wrote an opinion in favor of granting a new trial.)

PEOPLE v. VOGEL

Supreme Court of California, In Bank, 1956.
46 Cal.2d 798, 299 P.2d 850.

[In a bigamy trial the court refused to admit evidence to show that defendant's wife had told him she was going to get a divorce, and that some time thereafter she married Earl Heck, lived with him, and received mail and telephone calls as Mrs. Earl Heck. The reason for the refusal was that "defendant's good faith belief that she had divorced him and married Heck was immaterial".]

TRAYNOR, JUSTICE. Defendant appeals from a judgment of conviction entered on a jury verdict finding him guilty of bigamy and from an order denying his motion for a new trial. . . .

We have concluded that defendant is not guilty of bigamy, if he had a bona fide and reasonable belief that facts existed that left him free to remarry. As in other crimes, there must be a union of act and wrongful intent. So basic is this requirement that it is an invariable element of every crime unless excluded expressly or by necessary implication. Sections 281 and 282 do not expressly exclude it nor can its exclusion therefrom be reasonably implied.

Certainly its exclusion cannot be implied from the mere omission of any reference to intent in the definition of bigamy, for the commissioners' annotation to section 20 makes it clear that such an omission was not meant to exclude intent as an element of the crime but to shift to defendant the burden of proving that he did not have the requisite intent. The commissioners quote at length from People v. Harris, 29 Cal. 678, 681–682. That case involved a conviction for twice voting at the same election. The defendant sought to defend upon the ground that he was so drunk at the time he voted the second time that he did not know what he was doing and that he therefore had no criminal intent. The court held that the trial court erred in excluding from the jury any consideration of the mental state of the defendant by reason of his intoxicated condition, stating: "It is laid down in the books on the subject, that it is a universal doctrine that to constitute what the law deems a crime there must concur both an evil act and an evil intent. *Actus non facit reum nisi mens sit rea.* —1 Bish. on Cr.Law, Secs. 227, 229; 3 Greenl.Ev., Sec. 13. Therefore the intent with which the unlawful act was done must be proved as well as the other material facts stated in the indictment; which may be by evidence either direct or indirect, tending to establish the fact, or by inference of law from other facts proved. When the act is proved to have been done by the accused, if it be an act in itself unlawful, the law in the first instance presumes it to have been intended, and the proof of justification or excuse lies on the defendant to overcome this legal and natural presumption. . . .

The "correct and authoritative exposition of Sec. 20" as applied in People v. Harris to the crime of twice voting in the same election applies with even greater force to the crime of bigamy and compels the conclusion that guilty knowledge, which was formerly a part of the definition of bigamy was omitted from section 281 to reallocate the burden of proof on that issue in a bigamy trial. Thus, the prosecution makes a prima facie case upon proof that the second marriage was entered into while the first spouse was still living, and his bona fide and reasonable belief that facts existed that left the defendant free to remarry is a defense to be proved by the defendant.

Sec. 1   IGNORANCE OR MISTAKE   527

Nor must the exclusion of wrongful intent be implied from the two exceptions set forth in section 282. Obviously they are not all inclusive, for it cannot be seriously contended that an insane person or a person who married for the second time while unconscious, Pen. Code, § 26, subds. 3, 5, could be convicted of bigamy. Moreover, the mere enumeration of specific defenses appropriate to particular crimes does not exclude general defenses based on sections 20 and 26 (see, 2 Lewis' Sutherland, Statutory Construction, § 495, p. 924; 23 Cal.Jur., Statutes, § 118, p. 742), for the enumerated defenses in no way conflict with such general defenses. . . .

The foregoing construction of sections 281 and 282 is consistent with good sense and justice. (See, dissenting opinion of McComb, J., in People v. Kelly, 32 Cal.App.2d 624, 628, 90 P.2d 605.) The severe penalty imposed for bigamy, the serious loss of reputation conviction entails, the infrequency of the offense, and the fact that it has been regarded for centuries as a crime involving moral turpitude, make it extremely unlikely that the Legislature meant to include the morally innocent to make sure the guilty did not escape. . . .

In a prosecution for bigamy evidence that a person is generally reputed to be married is admissible as tending to show actual marriage. The same evidence that would tend to prove an actual marriage, if offered by the People, could reasonably form the basis for an honest belief by a defendant that there was such marriage, that it was legally entered into, and that he was, therefore, free to remarry. The evidence offered to show that Peggy had married Earl Heck should therefore have been admitted. The statement allegedly made by Peggy that she was going to divorce defendant was admissible on the issue of his belief that she had done so and it was also admissible to impeach her testimony that she did not tell him that she was going to divorce him. The exclusion of this evidence was clearly prejudicial, for it deprived defendant of the defense of a bona fide and reasonable belief that facts existed that left him free to remarry. . . .

The judgment and order are reversed.[1]

GIBSON, C. J., and CARTER, SCHAUER, SPENCE and MCCOMB, JJ., concur.

SHENK, JUSTICE. I dissent. . . .

Bigamy is a statutory crime, defined in section 281 of the Penal Code, as follows: "Every person having a husband or wife living, who marries any other person, except in the cases specified in the

---

1. Contra, State v. Hendrickson, 67 Utah 15, 245 P. 375, 57 A.L.R. 786 (1926).

next section, is guilty of bigamy." The exceptions contained in section 282 are as follows:

"The last section does not extend—

"1. To any person by reason of any former marriage, whose husband or wife by such marriage has been absent for five successive years without being known to such person within that time to be living; nor

"2. To any person by reason of any former marriage which has been pronounced void, annulled, or dissolved by the judgment of a competent Court."

While the legislature has provided a condition and a term of years after which a person may in good faith reasonably conclude that an absent spouse is dead, it has provided no such condition or term for concluding that an absent spouse has procured a divorce. The legislature has not, either expressly or by reasonable implication, made a mere belief in the existence of a prior divorce a defense to a bigamy prosecution. . . .

STATE v. RUHL

Supreme Court of Iowa, 1859.
8 Iowa 447.

WRIGHT, C. J. Several errors are assigned, and they will be briefly noticed in their order. . . .

The second bill of exceptions shows, that the defendant proposed to prove that the said Matilda had, before the alleged enticing, told him that she was over fifteen years of age, which was objected to, and the objection sustained.

The language of the section (2584) under which this indictment was found is, that "if any person take or entice away an unmarried female, under the age of fifteen years, from her father or mother, guardian, or other person having the legal charge of her person, without their consent, he shall upon conviction, &c." The object of the proposed testimony, was to show that defendant believed, or had good reason to believe, that the prosecuting witness was, at the time of taking or enticing away, over fifteen years of age. Would such proof aid the defendant, if in fact the female was under the age named? We think not. It is not like the case stated by appellant, and found in the books, of a married man, through a mistake of the person, having intercourse with a woman whom he supposed to be his wife, when she was not. In such a case there is no offense, for none was intended either in law or morals. In the case at bar, however, if defendant enticed the female away, for the purpose of defilement or prostitution, there existed a criminal or wrongful intent—even though she was over the age of fifteen. The testimony offered was, therefore, irrelevant—for the only effect of it would have been, to show

Sec. 1   *IGNORANCE OR MISTAKE*   529

that he intended one wrong, and by mistake committed another. The wrongful intent to do the one act, is only transposed to the other. And though the wrong intended is not indictable, the defendant would still be liable, if the wrong done is so. Bishop's Cr.Law, secs. 247, 249, 252, 254, (note 4). In this last section, the rule is thus briefly stated: "The wrong intended, but not done, and the wrong done, but not intended, coalesce, and together constitute the same offense, not always in the same degree, as if the prisoner had intended the thing unintentionally done."

(For other reasons the judgment was reversed.)

REGINA v. TINKLER
Norfolk Circuit, 1859.
1 Fost. & F. 513, 175 Eng.Rep. 832.

The prisoner was indicted, under the 9 Geo. 4, c. 31, s. 20, for unlawfully taking one Sarah Thompson, she being then unmarried, and under the age of sixteen years, out of the possession and against the will of Jane Barnes, her lawful guardian.

It appeared that the prisoner, who was a widower, had married the elder sister of Sarah Thompson, and up to the time of his wife's death, Sarah Thompson, who was an orphan, had lived in the prisoner's house. On that occasion, Mary Johnson, another married sister of Sarah Thompson, caused her to be placed under the care of Jane Barnes.

No improper motive was alleged against the prisoner, he having asserted, as his reason for taking the child away, that he had promised her father, on his deathbed, to take care of her.

The Chief Justice told the jury that it was clear the prisoner had no right to act as he had done in taking the child out of Mrs. Barnes's custody. But inasmuch as no improper motive was suggested on the part of the prosecution, it might very well be concluded, that the prisoner wished the child to live with him, and that he meant to discharge the promise which he alleged he had made to her father, and that he did not suppose he was breaking the law when he took the child away. This being a criminal prosecution, if the jury should take this view of the case, and be of opinion that the prisoner honestly believed that he had a right to the custody of the child, then, although the prisoner was not legally justified, he would be entitled to an acquittal upon this charge.

The jury found the prisoner not guilty.[1]

---

1. The Texas statute (Vernon's Ann. Pen.Code art. 41) provides that for an act, otherwise criminal, to be excusable because of mistake of fact, it must be a mistake that "does not arise from a want of proper care on the part of the person so acting." Even under this statute one who takes what he honestly believes to be his is not guilty of theft whether this belief did

Perkins Cs.Crim.Law & Procedure 3rd Ed.–UCB—34

PEOPLE v. HERNANDEZ

Supreme Court of California, In Bank, 1964.
61 Cal.2d 529, 39 Cal.Rptr. 361, 393 P.2d 673.

PEEK, JUSTICE. By information defendant was charged with statutory rape. (Pen.Code, § 261, subd. 1.) Following his plea of not guilty he was convicted as charged by the court sitting without a jury and the offense determined to be a misdemeanor.

Section 261 of the Penal Code provides in part as follows: "Rape is an act of sexual intercourse, accomplished with a female not the wife of the perpetrator, under either of the following circumstances: 1. Where the female is under the age of 18 years; . . .."

The sole contention raised on appeal is that the trial court erred in refusing to permit defendant to present evidence going to his guilt for the purpose of showing that he had in good faith a reasonable belief that the prosecutrix was 18 years or more of age.

The undisputed facts show that the defendant and the prosecuting witness were not married and had been companions for several months prior to January 3, 1961—the date of the commission of the alleged offense. Upon that date the prosecutrix was 17 years and 9 months of age and voluntarily engaged in an act of sexual intercourse with defendant.

In support of his contention defendant relies upon Penal Code, § 20, which provides that "there must exist a union, or joint operation of act and intent, or criminal negligence" to constitute the commission of a crime. He further relies upon section 26 of that code which provides that one is not capable of committing a crime who commits an act under an ignorance or mistake of fact which disproves any criminal intent.

Thus the sole issue relates to the question of intent and knowledge entertained by the defendant at the time of the commission of the crime charged.

Consent of the female is often an unrealistic and unfortunate standard for branding sexual intercourse a crime as serious as forcible rape. Yet the consent standard has been deemed to be required by important policy goals. We are dealing here, of course, with statutory rape where, in one sense, the lack of consent of the female is not an element of the offense. In a broader sense, however, the lack of consent is deemed to remain an element but the law makes a

---

or did not result from want of due care. Green v. State, 153 Tex.Cr.R. 442, 221 S.W.2d 612 (1949).

It is beyond the power of the legislature to punish a junk dealer who purchases stolen property, without knowing it is stolen and without even a failure to use due diligence in this regard. People v. Estreich, 272 App. Div. 698, 75 N.Y.S.2d 267 (1947). Affirmed without opinion: 297 N.Y. 910, 79 N.E.2d 742.

See Vernon's Ann.Texas Pen.Code, art. 41 (1952).

conclusive presumption of the lack thereof because she is presumed too innocent and naive to understand the implications and nature of her act. The law's concern with her capacity or lack thereof to so understand is explained in part by a popular conception of the social, moral and personal values which are preserved by the abstinence from sexual indulgence on the part of a young woman. An unwise disposition of her sexual favor is deemed to do harm both to herself and the social mores by which the community's conduct patterns are established. Hence the law of statutory rape intervenes in an effort to avoid such a disposition. This goal, moreover, is not accomplished by penalizing the naive female but by imposing criminal sanctions against the male, who is conclusively presumed to be responsible for the occurrence.

The assumption that age alone will bring an understanding of the sexual act to a young woman is of doubtful validity. Both learning from the cultural group to which she is a member and her actual sexual experiences will determine her level of comprehension. The sexually experienced 15-year old may be far more acutely aware of the implications of sexual intercourse than her sheltered cousin who is beyond the age of consent. A girl who belongs to a group whose members indulge in sexual intercourse at an early age is likely to rapidly acquire an insight into the rewards and penalties of sexual indulgence. Nevertheless, even in circumstances where a girl's actual comprehension contradicts the law's presumption, the male is deemed criminally responsible for the act, although himself young and naive and responding to advances which may have been made to him.[1]

The law as presently constituted does not concern itself with the relative culpability of the male and female participants in the prohibited sexual act. Even where the young woman is knowledgeable it does not impose sanctions upon her. The knowledgeable young man, on the other hand, is penalized and there are none who would claim that under any construction of the law this should be otherwise. However, the issue raised by the rejected offer of proof in the instant case goes to the culpability of the young man who acts *without* knowledge that an essential factual element exists and has, on the other hand, a positive, reasonable belief that it does not exist.

---

1. The inequitable consequences to which we may be led are graphically illustrated by the following excerpt from State v. Snow (Mo.1923) 252 S.W. 629 at page 632: "We have in this case a condition and not a theory. This wretched girl was young in years but old in sin and shame. A number of callow youths, of otherwise blameless lives . . . fell under her seductive influence. They flocked about her, . . . like moths about the flame of a lighted candle and probably with the same result. The girl was a common prostitute . . . . The boys were immature and doubtless more sinned against than sinning. They did not defile the girl. She was a mere 'cistern for foul toads to knot and gender in.' Why should the boys, misled by her, be sacrificed? What sound public policy can be subserved by branding them as felons? Might it not be wise to ingraft an exception in the statute?"

The primordial concept of *mens rea*, the guilty mind, expresses the principle that it is not conduct alone but conduct accompanied by certain specific mental states which concerns, or should concern the law. In a broad sense the concept may be said to relate to such important doctrines as justification, excuse, mistake, necessity and mental capacity, but in the final analysis it means simply that there must be a "joint operation of act and intent," as expressed in section 20 of the Penal Code, to constitute the commission of a criminal offense. The statutory law, however, furnishes no assistance to the courts beyond that, and the casebooks are filled to overflowing with the courts' struggles to determine just what state of mind should be considered relevant in particular contexts. In numerous instances culpability has been completely eliminated as a necessary element of criminal conduct in spite of the admonition of section 20 to the contrary. More recently, however, this court has moved away from the imposition of criminal sanctions in the absence of culpability where the governing statute, by implication or otherwise, expresses no legislative intent or policy to be served by imposing strict liability. (People v. Stuart, 47 Cal.2d 167, 302 P.2d 5, 55 A.L.R.2d 705; People v. Vogel, 46 Cal.2d 798, 299 P.2d 850; People v. Winston, 46 Cal.2d 151, 293 P.2d 40.)

Statutory rape has long furnished a fertile battleground upon which to argue that the lack of knowledgeable conduct is a proper defense. The law in this state now rests, as it did in 1896, with this court's decision in People v. Ratz, 115 Cal. 132, at pages 134 and 135, 46 P. 915, at page 916, where it is stated: "The claim here made is not a new one. It has frequently been pressed upon the attention of courts, but in no case, so far as our examination goes, has it met with favor. The object and purpose of the law are too plain to need comment, the crime too infamous to bear discussion. The protection of society, of the family, and of the infant, demand that one who has carnal intercourse under such circumstances shall do so in peril of the fact, and he will not be heard against the evidence to urge his belief that the victim of his outrage had passed the period which would make his act a crime." The age of consent at the time of the Ratz decision was 14 years, and it is noteworthy that the purpose of the rule, as there announced, was to afford protection to young females therein described as "infants." The decision on which the court in Ratz relied was The Queen v. Prince, L.R. 2 Crown Cas. 154. However England has now, by statute, departed from the strict rule, and excludes as a crime an act of sexual intercourse with a female between the ages of 13 and 16 years if the perpetrator is under the age of 24 years, has not previously been charged with a like offense, and believes the female "to be of the age of sixteen or over and has reasonable cause for the belief." (Halsburg's Statutes of England, 2d Ed., Vol. 36, Continuation Volume 1956, at page 219.)

The rationale of the Ratz decision, rather than purporting to eliminate intent as an element of the crime, holds that the wrongdoer must assume the risk; that, subjectively, when the act is committed, he consciously intends to proceed regardless of the age of the female and the consequences of his act, and that the circumstances involving the female, whether she be a day or a decade less than the statutory age, are irrelevant. There can be no dispute that a criminal intent exists when the perpetrator proceeds with utter disregard of, or in the lack of grounds for, a belief that the female has reached the age of consent. But if he participates in a mutual act of sexual intercourse, believing his partner to be beyond the age of consent, with reasonable grounds for such belief, where is his criminal intent? In such circumstances he has not consciously taken any risk. Instead he has subjectively eliminated the risk by satisfying himself on reasonable evidence that the crime cannot be committed. If it occurs that he has been misled, we cannot realistically conclude that for such reason alone the intent with which he undertook the act suddenly becomes more heinous.

While the specific contentions herein made have been dealt with and rejected both within and without this state, the courts have uniformly failed to satisfactorily explain the nature of the criminal intent present in the mind of one who in good faith believes he has obtained a lawful consent before engaging in the prohibited act. As in the Ratz case the courts often justify convictions on policy reasons which, in effect, eliminate the element of intent. The Legislature, of course, by making intent an element of the crime, has established the prevailing policy from which it alone can properly advise us to depart.

We have recently given recognition to the legislative declarations in sections 20 and 26 of the Penal Code, and departed from prior decisional law which had failed to accord full effect to those sections as applied to charges of bigamy. (People v. Vogel, supra, 46 Cal.2d 798, 299 P.2d 850.) . . .

We are persuaded that the reluctance to accord to a charge of statutory rape the defense of a lack of criminal intent has no greater justification than in the case of other statutory crimes, where the Legislature has made identical provision with respect to intent. " 'At common law an honest and reasonable belief in the existence of circumstances, which, if true, would make the act for which the person is indicted an innocent act, has always been held to be a good defense. . . . So far as I am aware it has never been suggested that these exceptions do not equally apply to the case of statutory offenses unless they are excluded expressly or by necessary implication.' " (Matter of Application of Ahart, 172 Cal. 762, 764–765, 159 P. 160, 161–162, quoting from Regina v. Tolson, [1889] 23 Q.B.D. 168, s. c., 40 Alb.L.J. 250.) Our departure from the views expressed in Ratz is in no manner indicative of a withdrawal from the sound policy that it is in the public interest to protect the sexually naive female from exploitation. No responsible person would hesitate to condemn as untenable a claimed good faith belief in the age of consent of an "infant" female whose obviously tender years preclude the existence of reasonable grounds for that belief. However, the prosecutrix in the instant case was but three months short of 18 years of age and there is nothing in the record to indicate that the purposes of the law as stated in Ratz can be better served by foreclosing the defense of a lack of intent. This is not to say that the granting of consent by even a sexually sophisticated girl known to be less than the statutory age is a defense. We hold only that in the absence of a legislative direction otherwise, a charge of statutory rape is defensible wherein a criminal intent is lacking.

For the foregoing reasons People v. Ratz, supra, 115 Cal. 132, 46 P. 915, and People v. Griffin, supra, 117 Cal. 583, 49 P. 711 are overruled, and People v. Sheffield, 9 Cal.App. 130, 98 P. 67, is disapproved to the extent that such decisions are inconsistent with the views expressed herein.

Some question has been raised that the offer of proof of defendant's reasonable belief in the age of the prosecutrix was insufficient to justify the pleading of such belief as a defense to the act. It is not our purpose here to make a determination that the defendant entertained a reasonable belief. Suffice to state that the offer demonstrated a sufficient basis upon which, when fully developed, the trier of fact might have found in defendant's favor. We conclude that it was reversible error to reject the offer.

The judgment is reversed.

GIBSON, C. J., and TRAYNOR, SCHAUER, MCCOMB, PETERS and TOBRINER, JJ., concur.

MODEL PENAL CODE

Section 213.6. Provisions Generally Applicable to Article 213. [Sexual Offenses.]

(1) Mistake as to Age. Whenever in this Article the criminality of conduct depends on a child's being below the age of 10, it is no defense that the actor did not know the child's age, or reasonably believed the child to be older than 10. When criminality depends on the child's being below a critical age other than 10, it is a defense for the actor to prove by a preponderance of the evidence that he reasonably believed the child to be above the critical age.

. . .

Section 230.1. Bigamy and Polygamy.

(1) Bigamy. A married person is guilty of bigamy, a misdemeanor, if he contracts or purports to contract another marriage, unless at the time of the subsequent marriage:

(a) the actor believes that the prior spouse is dead; or

(b) the actor and the prior spouse have been living apart for five consecutive years throughout which the prior spouse was not known by the actor to be alive; or

(c) a Court has entered a judgment purporting to terminate or annul any prior disqualifying marriage, and the actor does not know that judgment to be invalid; or

(d) the actor reasonably believes that he is legally eligible to remarry.

(2) *Polygamy*. A person is guilty of polygamy, a felony of the third degree, if he marries or cohabits with more than one spouse at a time in purported exercise of the right of plural marriage. The offense is a continuing one until all cohabitation and claim of marriage with more than one spouse terminates. This section does not apply to parties to a polygamous marriage, lawful in the country of which they are residents or nationals, while they are in transit through or temporarily visiting this State.

(3) *Other Party to Bigamous or Polygamous Marriage*. A person is guilty of bigamy or polygamy, as the case may be, if he contracts or purports to contract marriage with another knowing that the other is thereby committing bigamy or polygamy.

SECTION 2. COMPULSION OR NECESSITY

A command or order, not backed by public authority, will not excuse a deed which would otherwise be a crime (except to the decreasing extent that a husband's command may excuse his wife). Under certain circumstances one who has carried out a private command or order may be free from guilt although the criminal law was violated, but the excuse will be based upon some other ground. If, for example, the thing commanded is not obviously wrongful, and the order is carried out in innocence of the criminal purpose intended, the "innocent agent" is not guilty of crime. This may happen in various ways, such as where an employer commits larceny by directing an employee to take a certain chattel (which actually belongs to another) and place it in the employer's house or store. The employee is not guilty of crime if he carries out this order in the innocent belief that the chattel belongs to his employer. In such cases, however, it is the mistake of fact, and not the command, which constitutes the excuse.

If a command or order is accompanied by violence or threat of violence, the real problem is not the command but the compulsion. An "act" is a willed movement. Hence if one's body is propelled against his will, this is not his act. The classic example is this: A, B and C are standing near the edge of a precipice. Suddenly A shoves B violently against C, causing C to fall to his death. A has caused the death of *C*, but *B* whose body was used as a tool by *A*, so to speak, has not caused this death. *B* did not act, he was acted upon.

Such a situation is mentioned to avoid any possible misunderstanding, but "compulsion" has quite a different meaning. "Compulsion," as used in this connection, applies where it is the *will* rather than the *body* which is coerced. If, in a case similar to the one mentioned, *A* had not touched *B*, but had pointed a loaded pistol at him and threatened to kill him unless he pushed *C* over the edge, and *B* had done this to save his own life, it would have been a case of compulsion. In this case *B* had a choice. It was not an easy choice, to be sure, but when he decided to push *C* to his death rather than risk his own life, this was a willed movement and hence an "act." And the resulting death is legally imputable to him as well as to *A*. Whether he is criminally responsible for this death he has caused depends upon whether or not this compulsion will be recognized as an excuse.

Statements can be found by some of the early writers indicating that no man is ever criminally answerable for what he was compelled to do in order to save his own life. And unquestionably such compulsion or necessity will be recognized as an excuse for most deeds which would otherwise be criminal. But Blackstone asserted: ". . . though a man be violently assaulted, and hath no other possible means of escaping death but by killing an innocent person, this fear and force shall not acquit him of murder; for he ought rather to die himself than escape by the murder of an innocent."[1] No sound analogy can be drawn from the "self defense" cases because such defense does not involve the killing of an *innocent* person. And the very few cases of this nature which have reached the courtroom show that the common law does not justify or excuse such a killing.[2] Strangely enough the possibility of manslaughter rather than murder in such cases seems never to have had adequate consideration. The killing is intentional, to be sure, and there is no legally recognized *provocation*. But the circumstances are extremely *mitigating*. The mitigation in such a case is entitled to greater recognition than that in most instances of voluntary manslaughter committed in the sudden heat of passion. The state of mind of one who reluctantly takes the life of an innocent person as the only means of saving his own, while not guiltless, is certainly not malice aforethought.

One of the most sordid cases of compulsion is that of the brute who tried, at the point of a gun, to force his wife and another man to have sexual intercourse. He was convicted of an assault with intent to commit rape on his own wife. On appeal it was urged that the male victim of the assault would not have been guilty of rape had the

---

[1] 4 Bl.Comm. 30.

[2] The leading case is Brewer v. State, 72 Ark. 145, 78 S.W. 773 (1904). An Alabama opinion goes into the subject rather thoroughly although the actual decision turns on another point. Arp v. State, 97 Ala. 5, 12 So. 301 (1893).

act been completed and hence there was no intent to commit rape. The court, in affirming the conviction, did not rest the decision entirely upon this point but was inclined to the view that not even the fear of immediate death would be a defense to a charge of rape.[3]

For most offenses, however, a well-grounded fear of immediate death or great bodily injury is recognized as an excuse. One is not punishable for robbery because of having driven the get-away car for robbers if it is done at the point of a pistol and under the threat of immediate death.[4] And one who damaged a threshing machine with a sledge hammer was held not guilty of crime when it was found that he had been compelled to do so by a violent mob.[5] It was even recognized that one who joins the enemy forces in time of war is not guilty of treason if he does so in fear of death or great bodily injury, and escapes at the first reasonable opportunity [6]—provided he has not caused death in the meantime.[7]

It has been argued that if such compulsion will excuse treason it should excuse any crime, and therefore murder.[8] The answer, however, is obvious. Joining enemy forces, with mental reservation, and leaving at the earliest opportunity causes no lasting harm. Homicide does.

The word "compulsion," as it is used in the criminal law, is limited usually to situations in which the unwilling action is compelled by some other person. Quite similar emergencies may arise in which the pressure is exerted by some other agency, and the result is the same. Here also it is necessary to distinguish between forcing the body and forcing the will. Treating physical impossibility and extreme pressure of circumstances as if they were identical "is one of the oldest fallacies of the law."[9] If a tornado hurls the body of A against B, with fatal results to B, this death is not caused by the act of A. But if A and B are adrift in a small boat 1000 miles from land and without food, and A kills B and eats his flesh as the only means of saving

---

3. State v. Dowell, 106 N.C. 722, 11 S. E. 525 (1890).

4. People v. Merhige, 212 Mich. 601, 180 N.W. 418 (1920).

5. Rex v. Crutchley, 5 Car. & P. 133, 172 Eng.Rep. 909 (1831).

6. Oldcastle's Case, 3 Co.Inst. *10, 1 Hale, P.C. 50, 1 East, P.C. 70. "An American . . . charged with playing the role of the traitor may defend by showing that force or coercion compelled such conduct". Kawakita v. United States, 343 U.S. 717, 736, 72 S.Ct. 950, 962, 96 L.Ed. 1249 (1952). As to what constitutes compulsion see D'Aquino v. United States, 192 F.2d 338 (9th Cir. 1951).

Respublica v. McCarty, 2 Dallas 86, 1 L.Ed. 300 (Pa.1781). In this case defendant was not excused because he was still with the British forces eleven months after he claimed to have been compelled to join them.

7. The soldier "who commanded the guards at the king's tryal, and at his murder" had no defense although "all that he did was as a soldier, by the command of his superior officer, whom he must obey or die". Axtell's Case, Kelyng 13, 84 Eng.Rep. 1060 (1660).

8. 1 East, Pleas of the Crown 294 (1803).

9. Per Mr. Justice Holmes in the Eliza Lines, 199 U.S. 119, 130, 26 Sup.Ct. 8, 10, 50 L.Ed. 115 (1905).

his own life, this death is caused by *A*. Furthermore, no matter how great the necessity, the law will not excuse the intentional killing of an *innocent* person on the plea that it was necessary to save the life of the slayer. In the boat case mentioned the English court insisted that the crime was murder and pronounced sentence of death,[10] but the sentence was afterward commuted by the crown to six months' imprisonment. It would seem that circumstances so obviously and extremely mitigating as to cause such a reduction by the pardoning power should have been recognized by the court as reducing the grade of the crime itself. In the famous case of "human jettison," the actual verdict was guilty of manslaughter. In this case a leaking boat loaded with survivors after a ship-wreck was in grave danger of sinking in a storm. It was not a modern life-boat and all would have been lost if it had gone down. The sailors threw some passengers overboard to lighten the load. As thus lightened the boat was kept afloat during the storm and the survivors were picked up by a passing vessel the following day. The judge charged the jury that the sailors had no privilege to sacrifice passengers even in such extreme peril.[11] He intimated, although it was quite beside the point, that if several are in such peril that some must be sacrificed in order for any to be saved—and none of the group owes any duty to others in this emergency—choice by lot would be proper.

What seems to be the accepted view today, although the cases are very few, is that no one is privileged to choose the death of some other innocent person in order to preserve his own life. In extreme emergencies, however, the field of legally-recognized causation may be somewhat narrow. One may not wilfully plunge a knife into an obviously guiltless breast, but it does not follow that in a race, or even a struggle, for means of safety, adequate to preserve the life of only one, the winner shall under all circumstances be said to have killed the loser.

On the other hand, where the necessity is great a deed not involving death or great bodily harm may be excused, even if otherwise it would be a crime. For example, if merchant vessels are forbidden to enter a certain port, and such a ship is forced to take refuge there during a violent storm, for the safety of the vessel and those on board, there has been no violation of the embargo.[12] And what might otherwise constitute attempted revolt by sailors on the high seas may be excused by the unseaworthiness of the vessel.[13]

The problem that seems to have aroused the most discussion and the least litigation is that of taking food to avoid starvation. Al-

10. Regina v. Dudley and Stephens, 14 Q.B.D. 273 (1884).

11. United States v. Holmes, 1 Wall.Jr. 1, Fed.Cas.No.15,383 (1842). The judge emphasized the duty owed by sailors to passengers.

12. The William Gray, 1 Paine 16, Fed. Cas.No.17,694 (1810). Compare Commonwealth v. Brooks, 99 Mass. 434 (1868).

13. United States v. Ashton, 2 Sumn. 13, Fed.Cas.No.14,470 (1834).

though Lord Bacon said that "if a man steals viands to satisfy a present hunger, this is no felony nor larceny," [14] the books are full of statements indicating that "economic necessity" is no defense to a criminal charge. And it has been so held.[15] But "economic necessity," as this phrase has been used, falls far short of an actual need to prevent starvation. And mere convenience will not excuse the intentional deprivation of another's property. Under ordinary circumstances in the modern community it is not *necessary* to take another's food, without his consent, because an appeal may be made to the public authorities. But if a ship should be disabled on the high seas and its wireless destroyed, and those on board, after exhausting the ship's provisions, should find that part of the cargo was food and should break open boxes of freight and eat the contents as the only means of saving themselves from starvation, they would not be guilty of larceny. Doubtless the lack of any case holding such an appropriation not to be larceny (or *contra*) is because the result is too obvious to have resulted in prosecution.

The bank cashier who hands over money to an armed bandit, under threat of immediate death if he refuses, thereby appropriates the bank's money to save his own life. But this is not embezzlement.[16]

NALL v. COMMONWEALTH

Court of Appeals of Kentucky, 1925.
208 Ky. 700, 271 S.W. 1059.

CLAY, J. Appellant, who was 18 years of age when the crime was committed, was convicted of the offense of breaking and entering a storehouse with intent to steal, and his punishment fixed at one year's imprisonment.

According to the evidence for the commonwealth, the Hawk Eye Oil Company conducts a gasoline and oil filling station at the northeast intersection of Seventh and Broadway streets in Paducah. On the night of August 15, 1923, Mattie Culver, a woman 45 years of age, drove appellant in an automobile to a point near the station. Appellant then left the car, broke into the oil station, and took from the cash register a quantity of cash and checks. Some one notified the police, and on their arrival appellant escaped from the filling station through a window. He afterwards met Mattie Culver, who had driven away, and turned over to her the money and checks except a portion which he had dropped in the yard of a residence while making his escape. Appellant admitted the offense, but defended on the ground

---

14. Bacon: Maxims, reg. 5.
15. State v. Moe, 174 Wash. 303, 24 P.2d 638 (1933).
16. State v. McGuire, 107 Mont. 341, 88 P.2d 35 (1938).

that he was the victim of coercion or compulsion. In support of this claim he testified that he had worked at Floyd Culver's garage a while and became acquainted with him and his wife, Mattie Culver.

On the night in question he was at Wallace Park when Mattie Culver came by in an automobile and asked him to go down town with her. While driving along she told him that she wanted him to break into the filling station. She also drew a pistol and told him that if he did not do so she would kill him. She had the pistol on him until the automobile stopped across the street. She then got out of the car and followed him to the station and kept the pistol pointed at him until he broke into the station. He did not want to break in, but was afraid of Mattie Culver. Mrs. J. L. Nall, the mother of appellant, testified that after her son was arrested Mattie Culver came to her home and told her that it was all her fault; that she had told her son that if he did not break into the building she would blow his brains out, and showed witness the gun she had used. Mrs. Nall was corroborated by her daughter, who claims to have been present when the conversation occurred.

The failure of the court to give an instruction on coercion is the sole ground urged for reversal. Though the question has not arisen in this state, it seems to be settled in other jurisdictions that the law will excuse a person when acting under coercion or compulsion for committing most, if not all, crimes, except taking the life of an innocent person. However, a threat of future injury is not enough to excuse a criminal act,[1] but the compulsion must be present, imminent, and impending, and of such a nature as to induce a well-grounded apprehension of death, or serious bodily harm if the act is not done. The rule seems to be a sound one, and we perceive no reason why it should not prevail in this state.

It is suggested that the defense of coercion in this case is a mere sham or subterfuge. That may be, but where it is supported by substantial evidence the question is for the jury and not for the court. Having this view of the case, it follows that the court should have instructed on the question of coercion.

Judgment reversed, and cause remanded for a new trial consistent with this opinion.

---

1. A seventeen-year-old boy in an Industrial School who submitted to an act of sodomy with a guard, under threats that the guard would "slap him down" every time he saw him, acted under compulsion. Perryman v. State, 63 Ga.App. 819, 12 S.E.2d 388 (1940).

One is not guilty of killing moose without a license and out of season if this was reasonably necessary to protect his property. Cross v. State, 370 P.2d 371, 93 A.L.R.2d 1357 (Wyo.1962).

MODEL PENAL CODE

Section 2.09. Duress.

(1) It is an affirmative defense that the actor engaged in the conduct charged to constitute an offense because he was coerced to do so by the use of, or a threat to use, unlawful force against his person or the person of another, which a person of reasonable firmness in his situation would have been unable to resist.

(2) The defense provided by this Section is unavailable if the actor recklessly placed himself in a situation in which it was probable that he would be subjected to duress. The defense is also unavailable if he was negligent in placing himself in such a situation, whenever negligence suffices to establish culpability for the offense charged.

. . .

(4) When the conduct of the actor would otherwise be justifiable under Section 3.02, this Section does not preclude such defense.

Section 3.02. Justification Generally: Choice of Evils.

(1) Conduct which the actor believes to be necessary to avoid a harm or evil to himself or to another is justifiable, provided that:

    (a) the harm or evil sought to be avoided by such conduct is greater than that sought to be prevented by the law defining the offense charged; and

    (b) neither the Code nor other law defining the offense provides exceptions or defenses dealing with the specific situation involved; and

    (c) a legislative purpose to exclude the justification claimed does not otherwise plainly appear.

(2) When the actor was reckless or negligent in bringing about the situation requiring a choice of harms or evils or in appraising the necessity for his conduct, the justification afforded by this Section is unavailable in a prosecution for any offense for which recklessness or negligence, as the case may be, suffices to establish culpability.

SECTION 3. CONSENT OF THE OTHER PARTY

The problem of consent in the criminal law requires particular attention to two different matters: (1) What is the legal effect of consent or non-consent? (2) What will be regarded as consent within the legal meaning of the term?

In studying the legal effect of consent or non-consent it is important to recognize three different categories of crime.

(1) In certain offenses the *want* of consent of the person harmed is an essential ingredient of the crime by the very words of the definition, or the necessary implication of other terms. Thus in common-

law rape the phrase "without her consent" (or "against her will") is found in the definition itself. The finding of consent on the part of the person alleged to have been harmed completely disproves the commission of such a crime.

(2) At the other extreme will be found those offenses which can be committed even with the consent of the person harmed, such as "statutory rape" (carnal knowledge of a child) or murder. Furthermore, touching a girl under the age of consent with intent to have intercourse with her is an assault with intent to commit rape,[1] or an attempt to commit rape[2] although no force or violence is intended and she is entirely willing. And the sound view is that such a girl is just as incapable of giving a legally-recognized permission to an indecent fondling of her person as she is of giving such license to the act of intercourse itself, and hence her consent to such liberties is no defense.[3] A girl under the age of consent is frequently said to be incapable of giving consent to such misdeeds. What is meant, of course, is that her consent is incapable of giving a legally-recognized permission.

(3) Between these two extremes is a third category in which consent or non-consent will determine whether the conduct was lawful or unlawful within certain limits,—but not beyond. The typical example is battery. What is called a "fond embrace" when gladly accepted by a sweetheart is called "assault and battery" when perpetrated upon another without her consent. And the act of one who grabs another by the ankles and causes him to fall violently to the ground may result in a substantial jail sentence under some circumstances, but receive thunderous applause if it stops a ball carrier on the gridiron. The difference is because one who engages in a game such as football consents to such physical contact as is normally and properly to be expected in playing the game.

There are limits, however, to the extent to which the law will recognize a license based on such consent. Just as there can be no legally-valid permission to be killed, so the law will not recognize a license unnecessarily to be maimed. One may permit an amputation made necessary by accident or disease. But he who struck off the hand of a "lustie rogue" to enable him to beg more effectively was guilty despite the other's request.[4] A wrongdoer effectively may give consent to moderate chastisement and he who inflicts such permitted

---

1. People v. Babcock, 160 Cal. 537, 117 P. 549 (1911); Commonwealth v. Murphy, 165 Mass. 66, 42 N.E. 504 (1895); Fannin v. State, 65 Okl.Cr. 444, 88 P.2d 671 (1939); Steptoe v. State, 134 Tex.Cr.R. 320, 115 S.W.2d 916 (1938). Contra: State v. Pickett, 11 Nev. 255 (1876).

2. Alford v. State, 132 Fla. 624, 181 So. 839 (1938); Rainey v. Commonwealth, 169 Va. 892, 193 S.E. 501 (1937); Regina v. Martin, 9 Car. & P. 213, 169 Eng.Rep. 49 (1840).

3. People v. Gibson, 232 N.Y. 458, 134 N.E. 531 (1922); Carter v. State, 121 Tex.Cr. 493, 51 S.W.2d 316 (1932).

4. Wright's Case, Co. Litt. 127a (1604).

punishment is not guilty of assault and battery although he would be guilty without consent.[5] On the other hand, if two engage in a fist fight, by mutual consent, exchanging blows intended or likely to cause great bodily injury, both are guilty of assault and battery.[6]

In a prosecution for any offense falling within the second category, or one beyond the permitted limits in the third category, it is futile to talk of consent because this will not be exculpating even if established. If the crime falls within the first category the prosecution must negative consent to make out even a prima-facie case. A prima-facie case does not necessarily require positive evidence of nonconsent, if the offense is within the third category, but within the limits permitted by law proof of consent will disprove the charge. This invites inquiry as to just what will be regarded as consent within the legal meaning of the term.

It has been said: "A 'compelled consent' is in law no consent at all."[7] And this is beyond question if the duress employed was sufficient. Submission under extreme pain or fear is not that positive concurrence with the desire of another which is implied by the word "consent" as it is used in the law. What is claimed to have been duress in a particular case may be inadequate for this purpose. This will depend upon all the circumstances including the offense alleged to have been committed. In no case, however, will "consent" be recognized if it was induced by threats of immediate death or great bodily harm imposed by one apparently able and willing to enforce his threats if frustrated.

Certain of the statutory additions to the crime of extortion are enlightening on this point. They provide a punishment for the obtaining of property from another "with his consent, induced by a wrongful use of force or fear."[8] The fear may be induced by a threat to harm the person or his relative or member of his family, by injury to person or property, accusation of crime, imputation of deformity or disgrace, exposure of a secret, or kidnaping.[9] If the force or fear generates a well-grounded belief that the property must be handed over to avoid immediate death or great bodily injury, the submission thereto is not "consent," in the legal view, and the obtaining of the property by such means is robbery,—not extortion. If the property is freely and voluntarily handed over without any coercion it is a gift,—not extortion. Only between these extremes is

5. State v. Beck, 19 S.C.L. (1 Hill) 363 (1833).

6. State v. Newland, 27 Kan. 764 (1882); Commonwealth v. Collberg, 119 Mass. 350 (1876); King v. Donovan, [1934] 2 K.B. 498.

7. Shehany v. Lowry, 170 Ga. 70, 72, 152 S.E. 114, 115 (1929).

8. New York Penal Law, § 850. The section adds "or under color of official right," which is common-law extortion.

9. Id. at § 851.

the other's property obtained "with his consent by a wrongful use of force and fear."

Conditional consent is no consent beyond the terms of the condition. If one places an article in the hands of another for inspection with the understanding that he will either return it or pay for it now, there is no consent for him to run off with it without payment.[10] And the proprietor of a store who placed a large box of matches on the counter, for the convenience of customers in lighting pipes and cigars in the store, did not consent that the whole box of matches should be carried away.[11] Consent to one thing, moreover, is not consent to a different or additional thing. The girl who willingly ate a fig did not consent to eat a deleterious drug added without her knowledge.[12] Nor would her consent have included some entirely different article if it had been substituted by sleight of hand undetected by her.

Consent obtained by fraud has given rise to some of the most difficult problems in this field.

REX v. TURVEY

Court of Criminal Appeal, 1946.
[1946] 2 All E.R. 60.

LORD GODDARD, L. C. J. [delivering the judgment of the court]: In this case the court is of the opinion that the conviction must be quashed. The appellant appeals against his conviction on count 1 of the indictment only.

The circumstances were these: The appellant was charged that on Dec. 12, 1945, being a servant of His Majesty's Minister of Works, he stole from the Minister a considerable number of table knives, spoons, and so forth. He had got into touch with some foreigner living at Newton Abbot, and found that he would be a ready receiver of goods which could be stolen from the Ministry of Works. Then, being in charge at that time of a depot of the Ministry of Works at Torquay, he approached one Ward, who was in charge of a depot at Exeter. Ward was tempted to steal the property of the Ministry of Works and hand it to the appellant, who would in turn hand it to the man at Newton Abbot. Ward at once communicated with his superiors at Bristol, the people who were really in control of the property, and told them of this plan which had been suggested to him. The officials of the Ministry of Works said it would be a good thing to let this plan go on and catch them at a suitable time, which would enable them to prosecute this appellant for stealing. What they did

---

10. Rex v. Chisser, T.Raym. 275, 83 Eng.Rep. 142 (1678).

11. Mitchum v. State, 45 Ala. 29 (1871).

12. Commonwealth v. Stratton, 114 Mass. 303 (1873).

Sec. 3   CONSENT OF THE OTHER PARTY   545

was this: They told Ward to hand over the property to the appellant, and Ward handed over the property to the appellant. He intended to hand it to the appellant and did hand it to the appellant.

That being so, the question arose whether or not the appellant could be charged with stealing. He could have been charged with conspiracy that he was inciting to commit a felony and other charges, there is no doubt, but could he be charged with the felony of stealing? In this case it is perfectly clear that if he stole the goods, he stole them at Exeter, but he did not take them there against the will of the owner because the owner handed them to him and meant to hand them to him. The chairman in his ruling, when counsel submitted no case, set out his findings, and it appears that he decided principally on the authority of R. v. Eggington [sic] (1), an old case, but perfectly good law, and also because he took a certain view with regard to the control the owner was exercising over the goods.

R. v. Egginton[1] was a case in which a servant told his master that someone was going to rob the premises. "Very well," said the master, "let them rob the premises and we will catch them"; in other words, to put a homely illustration, a man, knowing that somebody is going to break into his house, leaves the bolts drawn and so makes it easy for the man to come into the house, and when he comes in he catches him and a crime has been committed; he commits the crime none the less that the servant has been told to make things easy.[2] In this case, if Ward had been told by the person who really had control of these matters, "Let the appellant come in and take the goods," that would have been one thing, but he told him to take the goods and hand them to the appellant, and that makes all the difference.

One matter to which the chairman seems to have attached considerable importance was this, that Ward said to the appellant at the time when he was handing over the goods: "You must give me a receipt, I must have a receipt for these goods," and the appellant said he quite understood that and he would give a receipt for the goods. Thereupon, a perfectly fictitious document is made out, which both parties knew and intended to be fictitious, under which it is made to look as though the goods were handed over to the appellant to take to the Palace Hotel at Torquay, but, of course, that was not an authority by Ward to the appellant to take the goods to Torquay because everybody knew that the appellant was meaning to steal these goods and they were to go to the receiver at Newton Abbot. No one intended that they were to go to Torquay, and this document was simply manufactured as a blind, or whatever word you like to use; it is not a genuine document, and therefore it is as if it did not exist.

1. R. v. Egginton (1801), 2 Bos. & P. 508; 15 Digest 883, 9693.

[By the Compiler.]

2. But it is otherwise if the servant opened the door for D at the master's direction. Smith v. State, 362 P.2d 1071 (Alaska 1961).

The other point on which the chairman in his direction to the jury, as we think, went wrong was that he told the jury that these goods always remained under the control of the Ministry, because apparently the police had been warned, and the police were to follow the prisoner once he had stolen them, either to follow him or go immediately to Newton Abbot and find them in the possession of the receiver. But that will not do. Once the goods were handed over to the appellant the goods were under his control and nobody else's. What was to happen supposing, while he was driving along being followed by the police, the police car broke down? Of course, he would cheerfully drive away with these goods. Of course the goods were under the appellant's control as soon as he went away with the goods.

The charge that was put against the appellant was the wrong charge, a charge of which he could not have been convicted because there was no evidence here of what, to use a technical expression, is termed asportation. He did not carry away the goods against the will of the owner but because the owner was willing that he should have the goods and gave them to him. In those circumstances, the conviction will be quashed, so far as this charge is concerned, and the appeal allowed on count 1.

Appeal allowed.

PEOPLE v. COOK

District Court of Appeal, Second District, Division 4, California, 1964.
228 Cal.App.2d 716, 39 Cal.Rptr. 802.

BURKE, PRESIDING JUSTICE. Frank Billy Ray Cook, defendant, was charged by information with violation of section 487, subd. 3 of the Penal Code (Grand Theft Auto) and Vehicle Code, section 10851. He was acquitted by a jury of Grand Theft Auto, but found guilty of violating Vehicle Code, section 10851. A new trial was denied, probation was denied, and defendant was sentenced to the state prison for the term prescribed by law. . . .

The first ground of appeal is that the Mercury was taken with the consent of Frahm Pontiac, and even though such consent be deemed to have been induced by trick and device and under false pretenses, nevertheless, it constituted consent. The arrangements were made to register the Mercury in the buyer's name which would entitle him to possession and use of the vehicle. Frahm Pontiac acquired defendant's Buick as a trade-in and part consideration for the Mercury. Having acquired the Mercury with Frahm's consent, possession cannot be held to have been obtained in violation of section

10851 of the Vehicle Code.[1] The point appears to be novel in California but defendant offers persuasive authority from other jurisdictions to the effect that fraudulent inducement does not vitiate the consent given to the extent of creating the crime of auto theft.

In Perkins on Criminal Law, p. 859, it is stated:
"It has been held, it may be emphasized, that one who obtains the owner's consent to drive his car by fraudulently misrepresenting the use to be made of it, is not guilty of operating a car without the consent of the owner although the owner would not have consented to the use actually made."

One of the earliest cases holding that fraudulently induced consent is consent nonetheless and that such consent prevents a violation of a vehicle joy ride statute is State v. Boggs, 181 Iowa 358, 164 N.W. 759 (1917), the court stating: "The gist of the offense charged is taking and driving of the motor car in question without the consent of the owner."

The court then noted: "It is contended on behalf of appellant that consent obtained by trick, deceit, or misrepresentation is not consent in fact." In rejecting this contention, the court concluded: "The statute was not designed to punish one who [by misrepresentation or for a fraudulent purpose], obtains consent of the owner to take and operate his motor vehicle . . .."

In State v. Mularky, 195 Wis. 549, 218 N.W. 809 (1928), State v. Boggs, supra, was discussed with approval, and the court there held that consent, however obtained, prevented a violation of the Wisconsin Joy Ride Statute.

In United States v. One 1941 Chrysler, 74 F.Supp. 970 (E.D. Mich.1947), the court was called upon to construe sections 413 and 414 of the Michigan Penal Statutes. These two sections are the equivalent of California's Penal Code, section 499b (the Misdemeanor Joy Ride Statute) and Vehicle Code, section 10851, the court holding:

"The provisions of such statutes as Sections 413 and 414 are not designed to punish one who obtains consent of the owner to take and operate his motor vehicle by misrepresentations or for a fraudulent purpose. They are directed against one who takes possession of such a vehicle without the consent of the owner." (See also People v. Smith, 213 Mich. 351, 182 N.W. 64.)

[1]. Section 10851 of the Vehicle Code reads in part as follows:
"Any person who drives or takes a vehicle not his own, without the consent of the owner thereof, and with intent either permanently or temporarily to deprive the owner thereof of this title to or possession of the vehicle, whether with or without intent to steal the same, or any person who is a party or accessory to or an accomplice in the driving or unauthorized taking or stealing is guilty of a felony, ..." (Stats.1959, c. 3, p. 1597, § 10851.)

The above mentioned cases constitute specific applications of the basic common law rule that, unless there is statutory language to the contrary, whenever lack of consent is a necessary element of a crime, the fact that consent is obtained through misrepresentation will not supply the essential element of non-consent.

Perkins on Criminal Law, at page 859, states:
"Except for this, (larceny by trick) if it is truly an exception, and except where the result has been changed by statute, an offense which requires the absence of consent is not committed if there was consent to exactly what was done, even if such consent was induced by fraud." . . .

People v. Perez, 203 Cal.App.2d 397, 21 Cal.Rptr. 422, has been cited as supporting defendant's conviction of a violation of Vehicle Code, § 10851. In that case, the defendant attained possession of an automobile under the false representation that he had a buyer for it. He was given permission by the owner to keep the car for three days to make the sale to his buyer. Defendant never returned the car. The court stated (p. 399, 21 Cal.Rptr. p. 424): "Even though his original possession had been lawful, he had no authority to keep [the automobile] more than three days and then only for the purpose of consummating a sale to [his purported buyer.] . . . Actually, his original possession, his keeping the car beyond three days, his driving the car to Arizona . . . were all unlawful and, . . . if believed, could not be construed in any other way than intentionally taking and depriving the owner of possession, to say the least. Intent to deprive the owner may be established from the circumstances of the case, [citation] and is a question for the trier of fact. [Citations.] Each time defendant drove the car without the consent of the owner it was a violation of the statute. [Citation.]"

There is a generally recognized distinction, however, between *fraud in the factum*, which gives rise to no consent at all, and *fraud in the inducement*, which does not vitiate consent. Perez, supra, is an example of *fraud in the factum*, since the owner never intended that the defendant would acquire possession of the car for his own use.

Here, there was *fraud in the inducement*; the owner intended to sell defendant the car and consented to the taking of possession of it by him and, unlike Perez, the fraud did not vitiate consent.

No authorities are cited in opposition to defendant's contentions that consent, albeit falsely induced, bars prosecution under such section 10851 of the Vehicle Code. Respondent argues only that the facts conclusively establish an intent on defendant's part, defendant having been an accomplice, to deprive Frahm Pontiac of its title or possession of the 1959 Mercury, which is the essence of the charge; that the fraud in obtaining consent vitiates the consent and does not excuse the criminal act.

Fraud, vitiating consent, as indicated, is a completely tenable principle in contract law, and when specifically incorporated in a penal statute determines the operation of the section, as in the case of Penal Code, section 484. However, section 10851 of the Vehicle Code makes no reference to fraud, false pretense or trick and device but is specifically based upon the taking without consent. . . .

The judgment of conviction is reversed and the cause remanded to the trial court with directions to dismiss.

JEFFERSON and KINGSLEY, JJ., concur.

STATE v. LANKFORD

Court of General Sessions of Delaware, Sussex County, 1917.
6 Boyce 594, 102 A. 63.

. . . Harry S. Lankford was indicted for an assault upon Alice M. Lankford, his wife. Verdict guilty. . . .

BOYCE, J., charging the jury, in part: It is admitted that the accused and the prosecuting witness were married on the tenth day of June, 1916, and that the former communicated syphilis to his wife.

A husband may commit an assault and battery upon his wife, notwithstanding the marriage relation. State v. Buckley, 2 Har. 552.

A wife in confiding her person to her husband does not consent to cruel treatment, or to infection with a loathsome disease. A husband, therefore, knowing that he has such a disease, and concealing the fact from his wife, by accepting her consent, and communicating the infection to her, inflicts on her physical abuse, and injury, resulting in great bodily harm; and he becomes, notwithstanding his marital rights, guilty of an assault, and indeed, a completed battery. 2 Bish.Crim.Law, § 72b(2).

If the accused knew he was infected with syphilis, and his infection was unknown to his wife, the intent to communicate the disease to her by having sexual intercourse with her, may be inferred from the actual results.

If the jury should find from the evidence that the accused, knowing that he was infected with a venereal disease, and, without informing his wife of the fact, had sexual intercourse with her after such knowledge had been communicated to him, and thereby infected her with the disease, their verdict should be guilty.

If the jury should find that the accused, during the period he had sexual relations with his wife, did not know that he was infected with a venereal disease, and that he did not communicate with his wife after being informed that he was infected, their verdict should be not guilty.

Verdict, guilty.[1]

REGINA v. DEE

Court for Crown Cases Reserved, Ireland, 1884.
15 Cox C.C. 579.

MAY, C. J. The question which arises on the case is whether, in point of law, the prisoner should be considered as guilty of rape. There is not, I think, any doubt or dispute as to the facts and circumstances of the case. Upon the report of the judge, who was myself, and the findings of the jury, it is, I think, established, that Judith Gorman, the wife of one J. Gorman, who was absent, having gone out to fish, lay down upon a bed in her sleeping room in the evening when it was dark; that the prisoner came into the room, personating her husband, lay down upon her and had connection with her; that she did not at first resist, believing the man to be her husband, but that on discovering that he was not her husband, which was after the commencement, but before the termination of the proceeding, her consent or acquiescence terminated, and she ran downstairs. It appeared, I think manifestly, that the prisoner knew the woman was deceived, as she said to the prisoner in his presence and hearing when he came into the room, "You are soon home to-night," to which he made no reply. At the time my own opinion, founded upon well-known cases in England, was that the prisoner was not guilty of rape, but at the request of the counsel for the Crown I left certain questions to the jury, and upon their findings directed them to find a verdict of guilty, reserving the case for the consideration of this court, which is now called upon to decide the question which arises. There have been several cases in England which have arisen on the point, whether the having connection with a married woman by personation of her husband amounts to the crime of rape. Rape may be defined as sexual connection with a woman forcibly and without her will: (Reg. v. Fletcher, 8 Cox C.C. 134). It is plain, however, "forcibly" does not mean violently, but with that description of force which must be exercised in order to accomplish the act, for there is no doubt

---

[1]. A doctor of theology, by falsely pretending to be a surgeon, induced a woman to permit him to make an intimate examination of her body under pretense of examining the working of an artificial limb. A conviction of assault and battery, and indecent assault, was affirmed on the ground that her consent was obtained by fraud. Commonwealth v. Gregory, 132 Pa.Super. 507, 1 A.2d 501 (1938).

D obtained a woman's consent to sexual intercourse with her under the false and fraudulent pretense that he was an officer and would otherwise arrest her. It was held that this was not rape because of her consent to the act. People v. Cavanaugh, 30 Cal.App. 432, 158 P. 1053 (1916).

that unlawful connection with a woman in a state of unconsciousness, produced by profound sleep, stupor, or otherwise, if the man knows that the woman is in such a state, amounts to a rape. The case which the court has to deal with is that of connection with a married woman obtained by personation of the husband while the woman is awake. On this point subtle distinctions have been drawn. The earliest reported case appears to be that of Rex v. Jackson (Russ. & Ry. 487). There the prisoner was convicted of burglary with intent to commit a rape on a married woman. It appeared in evidence that the prisoner got into the woman's bed as if he had been her husband, and had partial connection with her. The case was considered by the twelve judges. Four of the judges thought having carnal knowledge of a woman whilst she was under the belief that the man is her husband would be a rape, but the other eight judges thought it would not; but several of the eight judges intimated that if the case should occur again they would advise the jury to find a special verdict. This case cannot be regarded as one of much authority. Doubts seem to have existed in the minds even of the majority. However, in Reg. v. Saunders (8 C. & P. 265), in the year 1838, a married woman, a Mrs. Cleasby, in like manner submitted to connection with a man believing him to be her husband, but on discovering the mistake she ran and hanged herself, but was cut down and recovered. Gurney, B. directed the jury that the evidence did not establish a rape, as she consented, but that if they found that it was a fraud on her, and that she did not consent as to the person, they might find the prisoner guilty of an assault, which was accordingly so found, the court proceeding on the enactment of 7 Will. 4 & 1 Vict. c. 85, s. 11, which provides that on the trial of any person for any felony which includes an assault, the jury may acquit of the felony and find the party guilty of an assault, if the evidence should warrant such finding. I do not myself understand the application of the statute. If the consent of the woman prevented the crime being a rape, it would seem that it would also prevent it being an assault, which consent excludes. The same point arose in the case of Reg. v. Clarke (1 Dears.C.C. 397), where, under similar circumstances, the jury having found the prisoner guilty, the judge reserved the case, and upon argument the judges held that they were bound by the decision in R. v. Jackson, and that they ought not to allow the question to be opened, and the conviction was quashed. Reg. v. Barrow is reported in 1 L.Rep.C.C.R. 156. All the judges, Bovill, C. J., Channell, B., Byles, Blackburn, and Lush, JJ., there held, under similar circumstances, that when the consent is obtained by fraud, the act does not amount to rape; contrary, however, to the opinion of Kelly, C. B., before whom the case was tried, expressed at the trial. The case of Reg. v. Flattery was not a case of personation of a husband, but of sexual connection by a medical man, under pretence of his performing a surgical operation on a woman. In that case the prisoner was adjudged guilty of rape, it being clear that the woman did not submit knowingly to connection but to a different act, Kelly, C. B. saying "the case is therefore not within the authority of those cases which have been decided, decisions which I regret, that where a man by fraud induces a woman to submit to sexual connection it is not rape." Mellor, Denman, and Field, JJ. and Huddleston, B. all expressed their dissatisfaction with the dictum of Rex v. Jackson, and their desire that the case should be reconsidered. The last case on the subject of personation appears to be that of Reg. v. Young (14 Cox C.C. 114). Though the prisoner was held to have been properly convicted in that case, it does not clearly illustrate the precise point which is now before us, for on the facts as explained by the judge who tried the case it appeared that the commencement of the sexual connection in that case, which was one of personation, took place while the woman was asleep. Before its completion, however, she awoke and called out to her husband. It would seem that the criminal and felonious act of penetration was completed while the woman was asleep, and therefore unconscious. It is well settled, as I have observed, that connection with a woman while unconscious does constitute rape. The question arises now for our consideration, are we bound to follow the decisions in England to which I have referred? The series of cases to which I have drawn attention appear to be an echo of the first case of Rex v. Jackson. The others followed, no further argument being treated as necessary. Nevertheless, if the doctrine thus established had been adopted by the judges in England without objection, I do not think that this court should establish a different legal determination, unanimity on such points being of great importance. In its inception, however, that original case of Rex v. Jackson was dissented from by four of the twelve judges who heard it, while on the majority several apparently doubted the doctrine there contended for. In the case of Reg. v. Flattery all the judges desired that this doctrine should be reconsidered. In Ireland, until the present case, no similar question seems to have arisen; and it appears to me, under all the circumstances, that it is competent for us, and it is our duty, to consider the doctrine of those English decisions upon their merits. Now, rape being defined to be sexual connection with a woman without her consent, or without and therefore against her will, it is essential to consider what is meant and intended by consent. Does it mean an intelligent, positive concurrence of the will of the woman, or is the negative absence of dissent sufficient? In these surgical cases it is held that the submission to an act believed to be a surgical operation does not constitute consent to a sexual connection, being of a wholly different character; there is no *consensus quoad hoc*. In the case of personation there is no *consensus quoad hanc personam*. Can it be considered that there is a consent to the sexual connection, it being manifest that, had it not been for the deceit or fraud, the woman would not have submitted to the act? In the cases of idiocy, of stupor, or of infancy, it is held that there is no legal consent, from the want of an intelligent and discerning will. Can a woman, in the case of personation, be regarded as consenting to the act in the exercise of an intelligent will? Does she consent, not knowing the real nature of the act? As observed by Mr. Curtis, she intends to consent to a lawful and marital act, to which it is her duty to submit. But did she consent to an act of adultery? Are not the acts themselves wholly different in their moral nature? The act she permitted cannot properly be regarded as the real act which took place. Therefore the connection was done, in my opinion, without her consent, and the crime of rape was constituted. I therefore am of opinion that the conviction should stand confirmed.

PALLES, C. B. . . . The person by whom the act was to be performed was part of its essence. The consent of the intellect, the only consent known to the law, was to the act of the husband only, and of this the prisoner was aware. As well put by Mr. Curtis, what the woman consented to was not adultery, but marital intercourse. The act consented to was not a crime in law; it would not subject her to a divorce. Were adultery criminally punishable by our law she would not be guilty. Compare the case now with Reg. v. Flattery (2 Q.B. Div. 410), a decision subsequent to any of those relied on for the prisoner. In it the act to which the consent was given, one of medical treatment, was different in nature from the act committed, and on this difference in nature the case turned. Viewing man as an animal, it might be said that the act here consented to and the act committed were of the same nature. Thus, the case might be distinguished from Reg. v. Flattery, and the animal instinct of the idiot held to be consent. But if I be right in holding that, in determining the legal relations of man to man, we regard him not as the animal but as the rational being, and if in administering the common law of this country, we are, as I believe us to be, at liberty to remember that it is the law of a Christian country, the growth of centuries of Christian wisdom—a law which, on the one hand, constituted the crime of rape as the protection of virtue, and on the other hand gave effect to the divine institution of marriage, by subjecting the wife to the will of the husband—I cannot entertain any doubt that the violation by a stranger of the person of a married woman is, in the view of that law, as it is in morality, an act different in nature from the lawful act of the husband. If this be so, Reg. v. Flattery (2 Q.B.Div. 410) rules this case. For these reasons, I am of opinion that the conviction should stand. . . . [1]

(LAWSON, O'BRIEN, ANDREWS, and MURPHY, JJ., also give opinions affirming the conviction.)

[1]. "If a woman be beguiled into her consent by marrying a man who had another wife living, or by causing the nuptials to be illegally celebrated, and persuading her that the directions of the law had been observed; in neither case will the pretended husband be guilty of a rape." State v. Murphy, 6 Ala. 765, 770 (1844).

Procuring sexual intercourse with a single woman by the device of a sham marriage is rape by fraud under the Texas statute. Lee v. State, 44 Tex. Cr. 354, 72 S.W. 1005 (1902). Okla-

MODEL PENAL CODE

Section 2.11. Consent.

(1) In General. The consent of the victim to conduct charged to constitute an offense or to the result thereof is a defense if such consent negatives an element of the offense or precludes the infliction of the harm or evil sought to be prevented by the law defining the offense.

(2) Consent to Bodily Harm. When conduct is charged to constitute an offense because it causes or threatens bodily harm, consent to such conduct or to the infliction of such harm is a defense if:

(a) the bodily harm consented to or threatened by the conduct consented to is not serious; or

(b) the conduct and the harm are reasonably foreseeable hazards of joint participation in any concerted activity of a kind not forbidden by law; or

(c) the consent establishes a justification for the conduct under Article 3 of the Code.

(3) Ineffective Consent. Unless otherwise provided by the Code or by the law defining the offense, assent does not constitute consent if:

(a) it is given by a person who is legally incompetent to authorize the conduct charged to constitute the offense; or

(b) it is given by a person who by reason of youth, mental disease or defect or intoxication is manifestly unable or known by the actor to be unable to make a reasonable judgment as to the nature or harmfulness of the conduct charged to constitute the offense; or

(c) it is given by a person whose improvident consent is sought to be prevented by the law defining the offense; or

(d) it is induced by force, duress or deception of a kind sought to be prevented by the law defining the offense.

Section 3.08. Use of Force by Persons with Special Responsibility for Care, Discipline or Safety of Others.

The use of force upon or toward the person of another is justifiable if:

. . .

(4) the actor is a doctor or other therapist or a person assisting him at his direction, and:

(a) the force is used for the purpose of administering a recognized form of treatment which the actor believes to be adapted to promoting the physical or mental health of the patient; and

(b) the treatment is administered with the consent of the patient or, if the patient is a minor or an incompetent person, with the consent of his parent or guardian or other person legally competent to consent in his behalf, or the treatment is administered in an emergency when the actor believes that no one competent to consent can be consulted and

homa held otherwise on the ground that the artifice meant by the statute is such as deceives the woman as to the identity of the man with whom she is having intercourse. Draughn v. State, 12 Okl.Cr. 479, 158 P. 890 (1916).

Sec. 4   GUILT OF THE INJURED PARTY   555

that a reasonable person, wishing to safeguard the welfare of the patient, would consent; or. . . .

Section 213.1.   Rape and Related Offenses. . . .

(2) Gross Sexual Imposition. A male who has sexual intercourse with a female not his wife commits a felony of the third degree if: . . .

> (c) he knows that she is unaware that a sexual act is being committed upon her or that she submits because she falsely supposes that he is her husband.

SECTION 4. GUILT OF THE INJURED PARTY

Guilt of the injured party will be a complete defense as to acts, which would otherwise be criminal, if such acts were committed in self-defense or otherwise to prevent crime and did not exceed the privilege recognized by law for such a purpose. In such a case the person has no wrongful purpose in mind but is merely seeking to frustrate a crime attempted by another. On the other hand it is an established principle of law that one crime is no excuse for another. The fact that the person killed was himself a murderer is no defense to a charge of murder. And it is just as much larceny to steal from a thief as to steal from anyone else,—[1] although needless to say the recapture of stolen property from the thief, by or for the lawful owner, is not stealing. It is also larceny to steal whiskey from one who violated the law by possessing it.[2] And the fact that counterfeit coin was paid to a prostitute for unlawful intercourse is no defense to a charge of uttering counterfeit coin.[3]

COMMONWEALTH v. MORRILL & ANOTHER

Supreme Judicial Court of Massachusetts, 1851.
62 Mass. 571.

This was an indictment, which alleged that the defendants, Samuel G. Morrill and John M. Hodgdon, on the 17th of September, 1850, at Newburyport, "devising and intending one James Lynch by false pretences to cheat and defraud of his goods, did then and there unlawfully, knowingly and designedly falsely pretend and represent to said Lynch that a certain watch which said Morrill then and there had, and which said Morrill and Hodgdon then and there proposed

---

1. Ward v. People, 3 Hill 395 (N.Y. 1842). And it is no defense to a charge of embezzling money from a city that the city acquired the money illegally. State v. Patterson, 66 Kan. 447, 77 P. 860 (1903).

2. State v. Donovan, 108 Wash. 276, 183 P. 127 (1919). And it is malicious mischief wilfully to destroy liquor so held by another. State v. Stark, 63 Kan. 529, 66 P. 243 (1901).

3. The Queen v. ———, 1 Cox C.C. 250 (1845).

and offered to exchange with said Lynch for two other watches belonging to said Lynch, was a gold watch of eighteen carats fine, and was of great value, to wit, of the value of eighty dollars; and the said Lynch, then and there believing the said false pretences and representations so made as aforesaid by said Morrill and Hodgdon, and being deceived thereby, was induced by reason of the false pretences and representations so made as aforesaid to deliver, and did then and there deliver, to the said Morrill the two watches aforesaid, belonging to said Lynch, and of the value of twenty dollars, and the said Morrill & Hodgdon did then and there receive and obtain the two said watches, the property of said Lynch, as aforesaid, in exchange for the said watch, so represented as a gold watch as aforesaid, by means of the false pretences and representations aforesaid, and with intent to cheat and defraud the said Lynch of his said two watches, as aforesaid; whereas in truth and in fact said watch so represented by said Morrill and Hodgdon as a gold watch, eighteen carats fine, and of the value of eighty dollars, was not then and there a gold watch, and was not then and there eighteen carats fine, and was then and there of trifling value," &c.

At the trial in the court of common pleas, before Hoar, J., it appeared in evidence, that Lynch represented his watches, one of which was of silver, and the other of yellow metal, as worth fifty dollars; and on the testimony of the only witness for the commonwealth, who was a judge of the value of watches, they were worth not exceeding fifteen dollars. Lynch testified, that his silver watch cost him fifteen dollars; that he received the other in exchange for two, which cost him respectively seven dollars and thirteen dollars; and that he believed it to be worth thirty dollars.

The defendant requested the presiding judge to instruct the jury, that if Lynch's watches were not worth fifty dollars, or some considerable part of that sum, but were of merely trifling value, this indictment could not be maintained. But the judge instructed the jury, that if they supposed that each of the parties was endeavoring to defraud the other, and Lynch knew that his watches were of little value, the jury should not convict the defendants merely because they had the best of the bargain; but that if the defendants made the false representations charged in the indictment, with the intent to defraud, knowing them to be false, and they were such as would mislead and deceive a man of ordinary prudence, and Lynch, by reason of the representations, and trusting in them, parted with his property and was defrauded, it was not necessary to show that he was defrauded to the extent charged in the indictment, provided he, in good faith, parted with property which he believed to be valuable, and was defrauded to any substantial amount, for example, to the amount of five dollars; and that the defendants might be convicted, although from the mistake of Lynch, in over-estimating his property, he might not have been cheated to so great an extent as he at the time supposed.

The jury found the defendants guilty, who thereupon moved in arrest of judgment, on the ground that the indictment was insufficient; and this motion being overruled, they alleged exceptions to the order of the court, overruling the same, and also to the instructions aforesaid.

DEWEY, J. The exceptions taken to the instructions of the presiding judge cannot be sustained. If it were true that the party, from whom the defendants obtained goods by false pretences, also made false pretences as to his goods, which he exchanged with the defendants, that would be no justification for the defendants, when put on trial upon an indictment, charging them with obtaining goods by false pretences, knowingly and designedly in violation of a statute of this commonwealth. Whether the alleged misrepresentation of Lynch, being a mere representation as to the value or worth of a certain watch, and an opinion rather than a statement of a fact, would be such false pretence as would render him amenable to punishment under this statute, might be questionable, but supposing that to be otherwise, and it should appear that Lynch had also violated the statute, that would not justify the defendants. If the other party has also subjected himself to a prosecution for a like offence, he also may be punished. This would be much better than that both should escape punishment, because each deserved it equally. . . .[1]

Judgment on the verdict.

---

1. Prosecutions for obtaining money or property by false pretenses have raised this issue frequently. The leading case for the minority view (although the New York rule is now otherwise as a result of legislation) is McCord v. People, 46 N.Y. 470 (1871). In this case defendant obtained a gold watch and a diamond ring as a "bribe" by falsely pretending to be an officer with a warrant for the victim's arrest. In reversing a conviction of false pretenses the court said that neither law nor public policy designs the protection of rogues in their dealing with one another. The Wisconsin court reached a similar result under other facts. State v. Crowley, 41 Wis. 271 (1876). The majority view is that *particeps criminis* applies only to civil actions, and that the guilt of one is not sufficient to establish the innocence of the other in a criminal prosecution. Horton v. State, 85 Ohio St. 13, 96 N.E. 797 (1911). Thus convictions have been upheld where money was obtained by altering a number punched from an illegal punch board, State v. Mellenberger, 163 Or. 233, 95 P.2d 709 (1939); by falsely pretending to have an unlawful plan to tap wires coming from horse races, Gilmore, Munger and Klein v. People, 87 Ill.App. 128 (1899); and by a confidence game in which the victim was induced to place a bet under the belief that a trick had been practiced whereby he was to cheat the other party, Regina v. Hudson, 8 Cox C.C. 305 (1860). In another case the suggestion that the victim of false pretenses thought he was buying stolen property was rejected as unimportant. Frazier v. Commonwealth, 291 Ky. 467, 165 S.W.2d 33 (1942).

The New York court felt bound to follow McCord, but suggested to the legislature that the rule be changed. People v. Thompkins, 186 N.Y. 413, 417, 79 N.E. 326, 327 (1906). The change was made the following year. N.Y.Laws 1907, c. 581, § 1. See now N.Y.Pen.Code § 1290. The rule was changed by statute in Wisconsin much more recently. W.S.A. 939.14 (1955). "It is no defense to a prosecution for crime that the victim also was guilty of crime. . . ."

SECTION 5. CONDUCT OF THE INJURED PARTY

The rules of law concerning negligence as a defense in civil actions for personal injuries have no application to criminal prosecutions.[1] "It is enough to say that contributory negligence, if shown, is never a defense or excuse for crime, nor can it in any degree serve to purge an act otherwise constituting a public offense of its criminal character."[2] In one case a man threw a handful of blasting powder into an open fireplace. A resulting explosion set fire to the building and the wife and 19 year old son of the host were burned to death. Several others, some of them younger and less able to take care of themselves than those who were killed, were able to get out of the house in safety. But this did not entitle defendant to an instruction that he was excused if those who did not reach safety had failed to use due care in the effort.[3] In another case defendants had run over and killed a pedestrian while they were driving a horse and carriage at an excessive rate and were somewhat intoxicated. They thought they should be excused because deceased, who was deaf, had the habit of walking in the middle of the road at various times of the day and night. But the court held otherwise.[4]

It does not follow, however, that the conduct of the injured party must be ignored. His conduct may have a bearing on whether or not the one who caused the injury was culpably negligent.[5] Or it may be found that the negligence of the injured party was the *sole* cause of his injury.[6] "If the decedents were negligent," said the Washington court, "and such negligence was the sole cause of their death, then the appellant would not be guilty of manslaughter."[7]

---

1. Bowen v. State, 100 Ark. 232, 140 S.W. 28 (1911); People v. McKee, 80 Cal.App. 200, 251 P. 675 (1926); State v. Campbell, 82 Conn. 671, 74 A. 927 (1910); State v. Medlin, 355 Mo. 564, 197 S.W.2d 626 (1946); Click v. State, 144 Tex.Cr.R. 468, 164 S.W.2d 664 (1942).

2. State v. Moore, 129 Iowa 514, 519, 106 N.W. 16, 17 (1906). Accord: Penix v. Commonwealth, 313 Ky. 587, 233 S.W. 2d 89 (1950).

3. Embry v. Commonwealth, 236 Ky. 204, 32 S.W.2d 979 (1930).

4. Regina v. Longbottom and Another, 3 Cox C.C. 439 (1849). See also Regina v. Kew, 12 Cox C.C. 355 (1872).

5. Held v. Commonwealth, 183 Ky. 209, 208 S.W. 772 (1919); People v. Campbell, 237 Mich. 424, 212 N.W. 97 (1927).

6. Cain v. State, 55 Ga.App. 376, 190 S.E. 371 (1937). And see State v. Diamond, 16 N.J.Super. 26, 83 A.2d 799 (1951).

7. State v. Ramser, 17 Wash.2d 581, 590, 136 P.2d 1013, 1017 (1943). And see Commonwealth v. Aurick, 138 Pa. Super. 180, 10 A.2d 22 (1939).

CARBO v. STATE

Court of Appeals of Georgia, 1908.
4 Ga.App. 583, 62 S.E. 140.

Carbo and Simpson were indicted for involuntary manslaughter in the commission of an unlawful act, by using, within the corporate limits of the City of Savannah, a certain detonating and fulminating preparation to the grand jurors more particularly unknown, contrary to an ordinance of that city making it unlawful to sell or use any detonating or fulminating preparation, or instrument made or composed wholly or in part of nitroglycerine or other detonating or fulminating substance whatever. After conviction a new trial was granted on the ground that the homicides resulted from the mere having or keeping, and not from the using of the prohibited articles. A nolle prosequi was entered, and another special presentment was returned, charging involuntary manslaughter in the commission of a lawful act without due caution and circumspection, by assembling a large quantity of explosives in the city so negligently and improperly as probably to produce the unlawful homicide of the persons killed. The evidence showed, that the accused made torpedoes on premises at the corner of Anderson and Burroughs streets in Savannah, a thickly populated part of the city, and stored them, in large quantities, in a small wooden house or shanty on the same premises. On one occasion he had requested a woman living near to watch the house and turn away any boys or children she might see there, and answered affirmatively her suggestion that it would be dangerous if a spark or cigarette fell among the papers. On an evening in December, 1906, while Carbo and Simpson were in this house, an explosion occurred that burned them severely. They ran for relief to a house near by, where Carbo gave a key to a boy, or young man, and told him to lock up the place where the explosion occurred. In the meantime a fire alarm had been given, and firemen had come and extinguished some fire inside of the house. A little boy on the street said to one of them, "Mister, don't go in there; the thing is full of dynamite." This one went (after extinguishing the fire) to where Carbo and Simpson were, and asked Carbo if there were any high explosives in the house in question. He answered, "No," and said, "For God's sake, don't put any water there, nor allow any one to go in there." The fireman told him that he (fireman) had been in there and had put water in there. Carbo said no more after that; and the fireman went out and telephoned to his chief to come, as it looked dangerous. He came in about twenty minutes, and was told that the place looked bad; that he had better be careful how he went in there; that the boys said it was full of dynamite. He replied that they would have to make an investigation, and went into the house, followed by three firemen. There were some trunks and lots of rubbish. Packages were scattered over the floor, and a pile of stuff that looked like paper. The chief pulled down some of it, and was told, "You had better not do that; you don't know what you are handling." He said, "We have to make an investigation." A boy came to the door, picked up something, and said it was the cause of the explosion that had taken place. He was told to put it down; and suddenly there was a flash and an explosion, followed by another or others, that killed one of the firemen outright and so badly burned and wounded two others that they died from the injuries so received. The force of it was such as to throw down men in the street. . . .

(Syllabus by the Court:)

RUSSELL, J. 1. There can be no conviction of the offense of involuntary manslaughter, either in the commission of an unlawful act, or in the commission of a lawful act without due caution and circumspection, where the homicide is directly due to an independent intervening cause in which the accused did not participate and which he could not foresee.

2. To constitute a crime there must be either the joint operation of act and intention, or criminal negligence. Criminal negligence necessarily implies, not only knowledge of probable consequences which may result from the use of a given instrumentality, but also wilful or wanton disregard of the probable effects of such instrumentality upon others likely to be affected thereby.

3. Consequently, criminal negligence is not shown as against a defendant who uses every means in his power for the safety of those whom it is alleged his negligence has affected.

4. One who has an object of danger or a dangerous instrument of any kind upon his premises owes no duty with reference to the safety of others, except as to those likely to be affected thereby. And upon his trial for crime, it must appear that the injury to those affected by such dangerous instrument was due to such negligence on his part.

5. One who, with full knowledge of a danger of which he has been warned, encounters such danger himself, assumes all risks; and a resulting injury can not be made chargeable to another, where it appears that the injured person being of sound mind and of the age of discretion, by the exercise of ordinary diligence could have avoided the injury.

6. Before one can be held criminally liable for the result of negligence, it must be shown, beyond reasonable doubt, that the result, though caused by the accused unintentionally, injuriously affected one who, but for his ignorance of the danger, might have escaped harmless. There can be no conviction where it appears that the person injured was apprised of the danger, and unnecessarily, and over the protest of the defendant, exposed himself thereto.

Judgment reversed.

HUBBARD v. COMMONWEALTH

Court of Appeals of Kentucky, 1947.
304 Ky. 818, 202 S.W.2d 634.

Opinion of the court by STANLEY, COMMISSIONER—Reversing.

R. W. Dyche died of a heart attack. Robert Hubbard has been adjudged guilty of killing him and sentenced to two years' imprisonment on a charge of voluntary manslaughter. The trial was had in Jackson County on a change of venue.

Hubbard was at home on furlough from the army in August, 1945. He was arrested for being drunk in a public place and taken before the County Judge of Laurel County. Being too drunk to be tried, he was ordered to jail, but refused to go peaceably. Dyche, the jailer, and Newman, a deputy, took hold of him. The prisoner resisted and struck Newman. In the scuffle both fell to the floor and Hubbard lay on his back "kicking at" anybody or anything within reach. Dyche had hold of him. He said, "I have done all I can; you will have to help me," or "Somebody is going to have to take my place; I am done." Judge Boggs took hold of the prisoner and persuaded him to get up; but he continued to resist as he was being taken to jail by Newman and another person. Dyche followed them out of the courthouse. He put his hand over his heart and sat down. In a few minutes he got down on the ground where he "rolled and tumbled" until he died within a half hour. Hubbard never struck Dyche at all, and he received no physical injury. He had been suffering for some time with a serious condition of the heart, and had remarked to a friend several hours before that he was feeling bad. Three doctors testified that his death was due to acute dilation of the heart, but that the physical exercise and excitement was calculated to accelerate his death.

The defendant testified that he had no memory of what had occurred. He and the deceased were friends.

The only inquiry we need make is whether the facts constitute involuntary manslaughter. It seems manifest that under any proper view of the case the defendant could be guilty of no higher degree of homicide, although the court did not give an instruction on that offense. The death of Dyche was charged to have resulted from the commission by Hubbard of a misdemeanor not of a character likely to endanger life. The Attorney General frankly concedes that the defendant was at least entitled to an instruction on involuntary manslaughter, and expresses grave doubt whether he is guilty of any culpable homicide. The only theory of guilt is that his unlawful act in resisting arrest contributed to Dyche's death or accelerated it.

There is a close line of distinction between criminal responsibility and innocence where the facts approach or are similar to those presented here. One cannot escape culpability because factors other than his act contributed to the death of another or hastened it, such as where he was suffering from some fatal malady or had a predisposed physical condition, as being in feeble health, without which a blow or other wound would not have been fatal. Under most modern decisions death caused or accomplished through fright, fear or nervous shock may form a basis for criminal responsibility. On the other hand, it is held that to warrant a conviction of homicide the act of the accused must be the proximate cause of death; that if there was an intervening cause for which the accused was not responsible and but for which death would not have occurred, he is blameless. . . .

In the present case the misdemeanor of the defendant must be regarded as too remote—not in time, to be sure, but as the cause. The failure of the man's diseased heart was the cause. The deceased knowing he had a serious condition of the heart undertook a task which he knew would excite him or create an emotional state of mind, which he also well knew he should have avoided. The evidence is that he had theretofore exercised such wise discretion. His intervening act in rolling and tumbling in pain on the courthouse yard, instead of lying quiet and still, was probably as much responsible for his ensuing death as was the initial excitement caused by the conduct of the accused. It was suggested in reference to the death of the woman in the Couch case that it may have been due to improper or want of attention following her confinement, or to some unrelated disease, hence the indictment which described the facts in detail was held not to state a criminal offense. It is, at least, speculative to say that the act of the defendant in this case was sufficiently proximate to impose criminal responsibility upon him for the unfortunate death. We are of opinion, therefore, that the court should have directed an acquittal.

The judgment is reversed.

REGINA v. HOLLAND

Liverpool Assizes, 1841.
2 Moody & R. 351, 174 Eng.Rep. 313.

Indictment for murder. The prisoner was charged with inflicting divers mortal blows and wounds upon one Thomas Garland, and (amongst others) a cut upon one of his fingers.

It appeared by the evidence that the deceased had been waylaid and assaulted by the prisoner, and that, amongst other wounds, he was severely cut across one of his fingers by an iron instrument. On being brought to the infirmary, the surgeon urged him to submit to the amputation of the finger, telling him, unless it were amputated, he considered that his life would be in great hazard. The deceased refused to allow the finger to be amputated. It was thereupon dressed by the surgeon, and the deceased attended at the infirmary from day to day to have his wounds dressed; at the end of a fortnight, how-

Sec. 6　　　CONDONATION BY INJURED PARTY　　　563

ever, lockjaw came on, induced by the wound on the finger; the finger was then amputated, but too late, and the lockjaw ultimately caused death. The surgeon deposed, that if the finger had been amputated in the first instance, he thought it most probable that the life of the deceased would have been preserved.

For the prisoner, it was contended that the cause of death was not the wound inflicted by the prisoner, but the obstinate refusal of the deceased to submit to proper surgical treatment, by which the fatal result would, according to the evidence, have been prevented.

MAULE, J., however, was clearly of opinion that this was no defence, and told the jury that if the prisoner wilfully, and without any justifiable cause, inflicted the wound on the party, which wound was ultimately the cause of death, the prisoner was guilty of murder; that for this purpose it made no difference whether the wound was in its own nature instantly mortal, or whether it became the cause of death by reason of the deceased not having adopted the best mode of treatment; the real question is, whether in the end the wound inflicted by the prisoner was the cause of death?

Guilty.[1]

SECTION 6.　CONDONATION BY INJURED PARTY

"Of a nature somewhat similar to the two last is the offence of *theft bote*, which is where the party robbed not only knows the felon, but also takes his goods again, or other amends, upon agreement not to prosecute. This is frequently called compounding of felony, and formerly was held to make a man an accessory; but is now punished only with fine and imprisonment. . . . By statute 25 Geo. II, c. 36, even to advertise a reward for the return of things stolen, with no questions asked, or words to the same purport, subjects the advertiser and the printer to a forfeiture of 50*l*. each." 4 Bl.Comm. 133–4.

The owner's reacquisition of a chattel previously stolen from him is not of itself sufficient to taint him with criminal guilt. It is his act of obtaining it under agreement or understanding to abstain from prosecution or to withhold evidence of the larceny that is illegal. This is merely a particular instance of a general crime. For anyone to obtain anything of value, or a promise thereof, upon such an agree-

---

[1]. The victim of a criminally negligent traffic accident was moved from the hospital, by his mother, contrary to the doctor's orders. There was no evidence that this actually hastened the death but the court indicates that it would not have been superseding had it done so. People v. Clark, 106 Cal.App.2d 271, 235 P.2d 56 (1951).

For the rule under the Texas statute see Noble v. State, 54 Tex.Cr.R. 436, 113 S.W. 281 (1908).

ment or understanding in regard to any felony is a common-law offense known as compounding a felony. The ancient classification of such an offender as an accessory to the crime after the fact suggests that it was limited to cases of felony in the early days. But that limitation has tended to disappear. It has been said that to take a reward to forbear or stifle a criminal prosecution for a misdemeanor is also indictable at common law, except for offenses largely of the nature of private injuries or of low grade.[1] And it has not been uncommon for statutes to forbid the compounding of any criminal offense.[2]

Discussions of the subject often suggest that an attempt by the offender and the offended to settle the offense outside of the criminal court room is usually a crime and always quite ineffective. This is far from the true picture.[3] To begin with, a multitude of offenses, including a substantial number of serious crimes, are not prosecuted because they are settled between the two persons involved and never reach the attention of the prosecuting authorities. This, of course, is merely a factual matter and does not dispute the statement as to the law. The law itself, however, has taken definite strides in this direction. The most sweeping provision of this nature is a statute expressly authorizing the compromise of a misdemeanor for which the injured person has a civil action (unless there are special circumstances of aggravation).[4] The court may have discretion to permit the prosecution to proceed notwithstanding such a compromise,[5] but it will be exercised rarely and only under unusual circumstances.

There are also certain specific provisions to be considered. The most common is the statute providing that intermarriage of the parties shall bar a prosecution for seduction.[6] Much rarer is the enactment under which such marriage will bar a prosecution for rape.[7] Some statutes invite a settlement by the parties, such as a bad check act providing a penalty for the issuance of such an instrument unless it is paid within three days after written notice;[8] or a statute making the refusal of an officer, clerk or agent to hand over money or

---

1. State v. Carver, 69 N.H. 216, 39 A. 973 (1897).

2. For example, Ill.Rev.Stats. c. 38, § 135 (1957); New York Penal Law, § 570.

3. For an elaborate consideration of the field see Miller, The Compromise of Criminal Cases, 1 So.Cal.L.Rev. 1 (1927).

4. For example, West's Ann.Cal.Pen. Code, § 1377.

5. Id. at § 1378.

6. West's Ann.Cal.Pen.Code, § 269 (1949); Ill.Rev.Stats., c. 38, § 537 (1957); New York Penal Law § 2176. As to an offer of marriage see Lasater v. State, 77 Ark. 468, 94 S.W. 59 (1906).

7. Ill.Rev.Stats., c. 38, § 490 (1957).

8. Tenn.Code Ann. § 39–1904 (1955). Under some of the statutes payment on written notice does not bar the prosecution but merely negatives the presumption of fraudulent intent. Cook v. Commonwealth, 178 Va. 251, 16 S.E.2d 635 (1941).

property in his care, on demand, prima-facie evidence of embezzlement.[9]

Any such provision gives to the person harmed by a crime more or less power to control whether prosecution shall or shall not be brought. Beyond any of the foregoing in this regard is the enactment found in some states providing that no prosecution for adultery shall be brought except upon complaint of the aggrieved spouse.[10]

These exceptions have been mentioned because of their importance, but they are definitely exceptions. A criminal offense is a public wrong. The act which constitutes a crime may also be a private wrong, such as larceny or battery, or be a public wrong only, such as joining enemy forces in time of war or making fraudulent misstatements in an income tax return. Insofar as an act constitutes a private wrong the injured individual is free to make a settlement with the wrongdoer, or to forgive him entirely without any reparation. But the general rule is that a private individual has no power to ratify, settle or condone a public wrong even if it was a wrong which injured his person or harmed his property. If he is able to do so it is only because of some exception to the general rule and in the exact manner provided.[11] In the absence of such exception the victim of rape cannot excuse the ravisher by ratifying or forgiving the act[12] or even by marrying him.[13] The owner of money or property, even after complete restitution has been made, cannot forgive the crime of embezzlement[14] or larceny.[15] It is even beyond the power of a mother's love to wipe out the criminal guilt of a son who maliciously burned her barn.[16]

HOLSEY v. STATE

Court of Appeals of Georgia, 1908.
4 Ga.App. 453, 61 S.E. 836.

POWELL, J. The defendant, who did odd jobs around a livery stable, drove one of the horses on a certain Sunday without the consent of the proprietor. On the next day, when the proprietor discovered this fact, he gave the defendant the choice of taking a whip-

---

9. Id. at § 39-4233 (1955).

10. For example, Iowa Code Ann. § 702.1. Whether or not consent given by filing the complaint can be withdrawn later, so as to stop the prosecution, is discussed in State v. Allison, 175 Minn. 218, 220 N.W. 563 (1928).

11. Commonwealth v. Heckman, 113 Pa.Super. 70, 172 A. 28 (1934).

12. Commonwealth v. Slattery, 147 Mass. 423, 18 N.E. 399 (1888).

13. State v. Newcomer, 59 Kan. 668, 54 P. 685 (1898).

14. Fleener v. State, 58 Ark. 98, 23 S.W. 1 (1893).

15. Breaker v. State, 103 Ohio St. 670, 134 N.E. 479 (1921).

16. State v. Craig, 124 Kan. 340, 259 P. 802 (1927).

ping or paying for the horse; the defendant chose the latter horn of the dilemma and bought the horse on satisfactory terms. Afterwards his prosecution was instituted and the defendant was convicted.

The old and well-recognized rule is that where one person interferes with the property of another and converts it to his own use, the latter, upon discovery of the fact, may elect to reclaim the property, treating the taking as wrongful, or he may waive the wrongful character of the taking and treat the matter as a purchase of the property by the taker, and sue him for the price. In the latter event the law looks upon the transaction just as if it were originally a regular sale between the parties. In the case at bar, when the owner of the animal discovered that it had been used,—that is to say, that the defendant had made a wrongful interference with it, and then took pay for the entire value of the animal, neither law nor justice should give the transaction any other interpretation than that it was the intention of the owner of the animal to acquiesce in the defendant's act of using it on the day before. Indeed, we think it may be said, as a general rule, that in no event will a prosecution under section 225 of the Penal Code lie, where, before the institution of the prosecution, the owner of the animal, either for or without a consideration, has given acquiescence, or, so to speak, ex post facto consent to the previously unauthorized use of his property. This ruling is to be taken, however, with the understanding that the principle is applicable only in that class of cases where the offense involves no crime against society or good morals, but relates solely to the redressing of private-property wrongs. Of course the ex post facto consent of the owner could not render a larceny, with all its elements complete, any the less a crime; but as to the offenses of the nature involved in § 225 of the Penal Code there is a different principle.

Judgment reversed.[1]

PEOPLE v. GOULD

Supreme Court of Michigan, 1888.
70 Mich. 240, 38 N.W. 232.

LONG, J. The respondent in this cause was convicted in the circuit court for the county of Shiawassee, for seducing and debauching one Kate Morrow, and brings the case here on writ of error.

The action was brought under section 9283, How.Stat., which provides:

"If any man shall seduce and debauch any unmarried woman, he shall be punished by imprisonment in the State prison not more than five years," etc.

---

[1]. As to the effect of the termination of a criminal proceeding because of a compromise see Restatement, Torts § 660 and comment c (1938); Orndorff v. Bond, 185 Va. 497, 39 S.E.2d 352 (1946); Leonard v. George, 178 F.2d 312 (4th Cir. 1949).

The information charges—

"That on October 10, 1886, at the township of Shiawassee, in the county of Shiawassee, [said William Gould] did seduce and debauch one Kate Morrow; she, the same Kate Morrow, being then and there an unmarried woman," etc.

The cause was tried before a jury.

It appeared on the trial of the case that on April 19, 1887, said Kate Morrow made complaint, under How.Stat. § 9283, before George A. Parker, a justice of the peace of the township of Shiawassee, in said county, charging the respondent with seducing and debauching her. A warrant was issued on said complaint; the respondent was arrested, and brought before said justice; and the examination set down for April 27, 1887. On said day the case was called, the respondent being present, and a recess taken to 1 o'clock in the afternoon of the same day. During such recess the respondent sought and obtained an interview with Kate and her mother, and finally went to their home, where Kate and respondent were married, during such recess, by Mr. Carruthers, a justice of the peace of said township. On the afternoon of the same day, about 7 o'clock, the respondent took the east-bound train for Port Huron, and deserted and abandoned his wife, and did not live or cohabit with her after said marriage, nor did he return to said county of Shiawassee till brought there under arrest as a disorderly person, under How.Stat. § 1985. . . .

The court voluntarily charged the jury, among other matters, as follows:

"On this subject of marriage, I charge you that, if the marriage (and there is no dispute about that) took place, with the intention on respondent's part, at that time, to perform in good faith all the duties which the relation of marriage imposed, and which naturally grew out of such relation, then the complaint would not be warranted; but if the marriage was resorted to as a piece of legal trickery to stop the voice of the girl, Kate, and prevent her from being a witness, with the intention, fixed and determined on in his mind at that time, not to live with her, nor to assume any of the duties and obligations of the marriage relation, and with the intention to abandon this girl, then the offense would be one against public decency and order, and would not be condoned by such marriage, and would be subject to prosecution."

We do not agree with the learned circuit judge in what he states the law to be, or in the reasons which he gives for so holding. Under this charge the jury were told that the guilt or innocence of the respondent must be made to depend, not upon the facts which go to make up the offense charged,—the seducing and debauching, and, as in this case, the surrender by Kate Morrow of her person to the respondent, in reliance upon his promise of marriage,—but upon the good faith or want of good faith of the respondent in entering into the marriage relation with her after the offense with which he was charged was committed.

It would not be claimed that, had the respondent married this girl at any time previous to the complaint being made against him, public policy or public decency would have required his prosecution. But, on the other hand, it will be conceded that public morals and public decency would be much better subserved by the marriage of the parties in this class of cases, as well as in bastardy proceedings under the statute, and thus make legitimate the children begotten by such illicit intercourse, and save, in part at least, the shame and disgrace of the injured female. The statute, in other sections, provides some punishment for the offense of deserting and abandoning the female after such marriage.

The *gravamen* of the offense under the statute under which respondent was convicted, is not the mere fact of intercourse. Two elements enter into it, and both must concur and exist at the same time,—seduction and debauchery; and, if there is no such concurrence, the offense would not be complete. Debauchery and carnal intercourse, without seduction, is no offense under this statute. The offense which this statute is aimed at is the seduction and debauchery accomplished by the promises and blandishments the man brings to his aid in effecting the ruin and disgrace of the female; and where the seduction and debauchery is accomplished by promises of marriage, upon which the female relies, and thus surrenders her person, and gives to the man the brightest jewel in the crown of her womanhood, it is the broken promise which the law will regard as the *gravamen* of the offense. It must therefore be held that, where seduction and debauchery is accomplished under promise of marriage, and the promise has been kept and performed, no prosecution can be allowed or conviction had after such marriage; and the question of the good faith or want of good faith upon the part of the man in entering into such marriage cannot enter into the question of his guilt or innocence. The promise has been kept and performed, and it would be against public policy and public decency to permit prosecutions to be carried forward in the courts of justice thereafter.

This question came before the courts of Pennsylvania in Com. v. Eichar, 1 Am.Law Jour. 551. In that case, Knox, P. J., delivering the opinion of the court, says:

"Can he now be convicted and punished for her seduction before marriage? It is not the carnal connection, even when induced by the solicitation of the man, that is the object of this statutory penalty, but it is the *seduction under promise* of marriage, which is an offense of so grievous a nature as to require this exemplary punishment. What promise? One that is kept and performed? Clearly not, but a false promise, broken and violated after performing its fiendish purpose. The evil which led to the enactment was not that females were seduced, and then made the wives of the seducers; but that, after the ends of the seducer were accomplished, his victim was abandoned to her disgrace. An objection to this construction is that it places within the power of the seducer a means of escaping the penalty. So be it. This is far better than, by a contrary construction, to remove the inducement to a faithful adherence to the promise which obtained the consent."

Prosecutions under similar statutes in New York are prohibited by statute after the marriage of the parties. 3 Rev.St.N.Y. (5th ed.) 942.

We think this better reasoning than that of the learned circuit judge before whom this case was tried.

The respondent's fifth request to charge should have been given. It follows that the verdict and judgment of the court below must be reversed, and set aside, and the respondent discharged.[1]

CHAMPLIN and MORSE, JJ., concurred with LONG, J.

SHERWOOD, C. J. I concur in the result in this case, on the ground that the marriage is not repudiated by the wife, nor claimed to be fraudulent. Were it otherwise, I should agree with the circuit judge.

CAMPBELL, J., did not sit.

---

1. "It is true, as stated, that society approves the act of defendant when he endeavors to make amends for the wrong done the injured female, by marrying her, and usually a good faith marriage between the parties to the wrong, prevents or terminates a prosecution; but the statute which defines the offense and declares the punishment therefor, makes no such provision. If the defendant has acted in good faith in marrying the girl, and honestly desires to perform the marital obligations resting upon him, and is prevented from doing so by the influence and interference of persons other than his wife, it may constitute a strong appeal to the prosecution to discontinue the same, or to the governor for the exercise of executive clemency, but as the law stands it furnishes no defense to the charge brought against the defendant.
"The judgment of the District Court will be affirmed." State v. Newcomer, 59 Kan. 668, 670, 54 P. 685, 686 (1898).

"If any man against whom a prosecution has begun, either before a justice of the peace or by indictment by a grand jury, for the crime of seduction, shall marry the female alleged to have been seduced, such prosecution shall not then be terminated, but shall be suspended; provided, that if at any time thereafter the accused shall wilfully and without such cause, as now constitutes a legal cause for divorce, desert and abandon such female, then at such time said prosecution shall be continued and proceed as though no marriage had taken place between such female and the accused." Ark. Stats. § 41–3409 (1947). The following section expressly provides that the wife shall be competent as a witness against the accused.

Compare Harp v. State, 158 Tenn. 510, 14 S.W.2d 720 (1928).

If the victim of rape marries the offender before trial she is incompetent, under the Iowa statute, to be a witness against him. State v. McKay, 122 Iowa 658, 98 N.W. 510 (1904).

MODEL PENAL CODE

Section 213.3. Corruption of Minors and Seduction.

(1) Offense Defined. A male who has sexual intercourse with a female not his wife, or any person who engages in deviate sexual intercourse or causes another to engage in deviate sexual intercourse, is guilty of an offense if: . . .

> (d) the other person is a female who is induced to participate by a promise of marriage which the actor does not mean to perform.

Chapter 10

SPECIAL DEFENSES

SECTION 1. PUBLIC AUTHORITY

Nothing done under valid public authority is a crime if such authority is in no way exceeded or abused. Deeds which would otherwise be crimes, such as taking or destroying property, taking hold of a person by force and against his will, placing him in confinement, or even taking his life, are not criminal if done with proper public authority. The typical instances in which even the extreme act of taking human life is done by public authority are (1) the killing of an enemy as an act of war and within the rules of war, and (2) the execution of a sentence of death pronounced by a competent tribunal.

Any unauthorized departure from the authority given destroys the privilege which would otherwise be present. Even in time of war an alien enemy may not be killed needlessly after he has been disarmed and securely imprisoned.[1] No one other than the proper officer or his duly appointed deputy may lawfully execute the sentence of death.[2] And that officer may not substitute one method of execution for another.[3] Suppose, for example, in a state in which the electric chair is used for capital punishment, the officer in charge should discover that no electric current was available at the time set for execution. The sentence of the court would specify that particular means of carrying out the sentence, and if the officer should shoot the prisoner, or hang him, the officer would be guilty of criminal homicide.

"And, further, if judgment of death be given by a judge not authorized by lawful commission, and execution is done accordingly, the judge is guilty of murder. And upon this account Sir Matthew Hale himself, though he accepted the place of a judge of the common pleas under Cromwell's government, (since it is necessary to decide the disputes of civil property in the worst of times,) yet declined to sit on the crown side at the assizes and try prisoners, having very strong objections to the legality of the usurper's commission; a distinction

---

1. "That it is legal to kill an alien enemy in the heat and exercise of war, is undeniable; but to kill such an enemy after he has laid down his arms, and especially when he is confined in prison, is murder." State v. Gut, 13 Minn. (Gil. ed.) 315, 330 (1868).

2. ". . . even though it be the judge himself." 4 Bl.Comm. 179.

3. "If an officer beheads one who is adjudged to be hanged, or *vice versa*, it is murder, . . ." Ibid.

perhaps rather too refined, since the punishment of crimes is at least as necessary to society as maintaining the boundaries of property." [4]

Wilful abuse of authority will also destroy the privilege. Thus obviously excessive flogging of a disobedient convict, by a guard, constituted criminal assault and battery.[5]

The exercise of public authority most commonly resulting in an application of force to the person is the making of an arrest, or the detention of one already in custody who seeks to depart without lawful authority. A peace officer, or even a private person, may have authority to arrest a certain individual. This authority is sometimes under a warrant and at other times without a warrant.[6] The amount

of force that may lawfully be used in the apprehension depends upon all of the facts in the particular case, including the conduct of the arrestee and the nature of the offense for which the arrest is being made. If the arrest itself is authorized, and the force used in making it is not excessive, there is no assault, battery or false imprisonment.[7] On the other hand, a battery results from any laying on of hands to make an unauthorized arrest,[8] or from the use of excessive force in making an arrest that would otherwise be lawful.[9]

---

4. Id. at 178.

5. State v. Mincher, 172 N.C. 895, 90 S.E. 429 (1916).

6. Professor Wilgus, in his very scholarly analysis, has reached this conclusion: At common law either officer or private person was privileged to arrest without a warrant for treason, felony or breach of the peace committed in his presence,—except that the arrest for breach of the peace was not privileged without a warrant unless it was effected while the breach was being committed or on immediate and continuous pursuit thereafter. Wilgus, Arrest Without a Warrant, 22 Mich.L.Rev. 673 (1924). Compare Restatement, Second, Torts §§ 119, 121 (1965).

At common law, moreover, either officer or private person is privileged, without a warrant, to arrest one who is reasonably believed to be guilty of felony, with one important distinction: The officer is protected if he believes upon reasonable grounds (1) that a felony has been committed and (2) that the arrestee is the guilty person; whereas for the protection of a private person it is necessary (1) that a felony has in fact been committed and (2) that he has reasonable grounds for believing the arrestee guilty of committing it. Ibid; A.L.I. Code of Criminal Procedure, 236–40 (official draft with commentaries, 1931).

Changes have been made by statutes, usually enlarging the scope of the privilege to arrest without a warrant.

7. State v. Fuller, 96 Mo. 165, 168, 9 S.W. 583, 584 (1888).

8. Restatement, Second, Torts § 118, comment b (1965).

9. Moody v. State, 120 Ga. 868, 48 S.E. 340 (1904); Reynolds v. Griffith, 126 W.Va. 766, 30 S.E.2d 81 (1944).

REGINA v. LESLEY

Court for Crown Cases Reserved, 1860.
Bell C.C. 220, 169 Eng.Rep. 1236.

ERLE, C. J. In this case the question is, whether a conviction for false imprisonment can be sustained upon the following facts.

The prosecutor and others, being in Chili, and subjects of that state, were banished by the government from Chili to England.

The defendant, being master of an English merchant vessel lying in the territorial waters of Chili, near Valparaiso, contracted with that government to take the prosecutor and his companions from Valparaiso to Liverpool, and they were accordingly brought on board the defendant's vessel by the officers of the government, and carried to Liverpool by the defendant under his contract. Then, can the conviction be sustained for that which was done within the Chilian waters? We answer no.

We assume that in Chili the act of the government towards its subjects was lawful; and, although an English ship in some respects carries with her the laws of her country in the territorial waters of a foreign state, yet in other respects she is subject to the laws of that state as to acts done to the subjects thereof.

We assume that the government could justify all that it did within its own territory, and we think it follows that the defendant can justify all that he did there as agent for the government, and under its authority. In Dobree v. Napier (2 Bing.N.C. 781) the defendant, on behalf of the Queen of Portugal, seized the plaintiff's vessel for violating a blockade of a Portuguese port in time of war. The plaintiff brought trespass; and judgment was for the defendant, because the Queen of Portugal, in her own territory, had a right to seize the vessel and to employ whom she would to make the seizure; and therefore the defendant, though an Englishman seizing an English vessel, could justify the act under the employment of the Queen.

We think that the acts of the defendant in Chili become lawful on the same principle, and therefore that there is no ground for the conviction.

The further question remains, can the conviction be sustained for that which was done out of the Chilian territory? And we think it can.

It is clear that an English ship on the high sea, out of any foreign territory, is subject to the laws of England; and persons, whether foreign or English, on board such ship, are as much amenable to English law as they would be on English soil. In Regina v. Sattler (Dears. & Bell's C.C.R. 525) this principle was acted on, so as to make the prisoner, a foreigner, responsible for murder on board an

English ship at sea: the same principle has been laid down by foreign writers on international law, among which it is enough to cite Ortolan, sur la Diplomatic de la Mer, liv. 2, cap. 13.

The Merchant Shipping Act, 17 & 18 Vict. c. 104, s. 267, makes the master and seamen of a British ship responsible for all offences against property or person committed on the sea out of her Majesty's dominions as if they had been committed within the jurisdiction of the Admiralty of England.

Such being the law, if the act of the defendant amounted to a false imprisonment he was liable to be convicted. Now, as the contract of the defendant was to receive the prosecutor and the others as prisoners on board his ship, and to take them, without their consent, over the sea to England, although he was justified in first receiving them in Chili, yet that justification ceased when he passed the line of Chilian jurisdiction, and after that it was a wrong which was intentionally planned and executed in pursuance of the contract, amounting in law to a false imprisonment.

It may be that transportation to England is lawful by the law of Chili, and that a Chilian ship might so lawfully transport Chilian subjects; but for an English ship the laws of Chili, out of the state, are powerless, and the lawfulness of the acts must be tried by English law.

For these reasons, to the extent above mentioned, the conviction is affirmed.

Conviction confirmed accordingly.[1]

COMMONWEALTH ex rel. WADSWORTH v. SHORTALL

Supreme Court of Pennsylvania, 1903.
206 Pa. 165, 55 A. 952.

[Wadsworth was a private in a division of the National Guard that had been ordered out by the governor to suppress disorder and violence which was beyond the control of local authorities. He was posted to guard a house at night and told to halt all prowlers or persons approaching the house. He was ordered to "shoot to kill" any person who refused to halt when challenged. About 11:30 o'clock a stranger approached the house. Wadsworth called "halt" four times. The stranger ignored the command, opened the gate, continued into the yard, and was then shot and killed by Wadsworth. Wadsworth was arrested and held in custody on a charge of manslaughter. To

---

1. The ship went very near Peru and the prosecutor asked to be put ashore there offering to pay the captain the amount the Chilian government paid him. The captain refused on the ground that he was under contract to take him to Liverpool. The ship touched at the Azores and the captain had holes made in the boats to prevent the men getting away.

Sec. 1 *PUBLIC AUTHORITY* 575

inquire into the legality of his imprisonment the presiding justice of this court allowed a writ of habeas corpus.]

Opinion by Mr. Justice Mitchell, April 17, 1903: . . .

And while the military are in active service for the suppression of disorder and violence, their rights and obligations as soldiers must be judged by the standard of actual war. No other standard is possible, for the first and overruling duty is to repress disorder, whatever the cost, and all means which are necessary to that end are lawful. The situation of troops in a riotous and insurrectionary district approximates that of troops in an enemy's country, and in proportion to the extent and violence of the overt acts of hostility shown is the degree of severity justified in the means of repression. The requirements of the situation in either case, therefore, shift with the circumstances, and the same standard of justification must apply to both. The only difference is the one already adverted to, the liability to subsequent investigation in the courts of the land after the restoration of order.

Coming now to the position of the relator, in regard to responsibility, we find the law well settled. "A subordinate stands as regards the application of these principles, in a different position from the superior whom he obeys, and may be absolved from liability for executing an order which it was criminal to give. The question is, as we have seen, had the accused reasonable cause for believing in the necessity of the act which is impugned, and in determining this point, a soldier or member of the posse comitatus may obviously take the orders of the person in command into view as proceeding from one who is better able to judge and well informed; and if the circumstances are such that the command may be justifiable, he should not be held guilty for declining to decide that it is wrong with the responsibility incident to disobedience, unless the case is so plain as not to admit of a reasonable doubt. A soldier, consequently, runs little risk in obeying any order which a man of common sense so placed would regard as warranted by the circumstances:" Hare, Const. Law, p. 920.

The cases in this country have usually arisen in the army and been determined in the United States courts. But by the Articles of War (art. 59) under the acts of congress, officers or soldiers charged with offenses punishable by the laws of the land, are required (except in time of war) to be delivered over to the civil (i. e., in distinction from military) authorities; and the courts proceed upon the principles of the common (and statute) law: 31 F. 711. The decisions therefore are precedents applicable here.

A leading case is U. S. v. Clark, 31 F. 710. A soldier on the military reservation at Fort Wayne had been convicted by court martial and when brought out of the guardhouse with other prisoners at "retreat," broke from the ranks and was in the act of escaping when

Clark, who was the sergeant of the guard, fired and killed him. Clark was charged with homicide and brought before the United States district judge, sitting as a committing magistrate. Judge Brown, now of the Supreme Court of the United States, delivered an elaborate and well considered opinion, which has ever since been quoted as authoritative. In it he said, "The case reduces itself to the naked legal proposition whether the prisoner is excused in law in killing the deceased." Then after referring to the common-law principle that an officer having custody of a prisoner charged with felony may take his life if it becomes absolutely necessary to do so to prevent his escape, and pointing out the peculiarities of the military code which practically abolish the distinction between felonies and misdemeanors, he continued, "I have no doubt the same principle would apply to the acts of a subordinate officer, performed in compliance with his supposed duty as a soldier; and unless the act were manifestly beyond the scope of his authority, or were such that a man of ordinary sense and understanding would know that it was illegal, that it would be a protection to him, if he acted in good faith and without malice."

In McCall v. McDowell, 1 Abb. (U.S.) 212, where an action was brought by plaintiff against Gen. McDowell and Capt. Douglas for false imprisonment under a general order of the former for the arrest of persons publicly exulting over the assassination of President Lincoln, the court said, "Except in a plain case of excess of authority, where at first blush it is apparent and palpable to the commonest understanding that the order is illegal, I cannot but think that the law will excuse a military subordinate, when acting in obedience to the order of his commander, otherwise he is placed in a dangerous dilemma of being liable to damages to third persons, for obedience to the order, or for the loss of his commission and disgrace for disobedience thereto. . . . Between an order plainly legal and one palpably otherwise there is a wide middle ground where the ultimate legality and propriety of orders depends or may depend upon circumstances and conditions, of which it cannot be expected that the inferior is informed or advised. In such cases justice to the subordinate demands, and the necessities and efficiency of the public service require that the order of the superior should protect the inferior, leaving the responsibility to rest where it properly belongs, upon the officer who gave the command." The court sitting without a jury accordingly gave judgment for Capt. Douglas, though finding damages against Gen. McDowell.

In U. S. v. Carr, 1 Woods 480, which was a case of the shooting of a soldier in Fort Pulaski by the prisoner who was sergeant of the guard, Woods, J., afterwards of the Supreme Court of the United States, charged the jury: "Place yourselves in the position of the prisoner at the time of the homicide. Inquire whether at the moment he fired his piece at the deceased, with his surroundings at the time, he had reasonable ground to believe, and did believe, that the killing or serious wounding of the deceased was necessary to the suppression of a mutiny then and there existing, or of a disorder which theatened to ripen into mutiny. If he had reasonable ground so to believe, then the killing was not unlawful. But if on the other hand the mutinous conduct of the soldiers, if there was any such, had ceased, and it so appeared to the prisoner, or if he could reasonably have suppressed the disorder without the resort to such violent means as the taking of the life of the deceased, and it would so have appeared to a reasonable man under like circumstances, then the killing was unlawful. But it must be understood that the law will not require an officer charged with the order and discipline of a camp or fort to weigh with scrupulous nicety the amount of force necessary to suppress disorder. The exercise of a reasonable discretion is all that is required."

In Riggs v. State, 4 Cold. 85, the Supreme Court of Tennessee held to be correct an instruction to the jury that "any order given by an officer to his private which does not expressly and clearly show on its face, or in the body thereof, its own illegality, the soldier would be bound to obey, and such order would be a protection to him."

These are the principal American cases and they are in entire accord with the long line of established authorities in England.

Applying these principles to the act of the relator, it is clear that he was not guilty of any crime. The situation as already shown was one of martial law, in which the commanding general was authorized to use as forcible military means for the repression of violence as his judgment dictated to be necessary. The house had been dynamited at night and threatened again. With an agent so destructive, in hands so lawless, the duty of precaution was correspondingly great. There was no ground therefore for doubt as to the legality of the order to shoot. The relator was a private soldier and his first duty was obedience. His orders were clear and specific, and the evidence does not show that he went beyond them in his action. There was no malice for it appears affirmatively that he did not know the deceased, and acted only on his orders when the situation appeared to call for action under them. The unfortunate man who was killed was not shown to have been one of the mob gathered in the vicinity, though why he should have turned into the gate is not known. The occurrence, deplorable as it was, was an illustration of the dangers of the lawless condition of the community, or of the minority who were allowed to control it, and must be classed with the numerous instances in riots and mobs, where mere spectators and even distant non-combatants get hurt without apparent fault of their own. . . .

The relator, Arthur Wadsworth, is discharged from further custody under the warrant held by respondent.[1]

---

[1]. If a military detail was sent to kill an officer unlawfully the order given would not excuse the killing. But a member of the detail who did *not* know the mission and did not participate in the killing would not be guilty of the homicide. The rule that all conspirators are guilty by reason of

the act of one in carrying out their unlawful agreement has no application to a soldier obeying orders with no knowledge of an intended unlawful purpose. Riggs v. State, 43 Tenn. 85 (1866). An order to a sentry to kill anyone using opprobrious words to him would be obviously illegal and void, and would not justify or excuse such a killing. United States v. Bevans, 24 Fed.Cas. 1183, No. 14,589 (1816), reversed on other grounds 3 Wheat. 336 (1818). An order to assist in the perpetration of rape is not a military command. State v. Roy, 233 N.C. 558, 64 S.E.2d 840 (1951).

An officer may shoot, if necessary, to arrest one who has committed a felony in his presence. Stinnett v. Virginia, 55 F.2d 644 (4th Cir. 1932). Even under the statute an officer is not privileged to shoot a fleeing misdemeanant who cannot otherwise be arrested. The statute reads: "If, after notice of the intention to arrest the defendant, he either flee or forcibly resist, the officer may use all the necessary means to effect the arrest." Johnson v. State, 173 Tenn. 134, 114 S.W. 819 (1938).

One being arrested for a misdemeanor resisted the officer and was shot. For this shooting the officer was convicted of assault and battery. This conviction was reversed because of an instruction to the effect that an officer arresting for a misdemeanor has no right to go to the extremity of shedding blood except in self-defense. Territory v. Machado, 30 Haw. 487 (1928).

"If he have a warrant for any crime, from the highest to the lowest, whether a felony or a misdemeanor, and the party resist, and the constable have no means of making him amenable except by killing him, he is justified in so doing. But the case of flight is different from resistance. If the warrant be for felony, flight is tantamount to resistance, and the flying felon may be justifiably killed, if he cannot be otherwise secured. In cases of misdemeanor, resistance will justify killing, though flight will not; for in such cases the law considers it better, that the accused should escape than that a life should be taken." Rex v. Finnerty, 1 Cr. & Dix 167, n. (Ireland, 1830). This is dictum as to the misdemeanant since the person to be arrested was charged with a felony. A number of cases which seem to authorize deadly force to overcome resistance on the part of one being arrested for a misdemeanor, were actually self-defense cases. Pearson, The Right to Kill in Making Arrests, 28 Mich.L.Rev. 957 (1930).

In a study of this subject it is helpful to compare different provisions of the statutes such, for example, as the following sections of the California Penal Code:

§ 843. "When the arrest is being made by an officer under the authority of a warrant, after information of the intention to make the arrest, if the person to be arrested either flees or forcibly resists, the officer may use all necessary means to effect the arrest."

§ 196. "Homicide is justifiable when committed by public officers and those acting by their command in their aid and assistance, either— . . .

"2. When necessarily committed in overcoming actual resistance to the execution of some legal process, or in the discharge of any other legal duty; or,

"3. When necessarily committed in retaking felons who have been rescued or have escaped, or when necessarily committed in arresting persons charged with felony, and who are fleeing from justice or resisting such arrest."

One who responds to the call of an officer to aid in making an arrest, and uses such force as is reasonably necessary to carry out the officer's orders, is justified even if the officer is not. Commonwealth v. Sadowsky, 80 Pa. Super. 496 (1923).

Section 131(a) of the Restatement of Torts limited the use of deadly force in making an arrest to cases where "the arrest is made for treason or for a felony which normally causes or threatens death or serious bodily harm, or which involves the breaking and entry of a dwelling place". This was so far out of line with existing law that it was amended to read "treason or felony" without restriction as to the type of felony. Restatement, 1948 Supp. 628. See now Restatement, Second, Torts § 131 (1965).

MODEL PENAL CODE

Section 2.10. Military Orders.

It is an affirmative defense that the actor, in engaging in the conduct charged to constitute an offense, does no more than execute an order of his superior in the armed services which he does not know to be unlawful.

Section 3.03. Execution of Public Duty.

(1) Except as provided in Subsection (2) of this Section, conduct is justifiable when it is required or authorized by:

(a) the law defining the duties or functions of a public officer or the assistance to be rendered to such officer in the performance of his duties; or

(b) the law governing the execution of legal process; or

(c) the judgment or order of a competent court or tribunal; or

(d) the law governing the armed services or the lawful conduct of war; or

(e) any other provision of law imposing a public duty.

(2) The other sections of this Article apply to:

(a) the use of force upon or toward the person of another for any of the purposes dealt with in such sections; and

(b) the use of deadly force for any purpose, unless the use of such force is otherwise expressly authorized by law or occurs in the lawful conduct of war.

(3) The justification afforded by Subsection (1) of this Section applies:

(a) when the actor believes his conduct to be required or authorized by the judgment or direction of a competent court or tribunal or in the lawful execution of legal process, notwithstanding lack of jurisdiction of the court or defect in the legal process; and

(b) when the actor believes his conduct to be required or authorized to assist a public officer in the performance of his duties, notwithstanding that the officer exceeded his legal authority.

Section 3.07. Use of Force in Law Enforcement.

(1) Use of Force Justifiable to Effect an Arrest. Subject to the provisions of this Section and of Section 3.09, the use of force upon or toward the person of another is justifiable when the actor is making or assisting in making an arrest and the actor believes that such force is immediately necessary to effect a lawful arrest.

(2) Limitations on the Use of Force.

(a) The use of force is not justifiable under this Section unless:

(i) the actor makes known the purpose of the arrest or believes that it is otherwise known by or cannot reasonably be made known to the person to be arrested; and

(ii) when the arrest is made under a warrant, the warrant is valid or believed by the actor to be valid.

(b) The use of **deadly force is not** justifiable under this Section unless:

(i) the arrest is for a felony; and

(ii) the person effecting the arrest is authorized to act as a peace officer or is assisting a person whom he believes to be authorized to act as a peace officer; and

(iii) the actor believes that the force employed creates no substantial risk of injury to innocent persons; and

(iv) the actor believes that:

(1) the crime for which the arrest is made involved conduct including the use or threatened use of deadly **force;** or

(2) there is a substantial risk that the person to be arrested will cause death or serious bodily harm if his apprehension is delayed.

(3) Use of Force to Prevent Escape from Custody. The use of force to prevent the escape of an arrested person from custody is justifiable when **the force** could justifiably have been employed to effect the arrest under **which** the person is in custody, except that a guard or other person authorized **to act as** a peace officer is justified in using any force, including deadly **force,** which he believes to be immediately necessary to prevent the escape **of a person** from a jail, prison, or other institution for the detention of persons charged with or convicted of a crime.

(4) Use of Force by Private Person Assisting an Unlawful Arrest.

(a) A private person who is summoned by a peace officer to assist in effecting an unlawful arrest, is justified in using any force which he would be justified in using if the arrest were lawful, provided that he does not believe the arrest is unlawful.

(b) A private person who assists another private person in effecting an unlawful arrest, or who, not being summoned, assists a peace officer in effecting an unlawful arrest, is justified in using any force which he would be justified in using if the arrest were lawful, provided that (i) he believes the arrest is lawful, and (ii) the arrest would be lawful if the facts were as he believes them to be.

Section 3.09. Mistake of Law as to Unlawfulness of Force or Legality of Arrest; Reckless or Negligent Use of Otherwise Justifiable Force; Reckless or Negligent Injury or Risk of Injury to Innocent Persons.

(1) The justification afforded by Sections 3.04 to 3.07, inclusive, is unavailable when:

(a) the actor's belief in the unlawfulness of the force or conduct against which he employs protective force or his belief in the lawfulness of an arrest which he endeavors to effect by force is erroneous; and

(b) his error is due to ignorance or mistake as to the provisions of the Code, any other provision of the criminal law or the law governing the legality of an arrest or search.

(2) When the actor believes that the use of force upon or toward the person of another is necessary for any of the purposes for which such belief

would establish a justification under Sections 3.03 to 3.08 but the actor is reckless or negligent in having such belief or in acquiring or failing to acquire any knowledge or belief which is material to the justifiability of his use of force, the justification afforded by those Sections is unavailable in a prosecution for an offense for which recklessness or negligence, as the case may be, suffices to establish culpability.

(3) When the actor is justified under Sections 3.03 to 3.08 in using force upon or toward the person of another but he recklessly or negligently injures or creates a risk of injury to innocent persons, the justification afforded by those Sections is unavailable in a prosecution for such recklessness or negligence towards innocent persons.

SECTION 2. DOMESTIC AUTHORITY

References may be found to an ancient authority of a husband to chastise his wife [1] with a "whip or rattan no bigger than my thumb, in order to inforce the salutary restraints of domestic discipline." [2] This was doubted in Blackstone's time,[3] and is definitely not recognized in the modern common law. Hence a husband who strikes his wife, even to enforce obedience to his just commands, is guilty of battery,[4] although he may use moderate force to *restrain* her from committing crimes or torts.[5] Wife beating is sometimes made punishable by express statutory provision. In some instances this seems merely to emphasize the fact that it is unlawful; [6] in others it is to provide a special penalty for this type of battery.[7]

Firmly recognized in the law, however, is the right of the parent to discipline his minor child by means of moderate chastisement.[8] The right to correct an adopted child is the same as the right of a natural parent in this regard; [9] and this authority has been extended even to one who has taken a child into his home to be brought up as a member of the family without formal adoption.[10] Similarly, a guard-

1. "They refuse to bind him to keep the peace at her suit unless her life be in danger, because by the law he hath the power of castigation; . . ." Bradley v. His Wife, 1 Keb. 637, 83 Eng.Rep. 1157 (1663).

2. Bradley v. State, Walker 156, 157 (Miss.1824).

3. 1 Bl.Comm. 444–5.

4. Fulgham v. State, 46 Ala. 143 (1871).

5. See People v. Winters, 2 Park.Cr. 10 (N.Y.1823).

6. Georgia Code § 26–1410 (1953).

7. West's Ann.Cal.Pen.Code § 273d.

8. Richardson v. State Board, 98 N.J.L. 690, 121 A. 457 (1923).

9. State v. Koonse, 123 Mo.App. 655, 101 S.W. 139 (1907).

10. See the instruction in State v. Gillett, 56 Iowa 459, 9 N.W. 362 (1881).

ian may lawfully administer moderate chastisement for the correction of his ward.[11]

The common law authorized a master to punish his apprentice in the same manner; but true apprenticeship is a special relation. An employer has no authority to administer corporal punishment to an ordinary servant merely because the particular employee happens to be a minor.[12] The father's authority to punish a minor child may be delegated to an employer; but the employer has no such privilege unless he has received permission from the parent.[13]

"By law, as well as immemorial usage, a schoolmaster is regarded as standing in loco parentis, and like the parent, has the authority to moderately chastise pupils under his care."[14] Hence the ordinary whipping of a pupil, for wilful disobedience of lawful rules, is not an assault and battery by the teacher, if administered for discipline and not in anger or with undue severity.[15]

The existence of such private authority, needless to say, will not justify immoderate punishment.[16] On the other hand unintentional harm may be excused even if it goes beyond that actually authorized. Thus an act by a teacher in the exercise of his authority, not prompted by malice, is not a battery even if it causes a permanent injury if the injury was quite unexpected and without negligence.[17]

Those in charge of trains, boats, theaters, stadia and similar places, while without authority to punish members of the public for misbehavior, may use reasonable and moderate force to expel a person who refuses to pay his fare or admission,[18] or is guilty of serious misconduct even after he has paid. But even one with authority to remove such a person will be guilty of assault and battery if he does so improperly as by ejecting a passenger from a moving train.[19]

11. Stanfield v. State, 43 Tex. 167 (1875).

12. Tinkle v. Dunivant, 84 Tenn. 503 (1886). "The rule obtaining in this state is that a master has no authority to chastise his servant, no matter how flagrant his violation of duty may be." Cook v. Cook, 232 Mo.App. 994, 996, 124 S.W.2d 675, 676 (1939).

13. Cooper v. State, 67 Tenn. 324 (1874).

14. Roberson v. State, 22 Ala.App. 413, 414, 116 So. 317 (1928).

15. Danenhoffer v. State, 69 Ind. 295 (1879).

16. Clasen v. Pruhs, 69 Neb. 278, 95 N.W. 640 (1903).

17. Drum v. Miller, 135 N.C. 204, 47 S.E. 421 (1904).

18. Carpenter v. Washington & G. R. Co., 121 U.S. 474, 7 S.Ct. 1002, 30 L.Ed. 1015 (1887).

19. State v. Kinney, 34 Minn. 311, 25 N.W. 705 (1885).

EVERSOLE v. COMMONWEALTH

Court of Appeals of Kentucky, 1914.
157 Ky. 478, 163 S.W. 496.

SETTLE, J. The appellant, Emma Eversole, was tried in the court below under an indictment charging her with the murder of her husband, Mack Eversole, but by the verdict of the jury was found guilty of voluntary manslaughter, upon which judgment was duly entered fixing her punishment at confinement in the penitentiary for not less than 2 nor more than 21 years, and, from that judgment, she has appealed. . . .

Appellant's fourth and final contention must be overruled in part and sustained in part. In so far as it complains of the instructions that were given by the trial court, it is without merit, for by them the jury were correctly told in what state of case they would be authorized to find the appellant guilty of murder or voluntary manslaughter, and what punishment they might inflict for the first-named crime, also what would justify the application of the law of self-defense as to one of appellant's grounds of defense; while in and through them, separately and as a whole ran the admonition to the jury to allow the appellant the benefit of every reasonable doubt in the matter of determining her guilt or innocence, or, if they found her guilty, in determining the degree of her offense. But in view of the evidence furnished by appellant's testimony and that of several of her witnesses, that deceased ordered her to at once leave the house, threatened to kill her if she did not do so, and, upon her refusing to go, immediately assaulted and struck her with the gun as if to forcibly compel her to leave the house, or to kill her, the court should have given the following additional instruction: The jury are further instructed that appellant had the right, equally with her husband, Mack Eversole, to live and remain in the house occupied by them as a home, and the husband had no right to forcibly evict her therefrom, and, if they believe from the evidence that the husband ordered defendant to immediately leave the house, and that upon her refusal to leave it, if she did so refuse, he attempted to drive her from the house by threatening to kill her, and forcibly assaulting and striking her with a gun, she had the right to resist and prevent such assault or attempted ejection by the use of such force, and no more, as was necessary or appeared to her to be reasonably necessary to that end, and if in so doing she had reasonable grounds to believe and did believe she was in imminent danger of death or great bodily harm at the hands of her husband, and that she had no other safe or to her apparently safe means of escape from such danger, then she had the right to use such force or means as to her appeared to be reasonably necessary to protect her life or person from such danger or to her apparent danger, even to the extent of shooting or killing her husband; and, if the jury believe from the evidence that the latter met his death under such circumstances and in the manner predicated in this instruction, they should acquit the defendant.

"Whatever may have been the rule formerly, the authority on the part of the husband to even moderately chastise his wife is now expressly repudiated, and all such punishment is regarded as an assault and battery, for which he must answer criminally. The husband has no right to compel his wife by force to obey his wishes. Her person is as sacred as that of her husband, and the protection offered by law to the one should not be denied to the other; but he may defend himself against her, and may restrain her from acts of violence towards himself or towards others. The mother may interfere by force, if necessary to do so, to protect her child from cruel treatment, or wanton chastisement, or abuse by either the stepfather or father; but her right to interfere depends upon the fact whether the father has exceeded the just limits of parental authority in the extent and character of the chastisement which he is administering to the child. If he has, the wife, by interfering for the protection of the child, does not become an aggressor, and, should the husband repel such interference by an assault upon the wife, he is in the wrong, and must be regarded as an assailant, and treated as a wrongdoer. If, however, the chastisement of the child does not exceed the just limit of parental authority, the interference of the mother would be unwarranted, and the father is fully justified in using all reasonable and necessary force to protect himself and restrain and prevent her interference."

The wife is neither the husband's mistress nor slave, nor can she forcibly be compelled by him to submit to inhuman treatment at his hands, and, if the courts should sustain the husband in such conduct, it would be but a mockery of justice. As the case must again be tried, we express no opinion as to the weight or effect of the evidence.

For the reasons indicated, the judgment is reversed for a new trial consistent with the opinion.[1]

1. D slapped his wife who was drunk and insolent. She lost her balance and struck a chair as she fell, receiving fatal injuries. D was convicted of manslaughter and appealed. In affirming the conviction the court held there was no error in the judge's *refusal* to instruct that a husband has a right to administer due and proper chastisement to his wife. Commonwealth v. McAffee, 108 Mass. 458 (1871).

"We may assume that the old doctrine that a husband had a right to whip his wife, provided he used a switch no larger than his thumb, is not law in North Carolina. Indeed, the Courts have advanced from that barbarism until they have reached the position that the husband has no right to chastise his wife under any circumstances.

"But from motives of public policy, and in order to preserve the sanctity of the domestic circle, the Courts will not listen to trivial complaints.

"If no permanent injury has been inflicted, nor malice, cruelty nor dangerous violence shown by the husband, it is better to draw the curtain, shut out the public gaze, and leave the parties to forget and forgive." State v. Oliver, 70 N.C. 60 (1874). In this case, however, the conviction of assault and battery was affirmed.

CLEARY v. BOOTH

Queen's Bench Division, 1893.
[1893] 1 Q.B. 465.

LAWRENCE, J. The question in this case is not an easy one; there is no authority, and it is a case of first impression. The question for us is whether the head master of a board school is justified in inflicting corporal punishment upon one of his scholars for an act done outside the limits of the school, and the appellant's counsel has in his argument relied on what might happen if a boy were not punished by the master for such acts. The facts seem to be that a boy while coming to the appellant's school was assaulted by another boy belonging to the same school; that complaint was made to the appellant, who then and there punished the boy who had committed the assault and also the respondent, who was in his company. The first observation that occurs to one to make is that one of the greatest advantages of any punishment is that it should follow quickly on the offence. The cases cited to us shew that the schoolmaster is in the position of the parent. What is to become of a boy between his school and his home? Is he not under the authority of his parent or of the schoolmaster? It cannot be doubted that he is; and in my opinion among the powers delegated by the parent to the schoolmaster, such a power as was exercised by the appellant in this case would be freely delegated. If we turn to the Code we find that there are several things for which a grant may be given, including discipline and organization, and that the children are to be brought up in habits of good manners and language, and of consideration for others. Can it be reasonably argued that the only right of a schoolmaster to inflict punishment is in respect of acts done in the school, and that it is only while the boys are there that he is to see that they are well-mannered, but that he has exceeded all the authority delegated to him by the parent if he punishes a boy who within a yard of the school is guilty of gross misbehaviour? It is difficult to express in words the extent of the schoolmaster's authority in respect to the punishment of his pupils; but in my opinion his authority extends, not only to acts done in school, but also to cases where a complaint of acts done out of school, at any rate while going to and from school, is made to the schoolmaster. In the present case I think that weight may properly be placed on the fact that the act for which the boy was punished was done to another pupil of the same school. I think, therefore, that the justices were wrong in convicting the appellant as they did, and that the case must be sent back to them to find as a fact whether the punishment was excessive.

COLLINS, J. I am of the same opinion. It is clear law that a father has the right to inflict reasonable personal chastisement on his son. It is equally the law, and it is in accordance with very ancient practice, that he may delegate this right to the schoolmaster. Such a right has always commended itself to the common sense of mankind. It is clear that the relation of master and pupil carries with it the right of reasonable corporal chastisement. As a matter of common sense, how far is this power delegated by the parent to the schoolmaster? Is it limited to the time during which the boy is within the four walls of the school, or does it extend in any sense beyond that limit? In my opinion the purpose with which the parental authority is delegated to the schoolmaster, who is entrusted with the bringing up and discipline of the child, must to some extent include an authority over the child while he is outside the four walls. It may be a question of fact in each case whether the conduct of the master in inflicting corporal punishment is right. Very grave consequences would result if it were held that the parent's authority was exclusive up to the door of the school, and that then, and only then, the master's authority commenced; it would be a most anomalous result to hold that in such a case as the present the boy who had been assaulted had no remedy by complaint to his master, who could punish the assailant by a thrashing, but must go before the magistrate to enforce a remedy between them as citizens. Not only would such a position be unworkable in itself, but the Code, which has the force of an Act of Parliament, clearly contemplates that the duties of the master to his pupils are not limited to teaching. A grant may be made for discipline and organization, and it is clear that he is entrusted with the moral training and conduct of his pupils. It cannot be that such a duty or power ceases the moment that the pupil leaves school for home; there is not much opportunity for a boy to exhibit his moral conduct while in school under the eye of the master: the opportunity is while he is at play or outside the school; and if the schoolmaster has no control over the boys in their relation to each other except when they are within the school walls, this object of the Code would be defeated. In such a case as the present, it is obvious that the desired impression is best brought about by a summary and immediate punishment. In my opinion parents do contemplate such an exercise of authority by the schoolmaster. I should be sorry if I felt myself driven to come to the opposite conclusion, and am glad to be able to say that the principle shews that the authority delegated to the schoolmaster is not limited to the four walls of the school. It is always a question of fact whether the act was done outside the delegated authority; but in the present case I am satisfied, on the facts, that it was obviously within it. The question of excess is one for the magistrates.

STATE v. MIZNER

Supreme Court of Iowa, 1876.
45 Iowa 248.

DAY, J. The prosecuting witness, Ida Brumer, in substance testified that the defendant taught a district school in Rossville, and that she commenced attending his school in the forepart of November, 1874. That, on the 22nd day of December, 1874, whilst she was a pupil in defendant's school, defendant whipped her, in a manner which, from her testimony, appears to be unreasonable and immoderate. She further testified that, at the time she commenced going to school, which was about the 10th day of November, she told the defendant she was twenty years of age, and that, in fact, she was twenty-one years of age on the 25th day of that month.

No testimony was introduced on the part of the State but that of the prosecuting witness. The State having rested, the defendant made the following admissions and offer, to-wit: "It is hereby conceded by the defendant that he whipped Ida Brumer, at the time and place alleged in the information, and that he is guilty of an assault and battery, unless he can show, as he offers to do, that such whipping was reasonable chastisement of said Ida Brumer, in the school, as his pupil, for misconduct in school. Defendant further concedes that said Ida Brumer, at the time of such whipping, had attained her majority." Thereupon the court refused to allow the defendant to prove that the alleged whipping was reasonable chastisement of said Ida Brumer in school, as his pupil, for misconduct in school, holding that, as it was conceded that Ida Brumer had attained her majority at the time of the whipping, the facts which the defendant offered to prove constituted no defense. To this ruling the defendant excepted. No further evidence being introduced, the court instructed the jury as follows: "If you find from the evidence that the defendant committed an assault and battery upon the prosecutrix, and you further find from the evidence that at the time of the assault the prosecutrix had attained the age of twenty-one years, you are instructed that the defendant had not the lawful right to make the assault and battery as a punishment for disobedience of the orders of the teacher or of the rules of the school." The defendant excepted to this instruction.

The court seems to have recognized the general doctrine that a teacher may, for the maintenance of his authority and the enforcement of discipline, legally inflict reasonable chastisement upon a pupil. Whilst the authorities upon the subject are not numerous, there can, it seems to us, be no doubt of the existence of this right. In 3 Greenleaf on Evidence, section 63, it is said the criminality of a charge of assault and battery may be disproved by evidence showing that the act was lawful; as, if a parent in a reasonable manner corrects his child, or a schoolmaster his scholar.

The court denied the right of the defendant in this case to inflict corporal punishment to any extent upon the prosecuting witness, because she was twenty-one years of age. A parent may lawfully correct his child, being under age, in a reasonable manner. 1 Blackstone, 452; 2 Kent's Commentaries, 203. If the court intended to deny the right of the defendant to chastise the prosecuting witness because the same limitation is imposed upon a teacher as upon a parent, the right to inflict corporal punishment should, in this case, have been denied upon reaching the age of eighteen, for then the prosecuting witness attained her majority. Code, 2237. Schools are provided for the instruction of youth between the ages of five and twenty-one years. Code, section 1727. If the right of a teacher to inflict corporal punishment is correlative simply with the right of a parent, it follows that in every school there may be a privileged class of young ladies, between the ages of eighteen and twenty-one years, entitled to all the privileges of the school, but not subject to the same discipline and authority as the other pupils. It is quite apparent that such a condition of things might destroy the authority of the teacher and be utterly subversive of good order. But, as the court fixed the age of twenty-one years, it is probable that he had in view, not any analogy between teacher and parent, but the ages of those who might lawfully attend school. Only youth between the ages of five and twenty-one years are, of right, entitled to attend the public schools.

But, if a child a few months younger than five years should, by misrepresenting his age, or by mere sufferance, be allowed to attend school and enjoy its privileges and advantages, would a teacher be liable to a prosecution for assault and battery, if he should inflict reasonable and moderate chastisement upon such pupil for conduct tending to destroy the order of the school and lessen the means of imparting instruction to others? Manifestly, it seems to us, he would not. And, if a person a few months more than twenty-one years of age should, by the like sufferance or misrepresentation, be allowed to become a pupil in a school, upon what principle could such person claim all the privileges and advantages which belong only to persons under the age of twenty-one years, and at the same time be granted immunity from the reasonable corporal inflictions which may legally be imposed upon a person under twenty-one years of age? A person over twenty-one years of age becomes a pupil only of his own voluntary act. If he does so, and thus of his own will creates the relation of teacher and pupil, and claims privileges and advantages belonging only to those under age, he thereby waives any privilege which his age confers. These views are fully sustained by the case of Stevens v. Fassett, 27 Maine 266. In this case, on page 287, the court say: "But it is insisted that, if such is the authority of the teacher over one who is in legal contemplation a scholar, the same cannot apply to the case of one who has no right to attend the school as a pupil. It is not necessary to settle the question whether one living in the district and not being between the ages of four and twenty-one years can, with propriety, require the instruction of town schools. If such does present himself as a pupil, is received and instructed by the master, he cannot claim the privilege, and receive it, and at the same time be subject to none of the duties incident to a scholar. If disobedient, he is not exempt from the liability to punishment, so long as he is treated as having the character which he assumes. He cannot plead his own voluntary act, and insist that it is illegal, as an excuse for creating disturbances, and escape consequences which would attach to him either as a refractory, incorrigible scholar, or as one who persists in interrupting the ordinary business of the school."

The prosecuting witness in this case, although within fifteen days of being twenty-one years old, told the defendant that she was twenty years of age. This could have been done for no other purpose but that of deceiving the defendant as to her age, and securing privileges and advantages to which the law did not entitle her. She voluntarily assumed the position of pupil, claimed its rights, and took upon herself its duties, and she thereby conferred upon her teacher his correlative rights and duties. The court should have permitted the defendant to prove that the whipping was a reasonable chastisement of the prosecuting witness, as his pupil, for misconduct in school, and should have left it to the jury to determine whether or not the whipping was, under all the circumstances, reasonable.

In rejecting the testimony offered, and in giving the instruction complained of, the court erred.

Reversed.[1]

MODEL PENAL CODE

Section 3.08. Use of Force by Persons with Special Responsibility for Care, Discipline or Safety of Others.

The use of force upon or toward the person of another is justifiable if:

(1) the actor is the parent or guardian or other person similarly responsible for the general care and supervision of a minor or a person acting at the request of such parent, guardian or other responsible person and:

(a) the force is used for the purpose of safeguarding or promoting the welfare of the minor, including the prevention or punishment of his misconduct; and

---

[1]. On retrial Mizner was unable to prove that the whipping was reasonable chastisement and was again convicted of assault and battery. This conviction was affirmed. State v. Mizner, 50 Iowa 145 (1878).

(b) the force used is not designed to cause or known to create a substantial risk of causing death, serious bodily harm, disfigurement, extreme pain or mental distress or gross degradation; or

(2) the actor is a teacher or a person otherwise entrusted with the care or supervision for a special purpose of a minor and:

(a) the actor believes that the force used is necessary to further such special purpose, including the maintenance of reasonable discipline in a school, class or other group, and that the use of such force is consistent with the welfare of the minor; and

(b) the degree of force, if it had been used by the parent or guardian of the minor, would not be unjustifiable under Subsection (1) (b) of this Section; or . . .

[There are also provisions for certain other persons such as guardians, doctors, wardens, and persons responsible for the safety of vessels or aircraft, or authorized to maintain order or decorum in a train or in a place where others are assembled.]

SECTION 3. PREVENTION OF CRIME

Two important privileges overlap. They are the privilege (1) to intervene for the purpose of preventing the perpetration of crime and (2) to defend person or property. To the extent of the overlap both privileges are available to the one thus benefited. "It is not necessary that he should intervene solely for the purpose of protecting the public order or of protecting the private interests imperiled. His act, though a single one, may well be done for both purposes. If so, either privilege is available to him."[1]

Perhaps it should be said that any unoffending person may intervene for the purpose of preventing the commission or consummation of any crime if he does so without resorting to measures which are excessive under all of the facts of the particular case. No such statement has been found because, perhaps, the measures permissible for the prevention of minor misdemeanors are so mild as scarcely to require a privilege for their support.

In the absence of legislative authority, the privilege to intervene for the purpose of preventing the commission or consummation of a crime does not authorize the use of force in case of a misdemeanor which is not an affray or some other equally serious breach of the peace.[2] In considering statutory enlargements of this field it is important to bear in mind that the "privilege to use force to prevent the commission of crime is usually co-extensive with the privilege to make

---

1. Restatement, Second, Torts, Scope Note to c. 5, Topic 2 (1965).
2. Id. at § 140.

an arrest therefor without a warrant." [3] It is not uncommon for modern statutes to authorize either a peace officer [4] or a private person [5] to arrest without a warrant for any public offense committed or attempted in his presence. And such an enactment *may* be held to make a corresponding enlargement in the field of crime prevention.

No legislative authority is needed for the privilege other than that indicated in the preceding paragraph. The common law recognizes the privilege to use force to prevent the commission or consummation, not only of a felony, but also of a misdemeanor amounting to a breach of the peace.[6] As to all such offenses the question is not whether force may be used but only under what circumstances and to what extent.

The use of deadly force for crime prevention is narrowly limited. Restricting attention for the moment to force neither intended nor likely to cause death or serious bodily harm, and to offenses within the general scope of the preventive privilege (whether by common law or by legislative enlargement), the following generalization may be offered: Any amount of such force is privileged to prevent the commission or consummation of such an offense if it is reasonably believed to be necessary for this purpose by him who uses it.[7] The use of force, although not intended or likely to cause death or serious bodily harm, constitutes a battery if it is clearly in excess of that reasonably believed necessary for the prevention.

This takes us to the most difficult part of the field, which is the use of deadly force for crime prevention.[8]

3. Id. at § 140, comment *a*.

4. For example, West's Ann.Cal.Pen. Code, § 836.

5. Id. at § 837.

6. Ward v. De Martini, 108 Cal.App. 745, 292 P. 192 (1930); Spicer v. People, 11 Ill.App. 294 (1882). As so used a "breach of the peace" means a public offense done by violence or one causing or likely to cause an immediate disturbance of public order. Restatement, Second, Torts § 116 and § 140, comment *a* (1965).

7. Restatement Second, Torts §§ 141–143 (1965).

8. Statutes on this point differ widely. For example, compare the following:

West's Ann.Cal.Pen.Code, § 197. "Homicide is also justifiable when committed by any person in either of the following cases:

"1. When resisting any attempt to murder any person or to commit a felony, or to do some great bodily injury upon any person; . . ."

"The broad doctrine intimated by Lord Coke was, that a felon may be killed to prevent the commission of a felony without any inevitable cause, or as a matter of mere choice with the slayer. —3 Inst. 56. If such a rule ever prevailed, it was at a very early day, . . . for Blackstone states the principle to be, that 'where a crime, in itself *capital*, is endeavored to be committed *by force*, it is lawful to *repel that force* by the death of the party attempting.' . . . Both of these views, however, have been repudiated by the later authorities, each being to some extent materially modified. All admit that the killing can not be done from *mere choice*; and it is none the less certain that the felony *need not be a capital one* to come within the scope of the rule. . . . We find it often stated, . . . that one may, as Mr. Bishop expresses it, 'oppose another who is attempting to perpetrate *any felony*, to the extinguishment, if need be, of the felon's

COMMONWEALTH v. EMMONS

Superior Court of Pennsylvania, 1945.
157 Pa.Super. 495, 43 A.2d 568.

Opinion by ARNOLD, J., July 19, 1945:

The defendant, Mildred E. Emmons, on September 21, 1943 shot one Edward Gray with a rifle and seriously injured him. She was indicted in three counts,—assault and battery with intent to murder, aggravated assault and battery and simple assault and battery. The jury found her guilty of aggravated assault and battery. The court overruled defendant's motion for new trial and sentenced, and this appeal followed.

The defendant lived in a second floor apartment of a house in Sacone, Upper Darby, Delaware County, Pa. The apartment house fronted on a forty foot wide improved street known as Broadway Avenue. On the side of the house was an unopened street known as Beechwood Avenue, which was a cul-de-sac ending at the rear of the apartment house premises, and was used by the defendant as a way to a garage on the premises.

The defendant had purchased under a bailment lease a Chevrolet Sedan automobile, and on September 21, 1943 was in default thereunder in the amount of $115.66, being two monthly installments. The bailment lease gave the bailor the right to repossess upon default. The lease had been assigned by the seller-bailor to a finance company, which determined to repossess. Its representative came to defendant's second floor apartment on September 21, 1943 at about 11:00 o'clock A.M., knocked on the door and also rang the door bell. There was no response, the defendant later claiming she was asleep.

Defendant's automobile was at this time parked on the unopened cul-de-sac street called Beechwood Avenue. With the aid of Gray (an employe of a commercial garage) defendant's automobile was pushed backwards onto Broadway Avenue and parked near the curb, and the hood of the automobile was raised in order to check the serial numbers. Two shots were fired and the left femur bone in the leg of Edward Gray was badly shattered.

---

existence.' . . . The safer view is that taken by Mr. Wharton, that the rule *does not authorize the killing of persons attempting secret felonies, not accompanied by force.*" Storey v. State, 71 Ala. 329, 338-9 (1882).

"But the right to kill is based upon the law of necessity or apparent necessity. . . . The doctrine of the right to protect one's habitation gives no moral right to kill another, unless necessity or apparent necessity, for purposes countenanced by law, exists. . . . after the deceased had entered, though burglariously, and after he was in the house, the defendant had no right to kill him for the act of entry already committed. . . . The evidence shows that there was no property in the kitchen worthy of stealing, . . . The right of defendant, in other words, was limited (1) to the protection of himself, (2) to prevent a felony in the bedroom and, probably, (3) to prevent the deceased from entering that room at all." State v. Sorrentino, 31 Wyo. 129, 137-8, 224 P. 420, 422 (1924).

Circumstances led the police officers to interview the defendant who stated that she had fired with a .22 rifle, but did not recall how many shots. She said that she believed the men were stealing her automobile, and that she fired at a point near the intersection of the unopened street and Broadway Avenue, and did not aim at or intend to shoot anyone. There was, however, evidence on the part of the Commonwealth upon which the jury may well have found that the defendant intentionally shot Gray.

The various assignments of error raise but one question, viz.:—

Where in good faith and upon reasonable grounds, one believes her automobile is being stolen from where it was parked in broad daylight on an unopened street (or private way),—may one shoot the person believed to be the thief in order to prevent the supposed larceny? The learned court below answered this question in the negative, and so do we.

While it has been asserted that some rule of law exists which justifies killing in order to prevent the commission of a felony,—we are convinced that no such broadly stated rule exists. There is no right to kill in order to prevent *any* felony. To justify the killing it must be to prevent the commission of a felony which is either an atrocious crime or one attempted to be committed by force (or surprise) such as murder, arson, burglary, rape, kidnapping, sodomy or the like.

While we are unable to discover any Pennsylvania cases on the subject, all writers seem to be in accord, both where the death of the supposed felon results, and where some form of assault and battery is committed.

40 C.J.S., Homicide, Section 101, states the rule: "The taking of human life is justifiable when done for the prevention of any *atrocious* crime attempted to be committed with force. . . . A homicide is justifiable when committed by necessity and in good faith in order to prevent a felony attempted by *force* or surprise, such as murder, robbery, burglary, arson, rape, sodomy and the like. . . Killing to prevent a felony is not justifiable if the felony is a secret one, or *unaccompanied by force*, or if it *does not involve the security of the person or home*. . . . (Emphasis supplied.)

26 Am.Jur., Homicide, Section 172, states the rule: "In general, it may be said that the law countenances the taking of human life in connection with the defense of property *only where an element of danger to the person of the slayer* is present. . . ." (Emphasis supplied.) "The mere fact that such (personal) property is being wrongfully taken . . . does not justify a homicide committed in an attempt to prevent the taking or detention."

1 Bishop Criminal Law, 9th Ed., Section 876, states the rule: "A felonious homicide is committed by one who inflicts death in oppos-

ing an unlawful endeavor to carry away his property. There is here the right to resist, but not to the taking of life."

The rule is the same where the supposed felon does not die and the indictment is for some form of assault and battery: 6 C.J.S., Assault and Battery, Section 94, "It is only in extreme cases that a person is entitled to inflict great bodily harm or endanger human life in protecting (personal) property, although *where the defense of person or of a dwelling, is involved, it would seem that the use of a deadly weapon may sometimes be justified."* (Emphasis supplied.)

Likewise in 4 Am.Jur., Assault and Battery, Section 63: "While a man may use as much force as is necessary in the defense of his property, it is generally held *that in the absence of the use of force on the part of the intruder,* he is not justified in inflicting great bodily harm or endangering life." (Emphasis supplied.) "The preservation of human life and limb from grievous harm is of more importance to society than the protection of property." . . .

In the present case the defendant was not defending her person, or her home or "castle". There was no felony by force or any atrocious crime to be prevented. There was no danger to her or her habitation. There was no force by an intruder for her to repel. There was no justification in law for her infliction of grievous bodily harm.

The assignments of error are overruled, the judgment of the court below is affirmed, and defendant is directed to appear in the court below at such time as she may be there called, and that she be by that court committed until she has complied with her sentence or any part of it that had not been performed at the time the appeal was made a supersedeas.[1]

RHODES, DITHRICH and ROSS, JJ., dissent.

VILIBORGHI v. STATE
Supreme Court of Arizona, 1935.
45 Ariz. 275, 43 P.2d 210.

[Tried for murder, defendant was convicted of manslaughter. He conducted a store in the front of the building in which he lived. The evidence was conflicting but the testimony of defendant indicated

---

[1]. Compare State v. Metcalfe, 206 N.W. 620 (Iowa 1925), superseded by the opinion in State v. Metcalfe, 203 Iowa 155, 212 N.W. 382 (1927).

"The use of force or the imposition of a confinement intended or likely to cause death or serious bodily harm is privileged if the felony for the prevention of which the actor is intervening is of a type threatening death or serious bodily harm or involving the breaking and entry of a dwelling place."

Restatement, Second, Torts § 143(2) (1965).

To be within the privilege the force must be used for the purpose of preventing a felony. One who actually prevented the consummation of a felony by shooting the felon was not protected in a case in which the fact of the intended felony was unknown to the shooter at the time. Regina v. Dadson, 4 Cox C.C. 360 (1850).

the following: The store had been burglarized on several occasions, during one of which a shot had been fired at him. On the night in question he was awakened by noises in the front of the building and went to investigate, taking a revolver with him, thinking that burglars were attempting to break into the building. Seeing a human hand reaching through the front window, and believing that his life and property were in danger, he fired through the window and immediately heard footfalls of persons running away. After the noise ceased he investigated and found the body of deceased lying on the sidewalk and beside it a jar of preserves and a bottle of pickles which had evidently been taken from a shelf adjacent to the broken window through which he saw the hand entering. The defense was based upon a claim of justification, and an appeal was taken on the ground (among several others) that error was committed in the instructions to the jury.]

LOCKWOOD, CHIEF JUSTICE. . . . It was the contention of defendant, sustained by evidence offered in his behalf, that the deceased was, at the time the fatal shot was fired, actually engaged in a first-degree burglary, with the intent to commit petit larceny. Section 4746, R.C.1928. Petit larceny is the stealing of any goods under the value of $50, unless they belong to certain specified classes, regardless of value. Section 4757, R.C.1928. This offense of itself is merely a misdemeanor, and the killing of a thief who is engaged merely in a misdemeanor is not justifiable. It may be urged that, since under our statute the burglary is completed as soon as the felonious entry is made, the actual taking of property as a result of and immediately after the entry is not burglary, but merely petit larceny, and therefore the owner of the premises can only resist such taking in the manner allowed for the prevention of a misdemeanor. We think this is a most unreasonable limitation of the law of justifiable homicide. If this be the law, all a burglar needs to do is to complete his entry, and he may then with impunity continue his burglarious purpose without fear of being shot by the justly incensed home owner, so long as he tells the latter that he has no intention of taking more than $50 worth of property. We cannot conceive such to be the law, and hold that so far as the question of justifiable homicide is concerned, when goods are stolen during the commission of a burglary, the entire act from beginning to end is a felony, and any one who may kill the perpetrator before he has fully completed his purpose is to be tried by the rules applying to homicides committed to prevent felonies, and not those which govern misdemeanors. It therefore follows that the owner of the premises burglarized may, at any stage of a burglary, kill the burglar if it be reasonably necessary to prevent the final completion of his felonious purpose, regardless at what stage of the crime the shooting occurs. He may, even after the burglary has been completed, and the burglar is withdrawing from the scene of his crime, if the latter attempts to resist or flee from arrest, use such force as is reasonably necessary for the apprehension of the offender, even to the taking of life. Section 4590, R.C.1928. And in all of such cases the question of the necessity of the killing depends upon the reasonable apprehension and belief of the defendant, and not whether such apprehension and belief was justified by the facts as they actually existed. With these tests it clearly appears that the instructions complained of were erroneous in several respects.

The first one states positively that, regardless of what the circumstances would lead the defendant, as a reasonable man, to believe, if as a matter of fact the deceased was not actually engaged in an attempt to burglarize the defendant's store, the latter would be guilty of either murder or manslaughter in killing him. It omits entirely the test of reasonable grounds for belief, and directs the jury to return their verdict on the facts as they actually existed, and not as they appeared to the reasonable apprehension of the defendant.

The second instruction is correct, for under no circumstance may one person shoot another as a punishment for a crime which has been committed.

The third instruction is somewhat ambiguous in that it might be construed to mean that, after the entry had been completed, even though the burglary is still in progress, the owner of the premises may not kill to prevent the completion of the attempted crime. This, as we have said, is not the law. This instruction alone, however, in view of the general instructions, would probably not be reversible error, for the ambiguity is hardly of such a serious nature that, taking the instructions as a whole, it would mislead the jury.

The fourth instruction, however, is fatally erroneous. It states flatly that if the defendant killed the deceased to prevent the loss of the canned goods which are referred to in the evidence, even though the deceased was in the act of stealing them, he would be guilty of manslaughter. As we have stated, had the stealing been a simple misdemeanor, the instruction would have been correct, but the whole evidence shows beyond doubt that if the deceased did steal the canned goods referred to, it must have been done in the perpetration of a burglary, and the stealing was therefore part of a felony and the defendant was justified in killing the deceased if it was reasonably necessary to prevent its completion. In no possible way can this instruction be reconciled with the law, and it is obvious that it, considered with the evidence which appears in the record, was in the highest degree prejudicial, and could not be cured by a reference to the general instructions.

Because of the various errors which we have discussed, we are of the opinion that the defendant did not have that fair and impartial trial guaranteed him by the law, and the judgment of the superior court is therefore reversed, and the case remanded for a new trial.[1]

McAlister and Ross, JJ., concur.

MODEL PENAL CODE

Section 3.07. . . .

(5) Use of Force to Prevent Suicide or the Commission of a Crime.

(a) The use of force upon or toward the person of another is justifiable when the actor believes that such force is immediately necessary to prevent such other person from committing suicide, inflicting serious bodily harm upon himself, committing or consummating the commission of a crime involving or threatening bodily harm, damage to or loss of property or a breach of the peace, except that:

(i) any limitations imposed by the other provisions of this Article on the justifiable use of force in self-protection, for the protection of others, the protection of property, the effectuation of an arrest or the prevention of an escape from custody shall apply notwithstanding the criminality of the conduct against which such force is used; and

---

1. In affirming a conviction of murder the court said: "Concede the common law doctrine, that homicide is justifiable for the prevention of any forcible and atrocious crime, must there not be an apparent necessity, on the part of the slayer—yea, an absolute necessity for the act—to make the killing justifiable?" Mitchell v. State, 22 Ga. 211, 234 (1857). Compare State v. Beal, 55 N.M. 382, 234 P.2d 331 (1951).

It is reversible error to instruct that in order to establish a defense the defendant's act must have been to prevent a felony and the force used by him no more than necessary to prevent the felony. He might have been mistaken as to a felony actually impending, or as to the force needed to repel it. Spicer v. People, 11 Ill.App. 294 (1882).

X proposed sexual intercourse to Mrs. D which she refused. X said he would be back next morning to compel her. She told D. D pretended to leave for work next morning but returned and concealed himself near the bedroom. X came, found Mrs. D in the kitchen, led her to the bedroom; whereupon D stabbed X to death. D was indicted for murder and convicted of manslaughter. The conviction was affirmed because a killing to prevent a felony cannot be justified unless there was reason to believe it was necessary for that purpose. Luttrell v. State, 178 Miss. 877, 174 So. 53 (1937).

Mrs. Moore found deceased with his arm around her daughter and his other hand under her clothes. She shot and killed him. The daughter was under the age of consent and Mrs. Moore's defense was that she shot to prevent the crime of rape. A conviction of murder was reversed because the judge failed to instruct the jury that defendant was privileged to kill if necessary to prevent statutory rape. Moore v. State, 91 Tex.Cr.R. 118, 237 S.W. 931 (1922).

It was error to instruct that under no circumstances of aggravation would a man be justified in taking the life of another who attempts seduction of the slayer's wife. Biggs v. State, 29 Ga. 723 (1860).

A woman is not privileged to kill a man who is attempting to rape her if she is obviously and safely able to prevent the rape without the use of deadly force. Tolbert v. State, 31 Ala.App. 301, 15 So.2d 745 (1943).

(ii) the use of deadly force is not in any event justifiable under this Subsection unless:

(1) the actor believes that there is a substantial risk that the person whom he seeks to prevent from committing a crime will cause death or serious bodily harm to another unless the commission or the consummation of the crime is prevented and that the use of such force presents no substantial risk of injury to innocent persons; or

(2) the actor believes that the use of such force is necessary to suppress a riot or mutiny after the rioters or mutineers have been ordered to disperse and warned, in any particular manner that the law may require, that such force will be used if they do not obey.

(b) The justification afforded by this Subsection extends to the use of confinement as preventive force only if the actor takes all reasonable measures to terminate the confinement as soon as he knows that he safely can, unless the person confined has been arrested on a charge of crime.

Section 3.06. Use of Force for the Protection of Property. . . .

(3) Limitations on Justifiable Use of Force. . . .

(d) Use of Deadly Force. The use of deadly force is not justifiable under this Section unless the actor believes that: . . .

(ii) the person against whom the force is used is attempting to commit or consummate arson, burglary, robbery or other felonious theft or property destruction and either:

(1) has employed or threatened deadly force against or in the presence of the actor; or

(2) the use of force other than deadly force to prevent the commission or the consummation of the crime would expose the actor or another in his presence to substantial danger of serious bodily harm.

SECTION 4. SELF-DEFENSE

It is convenient to discuss problems of self-defense in terms of deadly force (force either intended or likely to cause death or great bodily injury) and nondeadly force (force neither intended nor likely to cause death or great bodily injury). It is important also to distinguish between reasonable force and unreasonable force, these being complex concepts dependent upon the nature of the force itself and the circumstances under which it is employed. It is misleading to speak of a division of the field into (1) deadly force and (2) reasonable force because these terms are neither mutually exclusive nor collectively exhaustive. Either deadly force or nondeadly force may

Sec. 4 **SELF-DEFENSE** 599

be either reasonable or unreasonable, depending upon the circumstances of its use. Deadly force is unreasonable if nondeadly force is obviously sufficient to prevent the threatened harm.[1] And nondeadly force is unreasonable if it is obviously and substantially in excess of what is needed for the particular defense.[2]

There are some indications of an original requirement of actual necessity [3] but they do not represent the modern common law of self-defense. The privilege to use force in the effort to avert harm threatened (actually or apparently) by the wrongful act of another is based upon the reasonable belief of the defender under the circumstances as they appear at the moment.[4] He is neither limited by, nor entitled to the benefit of, secret intentions or other unknown factors. One who has knocked down another, in the reasonable belief that this was necessary to prevent being stabbed, is not guilty of battery because it is learned later that the other intended no harm but was merely playing too realistic a joke with a rubber dagger.[5] On the other hand, proof that a fatal shot actually saved the life of the slayer is no defense if he fired in cold blood while utterly unaware of the impending danger.[6] One caution should be added. A bona-fide belief which is correct will not be held to be unreasonable merely because the defender is unable to paint a word-picture explaining exactly how he knew what the real facts were.[7]

One who is himself free from fault is privileged to use whatever nondeadly force reasonably seems to him to be necessary to prevent being harmed by the wrongful act of another.[8] This is true whether

---

1. Etter v. State, 185 Tenn. 218, 205 S.W.2d 1 (1947).

2. People v. Moody, 62 Cal.App.2d 18, 143 P.2d 978 (1943); Restatement, Second, Torts § 70 (1965). A kick is not a justifiable method of turning a trespasser out of the house. Wild's Case, 2 Lewin C.C. 214, 168 Eng.Rep. 1132 (1837).

3. Scott v. State, 203 Miss. 349, 34 So. 2d 718 (1948); Regina v. Smith, 8 Car. and P. 160, 173 Eng.Rep.. 441 (1837); Regina v. Bull, 9 Car. and P. 22, 173 Eng.Rep. 723 (1939).

4. People v. Anderson, 44 Cal. 65 (1872); People v. Toledo, 85 Cal.App.2d 570, 577, 193 P.2d 953 (1948); Territory v. Yadao, 35 Hawaii 198 (1939); Weston v. State, 167 Ind. 324, 78 N.E. 1014 (1906); State v. Anderson, 230 N.C. 54, 51 S.E.2d 895 (1949); United States v. Ah Chong, 15 Philippine, 448 (1910). One whose life has been threatened by another, and who sees that other apparently reaching for a weapon, may shoot in self-defense although the other does not have a weapon in hand or in sight at the moment. Lomax v. State, 205 Miss. 635, 39 So.2d 267 (1949). As to the rule under the Texas statute see Brown v. State, 152 Tex.Cr. R. 440, 214 S.W.2d 792 (1948).

5. Restatement, Second, Torts § 63, Illustrations 5, 9 (1965).

6. Trogden v. State, 133 Ind. 1, 32 N.E. 725 (1892); Josey v. United States, 77 U.S.App.D.C. 321, 135 F.2d 809 (1943); Restatement, Second, Torts § 63, Comment f (1965).

7. The American Law Institute has stated this result in other words: ". . . correctly or reasonably believes . . ." Restatement, Second, Torts §§ 63(2), 70 (1) (1965).

8. State v. Gough, 187 Iowa 363, 174 N.W. 279 (1919); State v. Evenson, 122 Iowa 88, 97 N.W. 979 (1904); People v. Katz, 263 App.Div. 883, 32 N.Y.

the threatened harm is deadly or nondeadly. And he may use this force without yielding ground unless the endangering conduct of the other is negligent rather than intentional.[9] Deadly force is not privileged in defense against nondeadly force.[10] One, for example, must submit to a box on the ear and seek redress in the courts if he is unable to prevent it by means other than resort to deadly force.[11] One who is at fault in bringing on the encounter, or in engaging in it, is not privileged to use any force to defend himself against nondeadly force.

There is a sharp split with reference to the privilege of using deadly force in self-defense. Some states follow the "retreat rule" and others the "no retreat rule." These labels are not precise because no jurisdiction either requires retreat, or permits a standing of ground, under all circumstances. To understand the difference between the two rules it is necessary to think in terms of three situations. (1) One, entirely free from fault, is the victim of an assault which was murderous from the beginning. (2) One who was the aggressor in an ordinary fist fight, or other nondeadly encounter, or who willingly engaged therein, finds that his adversary has suddenly and unexpectedly changed the nature of the contest and is resorting to deadly force. (3) One who started an encounter with a murderous assault upon another, or who willingly engaged in mutual combat of a deadly nature, changes his mind in the midst of the fight and would like to stop. According to Sir Michael Foster the common law made a different provision for each of the three.[12] Under his analysis the person identified above as "one" is in situation—(1) entitled to stand his ground and defend himself with deadly force if this reasonably seems necessary for his protection there; (2) required to retreat rather than to use deadly force in his defense if a reasonably safe retreat is available, unless in his "castle" at the time; (3) required to "withdraw" before resorting to deadly force. As to (3) there seems to be little disagreement. The murderous assailant has not lost his privilege of self-defense forever,[13] but he has forfeited it for the moment. He cannot reacquire it by "retreat to the wall." He must bring

---

S.2d 157 (1942); State v. Sherman, 16 R.I. 631, 18 A. 1040 (1889).

9. Restatement, Second, Torts § 64 (1965).

10. State v. Doherty, 52 Or. 591, 98 P. 152 (1908). Compare State v. Bartlett, 170 Mo. 658, 71 S.W. 148 (1902). As to the rule under a particular statute see Witty v. State, 150 Tex.Cr.R. 555, 203 S.W.2d 212 (1947).

11. Restatement, Second, Torts § 65, Illustration 1 (1965).

12. Foster, Crown Law 273–277 (1762).

13. State v. Goode, 271 Mo. 43, 195 S.W. 1006 (1917).

A murderous assailant who had abandoned his purpose, withdrawn from the conflict, and fled into his house had regained the privilege of self-defense and could use deadly force when the other broke into the house to kill him. Stoffer v. State, 15 Ohio St. 47 (1864). It is an assault for the victim of an attack to hunt up his assailant and strike him after he has withdrawn completely. Wendler v. State, 128 Fla. 618, 175 So. 255 (1937).

his attack to an end.[14]   And if he is unable to get entirely away from his adversary, he must in some manner convey to him the information that the fight is over.[15] If circumstances do not permit him to do so this is his own misfortune for bringing such a predicament upon himself.[16]

The chief controversy has been in regard to situation (1). Professor Joseph H. Beale took the position that the innocent victim of a murderous assault is always required to take advantage of an obviously safe retreat, rather than to resort to deadly force unless he is (a) the victim of attempted robbery, (b) attacked by a person he is lawfully attempting to arrest, or (c) in his "castle" at the time.[17]

The so-called "no retreat rule" jurisdictions tend to follow the analysis of Foster. The "retreat rule" jurisdictions tend to accept Beale's position with reference to situation (1). This has tended to cause confusion in regard to situation (2). Foster thought of one in this situation as having an "imperfect" right of self-defense because required to retreat rather than use deadly force if a safe retreat was available. Some courts have interpreted this "imperfect" right of self-defense to mean that it is only partly exculpatory. One killing under an "imperfect" right of self-defense is not guilty of murder, but is guilty of manslaughter, under this analysis.[18]

The phrase "retreat to the wall," although derived from the facts of an ancient case,[19] is used strictly as a metaphor. One who is subject to this requirement is bound to elect an obviously safe retreat in preference to the use of deadly force, if such an avenue of escape is available. Whenever the circumstances are such that no obviously safe retreat is available the person is "at the wall" and no retreat (or further retreat) is required.

PEOPLE v. LA VOIE

Supreme Court of Colorado, 1964.
— Colo. —, 395 P.2d 1001.

MOORE, JUSTICE. The defendant in error, to whom we will refer as defendant, was accused of the crime of murder in an information filed in the district court of Jefferson county. He entered a plea of not guilty and a jury was selected to try the case. At the conclusion of the evidence, the trial court, on motion of counsel for defendant,

---

14. People v. Button, 106 Cal. 628, 39 P. 1073 (1895). For the distinction between "retreat" and "withdrawal" see State v. Mayberry, 360 Mo. 35, 226 S.W.2d 725 (1950).

15. State v. Smith, 10 Nev. 106 (1875).

16. People v. Button, 106 Cal. 628, 39 P. 1073 (1895).

17. Beale, Retreat from a Murderous Assault, 16 Harv.L.Rev. 567 (1903).

18. State v. Partlow, 90 Mo. 608, 4 S.W. 14 (1887); People v. Filippelli, 173 N.Y. 509, 66 N.E. 402 (1903).

19. Anonymous, Fitzh.Abr.Corone, pl. 284 (1328).

602 SPECIAL DEFENSES Ch. 10

directed the jury to return a verdict of not guilty. It was the opinion of the trial court that the evidence was insufficient to warrant submission of any issue to the jury in that the sum total thereof established a clear case of justifiable homicide. The district attorney objected, and the case is here on writ of error requesting this court to render an opinion expressing its disapproval of the action of the trial court in directing the verdict of not guilty.

Eighteen witnesses testified during the trial; thirteen were called as witnesses for the prosecution and five for the defense, including the defendant himself. We have read the record and have found nothing therein which would warrant the submission of any issue to the jury for determination.

For purposes of focus and clarity we will summarize the pertinent facts leading up to the homicide. The defendant was employed as a pharmacist at the Kincaid Pharmacy, 7024 West Colfax Avenue, Lakewood, Colorado. His day's work ended at about 12:30 A.M. After leaving his place of employment, he obtained something to eat at a nearby restaurant and started on his way home. He was driving east on West Colfax Avenue, toward the city of Denver, at about 1:30 A.M. An automobile approached his car from the rear. The driver of this auto made contact with the rear bumper of defendant's car and thereupon forcibly, unlawfully, and deliberately accelerated his motor, precipitating the defendant forward for a substantial distance and through a red traffic light. There were four men in the automobile who were under the influence of intoxicating liquor in varying degrees. Prior to ramming the car of the defendant they had agreed to shove him along just for "kicks." The defendant applied his brakes to the full; but the continuing force from behind precipitated him forward, causing all four wheels to leave a trail of skid marks. When defendant's car ultimately came to a stop the auto containing the four men backed away a few feet. The defendant got out of his car and as he did so he placed a revolver beneath his belt. He had a permit to carry the gun. The four men got out of their auto and advanced toward the defendant threatening to "make you eat that damn gun," to "mop up the street with you," and also directed vile, profane and obscene language at him. The man who was in advance of his three companions kept moving toward defendant in a menacing manner. At this point the defendant shot him. As a result, he died at the scene of the affray.

In upholding the action of the trial court we think it sufficient to direct attention to the opinion of this court in People v. Urso, 129 Colo. 292, 269 P.2d 709, where we find, inter alia, the following pertinent language:

". . . It is our opinion, and we so state, that if it is within the power of a trial court to set aside a verdict, not supported by competent legal evidence, then it is equally within the province and power of the court to prevent such a verdict ever coming into existence. In either position, before or after the verdict, the trial court is compelled to survey and analyze the evidence, and from the same evidence, his analysis would undoubtedly be the same before or after a verdict. If it is to the end that the evidence is insufficient or incompetent, and no part of it is convincing beyond a reasonable doubt, then he should be courageous enough to prevent a miscarriage of justice by a jury. . . ."

The law of justifiable homicide is well set forth by this court in the case of Young v. People, 47 Colo. 352, 107 P. 274:

". . . When a person has reasonable grounds for believing, and does in fact actually believe, that danger of his being killed, or of receiving great bodily harm, is imminent, he may act on such appearances and defend himself, even to the extent of taking human life when necessary, although it may turn out that the appearances were false, or although he may have been mistaken as to the extent of the real or actual danger. . . .."

The defendant was a stranger to all four occupants of the auto. He was peaceably on his way home from work, which terminated after midnight. Under the law and the circumstances disclosed by the record, defendant had the right to defend himself against the threatened assault of those whose lawlessness and utter disregard of his rights resulted in the justifiable killing of one of their number.

The judgment is affirmed.

SUTTON and HALL, JJ., concur.

BROWN v. UNITED STATES

Supreme Court of the United States, 1921.
256 U.S. 335, 65 L.Ed. 961, 41 S.Ct. 501.

MR. JUSTICE HOLMES delivered the opinion of the court.

The petitioner was convicted of murder in the second degree committed upon one Hermes at a place in Texas within the exclusive jurisdiction of the United States, and the judgment was affirmed by the Circuit Court of Appeals. 257 F.R. 46. A writ of certiorari was granted by this Court. 250 U.S. 637, 39 S.Ct. 494, 63 L.Ed. 1183. . . .

The other question concerns the instructions at the trial. There had been trouble between Hermes and the defendant for a long time. There was evidence that Hermes had twice assaulted the defendant with a knife and had made threats communicated to the defendant that the next time one of them would go off in a black box. On the day in question the defendant was at the place above mentioned superintending excavation work for a postoffice. In view of Hermes's threats he had taken a pistol with him and had laid it in his coat upon a dump. Hermes was driven up by a witness, in a cart to be loaded, and the defendant said that certain earth was not to be removed, whereupon Hermes came toward him, the defendant says, with a knife. The defendant retreated some twenty or twenty-five feet to where his coat was and got his pistol. Hermes was striking at him and the defendant fired four shots and killed him. The judge instructed the jury among other things that "it is necessary to remember, in considering the question of self-defense, that the party assaulted is always under the obligation to retreat, so long as retreat is open to him, provided he can do so without subjecting himself to the danger of death or great bodily harm." The instruction was reinforced by the further intimation that unless "retreat would have appeared to a man of reasonable prudence, in the position of the defendant, as involving danger of death or serious bodily harm" the defendant was not entitled to stand his ground. An instruction to the effect that if the defendant had reasonable grounds of apprehension that he was in danger of losing his life or of suffering serious bodily harm from Hermes he was not bound to retreat was refused. So the question is brought out with sufficient clearness whether the formula laid down by the Court and often repeated by the ancient law is adequate to the protection of the defendant's rights.

It is useless to go into the developments of the law from the time when a man who had killed another no matter how innocently had to get his pardon, whether of grace or of course. Concrete cases or illustrations stated in the early law in conditions very different from the present, like the reference to retreat in Coke, Third Inst. 55, and elsewhere, have had a tendency to ossify into specific rules without much regard for reason. Other examples may be found in the law as to trespass *ab initio*. Rationally the failure to retreat is a circumstance to be considered with all the others in order to determine whether the defendant went farther than he was justified in doing; not a categorical proof of guilt. The law has grown, and even if historical mistakes have contributed to its growth it has tended in the direction of rules consistent with human nature. Many respectable writers agree that if a man reasonably believes that he is in immediate danger of death or grievous bodily harm from his assailant he may stand his ground and that if he kills him he has not exceeded the bounds of lawful self-defense. That has been the decision of this Court. Beard v. United States, 158 U.S. 550, 559, 15 S.Ct. 962, 39 L.Ed. 1086. Detached reflection cannot be demanded in the presence of an uplifted knife. Therefore in this Court, at least, it is not a condition of immunity that one in that situation should pause to consider whether a reasonable man might not think it possible to fly with safety or to disable his assailant rather than to kill him. Rowe v. United States, 164 U.S. 546, 558, 17 S.Ct. 172, 41 L.Ed. 547. The law of Texas very strongly adopts these views as is shown by many cases, of which it is enough to cite two. Cooper v. State, 49 Tex.Crim.Rep. 28, 38, 89 S.W. 1068. Baltrip v. State, 30 Tex.Ct.App. 545, 549, 17 S.W. 1106.

Sec. 4   *SELF-DEFENSE*   605

It is true that in the case of Beard he was upon his own land (not in his house), and in that of Rowe he was in the room of a hotel, but those facts, although mentioned by the Court, would not have bettered the defence by the old common law and were not appreciably more favorable than that the defendant here was at a place where he was called to be, in the discharge of his duty. There was evidence that the last shot was fired after Hermes was down. The jury might not believe the defendant's testimony that it was an accidental discharge, but the suggestion of the Government that this Court may disregard the considerable body of evidence that the shooting was in self-defence is based upon a misunderstanding of what was meant by some language in Battle v. United States, 209 U.S. 36, 38, 28 S.Ct. 422, 52 L. Ed. 670. Moreover if the last shot was intentional and may seem to have been unnecessary when considered in cold blood, the defendant would not necessarily lose his immunity if it followed close upon the others while the heat of the conflict was on, and if the defendant believed that he was fighting for his life.

The Government presents a different case. It denies that Hermes had a knife and even that Brown was acting in self-defence. Notwithstanding the repeated threats of Hermes and intimations that one of the two would die at the next encounter, which seem hardly to be denied, of course it was possible for the jury to find that Brown had not sufficient reason to think that his life was in danger at that time, that he exceeded the limits of reasonable self-defence or even that he was the attacking party. But upon the hypothesis to which the evidence gave much color, that Hermes began the attack, the instruction that we have stated was wrong.

Judgment reversed.[1]

MR. JUSTICE PITNEY and MR. JUSTICE CLARKE dissent.

[1] "The doctrine of 'retreat to the wall' had its origin before the general introduction of guns. Justice demands that its application have due regard to the present general use and to the type of firearms. It would be good sense for the law to require, in many cases, an attempt to escape from a hand to hand encounter with fists, clubs, and even knives, as a condition of justification for killing in self-defense; while it would be rank folly to so require when experienced men, armed with repeating rifles, face each other in an open space, removed from shelter, with intent to kill or to do great bodily harm. What might be a reasonable chance for escape in the one situation might in the other be certain death. Self-defense has not, by statute nor by judicial opinion, been distorted by an unreasonable requirement of the duty to retreat, into self-destruction." State v. Gardner, 96 Minn. 318, 104 N.W. 971 (1905).

One who finds trouble by going out of his way to look for it does not have the privilege of self-defense. Valentine v. State, 108 Ark. 594, 159 S.W. 26 (1913). But the mere fact that a man has been threatened and has reason to expect an assault does not deprive him of the right to go about his business as usual, even if this will take him where he has reason to expect the other. People v. Gonzales, 71 Cal. 569, 12 P. 783 (1887). And if he does meet the other, and is attacked by him, he has the privilege of self-defense, in spite of the fact that he took the precaution of arming himself to be prepared for such an emergency. State v. Evans, 124 Mo. 397, 28 S.W. 8 (1894). A man cannot be said to be seeking a difficulty, in the sense of being deprived of the privi-

PEOPLE v. LIGOURI

Court of Appeals of New York, 1940.
284 N.Y. 309, 31 N.E.2d 37.

SEARS, J. The defendants, Giro Ligouri and William Panaro, were indicted together for the crime of murder in the first degree. They have been found guilty by the verdict of a jury of the crime of murder in the second degree. Their convictions have been unanimously affirmed by the Appellate Division in the second department, and are brought before this court by an order granted by one of the judges of this court.

It is not disputed by either appellant that Ligouri, on October 24, 1938, shot and killed Nicholas Cosaluzzo. In fact, Ligouri, himself, sworn in his own behalf, testified to the shooting. The affair occurred about three o'clock in the afternoon in a public street in the borough of Brooklyn, New York City, at or near the corner of McDonald avenue and Avenue X. . . .

The defendant Ligouri urges that the trial court in its charge in respect to justification committed error. The court was requested on behalf of Ligouri to charge in this language: "If the defendant Ligouri was attacked feloniously by the deceased, Cosaluzzo, the defendant Ligouri had a right to shoot Cosaluzzo." The court declined to charge as requested, stating that it had already been covered. Defendant continued, "I ask Your Honor to charge the jury that a person who is feloniously attacked is under no obligation to retreat but may stand his ground, and if necessary, kill his opponent." This the court declined, saying, "If a person kills another whom he claims assaults him, he is under an obligation to retreat as far as possible, unless the circumstances are such that unless he acted as he did he would be the recipient of irreparable and grievous bodily harm." Exceptions were taken to the court's declining to charge as requested and to the charge. In the main charge the court had said on the subject of self-defense: "The defendant Ligouri claims that while he discharged these revolvers, what he did was done in self-defense. As I have already said, the law is that an act otherwise criminal is justified when done to protect the person committing it, or another whom he is bound to protect from inevitable and irreparable personal injury, and the injury could only have been prevented by the act, nothing

---

lege of self-defense, merely because he is attempting to restrain a trespasser from unwarranted control over his property. And this is true even if he armed himself with a weapon to be prepared to defend himself if necessary. Ayers v. State, 60 Miss. 709 (1883). The fact that one is carrying a weapon unlawfully does not deprive him of the privilege of using it if necessary to defend himself from death or great bodily injury. State v. Doris, 51 Or. 136, 94 P. 44 (1908). The fact that a difficulty arose out of an unlawful gambling game does not deprive the innocent victim of a muderous assault of the privilege of self-defense. State v. Leaks, 114 S.C. 257, 103 S.E. 549 (1919). Compare Shack v. State, 236 Ala. 667, 184 So. 688 (1938).

more being done than is necessary to prevent the injury. A person who is attacked before he can resort to acts which result in death, is bound to retreat and to avoid the attack, unless the circumstances be such that he believes that he is in such imminent danger of irreparable injury, and the only thing he could do to protect himself and prevent that injury being inflicted upon him, would be to act as he did, and to do no more to prevent it than was necessary. If the circumstances justified the belief on his part that he is in danger of inevitable and irreparable injury, although it should turn out he was mistaken, an ordinarily prudent man under the same circumstances would be justified in doing what he did, if he thinks he is in danger of death. If you believe that Nick unexpectedly pulled this gun and snapped it on him, and under those circumstances he felt the only thing for him to do was to do what he did, discharge and empty both of his guns into him, even though death resulted, that would be justifiable under the law, but he could not do more than necessary, more than what an ordinarily prudent man under the same circumstances would be justified in doing. He does not have to satisfy you that the situation existed, but if, upon considering all the evidence in the case, there is a reasonable doubt, he must have the benefit of it, and your verdict will be not guilty, because the People must establish to your satisfaction beyond a reasonable doubt that this was a wilful, wanton killing, and was not excusable and not justifiable. That is their burden."

The applicable statute, Penal Law, section 1055, contains the following language:

"Homicide is also justifiable when committed:

"1. In the lawful defense of the slayer, or of his or her husband, wife, parent, child, brother, sister, master or servant, or of any other person in his presence or company, when there is reasonable ground to apprehend a design on the part of the person slain to commit a felony, or to do some great personal injury to the slayer, or to any such person, and there is imminent danger of such design being accomplished; or,

"2. In the actual resistance of an attempt to commit a felony upon the slayer, in his presence, or upon or in a dwelling or other place of abode in which he is."

The language employed by the court in the main charge is that applicable in the usual case of self-defense and falls within the first subdivision as above cited. This is not, however, the ordinary case. Here, on the assumption in the request, a felony was in process of being committed. So in substance the court charged. To avoid the felonious aggression against his person, if it occurred, Ligouri was justified under the second division of the section in standing his ground and, if necessary, destroying the person making the felonious attack. . . .

We reach the conclusion that error occurred in the refusal of the trial court to charge as requested. It may be argued that the charge amounted to granting the request as no one could consider escape as reasonably possible from a pistol purposefully and directly aimed at the assailed. The charge, however, left this matter to deduction. The defendants were on trial for crimes punishable by death. They were entitled to have the judge charge the jury definitely and directly that if they found that the felonious assault, assumed in the request, was occurring, the defendant against whom it was being perpetrated was justified in killing the felonious aggressor if such were necessary in resisting the assault. This error goes to the very foundation of the defense, and necessitates a reversal of the conviction of Ligouri. . . .

For these reasons the judgments should be reversed and a new trial ordered as to both defendants. . . .

LEHMAN, CH. J., LOUGHRAN and RIPPEY, JJ., concur with SEARS, J.; LEWIS, J., dissents in opinion in which FINCH, J., concurs as to Ligouri but concurs in the grant of a new trial to Panaro; CONWAY, J., concurs in the opinion of LEWIS, J., as to Ligouri but votes to affirm as to both defendants.

Judgments reversed, etc.

STATE v. DAVIS

Supreme Court of South Carolina, 1948.
214 S.C. 34, 51 S.E.2d 86.

OXNER, JUSTICE. Appellant, Mack Davis, was indicted and tried for the murder of Norman Gordon, Jr. He sought to excuse the homicide on the ground of self-defense. The trial resulted in a verdict of guilty with recommendation to the mercy of the Court and he was sentenced to imprisonment for life. The only question to be determined on this appeal is whether in establishing his plea of self-defense, appellant had the right to claim immunity from the law of retreat.

About 11 o'clock on Saturday night, August 2, 1947, appellant shot the deceased in a cornfield near a filling station and store operated by W. H. Hinds in a rural section of Florence County. Some time late that afternoon these two Negroes had an argument at a tobacco barn where the deceased was working, as a result of which the deceased, apparently without much, if any, provocation, slapped or struck appellant and knocked him down. Appellant immediately left the scene. That night about 9 o'clock he came to the store of Mr. Hinds. About an hour and a half later the deceased arrived and asked Hinds to lend him a gun, stating, according to Hinds, "I believe Mack (appellant) is going to shoot me." Hinds refused to do so and told the deceased that he didn't "want any shooting around here." The deceased replied that he had a gun at the tobacco barn which he could get and then left. About the same time or shortly thereafter, appellant went across the road in the direction of his home. Approximately a half hour later Hinds and several of those in the store heard the sound of a shotgun. They made an investigation and found the deceased lying fatally wounded in the cornfield at a point about 25 or 30 yards from the store and about 15 feet from the road, with a rifle near his body. He died shortly thereafter while being carried to the office of a physician.

Appellant testified that after hearing the conversation between the deceased and Hinds, he became alarmed and went home for the purpose of securing his shotgun, intending to return to the store where he had several matters to attend to. He said that he planned to approach the store from the rear through the cornfield because the deceased might see him first if he entered through the front. According to his testimony, while in the cornfield he saw the deceased approaching and squatted to escape observation but that the deceased when within close range recognized him and raised his rifle, whereupon he (appellant) shot in defense of his life. The theory of the State was that appellant concealed himself in the cornfield for the purpose of shooting the deceased as the latter returned to the store.

Appellant lived at the home of his sister and brother-in-law, a distance of about four-tenths of a mile from the scene of the homicide. The field in question was owned by Hinds and cultivated by appellant's brother-in-law as a sharecropper. Appellant worked for him and had assisted in cultivating this corn, which had been laid by at the time of the homicide, but the record does not disclose whether his compensation was in the form of wages or a share in the crop. The deceased also worked on some farm in the same community.

Counsel for appellant requested the Court "to charge the jury that the defendant was on the premises on which he was working and the law of retreat would not apply to him." The request was refused and the jury was instructed that it was incumbent upon appellant to establish all of the elements of self-defense, including that of retreating, which the Court then qualified as follows: "I charge you as a matter of law that if a person is threatened with a gun, any kind of firearms, within shooting range, why, obviously there is no duty to retreat; and it is only in cases where a person can with safety avoid a difficulty that he is required to retreat under the law to avoid committing murder." . . .

It is now well established in this State that if a person is assaulted while on his own premises and is without fault in bringing on the difficulty, he is not bound to retreat in order to invoke the benefit of the doctrine of self-defense, but may stand his ground and repel the attack with as much force as is reasonably necessary. . . . This is true whether the attack occurs in defendant's home, place of business, or elsewhere on property owned or lawfully occupied by him. It was also held in State v. Marlowe, 120 S.C. 205, 112 S.E. 921, 922, that a member of a club, wrongfully attacked by another in the club rooms, was under no duty to retreat, the Court observing: "A man is no more bound to allow himself to be run out of his rest room than his workshop." In some jurisdictions the rule has been extended so as to relieve the defendant from the necessity of retreating if attacked in any place where he has a right to be, as when he is lawfully on a public street or highway. We have not gone that far. In State v. McGee, 185 S.C. 184, 193 S.E. 303, 306, the Court stated that "The fact that the defendant was on a public highway, where all men have equal rights, and in his automobile, did not constitute any one of those special privileges obviating the necessity of retreating before killing." It was held in State v. Gordon, supra [128 S.C. 422, 122 S.E. 503], that where a foreman on a farm was assaulted by one of the employees under him at the place where they were working, he was not required to retreat. The Court concluded that the place of work "was the defendant's place of business within the meaning of that term as employed in the law of retreat."

In the case at bar, we do not think under the circumstances that appellant is entitled to claim immunity from the law of retreat. The homicide did not occur at or within the curtilage of the home in which he resided. This house was located across the public road and at some distance from the scene of the shooting. Nor was appellant attacked while working at his "place of business". It is true that he had assisted during the year in cultivating the corn in this field but his presence there on the night in question was wholly unrelated to his employment. There is no showing that he even had any interest in the corn crop. Whether his brother-in-law, the sharecropper, would have been required to retreat if attacked in this cornfield under similar circumstances is a question that is not before us.

All exceptions are overruled and judgment affirmed.[1]

BAKER, C. J., and FISHBURNE, STUKES and TAYLOR, JJ., concur.

---

[1]. A garage owner, attacked in the private driveway to his garage, was under no duty to retreat. State v. Sipes, 202 Iowa 173, 209 N.W. 458 (1926).

When a man is on his own premises other than his house or within the curtilage thereof the reasons for not retreating do not apply. Lee v. State, 92 Ala. 15, 9 So. 407 (1890).

The right to stand his ground applies to one while in his dwelling house, office, or place of business, or within the curtilage thereof. Bryant v. State, 252 Ala. 153, 39 So.2d 657 (1949).

The house of a prostitute is her "castle" in spite of her immoral use of the place. Russell v. State, 61 Fla. 50, 54 So. 360 (1911).

While there is no duty to retreat from the dwelling, and this has been extended to the place of business, it does not include an illicit still set up at a place other than the dwelling. Hill v. State, 194 Ala. 11, 69 So. 941 (1915).

STATE v. GRIERSON

Supreme Court of New Hampshire, 1950.
96 N.H. 36, 69 A.2d 851.

Indictment for first degree manslaughter. Trial by jury after a view resulting in a verdict of guilty. The State's evidence tended to prove that the defendant, Leah W. Grierson, killed Charles A. Peabody by stabbing him in the heart with a paring knife in the kitchen of her home at 15 Brock Street in Rochester at about 10 o'clock on the evening of May 23, 1948. It appeared they had been drinking together at a club in Dover on the afternoon in question and had returned to the defendant's home shortly after 9:30 in the evening. According to the defendant soon after they arrived at her home the deceased began quarreling with her over an alleged friendship, which she denied, with another man. She testified Peabody came at her with a small kitchen or paring knife cursing her and threatening to "fix" her. She tried to seize the knife to prevent him from stabbing her. He then began to hit her, first on one side of the face, then on the other and also about the shoulders. That was the last she remembered of the quarrel. Her next recollection was of seeing Peabody lying on the floor and of trying to bring him to by putting a wet towel on his face. She claims she does not remember calling the police but according to Officer Levesque of the Rochester Police Department he received a call around 11 o'clock to come to her home right away. He did so and she came to meet him as he got out of the car crying "I think I killed him, Charlie, I think I killed him". Thereafter according to this officer and Marshal Redden, who arrived at the scene a few minutes later and who died before the trial, she repeatedly said "I killed him". . . .

BLANDIN, JUSTICE. . . . The respondent next takes issue with the Court's refusal to give requested instructions to the effect that she need not retreat if assaulted in her own home but could stand her ground and use such force as reasonably necessary to repel the attack. The Court charged the jury in substance that Mrs. Grierson must act as a reasonable person under the circumstances and if, as the State claimed by so doing, she could have avoided the attack by retreating she was bound to do so; if not then she had the right to use reasonable force in repelling Peabody's assault. We believe the charge applied the law correctly to the facts in this case. Unquestionably the general rule, which we follow in this state, is that one attacked in his home by an intruder need not retreat but may stand his ground and use reasonable force to repel the assault even though this may result in the death of the intruder. However, here, as shown by the defendant's own admission, the deceased was not an intruder but was residing in her home, if not permanently, at least temporarily as her guest. "Thus a man's house is the dwelling place of . . .

one who is residing, however temporarily, as a guest". Res.Torts, Vol. 1, § 65, p. 140. In such cases the privilege of the above rule does not exist and the person attacked must retreat if this is a reasonable means of avoiding the danger consistent with his own safety.[1] Although we find no cases in this State squarely on the point the tenor of our decisions and the modern authority supported by the better reason uphold this doctrine. Beale, Harv.Law Rev., p. 567. See also Restatement, Torts, Vol. 1, § 65, pp. 134–135, 140. The rule stated there is believed applicable to crimes as well as torts under present day conditions. See also State v. Elliott, 11 N.H. 540, 544–545 and Aldrich v. Wright, 53 N.H. 398, 404, 407, 422, 16 Am.Rep. 339, where Doe, C. J., after stressing the "immense value" which the law places on human life, 53 N.H. at page 407, says 53 N.H. at page 422, "It is reasonably necessary that the person who kills another in his own defence should have first retreated as far as he conveniently or safely can, to avoid the violence of the assault. . . . The party assaulted must therefore flee as far as he conveniently can, either by reason of some wall, ditch, or other impediment, or as far as the fierceness of the assault will permit him. . . . This maxim of retreating to the wall is a statement of fact properly illustrating the weight to be given to the sanctity of human life in determining the reasonable necessity of killing a human being . . .".

Exceptions overruled.

DUNCAN, J., dissented; the others concurred.

DUNCAN, JUSTICE (dissenting). The jury was instructed that if the respondent could reasonably have avoided the attack without us-

---

1. There is a duty to retreat if both live in the house. Commonwealth v. Johnson, 213 Pa. 432, 62 A. 1064 (1906). There is a duty to retreat if assailant entered as an invited guest. Oney v. Commonwealth, 225 Ky. 590, 9 S.W.2d 723 (1928). There is no duty to retreat if "he is attacked within his dwelling place which is not also the dwelling place of the other, . . ." Restatement, Second, Torts § 65(2) (a) (1965).

There is no duty to retreat even if both live in the same house. Jones v. State, 76 Ala. 8 (1884); People v. Tomlins, 213 N.Y. 240, 107 N.E. 496 (1914); State v. Phillips, 38 Del. 24, 187 A. 721 (1936). There is no duty to retreat from one who entered as an invited guest. State v. Bissonette, 83 Conn. 261, 76 A. 288 (1910). One is not required to retreat from his place of employment even if the assailant is also employed there. State v. Gorden, 128 S.C. 422, 122 S.E. 501 (1924).

An employee should retreat rather than kill an invited customer. Wilson v. State, 69 Ga. 224 (1882).

A roomer who was attacked in another part of the house by the owner had a duty to retreat. State v. Dyer, 147 Iowa 217, 124 N.W. 629 (1910).

A guest in the house of a friend is under no obligation to retreat from a third person. Lawler v. State, 22 Ala.App. 549, 117 So. 605 (1928).

"A is standing in the vestibule of his dwelling house. B starts toward A brandishing a razor and threatening to kill him. A is privileged to stand his ground, await B's attack and shoot or stab him, although A could with perfect safety avoid B's attack by retreating to an inner room or by closing and locking the door of the vestibule." Restatement, Second, Torts § 65, Illustration 6 (1965).

Sec. 4 SELF-DEFENSE 613

ing force to repel it, and failed to do so, then she was guilty. In my opinion this was error. If the view be taken that failure to retreat is merely "a circumstance to be considered with all the others in order to determine whether the defendant went farther than he was justified in doing", then it was error to impose a categorical duty. Id. If the view be taken that retreat is a positive requirement where apparently possible with reasonable safety, except that one attacked in his dwelling may stand his ground, then the respondent was improperly deprived of the benefit of the exception, which should not be restricted to cases of attack by intruders.[2]

STATE v. CLYDE

Supreme Court of Hawaii, 1964.
47 Haw. 345, 388 P.2d 846.

MIZUHA, JUSTICE. Defendant-appellant was convicted of murder in the first degree and as required by R.L.H.1955, § 291–5 (Supp.1961), sentenced to life imprisonment not subject to parole.

Defendant and the deceased, Ruperto Canto, had had several altercations prior to the date of the murder. On December 28, 1961, defendant broke into a friend's apartment and took a twelve gauge shotgun without permission and then drove to Canto's apartment. He walked into the Canto apartment with a jacket covering an object, "shook the jacket off the shotgun," pointed the shotgun at Canto and according to defendant told him "don't move." The victim's wife, Mrs. Bette Canto, screamed. The defendant testified that this scream distracted his attention, that he then caught a glimpse of the deceased leaping towards him and the shotgun went off. The deceased was shot three times. Defendant claimed that he fired in self-defense. According to Mrs. Canto's testimony, when the shotgun was revealed, she asked, "are you going to shoot him" or "are you going to kill him," and defendant said "yes" and almost simultaneously fired. . . .

Appellant contends next that the court erred in giving the instruction on self-defense. Instruction 37 read:

"The acts which a person may do in self-defense and justify under a plea of self-defense depend upon the conduct of those involved in the encounter and the circumstances attending it. No fixed rule

---

2. The judge instructed: "To justify a killing in self-defence, it was necessary that an *assault* should have been committed by the person killed; that it was not enough that the party killed had a pistol in his hand, but that there must have been a presentation of it, or some demonstration of shooting." In holding this to be reversible error the court said: "If such be the law, then there is no such thing as available self-defence—when the assailant makes his attack with a pistol, or other kind of firearm; for, the assault and discharge of the weapon are simultaneous, or so nearly so, that resistance would be almost impossible." Goodall v. State, 1 Or. 333, 336 (1861). See also Ludwick v. State, 151 Tex.Cr. R. 623, 210 S.W.2d 589 (1948).

is applicable to every case, but certain general principles are established as guides for the jury's determination.

"The law of self-defense is founded on the principle of necessity, either actual or apparent, and in order to justify the taking of human life on this ground the slayer, as a reasonable man, must have reason to believe and must believe that he is in danger of receiving great bodily harm; and further, the circumstances must be such that an ordinarily reasonable person, if he were in those circumstances and if he knew and saw what such person in real or apparent danger knows and sees, would believe that it was necessary for him to use, in his defense and to avoid great bodily injury to himself, such force or means as might cause the death of his adversary.

"A bare fear that a person's life or limb is in danger is not sufficient to justify a homicide. To justify taking the life of another in self-defense, the circumstances must be such as to excite the fears of a reasonable man placed in a similar position, and the party killing must act under the influence of such fears alone. The danger must be apparent and must be present and imminent, or must so appear at the time to the slayer as a reasonable man, and the killing must be done under a well-founded belief that it is necessary to save one's self from death or great bodily harm."

The trial court did not err. ". . . It is generally held that the apprehension of danger and belief of necessity which will justify killing in self-defense must be a reasonable apprehension and belief, such as a reasonable man would, under the circumstances, have entertained. . . ." 1 Wharton, Criminal Law and Procedure, § 215, p. 471. . . .

Likewise, "the question is not whether the jury believed the force used was necessary in self-defense, but whether the defendant, acting as a reasonable man, had this belief. . . ." Perkins, Criminal Law, c. 10, § 4, p. 884. People v. Miller, 403 Ill. 561, 87 N.E.2d 649; Wireman v. Commonwealth, 290 Ky. 704, 162 S.W.2d 557.

The instruction given in the present case, while not stated in the same words, expressed the same rule of law given in the instruction on self-defense in Territory v. Leong Kun, 29 Haw. 90.

Appellant . . . requested the following instruction (Defendant's Instruction No. 1):

"If you find from all the evidence, including defendant's mental condition and his prior mental history, that at the time defendant obtained the weapon and proceeded to the room of the deceased, defendant was acting upon an apparent danger as it reasonably appeared to him at that time, in that he believed his life was in danger and that when he fired the weapon he felt it was necessary to protect himself from defendant [sic] then you are instructed defendant acted in self defense and you must return a verdict of not guilty."

This instruction attempts to set forth a subjective test for the law of self-defense. . . .

We rejected the subjective test in Territory v. Aquino, supra, 43 Hawaii at 379, where this court approved the following instruction:

" 'I further instruct you that self-defense, in proper cases, is the right of every person. It may be resorted to by anyone who is violently assaulted by another in such a manner as to cause the person so assaulted in good faith to believe that he is in immediate danger of either being killed or of receiving great bodily harm from his assailant, however, it must appear that the circumstances were sufficient to excite the fear of a reasonable person similarly situated and that this defendant was acting in good faith during the situation and circumstances from his standpoint and that he really acted upon the influence of such a fear and not in the spirit of illwill, hatred or revenge.

" '. . . Circumstances justifying assault in the law of self-defense must be such as to render it unavoidable under all the circumstances, judged from the standpoint of a reasonable man placed in defendant's position, and if you believe from the evidence that this defendant could have avoided any conflict between himself and the deceased without increased danger to himself, it was his duty to avoid such conflict and so render his resort to the law of self-defense unnecessary.' " . . .

The judgment is affirmed.[1]

---

1. Accord: People v. Williams, 32 Cal. 280 (1867).

"In determining whether the actor's apprehension of the intentional infliction of bodily harm or an offensive contact is reasonable, the circumstances which are known, or should be known, to the actor must be such as would lead a reasonable man to entertain such an apprehension. In this connection the qualities which primarily characterize a 'reasonable man' are ordinary firmness and courage." Restatement, Second, Torts § 63, Comment *i* (1965).

The instruction should not speak in terms of an "ordinarily prudent and courageous man," but of an "ordinarily prudent and cautious man." State v. Sipes, 202 Iowa 173, 185, 209 N.W. 458, 463 (1926). Accord: People v. Smith, 164 Cal. 451, 129 P. 785 (1913).

". . . the fears of a reasonable man that his life is in danger, or that a felony is about to be perpetrated upon him." Jarrard v. State, 206 Ga. 112, 114, 55 S.E.2d 706, 709 (1949).

The question is not apparent danger as seen by the jury at the trial, but as it appeared to the defendant at the moment. Wireman v. Commonwealth, 290 Ky. 704, 162 S.W.2d 557 (1942); Patillo v. State, 22 Tex.App. 586, 3 S.W. 766 (1886).

The fact that defendant was intoxicated at the time would not justify a killing in alleged self-defense if the need for deadly force would not have seemed necessary to a reasonably prudent man under the circumstances. Springfeld v. State, 96 Ala. 81, 11 So. 250 (1892). Contra: His condition may be taken into account in considering whether he apprehended an assault. Regina v. Gamlin, 1 Fost. and F. 90, 175 Eng.Rep. 639 (1858).

If the defendant relies upon self-defense he has the burden of establishing this fact by a preponderance of the evidence. Commonwealth v. Palmer, 222 Pa. 299, 71 A. 100 (1908); State v. Ballou, 20 R.I. 607, 40 A. 861 (1898); State v. Dillard, 59 W.Va. 197, 53 S.E. 117 (1906). If the jury are in doubt up-

STATE v. BROADHURST

Supreme Court of Oregon, 1948.
184 Or. 178, 196 P.2d 407.

(Defendant, who had "married" Dr. Broadhurst although she was the wife of another, asked Williams to kill her "husband." Williams pretended to have car trouble at a spot on a lonely road where he knew Dr. Broadhurst would be driving. Dr. Broadhurst stopped to give help and Williams hit him over the head with a heavy wrench. At that point, according to Williams' testimony, he changed his mind and decided to leave without killing the other. But Dr. Broadhurst came at him and he was forced to kill to save his own life. Defendant was convicted of first degree murder and appeals.)

ROSSMAN, C. J. . . . Finally, under this contention the defendant argues that the testimony of Williams shows that he shot in self-defense and that Williams' testimony is binding upon the State. She, therefore, claims that the crime of murder was not committed.

In a preceding paragraph we showed that Williams swore that he struck Dr. Broadhurst only once with the wrench. He claimed that at that juncture he underwent a change of heart and decided to quit. His actual words were: "I had quit. . . . I decided I was going to leave the country right away." By reverting to the preceding paragraph, the testimony can be read upon which the defendant depends for a contention that two affrays occurred at the Succor Creek junction: (a) one in which Williams was the aggressor, and (b) a second in which Dr. Broadhurst was the aggressor. The defendant claims that Williams abandoned the first before the second purported affray was begun.

Dr. Joseph Beeman, whose qualifications are admitted, performed an autopsy upon Dr. Broadhurst's remains. He found three wounds upon the forehead. One was three-eighths of an inch in diameter, another was an inch and a half in diameter. He said: "This wound had gone down to the skull." The third wound "was one and five-eighths of an inch long and three-fourths of an inch wide." According to the witness it "had gone through the skull and had torn the frontal part . . . had fractured the skull bone over the right eye." We call attention to the fact that two of the blows penetrated the skull and that one of them fractured the skull bone. Dr. Beeman

on this point they should convict. State v. Byers, 100 N.C. 512, 6 S.E. 420 (1888). Contra: The burden is upon the prosecution to establish the guilt of the defendant beyond a reasonable doubt. People v. Duncan, 315 Ill. 106, 145 N.E. 810 (1924); People v. Downs, 123 N.Y. 558, 25 N.E. 988 (1890); Gravely v. State, 38 Neb. 871, 57 N.W. 751 (1894).

One who has received information of threats against his life made by another is justified in acting more quickly, and taking harsher measures for his protection against that other, than in the absence of such information. People v. Torres, 94 Cal.App.2d 146, 210 P.2d 324 (1949).

Sec. 4 SELF-DEFENSE 617

testified that the shotgun wounds were in the right chest. We quote from him:

"He had the shotgun wounds in his right chest which was going from left to right, just slightly upwards and slightly backwards."

. . .

An aggressor, in a combat which led to the death of the assaulted party, can not claim that he struck the fatal blow in self-defense unless, before the blow, he withdrew in good faith from the combat, and, in addition, brought home to the assaulted man notice of his intention in such a way that the adversary, as a reasonable man, must have known that the assault was ended. Abandonment of the assault and reasonable notice thereof are essential to restore to the aggressor the right of self-defense. Vol. 40, C.J.S., Homicide, § 121, page 995, in stating the rule to which we are adverting says:

". . . He must also in some manner make known his intention to his adversary; and if the circumstances are such that he cannot notify his adversary, as where the injuries inflicted by him are such as to deprive his adversary of his capacity to receive impressions concerning his assailant's design and endeavor to cease further combat, it is the assailant's fault and he must bear the consequences. As long as a person keeps his gun in his hand prepared to shoot, the person opposing him is not expected or required to accept any act or statement as indicative of an intent to discontinue the assault. . ."

In 26 Am.Jur., Homicide, § 135, page 247, we find:

". . . Nor is this all; the aggressor must inform his antagonist of his purpose to withdraw from the conflict. If the circumstances are such that he cannot do this, it is attributable to his own fault and he must abide by the consequences."

Both of the treatises from which we quoted cite in partial support of their statements People v. Button, 106 Cal. 628, 39 P. 1073, 28 L.R.A. 591, 46 Am.St.Rep. 259. That decision is carefully reasoned and fully supports the claims made for it.

If Williams had quit the combat before he shot Dr. Broadhurst, he did not manifest that fact in any way whatever, with the exception of walking a few steps to his automobile. But upon the seat of the car lay his gun ready to be fired. At the moment when he claims Dr. Broadhurst advanced upon him he still had the wrench in his hand. His own words are, "When he started after me I had the wrench in my hand." There is no evidence that Dr. Broadhurst, upon whose head three vicious blows had rained, one of which fractured his skull bone, had regained consciousness when he is said to have begun an attack upon his assailant. Unless Dr. Broadhurst in some miraculous manner had regained consciousness and had discovered the secret purpose of Williams to abandon the assault, the right of Williams to act in self-defense had not been restored. Williams was asked: "Was he pretty well recovered when you handed the shirt to him?" He answered, "No." The nearest he came to attributing consciousness to the battered, bloody victim of his brutal blows was made in the following answer: "I had just got to the door and he started to come after me, so I imagine he was coming out of it." If Dr. Broadhurst advanced upon Williams, then we think that the following, taken from People v. Button, supra, is applicable:

"While the deceased had eyes to see and ears to hear, he had no mind to comprehend, for his mind was taken from him by the defendant at the first assault. Throughout the whole affray, it must be conceded that the deceased was guilty of no wrong, no violation of the law. When he attempted to kill the defendant, he thought he was acting in self-defense, and, according to his lights, he was acting in self-defense."

We are certain that the fifth and sixth contentions are without merit. . . .

The judgment of the circuit court is affirmed.

(Certiorari denied 337 U.S. 906, 69 S.Ct. 1046, 93 L.Ed. 1718.)

MODEL PENAL CODE

Section 3.04. Use of Force in Self-Protection.

(1) Use of Force Justifiable for Protection of the Person. Subject to the provisions of this Section and of Section 3.09, the use of force upon or toward another person is justifiable when the actor believes that such force is immediately necessary for the purpose of protecting himself against the use of unlawful force by such other person on the present occasion.

(2) Limitations on Justifying Necessity for Use of Force.

(a) The use of force is not justifiable under this Section:

(i) to resist an arrest which the actor knows is being made by a peace officer, although the arrest is unlawful; or

(ii) to resist force used by the occupier or possessor of property or by another person on his behalf, where the actor knows that the person using the force is doing so under a claim of right to protect the property, except that this limitation shall not apply if:

(1) the actor is a public officer acting in the performance of his duties or a person lawfully assisting him therein or a person making or assisting in a lawful arrest; or

(2) the actor has been unlawfully dispossessed of the property and is making a re-entry or reception justified by Section 3.06; or

(3) the actor believes that such force is necessary to protect himself against death or serious bodily harm.

(b) The use of deadly force is not justifiable under this Section unless the actor believes that such force is necessary to protect himself against death, serious bodily harm, kidnapping or sexual intercourse compelled by force or threat; nor is it justifiable if:

(i) the actor, with the purpose of causing death or serious bodily harm, provoked the use of force against himself in the same encounter; or

(ii) the actor knows that he can avoid the necessity of using such force with complete safety by retreating or by surrendering possession of a thing to a person asserting a claim of right thereto or by complying with a demand that he abstain from any action which he has no duty to take, except that:

(1) the actor is not obliged to retreat from his dwelling or place of work, unless he was the initial aggressor or is assailed in his place of work by another person whose place of work the actor knows it to be; and

(2) a public officer justified in using force in the performance of his duties or a person justified in using force in his assistance or a person justified in using force in making an arrest or preventing an escape is not obliged to desist from efforts to perform such duty, effect such arrest or prevent such escape because of resistance or threatened resistance by or on behalf of the person against whom such action is directed.

(c) Except as required by paragraphs (a) and (b) of this Subsection, a person employing protective force may estimate the necessity thereof under the circumstances as he believes them to be when the force is used, without retreating, surrendering possession, doing any other act which he has no legal duty to do or abstaining from any lawful action.

(3) *Use of Confinement as Protective Force.* The justification afforded by this Section extends to the use of confinement as protective force only if the actor takes all reasonable measures to terminate the confinement as soon as he knows that he safely can, unless the person confined has been arrested on a charge of crime.

SECTION 5. DEFENSE OF OTHERS

"Ordinarily,—if not always," says Bishop, "one may do in another's defence whatever the other might in the circumstances do for himself."[1] But while this has been repeated now and then[2] it is broader than the special privilege granted to one to use force in the aid of another.[3] This special privilege seems to have had its roots in

---

1. Bishop, Criminal Law § 877 (9th ed. 1923).
2. Stanley v. Commonwealth, 86 Ky. 440, 6 S.W. 155 (1887).
3. Morrison v. Commonwealth, 74 S.W. 277, 24 Ky.Law Rep. 2493 (1903); Restatement, Second, Torts § 76 (1965).

the law of property.[4] The privilege of one to protect what is "his" was extended to include the protection of his wife, his children and his servants. In the course of time this privilege outgrew the property analogy and came to be regarded as a "mutual and reciprocal defence."[5] The household was regarded as a group. Any member of the family had the privilege of defending another member; the master could defend the servant, or the servant defend the master.[6] Even this concept of the privilege has been outgrown. It now includes the members of one's immediate family or household and any other whom he is under a legal or socially-recognized duty to protect.[7] Thus a conductor is privileged to defend his passenger, and a man is privileged to defend a lady friend whom he is escorting at the moment.[8]

The privilege to use force in defense of another is subject to the same general limitations and restrictions as the privilege to use force in self-defense. Hence deadly force may not be used to save another from non-deadly force,[9] and even non-deadly force must not be obviously in excess of what is needed for the purpose.[10]

This special privilege to use force in the defense of certain persons does not supersede the privilege to use force for the prevention of crime. It is in addition thereto.[11] One person may be in a position to claim both privileges.[12] Another may have the benefit of one only, —or of neither.

MITCHELL v. STATE

Supreme Court of Florida, 1901.
43 Fla. 188, 30 So. 803.

MABRY, J. Plaintiffs in error were tried and convicted in the Criminal Court of Record for Duval County of the crime of manslaughter, upon an information filed against them in that court charg-

---

4. Restatement, Second, Torts § 76, Comment *e* (1965).

5. 3 Bl.Comm. 3.

6. "A man may defend his family, his servants or his master, whenever he may defend himself." Pond v. People, 8 Mich. 150, 176 (1860).

7. Restatement, Second, Torts § 76, Comments *e, f* (1965).

8. Ibid.

9. Id. at Comment *b*.

10. Ibid.

11. In a case in which the relation between the parties was not emphasized the court said: "The law makes it the duty of every one, who sees a felony attempted by violence, to prevent it, if possible, and allows him to use the necessary means to make his resistance effectual. One may kill in defense of another under the same circumstances that he would have the right to kill in defense of himself." State v. Hennessey, 29 Nev. 320, 344, 90 P. 221, 227 (1907).

12. "As to the defendant Wendell Reed, the court failed to charge the law with respect to both (a) his right to fight in the necessary defense of his step-father, and (b) his right and duty as a private citizen to interfere to prevent a felonious assault. Each right is recognized in the decisions of this court." State v. Robinson, 213 N.C. 273, 281, 195 S.E. 824, 829–30 (1938).

ing them with the commission of that offence. They have sued out a writ of error to this court and have specified six assignments of error, only two of which—the fourth and fifth—have been argued. . . .

The fourth assignment of error imputes to the court error in refusing to give the seventh request on behalf of plaintiffs in error. This request sought to have the jury instructed that if they believed from the evidence the defendant Mitchell, at the time he fired the fatal shot that killed the deceased, the latter, from all indications present to the observations of said defendant, was in the act of striking at the sister of defendant with an open knife in an angry manner; and, further, that defendant had good reason to believe and did believe that his sister was then in imminent danger of being killed or of receiving great bodily harm from deceased, then, as matter of law, the defendant had the right to use whatever means he had at command to prevent the infliction of such harm upon his sister, and if in doing so it was necessary to take the life of deceased, defendant would be justified in doing so, and the verdict should be not guilty. The avowed object of this request was to place defendant Mitchell in a position to avail himself of the defence of justifiable homicide embraced in the second head of the second division of section 2378 Revised Statutes, to the effect that a homicide is justifiable when committed not only in lawful defence of the person killing, but also in defence of his or her husband, wife, parent, child, master, mistress, or servant, when there shall be reasonable ground to apprehend a design to commit a felony or to do some great personal injury, and there shall be imminent danger of such design being accomplished. Neither brother nor sister is included among the domestic relations enumerated in the statute in defence of whom life may be taken, not merely when an actual necessity to kill to prevent a felony, but when there shall be reasonable ground to apprehend a design to commit a felony or to do some great personal injury and there shall be imminent danger of such design being accomplished, but we are earnestly requested to include them by construction. In the specific enumeration of the persons in the statute the legislature has employed no terms under which the courts are authorized to include other persons of similar relation, and until the statute is amended, brother and sister cannot be included. We reached this conclusion after mature deliberation in the case of Richard v. State, decided at the last term, and still think our conclusion correct.

At common law any person might take the life of another to prevent him from committing a known forcible felony, and this right is recognized by our statute. By the third head of the second division of section 2378, homicide is justifiable when necessarily committed in attempting by lawful ways and means to apprehend any person for any felony committed, or in lawfully suppressing any riot, or in lawfully keeping and preserving the peace. The felony of unlawfully taking of life or inflicting serious bodily harm is a violent breach of the peace, and it may be prevented by slaying the perpetrator. A brother is not, of course, excluded from the right to slay to prevent the felony upon his sister, as he may to prevent it upon any other person. The right to slay in such case, however, rests upon necessity. It was so at common law when one not assaulted himself slayed to prevent a felony, and our statute expressly provides that homicide is justifiable "when necessarily committed . . . in lawfully suppressing any riot or in lawfully keeping and preserving the peace." When called upon to define the right to slay to prevent a felony by one not himself assaulted or endangered, and not standing within the relations enumerated by the statute, the court should not extend it beyond necessity, and a request broader than this should be refused. In this case the court instructed the jury, at the request of defendants, that the law "permits one who sees another in the act of committing a felony to use every means in his power to prevent its commission, and, if in doing so, it becomes necessary to take the life of the person so offending, the law holds him who so takes human life blameless." According to the testimony in the case the defendants, before Mitchell commenced to shoot at the deceased, were not assaulted or in any way threatened with injury. By the testimony of the State it appeared that deceased and a brother of Mitchell had a difficulty, and also the sister of deceased and the sister of Mitchell had quarreled, and that some ten or fifteen minutes after these disturbances had been stopped and quieted the defendants came up and Mitchell commenced to fire on deceased who was making no demonstrations of harm towards any one at the time. The deceased was shot twice in the back and once in the breast and [died] in a short time thereafter. Witnesses for the defence state that when the defendants came up the deceased was approaching the sister of Mitchell with a drawn knife in his hand and used language indicating a design to kill her. Some of the witnesses say that deceased was five or six feet from Mitchell's sister when the firing commenced, and others indicate that he was still closer. Mitchell said nothing, but entered the field by rapidly firing his pistol at deceased who soon fell mortally wounded. The correct view of the law upon the facts is whether the killing was necessarily done to prevent a felony, and as the seventh request was not entirely consistent with this view it was properly refused.

The next error assigned is that the verdict is not sustained by the evidence. It is conceded that the witnesses in the case for the respective parties are in direct conflict and about equal in number. If the testimony of the State is to be believed, defendants can have no ground of complaint for being convicted of manslaughter. The question of conflict in the evidence was for the jury, and there is no ground for disturbing the verdict on this account. . . .

The judgment must be affirmed, and it is so ordered.[1]

1. This subdivision of the Florida statute has been amended to include brother and sister (with other additions). F.S.A. § 782.02.

MURPHY v. STATE

Supreme Court of Tennessee, 1949.
188 Tenn. 583, 221 S.W.2d 812.

PREWITT, JUSTICE. Defendant, Joe Murphy, appeals from conviction of voluntary manslaughter for the homicide of Hubert Ray Cook and punishment of not less than two nor more than ten years in the State prison for the offense.

There is little conflict in the testimony. Deceased, Hubert Ray Cook, was a young man who weighed about 140 pounds. Defendant is a man about 45 years of age. Arthur D. Murphy, a son of defendant, was subject to epileptic fits, and from the record before us, it appears that he did about as he pleased with reference to the ordinary matters of life.

The homicide occurred on Saturday night, August 7, 1948, at a dance in a store building at Wilder. The proof shows that deceased had gone to the juke box to put in some nickels which would cancel the records that were furnishing the music for this dance. Arthur D. Murphy testified that the proprietor of the store had asked him to look after the juke box; that deceased came up to the juke box and started canceling the records and when he told him not to do this, he and deceased got into an argument which led to the homicide. Defendant testified that deceased made a motion to strike him, but his testimony is not corroborated in this respect. The weight of the evidence is that as a result of this argument Arthur D. Murphy hit deceased and knocked him backwards over a stack of soft drink bottles. When deceased came up he had a soft drink bottle in his hand and struck Arthur D. Murphy between the eyes. This cut on the latter's head seems to have addled him, and the testimony is that deceased reached for another bottle, or had another bottle in his hand. About this time defendant, who testified that he had come to the dance to look after his son, pulled his pistol, which he admitted carrying, and shot deceased one time behind the right ear, from the effects of which he died shortly.

The law in this State is well settled that where one is the aggressor in a difficulty he may not plead self-defense without withdrawing from the conflict and notifying his adversary of such withdrawal, unless the assault on him is so fierce and deadly that no time to withdraw is presented. When an intervenor puts himself in the same position of the person to be rescued, he acts at his own peril.

"The doctrine of freedom from fault in bringing on a difficulty as a condition precedent to a plea of self-defense applies with equal force to a case in which one person interferes in a difficulty between two others in behalf of, or to protect, one of them; and generally speaking a person who does this will not be allowed the benefit of the plea of self-defense, unless such plea would have been available to the person whose part he took in case he himself had done the killing, since the person interfering is affected by the principle that the party bringing on the difficulty cannot take advantage of his own wrong.[1] If the person sought to be protected provoked or brought on the difficulty, he must have clearly manifested a desire and intention to retire from the conflict; and even then the person interfering would not be justifiable if he struck the fatal blow in pursuance of a previous design to assist his friend in the event of a personal difficulty. And where one person interferes in behalf of another who was the aggressor, and there is opportunity to retreat after the interference and advantage is not taken of it, the person interfering can claim no greater right than the other, and neither of them can invoke the doctrine of self-defense. Thus, if a son fight in defense of his father, his act in doing so will receive the same construction as that of the father, and if the latter was the aggressor in bringing on the difficulty, and could not plead self-defense, the same rule applies to the son. And the son cannot rely upon his own freedom from fault in bringing on the difficulty, as a defense, where he knew the father had provoked the attack;[2] both must have been without fault in bringing it on. Nor is a father justified in killing the adversary of his son, where the son had provoked and brought on the conflict in which he was placed in imminent danger. And the plea of self-defense cannot be interposed by a father who kills an officer rightfully seeking to arrest his son, to prevent such arrest. Nor can one strike to relieve a brother from peril unless the brother was free from fault in bringing on the difficulty which placed him in peril. And if a person in whose defense a brother engaged was in fault, and had not retreated or attempted to retreat, the interference is not justifiable or excusable." Wharton on Homicide, 3d Ed., § 332, pp. 534–535.

1. Sherrill v. State, 138 Ala. 3, 35 So. 129 (1903); Utterback v. Commonwealth, 105 Ky. 723, 49 S.W. 479 (1899); State v. Cook, 78 S.C. 253, 59 S.E. 862 (1906); Cooper v. State, 123 Tenn. 37, 138 S.W. 826 (1909).

One who intervenes in behalf of his brother cannot avail himself of the right of self-defense unless both he and his brother were free from fault in bringing on the difficulty. Moore v. State, 25 Okl.Cr. 118, 218 P. 1102 (1923).

One who killed in defense of his son was not authorized to rely upon a reasonable belief that his son was free from fault. Nothing short of this actual fact would justify his act. Lovejoy v. State, 33 Ala.App. 414, 34 So.2d 692 (1948), certiorari denied 250 Ala. 409, 34 So.2d 700 (1948).

2. State v. Linney, 52 Mo. 40 (1873).

One who has seen the entire encounter is not privileged to intervene in behalf of the aggressor. People v. Travis, 56 Cal. 251 (1880); State v. Turner, 246 Mo. 598, 152 S.W. 313 (1912).

While two officers in plain clothes were attempting to make a lawful arrest D, who thought the men were wrongfully attacking an 18-year-old boy, went to the aid of the lad. In upholding a conviction of assault it was held that one who intervenes in a struggle does so "at his peril" and is not protected if the one he aids was in the wrong. People v. Young, 11 N.Y.2d 274, 229 N.Y.S.2d 1, 183 N.E.2d 319 (1962).

We are of opinion that the jury was justified in concluding that the son of defendant was the original aggressor in the trouble which took the life of deceased. The son would not have been entitled to rely on the right of self-defense until he had withdrawn from the difficulty and notified deceased of that fact, and not having done so, defendant was not justified in taking the life of deceased. . . .

All assignments of error are overruled and the judgment is affirmed.

All concur.

STATE v. CHIARELLO

Superior Court of New Jersey, Appellate Division, 1961.
69 N.J.Super. 479, 174 A.2d 506.

The opinion of the court was delivered by CONFORD, S. J. A. D.

This is an appeal from a conviction of the defendant for atrocious assault and battery with a dangerous weapon, contrary to N.J.S. 2A:90–1 and 2A:151–5, N.J.S.A. The defendant shot and seriously wounded Louis Walker and Roland Houle, in order, as he claims, to prevent their murdering William J. Edwards. All four were employees of Camp Harmony in Somerset County. An affray had begun among the others, who had been drinking, awakening the defendant. From his testimony, to be described later, a jury could have properly found that defendant in good faith reasonably deemed it necessary to physically disable Walker and Houle in order to save Edwards' life. But from proofs adduced as to what had transpired before defendant's attention was drawn to the melée, it might have been concluded by a jury that it was not in fact necessary to shoot Walker and Houle to prevent death or serious injury to Edwards, and that Edwards himself would not in the circumstances have been justified in using such measures as a matter of self-defense.

The principal question for resolution on this appeal is the correctness of the trial court's charge to the jury that the defendant's justification in defending Edwards in the manner he did depended upon whether Edwards himself would have been legally justified, on the basis of the circumstances known to Edwards, in using the same force and violence on Walker and Houle. It is and was the defendant's position at the trial that he had the right to act upon his own reasonable judgment on the basis of the appearances as manifested to him, without imputation to him of Edwards' peculiar knowledge of the circumstances. There is no completely satisfactory appellate decision on the point in this State. . . .

The portion of the charge of the trial court presently material, and to which defendant adequately specified his objections, was as follows:

"The defendant, while admitting the shooting, urges that his conduct was justified on the ground of defense of one William Edwards who was being assaulted. In proper circumstances, ladies and gentlemen of the jury, one may, without committing actionable assault and battery, intervene for the defense of a third person, using such means as he could employ to protect himself from a similar aggression. The doctrines, principles and rules of the right of self defense apply where a person resists an attack made in his presence on a relative, member of his family or social friends. But before one person has the right to use force in the defense or aid of another, the circumstances must be such that the person on whom the assault is being made has the right of self defense and, therefore, the right to use the same force and intervention must be necessary for the protection of the third person. . . ."

Burdick sums up the matter in this wise (2 Law of Crime, § 437, at pp. 136–137 (1946));

"It is, nevertheless, held in many cases that when one comes to the defense of another he stands in the same shoes as the person attacked, and that the same rules that would apply to one's own defense apply also to the defender. Consequently, it is held that a homicide is not justified in such a case if either the person defended or the defender is at fault in occasioning the difficulty; and despite the fact that a defender acts in good faith, some cases hold that he is not justified if, although unknown to him, the defended person was in fault. The more reasonable view is that one defending another in good faith and in ignorance of the other's fault is justified when acting upon reasonable appearances. While it is said that this latter rule 'would allow an innocent man who had been forced to strike in self-defense, to be killed with impunity merely because appearances were against him', yet the same objection could also be made to killing in the prevention of a forcible felony, the established rule in such cases being that one is justified if he acts in good faith upon a well-grounded belief that such a felony is being attempted. Moreover, when one is apparently in immediate danger of being killed by felonious attack, if a defender before he can lawfully act must wait until he ascertains who was in fault, then innocent men will be killed for lack of defenders." . . .

In the light of the foregoing considerations, we are satisfied that the application of sound principle in the area of crimes of assault precludes liability in the absence of either guilty intent or negligence. Consequently, we hold the charge of the trial court, in conditioning this defendant's exculpating justification for his acts upon the premise that Edwards would have been legally justified in taking like defensive measures on the facts as Edwards knew them to be, rather than excusing defendant if his conduct was justified upon the basis of the facts *as he reasonably concluded them to be*, both in relation to the gravity of the threat to Edwards and to the extent of the force necessary to protect him therefrom, was prejudicially erroneous. This must lead to a reversal of the conviction. . . .

Reversed and remanded for a new trial.[1]

PEOPLE v. CURTIS

Supreme Court of Michigan, 1884.
52 Mich. 616, 18 N.W. 385.

CAMPBELL, J. Curtis was tried in the Cass county circuit court and convicted of murder in the second degree. Errors are assigned on rulings during the trial and in instructions to the jury. Macon Wilson was the person killed. . . .

The respondent was entitled and bound to take an interest in the life and safety of his brother. There was no difference in the testimony as to his being in danger, and all the instructions which confined the right of respondent to helping him only when he was entirely without fault were unwarranted. The court refused to charge that a brother might interpose against a felonious or serious bodily harm, unless the assailed party was entirely blameless, and this was contrary to the well-settled principle that a dangerous felony may be prevented by one who is not himself in the wrong, directly or by complicity. . . .[1]

The judgment must be reversed and a new trial ordered. The prisoner must be remanded to the custody of the sheriff of Cass county, and must be allowed bail if he desires it, in a moderate amount.

The other Justices concurred.

---

[1]. Hathaway v. State, 32 Fla. 56, 13 So. 592 (1893); Williams v. State, 70 Ga. App. 10, 27 S.E.2d 109 (1943); State v. Minella, 177 Iowa 283, 158 N.W. 645 (1916); Carroll v. Commonwealth, 83 S.W. 552, 26 Ky.Law Rep. 1083 (1904); Pond v. People, 8 Mich. 150 (1860); Staten v. State, 30 Miss. 619 (1856); State v. Harrod, 102 Mo. 590, 15 S.W. 373 (1891). And see Reeves v. State, 153 Tex.Cr.R. 32, 217 S.W. 2d 19 (1949).

One is privileged to go to the defense of his brother if this reasonably seems to be necessary to save the brother from death or great bodily injury. And in doing so he is not charged with knowledge of the fact that the brother had no privilege to defend himself unless he knew or should have known that his brother was the aggressor. Snell v. State, 29 Tex.App. 236, 15 S.W. 722 (1890).

[1]. One may kill if necessary to save his brother's life even if the latter started the difficulty unless he did so with felonious intent. Little v. State, 87 Miss. 512, 40 So. 165 (1906).

MODEL PENAL CODE

Section 3.05. Use of Force for the Protection of Other Persons.

(1) Subject to the provisions of this Section and of Section 3.09, the use of force upon or toward the person of another is justifiable to protect a third person when:

(a) the actor would be justified under Section 3.04 in using such force to protect himself against the injury he believes to be threatened to the person whom he seeks to protect; and

(b) under the circumstances as the actor believes them to be, the person whom he seeks to protect would be justified in using such protective force; and

(c) the actor believes that his intervention is necessary for the protection of such other person.

(2) Notwithstanding Subsection (1) of this Section:

(a) when the actor would be obliged under Section 3.04 to retreat, to surrender the possession of a thing or to comply with a demand before using force in self-protection, he is not obliged to do so before using force for the protection of another person, unless he knows that he can thereby secure the complete safety of such other person; and

(b) when the person whom the actor seeks to protect would be obliged under Section 3.04 to retreat, to surrender the possession of a thing or to comply with a demand if he knew that he could obtain complete safety by so doing, the actor is obliged to try to cause him to do so before using force in his protection if the actor knows that he can obtain complete safety in that way; and

(c) neither the actor nor the person whom he seeks to protect is obliged to retreat when in the other's dwelling or place of work to any greater extent than in his own.

SECTION 6. DEFENSE OF PROPERTY

Criminal cases, in which defense of property has been relied upon as an exculpating circumstance, have seldom been entirely divorced from some other privilege, such as self-defense or crime prevention.[1] And the fact that the exercise of such other privilege may result incidentally in the protection of property, does not in any way narrow its scope. Hence property protection is usually overshadowed by self-defense, crime prevention or even the privilege of arrest. In fact, the chief importance of the privilege of protecting property is

---

1. For example, State v. Pollard, 139 Mo. 220, 40 S.W. 949 (1897).

Sec. 6   DEFENSE OF PROPERTY   629

frequently that its exercise does not make one an "aggressor", or in any way at fault, and hence leaves all other privileges unimpaired.[2]

One is privileged to use nondeadly force when this reasonably appears to be necessary to protect his property, real or personal, from unprivileged interference by another,—provided he does not employ more force than reasonably appears to be necessary for the purpose.[3] This privilege does not include the use of deadly force, at least if the habitation is not involved, even if the trespass cannot be prevented otherwise.[4] Bishop says, "it may now be deemed reasonably clear that, to prevent an unlawful entrance into a dwelling-house, the occupant may make defence to the taking of life, without being liable even for manslaughter."[5] But this seems not to be the accepted view

2. Ayers v. State, 60 Miss. 709 (1883).

3. Restatement, Second, Torts § 77 (1965). No force is privileged if a mere request would obviously be sufficient. Ibid.

"A man may use force to defend his real or personal property in his actual possession against one who endeavors to dispossess him without right, taking care that the force used does not exceed what reasonably appears to be necessary for the purpose of defense and prevention." Carpenter v. State, 62 Ark. 286, 310, 36 S.W. 900, 907 (1896). And see Turpen v. State, 89 Okl.Cr. 6, 204 P.2d 298 (1949).

If the reasonable use of nondeadly force unexpectedly results in accidental death, it does not constitute criminal homicide. Morgan v. Durfee, 69 Mo. 469 (1897); Hinchcliffe's Case, 1 Lewin 161, 168 Eng.Rep. 998 (1823).

It was held unreasonable to beat an old man with a cane merely because he was picking a few flowers. Chapell v. Schmidt, 104 Cal. 511, 58 P. 892 (1894).

The owner may use reasonable force to eject a trespasser from his home, after notice to withdraw is ignored. Phelps v. Arnold, 112 Cal.App. 518, 297 P. 31 (1931).

A kick is not a justifiable mode of putting a mere trespasser out of the house and death resulting from such unreasonable force is criminal homicide. Wild's Case, 2 Lewin 214, 168 Eng.Rep. 1132 (1837), and see Fortune v. Commonwealth, 133 Va. 669, 112 S.E. 861 (1922).

There is no justification for an assault in revenge for the breaking of a mirror, after the harm has been done.

State v. Allen, 131 W.Va. 667, 49 S.E. 2d 847 (1948).

4. Turpin v. State, 89 Okl.Cr. 6, 204 P.2d 298 (1949); State v. Patterson, 45 Vt. 308 (1873).

"But, in the absence of an attempt to commit a felony, he cannot defend his property, except his habitation, to the extent of killing the aggressor for the purpose of preventing the trespass; and if he should do so, he would be guilty of a felonious homicide." Carpenter v. State, 62 Ark. 286, 310, 36 S.W. 900, 907 (1896).

"Life being superior to property, no one has the right to kill in defence of the latter; yet by less extreme means, one may defend his own." 2 Bishop, Criminal Law § 706 (9th ed. 1923).

The defendant drew a knife which he threatened to use (but did not use) in defense of his property. A conviction of assault was reversed on the ground that a *threat* to use a weapon may be privileged when its actual use would not be. State v. Yancey, 74 N.C. 244 (1876).

The court said, *obiter*, that death resulting from the accidental discharge of a gun used only as a bluff, would not necessarily be criminal. People v. Hubbard, 64 Cal.App. 27, 220 P. 315 (1923).

5. 2 Bishop, Criminal Law § 707 (9th ed. 1923).

In speaking of the conduct of the prosecuting witness the court said: "It was his house and he had a right to protect it against any peace-disturbing, profane intruder, even if necessary to the taking of his life." State v. Raper, 141 Mo. 327, 329, 42 S.W. 935, 936

where the defender has no reason to fear that the trespasser intends to commit a felony or to inflict personal harm upon him or some other person in the house.[6] Clearly, if the defender reasonably believes that the intruder intends to kill him, or to inflict great bodily harm upon him, or upon anyone else in the house, he may make his defense at the threshold.[7] He is not bound to stay the use of deadly force until the other has gained the advantage of an entrance. But the accepted view does not permit the use of deadly force merely to prevent a relatively unimportant trespass, even if it takes the form of an entrance of the dwelling. The difference between this and Bishop's view is not so wide as might seem at first glance. When an intruder insists upon an unlawful entrance into the building with such violence that only deadly force can stop him, the defender will usually have good reason to fear for his safety or the safety of others. And no more than this is needed for his privilege to use deadly force. But he might know the facts to be otherwise. A householder who is on the outside, for example, and too far away at the moment to make use of nondeadly force would not be privileged to shoot to prevent the entrance of one he knew did not intend to commit a felony or to inflict personal harm.[8]

Deadly force is privileged, if apparently necessary, not only to prevent a felonious intrusion of the dwelling house, but also to pre-

(1897). The knife had actually been drawn but not used except as a bluff.

In affirming a conviction of murder for the shooting of a trespasser who refused to leave the house, the court said *obiter* that one may prevent an aggressor from entering his home when the door is closed, even to the extent of killing him. Russell v. State, 219 Ala. 567, 122 So. 683 (1929).

6. Carroll v. State, 23 Ala. 28 (1853); Miller v. Commonwealth, 188 Ky. 435, 222 S.W. 96 (1920); State v. Taylor, 143 Mo. 150, 44 S.W. 785 (1898); State v. Patterson, 45 Vt. 308 (1873).

"One is no more privileged to use such force to prevent another from intruding upon his dwelling place than he is to use similar force to prevent the other from intruding upon his possession of any other land. In either case, he may use such force if the intrusion threatens death or serious bodily harm to the occupiers or users of the land." Restatement, Second, Torts § 79, Comment *d* (1965).

"The broad rule invoked that one is justified in killing to prevent entrance of his residence against his protest is approved in this State in accordance with the weight of authority, subject to the qualification that the entrance is either with a felonious purpose to do bodily harm, or under circumstances justifying a reasonable apprehension of such purpose." Wooten v. State, 171 Tenn. 362, 365, 103 S.W.2d 324, 325 (1937).

"He can kill intentionally only in defense of life or person, or to prevent a felony." People v. Hubbard, 64 Cal. App. 27, 35, 220 P. 315, 319 (1923).

7. Bailey v. People, 54 Colo. 337, 130 P. 832 (1913); Cooper's Case, Cro.Car. 554, 79 Eng.Rep. 1069 (K.B. 1639).

8. "A comes to B's premises during a severe storm and asks permission to take shelter in B's dwelling house. B refuses to permit him to do so, although he knows that A neither intends nor is likely to harm any person or thing in the house. A, a much larger man than B, attempts to overcome B's resistance by physical force which B is unable to resist except by shooting A. B is not privileged to do so to prevent A from entering his dwelling place." Restatement, Second, Torts § 79, Illustration 1 (1965).

vent a felonious attack upon the house itself, such as an attempt to commit arson or malicious mischief.[9] But in all such cases the privilege is rather that of crime prevention than property protection.[10]

COMMONWEALTH v. DONAHUE

Supreme Judicial Court of Massachusetts, 1889.
148 Mass. 529, 20 N.E. 171.

HOLMES, J. This is an indictment for robbery, on which the defendant has been found guilty of an assault. The evidence for the Commonwealth was, that the defendant had bought clothes, amounting to twenty-one dollars and fifty-five cents, of one Mitchelman, who called at the defendant's house, by appointment, for his pay; that some discussion arose about the bill, and that the defendant went upstairs, brought down the clothes, placed them on a chair, and put twenty dollars on a table, and told Mitchelman that he could have the money or the clothes; that Mitchelman took the money and put it in his pocket, and told the defendant he owed him one dollar and fifty-five cents, whereupon the defendant demanded his money back, and, on Mitchelman refusing, attacked him, threw him on the floor, and choked him until Mitchelman gave him a pocket-book containing twenty-nine dollars. The defendant's counsel denied the receiving of the pocket-book, and said that he could show that the assault was justifiable, under the circumstances of the case, as the defendant believed that he had a right to recover his own money by force, if necessary. The presiding justice stated that he should be obliged to rule, that the defendant would not be justified in assaulting Mitchelman to get his own money, and that he should rule as follows: "If the jury are satisfied that the defendant choked and otherwise assaulted Mitchelman, they would be warranted in finding the defendant guilty, although the sole motive of the defendant was by this violence to get from Mitchelman by force money which the defendant honestly believed to be his own." Upon this the defendant saved his exceptions, and declined to introduce evidence; the jury were instructed as stated, and found the defendant guilty.

On the evidence for the Commonwealth, it appeared, or at the lowest the jury might have found, that the defendant offered the twenty dollars to Mitchelman only on condition that Mitchelman should accept that sum as full payment of his disputed bill, and that Mitchelman took the money, and at the same moment, or just afterwards, as part of the same transaction, repudiated the condition. If this was the case,—since Mitchelman, of course, whatever the sum due him, had no right to that particular money except on the conditions on which it was offered, Commonwealth v. Stebbins, 8 Gray 492,

---

9. State v. Couch, 52 N.M. 127, 193 P.2d 405 (1948).

10. Restatement, Second, Torts § 79, Comment c (1965).

—he took the money wrongfully from the possession of the defendant, or the jury might have found that he did, whether the true view be that the defendant did not give up possession, or that it was obtained from him by Mitchelman's fraud. . . .

It is settled by ancient and modern authority, that, under such circumstances, a man may defend or regain his momentarily interrupted possession by the use of reasonable force, short of wounding or the employment of a dangerous weapon. . . . To this extent the right to protect one's possession has been regarded as an extension of the right to protect one's person, with which it is generally mentioned. . . .

We need not consider whether this explanation is quite adequate. There are weighty decisions which go further than those above cited, and which hardly can stand on the right of self-defence, but involve other considerations of policy. It has been held, that, even where a considerable time had elapsed between the wrongful taking of the defendant's property and the assault, the defendant had a right to regain possession by reasonable force, after demand upon the third person in possession, in like manner as he might have protected it without civil liability. Whatever the true rule may be, probably there is no difference in this respect between the civil and the criminal law. The principle has been extended to a case where the defendant had yielded possession to the person assaulted, through the fraud of the latter. On the other hand, a distinction has been taken between the right to maintain possession and the right to regain it from another who is peaceably established in it, although the possession of the latter is wrongful. It is unnecessary to decide whether, in this case, if Mitchelman had taken the money with a fraudulent intent, but had not repudiated the condition until afterwards, the defendant would have had any other remedy than to hold him to his bargain if he could, even if he knew that Mitchelman still had the identical money upon his person.

If the force used by the defendant was excessive, the jury would have been warranted in finding him guilty. Whether it was excessive or not was a question for them; the judge could not rule that it was not, as matter of law. Therefore the instruction given to them, taken only literally, was correct. But the preliminary statement went further, and was erroneous; and coupling that statement with the defendant's offer of proof, and his course after the rulings, we think it fair to assume that the instruction was not understood to be limited, or, indeed, to be directed to the case of excessive force, which, so far as appears, had not been mentioned, but that it was intended and understood to mean that any assault to regain his own money would warrant finding the defendant guilty. Therefore the exceptions must be sustained.

It will be seen that our decision is irrespective of the defendant's belief as to what he had a right to do. If the charge of robbery had been persisted in, and the difficulties which we have stated could have been got over, we might have had to consider cases like Regina v. Boden, 1 C. & K. 395, 397; Regina v. Hemmings, 4 F. & F. 50; State v. Hollyway, 41 Iowa 200. There is no question here of the effect of a reasonable but mistaken belief with regard to the facts. The facts were as defendant believed them to be.

Exceptions sustained.[1]

STATE v. BECKHAM

Supreme Court of Missouri, Division Two, 1924.
306 Mo. 566, 267 S.W. 817.

RAILEY, C. . . . I. It is claimed by appellant that his demurrer to the evidence at the conclusion of the case should have been sustained. In passing upon this question, we have deemed it advisable to state in brief form the outstanding facts in the case.

Appellant was engaged in operating a chilli stand in Joplin, Missouri, where soft drinks were kept and lunches furnished to customers. When not engaged in the above business, he sometimes performed the services of a minister of the Gospel. He conducted his chilli business in a small room, but he and his wife lived elsewhere. No human being occupied this room at night. At the time of the killing, the above building contained a few bottles of soda pop and a little personal property, the total value of which did not exceed six dollars. According to defendant's testimony, his chilli stand had been robbed on several occasions. He was in possession of his son's gun and concluded to erect a spring, or trap-gun, in the north part of his building, where a window was located, to guard his property from the approach of robbers. This window had hinges at the top and, when left free and unfastened at the bottom, could be moved out for some distance. Appellant arranged the spring gun so that it would point to some part of this north window, and was so constructed that, when the lower part of the window was moved out from the bottom, it would cause the gun to explode and discharge its load through some part of the window. Appellant testified that he placed the gun so that its load, when discharged, would pass through the upper corner of the window, and that he had no intention of killing or injuring any one, but that he resorted to this plan in order to scare prospective robbers and keep them away. He said the gun become misplaced or slipped from its

---

1. "Force may be used by the owner to retake property from a person who has obtained possession of it by force or fraud and is overtaken while carrying it away." Riffel v. Letts, 31 Cal. App. 426, 428, 160 P. 845, 846 (1916).

The recaption must be by action promptly taken after dispossession or after timely discovery thereof. It must be only after a request for the chattel has been made and ignored, unless such request reasonably seems to be useless or hazardous. The force used must be nondeadly, and must not exceed what reasonably seems necessary for the purpose. Restatement, Second, Torts §§ 103, 104, 106 (1965).

position, in some manner, and that, by reason thereof, the load went through a pane of said window and killed deceased on the outside, instead of the load being discharged through the upper part of the window as he intended, and which would not have injured deceased. Appellant said he had been placing this gun at the above place for some time prior to the killing. He had closed his place of business, and had gone home with his wife the night of the homicide. He recognized deceased, after the homicide, as one of several boys who were in his chilli stand the day before the shooting, and paid for a lunch at that time. He said the lower part of the window was nailed securely when he went home that night.

W. F. Gibson, chief of detectives in said city, testified that when he got to the scene of the killing, between eight and nine o'clock in the morning, the gun was still in position, and that the hook used to fasten the window was not fastened and it came open.

On the morning of May 10, 1923, Aubry Windsor, a youth seventeen years of age, was found dead on the outside of defendant's building, and near said window. It was found on examination, that the shot from the gun placed there by defendant had passed through one of the window panes and struck deceased in the face. The father of deceased testified that the latter had gone through the high school at Lincoln City, Nebraska, and had started to the Nebraska University. He said deceased left home on April 17, 1923. There is nothing in the record tending to show that deceased was armed, when killed, with a gun, burglers' [sic] tools or even a pocket knife. It does not appear that he had a criminal record, nor that his reputation for honesty had ever been questioned. It is conceded by defendant that deceased was in the chilli stand the day before the homicide, eating a lunch and, hence, had an opportunity for observing that only five or six dollars' worth of property was in the building.

In the light of the foregoing facts, the appellant insists that he was justified in killing deceased with the spring gun under the circumstances aforesaid. The discussion of this subject has not been directly considered by this court, although it has assumed a wide range in other jurisdictions. Upon a careful consideration of the question we have reached the conclusion that when defendant placed this silent instrumentality of death in his building as heretofore detailed, he acted at his peril, and could not, on a demurrer to the evidence, successfully rely upon a plea of justification, unless it could be said as a matter of law, that if he had been personally present and killed deceased with said gun under the circumstances aforesaid he would have been justified in so doing. If defendant had been personally present and killed deceased under the circumstances aforesaid, in order to sustain his plea of justification he would have been compelled to satisfy the jury that he had used no more force than was reasonably necessary in repelling the assault of deceased in attempting to enter his premises to commit the crime of burglary, if such was his intention.

Sec. 6 DEFENSE OF PROPERTY 635

If the defendant had been personally in charge of the gun which killed deceased, and the latter was attempting to enter defendant's building to commit any kind of a crime, he would have been guilty of burglary in the second degree. Under such circumstances, the defendant would have had the legal right to arrest deceased for the commission of a felony, and the jury, in passing upon the plea of justification, might conclude that it was not reasonably necessary for appellant to kill deceased. Again, if defendant had been personally present, and had killed deceased with said gun, under the foregoing circumstances, the jury, in passing upon the plea of justification, might have concluded that there was no reasonable necessity for killing deceased until the latter had, at least, entered the building. We cannot say, as a matter of law, that defendant was justified in killing deceased with a spring gun in this case and, hence, the court committed no error in overruling the demurrer to the evidence. . . .

(a) If defendant had been personally present handling the gun which killed deceased, under the law of this State it would be a question for a jury as to whether, in killing deceased, he used more force than was reasonably necessary under the circumstances aforesaid. It is manifest that a mechanical death-trap like the one used in this case, would hardly be expected to refrain from using more force than was reasonably necessary in repelling the assault of a person trying to enter the building. On the contrary, it would kill all alike in its wake and, hence, its legitimate use could not be sustained, unless facts are conceded which would warrant the court in declaring as a matter of law that defendant was justified in killing deceased under the circumstances of the case.

On the record before us, the demurrer to the evidence was properly overruled. . . .

Appellant strenuously insists in his belief that we should declare, as a matter of law, that he was justified in killing deceased with the spring gun as shown by the testimony. We have disposed of this issue in the former paragraphs of the opinion. He contended, however, at the trial, that he placed the gun there for a scare if anybody started to break in, with no intention of hurting anybody. He testified further that he placed the gun so it did not point toward the window, but it pointed "up towards the top and to the right of the window." He said the gun "slipped from its position and fell to one side." Giving to defendant the full benefit of his testimony, the court properly submitted to the jury by Instruction Three supra, the question as to whether appellant was guilty of culpable negligence in so placing this manstrap [sic], that it slipped from the position in which he placed it, and killed a seventeen-year-old boy on the outside, when he had no intention of killing or injuring any one.

IV. It is evident, from the penalty inflicted in this case, that the jury accepted defendant's theory of the killing, to the effect that he did not intend to kill or injure any one; and that he attempted to place the loaded gun, so that the explosion of same would cause the shot to pass out at the top of the window and scare the intruder away, without inflicting any personal injury on him. In view of defendant's testimony in respect to this matter, the jury were justified in finding him guilty of manslaughter, on account of his placing so dangerous an agency as a loaded gun, where it would kill a human being in so careless and negligent a manner as that disclosed in this case. If he used the gun as above indicated, it was his duty in placing the same to exercise such care and caution as an ordinarily careful or prudent man would do under like circumstances. The very fact that the gun slipped of its own motion clearly indicated that it had been carelessly and negligently placed. On the undisputed facts the jury were authorized to convict defendant of criminal negligence, in a case where human life was at stake. Instruction Three properly advised the jury as to the law which should apply in passing upon the above issue.

It is unfortunate that a minister of the Gospel should have been so careless as to cause the death of this boy by negligently placing a death-trap to protect five or six dollars' worth of personal property, if he did not intend to kill or injure any one.

We are of the opinion that defendant had a fair and impartial trial; that he was properly convicted of culpable negligence on his own showing, and should suffer the consequences accordingly.

The judgment below was for the right party and is accordingly affirmed. HIGBEE, C., concurs.

PER CURIAM: The foregoing opinion of RAILEY, C., is adopted as the opinion of the court. All of the judges concur, except WALKER, J., absent.[1]

---

1. Defendant set a spring gun in an unoccupied building with the intent to kill anyone who should force an entrance. This was done to protect his furniture. Two brothers went to this building and one of them gained an entrance, merely to satisfy his curiosity, by breaking the lock. He was killed by the spring gun as he entered. A conviction of manslaughter was affirmed. State v. Green, 118 S.C. 279, 110 S.E. 145 (1921).

Defendant set a spring gun in his store to protect it against burglary. He failed to notify the police department of this precaution and a policeman was killed by the gun while he was testing the fastening of the door. A conviction of second degree murder was set aside for other reasons. But the court held that a conviction of either murder in the second degree or manslaughter would be affirmed if reached in a trial free from error. Pierce v. Commonwealth, 135 Va. 635, 115 S.E. 686 (1923).

The privilege to use deadly force by means of a spring gun, to protect property, is measured by the extent of the privilege the owner would have to use deadly force for this purpose, in person, if he were present. Restatement, Second, Torts, § 85 (1965).

A spring gun placed in a trunk in such a manner as to kill anyone who opened it, caused the death of a maid who looked in just as a matter of curiosity. A conviction of murder was reversed because the judge had approved the view of the prosecuting attorney that killing by means of a spring gun is privileged only to prevent the commission of a capital crime. State v. Marfaudille, 48 Wash. 117, 92 P. 939 (1907).

MODEL PENAL CODE

Section 3.06. Use of Force for the Protection of Property.

(1) Use of Force Justifiable for Protection of Property. Subject to the provisions of this Section and of Section 3.09, the use of force upon or toward the person of another is justifiable when the actor believes that such force is immediately necessary:

    (a) to prevent or terminate an unlawful entry or other trespass upon land or a trespass against or the unlawful carrying away of tangible, movable property, provided that such land or movable property is, or is believed by the actor to be, in his possession or in the possession of another person for whose protection he acts; or

    (b) to effect an entry or re-entry upon land or to retake tangible movable property, provided that the actor believes that he or the person by whose authority he acts or a person from whom he or such other person derives title was unlawfully dispossessed of such land or movable property and is entitled to possession, and provided, further, that:

        (i) the force is used immediately or on fresh pursuit after such dispossession; or

        (ii) the actor believes that the person against whom he uses force has no claim of right to the possession of the property and, in the case of land, the circumstances, as the actor believes them to be, are of such urgency that it would be an exceptional hardship to postpone the entry or re-entry until a court order is obtained.

(2) Meaning of Possession. . . .

(3) Limitations on Justifiable Use of Force.

    (a) Request to Desist. The use of force is justifiable under this Section only if the actor first requests the person against whom such force is used to desist from his interference with the property, unless the actor believes that:

        (i) such request would be useless; or

In refusing to convict defendant of a nuisance for guarding his shop with a spring gun, the court pointed out that breaking and entering the shop in the night with intent to steal would be burglary under the statute and the taking of life to prevent burglary would be justified. State v. Moore, 31 Conn. 479 (1863).

The setting of spring guns in open fields or outhouses, not within the curtilage of the dwelling house, without notice, will not justify or excuse resulting homicide. United States v. Gilliam, 25 Fed.Cas.1319, No. 15,205a (1882).

A trespasser in a vineyard, who was injured by a spring gun, was entitled to damages. Hooker v. Miller, 37 Iowa 613 (1873).

If one sets a deadly spring gun on open land and thereby kills a trespasser it is criminal homicide. But a device set merely to alarm a trespasser or to inflict slight chastisement is privileged. Simpson v. State, 59 Ala. 1 (1877).

A statute provided that whoever set a spring gun for the purpose of killing game "or for any other purpose" should be guilty of manslaughter in the second degree if it caused the death of any human being. Defendant set a spring gun in his orchard to prevent persons from stealing his apples. A trespasser, who pulled the wire just out of curiosity, was killed. The court affirmed a conviction of second degree murder. Schmidt v. State, 159 Wis. 15, 149 N.W. 388 (1914).

(ii) it would be dangerous to himself or another person to make the request; or

(iii) substantial harm will be done to the physical condition of the property which is sought to be protected before the request can effectively be made.

(b) *Exclusion of Trespasser.* The use of force to prevent or terminate a trespass is not justifiable under this Section if the actor knows that the exclusion of the trespasser will expose him to substantial danger of serious bodily harm.

(c) *Resistance of Lawful Re-entry or Recaption.* . . .

(d) *Use of Deadly Force.* The use of deadly force is not justifiable under this Section unless the actor believes that:

(i) the person against whom the force is used is attempting to dispossess him of his dwelling otherwise than under a claim of right to its possession; or

(ii) the person against whom the force is used is attempting to commit or consummate arson, burglary, robbery or other felonious theft or property destruction and either:

(1) has employed or threatened deadly force against or in the presence of the actor; or

(2) the use of force other than deadly force to prevent the commission or the consummation of the crime would expose the actor or another in his presence to substantial danger of serious bodily harm.

(4) *Use of Confinement as Protective Force.* . . .

(5) *Use of Device to Protect Property.* The justification afforded by this Section extends to the use of a device for the purpose of protecting property only if:

(a) the device is not designed to cause or known to create a substantial risk of causing death or serious bodily harm; and

(b) the use of the particular device to protect the property from entry or trespass is reasonable under the circumstances, as the actor believes them to be; and

(c) the device is one customarily used for such a purpose or reasonable care is taken to make known to probable intruders the fact that it is used.

(6) *Use of Force to Pass Wrongful Obstructor.* . . .

SECTION 7. ENTRAPMENT

Officers have sometimes gone too far in their zeal to secure convictions,—so far, in fact, as to defeat their own purpose. The most obvious cases are those in which the plot to trap an offender has been laid in such a manner as to leave out some element essential to

Sec. 7 ENTRAPMENT 639

guilt. In one case, for example, officers planned to catch the person who had been aiding prisoners of war to escape. A prisoner, who was willing to cooperate with the officers, was directed what to do. The defendant took this prisoner, in her vehicle, beyond the ordinary prison limits to a point where she was arrested under the prearranged plan. A conviction of aiding a prisoner of war to escape was held to be improper because there had been no escape,—since the prisoner had gone only where he was directed to go by those in charge.[1] Furthermore a detective who seemingly joins a criminal venture, not to promote its success but to secure evidence of the crime, is not a real conspirator and his acts cannot be imputed to the others.[2] And if such a detective himself unlocks and opens the door through which the others enter there can be no conviction of common-law burglary. Since his intent was to frustrate the crime, he is not guilty. And since he is not guilty, his opening of the door cannot be imputed to the others and hence an essential element of common-law burglary is lacking.[3] Or if a detective placed an obstruction on a railroad track, with authority from the company and with the intent to remove it before any harm was done, which he did, another could not properly be convicted on the theory that he was present aiding and abetting the commission of a crime.[4]

More difficult are those cases in which every element of the offense is present but it is claimed that there should be no conviction because of "entrapment" by a public officer. Providing an opportunity for those criminally inclined to perpetrate an offense in the presence of an officer will not bar conviction. It is no defense to an indictment for larceny, for example, that the money was stolen from a constable who feigned drunkenness with the intention of making an arrest if his money should be taken.[5]

The distinction is between detection and instigation. Traps may be laid or "decoys" employed to secure the conviction of those who intend to commit crime; but the zeal for enforcement must not induce officers to implant criminal ideas in innocent minds.[6] And for

1. Rex v. Martin, Russ. and R.C.C. 196, 168 Eng.Rep. 757 (1811).

2. State v. Neely, 90 Mont. 199, 300 P. 561 (1931).

"The defendant is not to be charged with what was done by the detective, as the two were not acting together for a common purpose." State v. Currie, 13 N.D. 655, 661, 102 N.W. 875, 877 (1905).

3. Love v. People, 160 Ill. 501, 43 N.E. 710 (1896).

An even clearer case was the one where the "burglar" waited on the outside while a supposed accomplice, acting under directions of the sheriff, opened the door, went in, took some money, marked it so it could be identified, and then went out and delivered it. People v. Collins, 53 Cal. 185 (1878).

4. State v. Douglass, 44 Kan. 618, 26 P. 476 (1890).

5. People v. Hanselman, 76 Cal. 460, 18 P. 425 (1888).

6. "Decoys are permissible to entrap criminals, but not to create them; . . ." United States v. Healy, 202 F. 349 (D.C.Mont.1913).

some reason the word "entrapment," which might well refer to the former situation, has come to be applied only to the second.[7] A conviction of conspiracy to rob will be reversed if the idea originated in the minds of officers who suggested the plan to the "conspirators" in order to secure the conviction.[8] But if the plan to break into a building originated in the mind of the burglar, the fact that a detective pretended to agree to help him, and went along in order to have evidence of the crime, will not bar a conviction.[9]

The mere fact that officers have led the defendant to furnish a specific instance of an habitual course of criminal conduct is not a defense.[10] Thus one may be convicted of using the United States mails to give information telling where obscene matter can be obtained, although his letter was in response to a request written by a post office inspector under a fictitious name.[11] And evidence of liquor purchased by officers may be used to convict the seller of a violation of the prohibition law.[12]

Instigation will bar conviction even in cases involving such offenses. In the Sorrells case [13] M, a prohibition agent, went to S's house to purchase liquor, posing as a tourist. His first request was without success. But learning that both had served in the same Division in World War I, M engaged S in extended reminiscences of their war experiences. And after at least two rejections of his proposal he pleaded with S for a third time for aid to a thirsty tourist. Then S

---

7. "Entrapment is the conception and planning of an offense by an officer and his procurement of its commission by one who would not have perpetrated it except for the trickery, persuasion, or fraud of the officer." People v. Lindsey, 91 Cal.App.2d 914, 916, 205 P.2d 1114, 1115 (1949). "The law does not frown upon the entrapment of a criminal but will not tolerate the seduction of innocent people into a career of crime by its officers." People v. Crawford, 105 Cal.App.2d 530, 536, 537, 234 P.2d 181, 185 (1951).

8. Connor v. People, 18 Colo. 373, 33 P. 159 (1893).

A conviction was reversed because of evidence that an immigration officer had suggested to defendant a plan to bring Chinese over the border illegally. Woo Wai v. United States, 223 F. 412, 137 C.C.A. 604 (9th Cir. 1915).

The Iowa court refused to reverse a conviction of burglary, although the plan had been suggested to defendant by a constable. But the court expressed disapproval of the practice and reduced the sentence from three years to six months. State v. Abley, 109 Iowa 61, 80 N.W. 225 (1899).

9. State v. Currie, 13 N.D. 655, 102 N.W. 875 (1905).

Compare Saunders v. People, 18 Mich. 218 (1878). In this case a policeman complied with defendant's request to leave a door to the courthouse unlocked so the defendant could remove public records. The officer had communicated the request to his superiors and had been directed to comply. This practice was denounced by the court, and two of the judges apparently would have been willing to reverse the conviction on this ground alone.

10. People v. Lindsey, 91 Cal.App.2d 914, 205 P.2d 1114 (1949).

11. Grimm v. United States, 156 U.S. 604, 15 S.Ct. 470, 39 L.Ed. 550 (1895).

12. Moss v. State, 4 Okl.Cr. 247, 111 P. 950 (1910).

13. Sorrells v. United States, 287 U.S. 435, 53 S.Ct. 210, 77 L.Ed. 413 (1932).

left the house, procured a half gallon of liquor and sold it to M for five dollars. There was no evidence of any prior violation by S, and his conviction was reversed by the Supreme Court. The majority seemed to ground the decision upon the theory that an offense induced by entrapment was beyond the scope of the statute. Mr. Justice Roberts took the view that the crime had been committed but that the conduct of the officer operated as an estoppel against the government. Mr. Justice Brandeis and Mr. Justice Stone concurred in this opinion. And the District Court had held that the use of a federal agent who was an Indian, but did not have the appearance of being one, to entrap defendant into the offense of selling intoxicating liquor to an Indian, "estops the government from a conviction." [14]

SCOTT v. COMMONWEALTH

Court of Appeals of Kentucky, 1946.
303 Ky. 353, 197 S.W. 774.

LATIMER, JUDGE. Darwin Scott and two companions were tried and convicted in the Catlettsburg Police Court on a warrant charging them with the unlawful possession of intoxicating beverages for purpose of sale in local option territory. They appealed to the Boyd Circuit Court. Upon their trial in the Boyd Circuit Court, the two co-defendants were acquitted but Scott was convicted and his punishment fixed at a fine of $100 and a confinement in jail for 30 days. From that judgment he files a motion in this court for the granting of an appeal.

Prior to the warrant and conviction in police court, the Chief of Police of Catlettsburg had searched the premises of Scott without a search warrant and had seized and taken possession of a considerable quantity of liquor. Scott was not put upon trial at that time and the Chief of Police was instructed by the City Attorney that the search was illegal, and that the property seized should be returned to Scott. Acting under these instructions, the Chief of Police took the liquor

---

14. United States v. Healy, 202 F. 349 (D.C.Mont.1913). The court said that ignorance of the essential fact would not be an excuse ordinarily, as far as this statutory offense is concerned, but that there should be no conviction of an offense procured by this stratagem. "These concerns flow from the doctrine of estoppel, . . ." United States ex rel. Hall v. Illinois, 329 F.2d 354, 358–59 (7th Cir. 1964).

Conviction in any such case would be "contrary to public policy." People v. Crawford, 105 Cal.App.2d 530, 536, 234 P.2d 181, 185 (1951). It has been suggested that whenever the officer solicits the act (sale of heroin in this case) there is almost always a question of entrapment for the jury to consider. United States v. Moses, 220 F.2d 166 (3d Cir. 1955). On the other hand, one court has held that it is an affirmative defense and defendant has the burden of showing that he was induced to commit the offense. People v. Terry, 44 Cal.2d 371, 282 P.2d 19 (1955).

Entrapment is not established if the evidence shows that the intent to commit the crime originated in the mind of the defendant. People v. Nunn, 46 Cal.2d 460, 296 P.2d 813 (1956).

back to Scott's house on February 8, 1946, and delivered it to him in the street, at which time Scott and a colored man working for him took possession of it, part of it being carried into the house by the colored man and a portion of it being taken into the house by Scott himself about one-half hour later that day. Shortly after delivering the liquor to Scott the Chief of Police obtained a search warrant apparently basing the affidavit upon what had occurred with respect to the redelivery of the liquor. Pursuant to the search warrant the premises were then searched and the liquor again taken into possession. Scott was tried for possessing the liquor illegally for the purpose of sale and convicted as above stated.

Appellant contends that his motion should be sustained and that the judgment of the lower court should be reversed for the following reasons: First, the trial court should have quashed the search warrant because the affidavit for the search warrant is insufficient on its face, and second, that the act of the Chief of Police in returning the liquor to Scott and subsequently searching the house for the same liquor constitutes entrapment and should not be upheld.

In view of the fact that the judgment must be reversed for the reason set out below, it will be unnecessary to discuss the sufficiency or insufficiency of the affidavit for the search warrant.

The claim that the act of the Chief of Police constituted entrapment presents the serious question herein. It seems to be the general rule, and the courts are agreed, that the criminality of the act depends on whether the criminal intent originated in the mind of the accused or originated in the mind of the entrapping person. Where it originates in the mind of the accused, the fact that the opportunity is furnished constitutes no defense. The real test seems to be that he must participate in all the acts necessary to constitute the crime, and unless he does, he should not be convicted. See Annotated Cases, 18 A.L.R. 146. This liquor had been previously taken illegally, that is, without search warrant. In order for Scott to get it back into his possession there must have been some act upon the part of the officer, no part of which the accused could participate in. To say that the accused and the officer acted together in initiating the act would be making the officer a party to a criminal act and thereby charging him with criminal responsibility. The officer in no way had such thing in mind. It does appear, however, that he did have in mind the obtaining of evidence for the purpose of prosecution, and the evidence he was seeking was the liquor, which he himself, under direction of his superiors, placed in the hands of the accused. This is obvious from the following testimony:

Q. 29. Now, Chief, when you took the whiskey up and delivered it to Mr. Scott, under orders from some of your superiors, for the reason it had been illegally seized in the first place, did you have in mind to get it back to him and then grab him for having it in his possession? A. I was looking for evidence.

"Q. 30. Did you have that in mind? A. I was looking for evidence.

"Q. 31. Will you answer the question? Did you have that in mind? A. I said I was looking for evidence.

"Q. 32. You refuse to answer the question?

"Mr. Burchett: I think we will admit he had it in mind."

We believe such deportment on the part of the officer constitutes an entrapment and such that should relieve the defendant from guilt.

Wherefore, the judgment is reversed.[1]

SHERMAN v. UNITED STATES

Supreme Court of the United States, 1958.
356 U.S. 369, 2 L.Ed. 848, 78 S.Ct. 819.

MR. CHIEF JUSTICE WARREN delivered the opinion of the Court.

The issue before us is whether petitioner's conviction should be set aside on the ground that as a matter of law the defense of entrapment was established. Petitioner was convicted under an indictment charging three sales of narcotics in violation of 21 U.S.C. § 174, 21 U.S.C.A. § 174. A previous conviction had been reversed on account of improper instructions as to the issue of entrapment. 2 Cir., 200 F.2d 880. In the second trial, as in the first, petitioner's defense was a claim of entrapment: An agent of the Federal Government induced him to take part in illegal transactions when otherwise he would not have done so.

In late August 1951, Kalchinian, a government informer, first met petitioner at a doctor's office where apparently both were being treated to be cured of narcotics addiction. Several accidental meetings followed, either at the doctor's office or at the pharmacy where both filled their prescriptions from the doctor. From mere greet-

---

[1]. Even if contraband evidence must be suppressed because obtained by illegal search and seizure it cannot properly be returned to the defendant. United States v. Yee Ngee How, 105 F.Supp. 517 (D.C.Cal.1952).

Money unlawfully seized by police may be subjected to a federal tax lien. The Fourth Amendment does not guarantee that such property will be returned to the owner. Welsh v. United States, 95 U.S.App.D.C. 93, 220 F.2d 200 (1955).

Detectives, pretending to be buyers of skins taken unlawfully, went to boys who had not been trapping beaver and suggested to them that they do so. The detectives were held guilty of a conspiracy to trap beaver. Reigan v. People, 120 Colo. 472, 210 P.2d 991 (1949). A detective sat in a game of poker and made a small bet to secure evidence against habitual gamblers. A conviction of the detective was reversed on the theory that he had no criminal intent. There was a vigorous dissent. State v. Torphy, 78 Mo. App. 206 (1899).

One who sold Jamaica ginger to a decoy, sent by police to get evidence, and who did not drink it or intend to do so, could not properly be convicted of selling it knowing, or with reasonable grounds to know, that it was bought for beverage purposes. Sherman v. United States, 10 F.2d 17 (6th Cir. 1926).

ings, conversation progressed to a discussion of mutual experiences and problems, including their attempts to overcome addiction to narcotics. Finally Kalchinian asked petitioner if he knew a good source of narcotics. He asked petitioner to supply him with a source because he was not responding to treatment. From the first petitioner tried to avoid the issue. Not until after a number of repetitions of the request, predicated on Kalchinian's presumed suffering, did petitioner finally acquiesce. Several times thereafter he obtained a quantity of narcotics which he shared with Kalchinian. Each time petitioner told Kalchinian that the total cost of narcotics he obtained was twenty-five dollars and that Kalchinian owed him fifteen dollars. The informer thus bore the cost of his share of the narcotics plus the taxi and other expenses necessary to obtain the drug. After several such sales Kalchinian informed agents of the Bureau of Narcotics that he had another seller for them. On three occasions during November 1951, government agents observed petitioner give narcotics to Kalchinian in return for money supplied by the Government.

At trial the factual issue was whether the informer had convinced an otherwise unwilling person to commit a criminal act or whether petitioner was already predisposed to commit the act and exhibited only the natural hesitancy of one acquainted with the narcotics trade. The issue of entrapment went to the jury,[1] and a conviction resulted. Petitioner was sentenced to imprisonment for ten years. The Court of Appeals for the Second Circuit affirmed. 240 F.2d 949. We granted certiorari. 353 U.S. 935, 77 S.Ct. 812, 1 L.Ed. 2d 758.

In Sorrells v. United States, 287 U.S. 435, 53 S.Ct. 210, 77 L.Ed. 413, this Court firmly recognized the defense of entrapment in the federal courts. The intervening years have in no way detracted from the principles underlying that decision. The function of law enforcement is the prevention of crimes and the apprehension of criminals. Manifestly, that function does not include the manufacturing of crime. Criminal activity is such that stealth and strategy are necessary weapons in the arsenal of the police officer. However, "a different question is presented when the criminal design originates with the officials of the government, and they implant in the mind of an innocent person the disposition to commit the alleged offense and induce its commission in order that they may prosecute." 287 U.S. at page 442, 53 S.Ct. at page 212. Then stealth and strategy become as objectionable police methods as the coerced confession and the unlawful search. Congress could not have intended that its statutes were to be enforced by tempting innocent persons into violations.

However, the fact that government agents "merely afford opportunities or facilities for the commission of the offense does not" con-

[Footnotes are by the Court.]
1. The charge to the jury was not in issue here.

stitute entrapment. Entrapment occurs only when the criminal conduct was "the product of the *creative* activity" of law-enforcement officials. See 287 U.S. at pages 441, 451, 53 S.Ct. at pages 212, 216. To determine whether entrapment has been established, a line must be drawn between the trap for the unwary innocent and the trap for the unwary criminal. The principles by which the courts are to make this determination were outlined in Sorrells. On the one hand, at trial the accused may examine the conduct of the government agent; and on the other hand, the accused will be subjected to an "appropriate and searching inquiry into his own conduct and predisposition" as bearing on his claim of innocence. See 287 U.S. at page 451, 53 S.Ct. at page 216.

We conclude from the evidence that entrapment was established as a matter of law. In so holding, we are not choosing between conflicting witnesses, nor judging credibility. Aside from recalling Kalchinian, who was the Government's witness, the defense called no witnesses. We reach our conclusion from the undisputed testimony of the prosecution's witnesses.

It is patently clear that petitioner was induced by Kalchinian. The informer himself testified that, believing petitioner to be undergoing a cure for narcotics addiction, he nonetheless sought to persuade petitioner to obtain for him a source of narcotics. In Kalchinian's own words we are told of the accidental, yet recurring meetings, the ensuing conversations concerning mutual experiences in regard to narcotics addiction, and then of Kalchinian's resort to sympathy. One request was not enough, for Kalchinian tells us that additional ones were necessary to overcome, first, petitioner's refusal, then his evasiveness, and then his hesitancy in order to achieve capitulation. Kalchinian not only procured a source of narcotics but apparently also induced petitioner to return to the habit. Finally, assured of a catch, Kalchinian informed the authorities so that they could close the net. The Government cannot disown Kalchinian and insist it is not responsible for his actions. Although he was not being paid, Kalchinian was an active government informer who had but recently been the instigator of at least two other prosecutions.[2] Undoubtedly the impetus for such achievements was the fact that in 1951 Kal-

---

2. "Q. And it was your (Kalchinian's) job, was it not, while you were working with these agents to go out and try and induce somebody to sell you narcotics, isn't that true?
 * * * * *
"A. No, it wasn't my job at all to do anything of the kind.
"Q. Do you remember this question (asked at the first trial)—. . . . 'Q. And it was your job while working with these agents to go out and try and induce a person to sell narcotics to you, isn't that correct? A. I would say yes to that.' Do you remember that?
"A. If that is what I said, let it stand just that way.
 * * * * *
"Q. So when you testify now that it was not your job you are not telling the truth? A. I mean by job that nobody hired me for that. That is what I inferred, otherwise I meant the same thing in my answer to your question." R. 100.

chinian was himself under criminal charges for illegally selling narcotics and had not yet been sentenced.[3] It makes no difference that the sales for which petitioner was convicted occurred after a series of sales. They were not independent acts subsequent to the inducement but part of a course of conduct which was the product of the inducement. In his testimony the federal agent in charge of the case admitted that he never bothered to question Kalchinian about the way he had made contact with petitioner. The Government cannot make such use of an informer and then claim disassociation through ignorance.

The Government sought to overcome the defense of entrapment by claiming that petitioner evinced a "ready complaisance" to accede to Kalchinian's request. Aside from a record of past convictions, which we discuss in the following paragraph, the Government's case is unsupported. There is no evidence that petitioner himself was in the trade. When his apartment was searched after arrest, no narcotics were found. There is no significant evidence that petitioner even made a profit on any sale to Kalchinian.[4] The Government's characterization of petitioner's hesitancy to Kalchinian's request as the natural wariness of the criminal cannot fill the evidentiary void.[5]

The Government's additional evidence in the second trial to show that petitioner was ready and willing to sell narcotics should the opportunity present itself was petitioner's record of two past narcotics convictions. In 1942 petitioner was convicted of illegally selling narcotics; in 1946 he was convicted of illegally possessing them. However, a nine year-old sales conviction and a five-year old possession conviction are insufficient to prove petitioner had a readiness to sell narcotics at the time Kalchinian approached him, particularly when we must assume from the record he was trying to overcome the narcotics habit at the time.

The case at bar illustrates an evil the defense of entrapment is designed to overcome. The government informer entices someone attempting to avoid narcotics not only into carrying out an illegal sale but also into returning to the habit of use. Selecting the proper time,

---

3. "Q. But you had made a promise, an agreement, though, to cooperate with the Federal Bureau of Narcotics before you received a suspended sentence from the court? A. (Kalchinian). I had promised to cooperate in 1951.
"Q. And that was before your sentence? A. Yes, that was before my sentence." R. 99.
Kalchinian received a suspended sentence in 1952 after a statement by the United States Attorney to the Judge that he had been cooperative with the Government. R. 89, 98.

4. At one point Kalchinian did testify that he had previously received the same amount of narcotics at some unspecified lower price. He characterized this other price as "not quite" the price he paid petitioner. R. 80.

5. It is of interest to note that on the first appeal in this case the Court of Appeals came to the same conclusion as we do as to the evidence discussed so far. See United States v. Sherman, 2 Cir., 200 F.2d 880, 883.

the informer then tells the government agent. The set-up is accepted by the agent without even a question as to the manner in which the informer encountered the seller. Thus the Government plays on the weaknesses of an innocent party and beguiles him into committing crimes which he otherwise would not have attempted.[6] Law enforcement does not require methods such as this.

It has been suggested that in overturning this conviction we should reassess the doctrine of entrapment according to principles announced in the separate opinion of Mr. Justice Roberts in Sorrells v. United States, 287 U.S. 435, 453, 53 S.Ct. 210, 217, 77 L.Ed. 413. To do so would be to decide the case on grounds rejected by the majority in Sorrells and, so far as the record shows, not raised here or below by the parties before us. We do not ordinarily decide issues not presented by the parties and there is good reason not to vary that practice in this case.

At least two important issues of law enforcement and trial procedure would have to be decided without the benefit of argument by the parties, one party being the Government. Mr. Justice Roberts asserted that although the defendant could claim that the Government had induced him to commit the crime, the Government could not reply by showing that the defendant's criminal conduct was due to his own readiness and not to the persuasion of government agents. The handicap thus placed on the prosecution is obvious.[7] Furthermore, it was the position of Mr. Justice Roberts that the factual issue of entrapment—now limited to the question of what the government agents did—should be decided by the judge, not the jury. Not only was this rejected by the Court in Sorrells, but where the issue has been presented to them, the Courts of Appeals have since Sorrells unanimously concluded that unless it can be decided as a matter of law, the issue of whether a defendant has been entrapped is for the jury as part of its function of determining the guilt or innocence of the accused.[8]

6. Cf. e. g., Lufty v. United States, 9 Cir., 198 F.2d 760, 33 A.L.R.2d 879; Wall v. United States, 5 Cir., 65 F.2d 993; Butts v. United States, 8 Cir., 273 F. 35, 18 A.L.R. 143.

7. In the first appeal of this case Judge Learned Hand stated: "Indeed, it would seem probable that, if there were no reply (to the claim of inducement), it would be impossible ever to secure convictions of any offences which consist of transactions that are carried on in secret." United States v. Sherman, 2 Cir., 200 F.2d 880, 882.

8. For example, in the following cases the courts have in affirming convictions, held that the issue of entrapment had been properly submitted to the jury. United States v. Lindenfeld, 2 Cir., 142 F.2d 829; United States v. Brandenburg, 3 Cir., 162 F.2d 980; Demos v. United States, 5 Cir., 205 F.2d 596; Nero v. United States, 6 Cir., 189 F.2d 515; United States v. Cerone, 7 Cir., 150 F.2d 382; Louie Hung v. United States, 9 Cir., 111 F. 2d 325; Ryles v. United States, 10 Cir., 183 F.2d 944; Cratty v. United States, 82 U.S.App.D.C. 236, 163 F.2d 844. And in the following cases the courts have reversed convictions where the issue of entrapment was either not submitted to the jury or was submitted on improper instructions. United States v. Sherman, 2 Cir., 200 F.2d 880; United States v. Sawyer, 3 Cir., 210 F.2d 169; Wall v. United States, 5 Cir., 65 F.2d 993;

To dispose of this case on the grounds suggested would entail both overruling a leading decision of this Court and brushing aside the possibility that we would be creating more problems than we would supposedly be solving.

The judgment of the Court of Appeals is reversed and the case is remanded to the District Court with instructions to dismiss the indictment.[9]

Reversed and remanded.

MR. JUSTICE FRANKFURTER, whom MR. JUSTICE DOUGLAS, MR. JUSTICE HARLAN, and MR. JUSTICE BRENNAN join, concurring in the result.

Although agreeing with the Court that the undisputed facts show entrapment as a matter of law, I reach this result by a route different from the Court's.

The first case in which a federal court clearly recognized and sustained a claim of entrapment by government officers as a defense to an indictment was, apparently, Woo Wai v. United States, 9 Cir., 223 F. 412. Yet the basis of this defense, affording guidance for its application in particular circumstances, is as much in doubt today as it was when the defense was first recognized over forty years ago, although entrapment has been the decisive issue in many prosecutions. The lower courts have continued gropingly to express the feeling of outrage at conduct of law enforcers that brought recognition of the defense in the first instance, but without the formulated basis in reason that it is the first duty of courts to construct for justifying and guiding emotion and instinct.

Today's opinion does not promote this judicial desideratum, and fails to give the doctrine of entrapment the solid foundation that the

---

Lufty v. United States, 9 Cir., 198 F. 2d 760, 33 A.L.R.2d 879; Yep v. United States, 10 Cir., 83 F.2d 41.

9. [Compiler's footnote.] Defendant was introduced to a government agent by an informer who did not reveal the agent's connection with the government. The agent then solicited the defendant for an introduction to a supplier of heroin. The factual situation was such as to allow an inference that the defendant needed no persuasion to commit the crime and hence the defense of entrapment was not established. Masciale v. United States, 356 U.S. 386, 78 S.Ct. 827 (1958). See also Marshall v. United States, 258 F.2d 94 (10th Cir. 1958).

It is to be noted that a conviction is to be upset (or barred) on the ground of entrapment only when defendant has been induced to commit the offense by public officers, or by persons working with or for such officers or whose actions have been adopted by them. In many cases of conspiracy, for example, considerable persuasion has been employed by one upon the other, but this is no defense to him who yielded to such temptation. If any analogy is to be drawn between entrapment and a coerced confession it must be emphasized that the prosecution cannot offer such a confession in evidence without seeking to take advantage of the misconduct (plus the fact that a coerced confession is untrustworthy). Thus it has been held that a conviction based upon a coerced confession must be reversed, the fact that the coercion was exercised by private persons rather than by officers being unimportant. People v. Berve, 51 Cal. 2d 286, 332 P.2d 97 (1958).

[Footnotes by Mr. Justice Frankfurter.]

Sec. 7   ENTRAPMENT   649

decisions of the lower courts and criticism of learned writers have clearly shown is needed.[1] Instead it accepts without re-examination the theory espoused in Sorrells v. United States, 287 U.S. 435, 53 S.Ct. 210, 77 L.Ed. 413, over strong protest by Mr. Justice Roberts, speaking for Brandeis and Stone, JJ., as well as himself. The fact that since the Sorrells case the lower courts have either ignored its theory and continued to rest decision on the narrow facts of each case, or have failed after penetrating effort to define a satisfactory generalization, see, e. g., United States v. Becker, 2 Cir., 62 F.2d 1007 (L.Hand, J.), is proof that the prevailing theory of the Sorrells case ought not to be deemed the last word. In a matter of this kind the Court should not rest on the first attempt at an explanation for what sound instinct counsels. It should not forego re-examination to achieve clarity of thought, because confused and inadequate analysis is too apt gradually to lead to a course of decisions that diverges from the true ends to be pursued.[2]

It is surely sheer fiction to suggest that a conviction cannot be had when a defendant has been entrapped by government officers or informers because "Congress could not have intended that its statutes were to be enforced by tempting innocent persons into violations." In these cases raising claims of entrapment, the only legislative intention that can with any show of reason be extracted from the statute is the intention to make criminal precisely the conduct in which the defendant has engaged. That conduct includes all the elements necessary to constitute criminality. Without compulsion and "knowingly," where that is requisite, the defendant has violated the statutory command. If he is to be relieved from the usual punitive consequences, it is on no account because he is innocent of the offense described. In these circumstances, conduct is not less criminal because the result of temptation, whether the tempter is a private person or a government agent or informer.

The courts refuse to convict an entrapped defendant, not because his conduct falls outside the proscription of the statute, but because, even if his guilt be admitted, the methods employed on behalf of the Government to bring about conviction cannot be countenanced. As Mr. Justice Holmes said in Olmstead v. United States, 277 U.S. 438, 470, 48 S.Ct. 564, 575, 72 L.Ed. 944 (dissenting), in another connec-

---

1. Excellent discussions of the problem can be found in Mikell, The Doctrine of Entrapment in the Federal Courts, 90 U.Pa.L.Rev. 245; Donnelly, Judicial Control of Informants, Spies, Stool Pigeons, and Agent Provocateurs, 60 Yale L.J. 1091, 1098–1115; Note, Entrapment by Government Officials, 28 Col.L.Rev. 1067.

2. It is of course not a rigid rule of this Court to restrict consideration of a case merely to arguments advanced by counsel. Presumably certiorari was not granted in this case simply to review the evidence under an accepted rule of law. The solution, when an issue of real importance to the administration of criminal justice has not been argued by counsel, is not to perpetuate a bad rule but to set the case down for reargument with a view to re-examining that rule.

tion, "It is desirable that criminals should be detected, and to that end that all available evidence should be used. It also is desirable that the government should not itself foster and pay for other crimes, when they are the means by which the evidence is to be obtained. . . . (F)or my part I think it a less evil that some criminals should escape than that the government should play an ignoble part." Insofar as they are used as instrumentalities in the administration of criminal justice, the federal courts have an obligation to set their face against enforcement of the law by lawless means or means that violate rationally vindicated standards of justice, and to refuse to sustain such methods by effectuating them. They do this in the exercise of a recognized jurisdiction to formulate and apply "proper standards for the enforcement of the federal criminal law in the federal courts," McNabb v. United States, 318 U.S. 332, 341, 63 S.Ct. 608, 613, 87 L.Ed. 819, an obligation that goes beyond the conviction of the particular defendant before the court. Public confidence in the fair and honorable administration of justice, upon which ultimately depends the rule of law, is the transcending value at stake. . . .

As Mr. Justice Roberts convincingly urged in the Sorrells case, such a judgment, aimed at blocking off areas of impermissible police conduct, is appropriate for the court and not the jury. "The protection of its own functions and the preservation of the purity of its own temple belongs only to the court. It is the province of the court and of the court alone to protect itself and the government from such prostitution of the criminal law. The violation of the principles of justice by the entrapment of the unwary into crime should be dealt with by the court no matter by whom or at what stage of the proceedings the facts are brought to its attention." 287 U.S. at page 457, 53 S.Ct. at page 218 (separate opinion). Equally important is the consideration that a jury verdict, although it may settle the issue of entrapment in the particular case, cannot give significant guidance for official conduct for the future. Only the court, through the gradual evolution of explicit standards in accumulated precedents, can do this with the degree of certainty that the wise administration of criminal justice demands.[10]

10. [Compiler's footnote.] "Police methods designed to tempt innocent persons into crime are as objectionable as the coerced confession and the unlawful search". Accardi v. United States, 227 F.2d 168, 172 (5th Cir. 1958).

" 'Entrapment' is the planning of an offense by an officer, or someone acting under his direction, and his procurement by improper inducement of its commission by one who would not have perpetrated it, except for the trickery of the *officer*." Crosbie v. State, 330 P.2d 602, 606 (Okl.Cr.1958).

"The controlling question in entrapment is whether an unwary innocent, having no disposition to commit a crime, is trapped into an offense that is the product of the creative activity of the government's own agents. Sorrells and Sherman hold that this is a question for the jury, unless the evidence is so clear that the Court should decide it as a matter of law." Lathem v. United States, 259 F.2d 393, 396 (5th Cir. 1958).

An informer, working with a government agent, asked D if he had narcotics for sale. D replied in the affirmative

MODEL PENAL CODE

Section 2.13. Entrapment.

(1) A public law enforcement official or a person acting in cooperation with such an official perpetrates an entrapment if for the purpose of obtaining evidence of the commission of an offense, he induces or encourages another person to engage in conduct constituting such offense by either:

 (a) making knowingly false representations designed to induce the belief that such conduct is not prohibited; or

 (b) employing methods of persuasion or inducement which create a substantial risk that such an offense will be committed by persons other than those who are ready to commit it.

(2) Except as provided in Subsection (3) of this Section, a person prosecuted for an offense shall be acquitted if he proves by a preponderance of evidence that his conduct occurred in response to an entrapment. The issue of entrapment shall be tried by the Court in the absence of the jury.

(3) The defense afforded by this Section is unavailable when causing or threatening bodily injury is an element of the offense charged and the prosecution is based on conduct causing or threatening such injury to a person other than the person perpetrating the entrapment.

and immediately produced a package from which he sold narcotic capsules to the agent and to the informer. This was held not to present any issue of entrapment. Berry v. United States, 116 U.S.App.D.C. 375, 324 F.2d 407 (1963). Separate counts had charged unlawful possession and unlawful sale of narcotics and one judge, while concurring as to the conviction of unlawful possession, thought that the issue of entrapment should have been presented to the jury with reference to the unlawful sale.

Part 2
PROCEDURE AND ENFORCEMENT

Chapter 11

THE LIMITATIONS OF PROSECUTION

SECTION 1. JURISDICTION

(A) THE EXTENT OF THE AUTHORITY OF THE STATE

Criminal prosecutions are subject to certain limitations. Four distinct kinds, namely, jurisdiction, lapse of time, former jeopardy and what is known as the *ex post facto rule*, are entitled to special consideration.

"The power of a sovereign to affect the rights of persons, whether by legislation, by executive decree, or by the judgment of a court, is called *jurisdiction*."[1] As relates to the power of a sovereign to affect the rights of persons by the judgment of a court, jurisdiction is the power to hear and determine a cause of action. Thus we use the word jurisdiction first, to mean the scope of authority of a state; and second, within the state, to signify the scope of authority of its various tribunals. To have jurisdiction over a criminal prosecution means to have power, first, to inquire into the facts; second, to apply the law to the facts; and third, if the law as applied to these facts requires it, to pronounce the appropriate sentence. Any given court may lack these powers either because they are not within the judicial machinery of the state at all, or because they are lodged exclusively in some other part of this machinery. If any such question arises we have first to decide whether the state has the power to try the accused for the alleged crime. The different theories of criminal jurisdiction are entitled to first consideration.

1. Beale, The Jurisdiction of a Sovereign State, 36 Harv.L.Rev. 241 (1923).

TITLE 18—UNITED STATES CODE
CRIMES AND CRIMINAL PROCEDURE

§ 1651. Piracy under law of nations [2]

Whoever, on the high seas, commits the crime of piracy as defined by the law of nations, and is afterwards brought into or found in the United States, shall be imprisoned for life

§ 1652. Citizens as pirates

Whoever, being a citizen of the United States, commits any murder or robbery, or any act of hostility against the United States, or against any citizen thereof, on the high seas, under color of any commission from any foreign prince, or state, or on pretense of authority from any person, is a pirate, and shall be imprisoned for life.

§ 2381. Treason

Whoever, owing allegiance to the United States, levies war against them or adheres to their enemies, giving them aid and comfort within the United States or elsewhere, is guilty of treason and shall suffer death, or be imprisoned not less than five years and fined not less than $10,000; and shall be incapable of holding any office under the United States.

§ 953. Private correspondence with foreign governments

Any citizen of the United States, wherever he may be, who, without authority of the United States, directly or indirectly commences or carries on any correspondence or intercourse with any foreign government or any officer or agent thereof, with intent to influence the measures or conduct of any foreign government or of any officer or agent thereof, in relation to any disputes or controversies with the United States, or to defeat the measures of the United States, shall be fined not more than $5,000 or imprisoned not more than three years, or both.

This section shall not abridge the right of a citizen to apply, himself or his agent, to any foreign government or the agents thereof for redress of any injury which he may have sustained from such government or any of its agents or subjects.

§ 2112. Personal property of United States

Whoever robs another of any kind or description of personal property belonging to the United States, shall be imprisoned not more than fifteen years.

---

2. Constitution of the United States, Art. I, § 8: 1. The Congress shall have power. . . . 10. To define and punish piracies and felonies committed on the high seas, and offenses against the law of nations.

§ 471. Obligations or securities of United States

Whoever, with intent to defraud, falsely makes, forges, counterfeits, or alters any obligation or other security of the United States, shall be fined not more than $5,000 or imprisoned not more than fifteen years, or both.

(i). IN GENERAL

IN RE CARMEN'S PETITION

United States District Court, N.D. California, S.D., 1958.
165 F.Supp. 942.

GOODMAN, CHIEF JUDGE. Petitioner is confined at the California State Penitentiary at San Quentin pursuant to a judgment of conviction of murder and a sentence of death imposed by the Superior Court of the State of California in and for the County of Madera, on October 30, 1951. By an application for the writ of habeas corpus, he seeks his discharge on the ground that the California Superior Court lacked jurisdiction to try him for the murder of which he was convicted because exclusive jurisdiction to try him for such offense was vested by federal statute in the United States District Court.

The statute relied upon by petitioner is often referred to as the Ten Major Crimes Act[2] and is now incorporated in Sections 1151, 1153, and 3242 of Title 18 of the United States Code. It provides in substance that an Indian who commits any of the ten listed crimes, among which is murder, in Indian Country shall be subject to the same laws and penalties and tried in the same courts as persons committing such crime within the exclusive jurisdiction of the United States. During petitioner's trial in the Superior Court apparently he and his counsel, the prosecution, and the court were all unaware of this statute. There was testimony at the trial indicating that both petitioner and his victim were Indians, but this testimony was given as background information and not for the purpose of questioning the court's jurisdiction. There was evidence that the scene of the crime was the victim's residence, but this evidence did not establish that his residence was in Indian Country. . . .

The testimony at petitioner's trial was that both he and his victim were Indians, and that the murder occurred at the victim's residence. Although these facts alone did not fully demonstrate the lack of jurisdiction in the trial court, they should have put the State Court on inquiry as to its own jurisdiction. The right to be tried in a Federal Court accorded petitioner by the Ten Major Crimes Act, was not a

---

2. As originally enacted in 1885, 23 Stat. 385, this Act dealt only with seven crimes and was then referred to as the Seven Major Crimes Act. In 1909, the crime of assault with a dangerous weapon was included. 35 Stat. 1151. And, in 1932, incest and robbery were added, 47 Stat. 337.

mere procedural right, waived unless asserted.[3] It could not have been waived even by express agreement. The Ten Major Crimes Act was enacted for the protection of the Indian wards of the United States. Both the trial court and the state's attorneys had a duty to uphold this federal statute. They had a responsibility to see to it that the court did not improperly assume jurisdiction over an Indian ward of the Federal government.

When the matter came to the attention of the United States, its representative promptly advised the California Supreme Court of the jurisdictional question while the appeal was pending. The stipulation of the parties that petitioner was an Indian by blood, and that the locus of the crime was an Indian allotment, the title to which was held in trust, constituted at the least a prima facie showing of the lack of jurisdiction in the State court. If, in the opinion of the California Supreme Court, the exclusive federal jurisdiction also depended upon the fact that petitioner was a tribal Indian and had not received a fee patent to an allotment under the Dawes Act, these were facts which were a matter of public record and easily ascertainable. They were in fact ascertained by the Referee appointed by the California Supreme Court upon petitioner's application for the writ of habeas corpus, which was promptly presented to that court after his unsuccessful appeal. Yet the California Supreme Court deemed itself powerless to remedy an assumption of jurisdiction clearly in violation of a federal statute.

Under these circumstances, it becomes the plain duty of this Court to protect the jurisdiction vested in the Federal Courts by the Ten Major Crimes Act. . . .

The writ of Habeas Corpus will issue and it is Ordered that petitioner be discharged from custody.[4]

[By the Compiler.]

3. "It has been repeatedly held in considering objections to the jurisdiction of the court in criminal prosecutions, a distinction must be made between those which involve jurisdiction of fundamental rights of the accused and those which involve mere personal privileges of the accused. The former cannot be waived, but the latter can." In re Duty, 318 P.2d 900, 902 (Okl.Cr. 1957).

4. The president of a national bank was charged with violation of a state statute which made it a felony for an officer of a bank to accept a deposit when his bank was insolvent and with knowledge of such insolvency. His conviction, affirmed by the state court, was reversed by the Supreme Court on the ground that Congress, having created a system of national banks, has the sole power to regulate and control the exercise of their operations. Easton v. Iowa, 188 U.S. 220, 23 S.Ct. 288, 47 L.Ed. 452 (1903).

Title 18 of the United States Code (Crimes and Criminal Procedure) has this provision:

Section 3231. District Courts.

The district courts of the United States shall have original jurisdiction, exclusive of the courts of the States, of all offenses against the laws of the United States.

Nothing in this title shall be held to take away or impair the jurisdiction of the courts of the several States under the laws thereof.

(ii) Basis of Criminal Jurisdiction

REGINA v. WAINA AND SWATOA

Supreme Court of New South Wales, 1874.
2 N.S.W.L.R. 403.

[The Plato, a British ship, was wrecked. The crew of ten men then rigged up the longboat of some eight tons, and sailed it into a harbor of the savage island of Mallatta or Mallantha. Six of the crew went on shore and while on the beach were attacked by natives, and killed before the eyes of the four men in the longboat, who immediately decided to leave. They were pursued by canoes full of natives who fired arrows at them, wounding the captain. The boat soon went ashore on a reef, and the natives waded out to plunder it. After taking what they wanted from the boat, they killed two more of the crew, stripped the captain and the remaining member of the crew, and then sank a tomahawk in the captain's skull.]

Sir J. Martin, C. J. . . . I am of opinion that the prosecution must fail for several reasons. If it depended simply on the point whether a boat is a "ship" within the meaning of the cases, I might reserve the decision. The case, however, does not depend on that alone. Whether a boat is a "ship" within the meaning of the cases there is no authority to show. My own opinion, however, is that a Judge would not be allowed to extend the law so as to stretch the jurisdiction of the Court in such a manner. The cases clearly show that the general principle is that a British ship is part of British territory, wherever she is *waterborne,* and that every foreigner on board, committing a crime on the high seas, is amenable to our law.[1] It is equally clear, however, that our jurisdiction does not extend one inch outside of the ship. It is strictly confined to the vessel, and there is no area surrounding the ship, however small, over which it can be made to extend. I admit that it is not the size of the vessel that would alone make it a ship, and I will not say that if this boat had started originally on a voyage, registered as a ship, that it would not

---

The fact that one is on probation under a federal conviction does not deprive the state, which has arrested him, of jurisdiction to try him for the state offense. Strand v. Schmittroth, 251 F.2d 590 (9th Cir. 1957).

1. Defendant, an American citizen, while a member of the crew of a vessel sailing under the British flag, killed another on board the vessel at a time when it was in the river Garonne, within the boundaries of the French empire. Having been charged with murder in England, the accused claimed there was no jurisdiction to try him there. He was convicted of manslaughter. This conviction was affirmed, the court saying: "Although the prisoner was subject to the American jurisprudence as an American citizen, and to the law of France as having committed an offence within the territory of France, yet he must also be considered as subject to the jurisdiction of British law, which extends to the protection of British vessels, though in ports belonging to another country." Regina v. Anderson, 11 Cox C.C. 198, 204 (1868).

be one within the meaning of the cases. I do not think, however, that a boat of the character disclosed in the evidence, sailing under the circumstances narrated, comes within the description of a ship. I have taken considerable trouble in looking into all the cases, and I can find none, either American or English, which would justify me in holding it to be a ship. Here, however, supposing it were a ship, was this boat on shore on this island? and under the circumstances described, could it be held to be within our jurisdiction? I am of opinion that it could not.

The Attorney-General had referred to the Merchant Seaman's Act as conferring jurisdiction, but the Imperial Parliament could not pass a statute affecting foreigners outside the British dominions. No foreign nation would allow such an assumption of authority, nor would the British nation allow a similar power to be assumed by foreigners. We might pass statutes affecting our own subjects wherever they might be; but where a foreigner committed an offence outside the British dominions, no statute of ours couid [sic] make him amenable to British laws. If the jurisdiction contended for could be extended to a boat there is no saying to what lengths the argument might lead. If the jurisdiction extended to a boat, it might be held to extend to a raft, or to anything that floated on the water. I am of opinion, supposing that the murder was committed in the boat whilst on shore on this island, and that the arrows were fired either from the shore or from the canoes, that the Court would have no jurisdiction—neither the shore nor the canoes being British territory. The onus of proving that the crime was committed within British territory lay upon the Crown; but here the evidence showed that the prisoners were foreigners in their own country, and there was no British law that could touch them. . . . Being of opinion, therefore, that this boat on shore on a foreign island was not a "ship on the high seas," and that the crime committed was by foreigners in their own country, I hold that this Court has no jurisdiction whatever to try the case.

His Honor then directed the jury to acquit the prisoners, which they at once did in compliance with his Honor's direction, and the prisoners were both *discharged*.

REGINA v. AZZOPARDI

Central Criminal Court, 1843.
1 Car. & K. 203, 174 Eng.Rep. 776.

Murder.—The prisoner was tried under a special commission founded on the stat. 9 Geo. IV, c. 31, s. 7, which authorizes the trial of any of her Majesty's subjects who shall be charged in England with any murder or manslaughter committed on land out of the United Kingdom, "whether within the king's dominions or without." The indictment charged that the prisoner, being a subject of her Majesty, had murdered Rosa Sluyk, at Smyrna. In some of the counts of the indictment, the deceased was stated to have been "in the peace of God and our said lady the Queen"; and in others, that allegation was omitted.

It appeared that the murder was committed at Smyrna, and that the prisoner was a native of Malta, of the age of about twenty-one, and was residing at Smyrna under a passport from the governor of Malta. The person murdered was a Dutch woman, and proof was given that Malta is part of her Majesty's dominions.

Ballantine, for the prisoner, submitted that it was necessary that the person alleged to have been murdered should have been a British subject, and should be described as such in the indictment.

GURNEY, B. (having conferred with COLTMAN, J.), reserved the point for the opinion of the fifteen Judges.

Verdict—Guilty. . . .

JUNE 19th, 1843

The prisoner being again brought up at the Central Criminal Court,

GURNEY, B., now delivered the judgment of the fifteen Judges as follows:—"Upon your trial your learned counsel took an objection to your case being within the Act of Parliament upon which you were tried; you a British subject committing a murder in a foreign country, upon a person who was not a British subject. I reserved the point for the consideration of the Judges, who have considered it, and they are all of opinion that your case does fall within the statute, and therefore, that the objection must be overruled. You, a British subject, living under the protection of the British government, are subject to the laws of Great Britain, and you have offended against those laws in the crime you have committed."

Sentence of Death was passed on the prisoner.[1]

---

1. Accord, Rex v. Sawyer, 2 Car. & K. 101, 175 Eng.Rep. 41 (N.P.1815). See 1 East P.C. 369.

In MacLeod v. Attorney General for New South Wales [1891] A.C. 455, the defendant, having first married in New South Wales and later married another wife in St. Louis, Missouri, was convicted of bigamy in the colony of New South Wales. The conviction was under this statute: "Whosoever being married marries another person during the life of the former husband or wife, wheresoever such second marriage takes place, shall be liable to penal servitude for seven years." This conviction was reversed by the Judicial Committee of the Privy Council. It was suggested that "whosoever" as here used means whosoever etc., "and who is amenable, at the time of the offence committed, to the jurisdiction of the colony of New South Wales," and that "wheresoever" as used in the statute means "wheresoever in this colony the offence is committed." If the ordinary meaning were given to the words, "it would have been beyond the jurisdiction of the colony to enact such a law."

UNITED STATES v. SMILEY

United States Circuit Court, N.D. California, 1864.
27 Fed.Cas. 1132, No. 16,317.

[The steamer Golden Gate, belonging to the Pacific Mail Steamship Company caught fire off the Mexican Coast and was completely destroyed. The underwriter sent a ship to recover lost treasure but this venture was unsuccessful. Then Thomas J. L. Smiley and others fitted up an expedition with complete equipment. They obtained from the Mexican government a license to explore for the lost treasure and recovered over three hundred thousand dollars in money. As Smiley and the original shippers were unable to agree upon what the recovering party should retain as compensation for the recovery of the specie, none of it was given up and Smiley and the others were indicted for plundering and stealing the treasure from the Golden Gate in violation of the federal statute against stealing money or goods from, or belonging to, a wrecked ship.]

FIELD, CIRCUIT JUSTICE. We are not prepared to decide that the statute does not apply to a case where the vessel has gone to pieces, to which the goods belonged, of which larceny is alleged. It would fail of one of its objects if it did not extend to goods which the officers and men of a stranded or wrecked vessel had succeeded in getting ashore, so long as a claim is made by them to the property, though before its removal the vessel may have been broken up. We are inclined to the conclusion that, until the goods are removed from the place where landed, or thrown ashore, from the stranded or wrecked vessel, or cease to be under the charge of the officers or other parties interested, the act would apply if a larceny of them were committed, even though the vessel may in the meantime have gone entirely to pieces and disappeared from the sea. But in this case the treasure taken had ceased to be under the charge of the officers of the Golden Gate, or of its underwriters, when the expedition of Smiley was fitted out, and all efforts to recover the property had been given up by them. The treasure was then in the situation of derelict or abandoned property, which could be acquired by any one who might have the energy and enterprise to seek its recovery. In our judgment the act was no more intended to reach cases where property thus abandoned is recovered, than to reach property voluntarily thrown into the sea, and afterwards fished from its depths.

Accord, State v. Stephens, 118 Me. 237, 107 A. 296 (1919) (indictment in a Maine court for a bigamous marriage contracted in New Brunswick); People v. Price, 250 Ill. 109, 95 N.E. 68 (1921); State v. Cutshall, 110 N.C. 538, 15 S.E. 261 (1892); Wilson v. State, 16 Okl.Cr. 471, 184 P. 603 (1919).

Compare Trial of Earl Russell, [1901] A.C. 446 (trial for bigamy of Earl Russell who had obtained in Nevada a divorce from his first wife and had there married a second wife, the English courts not recognizing the validity of the Nevada divorce).

But if the act covered a case where the property was recovered after its abandonment by the officers of the vessel and others interested in it, we are clear that the circuit court has no jurisdiction of the offense here charged. The treasure recovered was buried in the sand, several feet under the water, and was within one hundred and fifty feet from the shore of Mexico. The jurisdiction of that country over all offenses committed within a marine league of its shore, not on a vessel of another nation, was complete and exclusive.

Wheaton, in his treatise on International Law, after observing that "the maritime territory of every state extends to the ports, harbors, bays, and mouths of rivers and adjacent parts of the sea inclosed by headlands, belonging to the same state," says: "The general usage of nations superadds to this extent of territorial jurisdiction a distance of a marine league, or as far as a cannon-shot will reach from the shore, along all the coasts of the state. Within these limits its rights of property and territorial jurisdiction are absolute, and exclude those of every other nation." Part 2, c. 4, § 6.

The criminal jurisdiction of the government of the United States —that is, its jurisdiction to try parties for offenses committed against its laws—may in some instances extend to its citizens everywhere. Thus, it may punish for violation of treaty stipulations by its citizens abroad, for offenses committed in foreign countries where, by treaty, jurisdiction is conceded for that purpose, as in some cases in China and in the Barbary States; it may provide for offenses committed on deserted islands, and on an uninhabited coast, by the officers and seamen of vessels sailing under its flag. It may also punish derelictions of duty by its ministers or consuls, and other representatives abroad. But in all such cases it will be found that the law of congress indicates clearly the extraterritorial character of the act at which punishment is aimed. Except in cases like these, the criminal jurisdiction of the United States is necessarily limited to their own territory, actual or constructive. Their actual territory is co-extensive with their possessions, including a marine league from their shores into the sea.

This limitation of a marine league was adopted because it was formerly supposed that a cannon-shot would only reach to that extent. It is essential that the absolute domain of a country should extend into the sea so far as necessary for the protection of its inhabitants against injury from combating belligerents while the country itself is neutral. Since the great improvement of modern times in ordnance, the distance of a marine league, which is a little short of three English miles, may, perhaps, have to be extended so as to equal the reach of the projecting power of modern artillery. The constructive territory of the United States embraces vessels sailing under their flag; wherever they go they carry the laws of their country, and for a violation of them their officers and men may be subjected to punishment. But when a vessel is destroyed, and goes to the bottom, the jurisdiction of the country over it necessarily ends, as much so as it would over an island which should sink into the sea.

In this case it appears that the Golden Gate was broken up; not a vestige of the vessel remained. Whatever was afterwards done with reference to property once on board of her, which had disappeared under the sea, was done out of the jurisdiction of the United States, as completely as though the steamer had never existed.

We are of opinion, therefore, that the circuit court has no jurisdiction to try the offense charged, even if, under the facts admitted by the parties, any offense was committed. According to the stipulation, judgment sustaining the demurrer will be, therefore, entered and the defendants discharged.[1]

HANKS v. STATE

Texas Court of Appeals, 1882.
13 Tex.App. 289.

WHITE, P. J. There is but a single question which we think is involved in and requires discussion on this appeal.

Appellant and one P. F. Dillman were jointly indicted in the District Court of Travis county for the forgery of a transfer of a land

---

1. "If it be committed on board of a foreign vessel by a citizen of the United States, or on board of a vessel of the United States by a foreigner, the offender is to be considered, *pro hac vice*, and in respect to this subject as belonging to the nation under whose flag he sails. If it be committed, either by a citizen or a foreigner, on board of a piratical vessel, the offense is equally cognizable by the courts of the United States." United States v. Holmes, 5 Wheat. 412, 5 L.Ed. 122, (U.S.1820). "Whoever, on the high seas, commits the crime of piracy as defined by the law of nations, and is afterwards brought into or found in the United States, shall be imprisoned for life." 18 U.S.C.A. § 1651 (1948). Cf. § 1653.

The "absent voters law" is not rendered invalid by the penalty clause, because the state has power by statute to punish its own citizens for crimes committed beyond its territory. State ex rel. Chandler v. Main, 16 Wis. 398 (1863).

"The Right Hon. Lord Kingsdown, in the Adv.-Gen. of Bengal v. Ranee Surnomoye Dosee, 9 Moore, Indians Appeals 387, 424 says: 'Where Englishmen establish themselves in an uninhabited or barbarous country, they carry with them not only the laws, but the sovereignty of their own State; and those who live amongst them and become members of their community become also partakers of, and subject to the same laws.'

"Nevertheless, the subject has presented to publicists and legislators so many grave doubts on the score of expediency and justice, that few countries have attempted to require of their citizens a general observance of their criminal law outside of the national territory, except in particular places.

"These exceptions are barbarous lands, in which local law does not exist, and to which the doctrine of the sovereignty of each nation over all persons within its territory does not completely apply; and Mohammedan and other non-Christian countries, in which the citizens of many states enjoy a conventional immunity from the local law. In such places it is not only proper but necessary for each state to subject its citizens to its own regulations. The argument of expediency may also be applied to the punishment of citizens for offenses of a high grade, such as murder, wherever committed." 2 Moore, Digest of International Law 256 (1906).

certificate for a league and labor of land in the State of Texas. It is alleged in the indictment that the acts constituting the forgery were all committed in Caddo parish, in the State of Louisiana. No act or thing connected with the execution of the forgery is charged to have been done in Texas; but the crime and injury, so far as this State is concerned, are averred to consist in the fact that the said forgery in Louisiana "did then and there relate to and affect an interest in land in the State of Texas, . . . and would, if the same were true and genuine, have transferred and affected certain property, to-wit, a certain land certificate, number 222, for one league and labor of land in the State of Texas," etc.

This indictment was brought under Article 451 of the Penal Code.

By Article 454 of the Code it is declared that "persons out of the State may commit and be liable to indictment and conviction for committing any of the offenses enumerated in this chapter which do not in their commission necessarily require a personal presence in this State, the object of this chapter being to reach and punish all persons offending against its provisions, whether within or without this State," etc.

It was made a ground both in the motion to quash the indictment and in arrest of judgment, and is again urgently insisted upon in the able brief of counsel for appellant, that the facts alleged, if true, would constitute an offense against the sovereign State of Louisiana alone, and one of which the courts of this State would have no jurisdiction.

If the position thus assumed in behalf of appellant be correct, then the Legislature had no authority to pass the act quoted, and the same is an absolute nullity. Can this proposition be maintained? It certainly cannot be found in any constitutional inhibition, State or Federal, depriving the Legislature of the authority, and unless there is some authority of law superior to the right of a State Legislature, which could and should control the action of the latter within the scope of its constitutional powers, we cannot well conceive how its enactments, if reasonable and consistent with that power, could be held inoperative and nugatory.

Two authorities, which are to the effect that "the Legislature of one State cannot define and punish crimes committed in another State," are mainly relied upon. The leading one is the case of The State v. Knight, taken from 2 Haywood, and reported in Taylor's North Carolina Reports, page 44. The other is People v. Merrill, 2 Park's Criminal Reports, 590. The defendant in the first case was indicted under a statute the words of which were: "And whereas there is reason to apprehend that wicked and ill disposed persons resident in the neighboring States make a practice of counterfeiting the current bills of credit of this State, and by themselves or emissaries utter or vend the same, with an intention to defraud the citizens of this State: Be it enacted, etc., that all such persons shall be subject to the same mode of trial, and on conviction liable to the same pains and penalties as if the offense had been committed within the limits of this State and prosecuted in the superior court of any district of this State." It was held that the jurisdiction to try in North Carolina was doubtful, and the prisoner was discharged.

Mr. Wharton, in his work on the Conflict of Laws, says: "The sturdiest advocates of the hypothesis that the *locus delicti* alone confers jurisdiction have admitted that there are cases in which a person whose residence is outside the territory may make himself, by conspiring extra-territorially to defeat its laws, infra-territorially responsible. If, for instance, a forger should establish on the Mexican side of the boundary between the United States and Mexico a manufactory for the forgery of United States securities, for us to hold that when the mischief is done he can take up his residence in the United States without even liability to arrest, would not merely expose our government to spoliation, but bring its authority into contempt. To say that in such a case the Mexican government can be relied upon to punish is no answer; because, first, in countries of such imperfect civilization, penal justice is uncertain; secondly, in cases where, in such country, the local community gains greatly by the fraud and suffers by it no loss, the chances of conviction and punishment would be peculiarly slight; and, thirdly, because all that the offender would have to do to escape justice in such a case would be to walk over the boundary line into the United States, where on this hypothesis he would go free." (Whart. Conflict of Laws, sec. 876.) Again he says: "Thus it has been held that the originator of a nuisance to a stream in one country which affects such stream in another country is liable to prosecution in the latter country; that the author of a libel uttered by him in one country and published by others in another country from which he is absent at the time is liable in the latter country; that he who on one side of a boundary shoots a person on the other side is amenable in the country where the blow is received; that he who in one State employs an innocent agent to obtain goods by false pretenses in another State is amenable in the latter State; and that he who sells through agents, guilty or innocent, lottery tickets in another State is amenable in the State of the sale, though he was absent from such State personally. In England we have the same principle affirmed by the highest judicial authority." And he quotes Lord Campbell as saying, "that a person may, by the employment as well of a conscious as of an unconscious agent, render himself amenable to the law of England when he comes within the jurisdiction of our courts;" and Cir. R. Phillimore as saying, "It is a monstrous thing that any technical rule of venue should prevent justice from being done in this country on a criminal for an offense which was perpetrated here but the execution of which was concocted in another country." (Whart. Conflict of Laws, sec. 877.)

Mr. Cooley, in his great work on Constitutional Limitations, treating of territorial limitation to legislative authority, says: "The legislative authority of every State must spend its force within the territorial limits of the State. . . . It cannot provide for the punishment as crimes of acts committed beyond the State boundary, because such acts, if offenses at all, must be offenses against the sovereignty within whose limits they have been done." But, after laying down this doctrine, in the very next sentence he says: "But if the consequences of an unlawful act committed outside the State have reached their ultimate and injurious result within it, it seems that the perpetrator may be punished as an offender against such State." (Cooley's Const. Lim., 4 ed., pp. 154–5.) If this latter rule be the law, then it is a solecism to say that the Legislature cannot so declare it by express enactment.

Story, in his Conflict of Laws, says: "Although the penal laws of every country are in their nature local, yet an offense may be committed in one sovereignty in violation of the laws of another, and if the offender be afterwards found in the latter State, he may be punished according to the laws thereof, and the fact that he owes allegiance to another sovereignty is no bar to the indictment." (Story on the Conflict of Laws, 4 ed., section 625b.)

The offense charged in the indictment against appellant comes clearly within the terms of Article 454 of the Penal Code. Had it been committed by one of our own citizens within this State, there then could be no question as to his liability. Here, the defendant in effect says: "You may try and convict your own citizens for the same act I have committed, but you cannot try and punish me, because what I have done, though equally as violative of the spirit and letter of the law, is still not triable in your court because it was committed in another State, and your Legislature could not pass a law which could embrace me within its pains and penalties." We can see no valid reason why the Legislature of the State of Texas could not assert, as it has done in Article 454 supra, her jurisdiction over wrongs and crimes with regard to the land titles of the State, no matter whether the perpetrator of the crime was at the time of its consummation within or without her territorial limits. Such acts are offenses against the State of Texas and her citizens only, and can properly be tried only in her courts. It may in fact be no crime against the State in which it is perpetrated; and if it is under such circumstances as we are considering, that other State would have no interest in punishing it, and would rarely, if ever, do so. When this forgery was committed in Louisiana, *eo instanti* a crime was committed against, and injury done to, the State of Texas, because it affected title to lands within her sovereignty.

Our conclusion is that the Legislature had authority to adopt the act in question; that the same is in violation of no law superior thereto; and that the jurisdiction thereby conferred can be rightly exercised by the courts of this State. The defendant appears to us to come clearly within the scope of that jurisdiction. He has been, as far as we can see, fairly and impartially tried under the law, and legally convicted according to the evidence exhibited in the record. We have found no error for which a reversal of the judgment should be had, and it is therefore affirmed.

Affirmed.[1]

HURT, J., dissents upon the ground that the Legislature had no authority to pass Article 454, Penal Code.

Opinion delivered November 22, 1882.

(iii) THE SITUS OF CRIME

STATE v. HALL

Supreme Court of North Carolina, 1894.
114 N.C. 909, 19 S.E. 602.

INDICTMENT for murder, tried at Spring Term, 1893, of Cherokee, before GRAVES, J., and a jury.

The defendants (Hall, as principal and Dockery, as accessory before the fact), were charged with the killing of Andrew Bryson on 11 July, 1892, in Cherokee County. The testimony tended to show that when the shooting occurred by which deceased was killed the defendants were in North Carolina and the deceased in Tennessee.

The defendants asked for the following instructions (among others):

"1. That it devolves upon the State to satisfy the jury beyond a reasonable doubt that the killing took place in the State of North Carolina; and if the State has failed to satisfy the jury beyond a rea-

---

1. A. K. Cutting, a citizen of the United States, was imprisoned in Mexico, for having published in a newspaper in Texas, certain matters regarding a citizen of Mexico. On the ground of lack of jurisdiction to proceed against him there under these facts, his release was demanded by the United States. In President Cleveland's Annual Message, December 6, 1881, a reference to this case included the following statement: "A sovereign has jurisdiction of offenses which take effect within his territory, although concocted or commenced outside of it; but the right is denied of any foreign sovereign to punish a citizen of the United States for an offense consummated on our soil in violation of our laws, even though the offense be against a subject or citizen of such sovereign."

As to Cutting's Case, see 2 Moore, Digest of International Law § 201 (1906). Cf. Commonwealth v. Blanding, 20 Mass. 304 (1825); State v. Piver, 74 Wash. 96, 132 P. 858 (1913). A state has power to govern the conduct of its citizens upon the high seas with respect to matters in which the state has a legitimate interest and where there is no conflict with Acts of Congress. Skiriotes v. Florida, 313 U.S. 69, 61 S.Ct. 924 (1941).

sonable doubt that the deceased received the wound from which he died whilst he was in the State of North Carolina, the defendants are not guilty.

"2. That if the prisoners were in North Carolina and the deceased was in Tennessee and the prisoners, or either of them, shot the deceased whilst he, the deceased, was in the State of Tennessee, and the deceased died from the effects of the wounds so received, the defendants are not guilty."

The instructions were refused, and after a verdict of guilty the defendants appealed from the judgment rendered thereon.

SHEPHERD, C. J. . . . It is a general principle of universal acceptation that one State or sovereignty can not enforce the penal or criminal laws of another, or punish crimes or offenses committed in and against another State or sovereignty. . . .

It seems to have been a matter of doubt in ancient times whether, if a blow was struck in one county and death ensued in another, the offender could be prosecuted in either, though according to Lord Hale (Pleas of the Crown, 426) "the more common opinion was that he might be indicted where the stroke was given." This difficulty, as stated by Mr. Starkie, was sought to be avoided by the legal device "of carrying the dead body back into the county where the blow was struck, and the jury might there," he adds, "inquire both of the stroke and death." 1 Starkie Cr.Pl., 2 Ed., 304; 1 Hawk, P.C., ch. 13; 1 East, 361. But to remove all doubt in respect to a matter of such grave importance, it was enacted by the statute 2 and 3 Edward VI that the murder might be tried in the county where the death occurred.[1] This statute, either as a part of the common law or by reenactment, is in force in many of the States of the Union, and as applicable to counties within the same State its validity has never been questioned, but where its provisions have been extended so as to affect the jurisdiction of the different States its constitutionality has been vigorously assailed. Such legislation, however, has been very generally, if not indeed uniformly, sustained. . . .

---

1. Where defendant inflicted injuries upon a victim in New York which resulted in the latter's death two days later, in New Jersey, the crime was not punishable in New Jersey. State v. Carter, 27 N.J.L. 499 (1859).

Where deceased died in Texas as a result of a blow struck by defendant in Quay County, New Mexico, venue of murder prosecution was properly laid in Quay County. State v. Justus, 65 N.M. 195, 334 P.2d 1104 (1959).

Under a statute providing: "If any such mortal wound shall be given, or other violence or injury shall be inflicted, or poison administered, on the high seas, or on any other navigable waters, or on land, either within or without the limits of this state, by means whereof death shall ensue in any county thereof, such offense may be prosecuted and punished in the county where such death may happen," defendant was convicted of murder, for inflicting, outside of Michigan, wounds of which the victim died within the state. Tyler v. People, 8 Mich. 320 (1860).

Statutes of this character "are founded upon the general power of the Legislature, except so far as restrained by the Constitution of the Commonwealth and the United States to declare any willful or negligent act which causes an injury to person or property within its territory, to be a crime." Kerr on Homicide, 47. In many of the States there are also statutes substantially providing that where the death occurs outside of one State, by reason of a stroke given in another, the latter State may have jurisdiction. See our act, The Code, sec. 1197. The validity of these statutes seems to be undisputed, and indeed it has been held in many jurisdictions that such legislation is but in affirmance of the common law. It is manifest that statutes of this nature are only applicable to cases where the stroke and the death occur in different jurisdictions, and it is equally clear that where the stroke and the death occur in the same State the offense of murder at common law is there complete, and the courts of that State can alone try the offender for that specific common law crime.

The turning point, therefore, in this case is whether the stroke was, in legal contemplation, given in Tennessee, the alleged place of death; and upon this question the authorities all seem to point in one direction. . . .

In Simpson v. State, 92 Ga. 41, 17 S.E. 984, it was held by the Supreme Court of Georgia that one who, in the State of South Carolina, aims and fires a pistol at another who at the time is in the State of Georgia, is guilty of the offense of "shooting at another" although the ball did not take effect, but struck the water in the latter State. The Court said: "Of course the presence of the accused within this State is essential to make his act one which is done in this State, but the presence need not be actual; it may be constructive. The well-established theory of the law is that where one puts in force an agency for the commission of crime, he in legal contemplation accompanies the same to the point where it becomes effectual. . . . So, if a man in the State of South Carolina criminally fires a ball into the State of Georgia the law regards him as accompanying the ball and as being represented by it up to the point where it strikes. If an unlawful shooting occurred while both the parties were in this State the mere fact of missing would not render the person who shot any the less guilty; consequently, if one shooting from another State goes, in a legal sense, where his bullet goes, the fact of his missing the object at which he aims can not alter the legal principle." . . .

In view of the foregoing authorities it can not be doubted that the place of the assault or stroke in the present case was in Tennessee, and it is also clear that the offense of murder at common law was committed within the jurisdiction of that State. If this be so it must follow that unless we have some statute expressly conferring jurisdiction upon the courts of this State, or making the act of shooting under the circumstances a substantive murder, the offense with which the prisoners are charged can only be tried by the tribunals of Tennessee. . . .

The fact that the prisoners and the deceased were citizens of the State of North Carolina can not affect the conclusion we have reached. If, as we have seen, the offense was committed in Tennessee, the personal jurisdiction generally claimed by nations over their subjects who have committed offenses abroad or on the high seas can not be asserted by this State. Such jurisdiction does not exist as between the States of the Union under their peculiar relation to each other (Rorer Interstate Law, 308), and even if it could be rightfully claimed it could not in a case like the present be enforced in the absence of a statute providing that the offense should be tried in North Carolina. Even in England, where it seems the broadest claim to such jurisdiction is asserted, a statute (33 Hen. VIII) appears to have been necessary in order that the courts of that country could try a murder committed in Lisbon by one British subject upon another. In People v. Merrill, 2 Parker Cr.Cases, 600, it is said that by the common law offenses were local and the jurisdiction in such case depends upon statutory provisions. Granting, however, that in some instances the jurisdiction may exist without statute, it is not exercised in all cases. Dr. Wharton says: "It has already been stated that as to crimes committed by subjects in foreign civilized States, with the single exception in England of homicides, the Anglo-American practice is to take cognizance only of offenses directed against the sovereignty of the prosecuting State; perjury before consuls and forgery of government documents being included in this head." To the same effect is 3 A. & E. Enc., 539, in which it is said: "As to offenses committed in foreign civilized lands the country of arrest has jurisdiction only of offenses distinctively against its sovereignty." See also Dr. Wharton's article upon the subject in 1 Criminal Law Magazine, 715. As between the States the question is so clear to us that we forbear a general discussion of the subject. We may further remark that, while it is true that the criminal laws of a State can have no extra-territorial force, we are of the opinion that it is competent for the Legislature to determine what acts within the limits of the State shall be deemed criminal, and to provide for their punishment. Certainly, there could be no complaint where all the parties concerned in the homicide are citizens of North Carolina. It may also be observed that in addition to its common-law jurisdiction the State of Tennessee has provided by statute for the trial of an offender under the circumstances of this case.

For the reasons given we are constrained to say that the prisoners are entitled to a

New Trial.[2]

---

2. Accord, State v. Carter, 27 N.J.L. 499 (1859).

The same principle applies to other offenses. Thus the offense of obtaining property by false pretenses is committed where the property is obtained and not where the false pretense is made, Connor v. State, 29 Fla. 455, 10

BEATTIE v. STATE

Supreme Court of Arkansas, 1904.
73 Ark. 428, 84 S.W. 477.

George Beattie, a resident of Missouri, was arrested, tried and convicted on a charge that, being a resident of the State of Missouri, he did, in the county of Sharp and State of Arkansas, in May, 1904, herd, graze and permit to run at large about nineteen head of cattle. He was convicted and fined $100 before a justice of the peace. . . .

RIDDICK, J., (after stating the facts.) This is an appeal from a judgment convicting a nonresident defendant and assessing a fine of $100 against him for permitting his cattle to run at large in this State.

Now, it is clear that our statute on that subject does not forbid a nonresident, whose cattle have strayed or come of their own volition into this State, from driving them out again. It is equally clear that it does not subject a resident of Missouri, who turns his cattle at large in that State, to a criminal prosecution and fine if the cattle afterwards come into this State; for the Legislature of this State has no power to punish a resident of Missouri for a lawful act done in that State. Nor do we think that it would alter the case if the defendant knew, at the time he turned them at large in Missouri, that they would probably come into Arkansas, for the Legislature of this State cannot compel the residents of Missouri who live near the State line to keep their cattle in inclosed lots or fields in order to prevent them from coming into this State, and we do not think that it was the intention of this statute to do so. The people of Missouri have the right to permit their cattle to run at large in that State, unless forbidden by the law of that State; and if the people of this State desire to keep such

---

So. 891 (1892); robbery is committed where the property is taken from the person, not where the person is first seized, if he is carried to another place before compelled to surrender his property, Sweat v. State, 90 Ga. 315, 17 S.E. 273 (1892), nor where the property is carried subsequently, 2 Hale P.C. *163; forgery is committed where the false instrument is made and the offense of uttering a forged instrument is committed where the instrument is uttered, State v. Hudson, 13 Mont. 112, 32 P. 413 (1893); the offense of receiving stolen goods is committed where they are received, State v. Rider, 46 Kan. 332, 26 P. 745 (1891); libel is committed at the place of publication, Commonwealth v. Blanding, 20 Mass. 304 (1825); contra: United States v. Smith, 173 F. 227 (D.Ind.1909); and bigamy is committed where the bigamous marriage is performed, 1 Hale P.C. *693.

"Thus it appears that, not only at the common law, but in states where the question of jurisdiction is regulated by statute, courts have with a degree of uniformity held that the crime is committed at the place where the act is done which results in the injury or death, and that the prosecution for such act is properly conducted at the place where the act is done, and not where the death may occur. Here it is conceded that the assault was made and the poison administered in the city of Cincinnati, state of Ohio. At that time both the victim and the wrongdoer were in the state of Ohio. The wrong was done there. It was a completed transaction so far as the appellee was concerned, as much so as though he had shot her or otherwise inflicted upon her person a mortal

cattle from entering this State, they can do so by putting up a fence along the line between this State and Missouri or by a statute authorizing the cattle of nonresidents which stray into this State to be impounded and kept at the costs of the owners. But to undertake to arrest and fine a resident of Missouri because he does not prevent his cattle from straying into this State would be to assume a jurisdiction over the residents of that State never intended by the statute and beyond the power of the Legislature to confer.

The evidence in the case was conflicting, and some of it, if true, might have warranted a finding that the defendant was guilty, but the finding of facts by the court has evidence to support it, and, taking that as true, no crime was committed.

The judgment will therefore be reversed, and the cause remanded for a new trial.

PEOPLE v. BOTKIN

Supreme Court of California, In Bank, 1901
132 Cal. 231, 64 P. 286.

GAROUTTE, J. Defendant has been convicted of the crime of murder, and prosecutes this appeal. The charge of the court given to the jury upon the law contained declarations which were held to be unsound in People v. Vereneseneckockockhoff, 129 Cal. 497, 58 P. 156. In view of the decision in that case, the attorney-general concedes that the judgment should be reversed and the cause remanded to the trial court for further proceedings. But defendant claims that she is not triable at all by the courts of this state, and this contention should now be passed upon. For if maintainable, a second trial becomes a useless expenditure of money, time, and labor, and necessarily should not be had.

For the purposes of testing the claim of lack of jurisdiction in the courts of California to try defendant, the facts of this case may be deemed as follows: Defendant, in the city and county of San Francisco, state of California, sent by the United States mail to Elizabeth Dunning, of Dover, Delaware, a box of poisoned candy, with intent that said Elizabeth Dunning should eat of the candy and her death be caused thereby. The candy was received by the party to whom ad-

---

wound, and, according to the well-recognized rule, the courts of that state alone have jurisdiction to punish the offense. The trial court correctly so held. Judgment Affirmed." Commonwealth v. Apkins, 148 Ky. 207, 146 S.W. 431, 434 (1912).

The defendants were indicted for manslaughter of a man who died within the county in consequence of injuries inflicted by them upon him in a British merchant ship on the high seas. The statute provided "if a mortal wound is given, or other violence or injury inflicted, or poison is administered, on the high seas, or on land either within or without the limits of this state, by means whereof death ensues in any county thereof, such offence may be prosecuted and punished in the county where the death happens." This statute was upheld. Commonwealth v. Macloon, 101 Mass. 1 (1869).

dressed, she partook thereof, and her death was the result. Upon these facts may the defendant be charged and tried for the crime of murder in the courts of the state of California? We do not find it necessary to declare what the true rule may be at common law upon this state of facts, for, in our opinion, the statute of this state is broad enough to cover a case of the kind here disclosed. There can be no question but that the legislature of this state had the power to declare that the acts here pictured constitute the crime of murder in this state, and we now hold that the legislative body has made that declaration.

Section 27 of the Penal Code reads as follows:—
"The following persons are liable to punishment under the laws of this state:— [1]

"1. All persons who commit, in whole or in part, any crime within this state;

"2. All who commit larceny or robbery out of this state, and bring to, or are found with the property stolen, in this state;

"3. All who, being out of this state, cause or aid, advise or encourage, another person to commit a crime within this state, and are afterwards found therein."

Subdivision 1 covers the facts of this case. The acts of defendant constituted murder, and a part of those acts were done by her in this state. Preparing and sending the poisoned candy to Elizabeth Dunning, coupled with a murderous intent, constituted an attempt to commit murder, and defendant could have been prosecuted in this state for that crime, if, for any reason, the candy had failed to fulfill its deadly mission. That being so—those acts being sufficient, standing alone, to constitute a crime, and those acts resulting in the death of the person sought to be killed—nothing is plainer than that the crime of murder was in part committed within this state. The murder being committed *in part* in this state, the section of the law quoted declares that persons committing murder under those circumstances "are liable to punishment under the laws of this state." The language quoted can have but one meaning, and that is: a person committing a murder in part in this state is punishable under the laws of this state, the same as though the murder was wholly committed in this state.

Counsel for defendant insist that this section contemplates only offenses committed by persons who, at the time, are without the state. This construction is not sound. For as to subdivision 1, it is not at all plain that a person without the state could commit, in whole, a crime within the state. Again, if the crime in whole is committed

---

1. Cal.Pen.Code, § 778a. "Whenever a person with intent to commit a crime, does any act within this state in execution or part execution of such intent, which culminates in the commission of a crime, either within or without this state such person is punishable for such crime in this state in the same manner as if the same had been committed entirely within this state". (Added in 1905.)

within the state by a person without the state, such a person could not be punished under the laws of this state, for the state has not possession of his body, and there appears to be no law by which it may secure that possession. Indeed, all of the subdivisions of the section necessarily contemplate a case where the person is, or comes, within the state. If the framers of the section had intended by subdivision 1 to cover the case of persons only who were without the state when the acts were committed which constitute the crime, they would have inserted in the section the contingency found in the remaining subdivisions, which subdivisions contemplate a return to the state of the person committing the crime. It is plain that the section, by its various provisions, was intended to embrace *all persons* punishable under the laws of the state of California. The defendant, having committed a murder in part in the state of California, is punishable under the laws of the state, exactly in the same way, in the same courts and under the same procedure, as if the crime was committed entirely within the state.

For the foregoing reasons the judgment and orders are reversed and the cause remanded.[2]

McFarland, J., Van Dyke, J., Henshaw, J., Beatty, C. J., and Temple, J., concurred.

STATE v. BENNETT

Supreme Court of Iowa, 1863.
14 Iowa 479.

The defendant was indicted for stealing a horse. The Court below charged the jury, that if the horse was stolen by the defendant in the State of Missouri, and brought by him into Wapello county, that he might be indicted and convicted in this State. This ruling is the error assigned. . . .

Baldwin, C. J. . . . Mr. Bishop, in his late work on Criminal Law, refers to the conflict of authorities on this question, and shows clearly the fallacy of the reasoning of the judges who hold that the

---

2. Cf. People v. Licenziata, 199 App. Div. 106, 191 N.Y.S. 619 (2nd Dep't 1921). In this case the defendant purchased a large quantity of wood alcohol in New York. This he put into mixtures called "whisky" and "brandy", which he sold for beverage purposes. A customer from Connecticut purchased part of it and this purchase found its way to a hotel at Chicopee Falls, Massachusetts, where a man died as a result of drinking it. It was shown that defendant knew of the poisonous nature of the mixture when he sold it in New York. A conviction of manslaughter in the first degree in New York was affirmed under the statutes of that state.

In People v. Zayas, 217 N.Y. 78, 111 N. E. 465 (1916), defendant was held triable in New York for there making false pretenses by means of which he obtained property which was delivered to him in Pennsylvania.

See Cook, The Logical and Legal Bases of the Conflict of Laws, 33 Yale L.J. 457, 462 (1924).

Courts of the State to which the stolen property has been taken cannot take jurisdiction of the offense. He says:

"Our courts can try all offenses against our laws, and if a man has property in his hands here, they can inquire what legal relation he sustains to this property; and if it came with him from a foreign country, the relation he sustained to it there establishes his relation to it here. This is familiar law, undisputed, practised upon daily in all our tribunals in the ordinary matters of litigation. The proposition that a man is to escape punishment for the violation of our laws because he first violated the laws of a foreign country is absurd in itself, and mischievous in its practical application. Nothing is plainer than that when a man is found here with property, our Courts will inquire after the owner of it, equally, whether such owner is alleged to be a foreigner or citizen, present personally or absent. Nothing is plainer than that our Courts will protect the right of property, equally whether the property is in the owner's grasp, or wrongfully found in the grasp of the felon. And no principle is better established as a general doctrine than that any physical removal, however slight, of the entire physical substance of the thing alleged to be stolen, to which physical substance the remover has not the right of possession, even though he has it in his custody, lawfully or unlawfully, is, where the felonious intent exists, larceny. If, therefore, the complete offense is not committed here, by one bringing here from a foreign country personal goods which he has there stolen, using them here as his own, meaning at the same time here to deprive the owner of his ownership therein, then it is impossible for any man, under any circumstances, to do acts completely falling within all the descriptions and definitions given in the books of this offense."

In answer to the objection that it renders the prisoner liable to be twice convicted and punished for one offense, in violation of the spirit of the common law, the author says: "The common law either admits of two convictions in such a case or it does not; if it does, there is nothing in the objection; if it does not, then the first conviction, in whatever locality it takes place, may be plead in bar of the second. The common law, however, knows no such plea in defense of a prosecution as *liability to an indictment elsewhere.*" 1 Bish.Crim. Law, 596, 597.

Affirmed.[1]

---

[1]. Accord, State v. Ellis, 3 Conn. 185 (1819); Ferrill v. Commonwealth, 62 Ky. 153 (1864); Thomas v. Commonwealth, 15 S.W. 861, 12 Ky.L.Rep. 903 (1891); Cummings v. State, 1 Harr. & J. 340 (Md.1802); Worthington v. State, 58 Md. 403 (1882); Commonwealth v. Andrews, 2 Mass. 14 (1806); Commonwealth v. Holder, 75 Mass. 7 (1857); Hamilton v. State, 11 Ohio 435 (1842); State v. Johnson, 2 Or. 115 (1864); State v. Hill, 19 S.C. 435 (1883).

Contra: Lee v. State, 64 Ga. 203 (1879); Beal v. State, 15 Ind. 378 (1860); State v. Reonnals, 14 La.Ann. 278 (1859); People v. Loughridge, 1 Neb. 11 (1871); State v. LeBlanch, 31 N.J. L. 82 (1864); People v. Gardner, 2 Johns. 477 (N.Y.1807); People v. Schenck, 2 Johns. 479 (N.Y.1807);

Sec. 1 *JURISDICTION* 675

(iv) Jurisdiction Over Boundary Rivers

NIELSON v. OREGON

Supreme Court of the United States, 1909.
212 U.S. 315, 53 L.Ed. 528, 29 S.Ct. 383.

[Nielson, a citizen of Washington, had a license from the Fish Commissioner of Washington to operate a purse net on the Columbia River and was on said river, within the limits of the State of Washington, operating a purse net when he was arrested by Oregon officers. An Oregon statute prohibited fishing with a purse net on the Columbia River and Nielson was convicted for a violation of that law. From that judgment the case was taken to the Supreme Court on error.

Before the territories had been admitted into the Union it had been provided by Act of Congress "that the Territory of Oregon and the Territory of Washington, shall have concurrent jurisdiction over all offenses committed on the Columbia River, where said river forms the common boundary between said territories". And the Act of Congress admitting Oregon into the Union provides that it shall have "jurisdiction in civil and criminal cases upon the Columbia River and Snake River, concurrently with the states and territories of which those rivers form a boundary in common with this State".]

Mr. Justice Brewer. . . . Undoubtedly one purpose, perhaps the primary purpose, in the grant of concurrent jurisdiction was to avoid any nice question as to whether a criminal act sought to be prosecuted was committed on one side or the other of the exact boundary in the channel, that boundary sometimes changing by reason of the shifting of the channel. Where an act is *malum in se* prohibited and punishable by the laws of both States, the one first acquiring jurisdiction of the person may prosecute the offense, and its judgment is a finality in both States, so that one convicted or acquitted in the courts of the one State cannot be prosecuted for the same offense in the courts of the other. But, as appears from the quotation we have just made, it is not limited to this. It extends to civil as well as criminal matters, and is broadly a grant of jurisdiction to each of the States.

State v. Brown, 2 N.C. 100 (1794); Simmons v. Commonwealth, 5 Binn. 617 (Pa.1813); Simpson v. State, 23 Tenn. 456 (1844). This has been changed by statute (now Tenn.Code Ann. § 11477) (Williams, 1934), see Henry v. State, 47 Tenn. 331 (1870).

Whatever may be the rule at common law, it is clear that a state statute may make it a punishable offense, under the name of larceny, for a thief to bring into the state, goods stolen elsewhere by him. State v. Adams, 14 Ala. 486 (1848); La Vaul v. State, 40 Ala. 44 (1866); McFarland v. State, 4 Kan. 68 (1866); People v. Williams, 24 Mich. 156 (1871); State v. Butler, 67 Mo. 59 (1877).

The present case is not one of the prosecution for an offense *malum in se*, but for one simply *malum prohibitum*. Doubtless the same rule would apply if the act was prohibited by each State separately, but where as here the act is prohibited by one State and in terms authorized by the other, can the one State which prohibits, prosecute and punish for the act done within the territorial limits of the other? Obviously, the grant of concurrent jurisdiction may bring up from time to time many and some curious and difficult questions, so we properly confine ourselves to the precise question presented. The plaintiff in error was within the limits of the State of Washington, doing an act which that State in terms authorized and gave him a license to do. Can the State of Oregon, by virtue of its concurrent jurisdiction, disregard that authority, practically override the legislation of Washington, and punish a man for doing within the territorial limits of Washington an act which that State had specially authorized him to do? We are of opinion that it cannot. It is not at all impossible that in some instances the interests of the two States may be different. Certainly, as appears in the present case, the opinion of the legislatures of the two States is different, and the one State cannot enforce its opinion against that of the other, at least as to an act done within the limits of that other State. Whether, if the act of the plaintiff in error had been done within the territorial limits of the State of Oregon, it would make any difference we need not determine, nor whether, in the absence of any legislation by the State of Washington authorizing the act, Oregon could enforce its statute against the act done anywhere upon the waters of the Columbia. Neither is it necessary to consider whether the prosecution should be in the names of the two States jointly. It is enough to decide, as we do, that for an act done within the territorial limits of the State of Washington under authority and license from that State one cannot be prosecuted and punished by the State of Oregon.

. . .

The judgment of the Supreme Court of the State of Oregon is reversed and the case remanded for further proceedings not inconsistent with this opinion.[1]

---

1. In many cases the courts of one state have punished crimes committed upon that part of the river within the boundaries of another state: Carlisle v. State, 32 Ind. 55 (1869); Dougan v. State, 125 Ind. 130, 25 N.E. 171 (1890); Lemore v. Commonwealth, 127 Ky. 480, 105 S.W. 930 (1907); State v. Cunningham, 102 Miss. 237, 59 So. 76 (1912); State v. Metcalf, 65 Mo.App. 681 (1896); State v. Cameron, 2 Pin. 490 (Wis.1850); see Commonwealth v. Garner, 3 Grat. 655 (Va.1846). In Wiggins Ferry Co. v. Reddig, 24 Ill. App. 260 (1887), the court at page 265 said: "Undoubtedly it would be held that the judicial tribunal first taking cognizance of the cause would, under well established and understood principles, retain its jurisdiction to the end of the controversy, applying the law of the *forum* to the facts of the case in settling the rights of the parties."

Defendant was charged in Minnesota with larceny from the person. The evidence showed that the offense was committed on a bridge which spans the Mississippi River, at a point be-

Sec. 1   JURISDICTION   677

(B) VENUE

If an alleged offense is triable within the state it is then necessary to determine which of the courts in the state may try it. To decide this it is necessary to ascertain the particular area (or areas) of the state within which it may be tried. This area will usually be a county, although in some states it may be some other subdivision such as a district. And the county (or other area) appropriate for this trial is called the "venue." The word "venue" originally meant the neighborhood from which the jurors were to come. It still has that meaning except that the place of trial is the same whether it is to be by a jury or without a jury.

Statutory provisions with reference to venue differ from state to state. The American Law Institute included the following suggestions in its proposed Code of Criminal Procedure, after an exhaustive study of all of the existing statutes:

Section 238. Right to try where offense committed within state. Any person who commits within this state an offense against this state, whether he is within or without the state at the time of its commission, may be tried in this state.

Section 239. Offense in or against aircraft. Any person who commits an offense in or against any aircraft while it is in flight over this state may be tried in this state. The trial in such case may be in any county over which the aircraft passed in the course of such flight.

Section 240. Place of trial generally. In all criminal prosecutions the trial shall be in the county where the offense was committed unless otherwise provided in this Code.

Section 241. Where accessory in one county and offense committed in another. Where a person in one county aids, abets or procures the commission of an offense in another county he may be tried for the offense in either county.

Section 242. Where offense committed partly in one and partly in another county. Where several acts are requisite to the commission of an offense, the trial may be in any county in which any of such acts occurs.

tween Minnesota and Wisconsin, and was committed on a part of the bridge over an island which is on the Wisconsin side of the main channel of the river. It was held that the Minnesota court had jurisdiction. State v. George, 60 Minn. 503, 63 N.W. 100 (1895).

Where a river which forms a boundary line between two states suddenly leaves its old bed and forms a new one by the process of avulsion there is no change of the boundary line. State v. Jacobs, 93 Ariz. 336, 380 P.2d 998 (1963).

Section 243. Where offense committed on or near county boundary. Where an offense is committed on or within five hundred yards of the boundary of two or more counties the trial may be in any one of such counties.

Section 244. Where person in one county commits offense in another. Where a person in one county commits an offense in another county the trial may be in either county.

Section 245. Where offense committed on railroad train or other vehicle. Where an offense is committed on a railroad train or other public or private vehicle while in the course of its trip the trial may be in any county through which such train or other vehicle passed during such trip.

Section 246. Where offense committed on vessel. Where an offense is committed on board a vessel in the course of its voyage, the trial may be in any county through which the vessel passed during such voyage.

Section 247. Where injury inflicted in one county and death occurs in another. Where a person inflicts an injury upon another person in one county from which the injured person dies in another county, the trial for the homicide may be in either county.

Section 248. Where stolen property brought into another county. Where a person obtains property by larceny, robbery, false pretenses or embezzlement in one county and brings the property so obtained into any other county or counties, he may be tried in the county in which he obtains the property or in any other county into which he brings it.

Section 249. Conviction or acquittal in one county bar to prosecution in another. Where a person may be tried for an offense in two or more counties, a conviction or acquittal of the offense in one county shall be a bar to a prosecution for the same offense in another county.

Where the evidence as to venue is disputed the jury should pass upon it as one of the issues of the case. If it is clear that the court has no jurisdiction over the offense the prosecution should be dismissed. But if the lack of jurisdiction is because the offense is within the exclusive jurisdiction of the court of some other county of the state the usual procedure is not to discharge the defendant, but to have him committed, or admitted to bail, to await transfer to the proper county for trial there.

STATE v. FAVORS

Supreme Court of Arizona, En Banc, 1962.
92 Ariz. 147, 375 P.2d 260.

UDALL, VICE CHIEF JUSTICE. Bobby Favors was convicted in the Superior Court of Pima County of the crime of wilfully and unlawfully robbing Jack Weylor on December 7, 1960. He appeals to this court.

With two other men Favors entered upon Weylor's property and with a 30–30 rifle forced him to give up his wallet along with its contents. The identity of Favors as one of the three men was established to the satisfaction of the jury, notwithstanding the fact that he claimed to have been elsewhere at the time of the commission of the crime.

The errors urged by the defendant relate to four different matters. First it is argued that the court erred in reopening the state's case to hear evidence on the question of venue, when the state failed to establish venue before the time that the court was to instruct the jury. When defendant had finished his own closing argument he asked the court to instruct the jury that there was no evidence in the trial that the crime had been committed in Pima County. Thereupon plaintiff moved the court for permission to reopen the case for the purpose of hearing evidence regarding the question of venue, which motion was granted. Deputy Sheriff Norman Ranger was recalled and he testified that the alleged robbery was committed in Pima County at the place specified in the information.

Such a ruling was within the sound discretion of the court. In State v. Cassady, 67 Ariz. 48, 190 P.2d 501, we said:

"Our rules of criminal procedure should be construed so as to promote justice—not to thwart it. To have refused to permit the state to reopen its case would have been an abuse of legal discretion and an 'assist' to the obstruction of justice." . . .

Judgment of conviction affirmed.[1]

BERNSTEIN, C. J., and STRUCKMEYER, JENNINGS and LOCKWOOD, JJ., concur.

---

1. Where defendant did not know that venue would not be proved he could move for an acquittal at the conclusion of the evidence. United States v. Brothman, 191 F.2d 70 (2d Cir. 1951).

"The venue was a jurisdictional fact, . . ." People v. Adams, 300 Ill. 20, 24, 132 N.E. 765, 767 (1921). ". . . it has always been the law requiring the government or state, as the case might be, to prove the venue in order to show jurisdiction of the court to try and determine the issue." State v. Jackson, 187 Ind. 694, 699, 121 N.E. 114, 116 (1918). " 'It is a maxim in the law that consent can never confer jurisdiction; by which is meant that the consent of parties cannot empower a Court to act upon subjects which are not submitted to its determination and judgment by the law.' Cooley on Const.Lim. p. 575. . . . The general rule undoubtedly is that the objection that a court has no jurisdiction of the person of the accused may be waived. . . . This court holds that 'the right to object to the

STATE v. REESE

Supreme Court of Washington, Department One, 1920.
112 Wash. 507, 192 P. 934.

MAIN, J. The defendant was charged by information, by the prosecuting attorney of Spokane county, with the crime of grand larceny. The trial resulted in a verdict of guilty. A motion in arrest of judgment was made and sustained. The state appeals.

The information, omitting the formal parts, is as follows:

"That on or about August 31st, 1919, on a railway train of the Northern Pacific Railroad, arriving in, and passing through, Spokane county, Washington, the said defendant, Arthur Reese, whose other or true name is to the prosecuting attorney unknown, then and there being, did then and there, wilfully, unlawfully and feloniously, take, steal and carry away one certain gold watch of the value of $50 and one certain gold bougat [sic] watch fob of the value of $50, the property of, and belonging to, Chas. E. Roediger, with the intent to deprive and defraud the owner thereof."

It should be noted that, in this charge, it is not alleged that the offense was committed in Spokane county. Upon the trial it appeared from testimony that the respondent was a porter on the Northern Pacific train leaving Tacoma, Washington, on the evening of the 30th or 31st of August, 1919. The train arrived in Spokane the following morning. Among the passengers on the train was one C. E.

---

locality of trial is a personal privilege which the party may waive and thereby confer jurisdiction.' Brown v. Brown, 155 Tenn. 530, at page 537, 296 S.W. 356, 358, citing cases." State ex rel. Lea v. Brown, 166 Tenn. 669, 694–5, 64 S.W.2d 841, 849 (1933). Accord, Hildebrand v. United States, 304 F.2d 716 (10th Cir. 1962).

The federal statute provides (18 U.S. C.A. § 3231): "The district courts of the United States shall have original jurisdiction, exclusive of the courts of the states, of all offenses against the laws of the United States". Hence the question in regard to a particular court of the United States is one of venue rather than jurisdiction. Bickford v. Looney, 219 F.2d 555 (10th Cir. 1955).

Where the only reference from which venue might be inferred was testimony relating to certain named streets and business establishments the conviction was reversed. Morris v. State, 363 P.2d 377 (Okl.Cr.1961). The court said it would take judicial notice of the boundaries of the counties and the geographical locations of the cities and towns of the state, but not of streets and buildings where there is no evidence as to the town or city in which they are located.

Permitting either trial or appellate court to decide venue from facts judicially noticed but not communicated to the jury would deprive defendant of trial by jury on the issue of fact alleged in the indictment. State v. Jones, — Or. —, 400 P.2d 524 (1965).

Venue for the trial of a criminal case need not be proved beyond a reasonable doubt, but only by a preponderance of the evidence, and it may be established by circumstantial evidence. People v. Erb, — Cal.App.2d —, 45 Cal.Rptr. 503 (1965). Contra, State v. Jones, — Or. —, 400 P.2d 524 (1965).

Roediger, who occupied a berth in a sleeping car just in front of the car which was in charge of the respondent. Roediger retired about midnight, and at the time the train was near Yakima, Washington. At this time he had in his vest pocket a watch and fob. He awoke near Lind, Washington, and his watch and fob were missing. About a month later the respondent pawned the watch in the city of Spokane. Thereafter he was arrested, with the result as above indicated. The charge in this case is laid under § 2293 of Rem. & Bal.Code, which provides:

"The route traversed by any railway car, coach, train or other public conveyance, and the water traversed by any boat shall be criminal districts; and the jurisdiction of all public offenses committed on any such railway car, coach, train, boat or other public conveyance, or at any station or depot upon such route, shall be in any county through which said car, coach, train, boat or other public conveyance may pass during the trip or voyage, or in which the trip or voyage may begin or terminate."

By this statute, it is attempted to make the route traversed by a railway train a criminal district and to provide that the court in any county through which the train may pass during its trip shall have jurisdiction of any offense committed upon the train, regardless of whether, at the time the crime was committed, the train was in the county where the prosecution is attempted to be had. If this statute is constitutional, the judgment of the superior court cannot be sustained. On the other hand, if the statute is unconstitutional, the trial court ruled correctly on the motion in arrest of judgment. It should be kept in mind that this is not a case where property stolen in one county is carried by the thief into another, and in the latter county is charged with having committed an offense therein. As already pointed out, the information in this case does not charge that the offense was committed in Spokane county. Neither is it a case where an act done in one county contributes to the offense in another. The question is the constitutionality of the law under which the accused was tried and convicted. Const., art. 1, § 22, provides:

"In criminal prosecutions, the accused shall have the right to . . . a speedy public trial by an impartial jury of the county in which the offense is alleged to have been committed. . . ."

Under this section of the constitution one accused of crime has a right to be tried in the county in which the offense is alleged to have been committed. It requires no argument to show that the offense, being alleged in a particular county, the proof must show that it was committed in that county. Comparing the provisions of the statute with the requirements of the constitution, it appears that the statute goes beyond the constitutional limitation. Under the statute, the route traversed by a railway train is made a criminal district, and an offender may be prosecuted in any county in such district. Under the constitution, he can only be prosecuted in the county where the offense has been committed. In State v. Carroll, 55 Wash. 588, 104 Pac. 814, 133 Am.St. 1047, the court had before it a statute providing that, when property taken by burglary in one county had been brought into another county, the jurisdiction was in either county. It was there held that the statute violated Const., art. 1, § 22, which guaranteed to the accused a right to a trial in the county in which the offense was alleged to have been committed. While that case can hardly be said to be exactly in point upon the question presented upon this appeal, yet the analogy is very close. . . . In People v. Brock, 149 Mich. 464, 112 N.W. 1116, the question was before the supreme court of Michigan, and it was there held that such a statute cannot be sustained under a constitutional provision which guarantees to the accused the right to a trial in the county in which the offense has been committed. It was there said:

"It would be a startling innovation should we say that the legislature has power to subject a person charged with crime to prosecution in any one of several counties, covering a strip of territory coextensive with the length or breadth of the state, at the prosecutor's election, and yet that is what this statute authorizes if it is valid. It cannot be said that this offense was in 'contemplation of law' committed in each of said counties, as in a case where property stolen in one county is carried by the thief into another, or possibly where an act done in one county contributes to the commission of the offense in another."

In Watt v. People, 126 Ill. 9, 18 N.E. 340, the question was before the supreme court of Illinois and a different conclusion was there reached, though not by a unanimous court. The holding in that case seems to be influenced by the fact that the constitutional provision there being considered was less restrictive than were the similar provisions in either of the two earlier constitutions, and this fact led to the conclusion that it was the intention "to release in some degree the rigid rule formerly prevailing." As already stated, none of the other cases cited in the notes of Corpus Juris, or in the brief, discuss or decide the question here presented. Under this state of the authorities, we are constrained to disagree with the writer of the text upon where the weight of authority lies. It seems to us that reason and authority both support the view that the statute cannot take away from an accused a right guaranteed by the constitution.

The judgment will be affirmed.[1]

HOLCOMB, C. J., MITCHELL, PARKER, and MACKINTOSH, JJ., concur.

---

[1]. In 1922 the constitution of the State of Washington was amended as follows: "The route traversed by any railway coach, train or public conveyance, and the water traversed by any boat shall be criminal districts; and the jurisdiction of all public offenses committed on any such railway car, coach, train, boat or other public conveyance, or at any station or depot upon such route, shall be in any county through which the said car, coach, train, boat or other public conveyance may pass during the trip or voyage, or in which the trip or voyage may begin or terminate." Art. I, § 22.

PUTNAM v. UNITED STATES

United States Circuit Court of Appeals, Tenth Circuit, 1964.
337 F.2d 313.

[Putnam was charged with transportation in interstate and foreign commerce from Toronto, Canada, to Las Cruces, New Mexico, of an automobile knowing it to have been stolen, and entered a plea of guilty. Later he moved to withdraw his plea of guilty and to have vacated and set aside his conviction. From the order denying this motion, he appealed.]

Before MURRAH, CHIEF JUDGE, and HILL and SETH, CIRCUIT JUDGES.

HILL, CIRCUIT JUDGE. . . . Appellant's remaining contention that venue was not in the District of New Mexico is patently without merit. He was transporting a stolen car in interstate and foreign commerce and under 18 U.S.C.A. § 3237 venue for an offense involving transportation in interstate or foreign commerce is " . . . in any district from, through, or into which such commerce . . . moves." See Penny v. United States, 4 Cir., 154 F.2d 629.

Affirmed.[1]

A statute authorizing trial in either county if the offense was committed within one-quarter mile of the county line was held to be unconstitutional. Armstrong v. State, 41 Tenn. 338 (1860).

Accord, State v. Montgomery, 115 La. 155, 38 So. 949 (1905); State v. Hatch, 91 Mo. 568, 4 S.W. 502 (1887). A similar statute was held valid in Michigan, but the constitutional provisions were different. People v. Donaldson, 243 Mich. 104, 219 N.W. 602 (1928). In Oregon a statute authorizing trial in either county, if the offense is committed within a mile of the county line, was held not to violate defendant's right to be tried in the county in which the crime was committed. This statute was said merely to enlarge the boundaries of the county for judicial purposes. State v. Lehman, 130 Or. 132, 279 P. 283 (1929).

1. "The petitioner relies on those provisions of the Constitution of the United States which declare that in all criminal prosecutions the accused shall have the right to be tried by an impartial jury of the State and District wherein the crime shall have been committed. Art. 3, § 2; Amendments, Art. 6. But the right thereby secured is not a right to be tried in the District where the accused resides, or even in the District in which he is personally at the time of committing the crime, but in the District 'wherein the crime shall have been committed'. . . . When a crime is committed partly in one District and partly in another it must, in order to prevent an absolute failure of justice, be tried in either District, or in that one which the legislature may designate; and Congress has accordingly provided, that 'when any offense against the United States is begun in one judicial District and completed in any other, it shall be deemed to have been committed in either, and may be dealt with, inquired of, tried, determined and punished in either District, in the same manner as if it had been actually and wholly committed therein'. Rev.Stat. § 731." Burton v. United States, 202 U.S. 344, 388, 26 S.Ct. 688, 701, 50 L.Ed. 1057 (1906). The Court was quoting from In re Palliser, 136 U.S. 257, 258, 10 S.Ct. 1034, 34 L.Ed. 514 (1890).

The statute referred to now reads: "Except as otherwise expressly provided by enactment of Congress, any offense against the United States begun in one district and completed in another, or committed in more than one district,

UNITED STATES v. DIXON

United States District Court, E. D. New York, 1947.
73 F.Supp. 683.

Theodore Dixon was charged by indictments with manslaughter and assault committed on board a merchant vessel of the United States, and he moves to dismiss both indictments.

Motion denied.

BYERS, DISTRICT JUDGE. This is a motion, pursuant to Rule 12 of the Federal Rules of Criminal Procedure, 18 U.S.C.A. following section 687, to dismiss both indictments, made after plea of not guilty as to each. The motion was permitted pursuant to paragraph (b) (3) of said Rule.

The grounds are:

1, 2 and 3. That both indictments fail to show jurisdiction in the court. The respective charges involve one transaction; and as to the first, the defendant is charged with manslaughter according to

---

may be inquired of and prosecuted in any district in which such offense was begun, continued, or completed". 18 U.S.C. § 3237(a).

The statute quoted in PUTNAM is another paragraph of the same section.

In Commonwealth v. Macloon, 101 Mass. 1 (1869), it was held that death within the state, resulting from injuries inflicted elsewhere, was sufficient to authorize trial and conviction in the state, under an express statutory provision to that effect. Accord, as to death in one county resulting from an injury inflicted in another county in the same state, under a statute expressly so providing. State v. Criqui, 105 Kan. 716, 185 P. 1063 (1919). In State v. Carter, 27 N.J.L. 499 (1859) it was held that an indictment charging a fatal assault committed in New York and resulting in death in New Jersey charged no crime in the latter state. Apparently New Jersey had a statute somewhat similar to the Massachusetts act, but the court held that it applied only to murder and not to manslaughter. The opinion indicates that it is beyond the power of the state to punish for acts done exclusively in another state, even if death results therefrom and occurs in New Jersey.

In Washington it was held that taking a girl from one county and placing her in another county authorized conviction (of placing a girl in a house of prostitution) in the county *from which* she was taken. State v. Ashe, 182 Wash. 598, 48 P.2d 213 (1935). And a prosecution for obtaining property by false pretenses could be maintained in the county in which the false and fraudulent representation was made, although the property was obtained in another county. State v. Knutson, 168 Wash. 633, 12 P.2d 923 (1932). Both of these decisions were under a statute declaring the venue to be in either county if the offense was committed partly in each.

But a similar statute was held not to authorize a prosecution for attempted abortion in the county in which the miscarriage occurred if the unlawful operation was performed in a different county. State v. Hollenbeck, 36 Iowa 112 (1873). And a statute, authorizing a prosecution for burglary in a county into which was taken the loot from a house broken into in another county, was held to be unconstitutional. State v. McGraw, 87 Mo. 161 (1885).

The offense of filing a false income-tax return may be tried either in the district in which the return was prepared or in the district in which it was filed. United States v. United States District Court, 209 F.2d 575 (6th Cir. 1954).

Title 18 U.S.C.A. § 453; as to the second, he is charged with assault under Title 18 U.S.C.A. §§ 451 and 455.

It will be assumed from the motion papers, pro and con, that the proof will show that the defendant is a citizen of Great Britain, who was chief cook on the S. S. Benjamin Silliman, a merchant vessel of the United States which on March 27, 1947, was in command of W. S. Evans as master, and was proceeding out of the port of Ceuta, Spanish Morocco.

That between midnight and 2:00 A.M. of that day a fracas occurred in defendant's cabin, during the course of which one Elmo Martin was shot and the defendant Dixon was wounded. The master at once arranged for a doctor and a launch to attend the two men and take them ashore.

That at about 8:00 A.M., the master gave the British Consul at that port written authority to place a guard over both men, and to make a formal report to the United States Consul at Tangier.

That on April 2, 1947, the British Vice-Consul handed over the defendant to the master of the United States merchant ship Richardson to transport him to this country. He was so brought to the port of New York and there arrested and taken into custody, on or about April 15, 1947, and is now held to answer these indictments which were filed in this court on August 27 and September 2, 1947, respectively.

The alleged crimes having been committed on the high seas or elsewhere out of the jurisdiction of any particular state or district, trial is proper in the district where the offender is found, or into which he is first brought, Title 28 U.S.C.A. § 102.

It is a reasonable inference that the master of the Silliman sought the aid of the British Consul in Ceuta in the absence of a United States Consul, and that the former acted on behalf of the master in keeping Dixon under guard, and in causing him to be transported to the United States, and there to answer to a charge of having committed a crime on a merchant ship of the United States.

The court is not called upon to inquire how the defendant got here, so long as he was found in or was first brought to this district.

It is the present view that the master of the Silliman could have brought Dixon here in custody, and that he merely accomplished that purpose by securing the assistance of the British Vice-Consul and that of the master of the Richardson.

Dixon was not entitled to any intervention of the courts of Spanish Morocco, or of Great Britain. He had signed on a merchant ship of the United States and thereby subjected himself to the laws of this country, and he has been duly indicted, and must stand trial.

The foregoing disposes as well of the second and third points urged for him as of the first.

He was never in the custody of the British Vice-Consul as such, but the latter was requested by the master of the defendant's ship to assist in the discharge of the latter's duty and authority; no necessity for extradition arose, as the defendant never sought asylum in any country.

4. That the indictments fail to set forth a crime under the laws of the United States. This is contradicted by the language of the Statutes to which reference has been made.

It is no answer to the manslaughter charge that the alleged victim died ashore in the hospital, and not on the ship where seemingly he was shot. Title 18 U.S.C.A. § 553. See also Bostic v. Rives, 71 App.D.C. 2, 107 F.2d 649, at page 651.

This court is not called upon to direct which indictment is to be tried first.

Motion to dismiss denied. Settle order.[a]

UNITED STATES v. CORES

Supreme Court of the United States, 1958.
356 U.S. 405, 78 S.Ct. 875.

MR. JUSTICE CLARK delivered the opinion of the Court.

The sole issue in this appeal is whether an alien crewman who willfully remains in the United States in excess of the 29 days allowed by his conditional landing permit, in violation of § 252(c) of the Immigration and Nationality Act,[1] is guilty of a continuing offense

---

a. Where two or more courts have concurrent jurisdiction of the same offense the established rule is that the court first acquiring jurisdiction of the prosecution, retains it to the end. State v. Parker, 234 N.C. 236, 66 S.E. 2d 907 (1951), unless it voluntarily dismisses or abandons the prosecution, Rogers v. State, 101 Miss. 847, 58 So. 536 (1912), or the defendant waives his right to insist upon trial there, State v. Van Ness, 109 Vt. 392, 199 A. 759 (1938). Actual jurisdiction of the prosecution (as distinguished from potential jurisdiction of the offense) ordinarily requires jurisdiction of the person. Sherrod v. State, 197 Ala. 286, 72 So. 540 (1916). Hence if indictments for the same offense are found properly in two or more counties the case normally will be tried in the court first acquiring jurisdiction of the person by arrest. Smithey v. State, 93 Miss. 257, 46 So. 410 (1908). If, however, in the absence of any collusion on the part of the defendant, he is tried and acquitted in a court other than the one first acquiring jurisdiction, this is a complete bar to a subsequent trial in the **first court.** State v. Howell, 220 S.C. 178, 66 S.E. 2d 701 (1951). On the other hand the state has a right to elect the forum in which it will proceed and is not to be deprived of this choice by the **machinations** of the defendant or his friends. McDaniel, Sheriff v. Sams, 259 Ky. 56, 82 S.W.2d 215 (1935).

[Footnotes by the Court.]

1. 66 Stat. 221, 8 U.S.C. § 1282(c), 8 U.S.C.A. § 1282(c). Subsection (a) authorizes immigration officers to grant permits, on certain conditions, allowing alien crewmen to land for periods up to 29 days. Subsection (b) details procedures for revocation of permits. Subsection (c) sets out the criminal penalties involved in this case:

"Any alien crewman who willfully remains in the United States in excess of the number of days allowed in any

Sec. 1　　　　　　　　*JURISDICTION*　　　　　　　　687

which may be prosecuted in the district where he is found. Discovering that appellee's permit had expired before he entered the district where he was apprehended and where the prosecution was begun, the District Court dismissed the criminal information, holding that a violation of § 252(c) was not a continuing crime. The Government brought direct appeal, 18 U.S.C. § 3731, 18 U.S.C.A. § 3731, and we noted probable jurisdiction. 1957, 355 U.S. 866, 78 S.Ct. 123, 2 L.Ed.2d 72. Since we conclude that the District Court was in error, the judgment is reversed and the case is remanded for further proceedings.

The information, filed in the United States District Court for the District of Connecticut, charged that appellee entered the United States at Philadelphia on April 27, 1955, and that 29 days later, at the expiration of his conditional landing permit, he "did wilfully and knowingly remain in the United States, to wit: Bethel, Connecticut," in violation of § 252(c) of the Immigration and Nationality Act. A plea of guilty was entered, but a government attorney informed the court prior to sentencing that appellee was not in Connecticut at the expiration of his permit as charged in the information, but that in fact he came to Connecticut only after spending about a year in New York. The judge permitted withdrawal of the guilty plea and dismissed the case. He cited an earlier decision of the same court holding that § 252(c) did not define a continuing crime. United States v. Tavares, No. 9407 Crim., May 6, 1957, and indicated that the information was brought in an improper district since appellee was not in Connecticut at the time his permit expired.[2]

The Constitution makes it clear that determination of proper venue in a criminal case requires determination of where the crime was committed.[3] This principle is reflected in numerous statutory enactments, including Rule 18, Fed.Rules Crim.Proc., which provides that except as otherwise permitted, "the prosecution shall be had in a district in which the offense was committed . . .." In ascertaining

conditional permit issued under subsection (a) of this section shall be guilty of a misdemeanor, and upon conviction thereof shall be fined not more than $500 or shall be imprisoned for not more than six months, or both."

2. Appellee suggests that the inconsistency in the date of the offense as alleged in the information and as represented by government counsel provides additional reason for upholding the dismissal. This phase of the case, however, is not before us, United States v. Borden Co., 1939, 308 U.S. 188, 206–207, 60 S.Ct. 182, 191–192, 84 L.Ed. 181, so we confine our opinion to the point of statutory construction which clearly prompted the dismissal. Any inconsistency may be asserted by appellee on remand. See Fed.Rules Crim.Proc. [Rule] 7(e), 18 U.S.C.A.

3. "The Trial of all Crimes, except in Cases of Impeachment, shall be by Jury; and such Trial shall be held in the State where the said Crimes shall have been committed . . .." U.S. Const. Art. III, § 2, cl. 3.

"In all criminal prosecutions, the accused shall enjoy the right to a speedy and public trial, by an impartial jury of the State and district wherein the crime shall have been committed . . .." U.S.Const. Amend. VI.

this locality we are mindful that questions of venue "raise deep issues of public policy in the light of which legislation must be construed." The provision for trial in the vicinity of the crime is a safeguard against the unfairness and hardship involved when an accused is prosecuted in a remote place. Provided its language permits, the Act in question should be given that construction which will respect such considerations.

Unlike some statutory offenses,[4] there is an absence here of any specific provision fixing venue, save the general language of the Act providing for venue "at any place in the United States at which the violation may occur . . .."[5] In such cases the Court must base its determination on "the nature of the crime alleged and the location of the act or acts constituting it." United States v. Anderson, 1946, 328 U.S. 699, 703, 66 S.Ct. 1213, 1216, 90 L.Ed. 1529, and if the Congress is found to have created a continuing offense, "the locality of [the] crime shall extend over the whole area through which force propelled by an offender operates."

Section 252(c) punishes "[a]ny alien crewman who willfully remains in the United States in excess of the number of days allowed." The conduct proscribed is the affirmative act of willfully remaining, and the crucial word "remains" permits no connotation other than continuing presence. Nor does the section necessarily pertain to any particular locality, such as the place of entry, for the Act broadly extends to willfully remaining "in the United States."[6] Appellee urges, however, that the offense is completed the moment the permit expires, and that even if the alien remains thereafter, he no longer commits the offense. It is true that remaining at the instant of expiration satisfies the definition of the crime, but it does not exhaust it. It seems incongruous to say that while the alien "wilfully remains"

---

4. See e. g., 18 U.S.C. § 659, 18 U.S.C.A. § 659 (theft of goods in interstate commerce); 18 U.S.C. § 1073, 18 U.S.C.A. § 1073 (flight to avoid prosecution or giving testimony); 18 U.S.C. § 3236, 18 U.S.C.A. § 3236 (murder or manslaughter); 18 U.S.C. § 3239, 18 U.S. C.A. § 3239 (transmitting or mailing threatening communications); 32 Stat. 847, 34 Stat. 587, 49 U.S.C. § 41(1), 49 U.S.C.A. § 41(1) (certain violations of Interstate Commerce Act). See Barron, Federal Practice and Procedure, § 2061.

5. § 279, Immigration and Nationality Act, 66 Stat. 230, 8 U.S.C. § 1329, 8 U.S.C.A. § 1329.

6. The offense here is unlike crimes of illegal entry set out in § 275 and § 276 of the Act. 66 Stat. 229, 8 U.S.C. §§ 1325, 1326, 8 U.S.C.A. §§ 1325, 1326. Those offenses are not continuing ones, as "entry" is limited to a particular locality and hardly suggests continuity. Hence a specific venue provision in § 279 of the Act was required before illegal entry cases could be prosecuted at the place of apprehension. 66 Stat. 230, 8 U.S.C. § 1329, 8 U.S.C.A. § 1329. This reasoning underlay the request for specific legislation by the Immigration and Naturalization Service. See Analysis of S. 3455, 81st Cong., prepared by the General Counsel of the Service, p. 276-2. In contrast to illegal entry, the § 252(c) offense of willfully remaining is continuing in nature. A specific venue provision would be mere surplusage, since prosecutions may be instituted in any district where the offense has been committed, not necessarily the district where the violation first occurred. The absence of such provision, therefore, is without significance.

on the 29th day when his permit expires, he no longer does so on the 30th, though still physically present in the country. Given the element of willfulness, we believe an alien "remains," in the contemplation of the statute, until he physically leaves the United States. The crime achieves no finality until such time. Since an offense committed in more than one district "may be inquired of and prosecuted in any district in which such offense was . . . continued," 18 U.S.C. § 3237, 18 U.S.C.A. § 3237, venue for § 252(c) lies in any district where the crewman willfully remains after the permit expires. Appellee entered Connecticut and was found there, so that district has venue for the prosecution.

The legislative history is not inconsistent with this interpretation of the statute. After a thorough investigation of our immigration laws completed some two years prior to the enactment of § 252(c), the Senate Committee on the Judiciary reported, "The problems relating to seamen are largely created by those who desert their ships, remain here illegally beyond the time granted them to stay, and become lost in the general populace of the country." S.Rep. No. 1515, 81st Cong., 2d Sess., 550. The tracing of such persons is complicated by the obscuration worked both by their own movement and by the passage of time. In this atmosphere the Congress sought to establish sanctions for alien crewmen who "willfully remain," the Senate Committee having observed that traditional remedies for the problem were inadequate because many crewmen "do not have the necessary documents to permit deportation." *Ibid.* It is hardly likely that the Congress would create the new sanction only to strip it of much of its effectiveness by compelling trial in the district where the crewman was present when his permit expired—a place which months or years later might be impossible of proof.

Moreover, we think it not amiss to point out that this result is entirely in keeping with the policy of relieving the accused, where possible, of the inconvenience incident to prosecution in a district far removed from his residence. Forcing an alien crewman to trial in the district where he was present at the expiration of his permit could entail much hardship. By holding the crime here to be a continuing one we make a valuable tool of justice available to the crewman. Rule 21(b) of the Federal Rules of Criminal Procedure provides for transfer of the proceeding to another district on motion of the defendant if it appears that the offense was committed in more than one district, and "if the court is satisfied that in the interest of justice the proceeding should be transferred to another district or division in which the commission of the offense is charged." The rule, with its inherent flexibility, would be inapplicable absent characterization of the offense as continuing in nature.

Reversed and remanded.[7]

[Added by the Compiler.]

7. The Taft-Hartley Act did not require union officers to file non-Communist affidavits but it did make such filing a condition precedent to a union's use of the procedures of the National La-

Mr. Justice Douglas, with whom The Chief Justice and Mr. Justice Black concur, dissenting.

The decision seems to me to be out of harmony with the statutory scheme of venue which Congress designed for immigration cases. We are here concerned with a crime under § 252 of the Immigration and Nationality Act of 1952, 66 Stat. 163, 220, 8 U.S.C. § 1282, 8 U.S.C.A. § 1282; *viz.* unlawfully remaining in the United States. Sections 275 and 276 describe crimes of unlawful entry. Section 279 gives the District Courts jurisdiction over the trial of both types of crimes; and as to venue it provides:

"Notwithstanding any other law, such prosecutions or suits may be instituted at any place in the United States at which the violation may occur or at which the person charged with a violation of sections 275 or 276 of this title may be apprehended."

When Congress wanted to lay venue in the district where the accused was "apprehended," it said so. It would seem, therefore, that venue may be laid in the district where the alien was "apprehended" only in case of the crimes of unlawful entry. All other crimes are to be prosecuted in the district where the violation first occurred. It is no answer to say that this crime is different because it was "continuous." See In re Snow, 120 U.S. 274, 281, 7 S.Ct. 556, 559, 30 L.Ed. 658. As District Judge Smith said, the distinction drawn by § 279 between venue at the place of violation and venue at the place of apprehension "would be meaningless if violations such as the one in issue were regarded as continuous." *

Moreover, the crime is completed when the conditional permit expires. All elements of the crime occur then. Nothing more remains to be done. It is then and there, Congress says, that the crime is "committed" in the sense that term is employed in Art. III, § 2, cl. 3 of the Constitution and in the Sixth Amendment.

I would affirm the judgment of the District Court.

bor Relations Board. Such affidavits were required to be filed in the District of Columbia. It was held that if a false affidavit was executed in Colorado, there deposited in the mail, received in the District of Columbia and there placed on file, the offense was committed only in the District of Columbia. Hence a trial in the federal district court of Colorado was invalid for lack of venue. Travis v. United States, 364 U.S. 631, 81 S.Ct. 358, 5 L.Ed.2d 340 (1961). It was intimated that the result would have been otherwise if the officers had been required to file non-Communist affidavits.

[Footnote by Mr. Justice Douglas.]

*. Congress has made its intent equally clear in analogous situations, see, e. g., 18 U.S.C. § 659, 18 U.S.C.A. § 659, where the possession of certain stolen goods, certainly a continuing illegal status similar to remaining, is made a crime. Section 659 provides in pertinent part: "The offense shall be deemed to have been committed . . . in any district in which the defendant may have taken or been in possession of the said money, baggage, goods, or chattels."

(C) COURTS

Having determined the county (or other area) in which the accused may be tried, the final inquiry in the matter of jurisdiction is to ascertain which one of the tribunals sitting there is the proper one for this particular case. This is seldom a difficult problem although differences in the various jurisdictions tend to complicate any generalized statement.

To speak in very broad terms we may say that the ordinary criminal case will be tried in the court of general jurisdiction unless some other tribunal has been provided for this purpose. The name will vary from state to state, the labels "circuit court", "district court" and "superior court" being the most common. In many of the large cities the trial will be in the "criminal court," which may be a separate tribunal, or may be merely the name applied to the division (or divisions), of the district, circuit or superior court to which the criminal cases are assigned.

If the prosecution is for the violation of a city ordinance it will be in a city tribunal which may be called a "police court" or "municipal court" or may have some other name. Such a court (or some other) may have concurrent jurisdiction with the circuit, district or superior court over part of the criminal field,—usually limited to misdemeanor cases.

If the accusation charges a petty offense it may be triable summarily before a magistrate, and in some states the magistrate may have exclusive jurisdiction over the case at this stage of the proceedings. Where this is true such a case can reach the court of general jurisdiction only on appeal,—although the provision may be for a trial *de novo* upon such appeal. It is important to distinguish the trial of a petty offense by a magistrate (which may or may not be appealed to the court of general jurisdiction) from a preliminary hearing by a magistrate which does not determine guilt or innocence but merely decides whether there is sufficient evidence of guilt to require that the accused be bound over to the other court.

If the defendant is a "juvenile" (a term having a special definition for this purpose which varies from state to state), and the misdeed charged is not expressly excluded by the statute authorizing this type of procedure, the case may be tried in the "juvenile court." Whether it *must* be tried there, or may be tried either there or in the ordinary courts, depends upon the legislation in the particular state. The more progressive statutes on the subject give the juvenile court exclusive jurisdiction over cases falling within its field.

STATE v. STEPHENS

Supreme Court of Louisiana, 1922.
150 La. 944, 91 So. 349.

William Stephens was convicted of entering a store with intent to commit a crime and stealing property, and he appeals. . . .

By the WHOLE COURT.

PROVOSTY, C. J. The indictment against accused reads that—

He did "willfully, knowingly and maliciously and feloniously and with intent to commit a crime, in the daytime, enter the store of one L. H. Johnson and did then and there feloniously steal, take and carry away with the intent to appropriate the same to his own use, one pair of shoes of the value of seven dollars and fifty cents the personal property of one L. H. Johnson."

He was found "guilty as charged," and was sentenced to the penitentiary for not less than two nor more than three years.

For larceny of less than $20 value, the punishment cannot exceed six months in the parish jail. Act 107, p. 161, of 1902. Hence the sentence of two or three years in the penitentiary must have been for entering in the daytime with intent to steal, under section 854 of the R.S., reading:

"Sec. 854. Whoever, with intent to kill, rob, steal, commit a rape, or any other crime, shall in the nighttime enter without breaking, or in the daytime break or enter any dwelling house, or outhouse thereto adjoining and occupied therewith, or any office, shop, or warehouse, or any vessel, and every person present aiding and or abetting in the commission of such offense, or who shall have counseled, hired or procured the same to have been committed, on conviction shall be imprisoned at hard labor not exceeding five years, and fined not exceeding one thousand dollars."

In this statute, the "or" between the words "break" and "enter," in the sentence, "Whoever with intent to steal shall break or enter a shop in the daytime," should be "and." The act designed to be punished is a breaking and entering; not a mere entering. . . .

No sentence at all can be imposed. For while the indictment is good for larceny, and the accused may be said to have been tried for, and found guilty of, that offense as well as of entering a store with intent to steal, it has been by an incompetent tribunal—a jury—whereas, by article 7, § 41, of the Constitution, "all cases in which the punishment may not be at hard labor shall . . . be tried by the judge without a jury," and the larceny charged, being of less than $20, is not so punishable. Act 107 of 1902, supra.

The verdict and sentence are therefore annulled, and the case is remanded for trial for larceny.

Rehearing refused by the WHOLE COURT.[1]

MODEL PENAL CODE

Section 1.03. Territorial Applicability.

(1) Except as otherwise provided in this Section, a person may be convicted under the law of this State of an offense committed by his own conduct or the conduct of another for which he is legally accountable if:

(a) either the conduct which is an element of the offense or the result which is such an element occurs within this State; or

(b) conduct occurring outside the State is sufficient under the law of this State to constitute an attempt to commit an offense within the State; or

(c) conduct occurring outside the State is sufficient under the law of this State to constitute a conspiracy to commit an offense within the State and an overt act in furtherance of such conspiracy occurs within the State; or

(d) conduct occurring within the State establishes complicity in the commission of, or an attempt, solicitation or conspiracy to commit, an offense in another jurisdiction which also is an offense under the law of this State; or

(e) the offense consists of the omission to perform a legal duty imposed by the law of this State with respect to domicile, residence or a relationship to a person, thing or transaction in the State; or

(f) the offense is based on a statute of this State which expressly prohibits conduct outside the State, when the conduct bears a reasonable relation to a legitimate interest of this State and the actor knows or should know that his conduct is likely to affect that interest.

(2) Subsection (1) (a) does not apply when either causing a specified result or a purpose to cause or danger of causing such a result is an element of an offense and the result occurs or is designed or likely to occur only in another jurisdiction where the conduct charged would not constitute an offense, unless a legislative purpose plainly appears to declare the conduct criminal regardless of the place of the result.

(3) Subsection (1) (a) does not apply when causing a particular result is an element of an offense and the result is caused by conduct occurring outside the State which would not constitute an offense if the result had

---

1. A conviction in the superior court must be reversed if the offense charged was in the exclusive jurisdiction of an inferior court. People v. Fiene, 226 Cal.App.2d 305, 37 Cal.Rptr. 925 (1964).

On a trial for felonious assault in the district court the defendant may be convicted of a simple assault, although had the information charged only a simple assault the jurisdiction to try this misdemeanor would have been in an inferior court. People v. Spreckels. 125 Cal.App.2d 507, 270 P.2d 513 (1954).

occurred there, unless the actor purposely or knowingly caused the result within the State.

(4) When the offense is homicide, either the death of the victim or the bodily impact causing death constitutes a "result", within the meaning of Subsection (1) (a) and if the body of a homicide victim is found within the State, it is presumed that such result occurred within the State.

(5) This State includes the land and water and the air space above such land and water with respect to which the State has legislative jurisdiction.

SECTION 2. EXTRADITION

If the courts of the state in which the accused is found have not the power to try him for the crime of which he is accused, the question arises whether the state or nation in which such person could be tried for the offense, has the right to ask the first state to arrest the accused and deliver him over to the second state for trial by it. The surrender of an accused person in this way is called "extradition;" and where it is between the states of the Union it is frequently referred to as "interstate rendition."[1] The demand for extradition is called a "requisition." The "demanding state" makes the demand upon the "asylum state,"—in which the fugitive has taken refuge.

The Constitution of the United States provides (Art. IV, § 2, cl. 2) that "[a] person charged in any State with Treason, Felony or other Crime, who shall flee from Justice, and be found in another State, shall on Demand of the executive Authority of the State from which he fled, be delivered up, to be removed to the State having Jurisdiction of the Crime", and Congress has enacted (18 U.S.C.A. § 3182 (1948)), that "Whenever the executive authority of any State or Territory demands any person as a fugitive from justice, of the executive authority of any State, District or Territory to which such person has fled, and produces a copy of an indictment found or an affidavit made before a magistrate of any State or Territory, charging the person demanded with having committed treason, felony, or other crime, certified as authentic by the governor or chief magistrate of the State or Territory from whence the person so charged has fled, the executive authority of the State, District or Territory to which such person has fled shall cause him to be arrested and secured, and notify the executive authority making such demand, . . . " (See also the following section.) In any case authorized by those provisions the governor of a state may appoint an agent to demand of the executive authority of another state or territory any fugitive from justice charged with any crime if its own statute is broad enough. The Tennessee statute, for example, authorizes the governor to "appoint an

---

[1] "Interstate rendition" was rejected in favor of the phrase "interstate extradition" in the uniform act on this subject.

agent to demand of the executive of any other state in the union any fugitive from justice, or any person charged with treason, or any other crime committed in this state." [2] The Iowa Code Ann., at one time, authorized the demand only in the case of a "fugitive from justice charged with treason of felony." [3] The Iowa statute authorized the governor to appoint agents to demand fugitives from justice, not only from the executive authority of another state or territory, but also "from the executive authority of a foreign government." But the clause just quoted was void. International extradition depends upon treaties and no state of the Union can enter into treaties with foreign nations. Furthermore international extradition is a matter of foreign relations, belonging exclusively to the national government.[4]

The Constitution and statutes of the United States authorize extradition of a fugitive from justice charged with "treason, felony or other crime," but this is only "on demand of the executive authority of the state from which he fled." The federal law imposes no duty upon the offended state to make a demand if it does not choose to do so. Hence a state statute limiting the authority of the governor, in his demand for the return of fugitives from other states, to

2. Tenn.Code Ann. § 40–1023 (1955).

3. Iowa Code Ann. § 759.1 (1946). This has been changed by enactment of the Uniform Criminal Extradition Act. See Iowa Code Ann. c. 759 (1958).

4. "The laws of nations embrace no provision for the surrender of persons who are fugitives from the offended laws of one country to the territory of another. It is only by treaty that such surrender can take place." 4 Moore, Digest of International Law 245, (1906) quoting Mr. Rush, Sec. of State, to Mr. Hyde de Newville, Apr. 9, 1817. As the state of Iowa cannot enter into a treaty with a foreign government (U.S. Const. Art. I, § 10, cl. 1) it would never be in a position to demand the surrender of a fugitive as a matter of right from a foreign government. Clearly it could do no more than to request it as a matter of comity. But, "[a]lthough the question whether the several States of the United States possess the power to surrender fugitive criminals to foreign governments has never been actually decided by the Supreme Court, yet it may now be regarded as settled doctrine that they do not possess such power, but that it belongs exclusively to the National Government. The question has, however, been by no means free from controversy, and the present accepted view is the result of a gradual evolution of opinion and practice." 4 Moore, Digest of International Law 240 (1906). If Iowa cannot surrender a fugitive to a foreign government it would have little ground upon which to make requisition as a matter of comity. But more than that, if it lacks the power to make such a rendition it would seem equally to lack the power to make the demand. As said by Mr. Justice Miller in United States v. Rauscher, 119 U.S. 407, 414, 7 S.Ct. 234, 30 L.Ed. 425 (1886): "[I]t can hardly be admitted that, even in the absence of treaties or acts of Congress on the subject, the extradition of fugitives from justice can become the subject of negotiation between a state of this Union and a foreign government."

The truth is that as far as we are concerned with foreign countries, extradition is governed exclusively by the treaties of the United States with such countries, and by Acts of Congress in furtherance of the provisions thereof. 18 U.S.C.A. §§ 752, 1502, 3051, 3181, 3185–6, 3188–93 (1948). As a matter of procedure all applications for requisitions should be addressed to the Secretary of State accompanied by the necessary papers. 18 U.S.C.A. § 3184 (1948).

those charged with treason or felony (as once did the Iowa statute) is entirely valid. The legislative body is free to establish a policy of not demanding the return of misdemeanants if it sees fit to do so. The mandate of the Constitution of the United States, however, does not permit a state legislature to establish a policy of not surrendering fugitive misdemeanants to other states. The Texas statute purports to do this [5] but the limitation is unconstitutional. Despite the wording of this statute a fugitive may be extradited from Texas for a misdemeanor as well as for a felony.[6]

STATE v. HALL

Supreme Court of North Carolina, 1894.
115 N.C. 811, 20 S.E. 729.

AVERY, J. The defendants were arrested, and are now held under the statute (The Code, sec. 1165), which provides that any one of certain judicial officers therein named, "on satisfactory information laid before him that any fugitive in the State has committed, out of the State and within the United States, any offense which by the law of the State in which the offense was committed is punishable, either capitally or by imprisonment for one year or upwards in any State prison, shall have full power and authority, and is hereby required to issue a warrant for said fugitive, and commit him to jail within the State for the space of six months, unless sooner demanded by the authorities of the State wherein the offense may have been committed, pursuant to the Act of Congress in that case made and provided," etc. It is manifest that the prisoners cannot be lawfully detained, under the unmistakable language of the law, unless it has been made to appear that they are liable to extradition under the Act of Congress, passed in pursuance of Art. IV, sec. 2, clause 2, of the Constitution of the United States, in order to provide for the surrender of persons charged with criminal offenses "who shall flee from justice and be found in another State."

The prisoners were tried for murder in Cherokee County, and, upon appeal, it was held (114 N.C. 909, 19 S.E. 602) that if the deceased, at the time of receiving the fatal injury, was in the State of Tennessee, and the prisoners were in the State of North Carolina, the courts of the former Commonwealth alone had jurisdiction of the offense. The prisoners, if such were the facts, were deemed by the law to have accompanied the deadly missile sent by them across the border, and to have been constructively present when the fatal wound was actually inflicted. As our statute confers no power to detain in

---

5. Vernon's Ann.Texas Code Crim.Proc. art. 997.

6. Ex parte Wells, 108 Tex.Cr.R. 57, 298 S.W. 904 (1927). Guilt or innocence of the fugitive cannot be determined in the asylum state. In re Wheeler, 46 Wash.2d 277, 280 P.2d 673 (1955).

custody, or to surrender at the demand of the Executive of another State, any person who does not fall within the definition of a fugitive from justice according to the interpretation given by the courts of the United States to the clause of the Federal Constitution providing for interstate extradition, and the Act of Congress passed in pursuance of it, the only question before us is, whether a person can, in contemplation of law, "flee from justice" in the State of Tennessee when he has never been actually but only constructively within its territorial limits. Upon this question there is abundant authority, emanating not only from the foremost textwriters and some of the ablest jurists of the most respectable State courts, but from the Supreme Court of the United States, whose peculiar province it is to declare what interpretation shall be given to the Federal Constitution and the statutes enacted by Congress in pursuance of its provisions, which are declared by that instrument to be the supreme law of the land. If we can surrender under our statute only fugitives within the meaning of the Act of Congress, it would seem sufficient to cite Ex-parte Reggel, where it is held that a person arrested as a fugitive has a right "to insist upon proof that he was within the demanding State at the time he is alleged to have committed the crime charged, and consequently withdrew from her jurisdiction so that he could not be reached by her criminal process." It is admitted that the prisoners have never withdrawn from the jurisdiction of the courts of Tennessee, and have never been, either at the time when the homicide was committed, or since, exposed to arrest under process issuing from them. . . .

To hold that a person, who is liable to indictment only by reason of his constructive presence, is a fugitive from the justice of a State within whose limits he has never gone since the commission of the offense, involves as great an error as to maintain that one who has stood still and never ventured within the reach of another has fled from him to avoid injury. One who has never fled cannot be a fugitive. 2 Moore Extradition, sec. 582, et seq., after quoting the extract already given from Reggel's case, cites a number of other cases wherein Governors of States, under well-considered opinions of their legal advisers, have recognized and acted upon the principle that a person cannot be said to flee from a place where he has never actually been, but to which, by a legal fiction, he is deemed to have followed an agency or instrumentality, put in motion by him, to accomplish a criminal purpose. Spear (Extradition, pp. 396 to 400) cites and discusses the authorities bearing upon the question whether a person can be a fugitive from a State into which he has never entered, and not only reaches the same conclusion at which we have arrived, but maintains *arguendo* that a person who has been extradited as a fugitive cannot be sent back from the demanding State on requisition of the Executive who surrendered him, to answer a crime committed while he was a fugitive, because one who is forcibly taken away does not, in contemplation of law or in fact, flee from justice. The author says that, to assume that an abduction by force, though under legal process, is fleeing, "is a gross absurdity, quite as bad as the theory of fugitives by construction." . . .

While a statute passed now, and making it murder to wilfully put in motion within the State of North Carolina any force which should kill a human being in a neighboring State, might not be amenable to such constitutional objection as that discussed in State v. Knight, 1 N.C. 143, it would, as to this case, be an *ex post facto* law. But in the exercise of its reserved sovereign powers the State may, as an act of comity to a sister State, provide by statute for the surrender, upon requisition, of persons who, like the prisoners, are indictable for murder in another State, though they have never fled from justice.[1] If it shall be proved that the prisoners were in fact in North Carolina and the deceased in Tennessee when the fatal wound was inflicted, a law may still be enacted giving the Governor the authority to issue his warrant and deliver them on requisition. Meantime, it may be asked, what can be done to provide for this *casus omissus?* We may answer, in the language of Spear, *supra*, p. 400: "Nothing by any extradition process, until there is some authority of law for it. . . . State statutes may be enacted to furnish a remedy not now supplied by either Federal or State law." Were the courts, without any semblance of right, to supply the legislative omission, it would be a criminal usurpation of authority, more pernicious to the public interests than the escape of, not two, but scores of criminals. Appellate courts cannot deliberately legislate for the punishment of crime without incurring a moral accountability as grave as that of the criminal who suffers by the usurpation. . .

In State v. Spier, 12 N.C. 491, the Supreme Court declared the prisoner entitled to his discharge upon a writ of *habeas corpus*, where the term of the Court expired pending his trial for murder, because he could not be again put in jeopardy for that offense. The defect in the law was subsequently remedied by statute, allowing the Court to continue into the next week if a felony were being tried when the week expired. But the Court, composed of *Taylor, Hall* and *Henderson,* did not hesitate for a moment because a guilty man might escape. On the contrary, *Judge Hall* said: "The guilt or innocence of the prisoner is as little the subject of inquiry as the merits of any case can be, when it is brought before this Court on a collateral question of law." Courts enforce laws not simply to punish the guilty, but as well to protect the innocent. The law which fails to provide for the extradition of a guilty man must be understood and adhered to, because it may be invoked as a protection to the innocent who are prosecuted without cause, against the annoyance, expense and inva-

---

1. In re Hayes, 101 Cal.App.2d 416, 225 P.2d 272 (1950); Ex parte Bledsoe, 93 Okl.Cr. 302, 227 P.2d 680 (1951).

Sec. 2 EXTRADITION 699

sion of a personal liberty involved in being extradited. There was error. The prisoners should have been discharged.

Error.[2]

(CLARK, J., filed a dissenting opinion in which MACRAE, J., joined.)

HYATT v. PEOPLE ex rel. CORKRAN

Supreme Court of the United States, 1903.
188 U.S. 691, 23 S.Ct. 456.

This proceeding by *habeas corpus* was commenced by the relator, defendant in error, to obtain his discharge from imprisonment by the plaintiff in error, the chief of police in the city of Albany, State of New York, who held the relator by means of a warrant issued in extradition proceedings by the governor of New York. The justice of the Supreme Court of New York, to whom the petition for the writ was addressed, and also upon appeal, the Appellate Division of the Supreme Court of New York, refused to grant the relator's discharge, but the Court of Appeals reversed their orders and discharged him.

---

2. Accord, In re Mohr, 73 Ala. 503 (1883).

In Kentucky v. Dennison, 24 How. 66, 16 L.Ed. 717 (U.S.1860), a motion was made in behalf of the State of Kentucky for a rule on the Governor of Ohio to show cause why a mandamus should not be issued by this Court, commanding him to cause Willis Lago, a fugitive from justice, to be delivered up, to be removed to the State of Kentucky. The charge was that Lago "a colored freeman" had aided and abetted a female slave of a citizen of Kentucky to escape from her master. This was a crime in Kentucky but no such offense was known to the laws of Ohio. After holding that notwithstanding this fact it was the duty of the Governor of Ohio to honor this requisition from the Governor of Kentucky, Mr. Chief Justice Taney speaking for the Supreme Court said at pages 109–110: "But if the Governor of Ohio refuses to discharge this duty, there is no power delegated to the General Government, either through the Judicial Department or any other department, to use any coercive means to compel him.

"And upon this ground the motion for a mandamus must be overruled."

"It is true, that under present legal conditions, the general government, as was decided in the case of the Commonwealth of Kentucky v. Dennison, 24 How. 66, cannot enforce the performance of this constitutional obligation. But this results entirely from the fact that the act of congress which regulates these proceedings, directs the constitutional demand to be made upon the governor of the state to which the fugitive has fled; but as the executive of a state is not a federal officer, the general government cannot compel the performance of a function which it has no right to annex to the office. This was the extent of the decision just referred to; but I can entertain no doubt of the power of congress to vest in any national officer the authority to cause the arrest in any state of a fugitive from the justice of another state, and to surrender such fugitive on the requisition of the executive of the latter state. The national right to require the surrender, under the terms of the constitution, seems to me to be clear, and all that is necessary to render such right enforceable, in every case, is the necessary organ of the federal government." Beasley, C. J., In re Voorhees, 32 N.J.L. 141, 145–6 (1867).

172 N.Y. 176, 64 N.E. 825. A writ of error has been taken from this court to review the latter judgment.

The relator stated in his petition for the writ that he was arrested and detained by virtue of a warrant of the governor of New York, granted on a requisition from the governor of Tennessee, reciting that relator had been indicted in that State for the crime of grand larceny and false pretences, and that he was a fugitive from the justice of that State; that the warrant under which he was held showed that the crimes with which he was charged were committed in Tennessee, and the relator stated that nowhere did it appear in the papers that he was personally present within the State of Tennessee at the time the alleged crimes were stated to have been committed; that the governor had no jurisdiction to issue his warrant in that it did not appear before him that the relator was a fugitive from the justice of the State of Tennessee, or had fled therefrom; that it did not appear that there was any evidence that relator was personally or continuously present in Tennessee when the crimes were alleged to have been committed; that it appeared on the face of the indictments accompanying the requisition that no crime under the laws of Tennessee was charged or had been committed. Upon this petition the writ was issued and served.

The return of the defendant in error, the chief of police, was to the effect that the relator was held by virtue of a warrant of the governor of New York, and a copy of it was annexed. . . .

Upon the hearing before the judge on March 17, 1902, the relator was sworn without objection, and testified that he had been living in the State of New York for the past fourteen months; that his residence when at home was in Lutherville, Maryland; that he was in the city of Nashville, in the State of Tennessee, on July 2, 1901, and (under objection as immaterial) had gone there on business connected with a lumber company in which he was a heavy stockholder; that he arrived in the city on July 2, in the morning, and left about half-past seven in the evening of the same day, and while there he notified the Union Bank and Trust Company (the subsequent prosecutor herein) that the resignation of the president of the lumber company had been demanded and would probably be accepted that day. That after such notification, and on the same day, the resignation was obtained, and the Union Bank and Trust Company was notified thereof by the relator before leaving the city on the evening of that day; that he passed through the city of Nashville on the 16th or 17th of July thereafter on his way to Chattanooga, but did not stop at Nashville at that time, and had not been in the State of Tennessee since the 16th day of July, 1901, at the time he went to Chattanooga; that he had never lived in the State of Tennessee, and had not been in that State between the 26th or 27th of May, 1899, and the 2d day July, 1901.

Upon this state of facts the judge, before whom the hearing was had, dismissed the writ and remanded the relator to the custody of the

Sec. 2   EXTRADITION   701

defendant Hyatt, as chief of police. This order was affirmed without any opinion by the Appellate Division of the Supreme Court, 72 App. Div. 629, but, as stated, it was reversed by the Court of Appeals, 172 N.Y. 176, and the relator discharged. . . .

MR. JUSTICE PECKHAM, after making the foregoing statement of facts, delivered the opinion of the court. . . .

The subsequent presence for one day (under the circumstances stated above) of the relator in the State of Tennessee, eight days after the alleged commission of the act, did not, when he left the State, render him a fugitive from justice within the meaning of the statute. There is no evidence or claim that he then committed any act which brought him within the criminal law of the State of Tennessee, or that he was indicted for any act then committed. The proof is uncontradicted that he went there on business, transacted it and came away. The complaint was not made nor the indictments found until months after that time. His departure from the State after the conclusion of his business cannot be regarded as a fleeing from justice within the meaning of the statute. He must have been there when the crime was committed, as alleged, and if not, a subsequent going there and coming away is not a flight.

We are of opinion that as the relator showed without contradiction and upon conceded facts that he was not within the State of Tennessee at the times stated in the indictments found in the Tennessee court, nor at any time when the acts were, if ever committed, he was not a fugitive from justice within the meaning of the Federal statute upon that subject, and upon these facts the warrant of the governor of the State of New York was improperly issued, and the judgment of the Court of Appeals of the State of New York discharging the relator from imprisonment by reason of such warrant must be

Affirmed.[1]

---

[1]. This rule does not prevail in international extradition. Rex v. Godfrey, 39 T.L.R. 5 (K.B.1922). For a discussion of the Godfrey case see 32 Yale L.J. 287 (1923).

"To be regarded as a fugitive from justice it is not necessary that one shall have left the State in which the crime is alleged to have been committed for the very purpose of avoiding prosecution." Hogan v. O'Neill, 255 U.S. 52, 56, 41 S.Ct. 222, 223, 65 L.Ed. 497, 500 (1921). Cf. Roberts v. Reilly, 116 U.S. 80, 97, 6 S.Ct. 291, 300, 29 L.Ed. 544, 549 (1885); Bassing v. Cady, 208 U.S. 386, 28 S.Ct. 392, 52 L.Ed. 540 (1907).

Ignorance of having violated the law does not prevent one who leaves the State from being a fugitive: Appleyard v. Massachusetts, 203 U.S. 222, 27 S.Ct. 122, 51 L.Ed. 161 (1906).

"It is upon the petitioner under such circumstances to prove that he is not in fact a fugitive from justice and the burden requires evidence which is practically conclusive." Seely v. Beardsley, 194 Iowa 863, 866, 190 N.W. 498, 500 (1922). The question of insanity will not be tried in such proceedings: Drew v. Thaw, 235 U.S. 432, 35 S.Ct. 137, 59 L.Ed. 302 (1914). Nor will the court pass on the statute of limitations. Biddinger v. Commissioner of Police of City of New York, 245 U.S. 128, 38 S.Ct. 41, 62 L.Ed. 193 (1917).

The court will not pass upon an alleged alibi of a fugitive who admits he was within the demanding state at the

APPLICATION OF ROBINSON

Supreme Court of Nevada, 1958.
74 Nev. 58, 322 P.2d 304.

EATHER, JUSTICE. . . . Upon two grounds appellant asserts that the court below was in error in denying him discharge from custody under his writ.

First he contends that he was not a fugitive from justice of the state of Oregon.

In May, 1942 appellant was convicted of burglary in Oregon and sentenced to a term of five years in the state prison. In June, 1944 he was granted parole under the terms of which he was released to the custody of officers of Lincoln County, Nebraska, for the purpose of standing trial for felony. He was convicted in Nebraska and sentenced to serve 20 months in the state prison. He was released in August, 1945. On January 3, 1946, with a balance of his Oregon sentence remaining to be served, the Oregon parole board revoked his parole. The record before us is silent as to the basis for the revocation. We may assume it was for violation of the conditions of the parole. It was for the purpose of requiring him to serve the balance of his sentence that his return to Oregon was sought by the executive warrant here in question.

Appellant contends that in delivering him to Nebraska, Oregon has waived further service of sentence; that since he was compelled to leave Oregon under these circumstances he cannot be regarded as a fugitive from justice of that state. In support of his contention he relies upon In re Whittington, 34 Cal.App. 344, 167 P. 404.

Authorities are divided upon this proposition. In our view the better rule and the weight of authority today is to the effect that the mode or manner of a person's departure from a demanding state generally does not affect his status as a fugitive from justice and that the fact that his departure was involuntary or under legal compulsion will not preclude his extradition. Brewer v. Goff, 10 Cir., 138 F.2d

---

time of the alleged offense. Edmunds v. Griffin, 177 Iowa 389, 156 N.W. 353 (1916).

With the principal case, cf. Leonard v. Zweifel, 171 Iowa 522, 151 N.W. 1054 (1915); Taylor v. Wise, 172 Iowa 1, 126 N.W. 1126 (1910).

One, constructively present only at the time of the crime, who enters the jurisdiction voluntarily, gives bail and then departs, has waived his immunity. Kay v. State, 34 Ala.App. 8, 37 So.2d 525 (1948), rehearing denied 251 Ala. 419, 37 So.2d 529 (1948).

If D was within the state when he took steps which were intended to, and did, result in a crime his departure from the state makes him a "fugitive" in the constitutional sense even if he left the state before the crime was complete. Strassheim v. Daily, 221 U.S. 280, 31 S.Ct. 558, 55 L.Ed. 735 (1911). If D left the state after setting a bomb to murder X, although before the fatal explosion, he is a "fugitive".

710, holding that the Whittington decision is against the weight of authority.[1]

The essential fact remains that having committed an act which the law of Oregon constitutes a crime and having been convicted and sentenced therefor, appellant departed from Oregon jurisdiction and, when sought for enforcement of his penal obligation to that state, was found in another state.

Nor do we feel that Oregon can be said to have waived its right to insist upon service of sentence. Delivery to Nebraska was under parole from Oregon. Under these circumstances appellant continued while in Nebraska and until revocation of parole to serve the Oregon sentence. It was for Oregon to fix the conditions under which its sentence might be served. Oregon's act was not a suspension of sentence or abandonment of the prisoner. The appellant was not prejudiced in any constitutional right by Oregon's action in aid of the administration of justice in a sister state.

Second: Appellant contends that Oregon's right of requisition is barred by res judicata. Following Oregon's revocation of parole in 1946, Oregon on two occasions (prior to the present proceeding) has laid claim to a right to take appellant into custody as a parole violator. On both occasions appellant has secured discharge through habeas corpus.

[Footnote by the Court.]

1. California amendment of Penal Code, § 1549 (St. 1937, p. 1583) destroyed the effect of the Whittington case by expressly giving authority to the Governor to surrender any person charged with crime in another state, even though such person left the demanding state involuntarily.

[Compiler's note]. A prisoner awaiting trial for crime in Texas was extradited to California where he was wanted on a much more serious charge (murder). For some reason the murder charge was dropped whereupon an effort was made to extradite him back to Texas, but he was released on habeas corpus. In re Whittington, 34 Cal.App. 344, 167 P. 404 (1917).

The Governor of Oregon honored a requisition made by the Governor of Texas for the delivery of the plaintiff in error for removal to Texas as a fugitive from the justice of that State. The accused was taken to Texas, tried for murder and a conspiracy to commit murder and acquitted. She was, however, not released from custody because she was ordered by the Governor of Texas under a requisition of the Governor of Georgia, to be held for delivery to an agent of the State of Georgia for removal to that State as a fugitive from justice. Held, that the failure of Congress when enacting the interstate extradition provisions to provide for the case of a fugitive from justice who has not fled into the state where he is found, but was brought into it involuntarily by a requisition from another state, does not take the matters within the unprovided area out of possible state action, but leaves the state free to deliver the accused to any state from whose justice he has fled. Innes v. Tobin, 240 U.S. 127, 36 Sup.Ct. 290, 60 L.Ed. 562 (1916). Accord: Hackney v. Welsh, 107 Ind. 253, 8 N.E. 141 (1886). Contra: In re Hope, 7 N.Y.Cr. 406, 10 N.Y.Supp. 28 (1889). See Spear, A Lawyer's Question, 13 Alb.L.Q. 230; Larremore, Inadequacy of the Present Federal Statute Regulating Interstate Rendition, 10 Col.L.Rev. 208 (1910).

See note, Fugitives from Justice under the Federal Rendition Clause, 18 Col. L.Rev. 70 (1918).

The first occasion was in Nebraska. Local authorities took appellant into custody at Oregon's request. Appellant sought habeas corpus. The writ was summarily denied. On appeal the Nebraska Supreme Court, Application of Robinson, 150 Neb. 443, 34 N.W.2d 887, directed the lower court to issue the writ and proceed to hearing. Oregon failed to press its rights. No hearing was had. Appellant was discharged, without hearing, on Oregon's default.

The second occasion was in Kansas. Appellant had been convicted of a federal offense and sentenced to the federal prison at Leavenworth. Oregon placed a detainer against him with the prison authorities. Appellant through habeas corpus attacked Oregon's right to custody. Oregon withdrew the detainer. No hearing was had.

It cannot be said that appellant's discharges under habeas corpus in these two occasions resulted from judicial determinations which now bar Oregon from asserting the right of requisition. Appellant's discharges resulted simply from Oregon's failure to press its rights. Although appellant contends that the failure of a state to assert or press its extradition rights at a given time would result in a waiver of these rights, no authority is cited in support of this contention, and none has come to the attention of the court. Never has any hearing been had upon the merits of appellant's contentions until the hearing before the court below. Never were those rights judicially determined until the present proceeding. Res judicata does not apply.[1]

On motion to dismiss: Motion denied.

On appeal: Affirmed.

BADT, C. J., and MERRILL, J., concur.

HARDY v. BETZ

Supreme Court of New Hampshire, 1963.
105 N.H. 169, 195 A.2d 582.

[D, a resident of New Hampshire, was indicted in Massachusetts for nonsupport of an illegitimate child. A requisition from Massachusetts was honored by the governor of New Hampshire, who issued his warrant of arrest and extradition. Pursuant thereto defendant arrested plaintiff, who petitioned for a writ of habeas corpus.]

DUNCAN, JUSTICE. These proceedings relate to the support of a minor male child born April 29, 1953 in Boston, Massachusetts, shortly

---

[1]. One who has been extradited from Florida to Connecticut can be brought back by extradition to serve the balance of a term for which he had received a conditional pardon that was later revoked. United States v. Matus, 218 F.2d 466 (2d Cir. 1954).

after his mother's removal thereto from Portsmouth, New Hampshire. Soon after the birth of the child the mother married, and has continued to reside in Boston. In 1962 as a result of a request for public support, a proceeding was brought in the Roxbury District Court in Massachusetts, seeking support for the child from the plaintiff herein under the provisions of the Uniform Reciprocal Enforcement of Support Act. RSA ch. 546. Following a hearing before the Superior Court in Rockingham County on November 26, 1962, the petition was denied upon the ground that the plaintiff herein was under no duty to support the child. See RSA 168:1 requiring a paternity charge to be instituted within one year of the birth of the child. Thereafter the proceedings culminating in the petition now before us were instituted.[1]

The reserved case states that the plaintiff "has at no time seen [the mother of the child] since she departed from Portsmouth," that he denies that he is the father of the child, and that "he is not and never has been a fugitive from justice in the Commonwealth of Massachusetts." His application for a writ of habeas corpus alleges that he "was not in Massachusetts on the thirtieth day of May 1959 [the date alleged in the indictment] or at any time subsequent thereto."

At the outset it may be pointed out that we are not concerned with the contention that the plaintiff is not a fugitive from justice. The requisition papers disclose that it is conceded that at the time of the commission of the alleged crime the plaintiff was in Portsmouth, and that it is alleged that acts committed by him in Portsmouth intentionally resulted in a crime in Massachusetts. The answer of the Commonwealth of Massachusetts to the plaintiff's petition clearly indicates that the extradition proceedings are grounded upon the provisions of section 6 of the Uniform Extradition Act. RSA ch. 612.

This section provides: "Extradition of Persons Not Present in Demanding State at Time of Commission of Crime. The governor of this state may also surrender, on demand of the executive authority of any other state, any person in this state charged in such other state in the manner provided in section 3 with committing an act in this state, or in a third state, intentionally resulting in a crime in the state whose executive authority is making the demand, and the provisions of this chapter not otherwise inconsistent, shall apply to such cases, even though the accused was not in that state at the time of the commission of the crime, and has not fled therefrom." RSA 612:6.

1. The threat of a criminal punishment is a coercive measure to induce a man to perform his civil duty by supporting his family, but execution of the threat tends to frustrate the purpose of such legislation because it usually makes it impossible for the support to be given. This led to the Uniform Reciprocal Enforcement of Support Act, which has been very widely adopted, and provides for an alternative demand in the form of a support order and permits extradition to be avoided by compliance with this support order. See West's Ann.Cal.Code Civ.Proc. §§ 1650–1690 (1953); 2 U.C.L.A. L.Rev. 267 (1955).

The recital in the warrant of the governor of this state that the plaintiff herein is "charged . . . with having fled from said Commonwealth of Massachusetts" may be regarded as surplusage and presents no issue for determination here. Additionally, no issue is presented with respect to the form of the requisition papers, which include the required copy of an indictment, and of an affidavit before a magistrate.

The issue to be determined is whether a crime under the law of Massachusetts is substantially charged. Mass.G.L., c. 273, § 15 provides in part: "Any father of an illegitimate child, whether begotten within or without the commonwealth, who neglects or refuses to contribute reasonably to its support and maintenance, shall be guilty of a misdemeanor." The section further provides that if there has been no final adjudication of paternity "the question of paternity shall be determined in proceedings hereunder." It thus appears that although it has never been determined that the plaintiff herein is the father of the minor child in question the Massachusetts statute provides for such determination upon trial of the indictment. Under the Massachusetts statute the offense alleged is a continuing one and establishment of paternity is not a prerequisite to indictment.

The essential question before us is whether the indictment returned in Massachusetts can be held to charge a crime committed in that jurisdiction, when the affidavits establish that the plaintiff was not there present at the time of the crime for which he was indicted. By the sworn statement of the District Attorney for Suffolk District the plaintiff is charged with "having committed in Portsmouth, New Hampshire an act or acts intentionally resulting in the commission of said crime in this Commonwealth." The papers contain no specification of the nature of the "act or acts" so alleged to have been committed in this state, but it is plainly inferable that reliance is placed upon "acts of omission" committed in this state which are claimed to have "intentionally resulted" in a crime in Massachusetts. . . .

It has already been found by the Superior Court in the 1962 proceedings that the plaintiff is under no duty here to support the child, his paternity never having been established. Under the law of this jurisdiction no obligation to support an illegitimate child exists where paternity has been neither established nor acknowledged. See RSA 168:1 requiring a paternity charge to be instituted within one year of the birth of the child.

We come then to the question of whether Massachusetts can by legislative act impose upon a resident of New Hampshire, not present in Massachusetts, an obligation to support an illegitimate child in Massachusetts; and more particularly, impose criminal liability for failure to support such a child, when the father has never been within the jurisdiction of that Commonwealth so that it could impose such an obligation or liability upon him. . . .

"The criminal law of a state or nation has no operation or effect beyond its geographical or territorial limits." 1 Anderson, Wharton's Criminal Law and Procedure, s. 23. Restatement, Conflict of Laws, s. 457. See Hartford v. Superior Court, 47 Cal.2d 447, 454, 304 P.2d 1. "The crime of failure to furnish support, however, is committed where the defendant should have furnished the support . . . if the defendant was once subject to the jurisdiction so that the obligation exists." 2 Beale, The Conflict of Laws, s. 428.4. . . .

An order should be entered discharging the plaintiff from custody.

Remanded.

BLANDIN and WHEELER, JJ., concurred.

KENISON, C. J., and LAMPRON, J., dissented.

KENISON, CHIEF JUSTICE (dissenting). . . . The majority opinion in effect holds that section 6 of the Uniform Extradition Act is unconstitutional and cannot be applied in support cases where it is most needed. If there was authority for this view in the rigid dogma of Beale (2 Beale, The Conflict of Laws, s. 428.4) or in the worry of Lord Ellenborough a century and a half ago ("Can the island of Tobago pass a law to bind the rights of the whole world?", Buchanan v. Rucker, 9 East. 192 [K.B.1808]), it is not impressive today. In re Harris, 170 Ohio St. 151, 163 N.E.2d 762. The continuing crime of neglecting to support an illegitimate child in Massachusetts "whether begotten within or without the commonwealth" (Mass.G.L., c. 273, § 15) is an extraditable offense under section 6 of the Uniform Extradition Act. RSA 612:6. Ehrenzweig, Conflict of Laws, s. 82 (1962).

LAMPRON, J., concurs in this dissent.

FRISBIE v. COLLINS

Supreme Court of the United States, 1952.
342 U.S. 519, 72 S.Ct. 509.

MR. JUSTICE BLACK delivered the opinion of the Court.

Acting as his own lawyer, the respondent Shirley Collins brought this habeas corpus case in a United States District Court seeking release from a Michigan state prison where he is serving a life sentence for murder. His petition alleges that while he was living in Chicago, Michigan officers forcibly seized, handcuffed, blackjacked and took him to Michigan. He claims that trial and conviction under such circumstances is in violation of the Due Process Clause of the Fourteenth Amendment and the Federal Kidnaping Act, and that therefore his conviction is a nullity.

The District Court denied the writ without a hearing on the ground that the state court had power to try respondent "regardless of how presence was procured." The Court of Appeals, one judge dissenting, reversed and remanded the cause for hearing. 6 Cir., 189 F.2d 464. It held that the Federal Kidnaping Act had changed the rule declared in prior holdings of this Court, that a state could constitutionally try and convict a defendant after acquiring jurisdiction by force. To review this important question we granted certiorari. 342 U.S. 865, 72 S.Ct. 112. . . .

This Court has never departed from the rule announced in Ker v. Illinois, 119 U.S. 436, 444, 7 S.Ct. 225, 229, 30 L.Ed. 421, that the power of a court to try a person for crime is not impaired by the fact that he had been brought within the court's jurisdiction by reason of a "forcible abduction." No persuasive reasons are now presented to justify overruling this line of cases. They rest on the sound basis that due process of law is satisfied when one present in court is convicted of crime after having been fairly apprized of the charges against him and after a fair trial in accordance with constitutional procedural safeguards. There is nothing in the Constitution that requires a court to permit a guilty person rightfully convicted to escape justice because he was brought to trial against his will.

Despite our prior decisions, the Court of Appeals, relying on the Federal Kidnaping Act, held that respondent was entitled to the writ if he could prove the facts he alleged. The Court thought that to hold otherwise after the passage of the Kidnaping Act "would in practical effect lend encouragement to the commission of criminal acts by those sworn to enforce the law." [189 F.2d 468] In considering whether the law of our prior cases has been changed by the Federal Kidnaping Act, we assume, without intimating that it is so, that the Michigan officers would have violated it if the facts are as alleged. This Act prescribes in some detail the severe sanctions Congress wanted it to have. Persons who have violated it can be imprisoned for a term of years or for life; under some circumstances violators can be given the death sentence. We think the Act cannot fairly be construed so as to add to the list of sanctions detailed a sanction barring a state from prosecuting persons wrongfully brought to it by its officers. It may be that Congress could add such a sanction. We cannot.

The judgment of the Court of Appeals is reversed and that of the District Court is affirmed.[1]

It is so ordered.

Judgment of Court of Appeals reversed.

---

[1] Accord, State v. Wise, 58 N.M. 164, 267 P.2d 992 (1954); People v. Garner, 57 Cal.2d 135, 18 Cal.Rptr. 40, 367 P.2d 680 (1961).

STATE v. KEALY

Supreme Court of Iowa, 1893.
89 Iowa 94, 56 N.W. 283.

ROTHROCK, J. The defendant was indicted for the crime of obtaining money under false pretenses. After the crime was committed, he left this state, and went to the state of New York. A requisition was made upon the governor of that state for the extradition of the defendant, upon the ground that he had been indicted in this state, and he was returned to this state in pursuance of the requisition. After he was brought to this state, and while he was in custody under that indictment, he was indicted for forging a promissory note. When he was brought into court on the last indictment, he made a motion to be discharged from restraint on the indictment for forgery, on the ground that he was not extradited on that charge, and that, being in restraint on the first charge, he could not be required to plead to the second indictment, nor could he be restrained of his liberty by reason thereof, he never having had an opportunity to return to the state of New York. The court overruled the motion, and required the defendant to plead to the indictment. A plea of guilty was entered, and the defendant was sentenced to imprisonment in the penitentiary for two years.

It appears from the abstract in the case that the two indictments were founded upon wholly different and distinct charges, and, as we understand it, they did not involve the same transaction. The record does not show what disposition was made of the indictment of obtaining money under false pretenses. It is stated in argument that the defendant was sentenced to imprisonment for one year on that charge.

The question presented for decision is stated by counsel for the appellant in the following language: "Can a party taken from one country or state to another, upon proceedings of extradition, legally be held to answer to another and different offense than that upon which he was so extradited, without being given an opportunity to return to the state of his asylum?"

This case does not involve any question of international extradition. The defendant's removal from the state of New York to this state was not procured by any fraudulent pretense or representation made to him for the purpose of bringing him within the jurisdiction of our courts. It is provided by section 2, article 4, of the constitution of the United States, that "a person charged in any state with treason, felony or other crime, who shall flee from justice and be found in another state, shall on demand of the executive authority of the state from which he fled be delivered up to be removed to the state having jurisdiction of the crime." There was no abuse of this constitutional provision in this case. Extradition was not resorted to as a means of procuring the presence of the defendant in this state for the purpose of serving him with process in a civil action. There can be no question that the grand jury of Jones county, in this state, had the power to find the second indictment against the defendant, and there was the same right of extradition upon that charge that there was on the first indictment. His counsel states in argument that he was sentenced to the penitentiary for one year on the first indictment, and the imprisonment of two years on the second indictment was to commence at the expiration of the imprisonment on the first. It will be observed that what the defendant demanded was that the second indictment should be held in abeyance until he was discharged from imprisonment on the first, and until a reasonable time and opportunity had been given him after his release on the first charge to return to New York, from which asylum he was forcibly taken on the first charge.

There is a conflict of authority upon this question. This court is committed to the doctrine that, when a person is properly charged with a crime, the courts will not inquire into the circumstances under which he was brought into this state, and within the jurisdiction of the court. State v. Ross, 21 Iowa 467. It is true that the defendants in that case were not brought to this state under a requisition upon the executive of another state. They were arrested in the state of Missouri without legal warrant, and after being forcibly brought to this state they were rearrested, and turned over to the civil authorities, and indicted. It is said in that case that, "the officers of the law take the requisite process, find the persons charged within the jurisdiction, and this, too, without force, wrong, fraud, or violence on the part of any agent of the state, or officer thereof. And it can make no difference whether the illegal arrest was made in another state or another government. The violation of the law of the other sovereignty, so far as entitled to weight, would be the same in principle in the one case as the other. That our own laws have been violated is sufficiently shown by the indictment. For this the state had a right to detain the prisoners, and it is of no importance how or where their capture was effected." In the case at bar the defendant was properly indicted, and when process was issued on the indictment, it is of no importance by what authority he was brought into this state. In support of this doctrine: State v. Stewart, 60 Wis. 587, 19 N.W. 429; Ham v. State, 4 Tex.App. 645; State v. Brewster, 7 Vt. 118; Dow's Case, 18 Pa.St. 37; State v. Wensel, 77 Ind. 428; Kerr v. People, 110 Ill. 627. The first two cases above cited are founded on facts substantially the same as the case at bar. As we have said, there is a conflict of authority upon the question. The cases will be found collected in 7 Am. and Eng. Encyclopedia of Law, 648. We have no disposition to depart from the rule adopted by this court in State v. Ross, supra, and the judgment of the district court is Affirmed.[1]

1. Accord, Lascelles v. Georgia, 148 U.S. 537, 13 S.Ct. 687, 37 L.Ed. 549 (1893); State v. Rowe, 104 Iowa 323, 73 N.W. 833 (1898); Knox v. State, 164 Ind. 226, 73 N.E. 255 (1905); In re Flack, 88 Kan. 616, 129 P. 541

BLOOM v. MARCINIAK

Kansas City Court of Appeals, Missouri, 1934.
76 S.W.2d 712.

SHAIN, PRESIDING JUDGE. . . . There is a question which presents itself to this court in this cause that, in so far as this court has been able to ascertain, presents in some respects a question of first impression not only in this state but in the other states of the Un-

(1913) overruling State v. Hall, 40 Kan. 338, 19 P. 918 (1888); People v. Martin, 188 Cal. 281, 205 P. 121 (1922).

"In Knox v. State, at page 231, Montgomery, J., stated the following: 'The right of the person extradited to return to the country from which he has been surrendered is not a natural and inherent right of his own, but is based upon the right of his adopted sovereign to afford asylum to the fugitive, and to refuse to give him up to another except upon such terms as it is pleased to impose. The criminal himself never acquires a personal right of asylum or refuge anywhere, but all such rights as he may claim in this respect flow entirely out of the rights of the government to whose territory he has fled.'

"Compare Innes v. Tobin, 240 U.S. 127, 36 S.Ct. 290, 60 L.Ed. 562 (1916) discussed in 16 Col.Law Rev. 522.

"Before the decision of the Supreme Court in Lascelles v. Georgia a contrary view was held in a number of jurisdictions. See In re Cannon, 47 Mich. 481, 11 N.W. 280 (1882); Ex parte McKnight, 48 Ohio St. 588, 28 N.E. 1034 (1891); In re Fitton, 45 F. 471 (1891). In Ex parte McKnight, at page 603, Williams, C. J. stated the following: 'There could be no reason for the particularity required in the investigation of the specific crime charged in the warrant for the arrest, previous to the surrender, if the accused, when extradited, might be put upon trial for any other offense.'

"See note, Extradition-Prosecution for Other Offenses, 61 U. of Pa.Law Rev. 496 (1913).

"See Ex parte Wilson, 63 Tex.Cr.R. 281, 140 S.W. 98 (1911); Dominguez v. State, 90 Tex.Cr.R. 92, 234 S.W. 79 (1921); In re Jones, 54 Cal.App. 423, 201 P. 944 (1921)." Keedy, Cases on the Administration of The Criminal Law, 272–3, n. 14 (1928).

In United States v. Rauscher, 119 U.S. 407, 7 S.Ct. 234, 30 L.Ed. 425 (1886), it was held that one extradited from England on an indictment for murder could not be put on trial for inflicting cruel and unusual punishment. Apparently it was assumed, when extradition was demanded, that the victim would die, but the death did not occur. Miller, J., said:

"That right, as we understand it, is that he shall be tried only for the offence with which he is charged in the extradition proceedings, and for which he was delivered up, and that if not tried for that, or after trial and acquittal, he shall have a reasonable time to leave the country before he is arrested upon the charge of any other crime committed previous to his extradition." Id. at 424.

See Jacob, International Extradition: Implications of the Eisler Case, 59 Yale L.J. 622 (1950).

See In re Hope, 7 N.Y.Cr. 406, 10 N.Y.S. 28 (1889). See note, Limitations in Trial of Extradition and Interstate Rendition Prisoners, 6 Col.L.Rev. 522 (1906).

Until an extradited person has had reasonable time in which to return to the state from which he was brought, he is privileged from the service of civil process. Murray v. Wilcox, 122 Iowa 188, 97 N.W. 1087 (1904); Compton, Ault & Co. v. Wilder, 40 Ohio St. 130 (1883). In some jurisdictions an extradited person is not immune from civil process. Reid v. Ham, 54 Minn. 305, 56 N.W. 35 (1893); In re Walker, 61 Neb. 803, 86 N.W. 510 (1901), especially where extradition was not procured by connivance or in bad faith. Williams v. Bacon, 10 Wend. 636 (N.Y.1834). Where one who was brought here on extradition, is admitted to bail and returns to his home state, he is exempt here from civil process when he comes back for his trial. Murray v. Wilcox, supra.

ion as well, and, in so far as our research of the federal authorities is concerned, we have been unable to find any precedent directly in point.

The facts before us are clearly to the effect that a requisition regular in every respect has been made by the Governor of the state of Michigan on the Governor of the state of Kansas for the return from Kansas, the asylum state, of the petitioner, Bloom. It further is shown that the Governor of the state of Kansas has honored the requisition of the Governor of the state of Michigan and made a finding of fact to the effect that petitioner, Bloom, is a fugitive from justice, and in accordance with due form and due process has turned the petitioner over to the accredited agent of the state of Michigan, who in fulfillment of this lawful mission brings the petitioner en route into the state of Missouri, where his progress has been interrupted by the process issued out of this court.

This question presents itself: What authority have the courts of Missouri to interrupt this process of law so set in force and so being executed?

This court recognizes that a writ of habeas corpus is a writ of right, and we are not unmindful of the rights of citizenship.

In this case the usual feature, to wit, a requisition granted by the Governor of our own state, is absent. Had the Governor of our own state honored a requisition for the petitioner, then the issue of fact as to whether or not the petitioner is a fugitive could be determined by this court and the petitioner released if the finding of this court was to the effect that the petitioner was not a fugitive from justice.[1] Under the facts as above set forth, Missouri would unquestionably be the asylum state, and it is universally held that the courts of the asylum state have full jurisdiction to determine the issue involved.

As between the states of this Union, the Federal Constitution and the laws passed by Congress must control. The courts of this state, as well as the courts of all the states of this Union, should respect the laws of other states or else the very purposes of the Union of states must fail. It is especially important that the above course be followed concerning such laws and process of laws as are controlled by our national Constitution and acts of Congress.

While, as between a demanding and an asylum state, questions of comity must yield to the questions of the constitutional rights of the citizen of the asylum state, still we conclude that, as to the constitutional rights of one en route from an asylum state to a demand-

---

1. It is settled law in California that one cannot be guilty of theft of partnership funds of a partnership of which he is a partner. Hence a requisition sent from California based upon such an alleged "offense" does not charge a crime, and one in custody in Washington on such extradition proceedings is entitled to his release. Application of Varona, 38 Wash.2d 833, 232 P.2d 923 (1951).

ing state in due course of law and procedure, the courts of this state have no jurisdiction to disturb or overthrow the quasi judicial procedure of the sister asylum state.

While we find no expression of authority on all fours with the language above, still we conclude that our language is in logical sequence with well-established principles of law. While some earlier decisions are to the contrary, it is now a well-settled principle of law that the defense that a prisoner is not a fugitive from justice must be raised before he is taken from the asylum state.

For the law to be other than above would bring confusion. The authorities of one state must indulge in the presumption that the authorities of a sister state have awarded to a prisoner apprehended within its borders all due process of law to which he is entitled under the Constitution.

The documents presented in this case all bear evidence of regularity, and there is nothing from which we can conclude that the petitioner was not awarded every opportunity in Kansas, the fugitive state, to avail himself of his every constitutional right.

Based upon the conclusions above, the release of the petitioner is denied, our writ is quashed, and the said H. Henry Bloom, petitioner herein, is remanded to the custody of W. J. Marciniak, agent of the state of Michigan, free from interference in the performance of his official duty.[2]

2. Johnson was convicted of murder in Georgia and sentenced to life imprisonment. He escaped from a chain gang and fled to Pennsylvania. The governor of Pennsylvania, honoring a requisition from the governor of Georgia, issued a warrant of extradition under which Johnson was arrested. Failing to secure his release by resort to the state court, Johnson brought habeas corpus proceedings in the federal court. He claimed, among other assertions, that he had been subjected to cruel and unusual punishment by the Georgia authorities, and that there was reason to fear for his life if he should be returned to that state. The district court refused to order his release, but this was reversed by the United States Court of Appeals. Johnson v. Dye, Warden, 175 F.2d 250 (3d Cir. 1949). This, in turn, was reversed by a *per curiam* decision of the Supreme Court, because state remedies had not been exhausted. Dye, Warden v. Johnson, 338 U.S. 864, 70 S.Ct. 146, 94 L.Ed. 530 (1949).

It is unnecessary to determine, in the asylum state, whether the constitutional rights of the fugitive will be protected in the demanding state, because he can have recourse to the federal courts if the courts of that state fail to protect him. Ross, Sheriff v. Middlebrooks, 188 F.2d 308 (9th Cir. 1951); In re Quilliam, 88 Ohio App. 202, 89 N.E.2d 493 (1949), appeal denied 152 Ohio 368, 89 N.E.2d 494 (1949), certiorari denied 339 U.S. 945, 70 S.Ct. 790, 94 L.Ed. 1360 (1950). Ex parte Wallace, 38 Wash.2d 67, 227 P. 2d 737 (1951). See The Case of the Fugitive from a Chain Gang, 2 Stanford L.Rev. 174 (1949).

Compare Harper v. Wall, 85 F.Supp. 783 (D.C.N.J.1949), in which the United States District Court of New Jersey ordered the release of a fugitive from Alabama after the Alabama authorities declined to appear at the hearing. The court relied upon the decision of Johnson v. Dye, Warden, which had not been reversed by the Supreme Court when Harper v. Wall was decided.

See DeGraffenreid, The Law of Extradition, 2 Ala.L.Rev. 207 (1950).

See a case note in 34 Minn.L.Rev. 565 (1950).

SECTION 3. STATUTE OF LIMITATIONS

"With regard to limitations as to time, it is one of the peculiarities of English law that no general law of prescription in criminal cases exists among us. The maxim of our law has always been 'Nullum tempus occurrit regi,' and as a criminal trial is regarded as an action by the king, it follows that it may be brought at any time. This principle has been carried to great lengths in many well-known cases. In the middle of the last century Aram was convicted and executed for the murder of Clarke, fourteen years after his crime. Horne was executed for the murder of his bastard child (by his own sister) thirty-five years after his crime. In 1802 Governor Wall was executed for a murder committed in 1782. Not long ago a man named Sheward was executed at Norwich for the murder of his wife more than twenty years before; and I may add as a curiosity that, at the Derby Winter Assizes in 1863, I held a brief for the Crown in a case in which a man was charged with having stolen a leaf from a parish register in the year 1803. In this instance the grand jury threw out the bill."[1]

But although this was true at common law,[2] statutory limitations of the time in which prosecutions may be instituted, are quite general.[3]

---

1. 2 Stephen, History of the Criminal Law of England 1–2 (1883).

2. See the statement in Brightman v. Hatzel, 183 Iowa 385, 395, 167 N.W. 89, 92 (1918).

3. In 1944 Patriarca was indicted as an accessory before the fact to the murders of two persons in 1930. The statute provided that "no person shall be convicted of any offense, except treason against the state, murder, arson, burglary, counterfeiting, forgery, robbery, larceny, rape, or bigamy, unless indictment be found against him therefor within 3 years from the time of committing the same." The indictment was held to be too late on the ground that "a felony and being accessory before the fact to that felony are two separate and distinct offenses." State v. Patriarca, 71 R.I. 151, 43 A.2d 54, 57 (1945). The court emphasized that under Rhode Island law an accessory before the fact must be indicted as such and not as a principal. In People v. Mather, 4 Wend. 229 (N.Y.1830) it is said at page 255: "Whatever is murder is included in it. If the crime of accessory to a murder before the fact is not a murder, it is without a specific name." For this reason the statutory exception was held to include the accessory to murder before the fact and not to bar such a prosecution.

A statute limiting the time within which indictments may be found and filed has no reference to prosecutions in the police courts of municipalities. And such a prosecution will not be barred by lapse of time unless some statute or ordinance so provides. Battle v. Mayor, Etc., of City of Marietta, 118 Ga. 242, 44 S.E. 994 (1903).

An indictment charged that defendant made a false statement in a naturalization proceeding and thereby procured naturalization unlawfully. It was held that this indictment was not controlled by the three-year period of the general statute relating to non-capital offenses, but came under the five-year period of the Nationality Act. United States v. Bridges, 86 F. Supp. 922 (N.D.Cal.1949).

CALIFORNIA PENAL CODE

§ 799. [No limitation for murder, embezzlement of public moneys or falsification of public records: When prosecution may be commenced.] There is no limitation of time within which a prosecution for murder, the embezzlement of public moneys, and the falsification of public records must be commenced. Prosecution for murder may be commenced at any time after the death of the person killed, and for the embezzlement of public money or the falsification of public records, at any time after the discovery of the crime.

§ 800. [Limitations for other felonies: Three years: Six years.] An indictment for any other felony than murder, the embezzlement of public money, the acceptance of a bribe by a public official or a public employee, or the falsification of public records, must be found, and information filed, or case certified to the superior court, within three years after its commission. An indictment for the acceptance of a bribe by a public official or a public employee, a felony, must be found, and the information filed, or case certified to the superior court, within six years after its commission.

§ 801. [Misdemeanors: One-year limitation.] An indictment for any misdemeanor must be found or an information or complaint filed within one year after its commission.

§ 802. [Limitation where defendant out of State when or after offense was committed: Time of absence from State excluded.] If, when or after the offense is committed, the defendant is out of the State, an indictment may be found, a complaint or an information filed or a case certified to the superior court, in any case originally triable in the superior court, or a complaint may be filed, in any case originally triable in any other court, within the term limited by law; and no time during which the defendant is not within this State, is a part of any limitation of the time for commencing a criminal action.

§ 803. Indictment found, when presented and filed. An indictment is found, within the meaning of this chapter, when it is presented by the grand jury in open court, and there received and filed.

PEOPLE v. McGEE

Supreme Court of California, In Bank, 1934.
1 Cal.2d 611, 36 P.2d 378.

LANGDON, J. On November 3, 1930, an information was filed charging defendant with the crime of rape, and alleging the commission of the offense on or about March 30, 1926. A prior conviction of second degree burglary was also charged. Defendant appeared without counsel, pleaded guilty and was sentenced to imprisonment in the state prison. On March 18, 1933, defendant filed a motion to set aside the judgment, which was denied. This appeal is from the order denying the motion.

Section 800 of the Penal Code provides: "An indictment for any other felony than murder, the embezzlement of public money, or the falsification of public records, must be found, or an information filed, within three years after its commission." Section 802 of the same code provides: "If, when the offense is committed, the defendant is out of the state, indictment may be found or an information filed within the term herein limited after his coming within the state, and no time during which the defendant is not an inhabitant of, or usually resident within this state, is part of the limitation." On the face of the information herein it clearly appears that it was not filed within the period of the statute of limitations, and no allegations setting forth an exception to the running of the statute are made. If defendant had set up the bar of limitation, he would, so far as the record shows, have been entitled to a dismissal. But he failed to do so and raises the defense now for the first time after conviction and sentence. His contention is that the court lacked jurisdiction after the expiration of the three-year period, and that the judgment was therefore void.

Whether the statute of limitations in criminal cases is jurisdictional, or a matter of defense to be affirmatively pleaded by the defendant, is a question upon which there exists some diversity of opinion. In California the law is in a most confused state. This court, in Ex parte Blake, 155 Cal. 586 [102 P. 269, 18 Ann.Cas. 815], declared that the statute was a mere matter of defense, and not ground for discharge on habeas corpus. The District Court of Appeal, in Ex parte Vice, 5 Cal.App. 153 [89 P. 983], came to the opposite conclusion; and in People v. Hoffman, 132 Cal.App. 60 [22 P.2d 229], the court held that a motion to set aside a judgment would lie where the information showed on its face that the statute had run. A hearing in the Hoffman case was denied by this court. The early case of People v. Miller, 12 Cal. 291, also lends support to this conclusion.

It is necessary that this confusion be eliminated, and that the rule which shall govern prosecutions in this state be declared. In our view, the more desirable rule is that the statute is jurisdictional, and that an indictment or information which shows on its face that the prosecution is barred by limitations fails to state a public offense. The point may therefore be raised at any time, before or after judgment.

This is, of course, a rule essentially different from that governing civil actions, and it results from the different character of the statute in the two kinds of proceedings. In civil actions the statute is a privilege which may be waived by the party. In criminal cases, the state, through its legislature, has declared that it will not prosecute crimes after the period has run, and hence has limited the power of the courts to proceed in the matter. It follows that where the pleading of the state shows that the period of the statute of limitations has run, and nothing is alleged to take the case out of the statute, for example, that the defendant has been absent from the state, the power to proceed in the case is gone. . . .

The order appealed from is reversed.[1]

SEAWELL, J., CURTIS, J., WASTE, C. J., SHENK, J., and PRESTON, J., concurred.

STATE v. DISBROW

Supreme Court of Iowa, 1906.
130 Iowa 19, 106 N.W. 263.

The defendant, having been convicted of the crime of larceny by embezzlement, appeals. . . .

WEAVER, J. The indictment which was presented by the grand jury January 19, 1905, charges that defendant on October 16, 1896, being the guardian of one B. F. Smith, received into his possession by virtue of said trust the sum of $723.78, and afterward, on the 23d day of February, 1904, did embezzle and unlawfully and feloniously convert to his own use the said sum of money so received. Upon this indictment the defendant was found guilty and sentenced to a term of imprisonment in the penitentiary. . . .

It is said, however, on the part of the State, that even if this be true it is settled law that "the time during which an indictment which has been quashed or set aside was pending is not, in case a new indictment is found, computed as a part of the period of limitation, provided the same offense and the same offender are charged in both indictments." We find this general proposition stated in some of the text-books and cyclopedias; but reference to the cases relied upon, so far as we have been able to examine them, reveals in each instance that the decision turns upon a local statute expressly or impliedly providing that upon the setting aside of an indictment or the entry

---

1. "[I]n the administration of criminal justice, the statute of limitations must be held to affect not only the remedy, but to operate as a jurisdictional limitation upon the power to prosecute and punish". Waters v. United States, 328 F.2d 739, 743 (10th Cir. 1964).

The statute of limitations is merely one of repose. It gives a right that is waived if not asserted. Hence the indictment need not negate the running of the period. People v. Brady, 257 App.Div. 1000, 13 N.Y.S.2d 789 (1939).

One may be a person "fleeing from justice" so as to toll the federal statute of limitations although he was not within the federal district when the crime was committed. Brouse v. United States, 68 F.2d 294 (1st Cir. 1933).

of a *nol. pros.* the right of the State to present a new indictment within a limited time shall not be prejudiced. . . .

It seems to us a reasonable and just proposition that, in the absence of any statute saving such right to the State, the running of the statute of limitations ought not to be interrupted or suspended by the return and pendency of an indictment upon which no valid conviction or judgment can be founded. Such an indictment is no indictment. It is a nullity, and while it may serve as authority for the trial court to continue the defendant in custody and cause a resubmission of the case to the grand jury, such order is in effect the mere direction that the original inquiry shall be resumed as if the defective indictment had never been voted or returned into court. It is no more than a restoration of the case to the status it occupied at the time it was originally submitted. The grand jury takes it up anew, and may present or ignore the bill, without any reference whatever to the fact that one indictment has been presented and set aside. Cases are not wanting which tend to sustain this view. . . . But, without reference to the precedents from other States, our statute admits of no other conclusion than the one we have indicated. . . .

Other questions argued are not likely to arise on a retrial and we need not discuss them. For the reasons stated, the case must be remanded to the district court for a new trial.

Reversed.[1]

---

1. The statute is tolled while an indictment for the offense is pending, even if it is defective. Hickey v. State, 131 Tenn. 112, 174 S.W. 269 (1915).

"Whenever an indictment is dismissed for any error, defect or irregularity . . . after the period prescribed by the applicable statute of limitations has expired, a new indictment may be returned not later than the end of the next succeeding regular term of such court, following the term at which such indictment was found defective or insufficient, during which a grand jury shall be in session which new indictment shall not be barred by any statute of limitations." 18 U.S.C.A. § 3288.

Reinstating an inadvertently dismissed information reinstates the standing which such information had prior to the dismissal, even though such reinstatement was made at a time when more than a year had elapsed since the commission of the offense. City of Keokuk v. Shultz, 188 Iowa 937, 176 N.W. 946 (1920). The due filing of an information arrests the statute of limitations and it is not necessary that the trial be held within the prescribed period. Ibid.

E and three fellow-employees of a bank co-operated in the embezzlement of its money and the falsification of its records to conceal the shortages. This continued year after year until E, no longer with the bank, was not in a position to aid in the concealment. At that time he told the others that he "was absolutely through and would have nothing further to do with the shortage at the" bank. Having been indicted for embezzlement, E claimed that the prosecution was barred because more than the period of limitations had elapsed since the communication. The others had continued their unlawful activities until just a few weeks prior to the indictment. It was held that if a conspirator effectively withdraws from a conspiracy he is not liable for the further acts of his former associates and the statute of limitations begins to run from the date of his withdrawal. But E's withdrawal was not effective. Although he received no part of the money embezzled after the communication, he did not tell his co-conspirators

UNITED STATES v. GANAPOSKI

District Court of the United States, M.D. Pennsylvania, 1947.
72 F.Supp. 982.

[After Ganaposki, a bankrupt, had fraudulently concealed his assets from the trustee in bankruptcy in violation of federal law, the applicable statute of limitations which had provided that the indictment must be found "within three years after the commission of the offense", was amended to read that such concealment "shall be deemed to be a continuing offense until the bankrupt shall have been finally discharged, and the period of limitations herein provided shall not begin to run until such final discharge". Eight years after the concealment Ganaposki, who had been denied a discharge in bankruptcy, was indicted for that offense.]

MURPHY, DISTRICT JUDGE. . . . Defendant argues that the statute of limitations had expired long before the date of the indictment; that although the bankruptcy proceedings were pending when the Chandler Act of 1938 went into effect on September 22, 1938, the proviso of Section 52, sub. d, should not affect proceedings then pending. Says defendant, if it did affect the proceedings it was an ex post facto law and invalid; also because it did not treat all debtors alike. With this we cannot agree.

When a right of acquittal has not been absolutely acquired by the completion of the period of limitation, that period is subject to enlargement without being obnoxious to the constitutional prohibition against ex post facto laws.

Such an extension makes no change in the rules of evidence or quantum of proof. An act of limitation is an act of grace purely on

---

to stop falsifying the records. He did not want them to stop because that would have resulted in an immediate disclosure of the crime. Hence their continuing wrongful acts were imputable to him and he is not protected by the statute. Eldredge v. United States, 62 F.2d 449 (10th Cir. 1932).

Nearly four years after the alleged offense D was indicted for a crime having a five-year period of limitation. His claim that this violated his right to a speedy trial was rejected on the ground that this right applies only to one who has been charged with crime. Venus v. United States, 287 F.2d 304 (9th Cir. 1960). Accord: Harlow v. United States, 301 F.2d 361 (5th Cir. 1962).

But an unnecessary delay may be so oppressive as to constitute a denial of due process and hence bar a conviction. Ross v. United States, 349 F.2d 210 (D.C.Cir. 1965). In this case, although D was at all times available, seven months elapsed between an alleged illegal sale of narcotics and the filing of the complaint. At the trial no one actually remembered what had happened. The officer "refreshed his recollection" by referring to notes he had made at the time, but D having kept no notebook was unable to give an account of his actions on the day in question.

An unexplained delay of 140 days between the filing of a misdemeanor complaint for a traffic violation and D's arrest was an unreasonable deprivation of his right to a speedy trial, and a writ of prohibition was issued to bar the prosecution. Rost v. Municipal Court, 184 Cal.App.2d 507, 7 Cal.Rptr. 869, 85 A.L.R.2d 974 (1960).

the part of the sovereign and especially is this so in the matter of criminal prosecution. Such enactments are measures of public policy. They are entirely subject to the will of Congress. . . .

Defendant finally relies upon the case of United States v. Fraidin, supra, and particularly the reasoning and conclusion of that court. Confronted with a situation similar to that before us, the court in a very learned and exhaustive opinion referred to the discussion in 2 Collier on Bankruptcy, 14th Ed., Section 29.15, p. 1206, where the author in discussing Section 29, sub. d, states: "Now the period of limitations is governed completely by events outside the acts of the defendant in concealing his property, namely, discharge. In view of the fact that a discharge might be refused because there was concealment, or for numerous other reasons, it is quite possible that the period in which an indictment could be brought for concealment of assets might run interminably. It would seem that the general objective sought by the proviso *could have been attained* by making the concealment of assets a continuing offense until discharged or *denial thereof*." (Italics supplied.) It will be noted that the author states that "the general objective sought by the proviso could have been attained by making the concealment of assets a continuing offense until discharge or denial thereof." We do not disagree with the able author of the text of that valuable book, but surely it was not made as a suggestion to the courts to make an addition to the legislation as it was written by Congress.

The Court in the Fraidin case reasoned that it was proper to make such an addition and concluded (see Id., 63 F.Supp. at page 285) that "the proviso in this section as amended should be construed as though the words 'or until denial thereof' appeared at the very end of the proviso." We do not feel the court had the right to make such an addition. We refuse to do so.

In United States v. Newman, supra, 63 F.Supp. at page 270, the court stated inter alia, construing Section 29, sub. d;

"(3) Difficulties such as are anticipated are an insufficient justification for refusing to adopt an interpretation of Section 29 which its language plainly demands. (4) Unwise public policy is not the equivalent of lack of power or if (as here) Congress possess the authority to legislate as it has done in the two sections named, that is not the business of this court."

United States v. Nazzaro, supra, 65 F.Supp. 457: "The provisions of Section 29, sub. d, are not ambiguous. Congress and not the courts must determine if and when prosecution for an offense should be barred by limitation. No legislative history has been found or called to the attention of the court indicating that Congress intended otherwise than it expressly provided." The court followed United States v. Newman, supra, in the conclusion that the only remedy available for any asserted injustice or hardship created by this provision is an appeal to Congress to modify the statute.

"The general rule respecting statutes of limitation is that the language of the act must prevail, and no reasons based on apparent inconvenience or hardship can justify a departure from it." Amy v. Watertown, 1889, 130 U.S. 320, 9 S.Ct. 537, 538, 32 L.Ed. 953. . . .

For the foregoing reasons, we feel that the defendant's motion to dismiss should be denied. An order to that effect will be filed forthwith.[1]

PEOPLE v. SIEGEL

District Court of Appeal, Second District, Division 2, California, 1965.
235 Cal.App.2d 522, 45 Cal.Rptr. 530.

FLEMING, JUSTICE. May a probationer who received a suspended sentence in 1946 and whose probation was revoked in 1948 be required to serve his sentence in 1965?

In April 1946 defendant Siegel pleaded guilty to the crime of issuing a check without sufficient funds. He was sentenced to imprisonment for one year in the Los Angeles county jail, sentence was suspended, and he was placed on three years' probation. By the terms of his probation Siegel was ordered to follow all rules and regulations of the probation department and was granted permission to leave the state.

Subsequently Siegel left the state—with assurances, he now claims, that he need not report periodically to the probation department in order to remain in good standing. Since the original probation records in this case have been destroyed—Penal Code, § 1203.10, permits destruction of probation papers five years after the termination of probation—the only evidence of this alleged assurance consists of Siegel's own statement to that effect.

In May 1948 Siegel's probation officer recommended that the court revoke probation on the ground of desertion and issue a bench warrant for his arrest. The officer's report stated, "Probationer last reported on Jan. 2, 1948 . . . and Probation Officer has been unable to locate said probationer since that time. It now appears that

---

[1] A statute is unconstitutional if it authorizes punishment for an offense as to which the statute of limitations has already run, or an amnesty been given. Thompson v. State, 54 Miss. 740 (1887); State v. Keith, 63 N.C. 140 (1869); State v. Sneed, 25 Tex.Supp. 66 (1860).

The most elaborate discussion of this point to be found in the cases is in two opinions involving the same case. State v. Hart Moore, 42 N.J.L. 208 (1880); Moore v. State, 43 N.J.L. 203 (1881). The statute of limitations on a charge of conspiracy to violate the Internal Revenue Law begins to run from the last overt act alleged in the indictment. United States v. Albanese, 123 F.Supp. 732 (D.C.N.Y.1954), affirmed 224 F.2d 879 (2d Cir. 1955), certiorari denied 350 U.S. 845, 76 S.Ct. 87, 100 L.Ed. 753 (1955).

said probationer has deserted." On the recommendation of the probation officer probation was revoked in May 1948 and a bench warrant issued for defendant's arrest.

Fifteen years passed.

In July 1963 Siegel again appeared before the Superior Court to answer a charge of issuing checks without sufficient funds, and at that time his 1946 sentence and 1948 revocation of probation were brought before the court. The court ordered a supplemental probation report to cover Siegel's activities during the intervening years. This report showed that in February 1948 Siegel had been convicted in Florida of vagrancy; in November 1948, convicted in Chicago of passing bad checks; in August 1949, convicted in New York of grand larceny; in June 1952, convicted in Chicago federal court of transporting bad checks across state lines; in September 1958, again convicted of a federal offense involving bad checks; in October 1961, again convicted in a Florida federal court of transporting forged checks across state lines. In July 1963, as previously noted, he appeared before the California Superior Court on bad check charges.

After considering this report the court found that the defendant had violated the terms of his probation, the revocation of probation was confirmed, and the 1946 sentence of one year in the county jail was ordered into execution.

Siegel appeals from the order requiring him to serve his original sentence, and he has obtained bail pending appeal. He contends the trial court was without jurisdiction to sentence him some 17 years after the original judgment, and that in any event the trial court abused its discretion in so doing.

(1) *The Court Had Jurisdiction*

The law is settled that when a court revokes probation within the probationary period, the defendant may be arrested and sentenced any time thereafter even though the probationary period has expired. The jurisdictional fact is the timely revocation of probation. Resentencing or execution of the judgment may occur at any time after revocation of probation, regardless of lapse of time. In People v. Brown, 111 Cal.App.2d 406, 244 P.2d 702, resentencing occurred 15 years after defendant had been placed on probation; in People v. Daugherty, 233 A.C.A. 333, 43 Cal.Rptr. 446, 11 years after judgment; and in People v. Mason, 184 Cal.App.2d 182, 7 Cal.Rptr. 525, 11 years after judgment.

Siegel's probation was revoked in 1948 while the original three-year probationary term was in effect, and thus the court in 1963 possessed jurisdiction to order the sentence into execution, even though 17 years had elapsed from the date of the original sentence.

(2) *No Abuse of Discretion*

The trial court did not abuse its legal discretion in revoking probation. When judgment has been pronounced and sentence suspended upon the grant of probation, probation may be revoked without notice and hearing, and defendant ordered committed pursuant to the judgment.[1] Although the court may not arbitrarily revoke probation, it is not required to hold a hearing under rules which are applicable to formal trials and revocation may be based upon the probation officer's report alone.

The supplemental probation report on Siegel showed violations of probation during the probationary period, for example, the conviction for vagrancy in Florida in February 1948. Since the commission of further crimes within the probationary period is good ground for revocation of probation the court acted within its authority in confirming the revocation of probation and ordering the previously-imposed sentence into execution.

There remains the question whether as a matter of sound public policy stale proceedings such as these should be further pursued. At some point every old judgment, even in criminal cases, becomes archaic and obsolete. Judgments should not be asserted to the surprise of the parties or their representatives when all proper vouchers of evidence are destroyed and facts have become obscured by lapse of time or death of witnesses. Obviously at some point the books must be balanced, and old debts written off. Thus, the doctrine of laches, the rule of adverse possession, the ten-year statute of limitations for execution on a civil judgment (Code Civ.Proc. § 681), and the three-year statute of limitations for commencing most felony actions (Penal Code, § 800), all reflect a policy of repose in dealing with past events.

Here we are concerned with a one-year sentence of imprisonment ordered into execution 17 years after the original judgment. The probation files in the case have been destroyed, the original probation officer is dead, and the reasons for the original revocation of probation cannot be ascertained by direct evidence. Although during the intervening years the defendant bounced from bad check to bad check and from prison to prison, for these other crimes he has paid his penalty. In the light of these considerations the trial court might well have determined that the public interest would be better served by the application of a general policy of repose to stale criminal judgments, no matter how unworthy the individual beneficiary of such a policy might be, rather than by enforcement of an antiquated criminal sentence which through lapse of time carries substantial risk of injustice and can have little deterrent effect on crime.

Yet, presumptively, these considerations were fully weighed by the trial court and its decision went the other way. As an appellate

---

1. Contrast the situation where no judgment has been given and pronouncement of sentence has been suspended; in that event there is no basis on which a defendant could be directly committed to prison on revocation. He is therefore entitled to notice and hearing and counsel in what is equivalent to an arraignment for judgment. (In re Levi, 39 Cal.2d 41, 244 P.2d 403; In re Klein, 197 Cal.App.2d 58, 17 Cal.Rptr. 71.)

court we cannot say on this record that the result reached was clearly erroneous.

Judgment affirmed.

ROTH, P. J., and HERNDON, J., concur.

MODEL PENAL CODE

Section 1.06. Time Limitations.

(1) A prosecution for murder may be commenced at any time.

(2) Except as otherwise provided in this Section, prosecutions for other offenses are subject to the following periods of limitation:

(a) a prosecution for a felony of the first degree must be commenced within six years after it is committed;

(b) a prosecution for any other felony must be commenced within three years after it is committed;

(c) a prosecution for a misdemeanor must be commenced within two years after it is committed;

(d) a prosecution for a petty misdemeanor or a violation must be commenced within six months after it is committed.

(3) If the period prescribed in Subsection (2) has expired, a prosecution may nevertheless be commenced for:

(a) any offense a material element of which is either fraud or a breach of fiduciary obligation within one year after discovery of the offense by an aggrieved party or by a person who has legal duty to represent an aggrieved party and who is himself not a party to the offense, but in no case shall this provision extend the period of limitation otherwise applicable by more than three years; and

(b) any offense based upon misconduct in office by a public officer or employee at any time when the defendant is in public office or employment or within two years thereafter, but in no case shall this provision extend the period of limitation otherwise applicable by more than three years.

(4) An offense is committed either when every element occurs, or, if a legislative purpose to prohibit a continuing course of conduct plainly appears, at the time when the course of conduct or the defendant's complicity therein is terminated. Time starts to run on the day after the offense is committed.

(5) A prosecution is commenced either when an indictment is found [or an information filed] or when a warrant or other process is issued, provided that such warrant or process is executed without unreasonable delay.

(6) The period of limitation does not run:

(a) during any time when the accused is continuously absent from the State or has no reasonably ascertainable place of abode or work within the State, but in no case shall this provision extend the period of limitation otherwise applicable by more than three years; or

(b) during any time when a prosecution against the accused for the same conduct is pending in this State.

SECTION 4. FORMER JEOPARDY

Litigation would never end if the issues determined in one action could be raised anew between the same parties by the mere commencement of another proceeding. In the words of the ancient maxim: *"Nemo debet bis vexari pro eadem causa"* (No one ought to be twice tried for the same cause). This found expression in the common law in the form of the plea of *res judicata* in civil suits and in the pleas of the *autrefois acquit* and *autrefois convict* in criminal prosecutions. Such a plea in a criminal case, in the words of Blackstone, "is grounded on this universal maxim of the common law of England, that no man is to be brought into jeopardy of his life more than once for the same offence." 4 Bl.Comm. *335. The actual foundation is the broader maxim mentioned above, but it is from statements such as Blackstone's that we derive our phrases "former jeopardy," "double jeopardy" and "twice in jeopardy."

The Fifth Amendment says: ". . . nor shall any person be subject for the same offense to be twice put in jeopardy of life or limb; . . ." Similar language is to be found in the constitutions of many states, but it is important to keep in mind that there was no such common-law plea as "former jeopardy." The plea was either "former acquittal" (autrefois acquit) or "former conviction" (autrefois convict). There is no reason to believe that the phrase "twice put in jeopardy" was used in the Fifth Amendment for the purpose of introducing a change into this department of the law. In all likelihood the framers of the Constitution had no more in mind than embodiment of the common-law prohibition against placing a defendant in jeopardy a second time for the same offense after *acquittal* or *conviction*. An enlargement has resulted from judicial interpretation, however. The courts have tended to hold that a defendant is "in jeopardy" as soon as the jury has been impaneled and sworn (if the court has jurisdiction and the indictment is sufficient to support a conviction) and that the bar against a second trial begins at this point. This position has tended to introduce new difficulties into this branch of the law. The common-law principle (to repeat) was that an accused person should not be prosecuted again for the same offense after he had once been convicted or acquitted thereof. The word "jeopardy" merely happened to be used by Blackstone and others in explanation of this principle. The principle itself was quite independent of the meaning of the word "jeopardy." And this word, apart from the meaning engrafted upon it by the courts, signifies danger or peril. It comes from the same source as the word "jeopardize" which means "to expose to loss or injury." In a very real sense a man is in jeopardy when he has been charged with crime by a valid indictment. Neither precedent nor policy forbids a second indictment for the same offense merely because of the finding of a prior one, and the bar of "former jeopardy" has never been carried to that extent.[1]

The bar known as "former jeopardy" is grounded partly upon expediency and partly upon "fair play." Expediency alone requires some device which will prevent the same issues being tried time and again by the same parties. "Fair play" may require more than this. It would be quite unfair to the defendant in a criminal case, for example, if either the prosecuting attorney or the judge could arbitrarily withdraw the case from the jury after the trial started, merely in the hope of obtaining another jury which might be more likely to find a verdict of guilty. Any such unfairness could have been prevented, without material change from the common-law concept, by treating as the "equivalent of an acquittal" any disposition of a criminal case by which a jury which had been duly impaneled and sworn to try it was not permitted to bring in a verdict, by any act of the prosecuting attorney, or by any violation of judicial discretion on the part of the judge. Some of the cases approach the problem from this point of view.

Another solution, however, was reached by many courts. This was grounded upon the premise that a defendant was "in jeopardy" when a jury was duly impaneled and sworn to try his case and that the trial of this same case by any other jury would be placing him "twice in jeopardy." Such a position required certain exceptions to avoid obvious miscarriages of justice. The two views reach the same result in most cases but there are important shades of difference.

Because of these facts some of the problems in this field arise out of peculiarities in the proceedings themselves,—of which the following are merely examples. Was the case withdrawn from the jury after it had been duly impaneled and sworn but before it had rendered a verdict, and if so why? Has a retrial been ordered after a verdict was rendered, and if so what was the verdict and why was the retrial ordered?

Apart from problems arising out of the peculiarities of procedure in the particular case are those arising out of interpretations of

---

1. Statutes sometimes impose limitations that go beyond former jeopardy. For example: "An act or omission which is made punishable in different ways by different provisions of this code may be punished under either of such provisions, but in no case can it be punished under more than one; an acquittal or conviction and sentence under either one bars a prosecution for the same act or omission under any other . . . ." Cal.Pen. Code, § 654. D threw gasoline into the bedroom of Mr. and Mrs. R and ignited it. He was convicted of two counts of attempted murder and one count of arson. It was held that arson was the means used in the attempt to murder and hence D could not be punished for both. But an act depends upon the objective and if the intent is to kill two persons unlawfully the result is two offenses. Hence D could properly be punished for the two attempts to commit murder. Neal v. State of California, 55 Cal.2d 11, **9** Cal.Rptr. 607, 357 P.2d 839 (1961).

Sec. 4   FORMER JEOPARDY

the phrase "the same offense" as used in the former jeopardy rule. These two sets of problems require separate attention although both may happen to be involved in the same case.

(A) PROBLEMS PECULIAR TO THE PROCEEDINGS

No "jeopardy" is involved if the court lacked jurisdiction to try the case or if the indictment was insufficient to support a conviction. If, because of some fatal defect the indictment was quashed before trial [1] or set aside during the trial or afterwards, the defendant may be prosecuted upon a proper indictment subsequently found against him [2] (provided it is not barred for some other reason such as the statute of limitations).

Furthermore, jeopardy attaches only when there has been a real prosecution for crime. If a wrongdoer, not having been accused, hastens before a magistrate, confesses to having committed a certain offense and pays the fine imposed, the state is not barred from a subsequent prosecution. Such voluntary confession and payment of fine is not a criminal prosecution.[3] The burden of proof is upon the prosecution when it seeks to avoid a plea of former jeopardy on the claim of fraud or collusion.[4] And where the prosecuting attorney starts the prosecution, and carries it through, this has been held to bar a subsequent prosecution even if the prosecuting attorney was corrupted during the pendency of the prosecution. Such a judgment may be voidable, but it is not void and cannot be attacked in a collateral proceeding.[5]

ETTER v. STATE
Supreme Court of Tennessee, 1947.
185 Tenn. 218, 205 S.W.2d 1.

Mr. Justice Burnett delivered the opinion of the Court.

Etter was indicted, tried and convicted for the homicide of William Masters. He was convicted of voluntary manslaughter with his punishment fixed at two years' imprisonment.

On the night of March 8, 1946, Etter, the deceased and others were drinking whiskey and shooting craps in one of the men's dormi-

---

1. Reddan v. State, 4 G. Greene 137 (Iowa, 1853); State v. Scott, 99 Iowa 36, 68 N.W. 451 (1896).

2. State v. Smith, 88 Iowa 178, 55 N.W. 198 (1893).

3. State v. Bartlett, 181 Iowa 436, 164 N.W. 757 (1917).

4. State v. Maxwell, 51 Iowa 314, 1 N.W. 666 (1879).

5. Shideler v. State, 129 Ind. 523, 28 N.E. 537, 29 N.E. 36 (1891).

tories at Oak Ridge. Before the crap game started, Etter did not know Masters. After shooting craps until after midnight the occupant of the room where they were asked them to leave. They went to Etter's room and there continued the game. Masters soon lost all his money. He then prepared to leave when Etter gave him $5. because he did not want Masters to leave broke and because Masters lived several miles away and it was necessary that he get a cab home.

Etter then ate some cheese and crackers and retired to the wash room. While he was in the wash room, Masters returned and pushed open the door to the wash room and said: "You are going to give my money back, you damn son-of-a-bitch." At this time Masters had something in his hand and drew back to strike Etter, Etter ducked and the rock Masters threw missed Etter. Masters then struck Etter with his fist. He said he was going to kill Etter.

As the above was happening, Etter drew a pocket knife from his pocket and stabbed Masters in the abdomen. Masters then left and went up into the lobby of the dormitory. Etter washed his hands and left his knife by the drinking fountain and then also went up into the lobby. Masters was lying on the floor. He soon died as a result of this knife wound. Etter made no further assault but soon gave himself up to the officers who shortly arrived on the scene.

The above facts are almost wholly gathered from voluntary statements Etter gave the officers. He testified herein in his own defense and to all intents and purposes tells the same story. Etter was a larger man than Masters, weighing about 30 pounds more. Etter is a man 44 years of age while the deceased was 34 years of age. After the homicide the officers say Etter was intoxicated. In one of the statements made by the plaintiff in error he says the deceased had his hand in his pocket, in the other statement he did not so claim.

On June 7, 1946, the plaintiff in error was arraigned and brought to trial. The jury was selected and sworn and testimony introduced. At the noon recess one of the jurors became separated from the others and the officer. Defense counsel was informed of this fact. Apparently the trial Judge was also informed of the fact because after court had convened after lunch the trial judge called defense counsel to the bench and was in the process of asking counsel if he would waive the matter when counsel responded, "we are not in a position to waive any possible defense which our client might have in this case." This was also the position of the defense after conferring with the plaintiff in error. There was no "public statement" (meaning no announcement from the bench to those in the court room of what was going on or said) by the judge as to what he conferred with counsel for the respective parties about. After the statement of counsel that they would waive no rights the trial judge declared a mistrial.

The case came on for trial again on October 9, 1946, when the conviction here complained of was had. On September 23, 1946, a plea

Sec. 4 FORMER JEOPARDY 729

of former jeopardy, based on the above detailed happenings of June 7, 1946, was filed. Necessary proof in support of this plea was heard and the plea overruled.

This appeal is based on two alleged errors: (1) That the plea of former jeopardy should have been sustained and (2) the evidence "preponderates in favor of the innocence of the defendant and against the verdict of the jury."

It is axiomatic that the unexplained separation of the jury in this kind of a case *prima facie* vitiates the verdict. When a separation is shown it would be incumbent on the State or prosecution to show definitely that no communication was had with the juror (this showing must be positive and clear cut) during his absence from his brother jurors.

Practically all authorities agree that jeopardy begins when the accused is put upon trial before a court of competent jurisdiction, upon an indictment sufficient in form and substance to sustain a conviction, and the jury has been impaneled and sworn.[1] In ancient times it was said that a jury once sworn in a "case of life or member" could not be discharged by the court, but must render a verdict. We are not advised as to whether or not this requirement was ever extended to its extreme. Blackstone early realized the absurdity of the extreme when he recognized that juries in criminal cases might be

---

1. In a case in which trial by jury had been waived by D it was said: "So far as jeopardy is concerned, the commencement of a trial without a jury must be deemed the equivalent of one begun with a jury. The peril of jeopardy arises before a judge acting alone under the same circumstances as before a judge and jury". State v. Pittsburg Paving Brick Co., 117 Kan. 192, 230 P. 1035, 1037 (1924). And if D pleads guilty in good faith and this plea is duly entered and not withdrawn, the information or indictment being valid, jeopardy is complete. Markiewicz v. Black, 138 Colo. 128, 330 P.2d 539, 75 A.L.R.2d 678 (1958). In this case the judge had set a hearing for evidence to be considered on an application for probation. At this hearing the district attorney offered evidence of another crime by D but no evidence of the crime to which the plea of guilty had been entered, whereupon the judge ordered the case dismissed and D discharged. Thereafter the district attorney filed another information charging D with the identical offense charged in the first. It was held that the trial was barred by former jeopardy.

After the state had presented its evidence in a trial on a charge of second-degree murder, the court granted the state's motion to dismiss on the ground that the evidence disclosed an offense of a higher nature. The statute expressly authorized this procedure and declared that it should not constitute former jeopardy. It was held, however, that defendant could not thereafter be tried for first-degree murder because the evidence sufficient to convict him of that offense would also have been sufficient to convict him of the crime of second-degree murder of which he had been in jeopardy when the jury was sworn in the first case. The statute cannot overcome the express prohibition of the state constitution. The effective scope of the statute, said the court, is limited to other situations such as where the evidence in a trial for disturbing a meeting discloses an assault with a deadly weapon. Former jeopardy would not be involved there because the elements of the two offenses are different. Application of Williams, 85 Ariz. 109, 333 P.2d 280 (1958).

discharged during the trial in cases of "evident necessity." 4 Bl.Com. P. 361.

The expression "evident necessity" has been expanded and defined in modern times and practice in the necessities of justice to the point where "the court may discharge a jury without working an acquittal of the defendant in any case when the ends of justice, under the circumstances, would otherwise be defeated." 15 Am.Jur.P. 75, sec. 406.

It was early recognized in American jurisprudence that the court is to exercise a *sound discretion* on the subject and that this discretion rests in a large measure on the responsibility of the trial judges under their oaths of office. . . .

Certain conditions, if arising in the trial of a case, have come to be well recognized as constituting the occasion which will warrant the discharge of a jury, and, if they appear of record, will bar a plea of former jeopardy. These conditions are set forth in Wharton's Criminal Law, Vol. I, page 549, as: "(1) Consent of the prisoner: (2) illness of (a) one of the jurors, (b) the prisoner, or (c) the court: (3) absence of a juryman: (4) impossibility of the jurors agreeing on a verdict: (5) some untoward accident that renders a verdict impossible; and (6) extreme and overwhelming physical or legal necessity." . . .

For the reasons given, all assignments must be overruled and the judgment below must be affirmed.[2]

All concur.

GROGAN v. STATE

Supreme Court of Alabama, 1870.
44 Ala. 9.

PETERS, J. The appellant, Grogan, was indicted in the circuit court of Wilcox county, on the 28th day of May, 1868, for an assault on Robert Hinton, with intent to murder him. This cause came on to

---

2. V was indicted for a violation of the Primary Election Law. He pleaded not guilty and the case came on for trial. At the close of the case, the judge having charged the jury and the jury having retired to consider its verdict, the judge left the courtroom, directing that the court should remain open for the purpose of taking the verdict and that the clerk should receive it. Some eight hours later the jury came into the room, in the absence of the judge and stated to the deputy clerk that they were unable to agree. Thereupon the deputy clerk, without the consent of the defendant, discharged the jury from further service. The deputy clerk had a right to receive a verdict under the law of the jurisdiction, but he had no authority to discharge the jury. Later the case came on for trial again by another jury. The former proceeding was held not to be a bar to this second trial. State v. Van Ness, 82 N.J.L. 181, 83 A. 195 (1912).

If the need arises an alternate juror, who has been properly selected, may be substituted for one of the original twelve. People v. Hess, 104 Cal.App. 2d 642, 234 P.2d 65 (1951).

be tried in said court, at the October term thereof, in 1869, when the defendant, having pleaded not guilty, went to trial, with a jury, on that plea. For the purpose of trying the said defendant, a jury of good and lawful men were duly sworn and empanneled by the court, "to try the issue joined." The record then states that, "after the evidence had been gone through with, and the solicitor for the State had opened the case to the jury, and the counsel for the defendant, Grogan, had made their arguments to the jury, the counsel for the defendant, Grogan, having made their point of law to the court, that the circuit court of Wilcox county had no jurisdiction to try this cause," and the point thus made was sustained by the court, "the solicitor, on behalf of the State, moved the court to enter a *nolle prosequi* in this case, and further moved the court, that the defendant, Patrick T. Grogan, be bound over to appear at the next term of the city court to be held in and for the county of Dallas, in the State of Alabama, to answer such indictment as may be found against him by the grand jury of the circuit court of said Dallas county." To these motions the defendants objected, and insisted, "that the jury be required to render a verdict in said cause." These motions being heard, and argument thereon being had before the court, they were granted, and a *nolle prosequi* was entered by the court against the consent and objection of the defendant, said Grogan. And said Grogan was thereupon required by the court to enter into bond, with security, in the sum of five hundred dollars, conditioned that he appear at the next term of the circuit court of said county of Dallas, and from term to term thereafter until discharged by law, to answer the offense of assault with intent to murder. Said bond being given as required, said defendant was discharged by the court. The court then further ordered, that the clerk of the circuit court of Wilcox county forward to the clerk of the circuit court of Dallas county a certified copy of the judgment and proceedings in the case, which had been entered in said circuit court of Wilcox county. These were recitals made in the judgment of *nolle prosequi*.

There was also a bill of exceptions taken by the defendant on the trial, which shows the same facts as those set out in the judgment of the court above recited; and also, that after the cause had been submitted to the jury, and all the testimony had been closed and the cause partly argued by counsel on both sides, "the State moved to enter a *nolle prosequi*, and to bind the prisoner over to answer the *same charge* in Dallas county. To this motion the prisoner objected, and insisted that the jury be allowed to pass upon the case, and to return a verdict of guilty or not guilty." The court sustained the motion, and refused to permit the jury to bring in a verdict, and discharged them, and bound the defendant over to answer the same charge in Dallas county. To all which the defendant excepted, and reserved the same in his bill of exceptions.

From this judgment of the court below the said defendant, Grogan, has appealed to this court, and he here assigns the proceedings in the court below for error; and also moves this court for a *mandamus*, or other proper writ, "to the end that the supreme court will direct the discharge of the said Patrick T. Grogan, as upon a final trial and acquittal on the issues joined on the indictment in the circuit court of Wilcox county."

It also appears from the bill of exceptions, that there was some testimony offered by defendant, that the offense with which the defendant below was charged, had been committed in the county of Dallas, and not within a quarter of a mile of the boundaries of the two counties of Dallas and Wilcox; and also, some testimony offered by the State, showing that the offense was committed within a quarter of a mile of said boundaries.

At the last term of this court, the validity of section 3945 of the Revised Code was considered. It was then declared to be a constitutional law; and we have not since discovered any sufficient reason why that determination should not be adhered to. We are, therefore, satisfied with that exposition of the law, and it is here now again affirmed. Hill v. The State, at June term, 1869; Const.Ala. of 1867, § 8; Revised Code, § 3945.

The constitutional guaranty against a second trial for the same offense is in these words, to-wit: "No person shall, for the same offense, be twice put in jeopardy of life or limb."—Const.Ala.1867, art. 1, § 11.

The question of difficulty is to ascertain when this jeopardy begins; because, until it does begin, it can not be said to exist, and the constitutional protection can not be invoked. Happily, the embarrassment that once encumbered this question has been long since removed. At an early day in the judicial history of this State, this court settled the law to be, that "the unwarrantable discharge of a jury, after the evidence is closed, in a capital case, is equivalent to an acquittal."—Ned v. The State, 7 Por. 187, 203. This decision is in conformity with the law as settled at this day. A recent and carefully prepared work upon the subject of criminal law, lays down the rule in the following terms: "But when, according to the better opinion, the jury, being full, is sworn and added to the other branch of the court, and all the preliminary things of record are ready for the trial, the prisoner has reached the jeopardy from the repetition of which our constitutional rule protects him. During the trial, the prosecuting officer is not authorized to enter a *nolle prosequi*; or, if he enters it, even with the consent of the judge; or, if he withdraws a juryman, and so stops the hearing, the legal effect is an acquittal." —1 Bish.Cr.Law, §§ 856, 858, (3d ed. 1865.) Such a procedure as that shown by the record in this case entitles the defendant to have a verdict of not guilty returned by the jury, and he cannot be again brought into jeopardy for the same offense.

Here the jury was regularly sworn and empanneled, the defendant went to trial on his plea, the evidence was closed on both sides, and the argument for the defense was finished. The trial was then stopped, and a *nolle prosequi* was entered without the consent of the defendant and against his objection. Under such a state of facts, the discharge of the jury was an acquittal of the defendant. This is the law, and it must be enforced. The defendant should have been discharged as soon as the *nolle prosequi* was entered. The court erred in failing to do so. And, as he can not be again tried for the same offense, to answer which he was bound over to appear at the Dallas circuit court, the proceedings in the court below are reversed, back to the judgment of *nolle prosequi,* and it is ordered and adjudged by this court, that the appellant, said Patrick T. Grogan, the defendant below, be discharged from further prosecution upon the charge of assault on said Robert Hinton, with the intent to murder him, said Hinton, as made and set forth in said indictment, found in said circuit court of Wilcox county, on said 28th day of May, 1868, and herein above referred to.

There will be no need for a *mandamus* if the order of the court in its judgment in this case is obeyed, as it doubtless will be. Therefore, the questions arising on a consideration of the motion for that writ are not discussed in this opinion.[1]

---

1. Accord, State v. Callendine, 8 Iowa 288 (1859); State v. Spayde, 110 Iowa 726, 80 N.W. 1058 (1899); People v. Taylor, 117 Mich. 583, 76 N.W. 158 (1898). Cf. Maddox v. State, 230 Ind. 92, 102 N.E.2d 225 (1951).

Burton and Mack were charged jointly with robbing Sam Lawhon. They elected to be tried separately. Burton was tried first and was acquitted. During the trial of Mack, his attorney questioned the alleged victim of the robbery in regard to his testimony in Burton's trial, and then said: "and in spite of your testimony he was acquitted?" The prosecuting attorney immediately moved to discharge the jury and this motion was sustained. Mack was later tried and convicted by another jury over his objection that the proceeding before the first jury barred any subsequent trial for the same offense. In affirming the conviction the court said that the second trial resulted from the prejudicial misconduct of defendant's attorney. Mack v. Commonwealth, 177 Va. 921, 15 S.E. 2d 62 (1941).

A soldier was charged with rape and put on trial before a general court-martial in time of war. After hearing evidence and arguments of counsel, the court-martial closed to consider the case. Later the same day the court-martial re-opened and announced that it would be continued until a later day to hear other witnesses not then available. A week later the commanding general of the division withdrew the charges from the court-martial and transferred them to the commanding general of the Third Army with recommendations for trial by a new court-martial. The reason given was that the "tactical situation" made it impracticable to complete the case within a reasonable time. For a similar reason it was transferred on to the commanding general of the Fifteenth Army, who convened a court-martial to try the case. The soldier was convicted after his plea of former jeopardy had been overruled. The case was then taken to the federal court by habeas corpus proceedings. In upholding the conviction the court said: "The double-jeopardy provision of the Fifth Amendment, however, does not mean that every time a defendant is put to trial before a competent tribunal he is entitled to go free if the trial fails to end in a final judgment. Such a rule would create an insuperable obstacle to the administration of justice in

UNITED STATES v. TATEO

Supreme Court of the United States, 1964.
377 U.S. 463, 84 S.Ct. 1587.

[A five-count indictment included four charges under the federal bank-robbery statute and one of kidnaping. After four days of trial the judge told Tateo that if he was convicted by the jury he would receive "the absolute maximum sentence", explaining that this would mean he would not be eligible for parole but would "have to stay in jail for the rest of your life". This so alarmed Tateo that he pleaded guilty to four counts whereupon the jury was discharged and the kidnaping count dismissed. The sentence was to a total of 22 years and six months. Later the judgment of conviction was vacated on the ground that the plea of guilty had been coerced by the judge's statement. Thereafter defendant was re-indicted and brought for retrial on all five counts. The District Court sustained a motion to dismiss the indictment and ordered that Tateo be discharged, on the ground that the second trial was barred by the Fifth Amendment. The Government took a direct appeal to the Supreme Court as authorized by 18 U.S.C.A. § 3731.]

many cases in which there is no semblance of the type of oppressive practices at which the double-jeopardy prohibition is aimed. There may be unforeseeable circumstances that arise during a trial making its completion impossible, such as the failure of a jury to agree upon a verdict. In such event the purpose of the law to protect society from those guilty of crimes frequently would be frustrated by denying courts power to put the defendant to trial again." Wade v. Hunter, Warden, 336 U.S. 684, 688–9, 69 S.Ct. 834, 837, 93 L.Ed. 974 (1949). Mr. Justice Murphy, Mr. Justice Douglas and Mr. Justice Rutledge dissented.

Holt was charged with inflicting injury while engaged in the commission of robbery. He filed notice of his intention to prove an alibi and called upon the state to fix the time and place of the alleged crime. The prosecuting attorney did not file an answer to this request until the day of the trial (although he had given defense counsel a copy the day before). After the jury was impaneled and two witnesses examined, Holt's attorney asked for a continuance for eight days in order that he might prepare his case and secure the attendance of his witnesses. The court granted this request, discharged the jury, and reset the case for a later date. The defendant then filed a plea of former jeopardy. A demurrer to this plea was sustained, whereupon defendant was placed on trial and convicted. In affirming this conviction the court said that the discharge of the jury was part of the relief granted on defendant's motion although he did not ask for the discharge, and that his failure to object to the discharge of the jury constituted a waiver. Holt v. State, 223 Ind. 217, 59 N.E.2d 563 (1945).

The quashing of a bad indictment is no bar to a prosecution upon a good one. And if the first indictment was quashed upon defendant's motion, he cannot later maintain that it was valid. He cannot "blow hot and cold". United States v. Narvaez-Granillo, 119 F.Supp. 556 (D.C.Cal.1954).

If a conviction was vacated because defendant was not competent to stand trial there is no bar to another trial after he becomes competent. Flynn v. United States, 217 F.2d 29 (9th Cir. 1954) cert. denied, 348 U.S. 930, 75 S.Ct. 344 (1955).

MR. JUSTICE HARLAN delivered the opinion of the Court.

This case presents the question whether a federal criminal defendant who has had his conviction overturned in collateral proceedings on the ground that a guilty plea entered by him during trial was not voluntary but induced in part by comments of the trial judge, may be tried again for the same crimes or is protected against such a prosecution by the Double Jeopardy Clause of the Fifth Amendment. We hold that under these circumstances retrial does not infringe the constitutional protection against double jeopardy. . . .

The Fifth Amendment provides that no "person [shall] be subject for the same offence to be twice put in jeopardy of life or limb . . . ." The principle that this provision does not preclude the Government's retrying a defendant whose conviction is set aside because of an error in the proceedings leading to conviction is a well-established part of our constitutional jurisprudence. In this respect we differ from the practice obtaining in England. The rule in this country was explicitly stated in United States v. Ball, 163 U.S. 662, 671–672, 16 S.Ct. 1192, 1195, 41 L.Ed. 300, a case in which defendants were reindicted after this Court had found the original indictment to be defective. It has been followed in a variety of circumstances; see, e. g., Stroud v. United States, 251 U.S. 15, 40 S.Ct. 50, 64 L.Ed. 103, (after conviction reversed because of confession of error); Bryan v. United States, 338 U.S. 552, 70 S.Ct. 317, 94 L.Ed. 335 (after conviction reversed because of insufficient evidence); Forman v. United States, 361 U.S. 416, 80 S.Ct. 481, 4 L.Ed.2d 412 (after original conviction reversed for error in instructions to the jury).[1]

That a defendant's conviction is overturned on collateral rather than direct attack is irrelevant for these purposes. Courts are empowered to grant new trials under 28 U.S.C. § 2255, and it would be incongruous to compel greater relief for one who proceeds collaterally than for one whose rights are vindicated on direct review.

While different theories have been advanced to support the permissibility of retrial, of greater importance than the conceptual abstractions employed to explain the Ball principle are the implications of that principle for the sound administration of justice. Corresponding to the right of an accused to be given a fair trial is the societal interest in punishing one whose guilt is clear after he has obtained such a trial. It would be a high price indeed for society to pay were every accused granted immunity from punishment because of any defect sufficient to constitute reversible error in the proceedings leading to conviction. From the standpoint of a defendant,

---

[Footnotes by the Court.]

1. Green v. United States, 355 U.S. 184, 78 S.Ct. 221, 2 L.Ed.2d 199, does not undermine this settled practice; it holds only that when one is convicted of a lesser offense included in that charged in the original indictment, he can be retried only for the offense of which he was convicted rather than that with which he was originally charged.

it is at least doubtful that appellate courts would be as zealous as they now are in protecting against the effects of improprieties at the trial or pretrial stage if they knew that reversal of a conviction would put the accused irrevocably beyond the reach of further prosecution. In reality, therefore, the practice of retrial serves defendants' rights as well as society's interest. The underlying purpose of permitting retrial is as much furthered by application of the rule to this case as it has been in cases previously decided.

Tateo contends that his situation must be distinguished from one in which an accused has been found guilty by a jury, since his involuntary plea of guilty deprived him of the opportunity to obtain a jury verdict of acquittal. We find this argument unconvincing. If a case is reversed because of a coerced confession improperly admitted, a deficiency in the indictment, or an improper instruction, it is presumed that the accused did not have his case fairly put to the jury. A defendant is no less wronged by a jury finding of guilt after an unfair trial than by a failure to get a jury verdict at all; the distinction between the two kinds of wrongs affords no sensible basis for differentiation with regard to retrial.[2] Appellee's argument is considerably less strong than a similar one rejected in Bryan v. United States, supra. In that case the Court held that despite the Court of Appeals' determination that defendant had been entitled—because of insufficiency in the evidence—to a directed verdict of acquittal, reversal of the conviction with a direction of a new trial was a permissible disposition.

Downum v. United States, 372 U.S. 734, 83 S.Ct. 1033, 10 L.Ed. 2d 100, is in no way inconsistent with permitting a retrial here. There the Court held that when a jury is discharged because the prosecution is not ready to go forward with its case, the accused may not then be tried before another jury. The opinion recognized, however, that there are circumstances in which a mistrial does not preclude a second trial. In Gori v. United States, 367 U.S. 364, 81 S.Ct. 1523, 6 L.Ed.2d 901, we sustained a second conviction after the original trial judge declared a mistrial on the ground of possible prejudice to the defendant, although the judge acted without defendant's consent and the wisdom of granting a mistrial was doubtful. If Tateo had *requested* a mistrial on the basis of the judge's comments, there would be no doubt that if he had been successful, the Government would not have been barred from retrying him.[3] Although there may be good reasons why Tateo and his counsel chose not to make such a motion before the trial judge, it would be strange were Tateo to benefit because of his delay in challenging the judge's conduct.[4]

2. See Note, Double Jeopardy: The Reprosecution Problem, 77 Harv.L.Rev. 1272, 1278–1279 (1964).

3. If there were any intimation in a case that prosecutorial or judicial impropriety justifying a mistrial resulted from a fear that the jury was likely to acquit the accused, different considerations would, of course, obtain.

4. E. g., Downum v. United States, 372 U.S. 734, 83 S.Ct. 1033, 10 L.Ed.2d 100; Cornero v. United States, 9 Cir., 48

We conclude that this case falls squarely within the reasoning of Ball and subsequent cases allowing the Government to retry persons whose convictions have been overturned. The judgment below is therefore reversed and the case remanded to the District Court with instructions to reinstate the four bank robbery counts.

It is so ordered.

Judgment reversed and case remanded to the District Court with instructions.[5]

MR. JUSTICE GOLDBERG, with whom MR. JUSTICE BLACK and MR. JUSTICE DOUGLAS join, dissenting.

I would affirm the District Court's holding, 216 F.Supp. 850, that under our decision last term in Downum v. United States, 372 U.S. 734, 83 S.Ct. 1033, 10 L.Ed.2d 100, the Double Jeopardy Clause of the Fifth Amendment protects Tateo against reprosecution. The Court today departs from Downum and in so doing substantially weakens the constitutional guarantee. Downum was correctly decided and deserves a life longer than that accorded it by the decision

---

F.2d 69, 74 A.L.R. 797; compare, e. g., Bassing v. Cady, 208 U.S. 386, 28 S.Ct. 392, 52 L.Ed. 540; United States v. Dickerson, 106 U.S.App.D.C. 221, 271 F.2d 487.

[Added by the Compiler.]

5. On retaking the stand after the noon recess, a government witness changed his testimony in regard to a certain date. On cross examination he admitted that the error had been called to his attention by the prosecuting attorney. After excoriating the attorney, the judge directed a verdict of acquittal. It was held that after the judgment of acquittal had been entered the defendants could not be put on trial again for the same offense even if the judgment was directed by a judge who had no power to make such a direction under the circumstances. Fong Foo v. United States, 369 U.S. 141, 82 S.Ct. 671, 7 L.Ed.2d 629 (1962).

A defendant at whose instance an indictment is dismissed on the ground that no crime is charged has not been in prior jeopardy, and hence cannot complain if a second indictment charges a more serious crime than that attempted to be charged in the first. State v. Nichols, 236 Or. 521, 388 P.2d 739 (1964).

"There is no doubt therefore that under the Criminal Code the Crown has the same privilege as an accused person, of contesting the correctness in point of law of a decision or direction of the presiding Judge, and of securing a new trial, if the Court of Appeal is of opinion that a mistake has been made and that, in consequence of that mistake, there has been a miscarriage of justice in the sense that some substantial wrong has been done, not, of course, necessarily in the final result but in the method by which that result was arrived at so that it might well have been that a different result would have been arrived at if the mistake had not been made." Rex v. Nickle, 34 Can.Cr.Cas. 15, 16 (1920).

Acquittal of a criminal charge of wilful tax evasion does not bar the government's suit for 50% of a deficiency, in addition to the deficiency because it was due to a fraudulent intent to evade the tax. The doctrine of *res judicata* is inapplicable because of the difference in quantum of proof in civil and criminal cases; the acquittal was merely an adjudication that the proof was insufficient to overcome all reasonable doubt of guilt. The doctrine of double jeopardy is inapplicable because the 50% addition to the tax is not primarily punitive but is a remedial sanction imposed as a safeguard for protection of the revenue and to reimburse the Government for expense and loss resulting from the taxpayer's fraud. Helvering v. Mitchell, 303 U.S. 391, 58 S.Ct. 630, 82 L.Ed. 917 (1938).

today. . . . I agree with my Brother Douglas dissenting in Gori v. United States, 367 U.S., at 373, 81 S.Ct. at 1528 that: "The question is not . . . whether a defendant is 'to receive absolution for his crime.' . . . The policy of the Bill of Rights is to make rare indeed the occasions when the citizen can for the same offense be required to run the gantlet twice. The risk of judicial arbitrariness rests where, in my view, the Constitution puts it—on the Government." As in Downum I would "resolve any doubt 'in favor of the liberty of the citizen.'"

For these reasons, I dissent.

PEOPLE v. HENDERSON

Supreme Court of California, In Bank, 1963.
60 Cal.2d 482, 35 Cal.Rptr. 77, 386 P.2d 677.

TRAYNOR, JUSTICE. A jury found defendant guilty of murder of the first degree and fixed the penalty at death.[1] This appeal is automatic. (Pen.Code, § 1239(b).) In a previous trial for the same offense defendant waived trial by jury and pleaded guilty to murder, which the court found to be of the first degree. The court sentenced him to life imprisonment. On defendant's appeal the District Court of Appeal reversed the judgment and remanded the case for a new trial pursuant to a stipulation of defendant and counsel for the respective parties on the ground that defendant was improperly allowed to withdraw his plea of not guilty and to enter a plea of guilty after the court had ordered defendant's counsel discharged on defendant's motion. (Pen.Code, § 1018.) . . .

Defendant contends that the prohibition against double jeopardy precludes imposing the death sentence after reversal of the first judgment sentencing him to life imprisonment. Article I, section 13 of the California Constitution provides that "No person shall be twice put in jeopardy for the same offense . . .." It states a fundamental principle limiting the state's right repeatedly to prosecute a defendant. It is not an absolute prohibition, for although jeopardy may have attached, legal necessity or the real or implied consent of the defendant permits a retrial. In the present case, we must determine the extent to which a defendant who attacks an erroneous conviction thereby opens the door to being again placed in jeopardy.

He does not gain immunity, for by successfully attacking the judgment he at least subjects himself to a retrial that may reach the same result. There is a sharp conflict in the cases, however, whether

---

1. In a trial to determine whether the penalty shall be life imprisonment or death it is reversible error for the district attorney, in his argument to the jury, to mention that one under a life sentence will be eligible for parole after seven years under California law. People v. Morse, 60 Cal.2d 631, 36 Cal. Rptr. 201, 388 P.2d 33 (1964).

such an attack opens the door to the imposition of a more severe sentence on retrial. The question usually arises when a defendant has successfully attacked a conviction of a lesser included offense or a conviction of a lower degree of the crime charged.

Before this court's decision in Gomez v. Superior Court, 50 Cal. 2d 640, 328 P.2d 976, there was a curious distinction between a conviction of a lesser included offense and a conviction of a lesser degree of a crime divided into degrees. A conviction of a lesser included offense was deemed a final acquittal of the offense charged, which was not affected by a subsequent reversal of the conviction. A conviction of the lesser degree of a crime divided into degrees was not deemed an acquittal of guilt of the higher degree, and after reversal the defendant could be convicted of the higher degree on retrial. In the Gomez case, however, we found this distinction to be logically indefensible and held that the double jeopardy clause precluded convicting a defendant of a higher degree of a crime after he had secured reversal of his conviction of the lower degree. In Green v. United States, 355 U.S. 184, 78 S.Ct. 221, 2 L.Ed.2d 199, the United States Supreme Court reached the same conclusion with regard to a conviction of first degree murder after reversal of a conviction of second degree murder. In holding that a defendant is not required to elect between suffering an erroneous conviction to stand unchallenged and appealing therefrom at the cost of forfeiting a valid defense to the greater offense, we agreed with the reasoning in the Green case, that " 'a defendant faced with such a "choice" takes a "desperate chance" in securing the reversal of the erroneous conviction. The law should not, and in our judgment does not, place the defendant in such an incredible dilemma.' " This reasoning applies with equal force to the present case.

The Attorney General contends, however, that under the double jeopardy clause in the United States Constitution and the California Constitution the death penalty can be imposed on a conviction of first degree murder following reversal of a conviction for the same offense with punishment fixed at life imprisonment. (Stroud v. United States, 251 U.S. 15, 18, 40 S.Ct. 50, 64 L.Ed. 103; People v. Grill, 151 Cal. 592, 598, 91 P. 515; . . .)

When Stroud v. United States and People v. Grill were decided, it had been held by the United States Supreme Court and by this court that a reversed conviction of a lesser degree of a crime did not preclude conviction of the higher degree on retrial. (Trono v. United States, 199 U.S. 521, 533–534, 26 S.Ct. 121, 50 L.Ed. 292; People v. Keefer, 65 Cal. 232, 235, 3 P. 818.) A fortiori that rule would apply to different punishments for the same crime. Since the Green and Gomez cases have now established that a reversed conviction of a lesser degree of a crime precludes conviction of a higher degree on retrial, the rationale of the Stroud and Grill cases has been vitiated. It is immaterial to the basic purpose of the constitutional provision against double jeopardy whether the Legislature divides a crime into different degrees carrying different punishments or allows the court or jury to fix different punishments for the same crime. Thus, Mr. Justice Frankfurter dissented in the Green case arguing that the Court's decision in Stroud v. United States, supra, controlled the decision: "As a practical matter and on any basis of human values, it is scarcely possible to distinguish a case in which the defendant is convicted of a greater offense from one in which he is convicted of an offense that has the same name as that of which he was previously convicted but carries a significantly different punishment, namely death rather than imprisonment." (355 U.S. 184, 198 at p. 213, 78 S.Ct. 221, at p. 237, 2 L.Ed.2d 199.) Agreeing with Mr. Justice Frankfurter's reasoning, we overrule People v. Grill, 151 Cal. 592, 91 P. 515. A defendant's right to appeal from an erroneous judgment is unreasonably impaired when he is required to risk his life to invoke that right. Since the state has no interest in preserving erroneous judgments, it has no interest in foreclosing appeals therefrom by imposing unreasonable conditions on the right to appeal.

The judgment is reversed.

GIBSON, C. J., and PETERS, TOBRINER and PEEK, JJ., concur.

SCHAUER, JUSTICE (dissenting). . . .

PALKO v. CONNECTICUT

Supreme Court of the United States, 1937.
302 U.S. 319, 58 S.Ct. 149.

MR. JUSTICE CARDOZO delivered the opinion of the Court.

A statute of Connecticut permitting appeals in criminal cases to be taken by the state is challenged by appellant as an infringement of the Fourteenth Amendment of the Constitution of the United States. Whether the challenge should be upheld is now to be determined.

Appellant was indicted in Fairfield County, Conn., for the crime of murder in the first degree. A jury found him guilty of murder in the second degree, and he was sentenced to confinement in the state prison for life. Thereafter the State of Connecticut, with the permission of the judge presiding at the trial, gave notice of appeal to the Supreme Court of Errors. This it did pursuant to an act adopted in 1886 which is printed in the margin.[1] Public Acts 1886, p. 560,

---

[1] "Sec. 6494. *Appeals by the state in criminal cases.* Appeals from the rulings and decisions of the superior court or of any criminal court of common pleas, upon all questions of law arising on the trial of criminal cases, may be taken by the state, with the permission of the presiding judge, to the supreme court of errors, in the same manner and to the same effect as if made by the accused."

Sec. 4 FORMER JEOPARDY 741

now section 6494 of the General Statutes. Upon such appeal, the Supreme Court of Errors reversed the judgment and ordered a new trial. State v. Palko, 121 Conn. 669, 186 A. 657. It found that there had been error of law to the prejudice of the state (1) in excluding testimony as to a confession by defendant; (2) in excluding testimony upon cross-examination of defendant to impeach his credibility; and (3) in the instructions to the jury as to the difference between first and second degree murder.

Pursuant to the mandate of the Supreme Court of Errors, defendant was brought to trial again. Before a jury was impaneled, and also at later stages of the case, he made the objection that the effect of the new trial was to place him twice in jeopardy for the same offense, and in so doing to violate the Fourteenth Amendment of the Constitution of the United States. Upon the overruling of the objection the trial proceeded. The jury returned a verdict of murder in the first degree, and the court sentenced the defendant to the punishment of death. The Supreme Court of Errors affirmed the judgment of conviction.

1. The execution of the sentence will not deprive appellant of his life without the process of law assured to him by the Fourteenth Amendment of the Federal Constitution.

The argument for appellant is that whatever is forbidden by the Fifth Amendment is forbidden by the Fourteenth also. The Fifth Amendment, which is not directed to the States, but solely to the federal government, creates immunity from double jeopardy. No person shall be "subject for the same offense to be twice put in jeopardy of life or limb." The Fourteenth Amendment ordains, "nor shall any State deprive any person of life, liberty, or property, without due process of law." To retry a defendant, though under one indictment and only one, subjects him, it is said, to double jeopardy in violation of the Fifth Amendment, if the prosecution is one on behalf of the United States. From this the consequence is said to follow that there is a denial of life or liberty without due process of law, if the prosecution is one on behalf of the people of a state. Thirty-five years ago a like argument was made to this court in Dreyer v. Illinois, 187 U.S. 71, 85, 23 S.Ct. 28, 47 L.Ed. 79, and was passed without consideration of its merits as unnecessary to a decision. The question is now here.

We do not find it profitable to mark the precise limits of the prohibition of double jeopardy in federal prosecutions. The subject was much considered in Kepner v. United States, 195 U.S. 100, 24 S. Ct. 797, 49 L.Ed. 114, 1 Ann.Cas. 655, decided in 1904 by a closely divided court. The view was there expressed for a majority of the

A statute of Vermont (G.L. 2598) was given the same effect and upheld as constitutional in State v. Felch, 92 Vt. 477, 105 A. 23.

Other statutes, conferring a right of appeal more or less limited in scope, are collected in the American Law Institute Code of Criminal Procedure, June 15, 1930, p. 1203.

court that the prohibition was not confined to jeopardy in a new and independent case. It forbade jeopardy in the same case if the new trial was at the instance of the government and not upon defendant's motion. All this may be assumed for the purpose of the case at hand, though the dissenting opinions show how much was to be said in favor of a different ruling. Right-minded men, as we learn from those opinions, could reasonably, even if mistakenly, believe that a second trial was lawful in prosecutions subject to the Fifth Amendment, if it was all in the same case. Even more plainly, right-minded men could reasonably believe that in espousing that conclusion they were not favoring a practice repugnant to the conscience of mankind. Is double jeopardy in such circumstances, if double jeopardy it must be called, a denial of due process forbidden to the States? The tyranny of labels must not lead us to leap to a conclusion that a word which in one set of facts may stand for oppression or enormity is of like effect in every other. . . . Is that kind of double jeopardy to which the statute has subjected him a hardship so acute and shocking that our polity will not endure it? Does it violate those "fundamental principles of liberty and justice which lie at the base of all our civil and political institutions"? The answer surely must be "no." What the answer would have to be if the state were permitted after a trial free from error to try the accused over again or to bring another case against him, we have no occasion to consider. We deal with the statute before us and no other. The state is not attempting to wear the accused out by a multitude of cases with accumulated trials. It asks no more than this, that the case against him shall go on until there shall be a trial free from the corrosion of substantial legal error. This is not cruelty at all, nor even vexation in any immoderate degree. If the trial had been infected with error adverse to the accused, there might have been review at his instance, and as often as necessary to purge the vicious taint. A reciprocal privilege, subject at all times to the discretion of the presiding judge has now been granted to the state. There is here no seismic innovation. The edifice of justice stands, its symmetry, to many, greater than before.

2. The conviction of appellant is not in derogation of any privileges or immunities that belong to him as a citizen of the United States.

There is argument in his behalf that the privileges and immunities clause of the Fourteenth Amendment as well as the due process clause has been flouted by the judgment.

Maxwell v. Dow, supra, 176 U.S. 581, at page 584, 20 S.Ct. 448, 494, 44 L.Ed. 597, gives all the answer that is necessary.

The judgment is affirmed.

Mr. Justice Butler dissents.

(B) "THE SAME OFFENSE"

The underlying principle is that when an issue has once been settled between two parties as the result of a fair trial it should not be possible to reopen it by starting a new proceeding. Much of the difficulty in this field would have been avoided if attention had been focused upon this basic precept. But the precept has often been concealed behind words which were intended to express it. And just as the other aspect of the field was confused by overemphasis upon the word "jeopardy," so this part has been complicated by the use of the words "the same offense." [1]

WINN v. STATE

Supreme Court of Wisconsin, 1892.
82 Wis. 571, 52 N.W. 775.

LYON, C. J. 1. The special plea in bar of this prosecution sufficiently avers that the charge of the murder of Coates in the first information, and the charge of an assault with intent to murder Defoy in the present information, are predicated upon one and the same act of *Winn*. It is correctly argued in the plea, as it was at the bar, that if he committed the alleged felonious assault upon Defoy, and in doing so killed Coates, although unintentionally, he is guilty of murder. But the jury acquitted him of the crime of murder, and from that fact the inference is plausibly drawn that the jury must necessarily have negatived the alleged felonious assault upon Defoy, for otherwise they would have convicted *Winn* of the murder charged. It was very earnestly and ingeniously contended in argument by the learned counsel for *Winn* that in substance and legal effect such acquittal is an acquittal of the charge of felonious assault in the present information, and that by compelling the accused to trial therefor he was put twice in jeopardy of punishment for the same offense, in violation of the constitutional and statutory declaration of rights in that behalf. Const. art. I, sec. 8; R.S. sec. 4610.

The arguments for and against the sufficiency of this special plea are very full and able, and numerous adjudications are cited on either side in support of the respective propositions of counsel. To review the cases would call for a treatise on this branch of the law. We do not feel called upon to undertake the task of writing one. We adopt as the law on this subject the rule laid down by Chief Justice Shaw in Comm. v. Roby, 12 Pick. 496. The rule is that the offenses

---

[1]. Extrinsic evidence is admissible on the trial to identify the crime of which defendant has been convicted previously. People v. Braddock, 41 Cal.2d 794, 264 P.2d 521 (1953).

charged in two indictments are not identical unless they concur both in *law* and in *fact,* and that the plea of *autrefois acquit* or *convict* is bad if the offenses charged in the two indictments be distinct in law, no matter how closely they are connected in fact. In order to determine whether there is a concurrence in law, that is, whether a conviction or acquittal on one indictment is a good bar to a prosecution on another, the true inquiry is whether the first indictment was such that the accused might have been convicted under it by proof of the facts alleged in the other indictment.[1] If he could not, the conviction or acquittal under the first indictment is no bar. The result of an application of this test to the present inquiry is obvious. *Winn* could not have been convicted of the murder of Coates merely upon proof that he made a felonious assault upon Defoy. Proof that he killed Coates would also be required. Hence an acquittal on the information charging the murder of Coates is no bar to this information for a felonious assault on Defoy, and the special plea was properly overruled. To the same effect is the English case of Queen v. Morris, L. R. 1 Cr.Cas. 90, in which the accused was convicted of an assault and battery, and suffered punishment therefor, and afterwards, the injured party died of the wounds inflicted upon him by the accused. A subsequent indictment for manslaughter was upheld on the ground that the two prosecutions, though founded on the same assault, were for different offenses. The same question has frequently arisen in prosecutions for violations of excise laws, and the rule above stated seems to have been invariably applied by the courts. Black, Intox.Liq. 648, ch. 21, § 555, and cases cited in notes.

The reasonableness and justice of the above rule is shown and emphasized by the testimony on the trial of this case. It appears quite satisfactorily, if not conclusively, therefrom that *Winn* made a distinct felonious assault upon Defoy when he pointed his loaded revolver at him and snapped it, which had no connection with the killing of Coates, and that such killing resulted from the struggle to disarm *Winn,* and was purely accidental. Very likely *Winn* was acquitted of the murder of Coates on similar proofs, and the jury may not have considered,—probably did not consider,—whether *Winn* intended to kill Defoy or not when the revolver missed fire. Had issue been taken upon the special plea, and tried on the testimony in this record, we should expect the jury to find that the first assault, to wit, the attempt by *Winn* to shoot Defoy, had nothing to do with

---

1. Theft of a letter from a house letterbox and removal of the contents of the letter are separate offenses. Kinsella v. Looney, 217 F.2d 445 (10th Cir. 1954).

Although entering a bank with intent to steal has been made punishable it merges into the completed robbery if the robbery is consummated. Heflin v. United States, 358 U.S. 415, 79 S.Ct. 451, 3 L.Ed.2d 407 (1959).

If a single sale of narcotics violates two sections of the Internal Revenue Code, and one section of the Narcotic Drugs Import and Export Act, it will support three convictions and three sentences. Gore v. United States, 357 U.S. 386, 78 S.Ct. 1280, 2 L.Ed.2d 1405 (1958).

the acquittal of *Winn* of the murder of Coates, and that the question whether such attempt was or was not a felonious assault upon Defoy was not involved in such acquittal. This shows that *Winn* may be guilty of the felonious assault on Defoy and yet not guilty of the murder of Coates. A rule which would absolve *Winn* from conviction and punishment for the assault upon Defoy, of which he was guilty, merely because he was acquitted of the murder of Coates, of which he was not guilty, would be a most vicious one, and would shock all sensible and just ideas of the proper administration of criminal justice. We do not hesitate to reject such a rule. The demurrer to the special plea was properly sustained. . . .

By the Court.—The judgment of the circuit court is affirmed.[2]

SPANNELL v. STATE

Court of Criminal Appeals of Texas, 1918.
83 Tex.Cr.R. 418, 203 S.W. 357.

MORROW, JUDGE. Appellant was convicted of the murder of M. C. Butler. Appellant, his wife and deceased were in an automobile together, at night, and Major Butler and Mrs. Spannell were killed. Appellant claimed, and testified, that Major Butler assaulted him, and that several shots were fired by him at Major Butler with no intent to injure Mrs. Spannell. He was indicted in separate indictments for each of the homicides, was tried and acquitted for the murder of his wife, and filed in this case a plea of former acquittal based upon the proposition that the two homicides, resulting from a single act and volition, constituted but one offense. The court's refusal to submit the plea to the jury is made the basis of complaint. If in shooting at Major Butler with malice appellant unintentionally killed his wife, he would be guilty and could be prosecuted for murdering her. Richards v. State, 35 Tex.Cr.R. 38, 30 S.W. 805; McCullough v.

---

[2]. "Manifestly, appellee, if first tried for the shooting and wounding of Caywood, could not be convicted on proof that he shot Stewart, though both Caywood and Stewart were wounded by one and the same shot. As well might it be argued that, in the killing of several members of the same family by putting poison in the food eaten by them, conviction of the poisoner for the death of one of them would bar a prosecution for the killing of the others.

"If one should throw a bomb into a crowd, and kill several persons, it could not be maintained that his conviction for the death of one of them would bar a prosecution against him for the killing of any of the others. It seems to us that the mere statement of appellee's contention constitutes its refutation.

"The offenses committed by appellee were not included within one another, though resulting from the same act, but were separate and distinct offenses." Commonwealth v. Browning, 146 Ky. 770, 772–3, 143 S.W. 407, 408 (1912).

Where the same act constitutes a violation of two distinct statutes the test to determine whether there are two offenses or only one is whether each requires proof of a fact which the other does not. United States v. Brisbane, 239 F.2d 859 (3d Cir. 1956).

State, 62 Tex.Cr.R. 126, 136 S.W. 1055, in which the court says: "If appellant shot at Ollie Jamison with either his express or implied malice, and killed his wife without intending to kill her, his offense would be murder in the second degree."

If in defending his life against an unlawful attack by Major Butler appellant accidentally killed his wife, he was guilty of no offense. Plummer v. State, 4 Tex.App. 310; Clark v. State, 19 Tex.App. 495; Vining v. State, 66 Tex.Cr.R. 316, 146 S.W. 909. From the Plummer case, supra, we quote, as follows:

"We take the law to be that if the jury believed that the defendant found himself in a condition where he would have been justified in taking the life of Smelser in order to save himself from death or the infliction of great bodily harm, and, in so defending himself from such danger, he, by mistake or accident, shot Mrs. Smelser, then he would not only not be guilty of an assault with intent to murder Mrs. Smelser, but he would not be guilty of any offense whatever."

If he shot at Butler and in the same act killed Mrs. Spannell unintentionally, his guilt or innocence of each of the homicides would depend on whether in shooting at Butler he acted with malice or in self-defense. Assuming that the shots were fired at Butler only, and killed Mrs. Spannell, appellant having no intent, or volition to injure her, to determine whether he was guilty or innocent on his trial for her murder, it was necessary to decide whether in shooting at Butler he acted in self-defense or with malice. On this state of facts the decision that he was innocent of the murder of Mrs. Spannell necessarily involves the finding that appellant's act in firing at Butler was not such as to constitute murder.

It follows that, whether in shooting at Butler appellant acted with malice, or was justified, if in the same act, with no volition to injure his wife, he killed her, there could be but one offense, and the State, prosecuting under separate indictments for each of the homicides, would be concluded as to both by the judgment rendered in one of them. . . .

Where two persons are killed or injured in one transaction, the fact that more than one shot was fired does not, as a matter of law, render it insusceptible of proof that they were both killed by one act. A series of shots may constitute one act, in a legal sense, where they are fired with one volition. In cases where two persons have been killed or wounded by a series of shots, and under the general issue of not guilty it is urged as a defense that one of the homicides or injuries resulted from shots aimed at one striking another, the issue of singleness of the act and intent bringing the double result has not been made to depend on the number of shots fired.

If Major Butler killed Mrs. Spannell, or if appellant, with separate acts and volition, killed her, the offenses were not identical. The statute, article 572, C.C.P., designates as the special pleas available,

Sec. 4   FORMER JEOPARDY   747

former conviction, former acquittal, which include former jeopardy. Powell v. State, 17 Tex.App. 345. We infer that the plea of res adjudicata, in so far as it is distinct from these, is not to be entertained. This per force of the statute, article 572, supra, which names as one of the two special pleas permitted, "that he has been before acquitted by a jury of the accusation against him, in a court of competent jurisdiction, whether the acquittal was regular or irregular." It is the judgment of acquittal for the identical act and volition which will operate to sustain his plea, and the evidence, lack of evidence or reasons which impelled the court to enter the judgment are not important further than as they bear on the issue of identity. . . .

The failure of the court to admit evidence and submit to the jury the issues raised by the plea of former acquittal requires a reversal of the judgment, which is ordered.

Reversed and remanded.[1]

(The concurring opinion of DAVIDSON, P. J., and the opinions given in overruling a motion for a rehearing are omitted.)

1. A conviction of assault with a deadly weapon was held not to bar a subsequent trial for attempt to commit robbery, although based upon the same facts. "The essential elements of the two offenses are not the same." People v. Bentley, 77 Cal. 7, 9, 18 P. 799, 800 (1888).

A conviction of manslaughter, based upon a traffic accident, was held to bar a conviction of assault and battery on another person injured in the same accident, but not to bar a conviction of driving while intoxicated. Smith v. State, 159 Tenn. 674, 21 S.W.2d 400 (1929).

A traffic accident resulting in the death of two persons was held to entitle the state to two trials. The defendant was not entitled to the plea of former jeopardy when placed on trial for the killing of the second victim. State v. Fredlund, 200 Minn. 44, 273 N.W. 353 (1937).

The "state cannot divide an offense consisting of several trespasses into as many indictments as there are acts of trespass that would separately support an indictment and afterwards indict for the offence compounded of them all; as, for instance, just to indict for an assault, then for a battery, then for imprisonment, then for a riot, then for a mayhem, etc. . . ." State v. Ingles, 3 N.C. 4, 5 (1797).

"The distinctive ingredients of the crime of incest is the relationship of the parties, while the distinctive ingredient of the crime of statutory rape is the youthfulness of the female. The evidence necessary to convict of incest would not be sufficient to convict of statutory rape, as there need be no evidence as to the age of the female. On the other hand, evidence that would convict of statutory rape would not be sufficient to convict of incest, as the relationship is wanting. Hence the crimes, although committed by the same act, are different crimes; and a prosecution for one is no bar to a prosecution for the other. (The State v. Patterson, 66 Kan. 447, 71 P. 860)." State v. Learned, 73 Kan. 328, 331, 85 P. 293, 294 (1906). Contra, State v. Price, 127 Iowa 301, 103 N.W. 195 (1905). Cf. Burdue v. Commonwealth, 144 Ky. 428, 138 S.W. 296 (1911); Stewart v. State, 35 Tex.Cr.R. 174, 32 S.W. 766 (1895).

Acquittal of contributing to the moral delinquency of a child was held not to bar a prosecution for unlawful intercourse with her based upon the same transaction. State v. Rose, 89 Ohio St. 383, 106 N.E. 50 (1914).

It was held that the subsequent prosecution was barred in these cases: State v. Waterman, 87 Iowa 255, 54 N.W. 359 (1893), (obstruction of a highway shown by parol to be the same obstruction in both cases); State v. Stout, 75 Iowa 215, 39 N.W. 275 (1888), (uttering as true a forged note and mortgage and obtaining property under false pretenses by the same instruments); State v. Egglesht, 41 Iowa 574 (1875), (uttering forged checks, the former conviction having been for uttering one at the same time and in the same transaction, though another check); State v. Sampson, 157 Iowa 257, 138 N.W. 473 (1912), (holding to the same effect in case of several articles stolen at the same time, even though the articles were owned by different persons).

It was held that the subsequent prosecution was not barred in these cases: State v. Blodgett, 143 Iowa 578, 121 N.W. 685 (1909), (forgery and uttering forged instrument); State v. White, 123 Iowa 425, 98 N.W. 1027 (1904), (gambling and keeping a gambling house); State v. Graham, 73 Iowa 553, 35 N.W. 628 (1887), (maintaining a nuisance in the form of a building used for the unlawful sale of liquor and keeping liquor for the purpose of unlawful sale); State v. Brown, 75 Iowa 768, 39 N.W. 829 (1888), (follows State v. Graham, supra); State v. Boever, 203 Iowa 86, 210 N.W. 571 (1926), (maintaining a liquor nuisance and unlawful possession of the same liquor); State v. Cleaver, 196 Iowa 1278, 196 N.W. 19 (1923), (maintaining liquor nuisance and bootlegging); State v. Ingalls, 98 Iowa 728, 68 N.W. 445 (1896), (larceny and breaking and entering); State v. Broderick, 191 Iowa 717, 183 N.W. 310 (1921), (breaking and entering a building and feloniously receiving property stolen from the same building by means of breaking and entering); State v. Brown, 95 Iowa 381, 64 N.W. 277 (1895), (acquittal of a crime does not bar a prosecution for conspiracy to commit the crime); State v. Dericks, 42 Iowa 196 (1875), (permitting W, a minor, to play billiards in a saloon at one time and permitting M, another minor, to play in the saloon at another time); State v. Norman, 135 Iowa 483, 113 N.W. 340 (1907), (larceny of fowls from the premises of A and larceny of fowls from the premises of B).

State v. Moore, 143 Iowa 240, 121 N.W. 1052 (1909), (holding that conviction and punishment of the defendant under the federal statutes for breaking and entering a postoffice with intent to commit larceny is no bar to a subsequent prosecution by the state for burglary under an indictment which charges the same facts). Furthermore, "the same act may constitute an offense against both the State and the municipal corporation, and may be punished under both without a violation of any constitutional principle." Town of Bloomfield v. Trimble, 54 Iowa 399, 6 N.W. 586, 587 (1880). The local ordinance may regulate local affairs and provide a fine for a violation thereof (to be collected by a civil action), but may not create a crime or impose a criminal punishment. State ex rel. Keefe v. Schmiege, 251 Wis. 79, 28 N.W.2d 345 (1947).

During national prohibition it was held that a conviction of manufacture, transportation, and possession of liquor in violation of the state law did not bar a subsequent prosecution in the federal court for a violation of the National Prohibition Act, based upon the same manufacture, transportation and possession. Each such act violated the law of (1) the United States and (2) the state, and hence resulted in two offenses. United States v. Lanza, 260 U.S. 377, 43 S.Ct. 141, 67 L.Ed. 314 (1922).

It was held that an acquittal of murder by a court-martial did not bar a trial for murder in the state court, based upon the same homicide, because the United States and the State of Tennessee are distinct sovereignties. Each may punish for the violation of its own laws and neither may deprive the other of the right to try those charged with such violations. State v. Rankin, 44 Tenn. 145 (1867).

But an acquittal by a court-martial in the Philippines barred a subsequent trial for the same homicide in the civil courts of the Islands, when they were under the jurisdiction of the United States, because only the laws of the United States were involved. The court rejected the argument that one killing might constitute two separate offenses against the United States,—one against the civil law and the other against the military law. Grafton v. United States, 206 U.S. 333, 27 S.Ct. 749, 51 L.Ed. 1084 (1907).

Congress may impose both a criminal and a civil sanction in respect to the same act or omission since the double jeopardy clause prohibits merely punishing twice or attempting a second time to punish criminally. Rex Trailer Co. v. United States, 350 U.S. 148, 76 S.Ct. 219 (1956).

Sec. 4   FORMER JEOPARDY   749

HOAG v. NEW JERSEY

Supreme Court of the United States, 1958.
356 U.S. 464, 2 L.Ed.2d 913, 78 S.Ct. 829.

MR. JUSTICE HARLAN delivered the opinion of the Court.

In this case we are asked to set aside, under the Due Process Clause of the Fourteenth Amendment, a state conviction secured under somewhat unusual circumstance.

On June 26, 1951, a Bergen County, New Jersey, grand jury returned three indictments against the petitioner charging that on September 20, 1950, in concert with two others, he robbed three individuals, Cascio, Capezzuto and Galiardo, at Gay's Tavern in Fairview, New Jersey. These indictments were joined for trial. The State called five witnesses: the three victims named in the indictment, and two other persons Dottino and Yager. Dottino and Yager were also victims of the robbery, but they were not named in the indictment. All the witnesses, after stating that they were in Gay's Tavern on September 20, testified to the elements of a robbery as defined in the New Jersey statute:[1] that they were put in fear and that property was taken from their persons. The petitioner, who claimed that he was not at the tavern on the fateful day and testified to an alibi, was the sole witness for the defense. Although Galiardo and Dottino had both identified petitioner from a photograph during the police investigation, only one of the witnesses, Yager, identified him at the trial as one of the robbers. On May 27, 1952, the jury acquitted the petitioner on all three indictments.

Subsequently, on July 17, 1952, another Bergen County grand jury returned a fourth indictment against petitioner, which was the same as the first three in all respects except that it named Yager as the victim of the robbery at Gay's Tavern. At the trial upon this indictment the State called only Yager as a witness, and he repeated his earlier testimony identifying petitioner. The defense called Cascio, Capezzuto, Galiardo and Dottino, and they each once again testified either that petitioner was not one of the robbers or that a positive identification was not possible. Petitioner repeated his

---

Where basically the same evidence was used in a prosecution for criminal negligence in the operation of a vehicle resulting in death as had been introduced in a prior prosecution for driving while intoxicated, reckless driving and leaving the scene of an accident, which prior prosecution had resulted in an acquittal, the second prosecution was barred by double jeopardy. People v. Martinis, 46 Misc.2d 1066, 261 N.Y.S.2d 642 (1965).

[Footnotes by the Court.]

1. Section 2:166–1 of the Revised Statutes of New Jersey, under which petitioner was indicted, provided:

"Any person who shall forcibly take from the person of another, money or personal goods and chattels, of any value whatever, by violence or putting him in fear . . . shall be guilty . . . ." This section was subsequently repealed and substantially re-enacted. N.J.Stat.Ann.1953, § 2A:141–1.

alibi. This time the jury returned a verdict of guilty. The conviction was sustained on appeal in both the Superior Court of New Jersey, 35 N.J.Super. 555, 114 A.2d 573, and the Supreme Court of New Jersey, 21 N.J. 496, 122 A.2d 628. We granted certiorari to consider petitioner's claim, timely raised below, that he was deprived of due process. 352 U.S. 907, 77 S.Ct. 150, 1 L.Ed.2d 116.

Petitioner contends that the second prosecution growing out of the Gay's Tavern robberies infringed safeguards of the Double Jeopardy Clause of the Fifth Amendment which are "implicit in the concept of ordered liberty" and that these safeguards as such are carried over under the Fourteenth Amendment as restrictions on the States. Palko v. State of Connecticut, 302 U.S. 319, 58 S.Ct. 149, 152, 82 L.Ed. 288. More particularly, it is said that petitioner's trial for the robbery of Yager, following his previous acquittal on charges of robbing Cascio, Capezzuto, and Galiardo, amounted to trying him again on the same charges. However, in the circumstances shown by this record, we cannot say that petitioner's later prosecution and conviction violated due process.

At the outset it should be made clear that petitioner has not been twice put in jeopardy for the same crime. The New Jersey courts, in rejecting his claim that conviction for robbing Yager violated the Double Jeopardy Clause of the State Constitution,[2] have construed the New Jersey statute as making each of the four robberies, though taking place on the same occasion, a separate offense. This construction was consistent with the usual New Jersey rule that double jeopardy does not apply unless the same evidence necessary to sustain a second indictment would have been sufficient to secure a conviction on the first. Certainly nothing in the Due Process Clause prevented the State from making that construction.

But even if it was constitutionally permissible for New Jersey to punish petitioner for each of the four robberies as separate offenses, it does not necessarily follow that the State was free to prosecute him for each robbery at a different trial. The question is whether this case involved an attempt "to wear the accused out by a multitude of cases with accumulated trials." Palko v. State of Connecticut, supra, 302 U.S. at page 328, 58 S.Ct. at page 153.[3]

We do not think that the Fourteenth Amendment always forbids States to prosecute different offenses at consecutive trials even though

---

2. Article I, par. 11, of the New Jersey Constitution provides in part that "No person shall, after acquittal, be tried for the same offense."

3. Indeed, the New Jersey Superior Court recognized this problem under the double jeopardy clause of the State Constitution when it said in the present case: "Assuredly our prosecutors are aware that the concept of double jeopardy is designed to prevent the government from unduly harassing an accused, and we are confident that they will not resort unfairly to multiple indictments and successive trials in order to accomplish indirectly that which the constitutional interdiction precludes." 35 N.J.Super. at pages 561–562, 114 A.2d at page 577.

they arise out of the same occurrence. The question in any given case is whether such a course has led to fundamental unfairness. Of course, it may very well be preferable practice for a State in circumstances such as these normally to try the several offenses in a single prosecution, and recent studies of the American Law Institute have led to such a proposal. See Model Penal Code § 1.08(2) (Tent.Draft. No. 5, 1956).[4] But it would be an entirely different matter for us to hold that the Fourteenth Amendment always prevents a State from allowing different offenses arising out of the same act or transaction to be prosecuted separately, as New Jersey has done.[5] For it has long been recognized as the very essence of our federalism that the States should have the widest latitude in the administration of their own systems of criminal justice. . . . In the last analysis a determination whether an impermissible use of multiple trials has taken place cannot be based on any overall formula. Here, as elsewhere, "The pattern of due process is picked out in the facts and circumstances of each case." Brock v. State of North Carolina, 344 U.S. 424, 427–428, 73 S.Ct. 349, 350–351, 97 L.Ed. 456. And thus, without speculating as to hypothetical situations in which the Fourteenth Amendment might prohibit consecutive prosecutions of multiple offenses, we reach the conclusion that the petitioner in this case was not deprived of due process.

In Brock v. State of North Carolina, supra, this Court upheld a state conviction against a somewhat similar claim of denial of due process. In Brock two of the State's key witnesses had previously been tried and convicted of crimes arising out of the same transaction which formed the basis of the charge against the petitioner. Before judgments were entered on their convictions they were called by the State to testify at petitioner's trial. Because of their intention to appeal their convictions and the likelihood of a new trial in the event of reversal, the two witnesses declined to testify at petitioner's trial on the ground that their answers might be self-incriminatory. At this point the State was granted a mistrial upon its representation that the evidence of the two witnesses was necessary to its

---

4. See also Horack, The Multiple Consequences of a Single Criminal Act, 21 Minn.L.Rev. 805; Kirchheimer, The Act, The Offense and Double Jeopardy, 58 Yale L.J. 513; Gershenson, Res Judicata in Criminal Prosecutions, 24 Brooklyn L.Rev. 12.

5. The New Jersey Rules in force during 1952 provided:
"(Rule) 2:4–15 Joinder of Offenses (now Revised Rule 3:4–7):
"Two or more offenses may be charged in the same indictment or accusation in a separate count for each offense if the offenses charged, whether high misdemeanors or misdemeanors or both are of the same or similar character or are based on the same act or transaction or on two or more acts or transactions connected together or constituting parts of a common scheme or plan."

"(Rule) 2:5–4 Trial of Indictments or Accusations Together (now Revised Rule 3:5–6):
"The court may order two or more indictments or accusations to be tried together if the offenses and the defendants, if there is more than one, could have been joined in a single indictment or accusation."

case and that it intended to procure their testimony at a new trial of the petitioner. This Court held that a second trial of the petitioner did not violate due process.

Remembering that the Yager robbery constituted a separate offense from the robberies of the other victims, we find no basis for a constitutional distinction between the circumstances which led to the retrial in Brock and those surrounding the subsequent indictment and trial in the present case. It is a fair inference from the record before us that the indictment and trial on the charge of robbing Yager resulted from the unexpected failure of four of the State's witnesses at the earlier trial to identify petitioner, after two of these witnesses had previously identified him in the course of the police investigation. Indeed, after the second of the two witnesses failed to identify petitioner, the State pleaded surprise and attempted to impeach his testimony. We cannot say, that after such an unexpected turn of events, the State's decision to try petitioner for the Yager robbery, was so arbitrary or lacking in justification that it amounted to a denial of those concepts constituting " 'the very essence of a scheme of ordered justice,' which is due process." Brock v. State of North Carolina, supra, 344 U.S. at page 428, 73 S.Ct. at page 351. Thus, whatever limits may confine the right of a State to institute separate trials for concededly different criminal offenses, it is plain to us that these limits have not been transgressed in this case.

Petitioner further contends that his conviction was constitutionally barred by "collateral estoppel." [6] His position is that because

---

6. [Compiler's footnote.] Petitioner was tried and acquitted on a charge of conspiracy to defraud the United States by presenting false invoices and making false representations to a ration board to the effect that certain sales of sugar products were made to exempt agencies. Thereafter he was tried and convicted for aiding and abetting the uttering and publishing of the false invoices introduced in the conspiracy trial. Since, under the unique circumstances of the case, the jury in the second trial could not convict without finding against petitioner the very fact that was found in his favor in the first, this was *"res judicata"* and a valid defense to the second prosecution. Conviction reversed. Sealfon v. United States, 332 U.S. 575, 68 S.Ct. 237 (1948). The court points out that the doctrine of *"res judicata"* is applicable to criminal as well as civil proceedings, and operates to conclude those matters in issue which have been determined by a previous verdict, even though the offenses be different. The position is very sound but the label "collateral estoppel" is more appropriate and the present tendency is to employ it for this purpose. It is to be expected that the doctrine of collateral estoppel will be expanded and will remove much of the confusion which resulted from the effort to make all determinations of this nature in terms of "former jeopardy" and the "same offense". Much of the injustice resulting from the old method may also be removed by the application of collateral estoppel.

For example: While the same act may constitute both a federal offense and a state offense so that a conviction of one is no bar to a trial for the other (United States v. Lanza, 260 U.S. 377, 43 S.Ct. 141 (1922)), the doctrine of collateral estoppel has yet to be tested in the event of an acquittal in the first trial. Since the parties are not the same there is no former jeopardy unless so provided by special statute (such as West's Ann.Cal.Pen. Code, § 656, quoted below, which bars the state trial after a federal trial in such a case). But as collateral es-

Sec. 4 **FORMER JEOPARDY**

the sole disputed issue in the earlier trial related to his identification as a participant in the Gay's Tavern robberies, the verdict of acquittal there must necessarily be taken as having resolved that issue in his favor. The doctrine of collateral estoppel, so the argument runs, is grounded in considerations of basic fairness to litigants, and thus for a State to decline to apply the rule in favor of a criminal defendant deprives him of due process. Accordingly, it is claimed that New Jersey could not relitigate the issue of petitioner's "identity," and is thus precluded from convicting him of robbing Yager.

A common statement of the rule of collateral estoppel is that "where a question of fact essential to the judgment is actually litigated and determined by a valid and final judgment, the determination is conclusive between the parties in a subsequent action on a different cause of action." Restatement, Judgments, § 68(1). As an aspect of the broader doctrine of res judicata, collateral estoppel is designed to eliminate the expense, vexation, waste, and possible inconsistent results of duplicatory litigation. See Developments in the Law—Res Judicata, 65 Harv.L.Rev. 818, 820. Although the rule was originally developed in connection with civil litigation, it has been widely employed in criminal cases in both state and federal courts. . . .

Despite its wide employment, we entertain grave doubts whether collateral estoppel can be regarded as a constitutional requirement. Certainly this Court has never so held. However, we need not decide that question, for in this case New Jersey both recognized the rule of collateral estoppel and considered its applicability to the facts of this case. The state court simply ruled that petitioner's previous acquittal did not give rise to such an estoppel because "the trial of the first three indictments involved several questions, not just [petitioner's] identity, and there is no way of knowing upon which question the jury's verdict turned." 21 N.J. at page 505, 122 A.2d at page 632. Possessing no such corrective power over state courts as we do over the federal courts, we would not be justified in substituting a different view as to the basis of the jury's verdict.

---

toppel is applied on principles of equity rather than strict law, so to speak, it is arguable that the state and the United States are sufficiently related under our federal plan so that no man should be required to stand trial in either if he could not be convicted without finding against him on the very point which was found in his favor in a trial by the other.

Former jeopardy involves identity of offenses while collateral estoppel operates to render a prior judgment conclusive between the parties as to matters actually litigated. Cosgrove v. United States, 224 F.2d 146 (9th Cir. 1955).

"Whenever on the trial of an accused person it appears that upon a criminal prosecution under the laws of another state, government or country, founded upon the act or omission in respect to which he is on trial, he has been acquitted or convicted, it is a sufficient defense". West's Ann.Cal.Pen.Code, § 656 (1949).

Conviction of conspiracy in a state court will not bar a federal conviction based upon the same unlawful combination. Since it violated both state and federal law it constituted two offenses. Abbate v. United States, 359 U.S. 187, 79 S.Ct. 666, 3 L.Ed.2d 729 (1959). Compare Bartkus v. Illinois, 359 U.S. 121, 79 S.Ct. 676, 3 L.Ed.2d 684 (1959).

It is of course true that when necessary to a proper determination of a claimed denial of constitutional rights this Court will examine the record in a state criminal trial and is not foreclosed by the conclusion of the state court. . . . But this practice has never been thought to permit us to overrule state courts on controverted or fairly debatable factual issues. "On review here of State convictions, all those matters which are usually termed issues of fact are for conclusive determination by the State courts and are not open for reconsideration by this Court. Observance of this restriction in our review of State courts calls for the utmost scruple." Watts v. State of Indiana, supra, 338 U.S. at pages 50–51, 69 S.Ct. at page 1348.

In this case we are being asked to go even further than to overrule a state court's findings on disputed factual issues. For we would have to embark on sheer speculation in order to decide that the jury's verdict at the earlier trial necessarily embraced a determination favorable to the petitioner on the issue of "identity." In numerous criminal cases both state and federal courts have declined to apply collateral estoppel because it was not possible to determine with certainty which issues were decided by the former general verdict of acquittal. . . . Keeping in mind the fact that jury verdicts are sometimes inconsistent or irrational, . . . we cannot say that the New Jersey Supreme Court exceeded constitutionally permissible bounds in concluding that the jury might have acquitted petitioner at the earlier trial because it did not believe that the victims of the robbery had been put in fear, or that property had been taken from them, or for other reasons unrelated to the issue of "identity." For us to try to out-guess the state court on this score would be wholly out of keeping with the proper discharge of our difficult and delicate responsibilities under the Fourteenth Amendment in determining whether a State has violated the Federal Constitution. . . .

Affirmed.[7]

---

7. [Footnote by the Compiler.] Multiple trials for murder were involved in Ciucci v. Illinois, 356 U.S. 571, 78 S.Ct. 839 (1958). C was charged in four separate indictments with the murder of his wife and three children all of whom were found in a burning building with bullet wounds in their heads. Under Illinois law the jury is charged with the responsibility of fixing the penalty for first-degree murder from 14 years' imprisonment to death. C was tried for the murder of his wife, the jury finding him guilty and fixing the penalty at 20 years. He was then placed on trial for the murder of one of his daughters, this jury finding him guilty and fixing the penalty at 45 years. The prosecution then placed C on trial for the murder of his son and in this case obtained not only a verdict of guilty but the sentence of death. This judgment was affirmed by the Supreme Court of Illinois and the Supreme Court granted certiorari to consider the claim that this third trial violated the Due Process Clause of the Fourteenth Amendment. It was held that since these four homicides constituted separate crimes under Illinois law the state was constitutionally entitled to prosecute them at separate trials and to utilize all relevant evidence in each. Four justices dissented, three on the ground that the separate trials constituted unreasonable harassment in violation of Due Process and Mr. Justice Black on the ground that C was placed twice in jeopardy for the same offense.

Mr. Justice Brennan took no part in the consideration or decision of this case.

Mr. Chief Justice Warren, dissenting.

I think the undisputed facts disclosed by this record plainly show that the conviction of this petitioner has been obtained by use of a procedure inconsistent with the due process requirements of the Fourteenth Amendment. . . .

The issue is whether or not this determination of guilt, based as it is on the successive litigation of a single issue that had previously been resolved by a jury in petitioner's favor, is contrary to the requirements of fair procedure guaranteed by the Due Process Clause of the Fourteenth Amendment. The issue is not whether petitioner has technically committed five offenses, nor whether he could receive a total of five punishments had he been convicted in a single trial of robbing five victims. . . .

Evaluating the record in this case requires no speculation. The only *contested* issue was whether petitioner was one of the robbers. The proof of the elements of the crime of robbery was overwhelming and was not challenged. The suggestion that the jury might have acquitted because of a failure of proof that property was taken from the victims is simply unrealistic. The guarantee of a constitutional right should not be denied by such an artificial approach. The first jury's verdict of acquittal is merely an illusion of justice if its legal significance is not a determination that there was at least a reasonable doubt whether petitioner was present at the scene of the robbery. . . . To convict petitioner by litigating this issue again before 12 different jurors is to employ a procedure that fails to meet the standard required by the Fourteenth Amendment.

Mr. Justice Douglas, with whom Mr. Justice Black concurs, dissenting. . . .

CARMODY v. SEVENTH JUDICIAL DISTRICT COURT IN AND FOR LINCOLN COUNTY

Supreme Court of Nevada, 1965.
— Nev. —, 398 P.2d 706.

McNamee, Chief Justice. This is an original petition for a writ of prohibition.

On May 31, 1964 R. B. Free was beaten and robbed in his place of business at Pioche, Nevada. Later on the same day petitioners were arrested and charged with the robbery. On June 8, 1964 at their arraignment on the robbery charge petitioners each entered a guilty plea and were sentenced to the state prison.

On June 13, 1964 Free, the robbery victim, died from the injuries received during the robbery. On July 8, 1964 the grand jury returned an indictment against the petitioners charging them with murder alleged to have been committed during the robbery. At their arraignment on said murder charge petitioners entered pleas of former jeopardy. The pleas were overruled, petitioners stood mute, and the court entered a plea of not guilty for each of them. Prior to the time set for trial this proceeding was filed and an alternative writ of prohibition issued.

No factual issue exists because the parties have agreed to the facts in a written stipulation filed herein.

The only question for determination is whether under the circumstances of this case the petitioners have already been in jeopardy by reason of their plea of guilty to the robbery charge.

Cases in two states, New Jersey and Texas, hold that a conviction of robbery is a bar to a subsequent prosecution for murder done in perpetration of the robbery. The basis for the New Jersey and Texas rule that the plea of double jeopardy would be sustained is that both crimes were products of the same act.

On the other hand, the majority rule is that although robbery and murder may both arise out of the same act a conviction or acquittal of one offense will not bar a prosecution for the other.

Where the death of the victim occurs after the conviction for robbery the cases are unanimous that the crime of murder is a separate and distinct offense and changes the character of the offense of robbery.

The Nevada statute relating to double jeopardy is NRS 174.390 which states: "When the defendant is convicted or acquitted, or has been once placed in jeopardy upon an indictment or information, the conviction, acquittal or jeopardy is a bar to another indictment or information for the offense charged in the former, or for an attempt to commit the same, or for an offense necessarily included therein, of which he might have been convicted under that indictment or information."

It is readily apparent that robbery and murder are separate and distinct offenses under this statute.

Petitioners argue that by reason of their plea of guilty to the robbery charge the crimes of robbery and murder became merged under NRS 200.030. This contention is without merit. A merger could take place only where a crime includes other offenses. Neither robbery nor murder includes the other.

Petitioners urge that inasmuch as the doctrine of res judicata is applicable in criminal prosecutions, 147 A.L.R. 991, the defense of double jeopardy properly lies.

Because of their conviction of robbery by reason of their pleas of guilty, under the doctrine of res judicata they may be precluded in the trial for murder from contending that they did not commit the robbery. Even so, no fundamental unfairness would result to petitioners in their trial for murder. Furthermore petitioners have cited no authority which would permit the defense of double jeopardy merely because the doctrine of res judicata might be applicable.

Alternative writ of prohibition vacated and the proceeding is dismissed.

THOMPSON and BADT, JJ., concur.

MODEL PENAL CODE

Section 1.08. When Prosecution Barred by Former Prosecution for the Same Offense.

When a prosecution is for a violation of the same provision of the statutes and is based upon the same facts as a former prosecution, it is barred by such former prosecution under the following circumstances:

(1) The former prosecution resulted in an acquittal.* There is an acquittal if the prosecution resulted in a finding of not guilty by the trier of fact or in a determination that there was insufficient evidence to warrant a conviction. A finding of guilty of a lesser included offense is an acquittal of the greater inclusive offense, although the conviction is subsequently set aside.

(2) The former prosecution was terminated, after the information had been filed or the indictment found, by a final order or judgment for the defendant, which has not been set aside, reversed, or vacated and which necessarily required a determination inconsistent with a fact or a legal proposition that must be established for conviction of the offense.

(3) The former prosecution resulted in a conviction. There is a conviction if the prosecution resulted in a judgment of conviction which has not been reversed or vacated, a verdict of guilty which has not been set aside and which is capable of supporting a judgment, or a plea of guilty accepted by the Court. In the latter two cases failure to enter judgment must be for a reason other than a motion of the defendant.

(4) The former prosecution was improperly terminated. Except as provided in this Subsection, there is an improper termination of a prosecution if the termination is for reasons not amounting to an acquittal, and it takes place after the first witness is sworn but before verdict. Termination under any of the following circumstances is not improper:

(a) The defendant consents to the termination or waives, by motion to dismiss or otherwise, his right to object to the termination.

---

* States like Connecticut and Wisconsin which give the prosecution a broad right of appeal will want to add a clause at this point substantially as follows: "unless such acquittal has been set aside because of an error of law prejudicial to the prosecution".

(b) the trial court finds that the termination is necessary because:

(1) it is physically impossible to proceed with the trial in conformity with law; or

(2) there is a legal defect in the proceedings which would make any judgment entered upon a verdict reversible as a matter of law; or

(3) prejudicial conduct, in or outside the courtroom, makes it impossible to proceed with the trial without injustice to either the defendant or the State; or

(4) the jury is unable to agree upon a verdict; or

(5) false statements of a juror on voir dire prevent a fair trial.

Section 1.09. When Prosecution Barred by Former Prosecution for Different Offense.

Although a prosecution is for a violation of a different provision of the statutes than a former prosecution or is based on different facts, it is barred by such former prosecution under the following circumstances:

(1) The former prosecution resulted in an acquittal* or in a conviction as defined in Section 1.08 and the subsequent prosecution is for:

(a) any offense of which the defendant could have been convicted on the first prosecution; or

(b) any offense for which the defendant should have been tried on the first prosecution under Section 1.07, unless the Court ordered a separate trial of the charge of such offense; or

(c) the same conduct, unless (i) the offense of which the defendant was formerly convicted or acquitted and the offense for which he is subsequently prosecuted each requires proof of a fact not required by the other and the law defining each of such offenses is intended to prevent a substantially different harm or evil, or (ii) the second offense was not consummated when the former trial began.

(2) The former prosecution was terminated, after the information was filed or the indictment found, by an acquittal or by a final order or judgment for the defendant which has not been set aside, reversed or vacated and which acquittal, final order or judgment necessarily required a determination inconsistent with a fact which must be established for conviction of the second offense.

(3) The former prosecution was improperly terminated, as improper termination is defined in Section 1.08, and the subsequent prosecution is for an offense of which the defendant could have been convicted had the former prosecution not been improperly terminated.

Section 1.10. Former Prosecution in Another Jurisdiction: When a Bar.

When conduct constitutes an offense within the concurrent jurisdiction of this State and of the United States or another State, a prosecution in any such other jurisdiction is a bar to a subsequent prosecution in this State under the following circumstances:

(1) The first prosecution resulted in an acquittal or in a conviction as defined in Section 1.08 and the subsequent prosecution is based on the

---

* See footnote, supra, Sec. 1.08(1).

same conduct, unless (a) the offense of which the defendant was formerly convicted or acquitted and the offense for which he is subsequently prosecuted each requires proof of a fact not required by the other and the law defining each of such offenses is intended to prevent a substantially different harm or evil or (b) the second offense was not consummated when the former trial began; or

(2) The former prosecution was terminated, after the information was filed or the indictment found, by an acquittal or by a final order or judgment for the defendant which has not been set aside, reversed or vacated and which acquittal, final order or judgment necessarily required a determination inconsistent with a fact which must be established for conviction of the offense of which the defendant is subsequently prosecuted.

Section 1.11. Former Prosecution Before Court Lacking Jurisdiction or When Fraudulently Procured by the Defendant.

A prosecution is not a bar within the meaning of Sections 1.08, 1.09 and 1.10 under any of the following circumstances:

(1) The former prosecution was before a court which lacked jurisdiction over the defendant or the offense; or

(2) The former prosecution was procured by the defendant without the knowledge of the appropriate prosecuting officer and with the purpose of avoiding the sentence which might otherwise be imposed; or

(3) The former prosecution resulted in a judgment of conviction which was held invalid in a subsequent proceeding on a writ of habeas corpus, coram nobis or similar process.

SECTION 5. EX POST FACTO LAWS

Another limitation placed upon criminal prosecutions is that a person shall not be punished on a criminal charge for an act which was no offense at the time it was performed. Such a law is known as an *ex post facto* law and is prohibited both by The Constitution of the United States and by State Constitutions.[1] The term *ex post facto* "applies only to criminal laws; such laws as make acts, innocent when done, criminal; or, if criminal when done, aggravate the crime, or increase the punishment, or reduce the measure of proof. Every *ex post facto* law is necessarily retrospective; but the converse is not true. . . . Retrospective laws, as distinguished from *ex*

---

1. "No . . . ex post facto Law shall be passed." U.S.Const. Art. I, § 9, cl. 3. "No State shall . . . pass any . . . ex post facto Law . . ." U.S.Const. Art. I, § 10. "No . . . ex post facto law . . . shall ever be passed." Iowa Const. Art. I, § 21.

post facto laws, are not in conflict with the United States Constitution, nor are they in conflict with our State Constitution." [2]

2. State v. Squires, 26 Iowa 340, 346–7 (1868). Cf. Polk Co. v. Hierb, 37 Iowa 361 (1873); Kring v. Missouri, 107 U.S. 221, 2 S.Ct. 443, 27 L.Ed. 506 (1882); In re Medley, 134 U.S. 160, 10 S.Ct. 384, 33 L.Ed. 835 (1890); Duncan v. Missouri, 152 U.S. 377, 14 S.Ct. 570, 38 L.Ed. 485 (1894). A statute which increases the punishment for an existing offense is not applicable to a violation occurring prior to the enactment of the punishment. State v. Marx, 200 Iowa 884, 205 N.W. 518 (1925). Hence a jail sentence on conviction of maintaining a liquor nuisance, at a time before the statute authorizing such jail sentence became effective, was erroneous. Ibid. A change in the law relating to murder, by which degrees of murder with fixed penalties are substituted for the prior rule under which the jury determined whether the punishment should be death or life imprisonment, is *ex post facto*. Marion v. State, 16 Neb. 349, 20 N.W. 289 (1884). A change from death to one year's imprisonment at hard labor, followed by death, or from death to death preceded by solitary confinement is *ex post facto* as to offenses committed prior to the statutory change. Hartung v. People, 22 N.Y. 95 (1860), 26 N.Y. 167 (1863); In re Petty, 22 Kan. 477 (1879); In re Medley, 134 U.S. 160, 10 S.Ct. 384, 33 L.Ed. 835 (1890). Cf. State v. Rooney, 12 N.D. 144, 95 N.W. 513 (1903), in which a change of place of incarceration pending execution and a longer period of imprisonment prior to execution was held to be a mitigation of sentence. A change from fine "or" imprisonment to fine "and" imprisonment is *ex post facto*. Flaherty v. Thomas, 94 Mass. 428 (1866); Commonwealth v. McDonough, 95 Mass. 581 (1866). As to past offenses the legislative body cannot take away the right to deductions of time for good behavior. State v. Tyree, 70 Kan. 203, 78 P. 525 (1904); In re Canfield, 98 Mich. 644, 57 N.W. 807 (1894). The amount allowed to a prisoner per day, as a credit on his fine and costs when he is working them out, cannot be reduced as to past offenses. In re Hunt, 28 Tex.App. 361, 13 S.W. 145 (1890).

A statute reducing the punishment, which was enacted after the offense but prior to the conviction, applies to that conviction. People v. McGowan, 199 Misc. 1, 104 N.Y.S.2d 652 (1951).

A statute is not *ex post facto* because it attaches to a subsequent crime an increased punishment on account of former convictions, even though such former convictions were had prior to the enactment of the statute. State v. Dowden, 137 Iowa 573, 115 N.W. 211 (1908); State v. Norris, 203 Iowa 327, 210 N.W. 922 (1926); McDonald v. Massachusetts, 180 U.S. 311, 21 S.Ct. 389, 45 L.Ed. 542 (1901); People v. Stanley, 47 Cal. 113 (1874); Commonwealth v. Marchand, 155 Mass. 8, 29 N.E. 578 (1891); Commonwealth v. Graves, 155 Mass. 163, 29 N.E. 579 (1891); Ex parte Allen, 91 Ohio St. 315, 110 N.E. 535 (1915).

A statute denying to convicts under sentence for a second offense the same reductions from their sentence for good behavior that are allowed to other convicts is not *ex post facto* as applied to the punishment of an offense subsequently committed, although the offender had been convicted of his first offense before the passage of the act. In re Miller, 110 Mich. 676, 68 N.W. 990 (1896).

A law which, in providing for punishment of future offenses, authorizes the past conduct of the offender to be taken into account and punishment to be graduated accordingly, is not *ex post facto*, even as to a prior conviction. Armstrong v. Commonwealth, 177 Ky. 690, 198 S.W. 24 (1917).

A statute providing for a determination of guilt and then a separate determination as to penalty where the sentence may be death or imprisonment for life, is not *ex post facto* as to murder previously committed. People v. Ward, 50 Cal.2d 702, 328 P.2d 777 (1958).

A change of the penalty from death to imprisonment for life at hard labor is *ex post facto* as to arson committed prior to the change. Shepherd v. People, 25 N.Y. 406 (1862).

FLAHERTY v. THOMAS

Supreme Judicial Court of Massachusetts, 1866.
94 Mass. 428.

[Defendant was convicted of maintaining a place for the illegal sale of intoxicating liquors and sentenced to one year in the house of correction. Several months had elapsed between the conviction and the sentence and in the meantime a new statute had been enacted which provided a punishment for such conduct. Although the new statute made no reference to the old it was held to have resulted in a repeal by implication. The sentence pronounced did not exceed that which had been authorized under the earlier statute. As defendant was in custody under the sentence he sued out a writ of habeas corpus.]

GRAY, J. . . . The result is, that the old rule of punishment, laid down in the previous statutes, having been superseded and repealed, without any saving of prosecutions pending or offences already committed, did not justify the defendant's sentence after the repealing statute took effect; the St. of 1866, c. 280, §§ 1, 3, establishing a new rule of punishment, in aggravation of the rule in force when his offence was committed, could not constitutionally apply to his case; and there being therefore no law to authorize him to be punished, he is entitled to be discharged.

Prisoner discharged.[1]

PLACHY v. STATE

Court of Criminal Appeals of Texas, 1922.
91 Tex.Cr.R. 405, 239 S.W. 979.

LATTIMORE, JUDGE. Appellant was convicted in the District Court of Wharton County of the offense of selling intoxicating liquor, and his punishment fixed at four years in the penitentiary. . . .

It was alleged and proved on the trial that whisky was sold by appellant to said Wooley. The latter testified as a witness for the State. The Dean Law which was in operation on November 2, 1921,

---

[1]. Frequently the state has a general saving clause to the effect that where a penal statute is repealed, or amended to reduce the punishment, after a defendant has violated a statute and before his conviction therefor has become final, the defendant is punishable under the law as it read when his offense was committed. Where there is such a general saving clause, an amendatory statute mitigating punishment operates prospectively only unless the enactment itself declares otherwise. People v. Harmon, 54 Cal. 2d 9, 4 Cal.Rptr. 161, 351 P.2d 329 (1960). Thus where the death penalty was mandatory at the time the offense was committed D was not entitled to the benefit of an amendment which provided that the penalty might be either death or imprisonment for life at the discretion of the court or jury trying the case.

made the purchaser of intoxicating liquor punishable, and when used as a witness this court has uniformly held such purchaser to be an accomplice. This construction of the law must continue to prevail as to all violations thereof which occurred prior to the taking effect of said Chapter 61, supra. An examination of said amendatory statute discloses that Sec. 2c thereof reads as follows:

"Upon a trial for a violation of any of the provisions of this Chapter, the purchaser, transporter, or possessor of any of the liquors prohibited herein shall not be held in law or in fact to be an accomplice, when a witness in any such trial." Said amendatory Act became effective November 15, 1921, or about two weeks after date of the alleged offense herein charged against appellant. An exception was taken to the charge of the court below in this case because same did not submit to the jury the law of accomplice testimony as applicable to the witness Wooley, and in this connection we observe that the trial court refused a special instruction on the law of accomplice testimony telling the jury that the witness Wooley was an accomplice and must be considered by them as such. We are not informed by any qualification to any bill of exceptions as to the reason for such failure and refusal on the part of the trial court. It may have been that the learned trial judge was of the opinion that the amendatory act, supra, having gone into effect prior to the time of the instant trial, that Sec. 2c above quoted was applicable. We are of opinion that such a conclusion would be error.

It seems well settled in this State that a law which alters the rules of evidence applicable in a given case, so that under the new law less or different testimony is required to convict the offender than was required at the time of the commission of the offense, must be held an ex post facto law and not applicable upon the trial of one for an offense committed prior to the taking effect of such new enactment.

Section 16, Article 1 of our Constitution inhibits ex post facto laws. Supporting its definition by reference to numerous decisions of most of the states of the Union, as well as of the Supreme Court of the United States, Cyc. gives the following: "An ex post facto law is one which imposes a punishment for an act which was not punishable when it was committed, or imposes additional punishment, or changes the rules of evidence by which less or different testimony is sufficient to convict." See 8 Cyc. p. 1027. In Hart v. State, 40 Ala. 32, 88 Am.Dec. 752, the passage of a statute doing away with the requirement that an accomplice be corroborated, was held ex post facto in a prosecution for an offense committed prior to the enactment of such law. So in Goode v. State, 50 Fla. 45, 39 So. 461, a law which modified an existing rule of evidence by making proof of delivery of intoxicating liquor to a person by the accused, prima facie proof of ownership, was held to be ex post facto. So also in State v. Grant, 79 Mo. 113, 49 Am.Rep. 218, a law removing the incompetence to testify of one who had been convicted of petty larceny was held ex post

Sec. 5   EX POST FACTO LAWS   763

facto when such evidence was offered on the trial of one for an offense committed prior to the enactment of such statute.

Agreeing to the definition of ex post facto law as above given, and applying the rule of reason to its application in the instant case, we observe that the removal of the purchaser of intoxicating liquor from the ranks of accomplice testimony by statute, clearly makes possible a conviction on less evidence. A, the seller, could not formerly be convicted on the testimony of B, the purchaser, except some other person corroborate B. Under the rule now obtaining since the passage of said amendatory act, supra, A, the seller, can be convicted on the testimony of B, the purchaser, alone. This brings the instant case squarely within the rule laid down in Calloway et al. cases, supra, and will necessitate a reversal herein because of the failure and refusal of the court to apply the law of accomplice testimony to the witness Wooley. . . .

For the error above mentioned the judgment of the trial court will be reversed and the cause remanded.[1]

Reversed and remanded.

THOMPSON v. MISSOURI

Supreme Court of the United States, 1898.
171 U.S. 380, 43 L.Ed. 204, 18 S.Ct. 922.

MR. JUSTICE HARLAN delivered the opinion of the court.

The record suggests many questions of law, but the only one that may be considered by this court is whether the proceedings against the plaintiff in error were consistent with the provision in the Constitution of the United States forbidding the States from passing *ex post facto* laws.

Thompson was indicted in the St. Louis Criminal Court at its November term 1894 for the murder, in the first degree, of one Joseph M.

---

1. Accord, Phillips v. State, 92 Tex.Cr. R. 317, 244 S.W. 146 (1922); Hart v. State, 40 Ala. 32 (1866). A law which changes the rules of evidence in such a way as to allow a conviction on less evidence or proof than was previously required, is unconstitutional. Calder v. Bull, 3 Dall. 386, 1 L.Ed. 648 (U.S. 1798); Duncan v. Missouri, 152 U.S. 377, 14 S.Ct. 570, 38 L.Ed. 485 (1894); Cummings v. Missouri, 4 Wall. 277, 325, 18 L.Ed. 356 (U.S.1866).

If, under the law at the time of a homicide, a conviction and sentence for murder in the second degree amount to an acquittal of first degree murder notwithstanding a reversal of the conviction, it is *ex post facto* to change the law thereafter so as to allow another prosecution for first degree murder. Kring v. Missouri, 107 U.S. 221, 2 S.Ct. 443, 27 L.Ed. 506 (1882).

And a provision in the constitution of the state of Utah for the trial of criminal cases (other than capital) by a jury of eight persons only, was held to be *ex post facto* as to offenses committed before the territory became a state. Thompson v. Utah, 170 U.S. 343, 18 S.Ct. 620, 42 L.Ed. 1061 (1898).

A statute excluding those serving life sentences from the benefits of parole cannot be applied to those who were sentenced for life at a time when the parole law applied to such sentences. State ex rel. Woodward v. Board of Parole, 155 La. 699, 99 So. 534 (1924).

Cunningham, a sexton at one of the churches in the city of St. Louis. Having been tried and convicted of the offence charged, he prosecuted an appeal to the Supreme Court of Missouri, and by that court the judgment was reversed and a new trial was ordered. State v. Thompson, 132 Mo. 301, 34 S.W. 31. At the second trial the accused was again convicted; and a new trial having been denied, he prosecuted another appeal to the Supreme Court of the State. That court affirmed the last judgment, and the present appeal brings that judgment before us for reëxamination. State v. Thompson, 141 Mo. 408, 42 S.W. 949.

The evidence against the accused was entirely circumstantial in its nature. One of the issues of fact was as to the authorship of a certain prescription for strychnine, and of a certain letter addressed to the organist of the church containing threatening language about the sexton. The theory of the prosecution was that the accused had obtained the strychnine specified in the prescription and put it into food that he delivered or caused to be delivered to the deceased with intent to destroy his life. The accused denied that he wrote either the prescription or the letter to the organist, or that he had any connection with either of those writings. At the first trial certain letters written by him to his wife were admitted in evidence for the purpose of comparing them with the writing in the prescription and with the letter to the organist. The Supreme Court of the State, upon the first appeal, held that it was error to admit in evidence for purposes of comparison the letters written by Thompson to his wife, and for that error the first judgment was reversed and a new trial ordered.

Subsequently, the general assembly of Missouri passed an act which became operative in July, 1895, providing that "comparison of a disputed writing with any writing proved to the satisfaction of the judge to be genuine shall be permitted to be made by witnesses, and such writings and the evidence of witnesses respecting the same may be submitted to the court and jury as evidence of the genuineness or otherwise of the writing in dispute." Laws Missouri, April 8, 1895, p. 284.

This statute is in the very words of section 27 of the English Common Law Procedure Act of 1854, 17 & 18 Vict. c. 125. And by the 28 Vict. c. 18, §§ 1, 8, the provisions of that act were extended to criminal cases.

At the second trial, which occurred in 1896, the letters written by the accused to his wife were again admitted in evidence, over his objection, for the purpose of comparing them with the order for strychnine and the letter to the organist. This action of the trial court was based upon the above statute of 1895.

The contention of the accused is that as the letters to his wife were not, *at the time of the commission of the alleged offence*, admissible in evidence for the purpose of comparing them with other writings charged to be in his handwriting, the subsequent statute of Missouri changing this rule of evidence was *ex post facto* when applied to his case.

It is not to be denied that the position of the accused finds apparent support in the general language used in some opinions. . . .

Applying the principles announced in former cases—without attaching undue weight to general expressions in them that go beyond the questions necessary to be determined—we adjudge that the statute of Missouri relating to the comparison of writings is not *ex post facto* when applied to prosecutions for crimes committed prior to its passage. If persons excluded, upon grounds of public policy, at the time of the commission of an offence, from testifying as witnesses for or against the accused, may, in virtue of a statute, become competent to testify, we cannot perceive any ground upon which to hold a statute to be *ex post facto* which does nothing more than admit evidence of a particular kind in a criminal case upon an issue of fact which was not admissible under the rules of evidence as enforced by judicial decisions at the time the offence was committed. The Missouri statute, when applied to this case, did not enlarge the punishment to which the accused was liable when his crime was committed, nor make any act involved in his offence criminal that was not criminal at the time he committed the murder of which he was found guilty. It did not change the quality or degree of his offence. Nor can the new rule introduced by it be characterized as unreasonable—certainly not so unreasonable as materially to affect the substantial rights of one put on trial for crime. The statute did not require "less proof, in amount or degree," than was required at the time of the commission of the crime charged upon him. It left unimpaired the right of the jury to determine the sufficiency or effect of the evidence declared to be admissible, and did not disturb the fundamental rule that the State, as a condition of its right to take the life of an accused, must overcome the presumption of his innocence and establish his guilt beyond a reasonable doubt. Whether he wrote the prescription for strychnine, or the threatening letter to the church organist, was left for the jury, and the duty of the jury, in that particular, was the same after as before the passage of the statute. The statute did nothing more than remove an obstacle arising out of a rule of evidence that withdrew from the consideration of the jury testimony which, in the opinion of the legislature, tended to elucidate the ultimate, essential fact to be established, namely, the guilt of the accused. Nor did it give the prosecution any right that was denied to the accused. It placed the State and the accused upon an equality; for the rule established by it gave to each side the right to have disputed writings compared with writings proved to the satisfaction of the judge to be genuine. Each side was entitled to go to the jury upon the question of the genuineness of the writing upon which the prosecution relied to establish the guilt of the accused. It is well known that the adjudged cases have not been in harmony touching the rule relating to the comparison of handwritings: and the object of the legislature, as we may assume, was to give the jury all the light that could be thrown upon an issue of that character. We cannot adjudge that the accused had any vested right in the rule of evidence which obtained prior to the passage of the Missouri statute, nor that the rule established by that statute entrenched upon any of the essential rights belonging to one put on trial for a public offence.

Of course, we are not to be understood as holding that there may not be such a statutory alteration of the fundamental rules in criminal trials as might bring the statute in conflict with the *ex post facto* clause of the Constitution. If, for instance, the statute had taken from the jury the right to determine the sufficiency or effect of the evidence which it made admissible, a different question would have been presented. We mean now only to adjudge that the statute is to be regarded as one merely regulating procedure and may be applied to crimes committed prior to its passage without impairing the substantial guarantees of life and liberty that are secured to an accused by the supreme law of the land.

The judgment of the Supreme Court of Missouri is affirmed.[1]

---

1. A law is not *ex post facto* which makes certain matters admissible in evidence. State v. Dowden, 137 Iowa 573, 115 N.W. 211 (1908). A law is not *ex post facto* which enlarges the class of persons who can testify. Hopt v. Utah, 110 U.S. 574, 4 S.Ct. 202, 28 L.Ed. 262 (1884). Cf. Mrous v. State, 31 Tex.Cr.R. 597, 21 S.W. 764 (1893); Wester v. State, 142 Ala. 56, 38 So. 1010 (1905).

Laws do not come within the *ex post facto* rule if they merely regulate the mode of procedure in criminal cases and do not interfere with substantial protections theretofore granted to the accused. Cooley, Constitutional Limitations 372–83 (7th ed., Lane, 1903); Kring v. Missouri, 107 U.S. 221, 2 S.Ct. 443, 27 L.Ed. 506 (1882); People v. Mortimer, 46 Cal. 114 (1873); Marion v. State, 20 Neb. 233, 29 N.W. 911 (1886). Thus the legislature may change the place of trial or the tribunal. Cook v. United States, 138 U.S. 157, 11 S.Ct. 268, 34 L.Ed. 906 (1891); Commonwealth v. Phelps, 210 Mass. 78, 96 N.E. 349 (1911); Commonwealth v. Phillips, 28 Mass. 28 (1831); State v. Jackson, 105 Mo. 196, 16 S.W. 829 (1891); People v. Green, 201 N.Y. 172, 94 N.E. 658 (1911); State v. Cooler, 30 S.C. 105, 8 S.E. 692 (1889); State v. Welch, 65 Vt. 50, 25 A. 900 (1892). A statute authorizing an appeal by the State in proceedings for condemnation of liquors, relates only to procedure, and is not *ex post facto* as to such proceedings instituted before the act went into effect. State v. Taggart, 186 Iowa 247, 172 N.W. 299 (1919). It is not *ex post facto* to substitute proceedings by information for indictment. Lybarger v. State, 2 Wash. 552, 27 P. 449 (1891); In re Wright, 3 Wyo. 478, 27 P. 565 (1891). Contra: State v. Kingsly, 10 Mont. 537, 26 P. 1066 (1891); McCarty v. State, 1 Wash. 377, 25 P. 299 (1890). These two cases hold otherwise as to crimes committed when the state was a territory and hence governed by the federal constitution.

The statute conferring authority on the board of parole to mitigate sentences and grant paroles to persons convicted before the law took effect is not objectionable as *ex post facto*. Ware v. Sanders, 146 Iowa 233, 124 N.W. 1081 (1910); People ex rel. Liebowitz v. Warden, 186 App.Div. 730, 174 N.Y.S. 823 (1st Dep't 1919). An indeterminate sentence law is not *ex post facto* if it does not increase prior maximum and minimum penalties. Davis v. State, 152 Ind. 34, 51 N.E. 928 (1898); Commonwealth v. Kalck, 239 Pa. 533, 87 A. 61 (1913). The same is true of a law which merely remits a portion of the punishment or otherwise mitigates it. Commonwealth v. Wyman, 66 Mass. 237 (1853); Commonwealth v. Gardner, 77 Mass. 438 (1858); People v. Hayes, 140 N.Y. 484, 35 N.E. 951 (1894). Thus a change may be made from fine "and" imprisonment to fine "or" imprisonment. Hartung v. People, 22 N.Y. 95 (1860). And the death penalty may be changed to imprisonment for life at hard labor. Commonwealth v. Wyman, 66 Mass. 237 (1853); Commonwealth v. Gardner, 77 Mass. 438 (1858). See McInturf v. State, 20 Tex.App. 335 (1886). The contrary was held in New York. Shepherd v. People, 25 N.Y. 406 (1862). Removal of the minimum limit of a penalty is not *ex post facto*. People v. Hayes, 70 Hun 111, 24 N.Y.S. 194 (1893). And mere changes in the details of carrying out the punishment are unobjectionable if no substantial right of the prisoner is affected. Holden v. Minnesota, 137 U.S. 483, 11 S.Ct. 143, 34 L.Ed. 734 (1890). In re Tyson, 13 Colo. 482, 22 P. 810 (1889); State v. Rooney, 12 N.D. 144, 95 N.W. 513 (1903); Gilreath v. Commonwealth, 136 Va. 709, 118 S.E. 100 (1923).

Mere changes of prison discipline or penal administration are not *ex post facto*. People v. Bodjack, 210 Mich. 443, 178 N.W. 228 (1920); Commonwealth v. Kalck, 239 Pa. 533, 87 A. 61 (1913).

A change in the method of selecting grand jury lists is not unconstitutional as applied to a crime already committed. State v. Pell, 140 Iowa 655, 119 N.W. 154 (1909). Nor is a change in the number of grand jurors. State v. Ah Jim, 9 Mont. 167, 23 P. 76 (1890); Hallock v. United States, 185 F. 417 (8th Cir. 1911). Nor is a law which changes the mode of summoning or impaneling the jury. Gibson v. Mississippi, 162 U.S. 565, 16 S.Ct. 904, 40 L.Ed. 1075 (1896); Stokes v. People, 53 N.Y. 164 (1873). Nor is one which limits the time for challenging the jurors. State v. Taylor, 134 Mo. 109, 35 S.W. 92 (1896). Nor is one which gives the state additional peremptory challenges. State v. Ryan, 13 Minn. 370 (1868); Walston v. Commonwealth, 16 B.Mon. 15 (Ky.1855). Nor is one which gives the accused fewer peremptory challenges. South v. State, 86 Ala. 617, 6 So. 52 (1889); Mathis v. State, 31 Fla. 291, 12 So. 681 (1893). Nor is one which changes the grounds for challenge. Stokes v. People, 53 N.Y. 164 (1873). Nor is one which changes the requirements as to the pleadings. State v. Manning, 14 Tex. 402 (1855); Perry v. State, 87 Ala. 30, 6 So. 425 (1889). Nor is one which regulates the procedure on appeal. Jacquins v. Commonwealth, 63 Mass. 279 (1852).

An act providing that when a convict serving a life sentence commits murder in the first degree, he must upon conviction be sentenced to death, is not *ex post facto*. Bailey v. State, 211 Ala. 667, 101 So. 546 (1924).

A law which provides for separate trials of persons jointly indicted, only when granted by the court for good cause shown, is not *ex post facto* as to pending prosecutions, although the prior law authorized separate trials as a matter of right. Beazell v. Ohio, 269 U.S. 167, 46 S.Ct. 68, 70 L.Ed. 216 (1925).

The change in the mode of execution from hanging to electrocution, though after a verdict of guilty and before sentence does not come within the *ex post facto* rule. Ex parte Johnson, 96 Tex.Cr.R. 473, 258 S.W. 473 (1924).

A statute providing for the seizure and destruction of liquor is not *ex post facto* as to liquor which was lawfully acquired before the law was passed. Samuels v. McCurdy, 267 U.S. 188, 45 S.Ct. 264, 69 L.Ed. 568 (1925).

A statute authorizing the admission of evidence of defendant's history and background, and other matters, in mitigation or aggravation may be applied to an offense committed prior to its enactment without violating the constitutional prohibition against *ex post facto* laws. People v. Feldkamp, 51 Cal.2d 237, 331 P.2d 632 (1958).

PEOPLE v. GILL

Supreme Court of California, 1856.
6 Cal. 637.

Mr. Chief Justice Murray delivered the opinion of the Court. Mr. Justice Terry concurred.

The prisoner was indicted for murder, charged to have been committed on the 22d day of March, 1856, and was found "guilty of the crime of murder in the second degree."

At the time of the killing, charged in the indictment, there was no such crime known to the law as murder in the second degree, and the party could only have been convicted of murder or manslaughter.

The Act defining the offence of which the prisoner is found guilty, was not passed until the 16th of April, 1856, and provides that, upon trials for crimes committed previous to its passage, the party shall be tried by the laws in force at the time of the commission of such crime.

It is supposed, however, that this case presents an exception to the rule thus established. The blow was given before, but the death ensued after, the passage of the last statute. The death must be made to relate back to the unlawful act which occasioned it, and as the party died in consequence of wounds received on a particular day, the day on which the act was committed, and not the one on which the result of the act was determined, is the day on which the murder is properly to be charged.

Besides this, although it is not absolutely necessary to state the precise day on which the killing took place, still, a conviction in a case like the present, where the party was called upon, by the indictment, to answer an offence under one statute, and was found guilty under another, would be bad, and ought to be arrested on motion.

The judgment is reversed, and the Court below directed to re-try the prisoner for murder.[1]

---

[1]. On the second trial the defendant was convicted of manslaughter. He appealed on the claim that the old law had been repealed. This contention was rejected because the repealing statute contained a saving clause. The conviction was affirmed. People v. Gill, 7 Cal. 356 (1857).

The statute of limitations does not begin to run on the crime of manslaughter until the death of the victim. People v. Rehman, 62 Cal.2d 135, 41 Cal.Rptr. 457, 396 P.2d 913 (1964).

Chapter 12

PROCEEDINGS PRELIMINARY TO TRIAL

SECTION 1. STEPS BY THE PROSECUTION PRIOR TO INDICTMENT

(A) INTRODUCTION

The presence of one accused of crime is not essential to the finding of an indictment against him and he has no right to be present during this stage of the proceedings. The grand jury can decide whether he should be tried for some particular crime even if he is still at large,—and this is frequently done. On the other hand it is not necessary to wait for the indictment before making an arrest and frequently it is not wise to do so because the one accused might disappear during the deliberations of the grand jury.

If the indictment is found before the accused has been taken into custody a bench warrant will be issued for his arrest. If it is deemed desirable to have the arrest precede the indictment it will be necessary to have a complaint or information made before a magistrate to secure the issuance of a warrant, unless the circumstances are such as to authorize an arrest without a warrant. If the arrest precedes the indictment, and is made in obedience to a warrant, the procedure may follow this general outline (although variations will be found in some jurisdictions): (1) A complaint (or information or affidavit—the procedure varies in different jurisdictions) will be made or filed before a magistrate (or other officer having authority to issue warrants) charging the accused with a specified crime. (2) If the jurisdiction does not require the complaint itself to be in the form of a sworn written document the magistrate will put the complainant under oath while the facts are being stated, after which he may have the statement reduced to writing in the form of an affidavit. In any event the magistrate may require the complainant to answer questions, under oath, and may obtain the sworn statements of other witnesses if available. (3) If the magistrate finds "probable cause" for the charge made against the accused he will issue a warrant for his arrest (unless the magistrate decides that a summons will be sufficient to cause the accused to be present for trial and the law of the jurisdiction authorizes the use of a summons under the facts of the particular case.) (4) This warrant will be delivered to some peace officer for execution. (5) This officer will arrest the accused by virtue of this warrant. (6) The accused will then be taken before the magistrate for preliminary examination. (7) The result of the preliminary examination will be that the defendant is either discharged or "held to answer." (8) If held to answer he will be either bailed or committed to jail. (9) If he is committed to jail the magistrate (in many jurisdictions) will make out a warrant of commitment which he will deliver with the defendant to the officer. (10) The prosecuting attorney (unless he files an information against the accused, if the law of the jurisdiction permits such procedure) will file a bill of indictment to be presented to the grand jury. (11) The grand jury will hear evidence in support of the charge against the accused and will either find it to be a "true bill" or they will "ignore" it (fail to find it to be a true bill). (12) If the bill of indictment is found by the grand jury to be a "true bill" it will be properly indorsed and filed (whereupon the accused stands indicted for the crime charged against him). (13) The defendant (he was not strictly speaking a "defendant" until a formal pleading had been filed against him by the state) will be arraigned (called to the bar of the court to answer to the accusation contained in the indictment). (14) If the defendant pleads not guilty he will be tried by a petit jury (unless the jurisdiction authorizes the waiver of a jury in such a case and the jury is waived by defendant,—in which event he will be tried by the judge without a jury). (15) As a result of this trial the jury (if able to agree) will bring in a verdict of "guilty" (of the offense charged or of some lesser "included" offense) or "not guilty." (16) After the verdict of the jury the judge will pronounce the judgment (unless the verdict was "guilty" and the judgment is "arrested," or the pronouncement of judgment is suspended,—where this is permitted). The judgment will be one of acquittal if the verdict was "not guilty," and of conviction if the verdict was "guilty."

Various other steps may follow if the judgment is one of conviction, depending upon whether the defendant accepts this pronouncement as final or asks for a new trial or an appeal or a pardon, and so forth. But it is not necessary for the moment to carry this outline beyond the judgment of the trial court. It should be added that if the judgment is one of conviction the judge will also pronounce the penalty imposed upon the convicted defendant, unless a new trial has been granted or an appeal taken. This is the "sentence." In some jurisdictions, if the conviction is for felony, the "sentence" pronounced by the court may be in general terms and the actual term of incarceration may be determined later by some board or "authority."

Under sound theory these two pronouncements—(i. e. that of conviction and the sentence) are both judgments, although they are frequently referred to as "judgment and sentence." Both may be pronounced at the same time or the judgment of conviction may be entered at once and the sentence be pronounced at a later time.

It should also be mentioned that other steps may or may not be involved, such as an application for bail, an attack upon the validity of the indictment, an application for a change of venue, and so forth.

In some jurisdictions, if probation is indicated after guilt has been established by verdict or plea, the judge may either pronounce sentence and suspend the execution thereof, or he may postpone the pronouncement of sentence. One judge, years ago before probation officers had been provided for him, began the practice of suspending the sentence on condition that the defendant get a job, go to work and save his earnings above his reasonably necessary expenses by depositing a stipulated amount each week with the clerk, to be returned to him later if he lived up to the condition. Willingness or unwillingness to work, he concluded, was the best test to divide the sheep from the goats. His study of nonsupport cases brought to light the fact that frequently failure to support the family resulted from getting drunk after receiving the week's pay and spending the money while in that condition. If, as was frequently the fact, the man did not indulge in excessive drinking during the week, the judge added special conditions to his probation. His pay check was to be delivered to some responsible agency to be used for the benefit of the entire family, including himself. And from the end of the work week until Monday morning he was to be in jail.[1]

(B) THE COMPLAINT

To secure the issuance of a warrant of arrest (of one who has not been indicted) it is necessary to go before a magistrate or other officer authorized to issue a warrant, and satisfy him in the manner prescribed by law that proper ground exists.

GIORDENELLO v. UNITED STATES

Supreme Court of the United States, 1958.
357 U.S. 480, 78 S.Ct. 1245.

MR. JUSTICE HARLAN delivered the opinion of the Court.

Petitioner was convicted of the unlawful purchase of narcotics, see 26 U.S.C. (Supp. V) § 4704, 26 U.S.C.A. § 4704, after a trial without a jury before the Federal District Court for the Southern District of Texas. A divided Court of Appeals affirmed. 5 Cir., 241 F.2d 575. We granted certiorari to consider petitioner's challenge to the legality of his arrest and the admissibility in evidence of the narcotics seized

---

[1]. For an interesting study of probation see Gwyn, Work, Earn and Save, published by Institutes for Civic Education, Extension Division, University of North Carolina, Chapel Hill.

from his person at the time of the arrest. 355 U.S. 811, 78 S.Ct. 66, 2 L.Ed.2d 30.

Agent Finley of the Federal Bureau of Narcotics obtained a warrant for the arrest of petitioner from the United States Commissioner in Houston, Texas, on January 26, 1956. This warrant, issued under Rules 3 and 4 of the Federal Rules of Criminal Procedure, 18 U.S.C.A. (see note 3, *infra*), was based on a written complaint, sworn to by Finley, which read in part:

"The undersigned complainant [Finley] being duly sworn states: That on or about January 26, 1956, at Houston, Texas in the Southern District of Texas, Veto Giordenello did receive, conceal, etc., narcotic drugs, to-wit: heroin hydrochloride with knowledge of unlawful importation; in violation of Section 174, Title 21, United States Code.

"And the complainant further states that he believes that ———— ———— are material witnesses in relation to this charge." . . .

II.

Petitioner challenges the sufficiency of the warrant on two grounds: (1) that the complaint on which the warrant was issued was inadequate because the complaining officer, Finley, relied exclusively upon hearsay information rather than personal knowledge in executing the complaint; . . .

It appears from Finley's testimony at the hearing on the suppression motion that until the warrant was issued on January 26 his suspicions of petitioner's guilt derived entirely from information given him by law enforcement officers and other persons in Houston, none of whom either appeared before the Commissioner or submitted affidavits. But we need not decide whether a warrant may be issued solely on hearsay information, for in any event we find this complaint defective in not providing a sufficient basis upon which a finding of probable cause could be made.

Criminal Rules 3 and 4 provide that an arrest warrant shall be issued only upon a written and sworn complaint (1) setting forth "the essential facts constituting the offense charged," and (2) showing "that there is probable cause to believe that [such] an offense has been committed and that the defendant has committed it . . . ."[3] The provisions of these Rules must be read in light of the constitutional requirements they implement. The language of the Fourth Amendment, that ". . . no Warrants shall issue, but upon probable

3. [Footnote by the Court.] Rule 3: "The complaint is a written statment of the essential facts constituting the offense charged. It shall be made upon oath before a commissioner or other officer empowered to commit persons charged with offenses against the United States."

Rule 4(a): ". . . If it appears from the complaint that there is probable cause to believe that an offense has been committed and that the defendant has committed it, a warrant for the arrest of the defendant shall issue to any officer authorized by law to execute it. . . ."

cause, supported by Oath or affirmation, and particularly describing . . . the persons or things to be seized . . .," of course applies to arrest as well as search warrants. The protection afforded by these Rules, when they are viewed against their constitutional background, is that the inferences from the facts which lead to the complaint " . . . be drawn by a neutral and detached magistrate instead of being judged by the officer engaged in the often competitive enterprise of ferreting out crime." Johnson v. United States, 333 U.S. 10, 14, 68 S.Ct. 367, 369, 92 L.Ed. 436. The purpose of the complaint, then, is to enable the appropriate magistrate, here a Commissioner, to determine whether the "probable cause" required to support a warrant exists. The Commissioner must judge for himself the persuasiveness of the facts relied on by a complaining officer to show probable cause. He should not accept without question the complainant's mere conclusion that the person whose arrest is sought has committed a crime.

When the complaint in this case is judged with these considerations in mind, it is clear that it does not pass muster because it does not provide any basis for the Commissioner's determination under Rule 4 that probable cause existed. The complaint contains no affirmative allegation that the affiant spoke with personal knowledge of the matters contained therein; it does not indicate any sources for the complainant's belief; and it does not set forth any other sufficient basis upon which a finding of probable cause could be made. We think these deficiencies could not be cured by the Commissioner's reliance upon a presumption that the complaint was made on the personal knowledge of the complaining officer. The insubstantiality of such an argument is illustrated by the facts of this very case, for Finley's testimony at the suppression hearing clearly showed that he had no personal knowledge of the matters on which his charge was based. In these circumstances, it is difficult to understand how the Commissioner could be expected to assess independently the probability that petitioner committed the crime charged. Indeed, if this complaint were upheld, the substantive requirements would be completely read out of Rule 4, and the complaint would be of only formal significance, entitled to perfunctory approval by the Commissioner. This would not comport with the protective purposes which a complaint is designed to achieve. . . . The judgment of the Court of Appeals is reversed.

Reversed.

MR. JUSTICE CLARK, with whom MR. JUSTICE BURTON and MR. JUSTICE WHITTAKER concur, dissenting. . . .

JONES v. UNITED STATES

Supreme Court of the United States, 1960.
362 U.S. 257, 80 S.Ct. 725.

MR. JUSTICE FRANKFURTER delivered the opinion of the Court. . . .

We come to consider the grounds upon which the search is alleged to have been illegal. The attack which was made in the District Court was one of lack of probable cause for issuing the search warrant. The question raised is whether sufficient evidence to establish probable cause to search was put before the Commissioner by the officer, Didone, who applied for the warrant. The sole evidence upon which the warrant was issued was an affidavit signed by Didone. Both parties urge us to decide the question here, without remanding it to the District Court which, because it found lack of standing, did not pass on it. We think it appropriate to decide the question. . . .

Didone was a member of the Narcotic Squad in the District of Columbia. His affidavit claimed no direct knowledge of the presence of narcotics in the apartment. He swore that on the day before making the affidavit he had been given information, by one unnamed, that petitioner and another "were involved in the illicit narcotic traffic" and "kept a ready supply of heroin on hand" in the apartment. He swore that his informant claimed to have purchased narcotics at the apartment from petitioner and another "on many occasions," the last of which had been the day before the warrant was applied for. Didone swore that his informant "has given information to the undersigned on previous occasion and which was correct," that "[t]his same information" regarding petitioner had been given the narcotic squad by "other sources of information" and that the petitioner and the other implicated by the informant had admitted being users of narcotics. On this basis Didone founded his oath that he believed "that there is now illicit narcotic drugs being secreated [sic] in the above apartment by Cecil Jones." . . .

In testing the sufficiency of probable cause for an officer's action even without a warrant, we have held that he may rely upon information received through an informant, rather than upon his direct observations, so long as the informant's statement is reasonably corroborated by other matters within the officer's knowledge. Draper v. United States, 358 U.S. 307, 79 S.Ct. 329, 3 L.Ed.2d 327. We there upheld an arrest without a warrant solely upon an informant's statement that the defendant was peddling narcotics, as corroborated by the fact that the informant's description of the defendant's appearance, and of where he would be on a given morning (matters in themselves totally innocuous) agreed with the officer's observations. We rejected the contention that an officer may act without a warrant only when his basis for acting would be competent evidence upon a trial to prove defendant's guilt. Quoting from Brinegar v. United States, 338

U.S. 160, 172, 69 S.Ct. 1302, 1309, 93 L.Ed. 1879, we said that such a contention "goes much too far in confusing and disregarding the difference between what is required to prove guilt in a criminal case and what is required to show probable cause for arrest or search. . . . There is a large difference between the two things to be proved [guilt and probable cause] . . . and therefore a like difference in the *quanta* and modes of proof required to establish them." . . .

What we have ruled in the case of an officer who acts without a warrant governs our decision here. If an officer may act upon probable cause without a warrant when the only incriminating evidence in his possession is hearsay, it would be incongruous to hold that such evidence presented in an affidavit is insufficient basis for a warrant. If evidence of a more judicially competent or persuasive character than would have justified an officer in acting on his own without a warrant must be presented when a warrant is sought, warrants could seldom legitimatize police conduct, and resort to them would ultimately be discouraged. Due regard for the safeguards governing arrests and searches counsels the contrary. In a doubtful case, when the officer does not have clearly convincing evidence of the immediate need to search, it is most important that resort be had to a warrant, so that the evidence in the possession of the police may be weighed by an independent judicial officer, whose decision, not that of the police, may govern whether liberty or privacy is to be invaded.

We conclude therefore that hearsay may be the basis for a warrant. . . .

Petitioner argues that the warrant was defective because Didone's informants were not produced, because his affidavit did not even state their names, and Didone did not undertake and swear to the results of his own independent investigation of the claims made by his informants. If the objections raised were that Didone had misrepresented to the Commissioner his basis for seeking a warrant, these matters might be relevant. Such a charge is not made. All we are here asked to decide is whether the Commissioner acted properly, not whether Didone did. We have decided that, as hearsay alone does not render an affidavit insufficient, the Commissioner need not have required the informants or their affidavits to be produced, or that Didone have personally made inquiries about the apartment, so long as there was a substantial basis for crediting the hearsay. . . .[1]

[For other reasons the judgment was:] Vacated and remanded.

Mr. Justice Douglas.

I join the part of the opinion which holds that petitioner had "standing" to challenge the legality of the search. But I dissent from

---

1. For a comparable case holding that a search warrant was properly issued—affidavit sufficient, see United States v. Ventresca, 380 U.S. 102, 85 S.Ct. 741, 13 L.Ed.2d 684 (1965).

the ruling that there was "probable cause" for issuance of the warrant. The view that there was "probable cause" finds some support in Draper v. United States, 358 U.S. 307, 79 S.Ct. 329, 3 L.Ed.2d 327. But my dissent in Draper gives, I think, the true dimensions of the problem. This is an age where faceless informers have been reintroduced into our society in alarming ways. Sometimes their anonymity is defended on the ground that revelation of their names would ruin counter-espionage or cripple an underground network of agents. Yet I think in these Fourth Amendment cases the duty of the magistrate is nondelegable. It is not sufficient that the police think there is cause for an invasion of the privacy of the home. The judicial officer must also be convinced; and to him the police must go except for emergency situations. The magistrate should know the evidence on which the police propose to act. Unless that is the requirement, unless the magistrate makes his independent judgment on all the known facts, then he tends to become merely the tool of police interests. Though the police are honest and their aims worthy, history shows they are not appropriate guardians of the privacy which the Fourth Amendment protects. . . .

(C) THE WARRANT

Criminal procedure stems from the machinery developed for the handling of felony cases when all felonies were punishable by death. Many important changes have been made but all too frequently the steps now taken are still dominated by theories which should have been modified when milder punishments were provided for most felonies and which never should have applied in misdemeanor cases. This is well illustrated at this point in our procedure in many jurisdictions.

If complaint has been made before a magistrate charging a person with a capital crime, and it is sufficient to constitute "probable cause" of his guilt thereof, the first effort should be directed toward getting the supposed felon into custody. This is important first because it may be necessary to protect the community from other felonies that might be perpetrated by the same offender and second because there is no other way to assure his presence when it may be needed for the trial.

Many offenses are committed, however, under such circumstances that no more is needed than an official communication to the person accused thereof to appear for trial at a specified time and place. Where this is true it is an unnecessary burden upon officers charged with the enforcement of the law to require them to arrest the accused and take him before a magistrate for the purpose of giving bail. It is also an unnecessary hardship to be inflicted upon the accused himself,—particularly if he happens to be innocent of the offense charged. Hence the time has long passed when a warrant of arrest should be regarded as the logical result of every complaint. Except in the case of more serious crimes it might well be regarded as the exception rather than the rule. More will be said of this in the subsection entitled "Summons."

Reflecting the ancient theory a number of the statutes make it mandatory upon the magistrate to issue a warrant of arrest if "probable cause" or "reasonable ground to believe" is established supported by oath or affirmation. The following is an example:

If the "magistrate is satisfied from the complaint that the offense complained of has been committed and that there is reasonable ground to believe that the defendant has committed it, he must issue his warrant for the arrest of the defendant." [1]

The model Code of Criminal Procedure recommends the issuance of a summons in certain situations and the direction that the magistrate issue a warrant has an appropriate exception.[2]

Anciently any official command or order which authorized an arrest was spoken of as a "warrant of arrest." This included the oral order of a magistrate to arrest one who had committed a felony or breach of the peace in his presence.[3] This usage has left a trace still to be observed. Many statutes make provision for arrest on the oral order of a magistrate for an offense committed in his presence and also for arrests without a warrant (as well as for arrests in obedience to a warrant). And an arrest on such an oral order of a magistrate is not within the limitations provided for an arrest *without a warrant*.

What is now known as a "warrant of arrest," however, must be in writing. It has been defined as a "written order directing the arrest of a person or persons, issued by a court, body or official, having authority to issue warrants." [4]

---

1. West's Ann.Cal.Pen.Code, § 813. The 1963 amendment provides that "when the magistrate is a judge of the justice court he may issue such a warrant only upon the concurrence of the district attorney" or the Attorney General. See also the statutes in Alabama, Arizona, Idaho, Maine, Nevada, North Dakota, Oklahoma, Oregon, South Dakota, Tennessee and Utah. And for mandatory provisions in somewhat different form see the statutes in Delaware, Florida, Indiana, Kansas, Louisiana, Michigan, Minnesota, Missouri, Nebraska, Nevada, New Mexico, Wisconsin and Wyoming.

2. American Law Institute, Code of Criminal Procedure, § 2 (1930).

3. Lord Hale, writing in the seventeenth century, speaks of such an oral order of a magistrate as "a good warrant without writing." 2 Hale P.C. *86.

4. Restatement, Second, Torts, § 113 (1965).

The American Law Institute, after an exhaustive study of various statutes included the following as section 3 of its model Code of Criminal Procedure:

> Section 3. *Form and contents of warrant.* The warrant of arrest shall
>
> (a) be in writing and in the name of the State [Commonwealth or People];
>
> (b) set forth substantially the nature of the offense;
>
> (c) command that the person against whom the complaint was made be arrested and brought before the magistrate issuing the warrant or, if he is absent or unable to act, before the nearest or most accessible magistrate in the same county;
>
> (d) specify the name of the person to be arrested or, if his name is unknown to the magistrate, shall designate such person by any name or description by which he can be identified with reasonable certainty;
>
> (e) state the date when issued and the municipality or county where issued; and
>
> (f) be signed by the magistrate with the title of his office.

The customary statutory provision is much more general than this with a suggested form to be followed in substance. The following are given in the Federal Rules of Criminal Procedure:

> *Rule 4.* . . . *(b) Form. (1) Warrant.* The warrant shall be signed by the commissioner and shall contain the name of the defendant or, if his name is unknown, any name or description by which he can be identified with reasonable certainty. It shall describe the offense charged in the complaint. It shall command that the defendant be arrested and brought before the nearest available commissioner.
>
> 2. . . .

Form 12

Warrant For Arrest Of Defendant

In the United States District Court for the _____ District _____ of _____ Division.

United States of America
   v.   No. _____
John Doe
To _____⁵

---

5. Insert designation of officer to whom warrant is issued, e. g., "any United States Marshal or any other authorized officer"; or "United States Marshal for _____ District of _____"; or "any United States Marshal"; or "any Special Agent of the Federal Bureau of Investigation"; or "any United States Marshal or any Special Agent of the Federal Bureau of Investigation" or "any agent of the Alcohol Tax Unit".

You are hereby commanded to arrest John Doe and bring him forthwith before the District Court for the _____ District of _____ in the city of _____ to answer to an indictment charging him with robbery of property of the First National Bank of _____ in violation of 12 U.S.C.A. § 588b.

Clerk
By _____
Deputy Clerk

The Fourth Amendment to the Constitution of the United States provides:

> The right of the people to be secure in their persons, houses, papers, and effects, against unreasonable searches and seizures, shall not be violated, and no Warrants shall issue, but upon probable cause, supported by Oath or affirmation, and particularly describing the place to be searched, and the persons or things to be seized.

Such a provision does not forbid every arrest (or search) without a warrant, since this part of it merely bars "unreasonable searches and seizures." It does forbid an arrest (or search) without a warrant wherever this would be unreasonable, and it places limitations upon the issuance of warrants.

The validity of a warrant is not dependent upon the fact of crime having been committed or the guilt of the person accused.[6] It is dependent entirely upon three other factors which are: (1) compliance with all of the legal requirements for the issuance of a warrant, (2) jurisdiction of the magistrate or other issuing authority, and (3) regularity in the form of the warrant.[7] For obvious reasons one who properly executes a valid warrant is fully protected.[8] The protection may go even beyond this. So far as the executing officer is concerned the inquiry is not whether the warrant was actually valid or not, but whether it was "fair on its face" or *obviously* invalid.[9] As said by the California Court: "Where a warrant valid in form and issued by a court of competent jurisdiction is placed in the hands of an officer for execution, it is his duty without delay to carry out its commands. The law is well settled that for the proper execution of such process the officer incurs no liability, however disastrous may be the effect of its execution upon the person against whom it is issued."[10]

---

6. Restatement, Second, Torts § 123, comment *a* (1965).

7. Id. at § 123.

8. Id. at § 122.

9. Id. at § 124.

10. Malone v. Carey, 17 Cal.App.2d 505, 506–7, 62 P.2d 166, 167 (1936).

A warrant can have no authority beyond the territorial boundaries of the issuing jurisdiction. Hence an arrest in Kansas by a deputy sheriff of Oklahoma under a warrant from a district court of Oklahoma was unlawful.

The constitutional provision quoted, and the corresponding clauses of the state constitutions, bar unreasonable searches and seizures of both persons and property, and the limitations upon the issuance of warrants apply to warrants of arrest and to search warrants. One type of warrant commands the seizure of a person, the other commands a search for property with the direction that it be seized if found. Aside from the purpose to be accomplished they have much in common. The most outstanding difference is in regard to the life of the warrant issued. A warrant of arrest is good until executed or withdrawn,[11] whereas a search warrant is valid for a very short period only, frequently expiring, if not executed, in three [12] or ten days.[13]

Where a bench warrant has been authorized by the court the actual issuance of the warrant is a ministerial act.[14]

COMMONWEALTH v. CROTTY & OTHERS

Supreme Judicial Court of Massachusetts, 1865.
92 Mass. 403.

INDICTMENT for a riot.

At the trial in the superior court, before BRIGHAM, J., the grounds on which the district attorney relied were as follows: Calvin Peaslee had made a complaint to the police court of Lee, charging that "John Doe or Richard Roe, whose other or true name is to your complainant unknown," had committed an assault and battery upon him; upon which complaint a warrant, which was attached to the complaint was issued against "John Doe or Richard Roe, whose other or true name is to your complainant unknown, named in the foregoing complaint." Neither the complaint nor the warrant contained any further description or means of identification of the person to be arrested. Upon this warrant, a deputy sheriff with assistants proceeded to arrest Morris Crotty, one of the present defendants, as the

---

Stuart v. Mayberry, 105 Okl. 13, 231 P. 491 (1924). But a Kentucky warrant charging a specified felony constituted "reasonable information" to a Virginia officer that accused was charged in the other state with a crime punishable by imprisonment for more than a year and authorized the officer to arrest the accused without a warrant. Mullins v. Sanders, 189 Va. 624, 54 S.E.2d 116 (1949).

11. "Such warrants do not expire by lapse of time, nor by being returned to the clerk unexecuted." McKay v. Woodruff, 77 Iowa 413, 415, 42 N.W. 428, 429 (1889).

It was held that a deportation warrant, which is a warrant of arrest and deportation, was prima facie valid although it had been outstanding for 11 years. Bellaskus v. Crossman, 164 F.2d 412 (5th Cir. 1947).

12. Swanson v. State, 113 Tex.Cr.R. 104, 18 S.W.2d 1082 (1929).

13. McClary v. State, 34 Okl.Cr. 403, 246 P. 891 (1926).

14. State v. Gordon, 18 La.Ann. 528 (1866).

real person chargeable. Crotty resisted the arrest on the ground that the warrant was invalid, and the other defendants aided him. The officer testified that he did not rely upon any description in the warrant, but upon information otherwise obtained, for the identification of Crotty.

The judge instructed the jury that the above warrant authorized the arrest of Crotty, provided he was the person accused in the complaint attached to the warrant, notwithstanding the complaint or warrant did not contain his name, any description of his person, or any statement of the reason why his person was not described, and notwithstanding the person accused was described as "John Doe or Richard Roe;" and that Crotty's assault upon and resistance of the officer were unlawful acts, and if Crotty, or either of the defendants with him, and with other persons, or said Crotty with other persons to the number of three or more in all, mutually assisted each other in assaulting and resisting said officer while attempting to arrest Crotty under said warrant, and they acted in a violent and tumultuous manner, such persons were guilty of a riot.

The jury returned a verdict of guilty against some of the defendants, and they alleged exceptions.

BIGELOW, C. J. We cannot entertain a doubt that the warrant on which the officer attempted to arrest one of the defendants at the time of the alleged riot was insufficient, illegal and void. It did not contain the name of the defendant, nor any description or designation by which he could be known and identified as the person against whom it was issued. It was in effect a general warrant, upon which any other individual might as well have been arrested, as being included in the description, as the defendant himself. Such a warrant was contrary to elementary principles, and in direct violation of the constitutional right of the citizen, as set forth in the Declaration of Rights, art. 14, which declares that every subject has a right to be secure from all unreasonable searches and seizures of his person, and that all warrants, therefore, are contrary to this right, if the order in the warrant to a civil officer to arrest one or more suspected persons or to seize their property be not accompanied with a special designation of the persons or objects of search, arrest or seizure. This is in fact only a declaration of an ancient common law right. It was always necessary to express the name or give some description of a party to be arrested on a warrant; and if one was granted with the name in blank, and without other designation of the person to be arrested, it was void.

This rule or principle does not prevent the issue and service of a warrant against a party whose name is unknown. In such case the best description possible of the person to be arrested is to be given in the warrant; but it must be sufficient to indicate clearly on whom it is to be served, by stating his occupation, his personal appearance and peculiarities, the place of his residence, or other circumstances by which he can be identified.

The warrant being defective and void on its face, the officer had no right to arrest the person on whom he attempted to serve it. He acted without warrant and was a trespasser. The defendant whom he sought to arrest had a right to resist by force, using no more than was necessary to resist the unlawful acts of the officer. An officer who acts under a void precept, and a person doing the same act who is not an officer, stand on the same footing; and any third person may lawfully interfere to prevent an arrest under a void warrant, doing no more than is necessary for that purpose.

The defendants, therefore, in resisting the officer in making an arrest under the warrant in question, if they were guilty of no improper or excessive force or violence, did not do an unlawful act by lawful means, or a lawful act by unlawful means, and so could not be convicted of the misdemeanor of a riot, with which they are charged in the indictment.

The instructions under which the case was submitted to the jury did not meet this aspect of the case. It must therefore go to a new trial.

Exceptions sustained.[1]

---

1. Accord, Alford v. State, 8 Tex.App. 545 (1880); People ex rel. Prisk v. Allison, 6 Colo.App. 80, 39 P. 903 (1895); Harwood v. Siphers, 70 Me. 464 (1880). In this case the warrant gave only this description of the accused: "A person whose name is unknown but whose person is well known, of Vassalboro, in the county of Kennebec." In holding this was a void warrant which gave no protection to the officer, Symonds, J., said: "The warrant in this case is in accordance neither with the requirements of the constitution nor with the precedents of the criminal law. . . . The omission of the name, as a means of identification, is justified only on the ground of necessity; and when this is not known the warrant must indicate on whom it is to be served in some other way, by a specification of his personal appearance, his occupation, his precise place of residence or of labor, his recent history, or some facts which give the special designation that the constitution requires." Id. at 466–7. This is quoted with approval in 2 Bishop, New Criminal Procedure, § 679 (2d ed., Underhill, 1913). See United States v. Doe, 127 F. 982 (N.D.Cal.1904). In this case it is said: "A warrant for the arrest of the person named therein as defendant, to wit, 'John Doe, a Chinese person, whose true name is unknown,' would be absolutely void, and afford no protection to an officer who should arrest any person in supposed obedience to its command, because from such a description no particular person could be identified as the one against whom it was issued." Id. at 983–4. See also 1 Wharton, Criminal Procedure, § 28 (10th ed., Kerr.1918), where it is stated: "Such a warrant must, in addition, contain the best descriptio personae possible to be obtained of the person or persons to be apprehended, and this description must be sufficient to indicate clearly the proper person or persons upon whom the warrant is to be served; and should state his personal appearance and peculiarities, give his occupation and place of residence, and any other circumstances by means of which he can be identified."

Where a magistrate signs warrants in blank, and delivers them to a police officer to be filled up with the names of persons to be arrested, as occasion may require, and the police officer fills up one of them for the arrest of an individual, without any charge under oath being first made, the warrant will be a nullity, as not issuing in the or-

HOLMES v. BLYLER

Supreme Court of Iowa, 1890.
80 Iowa 365, 45 N.W. 756.

ACTION to recover damages for false imprisonment. There was a trial by jury, and a verdict and judgment in favor of plaintiff. The defendants appeal.

ROBINSON, J. The defendant Blyler was a constable of Lee township in Polk county during the years 1887 and 1888, and defendant Eggleston was one of the sureties on his official bond. On the twentieth day of April, 1887, Blyler, acting as constable, arrested plaintiff in Dubuque, caused him to be confined in the Dubuque jail for several hours, carried him from the jail to the railway train, handcuffed him, and thence took him to Des Moines, where plaintiff was discharged without a hearing. When the arrest was made Blyler had in his possession for service a warrant, duly issued by a justice of the peace in Polk county, directing the arrest of one Julian Martin, and defendants claim that all the acts of which plaintiff complains were done by Blyler in good faith, and under the honest belief that plaintiff

---

dinary course of justice from a court or magistrate. Rafferty v. People, 69 Ill. 111 (1873). A warrant issued with a blank for the name is not illegal where the name is unknown. Bailey v. Wiggins, 5 Har. 462 (Del.1854). A warrant must either name or describe the person to be arrested. Robison v. United States, 4 Okl.Cr. 336, 111 P. 984 (1910). A warrant for the arrest of an unnamed person is void unless it contains such a *descriptio personae* as will supply the lack of the name by which the accused is known. People ex rel. Prisk v. Allison, 6 Colo. App. 80, 39 P. 903 (1895).

A "John Doe" warrant which adequately describes the person to be arrested is valid. United States v. Altiere, 343 F.2d 115 (7th Cir. 1965).

"Appellant's contention that the place of possession to be searched was not sufficiently described in the search warrant is not well founded. It was described in both the affidavit and search warrant as a 'Scripps-Booth automobile touring car, license No. 232504'. . . . It is difficult to imagine a more definite description of the thing or possession to be searched under this search warrant than that given.

"Appellant insists that since the search warrant commanded the search of the automobile 'now being used and occupied and controlled by John Doe et al.,' there is not a sufficient description of the person to make the search warrant valid. That contention cannot be sustained because this search warrant did not command that any person be searched, and, acting under it, the peace officers did not search the person of any one." Prater v. Commonwealth, 216 Ky. 451, 287 S.W. 951 (1926). Accord as to a warrant for the search of a building, adequately described but said to belong to "John Doe." State ex rel. Henderson v. Cuniff, 30 Tenn.App. 347, 206 S.W.2d 32 (1947).

If the name of the owner or occupant is unknown no name is required in a search warrant. Harvey v. Drake, 40 So.2d 214 (Fla.1949).

A warrant ordering officers to search for and seize "books, records, pamphlets, cards, receipts, lists, memoranda, pictures, recordings, and other written instruments concerning the Communist Party of Texas and the operations of the Communist Party in Texas", is a general warrant and violates the constitutional requirement that a warrant particularly describe the things to be seized. Stanford v. Texas, 379 U.S. 476, 85 S.Ct. 506, 13 L.Ed.2d 813 (1965).

was Martin, and that as soon as the mistake was discovered plaintiff was released. On the trial plaintiff waived all claim against defendants except for compensatory damages.

I. Appellants complain of the refusal of the court to allow them to show that Blyler believed plaintiff was the person named in the warrant at the time of the arrest, and that plaintiff answered, substantially, to the description of Martin given by those who knew him. It is well settled that ministerial officers or sheriffs and constables act at their peril in serving judicial process, and that they cannot justify an abuse of process by showing that they acted in good faith, excepting in mitigation of damages. The plaintiff had waived claims for all but actual damages. He was entitled to recover those for the reason that his arrest was wholly unauthorized by the warrant, and the good faith of the officer would not exempt him from liability for the actual damages caused by his unauthorized act.

II. The appellants contend that the rejected evidence would have tended to show that Blyler was justified in arresting plaintiff without a warrant. But Blyler does not pretend that he acted under any provision of law which authorized such an arrest. Section 4200 of the Code authorizes a peace-officer to make an arrest without a warrant "when a public offense has in fact been committed, and he has reasonable ground for believing that the person to be arrested has committed it." In this case, however, the officer was acting, as he claimed, by virtue of the warrant which he held for the arrest of Martin. No claim to the contrary is made by his answer, nor by the evidence. That he might have made the arrest by authority other than that under which he claimed to act is wholly immaterial.[1]

III. The conclusions we have reached make a determination of other questions discussed by counsel unnecessary. The judgment of the district court is Affirmed.[2]

---

1. The fact that the sheriff held a void *search* warrant did not make the *arrest* unlawful if he had authority under the circumstances to arrest without a warrant. Keel v. State, 176 Miss. 867, 169 So. 653 (1936).

The arrest of D for felony was valid since the officer had reasonable cause to believe D guilty thereof, although the officer purported to make the arrest under an invalid warrant. Di Bella v. United States, 284 F.2d 897 (2d Cir. 1960); Willis v. United States, 106 U.S.App.D.C. 211, 271 F.2d 477 (1959); United States v. White, 342 F.2d 379 (4th Cir. 1965).

"There shall be no liability on the part of and no cause of action shall arise against any peace officer who makes an arrest pursuant to a warrant of arrest regular upon its face if such peace officer in making the arrest acts without malice and in the reasonable belief that the person arrested is the one referred to in the warrant". West's Ann.Cal.Civ.Code, § 43.5a.

2. Accord, Simpson v. Boyd, 212 Ala. 14, 101 So. 664 (1924).

"When a warrant issues for the arrest of W. and R. is arrested under it, although W. and R. may be the *same person*, all who are concerned in the arrest are trespassers. . . . To constitute a justification in such a case, the defendant must allege in his plea, and prove that W. and R. are the same person, that R. is as *well known by the name of W. as by the name of R., or that R. represented his name to be W. at the time of the commission*

PEOPLE v. WARREN

Supreme Court of New York, 1843.
5 Hill 440.

CERTIORARI to the Oneida general sessions, where the defendant was convicted of an assault and battery upon one Johnson, a constable. Johnson arrested the defendant on a warrant issued by the inspectors of election of the city of Utica for interrupting the proceedings at the election by disorderly conduct in the presence of the inspectors. (1 R.S. 137, § 37.) The warrant was regular and sufficient upon its face. The defendant resisted the officer, and for that assault he was indicted. The defendant offered to prove that he had not been in the presence or hearing of the inspectors at any time during the election, and *that Johnson knew it*. The court excluded the evidence, and the defendant was convicted. He now moved for a new trial on a bill of exceptions.

W. Hunt, for the defendant, said the evidence should have been admitted. It would have shown that the inspectors had no jurisdiction of the subject matter; and if the officer knew it, his process was no justification of the arrest. But,

PER CURIAM. Although the inspectors had no jurisdiction of the subject matter, yet as the warrant was regular upon its face, it was a sufficient authority for Johnson to make the arrest, and the defendant had no right to resist the officer. The knowledge of the officer that the inspectors had no jurisdiction is not important. He must be governed and is protected by the process, and cannot be affected by any thing which he has heard or learned out of it. There are some *dicta* the other way; but we have held on several occasions that the officer is protected by process regular and legal upon its face, whatever he may have heard going to impeach it.

And without hearing *T. Jenkins*, (district attorney,) who was to have argued for the people,

New trial denied.[3]

---

of the crime for which he is arrested." Johnston v. Riley, 13 Ga. 97, 137 (1853).

An officer who, under a warrant, arrests the very person intended to be arrested will be liable for false imprisonment if the warrant names another person. West v. Cabell, 153 U.S. 78, 14 S.Ct. 752, 38 L.Ed. 643 (1894).

"If there are two or more persons, within the bailiwick of the officer in whose hands the warrant is placed, bearing the same name, the officer is charged with the duty of ascertaining, before making an arrest, which of such persons the warrant was intended for. If he decides this question in good faith, he is not a trespasser in making the arrest, although he may make a mistake and arrest the wrong person." Blocker v. Clark, 126 Ga. 484, 488–9, 54 S.E. 1022, 1023–4 (1906).

See notes, 44 Am.Dec. 291 (1910); 51 L.R.A. 193, 219 (1901).

3. According to the definition of a warrant "fair on its face" adopted by the American Law Institute in Restatement, Second, Torts § 124 (1965), such a warrant is always protection to the

(D) ARREST

The "slightest touching of another, or of his clothes, or cane, or anything else attached to his person" is a battery unless privileged.[1] In one case the privilege may have been granted by consent (and within the field in which consent to physical contact is recognized by law), such as the consent impliedly given by a football player to the rather violent physical contact properly incident to the game, or the consent of one who mingles in a crowd to the less violent jostling which must be expected when many people are very close together. In other situations the privilege may exist notwithstanding the lack of consent of the one concerned, as where another is authorized by law to arrest him. But anyone, even an officer, "who would justify laying hands on a person for the purpose of making an arrest, must come protected by the shield provided by law."[2] In fact, even without touching the other, the officer may subject himself to liability for assault or false imprisonment if he undertakes to make an arrest without being privileged by law to do so.[3]

(i) What Constitutes Arrest

"An arrest is the taking of another into . . . custody . . . for the actual or purported purpose of bringing the other before a court, or of otherwise securing the administration of the law."[4] It is made by an actual restraint of the person arrested, or by his submission to the custody of the person making the arrest. As explained by an English court: "Mere words will not constitute an arrest; and if the officer says, 'I arrest you,' and the party runs

---

officer executing it. However, a "warrant" which names a person over whom or states a crime over which the court or body issuing it does not have jurisdiction is not a warrant "fair on its face," by definition, and offers no protection to the officer executing it. This results from the fact that the person undertaking the execution of the warrant takes the risk of knowing the general nature of the jurisdiction of the court or body whose process he serves.

1. Crosswhite v. Barnes, 139 Va. 471, 477, 124 S.E. 242, 244 (1924).

2. Ibid; State v. Small, 184 Iowa 882, 885, 169 N.W. 116, 117 (1918).

3. For example, an officer might be guilty of an assault because of an attempted arrest, without privilege, even if the other succeeded in avoiding him without being touched. Furthermore, if the other submitted to such an arrest without physical contact, the officer would be liable for false imprisonment. See Gold v. Bissell, 1 Wend. 210 (N.Y.1828).

4. Restatement, Second, Torts § 112 (1965).

"To constitute an arrest, there must be an actual or constructive seizure or detention of the person, performed with the intention to effect an arrest, and so understood by the person detained." Jenkins v. United States, 161 F.2d 99, 101 (10th Cir. 1947); Brinegar v. United States, 165 F.2d 512, 514 (10th Cir. 1948).

away, it is no escape; but if the party acquiesces in the arrest, and goes with the officer, it will be a good arrest."[5] The court had in mind a case in which the officer did not touch the other, because touching for the manifested purpose of arrest by one having lawful authority completes the apprehension, "although he does not succeed in stopping or holding him even for an instant."[6] Stated in other terms, words alone, however appropriate, will not be sufficient for an arrest unless accompanied either by actual physical contact or by submission of the other person.

The word "arrestee," although not found in many of the dictionaries, at least with this meaning, is a very useful term employed to signify the person who has been arrested or whose arrest is being sought or attempted.[7] The one making or attempting the arrest, whether an officer or a private person, may be spoken of as the "arrester."

An arrest must be for the actual or purported *purpose* of bringing the other before a court, body, or official or of otherwise securing the administration of the law. If there is no intent to take the other anywhere and his detention is a mere incident to the proper exercise of some other privilege, it is not an arrest.[8] If, for example, a peace officer is privileged by law to require a motorist to show his operator's license,[9] and requires a driver to stop his car for this purpose,[10]

---

5. Russen v. Lucas, 1 Car. and P. 153, 171 Eng.Rep. 1141 (N.P.1824).

On the other hand one who goes with an officer at the latter's request is not necessarily under arrest. Williams v. United States, 189 F.2d 693 (D.C.Cir. 1951).

6. State ex rel. Sadler v. District Court, 70 Mont. 378, 386, 225 P. 1000, 1002 (1924).

7. See State ex rel. Wong You v. District Court, 106 Mont. 347, 351, 78 P. 2d 353, 354 (1938).

8. "Arrest connotes restraint and not temporary detention for routine questioning." Shook v. United States, 337 F.2d 563, 566 (8th Cir. 1964).

The act of a policeman in stopping a motorist to see if he has a driver's license is a permissible police practice not amounting to an arrest. Commonwealth v. Mitchell, 355 S.W.2d 686 (Ky.1962).

An officer was privileged to stop a minor driving a car with out-of-state license plates to determine if he had a driver's license, and finding that he did not, had probable cause to arrest the minor for driving without a license. Lipton v. United States, 348 F.2d 591 (9th Cir. 1965).

It was implied that if officers approached a standing car for the purpose of routine investigation, with no intent to detain the person beyond the momentary requirements of such a mission, this would not constitute an arrest. Rios v. United States, 364 U.S. 253, 262, 80 S.Ct. 1431, 1437, 4 L.Ed.2d 1688 (1960).

If police stop a moving car, not for a routine investigation but to question the occupants about a suspected felony, this is an arrest and is unlawful if made without probable cause. Bowling v. United States, 350 F.2d 1002 (D.C.Cir.1965).

See, infra, under The Frisk and Held for Questioning.

9. Uniform Motor Vehicle Operators' and Chauffeurs' License Act, § 15(b); West's Ann.Cal.Vehicle Code § 274 (b); Tenn.Code Ann. § 59–709 (1956).

10. A state highway patrolman is empowered by the Tennessee statute to stop a car at any time and require the driver to show his license. Cox v.

whereupon he examines the license, finds it in order, and permits the driver to proceed on his way without undue delay, there has been no arrest. There has been "confinement" in the technical sense because the driver was detained by authority of an officer; but since it was momentary and a mere incident to the proper exercise of a privilege, the word "arrest" is not used. It would have constituted an arrest if the officer had violated his privilege in requiring the motorist to stop.[11]

(ii) Who May Arrest

Arrests are made either (1) in obedience to a warrant, (2) upon the oral order of a magistrate for an offense committed in his presence, (3) in aid of an officer who has requested assistance in making an arrest, or (4) "without a warrant" which has survived as an inept phrase meaning an arrest under circumstances other than any of the three first mentioned.

(1) Under a Warrant

At common law a warrant of arrest might be directed either to an officer or to a private person.[1] Modern statutes frequently authorize the issuance of warrants directed to "any peace officer."[2] At one time it was not uncommon to authorize direction to a private person.[3] Few of the statutes now have this express authorization but the common-law authority will not be abrogated unless the statute is very clear upon this point.[4]

The common law required one arresting under a warrant to have the warrant in his possession at the time,[5] unless he was assisting

---

State, 181 Tenn. 344, 181 S.W.2d 338 (1944). Cf. Robedeaux v. State, 94 Okl.Cr. 171, 232 P.2d 642 (1951).

11. Robertson v. State, 184 Tenn. 277, 198 S.W.2d 633 (1947). In this case the officers stopped the car and asked to see the driver's license, not because they wanted to inspect the license but merely as a device to enable them to see what was in the car.

1. 2 Hale P.C. *110.

2. Ariz.Rev.Stats., Crim.Proc.Rule 4 (1956); Louisiana—LSA–R.S. 15:51.

3. Tenn.Code Ann. § 11529 (Williams, 1934).

4. Meek v. Pierce, 19 Wis. 300, 318 (1865).

5. 1 Hale P.C. *583. An officer with a warrant for the arrest of Shaw on a misdemeanor charge left the warrant in his buggy while he went to Shaw's house about 150 or 200 yards away and arrested him. The arrest was effected only after a struggle, and Shaw was found guilty of resisting an officer and assault and battery. On defendant's motion this verdict was set aside "on the ground that at the time of making the arrest the officer had not such possession of the warrant as is required by law." This order was reversed on appeal and the case was remanded for the purpose of having sentence imposed. State v. Shaw, 104 S.C. 359, 89 S.E. 322 (1916).

When a valid warrant has been issued for the arrest of the accused for a misdemeanor and police officers make

another who had the warrant and who was then actively cooperating in the effort to make the arrest, and was actually or constructively present at the time.[6] This may have been suited to the conditions of the time in which the rule developed, but it is quite unsuited to the needs of the present day. Some of the modern statutes provide that "the officer need not have the warrant in his possession at the time of the arrest, but after the arrest, if the person arrested so requires, the warrant shall be shown to him as soon as practicable."[7] Some statutes authorize a telegraphic copy of a warrant of arrest.[8]

(2) On Oral Order of a Magistrate

Under the common law a magistrate who saw the commission of a felony or a breach of the peace was authorized either to arrest the offender himself or to order any peace officer or private person to do so.[1] This order might be given orally and was sufficient authority for the arrest. Such authority is seldom exercised but it is commonly included in modern statutes on arrest, frequently being enlarged to permit the magistrate to order the arrest of one who has committed any "public offense" in his presence.[2]

the arrest but do not have the warrant in their possession, the arrest is unlawful; and the officers are liable in damages to the accused. Crosswhite v. Barnes, 139 Va. 471, 124 S.E. 242 (1924). However, in Cabell v. Arnold, 86 Tex. 102, 23 S.W. 645 (1893), a valid warrant was issued and retained by a United States marshal, who telegraphed his deputy to make the arrest. The deputy, without the warrant in his possession and after informing the arrestee that a warrant had been issued, made the arrest. The court held that the one arrested could recover no damages in a civil action against the marshal.

See notes, Necessity of possession of warrant by officer claiming arrest privileged as under warrant, 25 Iowa L.Rev. 660 (1940); Necessity of showing warrant upon making arrest under warrant, 40 A.L.R. 62 (1926); 100 A.L.R. 188 (1936); What information is the accused person entitled to at the time of his arrest, 42 L.R.A. 673 (1899); and Using handcuffs in arresting for a misdemeanor, 3 A.L.R. 1172 (1919).

6. G, a policeman in Kalamazoo, Michigan, had a warrant for the arrest of M on a misdemeanor charge. Learning that M was in Battle Creek, G telephoned to an officer there to hold M until G reached that city. This was done and M was held for about three hours and then turned over to G. It was held that M was falsely imprisoned until G arrived with the warrant. McCullough v. Greenfield, 133 Mich. 463, 95 N.W. 532 (1903).

7. This is the provision of A.L.I. Code of Criminal Procedure, § 24. The provision of the Federal Rules of Criminal Procedure is the same in substance. Rule 4.

8. West's Ann.Cal.Pen.Code, §§ 850, 851.

1. 4 Bl.Comm. *292.

2. See, for example, West's Ann.Cal. Pen.Code, § 838. Defendant, a magistrate, on seeing the plaintiff commit a misdemeanor in his presence, ordered a policeman to arrest plaintiff and to "take him to the station house." Plaintiff was so arrested and imprisoned and brings an action for false imprisonment against the defendant. The court said: "While, therefore, a magistrate may order the arrest of any one for a public offense committed in his presence, he has no power to at once, without an examination or hearing, or without informing the offender of the charge against him,

(3) Assisting an Officer

The sheriff, being the officer particularly charged by common law with keeping the peace and apprehending wrongdoers, was authorized, whenever necessary for such purposes, to "command all the people of his county to attend him; which is called the *posse comitatus*, or power of the county; . . ."[1] The power to require such assistance by all able-bodied males, over the age of fifteen and under the rank of Peer, included the power to call upon any such individual. In the course of time it was recognized that any peace officer is authorized to call upon private persons to aid him in making arrests or preventing crimes.[2] And a person so required to give such assistance is guilty of a misdemeanor if he wrongfully refuses to comply.[3] Such a provision is frequently included in the modern statutes.[4] Some of the enactments speak only in terms of aid to an officer in executing a warrant,[5] whereas others codify the common-law rule,[6] and still others go to the length of authorizing any person making a lawful arrest to summon assistance.[7]

commit him to prison. If there be good cause for postponing the hearing, and the offender fail to give bail in a bailable case, then he may be committed until the hearing. But for a magistrate to order the arrest of any one for a misdemeanor committed in his presence, and at once without a hearing, or without cause postponing the hearing to another time, or giving him an opportunity to have counsel or give bail, peremptorily order him to prison is contrary to the very spirit of our bill of rights and the pointed provisions of our statutes." Toughey v. King, 77 Tenn. 422, 428 (1882).

1. 1 Bl.Comm. *343.

2. 1 Wharton, Criminal Procedure, § 41 (10th ed., Kerr, 1918).

3. 1 Hale P.C. *588; 1 Bl.Comm. *343.

4. The provision in the American Law Institute's Code of Criminal Procedure is as follows:
   Section 27. *Officer may summon assistance.* Any officer making a lawful arrest may orally summon as many persons as he deems necessary to aid him in making the arrest. Every person when required by an officer shall aid him in the making of such arrest.

5. This is true of the statutes in Georgia, Indiana, Nebraska, Oklahoma, Oregon, South Dakota and Tennessee.

6. Alabama, Arkansas, Illinois, Kentucky, Mississippi, New Hampshire, North Carolina, North Dakota.

7. Arizona, California, Idaho, Iowa, Louisiana, Montana, Nevada, Utah. Note, Right and duty of bystander, when summoned either directly or by hue and cry, to assist officer in making arrest without warrant, 18 Am. and Eng.Ann.Cas. 932 (1911). Note, Posse Comitatus, 44 Am.St.Rep. 136 (1895).

"If the officer has no warrant, or authority that will justify him, he may be liable as a trespasser; but the person who is called upon for aid, having no means of knowing what the warrant is by which the officer acts, and who relies upon the official character and call of the sheriff as his security for doing what is required, is clearly entitled to protection against suits by the person arrested." McMahan v. Green, 34 Vt. 69, 70 (1861).

But where the party making the arrest is not a known public officer, the person aiding him is not protected under this rule if the arrest is unauthorized. Dietrichs v. Schaw, 43 Ind. 175 (1873). See note, Liability for assisting in unlawful arrest or subsequent detention, 14 L.R.A.,N.S., 1123 (1908). There is authority contra. In Mitchell v. State, 12 Ark. 50 (1851) the court speaking of the rights of one summoned to assist an officer said, "It is most clearly his right to refuse in case

(4) "Without a Warrant"

Three special types of authority to make an arrest have been shown: (1) A warrant in the strict sense of written process issued by a magistrate, judge, or other official or body having authority to issue warrants; (2) the oral order of a magistrate to arrest for an offense committed in his presence and (3) the request for assistance by an officer who is himself undertaking to make the arrest. The common law recognized the authority of an officer to arrest, under certain other circumstances. Four types of circumstances were recognized as giving an officer a general power to arrest without any special authorization: (1) For a felony or a breach of the peace committed or attempted in his presence; (2) on a "charge" of felony made to the officer by a private person accusing another of a felony; (3) upon reasonable grounds for believing that a felony has been commited by the arrestee (often spoken of as "reasonable suspicion of felony" or "probable cause"); (4) for a felony actually committed by the arrestee but not in the officer's presence. These four are commonly included in the modern statute, in modified form. Even others are beginning to make their appearance, such as on "official information."

(a) Committed in his presence

At common law either an officer [1] or a private citizen [2] was authorized to arrest, without a warrant, for a felony committed in his presence. Either might also arrest, without a warrant, for a misdemeanor committed in his presence provided (1) the misdemeanor constituted a breach of the peace (in the narrow sense of the phrase, meaning a public offense done by violence or one causing or likely to cause an immediate disturbance of public order) and (2) the arrest was made immediately or on fresh pursuit.[3] The statutes in most

---

the officer has no legal authority to do the act, and it is equally clear that he has no such right in case the officer has such authority. He must, therefore, act or decline to act at his peril. If it be a hardship for a person, called by an officer to assist him, to decide at his peril, it is quite as hard that the rights of innocent individuals should be invaded with impunity." Id. at 59.

A private person has no right to refuse to assist an officer in making an arrest merely because some danger is involved; but if the effort would be dangerous and futile he may be entitled to refuse under extreme circumstances. Dougherty v. State, 106 Ala. 63, 17 So. 393 (1895).

An officer who assists another in an obviously unlawful arrest is not protected by the mere fact that the other requested his assistance. Roberts v. Commonwealth, 284 Ky. 365, 144 S.W. 2d 811 (1940).

1. A.L.I. Code of Criminal Procedure 231 (Official Draft with Commentaries, 1931).

2. Id. at 238.

3. 9 Halsbury, Laws of England 86-9 (2nd ed., Hailsham, 1933).

of the states now permit an officer to arrest, without a warrant, for any public offense (felony or misdemeanor) committed in his presence.[4] About twenty states have legislation extending this same authority to any private person.[5] In other states the authority of a private person to arrest for an offense committed in his presence is either retained as it was at common law (felony or a misdemeanor amounting to a breach of the peace),[6] broadened a little to include also a misdemeanor in the form of petit larceny,[7] or narrowed by being limited to felony cases only.[8]

4. A.L.I. Code of Criminal Procedure 232–3 (Official Draft with Commentaries, 1931). The Institute lists all of the states as having such legislation *except* Colorado, Maryland, Massachusetts, New Mexico, North Carolina, Texas, Vermont, West Virginia and Wisconsin.

5. Id. at 239. The states listed are Alabama, Arizona, California, Georgia, Idaho, Illinois, Iowa, Michigan, Minnesota, Mississippi, Montana, Nevada, New York, North Dakota, Oklahoma, Oregon, Rhode Island, South Dakota, Tennessee, Utah.

6. Id. at 239.

7. Ibid.

8. Id. at 238. The reasonable mistake of fact doctrine applies, and the officer is protected if he acts on a bona fide belief, based upon reasonable grounds, that an offense is being committed in his presence, even if no offense is in fact committed. Cave v. Cooley, 48 N.M. 478, 152 P.2d 886 (1944). An officer who makes an arrest for public drunkenness, without a warrant, is protected if the arrestee appears to be drunk even if not drunk as a matter of fact. Goodwin v. State, 148 Tenn. 682, 257 S.W. 79 (1924); Morris v. Combs' Administrator, 304 Ky. 187, 200 S.W.2d 281 (1947); see Kelley v. State, 184 Tenn. 143, 149, 197 S.W.2d 545, 547 (1946).

"In passing upon the right of an officer to make an arrest of one who is in possession of a pistol on the public street of a city, where the possession of a pistol makes a prima facie case, the possession in the presence of an officer determines the right of the officer to make an arrest, even though upon the trial of the case the accused might present a legal defense." Reed v. State, 195 Ga. 842, 851, 25 S.E. 2d 692, 698 (1943).

"We therefore conclude that . . . the act of fishing was committed by plaintiff (who admitted that he had no license) in the presence of defendants and that they were not required to know that the admitted fishing was done at a place or under circumstances where a license was not required under some exemption contained in the statute," and hence they were authorized to arrest the plaintiff without a warrant. Giannini v. Garland, 296 Ky. 361, 367, 177 S.W.2d 133, 136 (1944).

In Stearns v. Titus, 193 N.Y. 272, 85 N.E. 1077 (1908), it is stated: "To justify an arrest without a warrant for the commission of that offense, the crime must be actually committed or attempt be made to commit it in the presence of the officer. Reasonable suspicion, or probable cause to believe its commission is not sufficient." Also the misdemeanor is not committed in the "presence" of the officer unless he knows it is committed. State v. Gartland, 304 Mo. 87, 263 S.W. 165 (1924).

"A peace officer cannot legally make an arrest without a warrant for an offense claimed to have been committed in his presence which he himself provokes or brings about." Scott v. Feilschmidt, 191 Iowa 347, 351, 182 N.W. 382, 384 (1921).

PRICE v. TEHAN

Supreme Court of Errors of Connecticut, 1911.
84 Conn. 164, 79 A. 68.

The defendant Tehan was a policeman on duty in the city of Waterbury. An ordinance of that city enacted under authority of the city charter, which made the offense created by the ordinance a misdemeanor, forbade the assembly of persons idly and in crowds upon any footway, sidewalk, or crosswalk, in any street, or in the public squares of the city, and provided that "all persons to the number of three or more assembled and refusing to disperse when commanded to do so by a police officer, special constable, alderman or mayor of said city, shall forfeit and pay a penalty of not more than fifty dollars for every such offense." The plaintiff, who was then a minor, met two friends upon a sidewalk in the center of the city about 8 o'clock one Saturday evening, and there stood in conversation for several minutes with them. His meeting with one of these friends was by appointment; with the other by chance. The sidewalk was at the time crowded. Tehan, who had been specially detailed by the defendant Beach, who was the superintendent of police of the city, to keep clear the streets and walks in the vicinity, noticed from the opposite side of the street, where he was, the three young men standing as stated, and thereby interfering with free passage along the walk. He crossed the street and directed them to move on. They did not move immediately, and the plaintiff who was intending to go to a theater with one of the group, and might with equal propriety take either of two streets to reach there, asked this friend which way they should go. Tehan hearing this inquiry, and supposing that it was addressed to him, and because the plaintiff did not move at once, answered by saying, "I will show you which way to go," and arrested him and took him as a prisoner to the police station. The arrest was made for the violation of the ordinance. There was no such violation by either of the three young men, and the plaintiff was not allowed a reasonable time within which to comply with the officer's direction, before his arrest. Tehan believed that there was a violation of the ordinance, and acted in good faith. Tehan took the plaintiff directly to the station house, and there reported to the sergeant on duty at the desk. . . .

PRENTICE, J. (after stating the facts above). The plaintiff's arrest was at the hands of a police officer, without a warrant, and for the commission of a statutory misdemeanor created and defined by a municipal ordinance. The common law has long recognized the right of a peace officer to arrest without a warrant one whom he had reasonable or probable ground to suspect of having committed a felony, even though the suspected person was innocent, and although no felony had been committed. Power to the same extent has not been recognized in the case of misdemeanors. In many jurisdictions statutes have been enacted regulating that subject in a manner deemed to be more suited to modern conditions than does the common law. Section 1770 of our General Statutes is such a statute, and its provisions define and prescribe the limits of the powers of officers in making arrests for offenses such as that for which this arrest was made. The common-law power was less comprehensive, and there is no statute, general or special, which we have discovered, conferring a broader one upon this policeman. Section 21 of chapter 56 of the Special Acts of 1895 (12 Sp.Laws, p. 65) deals with the subject of arrests by members of the Waterbury police department for certain offenses; but it goes no further than the general statute, and the offenses enumerated do not embrace the present. The general statute referred to authorizes police and other peace officers to "arrest, without complaint and warrant, any person for any offense in the jurisdiction, when the offender shall be taken or apprehended in the act, or on the speedy information of others." It further provides that "all persons so arrested shall be immediately presented before proper authority."

The plaintiff's arrest was not upon the information of others. It was made upon the strength of the officer's own knowledge gained from his personal observation. The authority conferred in such cases is to arrest "when the offender is taken or apprehended in the act." This implies an offender and an act of offense which is not in the past. It does not justify an arrest of one who is not offending. Such a person cannot be taken in the act of offending, since he is not offending. The court below held, and rightly upon the facts before it, that the plaintiff was not committing, and had not committed, the offense created by the ordinance. The three young men, who met casually upon the walk, and stopped for a friendly and orderly conversation with each other, were certainly not subject to the penal provisions of the ordinance before they were requested to move on. Tehan's command did not instantly convert them into persons against whom a criminal charge could be made. That result could not be accomplished until they should, in the language of the ordinance, have refused to disperse in obedience to such command. That necessarily implies a reasonable time and opportunity to do as directed. Such time and opportunity Tehan did not give them before the arrest was made. It is evident that he acted hastily and impulsively, and that he was prompted to make the arrest because he was piqued, and quite possibly because his temper was aroused, by an innocent remark of the plaintiff, misunderstood or misconstrued. He failed to keep himself under that control which is required of an officer and to act with that regard for the rights of the individual which the law demands before he deprives a person of his liberty. The law seeks to give to those who are charged with the important duty of maintaining peace and good order in the community all reasonable protection in its discharge. But it cannot overlook the rights of private individuals, and justify arrests made as this was.

When authority over the plaintiff passed to the defendant Beach, he proceeded to exercise it by making terms with the plaintiff's friends as a condition of his liberation. This conduct was without possible justification. Upon what theory he assumed to act it is difficult to imagine. Whatever it was, it was a false one, and can afford him no protection for the wrong done the plaintiff by his unlawful restraint.

There is no error. The other Judges concurred.[1]

DILGER v. COMMONWEALTH

Court of Appeals of Kentucky, 1889.
88 Ky. 550, 11 S.W. 651.

JUDGE HOLT delivered the opinion of the court.

The appellant, Charles Dilger, is under sentence of death. His counsel urge that the verdict is not the result of a fair trial, but of popular clamor. In a case like this one, where, apparently at least, affluent circumstances and influential friends are lacking, those who administer the law should be especially alert, and stand like a wall between the passion of the hour and the object of it, insuring to him, however humble, an impartial trial. Without this barrier no citizen is safe. Remove it and the liberty, or what is more, the life of every individual is in danger. If the accused be given but the mere form of a trial, and made the victim of excited public sentiment or maddened popular feeling, then a degrading judicial farce is enacted,

---

[1]. In re Kellam, 55 Kan. 700, 41 P. 960 (1895), held that a statute authorizing police officers to arrest for a misdemeanor without a warrant "upon reasonable suspicion that an offense has been committed" was unconstitutional. "The liberties of the people do not rest upon so uncertain and insecure a basis as the surmise or conjecture of an officer that some petty offense has been committed. . . . This provision ['the right of the people to be secure in their persons and property against unreasonable searches and seizures shall be inviolate'] guaranties protection against unreasonable arrests, and when it was placed in the constitution, . . ., an arrest for a minor offense without a warrant, and not in the view of the officer, was deemed to be unreasonable and unlawful. . . . Felonies were excepted on account of the gravity of such offenses, and because the public safety and the prompt apprehension of criminals charged with offenses so heinous seemed to require that such arrests should be made without warrant."

See note on arrest in general, 84 Am.St. Rep. 679, 689 (1902). In accord with this view on the constitutionality of such statutes see Ex parte Rhodes, 202 Ala. 68, 79 So. 462 (1918); Orick v. State, 140 Miss. 184, 105 So. 465 (1925).

But the weight of authority seems to be contra. ". . . it is expressly declared in all of the authorities that the constitutional provision against search and seizure has reference only to general searches for the purpose of obtaining evidence, and has no reference to, nor does it prevent, arrests in proper cases without warrant." United States v. Rembert, 284 F. 996, 1001 (S.D.Tex.1922); Commonwealth v. Phelps, 209 Mass. 396, 95 N.E. 868 (1911). See note, 1 A.L.R. 585 (1919).

and an example furnished likely to be far-reaching for evil. Moved by these considerations, we have given this case as careful an examination as lies within our power.

Upon the night of August 15, 1888, and at about the midnight hour, the appellant was beating his mistress, Mary Burns, in an upstairs room occupied by them, in the city of Louisville. Her cries attracted the attention of Joseph Rosenberg and James W. Jones, who were the two policemen upon that beat, and they at once hastened to the house. They located the room where the offense was being committed by the noise, but just before they entered it the appellant stopped beating her, the cries ceased, and they knew of it, therefore, only by hearing and not by sight. The accused declined to be arrested by them, claiming that he had done nothing in their presence, and that therefore they could not arrest him without a warrant, since section 36 of our Criminal Code provides:

"A peace officer may make an arrest—
"1. In obedience to a warrant of arrest delivered to him.
"2. Without a warrant, when a public offense is committed in his presence, or when he has reasonable grounds for believing that the person arrested has committed a felony."

The appellant testifies that upon this mere objection to arrest being made by him, and without any action upon his part, they commenced beating him with their "billies." His defense, therefore, was, that the attempted arrest was unlawful; and if not, that unnecessary force was used, and that he acted in self-defense. His testimony is, to some extent, sustained by other evidence, but in our opinion it is overborne by other positive and circumstantial testimony, showing clearly that upon their offering to arrest him he at once began to use his deadly bowie-knife, driving it into the brain of the one and the heart of the other, and killing them both almost instantly. It is plain, from the verdict that the jury accepted this latter view of the bloody transaction.

The officers were dressed in their police uniform, and well known to the appellant to be policemen.

Unquestionably they had a right to make the arrest. While the offense of beating the woman was not committed in their sight, yet it was within their hearing, and when they were so near that they could not be mistaken as to the offender. This was in their presence, as contemplated by the law. Moreover, the instructions given to the jury told them that the offense for which the arrest was attempted must have been committed in the presence of the officers. . . .

The appellant has had two trials. There were four postponements of the case before the first trial and one thereafter. A careful inspection of the record satisfies us that he is guilty under the law; that he has been tried in accordance with it by an impartial jury; and

Sec. 1   STEPS PRIOR TO INDICTMENT   797

it only remains for us, unpleasant as is the duty, to affirm the judgment, which is accordingly done.[a]

(b) On charge preferred by another

At one time in the development of the law of arrest it seemed as if the authority of an officer to arrest on a charge of felony preferred by another person would be given almost the scope of that arising under a warrant. Lord Hale says: "And it appears by the books before-mentioned that in cases of arrests of this or like nature, the constable may execute his office upon information and request of others, that suspect and charge the offenders, . . ."[1] The most extreme statement of the point is by Mr. Justice Buller, in Williams v. Dawson,[2] to the effect that if an officer "received a person into custody, on a charge preferred by another of felony or a breach of the peace, there he is to be considered as a mere conduit; and if no felony or breach of the peace was committed, the person who preferred the charge alone is answerable." The phrase "receives a person into custody" suggests that the arrest may have been made by a private per-

---

a. "Where an officer is apprised by any of his senses that a crime is being committed, it is committed in his presence so as to justify an arrest without a warrant." (It was the sense of smell in this case.) Massa v. State, 159 Tenn. 428, 430, 19 S.W.2d 248, 249 (1929). See note, 15 Minn.L.Rev. 359 (1931).

But in People v. Johnson, 86 Mich. 175, 48 N.W. 870 (1891) shouting on the public street amounting to a breach of the peace, which was heard by a policeman 150 feet away was not committed in the "presence" of the officer because the one shouting was not in view.

The fact that the arrestee was carrying a concealed weapon at the time of the arrest will not justify the apprehension if the officer did not know of the presence of the weapon until a search was made. People v. Henneman, 373 Ill. 603, 27 N.E.2d 448 (1940), noted in 31 J.Crim.L. & Criminology 465 (1940). See note, 92 A.L.R. 490 (1934). Cf. James v. State, 94 Okl.Cr. 239, 234 P.2d 422 (1951).

Loud talking in the kitchen of one's home, heard by officers in passing but not a word of which was understood by them, was not the commission of an offense in their presence, there being no showing that the occupants were intoxicated or disorderly. Lucarini v. State, 159 Tenn. 373, 19 S.W. 2d 239 (1929).

One fleeing from another state to avoid prosecution for a robbery committed by him there is violating the federal Fugitive Felon Act. Hence an officer who finds him may arrest him for an offense committed in the presence of such officer. Bircham v. Commonwealth, 238 S.W.2d 1008 (Ky.1951).

1. 2 Hale P.C. * 89–90.

2. Nisi Prius (1788), quoted in Hobbs v. Branscomb, 3 Camp. 420, 421, 170 Eng.Rep. 1431, 1432 (K.B.1813).

Lord Mansfield had said much the same a few years earlier: ". . . if a man charges another with felony, and requires an officer to take him into custody, and carry him before a magistrate, it would be most mischievous that the officer should be bound first to try, and at his peril exercise his judgment on the truth of the charge. He that makes the charge should alone be answerable. The officer does his duty in carrying the accused before a magistrate, who is authorized to examine, and commit or discharge." Samuel v. Payne, 1 Dougl. 359, 360, 99 Eng.Rep. 230, 231 (K.B. 1780).

son who merely turned the arrestee over to an officer to take before a magistrate. If so the case is not unusual. Where an **arrest is made** by a private person upon his own responsibility the arrestee should be taken before a magistrate without undue delay and an officer who merely assists in causing this to be done does not incur liability thereby. This authority of the officer is frequently incorporated in a special statute.[3] The statement quoted from Mr. Justice Buller was approved, however, in Hobbs v. Branscomb [4] in which case the arrest had not been made by a private person but was made by the officers on a charge preferred by a private person. This seems to suggest complete protection to the officer who makes an arrest on a charge preferred by another with the sole responsibility resting upon that other. Some qualification was to be expected and was made very shortly. Just a few years after Hobbs v. Branscomb an officer, without a warrant, made an arrest for receiving stolen property on a charge preferred by a young thief. It was held unlawful for him to deprive a person of his liberty on such information, without further evidence.[5]

Thus the statement of the common law upon this point cannot be given in the unqualified terms suggested by Mr. Justice Buller, but must be in some such form as this: An officer arresting without a warrant upon a charge of felony preferred by another, and accusing the arrestee thereof, is protected if he acts reasonably.[6] This is expressly incorporated into a number of the statutes by including in the section authorizing an officer to arrest without a warrant, as one of the clauses: "On a charge made, upon reasonable cause, of the commission of a felony by the person arrested." [7] The word "charge" in such a statute, as at common law, does not mean a formal written charge made to a magistrate but an oral accusation made to the peace officer himself.[8]

An officer has reasonable ground for believing a person guilty of felony if he has received information to this effect from a person who is reasonably entitled to be believed.[9] This would seem to permit the inclusion of this basis for arrest without a warrant in the "probable cause" category and render a separate clause unnecessary. But because of a special limitation injected into the "probable cause" sec-

3. See Tenn.Code Ann. § 40–821 (1956).

4. See note 2 supra.

5. Isaacs v. Brand, 2 Stark. 167, 171 Eng.Rep. 609 (N.P.1817).

6. Mr. Justice Buller's reference to a "breach of the peace" as well as a felony is understandable if the arrest was actually made by a private person for such an offense committed in his presence and the officer merely received the custody of the person after the arrest had been made.

7. See the statutes in California, Idaho, Minnesota, Mississippi, Nevada, North Dakota, Oklahoma, South Dakota, Tennessee, and Utah.

8. Haggard v. First Nat. Bank of Mandan, 72 N.D. 434, 8 N.W.2d 5 (1942).

9. Vaughn v. State, 178 Tenn. 384, 158 S.W.2d 715 (1942); Lee v. State, 148 Tex.Cr.R. 220, 185 S.W.2d 978 (1945).

tion in many of the statutes (to be considered in the next subsection) this clause serves a useful purpose. "[W]e understand the law to be now well settled," said the Tennessee court, "that a *peace officer* may make an arrest on a charge of felony, upon a reasonable cause of suspicion, without a warrant, although it should afterwards turn out that no felony had, in fact, been committed. . . . And this principle of the common law is distinctly incorporated in our Code." [10]

An additional element is added by the Texas statute, to the effect that where it is shown by satisfactory proof to a peace officer, upon the representation of a credible person, that a felony has been committed, *and that the offender is about to escape, so that there is no time to procure a warrant, such peace officer may, without warrant, pursue and arrest the accused.*[11]

Many of the statutes have no such clause in any form.

(c) On probable cause

An arrest without a warrant on a bare suspicion, not supported by reasonable grounds, is clearly unlawful;[1] but both the common law and the statutes authorize an arrest on "reasonable suspicion of felony" subject to certain qualifications. What came to be the accepted view of the common law is that either an officer or a private person is privileged to arrest one who is reasonably believed to be guilty of felony, with this important distinction: the officer is protected if he believes, upon reasonable grounds (1) that a felony has been committed and (2) that the arrestee is the guilty party; whereas for the protection of a private person it is necessary (1) that a felony has in fact been committed and (2) that he has reasonable grounds for believing the arrestee guilty of committing it.[2] The reason for

---

10. Lewis v. State, 40 Tenn. 127, 146 (1859).

11. Vernon's Ann.Tex.Code Cr.Proc. art. 215.

1. People v. Chatman, 322 Ill.App. 519, 54 N.E.2d 631 (1944).

2. Holley v. Mix, 3 Wend. 350, 353 (N. Y.1829); Beckwith v. Philby, 6 B. & C. 635, 638–9, 108 Eng.Rep. 585, 586 (K.B. 1827); Walters v. Smith [1914] 1 K.B. 595; 1 Stephen, History of the Criminal Law 193 (1883); 9 Halsbury, Laws of England 84–87 (2d ed. Hailsham, 1933); A.L.I. Code of Criminal Procedure 236–42 (Official Draft with Commentaries, 1931).

Professor Jerome Hall has taken the position that the common law, prior to the Revolution, required an actual felony plus reasonable cause to believe the arrestee guilty thereof, to authorize an arrest without a warrant by an officer, as well as by a private person. Legal and Social Aspects of Arrest Without a Warrant, 49 Harv. L.Rev. 566 (1936). Without doubt the generalizations of the early writers lend support to this theory; but Professor Hall was unable to produce any early case in which an officer, having made an arrest on reasonable grounds for believing the arrestee guilty of felony, was held to have acted unlawfully because no felony had in fact been committed. Probably the most that can be said is that some of the early writers were thinking in terms of this requirement but that when the point was actually raised in the cases

this difference is that while either an officer or a private person is privileged to make an arrest for a felony not committed in his presence if he has reasonable grounds for believing the arrestee guilty thereof, —the private person is under no *duty* to do so.[3] To deter private persons from officious interference with the liberty of others it is quite proper to require them to act at their peril on the question whether a felony has or has not been committed, when they undertake to arrest for such an offense not occurring in their presence. With the officer it is different because in his case the privilege to arrest for felony carries with it a corresponding duty. Unfortunately, however, a number of the statutes authorizing an officer to arrest without a warrant have worded this part of the enactment in some such form as: "When a felony has in fact been committed, and he has reasonable cause to believe that the person to be arrested has committed it."[4]

It is in jurisdictions in which the general authority of an officer to arrest on reasonable suspicion of felony has such a limitation that there is real need for an additional clause authorizing him to arrest on a charge of felony preferred by another.[5]

Relatively few states have expressly codified the common-law rule whereby a peace officer is authorized to arrest without a warrant where he has reasonable cause to believe (a) that a felony has been committed and (b) that the person arrested committed it,[6] but the decisions have tended to recognize this rule where the courts have not been hampered by restrictive enactments.[7]

The common law tended to give an officer somewhat greater authority to arrest at night than in the daytime[8] and some of the statutes reflect this, in different form, by authorizing an officer to arrest at night where there is reasonable cause to believe the arrestee has committed a felony even though it afterward appears that the felony

---

it was held that a peace officer is not required to act at his peril on the question whether a felony has in fact been committed or not. See Restatement, Second, Torts § 121(b) (1965).

3. McCrackin v. State, 150 Ga. 718, 722, 105 S.E. 487, 489 (1920).

4. Idaho, North Dakota, Oklahoma. Compare subdivisions 3 and 5 of Idaho Code, § 19–603 (1948).

5. The states mentioned in the preceding note have this additional clause.

6. Alabama, Arkansas, Florida, Kentucky, Michigan, North Carolina, Ohio.

7. Doering v. State, 49 Ind. 56 (1874); Koscielski v. State, 199 Ind. 546, 158 N.E. 902 (1927); State v. Whitley, 183 S.W. 317 (Mo.1916); State v. Moore, 235 S.W. 1056 (Mo.1921); Diers v. Mallon, 46 Neb. 121, 64 N.W. 722 (1895); McCarthy v. DeArmit, 99 Pa. 63 (1881); State v. Hughlett, 124 Wash. 366, 214 P. 841 (1923); Allen v. Lopinsky, 81 W.Va. 13, 94 S.E. 369 (1917). See Scott v. Eldridge, 154 Mass. 25, 27 N.E. 677 (1891); Commonwealth v. Carey, 66 Mass. 246 (1853); Lee v. Jones, 44 R.I. 151, 116 A. 201 (1922); Crosswhite v. Barnes, 139 Va. 471, 124 S.E. 242 (1924).

8. "The constable may arrest suspicious nightwalkers . . . and men that ride armed in fair or markets or elsewhere." 2 Hale P.C. *89.

had not been committed.⁹ In other words, they extend the officer's authority at night (in this regard) to what it was at all times under the common law.

For the most part the statutes have not changed the authority of a private person to arrest on reasonable suspicion of felony but have left it as it was at common law with the requirement that (a) a felony has in fact been committed and (b) he has reasonable ground for believing the arrestee guilty. New York requires an actual felony by the arrestee himself, to authorize such an arrest by a private person;[10] a few statutes authorize the arrest on reasonable ground to believe the arrestee guilty of felony, even if no felony has in fact been committed,[11] while the Texas enactment does not authorize a private person without a warrant to arrest for an offense not committed in his presence.[12]

(d) For felony by arrestee

Under the English common law an officer arresting for felony who apprehended an innocent person was not justified unless he had probable ground to believe him guilty, but proof that the arrestee was the felon was justification in itself.[1] This has sometimes been codified, as in a statute providing that a peace officer "may, without a warrant, arrest a person; . . . (2) When a person arrested has committed a felony, although not in his presence. (3) Whenever he has reasonable cause to believe that the person to be arrested has committed a felony, whether or not a felony has in fact been committed."[2] At the present time, on the other hand, at least in the absence of express statutory authority therefor, it "is an elementary maxim that a search, seizure or arrest cannot be retroactively justified by what is uncovered".[3] And the trend of the case law is such as to cast serious doubt about the validity of a statute purporting to authorize an

---

9. Minnesta, Nevada, North Dakota, Oklahoma, and South Dakota. Statutes in the following states seem to reach the same result although they are not so specific: Idaho, and Utah.

10. N.Y.Code Cr.Proc. § 183.

11. Kentucky, Mississippi, Ohio and South Carolina.

12. Lacy v. State, 7 Tex.App. 403 (1879), construing the Texas statute which is now Vernon's Ann.Tex.Code Cr.Proc. art. 212.

For a collection of cases and a discussion of the subjects covered by footnotes 10, 11, and 12, see note, 133 A.L.R. 608 (1941).

Note, on arrest without warrant on suspicion for unlawful possession of weapons, 92 A.L.R. 490 (1934).

1. 2 Hale, P.C. *85. Even a private person was justified in the arrest if his arrestee was in fact the felon. Id. at *78. And see State v. Williams, 14 S.W.2d 434, 435–6 (Mo.1929).

2. West's Ann.Cal.Pen.Code, § 836.

3. United States v. Como, 340 F.2d 891, 893 (2d Cir. 1965).

"[A]n arrest is not justified by what the subsequent search discloses." Henry v. United States, 361 U.S. 98, 104, 80 S.Ct. 168, 4 L.Ed.2d 134 (1959).

arrest without either a warrant or probable cause to believe the arrestee guilty.

(e) On official information

The common law of arrest developed before the appearance of the telephone, the telegraph, the radio, and the official law-enforcement bulletin. These, together with changes such as the substitution of the automobile for the horse as the common means of transportation, require certain additions to the authority of an officer to arrest without a warrant.

It is commonplace today for important parts of the instructions issued by the headquarters of a law-enforcement unit to be sent to the various officers by radio and by an official bulletin issued periodically. It is also commonplace for one officer to receive an official communication from another officer by telephone, telegraph or letter. Due recognition should be given to such official communications. As yet very little has been done in this direction. Louisiana has pointed the way with a statute authorizing an officer to arrest without a warrant "when he has received positive information by written, telegraphic or other authoritative source that another official holds a warrant for such arrest." [a]

(iii) PLACE OF ARREST

The chief peace officer of the ancient village was a bailiff; and the village itself was called a "wick." In the course of time "bailiff's wick" was contracted into "bailiwick" and came to mean the territory or area throughout which a peace officer exercises his authority as such as a matter of law. Thus, in the absence of some special provision, the bailiwick of a member of the state police or state highway patrol is the state itself, the bailiwick of a sheriff is his county, and the bailiwick of a policeman is his town or city. The possibility of broader authority by some special provision of law must not be overlooked. The Alabama statute, for example, expressly authorizes a policeman or marshal to arrest anywhere within the limits of the county in which his city, town or village is situated; [1] and in some states, such as Iowa, it is expressly provided that although the constable is elected from a *township* he shall be a *county* officer.[2] It must not be assumed that an officer may never act in an official capacity outside of his bailiwick, because this may be authorized by some special statute. For example, some states expressly authorize a peace

---

a. Louisiana—LSA-R.S. 15:60(5).   2. Iowa Code Ann. § 39.21.

1. Ala.Code, tit. 15, § 152 (1940).

officer to execute a warrant anywhere in the state,[3] and any state having the Uniform Act on Fresh Pursuit expressly authorizes peace officers of other states to follow a fleeing felon across its boundary and arrest him within its territory. Any such special enactment will extend the authority of a peace officer in the particular situation specified, but it does not enlarge his bailiwick. It enables him to perform certain acts in an official capacity outside of his bailiwick. It is strictly construed, and hence legislative authorization for an officer to execute a warrant in any part of the state does not empower him to arrest *without a warrant* outside of his own bailiwick.[4]

Under the English common law a warrant issued by a judge of the King's Bench extended all over the kingdom, and was dated merely "England," but a warrant issued by a justice of the peace was good only in his county unless it was "backed" (endorsed) by the justice of another county, whereupon it could be executed therein.[5] In this country it is necessary to examine the statutes of each particular state. Some of these statutes are very similar to the English common law,[6] some require the warrant to be directed to a peace officer of the county in which the prosecution is brought but authorize him to execute it in any county in the state,[7] some authorize the direction to be to officers of the state generally so that the warrant may be executed in any county in the state, but limit each officer to his own bailiwick so far as execution is concerned,[8] while still others have the sweeping provision that a warrant of arrest may be executed in any part of the state by any peace officer of the state.[9]

By a rather common provision, if a person who has been lawfully arrested escapes, or is rescued, the person from whose custody he has unlawfully departed may immediately pursue him and retake him without a warrant in any place within the state.[10] An occasional suggestion for statutory change would authorize an officer, as such, to arrest without a warrant, outside of his bailiwick, for an offense committed in his presence, whether the officer was outside of his bailiwick when the offense was committed or was within his bailiwick at that time and followed the offender outside on fresh pursuit.[11]

3. Ga.Code § 27–209 (1933); Tenn.Code Ann. § 40–713 (1956).

4. Henson v. State, 120 Tex.Cr.R. 176, 49 S.W.2d 463 (1932).

5. 4 Bl.Comm. *291–2.

6. Or.Rev.Stats. 133.150, 133.160 (1957).

7. Del.Rev.Code, §§ 4468, 4477 (1935). And see the interpretation of the Washington statute in Nadeau v. Conn, 142 Wash. 243, 252 P. 913 (1927). The Delaware statute now authorizes the arrest "by any officer authorized by law". Del.Code Ann., Super.Court Rule 4(c) (1) (1953).

8. Such a provision was construed in York v. Commonwealth, 82 Ky. 360 (1884).

9. Ariz.Rev.Stats.; Cr.Proc.Rule 4.

10. See the statutes of Alabama, Arizona, California, Iowa and New York.

11. See United States v. Braggs, 189 F.2d 367 (10th Cir. 1951).

MALCOMSON v. SCOTT

Supreme Court of Michigan, 1885.
56 Mich. 459, 23 N.W. 166.

CAMPBELL, J. . . . But inasmuch as the other issue is raised, it is necessary to refer to that briefly. The extradition of criminals who are claimed to be fugitives from other states is governed entirely by the Constitution and laws of the United States. No state can deal with other states, under the express terms of the Constitution, without the approval of Congress, and what the state cannot do its policemen cannot do. An arrest here without compliance with the United States laws cannot be maintained. Michigan cannot treat foreign offenses as domestic, and there is nothing in our statutes which contemplates an arrest without warrant, for purposes of extradition.

Under the Constitution and Acts of Congress it is for the governor of the one state to determine whether he desires extradition, and for the governor of the other to decide whether he will grant it. Congress will not allow the demand to be made until the offender has either been indicted or otherwise complained of in the regular course of justice. There can be no demand before complaint. Rev.Stat.U.S. § 5278. Our statute in aid of such proceedings only allows an arrest where a complaint is made on oath, setting forth such matters "as are necessary to bring the case within the provisions of law," and on a full showing the person may be recognized to appear again before the magistrate at some future day, "allowing a reasonable time to obtain the warrant of the governor," and in default of bail there may be a commitment. How.Stat. §§ 9623, 9624–9626. But the statute further requires that the complainant shall be liable for costs and charges, and for the weekly support of the prisoner, and that the jailor may discharge him on default thereof.

The arrest, therefore, cannot be justified under this act, and the order of the commissioner was in clear violation of it, and could justify no further holding.

The views we have expressed leave it unnecessary to go into further details. The judgment must be reversed, with costs, and a new trial granted.[1]

SHERWOOD and CHAMPLIN, JJ., concurred. COOLEY, C. J., did not sit in this case.

[1.] In Simmons v. Vandyke, 138 Ind. 380, 37 N.E. 973 (1894) a writ of habeas corpus was sustained to release the plaintiff arrested by officers of state A without a warrant. A telegram had been received from officers of state B in which was set out the warrant for the arrest of the plaintiff on a charge of felony. The court did not specifically state the arrest was unauthorized, but held there was insufficient proof on which to hold the plaintiff.

Contra: A bench warrant was issued in the District of Wyoming for the arrest of plaintiff. Relying upon this warrant, a United States marshal for the District of Columbia arrested plaintiff without a warrant in the latter jurisdiction. The court, speaking through Brandeis, J., upheld the arrest: "The original arrest and detention were lawful. A person duly charged with a felony in one State, may, if he flees to another, be arrested, without a warrant, by a peace offi-

Sec. 1　　　STEPS PRIOR TO INDICTMENT　　　805

(iv) Time of Arrest

In the absence of some statutory restriction an arrest for crime, lawful in other respects, may be made on any day and at any hour of the day or night. Most of the statutes which mention time grant this authority, but a few of them make some restrictions in misdemeanor cases. Statutes in a few states do not authorize arrest for a misdemeanor at night unless upon the direction of the Magistrate endorsed upon the warrant;[a] a few others do not authorize arrest for a misdemeanor at night unless there is such authority in the warrant or the arrest is for an offense committed in the presence of the apprehending officer;[b] and a few do not authorize arrest for a misdemeanor either at night or on Sunday unless upon the direction of the Magistrate endorsed upon the warrant.[c]

(v) Rights, Privileges and Duties

(1) *Manifestation of Purpose and Authority*

Whatever crime one may have committed in the past, if he is engaged in no offense at the moment, he is privileged to use force if necessary to defend himself against any unlawful act which threatens him with death or injury or deprivation of his liberty.[1] And because of the mistake of fact doctrine it is important for him to know whether he is confronted with such danger or is dealing with a "minister of justice." Hence there is a common-law requirement that one about to be arrested is entitled to notice, if he does not already know, of (1) the intention to take him into the custody of the law, (2) the authority for the arrest, and (3) the reason therefor. This manifes-

---

cer in the State in which he is found and be detained for the reasonable time necessary to enable a requisition to be made. . . . The rule is not less liberal where the fugitive stands charged by an indictment found in one federal district and flees to another. . . . If the bench warrant issued in Wyoming was not effective as a warrant within the District of Columbia, the possession of it did not render illegal an arrest which could lawfully have been made without it. It would, at least serve as evidence that . . . [the marshal] . . . had reasonable cause to believe that a felony had been committed by [the plaintiff]." Stallings v. Splain, 253 U.S. 339, 341–2, 40 S.Ct. 537, 538, 64 L.Ed. 940 (1920). See notes, 46 Am.St.Rep. 414 (1895); 26 L.R.A. 33 (1895). As to a violation of the federal Fugitive Felon Act see Bircham v. Commonwealth, 238 S.W. 2d 1008 (Ky.1951).

a. Idaho Code Ann. § 19–607 (1948).

b. West's Ann.Cal.Pen.Code, § 840.

c. Minn.Stats.Ann. § 629.31. Cf. N.Y. Code Cr.Proc. § 180.

1. Starr v. United States, 153 U.S. 614, 14 S.Ct. 919, 38 L.Ed. 841 (1894); State v. Phillips, 118 Iowa 660, 92 N.W. 876 (1902); State v. Belk, 76 N.C. 10 (1877).

tation of purpose and authority is the so-called "Notice of arrest." The common law does not require this manifestation of purpose and authority if the making thereof is reasonably believed by the arrester to be: (a) dangerous to the arrester or to a third person, or (b) likely to imperil the making of the arrest or (c) useless or unnecessary.[2] A statutory provision substantially as follows is not uncommon:

"The person making the arrest must inform the person to be arrested of the intention to arrest him, of the cause of arrest, and the authority to make it, except when the person to be arrested is actually engaged in the commission of or attempt to commit an offense, or is pursued immediately after its commission, or after an escape. If the person making the arrest is acting under the authority of a warrant, he must show the warrant, if required."[3]

The American Law Institute, in restating the common law, says:
"If a peace officer makes an arrest without a warrant, the fact that he is in uniform, or so displays his badge of office as to be reasonably visible to the other, is a sufficient manifestation that he is making an arrest upon suspicion of felony or for a breach of the peace or other conduct for which by common law or by statute he is authorized to arrest the other."[4]

More than this, however, is required by many of the statutes.[5]

---

(2) Use of Force

The authority to arrest carries with it the privilege of using reasonable force if necessary to accomplish this purpose. Unless the arrester has authority to make the particular arrest, any force used by him to effect the apprehension will be unlawful. Hence it is necessary to distinguish between the authority to arrest and the authority to use force in accomplishing the arrest. The general rule is that the arrester is privileged to use reasonable force in order to make an authorized arrest. It assumes lawful authority for the arrest itself, and states in substance that in making or attempting such an arrest the arrester is privileged to make use of reasonable force, and is not privileged to employ any greater degree of force. Hence an arrester acts unlawfully if he uses more than reasonable force in making or attempting an arrest, however much authority he might have for the arrest itself.

---

2. Restatement, Second, Torts § 128 (1965).

3. For example, see the statutes in California, Idaho, Iowa, Nevada and Utah.

4. Restatement, Second, Torts § 128, comment *d* (1965).

5. Ala.Code, tit. 15, § 155 (1940); West's Ann.Cal.Pen.Code, § 841; N.Y.Code Cr. Proc. § 180; Tenn.Code Ann. § 40–806 (1956).

The courts should not, as stated by a federal judge, "lay down rules which will make it so dangerous for officers to perform their duties that they will shrink and hesitate from action which the proper protection of society demands."[1] Hence in distinguishing the degree of force permitted for the purpose of making an arrest from that which is unlawful the question is not whether it exceeded the actual necessity in some slight way, but whether it was reasonable under all of the circumstances or grossly excessive.[2] To quote from a Missouri case: "An officer in making an arrest should use no unnecessary violence; but it being his duty to make an arrest, the law clothes him with the power to accomplish that result. His duty is to overcome all resistance and bring the party to be arrested under physical restraint and the means he may use must be co-extensive with the duty, and so the law is written."[3]

In a very general way it is said to be lawful to kill if necessary to arrest for felony but not if the person is to be arrested for a misdemeanor only.[4] Defensive force must be distinguished from force employed solely for the purpose of apprehension. The arrester, if placed in danger by the violence of the arrestee, may use whatever force reasonably seems necessary to save himself from death or great bodily harm,—and he may do this without abandoning the effort to arrest, and whether the arrest is for felony or misdemeanor.[5] "The officer must of necessity be the aggressor; his mission is not accomplished when he wards off the assault; he must press forward and accomplish his object, he is not bound to put off the arrest until a more favorable time. Because of these duties devolved upon him the law throws around him a special protection".[6] Hence he may "freely and without retreating repel force by force".[7]

The American Law Institute originally took the position that no one, officer or private person, with or without a warrant, is privileged to use deadly force merely to stop the flight of one whose arrest is sought for a nondangerous felony.[8] This was so obviously not a restatement of the law that the Institute felt obliged to amend the wording in 1948.[9] The modern common law does not authorize a

1. Stinnett v. Virginia, 55 F.2d 644, 647 (4th Cir. 1932).

2. "It is when excessive force has been used maliciously, or to such a degree as amounts to a wanton abuse of authority that criminal liability will be imputed." State v. Dunning, 177 N.C. 559, 562, 98 S.E. 530, 531 (1919).

3. State v. Fuller, 96 Mo. 165, 168, 9 S.W. 583, 584 (1888).

4. 1 Bishop, New Criminal Procedure § 159 (2d ed., Underhill, 1913). See note, Homicide by official action or by officers of justice, 67 L.R.A. 292 (1905).

5. Restatement, Second, Torts §§ 65, 131, comment d (1965).

6. State v. Dierberger, 96 Mo. 666, 675, 10 S.W. 168, 171 (1888); State v. Ford, 344 Mo. 1219, 130 S.W.2d 635 (1939).

7. Foster, Crown Law 321 (2d ed. 1791).

8. Restatement, Torts § 131 and particularly illustration 1 (1934).

9. Restatement, 1948 Supp. p. 628. See now Restatement, Second, Torts § 131 (1965).

private person to use deadly force to effect an arrest unless it is for a felony of violence such as murder, arson, rape, robbery, burglary or mayhem. But it authorizes a peace officer to use deadly force if this reasonably seems necessary in making an arrest for felony. This goes too far and the Model Penal Code would limit the use of deadly force to the officer who is arresting for felony and believes that the arrestee has used or threatened to use deadly force or will probably cause death or serious bodily harm if his apprehension is delayed. (Section 3.7(2) (b).

An apprehending officer has the privilege of taking reasonable steps to protect himself from harm and to prevent escape of his prisoner. Hence if he believes, and has reasonable grounds for believing, such precaution necessary, he may handcuff or otherwise manacle his prisoner. This privilege depends upon all of the facts of each particular case, and an officer would be acting unlawfully if he should handcuff one arrested on a minor traffic charge if there was no resistance and no other reason for believing handcuffing necessary.[10]

The mere fact that the arrest is on a traffic charge, however, or for some other relatively minor offense, is not of itself conclusive of the precautions the officer may take. An officer has been killed by one arrested on a minor traffic charge who happened to be a gangster wanted for murder although not recognized as such by the arrester. Hence an apprehending officer is entitled to consider not only the offense for which the arrest is made, but the prisoner himself—his reputation if known, and in any case his appearance and his conduct—together with any other facts which may indicate whether violence or attempted escape is to be expected.

If the arrest is for felony the officer is privileged to handcuff his prisoner even if there has been no actual resistance or attempt to escape or evidence indicating the probability of either.[11]

Ex parte Warner, 21 F.2d 542, 543 (N.D. Okl.1927); Stinnett v. Virginia, 55 F. 2d 644, 646–7 (4th Cir. 1932); Jackson v. State, 66 Miss. 89, 5 So. 690, 692 (1888); Thompson v. Norfolk & W. R. Co., 116 W.Va. 705, 182 S.E. 880, 883 (1935). The Warner case involved a violation of the prohibition law. In the Jackson case the court did not deem it necessary to disclose what the felony was but the inference is that it was larceny. In the Stinnett case the court expressly referred to the limitation suggested (to dangerous felonies) and held that this is not the common law.

10. 1 Wharton, Criminal Procedure § 102 (10th ed., Kerr, 1918).

11. "There must be some discretion reposed in a sheriff or other officer, making an arrest for felony, as to the means taken to apprehend the supposed offender, and to keep him safe and secure after such apprehension:" Firestone v. Rice, 71 Mich. 377, 384, 38 N.W. 885, 888 (1888).

"The sheriff cannot stop, when the man is unknown to him, at the moment of arrest, to inquire into his character, or his intentions as to escape, or his guilt or innocence of the offense charged against him. His duty is to take him, to safely keep him, and to bring his body before a magistrate. If he does this without wantonness or malice, it is not for a jury to find that his precautions were useless and unnecessary in the light of after-acquired knowledge of the true character and intent of the accused, and to punish the sheriff in damages for what honestly appeared to him at the time

(3) Breaking Doors and Windows

It was well settled at a very early day that an arrest for crime by the sheriff under a warrant could be made in the house of the arrestee himself, or in the house of another; that the apprehending officer could open doors or windows to gain entrance if they were not opened upon his proper demand; and that he could break open locks if necessary when keys were not furnished at his request. All of this followed from the fact that such an arrest (as distinguished from an arrest in a civil case which was not uncommon in that period) was in the King's name and no man can have a castle against the King.[1] The authority of an officer to break into a house, if necessary, to arrest for a felony committed in his presence was also well established.[2] Although not entirely free from doubt, the better view is that an officer had similar authority in making an arrest on reasonable suspicion of felony,[3] or in making such an arrest for a breach of the peace committed in his presence.[4] As stated by the Massachusetts court: "The authority of a constable to break open doors and arrest without a warrant is confined to cases where treason or felony has been committed, or there is an affray or a breach of the peace in his presence."[5] Since the common-law authority to arrest without a warrant was subject to exactly the same limits, it seems that the common-law authority of an officer to break doors if necessary to make an arrest was coextensive with his authority to arrest.[6]

---

to be reasonable and right." Id. at 387, 38 N.W., at 889.

"Where a private person undertakes to arrest a felon or an escaped felon, and has made his purpose and reason for the arrest known, he must then proceed in a peaceable manner to make the arrest, and if he is resisted he may use such force as is necessary to overcome the resistance, if used for that purpose alone." State v. Stancill, 128 N.C. 606, 610, 38 S.E. 926, 928 (1901).

As to the liability of a state officer who deals with his prisoner in such a way as to violate the prisoner's rights under the Fourteenth Amendment see Lynch v. United States, 189 F.2d 476 (5th Cir. 1951).

1. "[T]he liberty or privilege of a house doth not hold against the King." Semayne's Case, 5 Co.Rep. 91a, 92a, 77 Eng.Rep. 194, 197 (K.B. 1604).

2. A.L.I. Code of Criminal Procedure 253 (Official Draft with Commentaries, 1931).

3. 1 Hale P.C. *583; Commonwealth v. Phelps, 209 Mass. 396, 95 N.E. 868 (1911). Hawkins cautiously suggests that such authority "seems" to be lacking in an arrest of this nature. 2 Hawkins P.C., c. 14, § 7 (6th ed., Leach, 1788).

4. 1 Hawkins, P.C., c. 63, § 16 (6th ed., Leach, 1788); See McCullough v. Commonwealth, 67 Pa. 30, 32 (1870).

5. McLennon v. Richardson, 81 Mass. 74, 77 (1860).

6. 1 Bishop, New Criminal Procedure §§ 196, 203 (2d. ed., Underhill, 1913). The Supreme Court seems to hold that an express statement of authority and purpose to arrest is a pre-requisite to the breaking of doors to accomplish this and even if the arrestee recognizes the officers and is aware of their purpose. Miller v. United States, 357 U.S. 301, 78 S.Ct. 1190 (1958).

The authority of a private person was not so broad. He was privileged to break doors to make an arrest only for a felony committed in his presence.[7] And the reason for this difference, explains Lord Hale, is that an arrest by a private person (in a proper case) is merely permitted whereas it is a matter of legal duty in the case of an officer.[8]

As to breaking open doors and windows, assuming this to be necessary to reach the place where the person to be arrested is, or is reasonably supposed to be, and that authority and purpose have been announced and admission demanded without avail, the common-law rule (where unchanged by statute) is this: If the building is *not* a dwelling house, the authority to arrest includes the authority to enter by force;[9] an officer seeking to arrest for any crime, either in obedience to a warrant or under lawful authority to arrest without a warrant,[10] may break doors or windows even of a dwelling house; a private person may break such doors or windows to make an arrest for a felony committed in his presence, but not to make an original arrest on probable cause for a felony committed elsewhere or for a misdemeanor;[11] any person may do so to recapture one who has escaped from his lawful custody;[12] and one who has lawfully entered a house for the purpose of making an arrest may break out if he is locked in.[13]

The statutes are variously worded. In some jurisdictions the authority of an officer to break doors or windows is limited by express enactment to (1) an arrest under a warrant or (2) an authorized arrest for felony without a warrant,[14] and in one state, at least, the authority does not apply to arrests for misdemeanor, with or without a warrant.[15] More frequently the statutory provisions codify what seems to be the common law on this point by according this privilege to the officer whenever he has lawful authority to arrest for crime,

---

7. 4 Bl.Comm. *293; Brooks v. Commonwealth, 61 Pa. 352 (1869).

8. 2 Hale P.C. *92.

9. 1 Bishop, op. cit. supra note 6, § 194.

10. An officer may not break into a house to execute civil process except to rearrest one who has escaped from his lawful custody. To arrest for crime he may break into the dwelling house, if necessary. 1 Bishop, op. cit. supra note 6, §§ 196, 203. If the arrest is without a warrant, for a misdemeanor not amounting to a breach of the peace, under statutes which have extended the authority of an officer to arrest without a warrant to include such a case but are silent as to authority to break doors, if necessary, the point is not free from question. Bishop's statement seems a logical conclusion. Since the common-law authority of an officer to break doors, if necessary, to arrest for crime was coextensive with his authority to make the arrest itself, a statute extending his authority to arrest should carry this incident with it unless denied by the same or some other statute.

11. A.L.I. Code of Criminal Procedure 255 (Official Draft with Commentaries, 1931).

12. Restatement, Second, Torts § 129, comment *d*, 135(2) (1965); 1 Bishop, op. cit. supra note 6, § 203.

13. 1 Bishop, op. cit. supra note 6, § 202.

14. Louisiana and Michigan.

15. Texas.

whether with or without a warrant—assuming this to be necessary after notice of authority and purpose, and a demand for admission.[16]

So far as private persons are concerned the statutes are almost unanimous in limiting this authority to felony cases; some keep it as at common law restricted to arrests for felony committed in the presence of the arrester;[17] while many more extend it to all cases in which the private person has lawful authority to arrest for felony.[18]

---

(4) Search of Prisoner

The common law authorizes any person making a lawful arrest to search the arrestee (unless such a search is obviously uncalled for) and to take from him any (a) offensive weapons or articles that might be useful in effecting an escape, or (b) fruits of the crime for which he was arrested or other evidence tending to prove him guilty thereof.[1] A very large discretion is extended to the arrester in this regard, particularly if he is an officer. Thus it has been held that an officer may remove the clothing of his prisoner if this is necessary under the circumstances for an effective search of his person.[2] Reasonable doubts must be resolved in favor of the officer, but obviously unreasonable steps must be avoided. It has been held, for example, that a male officer exceeded his privilege, after an arrest of a servant girl, on a charge of larceny, by requiring her to strip and stand naked before him.[3] Such procedure should be left to the police matron,—or to some matron called upon to assist the officer for this special purpose, if no police matron is available.

In extreme cases, where it is quite obvious that nothing properly to be seized would be disclosed, the mere search of an arrestee might be held unlawful. This should be limited to a situation in which the search was obviously to embarrass the arrestee and not in the expectation of finding anything subject to be seized.

---

16. Alabama, Arizona, Arkansas, California, Idaho, Iowa, Kentucky, Minnesota, Mississippi, Missouri, Montana, Nevada, New York, North Carolina, North Dakota, Oklahoma, Oregon, South Dakota, Tennessee, Utah, Washington.

17. Arizona, Louisiana, Michigan, North Dakota.

18. Alabama, California, Idaho, Iowa, Minnesota, Mississippi, Montana, Nevada, North Carolina, Oklahoma, South Dakota, Tennessee, Utah.

1. Hughes v. State, 145 Tenn. 544, 238 S.W. 588 (1922); Harris v. United States, 331 U.S. 145, 67 S.Ct. 1098, 91 L.Ed. 1399 (1947); Fischer v. State, 195 Md. 477, 74 A.2d 34 (1950).

2. "We think that the coroner, the sheriff, or a policeman, when he arrests a person charged with crime, has a right to search that person for evidences of his guilt, and if, in the prosecution of this search, it becomes necessary to remove the clothing of such person, the officer has a right to do so, . . ." Woolfolk v. State, 81 Ga. 551, 562, 8 S.E. 724, 728 (1889).

3. Hebrew v. Pulis, 73 N.J.L. 621, 64 A. 121 (1906). The girl was not under technical arrest when the search was ordered; however the court stated, "But, even if the case had been such that the officer would have been justified in arresting without a warrant, we think he was not justified in compelling the plaintiff to strip naked." 625, 64 Atl. at 122.

Few of the statutes express the full scope of the common law privilege of search and seizure incidental to a lawful arrest.[4] Many of the codes have no provision on the subject thus leaving it entirely to the common law. As said by the Missouri court: "We find no statute of this State giving the arresting officer authority to search a prisoner, but no statute is necessary. The power exists from the nature and objects of the public duty the officer is required to perform. Such authority is directly given to a committing magistrate by statute (section 4308), but unless the arresting officer has the authority immediately, on making the arrest, all evidence of crime and of identification of the criminal might be destroyed before the prisoner could be taken before the magistrate."[5]

Some of the statutes express part only of the common-law authority, such as this: "Any person making a lawful arrest may take from the person arrested all offensive weapons which he may have about his person and shall deliver them to the magistrate before whom he is taken."[6] "We do not think," said the Iowa court, "that an officer making an arrest is precluded by this statute from taking from the person of the prisoner any property other than 'offensive weapons.'"[7]

(5) The "Frisk"

It is common practice for an officer to pass his hands over the clothing of an arrestee in order to determine quickly whether or not

---

4. The Michigan statute provides for taking from the arrestee "all offensive weapons or incriminating articles," which seems to cover the field. Mich. Stats.Ann. § 28.884 (1954).

5. Holker v. Hennessey, 141 Mo. 527, 540, 42 S.W. 1090, 1093 (1897).

6. Such a provision, in substance, is found in the statutes of Arizona, California, Idaho, Iowa, Montana, Nevada, North Dakota, Oklahoma, South Dakota and Utah.

7. Commercial Exchange Bank v. McLeod, 65 Iowa 665, 667, 19 N.W. 329 (1884), 22 N.W. 919 (1885).

"It is a general rule that whenever officers have authority to conduct a search, their search can extend to portable effects, such as the contents of baggage, box, or bundle." Wright v. State, 177 Md. 230, 233, 9 A.2d 253, 255 (1939).

It may extend to the automobile the arrestee is driving at the time of the arrest. Arthur v. State, 227 Ind. 493, 86 N.E.2d 698 (1950); State v. Ragland, 171 Kan. 530, 233 P.2d 740 (1951); Callahan v. State, 42 Okl.Cr. 425, 276 P. 494 (1929); Fuqua v. State, 175 Tenn. 11, 130 S.W.2d 125 (1939).

Search of a house in which the arrest is made: United States v. Rabinowitz, 339 U.S. 56, 70 S.Ct. 430, 94 L.Ed. 653 (1950); Harris v. United States, 331 U.S. 145, 67 S.Ct. 1098, 91 L.Ed. 1399 (1947); People v. Conway, 225 Mich. 152, 195 N.W. 679 (1923); State v. Carenza, 357 Mo. 1172, 212 S.W.2d 743 (1948).

The search of D's home was not an incident to his arrest on the street nearly two blocks away and it was constitutional error to admit the fruits of this illegal search into evidence at his state court trial. James v. Louisiana, 382 U.S. 36, 86 S.Ct. 151, 15 L. Ed.2d 30 (1965).

As to the involuntary use of the stomach pump to obtain evidence see Rochin v. California, 342 U.S. 165, 72 S.Ct. 205, 96 L.Ed. 183 (1952).

any deadly weapons are concealed there. This is known as the "frisk." In one case a "frisk" may be preliminary to a thorough search; in another it may satisfy the officer that no more is needed. A "frisk" following a lawful arrest is clearly privileged—unless it is an arrest on a minor charge under circumstances showing plainly no reason for any search at all. The important question is whether "frisking" one who has not been arrested may be privileged in extreme situations.

The law dealing with the privilege of an officer to touch the person of another had its development before the invention of a tiny deadly weapon which might be concealed in the pocket and fired without even being removed therefrom. And rules quite suitable for the day when an armed man carried a sword or a "blunderbuss," plain for everyone to see, do not give the officer adequate opportunity to protect himself against a gangster armed with a concealed weapon.

Since the constitutional bar is only against unreasonable searches and seizures it would clearly not prohibit a "frisk" *reasonably* necessary for the officer's own protection. Such authority could be granted by statute and the uniform "Arrest Act", drafted by the Interstate Commission on Crime, includes a section which will authorize a peace officer, whenever he reasonably believes it necessary for his own protection, to "frisk" for dangerous weapons any person he is lawfully questioning as a criminal suspect.[1] Even without such a statute, since the common law is a living, growing body of rules rather than a dead thing, the courts might well hold that a "frisk" is privileged by common law whenever it is reasonably necessary for an officer to resort to this measure in order properly to perform his duty to the community without unreasonable risk to himself.[2]

---

(6) "Held for Questioning"

There is no authority (without consent or special statute) to lock a man in jail for questioning or for investigation if the circumstances are not sufficient to arrest him on a criminal charge, except that a court or magistrate may be authorized to commit a material

---

[1]. "A peace officer may search for a dangerous weapon any person whom he has stopped to question as provided in section 2, whenever he has reasonable ground to believe that he is in danger if the person possesses a dangerous weapon." The Uniform Arrest Act, § 3.

[2]. Gisske v. Sanders, 9 Cal.App. 13, 98 P. 43 (1908); People v. Didonna, 124 Misc. 872, 210 N.Y.S. 135 (Sp.Sess. 1925). Contra: People v. Beach, 49 Colo. 516, 113 P. 513 (1911); State v. McDaniel, 115 Or. 187, 231 P. 965 (1925).

See particularly People v. Rivera, 14 N.Y.2d 441, 252 N.Y.S.2d 458, 201 N.E.2d 32 (1964), certiorari denied 379 U.S. 978, 85 S.Ct. 679, 13 L.Ed.2d 568 (1965); People v. Pugach, 15 N.Y.2d 65, 255 N.Y.S.2d 833, 204 N.E.2d 176 (1964), certiorari denied 380 U.S. 936, 85 S.Ct. 946 (1965).

witness in a criminal case who refuses to enter into an undertaking to appear and testify in court after having been directed to do so.[1]

Under our system of justice no person is bound to incriminate himself, but there is no immunity which entitles a mere witness to refuse to give information relative to the guilt of some one else, unless there is some special protection in the particular case, as for example where the two are husband and wife.[2] Anciently, witnesses were punishable for a failure to give to officers outside of the courtroom, information of any felony known to them.[3] While this is not common at the present time it is still the right of the officer to demand such information, and the duty of the citizen to answer fully so long as what he says does not tend to incriminate himself or his spouse, or improperly to divulge a privileged communication.[4] The temporary detention of one being questioned for information in regard to a crime is not an arrest on the one hand, and if properly conducted is not unlawful, on the other.[5]

The "Arrest Act," drafted by the Interstate Commission on Crime includes a provision under which a peace officer may question any person abroad whom he has reason to suspect of committing a crime

---

1. Markwell v. Warren County, 53 Iowa 422, 5 N.W. 570 (1880).

2. Jin Fuey Moy v. United States, 254 U.S. 189, 41 S.Ct. 98, 65 L.Ed. 214 (1920).

3. 4 Bl.Comm. *119–21.

4. "The duty of every good citizen is, when called upon, to give all information in his power to the proper officers of the law as to persons connected with crime (Miller v. Fano, 134 Cal. 106, 66 P. 183; and this should be held to require that all proper information be given upon request of a personal nature, as affecting the one of whom inquiry is made, when the circumstances are such as to warrant an officer in making inquiry." Gisske v. Sanders, 9 Cal.App. 13, 16, 98 P. 43, 44–5 (1908). Accord, United States v. First National Bank of Mobile, 67 F.Supp. 616, 625 (S.D.Ala.1946).

5. "In Henry v. United States, 361 U. S. 98, 103 [80 S.Ct. 168, 4 L.Ed.2d 134, 139], the United States Supreme Court held that an arrest occurs when an automobile is stopped during a course of a criminal investigation. . . . In this state, however, we have consistently held that circumstances short of probable cause to make an arrest may still justify an officer's stopping pedestrians or motorists on the streets for questioning. If the circumstances warrant it, he may in self-protection request a suspect to alight from an automobile or to submit to a superficial search for concealed weapons. Should the investigation then reveal probable cause to make an arrest, the officer may arrest the suspect and conduct a reasonable incidental search. . . . We do not believe that our rule permitting temporary detention for questioning conflicts with the Fourth Amendment." People v. Mickelson, 59 Cal.2d 448, 450–51, 452, 30 Cal.Rptr. 18, 380 P.2d 658 (1963).

One who willingly accompanies officers to police headquarters and talks with them freely in the belief that he will be able to beguile them into exculpating him, is not under arrest. United States v. Vita, 294 F.2d 524 (2d Cir. 1961), certiorari denied 369 U.S. 823, 82 S.Ct. 837, 7 L.Ed.2d 788 (1962). Compare a case in which under somewhat similar facts it was held that a 19-year-old D considered that he was under restraint and therefore was under arrest. Seals v. United States, 117 U.S.App.D.C. 79, 325 F.2d 1006 (1963), certiorari denied 376 U.S. 964, 84 S.Ct. 1123, 11 L.Ed.2d 982 (1964).

See supra, under What Constitutes Arrest.

Sec. 1   *STEPS PRIOR TO INDICTMENT*   815

and may demand of him his name, address, business abroad and whither he is going. If such person does not satisfactorily identify himself and explain his actions, the officer shall have authority to detain him for two hours or less for further questioning and investigation.[6]

A few states have special statutes authorizing *arrest* on suspicion under certain conditions.[7]

(7) Disposition of Prisoner

Since the purpose of lawful arrest is to take the prisoner before a magistrate, court, body or official or otherwise secure the administration of the law, this is exactly what must be done. And even if an arrest is lawful when made the detention of the prisoner will become unlawful if this disposition is not made with reasonable promptness.

If the arrest is in obedience to a warrant the disposition of the prisoner will be directed therein, and this direction must be obeyed [a] unless the statute requires otherwise in some special situation. For example, if the warrant follows the familiar pattern it will command the officer to arrest the person named and take him before the issuing magistrate or some other magistrate of the same county. But a statute of the state may require that if the arrest is for a misdemeanor and is in a county other than that in which the warrant was issued, the officer *must*, upon request, take the prisoner before some magistrate or official of the county in which the arrest was made, to give him an opportunity to furnish bail there.[b]

If the arrest is without a warrant the arrester must, without unreasonable delay, take the prisoner before a magistrate of the county

6. The Uniform Arrest Act, § 2.

7. ". . . During the night time they (police officers) may examine all persons abroad whom they have reason to suspect of unlawful design, and may demand of them their business abroad and whither they are going; . . . Persons so suspected who do not give a satisfactory account of themselves . . . may be arrested by the police. . . ." Mass.Ann. Laws, c. 41, § 98 (Michie, 1944).

In New Hampshire the Uniform Arrest Act, note 5 supra, has been adopted, but the period of detention was extended to four hours: N.H.Rev.Laws, § 594.2 (1955). This act has also been adopted in Rhode Island: R.I.Pub. Laws 1941, c. 982.

"The municipal authorities of towns and cities may establish rules authorizing the arrest, without warrant, of persons found in suspicious places, and under circumstances which reasonably show that such persons have been guilty of some felony or breach of the peace, or threaten, or are about to commit some offense against the laws." Vernon's Ann.Tex.Code Cr. Proc. art. 214.

a. 2 Hale P.C. *119.

b. Iowa Code Ann. § 757.3.

in which the arrest is made.ᶜ The cases often speak of the arrester's duty in such terms as that he must take the prisoner before the magistrate "immediately" or "forthwith." ᵈ On the other hand, delay may be unavoidable, and hence unlawfulness at this point arises not from delay as such, but from unreasonable delay.ᵉ If an arrest is made at night, at an hour when the normal facilities for obtaining bail are not available, and the arrest itself is quite reasonable under the circumstances, the prisoner may be locked up for the night, and taken before the magistrate at a reasonable hour in the morning.ᶠ

---

(8) Rights and Duties of Arrestee

It is the duty of every person, whether guilty of any offense or not, to submit to arrest if the one arresting is duly authorized to do so under the circumstances and the arrest is made in a lawful manner.[1] An arrest which is unauthorized or is made in an unlawful manner may be resisted [2] unless there has been some statutory change in this regard such as is mentioned below. Where one has reason to believe that an unlawful attempt is being made to convey him by force beyond the reach of the law, or to carry him out of the country, he is justified in resisting, even to the death of his adversary if that becomes necessary.[3] But a man is not justified if he intentionally kills in defense against an illegal arrest of ordinary character.[4]

An unlawful arrest, however, may be such provocation as will reduce a killing in the resistance of such an arrest to manslaughter.[5]

---

c. If there is such great excitement at the time and place of arrest as to indicate the possibility of mob action there the arresting officer is privileged to carry the prisoner before a magistrate of some other county. Wiggins v. Norton, 83 Ga. 148, 9 S.E. 607 (1889).

d. Rutledge v. Rowland, 161 Ala. 114, 126–7, 49 So. 461, 466 (1909); Hogg v. Lorenz, 234 Ky. 751, 754, 29 S.W. 2d 17, 18 (1930).

e. Oxford v. Berry, 204 Mich. 197, 170 N.W. 83 (1918); State v. Freeman, 86 N.C. 683 (1882).

f. Ibid.; King v. Robertson, 227 Ala. 378, 150 So. 154 (1933); Tschuor v. Meck, 72 Ariz. 200, 232 P.2d 848 (1951).

1. King v. State, 89 Ala. 43, 8 So. 120 (1890).

2. "He [the officer] has no protection from his office, or from the fact that the other is an offender." 1 Bishop, Criminal Law § 868 (9th ed. 1923). As to the change made by the Uniform Arrest Act see footnote 6.

3. Ibid.

4. In resisting an unlawful arrest the citizen is not justified in taking the life of the trespasser, unless it is necessary to save his own life or to save his person from great bodily harm. Creighton v. Commonwealth, 84 Ky. 103 (1886).

5. Rex v. Chapman, 12 Cox C.C. 4 (1871). See note, Homicide in resisting arrest, 66 L.R.A. 353 (1905).
"And it is too well settled to be discussed, that an assault and resisting one in the execution of any authority or power, is indictable at common law." State v. Downer, 8 Vt. 424, 429 (1836).

An important change in regard to the privilege of resisting arrest is found in certain recent statutes such as the following:

"If a person has knowledge, or by the exercise of reasonable care, should have knowledge, that he is being arrested by a peace officer, it is the duty of such person to refrain from using force or any weapon to resist such arrest".[6]

No such provision is needed where the arrest is lawful because it has always been illegal to resist a lawful arrest. The purpose of such a provision is to impose upon the citizen a duty to submit to apprehension by a known officer, even if the latter is actually exceeding his authority, and seek redress in the courts, rather than to resort to self-help.[7] The arrestee's belief that the arrest is in excess of the officer's authority, it may be added, is often a mistaken notion and this provision discourages the attempt to settle such a dispute by force.

(vi) THE THIRD DEGREE

Any force or violence used for the purpose of extorting a confession from a prisoner is unlawful. The confession so obtained is not admissible in evidence,[1] and the officer who employed such force is guilty of assault and battery. He may be liable under the federal "Civil Rights Act,"[2] or under the corresponding provision of the federal criminal code.[3]

The Supreme Court has held that "real evidence" obtained from a defendant by the violent use of a stomach pump, to which he did not consent, may not be used to convict him even in a state court, because of the due process clause.[4]

---

6. West's Ann.Cal.Pen.Code, § 834a (1957 amendt.). This was adapted from section 5 of the Uniform Arrest Act. And see Model Penal Code Sec. 3.04(2) (a) (i).

7. See Warner, The Uniform Arrest Act, 28 Va.Law Rev. 315, 330–31 (1942).

1. Ammons v. State, 80 Miss. 592, 32 So. 9 (1902).

2. 8 U.S.C.A. § 43 (1946); Refoule v. Ellis, 74 F.Supp. 336 (N.D.Ga.1947). The federal courts have jurisdiction over suits brought under this section without allegation or proof of any jurisdictional amount. Douglas v. City of Jeannette, 319 U.S. 157, 63 S.Ct. 877, 87 L.Ed. 1324 (1943).

For an extensive review of the Civil Rights Act, see Note, 43 Ill.L.Rev. 105 (1948).

3. 18 U.S.C.A. § 242 (1948); Screws v. United States, 325 U.S. 91, 65 S.Ct. 1031, 89 L.Ed. 1495 (1945); Williams v. United States, 341 U.S. 97, 71 S.Ct. 576, 95 L.Ed. 774 (1951).

4. Rochin v. California, 342 U.S. 382, 72 S.Ct. 205, 96 L.Ed. 183 (1952).

(E) SUMMONS

The primitive method of bringing a defendant into court was by force, but as civilization advances there is an increasing tendency to procure his presence by persuasion whenever such procedure seems reasonably adequate for the purpose. Although almost forgotten now, arrest was anciently the normal procedure for procuring the presence of the defendant in a civil case.[1] Such usage has become so nearly obsolete that it is greatly restricted [2] if not entirely prohibited.[3] It is almost as absurd to rely upon arrest as the normal procedure in cases of minor infractions as it would be to do so in civil proceedings.

"It is provided by statute in England that upon complaint made of the commission of any offense the justice may, if he think fit, issue a summons instead of a warrant of arrest; and upon the failure of the person summoned to appear the justice may issue a warrant of arrest. 11 & 12 Vict. ch. 42, sec. 1.

"The summons is frequently used in England, even in felony cases if the magistrate is satisfied the person summoned will appear." [4]

The use of a summons on such a broad basis seems not to be authorized in any of the states of this country. In the relatively few jurisdictions in which this type of procedure is recognized by state law it is limited to misdemeanors (and usually to certain specified misdemeanors, determined by type or penalty), to violations of municipal ordinances, to offenses by juveniles, or to some combination of these.[5] One of the urgent needs for the improvement of the machinery of law enforcement is the enlarged use of the summons in lieu of

---

1. One author has insisted that a "discriminating and scholarly use of these terms" limits the words "arrest" and "arrested" to civil cases and employs "apprehend" and "apprehension" in criminal proceedings. 1 Wharton, Criminal Procedure, § 1 (10th ed., Kerr, 1918).

2. "No person shall be imprisoned for debt arising out of, or founded on a contract, express or implied, except in cases of fraud or breach of trust, ..." Mich.Const. Art. II, § 20.

3. Tenn.Code Ann. § 20–201 (1956).

4. A.L.I.Code of Criminal Procedure 217 (Official Draft with Commentaries, 1931).

5. Misdemeanors in general—Ohio.

Misdemeanors, after indictment or presentment—West Virginia.

Specified misdemeanors—New York—Pennsylvania.

Misdemeanors within jurisdiction of magistrate—Arkansas, Kentucky, Maryland.

Misdemeanors with specified limits as to penalty—Massachusetts—Virginia.

Violation of municipal ordinances—Colorado, Illinois, New Jersey.

Offenses by juveniles—Massachusetts.

arrest in all cases in which there is reason to believe it will be effective in having the defendant in court at the proper time.[6]

The greatest use of procedure of this general nature, in other than civil cases, has resulted from an extra-legal device,—the traffic ticket. While this special type of "summons" is strictly legal now as a result of municipal ordinance or state law [7] it seems to have had its origin and early development as a result of police practice in certain communities with no legislative foundation whatever.

The traffic "ticket" is not a true summons because it is not a writ issued by a court or magistrate. It is usually either a "notice" issued by the officer to the motorist, that he will be arrested if he does not appear, or it is an agreement, signed by the motorist, that he will do so. Some statutes or ordinances have provided for the release of a traffic violator, *after* arrest, by this device, but a much better provision authorizes the officer who has stopped such a motorist to release him *without* arrest if he will *agree* to appear voluntarily. The average traffic violator is not a "criminal" in any sense of the word, and anything which seems to place him in that category not only does him an injustice but is likely to confuse the attitude of the public toward those who commit true crimes.

The use of the traffic "ticket" saves so much time for the officer himself that the employment of some similar device might well be authorized for other cases of minor infractions where the of-

---

6. The American Law Institute, Code of Criminal Procedure, includes the following sections:

Section 12. *When summons shall be issued.* (1) Where the complaint is for the commission of an offense which the magistrate is empowered to try summarily he shall issue a summons instead of a warrant of arrest, unless he has reasonable ground to believe that the person against whom the complaint was made will not appear upon a summons, in which case he shall issue a warrant of arrest.

(2) Where the complaint is for a misdemeanor, which the magistrate is not empowered to try summarily, he shall issue a summons instead of a warrant of arrest, if he has reasonable ground to believe that the person against whom the complaint was made will appear upon a summons.

(3) The summons shall set forth substantially the nature of the offense, and shall command the person against whom the complaint was made to appear before the magistrate issuing the summons at a time and place stated therein.

Section 13. *How summons served.* The summons may be served in the same manner as the summons in a civil action.

Section 14. *Effect of not answering summons.* If a person summoned fails, without good cause, to appear as commanded by the summons, he shall be considered in contempt of court, and may be punished by a fine of not more than twenty dollars. Upon such failure to appear, the magistrate shall issue a warrant of arrest. If after issuing a summons the magistrate becomes satisfied that the person summoned will not appear as commanded by the summons he may at once issue a warrant of arrest.

7. Iowa Code Ann. § 321.485 (1946).

Rule 4(a) of the Federal Rules of Criminal Procedure reads:

"(a) Issuance. . . . Upon request of the attorney for the government a summons instead of a warrant shall issue. . . ."

fender is known or can be easily identified and the circumstances are sufficient to justify the conclusion that no more drastic step is needed.

(F) SUMMARY TRIAL AND PRELIMINARY EXAMINATION

Under English statutes, old enough to be common law in this country, magistrates were authorized to try certain petty offenses, without waiting for an indictment by the grand jury and without calling in the aid of a trial jury. Such a proceeding was spoken of as a summary trial. In this country magistrates, or other inferior courts, are authorized to try certain petty offenses without waiting for an indictment by the grand jury. And it is convenient to speak of these as "summary trials" although in many of them the defendant may demand a jury trial if he sees fit to do so.

The summary trial of a petty offense is quite different from a preliminary hearing or examination, although the two are sometimes confused by the layman. In a summary trial the magistrate is making a determination of guilt or innocence, and this determination is final unless an appeal is taken from a judgment of conviction. In a preliminary hearing or examination the magistrate has no power to make the determination of guilt or innocence and is merely called upon to determine whether there is sufficient ground to bind the defendant over to trial by a higher court. Sufficient ground to bind him over is found if it appears from the examination that a public offense, triable by a higher court, has been committed, and there is probable cause for believing the defendant guilty thereof.[1]

Two early English statutes [2] provided that the magistrate before whom a person was brought charged with felony, "shall take the examination of such prisoner and information of those that bring him, of the fact and circumstances thereof, and the same or as much thereof as shall be material to prove the felony, shall be put in writing within two days after the said examination." [3]

Under these statutes it was the practice of magistrates, for several centuries, to conduct secret inquisitions in which the accused, as well as others, was interrogated. In the early part of the nineteenth century this inquisitorial practice gave way in England to the custom of giving the accused the opportunity of making a voluntary statement after being cautioned that it might be used in evidence

---

1. People v. Sears, 124 Cal.App.2d 839, 269 P.2d 683 (1954).

2. 1 and 2 Phil. and M., c. 13, sec. 4 (1554); 2 and 3 Phil. and M., c. 10, sec. 2 (1555).

3. A.L.I.Code of Criminal Procedure 266 (Official Draft with Commentaries, 1931).

against him. This practice was crystallized in the statute of 1848 [4] which provided that the examination of all witnesses for the prosecution should precede this opportunity given to the accused, after caution, to make a voluntary statement if he should so desire.

Provisions against self-incrimination would prevent any inquisitorial practice in this country which included any pressure to compel the accused to answer questions. A rather common statutory provision is in substance as follows:

"When the accused is brought before the magistrate upon an arrest, either with or without a warrant, on a charge of having committed a public offense which the magistrate is not competent to try and determine, the magistrate shall immediately inform him of the charge against him, and of his right to the aid of counsel in every stage of the proceedings." [5]

The rights of an accused receive special attention in Chapter 13.

(G) DISCHARGE, COMMITMENT AND BAIL

If, as a result of a summary trial for a petty offense the defendant is acquitted, he must be discharged immediately and has the benefit of the rules of former jeopardy. But if the discharge is because, on preliminary examination, the magistrate does not find that an offense was committed, or finds that an offense was committed but that there is not sufficient reason to believe defendant guilty thereof, there has been no acquittal and the rules of former jeopardy do not apply. If as a result of a summary trial the defendant is found guilty (or if he entered a plea of guilty instead of standing trial) the magistrate renders such judgment as the case may require. And unless an appeal is taken this judgment is executed by an appropriate officer. When, as a result of a preliminary examination, the defendant is bound over to answer the charge filed against him,[1] he is admitted to bail unless the offense is not bailable. If the offense is not bailable, or defendant is unable to give bail, the defendant is committed to jail to await trial in the higher court.

---

4. 11 and 12 Vict., ch. 42, sec. 18. See now the Criminal Practice Act of 1925, 15 and 16 Geo.V., ch. 86, sec. 12.

5. See the statutes of Arizona, Arkansas, Idaho, Iowa, Kentucky, Missouri, Montana, Nevada, New Mexico, New York, North Dakota, Ohio, Oklahoma, Oregon, Tennessee. The right to a preliminary examination may be waived. Flowers v. State, 95 Okl.Cr. 27, 238 P.2d 841 (1951).

1. If the magistrate has jurisdiction over the subject matter he may bind the defendant over even if the complaint is insufficient as a matter of law. Tschuor v. Meck, 72 Ariz. 200, 232 P.2d 848 (1951).

All that is required to hold a defendant to answer to the superior court is a reasonable probability of guilt. People v. Platt, 124 Cal.App.2d 123, 268 P.2d 529 (1954).

SECTION 2. THE INDICTMENT OR INFORMATION

(A) THE GRAND JURY

The grand jury, one of the ancient English institutions, is a body of persons summoned from all parts of the county to pass upon accusations of crime therein. The number was variable at common law, but could not exceed twenty-three nor be less than twelve. It could not be less than twelve because a common-law indictment required the favorable vote of twelve grand jurors. It could not exceed twenty-three because the requirement of unanimity was limited to the trial jury and had no application to the grand jury. Since the vote of twelve grand jurors was sufficient to find an indictment it would not do to permit a body of such size that an indictment could be found although as many, or more, voted against than in favor. Some statutes have reduced the size of the grand jury and have substituted a new requirement as to the number of votes needed to find an indictment. Proceedings before the grand jury are secret except that some statutes permit a court to order public sessions of the grand jury when the subject matter of its investigation is one affecting the general public welfare,—such as corruption in public office or dereliction of duty by public officials.

A bill of indictment is a written accusation of crime submitted to the grand jury for its consideration. In this country this bill ordinarily is drawn by a prosecuting attorney, whose title varies from jurisdiction to jurisdiction, the more common being "district attorney," "county attorney," or in the federal system, "United States attorney." If this bill of indictment is found by the grand jury to be a "true bill," and is duly presented by them as such, it then becomes an indictment and the accused stands indicted. If the required number of grand jurors do not vote that the bill of indictment shall be found to be a true bill, the grand jury is said to "ignore" it. Such a bill does not become an indictment and the accused is not indicted.

If the grand jurors of their own knowledge, or of their own motion on information from others, take notice of a public offense, this is spoken of as a "presentment." In some jurisdictions such a presentment has been held sufficient to support a prosecution. The common practice, on the other hand, is for this presentment to be regarded as a mere instruction to the prosecuting attorney to draw a bill of indictment. Such a bill is submitted to the grand jury, the same as any other bill of indictment, and if found to be a true bill it becomes the basis of the prosecution.

Sec. 2   *THE INDICTMENT OR INFORMATION*   823

(B) THE INDICTMENT *

The legal mind of the sixteen and seventeen hundreds, together with other more worthy accomplishments, was master of the art of making two words grow where only one had ever been seen before. This art was applied with unusual diligence in the drawing of indictments and with the accretion of generations such pleadings became increasingly cumbersome. The ancient theory required every essential element of the offense charged to be stated directly and positively in the indictment and permitted no omission to be cured or aided by inference or intendment. So rigid were the requirements of technical exactness that many guilty defendants escaped on the most subtle distinctions.

Back of the apparent absurdity in these decisions there was in the beginning a useful purpose which was subsequently lost sight of entirely. Blackstone lamented the existence, in his day, of one hundred and sixty capital offenses. In the face of such atrocious severity of punishment one might well expect to find humane judges searching for technicalities merely to save miserable offenders from penalties which were outrageously excessive in particular cases. This practice seems not to have been uncommon. Furthermore, the procedure was scarcely less barbarous than the penalties. This was in the days when one who stubbornly refused to plead did not have a plea of not guilty entered for him. It was even prior to the time when a plea of guilty was entered in such a case. The practice then was to pass judgment that he suffer *peine fort et dure* by which he was slowly starved and crushed to death if his obstinancy continued. It is not surprising to find, associated with such methods, a procedure which did not permit the defendant to see the indictment or to have a copy of it, but forced him to rely entirely upon what he could gather from having the pleading read to him.[1] This was his sole source of information relative to the charge against him prior to the introduction of evidence in the trial itself. It was only natural for such rigorous procedure to receive an interpretation and application which was harsh from the standpoint of pleaders but mitigating so far as defendants were concerned. And when a judge occasionally went farther and required some mere evidentiary fact to be included in the indictment, it was not because this is required by good pleading (which in fact forbids it) but rather because a humane impulse had been forced to crack a piece of judicial machinery which would not yield otherwise to the proper administra-

---

* In part this section is adapted, by permission, from an article by the compiler of these cases, entitled "Short Indictments and Informations," 15 American Bar Association Journal 292, and to some extent from an article entitled "The Short Indictment Act," 14 Iowa Law Review 385.

1. Chitty, Criminal Law, 403.

tion of justice in the particular case. Unfortunately, however, every such decision became a precedent for all future cases, even after undue severity had been eliminated from the penal provisions and unreasonable harshness had been removed from the procedure itself. For every defendant who had been saved from paying the death penalty for some trivial offense by legalistic acumen, there remained an additional word, clause or phrase which all future indictments for such offenses would have to contain. More and more such pleadings became complicated and formidable. These fossilized relics of the age of punitive savagery were brought over to this country. Even the commonsense pioneers accepted them as a matter of course. Thus in a decision handed down in the middle of the last century,[2] reference is made to an indictment containing eight counts, only one of which is set forth in the opinion. This one contains over five hundred words. If the others were of equal length, as is more than probable, the entire pleading ran well over four thousand words. And the purpose of all this wilderness of language was merely to charge the defendants with the murder of Boyd Wilkinson.

The impetus in the direction of insisting upon technical perfection in criminal pleading—of "trying the record" instead of the defendant—not only outlived the original underlying purpose of serving as a safeguard against over-severity of punishment, but was carried to its most absurd extremes after the need for such manipulation had vanished. An outstanding example of justice being completely submerged in the formalism of the proceedings, is State v. Campbell, decided in 1907.[3] In this case a conviction of rape was reversed because the concluding sentence of the indictment was "against the peace and dignity of State" whereas the court held it should have been "against the peace and dignity of *the* State." Another verdict of guilty was set at naught because the indictment concluded "against the peace and dignity of the State of W. Virginia," the court being of the opinion that the word *West* should have been written in full.[4] Another classic, this time in the field of technical variance, is the case in which a conviction of stealing a pair of shoes was reversed because the proof established the larceny of two shoes both for the right foot and hence not a pair.[5] A fourth illustration of what should be avoided in the administration of criminal justice is the decision which upset a conviction under a statute making it grand larceny to steal any "cow or animal of the cow kind." The evidence had disclosed the theft of a steer, which was not "of the cow kind," said the appellate court, because a steer is a male.[6]

On the other hand, under statutes passed long ago it became possible to eliminate much of the needless verbosity and repetition with

2. State v. Shelledy, 8 Iowa 477 (1859).
3. 210 Mo. 202, 109 S.W. 706.
4. Lemons v. State, 4 W.Va. 755 (1870).
5. State v. Harris, 3 Har. 559 (Del. 1841).
6. Marsh v. State, 3 Ala.App. 80, 57 So. 387 (1912).

which common-law indictments were burdened. In fact the common legislative command was to use "ordinary and concise language, without repetition, and in such a manner as to enable a person of common understanding to know what is intended." But while the purpose was to simplify the wording of indictments to some extent, no change was made in the general plan, which required the indictment to include both the accusation of the offense itself and the particulars of the offense. The unfortunate result of retaining the same general plan was the retention of most of the verbosity and archaism of expression, because prosecuting attorneys preferred to follow the old precedents rather than to venture the use of simpler language which was authorized by the legislature, without any guiding suggestions.

The modern trend is in the direction of simplified indictments. The most progressive step in this direction reduces the indictment to a very simple and direct statement of the charge against the defendant, and entitles him to move for a bill of particulars if he wishes more information. This motion will be granted if additional information is needed. The brevity of such an indictment is well illustrated by one of the forms appended to the federal rules of criminal procedure.

Indictment for Murder in the First Degree of Federal Officer

In the District Court of the United States
for the _____ District of _____,

_____ Division

United States of America
v.
John Doe

No. _____

(18 U.S.C.A. §§ 1111, 1114)

The grand jury charges:

On or about the _____ day of _____ 19__, in _____ District of _____, John Doe, with premeditation and by means of shooting murdered John Roe, who was then an officer of the Federal Bureau of Investigation of the Department of Justice engaged in the performance of his official duties.[7]

A True Bill

_____
Foreman

_____
United States Attorney

Not all jurisdictions have simplified the indictment to this extent, but it is desirable that it should be done. The defendant gets more

---

7. "The specificity formerly held necessary to charge an offense is no longer required or sanctioned." Hence it was not necessary for the indictment to mention that the officer was a "human being." Donnelly v. United States, 185 F.2d 559 (10th Cir. 1950).

information from such a direct statement (plus a bill of particulars if there is any reason therefor) than he ever received from the most verbose indictment drawn in "legalistic" language.

(C) THE CORONER'S INQUEST

A coroner's inquest is an inquiry by the coroner, with the aid of a jury, into the death of a person. Under the English common law a person could be tried for murder or manslaughter on the finding of a coroner's jury, the same as upon indictment by a grand jury. This has not been the practice in this country. But the accusation returned by the coroner's jury usually authorizes the coroner to order the arrest and commitment of the accused, and is the equivalent of an examination and commitment by a magistrate.

(D) THE INFORMATION

An information is a written accusation of crime preferred by the public prosecuting officer without the intervention of the grand jury.

Under the English common law there could be no trial for felony on an information, because all felonies were punishable by death and it was felt that no man should be put on trial for his life except upon the sworn accusation of a jury,—either the grand jury or a coroner's jury. But the right of the attorney-general of Great Britain or of the solicitor-general during a vacancy in the other office, to file an information charging a misdemeanor was so well established that on several occasions Lord Mansfield denied applications by this official for leave to proceed in this way,—on the ground that he had the right *ex officio*, and no leave of court was needed. In this country the powers which were exercised by those officers in England are distributed to a large extent among the district attorneys (or county attorneys) of the state, an office which did not exist in England. Hence these officers are entitled to prosecute by information as a right inhering in their office, in the absence of some express limitation.

In most of the states there are constitutional limitations upon the power to prosecute by information. A few of the constitutions expressly authorize the legislature to modify or abolish the grand jury.[1] A few place the indictment and the information upon an equal basis,[2]

---

1. See, for example, the constitutions of Colorado, Illinois, Indiana, Iowa, Nebraska, North Dakota, South Dakota and Wyoming. Such legislation has been enacted in these states.

2. See, for example, the constitutions of Missouri, Nevada and Washington.

and a slightly larger number have a similar provision with the qualification that the prosecution by information shall be only after examination and commitment by a magistrate, or the waiver of such examination.[3]

At the other extreme the Fifth Amendment to the Constitution of the United States provides: "No person shall be held to answer for a capital, or otherwise infamous crime, unless on presentment or indictment of a grand jury, except in cases arising in the land or naval forces, or in the militia, when in actual service in time of war or public danger; . . ."

Whether a crime is infamous within the meaning of this Amendment is determined by the punishment provided for it,[4] and it has been held that any offense punishable by imprisonment in a penitentiary or at hard labor is infamous [5] (and any person sentenced to a term of more than one year for a federal offense may be imprisoned in a United States penitentiary).[6]

The Fifth Amendment is a limitation upon the federal government only, and does not apply to prosecutions in the state courts,[7] but very similar provisions are found in some of the state constitutions.[8] Under federal procedure, it may be added, the requirement that the prosecution for an infamous crime shall be only by indictment by a grand jury can be waived in other than capital cases. The rule is: "An offense which may be punished by imprisonment for a term exceeding one year or at hard labor may be prosecuted by information if the defendant, after he has been advised of the nature of the charge and of his rights, waives in open court prosecution by indictment." [9]

There has been a definite trend in modern times, with the aid of statutes and constitutional amendments, to make an increasingly larger use of the information.[10] This is entirely proper. The grand jury served a very important function in the transition from the rough and ready "justice" of the Hue and Cry to modern criminal procedure.

3. See, for example, the constitutions of Arizona, California, Idaho, Louisiana (except for a capital crime), Montana (or after leave granted by court), New Mexico, Oklahoma, Utah.

4. Ex parte Wilson, 114 U.S. 417, 5 S.Ct. 935, 29 L.Ed. 89 (1885).

5. United States v. Moreland, 258 U.S. 433, 42 S.Ct. 368, 66 L.Ed. 700 (1922).

6. 18 U.S.C.A. § 4083.

7. But see the concurring opinions in Rochin v. California, 342 U.S. 165, 72 S.Ct. 205, 96 L.Ed. 183 (1952).

8. See, for example, the constitutions of Maine, New York, Ohio and Rhode Island.

9. Federal Rules of Criminal Procedure, Rule 7(b), 18 U.S.C.A.

10. Where a criminal complaint in legal form is verified as true in positive terms, such verification constitutes a sufficient showing to authorize the issuance of a warrant of arrest. And if the defendant waives a preliminary hearing such verified complaint is sufficient to authorize holding him for trial and the filing of an information in the district court. State v. Hendricks, 80 Idaho 344, 330 P.2d 334 (1958).

It was also one of the safeguards of the subject against the king. But at the present time it should be reserved as a body to be called upon in emergencies rather than one whose action is needed in every felony prosecution.

SECTION 3. STEPS BY THE PROSECUTION AFTER INDICTMENT

After the indictment or the information for an indictable offense, there are several steps which may be taken by the prosecution before trial, one of which—the arraignment, is of such a nature that the trial cannot proceed without it unless it has been waived or the defendant is a corporation (or a different procedure has been established by statute).

(A) THE BENCH WARRANT

The person indicted, or informed against, may or may not be in the custody of the law at the time. If he is not, and does not voluntarily submit to the jurisdiction of the court, it is necessary that he be brought in. By the early English practice, if the offense charged was a misdemeanor only, *venire facias ad respondendum* was issued. This was a writ summoning the defendant to appear and be arraigned for the offense. If the offense charged was a felony, or if the defendant failed to respond to the *venire facias* issued in a misdemeanor case, the court issued a *capias* which commanded the sheriff to take the defendant and have him at the next assizes. If the magistrate had reason to believe one charged with a misdemeanor would not respond to a *venire facias*, a *capias* could be issued in the first instance as in felony cases. And, quite unfortunately it seems, the practice of issuing the *venire facias* tended to fall into disuse and the *capias* came to be used as the regular procedure for misdemeanors as well as for felonies. The *capias* satisfies the definition of an arrest warrant and this process frequently goes under the name of a "warrant" at the present time. The label "bench warrant" is common because this writ is issued from the bench, in legal theory, although ordinarily it is prepared and handed over by the clerk. By means of arrest or by summons or by merely transferring the accused from the jail if he is already in custody, he is brought before the court for arraignment.

(B) THE ARRAIGNMENT

"To arraign is nothing else but to call the prisoner to the bar of the court, to answer the matter charged upon him in the indictment." 4 Bl.Comm. 322.

The ancient ceremony consisted of four parts. First, the prisoner was called to the bar by name and commanded to raise his hand. The raising of the hand was merely for the purpose of identification and was not indispensable. Usually today the step by which the prisoner is brought before the bar of the court and identified is regarded as something preliminary to the arraignment rather than a part thereof. Second, the indictment was read to the prisoner distinctly in English, —and this was true in the early days when all other proceedings in court were in Latin. There was no thought of giving him a copy because usually he would not have been able to read it. The usual procedure today is to read the indictment or information, but a few of the statutes stipulate that it shall either be read or the substance stated. It is very generally provided that a copy shall be delivered to the defendant. Third, it was "demanded of him" whether he was guilty or not guilty of the crime charged. In form this seems inadequate since it has always been possible for the defendant to answer in some form other than a plea of guilty or a plea of not guilty. This was unimportant, however, because the form did not result in an actual limitation. And the usual provision today is that defendant shall be asked "whether he pleads guilty or not guilty." Fourth, (if the plea was "not guilty") the prisoner was asked how he would be tried.

This last part of the original arraignment goes back to the very origin of trial by jury. The more ancient method of trial for criminal offenses was trial by ordeal. In the words of Blackstone (4 Bl.Comm. 342–3): "Fire-ordeal was performed either by taking up in the hand, unhurt, a piece of red-hot iron of one, two, or three pounds' weight; or else by walking barefoot, and blindfold, over nine red-hot ploughshares laid lengthwise at unequal distances; and if the party escaped unhurt he was adjudged innocent; but if it happened otherwise, as without collusion it usually did, he was then condemned as guilty. . . .

"Water-ordeal was performed either by plunging the bare arm up to the elbow in boiling water, and escaping unhurt thereby, or by casting the person suspected into a river or pond of cold water; and if he floated therein without any action of swimming, it was deemed an evidence of his guilt, but if he sank he was acquitted."

The theory of trial by ordeal was that "God would always interpose miraculously to vindicate the guiltless." Hence, when trial by jury was added as a method of determining guilt or innocence, the defendant was given his choice of these methods of trial by asking him: "How will you be tried—by God or by country?" If he answered: "By God," he was tried by ordeal. If he answered: "By country," he was given a jury trial. After trial by ordeal became obsolete this question still was asked as a part of the arraignment although the defendant, at that time, had no choice as to how he would be tried for an indictable offense. Because there was no choice the approved answer of the defendant came to be: "By God and my country."

The fourth part of the ancient arraignment has tended to disappear in this country. In a few states the statutes expressly provide that it shall not be necessary to ask the prisoner how he will be tried. In the others this question is merely omitted from the statutory provisions for arraignment. On the other hand, there is very real reason for restoring this question to the arraignment,—in changed form. Today, in all but a very few states, one charged by indictment or equivalent information is permitted to waive the jury and be tried by the judge without a jury (either in all cases or in certain cases). In every instance in which this waiver is permitted the arraignment might well include this question (if the plea is not guilty): "How will you be tried—by a jury or without a jury?"

Under the early procedure the trial followed the arraignment very promptly if the defendant's plea was not guilty. In this country today the usual practice is to have the arraignment follow promptly after the indictment or information, if the defendant is available, although the trial may not be expected to be held until a later time. Many of the statutes permit the defendant to "appear" for arraignment by counsel if the indictment or information is for a misdemeanor.

Rule 10 of the Federal Rules of Criminal Procedure is as follows: "Arraignment shall be conducted in open court and shall consist of reading the indictment or information to the defendant or stating to him the substance of the charge and calling on him to plead thereto. He shall be given a copy of the indictment or information before he is called upon to plead."

(C) MOTIONS

A motion is an application made to a judge or court to obtain some rule or order deemed necessary or desirable in the progress of a cause. There are no peculiar motions by the prosecution, subject to special rules and provisions, but if an occasion arises which entitles the prosecution to some special rule or order it may file a motion therefor. If, for example, special circumstances should entitle the prosecution to a postponement of the date set for trial, this would be secured by the filing of an appropriate motion.[1]

(D) DEMURRER

If the defendant files a plea which, as a matter of law, is insufficient on its face for the purpose for which it is filed, the common law permitted a demurrer thereto. The modern statutory forms of pleas leave little occasion for a demurrer by the prosecution. Probably its most frequent use has been in connection with pleas of former conviction or former acquittal. Where the demurrer has been abolished, by statute or by rule, any objection to the defendant's plea is raised by motion.

(E) NOLLE PROSEQUI

At common law the prosecuting officer, at any time before judgment and without the consent of the defendant, may enter an order withdrawing the indictment or other accusation. This voluntary withdrawal of the prosecution by the prosecuting officer was known as a "nolle prosequi." It was customarily abbreviated to the form "Nol. pros." If the nolle prosequi resulted in the withdrawal of a legally sufficient indictment, after the trial commenced and without the consent of the defendant, it had the effect of an acquittal. Otherwise it was without prejudice to a further or fresh proceeding for the same offense.

In a number of the states today, no prosecution can be discontinued or abandoned, after the indictment or information has been filed, without an order of the court. In such a jurisdiction the prosecuting officer wishing to have the prosecution dismissed, after the filing of the indictment or information, files a "motion to dismiss." The frequency with which such a motion, by the prosecuting officer, is granted by the court as a matter of course causes it to have much the appearance of a nolle prosequi. And it frequently goes under that name, unofficially. But a dismissal by the court on motion of the prosecuting officer is quite different in fact from the common-law nolle prosequi,—which was a dismissal by that officer himself.

[1]. As to whether or not the prosecution may have a change of venue or of *venire* see Newberry v. Commonwealth, 192 Va. 819, 66 S.E.2d 841 (1951).

SECTION 4. STEPS BY THE DEFENDANT

(A) BAIL

Probably no step more frequently takes first place in the mind of one who finds himself in the custody of the law than that of being released on bail. It is properly considered at this point, therefore, although by no means limited to proceedings prior to the trial.[a]

The word "bail" comes from the Old French "baillier" (to deliver). As a verb (in this connection) it means the delivery of the accused. In its origin it meant the delivery of the body of the accused by the public officer to "private jailers" who were bound to produce him when required by the court. As a noun (in this connection) it refers to his "private jailers" (now commonly called his "sureties") and also to the security given for his release (more commonly called a "bail bond" or "recognizance"—depending upon the form—or simply an "undertaking").

The sureties of one who has been released on bail are not required or expected to keep him in confinement, but only to produce him when needed. But the ancient theory that they were "private jailers" prevailed to the extent of giving them authority to arrest the accused and surrender him to the public officer even before he was needed for purposes of the prosecution, if they deemed this necessary to insure his presence when required. This common-law authority is very generally incorporated in the statutes.

The purpose of committing to jail one who has been *charged* with crime is not to punish him. So far the state has no right to punish him because his guilt has not been established. The purpose is merely to secure his presence in order that he may be tried and, if found guilty, punished. The object of bail, therefore, is to provide a means of relief from an imprisonment which is imposed merely as a matter of precaution. From this it follows that it should be so regulated as reasonably to insure that the accused will be present when he is needed and that his liberty will not be restrained beyond the extent reasonably required for this purpose. Thus at common law, the matter of bail being entirely within the discretion of the magistrate or judge, it was felt that ordinarily there was no way to insure the appearance of one charged with a capital offense other than by keeping him in custody, and bail was commonly denied in these cases. On the other hand the probability that one charged with a misdemeanor could be produced by

---

a. As to bail after conviction see Herzog v. United States, 75 S.Ct. 349 (1955).

Sec. 4　　　　　*STEPS BY THE DEFENDANT*　　　　　833

friends, under sufficient financial pressure, was considered so great that bail was almost never denied to one so accused. When, beginning with the device of "benefit of clergy," it was possible to have one charged with a felony for which he would not be executed, there was not thought to be any definite indication either way.

In this country most of the states have a provision in their constitutions which is in substance as follows: All persons shall be bailable by sufficient sureties, unless for capital offenses when the proof is evident or the presumption great. This greatly narrows the discretion of the magistrate or judge in this field, but such discretion still exists in the matter of deciding what will be sufficient financial pressure to procure the presence of the accused when needed. This is subject to the general limitation that "excessive bail shall not be required" and in some jurisdictions to more specific restrictions.

Before an accused was delivered from the custody of the official jailer into the "friendly custody" of his "private jailers" at common law, security was required in the form of either a bail bond or a recognizance. A bail bond is a sealed instrument executed by the "bail" (now frequently by the accused, the principal, and his sureties), binding them to pay to the state a specified sum of money if the accused fails to appear as therein stipulated. A recognizance, at common law, was an obligation acknowledged by the obligor in open court and entered upon the order book. Being witnessed by the record itself it did not require the signature or seal of the obligor. A recognizance, when used in lieu of a bail bond, acknowledged an obligation to pay a specified sum of money if the accused failed to appear as therein specified. Anciently the accused himself was not a party to this acknowledgment, but this exclusion tended to disappear. In more recent times the acknowledgment—depending upon the jurisdiction and the gravity of the offense—might be by (1) both the accused and one or more sureties, (2) only the accused, (3) only a surety or sureties. In other words, the obligation is to pay a specified sum of money to the state if the accused fails to appear as specified,—whether it is in the form of a bail bond or a recognizance. The "undertaking" under some of the statutes is not exactly either the bail bond or the recognizance of the common law, but it is intended for the same purpose.

The so-called "cash bail," a deposit of money in lieu of a bail bond or recognizance, seems to have been unknown to the common law, but is quite common under the statutes. Rule 46 of the Federal Rules of Criminal Procedure expressly authorizes the deposit of cash, or bonds or notes of the United States.

Confusion will be avoided if care is taken to distinguish four phrases—(1) entitled to bail, (2) admitted to bail, (3) taking of bail, and (4) release on bail. In most of the jurisdictions one not charged with a capital offense is *entitled* to bail as a constitutional right before conviction. If the charge is a capital one he is still *entitled* to bail unless the "proof is evident or the presumption great." But as this must be determined by the court an order must be made *admitting* the defendant to bail or refusing to do so. If the defendant is *admitted* to bail, or *entitled* to bail as a matter of right without a hearing, and tenders an undertaking for this purpose, some authorized court or official must determine whether the offer is or is not satisfactory. The *taking* of bail is the acceptance of the tendered undertaking or cash deposit by an authorized court or official. The determination of whether such an offer is or is not sufficient does not have reference to the amount involved, which was fixed in advance, but depends upon whether or not the sureties can "qualify." If the bail is accepted and the prisoner is permitted to go at large he has then been *released* on bail. Sometimes the phrase is that he has been "enlarged" on bail.

If one who has been released on bail fails to appear at the stipulated time, steps will be taken to forfeit his undertaking or cash deposit. No final order of forfeiture will be entered at that time because the failure to appear may have resulted from excusable circumstances. In one form or another (the procedure varies under the different statutes) an opportunity will be given to show cause why the undertaking or cash deposit should not be forfeited. If such cause cannot be shown the actual forfeiture will follow.[a]

Even the final forfeiture of the undertaking or cash deposit does not interfere with the prosecution of the accused. If he is later brought into court he will be tried and, if convicted, punished.

If a prisoner is dissatisfied with an order refusing to admit him to bail, or refusing to accept an offer of bail made by him or in his behalf, or if he thinks the amount fixed for his bail is excessive, his remedy is by habeas corpus.

(B) HABEAS CORPUS

Habeas corpus is a Latin phrase meaning literally: "have the body." The import is that you have the man before the court in person (and explain by what authority you are detaining him). It is a legal device to give summary relief against illegal restraint of personal liberty. The legal process employed for this purpose is the *writ of habeas corpus*. It is a high prerogative common-law writ esteemed for centuries as the best and only sufficient safeguard of personal freedom. It has for its object the speedy release by judicial decree, of a person who is illegally restrained of his liberty, or is illegally de-

---

[a.] Under the Federal Rules of Criminal Procedure (Rule 46(f) (2)), 18 U.S.C.A. the surety on the bond becomes liable upon breach of condition. The district court, in its discretion, may set aside the forfeiture if justice does not require its enforcement. United States v. Davis, 202 F.2d 621 (7th Cir. 1953).

tained from the control of those entitled to his custody. It is a writ of inquiry directed to the person in whose custody the prisoner is detained, requiring the custodian to bring the prisoner before the judge or court, that appropriate judgment may be rendered upon judicial inquiry into the alleged unlawful restraint.

The Constitution of the United States provides (Art. I, sec. 9, par. 2): "The privilege of the writ of habeas corpus shall not be suspended, unless in cases of rebellion or invasion the public safety may require it."

An outline of the proceedings may be helpful to an understanding of the law of habeas corpus. The starting point is a petition. The person in custody or someone on his behalf, prepares a petition for a writ of habeas corpus and presents it to some court or the judge thereof. By so doing he "files a petition for a writ of habeas corpus." This petition may be either denied or granted, but it is important to bear in mind that granting the petition does not entitle the prisoner to a discharge. This is the preliminary step and the actual hearing does not take place until after the petition is granted. The petition must give the name or description of the custodian, the cause or pretense for the imprisonment (if known) and the ground upon which it is claimed to be illegal. The petition will be denied if it does not satisfy the legal requirements as to form, if it is not presented to the proper court or judge, or if it does not state facts sufficient to authorize release of the prisoner. On the other hand, if the petition is in proper form presented to a proper court or judge, and states a cause which if true, would entitle the prisoner to be released, it must be granted. The court or judge has very little discretion at this point of the proceedings. If the writ is granted, the petitioner is often said to have "sued out a writ of habeas corpus."

The writ of habeas corpus is directed to the custodian and commands him to have the body of the prisoner before the court or judge at a specifed time, and to bring with him the writ itself with a return thereon showing what he has been doing with the prisoner (meaning whether or not he has been detaining the person said to be a prisoner, and if so by what authority). If the return, or answer, of the custodian does not state a lawful authority for the confinement of the prisoner, his discharge will be ordered forthwith. If it states an adequate cause of detention the disputed facts will be determined at a hearing, and the court or judge, as a result of this hearing, will determine whether the detention is lawful or unlawful. If it is found to be lawful the prisoner will be remanded to the custody of the custodian. If it is found to be unlawful the discharge of the prisoner will be ordered, subject to the possibility that the court or judge may find proper cause for his commitment now despite the fact that his previous detention has been irregular.

Where one is deprived of his liberty without even the color of legal authority, the availability of the writ of habeas corpus is obvious. If the imprisonment is claimed to be by virtue of legal process, the validity and present force of such process are the only subjects of investigation in this type of proceeding. The dual nature of our government must be considered in this connection. If the imprisonment is claimed to be by virtue of federal authority, the validity and present force of such authority can be tested only by federal proceedings. Imprisonment claimed to be under state authority, on the other hand, may be inquired into by either state or federal proceedings, although it is only in rare instances that the federal courts or judges will discharge a prisoner held under color of state authority unless the prisoner has first exhausted his remedies in the state courts.[1]

A writ of habeas corpus cannot be used as a substitute for an appeal.[2] If a defendant has been convicted by a court having jurisdiction over the subject matter and the defendant, and he is in prison under a sentence which that court had lawful authority to pronounce, he cannot have the case reviewed by habeas corpus proceedings.[3]

If he claims that error was committed by the trial judge in admitting or excluding evidence or in giving or refusing instructions, or in any other manner, he must raise such an issue by a motion directed to the trial court or by an appeal to a higher court,—or in extreme cases by a writ of certiorari.

---

1. This does not require repetitious applications to state courts. Brown v. Allen, 344 U.S. 443, 73 S.Ct. 397 (1953). Denial of certiorari by the Supreme Court imports no expression of opinion on the merits of the case but means only that there were not four members of the Court who thought the case should be heard. Ibid.

2. In re Dixon, 41 Cal.2d 756, 264 P.2d 513 (1953); Jones v. Superior Court, 78 Ariz. 367, 280 P.2d 691 (1955).

The fact that the prisoner has not completed a proper sentence on one count does not preclude him from bringing habeas corpus on another count. In re Chapman, 43 Cal.2d 385, 273 P.2d 817 (1954).

3. Ex parte Hackett, 93 Okl.Cr. 82, 225 P.2d 184 (1950). As to what may be questioned by habeas corpus proceedings see Ex parte Drake, 38 Cal.2d 195, 238 P.2d 566 (1951).

As far as federal prisoners are concerned there has been a change of procedure in making a collateral attack based upon an alleged lack of jurisdiction. Under the "jurisdiction act", 28 U.S.C. § 2255, this is to be by motion rather than by resort to habeas corpus. With reference to this change of procedure see United States v. Hayman, 342 U.S. 205, 72 S.Ct. 263, 96 L.Ed. 232 (1952).

The availability of the writ of habeas corpus does not depend on actual detention in prison. One who has been released on parole is constructively a prisoner subject to restraint by penal authorities and the writ is available to him to test the validity of that restraint. In re Petersen, 51 Cal.2d 177, 331 P.2d 24 (1958).

A writ of habeas corpus does not entitle petitioner to a release if the only illegality of his detention is that he is being held in the wrong institution under a felony conviction when the sentence should have been for a misdemeanor. In such a case the order will direct that petitioner be taken before the district court to await a valid sentence. Lawton v. Hand, 183 Kan. 694, 331 P.2d 886 (1958).

There is, however, a margin of common ground on which a prisoner may question the legality of his imprisonment either by appeal or by habeas corpus. If his claim is that the court did not have jurisdiction over the subject matter, or over his person, or did not have authority to pronounce the sentence under which he is being confined, he may have the issue tested by either method,—with this limitation: ordinarily he must appeal if this remedy is still available to him.

Our criminal jurisdiction is based largely upon the so-called territorial theory of jurisdiction. If a particular criminal case did not involve any exception to the normal requirement, and a case should go to conviction although the crime clearly had not been committed within the territorial jurisdiction of the trial court, the defendant could be released from imprisonment under the sentence pronounced in such a case by habeas corpus proceedings, if necessary, because the trial, conviction, and sentence were utterly void by reason of lack of jurisdiction. The same might be true if the defendant had been indicted, tried, and convicted on a charge of a non-indictable offense. Although such an offense was committed within the territorial jurisdiction of the district court, for example, the law of the jurisdiction might be such that it would have to be prosecuted by complaint and summary trial before a magistrate and could come within the legal jurisdiction of the district court only on appeal. Hence a person in the penitentiary serving a sentence under a conviction based upon an indictment charging a non-indictable offense would be entitled to be released on a petition for habeas corpus [4] (if it is too late to appeal).

Furthermore, even though a court starts with jurisdiction over the subject matter and the defendant, it may lose that jurisdiction before sentence is pronounced. If it does lose such jurisdiction, the sentence is utterly void, and a prisoner serving such a sentence is entitled to release on habeas corpus if no other remedy is available.

A typical case is one in which a proper indictment was filed and the defendant arrested, after which the indictment was altered by an unauthorized amendment charging a different crime than that found by the grand jury. When the proper indictment was found the court had jurisdiction over the subject matter and when the defendant was arrested the court had jurisdiction over his person. At that point jurisdiction was complete so far as that case was concerned. But when the indictment was unlawfully altered to charge a different crime the court lost jurisdiction because there was no longer any lawful charge against the defendant. The alteration destroyed the original indictment and the altered writing had no standing in law. Hence the trial was of a man not legally charged with any crime and no court has jurisdiction to conduct such a criminal trial. For this reason he was able to secure his release by habeas corpus.[5]

---

[4]. Conkling v. Hollowell, 203 Iowa 1374, 214 N.W. 717 (1927).

[5]. In re Bain, 121 U.S. 1, 7 S.Ct. 781, 30 L.Ed. 849 (1877).

Another typical case of loss of jurisdiction is the Arkansas case in which a violent mob moved into the court room and completely dominated the trial, intimidating witnesses, counsel, jurors and even the judge himself so that no one dared to do anything other than let the case proceed to a hasty conviction. When this mob moved in and took over the situation the jurisdiction of the court moved out. What remained was the empty form of a trial having no legal validity whatever. The prisoner serving a sentence pronounced by that state court was released by federal habeas corpus proceedings.[6]

Furthermore, a court otherwise having jurisdiction of the case may pronounce a sentence it has no authority to pronounce under the law. The court acts without jurisdiction in the pronouncement of such a sentence, and the sentence itself is void and can be attacked either directly or indirectly. This is well illustrated in *Medley*. In that case the court inadvertently pronounced a sentence based on a statute passed after the crime was committed, and hence *ex post facto* as to that particular prosecution. So the prisoner serving that sentence was entitled to release on habeas corpus.[7]

This brings us to the most famous habeas corpus case of modern times: Mooney v. Holohan.[8] Tom Mooney had been convicted of first-degree murder in the California court, as a result of the fatal bombing of the San Francisco Preparedness Parade on July 22, 1916. After the conviction it was clearly established that perjury had been committed by witnesses for the prosecution during Mooney's trial. This would have entitled Mooney to a new trial, if the discovery had been made in time, but it was not a ground for release by habeas corpus because it did not affect the jurisdiction of the court or the authority of the court to pronounce sentence in the case.

The question may be asked: "If an innocent man has been convicted on perjured testimony, why should he not be released by habeas corpus?" But the flaw in this question is rather obvious. It cannot be determined judicially that perjury has been committed in a particular case without a thorough judicial investigation of the facts. Since the court is bound to issue a writ of habeas corpus if a petition presenting a proper ground therefor is presented in proper form to the appropriate court, it follows that every convict could secure a retrial of his case, in effect, by filing a petition for habeas corpus and alleging perjury by witnesses for the prosecution,—if this was recognized as a ground for release by this form of proceeding. Furthermore, a prisoner might be guilty of the crime of which he was convicted despite the fact that witnesses for the prosecution misstated facts on the witness stand in their zeal to put him "behind the bars." Hence it cannot be assumed that a convict is innocent merely because perjury

---

6. Moore v. Dempsey, 261 U.S. 86, 43 S.Ct. 265, 67 L.Ed. 543 (1923).

7. In re Medley, 134 U.S. 160, 10 S.Ct. 384, 33 L.Ed. 835 (1890).

8. Mooney v. Holohan, 294 U.S. 103, 55 S.Ct. 340, 79 L.Ed. 791 (1935). Cf. Coggins v. O'Brien, 188 F.2d 130 (1st Cir. 1951). Noted 65 Harv.L.Rev. 510 (1952).

on the part of prosecuting witnesses is established. For this reason, proof of such perjury should be used for other purposes. It should be used to secure a new trial if the discovery is made in time; and if not, it should be the basis of a petition for a pardon. Since the issuance of a pardon is within the discretion of the governor (or other pardoning authority,—depending upon the jurisdiction) it is possible for proper cases to be handled in this way without the risk of opening up every criminal case to a re-trial in collateral form.

Mooney was in the courts time and again, but the case which introduced a new element into the law of habeas corpus was when he filed an application in the Supreme Court of the United States for leave to file a petition for a writ of habeas corpus to be issued out of the High Court itself. His claim in this application was that he was being confined in violation of the "due process clause," of the Fourteenth Amendment to the Constitution of the United States, for the reason (as he alleged) that the *sole basis* of his conviction was perjured testimony *knowingly used by the prosecuting authorities* in order to obtain a conviction. The extreme nature of this claim must be emphasized: (1) The perjured testimony was alleged to be the sole basis of his conviction, which means in substance that he would have been entitled to an advice to the jury to acquit if this evidence had been lacking; (2) The perjured testimony was knowingly and purposely used against him by the prosecuting attorney. It may be added parenthetically that this extreme claim was never established and that Mooney was never released by habeas corpus; he was ultimately released by a governor who was satisfied that perjury had actually been committed by prosecuting witnesses and that there was at least grave doubt about his guilt.

The Supreme Court of the United States not only refused to order Mooney's release from imprisonment, it even refused to issue the writ of habeas corpus. It did not investigate the facts behind the extreme claim in his petition for the reason that he had not applied to the California courts for a writ of habeas corpus *on that ground*. But the Court said in substance, "If you can substantiate this claim and the California courts will not release you from imprisonment on that proof, *we will.*" The Court took the position that if the prosecuting authority of the state contrived to procure a criminal conviction through a deliberate deception of the court and the jury by the presentation of testimony known to be perjured, this was not due process of law but the mere pretense of a trial. And since, in such a case, there was no conviction based on due process of law, the judge would be wholly without authority to pronounce any sentence based upon such apparent conviction. Hence such a sentence, being beyond the jurisdiction of the court and utterly void, would give no authority for the defendant's confinement, so that a release might properly be ordered in habeas corpus proceedings,—even in the federal courts if the prisoner had exhausted his remedies in the state courts without avail.

This case will stand out in history as a landmark in the law of habeas corpus because it suggested that any conviction in a case in which any agency of the government had deprived the convict of his constitutional right to due process of law, is in legal effect utterly void and incapable of authorizing the judge to pronounce any valid sentence thereon, so that imprisonment under a sentence purporting to be based on such a conviction is without authority of law and will entitle the prisoner to release on habeas corpus proceedings if it is too late to raise the question by motion or appeal.

The Mooney case was decided only a few years after the famous *Scottsboro Rape* case.[9] This was not a habeas corpus case but had a bearing on the problem because it was held to show a violation of due process. Several young negroes were charged with rape in the state of Alabama. They were young and illiterate and obviously surrounded by hostile sentiment. The judge appointed all of the members of the bar to represent the accused. This had the appearance of a magnificent gesture; but what was everyone's business turned out to be nobody's business (as is so usually the case) and as a result no one of the trials lasted as long as a day although rape is a capital offense in that state. The conviction was affirmed on appeal by the Supreme Court of Alabama, and was taken to the Supreme Court of the United States by a writ of certiorari. The High Court reversed the Alabama court on the ground that the failure of the trial judge to make effective appointment of counsel to assist the defendants in their defense, coupled with the judge's failure to acquaint the defendants with their right to counsel, and his failure to give them time and opportunity to secure counsel, was a denial of due process of law in violation of the Fourteenth Amendment.

Scottsboro plus *Mooney* clearly suggested the possibility of habeas corpus in a case in which it was claimed the defendant had been denied the right of counsel, and this was soon put to the test. And the Supreme Court of the United States held, that while a defendant may waive his right of counsel and try his own case, he will be entitled to a release on habeas corpus if he was convicted in a case in which he was improperly denied the right of counsel, because such a conviction was based upon a violation of his constitutional right to due process of law and the court had no jurisdiction to pronounce any sentence upon such a void conviction.[10]

The Supreme Court has also held that if a confession and a plea of guilty have been obtained by threats made by officers of the law, the judge has no jurisdiction to pronounce judgment of conviction and sentence upon such a plea, and hence imprisonment under such a sentence may be terminated by habeas corpus proceedings if a more

---

9. Powell v. Alabama, 287 U.S. 45, 53 S.Ct. 55, 77 L.Ed. 158 (1932).

10. Johnson v. Zerbst, 304 U.S. 458, 58 S.Ct. 1019, 82 L.Ed. 1461 (1938); Walker v. Johnston, 312 U.S. 275, 61 S.Ct. 574, 85 L.Ed. 830 (1941).

direct remedy is not available.[11] The court also held that if prison officials suppress a convict's appeal documents until too late for him to perfect an appeal under state law, this amounts to a violation of his constitutional rights and will entitle him to have the validity of his conviction tested by habeas corpus proceedings.[12]

The result of these cases was to suggest that any one in a state penitentiary has a chance for release under federal habeas corpus proceedings, and a flood of such petitions followed. The vast majority of them were entirely without success. The federal courts had made it clear in the cases mentioned above that they intended to preserve and maintain the constitutional safeguards of persons accused of crime, by the use of federal habeas corpus if necessary. They next made it equally clear that this device is not a haven of refuge for those properly convicted of crime in the state courts.

It may be added that the Supreme Court has held that it is improper for prison authorities to require a petition for habeas corpus to be submitted for approval to some agency designated by them, such as the legal investigator of the parole board, and that such a regulation is invalid; but also, that such a regulation is not a ground for the release of an otherwise legally convicted and confined prisoner.[13]

The statute defining federal habeas corpus jurisdiction (28 U.S.C. A. section 2241) provides:

"Power to grant writ

"(a) Writs of habeas corpus may be granted by the Supreme Court, and any justice thereof, the district courts and any circuit judge within their respective jurisdictions. The order of a circuit judge shall be entered in the records of the district court of the district wherein the restraint complained of is had.

"(b) The Supreme Court, any justice thereof, and any circuit judge may decline to entertain an application for a writ of habeas corpus and may transfer the application for hearing and determination to the district court having jurisdiction to entertain it.

---

11. Waley v. Johnson, 316 U.S. 101, 62 S.Ct. 964, 86 L.Ed. 1302 (1942).

12. Cochran v. Kansas, 316 U.S. 255, 62 S.Ct. 1068, 86 L.Ed. 1453 (1942).

It was held that the prosecution's use of a coerced confession in a state case called for a reversal of a conviction obtained thereby. Brown v. Mississippi, 297 U.S. 278, 56 S.Ct. 461 (1936). And this is true whether the coercion is physical or mental. Payne v. Arkansas, 356 U.S. 560, 78 S.Ct. 844 (1958). On the other hand the mere evidence of a threat of lynching will not bar the use of a confession if it was freely and voluntarily given at another time and place in the absence of any coercive influence. Thomas v. Arizona, 356 U.S. 390, 78 S.Ct. 885 (1958).

13. Ex parte Hull, 312 U.S. 546, 61 S. Ct. 640 (1941). It has been held that 28 U.S.C.A. § 2255, which is the substantial equivalent of a writ of habeas corpus in more convenient form is not unconstitutional. To limit defendant to this remedy except where it is inadequate or ineffective does not suspend the writ of habeas corpus. United States v. Anselmi, 207 F.2d 312 (3d Cir. 1953).

"(c) The writ of habeas corpus shall not extend to a prisoner unless—

"(1) He is in custody under or by color of the authority of the United States or is committed for trial before some court thereof; or

"(2) He is in custody for an act done or omitted in pursuance of an Act of Congress, or an order, process, judgment or decree of a court or judge of the United States; or

"(3) He is in custody in violation of the Constitution or laws or treaties of the United States; or

"(4) He, being a citizen of a foreign state and domiciled therein is in custody for an act done or omitted under any alleged right, title, authority, privilege, protection, or exemption claimed under the commission, order or sanction of any foreign state, or under color thereof, the validity and effect of which depend upon the law of nations; or

"(5) It is necessary to bring him into court to testify or for trial."

(It should be observed that clause (5) provides for *habeas corpus ad testificandum* and has nothing to do with alleged unlawfulness of restraint. In such a case the prisoner is restored to the custody from which he was taken as soon as he is no longer needed as a witness.)

The most famous case under clause (2) of the federal statute is *In re Neagle*.[14] Neagle, a deputy United States marshal appointed to protect Mr. Justice Field of the United States Supreme Court while the Justice was on judicial duties in California, shot and killed one Terry while the latter was in the act of making a dangerous assault upon the Justice. Neagle was charged with murder in California and was arrested by state authorities there who insisted they were going to place him on trial for murder to determine whether or not the killing was under circumstances sufficient to justify the homicide. Upon federal habeas corpus proceedings it was held that the deputy marshal was acting under the authority of a law of the United States and hence not liable to answer to the courts of California for his act. He was therefore ordered released from the custody of the state authorities.

This case suggests two comments: (1) A federal officer committing homicide while in the performance of his duties as such officer is guilty of no offense if he is acting within the scope of his legal privilege under the circumstances, but is guilty of criminal homicide if he takes life by the use of deadly force which is clearly not privileged by the facts of the particular case. (2) The federal government has the right and power to determine this issue in its own courts, and it is quite proper that it should do so.

---

14. In re Neagle, 135 U.S. 1, 10 S.Ct. 658, 34 L.Ed. 55 (1890).

Sec. 4 STEPS BY THE DEFENDANT 843

It is very questionable, however, whether habeas corpus is the desirable remedy. Under one of the sections providing for the removal of causes (28 U.S.C.A. section 1442) the deputy marshal could have such a case removed to the federal court for trial there, as was done in the somewhat similar case of Tennessee v. Davis.[15]

(C) DEMURRER

A demurrer is a challenge by one party to his opponent's pleading. A demurrer to an indictment is a pleading by the defendant attacking the sufficiency of the indictment for a defect which is apparent from its face. This demurrer admits the truth of every fact sufficiently alleged but insists that as a matter of law the facts so alleged do not constitute an offense. In fact, at common law, this demurrer brings the whole record before the court so that any defect upon the face of either could be reached in this way.

In the early days a decision in favor of the defendant, on his demurrer to the indictment, resulted in his discharge unless the defect was obviously one of form rather than substance, in which case he was detained until a new indictment could be found. Even his discharge, however, did not bar the finding of a subsequent indictment charging the same offense as that intended by the first. Many of the modern statutes provide that the defendant shall not be discharged, as a result of sustaining his demurrer, if the judge orders the case resubmitted to the same or another grand jury;—or (if such procedure is available under the facts in the particular jurisdiction) if he orders or permits an amendment, or directs the filing of an information against the defendant.

Since the demurrer admits the truth of the allegations made, inquiry is invited as to what will happen if the court decides that the

---

15. Tennessee v. Davis, 100 U.S. 257, 25 L.Ed. 648 (1879).

The provision of 28 U.S.C.A. § 2255 which is the substantial equivalent of a writ of habeas corpus in more convenient form is not unconstitutional. To limit defendant to this remedy except where it is inadequate or ineffective does not suspend the writ of habeas corpus. United States v. Anselmi, 207 F.2d 312 (3d Cir. 1953), cert. denied, and a motion for leave to file a petition for a writ of habeas corpus was also denied. 345 U.S. 947, 73 S.Ct. 868 (1953).

It was held in one case that at least under certain circumstances the writ of habeas corpus is available to one who is at liberty on bail. Commonwealth ex rel. Levine v. Fair, 394 Pa. 262, 146 A.2d 834 (1958). Jones, C. J., dissented on the ground that the writ is not available to one who has been released on bail. The authority has been so strongly in favor of the position taken by the dissent that it has been held habeas corpus is not available to one who had been released on bail and surrendered himself into custody for the sole purpose of applying for the writ. Baker v. Grice, 169 U.S. 284, 18 S.Ct. 323 (1898); In re Ford, 160 Cal. 334, 116 P. 757 (1911).

indictment is legally sufficient and proper. There is no reason why this admission should be of any more force than "for the sake of argument" to determine the validity of the pleading, but anciently it was far more than this. It was said by an early writer: ". . . if a person be indicted or appealed of felony and he will demur to the appeal or indictment and it be judged against him, he shall have judgment to be hanged, for it is a confession of the indictment, ..."[1] The severity of this rule was modified in the course of time. Permission to enter a plea after the demurrer was overruled came to be granted commonly in felony cases. And modern statutes grant this permission in all cases,—felony or misdemeanor.

Even today it is possible to find, in some jurisdictions, a statutory provision traceable to the ancient rule that a decision against the defendant on a demurrer resulted in a judgment of conviction. Under modern statutes, if a defendant fails or refuses to answer an indictment or information against him, a plea of not guilty is entered in his behalf. But under some of the statutes if his original pleading is a demurrer, which is overruled, and he thereafter refuses to plead further, final judgment may be entered against him on the demurrer.[2]

The demurrer is a superfluous device,—at this point as elsewhere in procedure. It was pointed out in the Seventeenth Century that there was nothing to be accomplished by a demurrer to the indictment that could not be obtained in some other way.[3] Demurrers have been abolished in federal proceedings[4] and there is a trend in that direction.[5]

1. 2 Hale P.C. *257. ". . . if he demurre in law, and it be adjudged against him, he shall have judgment to be hanged." 2 Co.Inst. *178.

2. There is no uniformity in this regard. For example, final judgment is entered against the defendant in Iowa. Iowa Code Ann. § 777.10. In California a plea of not guilty must be entered. West's Ann.Cal.Pen.Code § 1124.

3. ". . . he may have all the advantages of exception to the insufficiency of the indictment or appeal by way of exception either before his plea of *not guilty*, or after his conviction and before judgment, . . ." 2 Hale P.C. *257. The original publication was in 1678. While Lord Hale is not specific at this point, what he has reference to is a *motion to quash* before his plea of not guilty, or a *motion in arrest of judgment* after conviction. At common law any objection which could be raised by a demurrer to the indictment could also be raised by either of these motions.

4. Federal Rules of Criminal Procedure, Rule 12, 18 U.S.C.A. Federal Rules of Civil Procedure, Rule 7(a), 28 U.S.C.A.

5. The American Law Institute has recommended that demurrers to the indictment or information be abolished. Code of Criminal Procedure § 209 (official draft, 1930).

(D) MOTIONS

(i) Motion to Quash

If it could be seen from the face of the indictment that it was insufficient as a matter of law a proper mode of attack was by a motion to quash. Any objection to the indictment which could be raised by demurrer could be raised also by the motion to quash, at common law.

The quashing of an indictment was not a bar to another indictment for the same offense. Hence the defendant gained no advantage by it, other than delay, unless it was a prosecution which should not have been brought at all. If defendant was indicted for the stealing of a dog, in the early days before this was a crime, the motion to quash was the proper remedy. It could be made at any time after the indictment was found (and before verdict) whereas a demurrer could not be filed prior to arraignment. And the motion did not involve any admission by the defendant. Hence it was more advantageous than a demurrer. If it was a different kind of case, on the other hand, and the objection raised by the motion could be cured by a new and more carefully drawn indictment, it was to the advantage of the defendant to wait before urging it. He could force the prosecution to disclose its case in full, he could take his chances, with one jury, and if the verdict was against him he could raise, by a motion in arrest of judgment, any objection he could have urged earlier by a demurrer or a motion to quash. Hence the motion to quash and the demurrer to the indictment tended more and more to fall into disuse while increased reliance was placed upon the motion in arrest of judgment. To prevent this statutes were passed in some states providing that the motion in arrest of judgment could not be sustained on any ground which could have been urged by a motion to quash or by a demurrer, other than lack of jurisdiction or the failure of the indictment or information to charge an offense. The net result of such a provision (sometimes expressly stated) is that any error or defect in the proceedings, other than lack of jurisdiction or failure to charge an offense, which properly could be raised by the defendant before going to trial, is waived by him if he goes to trial without objection. This is the provision of Rule 12 of the Federal Rules of Criminal Procedure except that the court is authorized to grant relief from the waiver for cause shown.

Another legislative effort to improve criminal procedure, in some jurisdictions, took the form of extending the motion to quash to cover other purposes and providing that it should not be used for any objection which could be raised by demurrer. The more modern trend, although it still has far to go, is to abolish both the demurrer and the motion to quash and substitute for both a motion to dismiss.

(ii) Motion to Dismiss

The motion to quash was greatly enlarged by statute. Some of the enactments changed the label to "motion to set aside the indictment" (or the information). But no motion under either label is appropriate for all of the possible need in this regard. Such a motion is completely ineffective, for example, if no indictment or information has been filed. But one arrested for crime cannot be kept in jail or on bail indefinitely by the mere absence of such formal accusation. After the lapse of too great a period of time (the statutory provisions differ) the defendant is entitled to be released from jail or to have his undertaking discharged (or his cash deposit returned) if he is on bail. And one device by which he obtains this relief has been a "motion to dismiss." The result, if the motion is granted, is the dismissal of the pending prosecution although it does not bar subsequent proceedings against him for the same offense unless this is so stated in the statute.

Some states have simplified the procedure by using the motion to dismiss not only for this purpose but also to quash the indictment or information. Simplification at this point has been carried to its logical conclusion in the Federal Rules of Criminal Procedure. Rule 12 abolishes the demurrer, the motion to quash, the plea in abatement, the plea to the jurisdiction, the plea of former conviction or former acquittal, and all other but the basic pleas. If there is *any* reason why a prosecution should be disposed of otherwise than on a plea of guilty, a plea of not guilty or a plea of *nolo contendere*, this is accomplished in a federal case by a motion to dismiss.

(iii) For Change of Venue

The common law permitted the defendant to obtain a change of the place of trial to an adjoining county if for any reason a fair and impartial trial could not be had in the county in which the offense was committed.[1] This transfer was known as a change of venue. For the most part now it is regulated by statute. The defendant's application for a change of venue is referred to as a "petition" in some of the statutes. Essentially it is a motion and under the more simplified types of procedure it is so called.

The defendant's petition or motion for a change of venue is a waiver of his right to have the trial in the county in which the offense is alleged to have been committed. Hence no such question is involved where the motion is filed by him. It is otherwise where the

---

1. ". . . the law is clear and uniform as far back as it can be traced . . . where an impartial trial cannot be had in the proper county, it shall be tried in the next." Rex v. Cowle, 2 Burr. 834, 859, 97 Eng.Rep. 587, 602 (1759). By the Crown and *a fortiori* by the defendant.

prosecution seeks a change of venue. In several states such a change is authorized by express constitutional provision. In the absence of such a provision in the constitution uniformity is lacking. In a number of states the need of having an impartial trial has been held sufficient to authorize a change on motion of the prosecuting attorney.[2] In others, even a statute providing for such a change has been held unconstitutional.[3]

(iv) For Change of Judge

A recusation is a challenge, directed against the judge before whom the case is to be tried, based upon the ground of prejudice or some other disqualification. In the beginning it was a request that the judge excuse (recuse) himself. Under modern statutes it is much more than this. The transfer of a case from one judge to another often has been called loosely a "change of venue." This inaccurate terminology has come about in part, no doubt, by reason of the fact that the judicial machinery in some parts of the country has been such that the simplest and most obvious method of obtaining a change of the judge to try the case has been by transferring it from one county to another. The proper designation is "change of judge." The defendant's effort to secure such a change in the early days was very definitely an "application" or a "petition," and it still, at times, carries such a label. But under the statutes it is essentially a motion and under the more simplified types of procedure it is designated a "motion for a change of judge."

(v) For Other Purposes

A motion, it should be remembered, must of necessity be an instrument that can be adapted to any peculiar need that arises. If the defendant is entitled to a postponement of the date set for trial, to a bill of particulars, or to relief of any other nature, his request therefor should be by motion. The desirable procedure would provide simply that if an occasion arises which entitles the defendant to some special rule or order he may file a motion therefor. This would include any of the motions mentioned above and any other for which a need might be found. Rule 12 of the Federal Rules of Criminal Procedure, for example, provides that except for the basic pleas, defendant's request for anything to which he thinks he is entitled "shall be raised only by motion to dismiss or to grant appropriate relief."[4]

---

2. See Newberry v. Commonwealth, 192 Va. 819, 66 S.E.2d 841 (1951). And see State v. Dryman, 127 Mont. 579, 269 P.2d 796 (1954).

3. Wheeler v. State, 24 Wis. 52 (1869).

4. This chapter deals with Proceedings Preliminary to Trial and the state-

(E) PLEAS

A trial, at law, is for the determination of an issue. And the issue, under our procedure, is formed by the pleadings. In a criminal case the pleading by the prosecution is the indictment or information, and that by the defendant is his plea. Without the defendant's plea there would be no issue and hence nothing to try.

In ancient times, if a person indicted for felony "stood mute," an inquest of office was taken to determine whether his silence was wilful or the result of incapacity to speak,—unless he had already spoken in court on the same day. If it was determined that he wilfully stood mute, judgment of *peine fort et dure* was given against him. This was: "That he be sent to the prison from whence he came, and put into a dark, lower room, and there to be laid naked upon the bare ground upon his back without any clothes or rushes under him or to cover him except his privy members, his legs and arms drawn and extended with cords to the four corners of the room, and upon his body laid as great a weight of iron, as he can bear, and more. And the first day he shall have three morsels of barley bread without drink, the second day he shall have three draughts of water, of standing water next the door of the prison, without bread, and this to be his diet till he die. . . .

"This judgment is given for his contempt in refusing his legal trial, and therefore he forfeits his goods, but it is no attainder, nor gives any escheat or corruption of blood. . . .

"The severity of the judgment is to bring men to put themselves upon their legal trial, and tho sometimes it hath been given and executed, yet for the most part men bethink themselves and plead." (2 Hale P.C. *319).

In the course of time the defendant who refused to plead was dealt with a little more humanely by the rule that the obstinate refusal to plead amounted to a plea of guilty. Under modern statutes such refusal by the defendant results in a plea of not guilty being entered for him by the court. In effect such refusal *is* itself a plea of not guilty and the entry by the judge is a mere matter of form.

At common law all of defendant's pleas, in a criminal case, were oral. Some of the statutes incorporate this requirement. Others permit the pleas to be either oral or in writing, and a few of them *require* certain pleas to be in writing.

ment in the text is made with this in mind. To correct a judgment that the court had no power to pronounce, if no other remedy is available, the defendant may apply for a writ of error coram nobis even after the sentence has been served. United States v. Morgan, 346 U.S. 502, 74 S.Ct. 247 (1954).

(i) Plea of Sanctuary

Anciently an offender who had fled to a church, or church yard, was immune from arrest while he remained in this sanctuary. And, unless his offense was treason or sacrilege, he was entitled to depart from the country if he took certain steps to confess his guilt and abjure the realm. He was given forty days to leave from a designated port. And if he was arrested and arraigned during this time his relief was by pleading his privilege of sanctuary. This saved his life, but by this abjuration his blood was attainted, and he forfeited all his goods and chattels. The plea of sanctuary was abrogated in the early 1600s.

(ii) Plea of Benefit of Clergy

In the very early days a cleric, charged with felony, was entitled to have his case transferred from the king's court to the ecclesiastical court. Originally this transfer was effected by a demand made by the bishop or ordinary. Later the procedure was for the cleric to file a plea of benefit of clergy and to support this plea by proof of his qualification. After the procedure of transferring such a case to the ecclesiastical court was abolished, benefit of clergy came to be a device by which one so entitled was spared the penalty of death in the king's court. It was extended, moreover, to include any man who could read. At this time the plea of benefit of clergy was available, but rapidly fell into disuse. A literate defendant could plead not guilty, with the possibility of acquittal, and still have the benefit of clergy, if convicted, by insisting upon it at the time of allocution. That is, when the judge asked him if he knew of any reason why judgment of death should not be pronounced against him, he could answer in the affirmative because entitled to benefit of clergy. Benefit of clergy is of historical interest only, but it is a mistake to assume that it was never recognized in this country.[1]

(iii) Plea to the Jurisdiction

By this plea the defendant questions the authority of the court to try him for the offense charged. If the lack of jurisdiction is shown on the face of the indictment, or information, it is demurrable or quashable. And if the lack is established by the evidence the defendant is entitled to an acquittal. This plea, therefore, was seldom used and has been omitted by many of the statutes. There is no prop-

---

1. It was allowed, for example, in State v. Sutcliffe, 4 Strob. 372 (S.C. 1850).

er place for it in simplified procedure. A motion should be adequate to raise any objection to the jurisdiction which can be determined without the aid of a jury. This is accomplished by Rule 12 of the Federal Rules of Criminal Procedure.

(iv). Plea in Abatement

At common law any objection to the prosecution which could not be raised properly by a plea in bar could be raised by a plea in abatement. This plea could be used for any defect, either apparent on the face of the indictment or founded on some matter extrinsic of the record. Thus to a large extent it tended merely to duplicate the demurrer or the motion to quash. It was purely a dilatory device for it was "a rule upon all pleas in abatement that he who takes advantage of a flaw must at the same time show how it may be amended" (4 Bl.Comm. 335). Its most frequent use came to be in cases of misnomer. If the defendant was indicted by the wrong name he could force a new indictment by filing this plea and proving his true name. Modern statutes have very generally simplified the procedure at this point. In one form or another they require defendant to state his true name at the time of arraignment, if he has been misnamed. If he fails to do so the prosecution may proceed under the name originally used. If he gives his true name this is duly entered in the record and included in subsequent proceedings without the delay of a new indictment or information. There is no room for a plea in abatement in simplified procedure, but it is still found in a few states.

(v) Plea of Pardon

It was a rule of the common law that an offender could not be tried for an offense for which he had been pardoned. But unless the pardon was in such form that the court could take judicial notice thereof, a special plea was required—the plea of pardon. If the defendant did not enter this plea he could be tried and convicted, though his pardon would still protect him from punishment. Only the most formalistic procedure would provide for such a plea because a pardon can be brought to the attention of the court in the most informal manner. It may be added that in some states the constitutional provision for pardon applies only "after conviction."

(vi) Pleas of Former Conviction, Former Acquittal or Former Jeopardy

The pleas of former conviction and former acquittal played an important part in the development of the law of "former jeopardy."

Some of the states added a third plea—the plea of former jeopardy. This addition was due to the notion that without it the protection to which a defendant was entitled might be defeated by the simple device of stopping the first prosecution before it reached the point of conviction or acquittal. Courts, however, have tended to reach the same results whether this third plea was included in the statute or not. Without the addition of this plea the tendency has been to hold that if the case is withdrawn from a jury, after it has been sworn and "charged with the deliverance of the defendant," and *without proper reason*, this is "equivalent to an acquittal" and bars a subsequent prosecution for that reason. Where this plea is included in the statute, on the other hand, the withdrawal of a case from a jury after "jeopardy has attached" has been held not to bar a subsequent prosecution if it was because of "evident necessity." Thus a plea of former jeopardy has been held not to bar a trial by a second jury if the case was withdrawn from the first because of illness of a juror, or of the defendant, or of the judge; because of impossibility of the jurors to agree upon a verdict; or because of other extreme physical or legal necessity.

There is no need, however, for any of these three pleas. The defendant is to be protected against double punishment and against an *improper* second trial, but no special plea is needed for this purpose. If the determination can be made without the aid of a jury a motion to dismiss should be sufficient to raise the point. And proper instructions to the jury in a trial under a plea of not guilty can complete the safeguard. These pleas (or at least the first two of them) are to be found in a number of the statutes but the trend is in the direction of abolishing them, as is done in Rule 12 of the Federal Rules of Criminal Procedure.

(vii) Plea of Agreement to Turn State's Evidence

Efficient enforcement of the law often makes it important for officers to enlist the aid of certain offenders in order to convict others. At times this has taken the form of an agreement by the prosecuting attorney not to prosecute a certain offender if he will testify against other parties to the same crime. This practice should be limited to cases of necessity and should be used with care to insure that the net result is the conviction of those most deserving punishment. The prosecuting attorney seldom will violate such an agreement on his part, but if he should the matter can be brought to the attention of the court. Since the prosecuting attorney has no pardoning power this cannot be an absolute bar to the prosecution, but it should be sufficient for the court to dismiss the prosecution if this is consistent with the ends of justice. Texas recognized a plea of agreement to turn state's evidence.[a] It was held that the plea was addressed solely to the court and did not present a jury question.[b] It is a matter much more appropriately handled by a motion to dismiss and this plea has had no general recognition.

(viii) Plea of Not Guilty by Reason of Insanity

Although the trend has been in the direction of reducing the pleas to be used in criminal cases, one new plea has been added by legislation [1] although it has not had widespread adoption. This is the plea of not guilty by reason of insanity. The hope was to simplify the trial by limiting this issue to a trial under this plea, and determining every other issue of guilt or innocence under the general plea of not guilty. It is doubtful that the added plea achieved the desired result. If this plea is joined with the plea of not guilty, under the California statutes, the defendant is tried first under the plea of not guilty and in that trial he is conclusively presumed to have been sane at the time of the alleged offense. If the verdict is guilty he is then tried on the plea of not guilty by reason of insanity, either before the same jury or a new jury.[2]

(ix) Plea of Not Guilty

Where a claim is made against the defendant in a civil action on certain alleged facts, the existence of which the defendant intends to deny on the trial, his pleading is framed in such a way as to deny generally the facts alleged against him. If, on the contrary, the defendant intends to admit that the facts alleged by the plaintiff are true, but to defend by proving other facts which constitute a defense under the particular circumstances, the common law of civil procedure requires him to disclose this by the nature of his pleading, called one of confession and avoidance. He is not entitled to introduce such proof under a plea which merely purports to deny the facts alleged. There was no such distinction in the common law of criminal procedure. If a defendant, charged with having feloniously stolen, taken and carried away the goods of another and so forth, intends to defend on the ground that he did not take the goods at all, his plea is "not guilty." But he enters the same plea if he intends to admit that he took and carried away the goods but did so (1) because they belonged to him and he had the right of immediate possession, (2)

---

a. Camron v. State, 32 Tex.Cr.R. 180, 22 S.W. 682 (1893).

b. Cameron [sic] v. State, 25 S.W. 288 (Tex.Cr.App.1894). See Prosecuting Attorney's Promise of Immunity, 46 Harv.L.Rev. 714 (1933).

1. See West's Ann.Cal.Pen.Code, § 1016.

2. Id. at § 1026.

Sec. 4   STEPS BY THE DEFENDANT   853

because he had the owner's consent to take them, (3) because he reasonably and in good faith believed that he had the owner's consent to take them, (4) because he took them as an officer of the law under proper authority to do so, or for any other reason which would constitute a defense to the charge. In truth, the plea of "not guilty" does not purport to say whether the facts charged in the indictment or information are untrue, or whether there are additional facts which nullify the effect of those charged so far as the defendant is concerned. It purports no more than its face value—that the defendant is "not guilty" of the offense charged.

The rule that a plea of not guilty in a criminal case raises every possible issue of guilt or innocence still prevails in general. Statutes creating some special plea such as "not guilty by reason of insanity" withdraw one particular issue from the general plea of "not guilty." But such special plea is not one of confession and avoidance. It admits nothing. (If this plea is filed without also the filing of a plea of not guilty, the net result is an admission that the defendant did the act charged.)

(x) Plea of Guilty

The plea of guilty does not give rise to any issue. It is a formal confession of guilt before the court, and is the equivalent of a verdict of guilty except for the possibility of withdrawal. At common law the court, *in its discretion,* might refuse or permit the withdrawal of a plea of guilty and the substitution of another plea therefor, at any time before sentence was pronounced. This is the general rule today, but an occasional decision (misinterpreting a statute intending to codify the common law rule) has held that the defendant has an absolute right to withdraw his plea of guilty, if he does so in time.[1] The most astounding case on this point is in Iowa. The defendant pleaded guilty. The judge, after assuring himself that defendant fully understood the charge against him and meant to confess his guilt, accepted the plea. Later the judge, after giving defendant an opportunity to offer any reason why judgment should not be pronounced against him, sentenced him to a term in the penitentiary. After the defendant had spent a few days in the penitentiary he formed a dislike for the place and appealed to his lawyer to get him out at once. The lawyer found that the sentence had not yet been entered in the court's record book and announced in open court that the defendant withdrew his plea of guilty. The judge refused to permit the withdrawal but he was reversed by the Supreme Court of Iowa.[2] The notion that the judgment of the court is not the official pronouncement from the bench, but the manual act of the clerk in entering it in the record

---

[1] State v. Hale, 44 Iowa 96 (1876).
[2] State v. Wieland, 217 Iowa 887, 251 N.W. 757 (1933).

book is questionable although as a matter of common law it is not a "final judgment" until such entry. Prior thereto it is within the control of the judge, but it should not be within the unlimited control of the defendant. In a later case the court soundly overruled its long list of cases giving the defendant an absolute right to withdraw his plea and gave the statute its proper interpretation, which leaves the granting or refusing of the withdrawal in the discretion of the court.[3]

At common law the defendant may plead guilty to any offense. The court cannot refuse to accept the plea even in a capital case. It may, however, advise him to withdraw a plea of guilty, and will usually do so in a case punishable by death. Moreover, the court may give the defendant an opportunity to consider the matter and retract his plea by postponing either the entrance of the plea or the judgment pronounced upon it. A few of the statutes do not permit the acceptance of a plea of guilty in a capital case.[4]

(xi). Plea of Nolo Contendere

If the defendant was indicted for a non-capital offense he might, at common law, offer a plea which did not expressly confess his guilt but impliedly did so by throwing himself on the king's mercy. This plea differed from the plea of guilty in two important respects. It could not be entered unless it was accepted by the court. Even if accepted by the court the filing of such a plea could not be used in a civil action for the same injury as a confession of guilt.[5] This plea is no longer recognized in England, in Canada, or (for the most part at least) in state cases in this country; but it has always been recognized in the federal courts. It is expressly included in Rule 11 of the Federal Rules of Criminal Procedure. In explaining this inclusion it was said:

"Historically the plea of *nolo contendere* was made only as a preliminary to an arrangement or an expectation that the punishment would be a fine and nothing more; but that, at least in recent years, has disappeared, and the plea of *nolo contendere* has exactly the same effect so far as punishment is concerned as a plea of guilty.

"However, it was thought by the Committee that this particular plea should be retained because of the effect of a plea of guilty in an antitrust case, for instance, and the implication that arises from the Clayton Act and all those things." [6]

---

3. State v. Machovec, 236 Iowa 377, 17 N.W.2d 843 (1945).

4. A statute may require the court to refuse to accept a plea of guilty in a capital case if defendant is not represented by counsel. People v. Ballentine, 39 Cal.2d 193, 246 P.2d 35 (1952).

5. 1 Hawk.P.C. c. 31, § 3.

6. VI New York University School of Law Institute Proceedings 162 (1946).

The official notes prepared by the committee add:

"While at times criticized as theoretically lacking in logical basis, experience has shown that it performs a useful function from a practical standpoint." [7]

(xii) PLEA OF GUILTY TO A LESSER OFFENSE

If the charge in the indictment or information is of a crime which has lower degrees, or other included offenses, the defendant may *offer* to plead guilty to any such offense of which he could be convicted on a trial under this indictment or information. Such a plea cannot be entered as a matter of right, and the judge ordinarily will refuse to accept it unless the prosecuting attorney so recommends.

If the defendant offers to plead guilty to some offense not named in the indictment, and not an "included offense," this is in substance a request that the original indictment or information be dismissed and a new one filed. This is entirely outside of the formal procedure.

The whole practice of "bargaining for pleas" has the possibility of abuse and should be handled with caution by prosecuting authorities.

(F) DISCOVERY *

The procedure by which one litigant is enabled to force his opponent to make certain of his evidence available for examination has come to be known as "discovery", and if this authorization is granted prior to the trial itself it is often referred to as "pre-trial discovery". The modern trend in civil cases has been to go very far in this direction.

Limiting our attention to criminal procedure it may be said without hesitation that the common law of England prior to the Revo-

---

7. Notes to Rule 11, Federal Rules of Criminal Procedure, 18 U.S.C.A.

Another form of this plea is *non vult contendere* (he does not wish to contend). In a California murder case the court refused to permit defendant to withdraw a plea of not guilty and plead *non vult contendere*, but later permitted him to withdraw his original plea and plead guilty. People v. Lennox, 67 Cal. 113, 7 P. 260 (1885).

The plea of nolo contendere was added to the California Penal Code by a 1963 amendment to section 1016.

* See Fletcher, Pretrial Discovery in State Criminal Cases, 12 Stan.L.Rev. 293 (1960); Louisell, Criminal Discovery, Real or Apparent, 49 Calif.L.Rev. 56 (1961); Louisell, The Theory of Criminal Discovery and Practice of Criminal Law, 14 Vand.L.Rev. 921 (1961).

lution made no provision for discovery by a criminal defendant. What seems to have been the first effort in this direction occurred shortly after the Revolution, when a motion was made for an order requiring the prosecution to make a report available for inspection by the defendant.[1] The Attorney-General said: "There never yet was an instance of such an application as the present, to give the defendant an opportunity of inspecting the evidence intended to be used against him upon a public prosecution". The motion was made upon two grounds: first, as a matter of right; and second, as within the discretion of the court. It was denied upon both grounds, Lord Kenyon saying: "There is no principle to warrant it . . .: and if we were to grant it, it would subvert the whole system of criminal law".

Some years later a different position was taken by the English court. Thus in 1833 the prosecution was directed to permit the defendant to examine a threatening letter allegedly written by him, in order to give his witnesses an opportunity to study the handwriting.[2] And in 1861 a defendant charged with false pretenses was given permission to inspect letters written by him to the alleged victim.[3] It is probable that in each case the court was thinking of this as something within its power to grant rather than a right belonging to the defendant. Without question this was the position taken in a recent Pennsylvania case.[4] The trial judge had ordered the prosecution to permit a pre-trial inspection by defendant of the alleged murder weapon, and pictures of the bedroom which was the scene of the killing, and the prosecution sought a writ of prohibition to prevent the carrying out of this order. In denying the writ the Supreme Court of Pennsylvania emphasized that the trial judge had exercised his discretionary power and was not enforcing any right of the defendant. A vigorous dissent asserted that even the recognition of such a discretionary power in the court was a "disastrous precedent-shattering decision".

The dissenting justice would have avoided this phrase if his research of the cases had been a little more extensive. As early as 1927 the Missouri court had recognized that the defendant in a criminal case has a right of discovery when circumstances make this important for the proper preparation of his defense.[5] This was a

1. The King v. Holland, 4 T.R. 691, 100 Eng.Rep. 1248 (K.B.1792).

2. Rex v. Harrie, 6 Car. & P. 105, 172 Eng.Rep. 1165 (1833).

3. Regina v. Colucci, 3 F. & F. 103, 176 Eng.Rep. 46 (1861).

4. In re Di Joseph's Petition, 394 Pa. 19, 145 A.2d 187 (1958).

5. State v. Tippet, 317 Mo. 319, 296 S. W. 132 (1927). In the same year the New York court, with an elaborate discussion of pre-trial discovery, refused to order the district attorney to make available to defendant documents and memoranda which were not themselves admissible in evidence. People ex rel. Lemon v. Supreme Court, 245 N.Y. 24, 156 N.E. 84, 52 A.L.R. 200 (1927).

prosecution for leaving the scene of a fatal traffic accident without stopping and an eye-witness had given the prosecution a written statement of the accident. The trial judge denied defendant's motion for a pre-trial inspection of the statement and this was held to be error. The defendant had a right to this discovery. Even earlier than this Iowa had a statute permitting such discovery but this had been held not to be mandatory.[6]

Probably no state has gone farther than California in recognizing the defendant's right to pre-trial inspection of evidence in the hands of the prosecution. In Powell [7], often regarded the leading California case on the point, D made a motion for an order authorizing D and his attorney to inspect and copy a signed statement made by D in the office of the Chief of Police, and also of a typewritten transcript of a tape recording made later in the same office. The motion was supported by affidavits of D and his attorney which set forth that D was not able to recall his statements nor relate them to his attorney; that the documents might be necessary to refresh D's recollection; that the evidence in the statements was material to the issue of liability, if any, and would be admissible at the trial. No counter affidavits were filed. The trial judge denied the motion on the ground that in a criminal prosecution the accused is not entitled to a pre-trial inspection of his written confession. The Supreme Court of California issued a writ of mandamus requiring the respondent court to set aside its original order and to issue an appropriate order of inspection with the right to make copies as requested.

Where discovery in a criminal case is recognized it has included not only confessions but such subjects as guns and bullets,[8] reports of scientific analyses,[9] autopsies [10] and photographs of persons and places [11].

Rule 16 of the Federal Rules of Criminal Procedure provides that upon motion of a defendant at any time after the filing of an indictment or information the court may order the attorney for the government to permit the defendant to inspect and copy or photograph designated books, papers, documents or tangible objects obtained from or belonging to the defendant, or obtained from others by seizure or process, upon a showing that the items sought may be material to the preparation of his defense and that the request is reasonable.[12]

6. State v. Howard, 191 Iowa 728, 183 N.W. 482 (1921).

7. Powell v. Superior Court In and For Los Angeles County, 48 Cal.2d 704, 312 P.2d 698 (1957).

8. State ex rel. Mahoney v. Superior Court, 78 Ariz. 74, 275 P.2d 887 (1954).

9. Walker v. Superior Court In and For Mendocino County, 155 Cal.App.2d 134, 317 P.2d 130 (1957).

10. State v. Thompson, 54 Wash.2d 100, 338 P.2d 319 (1959).

11. Norton v. Superior Court In and For San Diego County, 173 Cal.App. 2d 133, 343 P.2d 139 (1959).

12. For a somewhat similar rule see State v. Johnson, 28 N.J. 133, 145 A.2d 313 (1958).

It is noteworthy that this does not include signed or tape-recorded confessions or statements made by the defendant,[13] nor physical objects not belonging to the defendant which were found by the police or turned over to them voluntarily by others.

Jencks [14] established the right of the defendant in a criminal case to inspect written reports such as FBI records, *after the witness has testified in court*, to aid in cross-examination. And the so-called Jencks Act, 18 U.S.C.A. § 3500 provides: "In any criminal prosecution . . . no statement or report . . . made by a Government witness or prospective Government witness (other than the defendant) . . . shall be subject of subpoena, discovery or inspection until said witness has testified on direct examination in the trial of the case".[15]

Rule 16 of the Federal Rules of Criminal Procedure gives the defendant a substantial right of pre-trial discovery. It is now proposed to amend that rule to read as follows:

(a) Defendant's Statements; Reports of Examinations and Tests; Defendant's Grand Jury Testimony. Upon motion of a defendant the court may order the attorney for the government to permit the defendant to inspect and copy or photograph any relevant (1) written or recorded statements or confessions made by the defendant, or copies thereof, which are known by the attorney for the government to be within the possession, custody or control of the government, (2) results or reports of physical or mental examinations, and of scientific tests or experiments made in connection with the particular case, or copies thereof, which are known by the attorney for the government to be within the possession, custody or control of the

---

13. A defendant's oral statement, reduced to writing by a government stenographer, is not within the rule authorizing the court to order the government's attorney to permit the inspection and transcription of designated books and so forth. United States v. Peltz, 18 F.R.D. 394 (D.C. S.D.N.Y.1955). But compare United States v. Wider, 117 F.Supp. 484 (D. C.E.D.N.Y.1954).

14. Jencks v. United States, 353 U.S. 657, 77 S.Ct. 1007, 1 L.Ed.2d 1103 (1957).

A 600-word memorandum summarizing parts of a 3½-hour interrogation of witnesses is not a "statement" of the kind required to be produced by the so-called "Jencks Act" (18 U.S.C.A. § 3500). Palermo v. United States, 360 U.S. 343, 79 S.Ct. 1217, 3 L.Ed.2d 1287 (1959). An appendix to the opinion gives a partial summary of the legislative history bearing on the proper construction of the statute.

15. An FBI agent interviewed a witness, taking notes at the time. The agent then repeated back to the witness what had been said, referring to his notes. The witness indicated that the agent's oral presentation was correct. The agent then incorporated the substance of the notes in an "interview report" and destroyed the original notes. The trial judge found that this report was producible as a written statement made by said witness and adopted by him within the meaning of section 3500(e) (1). Prior to this finding the judge had denied a motion for the production of this statement in a trial resulting in conviction. The conviction was reversed. Campbell v. United States, 373 U.S. 487, 83 S.Ct. 1356, 10 L.Ed.2d 501 (1963).

Sec. 4 *STEPS BY THE DEFENDANT* 859

government, and (3) recorded testimony of the defendant before a grand jury.

(b) Other Books, Papers, Documents or Tangible Objects. Upon motion of a defendant the court may order the attorney for the government to permit the defendant to inspect and copy or photograph books, papers, documents or tangible objects, or copies or portions thereof, which are within the possession, custody or control of the government, upon a showing that the items sought may be material to the preparation of his defense and that the request is reasonable. This subdivision does not authorize the discovery or inspection of reports, memoranda, or other internal government documents made by government agents in connection with the investigation or prosecution of the case, or of statements made by government witnesses or prospective government witnesses (other than the defendant) to agents of the government except as provided in 18 U.S.C.A. § 3500.

(c) Discovery by the Government. If the court grants relief sought by the defendant under this rule, it may condition its order by requiring that the defendant permit the government to inspect, copy or photograph statements, scientific or medical reports, books, papers, documents or tangible objects, which the defendant intends to produce at the trial and which are within his possession, custody or control. . . .

It has often been assumed that the prosecution would have no right of pre-trial discovery in a criminal case, but the California court has held that where important it is entitled to such discovery as will violate neither defendant's privilege against self-incrimination nor the attorney-client privilege.[16] D, charged with rape, asked for a continuance on the ground that he needed time to gather medical evidence to prove he was impotent. After the continuance was granted the district attorney filed a motion requesting discovery of the names and addresses of physicians who would testify on behalf of D, the names and addresses of all physicians who had examined D prior to the trial, and all X-rays taken immediately following injuries which were claimed to have rendered D impotent. The motion having been granted by the trial court D sought prohibition on the ground that the forced disclosure of such information would violate his privilege against self-incrimination and also the attorney-client privilege. The order requiring discovery was upheld in part and reversed in part by the Supreme Court of California. The Court started with the premise that discovery should not be a "one-way street" and that the defendant in a criminal case has no valid interest in denying the prosecution access to evidence which will facilitate

16. Jones v. Superior Court of Nevada County, 58 Cal.2d 56, 22 Cal.Rptr. 879, 372 P.2d 919 (1962).

the ascertainment of the facts, except so far as necessary to protect his privilege against self-incrimination or some other recognized privilege. It held that the prosecution was entitled to discover the names of the witnesses who were to be called by D at the trial and such X-rays as he intended to introduce in evidence. The Court reasoned that this would violate no privilege of D since it did not require disclosure of anything that D did not himself intend to have brought out during the trial. But insofar as the trial court's order had required D to disclose the names of doctors he did not intend to use as witnesses and to furnish X-rays he did not intend to introduce as evidence, the forced disclosure would violate his privilege against self-incrimination and possibly also his attorney-client privilege.

Discovery was provided by an Act of Congress of 1874 which authorized a court in revenue cases, on motion of the government attorney, to require D to produce in court his private books, invoices and papers, or else the allegations of the attorney were to be taken to be confessed. The result would be a forfeiture of D's goods. It was held that such a compulsory production of a man's private papers, to be used in evidence against him, is in effect an unreasonable search and seizure in violation of the Fourth Amendment; and that it also compelled him to give evidence against himself in violation of the Fifth Amendment.[17] It is to be noted that the discovery approved in the California case was not to secure evidence to be used against D, but merely to see in advance evidence which D himself intended to use in the trial.

17. Boyd v. United States, 116 U.S. 616, 6 S.Ct. 524, 29 L.Ed. 746 (1886).

Chapter 13

CERTAIN RIGHTS AND PRIVILEGES OF THE ACCUSED

The voir dire examination, challenges to jurors, conduct of the trial, rules of evidence, instructions, and proceedings after verdict are matters normally dealt with in general practice and procedure courses, and in the course on evidence. Space limitations do not permit their inclusion here. Certain rights and privileges of the accused, however, are entitled to attention.

SECTION 1. THE RIGHT TO COUNSEL

Under the English common law one on trial for a capital crime had no right to the aid of counsel so far as matters of fact were concerned.[1] If a point of law arose it would be argued for him by counsel although originally this was due more to the desire of the judges to have the point clarified than to the recognition of any right belonging to the defendant. He did not have the aid of counsel in the examination or cross-examination of witnesses. In 1698 a statute was passed by which persons accused of high treason were given the right to have the assistance of counsel.[2] Not until 1836 did an English statute accord a similar right to those on trial for felony[3], although for some years prior to that time the judges had tended "to allow a prisoner counsel to instruct him what questions to ask, or even to ask questions for him, . . ."[4] In this country, however, the denial of assistance of counsel to those accused of crime, felony included, was rejected by the Colonies, and the right to such assistance was a part of our concept of due process of law at the time of the adoption of the Constitution.[5]

As it was not recognized under the early English law in felony cases, and no such right had been formally granted in England when the Sixth Amendment was proposed in 1789,[6] the assistance-of-counsel clause was added to insure that he should have such a right in federal prosecutions. For nearly one hundred and fifty years the right-to-

---

1. 4 Bl.Comm. *355.

2. 7 & 8 Wm. III, c. 3, sec. 1.

3. 6 & 7 Wm. IV, c. 114.

4. 4 Bl.Comm. 355–56.

5. Powell v. Alabama, 287 U.S. 45, 53 S.Ct. 55, 77 L.Ed. 158, 84 A.L.R. 527 (1932).

6. The first ten amendments, the first eight of which are known as the "Bill of Rights", were proposed on September 25, 1789, and ratified on December 15, 1791.

862   RIGHTS AND PRIVILEGES OF THE ACCUSED   Ch. 13

counsel guarantee of the Sixth Amendment was understood to mean only that an accused person who appeared with counsel was entitled to have the assistance of this attorney in his defense against the charge. When Congress, for example, enacted a statute in 1790 requiring the court to assign counsel to represent defendants in capital cases [7] no one doubted that this was something in addition to the constitutional guarantee. But in 1938 the Supreme Court took the position that the Sixth Amendment guarantee of assistance of counsel means not only that defendant's counsel must be permitted to assist him in his defense, but that an indigent defendant has the right to have counsel assigned to him.[8] This arose out of a trial for a non-capital felony. The right, it was explained, could be waived but the court lacked jurisdiction to try an uncounseled defendant who had not intelligently waived this right.

Rule 44 of the Federal Rules of Criminal Procedure, considered a restatement of case law as to proceedings in the federal courts [9] is as follows: "If the defendant appears in court without counsel, the court shall advise him of his right to counsel and assign counsel to represent him at every stage of the proceeding unless he elects to proceed without counsel or is able to obtain counsel."

For the most part the state courts took the position that a defendant who appeared with counsel could not be denied the right to have his assistance in the case, but that it was not necessary to assign counsel to an indigent defendant, at least in a non-capital case. And the Supreme Court held that the due-process requirement of the Fourteenth Amendment did not require a state to furnish counsel to the defendant in every criminal case in which he was unable to employ an attorney.[10] In other words, whether an indigent defendant in a non-capital case was entitled to have counsel assigned to him was held to depend upon the facts of the particular case.[11]

After several *dicta* to the effect that it would be a denial of due process to refuse to appoint counsel for an indigent defendant in a capital case in a state court, this was the square holding in

7. 1 Stat. 118. This statute is still in the books. 18 U.S.C.A. § 3005.

8. Johnson v. Zerbst, 304 U.S. 458, 58 S.Ct. 1019, 82 L.Ed. 1461, 146 A.L.R. 357 (1938).

9. Holtzoff, The Right of Counsel Under the Sixth Amendment, 20 N.Y. U.L.Q.Rev. 1 (1944).

10. Betts v. Brady, 316 U.S. 455, 62 S.Ct. 1252, 86 L.Ed. 1595 (1942). The conviction was affirmed in a robbery case in which the defendant did not have counsel and had not waived his right.

11. See, for example, Williams v. Kaiser, 323 U.S. 471, 65 S.Ct. 363, 89 L.Ed. 398 (1945); Tomkins v. Missouri, 323 U.S. 485, 65 S.Ct. 370, 89 L.Ed. 407 (1945); Uveges v. Pennsylvania, 335 U.S. 437, 69 S.Ct. 184, 93 L.Ed. 127 (1948); Bute v. Illinois, 333 U.S. 640, 68 S.Ct. 763, 92 L.Ed. 986 (1948); Crooker v. California, 357 U.S. 433, 78 S.Ct. 1287, 2 L.Ed.2d 1448 (1958); Cicenia v. Lagay, 357 U.S. 504, 78 S.Ct. 1297, 2 L.Ed.2d 1523 (1958).

Hamilton.[12] At this point the position seemed to be that except in a capital case an indigent defendant in a state criminal case was entitled to have counsel appointed for him if there were special circumstances which made this important, but not otherwise.[13]

GIDEON v. WAINWRIGHT

Supreme Court of the United States, 1963.
372 U.S. 335, 83 S.Ct. 792.

MR. JUSTICE BLACK delivered the opinion of the Court.

Petitioner was charged in a Florida state court with having broken and entered a poolroom with intent to commit a misdemeanor. This offense is a felony under Florida law. Appearing in court without funds and without a lawyer, petitioner asked the court to appoint counsel for him, whereupon the following colloquy took place:

"The COURT: Mr. Gideon, I am sorry, but I cannot appoint Counsel to represent you in this case. Under the laws of the State of Florida, the only time the Court can appoint Counsel to represent a Defendant is when that person is charged with a capital offense. I am sorry, but I will have to deny your request to appoint Counsel to defend you in this case.

"The DEFENDANT: The United States Supreme Court says I am entitled to be represented by Counsel."

Put to trial before a jury, Gideon conducted his defense about as well as could be expected from a layman. He made an opening statement to the jury, cross-examined the State's witnesses, presented witnesses in his own defense, declined to testify himself, and made a short argument "emphasizing his innocence to the charge contained in the Information filed in this case." The jury returned a verdict of guilty, and petitioner was sentenced to serve five years in the state prison. Later, petitioner filed in the Florida Supreme Court this habeas corpus petition attacking his conviction and sentence on the ground that the trial court's refusal to appoint counsel for him denied him rights "guaranteed by the Constitution and the Bill of Rights by the United States Government." Treating the petition for habeas corpus as properly before it, the State Supreme Court, "upon consideration thereof" but without an opinion, denied all relief. Since 1942, when Betts v. Brady, 316 U.S. 455, 62 S.Ct. 1252, 86 L.Ed. 1595, was decided by a divided Court, the problem of a defendant's federal constitutional right to counsel in a state court has been a continuing source of controversy and litigation in both state and federal courts. To give this problem another

---

12. Hamilton v. Alabama, 386 U.S. 52, 82 S.Ct. 157, 7 L.Ed.2d 114 (1961).

13. See Chewning v. Cunningham, 368 U.S. 443, 82 S.Ct. 498, 7 L.Ed.2d 442 (1962).

review here, we granted certiorari. Since Gideon was proceeding *in forma pauperis*, we appointed counsel to represent him and requested both sides to discuss in their briefs and oral arguments the following: "Should this Court's holding in Betts v. Brady, 316 U.S. 455, 62 S.Ct. 1252, 86 L.Ed. 1595, be reconsidered?" . . .

Treating due process as "a concept less rigid and more fluid than those envisaged in other specific and particular provisions of the Bill of Rights," the Court held that refusal to appoint counsel under the particular facts and circumstances in the Betts case was not so "offensive to the common and fundamental ideas of fairness" as to amount to a denial of due process. Since the facts and circumstances of the two cases are so nearly indistinguishable, we think the Betts v. Brady holding if left standing would require us to reject Gideon's claim that the Constitution guarantees him the assistance of counsel. Upon full reconsideration we conclude that Betts v. Brady should be overruled. . . .

We accept Betts v. Brady's assumption, based as it was on our prior cases, that a provision of the Bill of Rights which is "fundamental and essential to a fair trial" is made obligatory upon the States by the Fourteenth Amendment. We think the Court in Betts was wrong, however, in concluding that the Sixth Amendment's guarantee of counsel is not one of these fundamental rights. Ten years before Betts v. Brady, this Court, after full consideration of all the historical data examined in Betts, had unequivocally declared that "the right to the aid of counsel is of this fundamental character." Powell v. Alabama, 287 U.S. 45, 68, 53 S.Ct. 55, 63, 77 L.Ed. 158 (1932). While the Court at the close of its Powell opinion did by its language, as this Court frequently does, limit its holding to the particular facts and circumstances of that case, its conclusions about the fundamental nature of the right to counsel are unmistakable. . . .

Not only these precedents but also reason and reflection require us to recognize that in our adversary system of criminal justice, any person haled into court, who is too poor to hire a lawyer, cannot be assured a fair trial unless counsel is provided for him. This seems to us to be an obvious truth. Governments, both state and federal, quite properly spend vast sums of money to establish machinery to try defendants accused of crime. Lawyers to prosecute are everywhere deemed essential to protect the public's interest in an orderly society. Similarly, there are few defendants charged with crime, few indeed, who fail to hire the best lawyers they can get to prepare and present their defenses. That government hires lawyers to prosecute and defendants who have the money hire lawyers to defend are the strongest indications of the widespread belief that lawyers in criminal courts are necessities, not luxuries. **The right** of one charged with crime to counsel may not be deemed fundamental and essential to fair trials in some countries, but it is in ours. From the very beginning, our state and national constitutions and laws have laid great emphasis on procedural and substantive safeguards designed to assure fair trials before impartial tribunals in which every defendant stands equal before the law. This noble ideal cannot be realized if the poor man charged with crime has to face his accusers without a lawyer to assist him. A defendant's need for a lawyer is nowhere better stated than in the moving words of Mr. Justice Sutherland in Powell v. Alabama:

"The right to be heard would be, in many cases, of little avail if it did not comprehend the right to be heard by counsel. Even the intelligent and educated layman has small and sometimes no skill in the science of law. If charged with crime, he is incapable, generally, of determining for himself whether the indictment is good or bad. He is unfamiliar with the rules of evidence. Left without the aid of counsel he may be put on trial without a proper charge, and convicted upon incompetent evidence, or evidence irrelevant to the issue or otherwise inadmissible. He lacks both the skill and knowledge adequately to prepare his defense, even though he have a perfect one. He requires the guiding hand of counsel at every step in the proceedings against him. Without it, though he be not guilty, he faces the danger of conviction because he does not know how to establish his innocence." 287 U.S., at 68–69, 53 S.Ct., at 64, 77 L.Ed. 158.

The Court in Betts v. Brady departed from the sound wisdom upon which the Court's holding in Powell v. Alabama rested. Florida, supported by two other States, has asked that Betts v. Brady be left intact. Twenty-two States, as friends of the Court, argue that Betts was "an anachronism when handed down" and that it should now be overruled. We agree.

The judgment is reversed and the cause is remanded to the Supreme Court of Florida for further action not inconsistent with this opinion.

Reversed.[1]

[By the Compiler.]

1. The right to counsel means effective counsel. It is not sufficient that D was represented by a member of the bar, or even by a lawyer who is very competent in other fields. If the attorney was so unfamiliar with the crucial problems of the case as to be unable to make an effective defense D has been deprived of his right to counsel. People v. Ibarra, 60 Cal.2d 460, 34 Cal.Rptr. 863, 386 P.2d 487 (1963). The fact that counsel advised D to plead guilty although there were technical defenses that might have handicapped the prosecution was held not to entitle him to relief. Edwards v. United States, 103 U.S.App.D.C. 152, 256 F.2d 707 (1958).

"In every criminal case in which the defendant is charged with a felony or a misdemeanor, other than a petty offense, and appears without counsel, the United States commissioner or the court shall advise the defendant that he has a right to be represented by counsel and that counsel will be appointed to represent him if he is financially unable to obtain counsel. . . ." Criminal Justice Act of 1964, sec. 3006A(b).

Failure to notify accused of his constitutional right to assistance of coun-

Mr. Justice Douglas. . . . My Brother Harlan is of the view that a guarantee of the Bill of Rights that is made applicable to the States by reason of the Fourteenth Amendment is a lesser version of that same guarantee as applied to the Federal Government. Mr. Justice Jackson shared that view. But that view has not prevailed and rights protected against state invasion by the Due Process Clause of the Fourteenth Amendment are not watered-down versions of what the Bill of Rights guarantees.

Mr. Justice Clark, concurring in the result. . . .

Mr. Justice Harlan, concurring.

I agree that Betts v. Brady should be overruled, but consider it entitled to a more respectful burial than has been accorded, at least on the part of those of us who were not on the Court when that case was decided. . . .

In agreeing with the Court that the right to counsel in a case such as this should now be expressly recognized as a fundamental right embraced in the Fourteenth Amendment, I wish to make a further observation. When we hold a right or immunity, valid against the Federal Government, to be "implicit in the concept of ordered liberty" and thus valid against the States, I do not read our past decisions to suggest that by so holding, we automatically carry over an entire body of federal law and apply it in full sweep to the States. Any such concept would disregard the frequently wide disparity between the legitimate interests of the States and of the Federal Government, the divergent problems that they face, and the significantly different consequences of their actions. Cf. Roth v. United States, 354 U.S. 476, 496–508, 77 S.Ct. 1304, 1315–1321, 1 L.Ed.2d 1498 (separate opinion of this writer). In what is done today I do not understand the Court to depart from the principles laid down in Palko v. Connecticut, 302 U.S. 319, 58 S.Ct. 149, 82 L.Ed. 288, or to embrace the concept that the Fourteenth Amendment "incorporates" the Sixth Amendment as such.

On these premises I join in the judgment of the Court.

---

sel invalidated his guilty plea and rendered his conviction and incarceration for a misdemeanor constitutionally improper, in a state case. Harvey v. Mississippi, 340 F.2d 263 (5th Cir. 1965).

"The Supreme Court has indicated that **the right to have the assistance of** counsel carries with it a 'correlative **right to dispense with a lawyer's** help'. Adams v. United States ex rel. McCann, 1942, 317 U.S. 269, 279, 63 S.Ct. 236, 241. From that indication this and other Courts of Appeals have deduced that in a criminal prosecution the right to defend pro se is a constitutionally protected **right.**" Juelich v. United States, 342 F.2d 29, 31 (5th Cir. 1965).

DOUGLAS v. CALIFORNIA

Supreme Court of the United States, 1963.
372 U.S. 353, 83 S.Ct. 814.

Mr. Justice Douglas delivered the opinion of the Court. . . .

Although several questions are presented in the petition for certiorari, we address ourselves to only one of them. The record shows that petitioners requested, and were denied, the assistance of counsel on appeal, even though it plainly appeared they were indigents. In denying petitioners' requests, the California District Court of Appeal stated that it had "gone through" the record and had come to the conclusion that "no good whatever could be served by appointment of counsel." The District Court of Appeal was acting in accordance with a California rule of criminal procedure which provides that state appellate courts, upon the request of an indigent for counsel, may make "an independent investigation of the record and determine whether it would be of advantage to the defendant or helpful to the appellate court to have counsel appointed. . . . After such investigation, appellate courts should appoint counsel if in their opinion it would be helpful to the defendant or the court, and should deny the appointment of counsel only if in their judgment such appointment would be of no value to either the defendant or the court." People v. Hyde, 51 Cal.2d 152, 154, 331 P.2d 42, 43. . . .

In spite of California's forward treatment of indigents, under its present practice the type of an appeal a person is afforded in the District Court of Appeal hinges upon whether or not he can pay for the assistance of counsel. If he can the appellate court passes on the merits of his case only after having the full benefit of written briefs and oral argument by counsel. If he cannot the appellate court is forced to prejudge the merits before it can even determine whether counsel should be provided. At this stage in the proceedings only the barren record speaks for the indigent, and, unless the printed pages show that an injustice has been committed, he is forced to go without a champion on appeal. Any real chance he may have had of showing that his appeal has hidden merit is deprived him when the court decides on an *ex parte* examination of the record that the assistance of counsel is not required.

We are not here concerned with problems that might arise from the denial of counsel for the preparation of a petition for discretionary or mandatory review beyond the stage in the appellate process at which the claims have once been presented by a lawyer and passed upon by an appellate court. We are dealing only with the first appeal, granted as a matter of right to rich and poor alike (Cal.Penal Code §§ 1235, 1237), from a criminal conviction. We need not now decide whether California would have to provide counsel for an indigent seeking a discretionary hearing from the California Supreme Court after the District Court of Appeal had sustained his conviction (see Cal.Const., Art. VI, § 4c; Cal.Rules on Appeal, Rules 28, 29), or whether counsel must be appointed for an indigent seeking review of an appellate affirmance of his conviction in this Court by appeal as of right or by petition for a writ of certiorari which lies within the Court's discretion. But it is appropriate to observe that a State can, consistently with the Fourteenth Amendment, provide for differences so long as the result does not amount to a denial of due process or an "invidious discrimination." [1] Absolute equality is not required; lines can be and are drawn and we often sustain them. But where the merits of the one and only appeal an indigent has as of right are decided without benefit of counsel, we think an unconstitutional line has been drawn between rich and poor. . . .

The present case, where counsel was denied petitioners on appeal, shows that the discrimination is not between "possibly good and obviously bad cases," but between cases where the rich man can require the court to listen to argument of counsel before deciding on the merits, but a poor man cannot. There is lacking that equality demanded by the Fourteenth Amendment where the rich man, who appeals as of right, enjoys the benefit of counsel's examination into the record, research of the law, and marshalling of arguments on his behalf, while the indigent, already burdened by a preliminary

[By the Compiler.]

1. An indigent defendant who had counsel appointed to represent him on appeal was not subjected to invidious discrimination because neither that counsel nor the appellate court could discover a meritorious ground of appeal and the appellate court refused to appoint other counsel to represent him. In re Nash, 61 Cal.2d 491, 39 Cal.Rptr. 205, 393 P.2d 405 (1964). When an indigent prisoner has petitioned for a writ of error *coram nobis* it will often be readily apparent from the petition and the court's own records that the petition is without merit and should be summarily denied. In such a case appointment of counsel is not required. If, however, facts have been stated sufficient to satisfy the court that a hearing is required the petitioner is entitled to have counsel appointed to represent him. And he is entitled to have counsel appointed to represent him on appeal from an adverse determination at such hearing, subject to the limitations set forth in Nash. People v. Shipman, 62 Cal.2d 226, 42 Cal.Rptr. 1, 397 P.2d 993 (1965).

The state court is not required to appoint counsel for an indigent defendant to represent him in taking an appeal to the Supreme Court of the United States. Peters v. Cox, 341 F.2d 575 (10th Cir. 1965).

While the right to counsel under the Sixth Amendment extends through a direct appeal of the judgment of conviction it does not apply to a hearing under a motion to vacate the judgment. But if the circumstances were such that a fair and meaningful hearing could not be had without the aid of counsel the due process clause of the Fifth Amendment would require such aid. Dillon v. United States, 307 F.2d 445 (9th Cir. 1962).

Where counsel appointed for the purpose of appealing files notice of appeal and later requests permission to withdraw, on the ground that the record showed no prejudicial error, defendant was not entitled to have a second counsel appointed. Speers v. Gladden, 237 Or. 100, 390 P.2d 635 (1964). Contra, Hodge v. Reincke, 25 Conn. Sup. 207, 200 A.2d 252 (1964).

determination that his case is without merit, is forced to shift for himself. The indigent, where the record is unclear or the errors are hidden, has only the right to a meaningless ritual, while the rich man has a meaningful appeal.

We vacate the judgment of the District Court of Appeal and remand the case to that court for further proceedings not inconsistent with this opinion. It is so ordered.

Judgment of the District Court of Appeal vacated and case remanded.

MR. JUSTICE CLARK, dissenting.

I adhere to my vote in Griffin v. Illinois, 351 U.S. 12, 76 S.Ct. 585, 100 L.Ed. 891 (1956), but, as I have always understood that case, it does not control here. It had to do with the State's obligation to furnish a record to an indigent on appeal. There we took pains to point out that the State was free to "find other means of affording adequate and effective appellate review to indigent defendants." Id., at 20, 76 S.Ct., at 591. Here California has done just that in its procedure for furnishing attorneys for indigents on appeal. We all know that the overwhelming percentage of *in forma pauperis* appeals are frivolous. Statistics of this Court show that over 96% of the petitions filed here are of this variety.[1] California, in the light of a like experience, has provided that upon the filing of an application for the appointment of counsel the District Court of Appeal shall make "an independent investigation of the record and determine whether it would be of advantage to the defendant or helpful to the appellate court to have counsel appointed." People v. Hyde, 51 Cal.2d 152, 154, 331 P.2d 42, 43 (1958). California's courts did that here and after examining the record certified that such an appointment would be neither advantageous to the petitioners nor helpful to the court. It, therefore, refused to go through the useless gesture of appointing an attorney. In my view neither the Equal Protection Clause nor the Due Process Clause requires more. I cannot understand why the Court says that this procedure afforded petitioners "a meaningless ritual." To appoint an attorney would not only have been utter extravagance and a waste of the State's funds but as surely "meaningless" to petitioners.

With this new fetish for indigency the Court piles an intolerable burden on the State's judicial machinery. Indeed, if the Court is correct it may be that we should first clean up our own house. We have afforded indigent litigants much less protection than has California. Last Term we received over 1,200 *in forma pauperis* applications in none of which had we appointed attorneys or required a record.

[By Mr. Justice Clark.]

1. Statistics from the office of the Clerk of this Court reveal that in the 1961 Term only 38 of 1093 *in forma pauperis* petitions for certiorari were granted (3.4%). Of 44 *in forma pauperis* appeals, all but one were summarily dismissed (2.3%).

Some were appeals of right. Still we denied the petitions or dismissed the appeals on the moving papers alone. At the same time we had hundreds of paid cases in which we permitted petitions or appeals to be filed with not only records but briefs by counsel, after which they were disposed of in due course. On the other hand, California furnishes the indigent a complete record and if counsel is requested requires its appellate courts either to (1) appoint counsel or (2) make an independent investigation of that record and determine whether it would be of advantage to the defendant or helpful to the court to have counsel appointed. Unlike Lane v. Brown, 372 U.S. 477, 83 S.Ct. 768, decision in these matters is not placed in the unreviewable discretion of the Public Defender or appointed counsel but is made by the appellate court itself.

California's concern for the rights of indigents is clearly revealed in People v. Hyde, supra. There, although the Public Defender had not undertaken the prosecution of the appeal, the District Court of Appeal nevertheless referred the application for counsel and the record to the Los Angeles Bar Association. One of its members reviewed these papers, after which he certified that no meritorious ground for appeal was disclosed. Despite this the California District Court of Appeal made its own independent examination of the record.

There is an old adage which my good Mother used to quote to me, i. e., "People who live in glass houses had best not throw stones." I dissent.

Mr. Justice Harlan, whom Mr. Justice Stewart joins, dissenting.

In holding that an indigent has an absolute right to appointed counsel on appeal of a state criminal conviction, the Court appears to rely both on the Equal Protection Clause and on the guarantees of fair procedure inherent in the Due Process Clause of the Fourteenth Amendment, with obvious emphasis on "equal protection." In my view the Equal Protection Clause is not apposite, and its application to cases like the present one can lead only to mischievous results. This case should be judged solely under the Due Process Clause, and I do not believe that the California procedure violates that provision.

Equal Protection

To approach the present problem in terms of the Equal Protection Clause is, I submit, but to substitute resounding phrases for analysis. I dissented from this approach in Griffin v. Illinois, and I am constrained to dissent from the implicit extension of the equal protection approach here—to a case in which the State denies no one an appeal, but seeks only to keep within reasonable bounds the instances in which appellate counsel will be assigned to indigents.

The States, of course, are prohibited by the Equal Protection Clause from discriminating between "rich" and "poor" *as such* in the formulation and application of their laws. But it is a far different thing to suggest that this provision prevents the State from adopting a law of general applicability that may affect the poor more harshly than it does the rich, or, on the other hand, from making some effort to redress economic imbalances while not eliminating them entirely.

Every financial exaction which the State imposes on a uniform basis is more easily satisfied by the well-to-do than by the indigent. Yet I take it that no one would dispute the constitutional power of the State to levy a uniform sales tax, to charge tuition at a state university, to fix rates for the purchase of water from a municipal corporation, to impose a standard fine for criminal violations, or to establish minimum bail for various categories of offenses. Nor could it be contended that the State may not classify as crimes acts which the poor are more likely to commit than are the rich. And surely there would be no basis for attacking a state law which provided benefits for the needy simply because those benefits fell short of the goods or services that others could purchase for themselves.

Laws such as these do not deny equal protection to the less fortunate for one essential reason: the Equal Protection Clause does not impose on the States "an affirmative duty to lift the handicaps flowing from differences in economic circumstances." To so construe it would be to read into the Constitution a philosophy of leveling that would be foreign to many of our basic concepts of the proper relations between government and society. The State may have a moral obligation to eliminate the evils of poverty, but it is not required by the Equal Protection Clause to give to some whatever others can afford.

Thus it should be apparent that the present case is not one properly regarded as arising under this clause. California does not discriminate between rich and poor in having a uniform policy permitting everyone to appeal and to retain counsel, and in having a separate rule dealing *only* with the standards for the appointment of counsel for those unable to retain their own attorneys. The sole classification established by this rule is between those cases that are believed to have merit and those regarded as frivolous. And, of course, no matter how far the state rule might go in providing counsel for indigents, it could never be expected to satisfy an affirmative duty —if one existed—to place the poor on the same level as those who can afford the best legal talent available.

Parenthetically, it should be noted that if the present problem may be viewed as one of equal protection, so may the question of the right to appointed counsel at trial, and the Court's analysis of that right in Gideon v. Wainwright, 372 U.S. 335, 83 S.Ct. 792, is wholly unnecessary. The short way to dispose of Gideon v. Wainwright, in other words, would be simply to say that the State deprives the indigent of equal protection whenever it fails to furnish him with legal services, and perhaps with other services as well, equivalent to those that the affluent defendant can obtain. . . .

SECTION 2. THE PRIVILEGE AGAINST SELF-INCRIMINATION

The Fifth Amendment provides: "No person shall . . . be compelled in any criminal case to be a witness against himself, ..." It seems that this provision was "originally intended only to prevent return to the hated practice of compelling a person, in a criminal proceeding directed at him, to swear against himself".[1] It has been extended by interpretation, however, to protect not only the defendant, but also the witness, in all methods of interrogation before a court, grand jury or coroner's inquest, in investigations by a legislative body or administrative official.[2] The Fifth Amendment applies *per se* only in federal proceedings, but almost all state constitutions have a like or similar provision and this is one of the provisions of the Bill of Rights which is so basic to a free society that it is incorporated into the Due Process Clause of the Fourteenth Amendment and thereby made applicable to state proceedings.[3]

---

1. 8 Wigmore, Evidence, sec. 2252, p. 324 (McNaughton rev. 1961).

2. Id. at pp. 326–328.

3. D was held in contempt of court for refusing to answer certain questions in a state proceeding. He claimed that he was privileged not to answer because the questions called for answers that would tend to be incriminating. The state court upheld the conviction on a finding that the questions did not call for incriminating answers. The Supreme Court held that the questions did call for incriminating answers and reversed the conviction on the ground that the Fifth Amendment's exemption from self-incrimination is also protected by the Fourteenth against abridgment by the states. **Malloy v. Hogan,** 378 U.S. 1, 84 S.Ct. 1489, 12 L.Ed.2d 653 (1964).

The state may compel a witness to testify, notwithstanding the fact that such testimony might tend to incriminate him of a federal offense, but the federal government would not be permitted to make any use of the testimony thus compelled. **Murphy v. Waterfront Commission of New York Harbor,** 378 U.S. 52, 84 S.Ct. 1594, 12 L.Ed.2d 678 (1964). The Court held that the privilege protects either a state or a federal witness against incrimination under either state or federal law. It expressly **overruled** United States v. Murdock, 284 U.S. 141, 52 S.Ct. 63, 76 L.Ed. 210 (1933), which held that the federal government could compel a witness to give testimony that might incriminate him under state law. The implication is that the witness can be compelled to testify but that because of the privilege the state will not be permitted to make any use of compelled testi-

Sec. 2   *PRIVILEGE AGAINST SELF–INCRIMINATION*   873

In 1628 the King of England, Charles I, asked the lord chief justice if a reluctant prisoner in the Tower of London could be "racked" to make him talk. After consultation with all the judges the lord chief justice replied that the law did not permit a man to be tortured by the rack.[4] In this country today it is a matter of common knowledge (1) that any police brutality in the effort to coerce a confession is unlawful, and (2) that harsh police practices have not entirely disappeared. Years ago "the third degree" became a byword to symbolize violence by which officers extorted a confession. As such use of violence tended to disappear under the impact of public indignation some departments substituted other forms of torture, such as the "sweat-box". The prisoner was placed in a small box, which was kept entirely dark, and there he remained as long as necessary, which might be several days. He was allowed no communication with any person except an officer who would approach now and then to interrogate him. He was told he could get out whenever he was ready "to tell the truth"—nothing but a full confession being accepted as the "truth".[5] Then it was discovered that psychological torture might be as effective as physical torture. This often took the form of tiresome questioning carried on by officers acting in relays for excessively long hours, with the prisoner having little or no rest or refreshment.

It has long been the rule that an involuntary confession is not admissible in evidence against the defendant, and a confession is deemed involuntary if obtained by any form of compulsion, and also if it is obtained by promises.[6] Until recently the only explanation for exclusion was the fact that an involuntary confession is untrustworthy.

JACKSON v. DENNO, WARDEN

Supreme Court of the United States, 1964.
378 U.S. 368, 84 S.Ct. 1774.

[Some time after Jackson had robbed the desk clerk of a hotel, he encountered an officer on the street. They exchanged shots resulting in the death of the officer and the wounding of Jackson. At the hospital to which he was taken Jackson gave an oral confession and about two hours later a more complete and damaging written confession. Both confessions were introduced in evidence with-

---

mony. Compare Adams v. Maryland, 347 U.S. 179, 74 S.Ct. 442, 98 L.Ed. 608 (1954).

4. Proceedings Against John Felton for the Murder of the Duke of Buckingham, 3 How.St.Tr. 367 (1628).

5. See, for example, Ammons v. State, 80 Miss. 592, 32 So. 9 (1902).

6. An incriminating statement given on officer's promise that it would not be used against D is not admissible against him. Killough v. United States, 336 F.2d 929 (D.C.Cir. 1964).

out objection although there was a dispute as to the circumstances under which the latter was obtained.]

Mr. Justice White delivered the opinion of the Court.

Petitioner, Jackson, has filed a petition for habeas corpus in the Federal District Court asserting that his conviction for murder in the New York courts is invalid because it was founded upon a confession not properly determined to be voluntary. The writ was denied, 206 F.Supp. 759 (D.C.S.D.N.Y.), the Court of Appeals affirmed, 309 F.2d 573 (C.A.2d Cir.), and we granted certiorari to consider fundamental questions about the constitutionality of the New York procedure governing the admissibility of a confession alleged to be involuntary. . . .

In his closing argument, Jackson's counsel did not ask for an acquittal but for a verdict of second degree murder or manslaughter. Counsel's main effort was to negative the premeditation and intent necessary to first degree murder and to separate the robbery felony from the killing. He made much of the testimony tending to show a substantial interval between leaving the hotel and the beginning of the struggle with the policeman. The details of that struggle and the testimony indicating the policeman fired the first shot were also stressed.

Consistent with the New York practice where a question has been raised about the voluntariness of a confession, the trial court submitted that issue to the jury along with the other issues in the case. The jury was told that if it found the confession involuntary, it was to disregard it entirely, and determine guilt or innocence solely from the other evidence in the case; alternatively, if it found the confession voluntary, it was to determine its truth or reliability and afford it weight accordingly. . . .

II.

It is now axiomatic that a defendant in a criminal case is deprived of due process of law if his conviction is founded, in whole or in part, upon an involuntary confession, without regard for the truth or falsity of the confession, and even though there is ample evidence aside from the confession to support the conviction. Equally clear is the defendant's constitutional right at some stage in the proceedings to object to the use of the confession and to have a fair hearing and a reliable determination on the issue of voluntariness, a determination uninfluenced by the truth or falsity of the confession. In our view, the New York procedure employed in this case did not afford a reliable determination of the voluntariness of the confession offered in evidence at the trial, did not adequately protect Jackson's right to be free of a conviction based upon a coerced confession and therefore cannot withstand constitutional attack under the Due Process Clause of the Fourteenth Amendment. We therefore reverse the judgment below denying the writ of habeas corpus.

Under the New York rule, the trial judge must make a preliminary determination regarding a confession offered by the prosecution and exclude it if in no circumstances could the confession be deemed voluntary. But if the evidence presents a fair question as to its voluntariness, as where certain facts bearing on the issue are in dispute or where reasonable men could differ over the inferences to be drawn from undisputed facts, the judge "must receive the confession and leave to the jury, under proper instructions, the ultimate determination of its voluntary character and also its truthfulness." Stein v. New York, 346 U.S. 156, 172, 73 S.Ct. 1077, 1086, 97 L.Ed. 1522. If an issue of coercion is presented, the judge may not resolve conflicting evidence or arrive at his independent appraisal of the voluntariness of the confession, one way or the other. These matters he must leave to the jury.

This procedure has a significant impact upon the defendant's Fourteenth Amendment rights. In jurisdictions following the orthodox rule, under which the judge himself solely and finally determines the voluntariness of the confession, or those following the Massachusetts procedure, under which the jury passes on voluntariness only after the judge has fully and independently resolved the issue against the accused, the judge's conclusions are clearly evident from the record since he either admits the confession into evidence if it is voluntary or rejects it if involuntary. Moreover, his findings upon disputed issues of fact are expressly stated or may be ascertainable from the record. In contrast, the New York jury returns only a general verdict upon the ultimate question of guilt or innocence. It is impossible to discover whether the jury found the confession voluntary and relied upon it, or involuntary and supposedly ignored it. Nor is there any indication of how the jury resolved disputes in the evidence concerning the critical facts underlying the coercion issue. Indeed, there is nothing to show that these matters were resolved at all, one way or the other. . . .

A defendant objecting to the admission of a confession is entitled to a fair hearing in which both the underlying factual issues and the voluntariness of his confession are actually and reliably determined. But did the jury in Jackson's case make these critical determinations, and if it did, what were these determinations?

Notwithstanding these acknowledged difficulties inherent in the New York procedure, the Court in Stein found no constitutional deprivation to the defendant. The Court proceeded to this conclusion on the basis of alternative assumptions regarding the manner in which the jury might have resolved the coercion issue. Either the jury determined the disputed issues of fact against the accused, found the confession voluntary and therefore properly relied upon it; or it found the contested facts in favor of the accused and deemed the confession involuntary, in which event it disregarded the confession in accordance with its instructions and adjudicated guilt based solely on the other evidence. On either assumption the Court found no error in the judgment of the state court. . . .

It is now inescapably clear that the Fourteenth Amendment forbids the use of involuntary confessions not only because of the probable unreliability of confessions that are obtained in a manner deemed coercive, but also because of the "strongly felt attitude of our society that important human values are sacrificed where an agency of the government, in the course of securing a conviction, wrings a confession out of an accused against his will," and because of "the deep rooted feeling that the police must obey the law while enforcing the law; that in the end life and liberty can be as much endangered from illegal methods used to convict those thought to be criminals as from the actual criminals themselves." . . .

Under the New York procedure, the evidence given the jury inevitably injects irrelevant and impermissible considerations of truthfulness of the confession into the assessment of voluntariness. Indeed the jury is told to determine the truthfulness of the confession in assessing its probative value. As a consequence, it cannot be assumed, as the Stein Court did, that the jury reliably found the facts against the accused. This unsound assumption undermines Stein's authority as a precedent and its view on the constitutionality of the New York procedure. The admixture of reliability and voluntariness in the considerations of the jury would itself entitle a defendant to further proceedings in any case in which the essential facts are disputed, for we cannot determine how the jury resolved these issues and will not assume that they were reliably and properly resolved against the accused. And it is only a reliable determination on the voluntariness issue which satisfies the constitutional rights of the defendant and which would permit the jury to consider the confession in adjudicating guilt or innocence.

But we do not rest on this ground alone, for the other alternative hypothesized in Stein—that the jury found the confession involuntary and disregarded it—is equally unacceptable. Under the New York procedure, the fact of a defendant's confession is solidly implanted in the jury's mind, for it has not only heard the confession, but it has been instructed to consider and judge its voluntariness and is in position to assess whether it is true or false. If it finds the confession involuntary, does the jury—indeed, can it—then disregard the confession in accordance with its instructions? If there are lingering doubts about the sufficiency of the other evidence, does the jury unconsciously lay them to rest by resort to the confession? Will uncertainty about the sufficiency of the other evidence to prove guilt beyond a reasonable doubt actually result in acquittal when the jury knows the defendant has given a truthful confession? . . .

We turn to consideration of the disposition of this case. Since Jackson has not been given an adequate hearing upon the voluntariness of his confession he must be given one, the remaining inquiry being the scope of that hearing and the court which should provide it. . . .

However, we think that the further proceedings to which Jackson is entitled should occur initially in the state courts rather than in the federal habeas corpus court. Jackson's trial did not comport with constitutional standards and he is entitled to a determination of the voluntariness of his confession in the state courts in accordance with valid state procedures; the State is also entitled to make this determination before this Court considers the case on direct review or a petition for habeas corpus is filed in a Federal District Court. . . .

It is New York, therefore, not the federal habeas corpus court, which should first provide Jackson with that which he has not yet had and to which he is constitutionally entitled—an adequate evidentiary hearing productive of reliable results concerning the voluntariness of his confession. It does not follow, however, that Jackson is automatically entitled to a complete new trial including a retrial of the issue of guilt or innocence. Jackson's position before the District Court, and here, is that the issue of his confession should not have been decided by the convicting jury but should have been determined in a proceeding separate and apart from the body trying guilt or innocence. So far we agree and hold that he is now entitled to such a hearing in the state court. But if at the conclusion of such an evidentiary hearing in the state court on the coercion issue, it is determined that Jackson's confession was voluntarily given, admissible in evidence, and properly to be considered by the jury, we see no constitutional necessity at that point for proceeding with a new trial, for Jackson has already been tried by a jury with the confession placed before it and has been found guilty. True, the jury in the first trial was permitted to deal with the issue of voluntariness and we do not know whether the conviction rested upon the confession; but if it did, there is no constitutional prejudice to Jackson from the New York procedure if the confession is now properly found to be voluntary and therefore admissible. If the jury relied upon it, it was entitled to do so. Of course, if the state court, at an evidentiary hearing, redetermines the facts and decides that Jackson's confession was involuntary, there must be a new trial on guilt or innocence without the confession being admitted in evidence. . . .

Reversed.[1]

---

[1]. Oregon, which had followed the New York rule changed to the Massachusetts rule after Jackson. State v. Brewton, 238 Or. 590, 395 P.2d 874 (1964).

Mr. Justice Black, with whom Mr. Justice Clark joins as to Part I of this opinion, dissenting in part and concurring in part.

In Stein v. New York, 346 U.S. 156, 177–179, 73 S.Ct. 1077, 1089–1090, this Court sustained the constitutionality of New York's procedure under which the jury, rather than the trial judge, resolves disputed questions of fact as to the voluntariness of confessions offered against defendants charged with crime. I think this holding was correct and would adhere to it. While I dissented from affirmance of the convictions in Stein, my dissent went to other points; I most assuredly did not dissent because of any doubts about a State's constitutional power in a criminal case to let the jury, as it does in New York, decide the question of a confession's voluntariness. In fact, I would be far more troubled about constitutionality should either a State or the Federal Government declare that a jury in trying a defendant charged with crime is compelled to accept without question a trial court's factual finding that a confession was voluntarily given. Whatever might be a judge's view of the voluntariness of a confession, the jury in passing on a defendant's guilt or innocence is, in my judgment, entitled to hear and determine voluntariness of a confession along with other factual issues on which its verdict must rest. . . .

Mr. Justice Clark, dissenting. . . .

But even if the trial judge had instructed the jury to consider truth or falsity, the order here should be for a new trial, as in Rogers v. Richmond, supra. There the Court of Appeals was directed to hold the case a reasonable time "in order to give the State opportunity to *retry* petitioner . . .." 365 U.S. at 549, 81 S.Ct. at 744. (Emphasis supplied.) But the Court does not do this. It strikes down New York's procedure and then tells New York—not to retry the petitioner—but merely to have the trial judge hold a hearing on the admissibility of the confession and enter a definitive determination on that issue, as under the Massachusetts rule. This does not cure the error which the Court finds present. If the trial court did so err, this Court is making a more grievous error in amending New York's rule here and then requiring New York to apply it *ex post facto* without benefit of a full trial. Surely under the reasoning of the Court, the petitioner would be entitled to a new trial.

Believing that the constitutionality of New York's rule is not ripe for decision here, I dissent. If I am in error on this, then I join my Brother Harlan. His dissent is unanswerable.

Mr. Justice Harlan, whom Mr. Justice Clark and Mr. Justice Stewart join, dissenting.

Even under the broadest view of the restrictive effect of the Fourteenth Amendment, I would not have thought it open to doubt that the States were free to allocate the trial of issues, whether in criminal or civil cases, between judge and jury as they deemed best. The Court now holds, however, that New York's long-standing practice of leaving to the jury the resolution of reasonably disputed factual issues surrounding a criminal defendant's allegation that his confession was coerced violates due process. It is held that the Constitution permits submission of the question of coercion to the trial jury only if preceded by a determination of "voluntariness" by the trial judge—or by another judge or another jury not concerned with the ultimate issue of guilt or innocence.

The Court does make one bow to federalism in its opinion: New York need not retry Jackson if it, rather than the federal *habeas corpus* court, now finds, in accordance with the new ground rules, the confession to have been voluntary. I doubt whether New York, which in Jackson's original trial faithfully followed the teachings of this Court which were then applicable, will find much comfort in this gesture. . . .

McNABB v. UNITED STATES

Supreme Court of the United States, 1943.
318 U.S. 332, 63 S.Ct. 608.

[Acting upon information that the McNabb brothers planned an illegal sale of whiskey one night, federal officers went to the indicated place where they surprised the McNabbs in the forbidden act. The McNabbs fled and the officers postponed following them until they had poured out the illicit liquor. Then one officer went, with a flashlight, in the direction where noises were heard. The others followed when they heard a shot, and found the former fatally wounded. He died without having identified his assailant. Some hours later the McNabb brothers were arrested. They were not taken before a United States commissioner or a judge until some days later after they had confessed to the killing of the officer. Conviction resulted, based largely upon these confessions.]

Mr. Justice Frankfurter, delivered the opinion of the Court.

The petitioners are under sentence of imprisonment for forty-five years for the murder of an officer of the Alcohol Tax Unit of the Bureau of Internal Revenue engaged in the performance of his official duties. 18 U.S.C. § 253, 18 U.S.C.A. § 253. They were convicted of second-degree murder in the District Court for the Eastern District of Tennessee, and on appeal to the Circuit Court of Appeals for the Sixth Circuit the convictions were sustained. 123 F.2d 848. We brought the case here because the petition for certiorari presented serious questions in the administration of federal criminal justice. 316 U.S. 658, 62 S.Ct. 1305, 86 L.Ed. 1736. Determination of these questions turns upon the circumstances relating to the admission in evidence of incriminating statements made by the petitioners. . . .

In the view we take of the case, however, it becomes unnecessary to reach the Constitutional issue pressed upon us. For, while the power of this Court to undo convictions in state courts is limited to the enforcement of those "fundamental principles of liberty and justice", which are secured by the Fourteenth Amendment, the scope of our reviewing power over convictions brought here from the federal courts is not confined to ascertainment of Constitutional validity. Judicial supervision of the administration of criminal justice in the federal courts implies the duty of establishing and maintaining civilized standards of procedure and evidence. Such standards are not satisfied merely by observance of those minimal historic safeguards for securing trial by reason which are summarized as "due process of law" and below which we reach what is really trial by force. Moreover, review by this Court of state action expressing its notion of what will best further its own security in the administration of criminal justice demands appropriate respect for the deliberative judgment of a state in so basic an exercise of its jurisdiction. Considerations of large policy in making the necessary accommodations in our federal system are wholly irrelevant to the formulation and application of proper standards for the enforcement of the federal criminal law in the federal courts.

The principles governing the admissibility of evidence in federal criminal trials have not been restricted, therefore, to those derived solely from the Constitution. In the exercise of its supervisory authority over the administration of criminal justice in the federal courts, this Court has, from the very beginning of its history, formulated rules of evidence to be applied in federal criminal prosecutions. . . . And in formulating such rules of evidence for federal criminal trials the Court has been guided by considerations of justice not limited to the strict canons of evidentiary relevance.

Quite apart from the Constitution, therefore, we are constrained to hold that the evidence elicited from the petitioners in the circumstances disclosed here must be excluded. For in their treatment of the petitioners the arresting officers assumed functions which Congress has explicitly denied them. They subjected the accused to the pressures of a procedure which is wholly incompatible with the vital but very restricted duties of the investigating and arresting officers of the Government and which tends to undermine the integrity of the criminal proceeding. Congress has explicitly commanded that "It shall be the duty of the marshal, his deputy, or other officer, who may arrest a person charged with any crime or offense, to take the defendant before the nearest United States commissioner or the nearest judicial officer having jurisdiction under existing laws for a hearing, commitment, or taking bail for trial . . .." 18 U.S.C. § 595, 18 U.S.C.A. § 595. Similarly, the Act of June 18, 1934, c.

595, 48 Stat. 1008, 5 U.S.C. § 300a, 5 U.S.C.A. § 300a, authorizing officers of the Federal Bureau of Investigation to make arrests, requires that "the person arrested shall be immediately taken before a committing officer." Compare also the Act of March 1, 1879, c. 125, 20 Stat. 327, 341, 18 U.S.C. § 593, 18 U.S.C.A. § 593, which provides that when arrests are made of persons in the act of operating an illicit distillery, the arrested persons shall be taken forthwith before some judicial officer residing in the county where the arrests were made, or if none, in the county nearest to the place of arrest. Similar legislation, requiring that arrested persons be promptly taken before a committing authority, appears on the statute books of nearly all the states. . . .

In holding that the petitioners' admissions were improperly received in evidence against them, and that having been based on this evidence their convictions cannot stand, we confine ourselves to our limited function as the court of ultimate review of the standards formulated and applied by federal courts in the trial of criminal cases. We are not concerned with law enforcement practices except in so far as courts themselves become instruments of law enforcement. We hold only that a decent regard for the duty of courts as agencies of justice and custodians of liberty forbids that men should be convicted upon evidence secured under the circumstances revealed here. In so doing, we respect the policy which underlies Congressional legislation. The history of liberty has largely been the history of observance of procedural safeguards. And the effective administration of criminal justice hardly requires disregard of fair procedures imposed by law.

Reversed.[1]

MR. JUSTICE RUTLEDGE took no part in the consideration or decision of this case.

MR. JUSTICE REED, dissenting.

I find myself unable to agree with the opinion of the Court in this case. An officer of the United States was killed while in the performance of his duties. From the circumstances detailed in the

---

1. In a later case the lower courts felt that the delay in taking D before a commissioner was reasonable under the circumstances. In reversing the conviction the Court made it clear that any delay for the purpose of interrogation is forbidden so far as a federal prisoner is concerned. It said: "Circumstances may justify a brief delay between arrest and arraignment, as for instance, where the story volunteered by the accused is susceptible of quick verification through third parties. But the delay must not be of a nature to give opportunity for the extraction of a confession." Mallory v. United States, 354 U.S. 449, 77 S.Ct. 1356, 1 L.Ed.2d 1479 (1957). This rule is often referred to as the McNabb-Mallory rule.

If delay in taking an arrestee before a commissioner is due to the unavailability of that officer, a confession obtained during that delay, if otherwise admissible, is not rendered inadmissible under the McNabb-Mallory rule. United States v. Collins, 349 F.2d 296 (6th Cir. 1965).

Court's opinion, there was obvious reason to suspect that the petitioners here were implicated in firing the fatal shot from the dark. The arrest followed. As the guilty parties were known only to the McNabbs who took part in the assault at the burying ground, it was natural and proper that the officers would question them as to their actions.

The cases just cited show that statements made while under interrogation may be used at a trial if it may fairly be said that the information was given voluntarily. A frank and free confession of crime by the culprit affords testimony of the highest credibility and of a character which may be verified easily. Equally frank responses to officers by innocent people arrested under misapprehension give the best basis for prompt discharge from custody. The realization of the convincing quality of a confession tempts officials to press suspects unduly for such statements. To guard accused persons against the danger of being forced to confess, the law admits confessions of guilt only when they are voluntarily made. While the connotation of voluntary is indefinite, it affords an understandable label under which can be readily classified the various acts of terrorism, promises, trickery and threats which have led this and other courts to refuse admission as evidence to confessions.[2] The cases cited in the Court's opinion show the broad coverage of this rule of law. Through it those coerced into confession have found a ready defense from injustice.

Were the Court today saying merely that in its judgment the confessions of the McNabbs were not voluntary, there would be no occasion for this single protest. A notation of dissent would suffice. The opinion, however, does more. Involuntary confessions are not constitutionally admissible because violative of the provision of self-incrimination in the Bill of Rights. Now the Court leaves undecided whether the present confessions are voluntary or involuntary and declares that the confessions must be excluded because in addition to questioning the petitioners, the arresting officers failed promptly to take them before a committing magistrate. The Court finds a basis for the declaration of this new rule of evidence in its supervisory authority over the administration of criminal justice. I question whether this offers to the trial courts and the peace officers a rule of admissibility as clear as the test of the voluntary character of the confession. I am opposed to broadening the possibilities of defendants escaping punishment by these more rigorous technical requirements in the administration of justice. If these confessions are otherwise voluntary, civilized standards, in my opinion, are not advanced by setting aside these judgments because of acts of omission which are not shown to have tended toward coercing the admissions.

---

2. "In short, the true test of admissibility is that the confession is made freely, voluntarily and without compulsion or inducement of any sort." Wilson v. United States, 162 U.S. 613, 623, 16 S.Ct. 895, 899, 40 L.Ed. 1090; Lisenba v. California, 314 U.S. 219, 239, 62 S.Ct. 280, 291, 86 L.Ed. 166.

Our police officers occasionally overstep legal bounds. This record does not show when the petitioners were taken before a committing magistrate. No point was made of the failure to commit by defendant or counsel. No opportunity was given to the officers to explain. Objection to the introduction of the confessions was made only on the ground that they were obtained through coercion. This was determined against the accused both by the Court, when it appraised the fact as to the voluntary character of the confessions, preliminarily to determining the legal question of their admissibility, and by the jury. The Court saw and heard witnesses for the prosecution and the defense. The defendants did not take the stand before the jury. The uncontradicted evidence does not require a different conclusion. The officers of the Alcohol Tax Unit should not be disciplined by overturning this conviction.

GRIFFIN v. CALIFORNIA

Supreme Court of the United States, 1965.
380 U.S. 609, 85 S.Ct. 1229.

[Griffin was convicted of first-degree murder in a jury trial during which his failure to testify was the subject of comment by the district attorney and an instruction by the judge. The conviction having been affirmed by the Supreme Court of California was carried to this Court by certiorari.]

MR. JUSTICE DOUGLAS delivered the opinion of the Court. . . .

If this were a federal trial, reversible error would have been committed. Wilson v. United States, 149 U.S. 60, 13 S.Ct. 765, 37 L.Ed. 650, so holds. It is said, however, that the Wilson decision rested not on the Fifth Amendment, but on an Act of Congress. 18 U.S.C. § 3481. That indeed is the fact, as the opinion of the Court in the Wilson case states. But that is the beginning, not the end of our inquiry. The question remains whether, statute or not, the comment rule, approved by California, violates the Fifth Amendment.

We think it does. It is in substance a rule of evidence that allows the State the privilege of tendering to the jury for its consideration the failure of the accused to testify. No formal offer of proof is made as in other situations; but the prosecutor's comment and the court's acquiescence are the equivalent of an offer of evidence and its acceptance. The Court in the Wilson case stated:

" . . . the Act was framed with a due regard also to those who might prefer to rely upon the presumption of innocence which the law gives to every one, and not wish to be witnesses. It is not every one who can safely venture on the witness stand, though entirely innocent of the charge against him. Excessive timidity, nervousness when facing others and attempting to explain transactions of a suspicious character, and offenses charged against him, will often confuse and embarrass him to such a degree as to increase rather than remove prejudices against him. It is not every one, however, honest, who would therefore willingly be placed on the witness stand. The statute, in tenderness to the weakness of those who from the causes mentioned might refuse to ask to be witnesses, particularly when they may have been in some degree compromised by their association with others, declares that the failure of a defendant in a criminal action to request to be a witness shall not create any presumption against him." 149 U.S., p. 66, 13 S.Ct. p. 766.

If the words "Fifth Amendment" are substituted for "Act" and for "statute" the spirit of the Self-Incrimination Clause is reflected. For comment on the refusal to testify is a remnant of the "inquisitorial system of criminal justice," which the Fifth Amendment outlaws.[5] It is a penalty imposed by courts for exercising a constitutional privilege. It cuts down on the privilege by making its assertion costly. It is said, however, that the inference of guilt for failure to testify as to facts peculiarly within the accused's knowledge is in any event natural and irresistible, and that comment on the failure does not magnify that inference into a penalty for asserting a constitutional privilege. People v. Modesto, 62 A.C. 452, 468–469, 42 Cal.Rptr. 417, 398 P.2d 753. What the jury may infer given no help from the court is one thing. What they may infer when the court solemnizes the silence of the accused into evidence against him is quite another. That the inference of guilt is not always so natural or irresistible is brought out in the Modesto opinion itself:

"Defendant contends that the reason a defendant refuses to testify is that his prior convictions will be introduced in evidence to impeach him ([Cal.] Code Civ.Proc. § 2051) and not that he is unable to deny the accusations. It is true that the defendant might fear that his prior convictions will prejudice the jury, and therefore another possible inference can be drawn from his refusal to take the stand." Id., at 469, 42 Cal.Rptr. at 427, 398 P.2d at 763.

5. Our decision today that the Fifth Amendment prohibits comment on the defendant's silence is no innovation, for on a previous occasion a majority of this Court indicated their acceptance of this proposition. In Adamson v. People of State of California, 332 U.S. 46, 67 S.Ct. 1672, the question was, as here, whether the Fifth Amendment proscribed California's comment practice. The four dissenters (Black, Douglas, Murphy and Rutledge, JJ.) would have answered this question in the affirmative. A fifth member of the Court, Justice Frankfurter, stated in a separate opinion: "For historical reasons a limited immunity from the common duty to testify was written into the Federal Bill of Rights, and I am prepared to agree that, as part of that immunity, comment on the failure of an accused to take the witness stand is forbidden in federal prosecutions." Id., at 61, 67 S.Ct. at 1680. But, though he agreed with the dissenters on this point, he also agreed with Justices Vinson, Reed, Jackson, and Burton that the Fourteenth Amendment did not make the Self-Incrimination Clause of the Fifth Amendment applicable to the States; thus he joined the opinion of the Court which so held (the Court's opinion assumed that the Fifth Amendment barred comment, but it expressly disclaimed any intention to decide the point. Id., at 50, 67 S.Ct. at 1674).

We said in Malloy v. Hogan, supra, 378 U.S. p. 11, 84 S.Ct. p. 1495, that "the same standards must determine whether an accused's silence in either a federal or state proceeding is justified." We take that in its literal sense and hold that the Fifth Amendment, in its direct application to the federal government and its bearing on the States by reason of the Fourteenth Amendment, forbids either comment by the prosecution on the accused's silence or instructions by the court that such silence is evidence of guilt.[6]

Reversed.

THE CHIEF JUSTICE took no part in the decision of this case.

MR. JUSTICE HARLAN, concurring.

I agree with the Court that within the federal judicial system the Fifth Amendment bars adverse comment by federal prosecutors and judges on a defendant's failure to take the stand in a criminal trial, a right accorded him by that amendment. And given last Term's decision in Malloy v. Hogan, 378 U.S. 1, 84 S.Ct. 1489, 12 L.Ed.2d 653, that the Fifth Amendment applies to the States in all its refinements, I see no legitimate escape from today's decision and therefore concur in it. I do so, however, with great reluctance, since for me the decision exemplifies the creeping paralysis with which this Court's recent adoption of the "incorporation" doctrine is infecting the operation of the federal system. . . .

MR. JUSTICE STEWART, with whom Mr. JUSTICE WHITE joins, dissenting. . . .

Moreover, no one can say where the balance of advantage might lie as a result of counsels' discussion of the matter. No doubt the prosecution's argument will seek to encourage the drawing of inferences unfavorable to the defendant. However, the defendant's counsel equally has an opportunity to explain the various other reasons why a defendant may not wish to take the stand, and thus rebut the natural if uneducated assumption that it is because the defendant cannot truthfully deny the accusations made.

I think the California comment rule is not a coercive device which impairs the right against self-incrimination, but rather a means of articulating and bringing into the light of rational discussion a fact inescapably impressed on the jury's consciousness. The California procedure is not only designed to protect the defendant against unwarranted inferences which might be drawn by an uninformed jury; it is also an attempt by the State to recognize and articulate what it believes to be the natural probative force of certain facts. Surely no one would deny that the State has an important interest in throwing the light of rational discussion on that which transpires in the course of a

---

6. We reserve decision on whether an accused can require, as in Bruno v. United States, 308 U.S. 287, 60 S.Ct. 198, 84 L.Ed. 257, that the jury be instructed that his silence must be disregarded.

trial, both to protect the defendant from the very real dangers of silence and to shape a legal process designed to ascertain the truth.

The California rule allowing comment by counsel and instruction by the judge on the defendant's failure to take the stand is hardly an idiosyncratic aberration. The Model Code of Evidence, and the Uniform Rules of Evidence both sanction the use of such procedures.[6] The practice had been endorsed by resolution of the American Bar Association and the American Law Institute,[7] and has the support of the weight of scholarly opinion.[8] . . .

ULLMANN v. UNITED STATES

Supreme Court of the United States, 1956.
350 U.S. 422, 76 S.Ct. 497.

[The Immunity Act of 1954, 18 U.S.C. sec. 3486, authorized a United States attorney in certain investigations involving the national security, with the approval of the Attorney General, to "make application to the court that the witness shall be instructed to testify or produce evidence subject to the provisions of this section, and

---

6. Model Code of Evidence, Rule 201 (1942); Uniform Rules of Evidence, Rule 23(4) (1953).

7. 56 A.B.A.Rep. 137–159 (1931); 59 A.B.A.Rep. 130–141 (1934); 9 Proceedings A.L.I. 202, 203 (1931).

8. See Bruce, The Right to Comment on the Failure of the Accused to Testify, 31 Mich.L.Rev. 226; Dunmore, Comment on Failure of Accused to Testify, 26 Yale L.J. 464; Hadley, Criminal Justice in America, 11 A.B.A.J. 674, 677; Hiscock, Criminal Law and Procedure in New York, 26 Col.L.Rev. 253, 258–262; Note, Comment on Defendant's Failure to Take the Stand, 57 Yale L.J. 145.

[By the Compiler.]

Comment by prosecutor regarding the failure of accused to testify violates the federal constitutional privilege against self-incrimination but does not require a reversal unless it resulted in a miscarriage of justice. People v. Bostick, 62 Cal.2d 820, 44 Cal.Rptr. 649, 402 P.2d 529 (1965). Comment by court and prosecuting attorney on D's failure to testify violated his constitutional privilege against self-incrimination and requires reversal where it was so extensive as to suggest that without it the result might have been more favorable to him. People v. Odom, —— Cal.App.2d ——, 46 Cal.Rptr. 453 (1965). Improper argument and instruction on D's failure to testify constituted error but not such a denial of due process and fair trial that it could be raised retroactively on collateral attack by habeas corpus. In re Gaines, 63 Cal.2d ——, 45 Cal.Rptr. 865, 404 P.2d 473 (1965).

In a joint trial it is reversible error to permit counsel for one defendant to comment on co-defendant's failure to testify. De Luna v. United States, 308 F.2d 140 (5th Cir. 1962).

The Fifth Amendment gives a person a right to remain silent when another makes statements in his presence that tend to incriminate him. To use such silence as an implied admission of guilt would violate his protection. Ivey v. United States, 344 F.2d 770 (5th Cir. 1965). Argument and instruction in the penalty trial to the effect that one serving a life sentence may be pardoned or paroled and is eligible for parole after seven years constituted substantial and prejudicial error. It may be used to secure reversal of the death sentence in collateral proceeding on habeas corpus after judgment has been affirmed on appeal. In re Gaines, 63 Cal.2d ——, 45 Cal.Rptr. 865, 404 P.2d 473 (1965).

upon order of the court such witness shall not be excused from testifying or from producing books, papers, or other evidence on the ground that the testimony or evidence required of him may tend to incriminate him or subject him to a penalty or forfeiture. But no such witness shall be prosecuted or subjected to any penalty or forfeiture for or on account of any transaction, matter, or thing concerning which he is compelled, after having claimed his privilege against self-incrimination, to testify or produce evidence, nor shall testimony so compelled be used as evidence in any criminal proceeding (except prosecution described in subsection (d) hereof) against him in any court.

"(d) No witness shall be exempt under the provision of this section from prosecution for perjury or contempt committed while giving testimony or producing evidence under compulsion as provided in this section."

Petitioner was convicted of contempt for violating the court's order that he testify before a grand jury, after immunity under this statute had been extended to him. He claimed, *inter alia*, that the statute is unconstitutional and hence he was privileged not to testify. Questions asked him by the grand jury included those relating to his knowledge of activities of espionage and to his and other persons' membership in the Communist Party.]

MR. JUSTICE FRANKFURTER delivered the opinion of the Court.
. . .

It is in this spirit of strict, not lax, observance of the constitutional protection of the individual that we approach the claims made by petitioner in this case. The attack on the Immunity Act as violating the Fifth Amendment is not a new one. Sixty years ago this Court considered, in Brown v. Walker, 161 U.S. 591, 16 S.Ct. 644, 40 L.Ed. 819, the constitutionality of a similar Act, the Act of February 11, 1893, 27 Stat. 443. In that case, Brown, auditor for a railroad company, had been subpoenaed to testify before a grand jury which was investigating charges that officers and agents of the company had violated the Interstate Commerce Act. Invoking the privilege against self-incrimination, he refused to answer certain questions concerning the operations and the rebate policy of the railroad. On an order to show cause before the United States District Court for the Western District of Pennsylvania, he was adjudged in contempt. His petition for a writ of habeas corpus to the Circuit Court for the Western District of Pennsylvania was dismissed. Petitioner appealed to this Court, urging that the 1893 immunity statute was unconstitutional.

The Court considered and rejected petitioner's arguments, holding that a statute which compelled testimony but secured the witness against a criminal prosecution which might be aided directly or indirectly by his disclosures did not violate the Fifth Amendment's privilege against self-incrimination and that the 1893 statute did provide such immunity. "While the constitutional provision in question is justly regarded as one of the most valuable prerogatives of the citizen, its object is fully accomplished by the statutory immunity, and we are therefore of opinion that the witness was compellable to answer . . . ." 161 U.S. at page 610, 16 S.Ct. at page 652.

Petitioner, however, attempts to distinguish Brown v. Walker. He argues that this case is different from Brown v. Walker because the impact of the disabilities imposed by federal and state authorities and the public in general—such as loss of job, expulsion from labor unions, state registration and investigation statutes, passport eligibility, and general public opprobrium—is so oppressive that the statute does not give him true immunity. This, he alleges, is significantly different from the impact of testifying on the auditor in Brown v. Walker, who could the next day resume his job with reputation unaffected. But, as this Court has often held, the immunity granted need only remove those sanctions which generate the fear justifying invocation of the privilege: "The interdiction of the 5th Amendment operates only where a witness is asked to incriminate himself,—in other words, to give testimony which may possibly expose him to a criminal charge. But if the criminality has already been taken away, the amendment ceases to apply." Hale v. Henkel, 201 U.S. 43, 67, 26 S.Ct. 370, 376, 50 L.Ed. 652. Here, since the Immunity Act protects a witness who is compelled to answer to the extent of his constitutional immunity, he has of course, when a particular sanction is sought to be imposed against him, the right to claim that it is criminal in nature. . . .

Petitioner further argues that the immunity is not constitutionally sufficient so long as a witness is subject to the very real possibility of state prosecution. He urges that the statute does not, and constitutionally could not, grant such immunity. . . .

Here the State is forbidden to prosecute. But it cannot be contested that Congress has power to provide for national defense and the complementary power "To make all Laws which shall be necessary and proper for carrying into Execution the foregoing Powers, and all other Powers vested by this Constitution in the Government of the United States, or in any Department or Officer thereof." U.S. Const., Art. I, § 8, cl. 18. The Immunity Act is concerned with the national security. It reflects a congressional policy to increase the possibility of more complete and open disclosure by removal of fear of state prosecution. We cannot say that Congress' paramount authority in safeguarding national security does not justify the restriction it has placed on the exercise of state power for the more effective exercise of conceded federal power. We have already, in the name of the Commerce Clause, upheld a similar restriction on state court jurisdiction, Brown v. Walker, 161 U.S. at pages 606–607, 16 S.Ct. at pages 650–651, 40 L.Ed. 819, and we can find no distinction between the reach of congressional power with respect to commerce and its power with respect to national security. See also Hines v. Davidowitz, 312 U.S. 52, 61 S.Ct. 399, 85 L.Ed. 581.

Petitioner also urges that if Brown v. Walker is found nondistinguishable and controlling, then that case should be reconsidered and overruled. He also urges upon us a "return" to a literal reading of the Fifth Amendment. Brown v. Walker was the second case to deal with an immunity statute. Four years previously, in Counselman v. Hitchcock, 142 U.S. 547, 12 S.Ct. 195, 35 L.Ed. 1110, a unanimous Court had found constitutionally inadequate the predecessor to the 1893 statute because the immunity granted was incomplete, in that it merely forbade the use of the testimony given and failed to protect a witness from future prosecution based on knowledge and sources of information obtained from the compelled testimony. It was with this background that the 1893 statute, providing complete immunity from prosecution, was passed and that Brown v. Walker was argued and decided. . . .

We are not dealing here with one of the vague, undefinable, admonitory provisions of the Constitution whose scope is inevitably addressed to changing circumstances. The privilege against self-incrimination is a specific provision of which it is peculiarly true that "a page of history is worth a volume of logic." For the history of the privilege establishes not only that it is not to be interpreted literally, but also that its sole concern is, as its name indicates, with the danger to a witness forced to give testimony leading to the infliction of "penalties affixed to the criminal acts . . . ." Boyd v. United States, 116 U.S. 616, 634, 6 S.Ct. 524, 534, 29 L.Ed. 746. We leave Boyd v. United States unqualified, as it was left unqualified in Brown v. Walker. Immunity displaces the danger. Once the reason for the privilege ceases, the privilege ceases. We reaffirm Brown v. Walker, and in so doing we need not repeat the answers given by that case to the other points raised by petitioner.

The judgment of the Court of Appeals is affirmed.

Affirmed.

MR. JUSTICE REED concurs in the opinion and judgment of the Court except as to the statement that no constitutional guarantee enjoys preference.

MR. JUSTICE DOUGLAS, with whom MR. JUSTICE BLACK concurs, dissenting.

I would reverse the judgment of conviction. I would base the reversal on Boyd v. United States, 116 U.S. 616, 6 S.Ct. 524, 29 L.Ed. 746, or, in the alternative, I would overrule the five-to-four decision of Brown v. Walker, 161 U.S. 591, 16 S.Ct. 644, 40 L.Ed. 819, and adopt the view of the minority in that case that the right of silence created by the Fifth Amendment is beyond the reach of Congress.

First, as to the Boyd case. There are numerous disabilities created by federal law that attach to a person who is a Communist. These disabilities include ineligibility for employment in the Federal Government and in defense facilities, disqualification for a passport, the risk of internment, the risk of loss of employment as a longshoreman—to mention only a few. These disabilities imposed by federal law are forfeitures within the meaning of our cases and as much protected by the Fifth Amendment as criminal prosecution itself. But there is no indication that the Immunity Act, 68 Stat. 745, 18 U.S.C. (Supp. II) § 3486, 18 U.S.C.A. § 3486, grants protection against those disabilities. The majority will not say that it does. I think, indeed, that it must be read as granting only partial, not complete, immunity for the matter disclosed under compulsion. Yet, as the Court held in Counselman v. Hitchcock, 142 U.S. 547, 586, 12 S.Ct. 195, 206, 35 L.Ed. 1110, an immunity statute to be valid must "supply a complete protection from all the perils against which the constitutional prohibition was designed to guard . . . ."

(2) The guarantee against self-incrimination contained in the Fifth Amendment is not only a protection against conviction and prosecution but a safeguard of conscience and human dignity and freedom of expression as well. My view is that the Framers put it beyond the power of Congress to *compel* anyone to confess his crimes. The evil to be guarded against was partly self-accusation under legal compulsion. But that was only a part of the evil. The conscience and dignity of man were also involved. So too was his right to freedom of expression guaranteed by the First Amendment. The Framers, therefore, created the federally protected right of silence and decreed that the law could not be used to pry open one's lips and make him a witness against himself. . . .

The Court, by forgetting that history, robs the Fifth Amendment of one of the great purposes it was designed to serve. To repeat, the Fifth Amendment was written in part to prevent any Congress, any court, and any prosecutor from prying open the lips of an accused to make incriminating statements against his will. The Fifth Amendment protects the conscience and the dignity of the individual, as well as his safety and security, against the compulsion of government. . . .

It is no answer to say that a witness who exercises his Fifth Amendment right of silence and stands mute may bring himself into disrepute. If so, that is the price he pays for exercising the right of silence granted by the Fifth Amendment. The critical point is that the Constitution places the right of silence *beyond the reach of government*. The Fifth Amendment stands between the citizen and his government. When public opinion casts a person into the outer darkness, as happens today when a person is exposed as a Communist, the government brings infamy on the head of the witness when it compels disclosure. That is precisely what the Fifth Amendment prohibits. . . .

SECTION 3. THE RIGHT OF PRIVACY (TO BE FREE FROM UNREASONABLE SEARCH AND SEIZURE)

The Fourth Amendment provides: "The right of the people to be secure in their persons, houses, papers and effects, against unreasonable searches and seizures, shall not be violated, . . ." It was clear that any unlawful arrest, search or seizure by a federal officer was a violation of this constitutional right, but for a century and a quarter evidence which was relevant, material and otherwise competent was admitted against the defendant even if it had been obtained by such a violation. In 1914 *Weeks*[1] held that the Fourth Amendment barred the use of evidence, so procured, in a federal prosecution. This came to be known as the "exclusionary rule". In *Wolf*[2] the Supreme Court, for the first time, discussed the effect of the operation of the Due Process Clause of the Fourteenth Amendment upon such evidence. It held that security of privacy against unlawful intrusion by the police is implicit in the concept of ordered liberty and as such enforceable against the states under the protection of that Clause. Hence no state could affirmatively sanction such police intrusion. But finding that most of the English-speaking world did not regard the "exclusionary rule" as an essential ingredient of the right, it held that a state court was not required to exclude evidence merely because it was obtained by unlawful search and seizure. Twelve years later *Wolf* was expressly overruled by *Mapp*[3] wherein it was stated: "We hold that all evidence obtained by searches and seizures in violation of the Constitution is, by that same authority, inadmissible in a state court".[4]

The Court found at the time *Wolf* was decided that 30 states had rejected the "exclusionary rule". After that decision some of those states changed position as to this, such as *Cahan*[5] in California. Now, of course, the "exclusionary rule" applies in all our courts, state and federal.[6]

1. Weeks v. United States, 232 U.S. 383, 34 S.Ct. 341, 58 L.Ed. 652 (1914).

2. Wolf v. Colorado, 338 U.S. 25, 69 S.Ct. 1359, 93 L.Ed. 1782 (1949).

3. Mapp v. Ohio, 367 U.S. 643, 81 S.Ct. 1684, 6 L.Ed.2d 1081, 84 A.L.R.2d 933 (1961).

4. Id. at 655, 81 S.Ct. at 1691.

5. People v. Cahan, 44 Cal.2d 434, 282 P.2d 905, 50 A.L.R.2d 513 (1955).

6. *Mapp* does not apply retrospectively to state cases which had been finally decided before the Mapp decision was rendered. It applies to cases which were pending on direct review at that time (Ker v. California, 374 U.S. 23, 83 S.Ct. 1623, 10 L.Ed.2d 726 (1963), but not to those in which the point can be

WONG SUN v. UNITED STATES

Supreme Court of the United States, 1963.
371 U.S. 471, 83 S.Ct. 407.

[Toy and Wong Sun were convicted in the federal district court of the offense of fraudulent and knowing transportation and concealment of illegally imported heroin. Federal officers had broken into Toy's bedroom and searched for narcotics which were not found. Toy told the officers he had not been selling narcotics but that "Johnny" had. He took them to Johnny Yee's place where they found about an ounce of heroin. Yee then implicated Toy and Wong Sun who later made incriminating, unsigned statements. Over timely objections, the original statement by Toy, the heroin taken from Yee and the pre-trial statements were admitted in evidence. It was found that the officers' uninvited entrance into Toy's bedroom had been unlawful.]

Mr. Justice Brennan delivered the opinion of the Court. . . .

We believe that significant differences between the cases of the two petitioners require separate discussion of each. We shall first consider the case of petitioner Toy.

It is conceded that Toy's declarations in his bedroom are to be excluded if they are held to be "fruits" of the agents' unlawful action.

In order to make effective the fundamental constitutional guarantees of sanctity of the home and inviolability of the person, this Court held nearly half a century ago that evidence seized during an unlawful search could not constitute proof against the victim of the search. The exclusionary prohibition extends as well to the indirect as the direct products of such invasions. Silverthorne Lumber Co. v. United States, 251 U.S. 385, 40 S.Ct. 182, 64 L.Ed. 319. Mr. Justice Holmes, speaking for the Court in that case, in holding that the Government might not make use of information obtained during an unlawful search to subpoena from the victims the very documents illegally viewed, expressed succinctly the policy of the broad exclusionary rule:

"The essence of a provision forbidding the acquisition of evidence in a certain way is that not merely evidence so acquired shall not be used before the Court but that it shall not be used at all. Of course

---

raised only by collateral attack (habeas corpus in this case). Linkletter v. Walker, 381 U.S. 618, 85 S.Ct. 1731, 14 L.Ed.2d 601 (1965). "Thus the accepted rule today is that in appropriate cases the Court may in the interest of justice make the rule prospective. And 'there is much to be said in favor of such a rule for cases arising in the future.'" Id. at 628, 85 S.Ct. at 1737.

The Supreme Court has allowed certain errors to be raised retroactively by collateral attack. Indigent's right to counsel at the trial: Doughty v. Maxwell, 376 U.S. 202, 84 S.Ct. 702, 11 L.Ed.2d 650 (1964); Indigent's right to counsel on appeal: Smith v. Crouse, 378 U.S. 584, 84 S.Ct. 1929, 12 L.Ed.2d 1039 (1964); Use of a coerced confession: Reck v. Pate, 367 U.S. 433, 81 S.Ct. 1541, 6 L.Ed.2d 948 (1961).

this does not mean that the facts thus obtained become sacred and inaccessible. If knowledge of them is gained from an independent source they may be proved, like any others, but the knowledge gained by the Government's own wrong cannot be used by it in the way proposed." 251 U.S. at 392, 40 S.Ct. at 183.

The exclusionary rule has traditionally barred from trial physical, tangible materials obtained either during or as a direct result of an unlawful invasion. It follows from our holding in Silverman v. United States, 365 U.S. 505, 81 S.Ct. 679, 5 L.Ed.2d 734, that the Fourth Amendment may protect against the overhearing of verbal statements as well as against the more traditional seizure of "papers and effects." Similarly, testimony as to matters observed during an unlawful invasion has been excluded in order to enforce the basic constitutional policies. Thus, verbal evidence which derives so immediately from an unlawful entry and an unauthorized arrest as the officers' action in the present case is no less the "fruit" of official illegality than the more common tangible fruits of the unwarranted intrusion.[11] Nor do the policies underlying the exclusionary rule invite any logical distinction between physical and verbal evidence. Either in terms of deterring lawless conduct by federal officers, or of closing the doors of the federal courts to any use of evidence unconstitutionally obtained, the danger in relaxing the exclusionary rules in the case of verbal evidence would seem too great to warrant introducing such a distinction.

The Government argues that Toy's statements to the officers in his bedroom, although closely consequent upon the invasion which we hold unlawful, were nevertheless admissible because they resulted from "an intervening independent act of a free will." This contention, however, takes insufficient account of the circumstances. Six or seven officers had broken the door and followed on Toy's heels into the bedroom where his wife and child were sleeping. He had been almost immediately handcuffed and arrested. Under such circumstances it is unreasonable to infer that Toy's response was sufficently an act of free will to purge the primary taint of the unlawful invasion.

The Government also contends that Toy's declarations should be admissible because they were ostensibly exculpatory rather than incriminating. There are two answers to this argument. First, the statements soon turned out to be incriminating, for they led directly to the evidence which implicated Toy. Second, when circumstances are shown such as those which induced these declarations, it is immaterial whether the declarations be termed "exculpatory." Thus we

[Footnote by the Court.]

11. See Kamisar, Illegal Searches or Seizures and Contemporaneous Incriminating Statements: A Dialogue on a Neglected Area of Criminal Procedure, 1961 U. of Ill.Law Forum 78, 84–96. But compare Maguire, Evidence of Guilt (1959), 187–190.

find no substantial reason to omit Toy's declarations from the protection of the exclusionary rule.

We now consider whether the exclusion of Toy's declarations requires also the exclusion of the narcotics taken from Yee, to which those declarations led the police. The prosecutor candidly told the trial court that "we wouldn't have found those drugs except that Mr. Toy helped us to." Hence this is not the case envisioned by this Court where the exclusionary rule has no application because the Government learned of the evidence "from an independent source," nor is this a case in which the connection between the lawless conduct of the police and the discovery of the challenged evidence has "become so attenuated as to dissipate the taint." Nardone v. United States, 308 U.S. 338, 341, 60 S.Ct. 266, 268, 84 L.Ed. 307. We need not hold that all evidence is "fruit of the poisonous tree" simply because it would not have come to light but for the illegal actions of the police. Rather, the more apt question in such a case is "whether, granting establishment of the primary illegality, the evidence to which instant objection is made has been come at by exploitation of that illegality or instead by means sufficiently distinguishable to be purged of the primary taint." Maguire, Evidence of Guilt, 221 (1959). We think it clear that the narcotics were "come at by the exploitation of that illegality" and hence that they may not be used against Toy.

It remains only to consider Toy's unsigned statement. We need not decide whether, in light of the fact that Toy was free on his own recognizance when he made the statement, that statement was a fruit of the illegal arrest. Since we have concluded that his declarations in the bedroom and the narcotics surrendered by Yee should not have been admitted in evidence against him, the only proofs remaining to sustain his conviction are his and Wong Sun's unsigned statements. Without scrutinizing the contents of Toy's ambiguous recitals, we conclude that no reference to Toy in Wong Sun's statement constitutes admissible evidence corroborating any admission by Toy. We arrive at this conclusion upon two clear lines of decisions which converge to require it. One line of our decisions establishes that criminal confessions and admissions of guilt require extrinsic corroboration; the other line of precedents holds that an out-of-court declaration made after arrest may not be used at trial against one of the declarant's partners in crime.

It is a settled principle of the administration of criminal justice in the federal courts that a conviction must rest upon firmer ground than the uncorroborated admission or confession of the accused. . . .

We turn now to the case of the other petitioner, Wong Sun. We have no occasion to disagree with the finding of the Court of Appeals that his arrest, also, was without probable cause or reasonable grounds. At all events no evidentiary consequences turn upon that question. For Wong Sun's unsigned confession was not the fruit of that arrest, and was therefore properly admitted at trial. On the evidence that Wong Sun had been released on his own recognizance after a lawful arraignment, and had returned voluntarily several days later to make the statement, we hold that the connection between the arrest and the statement had "become so attenuated as to dissipate the taint." The fact that the statement was unsigned, whatever bearing this may have upon its weight and credibility, does not render it inadmissible; Wong Sun understood and adopted its substance, though he could not comprehend the English words. The petitioner has never suggested any impropriety in the interrogation itself which would require the exclusion of this statement.

We must then consider the admissibility of the narcotics surrendered by Yee. Our holding, supra, that this ounce of heroin was inadmissible against Toy does not compel a like result with respect to Wong Sun. The exclusion of the narcotics as to Toy was required solely by their tainted relationship to information unlawfully obtained from Toy, and not by any official impropriety connected with their surrender by Yee. The seizure of this heroin invaded no right of privacy of person or premises which would entitle Wong Sun to object to its use at his trial.

However, for the reasons that Wong Sun's statement was incompetent to corroborate Toy's admissions contained in Toy's own statement, any references to Wong Sun in Toy's statement were incompetent to corroborate Wong Sun's admissions. Thus, the only competent source of corroboration for Wong Sun's statement was the heroin itself. We cannot be certain, however, on this state of the record, that the trial judge may not also have considered the contents of Toy's statement as a source of corroboration.

Surely, under the narcotics statute, the discovery of heroin raises a presumption that someone—generally the possessor—violated the law. As to him, once possession alone is proved, the other elements of the offense—transportation and concealment with knowledge of the illegal importation of the drug—need not be separately demonstrated, much less corroborated. 21 U.S.C. § 174, 21 U.S.C.A. § 174. Thus particular care ought to be taken in this area, when the crucial element of the accused's possession is proved solely by his own admissions, that the requisite corroboration be found among the evidence which is properly before the trier of facts. We therefore hold that petitioner Wong Sun is also entitled to a new trial.

The judgment of the Court of Appeals is reversed and the case is remanded to the District Court for further proceedings consistent with this opinion.

It is so ordered.

Judgment of Court of Appeals reversed and case remanded to the District Court.[1]

MR. JUSTICE DOUGLAS, concurring.

While I join the Court's opinion I do so because nothing the Court holds is inconsistent with my belief that there having been time to get a warrant, probable cause alone could not have justified the arrest of petitioner Toy without a warrant. . . .

MR. JUSTICE CLARK, with whom MR. JUSTICE HARLAN, MR. JUSTICE STEWART and MR. JUSTICE WHITE join, dissenting.

The Court has made a Chinese puzzle out of this simple case involving four participants: Hom Way, Blackie Toy, Johnny Yee and "Sea Dog" Sun. In setting aside the convictions of Toy and Sun it has dashed to pieces the heretofore recognized standards of probable cause necessary to secure an arrest warrant or to make an arrest without one. Instead of dealing with probable cause as involving "probabilities," "the factual and practical considerations of everyday life on which reasonable and prudent men, not legal technicians, act," the Court sets up rigid, mechanical standards, applying the 20–20 vision of hind-sight in an area where the ambiguity and immediacy inherent in unexpected arrest are present. While probable cause must be based on more than mere suspicion, it does not require proof sufficient to establish guilt. The sole requirement heretofore has been that the knowledge in the hands of the officers at the time of arrest must support a "man of reasonable caution in the belief" that the subject had committed narcotic offenses. Carroll v. United States, 267 U.S. 132, 162, 45 S.Ct. 280, 288, 69 L.Ed. 543 (1925). . . .

[By the Compiler.]

1. Having probable cause to believe that Ker was illegally in possession of marijuana, officers went to his apartment to arrest him. Entering quietly by means of a key obtained from the building manager, they saw what appeared to be a package of marijuana and arrested Ker and his wife for the illegal possession of narcotics. A conviction resulted despite the claim that the evidence had been seized unlawfully and hence was inadmissible under the rule of Mapp v. Ohio, 367 U.S. 643, 81 S.Ct. 1684, 6 L.Ed.2d 1081 (1961). The crucial point was the method of entry which was without first demanding admittance and explaining the purpose as provided in section 844 of the California Penal Code. The state court held that the silent entry was lawful under a judicial exception which had been engrafted upon the statute by a series of decisions, namely that where the demand and notice might result in a danger of injury to the officer or the destruction of evidence, they may be omitted. The Supreme Court affirmed the conviction, finding that the state's interpretation of the statute was justified by the experience of arresting officers that narcotics are often disposed of during an attempted arrest. Ker v. California, 374 U.S. 23, 83 S.Ct. 1623, 10 L.Ed.2d 726 (1963). The court emphasized that the lawfulness of the arrest is to be determined by state law insofar as it is not violative of the federal constitution. Four justices dissented.

WAYNE v. UNITED STATES

United States Court of Appeals, District of Columbia Circuit, 1963.
115 U.S.App.D.C. 234, 318 F.2d 205.

[W, on trial under an indictment charging attempted abortion terminating in death, objected to the introduction in evidence of the autopsy report on the victim and expert testimony as to the cause of death. He claimed that these were the product of an unlawful entry into his apartment by the police. The evidence was admitted over his objection and a conviction resulted.]

BURGER, CIRCUIT JUDGE. . . .

(3)

(a) Appellant's third contention will be treated in two parts. The contention is that the entry of the police into his apartment, which had been found by a District Judge on a pre-trial motion to have been illegal, and the seizure of the body immediately following such illegal entry, precluded the introduction of the coroner's testimony about the condition of the body and the cause of death. The doctrine invoked is that commonly known as the "fruit of the poisonous tree." The government challenges the finding that the entry was illegal and argues further that, even if it was, it did not preclude the coroner from testifying.

Without now reaching the legality of the entry, we agree with the government that, in the circumstances of this case, the testimony objected to could not be considered as the "fruit of the poisonous tree." The Supreme Court has recently had occasion to discuss and clarify this difficult doctrine. Wong Sun v. United States, 371 U.S. 471, 83 S.Ct. 407, 9 L.Ed.2d 441 (1963). It stated that the exclusionary rule has no application when the government obtains evidence "from an independent source." Silverthorne Lumber Co. v. United States, 251 U.S. 385, 392, 40 S.Ct. 182, 64 L.Ed. 319 (1920). The Court added that the question to be asked in applying the doctrine is "'whether, *granting establishment of the primary illegality*, the evidence to which the instant objection is made has been come at by exploitation of that illegality or instead by means sufficiently distinguishable to be purged of the primary taint.' Maguire, Evidence of Guilt, 221 (1959)."

It appears to us that the standards set forth in Wong Sun call for admission of the coroner's testimony. It is undisputed that the deceased's sister had told the police, prior to their entry into appellant's apartment, that her sister was there. No one seeking entry "knew" as a fact that she was dead and no one had a right to assume it was a "body," rather than a dying or unconscious person, as the police thought. Accordingly, it is clear that this information came from an independent source, and it cannot reasonably be said that the evidence embodied in the coroner's testimony was acquired "by exploitation of

. . . [the] illegality," see Maguire, supra, or that it can be regarded as "gained by the Government's own wrong," Silverthorne, supra, 251 U.S. at 392, 40 S.Ct. at 183. It was inevitable that, even had the police not entered appellant's apartment at the time and in the manner they did, the coroner would sooner or later have been advised by the police of the information reported by the sister,[6] would have obtained the body, and would have conducted the post mortem examination prescribed by law. See D.C.Code Ann. § 11-1203 (1961). Thus, the necessary causal relation between the illegal activity and the evidence sought to be excluded is lacking in this case.

JUDGE WASHINGTON considers that the discussion in the preceding pages amply justifies the admission of the coroner's testimony, and that it is not necessary for us to pass upon the legality of the police entry, the reviewability of the pre-trial order, or the need (or not) to remand the case for further hearings on the circumstances of the entry. Accordingly, the discussion which follows reflects my own views. JUDGE WASHINGTON concurs in this opinion up to this point, and concurs in the affirmance of the conviction. . . . [1]

Affirmed.

EDGERTON, CIRCUIT JUDGE (dissenting).

It is hard for me to disregard the conduct and consider the rights of an unlicensed drunken doctor who seems to have bungled his work and killed his patient.

Since Judge Burger thinks the police entered Wayne's apartment legally and I think they entered illegally, while Judge Washington does not reach this question, it is not decided. Judge Washington and Judge Burger think the coroner's testimony was rightly admitted and therefore affirm the conviction. I disagree. . . .

[Footnote by the Court.]

6. Rules and Regulations of the Metropolitan Police, Chapter II, Section 55, p. 33, Chapter XXIV, Section 12, p. 104a (eff. Nov. 1948).

[Added by the Compiler.]

1. "Wong Sun v. United States, 371 U.S. 471, 83 S.Ct. 407, 9 L.Ed.2d 441, is the most recent case involving the extent of the 'poisonous tree' doctrine. There the Court held that the declarations of Toy made in his bedroom simultaneously with the arrest were inadmissible. In the same case the Court held that the unsigned confession of Wong Sun made upon his voluntary return to police headquarters several days after he had been released on his own recognizance was admissible. Following Nardone v. United States, 308 U.S. 338, 341, 60 S.Ct. 266, 268, 84 L.Ed. 307, the Court held that the connection between the arrest and the statement had 'become so attenuated as to dissipate the taint.' . . .
"In the Wong Sun case the statements of Toy made simultaneously with the illegal arrest and the unsigned confession of Wong Sun made several days thereafter are at opposite ends of the pole in considering the fruit of the poisonous tree. Between these two extremes there is a line, on one side of which the fruit is contaminated by the illegal arrest, and on the other side of which the taint has been dissipated. Where this line shall be drawn is a question of fact to be determined in each case." United States v. McGavic, 337 F.2d 317, 318-19 (6th Cir. 1964).

Since the body, which made it possible for the coroner to testify, was illegally obtained, I think his testimony should have been excluded. That the police learned legally from Joan that Jean was dead is immaterial because this knowledge did not, without the aid of the subsequent illegal entry, enable the coroner to testify. The "independent source" principle is simply that evidence obtained *without use of illegal means* is not excluded on the ground that the same evidence has also been obtained by use of illegal means. Since the body, and consequently the coroner's testimony, were not obtained without use of illegal means, the principle has no application here.

The majority of the court take the position that legal acquisition of information *leading to* an illegal entry makes evidence *resulting from* the illegal entry admissible, if by using the legally acquired information in a *different* way the government *could have* got the resulting evidence legally. . . .

LOPEZ v. UNITED STATES

Supreme Court of the United States, 1963.
373 U.S. 427, 83 S.Ct. 1381.

[A federal agent, investigating possible evasion of excise taxes on cabarets, was in L's office at L's request. Unknown to L the agent had a tape recorder in his pocket which recorded L's offer to bribe the agent. L was indicted for attempted bribery of a federal officer and at the trial the agent testified to what was said in the office on that occasion and, over timely objection, the tape recording thereof was admitted in evidence.]

Mr. Justice Harlan delivered the opinion of the Court. . . .

Petitioner's remaining contentions concern the admissibility of the evidence relating to his conversation with Davis on October 24. His argument is primarily addressed to the recording of the conversation, which he claims was obtained in violation of his rights under the Fourth Amendment. Recognizing the weakness of this position if Davis was properly permitted to testify about the same conversation, petitioner now challenges that testimony as well, although he failed to do so at the trial. His theory is that, in view of Davis' alleged falsification of his mission, he gained access to petitioner's office by misrepresentation and all evidence obtained in the office, i. e., his conversation with petitioner, was illegally "seized." . . .

We need not be long detained by the belated claim that Davis should not have been permitted to testify about the conversation of October 24. Davis was not guilty of an unlawful invasion of petitioner's office simply because his apparent willingness to accept a bribe was not real. He was in the office with petitioner's consent, and while there he did not violate the privacy of the office by seizing something surreptitiously without petitioner's knowledge. The only evidence obtained consisted of statements made by Lopez to Davis, statements which Lopez knew full well could be used against him by Davis if he wished. We decline to hold that whenever an offer of a bribe is made in private, and the offeree does not intend to accept, that offer is a constitutionally protected communication.

Once it is plain that Davis could properly testify about his conversation with Lopez, the constitutional claim relating to the recording of that conversation emerges in proper perspective. The Court has in the past sustained instances of "electronic eavesdropping" against constitutional challenge, when devices have been used to enable government agents to overhear conversations which would have been beyond the reach of the human ear. It has been insisted only that the electronic device not be planted by an unlawful physical invasion of a constitutionally protected area. The validity of these decisions is not in question here. Indeed this case involves no "eavesdropping" whatever in any proper sense of that term. The Government did not use an electronic device to listen in on conversations it could not otherwise have heard. Instead, the device was used only to obtain the most reliable evidence possible of a conversation in which the Government's own agent was a participant and which that agent was fully entitled to disclose. And the device was not planted by means of an unlawful physical invasion of petitioner's premises under circumstances which would violate the Fourth Amendment. It was carried in and out by an agent who was there with petitioner's assent, and it neither saw nor heard more than the agent himself.

The case is thus quite similar to Rathbun v. United States, 355 U.S. 107, 78 S.Ct. 161, 2 L.Ed.2d 134, in which we sustained against statutory attack the admission in evidence of the testimony of a policeman as to a conversation he overheard on an extension telephone with the consent of a party to the conversation. The present case, if anything, is even clearer, since in Rathbun it was conceded by all concerned "that either party may *record* the conversation and publish it." 355 U.S. at 110, 78 S.Ct. at 163. (Emphasis added.)

Stripped to its essentials, petitioner's argument amounts to saying that he has a constitutional right to rely on possible flaws in the agent's memory, or to challenge the agent's credibility without being beset by corroborating evidence that is not susceptible of impeachment. For no other argument can justify excluding an accurate version of a conversation that the agent could testify to from memory.[11] We think the risk that petitioner took in offering a bribe to Davis fairly included the risk that the offer would be accurately reproduced in court, whether by faultless memory or mechanical recording.

[Footnotes by the Court.]

11. The trustworthiness of the recording is not challenged.

It is urged that whether or not the recording violated petitioner's constitutional rights, we should prevent its introduction in evidence in this federal trial in the exercise of our supervisory powers. But the court's inherent power to refuse to receive material evidence is a power that must be sparingly exercised. Its application in the present case, where there has been no manifestly improper conduct by federal officials, would be wholly unwarranted.[12]

The function of a criminal trial is to seek out and determine the truth or falsity of the charges brought against the defendant. Proper fulfillment of this function requires that, constitutional limitations aside, all relevant, competent evidence be admissible, unless the manner in which it has been obtained—for example, by violating some statute or rule of procedure—compels the formulation of a rule excluding its introduction in a federal court.

When we look for the overriding considerations that might require the exclusion of the highly useful evidence involved here, we find nothing. There has been no invasion of constitutionally protected rights, and no violation of federal law or rules of procedure. Indeed, there has not even been any electronic eavesdropping on a private conversation which government agents could not otherwise have overheard. There has, in short, been no act of any kind which could justify the creation of an exclusionary rule. We therefore conclude that the judgment of the Court of Appeals must be affirmed.

Affirmed.

MR. CHIEF JUSTICE WARREN, concurring in the result.

I concur in the result achieved by the Court but feel compelled to state my views separately. As pointed out in the dissenting opinion of MR. JUSTICE BRENNAN, the majority opinion may be interpreted as reaffirming *sub silentio* the result in On Lee v. United States, 343 U.S. 747, 72 S.Ct. 967, 96 L.Ed. 1270. Since I agree with MR. JUSTICE BRENNAN that On Lee was wrongly decided and should not be revitalized, but base my views on grounds different from those stated in the dissent, I have chosen to concur specially. Although the dissent assumes that this case and On Lee are in all respects the same, to me they are quite dissimilar constitutionally and from the viewpoint of what this Court should permit under its supervisory powers over the administration of criminal justice in the federal courts.

I also share the opinion of MR. JUSTICE BRENNAN that the fantastic advances in the field of electronic communication constitute a great danger to the privacy of the individual; that indiscriminate use of such devices in law enforcement raises grave constitutional

---

12. Since Agent Davis himself testified to the conversation with petitioner which was the subject matter of the recording, the question whether there may be circumstances in which the use of such recordings in evidence should be limited to purposes of "corroboration" is not presented by this case.

questions under the Fourth and Fifth Amendments; and that these considerations impose a heavier responsibility on this Court in its supervision of the fairness of procedures in the federal court system. However, I do not believe that, as a result, all uses of such devices should be proscribed either as unconstitutional or as unfair law enforcement methods. One of the lines I would draw would be between this case and On Lee.

As MR. JUSTICE HARLAN sets out in greater detail, Agent Davis, upon entering the premises of the petitioner, gave full notice of both his authority and purpose—to investigate possible evasion or delinquency in the payment of federal taxes. In the course of this investigation, the petitioner offered Davis a bribe and promised more in the future if Davis would conceal the facts of the petitioner's tax evasion. Davis accepted the money and promptly reported it to his superiors. On a return visit to the petitioner's place of business to complete the investigation, Davis was outfitted with a concealed recorder to tape his conversation with the petitioner. At trial, Davis testified to both of his conversations with the petitioner, and the tape recording was introduced to corroborate this testimony. The petitioner did not claim he was entrapped into the bribery or that the purpose of the investigation from the start was to induce the bribe. On the contrary, he admitted giving the money to Davis but claimed that it was for the purpose of having the latter prepare his tax return. The only purpose the recording served was to protect the credibility of Davis against that of a man who wished to corrupt a public servant in the performance of his public trust. I find nothing unfair in this procedure. . . .

MR. JUSTICE BRENNAN, with whom MR. JUSTICE DOUGLAS and MR. JUSTICE GOLDBERG join, dissenting.

In On Lee v. United States, 343 U.S. 747, 72 S.Ct. 967, 96 L.Ed. 1270, the Court sustained the admission in evidence of the testimony of a federal agent as to incriminating statements made by the accused, a laundryman, on trial for narcotics offenses. The statements were made by the accused while at large on bail pending trial in a conversation in his shop with an acquaintance and former employee, who, unknown to the accused, was a government informer and carried a radio transmitter concealed on his person. The federal agent, equipped with a radio receiver tuned to the transmitter, heard the transmitted conversation while standing on the sidewalk outside the laundry. The Court rejected arguments invoking the Fourth Amendment and our supervisory power against the admissibility of the agent's testimony. I believe that that decision was error, in reason and authority, at the time it was decided; that subsequent decisions and subsequent experience have sapped whatever vitality it may once have had; that it should now be regarded as overruled; that the instant case is ra-

Sec. 4   RIGHTS AS TO THE TIME OF TRIAL   903

tionally indistinguishable; and that, therefore, we should reverse the judgment below. . . .

(6) The Olmstead decision caused such widespread dissatisfaction that Congress in effect overruled it by enacting § 605 of the Federal Communications Act, which made wiretapping a federal crime. . . . The passive and the quiet, equally with the active and the aggressive, are entitled to protection when engaged in the precious activity of expressing ideas or beliefs. Electronic surveillance destroys all anonymity and all privacy; it makes government privy to everything that goes on.

In light of these circumstances I think it is an intolerable anomaly that while conventional searches and seizures are regulated by the Fourth and Fourteenth Amendments and wiretapping is prohibited by federal statute, electronic surveillance as involved in the instant case, which poses the greatest danger to the right of private freedom, is wholly beyond the pale of federal law.[20] . . .

SECTION 4. RIGHTS AS TO THE TIME OF TRIAL

When the defendant has been indicted or informed against, has been arraigned and has entered his plea of not guilty (or had this plea entered for him by the court), the proceedings are in shape for trial. But although the proceedings are ready for trial the parties may not be. Two rights inhere in the defendant which protect him on both sides in this regard. The first of these is the right to a speedy trial; the other is the right not to be forced to trial until he has had due time for preparation.

[Footnote by Mr. Justice Brennan.]

20. Senator Hennings has termed electronic eavesdropping more insidious and more prevalent than wiretapping. The Wiretapping-Eavesdropping Problem: A Legislator's View, 44 Minn.L. Rev. 813, 815 (1960). Another observer has called the problem "far graver" than wiretapping. Williams, The Wiretapping-Eavesdropping Problem: A Defense Counsel's View, 44 Minn. L.Rev. 855, 862 (1960).

[Added by the Compiler.]

No fundamental rights are violated when officers, by means of an electronic device, listen in to a conversation relating to a crime to be committed in the future. State v. Pacheco, 98 Ariz. 377, 405 P.2d 809 (1965).

That evidence of a crime being committed, or to be committed, is recorded on tape without the knowledge of the wrongdoer does not constitute entrapment. United States v. Osborn, 350 F.2d 497 (6th Cir. 1965).

There is a tendency to extend the statutory prohibition of wire tapping to bar also electronic surveillance without physical contact. See West's Ann. Cal.Pen.Code, § 653j, added in 1963. This was interpreted not to apply to a communication if such surveillance was with the consent of one of the parties. People v. Fontaine, —— Cal.App.2d ——, 46 Cal.Rptr. 855 (1965).

The right of a person charged with a public offense to demand a speedy trial dates back to Magna Carta. A "speedy trial" does not necessarily mean a trial forthwith.[1] The machinery of justice is not so adapted that every man accused of crime can be tried on the very day he is taken into custody under an indictment or information,—or on the day the formal charge is filed if he is in custody at that time. Due regard must be given to the terms of court, in other than metropolitan areas. More than this, the prosecution is entitled to a reasonable time to prepare its case and get ready for trial. The purpose of this right is not to embarrass the prosecuting officer in the performance of his duty, but only to prevent unreasonable imprisonment without trial, which was anciently a means of great oppression. The defendant cannot insist that his trial be set at a date too early to allow a reasonable opportunity to prepare the case against him. Even after the date is set if, without the fault of the prosecution, delay becomes necessary in order to procure the attendance of material witnesses, or for some other proper purpose, a reasonable continuance will be granted. But negligence or want of due diligence in the preparation of its case will not entitle the prosecution to a delay in the setting of the case for trial or for a postponement of the date after it has been set.

At common law there was nothing to prevent the prosecution from putting the defendant on trial immediately after his arraignment unless he could show sufficient cause for a continuance. Statutes frequently entitle a defendant to a certain period after his plea is entered (such as three days or five days) without any showing on his part. And with or without such a statutory provision he will be given such reasonable time as he can show is necessary for the preparation of his defense. Upon proper showing he will be entitled to a continuance even after the date for the trial has been set. He is not entitled to a continuance just for the purpose of delay, but courts are reluctant to force a defendant to a criminal trial for which he insists he is not ready.

The right to a speedy trial applies only to one who has been accused of crime. The commencement of the proceedings is restricted only by the statute of limitations,[2] unless delay has been oppressive under the circumstances.[3]

1. A defendant serving a life term in California cannot complain of the failure to grant him a speedy trial in the United States Court in Oregon, having made no attempt to show how he could be present for trial there. Kyle v. United States, 211 F.2d 912 (9th Cir. 1954).

2. Harlow v. United States, 301 F.2d 361 (5th Cir. 1962), certiorari denied 371 U.S. 814, 83 S.Ct. 25, 9 L.Ed.2d 56; People v. Aguirre, 181 Cal.App.2d 577, 5 Cal.Rptr. 477 (1960).

3. See Ross v. United States, 349 F.2d 210 (D.C.Cir. 1965).

SECTION 5. RIGHT TO BE PRESENT DURING TRIAL

In all criminal prosecutions the defendant has a right to be present in person during the entire proceeding from arraignment to sentence. A statute denying this right would be an unconstitutional violation of due process. The only controversies or diversities with reference to the defendant's presence during trial have to do with the extent to which this is not merely a right belonging to him, but an absolute requirement. Insofar as this is merely one of defendant's rights it can be waived by him. If the trial cannot proceed during his absence, his presence is not only one of his rights but a requirement. It has not been uncommon to speak of this, and similar problems, in terms of the extent to which the defendant can or cannot waive his right.

Some courts have held that defendant's presence during trial is a requirement at common law in all felony cases, although others hold it to be merely one of the defendant's rights in non-capital felony trials. Almost without exception it is held to be a requirement in capital cases. There is some authority for the view that it is a requirement even in a misdemeanor case if corporal punishment may be imposed as the penalty for the particular offense, but the prevailing view holds it to be only a right in all cases less than felony. Where it applies, the requirement is limited to the trial itself, and certain essential preliminaries such as the arraignment, the plea, the calling, examining, challenging, impaneling and swearing of the jury,[a] plus the allocution and imposition of sentence if the verdict is guilty. It does not demand the defendant's presence when motions are being made or argued, or when an appeal is being heard.

While a statute would be unconstitutional if it purported to deprive the defendant of the right to be present during his trial on a criminal charge, an enactment does not deprive him of due process of law if it merely changes his presence during the trial, from what was formerly a requirement, to one of his rights. This would still entitle him to be present if he did not by his act or conduct waive his right. A defendant who escapes, or who otherwise voluntarily absents himself after the trial has been commenced in his presence, is generally regarded to have waived his right to be present.[b] Hence the trial may continue in his absence unless his presence in that particular trial is not merely a right but a requirement.

---

a. The selection of the jury often is referred to as a part of the trial and this is no doubt true in a sense. The trial proper, however, in common-law theory as well as in the layman's view, begins after the jury is sworn.

b. Diaz v. United States, 223 U.S. 442, 32 S.Ct. 250, 56 L.Ed. 500 (1912).

Many variations are found in the statutes dealing with this subject. Most of them provide that the defendant must be "personally present" if the prosecution is for a felony. A number of them authorize the defendant to appear by counsel for arraignment in a misdemeanor case and provide that the trial may be had in his absence. A few provide that if the defendant escapes after any trial has commenced it may continue to verdict. Rule 43 of the Federal Rules of Criminal Procedure adheres more closely to the common law than do many of the state statutes on this subject.[c] Rule 43 reads:

"The defendant shall be present at the arraignment, at every stage of the trial including the impaneling of the jury and the return of the verdict, and at the imposition of sentence, except as otherwise provided by these rules. In prosecutions for offenses not punishable by death, the defendant's voluntary absence after the trial has been commenced in his presence shall not prevent continuing the trial to and including the return of the verdict. A corporation may appear by counsel for all purposes. In prosecutions for offenses punishable by fine or by imprisonment for not more than one year or both, the court, with the written consent of the defendant, may permit arraignment, plea, trial and imposition of sentence in the defendant's absence. The defendant's presence is not required at a reduction of sentence under Rule 35."

SECTION 6. RIGHT TO A PUBLIC TRIAL

One accused of crime has a common-law right to a public trial [1] which has been embodied in the federal constitution and in the constitutions of most of the states. The public aspect of the trial has been considered almost exclusively from the standpoint of a right belonging to the defendant. It has been assumed that a public trial is not necessary if expressly waived by him.[2] And the right of a disinterested member of the public to attend, even if his presence is not desired by the defendant, has not been adequately tested, although it is clear that the defendant has no right to demand a secret trial.[3] The right to a public trial cannot be interpreted to require more than that the proceedings be open to the public. If they are so open there is no

---

[c.] For a summary of the statutes see American Law Institute, Code of Criminal Procedure 878–887 (official draft with commentaries, 1930).

[1.] Radin, The Right to a Public Trial, 6 Temp.L.Q. 381 (1932).

[2.] People v. Swafford, 65 Cal. 223, 3 P. 809 (1894). This case held, moreover, that failure to object constituted a waiver, but there is authority contra on this point. Wade v. State, 207 Ala. 1, 92 So. 101 (1921).

[3.] Carter v. State, 99 Miss. 435, 54 So. 734 (1911).

Sec. 6   RIGHT TO A PUBLIC TRIAL

requirement that the trial must stop merely because no member of the general public happens to be in attendance.

Neither the defendant nor anyone else has a right to require the judge to admit to the courtroom any unneeded person whose presence will interfere with the due and orderly conduct of the trial. Overcrowding will result in such interference. Hence if members of the general public are admitted until the seating capacity of the courtroom is exhausted, the exclusion of others is entirely proper. Furthermore, if all available space is taken by witnesses and other persons necessary to the trial or having some special and proper interest therein, the exclusion of disinterested members of the public is unavoidable.[4] Disorderly persons may be evicted, and if all who are not necessary to the trial are disorderly, all may be required to leave.[5] On the other hand it would be arbitrary and unreasonable if the judge, after having given such an order, should refuse to make any exceptions even upon a proper showing therefor. If the defendant's father, for example, or some other relative or friend whose presence was desired by him, should assure the judge that he had not participated in the disorder and would not in any way interfere with the due and orderly conduct of the trial, it would be prejudicial error to compel him to leave.

The chief controversy in this field has centered on the propriety of an order of exclusion based upon the salacious nature of the evidence to be introduced. An order excluding children from such a trial seems to have been free from question. So also is an order temporarily removing those having no special and proper interest in being present, if this is necessary to get the testimony of a very young witness who is so emotionally disturbed by the embarrassing nature of what she is to reveal that she cannot give a coherent account of the facts without it.[6] It is equally clear, on the other side, that an order of exclusion is improper if it is so sweeping in its scope as unnecessarily to keep from the courtroom every relative or friend of the defendant, or if an order which was proper when made is arbitrarily continued after the emergency which induced it has passed entirely.

The real difficulty lies between such extremes. One type of exclusion order in cases in which the evidence was to be particularly salacious has been this in substance: That no persons not needed for the trial itself be admitted to the courtroom except members of the press and those whose presence is desired by the defendant. Such an

---

4. Kugadt v. State, 38 Tex.Cr.R. 681, 44 S.W. 989 (1898).

5. Grimmett v. State, 22 Tex.App. 36, 2 S.W. 631 (1886).
It was held that the exclusion of the public except for members of the press and the bar was not unreasonable where it was apparent that D and his sympathizers were attempting to prevent an orderly presentation of the case. United States v. Fay, 350 F.2d 967 (2d Cir. 1965).

6. Moore v. State, 151 Ga. 648, 108 S.E. 47 (1921); State v. Callahan, 100 Minn. 63, 110 N.W. 342 (1907).

order has been upheld by some courts but held by others to be reversible error.[7] It is difficult to conceive how the defendant could be prejudiced by an order which permits the presence of any person desired by him. But some appellate judges, with minds well insulated from the atmosphere of the trial courtroom, have thought they could insure the presence of a number of the more substantial members of the community by forbidding such an exclusion. The indications are that such persons tend to shun trials of this nature, and that the chief result of such a rule is to provide an opportunity for some of the least desirable members of the community to satisfy very morbid impulses by hearing from the witness stand words so extreme they might not be permitted from across the footlights.[8]

"In cases like the one at bar, where the evidence is of a very immoral and disgusting nature, we do not think the court erred in excluding the general public from the courtroom during the trial. Of course, the friends of the defendant who desired to be present and officers of the court, including members of the bar, ought not to be excluded; but to exclude the general public who have only a curiosity to hear the revolting details of a rape case, does not deprive a defendant of a public trial as provided by the constitution and statutes above cited." [9]

In one case, the prosecution having acquiesced in defendant's motion that the public be excluded, the court granted the motion in the belief that the presence of the public would prevent the defendant from testifying freely and hence deprive her of a fair trial. A petition by newspaper publishers for a writ of mandate to compel vacation of the exclusion order was denied on the ground that they had no absolute right to be present and were properly excluded during her testimony. Such exclusion was upheld but the court added that the trial judge should not have excluded the public from the entire trial.[10]

An order "putting witnesses under the rule" [11] does not violate defendant's right to a public trial.[12]

7. The cases are cited in notes: 28 Tex. L.Rev. 265 (1949); 3 Vand.L.Rev. 125 (1949); 156 A.L.R. 265 (1945).

8. Radin, The Right to a Public Trial, 6 Temp.L.Q. 381 (1932).

9. State v. Johnson, 26 Idaho 609, 612-3, 144 P. 784, 785 (1914).

D, on trial for rape, was denied his constitutional right to a public trial by the exclusion from the courtroom of all spectators except members of the press, court officials and near relatives of the prosecutrix and of D. Thompson v. People, —— Colo. ——, 399 P.2d 776 (1965). In this case the prosecutrix was nearly twenty-one and there was no showing that she was emotionally upset. The court's order expressly excluded friends of D who were not close relatives.

10. Kirstowski v. Superior Court, 143 Cal.App.2d 745, 300 P.2d 163 (1956).

11. This order excludes all other witnesses from the courtroom while any one of them is on the witness stand.

12. State v. Worthen, 124 Iowa 408, 100 N.W. 330 (1904). Putting witnesses "under the rule" is within the discretion of the judge but it is error for

SECTION 7. RIGHT TO A TRIAL BY JURY

It has been said: "That the modern institution of trial by jury derives from Magna Carta is one of the most revered of legal fables." [1] "The 'judgment of his peers' there named is secured only to noblemen who are, by this provision, to be tried at the king's suit in the House of Lords." [2] But when we have shown that this protection was quite limited in its inception, and has since been broadened in its scope to include all people, we seem rather to have explained than to have contradicted the thought that this important benefit relates back to that great document. The right to trial by jury is still regarded by many as most important to liberty.

The usual common law classification of crimes recognizes three groups: (1) treason, (2) felony, and (3) misdemeanor. For certain important purposes of procedure, however, a different classification was employed. This emphasized the distinction between (1) indictable offenses and (2) petty offenses. Persons charged with very minor violations such as disorderly conduct, trivial breaches of the peace or infractions of municipal ordinances could be prosecuted without waiting for an indictment by the grand jury, and could be tried summarily without the aid of a trial jury. Except for such petty offenses the common law gives the defendant a right to a trial by jury in every prosecution for crime. This right is guaranteed by most of the constitutions. A few of the provisions seem to extend the right even beyond its common-law scope.[3]

---

the court to refuse to do so without exercising discretion under the theory that he has abandoned the practice. Charles v. United States, 215 F.2d 825 (9th Cir. 1954).

1. Frankfurter and Corcoran, Petty Federal Offenses and the Constitutional Guaranty of Trial by Jury, 39 Harv.L.Rev. 917, 922 (1926).

2. Beale, Criminal Pleading and Practice 253, note 1 (1899).

3. The Sixth Amendment provides: "In all criminal prosecutions, the accused shall enjoy the right to a speedy and public trial, by an impartial jury. . . ." Some of the state constitutions are similarly worded. But the phrase "criminal prosecutions," in such a constitutional clause, has been interpreted to include only what Blackstone refers to as "regular" proceedings as distinguished from the summary trial of petty offenses. 4 Bl.Comm. 280. In other words it is construed to preserve the right of trial by jury as it existed prior to the constitution and not to extend it to a broader field. Frankfurter and Corcoran, Petty Federal Offenses and the Constitutional Guaranty of Trial by Jury, 39 Harv.L.Rev. 917, 969 (1926).

But an occasional provision has an added phrase, such as that "in all criminal prosecutions, and in cases involving the life or liberty of an individual, the accused shall have the right to a speedy and public trial by an impartial jury." Iowa Const. Art. I, sec. 10. Since any imprisonment involves the liberty of an individual, and some of the petty offenses were punished by imprisonment for a short period, such a clause extends the right of trial by jury.

The constitutional right to a trial by jury means trial by a common-law jury unless otherwise specified. The common-law trial jury is a jury of twelve, and this number may be insisted upon unless a different one is provided. The constitution of Utah, for example, provides for the trial of felonies (other than capital) by a jury of eight.[4] The power of a state to provide for such a jury in its own courts is clear, but it is subject to one limitation: it cannot have retroactive effect. This constitutional provision, for example, was held to be *ex post facto* as to offenses committed before the territory became a state, because at that time the right to a common-law jury still prevailed.[5] So firm is the right to a jury of twelve that a verdict was set aside when it was discovered that it had been rendered by a jury of thirteen.[6] A number of the constitutions, it should be added, provide for the trial of certain grades of offenses by a jury of fewer than twelve.

(A) WAIVER

At one time the jury trial of an indictable offense was considered by many to be a requirement rather than a mere right. As it was expressed by one author some years ago, "the weight of authority, as well as the better opinion, is, that in prosecutions for crime other than minor misdemeanors and petty offenses, the defendant cannot waive his right to a trial by jury, or consent to a trial by a less number than twelve."[7] A similar view was expressed by others;[8] and a number of convictions were reversed because the trial was without a full panel of twelve, although it was with the express consent of the defendant. The theory was that a common-law jury was essential to the jurisdiction of the court in criminal cases.

In *Patton*[9] the Supreme Court rejected this view, disposing of the jurisdiction theory as follows:

"In the absence of a valid consent, the District Court cannot proceed except with a jury, not because a jury is essential to its jurisdiction, but because the accused is entitled by the terms of the Constitution to that mode of trial".

---

4. Utah, Const. Art. I, sec. 10.

5. Thompson v. Utah, 170 U.S. 343, 18 S.Ct. 620, 42 L.Ed. 1061 (1897).

6. Bullard v. State, 38 Tex. 504 (1873); State v. Hudkins, 35 W.Va. 247, 13 S.E. 367 (1891).

7. Rapalje, Criminal Procedure § 151 (1889).

8. Hughes, Criminal Law and Procedure § 2979 (1901); Cooley, Constitutional Limitations 674-5 (8th ed. by Carrington, 1927).

9. Patton v. United States, 281 U.S. 276, 50 S.Ct. 253, 74 L.Ed. 854, 70 A.L.R. 263 (1930).

Sec. 7 RIGHT TO A TRIAL BY JURY 911

And Rule 23 of the Federal Rules of Criminal Procedure expressly authorizes the waiver. On the other hand the defendant has no absolute right to demand a trial without a jury. The provision of the rule requiring the court and government to consent to the waiver of jury trial is valid, at least unless defendant can show some impelling reason in a particular case why he should be entitled to a trial by the judge alone.[10]

Today, the power of the judge to try a criminal case without a jury, when the jury has been waived, is accepted without question unless some state statute or constitution provides otherwise.

(B) ALTERNATE JURORS

While the verdict of a jury of thirteen will not support a judgment of conviction (in the absence of effective waiver by defendant), the mere presence of a thirteenth man on the panel is not necessarily fatal. It has been suggested, for example, that if the error is discovered before verdict the thirteenth member can be withdrawn and the trial proceed validly with the original twelve.[15] This suggested the possibility of one or more alternate jurors.

Now and then after the trial of a criminal case is well under way it becomes necessary to discontinue the proceedings and start all over again because a juror is unable to continue for some impelling reason such as illness. While not an everyday occurrence, a study of the records will disclose that this has happened time and again down through the years. It is particularly distressing to have this happen after the case has been in progress for many days, and perhaps weeks, whereas the longer the trial the greater is the likelihood of such a misfortune. The defendant can avoid the necessity of a fresh start by waiving his right to a full panel. This, however, is not a satisfactory solution because it places entirely too much control in his hands. The court and the prosecution, normally inclined to support the defendant in any offer to waive the jury (in whole or in part), would be extremely hesitant to block his waiver under these circumstances. The defendant on the other hand will not waive the full panel if he thinks he can gain the slightest advantage by insisting upon his rights (as he is fully entitled to do).

In the effort to improve the procedure at this point there has been a trend in the direction of authorizing the selection of alternate jurors for cases likely to be protracted. Statutes to this effect have been passed in a number of states. The most recent provision reflecting the result of an exhaustive study on a nation-wide basis is found in

---

10. Singer v. United States, 380 U.S. 24, 85 S.Ct. 783, 13 L.Ed.2d 630 (1965).

15. Bullard v. State, 38 Tex. 504 (1873).

Rule 24 of the Federal Rules of Criminal Procedure. This concludes with the following sub-division:

"(c) Alternate Jurors. The court may direct that not more than 4 jurors in addition to the regular jury be called and impanelled to sit as alternate jurors. Alternate jurors in the order in which they are called shall replace jurors who, prior to the time the jury retires to consider its verdict, become unable or disqualified to perform their duties. Alternate jurors shall be drawn in the same manner, shall have the same qualifications, shall be subject to the same examination and challenges, shall take the same oath and shall have the same functions, powers, facilities and privileges as the regular jurors. An alternate juror who does not replace a regular juror shall be discharged after the jury retires to consider its verdict. Each side is entitled to 1 peremptory challenge in addition to those otherwise allowed by law if 1 or 2 alternate jurors are to be impanelled, and 2 peremptory challenges if 3 or 4 alternate jurors are to be impanelled. The additional peremptory challenges may be used against an alternate juror only, and the other peremptory challenges allowed by these rules may not be used against an alternate juror." [16]

SECTION 8. RIGHT TO A FAIR AND IMPARTIAL TRIAL

The rather common constitutional clause guaranteeing the defendant a "trial by an impartial jury" does not exhaust the right to impartiality. The requirement of due process of law entitles the defendant to a fair and impartial trial in every respect.[1] The case in which a violent mob moved into the courtroom and completely dominated the trial, intimidating witnesses, counsel, jurors and even the judge himself so that no one dared to do anything other than let the case proceed to a hasty conviction,[2] requires no discussion. Much less than this may be sufficient to deprive the defendant of a fair and impartial trial. The case of Tumey v. Ohio is illuminating.[3] The defendant was arrested and brought before a village mayor charged

---

16. If the need arises an alternate juror, if he has been selected properly, may be substituted for one of the original twelve without placing the defendant in double jeopardy. People v. Hess, 104 Cal.App.2d 642, 234 P.2d 65 (1951).

1. "He is also entitled to a fair trial, which has been well defined as 'a trial before an impartial judge, an honest jury, and in an atmosphere of judicial calm.'" State v. Leland, 190 Or. 598, 608, 227 P.2d 785, 790 (1951). Cf. Robedeaux v. State, 94 Okl.Cr. 171, 232 P.2d 642 (1951). See Holtzoff, Relation Between the Right to a Fair Trial and the Right of Freedom of the Press, 1 Syracuse L.Rev. 369 (1950).

2. Moore v. Dempsey, 261 U.S. 86, 43 S.Ct. 265, 67 L.Ed. 543 (1923).

3. 273 U.S. 510, 47 S.Ct. 437, 71 L.Ed. 749 (1926).

Sec. 9   THE INTERPLAY OF RIGHTS AND PRIVILEGES   913

with unlawfully possessing intoxicating liquor. Ignoring a claim of disqualification, the mayor proceeded with a trial which resulted in a conviction. The judgment was reversed by the Court of Common Pleas on the ground that the mayor was disqualified as claimed, but this in turn was reversed by the Court of Appeals, and the State Supreme Court refused to disturb the conviction. The case was then taken to the Supreme Court of the United States upon a writ of error. The court discovered that under the relevant statutes and ordinances the mayor trying such a case was entitled to legal fees taxed in his favor in the event of a conviction but received nothing if an acquittal resulted. The court further found that the fees in this case amounted to $12.00 and that the mayor had been averaging about $100.00 a month from such fees in addition to his salary. In reversing the judgment the court said, speaking through Mr. Chief Justice Taft: "But it certainly violates the Fourteenth Amendment, and deprives a defendant in a criminal case of due process of law, to subject his liberty or property to the judgment of a court the judge of which has a direct, personal, substantial, pecuniary interest in reaching a conclusion against him in the case."

SECTION 9. THE INTERPLAY OF RIGHTS AND PRIVILEGES

MASSIAH v. UNITED STATES

Supreme Court of the United States, 1964.
377 U.S. 201, 84 S.Ct. 1199.

[M, who had been indicted for violation of the federal narcotics laws, had retained counsel and been released on bail. Thereafter a federal agent arranged with C, who had been jointly indicted with M, for the installation in C's car of a radio transmitter which would enable the agent in another car, parked out of sight, to listen to the conversation between M and C, during which M made several incriminating statements. Over timely objection the agent was permitted to testify as to these statements in the trial in which M was convicted.]

MR. JUSTICE STEWART delivered the opinion of the Court. . . .

Because of the way we dispose of the case, we do not reach the Fourth Amendment issue.

In Spano v. New York, 360 U.S. 315, 79 S.Ct. 1202, 3 L.Ed.2d 1265, this Court reversed a state criminal conviction because a confession had been wrongly admitted into evidence against the defendant at his trial. In that case the defendant had already been indicted for first degree murder at the time he confessed. The Court held that the defendant's conviction could not stand under the Fourteenth Amendment. While the Court's opinion relied upon the totality of the circumstances under which the confession had been obtained, four concurring Justices pointed out that the Constitution required reversal of the conviction upon the sole and specific ground that the confession had been deliberately elicited by the police after the defendant had been indicted, and therefore at a time when he was clearly entitled to a lawyer's help. It was pointed out that under our system of justice the most elemental concepts of due process of law contemplate that an indictment be followed by a trial, "in an orderly courtroom, presided over by a judge, open to the public, and protected by all the procedural safeguards of the law." 360 U.S., at 327, 79 S.Ct., at 1209, 3 L.Ed.2d 1265 (STEWART, J., concurring). It was said that a Constitution which guarantees a defendant the aid of counsel at such a trial could surely vouchsafe no less to an indicted defendant under interrogation by the police in a completely extrajudicial proceeding. Anything less, it was said, might deny a defendant "effective representation by counsel at the only stage when legal aid and advice would help him." 360 U.S., at 326, 79 S.Ct., at 1209, 3 L.Ed.2d 1265 (Douglas, J., concurring. . . .

This view no more than reflects a constitutional principle established as long ago as Powell v. Alabama, 287 U.S. 45, 53 S.Ct. 55, 77 L. Ed. 158, where the Court noted that " . . . during perhaps the most critical period of the proceedings . . . that is to say, from the time of their arraignment until the beginning of their trial, when consultation, thorough-going investigation and preparation [are] vitally important, the defendants . . . [are] as much entitled to such aid [of counsel] during that period as at the trial itself." Id., 287 U.S., at 57, 53 S.Ct., at 59, 77 L.Ed. 158. And since the Spano decision the same basic constitutional principal has been broadly reaffirmed by this Court.

Here we deal not with a state court conviction, but with a federal case, where the specific guarantee of the Sixth Amendment directly applies. We hold that the petitioner was denied the basic protections of that guarantee when there was used against him at his trial evidence of his own incriminating words, which federal agents had deliberately elicited from him after he had been indicted and in the absence of his counsel. It is true that in the Spano case the defendant was interrogated in a police station, while here the damaging testimony was elicited from the defendant without his knowledge while he was free on bail. But, as Judge Hays pointed out in his dissent in the Court of Appeals, "if such a rule is to have any efficacy it must apply to indirect and surreptitious interrogations as well as those conducted in the jailhouse. In this case, Massiah was more seriously imposed upon . . . because he did not even know that he was under interrogation by a government agent." 307 F.2d at 72–73.

The Solicitor General, in his brief and oral argument, has strenuously contended that the federal law enforcement agents had the right, if not indeed the duty, to continue their investigation of the petitioner and his alleged criminal associates even though the petitioner had been indicted. He points out that the Government was continuing its investigation in order to uncover not only the source of narcotics found on the S. S. *Santa Maria*, but also their intended buyer. He says that the quantity of narcotics involved was such as to suggest that the petitioner was part of a large and well-organized ring, and indeed that the continuing investigation confirmed this suspicion, since it resulted in criminal charges against many defendants. Under these circumstances the Solicitor General concludes that the government agents were completely "justified in making use of Colson's cooperation by having Colson continue his normal associations and by surveilling them."

We may accept and, at least for present purposes, completely approve all that this argument implies, Fourth Amendment problems to one side. We do not question that in this case, as in many cases, it was entirely proper to continue an investigation of the suspected criminal activities of the defendant and his alleged confederates, even though the defendant had already been indicted. All that we hold is that the defendant's own incriminating statements, obtained by federal agents under the circumstances here disclosed, could not constitutionally be used by the prosecution as evidence against *him* at his trial.

Reversed.[1]

MR. JUSTICE WHITE, with whom MR. JUSTICE CLARK and MR. JUSTICE HARLAN join, dissenting.

The current incidence of serious violations of the law represents not only an appalling waste of the potentially happy and useful lives of those who engage in such conduct but also an overhanging, dangerous threat to those unidentified and innocent people who will be the

---

1. Where an undercover agent was placed in the cell with D (with a concealed microphone) to see if D would make incriminating statements, a confession by D who had not been advised of his constitutional rights was inadmissible. People v. Flores, — Cal. App.2d —, 46 Cal.Rptr. 412 (1965).

This is similar to In re Lopez, 62 Cal.2d 368, 42 Cal.Rptr. 188, 398 P.2d 380 (1965) in which a stool pigeon was placed in D's cell. A confession made to him was inadmissible.

It is different from People v. Teale, 63 Cal.2d —, 45 Cal.Rptr. 729, 404 P.2d 209 (1965), where statements were made to a genuine cell mate; and People v. Ketchel, 59 Cal.2d 503, 30 Cal.Rptr. 538, 381 P.2d 394 (1963), where police listened to conversations between suspects.

Placing Ds in adjoining cells in which a microphone was hidden to record and monitor their conversations did not constitute a "process of interrogations" and thus entitle Ds to counsel. People v. Ross, — Cal.App.2d —, 46 Cal.Rptr. 41 (1965). It involved no physical trespass, no seizure and no invasion of the right of privacy because there is no right of privacy in jail.

It is made a felony to eavesdrop or record, by means of an electronic or other device, a conversation between a prisoner and his attorney. West's Ann.Cal.Pen.Code, § 653i.

victims of crime today and tomorrow. This is a festering problem for which no adequate cures have yet been devised. At the very least there is much room for discontent with remedial measures so far undertaken. And admittedly there remains much to be settled concerning the disposition to be made of those who violate the law. . . .

Applying the new exclusionary rule is peculiarly inappropriate in this case. At the time of the conversation in question, petitioner was not in custody but free on bail. He was not questioned in what anyone could call an atmosphere of official coercion. What he said was said to his partner in crime who had also been indicted. There was no suggestion or any possibility of coercion. What petitioner did not know was that Colson had decided to report the conversation to the police. Had there been no prior arrangements between Colson and the police, had Colson simply gone to the police after the conversation had occurred, his testimony relating Massiah's statements would be readily admissible at the trial, as would a recording which he might have made of the conversation. In such event, it would simply be said that Massiah risked talking to a friend who decided to disclose what he knew of Massiah's criminal activities. But if, as occurred here, Colson had been cooperating with the police prior to his meeting with Massiah, both his evidence and the recorded conversation are somehow transformed into inadmissible evidence despite the fact that the hazard to Massiah remains precisely the same—the defection of a confederate in crime.

ESCOBEDO v. ILLINOIS

Supreme Court of the United States, 1964.
378 U.S. 478, 84 S.Ct. 1758.

[E, a 22-year-old Mexican with no previous experience with the police, was arrested and interrogated about the fatal shooting of his brother-in-law. He retained a lawyer and was released by habeas corpus. Several days later D, who was in police custody and was later indicted for the murder jointly with E, told the police that E had fired the fatal shots. E was again arrested and urged to confess but said he wanted to see his lawyer. For hours E asked to see his lawyer and his lawyer asked to see him, but the police did not permit the meeting until they had E's statement. Ultimately confronted by D, E said: "I didn't shoot Manuel, you did it", and thus admitted some knowledge of the crime. Later he further implicated himself and then gave a written statement. During this time no one advised him in regard to his constitutional rights.]

MR. JUSTICE GOLDBERG delivered the opinion of the Court.

The critical question in this case is whether, under the circumstances, the refusal by the police to honor petitioner's request to con-

Sec. 9   *THE INTERPLAY OF RIGHTS AND PRIVILEGES*   917

sult with his lawyer during the course of an interrogation constitutes a denial of "the Assistance of Counsel" in violation of the Sixth Amendment to the Constitution as "made obligatory upon the States by the Fourteenth Amendment," and thereby renders inadmissible in a state criminal trial any incriminating statement elicited by the police during the interrogation. . . .

The interrogation here was conducted before petitioner was formally indicted. But in the context of this case, that fact should make no difference. When petitioner requested, and was denied, an opportunity to consult with his lawyer, the investigation had ceased to be a general investigation of "an unsolved crime." Petitioner had become the accused, and the purpose of the interrogation was to "get him" to confess his guilt despite his constitutional right not to do so. At the time of his arrest and throughout the course of the interrogation, the police told petitioner that they had convincing evidence that he had fired the fatal shots. Without informing him of his absolute right to remain silent in the face of this accusation, the police urged him to make a statement.[5] As this Court observed many years ago:

"It cannot be doubted that, placed in the position in which the accused was when the statement was made to him that the other suspected person had charged him with a crime, the result was to produce upon his mind the fear that, if he remained silent, it would be considered an admission of guilt, and therefore render certain his being committed for trial as the guilty person, and it cannot be conceived that the converse impression would not also have naturally arisen that, by denying, there was hope of removing the suspicion from himself." Bram v. United States, 168 U.S. 532, 562, 18 S.Ct. 183, 194, 42 L.Ed. 568.

Petitioner, a layman, was undoubtedly unaware that under Illinois law an admission of "mere" complicity in the murder plot was legally as damaging as an admission of firing of the fatal shots. Escobedo v. Illinois, 28 Ill.2d 41, 190 N.E.2d 825. The "guiding hand of counsel" was essential to advise petitioner of his rights in this delicate situation. This was the "stage when legal aid and advice" were most critical to petitioner. It was a stage surely as critical as was the arraignment in Hamilton v. Alabama, 368 U.S. 52, 82 S.Ct. 157, 7 L.Ed. 2d 114, and the preliminary hearing in White v. Maryland, 373 U.S. 59, 83 S.Ct. 1050, 10 L.Ed.2d 193. What happened at this interrogation could certainly "affect the whole trial," since rights "may be as irretrievably lost, if not then and there asserted, as they are when an accused represented by counsel waives a right for strategic purposes." It would exalt form over substance to make the right to counsel, under these circumstances, depend on whether at the time of the interroga-

---

5. Although there is testimony in the record that petitioner and his lawyer had previously discussed what petitioner should do in the event of interrogation, there is no evidence that they discussed what petitioner should, or could, do in the face of a false accusation that he had fired the fatal bullets.

tion, the authorities had secured a formal indictment. Petitioner had, for all practical purposes, already been charged with murder. . . .

It is argued that if the right to counsel is afforded prior to indictment, the number of confessions obtained by the police will diminish significantly, because most confessions are obtained during the period between arrest and indictment,[10] and "any lawyer worth his salt will tell the suspect in no uncertain terms to make no statement to police under any circumstances." This argument, of course, cuts two ways. The fact that many confessions are obtained during this period points up its critical nature as a "stage when legal aid and advice" are surely needed. The right to counsel would indeed be hollow if it began at a period when few confessions were obtained. There is necessarily a direct relationship between the importance of a stage to the police in their quest for a confession and the criticalness of that stage to the accused in his need for legal advice. Our Constitution, unlike some others, strikes the balance in favor of the right of the accused to be advised by his lawyer of his privilege against self-incrimination. . . .

We hold, therefore, that where, as here, the investigation is no longer a general inquiry into an unsolved crime but has begun to focus on a particular suspect, the suspect has been taken into police custody, the police carry out a process of interrogations that lends itself to eliciting incriminating statements, the suspect has requested and been denied an opportunity to consult with his lawyer, and the police have not effectively warned him of his absolute constitutional right to remain silent, the accused has been denied "the Assistance of Counsel" in violation of the Sixth Amendment to the Constitution as "made obligatory upon the States by the Fourteenth Amendment," and that no statement elicited by the police during the interrogation may be used against him at a criminal trial.

Crooker v. California, 357 U.S. 433, 78 S.Ct. 1287, does not compel a contrary result. In that case the Court merely rejected the absolute rule sought by petitioner, that "every state denial of a request to contact counsel [is] an infringement of the constitutional right *without regard to the circumstances of the case.*" Id., 357 U.S., at 440, 78 S.Ct., at 1292. (Emphasis in original.) In its place, the following rule was announced:

"[S]tate refusal of a request to engage counsel violates due process not only if the accused is deprived of counsel at trial on the merits, . . . *but also if he is deprived of counsel for any part of the pretrial proceedings*, provided that he is so prejudiced thereby as to infect his subsequent trial with an absence of 'that fundamental fairness essential to the very concept of justice.' . . . The latter

---

10. See Barrett, Police Practices and the Law—From Arrest to Release or Charge, 50 Cal.L.Rev. 11, 43 (1962).

Sec. 9   THE INTERPLAY OF RIGHTS AND PRIVILEGES   919

determination necessarily depends upon all the circumstances of the case." 357 U.S., at 439–440, 78 S.Ct., at 1292. (Emphasis added.) The Court, applying "these principles" to "the sum total of the circumstances [there] during the time petitioner was without counsel," id., 357 U.S., at 440, 78 S.Ct., at 1292 concluded that he had not been fundamentally prejudiced by the denial of his request for counsel. Among the critical circumstances which distinguish that case from this one are that the petitioner there, but not here, was explicitly advised by the police of his constitutional right to remain silent and not to "say anything" in response to the questions, id., 357 U.S., at 437, 78 S.Ct., at 1290, and that petitioner there, but not here, was a well-educated man who had studied criminal law while attending law school for a year. The Court's opinion in Cicenia v. La Gay, 357 U.S. 504, 78 S.Ct. 1297, 2 L.Ed.2d 1523, decided the same day, merely said that the "contention that petitioner had a constitutional right to confer with counsel is disposed of by Crooker v. California . . . ." That case adds nothing, therefore, to Crooker. In any event, to the extent that Cicenia or Crooker may be inconsistent with the principles announced today, they are not to be regarded as controlling.

Nothing we have said today affects the powers of the police to investigate "an unsolved crime," by gathering information from witnesses and by other "proper investigative efforts." We hold only that when the process shifts from investigatory to accusatory—when its focus is on the accused and its purpose is to elicit a confession—our adversary system begins to operate, and, under the circumstances here, the accused must be permitted to consult with his lawyer.

The judgment of the Illinois Supreme Court is reversed and the case remanded for proceedings not inconsistent with this opinion.

Reversed and remanded.[1]

MR. JUSTICE HARLAN, dissenting. . . .

Like my BROTHER WHITE, post, p. 1767, I think the rule announced today is most ill-conceived and that it seriously and unjustifiably fetters perfectly legitimate methods of criminal law enforcement.

MR. JUSTICE STEWART, dissenting. . . .

Supported by no stronger authority than its own rhetoric, the Court today converts a routine police investigation of an unsolved

---

[By the Compiler.]

1. D's voluntary confession after he had been taken before a commissioner and after he had been advised that he need not talk and warned that if he did talk his words might be used against him, was admissible although he had no counsel at the time of the confession since he had not requested counsel although advised of his rights thereto. Jackson v. United States, 119 U.S.App.D.C. 100, 337 F.2d 136 (1964).

It was held that Escobedo does not require exclusion of a confession made to a private person who was not a police agent or in any way connected with the police, the confession having been made prior to any police investigation, although D had not been advised of his right to remain silent and his right to counsel. Washington v. People, —— Colo. ——, 405 P.2d 735 (1965).

murder into a distorted analogue of judicial trial. It imports into this investigation constitutional concepts historically applicable only after the onset of formal prosecutorial proceedings. By doing so, I think the Court perverts those precious constitutional guarantees, and frustrates the vital interests of society in preserving the legitimate and proper function of honest and purposeful police investigation.

Like my BROTHER CLARK, I cannot escape the logic of my BROTHER WHITE'S conclusions as to the extraordinary implications which emanate from the Court's opinion in this case, and I share their views as to the untold and highly unfortunate impact today's decision may have upon the fair administration of criminal justice. I can only hope we have completely misunderstood what the Court has said.

MR. JUSTICE WHITE, with whom MR. JUSTICE CLARK and MR. JUSTICE STEWART join, dissenting.

In Massiah v. United States, 377 U.S. 201, 84 S.Ct. 1199, the Court held that as of the date of the indictment the prosecution is disentitled to secure admissions from the accused. The Court now moves that date back to the time when the prosecution begins to "focus" on the accused. Although the opinion purports to be limited to the facts of this case, it would be naive to think that the new constitutional right announced will depend upon whether the accused has retained his own counsel or has asked to consult with counsel in the course of interrogation. . . .

STATE v. NEELY

Supreme Court of Oregon, En Banc (1965).
239 Or. 487, 398 P.2d 482.

DENECKE, JUSTICE. The state petitioned for a rehearing and the Oregon District Attorneys' Association filed a brief in support of the petition. We granted the petition. . . .

[The court found that Neely had been effectively advised of his right to remain silent.]

Defendant also contended that his confession was inadmissible because it was obtained without his first being advised of his constitutional right to the assistance of counsel. In our initial opinion we specifically did not decide this issue. We must now so decide.

The state admits that defendant was not advised, prior to the making of the confession, of his right to counsel. . . .

The state admits, because of Escobedo, that if Neely had requested an opportunity to consult with his attorney and had been denied such request, his confession would be inadmissible. Escobedo unequivocally holds that a suspect in Neely's situation has a Fourteenth Amendment right to the assistance of counsel. The decisive issue

Sec. 9   *THE INTERPLAY OF RIGHTS AND PRIVILEGES*   921

remaining, therefore, is whether the state had an obligation to inform defendant that he had a right to the assistance of counsel. . . .

The state upon oral argument contended that a distinction should be made between the necessity of informing an accused of his right to counsel at the judicial stage of a criminal proceeding and prior thereto. The state acknowledged its obligation to inform an accused of his right to counsel at the judicial stage. The state contends it has no such obligation at the time of interrogation. We cannot agree.

Adoption of the distinction advanced by the state would lead to results contrary to the basic beliefs of the United States Supreme Court and of this court. Under the state's contention a suspect like Escobedo who has been previously jailed and, therefore, has previously needed the assistance of counsel, has a constitutional right to counsel because he knows through experience to demand counsel; however, a suspect who has never had any prior experience with the criminal process and, therefore, does not know by experience the assistance that a lawyer can give and, therefore, does not demand such assistance, has no constitutional right to counsel. If the state's distinction were accepted, we would grant the assistance of counsel to those educated enough to demand it and deny it to those too ignorant to ask for it. The United States Constitution demands equal treatment during the criminal process for the inexperienced and the uneducated.

We hold that the Sixth Amendment as made obligatory by the Fourteenth Amendment requires that before law enforcement officials can interrogate a person who is the focal suspect of a crime, such person must effectively be informed of his right to assistance of counsel as well as his right to remain silent. In the absence of such knowledge an accused can in no way be deemed to have intelligently waived his constitutional rights, and in the absence of such waiver a confession obtained by such interrogation is inadmissible.

Former opinion modified; reversed and remanded.[1]

1. Accord, the confession was inadmissible because (1) the investigation was no longer a general investigation into an unsolved crime but had passed to the accusatory stage and had begun to focus on a particular suspect, (2) who was in custody, (3) the officers carried out a process of interrogation that lent itself to the eliciting of incriminating statements, and (4) they had not informed the suspect of his absolute right to remain silent and of his right to counsel and no evidence established that he had waived these rights. People v. Dorado, 62 Cal.2d 338, 42 Cal.Rptr. 169, 398 P.2d 361 (1965); People v. Bostick, 62 Cal.2d 820, 44 Cal.Rptr. 649, 402 P.2d 529 (1965).

Contra, the police have no affirmative duty to warn an arrestee of his right to counsel and his right to remain silent, and a voluntary confession is not rendered inadmissible by the failure to give such warning. People v. Hartgraves, 31 Ill.2d 375, 202 N.E.2d 33 (1964); United States v. Childress, 347 F.2d 448 (7th Cir. 1965).

The admission of an excludable confession is *per se* prejudicial error and requires reversal, but the admission of incriminating statements other than a confession may be harmless error. People v. Dorado, 62 Cal.2d 338, 42 Cal.Rptr. 169, 398 P.2d 361 (1965). Such an admission does not require reversal if it was not the product of oppressive conduct and it is not probable that a different result would have been reached if it had not been admitted. People v. Robinson, 62 Cal.2d 889, 44 Cal.Rptr. 762, 402 P.2d 834 (1965). But such admission does require reversal in a homicide case where such admissions were the only direct evidence of the circumstances of the victim's death. People v. Forbs, 62 Cal.2d 847, 44 Cal.Rptr. 753, 402 P.2d 825 (1965).

The admission of illegally-obtained evidence which was prejudicial to D requires a reversal without regard to whether the other evidence might have been sufficient to support a conviction. The Court found it unnecessary to decide whether the introduction of such evidence could ever be subject to the rules of "harmless error". Fahy v. Connecticut, 375 U.S. 85, 84 S.Ct. 229, 11 L.Ed.2d 171 (1963).

Reversal of a conviction is not required by the admission of an inadmissible confession which was merely a repetition of earlier confessions made (1) to private persons and (2) to officers in what was a "clearly investigatory stage". People v. Jacobson, —— Cal.2d ——, 46 Cal.Rptr. 515, 405 P.2d 555 (1965). The sequence of the confessions was emphasized.

When a second confession, although otherwise unobjectionable, was due to the fact that D had already confessed, if the prior confession is inadmissible so is the second. Killough v. United States, 114 U.S.App.D.C. 305, 315 F.2d 241 (1962). "But this Court has never gone so far as to hold that making a confession under circumstances which preclude its use, perpetually disables the confessor from making a usable one after those conditions have been removed." United States v. Bayer, 331 U.S. 532, 540–41, 67 S.Ct. 1394, 1398, 91 L.Ed. 1654 (1947). The second confession was held to have been properly admitted under the facts of this case.

The use of a "truth serum" or its equivalent will not result in a voluntary confession. Townsend v. Sain, 372 U.S. 293, 83 S.Ct. 745, 9 L.Ed.2d 770 (1963).

The exclusionary rule does not apply to statements which were not elicited by any process of interrogation but were volunteered by the arrestee. People v. Vallarta, 235 Cal.App.2d ——, 45 Cal.Rptr. 631 (1965); People v. Propp, 235 Cal.App.2d 619, 45 Cal.Rptr. 690 (1965).

D, who was not in custody nor the focus of suspicion, voluntarily went to the office of the district attorney and made statements in the nature of an explanation by an apparently innocent person. The failure to advise him of his right to remain silent and his right to counsel did not render such statements inadmissible. People v. Garrett, 235 Cal.App.2d 134, 44 Cal. Rptr. 897 (1965).

Evidence of alleged rapist's confrontation with complainant (who identified him) was not improper on the theory that he was not represented by counsel or advised of his right to counsel. People v. Shaw, —— Cal.App.2d ——, 46 Cal.Rptr. 217 (1965).

The fact that D was identified by witnesses in a police lineup shortly after the crime and when he was without counsel did not deny him his constitutional right to the assistance of counsel. Williams v. United States, 345 F.2d 733 (D.C.Cir. 1965).

The Escobedo rule requires not only that the investigation had ceased to be a general investigation of an unsolved crime and had begun to focus on a particular suspect but also a process of interrogation that lends itself to eliciting incriminating statements. Hence a question intended merely to give an arrestee an opportunity to tell his side of the story, so to speak, does not come within the rule. United States v. Konigsberg, 336 F.2d 844 (3d Cir. 1964), cited with approval in People v. Stewart, 62 Cal.2d 571, 43 Cal.Rptr. 201, 400 P.2d 97 (1965).

If a person goes to the police station for the purpose of confessing guilt of an unsolved crime it is not necessary to advise him of his right to counsel before his statement is made. People v. Jenkins, 232 Cal.App.2d 323, 42 Cal.Rptr. 654 (1965).

"As we have noted the statement made by defendant to the reporter was in no way the result of police interrogation but was wholly voluntary, and hence no reason appears for excluding it". People v. Price, 63 Cal.2d ——, 46 Cal.Rptr. 775, 781, 406 P.2d 55, 61 (1965).

"So long as the methods used comply with due process standards it is in

Sec. 9   *THE INTERPLAY OF RIGHTS AND PRIVILEGES*   923

PERRY, JUSTICE (dissenting). I am unable to agree with that portion of the majority opinion which holds that, in the absence of informing the prisoner of his right to assistance of counsel, this is a denial of a constitutional right that prevents the use of a confession obtained.

In my opinion, Escobedo v. Illinois requires no such conclusion, nor do I believe that such a requirement would in a practical way protect any of the rights of an accused that should effect the admission of the confession if obtained without duress or fraud and voluntarily from the prisoner.

It should be noted that Mr. Justice Goldberg, writing for the majority in Escobedo v. Illinois, supra, commences the opinion with this statement:

"The critical question in this case is whether, *under the circumstances,* the refusal by the police to honor petitioner's request to consult with his lawyer during the course of an interrogation constitutes a denial of 'the Assistance of Counsel' in violation of the Sixth Amendment to the Constitution as 'made obligatory upon the States by the Fourteenth Amendment,' and thereby renders inadmissible in a state criminal trial any incriminating statement elicited by the police during the interrogation." (Emphasis supplied.)

PEOPLE v. PACK

District Court of Appeals, Second District, Division 2, California, 1962.
199 Cal.App.2d 857, 19 Cal.Rptr. 186.

[A collision between two cars travelling in opposite directions resulted in the hospitalization of all the occupants. When officers arrived the injured persons had been removed and no witnesses to the accident were found. From the position of the cars, which had not been moved, and from other evidence the officers concluded that one car, a Lincoln, had been travelling on the wrong side of the highway. On the floor of the Lincoln was found a "partially filled quart bottle of beer". One of the officers went to the hospital where he found defendant unconscious. At his request a blood sample was taken and tested and the result indicated that defendant had been intoxicated while driving. Based largely upon this evidence (People's Exhibit 5), admitted over timely objection, defendant was convicted of "felony drunk driving"—causing bodily injury as a result of driving while under the influence of liquor.]

the public interest for the police to encourage confessions and admissions during interrogation". People v. Garner, 57 Cal.2d 135, 164, 18 Cal. Rptr. 40, 57, 367 P.2d 680, 697 (1961).

Quoted with approval in People v. Dorado, 62 Cal.2d 338, 42 Cal.Rptr. 169, 179, 398 P.2d 361, 371 (1965); People v. Price, 63 Cal.2d —, 46 Cal. Rptr. 775, 780, 406 P.2d 55, 60 (1965).

Fox, Presiding Justice. . . . The second aspect of defendant's contention is that People's Exhibit 5 was obtained and admitted in violation of his constitutional rights. Pertinent to defendant's position is the statement of the court in People v. Duroncelay, 48 Cal.2d 766, 770–771, 312 P.2d 690, 693: "It is settled by our decision in People v. Haeussler, 41 Cal.2d 252, 257, 260 P.2d 8, that the admission of the evidence did not violate defendant's privilege against self-incrimination because the privilege relates only to testimonial compulsion and not to real evidence.[1] We also held in the Haeussler case that the taking of the defendant's blood for an alcohol test in a medically approved manner did not constitute brutality or shock the conscience and that, therefore, the defendant had not been denied due process of law under the rule applied in Rochin v. People of California, 342 U.S. 165, 72 S.Ct. 205, 96 L.Ed. 183 [25 A.L.R.2d 1396]. This holding is in accord with the recent decision of the United States Supreme Court in Breithaupt v. Abram, 352 U.S. 432, 77 S.Ct. 408, 411, 1 L.Ed.2d 448, where blood for an alcohol test was taken by a doctor while the defendant was unconscious. The court pointed out that blood tests had become routine in everyday life and concluded that 'a blood test taken by a skilled technician is not such "conduct that shocks the conscience," [2] Rochin, supra, 342 U.S. at page 172, 72 S.Ct.

---

1. Accord: State v. Ayres, 70 Idaho 18, 211 P.2d 142 (1949); State v. Sturtevant, 96 N.H. 99, 70 A.2d 909 (1950); State v. Cash, 219 N.C. 818, 15 S.E.2d 277 (1941); State v. Kroening, 274 Wis. 266, 79 N.W.2d 810 (1957); 8 Wigmore, Evidence, sec. 2263 (3d ed. 1940). The privilege against self-incrimination is not violated by requiring D to uncover his face so that a witness can identify him. People v. Clark, 18 Cal.2d 449, 116 P.2d 56 (1941). Or by the compulsory taking of his fingerprints. United States v. Kelly, 55 F.2d 67, 83 A.L.R. 122 (2d Cir. 1932); Shannon v. State, 207 Ark. 658, 182 S.W.2d 384 (1944); McGovern v. Van Ripper, 137 N.J.Eq. 548, 45 A.2d 842 (1946); McGarry v. State, 82 Tex.Cr.R. 597, 200 S.W. 527 (1918).

The Oklahoma Bill of Rights provides that "No person shall be compelled to give evidence which will tend to incriminate him. . . ." It was held that evidence of blood tests taken involuntarily violates this provision. Cox v. State, 395 P.2d 954 (Okl.Cr. 1964); Lorenz v. State, 406 P.2d 278 (Okl.Cr.1965).

One who has been arrested on a charge of intoxication has a right to have an opportunity to call his physician for the purpose of a blood-alcohol test and a denial of this right is a denial of due process which will prevent a conviction of the offense charged. In re Newbern, 175 Cal.App.2d 862, 1 Cal.Rptr. 80, 79 A.L.R.2d 901 (1959). Cited with approval, In re Newbern, 55 Cal.2d 500, 506, 11 Cal.Rptr. 547, 550, 360 P.2d 43, 46 (1961).

2. In *Rochin* officers choked D in the effort to prevent him from swallowing the evidence, and after this failed they extracted it by means of a stomach-pump applied apparently with brutality.

In another case, which may be useful by way of analogy, it was held that a search of the person, following a lawful arrest by federal officers, and a seizure of narcotics concealed in arrestee's rectum, the examination having been conducted by physicians under sanitary conditions with the use of medically approved procedures, was not unreasonable. Blackford v. United States, 247 F.2d 745 (9th Cir. 1957), certiorari denied 356 U.S. 914, 78 S.Ct. 672, 2 L.Ed.2d 586 (1958). See note, 106 U. of Pa.L.R. 1165 (1958).

In a lighter vein it may be mentioned that Melvin Belli (Bell eye) com-

Sec. 9   THE INTERPLAY OF RIGHTS AND PRIVILEGES   925

at page 209, nor such a method of obtaining evidence that it offends a "sense of justice," Brown v. State of Mississippi, 297 U.S. 278, 285, 286 [56 S.Ct. 461, 464–465, 80 L.Ed. 682].' There is no claim in the present case that the blood sample was not withdrawn in a medically approved manner. The blood was extracted by a registered nurse, and her testimony shows that she sterilized defendant's arm and used sterilized instruments.

"The question remains as to whether the taking of defendant's blood constituted an unreasonable search and seizure in violation of his constitutional rights." The court went on to answer this question in the negative. At page 772, 312 P.2d at page 694 it was stated: "The incidence of death and serious injury on the highways has undeniably assumed tragic dimensions and has been due in a significant degree to the effects of alcohol upon drivers. See National Safety Council Accident Facts—1955, pp. 43–71. So long as the measures adopted do not amount to a substantial invasion of individual rights, society must not be prevented from seeking to combat this hazard to the safety of the public. The extraction of blood for testing purposes is, of course, an experience which, every day, many undergo without hardship or ill effects. When this fact, together with the scientific reliability of blood alcohol tests in establishing guilt or innocence, is considered in the light of the imperative public interest involved, the taking of a sample for such a test without consent cannot be regarded as an unreasonable search and seizure where, as here, the extraction is made in a medically approved manner and is incident to the lawful arrest of one who is reasonably believed to have violated section 501 [now 23101] of the Vehicle Code."

Defendant attempts to distinguish this case by reference to the fact that the blood was taken "incident to a lawful arrest" (although the arrest followed the taking of the sample), while here there was no arrest at all. The distinction is not sound. Our courts have repeatedly stated that: "A search or seizure may be justified even though it is in no way related to an arrest." "The real criterion as to the reasonableness of a search is whether or not . . . under the facts, the police officer has reasonable grounds to believe that defendant may have committed a felony." [3]

mented facetiously that the lawfulness of extracting evidence from the alimentary canal depends upon which end is approached.

3. A difference is recognized between the search of a building or other fixed place and the search of a wagon or automobile because the vehicle can be moved quickly out of the jurisdiction. Hence officers who have probable cause to believe that contraband goods are being concealed and illegally transported in an automobile may search it without waiting for a warrant. Carroll v. United States, 267 U.S. 132, 45 S.Ct. 280, 69 L.Ed. 543, 39 A.L.R. 790 (1924).

In the early morning hours officers came upon the scene of a traffic accident. The position of the vehicles made it clear that H's car had been travelling on the wrong side of the street. As there was a strong odor of liquor on H's breath and the driver of the other car had been injured this gave the officers strong reason to be-

Here Officers Carlson and Ellis arrived at the scene of a collision between a Lincoln and an Oldsmobile on the evening of August 1, 1960. The Lincoln was on the wrong side of the highway; there were no skid marks. The officers found a partially filled quart bottle of beer on the front floor of the Lincoln. They checked with the Ventura police and learned that persons had been injured in the accident and taken to the Woodland Park Community Hospital. Investigation revealed that the Lincoln was registered in the name of defendant. Officer Ellis had previous experience in investigating automobile accidents. The position of the two cars indicated that the Lincoln was traveling east and the Oldsmobile in a westerly direction. He found marks on the highway and debris indicating the point of impact of the two cars. From this factual picture the officers had reasonable grounds to believe that the driver of the Lincoln went to the wrong side of the highway thereby causing the collision, and that the driver was under the influence of alcohol at the time. Therefore there was probable cause to believe that a felony had been committed. Hence the obtaining of a blood sample from defendant was not an unlawful search. Therefore the sample (Exhibit 5) together with its analysis was properly admitted in evidence.

It was important to get the sample as soon as possible in order that the analysis might the more accurately reflect the alcoholic content since such content became lower with the passage of time. It should also be pointed out that such tests are generally regarded as highly reliable and of substantial assistance in determining the issue of intoxication, and that a test of this kind may serve to exonerate as well as to convict.

Affirmed.[4]

ASHBURN and HERNDON, JJ., concur.

Hearing denied; SCHAUER and PETERS, JJ., dissenting.

---

lieve that H was guilty of felony drunk driving. Although H was unconscious a sample of his blood was taken under medically accepted conditions, and a test of this blood showed that he had in fact been intoxicated. The court recognized that the value of a blood test for alcohol depends upon the promptness with which the sample is taken. Hence it was held that there was such an emergency here that the search and seizure were lawful although there was no warrant, consent or arrest. People v. Huber, 232 Cal.App.2d 663, 43 Cal.Rptr. 65 (1965).

4. "It appears to be the consensus of the medical profession that when the blood alcohol concentrate of the driver of an automobile is 0.15% (by weight) such fact is conclusive evidence that the driver is under the influence of alcohol. (Committee on Tests for Intoxication of the National Safety Council, Chemical Tests for Intoxication (1938) p. 5; . . .)" Footnote in Lawrence v. City of Los Angeles, 53 Cal.App.2d 6, 9, 127 P.2d 931, 932 (1942).

Some persons have more tolerance for alcohol than is possessed by others. An amount which might impair the driving ability of one might not affect such ability of another. The interpretation of chemical tests for blood alcohol, based upon exhaustive study and research, makes due allowance for this difference. The analysis itself determines the per cent of al-

POINTER v. TEXAS

Supreme Court of the United States, 1965.
380 U.S. 400, 85 S.Ct. 1065.

[Pointer and Dillard were arrested in Texas on a charge of robbery and taken before a state judge for a preliminary hearing. Phillips, the chief witness, gave his version of the alleged robbery in detail, identifying Pointer as the man who had robbed him at gunpoint. The accused were both laymen and neither had a lawyer. Pointer did not attempt to cross-examine Phillips. Prior to the trial Phillips had moved to California and at the trial the state offered the transcript of Phillips' testimony given at the preliminary hearing as evidence. At the trial Pointer had counsel who objected that the use of this evidence would be "a denial of the confrontation of the witnesses against the Defendant". The objection was overruled and the trial resulted in

cohol in the blood by weight. If this percentage does not exceed 0.05 the presumption is that the person was not under the influence of intoxicating liquor. If the percentage amounts to 0.15 the presumption is that he was under the influence. Between these limits the amount of alcohol in the blood gives rise to no presumption either way but is merely a fact to be considered with other available evidence. This is the recommendation of various national organizations interested in traffic safety. It has been adopted by statute in several states and is the guide to the expert's opinion even where not so adopted.

The validity of chemical tests to determine impairment of the faculties is now widely accepted, but there are many hurdles to be cleared in a particular case. In the first place the expert must be prepared to prove that the sample to be tested was properly taken,—and particularly that the technique used precluded the possibility of the addition of any alcohol to the sample. The skin of the area from which a blood sample is to be taken must not be sterilized with an alcohol-containing antiseptic. And no such antiseptic must be used on instruments or containers. Next the expert must be prepared to establish the "chain of possession" of the sample used. He must be able to prove that the test was made of the sample taken from the defendant on trial with no possibility of substitution or tampering. And needless to say he must be prepared to establish his qualifications as an expert in this field and fully to explain the test made and its interpretation.

For a thorough examination of these problems see Donigan, Chemical Test Case Law (1950); Ladd and Gibson, The Medico-Legal Aspects of the Blood Test to Determine Intoxication, 24 Iowa Law Review 191 (1939); Monroe, The Drinking Driver—Problems of Enforcement, 8 Quarterly Journal of Studies on Alcohol 385 (1947); Mamet, Constitutionality of Compulsory Chemical Tests to Determine Alcoholic Intoxication, 36 Journal of Criminal Law and Criminology 132 (1945); Inbau, Self-Incrimination—What Can an Accused Person Be Compelled To Do, 28 Journal of Criminal Law and Criminology 261 (1937).

D, who drove on a federal parkway within Virginia while allegedly intoxicated, was prosecuted in the federal district court under the Virginia drunken driving statute made applicable by the Assimilative Crimes Act. It was held that the admission of a certificate showing that the alcoholic content of a sample of his blood had been determined by chemical analysis to be 0.15 per cent did not deprive him of his right of confrontation by witnesses, and that he was not deprived of any constitutional right by the jury's consideration of the statutory presumptions from such an alcoholic content. Kay v. United States, 255 F.2d 476 (4th Cir. 1958).

a conviction which was affirmed by the highest state court to which the case could be taken. The Supreme Court granted certiorari.]

MR. JUSTICE BLACK delivered the opinion of the Court.

The Sixth Amendment provides in part that:

"In all criminal prosecutions, the accused shall enjoy the right . . . to be confronted with the witnesses against him . . . and to have the Assistance of Counsel for his defence."

Two years ago in Gideon v. Wainwright, 372 U.S. 335, 83 S.Ct. 792, 9 L.Ed.2d 799, we held that the Fourteenth Amendment makes the Sixth Amendment's guarantee of right to counsel obligatory upon the States. The question we find necessary to decide in this case is whether the Amendment's guarantee of a defendant's right "to be confronted with the witnesses against him," which has been held to include the right to cross-examine those witnesses, is also made applicable to the States by the Fourteenth Amendment. . . .

In this Court we do not find it necessary to decide one aspect of the question petitioner raises, that is, whether failure to appoint counsel to represent him at the preliminary hearing unconstitutionally denied him the assistance of counsel within the meaning of Gideon v. Wainwright, supra. In making that argument petitioner relies mainly on White v. State of Maryland, 373 U.S. 59, 83 S.Ct. 1050, 10 L.Ed.2d 193, in which this Court reversed a conviction based in part upon evidence that the defendant had pleaded guilty to the crime at a preliminary hearing where he was without counsel. Since the preliminary hearing there, as in Hamilton v. State of Alabama, 368 U.S. 52, 82 S.Ct. 157, 7 L.Ed.2d 114, was one in which pleas to the charge could be made, we held in White as in Hamilton that a preliminary proceeding of that nature was so critical a stage in the prosecution that a defendant at that point was entitled to counsel. But the State informs us that at a Texas preliminary hearing such as is involved here, pleas of guilty or not guilty are not accepted and that the judge decides only whether the accused should be bound over to the grand jury and if so whether he should be admitted to bail. Because of these significant differences in the procedures of the respective States, we cannot say that the White case is necessarily controlling as to the right to counsel. Whether there might be other circumstances making this Texas preliminary hearing so critical to the defendant as to call for appointment of counsel at that stage we need not decide on this record and that question we reserve. In this case the objections and arguments in the trial court as well as the arguments in the Court of Criminal Appeals and before us make it clear that petitioner's objection is based not so much on the fact that he had no lawyer when Phillips made his statement at the preliminary hearing, as on the fact that use of the transcript of that statement at the trial denied petitioner any opportunity to have the benefit of counsel's cross-examination of the principal witness against him. It is that latter question which we decide here.

The Sixth Amendment is a part of what is called our Bill of Rights. In Gideon v. Wainwright, supra, in which this Court held that the Sixth Amendment's right to the assistance of counsel is obligatory upon the States, we did so on the ground that "a provision of the Bill of Rights which is 'fundamental and essential to a fair trial' is made obligatory upon the States by the Fourteenth Amendment." 372 U.S., at 342, 83 S.Ct., at 795. And last Term in Malloy v. Hogan, 378 U.S. 1, 84 S.Ct. 1489, 12 L.Ed.2d 653, in holding that the Fifth Amendment's guarantee against self-incrimination was made applicable to the States by the Fourteenth, we reiterated the holding of Gideon that the Sixth Amendment's right-to-counsel guarantee is " 'a fundamental right, essential to a fair trial,' " and "thus was made obligatory on the States by the Fourteenth Amendment." We hold today that the Sixth Amendment's right of an accused to confront the witnesses against him is likewise a fundamental right and is made obligatory on the States by the Fourteenth Amendment. . . .

There are few subjects, perhaps, upon which this Court and other courts have been more nearly unanimous than in their expressions of belief that the right of confrontation and cross-examination is an essential and fundamental requirement for the kind of fair trial which is this country's constitutional goal. Indeed, we have expressly declared that to deprive an accused of the right to cross-examine the witnesses against him is a denial of the Fourteenth Amendment's guarantee of due process of law. . . .

Under this Court's prior decisions, the Sixth Amendment's guarantee of confrontation and cross-examination was unquestionably denied petitioner in this case. As has been pointed out, a major reason underlying the constitutional confrontation rule is to give a defendant charged with crime an opportunity to cross-examine the witnesses against him. This Court has recognized the admissibility against an accused of dying declarations, and of testimony of a deceased witness who has testified at a former trial. Nothing we hold here is to the contrary. The case before us would be quite a different one had Phillips' statement been taken at a full-fledged hearing at which petitioner had been represented by counsel who had been given a complete and adequate opportunity to cross-examine. Compare Motes v. United States, supra, 178 U.S., at 474, 20 S.Ct., at 999. There are other analogous situations which might not fall within the scope of the constitutional rule requiring confrontation of witnesses. The case before us, however, does not present any situation like those mentioned above or others analogous to them. Because the transcript of Phillips' statement offered against petitioner at his trial had not been taken at a time and under circumstances affording petitioner through counsel an adequate opportunity to cross-examine Phillips, its introduction in a federal court in a criminal case against Pointer would have amounted to denial of the privilege of confrontation guaranteed by the Sixth Amendment. Since we hold that the right of an accused to be confronted with the witnesses against him must be determined by the same standards whether the right is denied in a federal or state proceeding, it follows that use of the transcript to convict petitioner denied him a constitutional right, and that his conviction must be reversed.

Reversed and remanded.

MR. JUSTICE HARLAN, concurring in the result. . . .

For me this state judgment must be reversed because a right of confrontation is "implicit in the concept of ordered liberty," reflected in the Due Process Clause of the Fourteenth Amendment independently of the Sixth. . . .

It is too often forgotten in these times that the American federal system is itself constitutionally ordained, that it embodies values profoundly making for lasting liberties in this country, and that its legitimate requirements demand continuing solid recognition in all phases of the work of this Court. The "incorporation" doctrines, whether full blown or selective, are both historically and constitutionally unsound and incompatible with the maintenance of our federal system on even course.

MR. JUSTICE STEWART, concurring.

I join in the judgment reversing this conviction, for the reason that the petitioner was denied the opportunity to cross-examine, through counsel, the chief witness for the prosecution. But I do not join in the Court's pronouncement which makes "the Sixth Amendment's right of an accused to confront the witnesses against him . . obligatory on the States." That questionable *tour de force* seems to me entirely unnecessary to the decision of this case, which I think is directly controlled by the Fourteenth Amendment's guarantee that no State "shall . . . deprive any person of life, liberty, or property, without due process of law." . . .

MR. JUSTICE GOLDBERG, concurring.

I agree with the holding of the Court that "the Sixth Amendment's right of an accused to confront the witnesses against him is . . . a fundamental right and is made obligatory on the States by the Fourteenth Amendment." . .

Appendix

THE AMERICAN LAW INSTITUTE

A MODEL CODE OF PRE-ARRAIGNMENT PROCEDURE

Tentative Draft No. 1 *

* Copyright 1966. Reprinted with the permission of the American Law Institute. (Most of the notes and all of the commentaries have been omitted).

ARTICLE 1. GENERAL PROVISIONS.

Section 1.01. Title and Effective Date.

This Act is called the [Code of Pre-Arraignment Procedure.] It shall become effective on

Section 1.02. Offenses to Which Code Is Inapplicable.

The provisions of this Code shall not supersede procedures specially provided by law with respect to the following offenses:

(a) [parking and minor traffic violations];
(b) ....
(c) ....

NOTE ON SECTION 1.02

Many jurisdictions have special provisions governing arrest, summons, and court appearance, in cases involving parking and minor traffic violations. See, e. g., CAL. VEHICLE CODE §§ 40300-307, 40311, 40500-517. These procedures are specially designed to meet the problem of a large volume of relatively minor offenses, and should not automatically be superseded by the provisions of this Code. In addition, in particular jurisdictions special procedures may exist with respect to other categories of cases, such as minor regulatory offenses. This section provides a form whereby the legislature may by specific exemption prevent the supersession of such procedures by this Code.

Section 1.03. Regulations.

(1) *Duty to Issue Regulations.* The chief law officer of the state [attorney general of the state] [   ] shall provide for the preparation and issuance of regulations implementing the provisions of this Code within each law enforcement agency and prosecution office in the state. Such regulations shall clearly designate the subordinate officers who are responsible for the enforcement of this Code in relation to persons in custody at each stage from arrest to release or court

appearance. Such regulations shall provide, so far as practicable, for uniform practices throughout the state.

(2) *Local Regulations.* The regulations issued pursuant to subsection (1) of this section shall provide, where appropriate, for the preparation and issuance of additional local regulations for use within particular law enforcement agencies. Such local regulations shall be subject to review and revision by the chief law officer of the state [attorney general of the state] [

(3) *Public Documents.* Regulations issued under this section shall be public documents.

Section 1.04. Station Officer.

The chief officer of each law enforcement agency shall assure that at all times there will be one or more officers in each police station specifically designated as station officers. The station officer shall be the most senior and responsible officer who reasonably can be made available for the purpose.

Section 1.05. Definitions.

[to be drafted]

NOTE ON SECTION 1.05

A number of terms repeatedly used in the Code will become defined terms under this section. These include: "Law Enforcement Officer," "Law Enforcement Agency," "Crime," "Offense," "Private Premises," and "Arrested Person."

ARTICLE 2. INVESTIGATION OF CRIME.

Section 2.01. Voluntary Cooperation With Law Enforcement Officers.

(1) *Authority to Request Cooperation.* A law enforcement officer may request any person to furnish information or otherwise to cooperate in the investigation or prevention of crime. The officer may request such person to respond to questions, to appear at a police station, or to comply with any other reasonable request. Compliance with a request for information or other cooperation hereunder shall not be deemed involuntary or coerced solely on the ground

    (a) that such request was made by one known to be a law enforcement officer; or

    (b) that such request was made to a person ordered to remain in the officer's presence under Section 2.02;

provided, that the officer shall not indicate to any person that such person is legally obliged to furnish information or otherwise cooperate hereunder if no such legal obligation exists.

(2) *Questioning of Suspects: Required Warning.* If a law enforcement officer, acting pursuant to this section, suspects or has reasonable cause to suspect that a person may have committed a crime, he shall, prior to engaging in sustained questioning of such person, take such steps as are reasonable under the circumstances to make clear to such person that no legal obligation exists to respond to such questioning. If any such questioning takes place at a police station, prosecutor's office, or other similar place, such person shall first be informed that he may promptly communicate with counsel, relatives or friends, and that counsel, relatives or friends may have access to him as provided in Section 5.07.

(3) *Warning to Persons Asked to Appear at a Police Station.* If a law enforcement officer acting pursuant to this section requests any person to come to or remain at a police station, prosecutor's office or other similar place, he shall take such steps as are reasonable under the circumstances to make clear to such person that there is no legal obligation to comply with such request.

(4) *Request to Make Search.* [Reporters' Note: This section will deal with requests to search and consents thereto; it will be drafted in connection with the search and seizure materials.]

Section 2.02. Stopping of Persons.

(1) *Stopping of Persons Having Knowledge of Crime.* A law enforcement officer lawfully present in any place may, if he has reasonable cause to believe that a felony or misdemeanor has been committed and that any person has knowledge which may be of material aid to the investigation thereof, order such person to remain in or near such place in the officer's presence for a period of not more than twenty minutes.

(2) *Stopping of Persons in Suspicious Circumstances.* A law enforcement officer lawfully present in any place may, if a person is observed in circumstances which suggest that he has committed or is about to commit a felony or misdemeanor, and such action is reasonably necessary to enable the officer to determine the lawfulness of that person's conduct, order that person to remain in or near such place in the officer's presence for a period of not more than twenty minutes.

(3) *Action to Be Taken During Period of Stop.* A law enforcement officer may require a person to remain in his presence pursuant to subsection (1) or (2) of this section only insofar as such action is reasonably necessary to

    (a) obtain the identification of such person;

    (b) verify by readily available information an identification of such person;

    (c) request cooperation pursuant to and subject to the limitations of Section 2.01; or

(d) verify by readily available information any account of his presence or conduct or other information given by such person.

(4) *Use of Force.* In order to exercise the authority conferred in subsections (1) and (2) of this section, a law enforcement officer may use such force, other than deadly force, as is reasonably necessary to stop any person or vehicle or to cause any person to remain in the officer's presence.

(5) *Search for Dangerous Weapons.* A law enforcement officer who has stopped or ordered any person to remain in his presence pursuant to this section may, if he reasonably believes that his safety so requires, search such person and his immediate surroundings, but only to the extent necessary to discover any dangerous weapons which may on that occasion be used against the officer.

(6) *Action to Be Taken After Period of Stop.* Unless an officer acting hereunder arrests a person during the time he is authorized by subsections (1) and (2) of this section to require such person to remain in his presence, he shall, at the end of such time, inform such person that he is free to go.

(7) *Records Relating to Persons Stopped.* A law enforcement officer, who has ordered any person to remain in his presence pursuant to this section, shall with reasonable promptness thereafter prepare and sign a report setting forth the name and address of such person; the place, time and purpose of the stop; the names of additional officers and other persons present; whether the person stopped objected thereto; whether force was used and, if so, the degree and circumstances thereof; and whether the person stopped was searched and, if so, a description of all items seized and their disposition.

(8) *Limitations to Prevent Abuse.* The authority to stop persons granted in subsections (1) and (2) of this section may not be used solely to aid in the investigation or prevention of the following crimes:

(a) any misdemeanor the maximum penalty for which does not include a sentence of imprisonment of more than thirty days;

(b) loitering;

(c) vagrancy;

(d) . . . [Note: There should be added to this list those felonies and misdemeanors, in connection with which the stop authority is unnecessary, or creates an undue risk of abuse or harassment, such as ordinances requiring permits for public parades or gatherings.]

Section 2.03. Order to Appear.

[Note: The Reporters are considering a provision granting a limited power to the prosecutor to order, under appropriate safeguards, the appearance of suspects and witnesses for specified purposes in connection with the investigation of crime. A draft of such a provision was discussed at the meetings of the Advisors and the Council, but is not presented at this time.]

ARTICLE 3. ARREST.

Section 3.01. Arrest Without a Warrant.

(1) *Authority to Arrest Without a Warrant.* A law enforcement officer may arrest a person without a warrant if the officer has reasonable cause to believe that such person has committed

    (a) a felony;

    (b) a misdemeanor, and the officer has reasonable cause to believe that such person

        (i) will not be apprehended unless immediately arrested; or

        (ii) may cause injury to himself or others or damage to property unless immediately arrested; or

    (c) a misdemeanor or petty misdemeanor in the officer's presence.

(2) *Reasonable Cause.* Reasonable cause exists under this section where there is a substantial objective basis for believing that the person to be arrested has committed a crime. An arrest shall not be deemed to have been made on insufficient cause hereunder solely on the ground that the officer is unable to determine the particular crime which may have been committed.

(3) *Determining Reasonable Cause.* In determining whether reasonable cause exists to justify an arrest under this section, a law enforcement officer may take into account all facts, including those based upon any expert knowledge which the officer in fact possesses, which a prudent officer would judge relevant to the likelihood that a crime has been committed and that the person to be arrested has committed it, including any failure to comply with an obligation imposed by this Code or with a lawful request for cooperation; *provided*, that no such failure shall alone be deemed sufficient to justify an arrest in any case where such failure does not itself constitute a crime.

(4) *Information From Others.* In determining whether reasonable cause exists to justify an arrest under this section, a law enforcement officer may rely on information he receives from any informant whom it is reasonable under the circumstances to credit, whether or not at the time of making the arrest the officer knows the informant's identity.

Section 3.02. Citation in Lieu of or in Connection With Arrest Without a Warrant.

(1) *Citation Without Arrest.* A law enforcement officer acting without a warrant who has reasonable cause to believe that a person

has committed an offense may, subject to the regulations to be issued pursuant to subsection (4) of this section, issue a citation to such person to appear in court in lieu of arresting him.

(2) *Citation After Arrest.* A law enforcement officer who has arrested a person without a warrant may, subject to the regulations to be issued pursuant to subsection (4) of this section, issue a citation to such person to appear in court in lieu of taking him to a police station as provided in Section 3.09.

(3) *Procedure for Issuing Citations.* In issuing a citation hereunder the officer shall proceed as follows:

    (a) He shall prepare a written citation to appear in court, containing the name and address of the cited person and the offense charged, and stating when the person shall appear in court. Unless the person requests an earlier date, the time specified in the citation to appear shall be at least three days after the issuance of the citation.

    (b) One copy of the citation to appear shall be delivered to the person cited, and such person shall sign a duplicate written citation which shall be retained by the officer.

    (c) The officer shall thereupon release the cited person from any custody.

    (d) As soon as practicable, one copy of the citation shall be filed with the court specified therein, and one copy shall be delivered to the prosecuting attorney.

At least 24 hours before the time set in the citation for the cited person to appear, the prosecuting attorney, or other person authorized by law to issue a complaint for the particular offense, shall either issue and file a complaint charging such person with an offense, or file with the court and deliver to such person a notice that a complaint has been refused and that such person is released from his obligation to appear. [Any person who wilfully violates a citation to appear in court hereunder is guilty of a misdemeanor.]

(4) *Regulations.* The regulations issued pursuant to Section 1.03 shall include regulations concerning the circumstances in which officers shall issue citations pursuant to this section. Those regulations shall be designed to provide the maximum use of citations, so that persons believed to have committed offenses will be taken into custody only when necessary in the public interest.

Section 3.03. Arrest Under a Warrant.

(1) *Authority to Arrest Under a Warrant.* Any law enforcement officer may arrest a person pursuant to a warrant in any county in the state.

(2) *Manner of Arrest Under a Warrant.* The law enforcement officer need not have the warrant in his possession at the time of the

arrest, but upon request he shall show the warrant to the defendant as soon as possible. If the officer does not have the warrant in his possession at the time of the arrest, he shall inform the defendant of the fact that a warrant has been issued.

Section 3.04. Service of Summons.

A summons may be served by any person authorized to serve a summons in a civil action. The summons shall be served upon a defendant by delivering a copy to him personally, or by leaving it at his dwelling house or usual place of abode with some person of suitable age and discretion then residing therein, or by sending it by certified mail to the defendant's last known address.

Section 3.05. Circumstances Implying Arrest.

(1) *Implied Restriction on Liberty.* If a law enforcement officer by specific order or by his conduct indicates that a person is obliged to remain in the officer's presence at any time when no such obligation exists under Section 2.02, or fails to inform a person who has been stopped that he is free to go when required to do so by Section 2.02(6), such person shall be accorded all the rights and protections afforded to arrested persons by this Code.

(2) *Requests to Appear at Police Station.* If a law enforcement officer, pursuant to Section 2.01, requests any person to come to or remain at a police station, prosecutor's office, or other similar place, and does not take such steps as are reasonable under the circumstances to make clear that no legal obligation exists to comply with such request, such person shall be accorded all the rights and protections afforded to arrested persons by this Code.

Section 3.06. Place of Arrest: Private Premises.

(1) *Demand That Person on Private Premises Submit to Arrest.* If a law enforcement officer believes that a person whom he is authorized to arrest is present on any private premises, he may, upon identifying himself as such, make a demand that such person either leave such premises and submit to arrest or admit the officer so that he may make the arrest.

(2) *Use of Force to Enter Private Premises.* If a demand lawfully made pursuant to subsection (1) of this section is not complied with, a law enforcement officer may use such force as is reasonably necessary to enter such private premises in order to effect the arrest, but only if the officer has reasonable cause to believe that a person whom he is authorized to arrest for a felony or misdemeanor is present on such premises, and the officer

    (a) is acting under a warrant for the arrest of such person; or

    (b) has reasonable cause to believe that such person would escape unless immediately arrested; or

(c) has reasonable cause to believe that such action is necessary to prevent harm to any person or damage to or loss of property.

(3) *Use of Force Without Prior Demand.* A law enforcement officer may, without making the demand required by subsection (1) of this section, use such force as is reasonably necessary to enter any private premises in order to effect an arrest, but only if the officer has reasonable cause to believe that a person whom he is authorized to arrest for a felony or misdemeanor is present on such premises, and that if such demand were made

(a) the person to be arrested would escape; or

(b) the officer would be subject to harm in effecting the arrest; or

(c) any person would be harmed or property would be damaged or lost.

(4) *Special Restrictions on Arrests at Night.* No law enforcement officer shall seek to enter any private premises in order to effect an arrest between 10 P.M. and 7 A.M. unless

(a) he is acting under a warrant of arrest and the warrant authorizes its execution during such hours; or

(b) he has reasonable cause to believe that such action is necessary to prevent

(i) the escape of the person to be arrested, or

(ii) harm to any person or damage to or loss of property.

(5) *Private Premises Defined.* For the purposes of this section, private premises shall mean any building or interior portion of a building which it would be unlawful, except by virtue of the authority in subsections (2) or (3) of this section, for a law enforcement officer to enter.

Section 3.07. Procedures on Arrest: Use of Force.

[to be drafted]

NOTE ON SECTION 3.07

It is contemplated that this section will be an adaptation of the provisions of the Model Penal Code governing the use of force on arrest.

Section 3.08. Procedures on Arrest: Warning.

Upon making any arrest, a law enforcement officer shall

(a) identify himself as such unless his identity is otherwise apparent;

(b) inform the arrested person that he is under arrest;

(c) as promptly as is reasonable under the circumstances, inform the arrested person of the cause of the arrest, unless the cause appears to be evident; and

(d) as promptly as is reasonable under the circumstances, and in any event before engaging in any sustained questioning, warn such person that he is not obliged to say anything or answer any questions, that anything he says may be used in evidence, and that upon arrival at the police station he will be permitted to communicate by telephone with counsel, relatives or friends.

Section 3.09. Procedures on Arrest: Prompt Taking to Police Station.

(1) *Prompt Taking to Police Station.* Any person arrested, if not released pursuant to subsection (2) of this section or Section 3.02, shall be brought promptly to a police station [; *provided*, that the arresting officer may first take such person to some other place if such person so requests or if such action is reasonably necessary for the purpose of having such person identified by a person in imminent danger of death or loss of faculties].

(2) *Release by Arresting Officer.* An officer shall promptly release from his custody any person who has been arrested without a warrant, if at any time prior to the appearance of such person at a police station the officer determines that he no longer has reasonable cause to believe that the arrested person has committed a crime for which such arrest is authorized.

NOTE ON SECTION 3.09

This section, like the preceding section, recognizes the serious change in the person's situation when he is arrested. The arrest is not for purposes of general investigation, but a step along the way to bringing a formal charge of crime. The Code adopts the premise that a person in custody and under serious suspicion should be accorded certain protections, such as a formal warning, telephone rights and access to counsel or family. These protections can only be afforded if the arrested person is brought to an official place of detention and his arrest duly recorded. The section, in using the term "promptly," does not intend to preclude a delay when this is necessitated by an emergency, such as a call to the arresting officer to rescue some person in the vicinity from danger or to proceed to the scene of another crime in the vicinity.

ARTICLE 4. DISPOSITION OF ARRESTED PERSONS.

Section 4.01. Preliminary Disposition of Arrested Persons; Warning.

(1) *Appearance Before Station Officer.* Any person arrested and brought to a police station shall forthwith be presented before the station officer, who shall make a record of the time when such person was brought before him.

(2) *Warning.* The station officer shall immediately inform the arrested person how long he may be held prior to the time that he is to be released or charged, and shall advise him in plain and understandable language

    (a) that if charged with crime, he will be released on bail or taken before a judicial officer as soon as possible;

    (b) that he is not obliged to say anything and that anything he says may be used in evidence;

    (c) that he may promptly communicate by telephone with counsel, relatives or friends and that, if necessary, funds will be provided to enable him to do so; and

    (d) that counsel or a relative or friend may have access to him as provided in Section 5.07. [Note: In any jurisdiction where counsel is provided for indigent persons at the stationhouse, the arrested person is to be so advised.]

The arrested person shall also forthwith be given a printed form which in plain and understandable language contains the substance of the matters listed in paragraphs (a)–(d) above, and he shall be asked to read it and to sign a statement at the bottom of such form which shall state: "I have read the warning given above and understand it." The station officer shall then countersign the form, recording thereon that he duly gave the warning required by this section. If the arrested person refuses to sign, the station officer shall make a written record, which he shall sign, that he gave the warning required by this section and that the arrested person refused to sign the form.

(3) *Warning to Illiterate Persons.* If the arrested person is unable to read or write, the station officer shall give the oral warning required by subsection (2) of this section in the presence of a witness; and the station officer shall make a written record, which he and such witness shall sign, that he gave the oral warning required by subsection (2) of this section and that no written warning was given on account of the illiteracy of the arrested person.

(4) *Incapacity to Understand Warning.* In any case where an arrested person is in such condition, on account of illness, injury, drink, or drugs, that, in the judgment of the station officer, he is incapable of understanding the warning, such warning shall be given as soon as such person is able to understand it.

(5) *Telephoning Rights.* Promptly after the warning the station officer shall afford the arrested person an opportunity, including if necessary funds in a reasonable amount, to use a telephone.

(6) *Information Concerning Location of Arrested Persons.* Information concerning the location of any arrested person upon his appearance at a police station under this section shall be promptly made available to a relative, attorney or friend upon a single inquiry at a centralized location.

Section 4.02. Disposition of Juveniles.

[to be drafted]

Section 4.03. Disposition of Persons Arrested Pursuant to a Warrant.

If a person has been arrested pursuant to a warrant, the station officer, after complying with the procedures required by Section 4.01, shall, in any case provided for in Section 8.01, release such arrested person on his own recognizance or admit him to bail. If the arrested person does not furnish bail, or if the crime charged in the complaint is not bailable under Section 8.01, further disposition of such person shall be in accordance with Section 4.06.

Section 4.04. Disposition of Persons Arrested Without a Warrant: The Period of Preliminary Screening.

(1) *Purpose, Definition and Duration of Period of Preliminary Screening.* If a person is arrested without a warrant, he may be detained for a period of preliminary screening for the purpose of determining whether a complaint should be issued charging him with crime. The period of preliminary screening shall commence when a person arrested without a warrant is first brought to the police station, and shall end with the disposition of such person made pursuant to subsections (2)–(6) of this section. The station officer shall make such disposition not later than four hours after a person arrested without a warrant was first brought to the police station.

(2) *Refusal of Complaint.* Notwithstanding any other provision of this section, if at any time during the period of preliminary screening the prosecuting attorney determines not to issue a complaint charging the arrested person with a crime, the station officer shall order the arrested person released forthwith.

(3) *Release.* If at any time during the period of preliminary screening the station officer concludes that there is no reasonable cause to believe that the arrested person has committed a crime, and no complaint charging such person with a crime has been issued, the station officer shall order the arrested person released forthwith.

(4) *Decision to Charge; Release on Bail.* If during the period of preliminary screening a complaint charging the arrested person with a crime is issued by the prosecuting attorney or any other person authorized by law to issue a complaint for the particular offense, the station officer shall, in any case provided for in Section 8.01, release the arrested person on his own recognizance or admit him to bail. If the arrested person does not furnish bail, or if the crime charged in the complaint is not bailable under Section 8.01, further disposition of such person shall be in accordance with Section 4.06.

(5) *Citation Procedure.* If the station officer concludes that there is reasonable cause to believe that the arrested person has com-

mitted a crime, but no complaint charging such person with a crime has been issued during the period of preliminary screening, he shall, unless an order is entered under subsection (6) of this section, proceed as follows:

    (a) He shall prepare a written citation to appear in court, containing the name and address of the arrested person and the crime charged, and stating when the person shall appear in court. Unless the arrested person requests an earlier date, the time specified in the citation to appear shall be at least three days after the arrest.

    (b) One copy of the citation to appear shall be delivered to the arrested person, and such person shall sign a duplicate written citation which shall be retained by the officer.

    (c) The station officer shall thereupon release the arrested person from custody.

    (d) As soon as practicable, one copy of the citation shall be filed with the court specified therein, and one copy shall be delivered to the prosecuting attorney.

At least 24 hours before the time set in the citation for the arrested person to appear, the prosecuting attorney, or other person authorized by law to issue a complaint for the particular offense, shall either issue and file a complaint charging such person with a crime, or file with the court and deliver to such person a notice that a complaint has been refused and that such person is released from his obligation to appear. [Any person who wilfully violates a citation to appear in court hereunder is guilty of a misdemeanor.]

    (6) *Detention for Further Screening for Certain Felonies.* If there is reasonable cause to believe that the arrested person has committed, or has conspired or attempted to commit, one or more of the following felonies:

    [(a) murder or manslaughter;
    (b) aggravated assault;
    (c) kidnapping;
    (d) rape;
    (e) arson;
    (f) burglary;
    (g) robbery;
    (h) grand larceny;
    (i) criminal sale of narcotics;
    (j) riot;
    (k) ....
    (*l*) ....
    (m) ....]

and that further investigation and custody are necessary in order to determine whether the arrested person should be charged with such a felony, the station officer may, in lieu of following the citation procedure set out in subsection (5) of this section, order the arrested person to be detained for a period of further screening. The station officer may also make such an order in the case of any other felony, but only if the arrested person is represented by counsel and both the arrested person and his counsel consent. The station officer shall make a record setting out the reasons for issuing an order hereunder and the time when such order was issued.

Section 4.05. Disposition of Persons Arrested Without a Warrant: The Period of Further Screening.

(1) *Purpose, Definition and Duration of Period of Further Screening.* If an order is issued under Section 4.04(6), a person arrested without a warrant may be detained for a period of further screening for the purpose of determining whether a complaint should be issued charging him with one of the felonies set forth in Section 4.04(6). The period of further screening shall commence when an order is made pursuant to Section 4.04(6), and shall end with the disposition of such person made pursuant to subsections (2)–(5) of this section. The station officer shall make such disposition not later than the times set out in paragraphs (a)–(c) hereof:

> (a) If the arrested person was first brought to the police station between 12 midnight and 8 A.M.—before 4 P.M. of the same day.
>
> (b) If the arrested person was first brought to the police station between 8 A.M. and 2 P.M.—before 10 P.M. of the same day.
>
> (c) If the arrested person was first brought to the police station between 2 P.M. and 12 midnight—before 12 noon of the following day.

(2) *Refusal of Complaint.* Notwithstanding any other provision of this section, if at any time during the period of further screening the prosecuting attorney determines not to issue a complaint charging the arrested person with a crime, the station officer shall order the arrested person released forthwith.

(3) *Release.* If at any time during the period of further screening the station officer concludes that there is no reasonable cause to believe that the arrested person has committed a crime, and no complaint charging such person with a crime has been issued, the station officer shall order the arrested person released forthwith.

(4) *Decision to Charge; Release on Bail.* If during the period of further screening a complaint charging the arrested person with a crime is issued by the prosecuting attorney or any other person authorized by law to issue a complaint for the particular offense, the

station officer shall, in any case provided for in Section 8.01, release the arrested person on his own recognizance or admit him to bail. If the arrested person does not furnish bail or if the crime charged in the complaint is not bailable under Section 8.01, further disposition of such person shall be in accordance with Section 4.06.

(5) *Citation Procedure.* If the station officer concludes that there is reasonable cause to believe that the arrested person has committed a crime, but no complaint charging such person with a crime has been issued during the period of further screening, he shall release the arrested person subject to a citation to appear in court in accordance with the provisions of Section 4.04(5); *provided*, that such person may be continued in custody if he is represented by counsel and he and his counsel both consent to such custody.

Section 4.06. Disposition of Arrested Persons Charged With Crime.

(1) *First Appearance Before a Judicial Officer.* In any case where a complaint charging an arrested person with a crime has been issued by the prosecuting attorney or other person authorized by law to issue a complaint for the particular offense, such arrested person, unless he has been released on his own recognizance or admitted to bail, shall be brought before a judicial officer at the earliest time after the issuance of such complaint that such an officer is available; *provided*, that any such person may be continued in custody if he is represented by counsel and he and his counsel both consent to such custody.

(2) *Filing of Complaint.* A complaint issued by the prosecuting attorney or other person authorized by law to issue a complaint for the particular offense shall be filed with the court at or prior to the first appearance of the arrested person before the judicial officer.

Section 4.07. Disposition of Incapacitated Persons.

[to be drafted]

Section 4.08. Interpreters.

[to be drafted]

Section 4.09. Records and Sound Recordings.

(1) *Obligation to Make Records Relating to Periods of Custody.* In accordance with regulations, to be issued pursuant to Section 1.03, law enforcement agencies responsible for making arrests or holding persons in custody before their first appearance in court shall make the full written and sound records required by subsections (2) and (3) of this section to assist in the resolution of disputes concerning the period of such custody.

(2) *Written Records.* The regulations relating to written records shall establish procedures for the making of a written record

covering the period of custody which will show actions taken by such agency with respect to each arrested person and the time such action was taken. Such record shall reflect as fully as possible the location of the arrested person throughout the period of his custody, the names of officers who sought information from him, and the officers responsible for his custody who can testify as to his location and the persons who communicated with him. Each item in such record shall be signed or initialed by the officer having responsibility for the arrested person when the action referred to in such item took place. The station officer shall be responsible for the completeness of such record.

(3) *Sound Recordings.* The regulations relating to sound recordings shall establish procedures to provide a sound recording of

    (a) the warning to arrested persons pursuant to Section 4.01(2); and

    (b) any questioning involving more than a few brief questions.

Such recording shall include an indication of the time of the beginning and ending thereof. The arrested person shall be informed that the sound recording required hereby is being made and the statement so informing him shall be included in the sound recording. The station officer shall be responsible for insuring that such a sound recording is made.

(4) *Arrested Person's Access to Records.* Law enforcement officers shall comply with reasonable requests to make available to the arrested person or his counsel any written record or sound recording made pursuant to this section or pursuant to Section 2.02(7). Such records shall be preserved for a reasonable time in accordance with regulations to be issued pursuant to Section 1.03.

ARTICLE 5. CONDITIONS OF INVESTIGATION DURING CUSTODY OF AN ARRESTED PERSON.

Section 5.01. Permitted Investigation.

    Subject to the provisions of this Code and other law, any law enforcement officer or other authorized person may

    (a) question an arrested person;

    (b) take the fingerprints and photograph of an arrested person;

    (c) conduct a lineup or subject an arrested person to other reasonable identification procedures;

    (d) confront an arrested person with a victim of or witness to or alleged accomplice in crime;

(e) confront an arrested person with any evidence or information acquired in the course of investigating the crime or the results of any test conducted in investigating the crime; and

may engage in any other lawful investigation.

Section 5.02. Deception as to Obligation to Cooperate.

No law enforcement officer shall attempt to induce an arrested person to make a statement or otherwise cooperate by indicating that such person is legally obliged to do so, if no such legal obligation exists.

Section 5.03. Abuse, Threats, Denial of Necessities.

No law enforcement officer shall attempt to induce an arrested person to make a statement or otherwise cooperate by subjecting, or threatening to subject, such person or any person in whom such person is interested to any form of abuse, or by depriving any arrested person of adequate food, water, medical attention, rest or other physical necessities.

Section 5.04. Unfair Inducement of Statements.

No law enforcement officer shall attempt to induce an arrested person to make a statement or otherwise cooperate by

(a) questioning of such unfair frequency, length or persistence as to constitute harassment of such person;

(b) persistent questioning after such person has made it clear that he is unwilling to make a statement or wishes to consult counsel before making a statement; or

(c) any other method which, in light of such person's age, intelligence and mental and physical condition, unfairly undermines his ability to make a choice whether to make a statement or otherwise cooperate.

Section 5.05. Use of Drugs, Hypnosis, Polygraph or Similar Techniques.

No law enforcement officer shall use drugs, hypnosis, polygraph tests or other similar techniques in connection with the questioning of any arrested person, unless such person has been informed that he is not obliged to submit thereto and has thereafter given his written consent.

Section 5.06. Creating Risk of Untrue Incriminatory Statements.

No law enforcement officer shall take any action which is designed to, or which under the circumstances creates a significant risk that it will, result in an untrue incriminating statement by an arrested person.

Section 5.07. Access, Consultation and Telephoning Rights.

(1) *Access to an Arrested Person.* Counsel for an arrested person shall have prompt access to him, by telephone, and in person on counsel's arrival at any place where such person is detained. Counsel for an arrested person shall not be prevented from staying at any such place and being allowed access to the arrested person whenever such person requests his presence. If no counsel for the arrested person is present, similar privileges must be accorded to a relative or friend of the arrested person.

(2) *Consultation and Telephoning Rights.* An arrested person shall be given reasonable opportunity from time to time during his detention to consult in private with counsel or any relative or friend present in lieu of counsel, and, upon request, to use the telephone.

Section 5.08. Questioning During the Period of Further Screening.

(1) *Prohibited Interrogation.* Except as authorized in subsection (2) of this section, no law enforcement officer shall question an arrested person or otherwise attempt to induce him to make a statement during any period of further screening, unless such person is represented by counsel, and his counsel is present or he and his counsel have consented thereto.

(2) *Permitted Investigation in the Absence of Counsel.* Notwithstanding the provisions of subsection (1) of this section, during any period of further screening a law enforcement officer may

(a) engage in the investigative procedures authorized in paragraphs (b)-(e) of Section 5.01, and, in connection with such procedures, ask the arrested person whether he wishes to make a statement; and

(b) ask the arrested person to clarify any statement he has made;

provided, that nothing herein shall be deemed to authorize any sustained questioning.

Section 5.09. Questioning of Arrested Persons Charged With Crime.

No law enforcement officer shall question an arrested person or otherwise attempt to induce him to make a statement during any period of custody between the time that a complaint is issued charging such person with a crime and the time such person is first brought before a judicial officer, unless such person is represented by counsel, and his counsel is present or he and his counsel have consented thereto.

Section 5.10. Applicability to Persons Appearing Voluntarily at Police Station.

The provisions of Sections 5.02 to 5.07 of this Article shall be applicable to persons who appear voluntarily, pursuant to request or otherwise, at a police station, prosecutor's office, or other similar place.

NOTE ON SECTION 5.10

This section, added to the Code to meet concerns expressed by the Advisors and members of the Council, applies the rules of the Code relating to unfair questioning and access by counsel, relatives and friends, to persons appearing voluntarily at a police station. See also Sections 2.01(2) and (3) for warnings to be issued to such persons.

ARTICLE 6. COMMENCEMENT OF PROCEEDINGS.

Section 6.01. Complaint.

The complaint is a written statement of the essential facts constituting the offense charged. It shall be made under oath subscribed by the complainant and filed with a judicial officer. It may be verified on information and belief.

Section 6.02. Issuance and Filing of Complaints.

(1) *Issuance and Filing by Prosecuting Attorney.* Except as otherwise provided in this section, a complaint charging a person with an offense shall be issued only by a prosecuting attorney having jurisdiction over the prosecution of the offense and shall be filed only with his approval.

(2) *Issuance and Filing by Chief Law Officer.* A complaint charging an offense may be issued and filed by the chief law officer of the state [attorney general of the state.]

(3) *Filing by Order of a Judicial Officer.* In any case in which a prosecuting attorney refuses to issue a complaint, a judicial officer may permit the filing of a complaint if, after hearing the complainant and the prosecuting attorney, he finds there is reasonable cause to believe that the person named in the complaint has committed the offense charged.

(4) *Complaint Hearings.* When a request is made for the issuance of a complaint, the prosecuting attorney may rule directly upon the request or may inform the person named in the proposed complaint that an application for a complaint has been made and that he may appear at the office of the prosecuting attorney at a time specified to show cause why a complaint should not issue.

(5) *Definitions.* A complaint is issued when it is approved for filing by the prosecuting attorney or other person authorized by law

to issue a complaint for the particular offense. A complaint is filed when it is lodged with the court having jurisdiction over the offense.

Section 6.03. Issuance of Warrant of Arrest.

If it appears from a complaint, or from an affidavit or affidavits filed with the complaint, that there is reasonable cause to believe that an offense has been committed and that the defendant has committed it, a judicial officer shall, except as otherwise provided in Section 6.04, issue a warrant for the arrest of the defendant unless he has already been arrested in connection with the offense charged and is in custody or has been released on obligation to appear in court. Before ruling on a request for a warrant the judicial officer may require the complainant to appear personally and may examine under oath the complainant and any witnesses he may produce. The warrant shall not authorize the arrest to be made on private premises between 10 P.M. and 7 A.M. unless there is reasonable cause to believe that such action is necessary to prevent the escape of the person to be arrested or harm to any person or damage to or loss of property.

Section 6.04. Issuance of Summons in Lieu of Warrant of Arrest.

(1) *When Summons May Issue.* In any case in which the judicial officer finds sufficient grounds for issuing a warrant pursuant to Section 6.03, he may issue a summons commanding the defendant to appear in lieu of a warrant.

(2) *When Summons Must Issue.* If the complaint is for the commission of a violation or a petty misdemeanor or one of the following crimes

    (a) ....

    (b) ....

    (c) ....

the judicial officer shall issue a summons instead of a warrant unless he has reasonable cause to believe that the defendant will not appear in response to a summons, in which case he may issue a warrant.

(3) *Summons on Request of Prosecuting Attorney.* In any case the judicial officer shall issue a summons in lieu of a warrant if the prosecuting attorney so requests. The prosecuting attorney shall request a summons whenever he is satisfied that there is no substantial risk that the defendant will fail to appear in response to the summons.

(4) *Failure to Appear on Summons.* If a person summoned fails to appear in response to the summons, a warrant for his arrest shall issue. [Any person who wilfully fails to appear in response to a summons is guilty of a misdemeanor.]

NOTE ON SECTION 6.04

The general purpose of this section is to reduce pretrial custody by providing for the maximum use of summons to appear in lieu of warrants of arrest. . . .

ARTICLE 7. FIRST APPEARANCE; PRELIMINARY HEARING.

[to be drafted]

ARTICLE 8. BAIL AND PRETRIAL RELEASE.

Section 8.01. Release by Station Officer.

(1) *Release on Own Recognizance.* When an arrested person has been brought before a station officer and a complaint has been issued charging him with a violation or a petty misdemeanor, the station officer shall release the defendant upon his written agreement that he will appear in court at the time and place specified.

(2) *Bail.* When an arrested person has been brought before a station officer and a complaint has been issued charging him with a misdemeanor or a felony, the station officer shall release the defendant upon his depositing bail, with a person authorized by law to accept bail, in the amount fixed in the warrant of arrest or, if no bail is fixed in the warrant or the arrest is without a warrant, the schedule of bail adopted as provided in Section 8.02. The bail shall be in cash or surety bond executed by a certified admitted surety insurer.

(3) *Modification of Bail.* If the prosecuting attorney believes that the bail provided in the warrant or schedule is insufficient to insure the appearance of the defendant, he may petition a judicial officer for an increase in the amount of bail. If the defendant believes that the bail is unnecessarily high, he may petition a judicial officer to reduce the amount of the bail or to release him on his own recognizance.

Section 8.02. Bail Schedules.

(1) *Misdemeanors.* It is the duty of the judges of the courts having jurisdiction of misdemeanors in each county to prepare and adopt, by majority vote, a schedule of bail for all misdemeanor cases. It shall contain a list of such offenses and the amounts of bail applicable thereto as the judges determine to be appropriate. If it does not list all misdemeanors specifically, it shall contain a general clause providing for a designated amount of bail for all misdemeanors not specifically listed in the schedule. The schedule of bail may be revised from time to time.

(2) *Felonies.* It is the duty of the judges of the courts having jurisdiction of felonies in each county to prepare and adopt, by a majority vote, a schedule of bail [for all bailable felonies] [for all felonies except the following:

(a) ....

(b) ....

(c) ....]

Such schedule shall contain a list of such offenses and the amounts of bail applicable thereto. The schedule of bail may be revised from time to time.

Section 8.03. Release by Judicial Officer.

[to be drafted]

Section 8.04. Penalty for Failure to Appear.

[to be drafted]

Section 8.05. Administrative Provisions.

[to be drafted]

ARTICLE 9. VIOLATIONS OF THE CODE: EXCLUSION OF EVIDENCE.

[Reporters' Note: This Article deals at present only with the exclusion of statements and (in Section 9.09) evidence derived from inadmissible statements. Provisions relating to the exclusion of other evidence (e.g., results of tests or identification procedures) will be drafted in connection with the search and seizure sections.]

Section 9.01. Statements Improperly Obtained in Seeking Voluntary Cooperation.

If a law enforcement officer requests any person to furnish information or otherwise cooperate pursuant to Section 2.01, and

(a) indicates that such person is legally obliged to comply with such request where no such legal obligation exists; or

(b) fails to give the warning required by Section 2.01(2),

no statement made in response to or as a result of such request, unless it is made in the presence of or upon consultation with counsel, shall be admitted in evidence against such person in a criminal proceeding in which he is the defendant.

Section 9.02. Statements Made After an Illegal Arrest.

If a law enforcement officer, acting without a warrant, arrests a person without the reasonable cause required by Section 3.01, and the court determines that such arrest was made without fair basis for the belief that such cause existed, no statement made by such person after such arrest and prior to his release, unless it is made in the presence of or upon consultation with counsel, shall be admitted in evidence against such person in a criminal proceeding in which he is the defendant.

Section 9.03. Statements Obtained After Improper Failure to Issue Warning.

(1) *Failure to Warn.* If an officer fails to issue the warning required by Section 3.08(d) or Section 4.01 to be given to an arrested person, no statement made by such person after he should have been so warned and prior to any time that such failure is cured, unless it is made in the presence of or upon consultation with counsel, shall be admitted in evidence against such person in a criminal proceeding in which he is the defendant.

(2) *Cure.* For purposes of this section, a failure to warn shall be deemed cured if after such failure

 (a) the omitted warning was subsequently issued; and

 (b) the court finds that the delay in issuing the warning did not substantially prejudice the arrested person.

Section 9.04. Statements Obtained During Delays in Disposition.

(1) *Failure to Take an Arrested Person to a Police Station.* In any case where an arrested person's production at a police station and before the station officer is delayed in violation of Section 3.09 or 4.01(1), no statement made by such person during such unlawful delay shall be admitted in evidence against such person in a criminal proceeding in which he is the defendant.

(2) *Failure to Release an Arrested Person.* In any case where the station officer fails to release an arrested person, whether outright, under a citation to appear, or on recognizance or bail, before the expiration of the time when such release is required by Section 4.03, 4.04 or 4.05, no statement made by such person after the expiration of such time and prior to his release shall be admitted in evidence against such person in a criminal proceeding in which he is the defendant.

(3) *Failure to Take an Arrested Person to a Judicial Officer.* In any case where an arrested person's production before a judicial officer is delayed in violation of Section 4.06(1), no statement made by such person during such unlawful delay shall be admitted in evidence against such person in a criminal proceeding in which he is the defendant.

(4) *Statements Made in the Presence of Counsel.* Nothing in this section shall be deemed to render inadmissible a statement made by an arrested person in the presence or with the consent of his counsel.

Section 9.05. Statements Obtained After Failure to Comply With Rules Relating to Telephoning, Access and Consultation.

(1) *Failure to Permit Telephoning.* If the station officer fails to afford any person an opportunity to use the telephone in violation of Section 4.01(5) or 5.07(2), no statement made by such person, in response to or as a result of any questioning which occurred after any such violation and before he has been given such an opportunity, shall be admitted in evidence against such person in a criminal proceeding in which he is the defendant; *provided*, that if such statement was made in the presence of or upon consultation with counsel, it shall not be rendered inadmissible by this subsection.

(2) *Failure to Permit Access or Consultation.* If at any time counsel, or a relative or friend, has been refused access to any person in violation of Section 5.07(1), or any person is denied a reasonable opportunity to consult with counsel, relative or friend, in violation of Section 5.07(2), no statement made by such person after any such violation and before he has had a reasonable opportunity to consult

    (a) with his counsel, where the violation involved counsel;

    (b) with the relative or friend, or with his counsel, where the violation involved a relative or friend,

shall be admitted in evidence against such person in a criminal proceeding in which he is the defendant.

Section 9.06. Statements Obtained by Violations of Rules Relating to Interrogation.

(1) *Deception as to Rights.* If a law enforcement officer attempts to induce any person to make a statement or otherwise cooperate by indicating that such person is legally obliged to do so, in violation of Section 5.02, no statement made in response to or as a result of any such attempt, unless it is made in the presence of or upon consultation with counsel, shall be admitted in evidence against such person in a criminal proceeding in which he is the defendant.

(2) *Improper Interrogation.* If a law enforcement officer attempts to induce any person to make a statement

    (a) by subjecting, or threatening to subject, such person or another to abuse or by depriving such person of physical necessities, in violation of Section 5.03; or

    (b) by questioning or any other method which violates Section 5.04, 5.05, or 5.06,

no statement made in response to or as a result of any such attempt shall be admitted in evidence against such person in a criminal proceeding in which he is the defendant.

(3) *Violation of Rules Relating to Questioning During the Period of Further Screening and After Complaint.* If a law enforcement officer questions an arrested person or otherwise attempts to induce him to make a statement

>(a) without complying, during any period of further screening, with the rules set out in Section 5.08; or

>(b) without complying, during any period of custody between the time that a complaint is issued charging such person with a crime and the time such person is first brought before a judicial officer, with the rules set out in Section 5.09,

no statement made in response to or as a result of such questioning or other attempt shall be admitted in evidence against such person in a criminal proceeding in which he is the defendant.

Section 9.07. Promises of Leniency.

If a law enforcement officer attempts to induce any person to make a statement by promising leniency for, or an improvement in the legal situation of, such person or another in whom such person is interested, no statement made in response to or as a result of any such attempt, unless it is made in the presence of or upon consultation with counsel, shall be admitted in evidence against such person in a criminal proceeding in which he is the defendant.

Section 9.08. Complex and Ambiguous Matters.

If an arrested person makes a statement in the absence of counsel which deals with matters of such complexity or ambiguity that, in light of such person's age, intelligence, and mental and physical condition, there is a substantial risk that such statement may be misleading or its use may be unfair, such statement shall not be admitted in evidence against such person in a criminal proceeding in which he is the defendant.

Section 9.09. Evidence Discovered as the Result of Statements Which Are Inadmissible.

If evidence is discovered as the result of information furnished by any person in a statement which is inadmissible by virtue of the provisions of this Article, and the prosecution fails to establish that it is likely that such evidence would have been discovered by law enforcement authorities in the absence of such statement, such evidence shall be inadmissible against such person in a criminal proceeding in which he is the defendant, unless the court finds that exclusion of such evidence is not necessary to deter violations of this Code. [The following factors shall be considered in determining whether exclusion is necessary to deter violations of this Code:

>(a) whether the violation involved a grave invasion of the defendant's rights;

(b) whether the violation was wilful, or the result of a failure on the part of a law enforcement officer or agency to attempt in good faith to insure compliance with this Code.]

Section 9.10. Inadvertent and Minor Violations.

A statement which would be inadmissible by virtue of Sections 9.01 to 9.06 of this Article shall not be excluded from evidence if the court finds that the violation which would render the statement otherwise inadmissible was insubstantial and resulted from error excusable under the circumstances.

Section 9.11. Preventive Action in Cases of Urgent Necessity.

(1) *Action Authorized in Cases of Urgent Necessity.* Notwithstanding the provisions of this Code, a law enforcement officer is authorized to take action, reasonable under the circumstances and not in violation of the constitutional rights or unduly oppressive of any person, which is urgently necessary to save life, prevent serious bodily harm, avert public catastrophe, or protect other individual or public interests of comparable magnitude, other than the public interest in securing the conviction of the person subjected to such action.

[*Alternative: (1) Action Authorized in Cases of Urgent Necessity.* Notwithstanding the provisions of this Code, a law enforcement officer is authorized to take action which is urgently necessary to avert serious injury to persons, or to safeguard important individual or public interests other than the interest in securing the conviction of the person subjected to such action; *provided,* that such action may be taken only if it is plainly justified in view of the seriousness of the harm or evil to be averted, and if it is not unduly oppressive or in violation of the constitutional rights of any person.]

(2) *Exclusion of Evidence.* Any evidence obtained by action rendered lawful by this section which is otherwise admissible shall not be rendered inadmissible by Sections 9.01 to 9.07 or Section 9.09 of this Code.

(3) *Compliance With Required Regulations.* No action otherwise unlawful by this Code shall be deemed to be lawful by virtue of this section unless there has been substantial compliance with regulations, to be promulgated pursuant to Section 1.03, which shall specify the circumstances under which action may be taken pursuant to this section, and which shall require that whenever practicable such action shall be authorized by one of a designated class of senior law enforcement officers. Full records shall be maintained as to the circumstances of any such action.

Section 9.12. Resolving Disputes Concerning Violations of the Code.

In any criminal proceeding where the admissibility of evidence is in question and there is conflicting testimony whether there has been compliance with the provisions of this Code, if the court finds that

    (a) the law enforcement agency involved has not taken steps in good faith to insure compliance by personnel in that agency with the provisions of this Code; or

    (b) law enforcement officers in the particular case have failed to comply diligently and in good faith with Section 4.09, relating to written and sound records, and as a result unexplained gaps or inconsistencies appear in such records,

the burden shall be on the prosecution to establish that there has been compliance with the relevant provisions of this Code.

Section 9.13. Savings Clause.

Nothing in this Article shall be deemed to render admissible any evidence which is inadmissible by virtue of the Constitutions of the United States and of this State, or by virtue of any other law not superseded by the provisions of this Code.

INDEX

References are to Pages

ABANDONMENT
Attempt, 246.
Child, 251, 256.
Conspiracy, 247.
Criminal attempt, 246.
Infant, 251.

ABATEMENT
Plea in, 850.

ABDUCTION
Discussed, 85.

ABORTION
Discussed, 86.
Mens rea, 350.

ABSOLUTE LIABILITY
See, also, Strict Liability.
For crime unconstitutional, 402, 405 n.
Statute should not require, 345.

ACCESSORY
See, also, Parties to Crime.
After the fact, 297.
At the fact, 297.
Before the fact, 297.
Completed felony only, 305.
Felony cases only, 296.
Principal distinguished, 297.
Procedural problems, 299.

ACCOMPLICE
See, also, Accessory; Principal.
Definition, 300.

ACCUSATION
See Complaint; Indictment; Information.

ACCUSATORY PLEADING
See Complaint; Indictment; Information.

ACCUSATORY PROCEDURE
Questioning in, 916, 920.

ACCUSED
Preliminary examination of, 820, 821.
Rights and privileges of, 861, 863, 867, 913, 916, 920, 927, 931.

ACQUITTAL
See, also, Former Jeopardy.
One conspirator, 276.

ACT
Conspirator imputed, 274.
Driving a car, 220.
Essential to crime, 217, 218.
Necessity of, 217, 218.
Possession as, 222 n.
What constitutes, 220.

ACTUS REUS
Battery, 345.
Burglary, 345.
Concurrence of mens rea, 438, 439.
Mens rea and, 344.
Murder, 345.
Physical part of crime, 344.
Resulting from mens rea, 439.

ADULTERY
Defined, 205.

ADVICE
See Counsel.

AFFRAY
Definition, 208.

AGENCY
See, also, Agent.
Section on, 283.

AGENT
Crime by, 283.
Liability of principal, 283, 284, 285.
Libel by, 285.
Principal liable for nuisance by, 388.

ALCOHOLISM
As a disease, 489.

ALLOCUTION
Benefit of clergy, 849.
Insanity at time of, 463.

ALTERATION
Indictment, 837.

ALTERNATE JUROR
Substitution during trial, 730 n.

AMENDMENT
Statute of Limitations, 719.

AMENTIA
See Insanity.

AMERICAN LAW INSTITUTE
See, also, Model Penal Code.
Code of Criminal Procedure,
    Authority to arrest, 571 n.
    Demurrer abolished, 844 n.
    Form and contents of warrant, 778.
    Officer may summon assistance, 790 n.
    Possession of warrant not required, 789 n.
    Summons in lieu of warrant, 790.
    Summons issued, 819 n.
    Venue, 677.
    Warrant defined, 777.
Youth Correction Authority Act, 458.

ANIMALS
Cruelty to, 262.

ANIMUS FURANDI
Fungible goods, 189.
In larceny, 187, 189, 191, 192.
Intent to,
    Deprive, 187, 189.
    Return, 187.
    Sell to owner, 191.
Taking by piece-worker, 192.
Taking to pawn, 194.

APPLICATION OF DECISION
Retrospective or prospective, 891 n.

APPREHENSION
Assault by placing in, 80, 82.

ARMED FORCES
Command by superior, 574.

ARRAIGNMENT
Definition, 829.
Insanity at time of, 463.
Pre-arraignment procedures, 931.

ARREST
See, also, Warrant of Arrest.
Assisting officer, 790, 791 n.
Authority to, 571 n.
Breaking doors to effect, 809.
By federal officer, 804.
By posse, 790.
Charge preferred by another, 797.
Deadly force in making, 807.
Disposition of prisoner, 815, 931.
Escaper, 803.
False imprisonment by, 783.
Felony by arrestee, 801.
Force used in making, 806.
Fourth Amendment requirement, 779.
Fugitive Felon Act, 797 n.
Fugitive from another state, 804.
Handcuffing arrestee, 808.

ARREST—Cont'd
"Held for questioning", 813.
Homicide by resisting, 39 n.
Manifestation of authority, 805.
"Notice of", 805.
Offense in "presence", 791, 793, 795.
Official information, 802.
On fresh pursuit, 803.
Oral order of magistrate, 789.
Place of, 802.
Possession of warrant, 788, 789 n.
Pre-arraignment procedures, 931.
Probable cause for, 799.
Purpose of, 787.
Resistance to, 795.
Resisting unauthorized, 816, 817.
Search of prisoner, 811.
Summons in lieu of, 818.
Time of, 805.
Under warrant, 788.
What constitutes, 786.
Who may, 788.
Without a warrant, 784 n, 791, 805, 806.
Wrong person under warrant, 783, 784 n.

ARRESTEE
Arrest for felony by, 801.
Defined, 787.
Disposition of, 815.
Duty of, 816.
Questioning, 813.
Rights of, 816.
Search of, 811.

ARREST WITHOUT WARRANT
Disposition of prisoner, 815, 931.

ARSON
Defined, 120.
Extortion by threat to accuse of, 373 n.
To injure insurer, 438.

ASPORTATION
See, also, Larceny.
Carrying away, 135.
Innocent buyer, 134.
Sufficient, 133.

ASSAULT
Aggravated, 241.
Attempt, 241, 244 n.
Consent obtained by fraud, 549, 550 n.
Included in battery, 75 n.
Intent in, 80, 82.
Intent to maim, 420.
Lawful touching is not, 77.
Mistake of fact, 520, 521.
Motor vehicle as cause, 79 n.
Placing in apprehension, 80, 82.
Threatening with weapon, 80.
What constitutes, 75.

INDEX

References are to Pages

ASSAULT AND BATTERY
Chapter on, 75.

ASSIGNMENT OF COUNSEL
To indigent, 863, 867, 868 n.

ATTEMPT
See, also, Assault; Conspiracy; Solicitation.
Abandonment, 246.
Elements of, 365.
Forgery, 225.
Impossibility, 231, 232, 235, **238.**
Intent necessary, 239.
Misdemeanor, 224.
Murder, 226.
Perpetrating act, 225.
Poison, 226.
Proximity, 226, 228.
Punishable, 224.
Rape, 238.
Receiving stolen property, 232, 235.
Section on, 224.
Specific intent necessary, **365.**
To assault, 241, 244 n.
To commit misdemeanor, 224, 225 n.

AUTOMOBILE
Homicide by, 31, 33 n, 38.

BAIL
Admitted to, 833.
After conviction, 832 n.
"Cash bail," 833.
Entitled to, 833.
Forfeiture of, 834.
Meaning of, 832.
Release on, 833.
Taking of, 833.

BAILEE
Embezzlement, 147, **148.**
Larceny, 142, 150 n.

BAILIWICK
Definition, 802.

BARRATRY
Defined, 213.

BATTERY
Actus reus, 345.
Assault included, 75 n.
By drug, 337.
Lawful touching is not, **77.**
Mens rea, 345.
Negligence, 78.
Without touching, 75.

BENCH WARRANT
Use of, 828.

BENEFIT OF CLERGY
Plea of, 849.

BESTIALITY
Defined, 206.

BIGAMY
Defined, 205.
Jurisdiction for, 660 n.
Mistake of fact, 525.
Mistake of law, 514.

BILL
Of indictment, 822.
Of particulars, 826.

BLACKMAIL
See Extortion.

BREACH OF PEACE
Discussed, 207.

BREAKING
See, also, Burglary.
Constructive, 103.
Into, 106.
Out, 107n.

BRIBERY
Definition, 210.

BUGGERY
Defined, 206.

BURGLARY
Actus reus, 345.
Authorized entry, 100.
Boring hole into building, 107, 109 n.
Breaking, 98, 100, 101, 103, 106.
    Authorized opening, 98, 100.
    Inside door, 106.
    Into, 107.
    Other than dwelling, 100, 101 n, 103.
    Out, 107 n.
    Partly open door or window, 101.
    Unlocked door opened, 99 n. 105.
Burglarious intent, 364.
Compulsion, 539.
Curtilage, building within, 93.
Deadly force to prevent, 594.
Dwelling,
    "Of another", 95, 103.
    "Therein", 112.
Dwelling house, 93.
Entry, 107.
    By instrument, 107.
Homicide by, 66, 68.
Inn, 93 n.
Intent, 111, 187.
    To steal inferred, 241 n.
Joint occupancy of dwelling, 95.

INDEX

References are to Pages

BURGLARY—Cont'd
Jurisdiction for, 692.
Meaning of, in statute, 114.
Mens rea, 345.
Nighttime, 109.
Opening inside door, 106.
Section on, 93.
Statutory, 100, 101 n, 103, 105.
With explosives, 114.

CASH BAIL
Forfeiture of, 834.
In lieu of bond, 833.
Meaning of, 833.

"CASTLE DOCTRINE"
Self-defense, 601, 610 n, 611, 612 n.

CAUSATION
Act of another, 326, 328, 329, 333, 337, 339, 340.
Cause of a cause, 325, 326.
Contributory cause, 315.
Death from medicine, 324.
Dependent intervening cause, 324–326.
Direct, 322.
Independent intervening cause, 314, 328, 336, 340.
Intended consequence, 339.
Negative act not superseding, 338.
Negligence not superseding, 324.
Section on, 312.
Superseding act, 314, 328, 336.
Unforeseeable harm, 322.

CHAMPERTY
Definition, 210.

CHEAT
See Larceny.

CHILD
See, also, Immaturity; Juvenile Delinquency.
Abandonment of, 251, 256.

CIVIL OFFENSE
Adulterated food, 391.
Distinguished from true crime, 388.

CIVIL RIGHTS ACT
Federal offense, 817.

CLASSIFICATION
Crimes, 4.

CODE OF CRIMINAL PROCEDURE
See American Law Institute.

COERCION
See, also, Compulsion, Extortion.
Doctrine of, 497.
Wife by husband, 497.

COLLATERAL ESTOPPEL
Discussed, 752.

COMMAND
By superior in armed forces, 574.

COMMON-LAW CHEAT
False token required, 161 n.

COMMUNIST PARTY
Conspiracy, 278.
Membership in, 278.

COMPLAINT
Contents of, 771, 774.
Issuance of, 769, 771.
Probable cause required for, 769, 771.

COMPOUNDING CRIME
Defined, 213.

COMPULSION
See, also, Coercion; Command; Coverture.
As excuse, 535, 539.
Burglary (statutory), 539.
Command, effect of, 535.
Excuse for treason, 537.
Explained, 535.
Homicide under, 536, 538 n.
Killing innocent person, 535.
Section on, 535.
Sodomy, 540 n.

CONCURRENCE
Actus reus and mens rea, 438, 439.

CONCURRENT JURISDICTION
Boundary rivers, 675.
Former jeopardy, 730.

CONDITIONAL
Intent, 367.

CONDONATION
By injured party, 563, 565, 566.

CONDUCT
Of injured party, 558, 559, 561, 562.

CONFESSION
Coerced by private person, 648 n.
Conviction on coerced, 841 n.
During illegal detention, 879.
Extrajudicial, 13, 15, 18, 21.
Infrajudicial, 21 n.
Involuntary,
  Excluded, 873.
  Procedure to determine, 873.
Right to counsel violated, 916, 920.
Uncorroborated, 14 n.

INDEX

References are to Pages

CONSENT
Affecting lawfulness of act, 541, 544.
Carnal knowledge of child, 88.
Fraudulently obtained, 546, 549, 550, 553 n.
"Joy riding", 546.
Larceny, 544.
Of other party, 541.

CONSPIRACY
Abandonment of, 247.
Acquittal of one, 276.
Acts imputed, 274.
Concert of action, 267.
Conviction of, and substantive crime, 264 n.
Corporations, 266.
Homicide from robbery, 310 n.
Husband and wife, 266 n.
Knowledge of unlawful purpose, 272, 273 n.
Manifested legislative intent, 269.
Mann Act, 269.
Mistake of law, 509.
Nolle prosequi of one, 270.
Overt act, 277 n.
Two guilty minds, 266.
Usury, 264.
Withdrawal from, 247.

CONSTITUTION
See Fifth Amendment; Fourteenth Amendment; Fourth Amendment; Sixth Amendment.

CONTEMPT
Criminal, 214.
Discussed, 214.

CONTINUING TRESPASS
In larceny, 184.

CONTRABAND
Larceny of, 128 n.

CONTRACEPTIVISM
Defined, 87.

CONTRIBUTORY
Cause, 315.

CONVICTION
Of conspiracy and substantive crime, 264 n.
On coerced confession, 841 n.

CORAM NOBIS
Writ of, 848 n.

CORONER'S INQUEST
Use of, 826.

CORPORATION
Conspiracy by, 266.
Criminal liability of, 288–290.
Liability of officer, 293.

CORPUS DELICTI
Corroboration, 13, 15, 18, 21.
Meaning of, 14 n.
Proof of, 13, 15, 18, 21.

COUNSEL
Assigned to indigent, 863, 867, 868 n.
Defendant's right to, 861, 863, 867, 916, 920, 927.
Defendant's right to,
On appeal, 867.
Erroneous advice of, 514.

COUNTERFEITING
Definition, 211.

COURTS
Jurisdiction of, 691, 692.

COVERTURE
See Coercion.

CRIME
Attempt to commit, 224.
By agent, 283.
Civil offense is not, 388.
Constituent parts of, 344.
Defined, 1.
Definition, Model Penal Code, 11.
Infamous, 6.
Juvenile delinquency distinguished, 447, 451.

CRIME PREVENTION
See Prevention of Crime.

CRIMINAL CAPACITY
See Coverture; Immaturity; Insanity; Intoxication; Presumption.

CRIMINAL INTENT
Meaning of, 343 n.

CRIMINAL JURISDICTION
See Jurisdiction.

CRIMINAL JUSTICE ACT
Right to counsel, 865 n.

CRIMINAL NEGLIGENCE
See, also, Negligence.
Cooperative undertaking, 355.
Epilepsy, effect of, 221.
Homicide by, 51, 54.
Ordinary negligence distinguished, 357.
Section on, 352.
What constitutes, 54.

CRUELTY
To animals, 262.

CURTILAGE
Burglary of building within, 93.

CUSTODY
See, also, Larceny.
Distinguished from possession, 143, 145, 147, 148.

DEADLY FORCE
Arresting for felony, 807.
Defense of others, 620.
Defined, 598.
Making arrest, 807.
Prevention of crime, 591, 592, 594.
Self-defense, 600.

DECENCY
Offenses against, 204.

DEFAMATION
Libel, 209.

DEFENDANT
Assigned counsel, 863, 867, 868 n.
Demurrer by, 843.
Motion by,
    Change of judge, 847.
    Change of venue, 846.
    To dismiss, 846.
    To quash, 845.
Plea by, see Plea.
Right of privacy, 891.
Right to counsel, 861, 863, 867, 916, 920, 927.
Standing mute, 823.

DEFENSE
See, also, Compulsion; Consent; Coverture; Domestic Authority; Entrapment; Immaturity; Insanity; Intoxication; Prevention of Crime; Public Authority; Self-Defense.
Of others,
    Force permitted, 620, 623, 625, 627.
    Necessity for use of force, 620.
    Other not privileged, 623, 625, 627 n.
    Section on, 619.
    What others, 620.
Of property, 628, 631, 633.
Spring-gun used, 633, 636 n.

DEFINITION
Accessory after the fact, 297.
Accessory before the fact, 297.
Accomplice, 300.
Adultery, 205.
Affray, 208.

DEFINITION—Cont'd
Arraignment, 829.
Arrestee, 787.
Arson, 120.
Bailiwick, 802.
Barratry, 213.
Bestiality, 206.
Bigamy, 205.
Bribery, 210.
Buggery, 206.
Champerty, 213.
Compounding crime, 213.
Contraceptivism, 87.
Counterfeiting, 211.
Crime, 1.
Deadly force, 598.
Demurrer, 843.
Disorderly house, 209.
Dueling, 92.
Embracery, 211.
Escape, 212.
Extortion, 211.
False imprisonment, 88.
Felony, 10 n.
Forcible entry, 209.
Fraudulent banking, 216.
Incest, 205.
Kidnaping, 89.
Libel, 209.
Maintenance, 213.
Mann Act, 206.
Manslaughter, 54.
Mayhem, 91.
Misconduct in office, 211.
Motion, 830.
Murder, 32.
Negligence, 352.
Nondeadly force, 597.
Obscenity, 206.
Obstruction of justice, 212.
Pandering, 206.
Perjury, 210.
Personal property, 124 n.
"Pimp", 206.
Piracy, 654.
Principal in first degree, 297.
Principal in second degree, 297.
Procurer, 206.
Prostitution, 206.
Rape, 88.
Recusation, 847.
Rescue, 212.
Riot, 208.
Rout, 208.
Seduction, 205.
Sodomy, 206.
Specific intent, 361.

INDEX

References are to Pages

DEFINITION—Cont'd
Subornation of perjury, 210.
Treason, 210, 654.
Unlawful assembly, 208.
Vague, 2.

DEGREE
Murder, 61–71.

DELIRIUM TREMENS
Insanity, 488.

DELUSION
Crime under insane, 471.

DEMURRER
Abolished by some statutes, 844.
Defendant, 843.
Definition, 843.
Discussed, 831.
Effect of overruling, 844.
Prosecution, 831.
Superfluous device, 844.

DISCOVERY
By defendant, 855.
By prosecution, 859.
Development of, 856.
Fifth Amendment, 860.
Pre-trial, 855.
Scope of, 857.

DISMISS
Motion to, 846.

DISORDERLY HOUSE
Definition, 209.

DOMESTIC AUTHORITY
As a defense, 581.
Guardian, 581.
Husband, 581, 583, 584 n.
Master over servant, 582.
Parent, 581.
Schoolmaster, 582, 585, 587.

DOUBLE JEOPARDY
See Former Jeopardy.

DRUNKENNESS
See Intoxication.

DUELING
Defined, 92.

DUE PROCESS CLAUSE
See Fourteenth Amendment.

DUE PROCESS OF LAW
Conviction without, 840.
Felon-registration ordinance, 511.
Fourteenth Amendment, 749.
Statute violates, 530 n.
Violation of, 402, 405 n, 511.

DURESS
See Compulsion.

DUTY
Essential to negative act, 254.
To care for one's own child, 256, 257.
To caution chauffeur to use care, 261.
To give information to officers, 814.

DWELLING
See, also, Arson, Burglary.
What constitutes, 93, 95.

EAVESDROPPING
Electronic devices, 901, 902.

ELECTRICITY
Larceny of, 124.

ELECTRONIC DEVICES
As corroboration, 899.
Crime being committed, 899.
Recording conversation, 899.
Right of counsel violated by, 913.
Without physical contact, 903 n.

EMBEZZLEMENT
Bailee, 147, 148.
Employee, 145, 147, 148.
English statute, 145.
Larceny distinguished, 145, 146.
Money illegally acquired, 555 n.
Specific intent necessary, 364 n.

EMBRACERY
Definition, 211.

EMPLOYEE
Embezzlement by, 145, 147, 148.
Larceny by, 145, 148.

EMPLOYER
Crime by employee, 261, 283–285.
Libel by employee, 285.
Nuisance by employee, 388.

ENFORCEMENT
See Procedure.

ENTRAPMENT
As a defense, 641, 643.
Instigation distinguished from detection, 639, 640 n.
Meaning of, 639, 640 n.
Section on, 638.

ENTRY
See Burglary.

EPILEPSY
Driving while subject to, 221.

ESCAPE
Definition, 212.
Permitting, 212.
Prison breach, 212.

964 INDEX

References are to Pages

EUTHANASIA
No excuse for homicide, 430 n.

EVIDENCE
Change of as ex post facto, 761, 763, 766 n.
"Fruit of poisonous tree", 892.

EXCUSE
Unknown fact is not, 435, 437.

EXECUTION
Change in mode of, not ex post facto, 767 n.
Insanity at time of, 463.

EX POST FACTO
Change between blow and death, 768.
Change of,
    Method of execution, 767 n.
    Procedure, 766 n.
    Rules of evidence, 761, 763.
Constitutional bar, 759.
Explained, 759.
Repeal of statute, 761.
Sentence, 838.
Statute,
    Changing penalty, 760 n.

EXTORTION
Definition, 211.
Mistake of law, 505.
Statutory (blackmail), 211.

EXTRADITION
"Asylum state", 694.
Constitutional provision, 694.
"Demanding state", 694.
"Fugitive", 694, 696, 699, 701 n.
Governor determines, 699 n.
Guilt of fugitive, 696 n.
Habeas corpus to test, 711.
International, 701 n.
Of one not a fugitive, 704.
Parolee, 702.
Requisition, 694.
Section on, 694.
Trial for another offense, 709.
Uniform, Act, 704.

FAILURE TO TESTIFY
Comment on defendant's, 883.

FALSE IMPRISONMENT
Defined, 88.
Public authority, 573.
Unlawful arrest, 783.

FALSE PRETENSES
By conditional vendee, 170.
By possessor, 169.

FALSE PRETENSES—Cont'd
False promise, 164, 165.
Falsity of statement, 196.
Guilt of other party, 555.
Jurisdiction for, 669 n.
Knowledge of falsity, 383.
Larceny distinguished, 157, 161, 172, 175.
Property must be obtained, 160.
Security misrepresented, 196.
Title obtained by fraud, 157, 160, 161, 169, 172, 175.

FEDERAL OFFENSES
    See, also, United States Code.
Civil Rights Act, 817.
Dyer Act, 175.
Fugitive Felon Act, 114, 115 n.
Hobbs Act, 119 n.
Interstate transportation of stolen car, 683.
Jones Act, 9.
Kidnaping Act, 90.
Mails violated, 87.
Mann Act, 206.
Misprision of felony, 114.
Motor Vehicle Theft Act, 175.
Piracy, 654.
Robbery, 654.
Smith Act, 278.
Treason, 210, 654.
White slave traffic law, 206.
Wiretapping, 903.

FEDERAL RULES OF CRIMINAL PROCEDURE
All but basic pleas abolished, 846.
Alternate juror, 912.
Arraignment, 830.
Cash bail, 833.
Defendant's presence at trial, 906.
Form of indictment, 825.
Form of warrant, 778.
Plea of nolo contendere, 854.
Rule 3, p. 772.
Rule 4, pp. 272, 274, 789 n.
Rule 4a, p. 819 n.
Rule 7(e), p. 687 n.
Rule 10, p. 830.
Rule 11, p. 854.
Rule 12, pp. 684, 844 n, 851.
Rule 16, pp. 857, 858.
Rule 18, p. 687.
Rule 23, p. 911.
Rule 24, pp. 846, 912.
Rule 35, p. 906.
Rule 43, p. 906.
Rule 44, p. 861.
Rule 46(f), (2), p. 834 n.

FELONY
Arrest for, 801.
Deadly force in arresting, 807.
Definition, 10 n.
Drunk driving, 923.
"Felony-misdemeanor", 10 n.
Force to prevent, 592, 593.
Misprision of, 114.
Penalty, 5.

FELONY-MURDER
Fatal, resistance to robbery, 329, 333.
Homicide in *res gestae*, 38.
What is, 38.

FIFTH AMENDMENT
Discovery, 860.
Effect of Fourteenth, 883.
Former jeopardy, 725, 734.
Indictment, 5, 827.
Procedure under, 5.
Self-incrimination, 872, 883.
Smith Act does not violate, 278.

FIGHTING
See Affray.

FOOD
Adulterated, 391, 394 n.

FORCE
    See, also, Deadly Force; Nondeadly Force.
In making arrest, 806.

FORCIBLE ENTRY
Definition, 209.

FORGERY
Attempt, 225.
Jurisdiction for, 670 n.
Knowledge required for uttering, 385.

FORMA PAUPERIS
Appeals, 869 n.
Defendant proceeding in, 864.

FORMER JEOPARDY
Additional statutory limitation, 726 n.
Appeal by state, 740.
Collateral estoppel, 752.
Concurrent jurisdiction, 730.
Constitutional bar, 725.
Conviction of lesser offense, 735 n.
Conviction vacated, 734.
Death sentence, 738.
Different victims, 743, 745, 749, 754 n.
"Evident necessity", 727.
Historical background, 725.
Incest—Statutory rape, 747 n.
Mistrial is not, 727, 730 n.

FORMER JEOPARDY—Cont'd
Multiple trials, 749, 754 n.
Plea of, 850.
Problems peculiar to proceedings, 727–742.
Res judicata, 752 n.
Robbery—Murder, 755.
"Same offense", 743–757.
Section on, 725.
State and federal, 753 n.
Test of, 743, 745, 749.
Victim dies after first trial, 755.
When jeopardy attaches, 727.
When jury waived, 729 n.

FORNICATION
Discussed, 205.

FOURTEENTH AMENDMENT
Arrest violating, 809 n.
Due process, 749.
Equal protection, 867, 870.
Former jeopardy, 740, 749.
Right to counsel, 862, 863, 867, 927.
    Before indictment, 916, 920.
Self-incrimination, 883.

FOURTH AMENDMENT
Arrest, 779.
Discovery, 860.
Effect of Fourteenth, 891.
Right of privacy, 891.

FRAUD
    See, also, Larceny, False Pretenses.
Consent obtained by, 546, 549, 550.
Goods obtained by, 157.
In the *factum*, 548.
In the inducement, 548.
Sexual intercourse obtained by, 550.
Use of motor vehicle by, 546.

FRAUDULENT BANKING
Defined, 216.
Knowledge of insolvency, 383.

FRESH PURSUIT
Uniform Act on, 803.

FRIGHT
Causing harm, 318.

FRISK
Of arrestee, 812.
Uniform Arrest Act, 813 n.

"FRUIT OF POISONOUS TREE"
Excluded, 892.
"Unpoisoned", 897.

FUGITIVE
Arrest of, from another state, 804.
Extradition of, 694, 696, 699, 701 n.

INDEX

References are to Pages

FUGITIVE FELON ACT
Amended, 115 n.
Arrest for, 797 n.

GRAND JURY
Indictment presented by, 822.
Presentment by, 822.
Size of, 822.

GUILT
Injured party, 555.
Plea of, 853.

HABEAS CORPUS
Ad testificandum, 842.
Constitutional provision, 835.
Conviction without due process, 840.
Discussion of, 834.
Extradition case, 711.
Federal statute, 841.
Lack of jurisdiction, 837.
Meaning of, 834.
Motion as substitute, 836 n.
Not substitute for appeal, 836.
Parolee, 836 n.
Petition for, 835.
State or federal proceeding, 836.
Writ of, 834.

HARD LABOR
Infamous crime, 7.

HOMICIDE
See, also, Manslaughter; Murder; Negligent Homicide.
Born alive, 27.
By,
    Co-conspirator, 310 n.
    Narcotic, 39 n.
    Negative act, 250, 252, 256 n.
    Negligence, 34.
Chapter on, 13.
Criminal negligence, 51, 54.
Driving without license, 414 n.
Euthanasia not an excuse, 430 n.
Fatal resistance to robbery, 329, 333.
From fright, 318.
Human being, 24.
Hunting accident, 411.
Infanticide, 28 n.
Jurisdiction, 666, 667 n, 671, 673 n.
Mitigation, 42, 45, 48.
    Other than provocation, 48 n.
Motive for, 435, 437.
Negative act causing, 250, 252, 254, 258, 261.
Negligence, 30, 31, 34.
Negligence of injured party, 559, 561, 562.
Of hemophiliac, 322.
Proof of corpus delicti, 13, 15, 18, 21.

HOMICIDE—Cont'd
Resisting arrest, 39 n, 795.
Sudden passion, 42, 45, 48.
Suicide attempt causing, 409.
To prevent larceny, 435.
Traffic accident causing, 31, 33 n, 413.
Under compulsion, 536, 538 n.
Unlawful act causing, 56, 58, 60.
While insane, 466, 469, 471.

HUE AND CRY
Reference to, 827.

HUSBAND
Coercion of wife, 497.
Conspiracy with wife, 266.
Domestic authority of, 581, 583, 584 n.

IDIOCY
See Insanity.

IGNORANCE
See Knowledge; Mistake of Fact; Mistake of Law.

ILLICIT COHABITATION
Discussed, 205.

IMMATURITY
    See, also, Juvenile Delinquency.
As a defense, 445.
Critical ages, 445.

IMMUNITY ACT
Effect of, 886.

IMPOSSIBILITY
See Attempt.

IMPRISONMENT
See False Imprisonment.

IMPUTABILITY
Chapter on, 217.

INCEST
Defined, 205.

INCORPORATION
    See, also, Corporation.
Section on, 288.

INDECENT EXPOSURE
Mens rea of, 347.

INDICTMENT
Alteration destroys, 837.
Bill of, 822.
By grand jury, 770.
Fifth Amendment, 5, 827.
Form of, 825.
Grand jury presents, 822.
Motion to quash, 845.
Simplification of, 825.
Steps by prosecution after, 828.

INDEX

References are to Pages

INDICTMENT—Cont'd
Steps by prosecution prior to, 769–827.
Technicalities of, 823.

INDIGENT DEFENDANT
Right to counsel, 861, 863, 867, 916, 920, 927.

INFAMOUS CRIME
Punishment determines, 6, 827.

INFANT
See, also, Immaturity.
Child stealing, 90.
Criminal capacity, 445.
Principal in second degree, 307.
Rape by, 307.

INFORMATION
See, also, Indictment.
Constitutional limitations, 826.
In lieu of indictment, 826.

INJURED PARTY
Condonation by, 563, 565, 566.
Conduct of, 558, 559, 561, 562.
Guilt of, 555.

INSANITY
Acquittal because of, 466 n.
Amentia, 464.
At time of,
    Alleged crime, 463, 466, 469, 471, 477, 479, 481.
    Allocution, 463.
    Arraignment, 463.
    Execution, 463.
    Trial, 463.
"Bifurcated trial", 486 n.
Constitutional limitations, 486 n.
Delirium tremens, 488.
Delusion, 471.
Dementia, 464.
Diminished responsibility, 466, 469, 479 n.
Homicide during, 466, 469, 471, 479, 481.
Irresistible impulse, 471, 479, 481, 483 n.
    "Almost unusable defense", 479 n.
Jury to decide, 486 n.
M'Naghten rule, 465.
"Moral insanity", 465.
Plea of not guilty because of, 852.
"Product rule", 473.
Proof of, 485.
Right-wrong test, 465, 481, 485.
Substantial capacity standard, 477, 479 n, 481.
Various meanings of, 464, 465.

INTENT
See, also, Larceny; Specific Intent.
Attempt, 239, 365.

INTENT—Cont'd
Burglarious, 111.
Conditional, 367.
Inferred from breaking in, 241 n.
Meaning, 359, 360 n.
Motive distinguished, 429.
Not "transferred", 418, 420.
To steal, see Animus Furandi.

INTERSTATE RENDITION
See Extradition.

INTERSTATE TRANSPORTATION
Mann Act, 269.
Stolen vehicle, 175.

INTOXICATION
Alcohol in blood, 926 n.
Alcoholism as a disease, 489.
As a defense, 490, 491.
Blood test for, 923.
By drugs, 490, 491.
Delirium tremens distinguished, 488.
Driving "under the influence", 220.
Felony drunk driving, 923.
In public place, 490.
Involuntary, 490, 491, 493.
Mistake resulting from, 495 n.
Section on, 487.
Specific intent disproved, 488.
"Under the influence", 496 n.
Voluntary, 488.

INVESTIGATORY PROCEDURE
Questioning in, 916, 920.

INVOLUNTARY
Intoxication, 490, 491, 493.
Manslaughter, 56, 58, 60, 353, 355, 360.

IRRESISTIBLE IMPULSE
See Insanity.

JENKS ACT
Discussed, 858.

JEOPARDY
See Former Jeopardy.

"JOHN DOE"
Warrant of arrest, 780.

"JOY RIDING"
Consent obtained by fraud, 546.

JURISDICTION
Basis of criminal, 657.
Bigamy, 660 n.
Boundary rivers, 675.
Burglary, 692.
Citizen, 666 n.
Citizen abroad, 658, 660.
Concurrent, 675.

INDEX

References are to Pages

JURISDICTION—Cont'd
Courts, 691, 692.
Extent of state's authority, 653.
Federal preemption, 655.
Foreigners abroad, 657.
Forgery, 670 n.
Habeas corpus where, wanting, 837.
Homicide, 666, 667 n, 671, 673 n.
Injured forum, 662, 670.
Larceny, 673.
Libel, 670 n.
Loss of by court, 837.
Nonresident, 704.
One brought in unlawfully, 707.
Piracy, 654.
Plea to, 849.
Probationer, 657 n.
Rights and privileges distinguished, 656 n.
Robbery, 670 n.
Roman theory, 666 n.
Section on, 653.
Sentence beyond, 838.
Situs of crime, 666, 667 n, 669 n, 671.
State and federal, 655, 656 n.
Statute of limitations, 715.
Ten major crimes act, 655.
Territorial, 666.
Venue, 677.
Vessel, 657 n, 662 n.
Where part committed, 671, 673 n.

JURY
Alternate jurors, 911.
Defendant's right to trial by, 909.
Waiver of, 910.

JUVENILE DELINQUENCY
Crime distinguished, 447, 451.
Record of, 455.

KIDNAPING
Defined, 89.
Mistake of law, 507.

KNOWLEDGE
As affecting mens rea, 380–384.
Conspiracy, 272, 273 n.
Distinguished from negligence, 381, 383 n.
False pretenses, 383, 385 n.
Fraudulent banking, 383.
Receiving stolen goods, 381, 383.
Uttering forged instrument, 385 n.

LARCENY
Appropriation by,
  Bailee, 142, 148, 186.
  Finder, 178, 180, 182.
  Servant, 145, 147, 148.
  Wife, 132 n.

LARCENY—Cont'd
Asportation, 134, 135.
  By innocent buyer, 134.
Automobile license plates, 128.
Breaking Bulk Doctrine, 150.
Caption, 132–134.
Chapter on, 124.
Consent of owner, 544.
Continuing trespass, 184.
Contraband, 128 n.
Custody vs. possession, 143, 145, 147, 148.
Delivered goods, 141–143.
Electricity, 124.
Embezzlement distinguished, 145.
False pretenses distinguished, 157, 161, 172, 175.
From illegal slot machine, 127.
Goods delivered by mistake, 150, 153, 154.
Goods obtained by fraud, 157, 158.
Homicide to prevent, 435.
Illegal lottery ticket, 125.
Intent, 161, 187, 189, 191, 192, 194.
  To force payment, 198.
  To pawn, 194.
  To sell to owner, 191.
Interstate transportation of stolen car, 683.
Jurisdiction, 673.
Lost property, 177, 180, 182.
Mistake of fact, 521.
Mistake of law, 502, 503.
No trespass *ab initio*, 186.
Personal property,
  Value, 125, 128, 130 n.
Possession necessary, 135.
Possession vs. custody, 143, 145, 147, 148.
Property,
  "Of another", 131.
Real estate severed, 139.
Statutory enlargement, 164.
Subject of, 124.
Theft (statutory) includes, 171.
Trespass, 137.
  Need of, 137–186.
Trespass required, 137–139, 141–143, 145, 147, 148.
Value for grand, 129 n.
Wild animals, 138.

LAW
Knowledge of, presumed, 501.

LIBEL
Definition, 209.
Jurisdiction for, 670 n.
Liability of principal, 285.
Malice, 377.

INDEX

LIMITATIONS
See, also, Statute of Limitations.
Of criminal capacity, See Coverture; Infant; Insanity; Intoxication.
Of prosecution, 653.

LINDBERGH LAW
Kidnaping, 90.

LOST PROPERTY
See Larceny.

MAGISTRATE
Arrest on oral order of, 789.
Preliminary examination by, 820.
Summary trial by, 820.

MAINTENANCE
Definition, 213.

MALICE
See, also, Malice Aforethought.
Discussed, 371.
Libel, 377.
Malicious mischief, 372, 375, 424, 426, 428.
Mayhem, 373.
Meaning of, 371.

MALICE AFORETHOUGHT
See, also, Malice.
Murder requires, 30, 31, 34.
Presumption of, 28, 30 n.
Wanton act dangerous to life, 30, 36, 38.
Without intent to kill, 30, 36, 38.

MALICIOUS MISCHIEF
Malice needed, 424, 426, 428.
Mens rea of, 424, 426, 428.
Property illegally held, 555 n.
What constitutes malice, 372, 375.

MALICIOUS TRESPASS
See Malicious Mischief.

MALUM IN SE
Attempted suicide, 409.
Malum prohibitum distinguished, 411.

MALUM PROHIBITUM
Homicide from, 411, 413.

MANN ACT
Conspiracy to violate, 269.
Defined, 206.
Motive for transportation, 433.

MANSLAUGHTER
See, also, Homicide; Provocation.
By negative act, 256 n, 258, 261.
Criminal negligence, 353, 355, 357.
Definition, 54.
Involuntary, 56, 58, 60, 353, 355, 360.
Medical treatment fatal, 353.

MANSLAUGHTER—Cont'd
Mens rea, 353, 355, 357.
Rule of provocation, 40.
Voluntary, 42, 45, 48.

MARRIAGE
As bar to prosecution for seduction, 566, 569 n.

MAYHEM
Defined, 91.
Malice, 373.

MEDICAL AID
Child, 252.
Not superseding cause, 324.

MENS REA
See, also, Concurrence; Criminal Negligence; Intent; Knowledge; Malice; Motive; Specific Intent; Strict Liability; Transferred Intent; Unlawful Conduct; Wilfulness.
Abortion, 350.
And actus reus, 344.
Battery, 345.
Burglary, 345.
Concurrence of actus reus, 438, 439.
General, 344.
Indecent exposure, 347.
Malicious mischief, 424, 426, 428.
Manslaughter, 353, 355, 357.
Meaning, 343.
Murder, 345.
Possession of obscene book, 394.
Resulting in actus reus, 439.
Section on, 343.
Statutory crime, 345.

MENTAL DISEASE OR DEFECT
See Insanity.

MERCY KILLING
Murder, 430 n.

MILITARY ORDERS
As excuse, 574.
Command of superior, 574.

MISCONDUCT IN OFFICE
Definition, 211.

MISDEMEANOR
Attempt to commit, 224.
Defined, 10 n.
"Felony-misdemeanor," 10 **n.**
Force used to prevent, 590.
Penalty, 5.

MISPRISION
Of felony, 114, 212.

MISTAKE

See, also, Mistake of Fact; Mistake of Law.
Due to intoxication, 495 n.
Larceny of goods delivered by, 150, 153, 154.

MISTAKE OF FACT

Assault, 520, 521.
Bigamy, 525.
Discussed, 520.
Excuse for act, 520, 521, 523, 525, 529, 530.
In defense of others, 623, 625, 627 n.
In self-defense, 599, 613.
Larceny, 521.
Obscene libel, 523.
Reasonable, 521.
Specific intent, 521.
Statutory rape, 530.
Unlawful act under, 528, 530.

MISTAKE OF LAW

Acting on court decision, 517.
Advice of counsel, 514.
Advice of government agent, 517 n.
Bigamy, 514.
Conspiracy, 509.
Extortion, 505.
Kidnaping, 507.
Knowledge presumed, 501.
Larceny, 502, 503.
Requiring registration, 511.
Section on, 501.
Specific intent lacking, 502.

MODEL PENAL CODE

Abandonment of attempt, 249.
Absolute liability, 443.
Arrest for felony, 808.
Arson, 122.
Assault, 84.
Attempt, 248.
Bigamy and polygamy, 534.
Burglary, 119.
Causation, 342.
Causing catastrophe, 123.
Classes of crimes, 11.
Complicity, 287, 310.
Compounding crime, 312.
Consent, 554.
Conspiracy, 281.
Corporate liability, 295.
Crime, 11.
Criminal homicide, 72.
Criminal mischief, 123.
Criminal trespass, 119.
Death sentence, 73.
Defiant trespasser, 120.
Duress, 500, 541.

MODEL PENAL CODE—Cont'd

Entrapment, 651.
Felony defined, 12.
Force in self-protection, 618.
Force to prevent crime, 597.
Force to protect property, 637.
Former jeopardy, 757.
Immaturity excluding criminal conviction, 457.
Inchoate crimes, 248.
Intoxication, 496.
Knowingly, 442.
Lost property, theft of, 202.
Manslaughter, 72.
Mental disease or defect, 486.
Military orders, 579.
Misdemeanor defined, 12.
Mistake as to age, 534.
Mistake of fact or law, 519.
Murder, 72.
Negative act, 264.
Negligent homicide, 73.
Negligently, 442.
Offenses against property, 122.
Protection of others, 628.
Purposely, 442.
Rape, 555.
Receiving stolen property, 202.
Reckless endangering, 84.
Recklessly, 442.
Requirement of culpability, 442.
Seduction, 570.
Services, theft of, 202.
Solicitation, 249.
Territorial applicability, 693.
Theft, 199.
Threats, 84.
Time limitations, 724.
Use of force for discipline, 589.
Violation defined, 12.
Voluntary act required, 223.
Young adult offenders, 457.

MORALITY

Offenses against, 204.

MOTION

Change of venue, 846.
Defined, 830.
Prosecution, 830.
To dismiss, 831, 846.

MOTIVE

For Mann Act violation, 433.
Homicide, 435, 437.
Intent distinguished, 429.
Mailing obscene matter, 432 n.
Mercy killing, 430 n.
Perjury, 430.
Section on, 429.

INDEX

References are to Pages

MURDER
See, also, Homicide, Malice.
Actus reus, 345.
Attempt,
    Specific intent, 365.
Attempt to commit, 226, 228, 231.
Burglary causing, 66, 68.
By automobile, 33 n, 38.
Death essential to, 305.
Decapitation after supposed death, 439.
Definition, 32.
Euthanasia not an excuse, 430 n.
First degree, 61, 64, 66, 68.
Indictment for, 825.
Mens rea, 345.
Mercy killing, 430 n.
Motive for, 435, 437.
Wanton act dangerous to life, 28, 30, 36.
Wilful, deliberate and premeditated, **61**, **64**.

NARCOTICS
Homicide by, 39 n.

NECESSITY
See, also, Compulsion.
Former jeopardy affected by, **727**.
For use of force,
    Crime prevention, 591.
    Self-defense, 599, 601.

NEGATIVE ACT
Cruelty to animals, 262.
Effect of, 438.
Homicide by, 250, 252, 256 n.
Legal duty, 250, 252, 254.
Manslaughter by, 256 n, 258, 261.
Not superseding, 338.
Section on, 250.

NEGLIGENCE
See, also, Criminal Negligence.
Defined, 352.
Homicide from, 30, 31, 34.
Of injured party, 557, 559, 562.

NEGLIGENT HOMICIDE
Statutory, 56.

NIGHTTIME
See Burglary.

NOLLE PROSEQUI
Discussed, 831.
One conspirator, 276.

NOLO CONTENDERE
Plea of, 854.

NONDEADLY FORCE
Crime prevention by, 591.
Defined, 597.

NOT GUILTY
Plea of, 852.

NUISANCE
Strict liability, 388.

OATH
False, 210.
Perjury, 210.

OBSCENE
Exposure, 347.
Mistake of fact, 523.
Motive for mailing, 432 n.
Possession of, book, 394.

OBSCENITY
Definition, 206.

OBSTRUCTION OF JUSTICE
Definition, 212.

OFFENSES
Affecting governmental functions,
    See Bribery; Champerty; Compounding Crime; Counterfeiting; Escape; Maintenance; Misconduct in Office; Obstruction of Justice; Perjury; Subordination of Perjury; Treason.
Against,
    Habitation,
        See Arson; Burglary.
    Morality,
        See Adultery; Bigamy; Incest; Prostitution; Seduction; Sodomy.
    Person,
        See Abduction; Abortion; Assault; Battery; Dueling; False Imprisonment; Homicide; Kidnaping; Manslaughter; Mayhem; Murder; Rape.
    Property, 124.
        See Embezzlement; False Pretenses; Larceny; Malicious Mischief.
    Public peace,
        See Breach of Peace; Disorderly House; Fighting; Forcible Entry; Libel; Riot; Rout; Unlawful Assembly.
Summary trial of petty, 820.

OFFICER
See, also, Arrest.
Assisting, to arrest, 790.
Bailiwick of, 802.
Pre-arraignment procedures, **931**.
Summons by, 819.

OMISSION
See Negative Act.

OTHERS
See Defense, of others.

PARDON
Plea of, 850.

PAROLE
Extradition of one released on, 702.
Violation of, 212.

PARTIES TO CRIME
Accessory after fact, 304, 305.
Accessory defined, 297.
Classified, 297.
Principal in first degree, 297.
Principal in second degree, 297.
Section on, 296.
Statutory changes, 301.

PASSION
Homicide in sudden, 42, 45, 48.

PEACE
Offenses against public, 207.

PEINE FORTE ET DURE
Ancient procedure, 848.
Discussed, 823.

PENALTY
Felony, 5.
Misdemeanor, 5.

PERJURY
Conviction on perjured testimony, 838.
Definition, 210.
Motive, 430.
Subornation of, 210.

PETTY OFFENSES
Trial of, 820, 909.

PIRACY
Definition, 654.
Federal offense, 654.

PLEA
Benefit of clergy, 849.
Defendant's refusal to enter, 823, 848.
Former jeopardy, 850.
Guilty, 853.
Guilty of lesser offense, 855.
In abatement, 850.
Issue joined by, 848.
Nolo contendere, 854.
Not guilty, 852.
Not guilty because of insanity, 852.
Oral at common law, 848.
Pardon, 850.
Sanctuary, 849.
To jurisdiction, 849.

POSSE
Arrest by, 790.

POSSESSION
See, also, Larceny.
As an act, 222 n.

PRELIMINARY EXAMINATION
Discussed, 820.
Right to counsel, 927.

PREMEDITATION
Killing with, 61, 64.
Time required for, 61, 64.

PRESENCE OF DEFENDANT
During trial, 905.

PRESUMPTION
Coercion of wife, 497.
Criminal incapacity of infant, 445.
Explained, 501.
Insanity, 476 n.
Knowledge of law, 501.
Malice aforethought, 28, 30 n.
Sanity, 486.
Specific intent not, 362 n.

PREVENTION OF CRIME
As a defense, 590.
Deadly force for, 592, 594.
Nondeadly force for, 591.
Section on, 590.

PRINCIPAL
See, also, Agent.
Accessory distinguished, 297.
Second degree, 297, 307.

PRIVATE PERSON
Arrest by, 572 n.
Assists officer to arrest, 790, 791 n.

PRIVILEGE
See Defense; Domestic Authority; Libel; Prevention of Crime; Public Authority; Self-Defense.

PROBABLE CAUSE
Arrest on, 799.
Complaint issued on, 769.
Not by what search discloses, 801.
What constitutes, 771, 774.

PROCEDURE
Ex post facto, 761, 763, 766 n.
Pre-arraignment, 931.
Problems of, 653.

PROMISSORY FRAUD
See False Pretenses.

PROPERTY
Force to defend, 628, 631, 633.

PROSPECTIVE
Application of decision, 891 n.

PROSTITUTION
Defined, 206.

INDEX

PROVOCATION
Effect of intoxication, 489.
Rule of, 40.
Words, 42, 60.

PUBLIC AUTHORITY
Armed forces, 573.
As defense, 571, 573, 574.
Foreign government, 573.

PUBLIC TORT
See Civil Offense.

PUBLIC TRIAL
Defendant's right to, 906.

PUBLIC WELFARE OFFENSE
See Civil Offense.

QUASH
Motion to, Indictment, 845.

QUESTIONING
Arrestee, 813.
In accusatory procedure, 916, 920.
In investigatory procedure, 916, 920.
Suspected person, 814.

RAPE
Age of consent, 88.
Attempt, 238.
By infant, 307.
Consent obtained by fraud, 550, 553 n.
Defined, 88.
Statutory, 88.
  Mistake of fact, 530.

RECEIVING STOLEN PROPERTY
Attempt, 232, 235.
Goods must be stolen, 158.
Knowledge, 381, 383.

RECUSATION
Definition, 847.

RESCUE
Definition, 212.

RES JUDICATA
See Former Jeopardy.

RESPONDEAT SUPERIOR
In civil offense, 405.
Not in true crime, 283, 406 n.
Nuisance, 388.
Tort law distinguished, 406 n.

RESPONSIBILITY
  See, also, Compulsion; Concurrence; Condonation; Conduct; Consent; Coverture; Criminal Negligence; Guilt; Ignorance; Infant; Injured Party; Insanity; Intoxication; Knowledge; Malice; Mens Rea; Motive; Necessity; Specific Intent; Strict Liability;

RESPONSIBILITY—Cont'd
  Transferred Intent; Unlawful Conduct; Wilfulness.
Chapter on, 343.

RETREAT
  See, also, Self-Defense.
By arrester, 807.

RETROSPECTIVE
Application of decision, 891 n.

RIGHT OF DEFENDANT
Fair and impartial trial, 912.
Presence during trial, 905.
Public trial, 906.
Right to confrontation, 927.
Right to counsel,
  At preliminary hearing, 927.
  At trial, 863.
  Before indictment, 916, 920.
  On appeal, 867.
  Violated, 913, 916, 920.
Time of trial, 903.
Trial by jury, 909.

RIGHT OF PRIVACY
See Electronic Devices; Search and Seizure.

RIOT
Defined, 208.

ROBBERY
Asportation, 135.
Federal offense, 654.
Intent to force payment, 198.
Jurisdiction for, 670 n.
Purse-snatching, 137 n.
Violence or putting in fear, 135, 137 n.

ROUT
Defined, 208.

RULE
Putting witnesses under, 908.

RULE OF PROVOCATION
Words as, 42.

SANCTUARY
Plea of, 849.

SCHOOLMASTER
Authority to discipline pupil, 582, 585, 587.

SEARCH
"Frisk", 812.
Incidental to arrest, 811, 812 n.
Of arrestee, 811.
Weapons by arrestee, 812.

SEARCH AND SEIZURE
  See also Search.
Blood test, 923.
Unreasonable, 891.

INDEX

References are to Pages

SEARCH WARRANT
Life of, 780.
Probable cause for issuance, 774, 775 n.

SEDUCTION
Defined, 205.
Marriage as bar to prosecution, 566, 569 n.

SELF-DEFENSE
See, also, Homicide; Justification.
Apparent danger, 437.
Apparent necessity, 599, 613.
As defense, 598.
"Castle doctrine", 601, 610 n, 611, 612 n.
Deadly force, 600.
Imperfect right of, 601.
Necessity for, 599, 601.
Reasonable force, 598.
Retreat "to the wall", 600, 603, 606, 607, 611, 612 n.
Unknown danger, 437.
Withdrawal from deadly conflict, 600 n, 601, 616.

SELF-INCRIMINATION
Blood test is not, 923.
Comment on failure to testify, 883.
Effect of Immunity Act, 886.
Privilege against, 872.
Sixth Amendment, 914.
Testimonial compulsion, 923.

SENTENCE
Judgment, 770.

SIXTH AMENDMENT
Effect of Fourteenth, 864, 917, 921, 929.
Right to counsel, 861, 862, 916.
Right to speedy trial, 909 n.
Right to trial by jury, 909 n.

SMITH ACT
Violation of, 278.

SODOMY
Compulsion, 540 n.
Defined, 206.

SOLICITATION
Criminal, 244.

SOVEREIGNTY
Offenses affecting, 210.

SPECIFIC INTENT
Burglary, 364.
Definition, 361.
Intoxication affecting, 488.
Mistake of fact, 521.
Misuse of, 371.
Not presumed, 362 n.

SPRING-GUN
Used to protect property, 633, 636 n.

STATUTE OF LIMITATIONS
Amendment of, 719.
Common law has none, 714.
Conspiracy, 721 n.
Defective indictment, 717.
Having run, 721 n.
Illustrative statute, 715.
Jurisdiction, 715.
Manslaughter, 768 n.
Pleading of, 715.
Probationer, 721.
Reinstatement of dismissed indictment, 718 n.
Starting of period, 718 n.
Tolling of, 718 n.

STATUTORY
See Burglary, Rape.

STEPS BY DEFENDANT
Bail, 832.
Demurrer, 843.
Discovery, 855.
Motions, 845.
Pleas, 848.

STOLEN
See Larceny.

STRICT LIABILITY
Limitation of, 408 n.
Not in true crime, 396, 402, 405 n.
Nuisance, 388.
Section on, 388.

SUBORNATION OF PERJURY
Definition, 210.

SUICIDE
Unlawful act, 409.

SUMMARY TRIAL
Of petty offenses, 820.
Preliminary examination distinguished, 820.

SUMMONS
In lieu of,
    Arrest, 790 n, 818.
    Warrant of arrest, 777.

SUPERSEDING CAUSE
Effect of, 336, 340.
Medical treatment is not, 324.

THEFT
See Larceny.

THIRD DEGREE
Confession by, 873.
Discussed, 817.

INDEX

References are to Pages

TICKET
Use of traffic, 819.

TIME
Arrest, 805.
Nighttime, 109.
Trial, 903.

TRAFFIC
Homicide by, accident, 31.

TRAFFIC ACCIDENT
Fatal, 357.
Homicide from, 413.

"TRANSFERRED INTENT"
Discussed, 418.
Not a criminal law concept, 418.

TREASON
Definition, 210, 654.

TRESPASS
See, also, Larceny; Malicious Mischief.
Doctrine of continuing, 184.

TRIAL
See, also, Right of Defendant.
Insanity at time of, 463.
Steps prior to indictment, 769–827.

TRUE BILL
By grand jury, 770.

UNCONSTITUTIONAL
Anti-miscegenation act, 433.
Denial of right to counsel, 863, 916, 920, 927.
Embezzlement without mens rea, 402.
Ex post facto law, 759.
Former jeopardy, 725.
Issuance of warrant, 772–73, 779.
Searches and seizures, 779, 891.
Taking insanity issue from jury, 486 n.
Treatment of prisoner, 809 n.
True crime without mens rea, 402, 530 n.
Use of illegally-obtained evidence, 892, 913, 916, 920.
Use of stomach pump, 812 n.
Venue statutes held, 680, 683 n.
Warrant of arrest, 780, 782 n.

UNIFORM ACT
Extradition, 704.
Fresh pursuit, 803.
Reciprocal Enforcement of Support, 704, 705 n.

UNIFORM ARREST ACT
"Frisk", 813 n.
Questioning suspected person, 814.
Resistance to unauthorized arrest, 817 n.

UNINTENDED CONSEQUENCES
See Criminal Negligence; Malum in Se; Malum Prohibitum; Negligence; Specific Intent.

UNITED STATES CODE ANNOTATED
5 U.S.C.A. § 300a, p. 881.
8 U.S.C.A. § 43, p. 817 n.
§ 1282(c), p. 686.
§§ 1325, 1326, p. 688 n.
§ 1329, p. 688 n.
18 U.S.C.A. § 88, pp. 10, 270.
§ 242, p. 817 n.
§ 253, p. 879.
§ 397, p. 269.
§ 398, p. 269.
§§ 451–55, p. 685.
§ 471, p. 655.
§ 541, p. 10.
§ 593, p. 881.
§ 595, p. 880.
§ 641, p. 397.
§ 659, pp. 688 n, **690 n.**
§ 752, p. 695 n.
§ 953, p. 654.
§ 1073, p. 688 n.
§ 1502, p. 695 n.
§ 1651, p. 654.
§ 1652, p. 654.
§ 2112, p. 654.
§ 2239, p. 688 n.
§ 2255, p. 836 n.
§ 2381, p. 654.
§ 2385, p. 278.
§ 2421, p. 433
§ 3051, p. 695 n.
§ 3181, p. 695 n.
§ 3184, p. 395 n.
§§ 3185–86, p. 695 n.
§§ 3188–93, p. 695 n.
§ 3231, pp. 656 n, **680 n.**
§ 3236, p. 688 n.
§ 3237, p. 683.
§ 3288, p. 718 n.
§ 3481, p. 883.
§ 3486, p. 886.
§ 3500, pp. 858, 859.
§ 3731, pp. 176, 734.
§ 5005, p. 450 n.
21 U.S.C.A. § 174, p. 895.
26 U.S.C.A. § 4704, p. 771.
27 U.S.C.A. §§ 91, 92, p. 9.
28 U.S.C.A. § 102, p. 685.
§ 1257(2), p. 512.
§ 1442, p. 843.
§ 2241, p. 841.
§ 2255, pp. 735, 836 n, 843 **n.**
49 U.S.C.A. § 41(1), p. 688 **n.**

INDEX

References are to Pages

UNLAWFUL ACT
Assault by, 78.
Causal relation necessary, 414.
Causing death, 409.
Conspiracy to commit, 264.
Homicide by, 56, 58, 60.
Malum in se, 409.
Malum prohibitum, 411.
Mistake of fact, 528, 530.
Resulting in prohibited act, 528, 530.
Suicide, 409.

UNLAWFUL ASSEMBLY
Definition, 208.
Disturbance of, 208.

UNLAWFUL CONDUCT
See, also, Unlawful Act.
Section on, 409.

USE
Car without owner's consent, 546.

USURY
Conspiracy to commit, 264.

UTTERING
Knowledge of forgery, 385 n.

VAGUE
Definition, 2.

VENUE
Change of,
  By defendant, 846.
  By prosecution, 831 n.
Illegal entry or stay, 686.
Interstate commerce, 683.
Motion for change of, 846.
Near boundary, 680, 683 n.
On ship, 684.
Place of death, 684 n.
Proof of, 679.
Train or vessel, 680, 682 n, 683 n.
What is, 677.

VIOLATION
Model Penal Code, 12.
Parole, 212.

VOLUNTARY
Intoxication, 488.
Manslaughter, 42, 45, 48.

WAIVER
Indictment, 827.
Right to counsel, 916, 920.
Trial by jury, 910.

WANTON ACT
Dangerous to life, 28, 30, 36.

WARRANT
  See, also, Search Warrant; Warrant of Arrest.
Bench warrant, 780, 828.

WARRANT OF ARREST
Arrest of wrong person, 783, 784 n, 785 n.
Arrest under, 788.
Arrest without, 791, 793, 795.
Authority of, 779 n.
Blank, a nullity, 782 n.
Execution of, 803.
"Fair on its face", 779, 785.
Form of, 778.
"John Doe", 780.
Life of, 780 n.
Possession of, 789.
Summons in lieu of, 777.
Validity of, 779, 780.
Void on its face, 780.

WEAPONS
Motive for carrying, 433 n.
Search of arrestee for, 811.
Threatening with, 80.

WHITE SLAVERY
Federal offense, 206.

WIFE
  See, also, Husband.
Authority of husband, 581, 583, 584 n.
Coercion by husband, 497.

WILFUL
Deliberate and premeditated killing, 61, 64.

WILFULNESS
Meaning of, 385.
Refusal to produce evidence, 386.

WIRETAPPING
Federal law, 903.

WITHDRAWAL
  See, also, Self-Defense.
From conspiracy, 247.
From deadly conflict, 600 n, 601, 616.

WORDS
Provocation, 42, 60.

WOUND
Neglect of, by injured party, 562.

YOUTH CORRECTION ACT
Federal, 450 n.

End of Volume